Programmer's Guide to the EGA and VGA Cards

Second Edition

Programmer's Guide to the EGA and VGA Cards

Second Edition

Richard F. Ferraro

Addison-Wesley Publishing Company, Inc.

Reading, Massachusetts • Menlo Park, California • New York • Don Mills, Ontario
Wokingham, England • Amsterdam • Bonn • Sydney
Singapore • Tokyo • Madrid • San Juan

Many of the designations used by manufacturers and sellers to distinguish their products are claimed as trademarks. Where those designations appear in this book, and Addison-Wesley was aware of a trademark claim, the designations have been printed in initial capital letters or all capital letters.

Ferraro, Richard F.
    Programmer's guide to the EGA and VGA cards / Richard F. Ferraro.
 -- 2nd ed.
        p.   cm.
    Includes index.
    ISBN 0-201-57025-4
       1. IBM Personal Computer--Programming.   2.   IBM Personal System / 2
(Computer system) --Programming.   3. Expansion boards (Computers)
I. Title.
    QA76.8.I2594F48   1990
    006.6' 765--dc20
                                                                            90-46498
                                                                              CIP

Cover design by Doliber Skeffington
Text design by Kenneth J. Wilson (Wilson Graphics & Design)
ISBN 0-201-57025-4

ABCDEFGHIJ-HA-943210
First printing, October 1990

Dedication

For my most wonderful mother, Jennie Ferraro, my most wonderful wife, Paula Lowe, my most wonderful son, Riccardo, and my most wonderful daughter, Georgia.

Contents

Chapter 4
The PC, C, and Assembly Language 72

Chapter 5
Principles of Computer Graphics 131

Chapter 15
ATI Technologies

Chapter 16
Chips and Technologies   766

Character Font Width • Gen-lock • Read/Modify/Write • Hardware Zoom and Pan • Multiple Soft Fonts

Preface

The Video Graphics Array (VGA) has clearly established itself as the color graphics card of choice for the PC family of computers. Millions of Enhanced Graphics Array (EGA) and VGA cards are in use worldwide. VGA controllers have penetrated every PC platform, from laptops to 80486s. Software applications have expanded from the early illustration and graphics packages. Now applications include workstation resolution CAD, desktop publishing, image processing, animation, and multi-media presentation systems.

When I wrote the first edition of this book, I wanted to find out which software packages used the VGA. Now, I doubt whether any software can be found that does not communicate through the VGA. The important question is "How much of the VGA is utilized?"

The VGA standard has produced a fertile graphics environment for the PC programmer. While it still reigns supreme in the PC graphics arena, the VGA has grown beyond its original scope. Nearly all VGA cards exceed the VGA standard in some significant way. I call these *Super VGAs*. While no standard exists for these Super VGA cards, advances have been made in the creation of a Super VGA standard by the Video Electronics Standards Association (VESA).

Few software applications fully use the advanced features of the Super VGAs. Most software developers have been largely on their own. Many software developers cannot resist programming the super cards in the standard VGA modes. This is unfortunate, since the Super VGA advances have become so pronounced that programmers can no longer afford to ignore their powerful new graphics features.

The motivation for a second edition of *The Programmer's Guide to the EGA and VGA Cards* is simple. I want to help programmers use the Super VGAs to the fullest extent possible.

This edition provides a comprehensive discussion of the complete VGA standards. Intended as reference material, the book elaborates on the PC graphics environment and includes information on the MDA, CGA, Hercules, EGA, VGA, 8514/A and the TIGA standards. I have also included a discussion of C and assembly language as it pertains to the code included in the book. Registers and their bits and the BIOS Calls and their parameters are illustrated.

The nine new chapters in this book explain every feature of the Super VGAs. Chapter 13 provides programmers with a detailed discussion of the Super VGAs. While there are many Super VGA cards available, most are based on the VGA chip of one of the following seven manufacturers. Chapters 15–21 thoroughly describe these VGA chips:

ATI Technologies	18800,28800
Chips and Technologies	82c451, 82c452, 82c453, 82c455, 82c456
Genoa Systems	5000 series, GVGA
Paradise/Western Digital	PVGA1A,WD90C00, WD90C10, WD90C11
Trident	8800, 8900
Tseng Labs	ET3000, ET4000
Video7/Headland Technologies	VEGA, V7VGA

Discussions focus on how to control, query, optimize, and write to and read from these cards. Armed with these tools, programmers can use the higher resolutions and improved capabilities of the Super VGA cards.

The book provides optimized program examples. The examples use many of the advanced features of these powerful cards. The features included are: control of the Super VGA's many display modes including the 1024 by 768 16- and 256-color modes; determination of the state of the VGA and graphics environment; control of alphanumerics; manipulation of character fonts; read- and write-to-display memory; draw points, lines and circles; read and write to the color tables; and control of the start address to allow panning and scrolling through the one megabyte of display memory.

Richard F. Ferraro   Seattle, Washington, 1990

Companion Software
Now Available

PROGRAMMER'S GUIDE COMPANION DISK AND
THE SUPER VGA TOOLBOX

Programmers will save time and assure typing accuracy by purchasing the companion software available with this book. *Programmer's Guide Companion Disk* includes all of the source code listings from this book. *The Super VGA Toolbox* offers a complete toolbox for the Super VGA cards in addition to this same source code.

Companion software may be purchased directly from the author. The special order coupon provided in the back of this book makes ordering by phone or mail quick and simple.

The Super VGA Toolbox

The Super VGA Toolbox is a comprehensive graphics toolbox that supports all Super VGA cards based on one of nineteen VGA chips discussed in this book. All VGA chips from IBM, ATI Technologies, Chips and Technologies, Genoa, Paradise/ Western Digital, Trident, Tseng, and Video7/Headland Technologies are supported.

The Super VGA Toolbox provides some 300 optimized functions that control and manipulate each of the chips indicated above. Each function is well-documented, and naming conventions are intuitive. A clearly written 100-page manual makes using the toolbox effortless. All source code is included, and the functions may be used royalty-free. The toolbox is designed so programmers can readily add additional functions, and software updates will be made available to handle new Super VGA chips as these are introduced.

The toolbox consists of a Standard VGA Library and a Global VGA Library. Together, these allow the programmer to write simple code that works on any of the above VGAs.

The Standard VGA Library consists of 150 functions that control the standard EGA/VGA cards. Functions perform alphanumerics, control the color palette, handle fonts, preset, read and write to rectangular windows, draw and clip lines and various shapes, and position the screen start and cursor position.

The 256-color 320 by 400 non-standard display mode is completely supported on all VGA implementations.

The Global VGA Library consists of 150 functions that control the super VGAs. These functions automatically detect the active VGA and adjust accordingly. Assembly language call tables allow the software to rapidly select the code suited to the VGA chip present. This allows the programmer the luxury of writing code without concern for the particular VGA chip present. It is simple to use, easy to modify and logically organized. Each function is completely documented within the source code and completely specified within the manual. No function is longer than one page. Each function in the toolbox is listed in a directory within the manual for easy reference. The directories briefly describe the function, the calling protocol, the function number, and which source file it can be found in.

The Super VGA Toolbox manual is complete, accurate and easy to use. It provides the programmer with a concise road map . Chapter One is the introduction. Chapter Two explains how to install the Super VGA Toolbox. Chapter Three describes the functions associated with the Standard VGA Library. All functions, their calling protocols, input and output parameters, and assumptions are described. Chapter Four describes all functions in the Specific VGA Libraries. Chapter Five describes all functions in the Global VGA Library. In addition, an appendix provides a complete set of cross-referenced lists for all of the alphanumeric and graphics display modes.

The following program example illustrates how easy it is to determine the active VGA card, set a graphics mode, and clear a rectangular window. This code uses the Global VGA Library and will execute properly on any VGA cards that support this Super VGA mode.

```
integer   VGA_id;        /*   VGA identification code */

main()
{ int width=800, height=600,  number_of_colors=16,  graphics=1, mode, x1=100,
y1=100, x2=500, y2=500,
                    bytes_per_row, page=0, row=10, column=5;
 char   box_color=50, line_color=4, string[100], attribute=1;  bytes_per_row=width;

Which_VGA();   /* determine the active VGA */

Build_Mode();                  /* build the mode tables */
mode = Find_Mode(width,height,number_of_colors,graphics);    /* Find the mode
number */
Set_Mode(mode);                /* set the mode to 800 by 600 256-color mode */

ClrWin_256(x1,y1,x2,y2,box_color,bytes_per_row);     /* Clear a window (256-
color) */
}
```

Acknowledgments

The challenge of writing this revised edition could not have been met without the support and assistance of many good people. Special thanks are due to:

Paula Lowe for her conceptual and editing assistance. She kept me on track and running during all phases of writing.

Julie Stillman and Abby Genuth from Addison-Wesley for their cheerful understanding and steadfast assistance in seeing this book through, from inception to publication.

John Klepper and Mark Moehring of the Institute of Applied Physiology and Medicine for their support in producing the first version of this book.

The VESA committee for their excellent technical documentation and, more importantly, for their noble efforts to bring order into the maelstrom.

And a special thanks for the technical support provided by the following people at the VGA chip manufacturers covered in this book:

ATI Technologies:
Edward Chu

Chips and Technologies:
    Bob Brummer
    Bob Conner
    Bo Ericsson

Genoa Systems:
    Darwin Chang

Paradise/Western Digital Imaging:
    Russell Chang
    Dave Foley

Trident Microsystems:
Kevin Walsh

Tseng Labs:
    Lou Aynet
    Joe Curley

Video7/Headland Technologies:
    Roger Uhlig

Chapter 1

Introduction to the Programmer's Guide

1.1 ABOUT COMPUTER GRAPHICS CARDS

For all of you who want to program graphics on your personal computers, the tools and means to use them are now available. No matter what your computer graphics applications, powerful graphics cards now enable you to generate sharp, effective graphic presentations on the video monitor.

An effective graphics system integrates graphics cards with a variety of graphics software, graphics peripherals, computer memory, and the DOS operating system. Graphics cards are used in personal computers to display data via images created by dots, lines, curves, arbitrary shapes, and alphanumeric characters on the video monitor. Monochrome cards, specifically the Hercules card, display data in black and white; the color graphics cards display the data in a variety of colors. The art of programming these graphics cards is known as computer graphics.

This book helps you harness the power of the most popular color graphics cards for your own applications. These include the Enhanced Graphics Adapter (EGA), the Video Graphics Array (VGA), and the Super VGA cards. The EGA/VGA standard provides a consistent foundation upon which to build your programs. Because of these standards, the programs you create today can enjoy long useful lifetimes on the millions of computers equipped with either the EGA or VGA cards. Furthermore, cards introduced in the future are bound to conform to the EGA/VGA and Super VGA standards. The time spent learning to program these cards today will benefit you for years to come. When new cards are introduced, you can focus on learning the improvements that expand upon the EGA/VGA standards.

The EGA and VGA computer graphics standards were developed by IBM for its Personal Computer (PC) and Personal System/2 (PS/2) computer families respectively. Although the Color Graphics Adapter (CGA) was introduced earlier, the CGA exhibited poor resolution and limited colors. The EGA standard and adapter board, developed in 1984, solved these problems. Since then, it has

1

become the third most popular color graphics standard for the PC. Manufacturers have produced several variations of the EGA, and nearly every software application has taken advantage of this powerful standard.

The VGA was introduced by IBM in 1987. It is built into the motherboard of models 50, 60, and 80 of the PS/2. This standard maintains downward compatibility to the EGA while adding some important new features. The most significant of these are the readability of the adapter registers, increased resolution, and a 256-color mode. The Super VGAs have been manufactured by several companies since 1987.

A second adapter released with the PS/2 family is the Multi-color Graphics Array (MCGA). The MCGA is incorporated into Model 30 of the PS/2 and is downwardly compatible to the Color Graphics Adapter (CGA) at the register and display memory level as well as at the BIOS level. This adapter has not been as popular at the EGA or VGA. Hence, this book focused exclusively on the EGA and VGA cards.

1.2   ABOUT THE NEED FOR THIS BOOK

Information detailing the operation of the EGA or VGA cards has been available only through a collection of technical manuals. Using these manuals is a frustrating process of "cut and paste" with the information being nearly impossible to decipher even for experienced graphics programmers. In addition, none of the references explained how a programmer would use the cards to perform computer graphics or rated one technique as better suited to a task than another. Graphics programming books presented a selection of graphics routines without providing essential details for programming.

As the capabilities, power, and flexibility of graphics systems increase, programming graphics becomes a more demanding, complex job. It is essential to know the capabilities of the graphics system, whether a programmer is using a preexisting graphics library or programming the graphic cards directly. To fully utilize the graphics system, the programmer must have a detailed understanding of computer graphics algorithms, the graphics system and how the graphics system integrates into the computer environment. Armed with an understanding of the graphics cards and a knowledge of computer graphics, the programmer can create a wide variety of graphics effects on the video monitor.

The VGA standard has been surpassed in performance by cards called "Super VGA." However, many programmers have chosen to ignore the advanced capabilities of these cards.

1.3   ABOUT THIS BOOK

This book provides a thorough, comprehensive guide for anyone who wants to program the Enhanced Graphics Adapter (EGA), the Video Graphics Array (VGA), or the Super VGAs. The goal of this book is to help each reader acquire the knowledge and skills necessary to program successfully with these graphics cards. Each chapter is a building block organized in a learning sequence. The chapters are also designed to stand alone. This blend of tutorial and reference manual gives the reader plenty of room for moving around, stopping, studying, and moving on.

The philosophy behind this book is that understanding optimizes programming. The features of the EGA/VGA are both numerous and hidden within the range of control registers and BIOS calls. There is more than one way to accomplish a task on the EGA/VGA. The programmer who is aware of the options within these adapters will be able to make the best choice.

It is difficult to recognize the significance and utility of several of the features on the EGA/VGA. Without an understanding of these features' underlying graphics functions, programmers may find many of these features obscure and therefore may not use them. This book unlocks the secrets of these features by providing a tutorial on relevant graphics devices, applications software, and principles.

Since the introduction of these graphics standards, several manufacturers have introduced EGA/VGA compatible cards. Many of these cards have enhanced features that extend the capabilities of the EGA and VGA. These Super VGA cards are discussed in detail in chapters 16-21.

1.4   TERMS AND STYLES USED IN THIS BOOK

The VGA and Super VGA are really an enhancement of the EGA, although there are some features on the EGA and VGA that differ. To minimize redundancy, the following terms are used: "EGA/VGA" is employed, and sentences are written with singular verbs, when information applies to either or both adapters. "EGA" is utilized when information relates only to the EGA. Similarly, "VGA" is used when the information applies only to the VGA.

Numbers are presented in either a decimal or a hexadecimal format. The decimal numbers are presented as the default case, and the hexadecimal numbers are followed by a "hex" qualifier. For example, "10" means the number 10, and "10 hex" means the number 16.

The EGA/VGA registers are described in Chapter 10. Each field is referenced both in the register illustration and in the descriptions. This referencing indicates which adapters are affected by each field. The register illustrations include a code name expressing which bits are used for each field. This code name is preceded by a small square if it applies to the EGA. It is followed by a small square if it applies to the VGA.

Some fields have different meanings depending on the adapter. Two codes are present in these fields separated by a slash. The first name refers to the EGA, and the code after the slash refers to the VGA. Codes that are neither preceded nor followed by a square apply to both the EGA and the VGA. A typical register is illustrated in Figure 1.1.

In Chapter 12, all program examples assume the Microsoft C and assembly

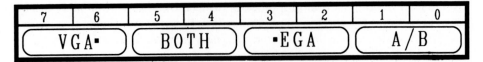

FIGURE 1.1   Typical Register Illustration

language conventions. The "large-model" compiler is used throughout the code, although the code can be readily changed to use the "medium-model" compiler option.

1.5   ABOUT THE CHAPTERS IN GENERAL

Chapters 2 through 5 equip the programmer with a thorough understanding of the features of the EGA/VGA and the relationships these adapters have to other display adapters, the PC computer, graphics devices, and graphics software. A tutorial supplies a background in C and assembly language for novice programmers. The graphics algorithms used in the program examples are introduced in the computer graphics tutorial.

Chapters 6 through 11 specify the functions of the EGA/VGA cards. These chapters offer clear, comprehensive information on the display modes, display memory, graphics processor, downloadable fonts, color processing, control registers, and BIOS calls.

This information is translated into programming examples in Chapter 12. Seventy program examples are included to illustrate the power and versatility of the EGA/VGA cards.

Chapters 13-21 provide detailed descriptions of the Super VGA chips. The scope and depth of this information allows the programmer to identify which chip is present; control, configure and fine tune the chip; invoke the advanced display modes; access up to one megabyte of display memory; and control the start address and cursor.

1.6   ABOUT THE CHAPTERS IN DETAIL

Chapter 2 reveals the EGA/VGA features so that the programmer is aware of the capacity of these adapters. Issues involving display resolution and color resolution are examined. Features of other graphics adapters are also reviewed.

Chapter 3 describes graphics hardware and software and the impact that they have on the EGA/VGA programmer. Hardware devices include interactive devices, graphics, adapters, monitors, data acquisition, and hardcopy devices. The requirements that popular graphics applications software place on the EGA/VGA adapters are discussed.

Chapter 4 examines the relationships between the EGA/VGA and the PC hardware and software. The aspects of the PC memory, input/output system, internal CPU registers, and BIOS calls that are critical to the performance of the EGA/VGA are introduced. A tutorial on C and assembly language teaches basic programming skills. These skills are applicable to the computer graphics programming examples presented in Chapter 12.

Chapter 5 explains the principles behind the computer graphics software examples presented in Chapter 12. Coordinate systems and transformations, characters, points, lines, and shapes are described. Special attention is given to the important line drawing, circle drawing, and clipping algorithms.

Chapter 6 furnishes the reader with the necessary tools to program alphanumerics on the EGA/VGA. The alphanumerics processing capabilities of the display adapter are established. Character shapes, sizes, and attributes are described. Each alphanumeric display mode is described and illustrated. The configurations of the display memory for these alphanumeric display modes are presented. Downloadable character sets are also discussed, including the organization of the fonts and techniques for reading, writing, and selecting the fonts.

Chapter 7 furnishes the reader with the necessary tools for programming graphics on the EGA/VGA. Characters, character attributes, and character fonts are described as they apply to the graphics display modes. Each of the graphics display modes is presented. The organization of the display memory for each of these graphics modes in provided. Details of the operation of the internal graphics processor offer the programmer important insights into how to speed up graphics operations. A brief description of video timing provides the programmer with some meaningful definitions.

Chapter 8 illustrates the color processing capabilities of the EGA/VGA. The palette registers and the color registers are described in detail, with special attention paid to techniques for reading and writing data from and to these registers. Techniques for converting data to colors as well as from one color scheme to another are presented.

Chapter 9 focuses on ascertaining the state of the graphics adapters. There are three ways to obtain this information: the registers can read directly, BIOS calls can be invoked, or the BIOS data area in host RAM memory can be interrogated. The register default values for the EGA/VGA are presented in table form. These values are useful to the programmer when trying to understand the operation of the display modes and the interaction of various display registers.

Chapter 10 presents the entire set of registers resident in the EGA/VGA cards. All of the parameters that pertain to the control of these adapters reside on the control registers. Most of the registers are segmented into fields. A single register can control several different graphics functions. Each field of every register is described in detail.

Chapter 11 presents the entire set of BIOS calls on the EGA/VGA cards. The input and output parameters of each call are provided. The effects that each call has on display memory, host registers, EGA/VGA registers, and the BIOS data area are included.

Chapter 12 provides the reader with 70 program examples that exercise the EGA/VGA cards. These examples span the text, font, graphics, and color sections of the adapters. Each program is well documented and simple to understand. These programs form the basis of a programmer's toolbox.

Chapter 13 describes the many features of the Super VGAs. Chapter 14 provides descriptions and several program examples of features and principles common to all of the Super VGAs.

Chapters 15-21 provide detailed descriptions and program examples for seven of the most popular Super VGA chip manufacturers' products. Seventeen separate Super VGA chips are thoroughly discussed.

1.7   PROGRAM EXAMPLES

The program examples found in Chapter 12 and Chapters 14-21 cover a broad variety of graphics topics. These include controlling the EGA/VGA, reading the state of the adapters, performing alphanumerics processing, handling graphics processing, manipulating color, downloading fonts, and using special effects. This collection of routines forms the foundation of a graphics toolbox.

The program examples are written in C and in assembly language. The C language was selected because of its popularity, structure, and speed. A variety of excellent C compilers are available, along with a large base of support tools for the C language. The C routines in this book can be translated readily into other high-level languages.

In many instances, the routines are written in assembly language. Each of the assembly language routines are short and well-documented. Even the novice assembly language programmer should have little trouble understanding the examples.

Several decisions had to be made regarding the routines included in this book. The programmer will have to make the same set of decisions as new programs are written. These decisions involved which routines to include, how complicated the routines should be, how specialized each routine should be, and what condition the adapters should be left in at the completion of each routine.

The routines selected for this book cover the entire scope of the EGA/VGA. These useful routines are valuable in the graphics setting and include string processing; point, line, and circle drawing; clipping; scrolling and panning; windowing; downloading fonts; and manipulating color. The routines illustrate principles taught in the book.

The selected routines are purposefully simple. This book is not the appropriate place to include multipage routines that perform complicated graphics functions. Each routine implements a specific function. The programmer can connect these routines to build more complicated functions. However, the line-drawing routine is a bit complicated because of its optimization. Line drawing is so important in the graphics environment that a very high speed implementation was selected. In addition, this optimization provides the programmer with several tricks that can be used to achieve high-speed graphics.

The degree of specialization for each routine depends upon the application. Routines that are too general can complicate the code and slow down the graphics process. Routines that are too specific also cause complications because the programmer must select from a large number of similar routines.

Some of the routines presented in Chapter 12 can handle a wide variety of applications. For example, the window routines can operate in any alphanumeric or graphics display mode. On the other hand, other routines are very specific. The line-drawing routine calls one of five specialized routines to actually draw the line.

Decisions regarding the condition of the adapter at the completion of each routine are critical to effective programming. For example, a particular routine may require several registers to set up. Modification of these registers will likely leave the adapter in an unpredictable state if the registers are not reset to their default values. It can be very time-consuming to set up these registers at the start of a routine and then reset them at the end of the routine. If a routine is called repetitively, with no other use being made of these registers, a great deal of time is wasted. Therefore, it is advantageous to set up the registers before the routine, call the routine repetitively, and then reset the registers. However, this leaves the adapter in an unpredictable state until the process is completed. The programmer must be aware of this condition and not interrupt the process before the registers are restored to their default values. Herein lies the tradeoff; performance versus programming complexity. Each application dictates the best solution to this problem.

1.8   COMPILERS AND ASSEMBLERS

The routines included in this book are written specifically for the Microsoft C compiler, version 4.0 or later; assembler, version 5.1 or later; and linker, version 3.0 or above. These C routines should be readily transportable to most C compilers. Assembly language programs are typically not as transportable as C programs, between different assemblers. Users of other assemblers may need to modify the assembly language code.

All program examples assume the Microsoft C and assembly language conventions for the large-model compiler. The assembler directives and references to parameters from within the assembly language programs may need to be altered if other compiler models are used.

Chapter 2

The Features of the EGA and VGA

2.1 EGA/VGA FEATURES

The EGA and VGA are implemented in Very Large Scale Integrated (VLSI) circuits. The EGA and VGA integrated circuits are used on several PC compatible graphics cards. These cards use low-cost, high-speed, high-density memory, and are inexpensive, compact, and easy to maintain. Hardware manufacturers have incorporated the EGA/VGA standard into commercially available graphics cards. In addition, several computers, including the IBM Personal System/2 computer family, incorporate the VGA on the PC motherboard.

The EGA/VGA standard is perhaps the single most important factor contributing to the success of these graphics boards. This standard has allowed software houses to develop programs that can reach a wide audience. The EGA and VGA boards include their own BIOS. The BIOS is a major factor contributing to compatibility. The routines resident in the BIOS make up for any subtle differences in the hardware implementations. Nearly all of the standard PC software applications are compatible with the EGA/VGA, including word processors, data base managers, spreadsheets, and utilities. Graphics programs including business graphics, computer-assisted design, desktop publishing, and illustration software have adopted the EGA as the color standard.

It is important to recognize that though the EGA/VGA standard is well-defined, the standard acts only as a minimum. Many EGA/VGA-compatible cards now improve upon the standard with better resolution, wider color selection, more memory planes, special character fonts, 132-character-wide screen formats, on-board arithmetic processors, and hardware zoom features. These additional features have unfortunately not been regulated by IBM or any standard; thus, drivers are necessary to incorporate these features into the above-mentioned software applications. For people that use several software packages, this can be a real nuisance because not every board has a driver for every software package. In addition, sometimes the driver for one package cannot reside in memory at the same time as a driver for a second package.

8

The abundant and flexible graphics features of the EGA/VGA provide the programmer with a powerful graphics tool. The EGA/VGA can be configured into one of several alphanumeric or graphics modes and can drive monochrome monitors, low- and high-resolution digital color monitors, and some EGAs and all VGAs can drive analog monitors.

This chapter includes descriptive information about the MDA/Hercules and CGA graphics adapters. These preceded the EGA/VGA. Many of the features on the EGA/VGA allow downward compatibility with these graphics adapters. Summary information is also provided on the MCGA, Professional Graphics Adapter (PGA), and 8514/A graphics adapters.

2.1.1 Read and Write Modes

A variety of read and write modes are implemented in the display processor. These modes augment the host processor, allowing many operations to occur within the EGA/VGA graphics processor, including display reads and writes of words that are 32 bits wide, as opposed to the standard 8-bit operation. This speeds many graphics applications by a factor of four. Other write modes allow logical operations to be performed with no host processor calculation. One read mode provides a color comparison. This compares a 4-bit color to the color of 8 neighboring pixels, all in one PC read instruction. Once the many hidden and important features of the EGA are understood, new doors open to the graphics programmer.

2.1.2 Display Memory

The programmer can read or write to display memory without having to wait for the horizontal or vertical retrace periods. This speeds up the graphics process significantly compared to that provided by other display adapters.

Memory is organized in a straightforward manner. Once the addressing is understood, the programmer can readily draw lines and shapes directly onto the screen, without relying on the BIOS calls.

The memory is mapped directly into the PC memory address space, allowing the programmer to utilize the PC assembly language *move* or *move string* instructions for rapid data transfers of data between host memory and display memory or between display memory and display memory. However, multiple wait states are common.

The display memory is mapped into the host address space at locations reserved for graphics memory. An EGA configured in a monochrome mode can coexist with a CGA. Similarly, an EGA configured in a color mode can coexist with an MDA.

The display memory is interfaced to the host processor through an 8-bit data bus, regardless of the width of the host data bus.

The display memory consists of up to 256 Kbytes of memory. It can be organized into a variety of resolutions depending on the display mode. It is

TABLE 2.1 Character Attributes

Mode	Attribute
Mono	Normal, Intensified, Reversed, Blinking, Underlined
Color	16 foreground, 16 background colors
Color	16 foreground, 8 background, blinking
Color	8 foreground, 8 background, 512 characters, blinking

possible to configure the display memory into several low-resolution pages or one high-resolution page.

The display memory is organized using a packed format or a bit-plane format, depending on the active display mode.

A 32-bit data bus is present in the EGA/VGA. The host can initiate a 32-bit host-to-memory data transfer in a single instruction. However, not all 32 bits can be unique. A data transfer that moves data from display memory to display memory can move 32 unique bits of data in a single instruction. This can provide up to a four-to-one increase in speed over the 8-bit data transfers.

2.1.3 Alphanumeric Modes

The display memory is organized so that it is compatible with the MDA and the CGA. This provides complete alphanumeric downward compatibility.

Each character is represented in display memory by two bytes. The ASCII character code describes which character is to be displayed, and the color of the character is determined by the character attributes. Transferring alphanumerics on the screen is very fast, because each character can be represented in the display memory by only two bytes.

In host memory, character and attribute bytes are stored in sequential memory locations. A special addressing mode is available in the EGA/VGA to cause the character and attribute to appear to be in sequential locations within the display memory. This allows the programmer to use the *move string* instruction for rapid alphanumeric data transfers.

Characters can be displayed using monochrome or color attributes. Typical attributes are listed in Table 2.1.

Up to eight pages of alphanumeric text can be stored in display memory at a time, depending on the amount of display memory installed.

Several display resolutions are possible in the alphanumerics modes. The default resolutions and characters sizes are listed in Table 2.2.

It is possible to define new character resolutions within the standard display modes by using the 8 by 8 character set. A few examples based on a color display mode are listed in Table 2.3.

TABLE 2.2 Default Alphanumeric Mode Resolutions

Mode	Adapter	Resolution (Characters)	Resolution (Pixels)	Characters (Pixels)
Color	EGA/VGA	40 by 25	320 by 200	8 by 8
Color	EGA/VGA	40 by 25	320 by 350	8 by 14
Color	VGA	40 by 25	360 by 400	9 by 16
Color	EGA/VGA	80 by 25	640 by 200	8 by 8
Color	EGA/VGA	80 by 25	640 by 350	8 by 14
Color	VGA	80 by 25	720 by 400	9 by 16
Mono	EGA/VGA	80 by 25	720 by 350	9 by 14
Mono	VGA	80 by 25	720 by 400	9 by 16

TABLE 2.3 Nonstandard Alphanumeric Mode Resolutions

Mode	Adapter	Resolution (Characters)	Resolution (Pixels)	Characters (Pixels)
Color	EGA/VGA	80 by 25	640 by 200	8 by 8
Color	EGA/VGA	80 by 43	640 by 350	8 by 8
Color	VGA	80 by 50	640 by 400	8 by 8

Character sets reside in display memory. Up to four character sets may reside simultaneously in the EGA, and eight can reside in the VGA.

2.1.4 Graphics Modes

The display memory is organized so that certain modes provide compatibility with the display memory of the CGA. This provides CGA graphics downward compatibility.

The monochrome modes utilize either two bits per pixel or one bit per pixel. When the program is emulating the Hercules, two bits per pixel are used for the various monochrome attributes. Other modes, called two-color modes, can also be thought of as monochrome modes because they can display two colors. The two colors do not need to be black and white.

The color modes utilize two, four, or eight bits per pixel. The "two bits per pixel" mode emulates the CGA, displaying up to four simultaneous colors per image. The "four bits per pixel" mode allows 16 simultaneous colors, and the "eight bits per pixel" mode allows 256 simultaneous colors.

There are several configurations of the display memory, depending on the active display mode. The standard resolutions are listed in Table 2.4.

TABLE 2.4 Standard Graphics Resolutions

Mode	Adapter	Resolution (Pixels)	Number of Colors	Typical Characters (Pixels)
Mono	EGA/VGA	640 by 200	2	8 by 8
Mono	EGA/VGA	640 by 350	4	8 by 14
Mono	VGA	640 by 480	2	8 by 16
Color	VGA	320 by 200	256	8 by 8
Color	EGA/VGA	640 by 200	16	8 by 8
Color	EGA/VGA	640 by 350	16	8 by 8
Color	VGA	640 by 480	16	8 by 16
Color	EGA/VGA	320 by 200	16	8 by 8

Character sets reside in host memory space, either in BIOS ROM or in RAM memory.

2.1.5 Downloadable Character Sets

Each display mode has an assigned default character set. The default character sets reside in the BIOS ROM.

The EGA/VGA can utilize user-defined downloadable character sets. Any style of character can be used. The character set can be up to 256 characters long. Each character can be up to 9 pixels wide and up to 32 scan lines high.

The EGA BIOS ROM contains three character sets with sizes of 8 by 8, 8 by 14, and 9 by 14 pixels. The 9-by-14 font is supplemental. It contains only the characters that differ in shape from the 8-by-14 character set.

The VGA BIOS ROM contains five character sets with sizes of 8 by 8, 8 by 14, 9 by 14, 8 by 16, and 9 by 16 pixels. The 9-by-14 and 9-by-16 fonts are supplemental. They contain only the characters that differ in shape from the 8-by-14 and 8-by-16 character sets.

Up to four character sets, each 256 characters long, can be resident simultaneously in the EGA display memory. Any two of these can be made active, providing the programmer with a character set that is 512 characters long.

Up to eight character sets, each 256 characters long, can be resident simultaneously in the VGA display memory. Any two of these can be made active, providing the programmer with a character set that is 512 characters long.

2.1.6 Control Registers

Certainly the most complicated aspect of the EGA/VGA is understanding the control registers. The registers are divided into five groups (see Table 2.5).

TABLE 2.5 EGA/VGA Register Groups

Number of Registers	Group Name
4	General registers
5	Sequencer registers
28	CRT controller registers
9	Graphics controller registers
22	Attribute controller
5	Color registers

Each register is one byte wide. Several of the registers are subdivided into fields. Often, individual bits within a register control entirely different functions. Some functions require fields that reside in more than one register.

The registers are accessed through the host I/O port address space. The I/O address of a subset of the registers changes depending on the configuration. If the EGA/VGA is in a monochrome mode, this subset is mapped into the addresses for the MDA. Similarly, if the EGA/VGA is in a color mode, this subset is mapped into the addresses for the CGA.

The register groups, as listed in Table 2.5, are each represented in the host I/O port space by two registers. The EGA/VGA registers are indexed by an addressing scheme through an index or address register and a data register.

On the EGA, the great majority of registers are write-only. This restricts the ability of the programmer to interrogate the display adapter. On the VGA, all but one register can be read by the host. The exception is the attribute control flip/flop.

2.1.7 Display Modes

The EGA/VGA can be configured in a variety of standardized display formats. These formats control the configuration of the display memory, the resolution of the display, the number of bits per pixel, the default character font, and the starting address of display memory.

All display modes are classified into alphanumeric or graphics modes. The graphics modes are also called *all-points-addressable*. There are important distinctions between these two types of modes.

The programmer can design new modes by manipulating the registers directly. However, this is not advised because of the complexity of the manipulations required to change a mode. A mistake could damage the monitor or the display adapter.

The Set Mode BIOS call changes the display mode simply and effectively.

Alphanumeric display modes are present that emulate the operation of the MDA monochrome system and the CGA color system.

2.1.8   EGA/VGA BIOS

The EGA/VGA BIOS is contained in ROM memory and present in all EGA/VGA implementations. Several alphanumeric and graphics functions can be performed through the BIOS calls.

The BIOS calls are invoked through assembly language calls. In some cases, these can be invoked directly from C routines.

The BIOS calls are organized into several classifications, as listed in Table 2.6.

Perhaps the most important aspect of the EGA/VGA is almost totally ignored. Few BIOS calls are provided to read and write data to the display memory. The calls available are restricted to those for reading and writing a pixel.

2.2   GRAPHICS READ AND WRITE MODES

Four write modes are available to the programmer. These can be used to improve the speed performance of the write operations. In addition, two read modes are available. One reads data directly from display memory, and the second reads the result of a comparison.

2.2.1   Write Mode 0

The programmer can write directly to the display memory through an 8-bit data bus.

The byte written by the host can be rotated any number of bits before being written to the display memory. This is useful for lining up bits in the byte with pixel locations.

The byte written by the host can be rotated and masked so that only specified bits in the byte affect the display memory. Up to eight pixels can occupy a single byte. This masking is useful when only a subset of the bits within a byte is to be modified. This operation requires a read/modify/write sequence. A read operation automatically reads all four display planes at the desired address into a 32-bit internal register. This register is used as one of the operands in the read/modify/write operations.

The byte written by the host can perform logical operations on the data that is resident in the display memory at the addressed byte. The logical operations include replacing, ANDing, ORing, and XORing. These operations require a read/modify/write sequence. A read operation automatically reads all four display planes at the desired address into a 32-bit internal register. This register is used as one of the operands in the read/modify/write operations.

Data can be written to multiple display memory bit planes simultaneously by using the Set/Reset and Enable Set/Reset Register. As many as four bit planes can be modified in a single operation. It is possible to write to eight neighboring horizontal pixels in all four bit planes in a single *move* instruction. This is effectively a 32-bit write operation, although only four bits are unique.

TABLE 2.6 EGA/VGA BIOS Calls

Control:

Card	Call
EGA/VGA	Mode Set
EGA/VGA	Select Active Display Page
EGA/VGA	Select Alternate Print Screen Routine
VGA	Video Enable/Disable
VGA	Display Switch
VGA	Video Screen On/Off

Return State:

Card	Call
EGA/VGA	Return Current Video State
EGA/VGA	Return Video Information
VGA	Read/Write Display Combination Code
VGA	Return Functionality/State Information
VGA	Save/Restore Video State

Interactive:

Card	Call
EGA/VGA	Set Cursor Type
EGA/VGA	Set Cursor Position
EGA/VGA	Read Cursor Position
EGA	Read Light Pen Position
VGA	Cursor Emulation

Alphanumerics:

Card	Call
EGA/VGA	Scroll Active Page Up
EGA/VGA	Scroll Active Page Down
EGA/VGA	Read Character/Attribute
EGA/VGA	Write Character/Attribute
EGA/VGA	Write Character Only
EGA/VGA	Write Teletypewriter to Active Page
VGA	Select Scan Lines for Alphanumeric Modes
EGA/VGA	Write String

Graphics:

Card	Call
EGA/VGA	Write Dot
EGA/VGA	Read Dot

TABLE 2.6 *(cont.)*

Palette:

Card	Call
EGA/VGA	Set Color Palette
EGA/VGA	Set Individual Palette Register
EGA/VGA	Set Overscan Register
EGA/VGA	Set All Palette Registers and Overscan
EGA/VGA	Toggle Intensity/Blinking Bit
VGA	Read Individual Palette Register
VGA	Read Overscan Register
VGA	Read all Palette Registers and Overscan
VGA	Default Palette Loading During Mode Set

Color Registers:

Card	Call
VGA	Set Individual Color Register
VGA	Set Block of Color Registers
VGA	Select Color Page
VGA	Read Individual Color Registers
VGA	Read Block of Color Registers
VGA	Read Current Color Page Number
VGA	Sum Color Values to Gray Scale
VGA	Default Palette Loading During Mode Set
VGA	Summing to Gray Scales

Character Generator:

Card	Call
EGA/VGA	User Alpha Load with Reset
EGA/VGA	ROM Monochrome Set with Reset
EGA/VGA	ROM 8x8 Character Set Load with Reset
EGA/VGA	Set Block Specifier with Reset
VGA	ROM 8x16 Character Set Load with Reset
EGA/VGA	User Alpha Load
EGA/VGA	ROM Monochrome Set
EGA/VGA	ROM 8x8 Character Set Load
VGA	ROM 8x16 Character Set Load
EGA/VGA	User Graphics Characters INT 1FH (8x8)
EGA/VGA	User Graphics Characters
EGA/VGA	Graphics Mode ROM 8x14 Character Set Load
EGA/VGA	Graphics Mode ROM 8x8 Character Set Load
EGA/VGA	Graphics Mode ROM 8x16 Character Set Load
EGA/VGA	Return Character Generator Information

2.2.2 Write Mode 1

All four display planes can be modified with the 32 bits of data in the EGA/ VGA internal 32-bit latch in a single *move* instruction. The 32-bit internal latch is loaded by a host-generated read operation. This mode provides very fast movement of data within the display memory. The display memory often contains storage that is not part of the active display. Data can be moved into and out of the active display region rapidly using this 32-bit write operation.

2.2.3 Write Mode 2

All four display planes can be modified with four bits of data. Each of the four display planes is written to with eight replicated bits. The byte moved from the host to display memory contains four significant bits, bits 0 to 3. Bit 0 is replicated eight times into bit plane 0, and bit 1 is replicated eight times into bit plane 1. The same holds for bits 2 and 3 into bit planes 2 and 3 respectively. This procedure is used in conjunction with the Bit Mask Register to modify selected bits within a byte without having to rotate the byte. It can also be effective for writing a block of eight identical values to the display.

2.2.4 Write Mode 3

This write mode is available on the VGA only and it is a bit complicated. Data is written to the display memory from the Set/Reset Register. Each bit in the Set/Reset Register, bits 0 to 3, is replicated eight times and written to the appropriate bit plane (Bit Planes 0 to 3). These bits are written through a bit mask. The bit mask is a logical AND of the byte written by the host after rotation and the value in the Bit Mask Register. This mode is effective for writing patterns of data to all four display planes when all of the pixels are the same color.

2.2.5 Read Mode 0

Read mode 0 reads a byte of data from the display memory. Only one bit plane can be active at a time. A read operation, while read mode 0 is in effect, will return the data in the active bit plane. If each pixel is represented by one bit in each bit plane, a read operation returns a bit from eight neighboring pixels.

2.2.6 Read Mode 1

Read mode 1 returns the result of a comparison. A four-bit value can be written into the Color Compare Register. Any or all of the four bit planes can be active in the comparison depending on the value of the Color No Care Register. All active planes are used in a process that compares the value in the addressed pixels of display memory with the value in the Color Compare Register. The byte returned to the host contains the result of eight comparisons, one comparison for each of the eight neighboring horizontal pixels represented in the byte.

2.3   EGA AND VGA RESOLUTION

Two issues that are always important in computer graphics are the amount of spatial resolution and the color resolution. The color resolution includes the total number of possible colors and the number of colors that can be displayed simultaneously.

2.3.1   Spatial Resolution

The resolution of the EGA/VGA in the low-resolution modes is 320 by 200 pixels. In the higher-resolution modes, the EGA/VGA features 640 by 350 pixels, and the VGA provides additional high-resolution modes of 640 by 480 pixels. These resolutions are ideal for a wide variety of color graphics applications, including many scientific and business graphics applications. The spatial resolving power of the human eye at normal screen viewing distances goes far beyond the 640-by-480 resolution of the EGA. In cases involving diagonal lines and curves, the eye can detect jagged lines at resolutions approaching 4,000 by 4,000 on a normal-size monitor. Thus, resolutions fifty times greater than the EGA/VGA's highest resolution could still be considered unsatisfactory. Laser printers can achieve resolutions up to 600 by 600 per inch. To match this resolution, if a normal viewing area of a monitor is 10 inches by 8 inches, the total screen resolution would need to be 6,000 by 4,800. Photosetting equipment can achieve over 1,000 by 1,000 per inch. To match this resolution, a monitor would require a resolution of 10,000 by 8,000.

The question arises: "How much resolution is enough?" The tradeoffs involved in adding resolution are not entirely based on cost. Higher-resolution images involve more processing time and greater storage requirements per image. If cost and processing speed were not issues, the answer clearly would be: "The higher the resolution, the better." As it is, cost and speed are big issues. The cost of high-resolution graphics adapters is easily surpassed by the cost of a compatible high-speed monitor. Each user must select the proper resolution for the application. The resolution of four popular display adapters is illustrated in Figure 2.1.

For business graphics, in which pie charts, bar charts, scatter plots, and simple two- and three-dimensional graphs represent the normal graphics employed, the EGA resolutions are adequate. This may be insufficient, however, if the business graphics are to be projected onto a screen directly from the monitor or if the monitor is to be photographed and put onto a slide. Often special slide-making software and hardware are utilized to create high-resolution slides, and the EGA is used to preview the slides. This is often the case in desktop publishing. The EGA/VGA resolutions are adequate to preview a page in a coarse mode or to view a portion of a page in nearly full resolution. Many

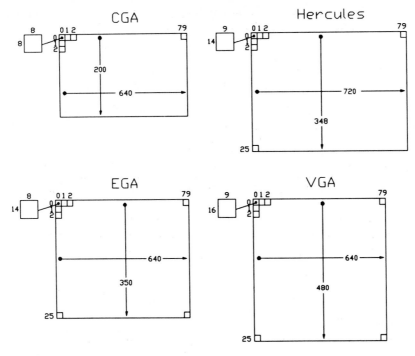

FIGURE 2.1   Resolution of Four Display Adapters

frequent desktop publishing users are purchasing WYSIWYG monitors. This acronym stands for "what you see is what you get"; these monitors generally represent a full page.

In computer-assisted design (CAD), high-resolution images are required. For some of the three-dimensional modeling packages, resolutions greater than the EGA are almost mandatory. However, the EGA/VGA performs admirably in most CAD applications. Zooming and panning techniques can be used to view the images in high resolutions. The speed at which graphics images can be drawn is significant when using panning and zooming because the image is redrawn frequently. In many packages, the resolution of the image is dictated by the resolution of the output device. Thus, supposing the hardcopy device is 2400 by 3150 per image, the image will be drawn to that resolution and a scaled-down version will be drawn on the display. This is often the case with two- and three-dimensional wire drawings; mechanical, electrical, and architectural schematic drawings; and printed circuit layout packages.

The graphic artist using one of the many painting and illustration packages available will usually find the EGA resolution sufficient for illustrations. Like the CAD packages, painting and illustration packages allow the user to zoom

TABLE 2.7 Number of Simultaneous Colors

Bits/Pixel	Number of Colors
1	2
2	4
4	16
8	256

and pan to view high-resolution portions of the screen. In fact, portions of the image can be blown up to resolutions of greater than one pixel per dot.

Scientific graphics software is similar to the software mentioned above. Although a higher resolution could represent more information on a single screen, zooming will usually adequately display the results. If the software package is flexible enough, the resolution of the EGA should be sufficient for most scientific applications.

2.3.2 Color Resolution

Several display modes in the EGA/VGA allow the display of 16 simultaneous colors. These 16 colors can be selected from a palette of 64 possible colors in the EGA and 256K colors in the VGA. One mode on the VGA allows 256 simultaneous colors from a palette of 256 Kcolors. (The term *Kcolors* is similar to *Kbytes* in that it actually represents a power of two. Thus, 256 Kcolors actually means 262,144 colors, just as 256 Kbytes means 262,144 bytes.)

The number of simultaneous colors is related to the number of bits associated with each pixel in the display memory. The more colors, the more bits. Table 2.7 lists the number of colors according to the number of bits per pixel.

The number of bits per pixel is always a power of two in the EGA/VGA, so that an integer number of pixels will fit into a single byte. The display memory is organized as bytes. In order to utilize memory fully, it is advantageous to pack the pixels evenly into the bytes.

The resolution of the display, in conjunction with the number of bits per pixel determine the total amount of display memory necessary. Table 2.8 lists some common configurations.

The number of bits per pixel dictates the number of simultaneous colors. These bits address a register within the color palette in the EGA or the Color Registers in the VGA. The register accessed by the display memory bits associated with a pixel determines the color output to the monitor. The wider the word in the Palette or Color Register, the more colors that are possible. Each of these registers is segmented into three parts. One part is assigned to represent the intensity of one of the three primary colors: red, green, or blue.

TABLE 2.8   Amount of Display Memory

Resolution	Bits/Pixel	Amount of Memory (Bytes)
320 by 200	1	8,000 bytes
320 by 200	2	16,000 bytes
320 by 200	8	64,000 bytes
640 by 200	2	32,000 bytes
640 by 350	1	28,000 bytes
640 by 350	2	56,000 bytes
640 by 350	4	112,000 bytes
640 by 480	1	38,400 bytes
640 by 480	4	153,600 bytes

The EGA Palette Registers are 6 bits wide; therefore, two bits are assigned to each color. This provides a selection of 64 colors. The VGA Color Registers are 18 bits wide; therefore, six bits are assigned to each color. This provides a selection of 256 Kcolors.

A number of techniques can be used to create more than 16 simultaneous colors. One technique is synchronous loading of the color lookup table. If the color table is modified at some point in the display refresh, a pixel with a value of six at one location of the display would not necessarily have the same color as another pixel with a value of 6 located at a different point of the display. This assumes that the color table was changed somewhere between the refreshing of the first and the second pixels. The easiest place to segment the display would be into horizontal sections. Each section would be separated by horizontal scan lines. The display is updated by counting through the display memory from the top to the bottom. In the 350-line configuration, there are 350 horizontal sync pulses corresponding to displayed lines per frame update. The status of the horizontal refresh can be monitored and the color table can be updated synchronous to the horizontal sync pulse. This would create horizontal windows across the screen, and each window could have its own set of 16 colors. However, the amount of time available during a horizontal retrace period is typically only a few microseconds.

Another technique that can effectively increase the number of simultaneous colors is *dithering*. Suppose a pattern of blue is interspersed with a random pattern of red dots. This would give the subjective effect of a color somewhere between red and blue. This technique is quite effective over large surfaces but falls apart as the area of color decreases. This technique creates more colors at the expense of resolution.

Many of the questions that exist for resolution also exist for color. The answer once again is application-specific. Having sixteen simultaneous colors is sufficient for most business graphics applications. Bar charts, pie charts, and line graphs of all kinds can usually be drawn effectively in fewer than sixteen colors.

Similarly, CAD and desktop publishing users are usually satisfied with sixteen simultaneous colors. However, these users often desire more than four planes of memory. It is often convenient to overlay drawings on separate planes during the construction of a drawing so that any plane can be modified independently. Most CAD packages maintain independent planes by utilizing host memory or disk storage. This often adds significantly to the processing time.

The output from CAD packages often is directed to color pen plotters; thus, the color on the monitor can be directly represented on the hardcopy. The output from desktop publishing packages, on the other hand, is primarily black and white. Color is often used to differentiate special formatting information. It is also used to differentiate areas of the screen that contain different elements such as messages, text, images, instructions, menus, and overlays.

Surface-shading CAD packages provide effective displays, turning line drawings into realistic representations. In order to achieve shading, subtle changes in color intensity are required. Broadcast standards require digital systems to represent color with 256 intensities per color.

Illustrators may or may not be satisfied with a limited number of colors. The number of colors required is usually directly related to the form the hardcopy output will take.

Scientists often require more than 16 colors. Being able to represent data with monotonic gray scale or color scale is very important to many scientists.

2.4 CONNECTORS AND SWITCHES

Several hardware switches and connectors on the motherboard and EGA display board are important for the programmer to understand. The switches include the motherboard configuration switches, the monitor-type switches, and special-purpose switches. Switches are also present on the monitors, which may be confusing to the user. The connectors include the monitor output connector, the mysterious video input and output connectors, the lightpen connector, and the feature connector. Specialized EGA boards also may have additional connectors such as a mouse connector.

In addition to the variety of hardware switches, AT-type computers will also require software set-up.

2.4.1 EGA Video Output Connector

The EGA uses a 9-pin D-Shell connector to interface with the monitor. The digital signals on this video output connector are meant to drive a digital monitor. The digital outputs are also called *direct drive outputs*. Through this connector, the EGA can interface to a monochrome display, an RGBI color monitor, or an enhanced color monitor. The outputs of this connector are listed, depending on the type of monitor installed, in Tables 2.9 to 2.11.

TABLE 2.9   EGA Output Connector: Monochrome Monitor

Pin	Signal Name
1	Ground
6	Intensity
7	Video
8	Horizontal Retrace
9	Vertical Retrace

TABLE 2.10   EGA Output Connector: RGBI Color Monitor

Pin	Signal Name
1	Ground
3	Red
4	Green
5	Blue
6	Intensity
8	Horizontal Retrace
9	Vertical Retrace

TABLE 2.11   EGA Output Connector: Enhanced Monitor

Pin	Signal Name
1	Ground
2	Secondary Red/Ground
3	Primary Red
4	Primary Green
5	Primary Blue
6	Secondary Green
7	Secondary Blue
8	Horizontal Retrace
9	Vertical Retrace

TABLE 2.12   Light Pen Connector

Pin	Signal
1	Light Pen Signal
3	Light Pen Switch
4	Ground
5	+ 5 volts
6	+ 12 Volts

2.4.2   EGA Light Pen Connector

The EGA is equipped with a light pen interface. The connector configuration is shown in Table 2.12.

2.4.3   EGA Feature Connector

The EGA has a 32-pin feature connector that can be used to interface with external devices. The signals on this connector are listed in Table 2.13.

2.4.4   VGA Video Output Connector

The VGA uses a 15-pin D-Shell Connector to interface with a monitor. The analog and digital signals on this connector are meant to drive an analog color or an analog monochrome monitor. The signals on this connector are listed in Table 2.14 for a monochrome monitor and in Table 2.15 for a color monitor. The monitor ID Bits 0–2 are found on pins 11, 12 and 4 respectively.

TABLE 2.13 EGA Feature Connector

Pin	Signal
1	Ground
2	-12 volts
3	+12 volts
4	J1 Auxiliary Jack 1
5	J2 Auxiliary Jack 2
6	Green Intensified Out
7	Red Intensified Out
8	Blue Intensified Out
9	Attribute Shift Load
10	Blue Out
11	Green Out
12	Green Input
13	Red Intensified
14	Blue Input
15	Red Input
16	Red Out
17	Feat1 Digital Input: Input Status #0 Register
18	Composite Horizontal and Vertical Blanking
19	Feat0 Digital Input: Input Status #0 Register
20	FC1 Digital Output: Feature Control Register
21	FC0 Digital Output: Feature Control Register
22	Green Intensified/Intensified
23	Blue Intensified/Video
24	Horizontal Sync Input
25	Vertical Sync Input
26	14 Mhz Clock Output
27	Disable Internal Drivers: Misc. Output Register
28	External Dot Clock Output
29	Vertical Sync Output
30	Horizontal Sync Output
31	Ground
32	+5 Volts

TABLE 2.14 VGA Output Connector: Enhanced Monochrome

Pin	Signal Name
2	Analog Monochrome
7	Analog Monochrome Return
10	Digital Ground
12	Digital Ground
13	Horizontal Sync
14	Vertical Sync

TABLE 2.15 VGA Output Connector: Enhanced Color

Pin	Signal Name
1	Analog Red
2	Analog Green
3	Analog Blue
6	Analog Red Return
7	Analog Green Return
8	Analog Blue Return
10	Digital Ground
13	Horizontal Sync
14	Vertical Sync

2.4.5 VGA Micro Channel Connector

The VGA is equipped with a Micro Channel. Also present is an Auxiliary Video Extension connector, which extends the Micro Channel for video adapter cards. The signals on this connector are listed in Table 2.16.

2.5 THE HERCULES MONOCHROME GRAPHICS CARD

The Hercules adapter is based on the Motorola MC6845 Graphics Controller Chip. The Hercules corporation quickly dominated the field of monochrome graphics and established the Hercules standard. The Hercules board provides a standard 80-character-by-25-row alphanumeric display and a relatively high resolution in the graphics mode of 720 horizontal by 348 vertical pixels. The outputs drive a digital monochrome monitor with sync frequencies of 50 Hz vertical and 18.4 kHz horizontal.

The Hercules board was the third display format standardized for the PC family of computers, following the Monochrome Display Adapter (MDA) and Color Graphics Adapter (CGA).

The Hercules adapter allows the programmer to position the cursor and subsequent characters anywhere on the screen. A maximum of 80 characters by 25 lines can be displayed. The columns are numbered from 0 on the far left column to 79 on the far right column of the screen. The rows are numbered from 0 on the top row to 23 on the bottom row. This requires a display buffer of 4,000 bytes, because each character is two bytes. A character is specified by a one-byte character code and a one-byte attribute code. The size of one character is 7 by 9 dots in a font block of 9 by 14 dots. The additional space in the font block is used for intercharacter spacing. A ROM character generator provides 256 simultaneous characters, including the 96 ASCII graphic characters and 16 word processor symbols. The attribute code specifies the relationship between foreground and background, underline, blink, and intensity level.

TABLE 2.16 Auxiliary Video Extension to Micro Channel

Pin	Signal
A-V1	Video Bus Output Enable
A-V2	Data Bus 7
A-V4	DAC Clock
A-V5	Enable DAC Clock
A-V6	Data Bus 6
A-V7	Ground
A-V8	Composite Blanking
A-V9	Horizontal Sync
A-V10	Vertical Sync
B-V1	Ground
B-V2	Data Bus 0
B-V3	Data Bus 1
B-V4	Data Bus 2
B-V5	Ground
B-V6	Data Bus 3
B-V7	Data Bus 4
B-V8	Data Bus 5
B-V9	Ground
B-V10	Video Signal Output Enable

2.5.1 Hercules Display Memory

The 4,000 bytes of memory addresses of the display buffer begin with B0000 hex. The characters are organized such that the first character is in the upper left corner of the screen, the second character to its immediate right and so on. The 81st character is directly under the first character on the second character line because there are 80 characters per row. The 2,000th character is displayed in the lower right corner of the screen.

In the alphanumerics mode the text buffer begins at PC memory address B000-B0FFF comprising 4K bytes. A single character is represented by two bytes, one for the character code and one for the attribute byte. To obtain the offset of a character code, use the equation $160 \times \text{Row} + 2 \times \text{Column}$. Remember that the columns are numbered from 0 to 79 starting at the left of the screen, while the rows are numbered from 0 to 24 starting at the top of the screen.

The character codes are contained in even addresses, and the attribute codes are contained in odd addresses. The attribute codes produce the character attributes listed in Table 2.17.

Bit 7 is for blinking or background intensity. If the blinker is off (display mode control port bit 5=0), then B=0 for normal background and B=1 for high-intensity background.

TABLE 2.17 Monochrome Character Attributes

Bit 7 6 5 4 3 2 1 0	Attribute Code
Bit B 0 0 0 I 0 0 0	Blank
B 0 0 0 I 0 0 1	Underline
B 0 0 0 I 1 1 1	Normal Display
B 1 1 1 I 0 0 0	Reverse Video

If the blinker is on (display mode control port bit 5=1), then B=0 for no blinking and B=1 for blinking with a normal-intensity background.

Bit 3 is for the intensity of the foreground; I=0 causes a normal foreground, and I=1 causes a high-intensity foreground.

2.5.2 Hercules Registers

The Input/Output (I/O) addresses occupy PC I/O port memory addresses from 3B0 to 3BF hex. In addition, a printer port is typically included on the display board. The printer port occupies I/O addresses in the range from 3BC to 3BF hex. The CRT control registers are accessed through an index register and a data register. The index register is located at address 3B4 hex and the data register is accessed at address 3B5 hex. This index/data register pair is common to many controllers that have several registers but cannot occupy several port addresses on the PC because of PC constraints. In addition to these two registers, a graphics control port is located at 3B8 hex and a monitor status register is located at port 3BA hex.

The internal registers include 14 registers used to control the display. These registers occupy sixteen-byte locations because two of the registers require sixteen-bit words. Ten of these registers are used for display hardware control. These include the following registers: Horizontal Total, Horizontal Displayed, Horizontal Sync Position, Sync Pulse Width, Vertical Total, Vertical Total Adjust, Vertical Displayed, Vertical Sync Position, Interlace Mode and Skew, and Scan Lines per Character Row. These registers are very similar, although not identical, to registers used in the EGA. The two remaining registers consist of the Cursor Top, Cursor Bottom, Upper Left Corner Memory Address, and Cursor Position Memory Address registers. The programmer can position and define the shape of the cursor using the cursor registers or can define the address of the upper left corner of the display using these two remaining registers. If the upper left address is varied, panning and scrolling of the display can be accomplished, however only 96 extra bytes are available for panning.

The Display Control Register enables the controller through bit 0, enables the display screen through bit 3, and enables the uppermost bit of the attribute code to control blinking through bit 5. The Monitor Status Register provides

TABLE 2.18 Monochrome Output Connector

Pin	Signal
1	Video Ground
2	Synchronization Ground
6	Signal Intensity
7	Video Signal
8	Horizontal Sync Signal
9	Vertical Sync Signal

information regarding the horizontal sync time in bit 0 and the presence of a video signal in bit 3.

2.5.3 Video Output Connector

The video output connector consists of the standard 9-pin connector. The signals carried on these pins are listed in Table 2.18.

This connector is mechanically identical to the connectors used for the CGA and EGA; however, it is not compatible because of the different electrical signals on the pins.

2.6 THE COLOR GRAPHICS ADAPTER

The Color Graphics Adapter (CGA) combines alphanumeric (A/N) modes and all-points-addressable (APA) graphics. The board provides direct video drive outputs capable of driving a color monitor. The monitor runs at either 7 MHz, for the low-resolution mode, or 14 MHz, for the high-resolution mode. Like the monochrome adapter described above, the CGA is based on the 6845 CRT controller.

The CGA's operation in the alphanumeric modes is similar to the monochrome adapter described above. The resolution is 40 or 80 columns by 25 rows. The 40-column low-resolution mode was designed for a low-resolution monitor or home television set. The size of one character is 7 by 7 dots in a font block of 8 by 8 dots. Because of the color processing, the characters can be displayed in one of 16 foreground colors and one of 8 or 16 background colors. Characters may also be blinked on a per-character basis.

2.6.1 CGA Display Memory

In the graphics mode, two resolutions, low and high, are available. Terminology that uses the qualifiers *low, medium,* and *high* is often confusing. One adapter's high resolution may be another's low resolution. In the CGA low-resolution mode, the memory is configured as 320 pixels horizontally by 200 pixels vertically. Each pixel can be drawn in one of four colors. Note that 320 times 200 is 64,000. Thus, for the entire display to fit into the 16 Kbyte memory restriction, each pixel can occupy only one-quarter of a byte or two bits. Thus, one pixel can display up to four different colors. In the high-resolution mode of 640 by 200 pixels, only one color per pixel is allowed because each pixel can occupy only one-eighth of a byte or one bit.

Each byte represents four pixels in the low-resolution mode. These four pixels are horizontal neighbors, with the far left pixel occupying the two leftmost bits in the byte, bits 7 and 6. The next neighboring pixel to the right is in bits 5 and 4, and so on. Note that care must be taken not to disturb the three neighboring pixels when only one pixel's value should be changed. This can be accomplished by "ORing" in ones and "ANDing" in zeros.

Each byte represents eight pixels in the high-resolution mode. These eight pixels are horizontal neighbors, with the leftmost pixel occupying the leftmost bit in the byte, bit 7. The next neighboring pixel to the right is in bit 6, and so on. Care must be taken not to disturb the seven neighboring pixels when only one pixel's value should be changed. Again, this can be accomplished by "ORing" in ones and "ANDing" in zeros.

The board contains 16 Kbytes of storage. This memory is mapped into the PC memory space beginning at B8000 hex. Because the maximum alphanumeric resolution of a screen is 80 columns by 25 rows by 2 bytes per character, one screen takes up 4K of memory. Thus, a board can store up to four pages at maximum alphanumeric resolution. The border can also be selected to be displayed in one of 16 colors. The character set contains the standard ASCII character set, foreign language support, Greek and scientific-notation characters, special characters for games and word processing, and characters for block graphics support.

In the high-resolution alphanumeric mode, the PC processor should access the display buffer only during vertical retrace time when the display is disabled. If this practice is not followed, random speckle will occur during the read or write times.

2.6.2 CGA Color Selection

There are traditionally two color palettes available. These palettes act as lookup tables; they decode a value from display memory into a color. These tables are used in the low-resolution graphics mode. One contains green, red, and brown; the other contains cyan, magenta, and white. This allows a pixel that contains only two bits to produce a color that requires 4 bits.

Color selection occurs in the alphanumeric mode through the attribute byte. The layout of the attribute byte is identical to the monochrome attribute byte, with the foreground and background representing colors. Bits 0–3 represent the foreground color and bits 4–6 represent the background color. The intensity

TABLE 2.19 CGA Color Codes

I R G B	Value	Color
0 0 0 0	0	Black
0 0 0 1	1	Blue
0 0 1 0	2	Green
0 0 1 1	3	Cyan
0 1 0 0	4	Red
0 1 0 1	5	Magenta
0 1 1 0	6	Brown
0 1 1 1	7	White
1 0 0 0	8	Grey
1 0 0 1	9	Blue (intensified)
1 0 1 0	10	Green (intensified)
1 0 1 1	11	Cyan (intensified)
1 1 0 0	12	Red (intensified)
1 1 0 1	13	Magenta (intensified)
1 1 1 0	14	Brown (intensified)
1 1 1 1	15	White (intensified)

bit (I) is in bit 7 and is used to highlight the foreground colors. The least significant bit in each of the foreground and background colors represents blue (B), the next significant bit represents green (G), and the next significant bit represents red (R). Table 2.19 illustrates the foreground and background colors.

2.6.3 CGA Control Registers

The 6845 registers are identical to the 6845 registers of the Hercules card described above. The index register is located at port address 3D4 hex and the data register is located at port address 3D5 hex.

Additional registers on the board include the Mode Control Register at 3D8 hex, the Color Select Register at 3D9 hex, the Status Register at 3DA, the Clear Light Pen Latch at 3DB hex, and the Preset Light Pen Latch at 3DC hex.

The Color Select Register contains color and control fields. The function of these fields varies depending on the active display mode. The Color Select Register fields are listed in Table 2.20.

Table 2.21 lists the functions controlled in the Mode Control Register.

Table 2.22 lists the functions of the Status Register.

The Clear Lightpen Latch clears the bit 1 of the Status Register, thereby resetting the light pen trigger status. Any output to this register causes the clearing of this bit.

TABLE 2.20   Color Select Register

Bit	40 by 25 A/N	320 by 200 APA	640 by 200 APA
0	Blue border	Blue background	Blue foreground
1	Green border	Green background	Green foreground
2	Red border	Red background	Red foreground
3	Bright border	Bright background	Bright foreground
4	Background colors	Alternate intensified colors	
5	No function	Selects Palette	

TABLE 2.21   Mode Control Register

Bit	Value	Function
0	0	40 by 25 alphanumeric mode
0	1	80 by 25 alphanumeric mode
1	0	Alphanumeric mode
1	1	320 by 200 APA mode
2	0	Color mode
2	1	Black and white mode
3	0	Disable video signal
3	1	Enable video signal
4	1	640 by 200 APA mode
5	0	Bit 7 in attribute controls blinking
5	1	Bit 7 in attribute controls background

TABLE 2.22   Status Register

Bit	Value	Function
0	1	Buffer memory may be accessed by the PC
1	1	Light pen trigger has occurred
2	0	Light pen switch is in on position
2	1	Light pen switch is in off position
3	1	Raster is in vertical retrace

TABLE 2.23 CGA Video Output Connector

Pin	Signal
1	Video Ground
2	Synchronization Ground
3	Red Signal
4	Green Signal
5	Blue Signal
6	Signal Intensity
7	Reserved
8	Horizontal Sync Signal
9	Vertical Sync Signal

TABLE 2.24 CGA RF Modulator Connector

Pin	Signal
1	12 volts
3	Composite Video
4	Logic ground

TABLE 2.25 Light Pen Interface Connector

Pin	Signal
1	Light Pen Input
3	Light Pen Switch
4	Chassis Ground
5	5 volts
6	12 volts

2.6.4 CGA Connectors

The video output connector consists of the standard 9-pin connector. The signals carried on these pins are listed in Table 2.23.

The composite video output connector is a standard RCA type phono jack, and it contains a 1.5 volt peak-to-peak amplitude composite video signal. The connector also has signal ground available.

The RF modulator connector contains the signals listed in Table 2.24.

The light pen interface connector contains the signals listed in Table 2.25. The light pen interface is rarely used in the PC environment because of the popularity of the mouse, joystick, and digitizing pad. The EGA includes the light pen interface, but it is not included on the VGA.

2.7 THE MULTICOLOR GRAPHICS ARRAY

The Multicolor Graphics Array (MCGA) and the VGA are the two primary adapters designed for the PS/2 series of personal computers. The MCGA is similar in function to the CGA, and the VGA is similar to the EGA. The MCGA is downwardly compatible to the CGA at the BIOS, control register, and display memory levels. Like the CGA, the MCGA can coexist with a monochrome adapter.

The control registers on the MCGA are identical to the 16 lower control registers of the CGA. These 16 registers control the video timing of the adapter. Although the registers are identical, the values loaded into these registers are different depending on whether a CGA or an MCGA is used. Therefore, programs that access these registers directly and that expect a CGA may disrupt the video performance of the MCGA. This problem can be alleviated by using the protection bit in the Mode Control Register. This protection write protects the first seven CRT controller registers which include the horizontal and vertical timing registers. This is identical to the protection method used with the VGA. The VGA can lock out these registers to protect the adapter and monitor from programs that expect an EGA.

The MCGA provides enhanced performance features that are similar to the VGA. Included are downloadable character sets and additional display modes. These features are programmed on the MCGA, as on the EGA and VGA, through the BIOS calls. The additional display modes include a 640-by-480 display mode capable of displaying two colors and a 320-by-200 display mode capable of displaying 256 simultaneous colors.

The MCGA is equipped with a set of 256 Color Registers that are identical to the VGA Color Registers. These store six bits of resolution for each of the three primary colors, red, green, and blue. This provides a total of 256 Kcolors.

The MCGA, like the VGA, drives either an analog monochrome or an analog RGB monitor.

2.8   THE PROFESSIONAL GRAPHICS ADAPTER

The Professional Graphics Adapter (PGA) is the next step up from the EGA in resolution, speed, depth, performance, and cost. The PGA operates at a graphics resolution of 640 by 480 with 256 simultaneous colors. The video output is analog RGB, providing a wide range of colors. Perhaps the most notable improvement over the EGA/VGA is the use of an on-board processor. This processor is capable of performing high-level graphics functions without relying on the host PC processor (that is, the 8088, 8086, 80286, or 80386). The IBM implementation uses a 6845 graphics controller with an 8088 on-board processor. This selection has been improved upon by several other manufacturers which are using more sophisticated processors such as the Texas Instrument 34010 VLSI circuit.

The color lookup table provides 256 simultaneous colors, and each location in the table is 12 bits deep. These 12 bits correspond to 4 bits of red, green, and blue each. Thus, there are 4,096 possible colors. The alphanumerics section is identical to the above-mentioned display adapters in that there are two bytes assigned to each color, one for the character value and one for the attribute byte. It uses an on-board character generator that produces a character matrix 16 pixels high by 8 pixels wide. Unlike the EGA, the PGA supports no downloadable soft character fonts.

Interfacing to the 6845 and to the other I/O ports on the PGA is similar to the Color Graphics Adapter. This includes the Mode-Select Register and the Status Register.

The on-board processor performs a wide variety of two- and three-dimensional graphics operations including windowing, clipping, viewing transformations, and modeling transformations. Primitives—such as drawing lines, arcs, circles, ellipses, filling enclosed areas, and moving to locations—are also implemented. A wide variety of text commands are also available; these allow control of text size and the placement and orientation of text strings.

These high-level graphics commands can be executed in a single command from the PC processor. Command lists consist of a series of high-level graphics commands, which can also be executed by a single host command.

2.9   THE 8514/A DISPLAY ADAPTER

This adapter is meant to plug into the PS/2 Micro Channel Auxiliary Video Extension Bus. It provides advanced graphics functions that can be used in parallel with the planar VGA. A graphics programming interface is provided, and the programmer is meant to interface with these BIOS type calls rather than programming the adapter directly. Two memory configurations are possible, allowing up to a 1,024-by-768 resolution with either four or eight bits per color. The color palette output is similar to the VGA in that each of the three primary colors has a 6-bit resolution, providing an 18-bit composite color.

Advanced graphics features are present to allow bit-block transfers, line drawing, area fills, pattern generation, color manipulation, and clipping.

Downloadable character sets include character fonts of 12 by 20 or 7 by 15, providing character resolutions of 85 by 38 and 146 by 51 respectively when the display is in a 1,024 by 768 resolution. An 8-by-14 character set is also available for use in the 640-by-480 mode.

Chapter 3

Graphics Hardware and Software

3.1 COMPUTER GRAPHICS HARDWARE

Graphics has always been an effective tool when used to display information. Trends in data that are obscured when displayed in columns of numbers become obvious when displayed in a graphical format. Since the first computers were used to analyze data, computer graphics has been employed to display the results.

In order to use computer graphics on the PC, the computer hardware, the graphics hardware, and the graphics software must be compatible. This chapter describes these three interrelated elements and emphasizes the impact they have on the programmer. Also provided is a detailed discussion of how the performance of the graphics system is affected by the computer hardware. The relationship among various graphics hardware components, including graphics adapters, monitors, and interactive and hard copy devices, is presented. Finally, a cross-section of graphics-related software is provided. These applications include programs for word processing, desktop publishing, charting, illustration, and computer-assisted design. Special attention is given to the hardware/software interface.

The hardware consists of the PC computer, interactive devices, hardcopy devices, the graphics adapter, the video cable, and the monitor. A typical computer system is illustrated in Figure 3.1.

3.1.1 The Computer System

The PC computer may be a PC, PC-XT, PC-AT, PC-386, or PS/2 model. The computer is typically constructed on a motherboard. This motherboard, also called the *planar* in the PS/2 family of computers, contains the microprocessor, memory, BIOS, interface circuitry, miscellaneous hardware, and card slots. The majority of computers require a video card if video output is desired. Some computers anticipate the need for the video hardware and actually include the video circuitry on the motherboard. No additional video card is necessary in these systems.

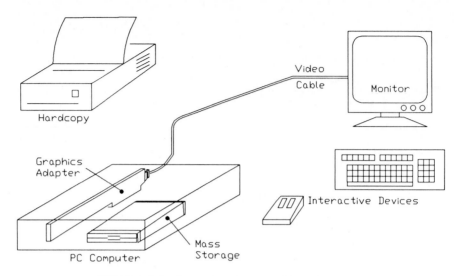

FIGURE 3.1   Computer System with Video Card

The PC graphics standards, including the Hercules, MDA, CGA, EGA, and VGA, have been implemented on the motherboard of several computers. These computers usually can be configured so that an additional or alternative display adapter can be used if desired. The PS/2 computer family (except Model 30) incorporates the VGA onto the motherboard. In the literature, this is referred to as the *planar VGA*. The planar VGA is shown in Figure 3.2.

A second adapter can be interfaced to the planar VGA hardware. Software control allows the user to select which of these video systems are active.

The key hardware features that affect computer graphics, besides the display adapter and monitor, are the microprocessor, coprocessor, the data bus word size, the amount and speed of the memory, and the amount of disk storage.

3.1.2   Microprocessors

There are several classes of computers within the PC family. Each class of computer is based on a different microprocessor. The microprocessor plays a large part in whether the computer is well-suited for a graphics application. Typical microprocessors include the 8088, 8086, 80286, and 80386. These integrated circuits can be further subdivided according to their operating speeds. The speed of the processor often plays a major role in the execution time of a graphics algorithm. Some versions are nearly four times as fast as others. Typical speeds include 4.7, 8, 10, 12, 14, 16, and 20 mHz.

The microprocessors used in the PC each have characteristic features. One of these features is the internal word length. Large amounts of data can be

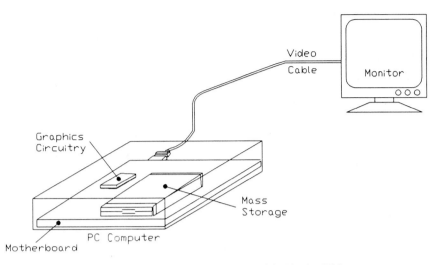

FIGURE 3.2 Computer System with Planar Video

Table 3.1 Microprocessors in the PC Family of Computers

Computer, PC Family	Microprocessor	Coprocessor	Word Width (Internal)	Word Width (External)
PC,PC/XT,PCjr	8088	8087	16	8
Model 30	8086	8087	16	16
PC/AT,PS/2	80286	80287	16	16, 8
PC386,PS/2 Model 80	80386	80387	32	32, 16, 8

handled better on a computer with a wide data bus than on one with a smaller data bus. The multiplexing of data onto a narrow bus is time-consuming because of hardware limitations.

Because of the large amount of data in graphics processing, a large address space is highly advantageous. Although the PC family of computers can address several megabytes of memory, much of this memory must be accessed indirectly through extended or expanded memory.

Graphics algorithms often transfer large data buffers. The word length of the processor dictates the internal width of the data path. The wider the data path, the more data can be transferred in a single operation. The microprocessors currently used in the PC family of computers are listed in Table 3.1.

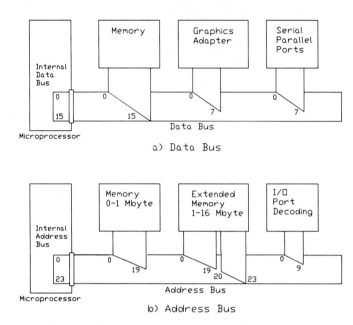

FIGURE 3.3 PC Computer Data and Address Bus

3.1.3 Coprocessors

Graphics algorithms often require sophisticated and repetitive mathematics. Great improvements in the speed of these algorithms can be achieved with the addition of a math coprocessor. Graphics algorithms often require floating-point calculations. These calculations operate orders of magnitude faster when a coprocessor is present and when the software utilizes it. Each class of microprocessor has a coprocessor associated with it, as listed in Table 3.1 above. Like the microprocessors, the coprocessor is available in different speed versions. Typical speeds include 4.7, 8, 10, 12, 14, 16, and 20 mHz.

3.1.4 Data Bus Size

Even though the microprocessor dictates the data bus word size, only a portion of the data bus might be sent to peripherals. This is the case with several of the graphics adapters. The PC sends an 8-bit data bus to several of the card slots. The graphics adapters are designed to utilize this byte-wide data bus but not the 16- or 32-bit data bus. Although the AT-class computers incorporate a 16-bit data bus and the 80386 computers incorporate a 32-bit data bus into their external adapter slots, the graphics adapters still interface to the host through the 8-bit bus. A typical PC data and address bus are illustrated in Figure 3.3.

3.1.5   Memory

Graphics is memory intensive. A single image can easily occupy over a megabyte of memory. The more memory available on the computer the better, because manipulating the images in memory is always faster than manipulating images on disk. The speed of the memory, the processor, and the wait states inserted by the devices dictate how fast the image data can be manipulated. The programs that operate in the computer also reside in this memory, and the speed of the memory dictates how fast these programs can operate. If the memory is slower than the processor, wait states are incorporated into the system. These wait states cause the microprocessor to wait, thereby reducing the processing speed.

3.2   INTERACTIVE DEVICES

In order for the user or programmer to interact with the computer and graphics system, some type of interactive input device is necessary. The keyboard is by far the most common interactive device. A pointing device allows the user to enter data spatially. The mouse is the most popular pointing device. Other devices include the trackball, digitizing pad, light pen, and joystick.

3.2.1   Keyboard

The keyboard is the primary device for operator interaction. It consists of the alphanumeric keys, the control keys, the function keys, and the cursor-control keys. In alphanumerics applications, the keyboard is an adequate tool. However, in graphics applications, the keyboard, a one-dimensional input device, lacks the ability to position items in a two-dimensional space. Characters are typed into the computer via the keyboard in a sequential fashion. Entering characters sequentially into the computer is adequate for text, which is sequential in nature. However, modifying the information once it has been entered requires two-dimensional processing capabilities. The computer text screen and the printed page are both two-dimensional, organized into rows and columns. To be effective, interactive screen processing must take advantage of this two-dimensional format. Typical programs that utilize this two-dimensional format are screen-oriented word processors and spreadsheets. Because the keyboard is the standard input device, special keys are provided to handle some of these two-dimensional positioning tasks.

Spatial positioning keys satisfy some of the two-dimensional processing requirements. These special keys provide a means of positioning a cursor into the two-dimensional page. The cursor indicates the position of a pointer onto the display page. Arrow keys on the keyboard allow the operator to position the cursor up, down, left, or right. "Page up" and "Page down" provide a means of jumping forward or backward through multiple-page documents. The "Home" and "End" keys allow jumping to the top or bottom of a page or a

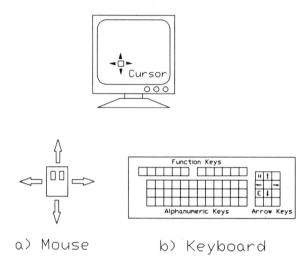

a) Mouse   b) Keyboard

FIGURE 3.4   Keyboard and Mouse Spatial Positioning

document. A set of function keys is also provided for application specific functions. The application software utilizes these keys to speed the operator interaction tasks. These spatially related keys are illustrated in Figure 3.4.

3.2.2   Mouse

A mouse is a pointing device that sends position information to the computer as it is moved on a surface. Internal to the mouse is sensing logic that converts the motion of the mouse into data streams that are input into the computer. This motion can be used to position the cursor on the screen. This provides a simple and understandable form of hand-eye communication for the user. A conflict occurs when the user attempts to use the mouse and the keyboard at the same time. The keyboard is designed for two hands, and the mouse requires one hand. Buttons are provided on the mouse so that some interaction, in addition to the position information, can be initiated from the mouse. The application software can interrogate these buttons and take action based upon their depressions. The spatial orientation of the mouse is illustrated in Figure 3.4.

With the advent of low-cost graphics systems, painting software packages have become popular. These programs provide an interactive way for the user to draw lines, shapes, and text onto the graphics display. The mouse has become the standard input device for these software packages.

There are two basic types of mouse hardware. One type utilizes a ball mounted inside the mouse body and extending out the bottom. The mouse rolls on a surface, and the motion of the ball is translated into codes that are sent to the computer. Lifting the mouse and moving it has no effect on the positioning hardware, because the ball is not rotated. Because this type of mouse relies on a moving part, the mouse is susceptible to inaccuracies.

A second type of mouse, called an *optical mouse*, relies on a flat plate that has accurate horizontal and vertical lines drawn onto its surface. The mouse consists of a light emitting diode (LED) and a photodetector. The LED shines a light onto the surface of the plate. Its reflection is detected by the photodetector, and each horizontal or vertical line that is crossed is counted. Similar to the mechanical mouse, this mouse will not detect when it is picked up and moved to another location on the plate. It is highly accurate, and precise motion control is possible.

Interfacing the mouse with the application software is accomplished through a software driver. A software driver, in a ".com" format, is a memory resident program also called terminate and stay resident. The driver interacts directly with the mouse hardware and with the applications software. The driver is invoked either directly from the application software or through an external event such as a keystroke. Differences in the hardware configurations of the mouse can be compensated for in the driver software. A mouse calling convention exists for the PC. Any mouse and mouse driver that are compatible with this convention can be used interchangeably. This mouse driver can be invoked from a high-level language or from assembly language.

3.2.3 Trackball

Similar to the mouse, the trackball provides a means of inputting position information. The trackball may be thought of as an upside-down mouse. The trackball assembly remains stationary on the table while the ball rotates freely within the assembly. Like that of the mouse, the motion of the trackball is monitored. The trackball is more accurate than the mouse and can rotate around its axis several times without requiring large arm movements. The ball is bigger and allowed to travel through greater excursions. These greater excursions can provide greater accuracy. In addition, the trackball is well-suited to limited desk space. The ball is usually positioned in the palm of the hand, and it can be rotated quickly and accurately. Video games, such as are found in arcades, often rely on trackballs for accurate motion control. The trackball drivers are typically designed to be compatible with the mouse software. Two or three buttons are provided.

One limitation of the trackball occurs when the palm is rotating. The fingers tend to move away from the buttons, and this makes pushing the buttons awkward. If the palm has to move to enable the fingers to reach the buttons, the ball moves and the position is modified.

3.2.4 Joystick

The joystick is an inexpensive, popular pointing device. It is most frequently used for personal computer games. The X and Y position of the stick is monitored and converted into positioning information. Most joysticks interface through a game port. The game port is optional on most PCs and is optionally included on multipurpose cards. The joystick is not popular with most graphics software, because of its lack of sensitivity.

3.2.5   Light Pen

The light pen is a pointing device that provides direct interaction between the hand and the screen. Any of the above-mentioned devices require an indirect translation between motion and screen position. The light pen, on the other hand, points directly at the screen.

The light pen consists of a photodetector inside a pen-like instrument. The light pen is held so that it points into the screen. As the electron beam scans across the screen, it eventually gets to the location of the light pen. The maximum time delay is 1/60th of a second on a noninterlaced and 1/30th of a second on an interlaced display. The light from the phosphor, being excited by the electron beam, is detected by the photodetector. This event triggers hardware on the light pen controller. The position of the electron beam at the time of the trigger determines the position of the light pen. Light pens can be very accurate and are easily manipulated across the screen. Further, the concept of pointing is simple for the user to understand.

A problem exists if the section of the screen to which the light pen is pointing is black. In this case, there will be no detection of the electron beam because no phosphor is excited. Tracking software or hardware can be installed to track the motion of the light pen across dark areas. The hardware or software attempts to anticipate the position of the light pen. A small block of pixels are turned on in the vicinity of the light pen. If the light pen position corresponds to the energized pixels, a trigger will occur. The original data, which was overwritten by the block of pixels, must be restored so that it is not corrupted.

The EGA has a built-in light pen port, including hardware registers and connector. No hardware-tracking ability is built into this interface. The VGA has no provision for a light pen.

3.2.6   Digitizing Pad

Perhaps the most sensitive and accurate of the pointing devices is the digitizing pad. This device uses a pad that can sense the position of a pointing device on its surface. As the pointing device is moved, its absolute position on the pad is monitored. Thus, if the pointing device is picked up and moved to another portion of the pad, its new absolute location will be monitored. These pads vary in size and resolving power. They are more expensive than the previously mentioned pointing devices and take up more desk space. However, their precision and performance are necessary in certain graphics applications.

One advantage of absolute position monitoring is that overlay sheets can be placed on the surface of the pad and used to store interactive menus. Thus, programs with several hundred special commands can reserve space on the overlay for each command. To invoke the command, the user positions the pointing device over the command and clicks one of the buttons on the pointing device. This eliminates the need to type in long commands or to memorize complex and annoying control codes. It also frees the display from drop-down menus.

Another advantage of a digitizing pad pertains to digitizing drawings. A drawing can be placed on the surface of the tablet and the positioning device can digitize points on the drawing. Some pads are transparent, allowing backlighting. This is effective when digitizing transparencies. Another popular application is to project onto the pad via a slide projector or video projector.

The digitizing pad is two dimensional. New techniques have been developed to digitize in three dimensions, and three-dimensional location sensors are available that can be scanned over the surface of objects. Laser beam scanners are highly accurate and can be completely automated. These devices are used in scanning parts for computer assisted design (CAD) or computer assisted manufacturing (CAM). Animators are currently using these devices to add realism to animations.

3.3 GRAPHICS ADAPTERS

Graphics adapters interface the computer to the video monitor. There are several standard graphics adapters used with the PC. The graphics adapters discussed in this book include the Monochrome Display Adapter (MDA), Hercules Graphics Adapter, Color Graphics Adapter (CGA), Enhanced Graphics Adapter (EGA), the Video Graphics Array (VGA), and the Professional Graphics Adapter (PGA). Both the MDA and the Hercules Adapter are monochrome systems, the CGA is a color system and the EGA, VGA and PGA may be either. A limited downward compatibility exists among these adapters. This limited compatibility is based upon the video BIOS calls, the port addresses, and the data addresses. Downward compatibility implies that software written for the simpler adapters can be executed on the more advanced adapters.

Although these adapters vary in performance, all have certain elements in common. These elements include the host interface, display memory, BIOS-related calls, and the video output circuitry. The elements of each adapter are listed in Table 3.2. The EGA and VGA adapters consist of several display modes, but only the unique display modes are listed.

3.3.1 Host Interface

The host can interact with the display adapter in two ways. The first is through the control registers, and the second is through the display memory. The control registers are assigned port addresses, whereas the display memory is mapped into the host memory address space. Both the registers and the display memory can be accessed directly through applications software or indirectly through the BIOS calls.

Table 3.2 Video Adapters

Adapter Type	Resolution pixels	Number Colors	Display Memory	BIOS
MDA	720 by 348	2/2	4 Kbytes	System
Hercules	720 by 348	2/2	4 Kbytes	System
CGA	320 by 200	4/16	16 Kbytes	System
CGA	640 by 200	2/16	16 Kbytes	System
EGA	640 by 350	16/64	256 Kbytes	Local
VGA	640 by 480	16/256K	256 Kbytes	Local
VGA	320 by 200	256/256K	256 Kbytes	Local

3.3.2 Display Memory

The display memory can be thought of as a giant shift register that is constantly sending a serial data stream to the monitor. All of the above-mentioned display adapters are raster scan displays. The serial data stream is necessary to refresh the monitor with the data in the display memory. This is illustrated in Figure 3.5.

In reality, a shift register memory is not effective, because data needs to be accessed by the host in a parallel fashion. The display memory is typically configured as parallel memory. Both the host and the video control logic must compete to gain access to the video memory.

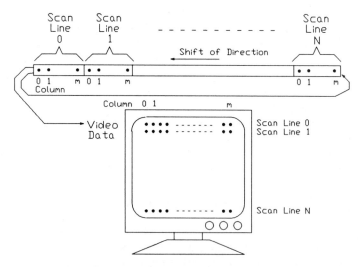

FIGURE 3.5 Shift Register Display Memory

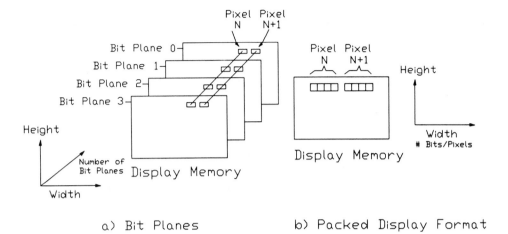

FIGURE 3.6 Bit-mapped versus Pixel-packed Display Format

Bit Planes versus Packed Display Format

There are two ways to segment the display memory. The first technique segments the memory into bit planes. A bit plane contains one bit for each pixel. The number of bit planes must equal the maximum number of bits per pixel, because only one bit exists per plane. The second technique is called *packed display format*. In this mode, there is only one memory plane, and the plane is segmented into elements, each being the number of bits in a pixel. Both of these techniques are identical if there is only one bit assigned to every pixel. These two modes are illustrated in Figure 3.6.

The EGA/VGA uses the top left corner of the display as the lowest display memory address. The advantage in using the top left corner becomes clear when alphanumerics are being displayed. The first character on a page would naturally be in the top left corner of the page. Similarly, the advantage in using the bottom left corner becomes clear when graphics are being displayed. The origin of a two-dimensional graph is usually in the bottom left corner. The process of drawing a line from a low vertical value to a higher vertical value is normally displayed as a line being drawn in an upward direction. If the lowest address corresponds to the upper left corner, this line would be drawn in a downward direction.

Mapping Data from Host Memory to Display Memory

Host memory in the PC can be thought of as two-dimensional. One dimension is the number of bits per element, and the second is the number of elements. In the PC, the common element is called the byte. A byte consists of eight bits. Therefore, host memory can be thought of as being two-dimensional, one dimension being very narrow—8 bits—and the second possibly being very long—1 megabyte.

Most programmers are accustomed to thinking of host memory as one-dimensional. However, for the examples below, two dimensions work out nicely. In some graphics processors, the basic element is the bit, and the addressing actually accesses single bits. This memory can be construed as being one-dimensional.

The graphics display memory can be thought of as three-dimensional. Later in this book, it is considered to be four-dimensional. The three dimensions are height (called *rows*), width (called *columns*), and depth (called *number of bits per pixel*). The two-dimensional host memory has to be segmented so that it maps into the three-dimensional display memory.

If there is one bit assigned to each pixel, the host two-dimensional memory would be eight pixels per element wide. The length of the memory can be determined from Equation 3.1.

Equation 3.1 Length of Host Memory Buffer

$$\text{Number of elements} = \frac{\text{Number of columns}}{\text{Number of pixels/element}} \times \text{Number of rows}$$

Since an element is equal to a byte, this equation would simplify to Equation 3.2.

Equation 3.2 Byte Length of Host Memory Buffer

$$\text{Number of bytes} = \frac{\text{Number of columns}}{8} \times \text{Number of rows}$$

To speed up the graphics process, the data-transfer rate between host memory and display memory must be maximized. The PC is effective at moving strings of data from one sequential block of memory to another block of memory. In the case of planed or bit-mapped memory, it would be advantageous to keep the data associated with each bit plane in a separate array. A *string move* operation can occur because both the host memory array and the display memory are sequential. Four arrays would be required in the above example, one for each bit plane. In the case of packed display memory, the host array should contain packed bytes, so once again the host memory and the display memory are sequential. The assembly language command that transfers sequential data rapidly is called the *move string byte* instruction (MOVSB). The source address is kept in the DS:SI register, the destination starting address is kept in the ES:DI

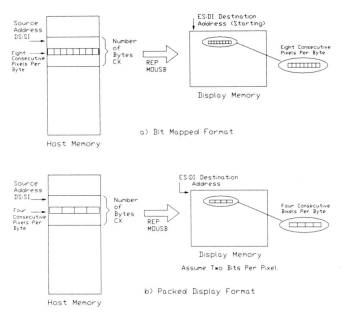

FIGURE 3.7 Transferring Data from Host Memory to Display Memory

register, and the number of bytes to move is kept in the CX register. This is illustrated in Figure 3.7. A similar procedure is followed if the data is to be transferred from display memory to host memory.

In Figure 3.7A, no assumption is made as to the number of bits per pixel, because each bit plane is loaded separately anyway. Each byte contains eight neighboring horizontal pixels. In Figure 3.7B, it is assumed that there are two bits per pixel. This is important because the two bits associated with the same pixel reside in the same byte.

The EGA and VGA adapters utilize both techniques. Several display modes are available to the programmer; each segments display memory into a bit-plane format or a packed-display format.

There are advantages and disadvantages to both types of implementations. Bit-plane mapping is advantageous when data is to be modified in a single plane. Eight pixels can be modified through a single byte. In the case of the packed format, this can be difficult. If only one plane is to be modified, the bits associated with the other planes have to be masked out of the write operation. In the EGA and VGA, this mapping is done in hardware to eliminate the need for read/modify/write operations. If there are four bits per pixel, three bits would be masked out of the write operation for each pixel. A byte write operation would therefore modify only two bits. In this case, the packed format operates at one-fourth the speed of the bit-mapped format.

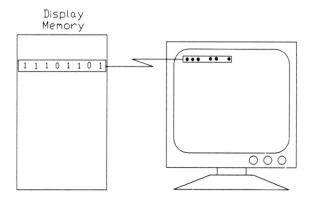

FIGURE 3.8   Mapping a Byte in Display Memory to the Monitor

The packed format is advantageous when a single pixel is modified. Again, if there are four bits per pixel, two pixels could be modified in a single byte write operation. In the bit-mapped format, four write operations would be necessary to modify the data in each of the display planes. This time, the bit-mapped format operates at one-fourth the speed of the packed format.

Transferring Data from Display Memory to the Monitor

The data in the display memory is output to the monitor through the video hardware section. Each byte in the display memory consists of a number of pixels. If there are eight pixels per byte, a byte in display memory would be translated onto the monitor as eight neighboring horizontal pixels, as shown in Figure 3.8.

Two consecutive bytes in display memory appear as horizontal neighbors on the monitor, if the end of the displayed row does not occur between the two bytes. This is illustrated in Figure 3.9.

Vertical neighbors are separated in display memory by the number of bytes per displayed scan row. In Figure 3.10, it is assumed that a scan line is 80 bytes wide. If there are 8 pixels per byte, the scan line is 640 pixels wide.

The data is output from the display memory to the monitor in a serial fashion. A byte is read out of display memory and parallel loaded into a shift register. The data is subsequently read out of the shift register in a serial bit stream that is output to the electron gun in the monitor. The monitor and the display memory are synchronized so that data read out of the display memory is displayed in the proper positions on the monitor. This data path is illustrated in Figure 3.11.

Virtual and Displayed Images

Data in the display memory is called a *virtual image*, and data on the monitor is called a *viewed image*. A starting address dictates which element in display memory corresponds to the upper left corner of the monitor. The width of the

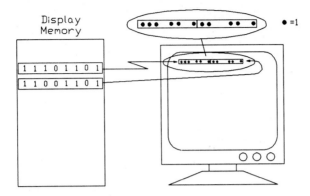

FIGURE 3.9 Horizontal Neighbors in Display Memory

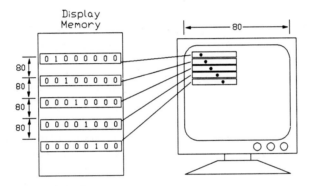

FIGURE 3.10 Vertical Neighbors in Display Memory

display is equal to the number of displayed elements per scan line. The width of the virtual image is equal to the number of elements reserved in display memory for a scan line. The virtual image does not have to be the same size as the viewed image.

The number of bytes in the display memory associated with an image is determined by Equation 3.2 above. It is repeated in Equation 3.3 with the new terminology.

Equation 3.3 Length of Host Virtual Buffer

$$\text{Number of bytes} = \frac{\text{Number of virtual columns}}{8} \times \text{Number of virtual rows}$$

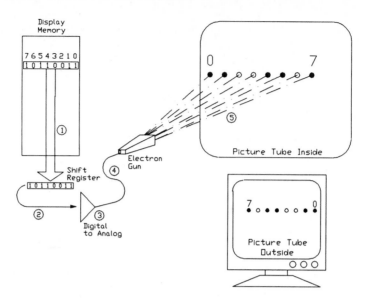

FIGURE 3.11 Parallel to Serial Conversion

Figure 3.12 illustrates a virtual image. In Figure 3.12A, the number of virtual rows is equal to the display height and the number of virtual columns is equal to the display width. In Figure 3.12B, the number of virtual rows is greater than the display height and the number of virtual columns is greater than the display width.

Window Mapping

The concept of a virtual image can be readily applied to the processing of a window. In the case of a window, the virtual size of the window is usually less than the size of the display. A typical window mapping from host memory to display memory and to the monitor is illustrated in Figure 3.13.

The window can fit compactly and sequentially in host memory with no wasted space, as shown in Figure 3.13A. The window is $J - L + 1$ elements per scan line wide and $M - N + 1$ scan lines high. It is to be displayed beginning at row N and column J. The window cannot be moved to the display memory with a single MOVSB instruction, because it is not in contiguous display memory. This occurs because the width of the window is less than the width of the display. The display memory is illustrated in Figure 3.13B. Only a segment of rows N through M is occupied by the window.

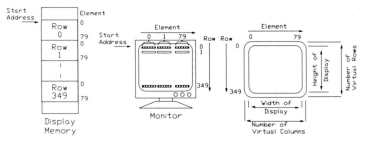

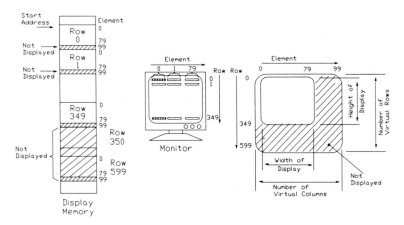

a) Number of Elements in a Row Equals Width of Display

b) Number of Elements in a Row less than Width of Display

FIGURE 3.12   Virtual Image

3.3.3   Graphics-related BIOS

Regardless of the memory configuration, most graphics systems have a facility for drawing to a single pixel without requiring in-depth knowledge of the display architecture. BIOS routines are provided on the system board to perform some basic display-related functions. On the EGA and VGA, a local BIOS ROM provides enhanced BIOS routines to further assist the programmer. Using the BIOS calls has advantages and disadvantages. They are easy to use, and new graphics boards can provide similar BIOS calls to insure compatibility. However, in many cases these calls are notoriously slow.

Even the BIOS calls require a certain amount of device-dependent code. Device-independent graphics standards, such as DGIS, provide a standardized set of routines that the graphics applications can call to control any display adapter.

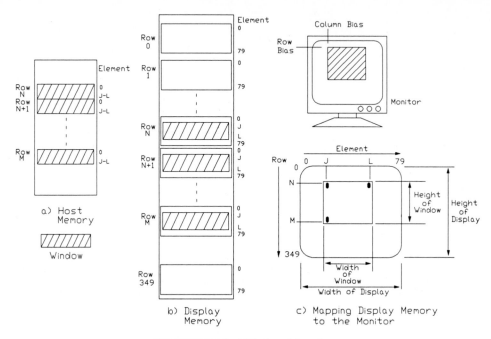

FIGURE 3.13 Window Mapping

3.3.4   Video Interface Cable

The video cable contains a number of shielded cables. The number of conductors and the pin numbers on the connectors depend on the graphics adapter and the monitor selected. The signals running inside the cable consist of video information and video control. These signals are listed in Table 3.3.

3.4   MONITORS AND DISPLAYS

The operation of a monitor is simple to understand. A scanning electron beam sweeps across the back face of the monitor. This beam scans across the screen in an orderly fashion. As the beam strikes the back face of the monitor screen, it excites the phosphor coating. The excited phosphor emits light, which is detected by the eye.

The monitor may be a digital or analog monochrome, RGBI or RrGgBb digital color, or an analog RGB color monitor. The resolution and performance of these monitors varies, as does the price. Monochrome monitors—used with the MDA, Hercules, or EGA—are less expensive than color monitors. Because of their simplicity, even inexpensive monochrome monitors are capable of handling high resolutions. A typical monochrome resolution is 720 by 348 pixels.

Color monitors vary in performance. RGBI monitors—used with the CGA

Table 3.3 Video Cable Signals

Adapter	Monitor	Video Signals	Sync Signals
MDA,EGA	Monochrome	Video, Intensity	Horizontal, Vertical
Hercules	Monochrome	Video, Intensity	Horizontal, Vertical
CGA,EGA	RGBI	Red, Green, Blue, Intensity	Horizontal, Vertical
EGA	RrGgBb	Red, Green, Blue, IRed, IGreen, IBlue	Horizontal, Vertical
VGA	Analog RGB	Analog Red, Green, Blue	Horizontal, Vertical
VGA	Analog Monochrome	Analog Green	Horizontal, Vertical

or EGA—accept digital color inputs, allowing the display of 16 unique colors. The resolution of these monitors is usually limited to 200 horizontal scan lines. RrGgBb monitors also accept digital color inputs and are used with the EGA. These monitors can display 64 unique colors and handle 350 horizontal scan lines.

Analog monitors must be used with the VGA. Analog RGB monitors can display an unlimited number of colors and typically can handle 480 horizontal scan lines. Analog monochrome monitors can display an unlimited number of shades of gray and, again, typically can handle 480 horizontal scan lines.

Multisync enhanced monitors commonly accept digital or analog color inputs and can display resolutions of 900 by 600 pixels. Advanced monitors, used with high-resolution graphics systems, can display resolutions of 2,000 by 2,000 pixels.

A variety of computer displays has evolved over the years to meet the growing needs of computer processing and computer graphics. Improvements include higher-resolution characters, more characters per line, more lines per screen, x,y addressable cursors, highlighted characters, graphics capabilities, and color.

There are several different types of display monitors, including vector displays, raster scan displays, storage and nonstorage monitors, and flat panel displays. Interfacing the wide variety of displays with the ever-growing number of computers has forced standards to emerge. Monitors are interfaced to the PC through a cable to the graphics hardware.

Storage displays, as in some oscilloscopes, use phosphors with extremely long decay times to store the electron beam's energy. Once the phosphor is excited, it remains excited and therefore does not need to be refreshed. When desired, a large field is energized that erases the entire screen. Selective portions of the screen cannot be erased. Nonstorage scopes use a phosphor with a faster decay time. Shortly after the electron beam leaves an area, that area naturally erases as the phosphor decays. In order for an image to remain on a short decay time

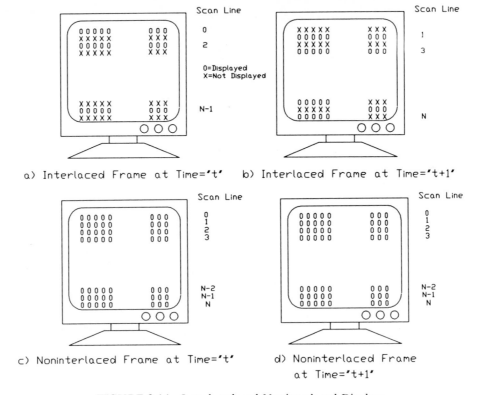

FIGURE 3.14 Interlaced and Noninterlaced Displays

phosphor, each area of the monitor's screen has to be refreshed at 50–70 Hz to avoid flicker before the phosphor decays.

3.4.1 Interlaced and Noninterlaced Displays

Displays are either interlaced or noninterlaced. Noninterlaced displays are used exclusively with the EGA/VGA. In an interlaced display, alternate scan lines are updated every frame. In a noninterlaced display, every scan line is updated every frame. This is illustrated in Figure 3.14.

In the interlaced mode, as the frame at *time* = t is displayed, only the even scan lines are updated. The odd scan lines still contain the data from the frame that was displayed at *time* = t − 1. This is illustrated in Figure 3.14A. Similarly, as the frame at *time* = t + 1 is displayed, only the odd scan lines are updated. The even scan lines still contain the data from the frame that was displayed at time t. This is illustrated in Figure 3.14B. In the noninterlaced mode, all of the scan lines are updated with new data as the frame at *time* = t and is displayed,

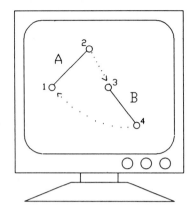

FIGURE 3.15   Vector Display Refresh

as shown in Figure 3.14C. Similarly, at *time = t + 1*, all of the scan lines are once again updated, as seen in Figure 3.14D.

Interlaced displays are used when the adapter or monitor hardware cannot keep up with the data rates required by the video system. The greater the resolution of the video system, the faster the hardware must be to keep up with the data rates. The interlaced hardware must be only half as fast as the non-interlaced hardware. The disadvantage of the interlaced hardware is that the eye can begin to detect the alternating frequencies on the screen, especially when these interact with the 60-cycle-per-second frequencies present in fluorescent lights.

3.4.2   Vector Displays

Vector displays were very popular in the early days of computer graphics because raster displays were very expensive due to the high cost of memory. Today, raster scan displays are popular because of the low cost of high-density, high-speed memory. Vector displays are currently used in systems that require extremely high speed vector processing.

Vector displays direct the electron beam across the screen as commanded by the display processor. The motion of the electron beam depends on the data being displayed. In Figure 3.15, two vectors represented by line A and line B are drawn on a screen. The commands in the vector processor list would be to draw line A, then line B, and repeat line A. The steps would be as follows: move to point 1, draw to point 2, move to point 3, draw to point 4, and repeat.

In contrast, the motion of the electron beam in a raster scan system occurs in an ordered fashion, regardless of the image. Raster scan systems move the electron beam from left to right and top to bottom, as illustrated in Figure 3.16.

Commands are stored in the memory of a vector display system. The amount

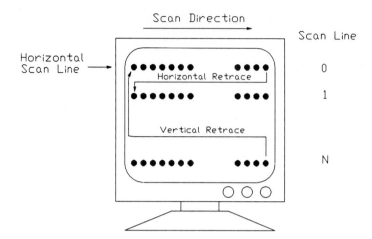

FIGURE 3.16 Raster Scan Display Refresh

of memory and the speed of the vector processor limit the number of commands that can be executed before the screen is refreshed. High-resolution displays can be implemented without requiring large amounts of digital memory. Unless the vector processor is very fast, only a small number of vectors will be displayed before the phosphor begins to decay. The phosphor must be fast-decaying for displays that simulate motion.

3.4.3 Raster Scan Displays

Raster scan displays rely on a memory buffer that contains a full frame of data. An entire picture is stored in this display memory. This memory may be thought of as a giant shift register. The data is read out of the shift register synchronously with the scanning electron beam. Thus, the electron beam is at the top left corner of the display when the shift register is outputting the first information. This is illustrated in Figure 3.5. As the electron beam scans across one horizontal line, the data which corresponds to the first horizontal line is output from the shift register. At the end of a horizontal line, the electron beam returns to the beginning of the next line. During this retrace time, no information is read out of the shift register. When the electron beam is ready for the second line, data once again is output from the shift register. This process continues until the last scan line is drawn. At this point, a vertical retrace occurs and the electron beam returns to the top left corner of the screen.

In reality, a shift register memory is not effective, because data needs to be accessed by the host in a parallel fashion. From the host's perspective, the display memory is configured as parallel memory.

Even though the display memory appears to be parallel, eventually it must be converted to a serial data stream in order to interface with the electron beam in the monitor.

3.4.4   Flat Panel Displays

Laptop computers and other portable display systems use flat displays because of size constraints. Liquid crystal displays (LCDs), plasma, and electroluminescent displays are three examples of the flat panel technology. Liquid crystals work in low voltage ranges, making them well suited for portable electronics. Electroluminescent and plasma displays work in the range from 110 to 200 volts. Problems inherent in the liquid crystal technologies include multiplexing difficulties, undesirable response times, and poor electro-optical characteristics, such as charge leakage. Display readability has been improved by twisted crystal techniques and low-power electroluminescent backlighting. Plasma displays are power hungry, but they provide straightforward multiplexing, and high resolutions are readily available. Electroluminescent displays, including ac-thin-film and dc-power displays, are popular in hand-held televisions. LCDs reflect light, whereas gas discharge and electroluminescent displays transmit light. This is a reason that LCDs require less power.

3.4.5   Monochrome Monitors

Monochrome monitors typically display data in a bi-stable format, which allows two colors to be displayed. A foreground of white, amber, or green on a black background are common color combinations used in bi-stable displays. Monochrome monitors can also display data in a gray scale format. The gray scale format requires a modulation of the video signal. As the electron beam is scanned across the phosphor, the amount of energy applied to the phosphor determines the level of brightness. More energy pumped into the phosphor at a given point results in a brighter intensity at that point. Monochrome gray scale monitors have special analog video inputs that control the gray scale. The enhanced monochrome monitor used with the VGA accepts the analog monochrome signal from the green analog output of the VGA.

The PC monochrome bi-stable monitors have an intensity signal that combines with the video signal to create a tri-stable display. The three intensity states correspond to off, on, and high-intensity on.

3.5   SIGNAL ACQUISITION

The information that is displayed using computer graphics has to originate somewhere. The data used in charts is either entered into the computer through a spreadsheet or data base program or entered into the computer through some input channel. The input channel may be analog or digital. Two-dimensional images are typically entered through an illustration or computer-assisted-design program through an analog or digital input channel.

3.5.1 Input Channels

The PC can input data via the serial ports, parallel ports, or the direct memory access (DMA) channel. The serial channel, running at 9,600 baud, can receive approximately 900 bytes per second. The parallel port can receive about 100,000 bytes per second. Using a DMA channel allows high-speed transfers of data into memory. Some data acquisition operations are so fast that intermediate high speed memory must be used to buffer the data. This buffer memory can hold bursts of information and then send the data to the computer at lower data rates that are consistent with the speed of the PC.

3.5.2 Analog-to-digital Converters

Because signals are measured in an analog format, they must be converted to a digital format before being entered into the computer. One source of information is obtained through direct data acquisition. A wide variety of analog-to-digital (A/D) converter boards are available for the PC family of computers. These boards vary in price and performance. The major issues relate to resolution, accuracy, speed, number of channels, available software, and special features.

Resolution is a measure of how precisely the input signal can be digitized. For example, an 8-bit digitization can resolve 256 steps in the input signal. The human eye can barely detect the difference between two adjacent gray scales that are 1/256th apart in intensity. A 12-bit digitization can resolve 4,096 steps, which is adequate for most data acquisition applications. A 16-bit A/D converter can resolve 32,768 steps. The human ear is amazingly sensitive, so 22 bits of resolution can be required for the accurate reproduction of sound.

Accuracy is a measure of how closely the digitized data actually resembles the analog data. Linearity and the signal-to-noise ratio are both key elements to accuracy. An analog-to-digital converter that has a resolution of 12 bits but is noisy or inaccurate may perform worse than a quiet, accurate 8-bit converter. The PC environment is electrically noisy because of the digital circuitry. As a result, care must be exercised when interfacing to the analog world.

The speed of an A/D converter is a measure of how fast successive samples can be taken; it also determines how fast the A/D can convert the analog data into a digital format. This speed is also called the *bandwidth*. Slow A/D converters may sample only 10 samples per second. Audio applications usually sample around 50,000 cycles per second. Video signals are typically sampled at around 3 million samples per second.

The speed of the A/D system must take into account the bandwidth of the entire system. If the A/D is digitizing data at 16 bits per sample, at a rate of 40,000 samples per second, the bandwidth of the system has to be 640,000 bits per second. Once the data is digitized, the resulting digital words must be stored somewhere. If the data is stored in memory, the memory must be large enough to hold all of the sampled data. If the A/D samples for 20 seconds, 12.8 million bits, or 1.6 million bytes, of memory are necessary. If the data is to be stored directly onto disk, the speed of the disk is critical. Some hard disks available for the PC can store sequential data at a rate of 400,000 bytes per second. Very high speed disks are capable of storing data at video rates of 3 million bytes per second. These disks are capable of digitizing real-time video signals.

3.5.3 Video Frame Grabbers

A common source of analog input for computer graphics is analog video signals. Video signals require external frame buffers because of their 3-mHz bandwidth. Video frame grabber boards are capable of digitizing video images. These video digitizers usually sample the video signals from an NTSC or RGB video source. The NTSC standard was developed in the United States as a broadcast standard.

A black-and-white video signal is traditionally sampled at a resolution of 8 bits and at a speed in excess of one million samples per second. A typical image might be 512 by 512 pixels, each pixel being represented by a byte. Thus, one video image would require approximately 32,000 bytes. The standard video rate of an interlaced signal is 30 frames per second. Thus, 960,000 bytes are acquired per second. This data rate includes the horizontal and vertical refresh time. During the refreshing no data is digitized, and the actual data rates surpass this 960,000 bytes per second rate. Typical frame buffers for the PC can store one full frame in a thirtieth of a second. Once acquired, the image can be downloaded into slower host memory or to disk. If the image is transferred to host memory, the speed of the host memory and the speed of the channel determine the rate at which the image can be transferred. If it is transferred to the disk, the speed of the disk also affects the transfer rate. Once the image has been downloaded, the buffer is free to acquire the next video frame.

3.5.4 Image Scanners

Certain applications require that static images be digitized. Image scanners perform this digitizing function. These consist of a row of photodetectors mounted in a mechanism that can scan a piece of paper. Facsimile machines may use this technique for transmitting images. Photocopy machines also use similar techniques for digitizing the original before the copy is made. Either the paper is moved across the scanner or the scanner is moved across the paper. Some scanners can scan a full page at once; others scan a line at a time. Line scanners can be hand-held or mounted in place of the print head. Printers can be used since they already have the accurate paper movement mechanism. This technique of acquiring images is especially popular in desktop publishing applications. Resolutions of 300 by 300 dots per inch and 600 by 600 dots per inch are common.

The images are digitized at a resolution of from one to eight bits per pixel. One bit per pixel produces bi-stable images, also referred to as black and white.

Dithering techniques are available that simulate gray scale or half tones. Optical filtering techniques are available that allow the scanning of color images. At 300 dots per inch, an 8.5-by-11-inch page requires 8,415,000 dots. If each dot is represented by one bit, 1.05 million bytes are necessary. If each dot is represented by eight bits, 8.4 million bytes are required. Thus, to utilize image scanners, a great deal of extended memory is required. To manipulate these images, even more memory is required. Indeed, maintaining two full-frame color buffers requires more than 16 Mbytes of storage.

An EGA or VGA operating at a resolution of 640 by 480 pixels can display only 1/350 of a full image at a time, given that the image was scanned at four bits per pixel. A VGA operating at 8 bits per pixel and a 320-by-200 resolution can display less than one thousandth of the entire image.

3.6   HARD-COPY DEVICES

The principal function of computer graphics is to communicate information. The combination of the computer graphics monitor and the graphics adapter provides an excellent means of interactively conveying information from the computer to the user. To share this information with others, some sort of hard copy is necessary. Many of the principles that apply to monitors also apply to hard-copy devices. Examples of graphics hard copy include the printed page, the output of pen plotters, photographs made using various techniques, and images stored in optical storage devices.

3.6.1   Printers

Common printers used with the PC family of computers include impact printers, ink jet printers, thermal printers, and laser printers. Impact printers transfer ink to paper by striking the paper through an inked ribbon. Color output is possible if a multicolor ribbon is used. Ink jet printers spray the ink onto the paper, and thermal printers burn the ink onto the paper. Laser printers transfer the ink to the paper through an optical technique.

3.6.2   Interfacing to Printers

Printers are commonly interfaced to computers through a serial or parallel port. All printers use the ASCII standard, but that is where the compatibility ends. Each printer seems to have its own technique for printing graphics. Printing graphics requires software that can translate the output from the graphics applications software into the appropriate control codes for the printer. These software translators are typically called *drivers*. High-level printer languages, such as PostScript, can alleviate many of the problems associated with the lack of graphic hard-copy standards.

3.6.3 Printer Drivers

The manufacturers of graphics software that interfaces with hard-copy devices must provide a wide variety of printer drivers. Without a special driver, the printer cannot be utilized to its fullest capacity. Memory resident software drivers called *terminate and stay resident* sometimes provide additional compatibility. These programs intercept the output of a graphics program and translate it so that it becomes compatible with the printer.

For example, assume that printer A is not compatible with the hard-copy codes used by a software application. A driver can be loaded into host memory to intercept all of the codes sent to the printer port by the applications software. The driver will translate these codes into printer codes that will be understood by printer A. The codes will then be sent out the printer port to printer A.

3.6.4 Impact Printers

Impact printers include daisy wheel printers and dot matrix printers. Daisy wheel printers use a wheel that contains a fixed number of character shapes, similar to the techniques used by typewriters. Only the character shapes included on the wheel can be printed. On many printers, the wheel is interchangeable, allowing additional character sets to be loaded. These wheels can be thought of as downloadable character sets.

A second type of impact printer is the dot matrix printer. This is by far the most popular printer used in the PC marketplace. The characters are formed on the page by a series of dots that are made when small hammers strike the paper through an inked ribbon. Any shape can be formed by commanding the proper hammers to strike the paper. These printers typically reproduce graphics at resolutions between 80 and 150 dots per inch. The hammers are usually configured on the print head in a vertical line, and the print head moves across the page horizontally. The number of hammers on a print head varies from 8 to 24. In line printers, the hammers are configured horizontally, and typically a single horizontal line is printed at a time. The paper moves vertically across the row of hammers.

Low-resolution dot matrix printers utilize a print head with eight hammers arranged vertically. Eight hammers are used because a typical character can be represented by eight vertical rows. Thus, an entire row of text can be printed in one pass by scanning the print head across the page. Because the hammers are rigidly mounted in the print head, good vertical tolerances are maintained within one character row. In addition, accurate motors and mechanical positioning techniques allow the print head to move across the page, maintaining a high degree of accuracy. This results in good horizontal tolerances per character row.

Tolerances start to get sloppy when the print head has to change direction. At the end of the print head travel, as it changes direction, a certain amount of looseness, called hysteresis, is present. This causes errors. Hysteresis is inherent in every mechanical mechanism. Errors are noticeable when vertical lines are printed, because the print head changes direction at the end of each scan. The vertical line will tend to shift horizontally back and forth by an amount equal to the hysteresis.

Accuracy problems are encountered when the paper is moved. Most printers rely on friction and perforated paper to provide accurate paper motion. Errors show up as slight variations in the vertical space between character rows. When graphic images are printed, inconsistencies along the vertical axis can be detected. If a solid block of black is printed, darker and lighter horizontal lines will be evident. These lines are signs of the paper-moving inaccuracies.

High-resolution dot matrix printers employ print heads with 24 pins. The diameter of each pin is twice the diameter of a human hair. The fineness of these pins provides high-resolution print. The details presented above for 8-pin heads apply to 24-pin heads as well. The sources of inaccuracies are the same. Because there are 24 pins fixed on a single head as opposed to 8, nearly one-third of the mechanical motion is necessary. This translates to higher tolerances. In addition, printers that incorporate the 24-pin heads are usually more expensive and are designed with high-quality mechanical components.

3.6.5 Ink Jet and Thermal Printers

Ink jet printers shoot the ink onto the page. Color ink jet printers can transfer several colors onto a page by shooting different color inks. Color ink jet printers have not been received very well in the PC marketplace.

Thermal printers are similar to impact printers except that the ink is transferred to the page by heating up an element on the print head rather than by striking a ribbon with a hammer. The increased temperature causes the ink to be deposited onto the page. Thermal printers can maintain a high degree of accuracy if the moving parts are minimized. Because the thermal elements can be small, it is possible to pack them very close to one another. Printers that position the elements in a horizontal line that spans the entire width of the page can achieve very high degrees of accuracy. The paper moves across the print heads in a line printer mode. If the mechanics of paper motion are handled properly, very high resolutions can be achieved. Special heat-sensitive paper is required for thermal printers.

3.6.6 Laser Printers

Laser printers have recently inundated the marketplace, producing near-publication-quality graphics hard copy. Resolutions up to 600 by 600 dots per inch are available on laser printers. Such printers cannot produce results equal to true publication-quality printouts produced by typesetters, which can achieve resolutions of 2,000 by 2,000 dots per inch, but the 600-dot-per-inch resolution is adequate in most situations. Currently, laser printers are restricted to black-and-white output, but the potential for color lasers certainly exists.

Laser printers contain an internal microprocessor and internal memory. Often, the printer has more memory and more powerful processors than are resident in the host computer. Two megabytes are common if a 300-dot-per-inch page of graphics is desired. An image printed on an 8½-by-11-inch page at 600 dots per inch requires over four megabytes of memory. The memory resident in the laser printer must be shared primarily between the bit-mapped page of data and the current resident character fonts. Character fonts can also require a large amount of data, especially the large font sizes. Several megabytes can be consumed if several fonts are actively resident.

Downloading fonts into the laser printer can be time-consuming. If the printer is interfaced through a serial channel operating at 9,600 baud, it can take more than 17 minutes to load one megabyte of fonts.

3.6.7 Plotters

Plotters provide accurate smooth drawings on paper using ink pens or heat-transfer devices. A pen plotter consists of a pen mounted in a holder that has two degrees of freedom. The pen is moved across the surface of a piece of paper by two *X* and *Y* motors. The placement of the pen on the paper is determined by control signals sent to the *X*-axis and *Y*-axis motors. A third control signal controls whether the pen comes in contact with the paper. If the pen comes into contact with the paper, a condition called *pen down*, ink is transferred. If the pen rides above the paper, a condition called *pen up*, no ink is transferred. The first case can be thought of as a *draw*, and the second case as a *move*. Plotters can be interfaced through an analog or digital interface. Digital interfaces are used almost exclusively in computer graphics applications.

The early plotters had analog inputs. With the help of digital-to-analog (D/A) converters, a computer could output data to these plotters by providing constantly changing horizontal and vertical position voltages. Analog signals are difficult to calibrate, cannot drive long cables, require D/A converters, and tie up the computer, requiring constant incremental outputs. Drawing a single line can require thousands of outputs from the computer through the D/A converters to the plotter.

Current plotters utilize a digital interface and incorporate a command language. A single *line draw* command can be used to draw a line. Most plotters come equipped with serial and/or parallel interfaces and conform to one of the popular command standards. Serial interfaces are popular with X/Y plotters, because the slow speed of the serial channel does not slow the X/Y plotters. This occurs because high-level commands are sent to the plotter. Serial channels also allow the plotters to be located a distance from the computer.

A single pen plotter can make multiple color plots. The software pauses the plotter at key points, and the user inserts a different color pen. Advanced plotters have pen holders that allow the plotter to select automatically from a variety of pens.

Plotters use fixed or moving paper. Large-format paper often requires the plotter to move the paper. In these plotters, the paper moves in one direction while the pen moves in a perpendicular direction. Each is restricted to one degree of freedom.

Several standards have been developed for the transfer of data to plotters. The plotters are equipped with internal processors that allow them to draw lines, curves, circles, and boxes; to shade areas; and to draw text automatically in a variety of fonts. Probably the most widely used standard was developed by Hewlett Packard and is called the Hewlett Packard Graphics Language (HPGL).

3.6.8   Photographic Slides

Photographic slides are very popular and effective for conveying information to a large audience. The high-resolution capability of slide film provides an excellent media for graphics hard copy. The slides can be created by photographing the monitor directly with a 35mm camera or by interfacing the computer with a slide maker. Although inexpensive, photographing the monitor has some bad side effects. Creating a slide on an inexpensive slide maker is easier than photographing the monitor directly, and the results are somewhat better in quality. Creating a slide on an expensive slide maker can produce incredible results, achieving resolutions as high as 4,000 by 4,000 dots per slide. A third approach, the most expensive, is to write directly to 35mm motion picture film using a laser beam.

Photographing the Monitor

A simple and inexpensive form of color hard copy can be obtained by mounting a camera on a tripod in front of the screen. A number of problems can arise that make this process difficult and the results less than optimal. The room must be completely dark to keep ambient light from reflecting off of the face of the monitor. It can be difficult to adjust the exposure, frame the photo, focus the camera, and shoot the picture in a darkened room. The curved monitor screens cause distortions, including a bowing of the image and a non-linear focal plane. In addition, color monitors align the red, green, and blue electron guns such that they converge on the monitor, as viewed from a perpendicular axis. Because the camera is close to the monitor, the angles are large, and the color can appear to be unconverged on the resultant slide. These distortions are exaggerated on a monitor the size of a standard 14-inch PC monitor. A smaller monitor, three inches in diameter with a flat face, produces far better results. However, this requires a second monitor to be attached to the system.

If a second monitor is used, it can be enclosed within a light-tight box. A camera mount in front of the monitor fixes the focal length and insures that ambient light will not cause reflections. This fixture will make the photographing task simpler as well as improve the quality of the slides.

Slide Makers

Commercial slide makers range from devices that are similar to the enclosed system mentioned above to sophisticated, high-resolution systems. The less expensive slide makers contain a small flat-screened color monitor, a camera, and an interface. The image is sent to the monitor in a color format, and the camera is triggered to take the photograph. Expensive slide makers rely on high-bandwidth black-and-white monitors. These monitors are capable of displaying resolutions of 4,000 dots per inch. It is possible to produce color slides from these black-and-white monitors by taking multiple exposures with different color filters in front of the shutter during each exposure. The red video signal is displayed on the monitor without the blue or green signals. Because the monitor is black and white, the red signal is displayed in white on a black background. A red filter is placed in front of the shutter, causing the video signal to be displayed in red. Similar techniques are used for the green and blue signals. The result is a high-resolution color slide.

Interfacing to slide makers, like interfacing to any hard-copy device, is confusing. Several standards are available to handle the input protocols of these devices. Any device that operates at the resolution of the PC graphics monitor does not require any additional software. The output that is directed to the computer monitor is also directed to the slide maker. Devices with higher resolutions must rely on software, because the resolution of the slide maker is higher than the resolution of the computer monitor. Two separate images must be generated, one for the monitor and one for the slide maker, to insure that the resolution of both are handled properly.

The slide maker may be thought of as a bit-mapped graphics system or as a vector graphics system. If it is treated as a bit-mapped system, the data output from the computer consists of each pixel or some data-compressed version of the display. If it is treated as a vector system, information is sent regarding the starting and ending coordinates and the color of the vector. In some ways, a slide maker resembles a color plotter; in fact, color plotter interface languages, such as HPIL, are commonly used as the interface protocol.

Video Recorders

Video reproductions of the screen can be accomplished via video recorders if the timing of the horizontal and vertical sync pulses are compatible. These video recordings can be made on video tape recorders or video disk recorders. Video recorders typically require an NTSC signal. The NTSC standard is very rigid regarding the variation in the synchronization timing. The EGA or VGA, operating at 640 pixels per scan line and 350 or 480 scan lines per frame, cannot be synchronized, because they exceed the limits of the NTSC. An additional problem is the interlaced requirement for NTSC signals.

Many of the CGA graphics implementations include an NTSC output. The CGA timing is based on a mode that uses 320 pixels per scan line by 200 pixels per scan line. The horizontal sync pulses of the CGA can be synchronized to the NTSC requirements. The 200-scan-line mode produces a vertical retrace frequency that is slower than the maximum retrace frequency of the NTSC. As a result, it is possible to design a converter that translates the CGA video output to an NTSC-compatible format.

Video projectors are available to project the video data from a monitor onto a screen. These projectors produce large images, thereby allowing effective presentations when a monitor screen is too small.

3.7 GRAPHICS-RELATED SOFTWARE

Software packages utilize the display adapter for text processing and for graphics processing. Popular packages include word processors; desktop publishers; charting, illustration, and computer-assisted-design packages; graphics programming environments; and font editors.

3.7.1 Word Processors

Word processors typically operate in the alphanumerics modes, because they process text and the alphanumeric modes are faster than the graphics modes. However, the demands on word processors have increased, and several word processors now utilize the graphics modes. Word processors operating in the alphanumeric modes have limited character fonts and cannot incorporate graphics into the documents. In addition, only one font size can be active at a time.

Graphics adapters typically display 80 characters per horizontal row and 25 horizontal rows of text on a screen. The printed page contains 80 or 135 characters per row by 60 lines. Thus, an entire printed page cannot be viewed on the monitor on a single screen.

Word processors in the alphanumeric mode have a limited ability to position space between characters. Some include proportional spacing, but this is restricted to placing additional character spaces between the characters. Advanced techniques, such as kerning and leading, are not possible in the alphanumeric modes.

One technique popular in word processors is the preview feature. This feature allows the operator to interact with the document while the display adapter is in an alphanumeric mode. In the regular text-entering mode, the text size is out of proportion, and graphics cannot be displayed. When the preview mode is invoked, the adapter switches to a graphics mode. The text and graphics are then viewed to scale. The amount of interaction that the user can have in the preview mode is often limited.

The term WYSIWYG, meaning "what you see is what you get," is often used with word processors. A true WYSIWYG word processor requires the word processor to operate in a graphics mode and to be capable of accurately displaying all fonts available to the printer. Such a program requires a graphics adapter and monitor capable of displaying an entire page of text. The resolution of a laser printer places severe demands on the WYSIWYG display adapter. A laser printer operating on an 8½-by-11-inch page at 600 dots per inch would require a full-screen monitor able to display 5,100 dots per line by 6,600 scan lines per page.

Typically, the hard-copy output of word processors is directed to printers. The printers can also be controlled in an alphanumeric or in a graphical format. Word processors use the alphanumeric format.

When color is employed, the screen is more readable. Color can be used to differentiate the menu and message areas from the text to provide a cleaner-looking display. When the word processor is in alphanumerics mode, color can highlight characters that have special attributes. These attributes include bolding, italics, underlining, superscripts, subscripts, and different font sizes and shapes.

Word processors code the special alphanumeric features into the text with control characters. Often one word processor needs to input text from another word processor. The word processor must understand the format of any formatted text files that it imports. Most word processors can import or export files that are in ASCII format. All control codes are stripped from an ASCII file, often referred to as an *unformatted file*. Exceptions are the tab and carriage return. These control codes are often specially handled, and each word processor may handle them differently.

The resolution of the display and the size of the character font affect the number of characters that can be displayed on a single monitor. The size of the monitor also affects the number of characters; even if the characters have high resolution, they still can be difficult to read if they are too slow. The speed of the graphics adapter affects how quickly the text can be panned and scrolled.

There is no advantage to using an alphanumeric mode as opposed to a graphics mode, other than processor speed and the resolution of the display memory. With advances in graphics controllers and memory, the alphanumeric modes will become extinct.

3.7.2 Desktop Publishers

Desktop publishers always operate in the graphics modes. These programs are meant to be used in conjunction with word processors and graphics programs. Desktop publishers are designed to incorporate text generated by word processors with graphics generated in a variety of ways, including through illustration packages, image scanners, CAD packages, or charting software.

The time-consuming text processing is done in a word processor, which operates in the fast alphanumeric modes. The output of the word processor is imported into the desktop publisher for touch-up work. Advanced text-processing features within the publishers include leading, kerning, and multiple font styles and sizes. Advanced page-formatting features include automatic columns per pages, automatic text flowing around figures, bulleting, headers and footers, borders, rules, and captions.

Because desktop publishers operate in the graphics modes, extensive text modifications can be time-consuming and are probably best done in the word processor. Interactive facilities within the publisher allow the user to touch up the document. These touch-ups usually involve moving figures or text, changing the style or size of text, or adding features that dress up the document. All of these steps require extensive calculation and screen manipulation.

It is possible to zoom a portion of the display data. Zooming in blows up a portion of the data, allowing the user to view areas in greater detail. Zooming out allows the user to see more of the picture. Some display adapters have high-speed zoom features incorporated into the hardware to allow rapid zooming.

Unless the adapter and display monitor can display a full page, a great deal of time is spent redrawing the figure as the viewing window is moved across the document. Panning, scrolling, and zooming all require extensive redrawing. The resolution of the graphics adapter, the speed of the graphics adapter, the speed of the host processor, the amount of memory in the host, and the speed of the disk drive are all key factors that determine the effectiveness of a desktop publisher.

The hardcopy output of desktop publishing software is directed to laser printers or to professional typesetting machines. Both of these outputs are traditionally black and white. Color printing can be accomplished by using color ink jet or color heat transfer printers; however, it is usually done at the printer. Color is used in desktop publishing to produce an easy-to-understand, ergonomic display. The text is readily differentiated from the menus and other special features present on the display.

3.7.3 Charting Software Packages

Charting programs display the data accepted in a graphical format on the monitor. Charting programs are forced to use the graphics modes to display the graphics. Some charting programs allow the user to modify data or enter data in a spreadsheet format. The spreadsheet format is typically displayed in alphanumeric mode.

Operator interaction is critical for optimal computer graphics. Seldom can a graph or chart be effective without some sort of operator interaction. The speed of the host computer and the display adapter are critical to responsive interaction.

Hard copy from these charting packages can be directed to printers, plotters, or slide makers. These packages typically operate in color and print in either monochrome or color. The resolution and color capacity of the display adapter determine the quality of the display as seen on the monitor. Similarly, the resolution and color capacity of the hard-copy device determine the quality of the hardcopy. Effective charting packages operate in the highest appropriate resolution, which typically corresponds to the hard-copy device.

Charting packages import data from a variety of sources. Many of these sources use their own formats. The charting program must understand the format of the data being imported. Most database or spreadsheet programs offer an ASCII output format. This ASCII format can be limiting, but it is widely supported. It uses commas and carriage routines to separate the fields and records associated with a spreadsheet or database file.

3.7.4 Illustration Packages

The key feature of an illustration package is effective operator interaction. Illustration or painting packages always operate in the graphics modes. The same issues that affect high-speed processing in the desktop publishing packages affect the illustration packages. These include the processor speed, the amount and speed of memory, and the adapter speed.

The resolution of the adapter determines how much of the illustration can be displayed on a single screen. Larger images, called *virtual images*, can be manipulated. Portions of these can be displayed on the monitor through panning and scrolling techniques, although these take time because of the image redrawing. In certain cases, if the virtual image fits into the adapter's display memory, panning and scrolling can occur without the image having to be redrawn. Usually, the more of an image that can be displayed at a time the better. The illustrator can see more of the illustration, and less panning and scrolling is required.

It is possible to zoom a portion of the display data. As previously described, zooming in blows up a portion of the data, allowing the user to view areas in greater detail. Zooming out allows the user to see more of the picture. Some display adapters have high-speed zoom features incorporated into the hardware to allow rapid zooming. When detailed illustrations are involved, it is often advantageous to work in a zoomed mode, because of the lack of hand/eye coordination inherent in using a pointing device.

Typical hard-copy devices supported by the illustration packages include printers and plotters. The images are typically stored in a raster format—that is, bit by bit. Data compression techniques are used to reduce the size of the files. Often the output of the illustration package is imported into another software program—for example, a desktop publisher. The data-compression technique used by the illustrator must be understood by the desktop publisher.

3.7.5 Computer Assisted Design

A wide variety of computer assisted design (CAD), software packages are available for the PC family of computers. Popular packages allow the user to create mechanical, architectural, and electronic drawings interactively. The features in the graphics environment that affect illustration packages also affect CAD packages.

One big difference between CAD and illustration packages is that CAD packages typically store the images in vector format rather than raster format. The CAD packages commonly generate line drawings, be these mechanical or electrical schematics or plans for a house. A vector format is used in order to process these lines quickly.

The hard-copy output of the CAD packages generally is sent to a printer or plotter. The vector format is readily translated to the format of the plotter, which expects a vector format. The vector format must be "rasterized" if the output is sent to a printer. The CAD packages can also import files from other software packages. If the file imported is in raster format, a "raster-to-vector" conversion must occur. Otherwise, a vector will be assigned to every pixel.

The output of CAD packages is often sent to other CAD packages, computer assisted manufacturing (CAM) packages, or desktop publishers. The vector format of the output must be understood by whatever programs import the CAD files.

3.7.6 Graphics Programming Environments

The programmer developing graphics applications may decide to purchase a graphics programming environment. As the variety and complexity of the graphics adapters increase, the task of the programmer becomes increasingly difficult. Each adapter has its own conventions and potentials. If the software is developed to provide complete compatibility across a family of graphics adapters, it must, in many ways, conform to the least powerful adapter. If the software takes advantage of the special features of each adapter, the programmer must become intimately familiar with all of the adapters. This can be intimidating to the programmer who wants to develop applications software, not to become a computer graphics expert.

Graphics toolboxes provide the programmer with a set of graphics routines. Depending on the toolbox implementation, the routines provided in the toolbox can interface to a number of different graphics adapters. The high-level graphics calls are incorporated into the applications software. These calls are primarily device-independent. A set of low-level routines, which are device-dependent, provide the hardware interface. These low-level routines may be incorporated into the applications program at compile or link time.

At compile time, the programmer selects the proper switches to conditionally compile the sections of code relating to the selected adapter. A second type of interface occurs at the driver level. A set of drivers are provided, one for each adapter. The applications program invokes the driver, with no knowledge of which driver is present. The proper driver is loaded into memory by the user. These drivers are called *terminate and stay resident* programs. Some drivers are loaded at run time, and others are loaded at bootstrap time through CON-

FIG.SYS. The disadvantage of loading a program at bootstrap time is that it occupies memory even if it is not being used.

There are tradeoffs between all of the graphics toolboxes. One might be too complicated for one user, yet not powerful enough for another. Some programmers will want an interface to all known graphics adapters, and others will desire optimized code for their own adapter. Standards that are as widely accepted as the EGA/VGA can provide a wide base of users and require only one graphics interface. The toolbox presented in this book is optimized for the EGA.

3.7.7 Font Editors

Some graphics adapters, such as the EGA and VGA, have the facility to download fonts. These graphics adapters can display user-generated fonts instead of the default fonts. With this feature, the user can select or create alternative font styles.

There are countless fonts available for the PC display adapters and for the printers. Usually, a standard font will suffice on the monitor unless the data output to the screen is destined to be printed. In this case, it is desirable to have the font on the monitor resemble the font to be printed. There are several font editor packages that allow the user to select the desired font style. These editors also allow the user to create their own fonts. Perhaps a few special symbols or a collection of symbols are desired.

These programs are generally interactive and operate in a graphics mode. They are typically undemanding of the graphics environment.

Chapter 4

The PC, C, and Assembly Language

4.1 PC HARDWARE

The PC hardware environment consists of the microprocessor and mathematical coprocessor, memory, input/output ports, mass storage devices, display, keyboard, and peripherals. The microprocessor is one of the integrated circuits in the Intel 8086, 8088, 80286, and 80386 family. The coprocessors generally used are the Intel 8087, 80287, or 80387 processors. The memory consists of either random access memory (RAM) or read only memory (ROM). The PC can address several million bytes of RAM and 256 Kbytes of ROM memory, also called *BIOS memory.*

The PC interfaces with peripherals through a set of input and output (I/O) ports. Typical peripherals include serial and parallel ports, programmable clocks, data-acquisition systems, and graphics adapters. The common mass-storage devices include floppy disks, hard disks, tape backups, and CD-ROM. Common graphics displays drive monochrome or color displays at a variety of resolutions. Typical display adapters include the MDA, CGA, EGA, MEGA, VGA, PGA, and specialized graphics systems. Keyboards are available in a number of configurations. They all share the alphanumeric keys, the function keys (F1–F10), the arrow keys, and specialized control keys, such as CTRL, ALT, and PrtSc. Besides the keyboard, the operator can interact with the computer through interactive devices. These include the mouse, joystick, trackball, and digitizing tablet. Common hard-copy devices include printers, plotters, and slide makers.

The microprocessor used in the PC dictates the word size of the processor. The 8088, 8086, and 80286 all rely on a 16-bit data path. Even though the 8088 has a 16-bit internal data path, it uses an external 8-bit bus to communicate with peripherals and memory. The 80386 uses a 32-bit data path. In addition, the 80386 computer systems interface to 16- and 8-bit buses.

Associated with each of these processors is a coprocessor. The coprocessor is specially designed to perform rapid mathematical calculations, especially floating-point operations. The host can be programmed to perform the same math-

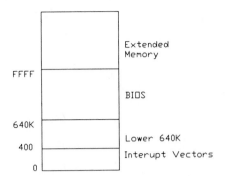

FIGURE 4.1   PC Memory Map

ematical calculations; however, the coprocessor will complete the same calculations in a fraction of the time. The 8087 coprocessor operates with either the 8088 or the 8086 host processor. Similarly, the 80287 and 80387 coprocessors operate with the 80286 and 80287 processors. Each computer can have one processor and one coprocessor. Because there are two processors, both may perform calculations at the same time.

Parallel processing enhances the computer's ability to process data quickly. The host processor passes a command and data to the coprocessor. The coprocessor performs the operation and alerts the host when the task is completed. The host, at its convenience, can return the result from the coprocessor. During the time it takes for the coprocessor to perform the task, the host can be operating on its own.

4.1.1   PC Memory

The PC memory is organized into three basic sections. The section that resides in lowest memory consists of up to 640 Kbyte of RAM memory. The memory space between the 640-Kbyte boundary and the 1-Mbyte boundary consists of several pages of special-purpose memory. This memory consists primarily of BIOS memory, display memory, and pages reserved for memory mapping. Together, these sections make up 1 Mbyte of memory. The programmer has easy access to this 1 Mbyte of memory through a 20-bit address bus. Two 16-bit words are required to form the 20-bit address.

The third section of memory is the expanded memory. This is by far the largest memory block, consisting of up to 16 Mbytes of storage. Accessing this memory is not as simple as accessing the lower 1 Mbyte of memory, because of the addressing. The EMS and EEMS standards give the programmer a means of accessing this memory. Typically, this memory is used for RAM disks. The memory configuration of the PC is illustrated in Figure 4.1.

The lower 640 Kbytes of memory consist of the system area in the lower

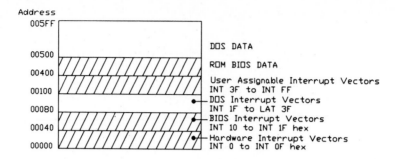

FIGURE 4.2 Low Memory Address Space

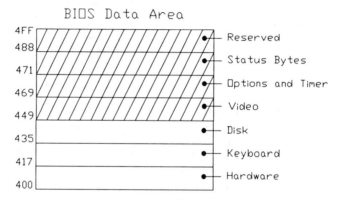

FIGURE 4.3 BIOS Data Area

1,536 bytes of storage and the operating system, (DOS) version 3.0 and above, and transient program area (TPA) in the remaining area. The system area is used for system data, interrupt vectors, BIOS data storage, and DOS data areas. This low memory address is shown in Figure 4.2. The memory areas denoted with cross-hatching in Figures 4.2–4.4 relate to the EGA/VGA.

The BIOS data area resides in this low memory address space between addresses 400 hex and 4FF hex. In this area, the BIOS routines store variables. In some cases, they can be accessed through BIOS calls. In other cases, they can be read directly. In keeping with the portability that BIOS provides, these variables should be read through the BIOS calls whenever possible. The three memory areas between 467 hex and 4FF hex are used for options—the timer, status bytes, and bytes reserved for future expansion. However, the EGA/VGA BIOS uses several of these memory locations to store its variables. Evidently, the 30 bytes reserved between 449 hex and 466 hex for the video parameters were not sufficient. The BIOS data area is illustrated in Figure 4.3.

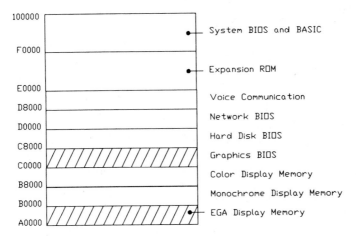

FIGURE 4.4 System-related Memory

The remaining memory below 640 Kbytes is used to hold device drivers, the DOS operating system, and the program area. The memory residing between 640 Kbytes and 1 Mbyte consists of the video area, disk and video BIOS, expansion ROM, system BIOS, and ROM Basic. The video area is reserved for RAM memory. The video memory is used to store the data that is displayed on the monitor. It resides on the video adapter board or on the motherboard. The BIOS areas reserved for expansion ROM include areas for graphics, hard disks, networking, voice communication, and specialized applications software. These areas are illustrated in Figure 4.4.

PC Input/Output

External devices are interfaced to the PC through memory I/O ports. Memory and I/O are controlled by different lines in the control bus of the computer, which, in turn, are controlled by different program instructions. The memory is composed of banks of RAM or ROM integrated circuits, usually in banks greater than 64 Kbytes. The I/O ports use hardware latches to interface the microprocessor with a wide variety of devices. A latch can represent a single I/O address. The PC hardware controls input and output ports differently from memory. The two configurations are illustrated in Figure 4.5.

Memory is accessed by a variety of program instructions. Nearly any instruction can access memory. Input/output ports are accessed by four instructions, two each for input and output. Ports are input to the host by the IN assembly language instruction and output by the OUT instruction. A typical interface requires data to be stored. Sometimes the data stored in the interface will be used to control the interface. Usually, ports are used instead of memory when only a few sequential storage locations are required for a given interface. In-

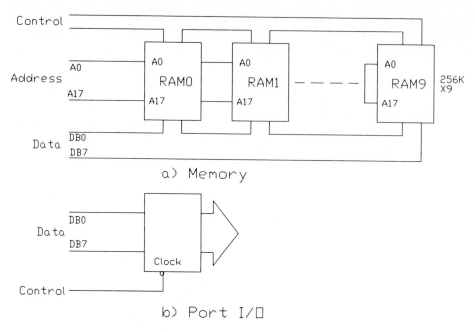

FIGURE 4.5 Memory versus Port I/O

tegrated circuits called *latches* are used to hold a single byte. In contrast, a single integrated circuit used in a memory bank can consist of 1 megabit of information per chip. Banks of nine of these memory chips implement a full megabyte of memory. Eight of the chips are used for the eight bits of data, and the ninth chip is used for the parity bit.

Interfacing with these memory integrated circuits is a technique that is well suited for large sequential blocks of data. This technique is wasteful, however, when a single byte of storage is required. In addition, accessing the memory system requires addressing and strobing. The information contained in a given memory cell is active on the bus for only a fraction of a second. This is not conducive to most I/O operations in which the information is required to control external functions.

A standard exists on the PC with regard to the input/output port locations for commonly used devices. Serial and parallel ports, display adapters, keyboards, timers, and disk drives have predetermined port addresses. Several addresses are reserved for user interfaces. The port I/O address range is limited compared to the memory addressing. Only ten bits are allocated in the port address space for I/O. Thus, only 1,024 unique locations exist. Because of the lack of space for expansion, a trend exists to increase this address space, using more of the 20 available address lines for port addressing. Figure 4.6 illustrates the port memory mapping.

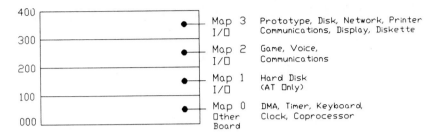

FIGURE 4.6   Port I/O Address Space

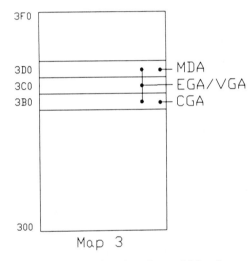

FIGURE 4.7   I/O Channel Map 3

Four maps are available, each being 256 locations long. The map 3 contains port space for the monochrome, color, and EGA/VGA adapters. These adapters have separate port address spaces. In order to be downwardly compatible, the EGA/VGA uses the port addresses associated with the monochrome or color systems. The I/O port locations dedicated to the display adapters are shown in Figure 4.7.

Indexed Port Addressing

Frequently, complicated devices require a number of ports. Because of the overcrowding of the host port address space, it is not possible for devices that require a large number of port addresses to assign one port address per register. The EGA/VGA has over 50 registers, yet it is allocated only 16 port I/O locations. To alleviate this problem, an indirect addressing scheme was designed to minimize the number of port addresses available to the host. With this addressing scheme, any device can use up to 256 ports, yet require only two addresses in the host port address space.

The indirect addressing scheme uses two host port addresses, one for an address port and a second for a data port. The host address port is loaded with an index number. Each of the device registers is assigned an index number. Before a register can be accessed by the host, the index number of this register must be loaded into the address register. Once the address register is loaded with an index value, the corresponding device register is selected. Only one device register can be accessed at a time. The host can access this device register through the data port register. The host data register provides an interface to the indexed device register. The host can read the contents of the device register or write to the device register through the host data register.

Some hardware implementations do not alter the index number in the address register. The index number in the address register will not change until the host writes into it again. It is not necessary to reload the address register with an index number until a device register with another index is desired. If two of the device registers need to be changed alternately, the index number in the address register will have to change with each access. This additional step can increase processing time, especially if the port I/O occurs inside a repetitive loop. To make matters worse, the limitation of the instruction set makes the IN and OUT instructions less flexible. This can drastically affect the speed at which port I/O can take place. Thus, a seemingly simple operation can involve a sizable number of instructions. The EGA/VGA uses this indirect addressing scheme to access the device registers. There are five groups of device registers in the EGA/VGA that are accessed by five sets of address and data register pairs.

Other hardware implementations automatically alter the index number in the address register after the host accesses the device registers through the data register. The index value is incremented so that the host can read or write to sequential device registers without having to modify the address register. This technique anticipates that the host will be loading a group of device registers sequentially. An example of this addressing scheme is found in the VGA Color Registers.

Accessing the Address and Data Registers

The I/O port registers are selected by a decoder on the host address bus. The data is presented to the registers by the host data bus. An 8-bit-wide processor can interface to an 8-bit-wide port register in a single machine cycle. A 16-bit-wide processor can interface to a 16-bit port register in a single machine cycle. Similarly, a 32-bit processor can interface with a 32-bit-wide port register in a single machine cycle.

The PC family of computers uses an 8-bit bus when the host processor is the 8088. The 8086 and 80286 processors can use a 16-bit data bus. The 80386 can use a 32-bit bus. Although a 16- or 32-bit processor is used, the port addresses are typically one byte wide.

The EGA and VGA boards are interfaced to the host processor through an 8-bit data bus, regardless of the processor. The VGA planar video systems and some VGA cards are interfaced to the host processor through a 16-bit bus.

It is possible to load the address register and the data register in a single output instruction with the EGA and VGA boards. The address register is located at a port address that precedes the data register. Thus, an address register port address of 3D0 hex would have an associated data register at port address 3D1 hex. This is the case with all five of the address and data register pairs in the EGA and VGA boards.

A single OUT instruction can output 16 bits on an 8-bit bus. It does this by multiplexing eight bits at a time onto the 8-bit-wide bus. The lower byte of the 16-bit word is output first, followed by the upper byte of the word. The time between these two output cycles is sufficient for hardware to access the EGA or VGA device registers. The lower byte, output first, corresponds to the index value to be loaded into the address register. The hardware has time to access the indexed device register and to respond to the following data on the bus by loading it into the selected device register. This technique will not work with a read operation because it is necessary to write data to the index register. This technique is not recommended in the case of the VGA planar display system. The VGA planar system is interfaced to the host through a 16-bit data bus.

Input/output ports may be *read-only, write-only* or *read and write*. If a port is read-only, the host microprocessor may only read this port. Writing to this port will have no effect. Similarly, the host processor will not be able to read a write-only port. Two registers, one read-only and one write-only, can occupy the same host port address, because one will be activated on every OUT instruction, and the other will be activated on every IN operation. No port conflict exists.

Write-only Ports

A severe limitation exists with write-only ports. The processor, and thus the software, has no way of determining what value is currently in a write-only register. This does not present a problem if only one application program is controlling the computer. The single program can keep a copy of the values in all of the write-only registers in read/write RAM. When a value of a register is desired, the applications program simply reads the value in the read/write RAM.

If more than one task is active, however, as is the case with event-driven memory resident programs, the state of the write-only registers can change without the knowledge of the application software. The memory resident program is not aware of the table that mirrors the write-only registers in read/write memory, which are maintained by the applications software. This limitation plagued the first-generation EGA implementations, because nearly all of the registers are write-only. The second generation of EGA adapters and the VGA adapters have alleviated this problem by not allowing any write-only registers.

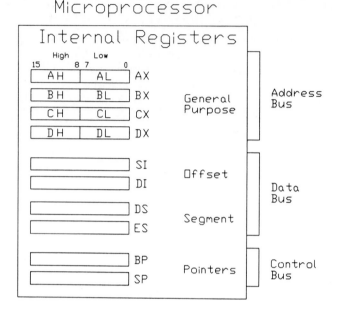

FIGURE 4.8 Internal Registers

4.1.2 Internal Registers

A third type of memory used by the processor is contained in the register file. The register file consists of several registers located on the microprocessor integrated circuit. The processor has a direct path to these registers and no external memory accesses are required. Nearly all instructions can access these registers directly. These registers include the control registers (such as the instruction counter and stack pointer), the index registers, the segment registers, and the general-purpose registers. These registers are illustrated in Figure 4.8.

The programmer controls the instruction pointer every time an instruction is executed or a jump is initiated. The stack pointer is used every time data is pushed or popped from the stack. The index registers are used in conjunction with the pointer registers to form a 20-bit address. These 20 bits can then span the entire lower 1 Mbyte of memory. The general-purpose registers are used to hold data and have special functions in several of the program instructions.

There are two segment registers, called the DS and the ES registers. They are used in conjunction with the index registers to form a 20-bit address. The index registers, SI and DI, contain the lower 16 bits of the address. This lower 16-bit field is called the offset. The segment registers contain the upper 16 bits of the address. Thus, a 20-bit address consists of two 16-bit addresses, called

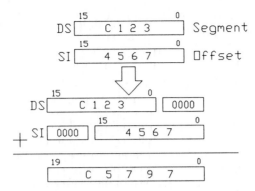

FIGURE 4.9 Creation of a 20-bit Address

the *segment* and the *offset*. The manner in which the 20-bit address is formed is illustrated in Figure 4.9.

In Figure 4.9 above, the segment address is shifted left by four positions before being added to the offset. This shift by four is equivalent to a multiplication by 16. This occurs because a 16-bit word, the offset, can access 64 Kbytes of storage, and there are 16 64-Kbyte sections in the lower 1 megabyte of memory.

The notation used when the segment and offset registers are combined is *DS:SI*. This terminology is frequently utilized in this book. Generally the DS segment register is associated with the SI index register, and the ES segment register is associated with the DI segment register. Whenever the SI or DI registers are used to form a 20-bit address without any specific reference to a segment register, the DS segment register is assumed.

The general-purpose registers include the AX, BX, CX, and DX registers. These 16-bit registers may be split into lower or higher bytes by using the convention *xL* or *xH*, where the *L* refers to the *lower* byte and the *H* refers to the *upper* byte of the 16-bit register. This allows 8-byte-wide data variables to be stored in these four registers.

Some of the registers have specific functions during the operation of program instructions. The CX register is often associated with counting tasks. The powerful move string (MOVS) instructions use the CX register as an input parameter indicating the number of bytes or words to move. The shift instruction uses the CX register to indicate the number of bit positions to shift. The multiply word instruction multiplies two 16-bit words, producing one 32-bit result. The data referenced in the source field of the instruction is always multiplied by the value in the AX register. The double-length result is returned in the DX and AX registers. These registers are typically used to hold data variables. They are often used by the BIOS routines to hold input and output parameters.

4.1.3 Processing Speed

The speed of the computer hardware plays a large part in the time required to execute a program. An instruction on a computer based on an 8088 microprocessor will take significantly longer to execute than will the same instruction on an 80386 microprocessor. The availability of a math coprocessor, such as the 8087, 80287 or 80387, also affects the operating speed. Graphics routines that require floating-point calculations will execute much more quickly if a math coprocessor is present. The processors are clocked by a crystal oscillator. The oscillator clock rate determines the hardware speed. An 8088 clocked at 4.7 mHz operates 40 percent more slowly than does an 8088 clocked at 8 mHz.

The speed of the memory can slow down the processing rate. If the memory is slower than the processor, the processor will have to wait for the memory. This delay, called a *wait state,* will be measured as a multiple of a machine cycle, because the processor and memory operate sychronously. The more wait states, the slower the processing.

In some cases, there are tradeoffs between processor speed and wait states. Suppose a processor can operate both at 8 mHz with memory operating at 0 wait states and at 10 mHz with memory operating at 1 wait state. It is unclear which mode to use to minimize processing time. Certain instructions require one memory access, whereas others require several memory accesses. Those which require multiple memory accesses will operate more slowly on a system whose memory causes wait states. For example, an instruction that fits into one 16-bit word and operates on data in an internal register will require one memory access. This access is required to fetch the instruction. Another instruction that operates on two data words in memory requires the instruction to be fetched, each of the data words to be read, and the result written back to memory. This totals four memory accesses.

The type of memory, RAM or ROM, also affects the processing speed. ROM memory is traditionally slower than RAM memory, requiring multiple wait states. The EGA/VGA BIOS is located in ROM memory. Thus, EGA/VGA programs that rely heavily on BIOS calls will operate more slowly than those that do not rely on BIOS. The 80386 computers have alleviated this problem by downloading the ROM code into RAM memory before processing.

The width of the data bus also affects processing speed. If an 8-bit data bus is used rather than a 16-bit data bus, it could take twice as long to send a 16-bit word across the bus. This is especially significant with the EGA/VGA. Many EGA and the VGA adapters—that is, a VGA that resides on a separate board—utilize an 8-bit bus. The planar VGA—that is, a VGA that resides on the motherboard, can utilize a 16-bit bus.

Many graphics programs have large memory requirements. If all of the relevant data required by a program fit into the available memory, no disk accesses are required. Disks operate significantly more slowly than memory. The number of disk accesses and the speed of the disk affect the processing speed.

4.1.4 BIOS

BIOS stands for Basic Input Output System. BIOS resides in ROM and provides a set of routines that interact directly with the PC hardware. The BIOS calls are invoked through the interrupt instruction of the CPU.

BIOS has two principle uses. The first is to provide compatibility despite variations in the PC implementation or family of microprocessors. This frees the programmer from the burdens of incompatible hardware. The second is to equip the programmer with a well-documented, easy-to-use set of routines that interact directly with the hardware. This eliminates the need for the programmer to understand the detailed operation of the hardware.

The PC has enjoyed increased popularity because of the availability of a wide range of software products. This software base is possible because of the compatibility shared between PCs. The BIOS programs help insure this compatibility. Hardware manufacturers utilize a variety of parts and system configurations to implement the PC. These implementation-specific variations can cause incompatibilities. The BIOS software routines resident on each PC take these variations into account and provide compatibility at the BIOS level.

The following example illustrates the importance of BIOS in insuring compatibility. Suppose a manufacturer builds a PC with a keyboard interface based on an integrated circuit. A second manufacturer builds the same keyboard interface but builds it using a different integrated circuit. Because each manufacturer provides the machines' BIOS, it is possible for each manufacturer to perform the same keyboard functions in different ways. Because of BIOS, the programmer has no need to be concerned with the hardware specifics.

The BIOS routines perform important and complicated tasks. Several of these routines will be useful to the programmer. By invoking a BIOS interrupt, the programmer can perform these tasks painlessly. The programmer must simply conform to the input and output constraints of the BIOS routines.

The BIOS routines allow the programmer to interface with the majority of input and output devices. The BIOS calls handle the video display, communications, printer, clock/calendar, keyboard, and disks. Special services include activating ROM BASIC and the start-up routine.

The programmer invokes the BIOS routines through a series of interrupts. The interrupts are organized into functional groups. These functional groups are listed in Table 4.1. The video display routines and the print screen routine are relevant to the EGA/VGA. The keyboard routines are useful when programs require operator interaction.

Families of hardware products evolve. Each evolution brings about change and improvements. BIOS insures that software will operate correctly for upgraded hardware. New versions of hardware will usually be downwardly compatible with the older implementations; this means that software that operates on the old system will operate correctly on the new system. However, the inverse is not true. Some new versions are so different from the previous versions that

TABLE 4.1 Host BIOS Routines

Interrupt # (Hex)	Hardware Serviced
10	Video display
13	Disk
14	Communications
16	Keyboard
17	Printer
11	Equipment status
12	Memory size
1A	Clock/calendar
5	Print Screen
18	ROM BASIC
19	Bootstrap start-up

creating complete compatibility would be prohibitively expensive. In these cases, the new versions are designed to be compatible at the BIOS level.

Display adapters have undergone such an evolution. The VGA is downwardly compatible at the BIOS level with the EGA, and both are downwardly compatible with the CGA at the BIOS level. This means that any software that interacts with the CGA exclusively through BIOS calls will operate correctly on either the EGA or the VGA. Likewise, any of the BIOS calls that operate on the EGA will operate correctly on the VGA. However, this compatibility does not insure that the adapters are compatible at the register level. It can be assumed that the boards are incompatible at the register level unless the board manufacturers specifically claim compatibility.

The BIOS routines are designed to be invoked by using interrupt calls. The interrupt calls utilize low memory interrupt vectors to determine the location of the start of the BIOS calls. Once the interrupt is invoked, the interrupt vector associated with the desired BIOS routine is interrogated to determine the starting address of the BIOS routine. This starting address consists of four bytes of information. The first two bytes correspond to the offset, or low-order, portion of the starting address; the second two bytes correspond to the segment, or high-order, portion of the starting address. The location of these four bytes corresponds to the interrupt number times four. Thus, the interrupt vector associated with interrupt 10 hex would be located at memory address 10 hex × 4 = 40 hex.

Table 4.2 lists two examples of the bytes that could be present beginning at 40 hex if the BIOS routine for interrupt 10 hex began at host address CA7C4 hex. The two examples illustrate that there is more than one way to produce a 20-bit address from two 16-bit addresses. Note that the low-order byte of a 16-bit word is always loaded preceding the high-order byte.

TABLE 4.2 Example Interrupt Vector for INT 10 Hex

Host Address (Hex)	Byte Value #1 (Hex)	Byte Value #2 (Hex)
0000:0040	00	12
0000:0041	C0	C2
0000:0042	C4	A4
0000:0043	A7	86

The system BIOS exists on the motherboard. However, the BIOS is resident on the adapter board on the hard disk controller, and the EGA/VGA graphics adapters. The system BIOS on the motherboard cannot anticipate which disk controller or display adapter will be present. The BIOS routines present in the ROM on the disk controller and on the EGA/VGA display adapters are responsible for loading the correct interrupt vectors for their BIOS routines. The remote BIOS ROMs are called by the system BIOS at bootstrap power-up to allow the remote BIOS routines to initialize the vectors and other important tasks.

It is often the case that an interrupt vector loaded by one BIOS will be overwritten with a different vector by a different BIOS. For example, the print-screen vector loaded by the system BIOS will be overwritten by the EGA/VGA BIOS. Two routines will exist that, when called, will print the screen. Because the EGA/VGA BIOS is invoked after the system BIOS, the interrupt vector will point to the EGA/VGA print-screen routine.

User-written software can also overwrite the vectors with pointers that access the applications software BIOS routine. This is often the case when terminate and stay resident (TSR) programs contain their own keyboard BIOS routines. When a keystrike occurs, the TSR program is invoked. It checks for a special key code, sometimes called a hot-key combination. If the TSR program determines that the last keystrike was the hot-key combination, it performs its function. If the keystrike was not the hot-key combination, the program passes control to the value previously loaded into the interrupt vector. In this manner, several TSR programs can interrogate a keystrike before control is passed to the system BIOS routine.

4.2 THE C LANGUAGE

The C language was chosen as the high-level language used in this book because it is a structured language, produces high-speed executable code, is popular in the PC environment, and is easily mixed with assembly language. This tutorial is not meant to teach the reader how to be an efficient C programmer. Rather, it defines the terminology used in this book to insure that all readers understand the programming examples. Care was taken to select the best graphics algorithms and to optimize their performance on the EGA/VGA. Of course, the experienced C programmer may find faster, more effective ways of implementing the algorithms than the examples provided here.

The nature and complexity of graphics algorithms beg for structure. Indeed, the graphics process itself is highly structured. Typical computer structures include the bit, byte, word, and string. Typical graphics structures include the pixel, horizontal line, and bit plane.

Graphics programming may be thought of as a translation process. Ideas are translated into codes that produce a result when executed on a computer. The better the translation between the ideas and the language, the easier the programming task becomes.

A structured language such as C is well-suited for graphics programming. Although it is not perfect, the C language provides an adequate translation. C is popular within the PC marketplace. This popularity has prompted manufacturers to create effective, fast, and easy-to-use compilers. In addition, a wide variety of program libraries are available to the programmer.

The C code is very readable, even to the novice user. The program examples in this book have comments interspersed throughout the code. Complete descriptions of the examples are provided in the text associated with the examples.

4.2.1 Other High-level Languages

The BASIC language has always been favored in the PC environment. This language was developed so that a line of BASIC code could be coded into a set of machine language instructions a line at a time. This type of decoding allows the use of interpreters instead of compilers. Interpreters are simple to use, and the programmer can see the results of the instruction immediately. However, BASIC code executes slowly, because every instruction must be decoded each time it is executed. In order to improve performance, BASIC compilers have been developed that perform admirably, although these still restrict the programmer to the constructs of the BASIC language.

FORTRAN is a popular language among scientific programmers. Developed as a formula-solving language, FORTRAN provides improved performance over BASIC but is not a structured language. The programmer is restricted to bytes, integers, and floating-point numbers. The most complicated structure possible in FORTRAN is the array. Character-string manipulation is awkward. Program control relies on *if* statements, *do* loops, and *goto* instructions. The programmer must use brute force to produce efficient graphics programs.

Pascal, like C, is a structured language, and there is no encompassing reason not to use it for graphics on the PC. In fact, the programs presented in this book can readily be translated into Pascal.

4.2.2 C and Assembly Language

In certain instances, assembly language routines are used in the examples in this book. To promote readability, these are used only where absolutely necessary. Certain BIOS calls require an assembly language interface. In other cases, assembly language routines are used in time-critical routines in which the C implementations would execute too slowly. The manufacturer of most C compilers anticipated the need for an assembly language interface and provide a simple means for combining these two languages.

Certain C compilers allow in-line assembly code. The programmer simply uses a compiler directive to indicate that assembly language instructions, instead of C language commands, follow. The assembly language statements are included in the midst of the C program. Most compilers, however, require that the assembly language routines be assembled independently using a macro assembler. The resulting object files are then linked to the C object files, creating the executable file.

A wide variety of C compilers is available for the PC. Each utilizes a different convention regarding the combination of C and assembly language. The interface is usually straightforward, once the specific rules are understood.

The examples in this book all follow a single protocol. The C routines call the assembly language routines. A set of parameters may be passed to the C program and, in certain cases, parameters may be passed back to the C program. At other times, assembly language routines call other assembly language routines. No assembly language routine ever calls a C routine.

The C programming examples in this book utilize a small percentage of the language's potential. In addition, the part used is actually the simplest to understand, which allows the reader to focus on the EGA/VGA function being implemented. The following discussion of the C language by no means covers the subject. Rather, these explanations offer a brief discussion of the basic structure of C as it applies to the programming examples.

The C program examples are presented as a selection of subroutines. The proper terminology for subroutines in the C language is *functions*. Because the word *function* has other meanings, the term *subroutine* is used in this book to avoid ambiguity. The hierarchy of subroutines includes a low-level set of primitive routines, implemented in either C or assembly language. These low-level primitives interact directly with the EGA/VGA hardware, either through BIOS calls or through direct manipulation of the display memory or the graphics registers.

4.2.3 Execution Speed

The time it takes for a program to execute depends on the number of instructions in the program and the execution time required by each instruction. When determining the number of instructions executed in a program, programmers must pay special attention to those instructions inside loops. Repetitive loops are used consistently in graphics applications. For example, up to 800 points are necessary to draw a diagonal line on the EGA/VGA. Graphics operations often deal with two-dimensional objects instead of lines. These dimensions greatly increase the number of pixels accessed in an operation. At the resolution of 640 by 480 pixels, there are 307,200 pixels on the screen. A routine used to output data to a single pixel would be called up to 307,200 times per image. Saving a little time in the routine that draws a pixel can add up to a significant performance improvement.

The amount of time required by the different machine instructions varies a great deal depending on the type of instruction. Some instructions can take one hundred times as long to execute as other instructions. For example, the divide instruction, IDIV, takes 100 times as long to execute as the shift right instruction, SHR. Instructions that occupy more than one word of program storage take longer to execute because of the additional words that have to be accessed from memory.

4.2.4   C Syntax

The C language syntax is flexible, but the programmer must take care to insure that the correct delimiters are always properly placed. The following are several rules relating to the C syntax.

1. Statements are terminated with a semicolon.

```
printf("Enter the desired color ? ");
```

2. More than one instruction can occupy a line.

```
color = red + blue;    red --;
```

3. The entry point of a subroutine is defined by a statement that includes the name of the subroutine and the parameters list associated with the subroutine. The name is followed by the parameter list. The parameter list can be empty. The parameter list must be preceded by a "(" preceding the parameter list and a ")" following the parameter list.

```
AddPnts(param_1,param_2,param_3)
```

4. A subroutine that has no parameters passed to it has the title delimited with a "()".

```
Reset()
```

5. The entry point and parameters of a subroutine are not terminated with a semicolon.

```
DrawPnt(page,x,y,color)
```

6. After the title and the parameter definitions, a subroutine is preceded by a "{". The subroutine is closed by a "}" following the last statement.

```
DrawPnt(page,x,y,color)
int x,y,color;  char page;
{ ...body of subroutine
}
```

7. A compound statement consists of multiple statements that are syntactically equivalent to a single statement. The group of statements are preceded with the delimiting "{" and followed with the delimiting "}".

```
if(x>=640)
  { x -= 640;
     wraparound = 1;
  }
```

8. Comments are delimited by a "/*" at the beginning and a "*/" at the end.

```
x -= 640;  /* subtract 640 from x for wrap around */
```

9. Comments may span more than one line.

```
/* this subroutine draws a point on the screen.
input parameters:
x = horizontal coordinate
y = vertical coordinate
color = color value */
```

10. Comments may not be nested. Comments may not be placed in the middle of an expression. The use of comments varies between different compilers.

Variables

Like any high-level language, C uses variables. There are global variables and local variables. Because the subroutines used in this book are self-contained, all variables are defined as local variables; no global variables are used. The following are several rules pertaining to the use of variables.

1. Variables may be constructed from lower-case or upper-case letters or numbers. The first character of a variable must be a letter. In some C compilers, only the first eight characters of a variable are significant. However, the character name can extend beyond eight characters.

```
TextFlag, param_1, retrace, r1213, miscellaneous
```

2. Variables are declared by indicating the type of each variable. The pre-defined data types used in the examples in this book are *int* for integer, *char* for character, and *float* for floating point.

```
int x,y,c;   char alpha,beta;   float scale;
```

3. All variables must be declared explicitly. Local variables are declared as the first expression in the subroutine. Variables passed as parameters are declared immediately following the title of the subroutine and before the beginning delimiting "{".

```
Horizontal(page,x1,x2,y,color)
 int xl,yl,color;  char page;  /* parameter variables */
{
 int x;  /* local variable "x" */
 for (x=x1; x<x2; x++)
    DrawPnt(page,x,y,color);
}
```

4. In most IBM PC C compilers, the integer constant or variable occupies two bytes. Signed integers range from -32768 to +32767. Unsigned integers range from 0 to +65535. Signed characters range from -128 to +127. Unsigned characters range from 0 to +255. The default declaration assumes the integer or characters are signed. The variables may be declared as unsigned by preceding the declaration with the modifier "unsigned".

```
unsigned int length;   unsigned char height;
```

5. The word length of integers can be extended to four bytes by preceding the declaration with the modifier "long". Long integers may be signed or unsigned.

```
long int   address;
```

6. As long as the limits of a variable type are not violated, one type of variable can be converted to a different type. The variable to be converted is preceded with the data type surrounded by parentheses.

```
int  code;   char eh;
code = 65;
/* convert the integer code, whose value is 65, to a
character. The character will be printed as a capital A since 65
is the ASCII code for an A. */
     eh = (char) code;  printf("\n eh = %c",eh)
```

7. Variables can be considered as a logical type if conditional expressions are used. A variable, either character or integer, with a value of 0 can be thought of as being false. Similarly, a variable with a nonzero value can be thought of as being true. The following two statements are identical.

```
/* in either case print the message if the value of flag is
non-zero */
     if(flag!=0) printf("The flag is true");
     if(flag) printf("The flag is true");
```

8. The "*" symbol preceding a variable in a TYPE declaration indicates that the variable is a pointer. The expression "int *point" defines the variable "point" to be a pointer to an integer. The "*" symbol preceding a variable in an expression yields the value pointed to by the variable. This assumes that the variable was previously declared as a pointer.

The "&" symbol preceding a variable yields the address of the variable. The expression "&alpha" evaluates as the address of the variable "alpha".

```
int alpha=10;  /* integer variable "alpha" is set to 10 */
int *tau,value;    /* "tau" is declared as a pointer to an
                     integer */
tau = alpha;  /* the pointer "tau" now points to the integer
                  variable alpha. */
value = *point;  /* "value" is loaded with the integer pointed
to by the "point" pointer, which is alpha. */
printf("Value = %2d",value);  /* prints out Value = 10 */
```

Constants

Constants are values that do not change throughout the execution of the program.

1. Constants are denoted in decimal, hexadecimal, octal, or binary format. The default format is assumed to be decimal. Hexadecimal format is indicated by preceding the number with a "0X" or "0x" prefix. Octal numbers are preceded with a "0" prefix.
int x,y,z; char alpha,beta;

```
/* these 3 variables are set to the same constant value */
x = 93;   y = 0x5D;   z = 0135;
/* Alpha is set to beta plus 30 hex */
alpha = 0x30 + beta;
```

2. Variables may be initialized to constants at the time of their declaration or during the course of the program.

```
Reset()
/* declare color as an integer whose value is 33 hex and declare
page as a character whose value is 0. Note that either color or
page can change value during the program. */
{ int x,y,color=0x33; char page=0;
/* set x equal to 600 and y = 300 */
x = 600;   y = 300;
```

3. Graphic characters can be represented in character constants by escape sequences. The notation used to indicate an escape sequence is the desired code preceded with a "\". Common escape sequences include "\n = linefeed", "\t = tab", "\0 = null", and "\f = formfeed".

```
/* precede the message with a line feed */
printf("\nEnter the length of the line ? ");
```

4. Long constants are declared by following the constant with an "L".

```
long address;
/* load address with a 32 bit long integer constant */
address = 0x0C1234L;
```

Data Structures

The C language utilizes a wide variety of data structures. The examples in this book use only one data structure, called the *array*. An array is a set of variables or constants organized in a sequential fashion. An array is composed of elements that can have only one type. The index of each element in the array is dictated by the position of the element and by the number of bytes occupied by a single element. Arrays of characters are called *strings*.

1. An array is declared by following the variable name with the number that represents the number of elements in the array.

```
/* delta is a character array which is 100 bytes long. Palette
is an array which is 16 integers, i.e., 32 bytes long. */
char delta[100];   int palette[16];
```

2. An element of an array is indicated by the array name followed by the index of the desired element. The element index must be preceded by a "[" and followed by a "]".

```
/* set the 11th element of the palette array to 33 hex */
palette[10] = 0x33;
```

3. The first element of an array is element 0. The second element is element 1, and the last element is N-1, where N is the length of the array.

```
int palette[16],i;
/* initialize all elements of the palette array. Note that the
first element of the array is palette[0], and the last element
is palette[15]. */
for (i=0; i<16; i++) palette[i] = 0x10;
```

4. Global arrays may be initialized in a declaration statement. Local arrays may be initialized in the MAIN portion of a program. Arrays may not be initialized in a declaration statement within a subroutine.

5. Under the proper conditions, an array can be initialized by providing the list of constants that are to be used to initialize the array. The list must be preceded with a "{" and ended with a "}". The number of elements in the initialization list must be equal to or less than the length of the array.

```
main()
/* initialize the three element color array to the constants
color[0]=10, color[1]=31, color[2]=15 */
{  int color[3] = {10, 31, 15};
```

6. Arrays of characters called *strings* store ASCII codes in an array. The string is normally terminated by a 0 byte. The 0 byte is declared within a string by a "\0". String initializations in declaration statements do not require the length of the array to be included.

```
/* the message array is terminated with a null character */
char message[] = "This is the End\0"
```

7. When an entire array is passed to a subroutine as a parameter, the declaration of the array within the subroutine does not need to include the length of the array. However, the declaration must indicate that the parameter is an array by following the array name with "[]"

```
WriteString(message)
/* message is an array whose length is unknown to this subroutine
WriteString */
char message[];
```

8. An individual element of an array passed to a subroutine causes a copy of the element to be passed to the subroutine. An entire array passed to a subroutine as a parameter causes a pointer that addresses the first element of the array to be passed to the subroutine.

```
/* declare message to be an array of 100 elements and palette to
be an array of 16 elements */
char message[100]; int palette[16];
/* call the subroutine ColorString and send it a pointer to the
first element in the message array along with a copy of the
10'th element of the palette array */
ColorString(message,palette[10]);
```

Operators

The C language provides the standard arithmetic and logical operators, along with a set of C-specific operators.

1. The standard arithmetic operators include those for addition ("+"), subtraction ("-"), multiplication ("*"), and division ("/") and ("%"). The first operator for division ("/") provides the true division, yielding a whole number and a fractional part. If integers are used, the fractional part is truncated. The "modulo" division operator ("%") yields only the fractional part. If integers are used, this fractional part represents the remainder of the integer division. This division can be used to generate modulo counters.

```
int x, y, side, inc;  float slope,length;
side = x * 3;  /* common integer multiply */
side = -y; /* side equals the negative of y */
/* "side" is a floating point number. It is divided by an
integer, "x", and the result is a floating point number in
"slope". */
slope = side / x;
/* both "side" and "x" are integers. The result of the division
is an integer in "inc" with the fractional part truncated. */
inc = y / x;
/* a rounded integer in "inc" results from the addition of .5 to
the integer division */
inc = (y / x) + .5;
/* the integer "length", is modulo divided by 640 to produce a
value which ranges from 0 to 639 in "x". */
x = length % 640;
```

2. The logical operators include those for ANDing ("&"), ORing ("|"), and exclusive ORing ("^"), as well as the one's complement ("~"). These logical operators cannot operate on floating-point or double floating-point variables.

```
int a,b,c;
a = c | b; /* "a" equals "c" OR "b" */
a = c & b; /* "a" equals "c" AND "b" */
```

3. The shift operators include those for shift left ("<<") and shift right (">>"). The variable preceding the shift operator will be shifted by the number of bits indicated in the variable or constant that follows the shift operator. Extreme care must be used when using this operator in complex expressions. The shift operations are processed after most other operators, and unless parentheses are used, the wrong data is often shifted. For example, the expression $a = b + c<<2$ is equivalent to $a = (b+c)<<2$, as opposed to $a = b + (c<<2)$.

```
int a,b,c=3;
a = b<<4; /* "a" equals "b" shifted left by 4 bits */
a = b<<c; /* "a" equals "b" shifted right by the number of bits
indicated by "c" */
```

4. Shifting left operations are similar to multiplications by a power of 2. A shift left by 1 bit is equivalent to a multiplication by two, a shift left by 2 bits is equivalent to a multiplication by 4, etc. Likewise, shifting right operations are similar to division by a power of 2. A shift right by 1 bit is equivalent to

a division by two, a shift right by 2 bits is equivalent to a division by 4, etc. Shift instructions are much faster than multiplication or division instructions.

```
a = b<<4; /* "a" equals "b" multiplied by 16. */
```

5. Arithmetic shifts are handled differently than are logical shifts. An arithmetic shift occurs when the integer value is signed. A logical shift occurs when the integer value is unsigned. An arithmetic left shift is different from a logical left shift. The sign bit does not shift out of the variable if the variable is signed. An arithmetic right shift is different from a logical right shift in that the signed bit is extended. The sign bit resides in the most significant bit of a value. In the case of a "char" variable, it resides in bit 7. In the case of an "integer" variable, it resides in bit 15. Care must be taken to insure that variables are declared as unsigned when a logical shift is desired.

```
int a = 0x8001, b;    unsigned int c=0x8001;
/* "b" equals "a" arithmetically shifted right by 2. Since "a"
is a 8001 hex, the result is b = E000 hex. */
b = a >> 2;
/* "b" equals "c" logically shifted right by 2. Since "c" is a
8001 hex, the result is b = 2000 hex. */
b = c >> 2;
/* "b" equals "a" arithmetically shifted left by 2. Since "a" is
a 8001 hex, the result is b = 8002 hex. */
b = a << 2;
/* "b" equals "c" logically shifted right by 2. Since "a" is a
8001 hex, the result is b = 0002 hex. */
b = c >> 2;
```

6. Special operators are used when a variable is modified by a variable or a constant. Any logical or arithmetic operator may be used to modify the variable. Special cases are the increment and decrement operations. In these cases, a variable is modified by +1 or -1.

```
a += 10; /* "a" = "a" plus 10 */
a *= 10; /* "a" = "a" times 10 */
a &= 0x1F; /* "a" = "a" ANDed with 001F hex */
a ++; /* increment a */
a --; /* decrement a */
```

7. Operator precedence is a major concern when coding expressions. The order used for operations on the variables and constants is critical to insure correct results. The order of precedence from highest to lowest is listed as follows:

1. Grouping expressions: parentheses ("()")

2. Associatives: incrementing ("++"), decrementing ("--"), type-changing ("(type)"), unary negate ("-"), logical NOT operation ("!")

3. Arithmetic: multiplication ("*"), division ("/"), modulo division ("%")

4. Arithmetic: addition ("+"), subtraction ("-")

5. Shifting: left shift ("<<"), right shift (">>")

6. Relational operators: greater than (">"), greater than or equal to (">="), less than ("<"), and less than or equal to ("<=")

7. Equality operators: equal to ("=="), not equal to ("!=")

8. Logical: AND ("&")

9. Logical: OR ("|")

10. Operate on self: addition ("+="), subtraction ("−="), etc.

Relational Operators

The C language provides a number of relational operators that are used to determine the condition of variables or expressions. Several program flow statements base their decisions upon these relational operators. The simplest program flow statement is the *if* statement. The syntax of the *if* statement is as follows:

```
if (condition is true) {expression}
```

The relational operators are used inside the conditional expression. These specify the condition that should be tested. The *if* statement is used as an example for the relational operators below.

1. Arithmetic operators: greater than (">"), greater than or equal to (">="), less than ("<"), and less than or equal to ("<=")

```
if (alpha>beta)
 printf("Alpha is greater than Beta");
if (alpha<=beta)
 printf("Alpha is less than or equal to Beta");
```

2. Equality operators: equal to ("=="), not equal to ("!=") Note that the relational equal consists of double equal symbols.

```
if (alpha==beta)
 printf("Alpha is equal to Beta");
if (alpha!=beta)
 printf("Alpha is NOT equal to Beta");
```

3. Logical negative operator: The negate operator called NOT ("!") can be used in place of implicitly stating "==0".

```
if (!alpha)
 printf("Alpha is false; that is, alpha is not equal 0");
```

Program Flow

The C language provides a number of program flow operations. These flow operations make decisions based on the conditional operators. The program flow statements include the *if, do, while, for, switch,* and *goto* commands.

1. The *if* statement is used to make decisions. Control passes to the statement or compound statements following the *if* expression when the expression evaluates to the logical value of true. The syntax is as follows:

```
if (expression==true) statement;
```

Optionally, the *else* clause may be added to the expression. It is added following the *if* statement. Control passes to the statement or compound statements following the *else* statement if the expression inside the *if* condition evaluates to false.

```
if (alpha)
 { flag = 1;
  printf("Alpha is true and alpha is NOT equal to 0");
 }
else
 { flag = 0;
  printf("Alpha is false and alpha is equal to 0");
 }
```

2. The *for* loop allows the statements or compound statements that follow the *for* loop declaration to be executed based on a starting and ending condition. A good deal of flexibility exists in this instruction. Only one type of conditional expression is used inside the *for* loop in this book. An index

variable is initialized to a value, and the statement or compound statements are executed. The index variable is then incremented or decremented by a specified amount until a final condition is reached. The general syntax of the *for* loop follows:

```
for (expression_1; expression_2; expression_3)
  { statement or compound statements }
```

The form of the *for* loop used in this book initializes the index variable in expression_1 and executes the statements following the expression list. It then modifies the index according to expression_3 while expression_2 is true. The *Break* statement can be used to divert program control out of the *for* loop.

```
/* execute the compound statements repetitively. The first
execution uses index = start. After the execution of the
compound statements, index is incremented. This process repeats
itself until index = end. At this time, program control resumes
after the compound statements. */
    for (index=start; index<end; index++)
     { printf("Executing the loop with index = %d",index);
       buf[i] = 3.3 * index;
     }
```

3. The *do...while()* construct executes a statement or compound statement repeatedly until a condition present in the *while* statement evaluates as false or zero. The *do...while()* construct is similar to the *while()* construct. The difference is that the statement or compound statements in the *do...while()* are executed before the first evaluation of the conditional expression is made. The conditional expression is evaluated before the statement or compound statements are evaluated in the *while()* statement. The *Break* statement can be used to divert program control out of the *while()* statement.

```
/* the print statement will be executed once */
alpha = 20;
do
 {
   printf("Executing the do construct");
   alpha ++;
 }
while(alpha<20);
```

4. The *while()* construct evaluates an expression and executes a statement or compound statements until the expression evaluates as false. The *while()*

construct is similar to the *do...while()* construct. The difference is that the statement or compound statements in the *do...while()* are executed before the first evaluation of the conditional expression is made. The conditional expression is evaluated before the statement or compound statements are evaluated in the *while()* statement. The *Break* statement can be used to divert program control out of the *do...while* statement.

```
/* the print statement will NOT be executed */
alpha = 20;
while(alpha<20)
  {
   printf("Executing the do construct");
   alpha ++;
  }
```

5. The *switch/case* statement is useful when multipath branching is desired. An expression present in the switch statement is evaluated and compared to a list of constant values contained in the *case* statements. The statements following a match between the *switch* expression and the *case* constant are executed. No statements are executed if a match does not occur. The *Break* statement can be used to divert program control out of the *switch* statement. This is frequently used in the *switch* statement when only one of the case paths should be executed. The *Default* statement is executed if none of the above case conditions are satisfied.

```
/* compare the variable "key" with the constants 1, 2, 3, 4, and
5 until a match occurs. The subroutines Sub3, Sub4, Sub5 and
Sub6 will be executed since the "key" variable is equal to 3. */
    key = 3;
    switch (key)
      {
         case 1: Sub1();
         case 2: Sub2();
         case 3: Sub3();
         case 4: Sub4();
         case 5: Sub5();
         default: Sub6();
      }
/* compare the variable "key" with the constants 1, 2, 3, 4, and
5 until a match occurs. The subroutine Sub3 alone will be
executed since the "key" variable is equal to 3 and the break
command will cause control to pass out of the switch command. */
    key = 3;
    switch (key)
```

```
    {
        case 1: Sub1(); break;
        case 2: Sub2(); break;
        case 3: Sub3(); break;
        case 4: Sub4(); break;
        case 5: Sub5(); break;
        default: Sub6();
    }
```

6. The *goto* LABEL statement is the most controversial control statement in the C language. Using this statement is considered by many to be poor programming practice in a structured language. Control is passed unconditionally to the program statements following the LABEL. The LABEL follows the same naming conventions as variables.

The *goto* command can be effective if an immediate abort is desired. In programs with complex, heavily nested code, it is sometimes useful to be able to exit without having to follow a path through the complicated program structure. Going through the program flow can be complicated and can make the code virtually unreadable. This is often unnecessary, and judicious use of the *goto* statement can help the programmer produce more readable code.

```
    /* control passes to the "Done" label if value>200 */
        INT value;
        if(value>200) goto Done;
        printf("Value less than or equal to 200");
        value ++;
    Done:
        printf("Value greater than 200");
```

Subroutines

Large computing tasks can be organized into sections of code. These sections are called *subroutines* in FORTRAN, *procedures* in Pascal, and *functions* in C. Although the term *function* is the accepted terminology for the C language, the terms *function, subroutine,* and *procedure* are used interchangeably throughout this book.

Subroutines are an essential part of effective programming, although additional overhead is required. A call to a subroutine requires *pushing* all parameters passed to the subroutine and the program counter on the stack before jumping to the subroutine location. The subroutine must *pop* any parameters off of the stack before executing. After executing, it must *pop* the program counter off of the stack and jump back to the calling program. This overhead is not significant if the subroutine is performing a number of calculations. However, it can be significant if the subroutine is short and called repeatedly.

Rules relating to subroutines are listed below.

1. The first line of a subroutine is the title. It consists of the name of the subroutine followed by a parameter list. The parameter list may be empty. The title is not followed by a semicolon.

```
SubTitle(param_1,param_2)  /* subroutine title */
 int param_1; real param_2;  /* parameter type statements */
 {  /* start of subroutine delimiter */
         /* body of subroutine */
    printf("Subroutine parameters %d %f",param_1,param_2);
         /* body of subroutine */
 }  /* end of subroutine delimiter */
```

2. The body of a subroutine is enclosed by delimiters. The "{" is used preceding the subroutine, and the "}" is used following the subroutine.

3. If parameters are passed to the subroutine, they must be defined in a type statement immediately after the title and before the opening "{" of the subroutine.

4. A return from the subroutine occurs when the ending "}" delimiter of the subroutine is encountered. It is also possible to exit from a subroutine using the *return* command.

```
/* If "param_1" is less than 0 control will pass back to the
calling program without any printout. */
SubTitle(param_1,param_2)
 int param_1; real param_2;
 {if(param_1<0) Return;
   printf("Subroutine parameters %d %f",param_1,param_2);
 }
```

5. A single parameter may be passed back to the calling program through the *return* instruction. An optional parameter may follow the *return* instruction. This parameter can be read by the calling program. The form of the *return* instruction is *return(parameter)*. The parameter returned to the host is read as if the subroutine were a function returning a variable.

```
/* calling program */
int param;
...
param = Sub(param_1); /* get parameter from subroutine */
...
/* subroutine */
```

```
Sub(param_1)
int param_1;
{ int send_back;
  send_back = param_1 * 10;
/* return to calling program with parameter */
 return(send_back);
}
```

The mechanism used in the PC family of computers to return a parameter to a calling program is to load the AX register with the value of the parameter. In the above example, the AX register is loaded with the value in send_back.

6. The technique employed to pass non-array parameters to a subroutine utilizes the stack. A copy of the parameters is *pushed* onto the stack. The subroutine, anticipating the parameters, will pull the copies of the parameters off of the stack. Because a copy of the data is placed on the stack, the subroutine cannot modify the value of the original data. If the subroutine modifies the parameter, it is merely changing the value of the copy of the parameter that resides on the stack.

```
/* calling program */
int param=1;
... /* param equals 1 */
Sub(param_1); /* get parameter from subroutine */
... /* param still equals 1 */
/* subroutine */
Sub(param_1)
int param_1;
{ param_1 = 0; /* change the copy of param to 0 */
}
```

7. Passing an array to a subroutine places a copy of the starting address of the array onto the stack. Because the parameter points to the actual array, the calling program and the subroutine reference the same data. If the subroutine modifies the array, the array will change with respect to the calling subroutine.

```
/* calling program */
int param[10], i;
...
/* all elements of the param buffer are set to "1" */
for (i=0; i<10; i++) param[i] = 1;
Sub(param_1);
/* all elements of the param array are now equal to "0" */
```

```
...
/* subroutine */
Sub(param_1)
int param_1[];
{
/* clear all elements of the param array */
for (i=0; i<10; i++) param_1[i] = 0;
}
```

8. Passing a single element of an array is equivalent to passing a value. A copy of the value is placed onto the stack. Therefore, the subroutine cannot modify the original array element.

9. It is possible for subroutines to modify nonarray variables. The technique employed has the calling routine send a pointer that points to the variable. As is true when an array is passed to a subroutine, the subroutine and the calling program both reference the same value. A pointer must be declared in the calling program and set to point to the desired variable. The pointer is passed as a parameter to the subroutine. The subroutine must declare this parameter as a pointer. If the subroutine modifies the value pointed to by the parameter, the original data variable in the calling program will be modified.

```
/* calling program */
int *tau /* "tau" is a pointer to an integer */
int alpha=10; /* "alpha" is an integer set to 10 */
tau = &alpha; /* "tau" points to alpha */
/* call subroutine "Sub" and send it the pointer "tau" */
Sub(&tau);
printf("The value of alpha is %d",alpha); /* alpha = 0 */
/* subroutine */
Sub(stau)
int *stau;        /* declare subroutine pointer */
  {
    /* clear the integer variable pointed to by "spoint" */
    *stau = 0;
  }
```

Input and Output

In this book, the input and output used by the C routines are limited to the terminal input and output.

1. The *printf* command is used to output data to the display at the current cursor position and in the color 07, where the background is 0 and the

foreground is 7. The *printf* command usually is not aware of the display configuration and does not necessarily respond to 43- or 50-line display formats.

2. The *scanf* command is used to input data from the keyboard. Values in this book are entered in either decimal format, using the "%d" indicator, or hexadecimal format, using the "%x" indicator. The variables contained within the *scanf* command are always preceded by an "&" sign indicating that a pointer is being passed to the *scanf* routine.

4.2.5 Memory Models

Most C compilers allow the use of small model, medium model, or large model compiler options. The small model compiler assumes that all code and data will reside in their own 64-Kbyte segment of memory. The medium model compiler assumes that the code and stack segments reside in one 64-Kbyte segment and the data segment resides in a second 64-Kbyte segment. The large model compiler makes no assumptions regarding the length of the code, stack, or data segments.

Small Model Compiler

In the small model compiler, the code is limited to one 64-Kbyte segment, and the data and stack are limited to another 64-Kbyte segment. Both the data and stack segment registers are initialized to the same value as the program is being loaded into memory. The code segment register is also initialized during the loading of the program. The code segment register may be initialized to a value different from the data and stack registers. The programmer need not be concerned with the values in the segment registers, because these will never change. All instructions that access data within the data/stack segment can use 16-bit addresses. Any memory location within the active 64-Kbyte segment of memory can be reached by a 16-bit offset value. An offset address of 0000 hex references the first byte of the data and stack segment. An offset address of FFFF hex references the last byte of the segment. The starting addresses of the data and stack segment are found in the data segment (DS) and the stack segment (SS) registers. The actual starting memory address is determined by shifting the value in the segment register left by four bits. The 20-bit memory address can be determined by shifting the value in the segment register left by four bits and adding the value in the offset register.

All of the code resides in a separate 64-Kbyte segment. The starting address of the code segment is found in the code segment (CS) register. As for the data and stack segment registers, the actual memory address is determined by shifting the value in the code segment register left by four bits. Any address in the code segment can be accessed through a 16-bit offset. The 20-bit byte memory address can be determined by shifting the value in the segment register left by four bits and adding the value in the offset register.

Medium Model Compiler

The medium model, like the small model, restricts the data and stack segments to 64 Kbytes. The rules that apply to the data and stack segments when using the small model also apply to the medium model. Data outside of the active data segment can be reached by explicitly calling for a *far* pointer. When a *far* keyword is used, a 32-bit address must be specified.

The code segment has no limitations other than the amount of memory resident in the lower 1 Mbyte in the computer. Instructions that modify the instruction pointer register (IP) must explicitly define the 20-bit address. Examples include the *jmp, call,* and *ret* instructions. Two words must be dedicated to the addresses referenced by these instructions. Two words are copied each time an address is *pushed* onto the stack by a *call* instruction or *popped* from the stack using a *ret* instruction.

Large Model Compiler

The code segment has no limitations other than the amount of memory resident in the lower 1 Mbyte in the computer. Rules that govern its behavior are identical to the small model compiler.

The data and stack segment are similarly unrestricted. Each time data is accessed, a 20-bit memory address must be used. Pointers passed onto the stack must also be 20 bits. The 20-bit addresses are stored in two registers, typically a segment and index register. If data resides in a 64-Kbyte area, it is not necessary to modify the data segment register. If the location of data is unclear, the full 20-bit address must be specified. When array pointers are passed as parameters to subroutines, two 16-bit words must be placed onto the stack. One is loaded into the segment register and the other is loaded into the offset register.

4.3 ASSEMBLY LANGUAGE

Assembly language is the closest a programmer can get to the hardware in the PC environment. The PC is controlled by an 8088, 8086, 80286, or 80386 processor. Each of these has its own set of commands. A common set of commands is understood by all of these processors. Only these common commands are used in the examples of this book. These commands, called *machine language instructions,* are located in the PC memory, either in the random access memory (RAM) or in the read only memory (ROM). An assembly language instruction is decoded into one machine language instruction. Each machine language instruction consists of one or more 16-bit words. Each instructs the processor regarding its next operation. Assembly language provides a tool to enable the programmer to write these machine instructions, thereby maintaining direct control over the processor. This tool frees the programmer from many of the ugly details surrounding machine language code.

Assembly language instructions interact directly with the computer's resources. These access RAM and ROM memory as well as the input/output (I/O) ports. Through the memory and I/O ports, the programmer has direct control over the processor, coprocessor, memory, and peripherals. This control over the computer is not absolute. The assembly language programmer must relinquish a small amount of control to the operating system.

Most C compilers translate the C instructions into assembly language instructions. Usually more than one assembly instruction is required to translate one C statement. Once instructions have been converted into assembly language, a macro assembler is used to further translate these assembly language statements into machine code. During the compilation process, the compiler decides which and how many assembly language instructions are to be used to implement the C commands. This selection process often results in more assembly language instructions than if the program were initially written in assembly language.

Understanding the assembly language program examples in this book does not require the reader to be a skilled assembly language programmer. Only a small subset of the potentials available in assembly language is utilized in the programming examples. All of the assembly language routines follow the same general form. Each is a relatively small subroutine usually called by a C routine. To understand or modify the examples, or to write similar programs, a programmer needs to understand only the syntax and instructions described in this section.

The microprocessor understands only one language called machine language. Each microprocessor has its own unique set of machine language instructions that it is capable of decoding and performing. The microprocessor manufacturer assigns instruction names to these machine-level commands. In addition, the fields and options associated with the instructions are formalized into a language structure. These commands and their respective parameters form the rudiments of assembly language. For example, one general type of instruction might be an *add* instruction. The microprocessor arithmetic unit will actually perform the add, but the microprocessor also needs to know which two words to add together. One or both of these two words might be contained in a local register or in memory. If one is in memory, it may be pointed to by a direct address, an indirect address pointed to by a register, or an immediate value that follows the instruction. (There are actually several more addressing modes, but these are not covered in the examples and are therefore not discussed here.) All of this information needs to be stored in the machine language instruction.

It is the task of the assembler to translate the symbolic notations used in the assembly language code into the proper machine code. A second important task of the assembler is to keep track of addresses. It is highly desirable to use symbols to keep track of program locations. It is simple to command the processor to jump to location "loop", but it is difficult to determine the actual address of the location of "loop". Symbols are also used to help document the code. It is easy to understand a command that loads a register with a value that represents the horizontal address if the value is referred to as "x_address" in the code. It is not as easy to understand the command if the address of the value is referred to as 43AC hex. Thus, the coding of instructions and the use of symbolic notation are the two prime purposes of an assembler.

Assemblers also provide a number of bells and whistles that make the programmer's job much easier. In order to keep the examples as portable as possible, the additional features of assemblers have not been utilized in the examples.

Reading an assembly language routine requires practice. The ability to determine that a group of assembly language instructions are performing a specific task can be difficult. The documentation associated with these assembly language routines is essential to understanding the meaning of the code. The associated text describes the function of the code in great detail. The program source code is also commented upon thoroughly. These comments reflect what the instruction is doing, how it is doing it, and how it fits in with the other instructions.

4.3.1 Assembly Language Syntax

Unlike the C syntax, the assembly language syntax is field-oriented. Strict rules applying to each of these fields must be adhered to in order for the assembler to operate correctly. Rules relating to the assembly language syntax are listed below.

1. The assembly language instruction must be contained on a single line.

2. The line consists of several fields including the label field, the instruction mnemonic field, the operand field, and the comment field. Each field may be a variable length and may start at any character position on the line, as long as the order is maintained.

```
Label: Instruction Operand Fields; Comments
Start: MOV AX,BX            ; Copy the BX register into AX
```

3. Labels are followed by a colon.

```
Label:
```

4. Comments may appear as the only item on a line or after the operand field. Comments are preceded by a ";".
This instruction adds the display pitch to the address contained in BX.

```
ADD     BX,Pitch              ; add pitch to the address in BX
```

5. The entry point of a subroutine must be a public symbol if C routines or other external assembly language routines call it. Several conventions are used by different C compilers for naming public assembly language labels. The Microsoft and Lattice C compilers require that the public labels be preceded with an underscore character ("_"). The Manx compiler requires that the public labels be followed by an underscore character. This causes a headache for those trying to create portable code. The examples used in this book assume the Microsoft and Lattice compiler conventions.

```
/* declare the entry point of the subroutine public */
public _Sub1
_Sub1      pro         far              /* title of subroutine */
```

4.3.2 Instruction Mnemonics

The instruction mnemonic describes the general function of the instruction. Typical instruction mnemonics include ADD, AND, MOV, and CALL. The assembly language reference manuals contain alphabetical listings of these instructions and details regarding their operation. A list of all instructions used in this manual is included below. The mnemonic field is located after the label, when a label is present. If no label is present, the mnemonic field is the first field on a line.

Most instructions require an operand field, but some do not. Others require that the operand consist of one field, but the majority require that there be two operand fields.

1. Examples of instructions that require no operand fields include the *return* (RET) and the *move string* (MOVS) instructions. The *move string* source and destination fields are implied in the instruction.

```
MOVS
RET        ;return from subroutine
```

2. Many instructions require one operand field. This field represents an address in the case of the CALL, LOOP, or the jump family of instructions. Other instructions require that the operand represent a source of data. These include the PUSH instruction and the multiply (MUL) and divide (DIV) instructions. Instructions that require the single operand field to be a source and destination include the POP instruction. Some instructions use the operand field to represent both the source and the destination. These include the *negate* (NEG), NOT, and *decrement* (DEC) instructions.

```
CALL SUB1        ;call subroutine 1
MUL  value       ;multiply the AX register by "value"
POP  AX          ;load the AX with the top of stack
NEG  BX          ;negate the BX register
```

3. Many operations require operands with two fields. These two fields usually represent the source and destination fields. Normally the destination field is followed by the source field, and the two are separated by a comma. Instructions that use the source and destination fields include the *move* (MOV), ADD, AND, *compare* (CMP), OR, and *load effective address* (LEA) instructions.

The shift instructions (SHL, SHR) and the rotate instructions (ROR, ROL) require two fields in the operand field. The first field corresponds to the source and destination field, and the second field is the count field that dictates how many bits to shift the instruction.

There are three instructions that have two destinations and one source field. These instructions are the *load* (LDS) and the LES instructions. The standard source/destination fields are used in the operand field, and the second destination is implied in the instruction itself. The LDS instruction uses the DS register, and the LES instruction uses the ES register as the second destination field. Two destination fields are required, because the source field points to a double word.

```
MOV  AX,BX       ;Copy the BX register to the AX register
ROR  AX,1        ;rotate right by 1
SHL  AX,CX       ;shift AX left by the # of bits in CX
LDS  SI,[bp]     ;load the DS register and the SI register with the
                 ;double word pointed to by the BP register.
```

4.3.3 Addressing Modes

There are three basic addressing modes used in the operand fields of the assembly language instructions. These addressing modes select the CPU registers, memory, immediates, or indirect addressing as the source and destination fields. Indirect fields may be indexed.

1. The hardware registers may be used as operands in the majority of instructions. If the AX, BX, CX, or DX registers are used, the operand is assumed to reference a word. If the AL, AH, BL, BH, CL, CH, DL, or DH registers are used, the operand is assumed to reference a byte.

```
MOV  AX,BX       ;move both bytes of the BX into AX
ROR  AL,1        ;rotate right the lower byte of AX
```

2. Memory locations may be used as operands in many instructions. Most of these instructions do not allow a memory field to be used in both of the two fields in a double field operand. Memory locations are usually referenced by symbolic names. Memory locations are often addressed through the indirect addressing modes, in which the pointer registers point to the desired memory location.

```
big:      DW   1        ;reserve one word of storage for "big"
small:    DB   1        ;reserve one byte of storage for "small"


          MOV  AX,big      ;move the word in memory location
                          ;"big" into the AX register
          MOV  small,AL    ;move the byte in AL into memory
                          ;location "small"
```

3. Immediate addressing references the instruction pointer. The value referenced in the operand field follows immediately after the instruction as the next word in memory. The immediate value is differentiated from a symbol by the fact that it begins with a number as opposed to a letter. It may be written in binary, octal, decimal, or hexadecimal notation.

```
MOV   AX,7344     ;load AX with the word 7344 decimal
MOV   AL,3Ah      ;load AL with the byte 3A hex
```

4. Indirect addressing uses the bracketed register in the operand field as a pointer to a memory location. The memory location is used as the operand. The indirect register must be bracketed (that is, it must be preceded with a "[" and followed by a "]".) If a segment register is included in the command, it precedes the bracketed indirect register. The two registers are separated by a colon. In this book, the source index register (SI), the destination index register (DI), or the base point register (BP) is used to reference a memory location. A 20-bit address is required to completely access the lower megabyte of memory. The data segment (DS) or extra segment (ES) register is used in conjunction with the index registers. If no segment register is indicated, the DS register is assumed. The stack segment (SS) register is used in conjunction with the base pointer register. Because it is the only segment register that may be used with the BP register, there is no reason to include it in the command line.

```
MOV   AX,[SI]     ;load AX with the value in memory pointed to by
                  ;the DS:SI register pair.
MOV   [DI],AX     ;load the value in the AX register into memory
                  ;as pointed to by the DS:DI register pair.
```

```
MOV  ES:[DI],AX  ;load the value in the AX register into memory
                 ;as pointed to by the ES:DI register pair.
MOV  AX,[BP]     ;load AX with the value in memory pointed to by
                 ;the SS:BP register pair.
```

5. Indexed addressing allows the programmer to add an offset to the indirect address. This addressing mode is used in this book to reference parameters resident on the stack. The indirect addressing mode causes a memory location to be used as an operand in an instruction. The address of the memory location is determined by adding a constant index value to the value in the indirect register. Note that this addition does not actually occur in the register; thus, the value of the indirect register does not change.

```
MOV  AX,[BP+6]   ;load AX with the value in memory pointed to
                 ;by the SS:BP register pair plus the constant
                 ;6.
```

6. At times, the length of an operand field is ambiguous. If an operand calls for the entire 16-bit register—for example, AX—the word nature of the instruction is evident. Likewise, if an operand calls for an 8-bit register—for example, AL—the byte nature of the instruction is evident. If, however, no statement is made as to the word or byte nature of an operand, the length must be defined. This is done with the BYTE PTR or WORD PTR prefixes. The BYTE PTR prefix precedes an operand when a byte is desired. The WORD PTR prefix precedes an operand when a word is desired.

```
MOV  WORD PTR [SI],12h  ;move the word 0012 hex to the word in
                        ;memory addressed by the DS:SI register
                        ;pair.
```

4.3.4 Assembly Language Instructions

All of the assembly language instructions used in this book are discussed in this section. The instructions have been organized into functional groups. These groups include the arithmetic, logical, data-move, stack-related, program-control, and input/output instructions.

Arithmetic Instructions

The arithmetic instructions include the ADD, CMP, INC, NEG, and SUB. All of these instructions affect the status flags located in the status register. These flags may subsequently be tested by the conditional branching instructions.

ADD <**destination**>,<**source**>. The add instruction adds the value referenced by the source field to the value referenced by the destination field and stores the result in the destination field.

CMP <**destination**>,<**source**>. The compare instruction subtracts the value referenced by the source field from the value referenced by the destination field. The flags in the processor status register are updated depending on the result. These flags include the zero flag and the sign flag. Neither of the values referenced by the source or destination fields are modified as a result of this instruction.

INC <**destination**>. The increment instruction adds one to the value referenced by the destination field.

SUB <**destination**>,<**source**>. The subtract instruction subtracts the value referenced by the source field from the value referenced by the destination field and stores the result in the destination field.

Logical Instructions

The logical instructions include AND, OR, ROL, RCL, ROR, RCR, SHL, SHR, and XOR. The shifting instructions are also commonly used to perform multiplications and divisions when one of the multiplicands is a power of 2.

AND <**destination**>,<**source**>. The logical AND instruction ANDs the value referenced by the source field to the value referenced by the destination field and stores the result in the destination field. The AND operation sets all bits in the destination to 1 when both of the associated bits in the input source and destination field are 1s.

OR <**destination**>,<**source**>. The logical OR instruction ORs the value referenced by the source field to the value referenced by the destination field and stores the result in the destination field. The OR operation sets all bits to 1 in the destination when either of the associated bits in the input source and destination are equal to 1.

Rotate and Shift Instructions

The rotate and shift instructions shift the data in a byte or word a specified number of bits. Zeros are shifted into the byte or word, and the data shifted out is lost for a shift instruction. In a rotate instruction, the data shifted out of the byte or word is shifted back into it from the opposing side. The shift count is the literal value, 1, or the CL register. The CL register is the lower byte of the CX register. The CX register is typically used as an index register. The value in the CX register determines the number of bits to shift the destination byte or word.

ROL <**destination**>,<**shift count**>. The rotate left instruction rotates a byte or word a specified number of bits to the left in the word referenced by the destination field. The leftmost bit of the byte or word is shifted into the rightmost bit.

RCL <**destination**>,<**shift count**>. The rotate left through the carry instruction utilizes the carry flag located in the status register. It is similar to the

ROL instruction. However, the leftmost bit is shifted into the carry, and the carry is shifted into the rightmost bit.

ROR <destination>,<shift count>. The rotate right instruction rotates a byte or word a specified number of bits to the right in the word referenced by the destination field. The rightmost bit of the byte or word is shifted into the leftmost bit.

RCR <destination>,<shift count>. The rotate right through the carry instruction utilizes the carry flag located in the status register. It is similar to the ROR instruction. However, the rightmost bit is shifted into the carry, and the carry is shifted into the leftmost bit.

SHL <destination>,<shift count>. The shift left instruction shifts a byte or word a specified number of bits to the left in the word referenced by the destination field. The rightmost bits of the byte or word are filled with zeros, and the leftmost bit is shifted out of the word and lost.

SHR <destination>,<shift count>. The shift right instruction shifts a byte or word a specified number of bits to the right in the word referenced by the destination field. The leftmost bits of the byte or word are filled with zeros, and the rightmost bit is shifted out of the word and lost.

XOR <destination>,<source>. The exclusive OR instruction exclusive ORs the value referenced by the source field to the value referenced by the destination field and stores the result in the destination field. The exclusive OR operation sets all bits that are the same to a 0 and all bits that are different to a 1. A number exclusive ORed with itself produces a 0.

Data Move Instructions

The data-moving instructions include the LDS, LES, MOV, MOVS, LODS and STOS instructions. These instructions move data from one location to another. A limitation on the MOV instruction is that it cannot move data from a source field that is a memory location to a destination field that is a memory location. The MOVS instruction moves a block of data exclusively from one memory location to another. The STOS and MOVS instruction codes are followed with a *B* for byte operation or a *W* for word operations. Because the memory requires greater than 16 bits of address, the segment and offset registers must be used. The segment registers are the DS and ES registers; the offset registers are the SI and DI registers. To address a byte or word in memory, the DS:SI pair of registers is used for the source memory address and the ES:DI pair of registers is used for the destination memory address. The MOVS or STOS instruction can move multiple bytes or words. This occurs if the MOVS or STOS instruction is preceded by a REP assembler directive. The CX register is used as the counter for the multiple bytes or words.

LDS <offset register>,<memory address>. The load data segment register is used to load the data segment register and the offset register with the four bytes pointed to by the memory address. The offset register is typically the SI register, because the DS:SI register pair is most often used to reference memory addresses. If C were sending an array's pointer to an assembly language routine in a large model, this instruction could be used to grab the 4-byte segment and offset register being transferred from the C routine.

LES <**offset register**>,<**memory address**>. The load extra segment register is used to load the extra segment register (ES) and the offset register with the four bytes pointed to by the memory address. The offset register is typically the DI register, because the ES:DI register pair is used to reference memory addresses in the string instructions. Other than the registers loaded, this instruction operates identically to the LDS instruction above.

MOV <**destination**>,<**source**>. The move instruction moves one byte or word, as addressed by the source field, into the byte or word addressed by the destination field. As was noted above, both fields cannot be memory addresses; one must be a register or a literal constant. There are several variations of this instruction depending on the addressing mode selected. This instruction is often used to load constants into registers or memory or to move data between registers and memory. One limitation of this instruction is that literal values cannot be moved directly into either the DS or the ES segment registers.

MOVS Moves data between memory locations. The source memory address is in the DS:SI register pair, and the destination memory address is in the ES:DI register pair. When the instruction is preceded by one of the repeat directives, the CX register is loaded with the number of bytes or words to move. MOVSB moves bytes of data, and MOVSW moves words of data. All examples of this instruction move the data in the positive direction. Thus, the SI and DI registers are incremented by 1 for the MOVSB byte instructions and by 2 for the MOVSW word instructions.

LODS Loads a data value into the AL or AX register from a memory location. The destination of the data is in the AL register for byte loads and in the AX register for word loads. The source memory address is in the DS:SI register pair. All examples of this instruction move the data in the positive direction. Thus, the address in the SI register is incremented by 1 for the LODSB byte instruction and by 2 for the LODSW word instructions.

STOS Stores the data value in the AL or AX register into a block of memory locations. The source of the data is in the AL register for byte stores and in the AX register for word stores. The destination memory address is in the ES:DI register pair. When the instruction is preceded by one of the repeat directives, the CX register is loaded with the number of bytes or words to move. STOSB stores bytes of data, and STOSW stores words of data. All examples of this instruction move the data in the positive direction. Thus, the address in the DI register is incremented by 1 for the STOSB byte instruction and by 2 for the STOSW word instruction. This instruction may be used to initialize a block of data.

Stack Instructions

Two stack instructions are used in the examples. The PUSH and POP instructions allow data to be put on and pulled off of the stack, respectively. There is no PUSHing and POPping of the status register, because there are no interrupt service routines included in the examples. These instructions are invoked at the start of each assembly language routine to save the stack pointer and the important registers that will be modified in the course of the routine. It is important to note that different C compilers require assembly language routines to leave different registers unmodified.

The top of the stack is actually the highest memory address that it may ever obtain, unless a stack error occurs. As items are PUSHed onto the stack, the stack pointer (SP) is decremented, thereby pointing to a lower memory address. As items are POPped from the stack, the SP is incremented.

When an assembly language subroutine is called from a C program, the C program PUSHes copies of the parameters being passed to the routine or pointers to the parameters on the stack. The program then PUSHes a copy of the return address on the stack. When the assembly language routine is finished, the return address is POPped from the stack and control returns to the calling C program. The assembly language routine may use the parameters located in the stack; it is not necessary, however, for the assembly language routine to actually POP the parameters off of the stack. The stack pointer must be saved at the start of the assembly language routine when it is pointing to the return address. During the course of the assembly language routine, the stack pointer may be modified without regard, because upon exit, the stack pointer can be restored to point to the return address. The assembly language routine must have *a priori* knowledge of where the various parameters will reside on the stack. Time can be saved by the assembly language routine, because it can reference the parameters without having to POP them from the stack.

POP <destination>. The POP instruction transfers a word from the top of the stack to the destination as indicated by the destination field. The destination may be a register or a memory location. The stack pointer register (SP) is incremented by 2 after the operation.

PUSH <source>. The push instruction transfers a word to the top of the stack from the source as indicated by the source field. The source may be a register or a memory location. The stack pointer register (SP) is decremented by 2 before the move operation.

Program Control Instructions

The program control registers include the jump, loop, and call instructions. The jump instructions include a wide variety of conditional branching instructions as well as the unconditional branch. Only one of the looping instructions, LOOP, is used in the examples. This instruction relies on the CX register as a loop counter and passes control back through a series of instructions until the CX register is decremented to 0. The subroutine call instruction is used exclusively to pass control to another assembly language subroutine. It PUSHes the return address onto the stack before relinquishing control. The called routine is always exited via a return instruction (RET), which POPs the return address off of the stack and then branches to that location.

JMP <**destination**>. The unconditional jump instructions pass control to the address referenced in the destination field. There are several different types of jumps depending on whether the jump is within a segment or into a different segment. If the jump is within a segment, only the instruction pointer register, IP, is modified. If the jump is to another segment, the code segment register, CS, is also modified.

Jxx <**destination**>. The conditional jump instructions pass control to the address referenced in the destination field depending on the condition of the status flags. The conditional jump instruction used in the examples includes jumps determined by the carry flag, JC & JNC, the zero flag, JZ & JNZ, the sign flag, JG, JGE, JL, JLE and the overflow flag, JO. In these examples, the *N* refers to *no*. Stated another way, JZ is jump if 0, and JNZ is jump if not 0. The "E" in JGE refers to including the equal condition. Thus, JG causes a jump if the flags indicate greater than, and JGE causes a jump if the flags indicate greater than or equal to. Several of these conditional jump instructions check the condition of multiple flags. For example, JG actually tests the zero, sign, and overflow flags.

CALL <**destination**>. The subroutine call instruction passes control to a subroutine. The subroutine call may be to a near or a far procedure. The stack pointer (SP) is decremented by 2, and the address of the next instruction is pushed onto the stack. The address referenced in the destination field is then loaded into the instruction pointer, and control is passed to that address. If an intersegment call is issued, two words must be PUSHed in order to save the code segment of the calling routine.

RET. The return instruction is used to return control to the calling program from a subroutine. The return instruction occurs as the final instruction executed in all of the assembly language routines. The data present on the top of the stack is loaded into the instruction pointer, and the stack pointer is decremented by 2. This effectively POPs the return address off of the stack and begins executing code at the returned address. If an intersegment return is issued, two words must be POPped in order to reload the code segment of the calling routine.

LOOP <**destination**>. The loop-until-complete instruction appears at the end of a loop. The CX register contains the number of iterations of the loop upon entry to the loop. At the LOOP instruction, the CX register is decremented. If the CX register is nonzero, control passes back to the destination address as indicated in the destination field. If the CX register is zero, control passes to the next instruction.

Input/Output Instructions

The input/output instructions are equivalent to move instructions. They move data to or from the I/O ports. The hardware decoding is handled separately for I/O ports from that for memory. The I/O instructions may input or output a byte or a word. If the address of the port is between 0 and 255, the port address can be included as a literal value. If the port address is greater than 255, the address must be provided in the DX register. The data transferred in or out always goes through the AX register. If a byte is transferred, the AL or AH bytes of the AX register may be used.

IN <**destination register Ax**>,<**source port address**>. The input from a port command inputs either a byte or a word into the AX register. If the port address is less than 256, the address may be included as a literal in the source port address. For example, the instruction IN AX,25 would input the data word on port number 25 into the AX register. If the address is greater than 255, the address must be called out in the DX register. For example, the instruction IN AX,DX would input the data word from the port as indicated by the value in the DX register into the AX register.

OUT <**source register Ax**>,<**destination port address**>. The output to a port command outputs either a byte or a word from the AX register. If the port address is less than 256, the address may be included as a literal in the source port address. For example, the instruction OUT AX,25 would output the data word on port number 25 from the AX register. If the address is greater than 255, the address must be called out in the DX register. For example, the instruction OUT AX,DX would output the data word from the AX register to the port indicated by the value in the DX register.

4.3.5 Interfacing C and Assembly Language

All of the assembly language routines in this book follow the same format. The steps taken by the assembly language routines are listed in Table 4.3 and discussed in the section below.

Assembly Language Routine Steps

Step 1. Because the base pointer register (BP) will be used to point to the parameters, it first needs to be saved by PUSHing it onto the stack as shown in the following instruction.

```
PUSH  BP     ;save the base pointer register
```

Step 2. The stack pointer is saved so that control will pass back to the C program correctly, regardless of the current state of the stack pointer. The stack pointer typically is saved in the base pointer register (BP). The base pointer

TABLE 4.3 Format of an Assembly Language Routine

Step #	Function
1	Save the base pointer register
2	Save the stack pointer
3	Save the host registers on the stack
4	Perform some action, accessing any parameters that might be on the stack
5	Restore the host registers from the stack
6	Restore the stack pointer
7	Restore the base pointer register
8	Return control to the calling routine

register may then be used to access the parameters on the stack. The following instruction saves the stack pointer.

```
MOV  BP,SP     ;save the stack pointer
```

Step 3. The C compiler requires that certain host registers be unmodified by the assembly language routine. The C program will depend on these values being unmodified, and nonrecoverable errors can occur if the registers are modified. Typically the registers that need to be saved are the index registers (SI and DI) and the segment registers (DS and ES). The compiler manual should be consulted to find out which registers must be unmodified. The easiest way to save these registers is to utilize the stack. The following instructions can be used to save the index and segment registers.

```
PUSH  DS     ;save the data segment
PUSH  ES     ;save the extra segment
PUSH  SI     ;save the source index
PUSH  DI     ;save the destination index
```

Step 4. The assembly language routine performs whatever function it was designed to perform. If parameters were passed by the C routine, these now reside on the stack. Because the stack pointer was copied into the base pointer register, the base pointer register is used to access the parameters.

Step 5. The subroutine is finished, and the saved registers need to be restored. Remember that the last item PUSHed onto the stack should be the first item POPped off of the stack. A critical assumption is that the stack pointer is at the same value as it was immediately after the registers were saved. Any items PUSHed onto the stack are assumed to have been POPped off of the stack. The following instructions restore the registers.

```
POP  DI        ;restore the destination index
POP  SI        ;restore the source index
POP  ES        ;restore the extra segment
POP  DS        ;restore the data segment
```

Only those registers modified in the assembly language routine need to be changed. However, to be on the safe side, all required registers can be saved as a matter of habit. This practice requires more time to PUSH and POP the unnecessary registers.

Step 6. Restoring the stack pointer is accomplished by copying the base pointer (BP) register into the stack pointer. This assumes that the BP register has not been modified since the stack pointer was saved. The following instruction restores the stack pointer.

```
MOV  SP,BP       ;restore the stack pointer
```

Step 7. The base pointer is restored by POPping it off of the stack as shown in the following instruction.

```
POP  BP          ;restore the base pointer register
```

Step 8. Control is passed back to the C calling routine by a return instruction as illustrated below.

```
RET          ;return to the calling program
```

In order to make the code more readable, two macro expansions were designed that can be used to eliminate the need for including all of the PUSH or POP instructions in the program listings. A macro entitled Prefix is used to save the stack pointer and the necessary host registers. It can be placed as the first instruction after the entry point. The Prefix macro expansion is listed below.

```
Prefix
PUSH BP        ;save the base pointer
MOV  BP,SP     ;copy and save the stack pointer
PUSH DS        ;save the data segment
PUSH ES        ;save the extra segment
PUSH SI        ;save the source index
PUSH DI        ;save the destination index
endm           ;end of macro
```

A second macro entitled Postfix is used to restore the host registers and the stack pointer and to return control to the C compiler. The Postfix macro expansion is listed on the following page.

TABLE 4.4 Passing Parameters from C

Step #	Function
1	Push the parameters onto the stack.
2	Push the return address onto the stack.
3	Pass control to the subroutine.

```
Postfix macro
POP    DI        ;restore the destination index
POP    SI        ;restore the source index
POP    ES        ;restore the extra segment
POP    DS        ;restore the data segment
MOV    SP,BP     ;restore the stack pointer
POP    BP        ;restore the base pointer
RET              ;return to the calling "C" routine
endm             ;end of macro
```

4.3.6 Passing Parameters

Parameters are passed to assembly language routines from C routines through the stack. Assembly language programming requires a detailed understanding of the operation of the stack, because the assembly language routines require the exact location of the parameters on the stack. A standard call to an assembly language routine has the following form:

```
Do_Something(parameter 1, parameter 2, ... ,parameter N);
```

In this example, the subroutine being called is named Do_Something. It is called with a list of parameters, although the parameters are optional. The C program follows a set of rules before passing control to the assembly language program. These steps are coded by the compiler, but they are important to understand. The C program follows the steps listed in Table 4.4 before calling an assembly language routine. These steps are discussed in the section below.

Steps for Passing Parameters from C

Step 1. The C program that is calling Do_Something PUSHes the parameters onto the stack, beginning with the last parameter in the list and ending with the first parameter in the list.

Elements PUSHed onto the stack cause the stack to grow toward lower memory. The last parameter, parameter N, is PUSHed first so it resides in the highest memory location of the parameter block. The stack pointer is decremented after every PUSH instruction. It always points to the next available

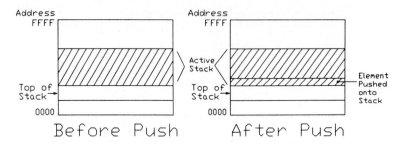

FIGURE 4.10 PUSHing Elements onto the Stack

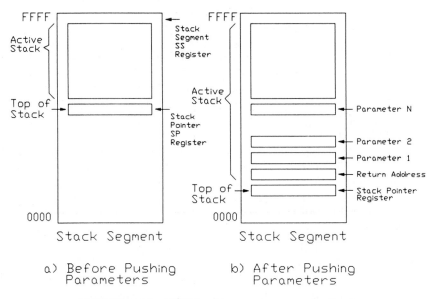

FIGURE 4.11 PUSHing Parameters onto the Stack

memory location, one word lower than the last element PUSHed onto the stack. The memory location pointed to by the stack pointer is referred to as the *top of stack*. No valid information resides at the top of stack. PUSHing an element onto the stack is illustrated in Figure 4.10.

Step 2. Before actually passing control to the assembly language routine, the C program PUSHes its return address onto the stack. The return address is the address of the instruction following the CALL instruction. This return address is the top element on the stack when the assembly language routine assumes control. The stack before and after the return address and the parameters are PUSHed is illustrated in Figure 4.11.

Step 3. Control is passed to the assembly language routine by modifying the instruction pointer with the entry point address of the called subroutine.

Receiving Parameters

In order for the assembly language routine to access the parameters, it is necessary for the routine to have *a priori* knowledge of the parameters being sent. This knowledge includes the number of parameters, the data type of each parameter, whether the parameter is a value or a pointer, and under which model the C code was compiled.

The technique employed by the assembly language routine to access the parameters on the stack utilizes the indexed, indirect addressing mode. This addressing mode is an efficient means for accessing the parameters on the stack. The stack pointer cannot be used in an indexed, indirect addressing mode.

The indexed, indirect addressing mode can be used with the base pointer register. The value in the stack pointer is copied to the base pointer register. The base pointer register then points to the parameter on the stack. When the assembly language routine requires the stack, the pointer to the parameters remains unchanged in the base pointer register. Any PUSH, PULL, or CALL instructions use the stack and modify the stack pointer. As soon as the stack pointer is modified, the pointer to the C parameter list is lost. The base pointer register maintains the pointer to the parameters, regardless of the stack pointer.

The assembly language routine should not POP the parameter elements off of the stack. This principle is consistent with the rule that each routine should be responsible for POPping any and all values it PUSHes onto the stack. Because the C routine PUSHed the parameters onto the stack, the routine should also POP them off of the stack. Therefore, the assembly language routine should not POP the parameters off of the stack.

In order to access the parameters on the stack without POPping them, the indexed, indirect address mode is used. This address mode determines an address by adding a constant to the value in the BP register. Because the BP register points to the top of the stack, any parameter can be accessed by providing the proper index.

The form of this addressing mode is [BP+n], where n is a constant called the *index*. The square brackets indicate that an address is contained in the expression, not the data itself. This is the indirect part of the address mode. The indirect addressing mode is illustrated in Figure 4.12.

The condition of the stack as the assembly language routine begins its operation is illustrated in Table 4.5. This table assumes that the return address was two words long and that all parameters on the stack are one word long.

The BP register points to the top of the stack. The return address is the first element on the stack, and it is assumed to be one 16-bit word. The first parameter in the list (parameter 1) is therefore the second element on the stack. In order to access the first parameter, it is necessary to add a constant value to the

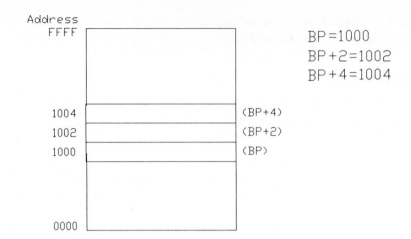

FIGURE 4.12 Indexed Indirect Addressing

TABLE 4.5 Stack Condition After a Call

Address	Value
[BP+4+(2*N)]	Parameter *N*
.	.
.	.
[BP+8]	Parameter 2
[BP+6]	Parameter 1
[BP+4]	Offset portion of return address
[BP+2]	Segment portion of return address
[BP]	Top of stack

BP register. This value is equal to the number of bytes occupied by the return address added to the number of bytes that the return address is located from the top of the stack. The top of the stack is one 16-bit word beneath the first element on the stack, which is the return address. Therefore, adding two bytes to the BP register points to the return address.

The number of bytes occupied by the return address depends on the C compiler model. Table 4.6 lists the storage requirement of the return address based on the C compiler model.

If the small C compiler model is used, all code addresses are assumed to reside in the same code segment. Therefore, the C routine resides in the same code segment as the assembly language routine. The C routine PUSHes one 16-bit word onto the stack. This word is the offset portion of the return address. The medium or large model requires that both the offset and the segment

TABLE 4.6 Return Address Length

C Compiler Model	Number of Bytes in Return Address
Small	2
Medium	4
Large	4

addresses be PUSHed onto the stack. Thus, the C routine PUSHes two 16-bit words onto the stack, representing the segment and offset return address.

The C programs in this book pass two types of parameters to the assembly language routines. These are data values and pointers. A data value requires one word if the variable is a character or integer type. Different compilers treat floating-point numbers in a variety of ways when they are passed as parameters. In this book, no floating-point variables are passed to assembly language routines. As listed in Table 4.6 above, a pointer variable requires either one or two 16-bit words.

Passing Variables

If a variable is passed to an assembly language routine, a copy of the current value of the variable is placed onto the stack. It is important to note that a copy of the value, not the value itself, is put onto the stack. The C calling program never interrogates the copy of the value on the stack to determine if it has been modified. The assembly language routine has no opportunity to alter the actual value itself. This is consistent with the guidelines of C, as proposed by Kernighan and Ritchie in *The C Programming Language,* Prentice Hall, 1978. The assembly language routine can modify the copy of the parameter that is located on the stack. Because this value on the stack is never copied back into the original C variable, modifications are lost once control passes back to the C program. This protects the C variable by insulating it from the assembly language routine. It also makes it difficult for the assembly language routine to modify C variables. Parameters are passed from one C routine to another C routine in a similar manner.

Passing Pointers

The C routine can pass a pointer to the assembly language routine as a parameter. This pointer contains a host memory address. The pointer will typically address a C variable or the first element of a C array. The assembly language routine can modify the C variables, because this pointer addresses these variables. Passing the pointer allows the subroutine to modify the parameter, treating the parameter as if it were public. The same is true if the subroutine is another C routine.

TABLE 4.7 Pointer Length

"C" Compiler Model	Number of Bytes in Pointer
Small	2
Medium	2
Large	4

Like the return address, the pointer must contain a 20-bit address. However, the pointer references the data segment pointer (DS), whereas the return address references the code segment register (CS). The length of the pointer is dependent on the compiler model. If a small or medium compiler model is used, it is assumed that the data segment for the C routine is the same as the data segment for the assembly language routine. As a result, the data segment register does not need to be modified. The large model makes no assumptions, and the data segment register must be modified to point to the proper segment. Table 4.7 lists the possible lengths of pointers.

If the small or medium C compiler model is used, all data is assumed to reside in the same data segment. Therefore, the C data variables reside in the same data segment as the assembly language variables. The C routine PUSHes one 16-bit word onto the stack. This word is the offset portion of the address to the variable. The following instruction can be used to load the offset portion of the pointer into the source index register.

```
MOV  SI,[BP+6]        ;load the offset into SI
```

If the large C compiler model is used, both the offset and the segment addresses are PUSHed onto the stack. Thus, the C routine PUSHes two 16-bit words onto the stack, representing the segment and offset address of the variable. The following instruction can be used to load the segment portion of the pointer into the data segment register and the offset portion of the pointer into the source index register.

```
LDS  SI,[BP+6]        ;load the segment into DS, and the offset
                      ;into SI
```

When the C calling routine passes an array to a subroutine, a pointer that addresses the first element of the array is passed as the parameter. This occurs whether the subroutine is written in assembly language or in C. The second element of the array could be accessed by incrementing the pointer. If the C array is a character-type array, the pointer would be incremented by 1. If the C array is an integer-type array, the pointer would be incremented by 2. The following instructions would load the first element of an array into the AL register and the second element of the array into the BL register, assuming that the array consists of byte elements. This example assumes that the pointer is at [BP+6].

```
LDS  SI,[BP+6]      ;get the pointer into DS:SI
MOV  AL,[SI]        ;get the first element
INC  SI             ;point to the second element
MOV  BL,[SI]        ;get the second element
```

The following instructions would load the first element of an array into the AX register and the second element of the array into the BX register, assuming that the array consists of integer elements. This example assumes that the pointer is at [BP+6].

```
LDS  SI,[BP+6]      ;get the pointer into DS:SI
MOV  AX,[SI]        ;get the first element into AX
INC  SI             ;add 2 in order to
INC  SI             ;point to the second element
MOV  BX,[SI]        ;get the second element
```

Returning an Argument

In the C language, an argument can be passed back to the calling routine without going through the parameter list. The routines that return arguments are typically called *functions*. The format used for a function call is listed in the statement below.

```
int argument;
argument = Function();
```

In this example, the function, named "Function", has no parameters but returns an argument named "argument". This argument is declared in the TYPE *int* statement. A function return argument is assumed to be a TYPE *int* by default, although any TYPE variable can be returned.

If the function being called is written in C, it returns the argument to the calling program through the return statement as follows. The argument is once again declared as a TYPE *int*.

```
return(argument);
```

If the function is written in assembly language, the argument is passed back to the calling C routine via the AX register. The assembly language routine loads

TABLE 4.8 The Assembly Language Form

Step #	Function
1	Declare any necessary macro expansions
2	Declare the entry point "public"
3	Define the code segment
4	Define the entry point
5	Body of the routine
6	Close the routine
7	Close the code segment

the AX register with the argument before exiting. This is illustrated in the following instruction.

```
MOV   AX,argument        ;return "argument" to the caller
RET
```

Sending parameters via the registers is a common technique used when one assembly language routine calls another assembly language routine. Any of the available general-purpose registers can be used to pass parameters. The stack is also a convenient way of passing parameters.

4.3.7 Typical Assembly Language Routines

The assembly language examples used in this book begin by declaring the entry point of the routine public. If a symbol is not declared public, no routines outside of the given module will be able to locate it. In the assembly language routines included in this book, the only symbol that needs to be considered public is the entry point of the routine.

The form of the assembly language examples provided in this book is consistent throughout. The steps followed in the design of the routines are listed in Table 4.8 and discussed in the section below.

Steps Used in Assembly Language Examples

Step 1. Any macro expansion files used in the assembly language routine must be included into the file so that the assembler can locate the expanded code. Typically, two-pass assemblers are used. The macros need only be included in pass 1. The assembler directive if1 ... ENDif is used to include the macro expansions in pass 1 only. The INCLUDE *name* assembler directive declares the external file that is to be included within the current file. The macro expansion file named macros.asm is included in the assembly language source file by the following conditional assembler directive statements.

```
if1
INCLUDE macros.asm
ENDif
```

Step 2. The Microsoft and Lattice naming conventions are adhered to in this book. Suppose that the entry point of a routine is "example". The Microsoft assembler requires that the name "example" be preceded with an underscore, producing "_example". The assembler pseudo-op PUBLIC is used to define the public symbols as follows:

```
PUBLIC _example
```

Step 3. The Microsoft/Lattice assembler requires that all assembly language routines define a code segment. In this book, no data storage is defined within the assembly language routines, so no data segment is defined. Compiler-related conventions regarding naming the code segment must be followed.

The following two statements define the code segment and align the code segment register (CS) to this segment. The code segment is named "codeseg". This is consistent with the name of the code segment in the C routines.

```
codeseg SEGMENT byte public 'code'
ASSUME cs:codeseg
```

Step 4. The entry point of the subroutine defines the subroutine entry point and declares this entry point as "near" or "far." Because the large C model is used in this book, any assembly language routines called by a C routine are given a far classification. Any assembly language routines called by other assembly language routines are given a near classification. The entry point is defined in the following statement. In this statement, the entry point is named "_example". This is identical to the name declared in the public statement.

```
_example    PROC    far
```

Step 5. The body of the assembly language routine contains the assembly language code.

Step 6. The subroutine ends by declaring the end of the procedure using an ENDP directive. The title and entry point of the routine are also included in this directive, as shown in the following statement.

```
_example    ENDP        ;end of procedure
```

Step 7. The code segment must be closed as the last step in the assembly language source code. This is accomplished by using the end segment directive,

ENDS. The name of the code segment being closed must be included in the directive, as shown in the following statement.

```
codeseg    ENDS        ;end of segment
```

Assembly Language Example

Consistent with the rules discussed above, the resultant form of all assembly language routines that are called by C routines is illustrated below. This is the form used in this book. The Prefix and Postfix macro expansions are included in the macros.asm file.

```
if1
INCLUDE macros.asm
ENDif
PUBLIC _example
codeseg SEGMENT byte public 'code'
ASSUME cs:codeseg

example    PROC    far             ;declare "example" as the
                                   ;entry point
Prefix                             ;save the stack pointer and
                                   ;push registers

Postfix                            ;restore the stack pointer
                                   ;body of procedure

                                   ;and pop registers

_example   ENDP            ;end of procedure "_example"
codeseg    ENDS            ;end of segment "codeseg"
```

Chapter 5

Principles of Computer Graphics

5.1 COORDINATE SYSTEMS

When wire drawings, graphs, or images are being drawn, some sort of coordinate reference system must be used. Data, extracted from the real world, is measured in a variety of coordinate systems. The range on the real-world data may vary between thousandths of an inch and light years. The numbers can be represented in integers or floating-point numbers. These numbering schemes are usually cumbersome to use in a graphics environment. It is necessary to translate this data to a coordinate system that is more conducive to graphics operations.

The data representing the "real world" is referenced as belonging to the *world coordinate system*. Because the data is to be represented graphically, a display coordinate system must be defined. Raster scan graphics systems, such as the EGA and VGA, are pixelated. Pixelated systems can be represented by an integer coordinate system because there are no fractions. The programmer can save a good deal of time and storage space if the data in the world system is converted to a graphics reference system.

The resolution of the *display coordinate system* should be well suited to the graphics hardware and to the data being displayed. The output of the display coordinate system is sent to a video monitor for display or to a hard-copy device for output. Because of the variety of resolutions available on these devices, each maintains its own coordinate system, called the *device coordinate system*.

The display coordinate system can be further subdivided. A single display may contain several images, referred to as *viewing windows*. The user views the data through these imaginary windows. It is convenient for each of these windows to maintain its own coordinate system, called the *window coordinate systems*.

The data, represented by pixels, may be organized into functional groups of pixels, called *objects*. These objects can have their own coordinate system, called the *object coordinate system*. An object can be positioned anywhere within the window, but the object definition would not change with respect to its own coordinate system.

5.1.1   World Coordinate System

The world coordinate system refers to the coordinates of the real world. This system exists independently of the graphics systems that represent it. World coordinates can be expressed in any measurement system using either integers or real numbers. The units may be seconds, inches, pounds, number of people, light years, or virtually anything that can be measured. Somewhere in the graphing process these world coordinates must be converted to a display coordinate system.

A transformation is required to convert the data in the real world coordinate system into the integer-pixelated display coordinate system. The transformation involves translation and scaling. Round-off errors usually occur during this process, because the display coordinate system rarely has adequate resolution to represent the world coordinate system.

5.1.2   Display Coordinate System

The display coordinate system relates to the actual resolution of the display memory. This system is measured in horizontal and vertical pixels. The total number of horizontal pixels times the total number of vertical pixels determines the number of pixels per image. Each pixel is represented by a magnitude. This magnitude is represented by a number of bits. The number of bits per pixel times the number of pixels determines the number of bits per image. The display coordinate system is not directly related to any hardware.

The display coordinate system can be larger than the display device coordinate system. In the case of the EGA/VGA, there are 256,000 bytes of display data available on the adapter. At four bits per pixel, this leaves 512,000 pixels per image or approximately 700 by 700 pixels. Zooming and panning allow the selective parts of the display coordinate system to be mapped to EGA/VGA active display. Even larger images can be maintained in host memory, with only sections loaded into the EGA/VGA display memory. Disks can also be utilized to store very large images. This hierarchy of image memory is illustrated in Figure 5.1.

5.1.3   Window Coordinate System

It has become popular to segment an image into separate areas, called *windows*. Each window can represent different data or different views of the same data. To allow programmers to work with these windows efficiently, each is referenced to its own coordinate system. Each window is defined by its shape, size, and position within the display. Windows are typically rectangular, so their size can be represented by a height and width. The window is positioned onto the display through some reference point. Generally, the display coordinates of the lower left corner or the upper right corner of the window define the placement of the window. Windows may be transparent or opaque depending on how the

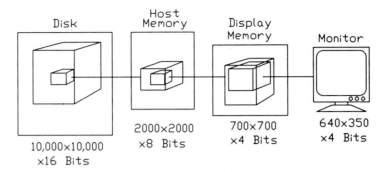

FIGURE 5.1 Hierarchy of the Display Coordinate System

software defines them. The EGA/VGA has no hardware facility for windows, and all window manipulations must be handled in software. A provision is made for split-screen operation, which may be thought of as two separate windows.

5.1.4 Device Coordinate System

A typical graphics system may use several device coordinate systems. A device coordinate system relates to the hardware device that will be used to process the data. The EGA/VGA display adapter, when operating in a display mode that features a resolution of 640 by 350 by 4 bits per pixel, has a display device coordinate system that ranges from 0 to 639 on the horizontal axis and from 0 to 349 on the vertical axis. The magnitude of each pixel ranges from 0 to 15.

The input and output of graphics systems also have their own device coordinate systems. A video frame grabber can have a resolution of 512 by 512 pixels at 8 bits per pixel. A dot matrix printer can have a resolution of 638 by 825. An image scanner can have a resolution of 2,550 by 3,300 by 8 bits deep. A laser printer's resolution can exceed 5,100 by 6,600. In the case of an ink jet printer, each dot may be represented by several bits; if a black-and-white printer is used, each dot is one bit. The relationship between the display coordinate system and the device coordinate systems is illustrated in Figure 5.2.

The concept of multiple coordinate systems is extremely important in computer graphics. Suppose the display had a device coordinate system of 640 by 480. If the graphics program operated in the device coordinate system, all of the data would have to be mapped into this resolution. Later, when the time comes to print this image, the image will be restricted to the display device coordinate system. This is true even though the printer has the capability for a higher resolution.

Suppose the display coordinate system is set to the resolution of the laser printer. Suppose further that the graphics software is vector-driven and that the memory available in the display device adapter is smaller than the maximum

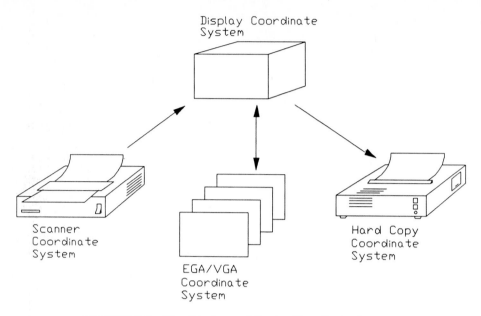

FIGURE 5.2 The Display and Device Coordinate Systems

resolution of the printer. The display device adapter can display only a portion of the total image at a time. This portion is commonly called a *window*.

5.1.5 Object Coordinate System

In an object-oriented display system, a series of dots, lines, and characters can be associated in such a way that they define an object. Each object maintains its own object coordinate system. If the object is moved or scaled, the entire object coordinate system is affected. These coordinate systems are associated with the display coordinate system or the device coordinate system through a set of reference parameters that are used to position the object in the larger reference system. Each object must have an origin. This origin is related to the origin of the display or device coordinate system by a set of coordinates, typically expressed as polar or rectangular coordinates. Figure 5.3 illustrates the relationship between an object coordinate system and a display coordinate system. The origin of the object coordinate system is referenced to the display coordinate system by the *XC, YC* coordinate pair.

Additional parameters may be necessary in order to map the object coordinate system into the display coordinate system. An object that is rotated by an angle *theta* is illustrated in Figure 5.4. It should be noted that the object did not rotate with respect to its own object coordinate system. Rather, the object coordinate system rotated with respect to the display coordinate system.

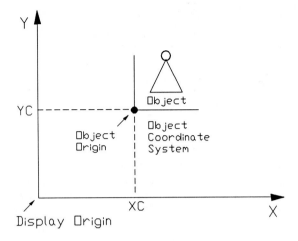

FIGURE 5.3   Object Coordinate Systems

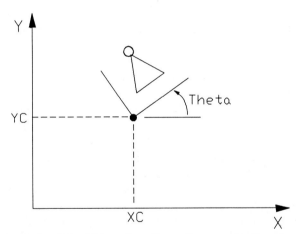

FIGURE 5.4   Object Coordinate System with Rotation

5.2   COORDINATE TRANSFORMATIONS

Coordinate transformations convert from one coordinate system to another. Common graphics linear transformations include scaling, translation, rotation, and polar-to-rectangular conversion. A single display coordinate system may be composed of several smaller display coordinate systems, called *windows*. These windows are constantly moved within the larger display space. Within a window there may be several object coordinate systems. Objects can associate and disassociate freely with several coordinate systems in a single operation.

Several transformations are discussed below, with equations given for each. Typically, in a graphics environment, matrix notation rather than equations is used to describe the transformations. These matrices can be combined to perform multiple transformations in a single operation. Graphics processors may include special-purpose hardware that can perform matrix calculations rapidly. The techniques involving two-dimensional and three-dimensional matrix notation are explained in many books that describe computer graphics.

5.2.1 Scaling Data

There are two types of scaling transformation: one operation scales the data; a second scales the coordinates of the data. If data in a two-dimensional space has magnitudes associated with it, the space can be considered to be three-dimensional. The first type of scaling operation changes the magnitudes of the data, and the second changes the size of the two-dimensional space.

Data passes through several stages in the graphics process: from digitization through coordinate transformations to the display system and hard-copy device. The data will likely be scaled in a different way at each of these stages.

5.2.2 Scaling the Magnitude of the Data

Data in the real world that has an associated magnitude must usually be scaled to fit in the limited dynamic range of the display system. An EGA can display a pixel in up to 4 bits, allowing 16 simultaneous colors. Thus, the data being displayed is limited to a dynamic range of 16. A VGA can display a pixel in up to 8 bits, allowing 256 simultaneous colors. This means that the data being displayed is limited to a dynamic range of 256.

The scaling operation is a multiplicative process that may incorporate a translation. The dynamic range of the data in the real world system is determined, shifted so that it is unipolar, and scaled so that it fits into the dynamic range of the display. This is illustrated in Equation 5.1

Equation 5.1 Scaling the Magnitude of Data

$$\text{Range\_of\_Display} = \text{Display\_Max} - \text{Display\_Min}$$

$$\text{Dynamic\_Range\_of\_Data} = \text{Data\_Max} - \text{Data\_Min}$$

$$\text{Scale\_Factor} = \frac{\text{Range\_of\_Display}}{\text{Dynamic\_Range\_of\_Data}}$$

$$\text{Scaled\_Data[i]} = (\text{Data[i]} - \text{Data\_Min}) \times \text{Scale\_Factor}$$

5.2.3 Scaling the Size of the Data

The transformation from the real-world coordinate system to the display coordinate system involves a coordinate scaling. This scaling is given in Equation 5.2.

Equation 5.2 Determining a Scale Factor

$$\text{X\_Scale} = \frac{\text{Integer Range of Display } X \text{ Coordinate}}{\text{Dynamic Range of Real World } X \text{ Coordinate}}$$

$$\text{Y\_Scale} = \frac{\text{Integer Range of Display } Y \text{ Coordinate}}{\text{Dynamic Range of Real World } Y \text{ Coordinate}}$$

The scaling transformation that incorporates these scale factors is listed in Equation 5.3.

Equation 5.3 Scaling Data

$$X \text{ new} = \text{X} \times \text{X\_Scale}$$

$$Y \text{ new} = \text{Y} \times \text{Y\_Scale}$$

Below are four examples that describe different scaling transformations.

Example 5.1   Real World Same as Display Space

The real-world coordinate system is measured in integers, the range consisting of 640 horizontal integers by 350 vertical integers. If the display coordinate system is also 640 horizontal by 350 vertical, no transformation is necessary. The transformation is considered one-to-one.

Example 5.2   Real World Measured in Integers

The real-world coordinate system is measured in integers, the range consisting of 1,280 horizontal integers by 700 vertical integers. If the display coordinate system is 640 horizontal by 350 vertical, a two-to-one transformation is necessary. The transformation is considered many-to-one, because it is four points in the real-world space map to one point in the display space.

Example 5.3   Real World Smaller than Display Space

The real-world coordinate system is measured in integers, the range consisting of 320 horizontal integers by 175 vertical integers. If the display coordinate system is 640 horizontal by 350 vertical, a one-to-two scaling transformation is necessary. The transformation is considered one-to-many, because one point in the real-world space can map to four points in the display space.

Example 5.4   Real World Measured in Reals

The real-world coordinate system is measured in real numbers, the range consisting of 640 horizontal integers by 350 vertical integers, with one significant fractional digit. If the display coordinate system is 640 horizontal by 350 vertical, a ten-to-one scaling transformation is necessary. The transformation is considered many-to-one, because 10 points in the real-world space map to one point in the display space.

5.2.4   Translation

Translation is used to move one coordinate system with respect to another. The translation can involve no rotations. Translation is an additive process, as shown in Equation 5.4.

Equation 5.4   Translation

$$X\_New = X + X\_translation$$

$$Y\_New = Y + Y\_translation$$

In Equation 5.4, a point, X, Y, is translated by an amount, X_translation and Y translation. Example 5.5 illustrates a transformation that requires a translation.

Example 5.5   Transformation Requiring Translation

The real-world coordinate system is measured in integers, ranging from 100 to 739 integers along the horizontal axis and 200 to 550 integers along the vertical axis. If the display coordinate system is 640 horizontal by 350 vertical, a translation is required. It would shift the real-world coordinate system so that the value of 100 on the real-world X axis would map to 0 on the display X axis. Similarly, 200 on the real-world Y axis maps to 0 on the display Y axis. No scaling transformation is necessary in conjunction with the translation. The transformation is considered one-to-one, because one point in the real-world space maps to one and only one point in the display space.

5.2.5   Rotation

Like translation, rotation moves an object coordinate system within a display or device coordinate system. The object rotates about its object origin by an angle *theta*, as indicated in Figure 5.4 above.

Rotating an object can be accomplished by Equation 5.5. These equations rotate a point X, Y by an angle *theta*. The transcendental functions Sine and

Cosine are used to perform the rotation. Rotations are treated like translations in a polar coordinate system.

Equation 5.5 Rotation

$$X\_new = X \times Cosine(\textit{theta})$$

$$Y\_new = Y \times Sine(\textit{theta})$$

5.2.6 Combining Transformations

It is possible to combine the linear operators. Scaling and translation equations are listed in Equation 5.6.

Equation 5.6 Scaling and Translation Transformation

$$X \text{ new} = (X\_Scale \times X) - \text{Translation of } X$$

$$Y \text{ new} = (Y\_Scale \times Y) - \text{Translation of } Y$$

Example 5.6 illustrates a transformation that requires both a translation and a scaling.

Example 5.6 Transformation Requiring Translation and Rotation

The real-world coordinate system is measured in bipolar integers, ranging from -640 to +639 horizontal integers and from -350 to +349 vertical integers. If the display coordinate system is 640 horizontal by 350 vertical, a two-to-one scaling transformation is necessary in conjunction with a translation. The translation would shift the real-world coordinate system so that the value of -640 on the real-world X axis maps to 0 on the display X axis. Similarly, -350 on the real-world Y axis maps to 0 on the display Y axis. The transformation is considered many-to-one, because four points in the real-world space map to one point in the display space. Both a scaling and a translation transformation are required.

5.2.7 Three-dimensional Transformations

A three-dimensional spatial coordinate system has all of the same transformations as discussed in the two-dimensional coordinate system. Often data that is present in a three-dimensional object coordinate system needs to be transformed so that it can be displayed in the two-dimensional display coordinate system. This transformation requires a projection of the three-dimensional space onto the two-dimensional space. A three-dimensional rectangular coordinate system

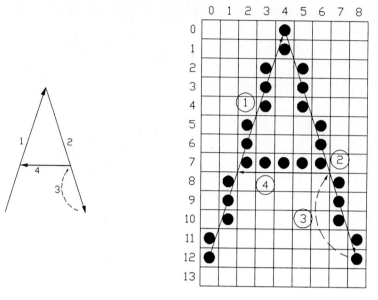

FIGURE 5.5 Script and Dot Matrix Characters

consists of an X axis, a Y axis, and a Z axis. Three-dimensional polar coordinate systems are also popular.

5.3 THE CHARACTER

The shape of a character can be represented by either script or dot matrix techniques. Script techniques represent characters as if they were drawn by a pen. Each character consists of a series of directives that represent line segments. A character is drawn into memory by a series of line segment commands. Script characters are compact and can be drawn rapidly if a fast vector processor is present. Dot matrix techniques consider the character to be a two-dimensional box of pixels. The character is drawn by copying the matrix into the display memory. Dot matrix character shapes tend to be long and contain a great deal of redundant information. Using them is simple and fast, because only a copy operation is necessary. No calculations have to be made to determine the shape of the character. A character drawn in each format is shown in Figure 5.5.

5.3.1 Script Characters

Script characters are represented by a sequence of plotting directives. Characters are drawn into a bit-mapped display by translating these plotting directives into foreground and background values. The characters are defined by a sequence of line segments. A line may be drawn in a color or may be invisible. Drawn lines correspond to moving the pen with it in contact with the paper. Curves would be drawn in a piecewise linear fashion.

Sophisticated script techniques employ shapes other than lines, such as curve segments. Script directives are very efficient when drawing straight lines, especially long straight lines. Also, by controlling the pen width, the character can be drawn in a variety of line widths. Script characters sets require minimal storage, because a font can be drawn in any size. All that is required to change the size of a character is a scaling factor.

The display adapters used on the PC utilize dot matrix character sets exclusively in the alphanumerics modes; dot matrix character sets are also used by default in the graphics modes. If script characters are available, the programmer can utilize them in the graphics modes.

5.3.2 Dot Matrix Characters

Dot matrix characters are represented by a rectangle of dots. The width of the character is equal to the width of the box; the height of the character is equal to the height of the box. Inter-character and inter-row space is usually reserved in the character box. In this case, the height and width of the characters must be smaller than the height and width of the character box. When the character matrix is small, 8 by 8, this technique is fast and efficient. A character may be stored with its attribute—color, for example—coded into it. It can also be stored with the attribute separate from it. The latter practice is far more popular and efficient.

The character matrix consists of a matrix of dots. If the character shape is separate from the character attribute, the dots are either "on" or "off". Each row consists of a set of horizontal dots, and each column consists of a set of vertical dots. Typically, the horizontal dots are represented by a byte in memory, each bit representing one of the dots. The vertical dimension of the matrix is represented by an array of these bytes. Character box sizes for the fonts available on the EGA/VGA are illustrated in Figure 5.6.

One character size can be used to draw characters of varying sizes. However, the characters take on a "pixelated" look. A large character can be derived from a small character by representing each dot in the small matrix by a block of dots in the large matrix. A character enlarged by this technique is compared to a character defined by a larger matrix size in Figure 5.7.

5.3.3 Character Sets

Character sets typically consist of 256 characters and symbols. Each set defines a particular font size and type. Typical font types include Gothic, Prestige, Pica, Times, Roman, Elite, and Mathematical, although there are countless others.

Font size is measured in points. A small font has a small point size—for example, 8 points—and a large font has a large point size—for example, 20

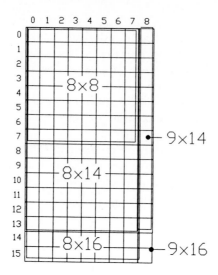

FIGURE 5.6 Dot Matrix Character Storage

points. It is difficult for the eye to distinguish between two fonts that are one point apart in size.

5.3.4   ASCII Standard

The ASCII standard insures that each of the common characters are assigned a unique code that is the same regardless of the keyboard, computer, or monitor. The common characters include the uppercase and lowercase characters of the alphabet, the numbers, the symbols, and a series of nonprintable characters, also referenced by control codes. The ASCII standard is probably the most important standard used in computers.

Typical nonprintable characters include carriage return, tab, backspace, form feed, null, and bell. The nonprintable characters can be accessed from the keyboard by holding the control key down while pressing a character key. For example, the bell code is 07 hex, and the G key is 47 hex. Holding down the control key and the G key simultaneously will issue, a Control-G. The code for a Control-G is 07 hex, which corresponds to the bell. Only some of the control codes have fixed meanings. The most common of these are found in the lower 32 characters.

The ASCII characters may be represented by a seven- or eight- bit code. The seven-bit code allows 128 unique characters, and the eight-bit code allows 256 characters. The seven-bit code is useful when data is being transmitted over a serial line, providing a 12.5-percent data reduction over the eight-bit code. When data is sent to a serial printer or across a modem, it might be helpful to use seven-bit codes. If the data is processed on a parallel bus, there is little

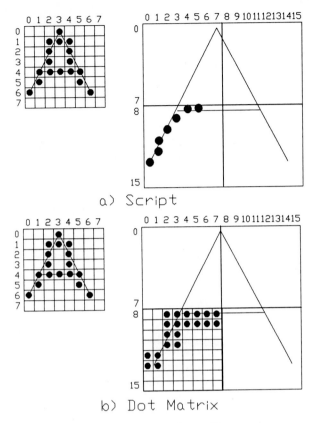

a) Script

b) Dot Matrix

FIGURE 5.7 Enlarging a Character

reason to use a seven-bit bus, because the bus is a multiple of eight bits wide. In the PC, an eight-bit code is used to represent the alphanumeric characters. The true ASCII standard refers only to the lower 128 character codes.

A second standard is called the *Extended ASCII standard*. These extended characters refer to key codes produced when multiple keys are held down. The Control, Shift, and Alt keys are considered the extended ASCII keys. The cold bootstrap can be initiated by holding down the Control, and Alt keys (to create an extended ASCII character set) in conjunction with the Del key. The two Shift keys, one on either side of the keyboard, actually have different codes, and holding both down simultaneously produces a unique code. These character codes are in the range of 128–256.

A standard was also developed to define the shapes of the characters that reside in character code positions 128–256. It is called the IBM Graphics Character Set, and it provides a standardized set of graphics symbols. These characters include specialized symbols, foreign accented characters, Greek characters, and line-drawing symbols. The special symbols are useful when common foreign characters are required or when mathematical symbols must be displayed. The line-drawing symbols are useful when primitive graphics must be drawn on a graphics system that is in an alphanumeric display mode.

5.3.5   Alphanumeric and Graphics Display Modes

The display adapters operate in alphanumeric modes for text processing and graphics modes for graphics processing. This optimizes the performance of the adapter to suit the needs of the software. The alphanumeric modes are faster but less flexible than the graphics modes. Only one of these display modes can be active at a time, because it is not possible to display characters in an alphanumeric mode at the same time as graphics are being displayed in the graphics mode. The software must pick one mode or the other.

The smallest element in the alphanumeric modes is a character position. The size of the character determines the number of characters that can fit on a screen. The smallest element in the graphics modes is the pixel. The resolution of the screen is dictated by the active display mode. The techniques used to display data in the alphanumerics modes are different from the techniques used in the graphics modes. In the alphanumeric modes, a code representing a character is loaded into display memory. This code is typically 16 bits wide, representing the character shape and the character attribute. In the graphics modes, a series of dots is drawn into the display memory, forming the character shape. These dots, representing the actual shape of the character, can require as many as 512 bits if the 16-color mode of the VGA is active, using a 8 by 16 character that occupies all four display planes.

Each adapter includes resident character sets. These character sets are used to produce the character patterns displayed on the screen. Each set includes 256 character shapes, consisting of alphabetical, numeric and special graphics characters. All of the characters in an individual character set have the same size. Some adapters are equipped with multiple character sets, allowing different font sizes. The smaller characters are used to display more characters on the screen, but the larger characters are more legible.

It is possible to draw primitive graphics in an alphanumeric mode. The graphics characters, contained in ASCII codes 128–255, contain line shapes. These allow the programmer to display continuous lines and boxes on the screen. Each graphic character must conform to the character size dictated by the selected character set. Thus, only limited graphics effects can be achieved. Although the graphics potential is limited, it allows the display to stay in an alphanumeric mode.

It is possible to display alphanumeric characters in a graphics mode. The same character sets used in the alphanumeric modes can be used in the graphics modes. The character shapes associated with each character are accessed from the active character set by their ASCII code. Using this technique, the programmer is limited to the character size and shape as loaded in the character set. In contrast, the programmer can draw alphanumeric characters on the screen without using the character sets. One way is to download user-specified character sets. This provides a great deal of flexibility, although the character size is still restricted by limitations in the display adapters. The programmer can draw the characters pixel by pixel, as if they were graphics elements. Any size or shape character can be drawn.

5.3.6   Drawing Characters in an Alphanumeric Mode

The alphanumerics modes represent characters in display memory by a character code and an attribute byte for that character. The actual pixel patterns of each character are not stored in display memory in the alphanumeric modes. Only the code and the attribute byte need to be written into display memory in order to display a character. Similarly, reading from an address in display memory returns the character code and attribute byte. Because only two bytes are stored per character, alphanumeric data transfers are fast. The BIOS routines are typically sufficient for most alphanumeric data transfers.

5.3.7   Drawing Characters in a Graphics Mode

Unlike the alphanumeric modes, the graphics modes store information in the display memory pixel by pixel. In order to display a character, a program must write every dot in the character box to display memory. The character shape and the attribute are joined when the character is written to display memory. If the foreground attribute of a character is red, the color red is written to each pixel in display memory that corresponds to the character foreground.

The character box consists of a number of horizontal scan lines, each the width of the character. The character width typically includes the horizontal and vertical intercharacter space. A display memory address must be provided to determine where the character will be drawn. Because the display is two-dimensional, the address is most easily defined in two dimensions, row and column. The pixel row and column number can correspond to any point of the character.

Assuming that the starting address refers to the top left corner of the pixel, the top scan line of the character is written to this starting address. Each vertical pixel is separated by a value equivalent to the width of the virtual image. If the virtual image is 80 bytes wide, 80 must be added to the starting address to determine the address of the second scan row. This process continues for each scan line, until the last scan line is written to the display.

5.4   THE POINT

A point is the most primitive structure in the graphics environment in a bit-mapped graphics system. All graphics structures are based on groups of points. A character, line, circle, or image can all be defined as a collection of points. A

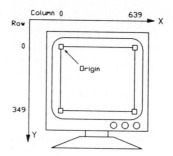

FIGURE 5.8   Screen Coordinate System

point may be represented in the graphics display system by one or more pixels. In the discussion that follows, it is assumed that a point is represented by one pixel. A pixel may be composed of one or more bits of information. A bit is the most primitive structure in the computer system, and a byte is the smallest addressable structure in the computer. In the EGA, a pixel is represented by one, two, or four bits of information. In the VGA, a pixel is represented by one, two, four, or eight bits of information.

The location of a point, as displayed on the monitor, is best described by a two-dimensional address. It can be described by a horizontal and vertical co-ordinate pair. The origin of the screen coordinate system, as viewed on the monitor, typically resides at the top left or bottom left corner of the monitor. All of the graphics adapters described in this book use the top left corner as the origin, as indicated in Figure 5.8.

From a programmer's perspective, this screen coordinate system is the easiest system to use. The screen and the printed page provide an obvious two-dimensional space. If the coordinate values of the pixel are specified and the limits of the horizontal and vertical axes are known, the position of the pixel on the screen can be visualized readily.

From the perspective of the display memory, the location of a pixel is more complex. The display memory is organized in either a bit-plane or a packed display format. The display memory is mapped into the host memory address space, organized into bytes. Each byte consists of eight bits, and these eight bits represent from one to eight pixels. Each display mode in the EGA and VGA organizes the data differently. To further complicate matters, a single display mode can allocate different numbers of bits to a pixel. The programmer must know the condition of the current display mode in order to understand where in display memory a pixel resides.

The graphics modes for the EGA and VGA are listed in Table 5.1. A description of the organization of the display memory for each mode is included.

Modes 4 and 5 utilize bit planes 0 and 1. The organization is termed *packed* because a single pixel resides in either bit plane 0 or bit plane 1. Alternate bytes

TABLE 5.1 Display Memory Organization

Mode (Hex)	Adapter	Format	Number of Colors	Pixels/Byte	Bit Planes
4,5	EGA/VGA	Packed	4	4	0,1 O/E
6	EGA/VGA	Packed	2	8	0,1 O/E
F	EGA/VGA	Bit mapped	2	8	0,2
11	VGA	Packed	2	8	0
D	EGA/VGA	Bit mapped	16	8	0,1,2,3
E	EGA/VGA	Bit mapped	16	8	0,1,2,3
10	EGA/VGA	Bit mapped	16	8	0,1,2,3
12	VGA	Bit mapped	16	8	0,1,2,3
13	VGA	Packed	256	1	0,1,2,3 chained

each byte containing four pixels, are loaded into bit plane 0 or bit plane 1 in an odd/even (O/E) fashion.

Mode F hex uses bit planes 0 and 2, organized in a bit-mapped format. The video bit is stored in bit plane 0, and the intensity bit is stored in bit plane 1.

Modes D, E, 10, and 12 hex use all four bit planes, in a bit-mapped format. A pixel can be represented by any or all of these bit planes. For example, a pixel can be represented by one bit in bit plane 0, 1, 2, or 5. Similarly, the pixel can be represented by two bits in bit planes 0 and 1, 0 and 2, 0 and 3, 1 and 2, 1 and 3, or 2 and 3. A pixel can also be represented by three bits in bit planes 0,1,2, bit planes 1,2,3, or bit planes 0,2,3.

Mode 13 hex uses all four bit planes. The bit planes are organized in a packed format because all eight bits associated with a single pixel reside in a single plane. The four planes are chained so that sequential bytes in host memory are loaded into alternating bit planes.

5.4.1 Bit Addressing

In all but mode 13 hex, more than one pixel is stored per byte. Thus, the smallest addressable structure in the computer, the byte, cannot resolve down to the lowest graphical structure, the pixel. It is not possible to address an individual pixel. Attempting to read a single pixel in modes 4, 5, or 6 will access four pixels from display memory. This occurs because a byte is read in a single instruction. The position of the desired pixel within the byte depends on the horizontal address of the pixel. Because there are four pixels per byte, a modulo 4 division will provide the pixel number within a byte. Figure 5.9 illustrates the pixel numbers within a typical byte.

The modulo 4 division is accomplished in C by the statement "address % 4", where address is an integer. The "%" symbol indicates modulo division. The

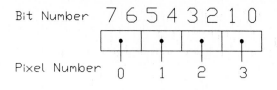

FIGURE 5.9   Pixel Numbers for Modes 4, 5, 6

address can be the horizontal coordinate of the pixel (0–639) or it can be the address relative to the start of display memory. In all of the standard display modes, the number of horizontal pixels per scan line is a multiple of four—either 320 or 640. Therefore, the modulo 4 division will provide the pixel position within a byte regardless of the vertical coordinate.

Suppose the pixel position within a byte is desired for a pixel located at $x=1$, $y=1$ in a mode in which there are 640 pixels per horizontal scan line. The horizontal address of the pixel is 1, and the address with respect to the start of the image is 641. Both 1 and 641 provide a pixel location of 1, as shown in Equation 5.7.

Equation 5.7   Determining Pixel Position

pixel position = address % 4

pixel position = 1 = 1 % 4

pixel position = 1 = 641 % 4

In modes D, E, F, 10, 11, and 12 hex, there are eight pixels per byte. The pixel location within a byte is determined by using a modulo 8 division. The technique used to determine the pixel position is similar to the technique described for modes 4, 5, and 6. Figure 5.10 illustrates the pixel numbers within a typical byte.

In mode 12 hex, one pixel occupies an entire byte. This is the simplest display mode to use when interacting with display memory. The pixel position is always 0, because the pixel occupies the entire byte.

5.4.2   Determining the Display Address

It is possible to determine the display memory address of a pixel given the horizontal coordinates of the pixel, the number of bits per pixel, and the virtual width of the image. The display address and the position of a pixel can be determined using the calculations in Equation 5.8.

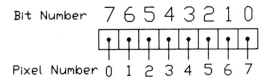

Typical Byte

FIGURE 5.10   Pixel Numbers for Modes D, E, F, 10, 11, 12

Equation 5.8   Determining a Display Address

$$\frac{\text{Display}}{\text{address}} = \frac{\text{Starting}}{\text{address}} + \frac{\text{Vertical}}{\text{component}} + \frac{\text{Horizontal}}{\text{component}}$$

$$\frac{\text{Vertical}}{\text{component}} = \left(\frac{\text{Virtual}}{\text{width}} \Big/ \text{Pixels per byte}\right) \times \frac{\text{Vertical}}{\text{coordinate}}$$

$$\frac{\text{Horizontal}}{\text{component}} = \frac{\text{Horizontal}}{\text{Coordinate}} \Big/ \text{Pixels per byte}$$

$$\frac{\text{Pixel}}{\text{Location}} = \frac{\text{Horizontal}}{\text{Coordinate}} \% \text{ Pixels per byte}$$

The display memory consists of 64 Kbytes per plane on most EGA and VGA adapters. The address begins at 0000 hex and extends to FFFF hex. The active display region begins at the *starting address*. The starting address may begin anywhere in this 64 Kbyte region. For the display modes with more than one page, the starting address is typically 0000 hex. Panning and scrolling can affect the position of the starting address. For the display modes in which more than one page is possible, the starting address can be determined from Equation 5.9.

Equation 5.9   Determining the Starting Address

$$\frac{\text{Starting}}{\text{address}} = \frac{\text{Page}}{\text{number}} \times \text{Bytes per page}$$

$$\text{Bytes per page} = \frac{\text{Vertical}}{\text{extent}} \times \left(\frac{\text{Horizontal}}{\text{extent}} \Big/ \text{Pixels per byte}\right)$$

The page numbers range from 0 to 7 depending on the mode, and the vertical and horizontal extents refer to the number of pixels in the virtual image.

5.4.3 Interacting with Pixels

Once the address and pixel location are determined, the pixel can be accessed in display memory. Reading a pixel really corresponds to reading a number of pixels, either 1, 4, or 8. In the bit-mapped cases, additional bits associated with the pixel might reside in other bit planes. In these cases, additional reads are necessary.

Writing to a pixel is more complex. Although the address and bit position are handled identically, writing to a pixel may mean writing to 1, 4, or 8 pixels. Additional masking is necessary to ensure that only the desired pixel is modified. In the case of four pixels per byte, three of the pixels have to be masked out. In the case of eight pixels per byte, seven of the pixels have to be masked out. When the display is in a bit-mapped mode, additional bits of a pixel may reside in more than one bit plane, and additional write operations may be required.

5.4.4 Reading a Pixel

In the following discussion, it is assumed that the display is in Read Mode 0. Read Mode 0 is the default read mode.

If the display memory is in a packed or bit-mapped format with one bit plane active, all of the bits associated with a single pixel are in a single plane. In order to read a pixel, the display address that accesses a byte containing the pixel must be determined. The display address is used to read a byte from the appropriate bit plane in display memory. This byte contains the desired pixel. Unfortunately, it also contains undesired pixels.

Once read, the byte from display memory resides in a variable in host memory. The pixel position can then be used to find the starting bit position of the desired pixel, within the variable. In order to obtain the value of the pixel, it is necessary to shift the bits associated with the pixel into the low-order bit positions of the byte. The bits in the variable that correspond to other pixels must be zeroed to provide the value of the desired pixel. Table 5.2 lists the number of bit positions to shift the variable and the value that should be used to zero out the unwanted bit positions. This value can be ANDed with the variable after shifting. A positive value in the "Number of Bits to Shift" column indicates a left shift; a negative value indicates a right shift.

In the modes that use a bit-packed format and which have multiple bit planes active, the read operation becomes more complicated. The modes that are bit packed have eight pixels per byte. In these modes, a pixel may be located in one, two, three, or four display planes. Each of the display planes that contains a bit for the pixel must be read before the value of the pixel can be determined. Mode F has data in bit planes 0 and 2, and all of the other modes may have data in all four bit planes.

TABLE 5.2 Reading a Pixel from Display Memory

Pixels/Byte	Pixel Position	Pixel in Bits	Number of Bits to Shift	ANDing Mask (hex)
4	0	6,7	−6	03
4	1	4,5	−4	03
4	2	2,3	−2	03
4	3	0,1	0	03
8	0	7	−7	01
8	1	6	−6	01
8	2	5	−5	01
8	3	4	−4	01
8	4	3	−3	01
8	5	2	−2	01
8	6	1	−1	01
8	7	0	0	01

5.4.5 Mode 6

In mode 6, data resides in both bit planes 0 and 2. The data in bit plane 0 refers to the *video* bit, and the data in bit plane 2 refers to the *intensify* bit. To determine the value of the pixel, the byte that contains the pixel in both display planes is read in a similar fashion to that described above. The display memory address is ascertained, and the byte is read from this address.

All of the display planes reside at the same address, and are differentiated by the Read Map Select Register, which chooses one of the bit planes during a read operation. In this example, the Read Map Select Register is loaded with a 0 and the byte containing the desired pixel is read from display memory into a variable in host memory called *Video*. The value in the Read Map Select Register is then changed to 2, and the byte at the same address in display memory is read into a second variable, called *Intensified*.

In order to determine a single value for the variable, these two variables must be joined. Although four values are possible for a pixel with two bits, in this case the values do not correspond to 0, 1, 2, and 3. Rather, the binary code with the two bits in bit positions 0 and 2 corresponds to values of 0, 1, 4 and 5. The *Video* variable must be shifted into bit position 0, and the *Intensify* variable has to be shifted into bit position 2. The number of bit positions to shift each variable is listed in Table 5.3. A positive shift value indicates a left shift, and a negative shift value indicates a right shift.

The undesired bits corresponding to the other seven pixels in these variables must be zeroed. The mask value is determined from Table 5.4 depending on the pixel position.

Once shifted and masked, the four variables are joined through an ORing

TABLE 5.3 Shifting the Video and Intensified Bits

				Pixel Position				
Variable	0	1	2	3	4	5	6	7
Video	-7	-6	-5	-4	-3	-2	-1	0
Intensified	-5	-4	-3	-2	-1	0	1	2

TABLE 5.4 Zeroing Unwanted Bits

Variable	Mask (Hex)	Comments
Video	01	Only bit 0 is significant
Intensified	04	Only bit 2 is significant

operation, as indicated in Equation 5.10. The "|" operator is the symbol used for the logical OR operation in the C language. The variables are denoted *newVideo* and *newIntensified*, because they represent the variables *Video* and *Intensified* after the shift and logical AND operation.

Equation 5.10 ORing the Attributes

Pixel value = newVideo | newIntensified

5.4.6 Multiple Bit Planes

In the modes that use a bit-packed format and that have multiple bit planes active, the read operation becomes more complicated. All of the display modes that are bit packed represent eight pixels in each byte. Each pixel may be represented by one, two, three, or four bits. These bits are located in one, two, three, or four display planes. Each of the display planes that contain a bit must be read before the value of the pixel can be ascertained. Mode F hex uses a format of two bits per pixel. It stores the two bits per pixel in bit planes 0 and 2; all of the other modes may have data in all four bit planes.

5.4.7 Modes F, 10, 11, and 12 hex

The bits associated with a pixel in modes F, 10, 11, and 12 hex can be located in any of the four bit planes. The value of the pixel depends on the convention being used. In the case of a pixel occupying a bit in all four bit planes, the value of the pixel ranges from 0 to 15. In the case of a pixel occupying one bit plane,

TABLE 5.5 Shifting the Variables from Four Bit Planes

Pixel Position	0	1	2	3	4	5	6	7
Data Bit Position	7	6	5	4	3	2	1	0
P0	−7	−6	−5	−4	−3	−2	−1	0
P1	−6	−5	−4	−3	−2	−1	0	1
P2	−5	−4	−3	−2	−1	0	1	2
P3	−4	−3	−2	−1	0	1	2	3

TABLE 5.6 Zeroing Unwanted Bits

Variable	Mask (Hex)	Comments
P0	01	Only bit 0 is significant
P1	02	Only bit 1 is significant
P2	04	Only bit 2 is significant
P3	08	Only bit 3 is significant

the value of the pixel is either 0 or 1. There is no set convention to determine the value of the pixel in any other cases. The case presented in mode 6 above illustrates this ambiguity. In mode 6, the values correspond to 0, 1, 4, and 5. It is up to the programmer to determine the convention when pixels occupy two or three bit planes.

An example is presented for determining the value of a pixel when the pixel occupies all four bit planes. The same technique can be applied when determining the value of a pixel occupying less than four bit planes. The programmer needs to ascertain the mask values and the number of bits to shift the variables.

Once the address of the byte in display memory that contains the desired pixel is determined, the four bytes from each display plane can be read into four variables called "p0", "p1", "p2", and "p3". These four variables correspond to the values read from bit planes 0, 1, 2, and 3, respectively. Each of the four variables must be shifted the proper amount before being joined into a single variable. Table 5.5 lists the amount of bits to shift the four variables. A positive value indicates a left shift, and a negative value indicates a right shift.

The undesired bits corresponding to the other seven pixels in these variables must be zeroed. The mask value is determined from Table 5.6 depending on the pixel position.

Once shifted and masked, the four variables are joined through an ORing operation, as indicated in Equation 5.11. The "|" operator is the symbol used for the logical OR operation in the C language. The variables are denoted "newP0", "newP1", "newP2", and "newP3" because they represent the four variables "P0", "P1", "P2", and "P3" after the shift and AND operation.

Equation 5.11 ORing the Four Variables

$$\text{Pixel value} = \text{newP0} \mid \text{newP1} \mid \text{newP2} \mid \text{newP3}$$

5.4.8 Writing a Pixel

Writing to a pixel in display memory requires a read/modify/write operation. In the following discussion, it is assumed that the EGA/VGA is in write mode 0, the default write mode. In all modes except mode 13 hex, there is more than one pixel per byte of display memory. However, the byte is the smallest structure that the host memory can access. Writing to one pixel without affecting the other pixels in the byte of display memory requires a masking operation. This insures that only the desired pixel is modified.

The address of the byte that contains the desired pixel is used to read the byte from display memory. This value is loaded into a variable, "read_val", in the host memory. A mask, called the "read mask" in Table 5.7, zeroes out the bits corresponding to the desired pixel. The value of the mask is determined by the number of pixels per byte and the pixel location within the byte. After the zeroing, the bit locations corresponding to the pixel value are 0 and therefore are ready for new data.

The value that is to be loaded into the desired pixel is resident in a variable, "write_val", in host memory. This value occupies the least significant bits of the variable. A mask value, called "write_mask" in Table 5.7, is used to zero all other bits in the variable. This prevents these bits from interfering with the subsequent operations. If the value in this variable does not exceed the maximum value that the pixel can obtain, the zeroing is unnecessary. Once zeroed, the variable "write_val" is shifted to the left so that the pixel value is placed in the bits corresponding to the pixel position. This resultant variable, "write_val", is ORed with the variable "read_val", which inserts the new pixel value into the byte read from display memory. The result is then written back to display memory at the same address that was used for the original read operation. This completes the read/modify/write operation. Table 5.7 contains the necessary constants for this operation. Positive values in the "Number of Bits to Shift" column indicate a left shift, and negative values indicate a right shift.

5.4.9 Using the Bit Mask and the Data Rotate Register

This time-consuming operation was anticipated by the designers of the EGA/VGA standard. Internal hardware is built into the EGA/VGA to perform the shifting and masking of the data automatically. A Bit Mask Register is provided in the EGA/VGA to act as a write mask register. A Data Rotate Register is

TABLE 5.7 Reading a Pixel from Display Memory

Pixels/Byte	Pixel Position	Pixel in Bits	Number of Bits to Shift	Read Mask	Write Mask
4	0	6,7	6	3F	03
4	1	4,5	4	CF	03
4	2	2,3	2	F3	03
4	3	0,1	0	FC	03
8	0	7	7	7F	01
8	1	6	6	BF	01
8	2	5	5	DF	01
8	3	4	4	EF	01
8	4	3	3	F7	01
8	5	2	2	FB	01
8	6	1	1	FD	01
8	7	0	0	FE	01

provided in the EGA/VGA to shift the data from the host. These two registers are used for the modify portion of the read/modify/write operation.

The Bit Mask Register is used to protect any bits within a byte of display memory from being modified. A byte of display memory can contain bits associated with more than one pixel. If one pixel needs to be modified, any bits associated with the other pixels have to be protected. Any bit positions within the Bit Mask Register that are reset to 0 are protect bits. A byte written from host memory will affect only those bits in display memory that correspond to a 1 in the Bit Mask Register. This provides the masking necessary for the modify operation. The mask values to load into the Bit Mask Register are determined by the pixel location bits and are listed in Table 5.7.

The Data Rotate Register shifts the byte written from host memory before it is written into display memory. The value that is to be written into a pixel must reside in the bit position associated with that pixel. If it resides in some other location, it must be shifted so that it resides in the proper pixel location. The value loaded into the Data Rotate Register corresponds to the number of pixels to left-shift the host byte. This register is called a *rotate register* because values greater than 8 but less than 16 are considered right shifts. The rotate values to load into the Data Rotate Register are also determined by the pixel location register and are listed in Table 5.8.

5.4.10 Multiple Bit Planes

In the modes that use a bit-packed format and that have multiple bit planes active, the write operation becomes more complicated. All of these bit-packed modes represent one bit from eight pixels in each byte. A pixel may be repre-

TABLE 5.8 Bit Mask and Data Rotate Register

Pixels/Byte	Pixel Position	Pixel in Bits	Data Rotate	Bit Mask (Hex)
4	0	6,7	6	C0
4	1	4,5	4	30
4	2	2,3	2	0C
4	3	0,1	0	03
8	0	7	7	80
8	1	6	6	40
8	2	5	5	20
8	3	4	4	10
8	4	3	3	08
8	5	2	2	04
8	6	1	1	02
8	7	0	0	01

sented by one, two, three, or four bits. These bits are located in one, two, three, or four display planes. Each of the display planes that contain a bit must be read before the value of the pixel can be determined. Mode F has data in bit planes 0 and 2; all of the other modes may have data in all four bit planes.

It is possible to write to a pixel in one of the bit planes using the techniques described above. The same techniques can be used. These techniques involving the Bit Mask and Rotate Registers are simply replicated, one for each of the desired bit planes.

It is necessary to understand the hardware in order to understand how to write to the display planes. Internal to the EGA/VGA adapter is a 32-bit-wide data bus. This data bus is segmented into four sections, each section being eight bits wide. Each of the four sections interfaces to one of the four bit planes. The host interfaces to the adapter through an 8-bit data bus. This 8-bit host bus is expanded to the 32-bit data bus. The eight bits from the host bus interface to each of the four EGA/VGA internal data buses, as shown in Figure 5.11.

5.4.11 Using the Map Mask Register

Each of the four latches comprising the 32-bit internal latch are enabled separately through signals E0, E1, E2, and E3. If signal E0 is active, the 8-bit data written from the host will affect bit plane 0. Likewise, if signal E1 is active, the 8-bit data written from the host will affect bit plane 1. It is possible for both E0 and E1 to be active. If this is the case, both bit plane 0 and bit plane 1 will be affected. Each will be modified with identical data. In fact, all four bit planes, or any combination of the four bit planes, can be written to simultaneously. This constitutes a 32-bit write operation in a single instruction. The limitation

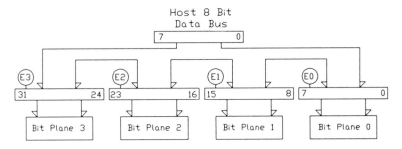

FIGURE 5.11 Host Eight-bit to EGA/VGA 32-bit Data Bus

is that the identical eight bits from the host are written to any of the enabled planes. The Map Mask Register determines which bit planes will be affected.

5.4.12 Writing to One Pixel in Multiple Planes

It is possible to write to one pixel in multiple display planes in a single host operation. This can be a big time-saver for the programmer who has to modify a single pixel. Hardware is provided in the EGA/VGA that can access one pixel location in each of the four bit planes. Two techniques can be used to accomplish this. The first utilizes the Set/Reset and Enable Set/Reset Registers. The second utilizes write mode 2.

5.4.13 Set/Reset and Enable Set/Reset Registers

The Set/Reset Register is used to interact with a single pixel in all four bit planes. A four-bit value is written into the Set/Reset Register. Each bit in this four-bit value accesses one of the display planes. Bit 0 accesses bit plane 0, bit 1 accesses bit plane 1, etc. The byte in display memory that contains the desired pixel is accessed by the address used in a host move operation. The individual pixel is enabled through the Bit Mask Register.

It is also possible to write to a pixel that does not occupy all four bit planes. Any number of bit planes can be accessed in a single operation by enabling only the desired bit planes. This is accomplished through the Enable Set/Reset Register. A four-bit value is loaded into this register. Each bit within this four-bit value enables one of the display planes. The enabled display plane is modified with the value in the corresponding bit position of the Set/Reset Register. Any bit in the Enable Set/Reset Register that contains a 1 causes the corresponding bit plane to be modified by the value in the Set/Reset Register. Any bit position in the Enable Set/Reset Register that contains a 0 causes the corresponding bit plane to be modified by the data being output from the host.

The technique employed to write a value to a pixel from one to four bit planes using the Set/Reset and Enable Set/Reset Register is complicated. The appropriate values are loaded into the Set/Reset and Enable Set/Reset Registers. A move operation sends an 8-bit data value to the display adapter. The value in the Map Mask Register determines which bit planes are active. Any bit planes enabled by the Map Mask Register and the Enable Set/Reset Register are modified by the value in the Set/Reset Register. Any bit planes enabled by the Map Mask Register but not enabled by the Enable Set/Reset Register are modified by the value sent by the host in the move operation.

5.4.14 Writing to Multiple Pixels in Multiple Planes

The data in one to eight pixels in each of the four display planes can be modified in a single operation. The Set/Reset Register and the Enable Set/Reset Register are used in an identical fashion, as was described previously. The byte in display memory that contains the desired pixel is accessed by the address referenced in the move instruction. When a single pixel is being modified, the Bit Mask Register enables just that one pixel. Additional pixels can be modified if their corresponding bit positions are enabled in the Bit Mask Register.

This technique effectively performs a 32-bit data transfer in a single host instruction. Each bit plane can be modified with different data, permitting up to eight pixels per bit plane to be altered. However, using the Set/Reset and the Enable Set/Reset Registers, all of the bits in a single bit plane can be modified only with the same data. This occurs because the Set/Reset Register contains only four bits, one bit destined for each display plane. Any pixels enabled by the Bit Mask Register will be modified by the same value, either a 0 or a 1, as loaded in the corresponding bit position of the Set/Reset Register.

5.4.15 Writing to All Planes Using Write Mode 2

Any combination of the four bit planes can be modified in a single host instruction by using write mode 2. Write mode 2 is made active by loading a 2 into the WM field of the Mode Register. The host move operation sends a four-bit word to the display adapter. With write mode 2 active, each of these four bits is associated with one of the four-bit planes. Bit 0 in the value sent by the host is associated with bit plane 0. Bits 1, 2 and 3 are associated with Bit Planes 1, 2, and 3, respectively. Each bit is replicated eight times and written to its respective display plane. Up to eight pixels in each bit plane can be modified with this replicated bit. The eight bits are accessed in display memory by the address used in the host move operation. The pixels that are affected depend on the value in the Bit Mask Register. This effectively produces a 32-bit write operation in a single host operation. However, the eight pixels in each plane can be modified only with an identical value, either 0 or 1.

5.5 THE LINE

A single image on the EGA/VGA can consist of thousands of lines. In an interactive graphics session, images can be redrawn hundreds of times. This results in an enormous number of lines being drawn. A line on the EGA/VGA

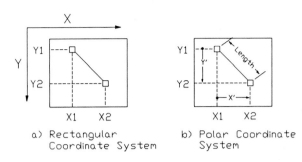

FIGURE 5.12   Defining a Line

can be composed of more than 600 dots. The line can be drawn by repeatedly calling a point-drawing routine. However, this puts a tremendous constraint on the point-drawing routine. Because it is called repeatedly, the point-drawing routine must be designed as efficiently as possible. Because the line-drawing routine is called repeatedly, it must also be designed as efficiently as possible.

There are several line-drawing algorithms available to the graphics programmer. Three important algorithms are discussed in the following sections. These include the solution of the linear equation, the incremental algorithm, and the Bresenham's line algorithm. The special cases of horizontal and vertical lines are also discussed. Bresenham's line algorithm is far superior to the other techniques when run in a PC environment.

5.5.1   Defining a Line

There are two popular ways to define a line. The first technique defines a line by its endpoints. This defines the line within a rectangular coordinate system. The second technique defines a line by one endpoint, a slope, and a length. This defines the line in a polar coordinate system. Both of these are illustrated in Figure 5.12.

In 5.12A, the endpoints are defined as the two coordinate pairs $(X1,Y1)$ and $(X2,Y2)$. In 5.12B, the one endpoint is defined as $(X1,Y1)$, the length is defined as LENGTH, and the slope is defined as (Y'/X'). The slope is a measure of the change along the vertical axis, Y', divided by the change along the horizontal axis, X'.

5.5.2   Determining the Length of a Line

The length of a line in one dimension can be determined by taking the absolute value of the difference between the endpoints. A line typically is drawn from one endpoint to another. If the position of the drawing device at the end of the line drawing is important, it is necessary to draw the line specifically from one coordinate to another. This is the case with pen plotters.

The length of a line in two dimensions can be determined by taking the length of the projection of that line onto each of two perpendicular axes. These values are squared and added. The square root of the result yields the length of the line. This equation is attributed to Pythagoras and is included in Equation 5.12.

Equation 5.12   Pythagorean Theorem

$$\text{Length} = (X^2 + Y^2)^{1/2}$$

The lengths of the projections X and Y, are often useful in themselves, and Equation 5.12 does not need to be solved. The lengths of the projections of the line along the X and Y axis are called X and Y. If these lengths are squared, it is not necessary to take the absolute value of the difference. The length does not have a direction, and thus it must always be possible. These lengths are described in Equation 5.13.

Equation 5.13   Lengths of Projections

$$X = \text{ABS}\ (X2 - X1)$$

$$Y = \text{ABS}\ (Y2 - Y1)$$

The programmer must take care when determining the length of a line in a discrete environment. A line that connects two adjacent pixels, say $X=1$ and $X=2$, occupies two pixels yet is only 1 pixel unit long. This is often a cause of confusion and inaccuracies. If a line having a length of 1 unit is drawn, two pixels will be involved.

5.5.3   Determining the Slope of a Line

The slope of a line is a measure of the line's direction. The slope of a line is a constant—that is, the slope of a line at one point on the line is equal to the slope of the line everywhere on the line. The slope can be determined by dividing the length of the projection of the line on one axis by the length of the projection of the line on the other axis. The slope of a line can be represented by the change of Y over the change of X or by the change of X divided by the change of Y, as shown in Equation 5.14.

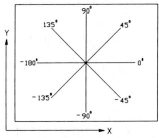 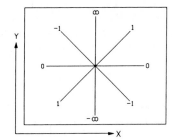

a) Measuring the Slope of a Line in Angles   b) Measuring the Slope of a Line in Lengths

FIGURE 5.13   Measuring the Slope of a Line

Equation 5.14   Slope of a Line

$$\text{Slope\_Y} = \frac{dy}{dx} = \frac{\text{length of } Y}{\text{length of } X}$$

$$\text{Slope\_X} = \frac{dx}{dy} = \frac{\text{length of } X}{\text{length of } Y}$$

These two slopes are not independent and are related by a reciprocal relationship, as shown in Equation 5.15.

Equation 5.15   Reciprocal Relationship of Slopes

$$\text{Slope\_X} = 1 / \text{Slope\_Y}$$

The angle of a slope is measured counterclockwise from the horizontal axis, as indicated in Figure 5.13A. A horizontal line has a slope of either 0 degrees or 180 degrees. A vertical line has a slope of 90 degrees or -90 degrees.

The slope can also be measured in terms of lengths by Equation 5.13. The slope of a line measured with Y as the independent variable is expressed in Equation 5.14. It should be noted that the vertical orientation is reversed in the EGA/VGA device coordinate system.

The slope corresponding to a horizontal line is 0 in this case, because the length of the projection along the vertical axis is 0. The slope corresponding to a 45-degree line is 1, because both projection lengths are equal. The slope of a vertical line is infinity, because the length of the projection along the Y axis is 0, and a scalar divided by 0 yields infinity, in this instance.

5.5.4 The Linear Equation

A line can be drawn by solving either of the linear equations in Equations 5.16 and 5.17.

Equation 5.16 Linear Equation: X Independent Variable

$$Y = (\text{Slope\_Y} \times X) + By$$

Equation 5.17 Linear Equation: Y Independent Variable

$$X = (\text{Slope\_X} \times Y) + Bx$$

In these equations, Y is the vertical coordinate, X is the horizontal coordinate, My and Mx are the slopes, By is the *y-intercept*, and Bx is the *x-intercept*. Equation 5.16 expresses a line with Y being the dependent variable and X being the independent variable. Equation 5.17 expresses a line with X being the dependent variable and Y being the independent variable.

The slope is defined in Equations 5.14. It is a measure of the amount of change that the dependent variable will incur due to an incremental change in the independent variable. The proper determination of which variable, X or Y, is independent is critical to effective line drawing.

5.5.5 Determining an Independent Variable

When drawing a line, care must be exercised when selecting whether the horizontal or the vertical axis, X or Y, should be the independent axis. In a continuous system, it makes no difference whether Equation 5.16 or 5.17, is selected. However, in a pixelated, discrete system, selecting the proper independent variable affects the quality of the line.

A line is typically drawn from one endpoint to the other. A line-drawing algorithm determines which axis is best thought of as being independent. It starts at the one endpoint with the coordinate of the independent axis plugged into Equation 5.16 or 5.17. This equation determines the value of the independent variable, and a point is drawn at the pixel located at this coordinate pair. The algorithm increments the independent variable, repeating this process until the second endpoint of the line is reached. The resulting line has only one point for each of the incremental values of the independent variable. It may have no point, one point, or many points for any value of the independent variable. This is illustrated in Figure 5.14.

In Figure 5.14, it is evident that the line in *b* is more filled in and looks continuous, while the line in *a* appears to be a dotted line. This occurs because in *b* the independent axis is X, and in *a* the independent axis is Y.

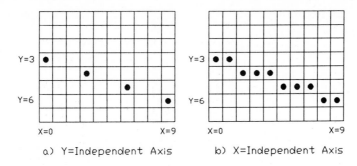

FIGURE 5.14 A Line Using Two Different Independent Axes

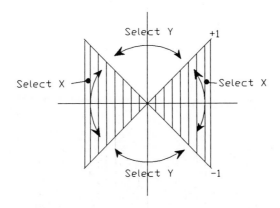

FIGURE 5.15 Selecting an Independent Axis

The criterion used to determine which axis to select as the independent axis involves the slope. If the slope is between -45 degrees and +45 degrees, X should be selected as the independent variable. If the slope is less than -45 degrees and greater then -135 degrees or greater than +45 degrees and less than 135 degrees, the Y axis should be selected. Measuring the slope in terms of lengths, this means that if the slope is between -1 and +1, select the X axis as the independent variable. Otherwise, the Y axis should be selected. In other words, if the change in Y is less than the change in X, select the X axis as the independent variable. The selection criterion is illustrated in Figure 5.15.

5.5.6 Drawing a Line Using the Linear Equation

The linear equation is listed in Equations 5.16 or 5.17. This algorithm is implemented by the following steps:

1. Determine the slope and intercept of the line.

2. Select the independent and dependent variable depending on the value of the slope.

3. Set the independent variable to the lesser of the two endpoints.

4. Solve the linear equation for the dependent variable.

5. Draw a point at the pixel selected by the two variables.

6. Increment the independent variable.

7. If the independent variable is not equal to the value at the second endpoint, repeat steps 4–7.

The linear equation requires a multiplication and an addition for every point. The multiplication must be a floating-point multiplication, because the slope is a real number. It is possible to estimate the floating-point multiplication with a fractional integer multiplication. Errors can occur unless the precision of the fractional part is high. The floating-point multiplication is time-consuming and slows down the line drawing. The addition requires a rounding operation, which can also be time-consuming. A coprocessor designed to perform rapid floating-point calculations does improve the performance, but these operations are still slow.

Because the display is pixelated, the result of this floating-point multiplication and integer addition must be converted to an integer so that a pixel can be selected. A round-off error will occur. Nevertheless, because the calculation is performed for every point drawn, the errors are usually insignificant. Only when these round-off errors accumulate do significant errors become apparent.

5.5.7 Drawing a Line Using an Incremental Algorithm

A second algorithm that is popular for drawing a line is the incremental technique. This algorithm bases itself on the linear equations in Equations 5.16 and 5.17, but the technique for solving the equation is different.

A slope can be thought of as an incremental change. If the slope is normalized, it represents the change incurred in the dependent variable based on an incremental change in the independent variable. In this case, the increment amount is equal to 1. For example, if a slope of length_Y/length_X is equal to 5.0, it can be said that for every step of 1.0 in X, a change of 5.0 occurs in Y. Thus, as the algorithm progresses, the value of the independent variable, in this case X, is incremented and the value in the dependent variable, in this case Y, is increased by 5.0.

This algorithm is implemented by the following steps.

1. The slope is calculated.

2. A decision is made based on the slope regarding which axis should be the independent variable.

3. An incremental slope is determined based on the change in the dependent variable based on a change of 1 in the independent variable.

4. Two floating-point or fractional integer accumulators are set up. These are loaded with the coordinate pair of one of the endpoints.

5. A point is drawn at the coordinate pair indicated by the rounded-off values of the two accumulators.

6. The independent variable is incremented, and the incremental slope is added to the dependent variable.

7. If the independent variable is not equal to the value at the second endpoint, repeat steps 5–7.

This algorithm requires no multiplications, either integer or floating point, inside the line-drawing loop. The slope must be considered as either floating point or fractional integer. Thus, either floating-point or fractional integer additions are required. The horizontal and vertical accumulators that keep track of the X and Y coordinates must be stored as floating-point or fractional integer variables to ensure that the round-off errors do not accumulate. This technique is usually faster than the previous technique, because it requires two floating-point or fractional integer additions per point instead of the one floating-point multiplication and one integer addition of the previous technique. This algorithm also requires a single round-off operation per point.

5.5.8 The Bresenham Line Algorithm

The Bresenham algorithm for drawing a line requires no multiplications and no floating-point or fractional integer variables. Because no real variables are necessary, the line-drawing algorithm exhibits no round-off errors. However, the transformation from the real-world coordinate system to the display coordinate system can still produce round-off errors.

The algebra related to the development of this algorithm is described in *Fundamentals of Interactive Computer Graphics*, by J. D. Foley and A. Van Dam (Addison Wesley, 1982). The derivation of the algorithm is complicated and will not be repeated here. The operation of the algorithm is straightforward.

This algorithm is called a heuristic algorithm, because it utilizes the natural constraints of the pixelated graphics system. Utilizing the discrete display space helps to speed the line-drawing processing. The two previous algorithms made calculations in a real number system and then rounded off to obtain the integer pixel values. The incremental algorithm, described in Section 5.5.7, could use an integer accumulator, thereby eliminating the floating-point operations. However, round-off errors accumulate over the length of the line, causing serious problems, especially with long lines. Bresenham's algorithm uses an integer accumulator but bases the accumulation upon a decision. The decision acts as an intelligent rounding off process. This eliminates accumulation errors.

As the incremental algorithm calculates the coordinate of the dependent variable, a round-off process selects between two pixels. Because the algorithm is solving the equation with X as the independent variable, the two pixels are immediate vertical neighbors. The following discussion assumes that the X axis represents the independent variable. As in the incremental algorithm described previously, the first point is drawn using the coordinates of one of the endpoints of the line. The X coordinate is incremented by 1. The Y coordinate may or may not be incremented depending on the result of a decision. To eliminate accumulation errors, a decision is made based on the error measured at every point. This limits both the error incurred at each individual point and the total accumulated error to half of one pixel. This is equivalent to the errors associated with round-off.

The decision is based upon a running accumulator called D. The initial value of D is obtained from Equation 5.18.

Equation 5.18 Determination of the Decision Value

$$D = (2 \times dY) - dX$$

In this equation, dY and dX are the incremental horizontal and vertical slopes. At each step, X is incremented by 1, and Y will either be incremented by 1 or not be incremented at all. This decision will be based on the current value of the D decision variable. At each step, D is updated by a value depending on the previous value of D. If the previous value of D is less than 0, Equation 5.19 is used to modify the decision variable.

Equation 5.19 Updating the Decision Variable If $D < 0$

$$D = D + (2 \times dY)$$

If the previous value of D is greater than or equal to 0, Equation 5.20 is used to modify the decision variable.

Equation 5.20   Updating the Decision Variable If D $>=$ 0

$$D = D + 2 \times (dY - dX)$$

Each step through the algorithm loop draws one point. Because the X axis is assumed to be the independent variable, this point is drawn one pixel to the right of the previous pixel. It resides at the same Y value or is above the previous Y value by 1. This inner loop requires one integer comparison and two integer additions per pixel. Over many lines, a stochastic analysis of the decisions would determine that less than two additions are occurring per point because decisions are sometimes made not to increment Y. The calculation of D requires a multiplication by 2, which can be accomplished by a shift left.

Although there are multiplications in this algorithm, they are all powers of 2 multiplications, which enables them to be implemented by shift instructions.

5.5.9   Aliasing

All of the line-drawing algorithms exhibit errors attributable to round off. These round-off errors are apparent on the display as jagged edges and are associated with undersampling. The terms *aliasing* and *anti-aliasing* are used to describe these jagged edges. These terms originate in sampling theory having to do with the digitization process. The digitization process involves the sampling of continuous signals.

A continuous signal is digitized at a sample rate of some number of samples per second. If the signal being sampled has frequencies present that are greater than half of the sample rate, aliasing occurs. This situation constitutes a one-dimensional example of aliasing. The same principle holds for the two-dimensional case. A continuous line has to be digitized in order to be displayed in a pixelated display format.

Representing a line, or any shape for that matter, on a discrete grid of points will likely result in aliasing. If the resolution of the display is high enough, the human eye might not be able to detect the aliasing errors. The EGA/VGA resolution of 640 by 350 is far too small to eliminate the visual perception of aliasing at normal viewing distances.

5.5.10   Anti-aliasing

It is possible to use a technique called *anti-aliasing*, which has the effect of removing these jagged edges. Short of adding more resolution, there is no way to truly remove the effects of aliasing. However, if the display adapter can display sufficient gray scale, the effects of aliasing can be diminished. This technique draws a line in different intensities, even though the line is meant to be drawn in one intensity.

Suppose a dot falls halfway between two pixels. The dot would be drawn in one or the other pixel at full intensity without anti-aliasing. With anti-aliasing, the dot is drawn in both pixels at half intensity. The resulting energy is the same and the result is quite impressive. This technique can be successful at enhancing the appearance of a display that is unappealing because of jagged lines. This enhancement occurs at the expense of blurring and additional processing time. It is usually faster to utilize a higher-resolution display than it is to perform anti-aliasing on a lower-resolution display.

5.5.11   Drawing Horizontal Lines

A special routine to draw horizontal lines can speed up the process of drawing lines. The Y coordinate of the line remains constant, and the line ranges between the X coordinates of the two endpoints. A pixel is drawn at each pixel position between these two endpoints on a single scan line of the display. A pixel is addressed in display memory by a byte address and a pixel location address. In a bit-mapped display, each byte contains up to eight bits from different pixels. A general point-drawing routine would access any of the bits within this byte independently, requiring a move operation per bit. A horizontal line-drawing routine can take advantage of the nature of the bit-map display. All bits within a byte that are included in the horizontal line can be updated in a single move operation.

5.5.12   Drawing Vertical Lines

A special routine to draw vertical lines can likewise speed up the process of drawing lines. The X coordinate of the line remains constant, and the line ranges between the Y coordinates of the two endpoints. A pixel is drawn on each scan line of the display, in one column between the endpoint scan lines. A pixel is addressed in display memory by a byte address and a pixel location address. The pixel location address refers to the bit position within the byte that contains the data relevant to the desired pixel. As the vertical line is drawn, this value will not change. Vertical neighboring pixels are separated in display memory by a number of bytes equal to the width of the virtual image. As each pixel is drawn, a new byte address is calculated. If the line is drawn from the smallest Y coordinate to the largest, the byte address is incremented by the virtual width. Vertical lines can be drawn rapidly, because only one addition is required per point.

5.5.13   Clipping

Keeping data within a window requires a technique called *clipping*. Clipping determines which lines should be drawn into a window, which should not be drawn, and which portions of a line should be drawn when the line is located partially within a window. Other data structures—for example, polygons—must also be calculated to determine which parts fit into a given window. In the case of bit-mapped graphics, all that is necessary to fit a portion of data into a window is to select the starting address and the height and width of the data and to move it into the window. This is much simpler than the situation in which data is being generated in a vector format.

The calculations involved in clipping lines can be difficult and time-consuming. One technique compares each point of the line to the endpoints of the window before it is drawn into the display. This is simple, although it requires four comparisons per point for every point on the line. If the line is much larger than the window, this technique can be extremely time-consuming. A better solution would be to determine where the line intersects the window and to calculate and draw only those points contained within the window.

The brute-force method to determine these intersection points involves calculating the intersection of the line and the edges of the window. If the endpoints of the line fall within the window, they should be used as the endpoints of the line. If the line crosses the window, the intersection points should be used as the line endpoint. Only those points inside the window should be calculated and drawn. This involves an inordinate amount of calculation, because both endpoints of every line must be checked. When the window is large and most lines fall completely within it, or when the window is small and both endpoints fall outside of it, this clipping procedure can be very inefficient.

A technique designed by Cohen-Sutherland uses an effective means of determining which lines fall entirely within the window and which fall entirely outside of the window. These lines can be drawn or not drawn without requiring the lengthy intersection calculations. Because the window is assumed to have horizontal and vertical edges, the equation for the line in question can be solved for the intersection point of the line and the horizontal or vertical border of the window. This calculation is far simpler than the calculation of the intersection of the actual window edge and the line in question.

In the Cohen-Sutherland technique, the line is continually subdivided until the remaining line may be trivially accepted or rejected. The standard linear equations $x = x + (1/m)y$ and $y = y + mx$ are used to calculate the intersection point of the line and the lines extended from the borders of the window. The slope of the line, m, is determined by dividing the vertical length of the line by the horizontal length of the line. The line is then translated upward, downward, to the left, or to the right in order to position the endpoint of the line at the intersection point of the extended border. Note that the intersection of the line and the extended border is not the same as the intersection of the line with the actual window edge. For example, the line may intersect with the extended left edge of the window above or below the actual window. Thus, additional decisions are necessary to determine if the new line can be trivially accepted or rejected. A description of this technique can be found in *Fundamentals of Interactive Computer Graphics*, Foley and Van Dam (Addison-Wesley, 1982).

5.6 THE CIRCLE

Several techniques are available for drawing circles. Unlike lines which have a constant slope, circles have slopes that are constantly changing, ranging from minus infinity through 0 to positive infinity. The constant slope of lines allows the programmer the luxury of deciding which coordinate is best suited to be the independent variable. This is not the case with circles.

A circle is defined by the sum-of-squares equation listed in Equation 5.21.

Equation 5.21 Equation of a Circle

$$\text{Radius}^2 = X^2 + Y^2$$

If the X coordinate is selected as the independent variable, Equation 5.22 can be used to solve this equation. It should be noted that for every value of X there are two values for Y, representing the positive and negative solution to the square root.

Equation 5.22 Solving the Circle Equation for X

$$Y = +/- (\text{Radius}^2 - X^2)^{1/2}$$

5.6.1 Utilizing Symmetry

Symmetry can be utilized to improve the speed of a circle-drawing program, because a circle is highly symmetric. Because it is symmetric about the X axis, only angles of 0 to 180 degrees need to be drawn. This symmetry is accounted for in the positive and negative solutions of Equation 5.22. Because the circle is symmetric about the Y axis, only angles of 0 to 90 degrees need to be handled independently. Similarly, the circle is symmetric about the 45-degree axis, requiring only 0 to 45 degrees to be handled. Thus, a circle can be completely drawn by replicating the arc from 0 to 45 degrees eight times. This can save a considerable amount of time. Symmetry about a circle is illustrated in Figure 5.16.

The equations that are used to determine the eight symmetric points given the calculated values of X and Y and the center coordinates X_Center,Y_Center are listed in Equation 5.23.

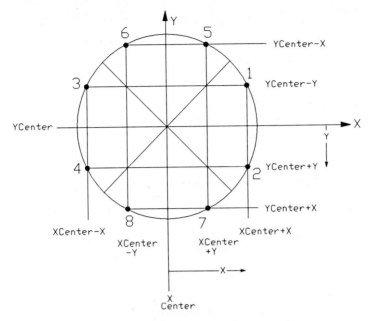

FIGURE 5.16 Symmetry about a Circle

Equation 5.23 Utilizing the Symmetry of a Circle

X1 = X_Center + X	Y1 = Y_Center + Y	original point
X2 = X_Center + X	Y2 = Y_Center − Y	X reflection
X3 = X_Center − X	Y3 = Y_Center + Y	Y reflection
X4 = X_Center − X	Y4 = Y_Center − Y	X/Y reflection
X5 = X_Center + Y	Y5 = Y_Center + X	45 reflection
X6 = X_Center − Y	Y6 = Y_Center + X	45,X reflection
X7 = X_Center + Y	Y7 = Y_Center − X	45,Y reflection
X8 = X_Center − Y	Y8 = Y_Center − X	45,X,Y reflection

5.6.2 Drawing a Circle Using the Circle Equation

Drawing a circle using Equation 5.22 uses techniques similar to the techniques used to draw a line. A coordinate is selected as the independent variable, and the equation is solved with respect to this variable.

The parameters of a circle usually include the center coordinates of the circle and the radius. The solution to Equation 5.22 will yield bipolar results if the center of the coordinate system is the same as the center of the circle. This is usually not the case, and the circle equation has to be translated to the desired center of the circle. The translation process is accomplished using the calculations in Equations 5.24.

Equation 5.24   Translating a Circle to a Center Point

$$X\_Circle = X + X\_Center$$

$$Y\_Circle = Y + Y\_Center$$

The circle is drawn utilizing the high degree of symmetry. The X axis is assumed to be the independent variable. In the following algorithm, it ranges from the X projection at 0 degrees to the X projection at 45 degrees. The X projections are determined from Equation 5.25.

Equation 5.25   Determining the X Limits

$$X\_Start = Radius \times Cos(theta) \text{ where } theta = 0 \text{ degrees}$$
$$X\_Start = Radius \times Cos(0) = Radius$$
$$X\_End = Radius \times Cos(theta) \text{ where } theta = 45 \text{ degrees}$$
$$X\_End = Radius \times Cos(45) = Radius \times .7071$$

Using the circle equation to draw a circle involves the following steps.

1. Determine the X_Start and X_End limits according to Equation 5.25.

2. Solve Equation 5.22 for the positive solution for Y, given X.

3. Translate the X index and the solution for Y to take advantage of the eight-way symmetry. This translation is indicated in Equations 5.23.

4. Draw the eight pixels as indicated in Step 4.

5. Increment the X variable.

6. Repeat steps 2 through 6 until the X value is greater than the value of X_End as determined in Step 1.

This method yields a poor image at locations on the circle where the slope is greater than 1, especially where the slope approaches infinity. The slope approaches infinity at 0 degrees and at 180 degrees. This solution requires two multiplications, an addition, and worst of all, a square root. The multiplications could require floating-point multiplications, because the value can exceed the dynamic range of an integer. There are several techniques for performing a square root, none of which are fast.

5.6.3   Drawing a Circle Using Parametric Equations

A second technique for drawing a circle utilizes the parametric equations for a circle. These equations are listed in Equation 5.26.

Equation 5.26   Parametric Equation for a Circle

$$X = \text{Radius} \times \text{Cos}(theta)$$

$$Y = \text{Radius} \times \text{Sin}(theta)$$

Theta is an angle that varies from 0 to 360 degrees. In these equations, *theta* is the independent variable. Drawing a circle is accomplished by incrementing *theta* by a constant value. The pixels drawn at the *X,Y* coordinate pair are subsequently drawn so that they are equally distributed around the circle. The smaller the incremental value, the greater the density of dots along the circle. The smaller the radius of the circle, the fewer dots are required. The circumference of a circle is $2 \times \text{PI} \times \text{radius}$. If the radius is 100 pixels, the circumference is 628 pixels. Therefore, at least 628 pixels should be drawn so that the circle appears to be a solid line. If the angular resolution of .5 degrees is selected, 720 pixels will be drawn. This might not be enough for many applications.

When working with these parametric equations, it is important to remember that the center of the circle must be considered as the origin. To draw a circle away from the origin, the center of the circle must be translated to the desired location before drawing occurs.

Another speed enhancer is to create sine and cosine tables and thereby reduce the *sin* and *cosine* calculations to table lookups. These tables can be lengthy, but they are often worth the sizable time savings.

A circle can be drawn using the parametric equations following these steps.

1. Set the *theta* value to 0.

2. Solve Equation 5.26 for *X* and *Y*, given *theta*.

3. Translate the solution *X* and *Y* to take advantage of the eight-way symmetry. This translation is indicated in Equation 5.23.

4. Draw the eight pixels, as indicated in Step 3.

5. Increment the *theta* variable by the desired amount.

6. Repeat Steps 2 through 6 until the *theta* value is greater than 45 degrees.

5.6.4 Bresenham's Circle Equation

A third technique was discovered by Bresenham, and it is similar to his line equation in that it requires no floating-point variables or multiplications. Like the line algorithm, this technique is also based on a decision variable. The decision is based on the value of a decision variable, D, where D is initialized according to Equation 5.27.

Equation 5.27 Initialization of the Decision Variable

$$D = 3 - (2 \times \text{Radius})$$

Either X or Y can be considered as the independent variable, because of the symmetry of the circle. Suppose that X is the independent variable. X is initialized to 0 and incremented in each iteration of the algorithm. The X variable ranges from 0 to a value less than Y. Y is initialized to a value equal to the radius. Each iteration through the algorithm draws one pixel. The sign of D determines whether Y should be decremented. It also dictates the adjustment that is to be made on the decision variable, D. The adjustment is indicated in Equation 5.28.

Equation 5.28 Adjustment to the Index Variable

$$D = D + (4 \times X) + 6 \qquad \text{if } D < 0$$

$$D = D + 4 \times (X - Y) + 10 \qquad \text{if } D >= 0$$

Because the X variable ranges from 0 to Y, only one-eighth of the circle is calculated. The symmetry is used to draw the remaining points. It should be noted that $X = Y$ at an angle of 45 degrees.

Although there are multiplications in this algorithm, they are all powers-of-two multiplications, which enable them to be implemented by shift instructions.

5.7 THE IMAGE

Images are different than line drawings, just as a photograph of a person is different from a stick figure. Line drawings are referred to as wire drawings, because they appear to be objects made from wires. Wire-model drawings are frequently done in two or three dimensions. Images are different from line drawings in that surfaces and shadings are used to give the appearance of realism. Images may or may not represent real-world objects.

The resolution restrictions that affect wire drawings also affect images. Images impose an additional constraint upon graphics systems that involve realistic gray scale or color scale. In order to obtain a lifelike representation of the color shadings of human skin, 24 bits of color may be required. These 24 bits are in contrast to the 6 bits of color available on the EGA and the 18 bits of color available on the VGA. Pseudocolor effects can be achieved using dithering techniques. A dithering technique does not rely on solid colors alone to represent shadings. One color can be scattered into a second color to produce a perceived third color. The patterns selected for the scattering are random. The programmer must be willing to sacrifice spatial resolution for the improved color. Black-and-white dithering techniques are common when images are portrayed on printers.

5.7.1   Writing Images

Images in a two-dimensional coordinate space are most commonly represented within a rectangular window. The images typically occupy more than one display plane, providing for gray scale or color scale. The image can be written into display memory a plane at a time or a pixel at a time.

5.7.2   Writing an Image a Bit Plane at a Time

Reading or writing an image a plane at a time is fast, because eight neighboring horizontal pixels can be written in a single byte move operation. Neighboring horizontal bytes in display memory occupy sequential location. Therefore, a block move instruction can be used to move one horizontal line at a time. This further speeds up the process. If the image being written is as wide as the virtual image, a single block move instruction can write an entire plane of the image. If four bit planes are active, four block moves are required.

A limitation to reading or writing an image a plane at a time arises when the data is not organized in a bit-mapped format. An image that possesses gray or color scale is often stored one pixel intensity at a time. A C array, for example, stores a two-dimensional array as a series of magnitudes, one magnitude per pixel. This format is called a packed display format. In order to translate the packed display format into a bit plane format, it is necessary to split the elements in the magnitude array into the desired number of bit plane arrays. This is accomplished by a series of shift operations, and it can be time-consuming.

5.7.3   Writing an Image a Pixel at a Time

A display that is organized in a packed display format is designed to be read or written to a pixel at a time. The EGA/VGA has a couple of packed display formats, but the majority are bit plane formats. It is possible to write packed data to the bit plane display a pixel at a time using the Set/Reset and Enable Set/Reset Registers.

This operation is not as fast as the plane-at-a-time technique, because only one pixel can be written at a time. If the image occupies all four display planes, four bits can be modified in a single operation. Both the OUT instruction and the move instructions are necessary to achieve this result, so it operates much slower. In addition, no block move instructions can be utilized because the Set/Reset function is implemented in a register, requiring the OUT instructions.

It is not possible to read the data from the display memory a pixel at a time in the EGA/VGA. The display memory is restricted to a bit plane organization during read operations. Although the Read Point BIOS call reads a byte at a time, it is actually reading each bit plane separately and accumulating the full resolution of the pixel in sequential accesses to each bit plane.

5.7.4 Image Data Compression

Bit-mapped images are large, and even the largest of disks can get overburdened. In addition, it takes a considerable amount of time to read and write this amount of data. Data-compression techniques are used to alleviate some of the storage and speed restrictions inherent in image manipulation. Effective data-compression techniques are highly desirable and most PC-based imaging software packages incorporate some compression technique. The problem is that no image compression standard was incorporated before all of the software houses selected their algorithms. Thus, communication between different packages is limited. There are several techniques used to perform image data compression. The run-length encoding technique is described below.

5.7.5 Run-length Encoding

Run-length encoding is a one-dimensional data-compression technique that is popular in PC-based graphics packages. Run-length encoding takes advantage of the fact that neighboring horizontal pixels often have the same value. Line drawings stored in a raster bit-mapped format usually have a large amount of space between the lines. This space is usually some consistent background color. Horizontal or nearly horizontal lines would also contain several horizontal neighbors with the same intensity. The compression technique selected the horizontal orientation, because display memory is usually oriented horizontally.

Run-length encoding stores sequences of repeated values. The number of repetitions of a particular value is stored along with the pixel value that is repeated. If a run consists of 100 pixels, all with an intensity of 10, instead of storing 100 consecutive values of 10, it is possible to store only two values. These values are the run count, which is 100, and the pixel value, which is 10. A data reduction of 50 is achieved. Because display memory is often organized so that one horizontal row directly follows a second horizontal row, two-dimensional blocks of similar value can also take advantage of this compression.

If pixels in a horizontal line are all different, the data-compression technique can work to a disadvantage. Suppose 100 horizontal pixels have no two adjacent pixels with the same value. The run-length encoding technique would have to store 200 values for these 100 pixels. A compression factor of .5 would occur.

It is possible and popular to use hybrid procedures that incorporate both techniques. If the algorithm is given some intelligence, it can search ahead and determine whether a run-length encoding scheme or a direct scheme is more efficient. Based on its decision, the next portion of the data is stored in one of the formats. A data structure is then necessary to insure that the resulting encoded data can be decoded when the image is redrawn. This structure incorporates some delimiter that indicates whether run-length encoded data or raw data follows. These data structures can be quite complicated, but they are deterministic and can be decoded exactly. This form of data compression does not degrade the image, because the reproduction is an exact duplicate of the original.

5.7.6 Image Processing

Image processing performs mathematical operations on two-dimensional images. Some popular operations include statistical analysis, filtering, edge detection, coordinate transformation, spectral analysis, contrast enhancement, and pattern recognition. Image-processing techniques operate on an entire image or on a window within the image. Many of these techniques are beginning to find their way into computer graphics applications. A primary requirement for many of these image-processing algorithms is a display buffer with a depth of at least eight bits per pixel. A fuzzy border exists between the fields of computer graphics and image processing. Computer graphics primarily involves the synthesis of images; image processing is concerned with the analysis of images. Often these fields overlap.

Statistical analysis algorithms include determining the number of pixels in a window, the intensity histogram, the mean intensity, the median intensity, the standard deviation, and the center of gravity within the window. All of these techniques involve counting and summing the intensities in a given window.

The number of pixels within a window is calculated by subtracting the lower coordinate in the horizontal and vertical directions from the respective higher value coordinate and adding 1. The addition of 1 is very important. Recall that if a window begins at pixel 2 and ends at pixel 3, the window is 2 pixels wide. These two numbers represent the height and width of the rectangle, and they would be multiplied together to determine the number of pixels per window. If the window were not oriented in the horizontal and vertical directions, more sophisticated techniques would have to be employed.

The intensity histogram is a measure of the magnitude distribution within a window. It is determined by building an array of numbers the length of which is equal to the number of possible intensities. Each pixel within the window is read and the corresponding counter is incremented. Array element 0 is incremented every time a pixel of 0 intensity is encountered. All other elements within the histogram array are similarly handled. When all pixels have been counted, the resulting array contains the intensity histogram.

The mean intensity of a window provides a measure of the average intensity within the window. The average intensity is obtained by accumulating the intensities of each pixel in the window and dividing the result by the total number of pixels in the window.

The standard deviation of a window is determined by summing the absolute values of the difference between each pixel intensity and the mean. This resultant value is divided by the total number of pixels in the window. It provides a measure of the spread of intensities within the window. A window of constant intensity would provide a standard deviation of 0.

5.8   COLOR THEORY

The computer graphics programmer uses color theory to help select colors to represent data. In the EGA, there are 64 possible colors, and in the VGA, there are 256 Kcolors. Selecting a color or color combination is made easier with even a cursory knowledge of color theory.

Gray scale or color scale is a monotonic progression of color based on intensity or brightness. A low value in the data would be represented by a low-intensity shade of gray. A high value in the data would be represented by a high-intensity shade of gray. Color can also be used to represent monotonic data. The shades of red could be used as effectively as the shades of gray. Color shading can also be used effectively to represent biphasic relationships. Monochrome gray scale can differentiate accurately between lower and higher intensities. However, gray scale cannot effectively display data that ranges from +10 through 0 to -10. In this case, the blue monotonic scale can be assigned to the negative numbers. The value 0 would be represented by no blue, -1 would be the minimum intensity blue, up to -10 would be the maximum intensity blue. Red can similarly be assigned to the positive values—the value 0 being represented by no red, +1 as minimum red, up to +10 as the maximum intensity red.

5.8.1   Describing Color

Colors are measured in a variety of ways. Artists have chosen the terms *tints, shade,* and *tones* to describe color. Other commonly used terms include *hue, saturation* or *chroma,* and *brightness* or *value.* Users of color select terminology that best suits their needs.

Artists are accustomed to pure saturated pigments. When they add black to the pigment to decrease its brightness, they use the term *shade.* In order to change the saturation of the color, they add white to the pigment. The resultant color is termed *tint,* and it relates to the pastel quality of the color. The color can also be modified by adding both white and black. This modifies the *tone* of the color. The addition of black and/or white to a pigment does not affect the *hue* of the color. Either a different pigment must be selected or pigments must be added to one another to affect the hue.

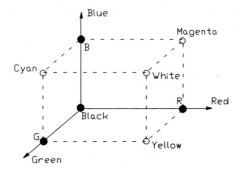

FIGURE 5.17 The Color Cube

5.8.2 Color Models

Several models are used to represent color. All of these models utilize a three-dimensional space. It is interesting to note that the human eye has three different types of color receptors on the retina. Perhaps four-dimensional models would be required if a fourth color receptor was present. Colors defined by one model can be transformed into other color coordinate systems. Each model is defined to describe colors effectively for specific applications. It would be clumsy to attempt to describe colors with a model that is unsuited for the application in question. As new applications of color arise, new models will be defined to suit the needs of the application.

5.8.3 The CIE Chromaticity Scale

The CIE chromaticity scale decomposes a color into three primary colors termed X, Y, and Z. This scale is used as a reference when colors are compared qualitatively. The CIE chromaticity diagram is used to determine the dominant wavelengths of a color or the complement of a color. The color is decomposed into dominant wavelengths that, when added together in the proper proportions, produce the color. The three CIE primary colors are not visible, but they can be combined to form any color that the eye can perceive.

5.8.4 The RGB Color Model

The RGB color model is based upon a three-dimensional Cartesian coordinate system. Color monitors and most color graphics systems utilize the RGB color model. A color cube represents these three dimensions in Figure 5.17.

Red is represented on one axis, blue is on a second and green is on a third. The origin of the color cube is red=0, green=0, and blue=0, which corresponds to black. Moving away from the origin along the cube diagonal produces gray scale, because equal parts of red, green, and blue are represented. The end of the diagonal is at red=maximum, blue=maximum, and green=maximum, which corresponds to white. Any color represented in an RGB format is represented by a dot somewhere within this color cube. The projections of the dot onto the three axes of the cube produce the intensity of each of the three colors.

5.8.5   The CMY Color Model

The three subtractive primary colors of cyan, magenta, and yellow are used in the CMY color model. These three colors are the complements of red, green and blue. When these three colors are subtracted from white light, red, green, and blue colors are produced. For example, cyan absorbs green and blue and therefore reflects red. This color model is useful when color devices that deposit colored pigments onto paper are used.

5.8.6   The YIQ Color Model

The YIQ model is used in color television. It is based on three coordinates that are especially well suited for coding color signals for display on a monochrome monitor. The YIQ model maximizes the amount of perceived information transmitted in a given frequency band. This was useful in the early days of television. Now that broadcast and receiving electronics have improved, it is easier to handle the higher frequencies. The encoding scheme used in the United States is called the NTSC standard. It is possible to convert from the YIQ model to and from the RGB model. As a result, RGB-to-NTSC converters are possible. This allows computer-based RGB signals that are operating in the proper frequency band to be converted to NTSC signals compatible with standard color televisions and video tape recorders.

5.8.7   The HSV and HLS Color Models

Although the models previously described are effective at implementing color processing equipment, they are awkward when trying to describe the colors in human terms. Two models that are better suited for description are called the HSV and the HLS models. The HSV model stands for hue, saturation, and value, and the HLS model utilizes hue, lightness, and saturation. Conversion techniques are available to convert the HSV or HLS models into the commonly used RGB model. These models are easier to describe. These models can be used during operator interaction and the selected values can then be converted to the RGB mode for the display hardware.

5.8.8   Color Dithering

When a limited color system is involved, it is difficult or impossible to represent accurately colors and color shadings found in the real world. The EGA can display only 16 simultaneous colors. If the programmer desires more colors, other techniques must be employed. One such technique is called *color dithering*.

In contrast, the VGA can provide a mode that displays 256 simultaneous colors. Color dithering may not be necessary or desirable in this mode.

Color dithering works in a similar fashion to black-and-white dithering. It trades off resolution for an increase in the number of perceived colors. A small box of pixels is selected to become the primitive pixel. The size of the box determines the total number of possible colors that can be represented in the pixel. A two-by-two pixel box would decrease the overall resolution of the display by a factor of four, but it would greatly increase the number of perceived colors. If the graphics system incorporates four display planes, sixteen simultaneous colors can be displayed. If four pixels are used per pixel box, the number of perceived colors is increased to 64 possible colors per pixel box.

In the high-resolution modes—640 by 350 or 640 by 480—this decrease in resolution may be acceptable. In the low-resolution modes—320 by 200—this decrease in resolution typically will be unacceptable. In a black-and-white system, hard-copy on a laser printer often employs dithering techniques. The high resolution of the laser can produce effective shadings using these techniques. The dot size is small enough that the dithering patterns cannot be detected. If a color high-resolution plotter is used, color dithering can also be effective.

Chapter 6

Alphanumeric Processing

6.1 EGA/VGA CHARACTER PROCESSING

Word processors, spreadsheets, database programs, desktop utilities, the DOS operating system, and user-written applications software are the most common and demanding text-related software products. In order to execute these programs rapidly, the EGA/VGA is designed for high-speed text manipulation. This speed is essential in all text-processing applications, because no one wants to wait while the screen is refreshed. The EGA/VGA provides the programmer with a flexible environment to achieve a wide variety of alphanumeric effects.

Alphanumerics may be displayed in a variety of colors or with various monochrome attributes. In the monochrome modes, characters may be represented in low or high intensity, in reversed intensity, with underlines, or blinking. In the color alphanumeric modes, one of 16 colors can be selected for the foreground and another for the background of each character. The character code selects a character shape from fonts of 512 characters. In addition, characters may be commanded to blink or be underlined.

6.1.1 Local Character Sets

The EGA/VGA contains character sets in the BIOS ROMS. A character set, once loaded and operational, consists of 256 characters. Two of these character sets may be active at a time, providing a combined character set that is 512 characters long. Because these fonts are downloadable, the programmer may load additional fonts. These fonts are termed *user fonts*.

The EGA is equipped with three character sets. Two of these, one having 8 by 8 characters and the other 8-by-14 characters, are complete 256-character fonts. The third is a 9-by-14 supplemental character set. Up to four character fonts, each 256 characters long, may be loaded into the EGA.

The VGA is equipped with five character sets. Three of these —one having 8-by-8 characters, another 8-by-14 and the third 8-by-16—are complete 256-character fonts. Two are supplemental character sets, one having 9-by-14 characters and the other 9-by-16. Up to eight character fonts, each 256 characters long, may be loaded into the VGA.

182

6.1.2 Special Alphanumeric Features

Complex alphanumeric screens can be generated utilizing the split screen, panning, and scrolling features. Selected windows within the screen can be programmed to scroll while others remain stationary. Tasteful and effective use of color in conjunction with these complex alphanumeric operations can produce user-friendly screens that are simple to understand and contain a great deal of information.

In order to process text with minimum delay, it is necessary to move large amounts of text rapidly about the screen. To facilitate this, the EGA/VGA incorporates alphanumeric display modes in addition to the graphics modes. Only characters that fit into the active character box size can be displayed during these alphanumeric modes. Although it is not possible to draw dots or lines in the alphanumeric modes, the IBM extended character set does provide a means of drawing horizontal lines, vertical lines, and symbolic characters. These can be used in the alphanumeric modes to perform primitive graphics. In addition, the programmer may select from several user fonts that contain graphic character patterns.

6.1.3 Processing Characters Quickly

Characters can be processed quickly in the alphanumeric modes because they are represented on the screen by a character code and an attribute code, both of which are one byte. As a result, a single character can be represented in two bytes. Suppose that a sixteen-color alphanumeric mode is active and the screen resolution is 25 lines of text by 80 characters per line. The 25-by-80 character resolution totals 2,000 characters per screen or 4,000 bytes per screen. Each character is represented by an 8-by-14 character box. If the characters are represented graphically, each character will be represented by 14 bytes per plane, because of the 8-by-14 character box. There are four bit planes. Thus, 14 times 4 produces 56 bytes per character. The total number of bytes needed to represent a full screen would be 56 bytes per character times 2,000 characters per screen, which totals 112,000 bytes per screen. The alphanumeric mode provides a 28-to-1 data-reduction advantage over the same data when represented in a graphics mode. Thus, although the alphanumeric modes are limited in their functionality, they allow rapid character manipulation.

6.1.4 Flexibility of the Alphanumeric Modes

The limited functionality of the alphanumeric modes is compensated for by the variety of features available within these modes. Resolution, character size, character color, special character attributes, large character sets, and downloadable character fonts provide a wide variety of excellent alphanumeric capabilities. These programming features give the programmer the flexibility to configure these boards to accommodate a wide variety of applications.

TABLE 6.1 Alphanumeric Display Modes

Mode (Hex)	Adapter	# Chars (X/Y)	Char Box	# of Pages	Resolution in Pixels
0 ,1	EGA/VGA	40/25	8 by 8	8	320 by 200
0*,1*	EGA/VGA	40/25	8 by 14	8	320 by 350
0+,1+	VGA	40/25	9 by 16	8	320 by 400
2 ,3	EGA/VGA	80/25	8 by 8	8	640 by 200
2*,3*	EGA/VGA	80/25	8 by 14	4/8	640 by 350
2+,3+	VGA	80/25	9 by 16	4/8	640 by 400
7	EGA/VGA	80/25	9 by 14	8	720 by 350
7+	VGA	80/25	9 by 16	8	720 by 400

The EGA/VGA can be programmed to operate in a number of different display resolutions. The display memory is organized so that a tradeoff exists between the resolution of an individual page and the total number of available pages. The screen resolution multiplied by the number of bits per pixel and by the number of available pages must fit within the amount of memory resident in the display memory. Therefore, the greater the screen resolution, the fewer the number of possible pages. Table 6.1 lists the standard EGA alphanumeric display modes and their associated alphanumeric resolutions, display formats, total number of pages, and pixel resolution.

The asterisk in the column entitled "Mode" refers to the operation of the adapter. It applies to the EGA when the EGA is configured with a high-resolution EGA monitor or a multisync monitor. It applies to the VGA when the VGA is programmed to operate in a 350-scan-line mode. This is accomplished by programming the Vertical Size (VS), field of the Miscellaneous Output Register. No such field exists for the EGA. In these cases, the vertical resolution of the display is 350 scan lines.

The plus in the column entitled "Mode" refers to the operation of the VGA adapter. It applies to the VGA when the VGA is programmed to operate in a 400-scan-line mode. This is accomplished by programming the VS field of the Miscellaneous Output Register. No such mode exists for the EGA. In these cases, the vertical resolution of the display is 400 scan lines.

Although these are the standard modes, other display modes are possible. Several manufacturers of EGA boards have programmed 640-by-480 and 800-by-600 display resolutions. Manufacturers will certainly program new display resolutions for the VGA as well. In addition, the programmer can set up specialized display modes. However, because of compatibility issues and the complexity of designing nonstandard display resolutions, programming display mode resolutions is not recommended. Details relating to specialized modes can be found in the register definitions in Chapter 10.

6.2 CHARACTER SHAPE

An alphanumeric character consists of a pattern contained within a rectangular box of dots. The larger the region, the more dots there are per character, resulting in greater character resolution. Given a fixed screen resolution, the price paid for added character resolution is fewer characters per screen. If both greater character resolution and more characters per screen are desired, additional display memory must be allocated and higher-speed display electronics, along with a higher-bandwidth monitor, must be provided.

6.2.1 Character Box Size

Each character font has a specified character box size. This size dictates the amount of memory necessary to store one character. In order to conserve space, the character shape is stored independently from the character attribute. This means that the character shape can be represented with one bit per pixel, even if the display is in a mode that uses four bits per pixel. Not until the last step before display is the attribute information added to the shape to produce the actual dot pattern output to the monitor.

6.2.2 Representing Characters in Memory

A character is represented in memory by a group of bytes. The EGA/VGA boards allow character widths of eight or nine pixels, and advanced EGA implementations allow characters up to 16 pixels. A character is represented by a group of horizontal scan lines. A horizontal scan line of a character is represented as a sequence of bytes. Each bit in each byte represents a dot within the character box. The height of the box is represented by consecutive bytes in host or display memory. The first byte corresponds to the top scan line of the character, and the last byte corresponds to the bottom scan line. The most significant bit in each of these bytes represents the far left pixel of the character. Likewise, the least significant bit represents the far right pixel. The standard notation for the bits in a byte is represented in Figure 6.1.

This notation allows a one-to-one correspondence between the far left bit in the byte and the far left pixel of the character when it is displayed on the screen. This convention is consistent within the many implementations of the EGA. However, it is by no means an industry standard. Many other graphics controllers consider bit 7, the most significant bit, to be the far right pixel when the character is displayed on the screen.

6.2.3 Character Tiling

These character boxes are laid onto the screen in a tiled fashion. No space exists between the character boxes, nor is there any overlap between character boxes when they are drawn onto the screen. This is illustrated in Figure 6.2.

Both horizontal and vertical intercharacter space must, therefore, be pro-

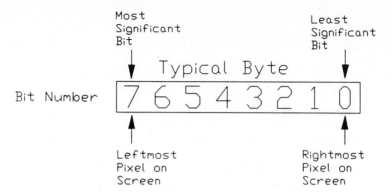

FIGURE 6.1 Bit and Pixel Relationship

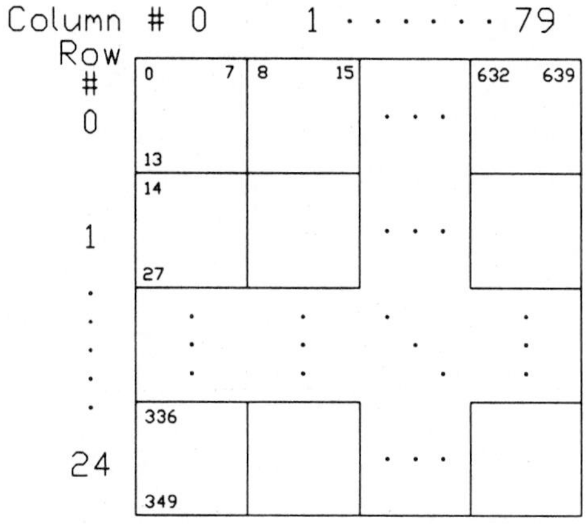

FIGURE 6.2 Character Tiling

vided in each character. Normally the intercharacter space is placed at the bottom and right of the character. Figure 6.3 illustrates the typical intercharacter spacing.

6.2.4 Downward-extending Characters

Some characters extend beneath the base of the characters—for example, the lowercase *y*. There are three ways of handling these downward-extending characters. The first two ways are used in small character fonts. The downward-extending portion of the *y* can extend into the intercharacter spacing at the bottom of the character box, or the baseline of the downward-extending character can be pushed up. In large character fonts, the downward extension of

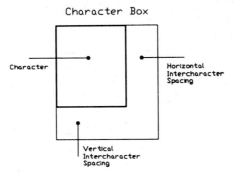

FIGURE 6.3 Intercharacter Spacing

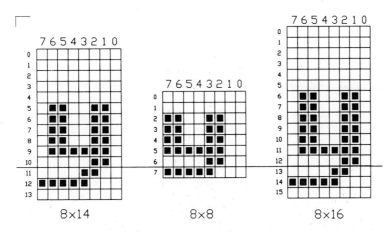

FIGURE 6.4 Downward-extending Characters

the characters can be accommodated by pushing the baseline of all of the characters higher. This provides improved legibility because the lower extending characters will not touch any tall characters positioned on the line directly above them. These three techniques are illustrated in Figure 6.4.

6.2.5 Character Layout Limitations

Advanced printsetting type functions are possible utilizing the EGA/VGA. Although the alphanumeric modes have no provisions for proportional fonts or kerning, the graphics mode allows software to produce any of these advanced printsetting type functions as long as the characters are drawn on a dot-by-dot basis.

Proportional fonts are desirable because they allow characters to have different widths. Thus the character *m* would have a wider character box than would the character *i*. Kerning actually takes into account neighboring pixels to determine the width of characters. For example, the letters *db* appear closer together than the characters *bd*, although the spacing is actually the same. Additional space could be placed between the *d* and *b* in *db* to maintain a uniform appearance. Kerning is effective when lines are justified. Because the EGA can have only one character box size per font but cannot have overlapping characters, neither of these techniques is applicable in the alphanumeric modes. Sophisticated desktop publishing programs utilize kerning techniques in the graphics modes to display alphanumerics on the screen. Again, the tradeoff is speed.

Within the character box, any bit set to 1 will be displayed in the foreground color. Likewise, any bit reset to 0 will be displayed in the background color. The characters are handled differently than in the graphics modes. In the graphics modes, the background or 0 bits are considered transparent, and the characters have no background color other than what was on the screen before the character was drawn.

6.2.6   The 8-by-8 Character Font

The 8-by-8 character font is the smallest of the three local fonts. The character size is typically 7-by-7 pixels within this box. The character is normally left-justified into the character box, leaving the bottom row and right column blank. Special graphics characters and lowercase characters with descenders can extend into these regions. Typically, character boxes are taller than they are wide. Because the 8-by-8 character box is square, additional space exists in the horizontal direction. This permits the characters to be drawn with fatter vertical lines. In most cases, for every pixel that is on, the pixel to the immediate left is turned on. This provides a broader-looking character and fills the extra width available in the character box. For this reason, this character set is often referred to as the *double-dot* character set.

The 8-by-8 character font is typically lacking in character clarity because of its small character box. However, it does allow 25 lines to be displayed on a 200-scan-line monitor or in a 200-scan-line mode. When more than 200 scan lines are available, more than the standard 25 lines may be displayed. At 350 scan lines, it is possible to display 43 character lines using the character font that is 8 scan lines high. The 400-scan-line implementations can display 50 lines, and the 480-line implementations can display 60 lines. A character from the 8-by-8 character font is portrayed in Figure 6.5.

6.2.7   The 8-by-14 Character Font

The 8-by-14 character font is similar to the 8-by-8 character font. The characters in this font fill a 7-by-9 area, left-justified in the box. The top two and bottom

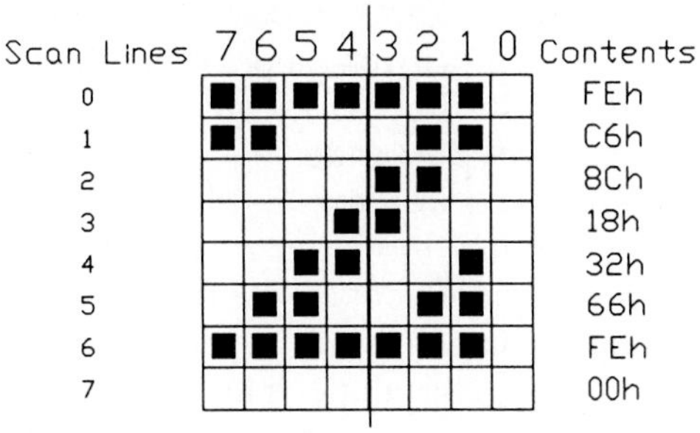

Scan Lines 7 6 5 4 3 2 1 0 Contents

FIGURE 6.5 Typical 8-by-8 Character

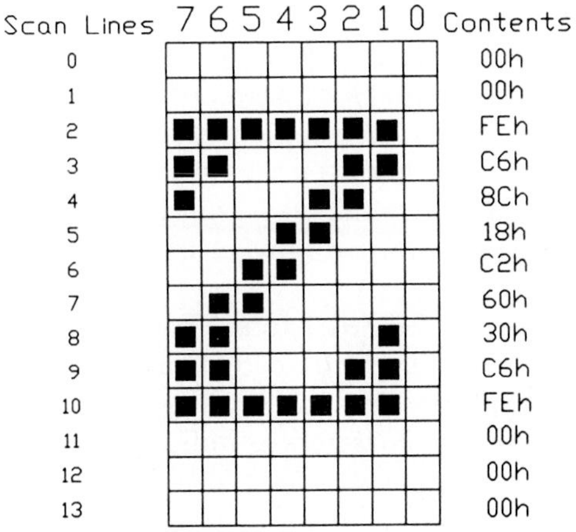

Scan Lines 7 6 5 4 3 2 1 0 Contents

FIGURE 6.6 Typical 8-by-14 Character

three scan lines of the character box typically are blank, with the exception of graphics characters and lowercase characters with descenders. The far right column is typically blank, providing intercharacter spacing.

This font is most often used when the adapter is in a 350-scan-line mode and resolution of 25 character lines per screen is desired. As was true for the 8-by-8 double-dot font, most horizontally neighboring pixels are turned on. A typical 8-by-14 character is represented in Figure 6.6.

6.2.8 The 9-by-14 Character Font

The 9-by-14 character font is the largest of the local fonts. It is actually represented within the BIOS character sets as a supplemental character set. It is called *supplemental* because not all of the 256 characters are provided. This is done to save space because only 8 of the 9 columns are unique for the majority of the characters. Most characters can be adequately represented within the 8-by-14 character box. In the monochrome alphanumeric display mode 7, there are 720 dots per horizontal scan line. If 80 characters per line are to be displayed, each character may be 9 dots wide.

The characters that look good in the 8-by-14 character set are displayed in the 9-by-14 format with the same dot patterns. The 9-by-14 format characters that could benefit from being wider contain dot patterns that are different from the 8-by-14 patterns. These characters are represented within the BIOS supplemental table with one byte per scan line. The ninth bit of the 9-by-14 format is always assumed to be a horizontal intercharacter space and is not represented in the character set. The character shape occupies an 8-by-9 character box, completely filling the width of the character box. The top two and bottom three scan lines of the character box are usually blank, like those of the 8-by-14 box. Typical characters that are included in the supplement are quotation marks (''), the plus sign (+), the minus sign (−), M, T, V, W, X, Y, Z, m, v, and w. Each character within the supplemental font is preceded by its ASCII code. An ASCII code of 00 indicates the end of the supplemental character set. When the 9-by-14 set is loaded, the 8-by-14 character set is first loaded into display memory. All of the character patterns contained within the supplemental character set are then written over the respective 8-by-14 characters. This results in the 9-by-14 character set.

The ninth column can be set either to the background color or to the same value as the eighth dot of the character code being displayed. This is controlled by the B/I field of the Mode Control Register. Setting the ninth dot to the background color is done for characters as indicated above. In the line graphics mode, ASCII characters between 128 and 255 are often used as pseudographics characters. Primitive lines may be drawn using these characters. In order for horizontal lines to be connected, the technique of assuming that the ninth pixel is background will not work. It would cause discontinuities. For these characters, the hardware will copy whatever is in the eighth dot position into the ninth dot position. If the eighth dot position is a 1, signifying a foreground pixel, the ninth dot will subsequently be displayed as a foreground pixel, thereby allowing continuous horizontal lines.

A typical character from the 9-by-14 character font is portrayed in Figure 6.7.

6.2.9   The 8-by-16 Character Font

In the VGA, an 8-by-16 character font is available. This font is used when the VGA is in a 400-scan-line mode, providing 25 character rows per screen. The character patterns are similar to those in the 8-by-14 font, with the exception of an additional two vertical scan lines. A typical 8-by-16 character is shown in Figure 6.8.

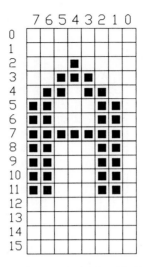

FIGURE 6.7   Typical 8-by-16 Character

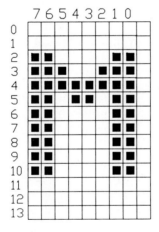

FIGURE 6.8   Typical 9-by-14 Character

6.2.10   The 9-by-16 Character Font

In the VGA, a 9-by-16 character font is available. Like the 8-by-16 character font, this font is used when the VGA is in a 400-scan-line mode, providing 25 character rows per screen. In the VGA, this font is used in display mode 7, which has 720 horizontal pixels per scan line. The 9-dot-wide character provides 80 characters per row. This font is a supplemental font because only a subset

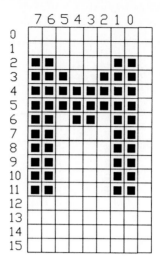

FIGURE 6.9   Typical 9-by-16 Character

of the ASCII character set is provided. The techniques employed to display this font are identical to the techniques used for the 9-by-14 font, with the exception of two additional vertical scan lines. A typical 9-by-16 character is shown in Figure 6.9.

6.3   CHARACTER ATTRIBUTES

The alphanumeric modes include modes 0, 1, 2, 3, and 7. Modes 0, 1, 2, and 3 are 16-color modes. Mode 7 is a monochrome mode.

In the alphanumeric modes, the attributes of each character are stored independently from the character shape. The character shapes are stored in the character sets resident in the BIOS or in a user-defined buffer. Once made resident, the character shapes from the character fonts are loaded into display memory. When the characters are displayed on the screen in alphanumeric modes, the character is represented by a one-byte ASCII character code followed by a byte-wide attribute. The attributes define the appearance of the character. The EGA/VGA is alerted to the display type by the Display Type (DT), field in the Mode Control Register. This field dictates whether the character attributes should be considered to be color display attributes or monochrome display attributes.

6.3.1   Monochrome Mode

The only alphanumeric monochrome mode is mode 7. It emulates the MDA or Hercules alphanumeric modes when a monochrome monitor is attached to the graphics system. In this mode, two bits are dedicated to each pixel. Thus, each

TABLE 6.2 Mode 7: Monochrome Attributes

Background (Bits 6–4)	Foreground (Bits 2–0)	Resulting Attribute
0	0	Black
0	1	Underline
0	7	Normal Video (white on black)
7	0	Reverse Video (black on white)
7	7	White

TABLE 6.3 Mode 7: Examples of Monochrome Attributes

Blink (Bit 7)	Backgrnd (Bits 6–4)	Intens (Bit 3)	Foregrnd (Bits 2–0)	Code (Hex)	Attribute
0	0	0	7	07	Normal
0	0	1	7	0F	Intense
0	0	0	1	01	Underline
0	0	1	1	09	Intense Underline
0	7	0	0	70	Reversed
1	7	0	0	F0	Blinking Reversed

character can be displayed with one of four attributes. The attributes associated with a character are derived from the three least significant bits of the foreground color and from the three least significant bits of the background color in the attribute byte.

If mode 7 is enabled when a monitor other than a monochrome monitor is installed, the EGA typically will not operate correctly with the monitor. The VGA is capable of driving the enhanced color monitor in mode 7.

The functions of the attribute byte, given that a monochrome monitor is attached, are listed in Table 6.2. The foreground field occupies bits 2–0, and the background field occupies bits 4–6.

These fields operate in conjunction with the two special attribute fields that control the intensity and blinking. Bit 3 contains the intensify field and bit 7 contains the blinking field. Some typical display attributes that combine the special fields with the foreground and background fields are listed in Table 6.3.

It should be noted that the underline function is normally disabled when any mode other than mode 7 is active. At Mode Set, the underline feature is disabled for all modes other than mode 7. The programmer must write the proper underline location into the Underline Location Register after a Mode Set. The Underline Location Register determines the scan line in the character box where this underlining occurs.

TABLE 6.4 Mode 7: Palette Registers

Register # (Hex)	Register Value (Hex)	Register # (Hex)	Register Value (Hex)
0	00	8	10
1	08	9	18
2	08	A	18
3	08	B	18
4	08	C	18
5	08	D	18
6	08	E	18
7	08	F	18

The monochrome monitor uses bit 3 for the video field and bit 4 for the intensify field. Thus, an 8 hex causes bit 3, the video bit, to be activated; a 10 hex causes bit 4, the intensified bit, to be activated. An 18 hex results in both being activated. Table 6.4 lists the default values present in the Palette Registers in mode 7.

Note that an attribute value of 0 maps to an output color of 00 hex. Any attribute value between 1 and 7 maps to an output color of 08 hex. An attribute value of 8 maps to an output color of 10 hex. Any attribute value between 9 and F hex maps to an output color of 18 hex.

6.3.2 Sixteen-color Mode

In the sixteen-color mode, the character has a variety of different attributes. One option allows the attribute byte to select from one of sixteen colors for the foreground and one of sixteen colors for the background of each character. A second option allows the attribute byte to select from one of sixteen colors for the foreground and one of eight colors for the background. In addition, the character may be programmed to blink. A third option allows the attribute byte to select from one of eight foreground colors, and the character may be represented by one of 512 character patterns. These 512 character patterns come from the chaining of two of the 256-long character sets. The background may be one of sixteen background colors or one of eight background colors; in addition, the option of blinking is available. These attribute options are illustrated in Figure 6.10.

The default colors loaded into the sixteen Palette Registers associated with the colors called out by the attribute byte are listed in Table 6.5.

6.4 DISPLAY MEMORY

The EGA/VGA display memory is organized into four bit planes, each up to 64 Kbytes long. These bit planes contain from one to eight pages, depending on the size of each display page and the total amount of display memory

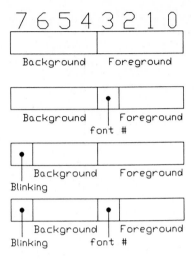

FIGURE 6.10 Attribute Byte in the 16-color Mode

TABLE 6.5 Default Colors for a 16-color Palette

Palette Register (Hex)	Color
0	Black
1	Blue
2	Green
3	Cyan
4	Red
5	Magenta
6	Brown
7	White
8	Gray
9	Light blue
A	Light green
B	Light cyan
C	Light red
D	Light magenta
E	Light brown (yellow)
F	Bright white

TABLE 6.6 Display Memory in Host Memory Address Space

Memory Map Field (MM Value)	Beginning Address (Hex)	Amount of Display Memory
0	A0000 – BFFFF	128 Kbytes
1	A0000 – AFFFF	64 Kbytes
2	B0000 – B7FFF	32 Kbytes
3	B8000 – BFFFF	32 Kbytes

available. When the EGA/VGA is in an alphanumeric mode, the display memory is used to store the character codes, the character attribute bytes, and the character fonts. The display memory is accessed indirectly by the hardware to obtain the actual character dot patterns for output to the monitor. This is quite different from the operation of the display in a graphics mode. In a graphics mode, the data in the bit planes is a bit-by-bit representation of the character dot patterns.

The four bit planes are accessed at the same address. The address referring to one byte in the host memory address space refers to four bytes in the display memory. Each of these four bytes resides at the same host address, and one byte is associated with each of the four bit planes. From the perspective of the host, the display memory can be thought of as a 32-bit-wide memory. In fact, a 32-bit data bus does exist inside the EGA/VGA and is used to access display memory.

6.4.1 Display Memory in Host Memory Address Space

The Memory Map (MM) field of the Miscellaneous Register dictates the host starting address of the display memory. The possible memory addresses and the associated Memory Map field values are listed in Table 6.6.

Invoking the Set Mode BIOS call (AH = 0) loads the Memory Map field with a starting address, as indicated in Table 6.7.

6.4.2 Bit Plane Utilization

In the alphanumeric modes, codes that represent the character and the character attribute are stored in memory. A single byte is dedicated to each character code, allowing 256 characters to be accessed. A single byte is also dedicated to the attribute of the character.

Bit plane 0 is used to store the character code, and bit plane 1 is used to store the character attribute. The character and attribute pair is stored in host memory, with the character code preceding the character attribute. When the

TABLE 6.7   Alphanumeric Display Mode Starting Addresses

Mode (Hex)	MM Field	Alpha Format	Address (Hex)
0	3	40 by 25	B8000
1	3	40 by 25	B8000
2	3	80 by 25	B8000
3	3	80 by 25	B8000
7	2	80 by 25	B0000

program needs to write to or read from the display memory, the character code should be written to an even address and the attribute should be written to an odd address. Data written to even addresses will be directed to bit plane 0; data written to odd addresses will be directed to bit plane 1.

Display plane 2 is used to store the character font bit patterns. The EGA display memory is segmented into four blocks, each separated by 16 Kbytes. The upper 8 Kbytes of each of these blocks are used to store the bit patterns, and the remaining 8 Kbytes of each block are unused. The VGA is segmented into eight blocks, each separated by 8 Kbytes. The dot patterns of one 256-character set can fit in each of these blocks. Thus, the EGA can hold four resident fonts, and the VGA can hold eight resident fonts.

6.4.3   Display Memory Address Compatibility

In order to maintain compatibility with older displays, it is desirable to begin the alphanumeric memory at the host address of B8000 hex for the Monochrome Display Adapter (MDA) or the Color Graphics Adapter (CGA). In order for the EGA to operate properly with software that produces text output, the default active page 0 of alphanumeric display memory must reside at B0000 hex. When the Monochrome Display Adapter (MDA) or the Hercules Graphics Standard is being emulated, the display memory begins at B0000 hex.

The host memory environment provides 128 Kbytes of address space for display adapters. The 64 Kbytes between host addresses A0000 and AFFFF are dedicated to the EGA, and the 64 Kbytes between host addresses A0000 hex and BFFFF hex are reserved for the MDA and CGA. A fully populated EGA contains 256 Kbytes of display memory organized into four bit planes, each being 64 Kbytes long. The memory will completely fill the space and must be physically strapped to begin at B0000 hex and end at BFFFF hex. This means that the first page of text does not correspond to the lowest address in the EGA display memory. Page 0 of text resides at B8000. Therefore, the first of text resides halfway through the display memory.

6.4.4 Fonts in Display Memory

The smallest character box used on the EGA/VGA is 8 pixels wide by 8 scan lines high. The maximum horizontal resolution of the EGA/VGA in a color mode is 640 pixels. Thus, 80 characters could exist on one horizontal line. The maximum resolution on the standard EGA is 350 scan lines. For the VGA, it is 480 scan lines. This means that 43 character lines can be displayed on one screen using the EGA, and 60 lines can be displayed on one screen using the VGA.

For the EGA, at 80 characters per line by 43 lines, a single screen can display 3,440 characters. At two bytes per character, this translates to 6,880 bytes per page. The specification calls for the EGA to support eight memory resident pages of text. Thus, 55,040 bytes must be reserved for the alphanumerics buffer. For the VGA, at 80 characters per line by 60 lines, a single screen can display 4,800 characters. At two bytes per character, this translates to 9,960 bytes per page. Multiplied by eight display pages, this is equivalent to 76,800 bytes for the alphanumeric buffer.

There are 32,768 bytes available between B8000 hex and the end of the buffer at BFFFF hex. It is therefore necessary to utilize two of the bit planes to store the character and attribute pairs. Using this technique, it is possible to store all eight bit planes of the EGA and seven full display pages of the VGA. One plane is used to store the ASCII character code, and the second plane is used to store the attribute byte associated with the character code. This requires 27,520 bytes for the EGA and 38,400 bytes for the VGA. The memory between A0000 hex and B7FFF hex in these two bit planes is not utilized in these modes.

In order to utilize downloadable character fonts, random access memory (RAM) is allocated to store the actual bit patterns of the characters. The EGA display memory, bit planes 2 and sometimes 3, holds the bit patterns. Host memory could have been used for this purpose, but accessing the bit patterns from host memory is time-consuming. The host memory is used to hold the bit patterns when the EGA/VGA is in a graphics mode because bit planes 2 and 3 are not available. In the EGA/VGA, internal hardware is provided to allow rapid accessing of the character code and the character attribute byte. Once accessed, the character code is quickly converted to an address that points into bit plane 2 and sometimes bit plane 3. The character bit pattern is retrieved from these bit planes and output to the monitor via the output logic. All of this occurs in hardware. If the bit patterns reside in host memory, however, this has to be done with software.

For the EGA, an 8-bit data bus exists between the host and the EGA. This is slow compared to the EGA 32-bit internal data bus. For the planar VGA, a 16-bit path exists between the host and the VGA. A planar VGA is a VGA that is physically located on the backplane of the host, as is true of the IBM System/2 computers. Even this 16-bit data path is slow compared to the internal 32-bit

TABLE 6.8 Odd/Even Address Bus Mapping

EGA/VGA Address	Host Memory Address
MA17	A17
MA16	A16
MA15	A15
MA14	A14
MA13	A13
MA12	A12
MA11	A11
MA10	A10
MA09	A09
MA08	A08
MA07	A07
MA06	A06
MA05	A05
MA04	A04
MA03	A03
MA02	A02
MA01	A01
MA00*	A14/A16
MA00†	A00

* word mode
† byte mode

data path. A VGA adapter plugged into a host backplane conforms to the 8-bit bus standard and again is limited by the 8-bit wide bus. Thus, planar VGA implementations are faster than VGA adapters.

6.4.5 Odd/Even Operation

A term that comes up repeatedly in the EGA/VGA documentation is *odd/even*. The Odd/Even (O/E) field of the Mode Register controls whether the odd/even or a sequential addressing mode is active. In a sequential mode, the least significant bit of the host address bus drives the least significant bit of the display memory address bus. In odd/even addressing, the least significant bit of the host address bus is not connected to the least significant bit of the display memory address bus. Rather, it is connected to a multiplexer that selects between odd or even planes. The least significant bit of the memory address bus is obtained from a higher-order host address bus bit, such as bit 14 or bit 16. All other bits of the host memory address bus map directly to the display memory bus. This address bus mapping is illustrated in Table 6.8.

The word mode or byte mode is selected by the Word/Byte (W/B) field in the Mode Control Register. Host address bit A14 or A16 is selected for use as EGA/VGA address bit MA00 by the Address Wrap (AW) field in the Mode Control Register.

This address-switching causes the EGA/VGA display memory to become segmented. A write of two consecutive bytes from host memory is mapped to the same address in the display memory space, but the two bytes are written to different bit planes. Data written to even host addresses is mapped to even bit planes—that is, bit planes 0 or 2. Data written to odd host addresses is mapped to odd bit planes—that is, bit planes 1 or 3.

In the textual convention established in the PC family of computers, the character code is stored first, followed immediately by the attribute byte. This character/attribute pair, when written to display memory, places all character codes into bit plane 0 and all attribute bytes into bit plane 1. Both reside at the same physical address. Thus, a single address in the display memory accesses both the character code and the character attribute. Strings composed of character/attribute pairs can be copied directly to the display memory using an assembly language move string word, MOVSW. No further software manipulations are necessary because the data is placed directly into the proper bit planes through address swapping. This is especially useful in view of the processing time necessary to load the character into plane 0 and the attribute into plane 1 using a brute-force method. The Map Mask Register would need to be loaded with a 1 to access plane 0 when writing the character code. The Map Mask Register would then need to be changed to a 2 in order for the attribute byte to be written into plane 1.

Two consecutive character codes in the host would occupy consecutive even addresses in the display memory. This occurs because the high-order host address line, bit A14 or bit A16, is used in place of host address bit 0. Thus, a high-order address bit is used to select either even or odd memory locations for the character/attribute pairs. If either A14 or A16 is low, all character/attribute pairs will be consecutive even memory locations. Likewise, if either A14 or A16 is high, the character/attribute pairs will be written to consecutive odd locations.

6.4.6   Reading Fonts in Odd/Even Modes

The odd/even addressing mode complicates the task of reading directly from display memory when the display is in an alphanumeric mode. It is still possible to read the character font bit patterns directly from display memory when the display is in an alphanumeric mode, although BIOS provides a call that will read the pattern. The technique to accomplish this is complicated because of the addressing protocol used in the alphanumeric modes, but it is useful to understand it because it helps clarify the operation of the odd/even modes.

TABLE 6.9 Font Size: Alphanumeric Modes

Mode (Hex)	Adapter	Columns/Rows	Address Page 0	Font Size
0 ,1	EGA/VGA	40/25	B8000	8 by 8
0*,1*	EGA/VGA	40/25	B8000	8 by 14
0+,1+	VGA	40/25	B8000	9 by 16
2 ,3	EGA/VGA	80/25	B8000	8 by 8
2*,3*	EGA/VGA	80/25	B8000	8 by 14
2+,3+	VGA	80/25	B8000	9 by 16
7	EGA/VGA	80/25	B0000	9 by 14
7+	VGA	80/25	B0000	9 by 16

TABLE 6.10 Typical Character String

Byte Location	Value
0	Character code for the first character
1	Attribute code for the first character
2	Character code for the second character
3	Attribute code for the second character
4	Character code for the third character
5	Attribute code for the third character

The alphanumeric display modes include modes 0, 1, 2, 3, and 7. The features of each of these modes are listed in Table 6.9.

The alphanumeric modes 0, 1, 2, and 3 all emulate the CGA color standard, and the alphanumeric mode 7 emulates the MDA monochrome standard. In all cases, the display memory is organized so that the character codes reside in bit plane 0, the character attributes reside in bit plane 1, and the character font bit patterns reside in bit plane 2.

Each character code occupies one byte, and each character attribute occupies another byte. In host memory, these bytes are ordered so that the character code is followed in the next higher memory byte address by its associated attribute byte. A typical string of three character/attribute pairs is shown in Table 6.10.

Note that this string of three characters occupies six bytes in host memory. To achieve fast data transfers, the move string instructions can be used to move the character/attribute string from host memory to display memory. This sequential transfer involves some address shuffling so that the character and attribute codes end up in the proper display bit planes.

The hardware that causes the odd/even shuffling during write operations also affects read operations. The odd/even addressing affects bit planes 0 and 1 as well as bit planes 2 and 3. Suppose that a string move operation is used to move a character font bit pattern consisting of eight sequential bytes into display memory bit plane 2. Because of the odd/even hardware, half of these bytes will end up in bit plane 2 and half in bit plane 3. Likewise, if a read operation from display memory bit plane 2 is attempted using a move string operation, half of the data will be read from bit plane 2 and half from bit plane 3. This is obviously undesirable.

To achieve correct results, it is necessary to employ alternative methods to load or read the bit patterns. One technique that works correctly places zero bytes between each of the character font bit pattern bytes. Loading an 8-byte-long font subsequently requires 16 bytes to be transferred to the display memory. When this technique is used, the character bit patterns are directed to bit plane 2, and the zero bytes are directed to bit plane 3.

In order for the bit pattern contained in bit plane 2 to be read, it is necessary to change the display mode from an alphanumeric mode to a graphics mode. The graphics mode does not utilize the odd/even automatic addressing shuffle. Once the system is in a graphics mode, it is possible to read bit plane 2 directly. However, the host addresses in which the fonts reside in the alphanumeric modes are different from the addresses in which the font resides in the graphics modes. In the alphanumeric modes, page 0 resides at host memory address B8000 hex; in graphics mode 10 hex, page 0 resides at address A0000.

6.4.7 Writing Directly to Memory

In order to write characters and or character attributes directly to memory, the programmer must keep track of the display configuration parameters. The alphanumeric display is normally considered to be composed of a grid of characters, each with a two-dimensional row and column address. It is necessary for the programmer to be able to calculate the physical display memory address from the row and column values. To do this, a number of other display parameters must be known. Typical parameters include the number of columns per character line, the number of character lines per page, the beginning address of each page, and the position of the cursor.

6.4.8 Determining a Physical Memory Address

The EGA/VGA display memory is mapped into a contiguous block of memory in the host address space. The lowest address of the display memory is called the *display memory base address*. The display memory is organized into display pages. The lowest address of each display page, referenced to the beginning of display memory, is called the *page offset*. A character occupies a byte location within this memory space. The address of the character, referenced to the

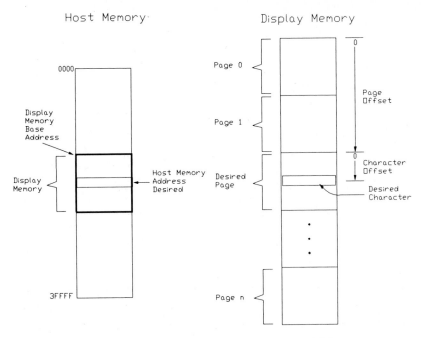

FIGURE 6.11 Calculating a Host Memory Address

display page, is called the *character offset*. These parameters are illustrated in Figure 6.11.

Equation 6.1 may be used to calculate the address of a character.

Equation 6.1 Determining the Host Address of a Character

$$\text{Host memory address} = \text{Display memory base address} + \text{Page offset} + \text{Character offset}$$

Each parameter in Equation 6.1 is described below.

Display Memory Base Address

The display memory base address is the address of the first byte of display memory mapped into the host address space. For a 256-Kbyte graphics system, this must be A0000. This value is determined by the Memory Map (MM) field in the Miscellaneous Register.

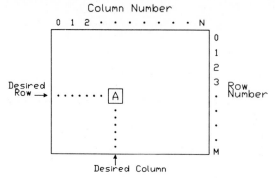

Two-dimensional Chapter Position

FIGURE 6.12 Two-dimensional Character Screen

Page Offset

The page offset is the address of the first byte of the desired display page with respect to the top of the display memory. The page offset is the distance from the beginning of display memory to the lowest address of the desired display page. It is a relative offset referenced to the top of display memory. A "relative" addressing scheme is used, so the lowest byte of display memory is considered to be address 0. In the EGA/VGA, for a given display mode, each page must be the same length. However, the display pages are not contiguous. This means that for a given display mode, the first byte of one page does not follow immediately after the last byte of the previous page. Therefore, it is necessary to keep track of the base address of each display page.

Character Offset

The character offset is the address of the desired character with respect to the top of the selected display page. The character offset is usually determined from a row and column value. The screen is typically perceived to be a two-dimensional grid of rows and columns, as shown in Figure 6.12.

In addition to the row and column, the number of characters per row is necessary. The display memory is organized so that the first byte in a display page corresponds to the character in the upper left corner of the monitor screen. The second byte represents the nearest right neighbor, and following bytes continue from right to left until the end of the scan row on the display monitor. The far right pixel displayed on the monitor is determined by the active display mode. Typical values are 320 or 640 pixels. These are loaded in the Horizontal Display End Register. The following byte may represent the next horizontal character or it may represent the far left character in the next row down the page. Which it represents is determined by the value in the Offset

Register. The Offset Register dictates the number of characters per line. This value may be thought of as the number of bytes separating two vertical neighboring pixels.

Vertical neighboring characters are thus separated by the number of characters in a row. Because there is one byte per character, this distance also corresponds to the number of bytes between vertically neighboring characters. The term *pitch* is often used to represent the number of bytes between successive vertical neighboring pixels. The address of the character with respect to the beginning of the page in which the character resides can be determined from the desired row number, column number, and number of characters per row, as shown in Equation 6.2.

Equation 6.2 Determining the Display Address of a Character

$$\begin{array}{c} \text{Character} \\ \text{address} \end{array} = \left(\begin{array}{c} \text{Row} \\ \text{number} \end{array} \times \begin{array}{c} \text{\# Characters} \\ \text{per row} \end{array} \right) + \begin{array}{c} \text{Column} \\ \text{number} \end{array}$$

Row Number

As seen in Figure 6.12 above, the row-numbering scheme begins with row number 0 as the top row. It is followed immediately by row number 1, row number 2, and so on, until the last row. The last row is equal to the number of rows per page minus one. The "minus one" is necessary because the first row is numbered 0. Thus, the fourth row of the display is actually row number 3.

Number of Characters Per Row

The number of characters per row determines how many characters are displayed on the monitor screen in a single character row. This value is found in the Horizontal Display End Register.

Column Number

The column-numbering scheme is similar to the row-numbering scheme. It begins with column number 0 as the far left column. The next column to the right is column number 1. The column number increments from left to right until the last column. The last column is equal to the number of characters per line minus one. Again, the "minus one" is necessary because the first column is numbered 0.

6.4.9 Writing Characters and Attributes

Once the host address of the desired character is determined, either a single byte representing the character code or two bytes representing the character code and the attribute byte can be written directly to memory.

A horizontal string of characters can be written to the display. An array could be moved to display memory using a move string command, such as the assembly language MOVSW instruction. The lower byte in each word would be the character code, and the upper byte would be the attribute byte. The array would consist of alternating bytes of character codes and attribute bytes.

The host PC protocol employed when copying a 16-bit word across an 8-bit bus is to copy the least significant byte first, followed by the most significant byte. The lower byte, which corresponds to the character code, is written to bit plane 0; the upper byte, the attribute byte, is written to bit plane 1. This occurs automatically through the odd/even hardware address shuffling.

It should be noted that the BIOS routines wait for a horizontal retrace period before modifying the display memory. This eliminates flicker in the alphanumeric modes. Usually one word can be written per horizontal retrace period. At 350 horizontal retrace periods per page and 60 pages per second, this means that 21,000 bytes, or 15,500 character/attribute pairs, can be written per second. A typical page consists of 80 columns by 25 rows, or 2,000 characters per page. Thus, nearly eight pages can be written per second. This seems to be more than adequate for most applications.

If no modification of the attribute byte is desired, a MOVS block move instruction cannot be used because the attribute bytes interleave the character codes. Software would have to write the character codes to even display memory addresses and increment the display address variable by 2 after each character code is written. This would skip over the attribute bytes and, therefore, would write only to bit plane 0, not to bit plane 1. Thus, it would modify only the characters. Likewise, the attributes can be changed without modifying the characters by writing the attribute bytes to odd display memory addresses. The attribute bytes are written to bit plane 1. A string of attributes can be written by writing the first attribute byte to the desired odd host address. After each write operation, the address is incremented by 2, skipping over the character attributes.

A vertical string of characters cannot be written using a single MOVS instruction because vertically neighboring characters do not occupy contiguous spaces in the display memory. It would be necessary to provide software that adds a constant to the address pointer as each character code and attribute byte pair is written to the display memory. This constant would be equal to the value in the Offset Register.

Writing character strings in other orientations is possible by simply adding the proper value to the display address variable after each character/attribute pair is output. Adding the value in the Offset Register plus 1 after every character causes the string to be written at a 45-degree angle in the downward direction. Subtracting the same offset produces a string written at a 45-degree angle in an upward direction.

Reading the character/attribute pair from display memory is done in a fashion similar to writing the pair. Again, the odd/even feature of the hardware auto-

TABLE 6.11 Character-manipulation BIOS Calls

BIOS	Code	Function
AH	AL	
05	—	Select active display page
08	—	Read attribute/character at current cursor position
09	—	Write attribute/character at current cursor position
0A	—	Write character only at current cursor position
0E	—	Write TTY character
13	0	Write character string, do not affect cursor position
13	1	Write character string, position cursor at end of string when done
13	2	Write character/attribute pair string, do not affect cursor position
13	3	Write character/attribute pair string, position cursor at end of string when done

matically accesses the character byte from page 0 and the attribute byte from page 1.

6.4.10 Reading and Writing Characters via BIOS

Another method for reading and writing characters, much simpler than that presented in the previous section, is to rely on the BIOS calls. There is a bit of overhead that must be accepted when using the alphanumeric BIOS calls. However, the simplicity of using BIOS may overcome the speed penalty. In reality, the BIOS calls are simply following the same algorithms described above. The overhead involved when using BIOS includes time spent on the interrupt response, ascertaining which BIOS routine to process, determining the current status of the display, and saving registers.

The BIOS routines dedicated to character manipulation are listed in Table 6.11, along with the BIOS codes used to call them. All of these calls are invoked through the interrupt INT 10 hex. Once the interrupt is invoked, the AH and sometimes the AL registers are used to distinguish which BIOS call to invoke.

6.5 ALPHANUMERIC DISPLAY MODES

In the alphanumeric modes, the EGA/VGA bit planes are used to store the character codes, the character attributes, and the character font bit patterns. There are four CGA-compatible display modes available in the EGA/VGA. The CGA can be configured in either a 40- or 80-column alphanumeric mode. Display modes 0 and 1 provide 40 columns, and display modes 2 and 3 provide an 80-column format. The difference between modes 0 and 1 and between

TABLE 6.12 Color Graphics Alphanumeric Modes

Display Mode (Hex)	Resolution in Characters	Number of Colors	Starting Address	Number of Pages
0,1	40 by 25	16	B8000	8
2,3	80 by 25	16	B8000	4/8

modes 2 and 3 has to do with the generation of a composite color signal on the CGA board. There is no distinction between these two modes at the direct drive color outputs on the EGA/VGA board.

The configuration sense switches on the EGA board alert the EGA as to the type of monitor in use. The VGA is software-configured via a batch file. In the CGA emulation modes, a standard PC-compatible color monitor is assumed to be connected to the EGA/VGA. These monitors are often called RGBI monitors because the red, green, and blue colors are each represented by one line. An intensity control bit can make the resultant color brighter. An RGBI monitor is capable of displaying 16 possible colors because there are four digital color control lines driving the color monitor.

In modes 0 through 3, if an enhanced color monitor is installed on the EGA/VGA board, a total of 16 out of 64 colors is possible. There are 64 possible colors because there are six digital color control lines driving the color monitor. Enhanced color monitors are sometimes called RrGgBb monitors because there are two lines dedicated to each color.

Both modes begin at host address B8000 hex. The color graphic alphanumeric modes are listed in Table 6.12.

There are several similarities found in these display modes. Details for each mode are described completely within each section.

6.5.1 Modes 0 and 1 (EGA/VGA)

Modes 0 and 1 are 40-column alphanumeric modes, compatible with the Color Graphics Adapter (CGA). As far as the EGA/VGA is concerned, there is no functional difference between modes 0 and 1.

In the EGA, these modes use 320 pixels per horizontal scan line. The EGA can operate with a resolution of 200 or 350 scan lines, as determined by the type of monitor connected to the EGA. The VGA uses 320 pixels per horizontal scan line in the modes with 200 and 350 scan lines and 360 pixels per horizontal scan line in the 400-scan-line mode. The VGA can operate with resolutions of 200, 350, or 400 scan lines, as determined by the setting of the number of scan lines in the BIOS call Select Scan Lines for Alphanumeric Mode.

The default character size for the EGA is an 8-by-8 character box in the 200-scan-line mode and an 8-by-14 character box for the 350-scan-line mode. The default character size for the VGA is an 8-by-8 character box in the 200-scan-

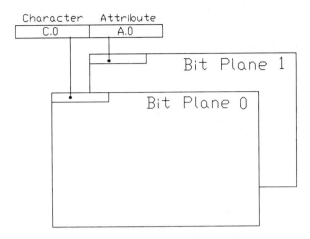

FIGURE 6.13   Modes 0,1: Mapping Character/Attributes into Display Memory

line mode, an 8-by-14 character box in the 350-scan-line mode, and an 8-by-16 character box in the 400-scan-line mode.

These modes allow a display resolution of 40 characters per row by 25 rows per screen, totaling $40 \times 25 = 1{,}000$ characters. Each character is represented by two bytes, one byte for the character code and one for the attribute byte. This is equivalent to 2,000 bytes per page. The character code is loaded into bit plane 0, and the attribute byte is loaded into bit plane 1, as shown in Figure 6.13.

When display memory is read from or written to, the transfer of data to the two display bit planes occurs automatically because of special hardware in the EGA/VGA. This addressing mode is called *odd/even* because data read from or written to even locations affects bit plane 0, and data read from or written to odd locations affects bit plane 1.

In Figure 6.14, a byte array in host memory called a *string* is copied to display memory. The array consists of alternating character codes and attribute bytes. In the array, the "C" refers to the character code, the "A" refers to the attribute byte, and the number following the "C" or "A" is the index number—that is, 0, 1, 2, . . . 79. The data in the string buffer is written to display memory bit planes 0 and 1, as indicated in Figure 6.14.

Although 2,000 bytes of memory are required per display page, only 1,000 bytes are required in each of the two bit planes because the character codes and attributes are loaded into separate bit planes. Because of the odd/even memory mapping in effect, only even addresses are accessible in bit plane 0, and only odd addresses are accessible in bit plane 1. A display page, therefore, requires 2,000 bytes and occupies 2,048 bytes of host memory address space. Up to eight display pages can be resident in display memory simultaneously. The mapping of display pages into memory is illustrated in Figure 6.15.

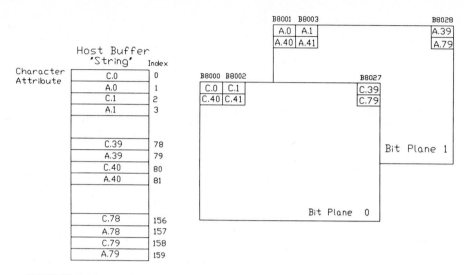

FIGURE 6.14 Modes 0,1: Moving Data from a Host Array to Display Memory

The EGA/VGA divides certain horizontal clocking signals by 2 in order to fill the entire screen with the 40 characters. Each character is twice as wide as the characters displayed in the 80-column modes.

6.5.2 Modes 2 and 3 (EGA/VGA)

Modes 2 and 3 are 80-column alphanumeric modes, compatible with the Color Graphics Adapter (CGA). As far as the EGA/VGA is concerned, there is no functional difference between modes 2 and 3.

In the EGA, these modes use 640 pixels per horizontal scan line. The EGA can operate with a resolution of 200 or 350 scan lines, as determined by the type of monitor connected to the EGA. The VGA uses 640 pixels per horizontal scan line in the modes that use 200 and 350 scan lines and 720 pixels per horizontal scan line in the 400-scan-line mode. The VGA can operate with a resolution of 200, 350, or 400 scan lines, as determined by the setting of the number of scan lines in the BIOS call Select Scan Lines for Alphanumeric Mode.

The default character size for the EGA is an 8-by-8 character box in the 200-scan-line mode and an 8-by-14 character box for the 350-scan-line mode. The default character size for the VGA is an 8-by-8 character box in the 200-scan-line mode, an 8-by-14 character box in the 350-scan-line mode, and a 9-by-16 character box in the 400-scan-line mode.

These modes allow a display resolution of 80 characters per row by 25 rows per screen, totaling $80 \times 25 = 2,000$ characters. Each character is represented by two bytes, one byte for the character code and one for the attribute byte.

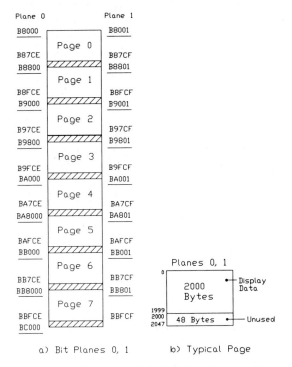

a) Bit Planes 0, 1   b) Typical Page

FIGURE 6.15 Modes 0,1: Display Memory Map

This is equivalent to 4,000 bytes per page. The character code is loaded into bit plane 0, and the attribute byte is loaded into bit plane 1, as shown in Figure 6.16.

When reading from or writing to display memory, the transfer of data to the two display bit planes occurs automatically because of special hardware in the EGA/VGA. This addressing mode is called *odd/even* because data read from or written to even locations affects bit plane 0, and data read from or written to odd locations affects bit plane 1.

In Figure 6.17, a byte array in host memory called *string* is copied to display memory. The array consists of alternating character codes and attribute bytes. In the array, the "C" refers to the character code, the "A" refers to the attribute byte, and the "X" is the index number—that is, 0, 1, 2, . . . 79. The data in the string buffer is written to display memory bit planes 0 and 1, as indicated in Figure 6.17.

Although 4,000 bytes of memory are required per display page, only 2,000 bytes are required in each of the two bit planes because the character codes and attributes are loaded into separate bit planes. Because odd/even memory mapping is in effect, only even addresses are accessible in bit plane 0, and only odd

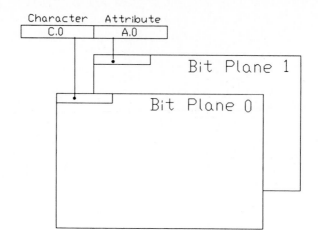

FIGURE 6.16   Modes 2,3: Mapping Character/Attributes into Display Memory

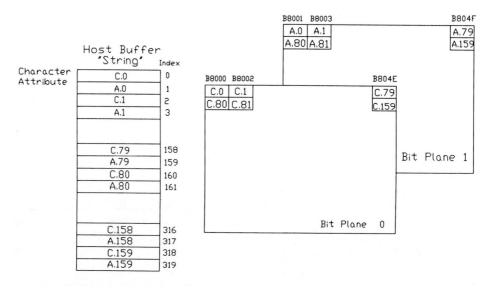

FIGURE 6.17   Modes 2,3: Moving Data from a Host Array to Display Memory

addresses are accessible in bit plane 1. A display page, therefore, requires 4,000 bytes and occupies 4,096 bytes of host memory address space. Up to eight display pages can be resident in display memory simultaneously. The mapping of display pages into memory is illustrated in Figure 6.18.

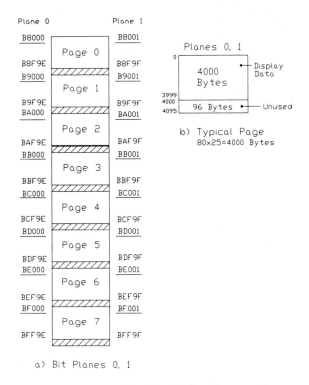

a) Bit Planes 0, 1

FIGURE 6.18   Modes 2,3: Display Memory Map

6.5.3   Mode 7 (EGA/VGA)

Mode 7 is an 80-column alphanumeric mode compatible with the Monochrome Display Adapter (MDA).

Mode 7 is the only mode that has the underline feature enabled at a Mode Set. All other modes disable this feature at a Mode Set. Underlining is enabled for a particular character when the attribute byte of a character is a 1 or a 9 for the foreground color and a 0 for a background color. The Underline Location Register must be programmed after a Mode Set occurs if underlining is desired.

In the EGA/VGA, this mode uses 720 pixels per horizontal scan line. The EGA can operate with a resolution of 350 scan lines. The VGA can operate with a resolution of 350 or 400 scan lines, as determined by the setting of the number of scan lines in the BIOS call Select Scan Lines for Alphanumeric Mode.

The default character size for the EGA is a 9-by-14 character box. The default

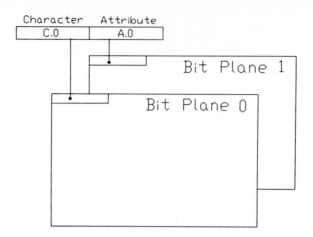

FIGURE 6.19 Mode 7: Mapping Character/Attributes into Display Memory

character size for the VGA is a 9-by-14 character box in the 350-scan-line mode and a 9-by-16 character box in the 400-scan-line mode.

This mode allows a display resolution of 80 characters per row by 25 rows per screen, totaling $80 \times 25 = 2,000$ characters. Each character is represented by two bytes, one byte for the character code and one for the attribute byte. This is equivalent to 4,000 bytes per page. The character code is loaded into bit plane 0, and the attribute byte is loaded into bit plane 1, as shown in Figure 6.19.

When display memory is being read from or written to, the transfer of data to the two display bit planes occurs automatically because of special hardware in the EGA/VGA. This addressing mode is called *odd/even* because data read from or written to even locations affects bit plane 0, and data read from or written to odd locations affects bit plane 1.

In Figure 6.20, a byte array in host memory called *string* is copied to display memory. The array consists of alternating character codes and attribute bytes. In the array, the "C" refers to the character code, the "A" refers to the attribute byte, and the "X" is the index number—that is, 0, 1, 2 . . . 79. The data in the string buffer is written to display memory bit planes 0 and 1, as indicated in Figure 6.20.

Although 4,000 bytes of memory are required per display page, only 2,000 bytes are required in each of the two bit planes because the character codes and attributes are loaded into separate bit planes. Because odd/even memory mapping is in effect, only even addresses are accessible in bit plane 0, and only odd addresses are accessible in bit plane 1. A display page, therefore, requires 4,000 bytes and occupies 4,096 bytes of host memory address space. Up to eight display pages can be resident in display memory simultaneously. The mapping of display pages into memory is illustrated in Figure 6.21.

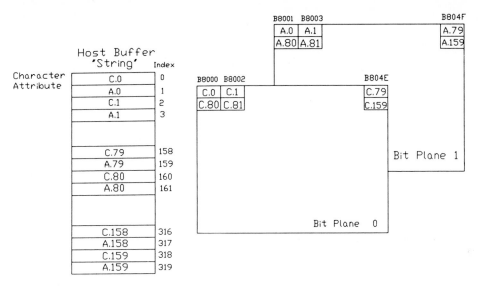

FIGURE 6.20   Mode 7: Moving Data from a Host Array to Display Memory

6.6   THE CURSOR

The cursor is used as a pointer on the display screen, bringing attention to a particular character position on the screen. Often it is used to indicate where text will be positioned on the screen as keys are typed on the keyboard. This is often the case when word processors are used or when users are responding to questions in application programs. The cursor can be thought of as a window through which characters will be entered onto the screen.

The cursor moves nondestructively across the screen, directed by program control. As it overwrites characters already on the screen, the characters that lay beneath the cursor change their attribute. In a color system, the characters switch foreground and background colors. In a monochrome system, the character foreground and background video and reversed video attributes are switched. As the cursor leaves a character position, the original character is restored.

The cursor blinks at a rate of 1/16th of the vertical frame rate. Because the vertical scan rate is 60 frames per second, the blink rate is nearly four on/off pairs, blinking at a rate of nearly two blinks per second.

6.6.1   Cursor-related BIOS Calls

There are several BIOS routines that interact with the cursor. The BIOS codes and their functions are listed in Table 6.13. All of the cursor BIOS calls are invoked through interrupt INT 10 hex. The AH register is used to distinguish which call is invoked.

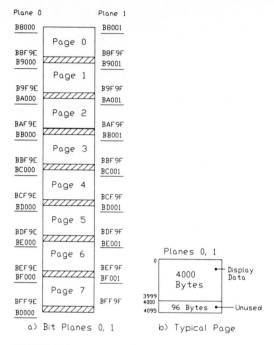

FIGURE 6.21 Mode 7: Display Memory Map

TABLE 6.13 Cursor-related BIOS Calls

BIOS Code AH (Hex)	Function
01	Set Cursor Type
02	Set Cursor Position
03	Read Cursor Position
12 BL=34	Cursor Emulation (VGA only)

6.6.2 Cursor Shape

The cursor shape is determined by the Cursor Start and the Cursor End Register. The cursor shape is always a rectangle that fills the scan lines of the character box beginning at the scan line number loaded in the Cursor Start Register and ending with the scan line loaded in the Cursor End Register. The BIOS call Set Cursor Type, AH = 01, loads these two registers. The cursor shape is illustrated in Figure 6.22.

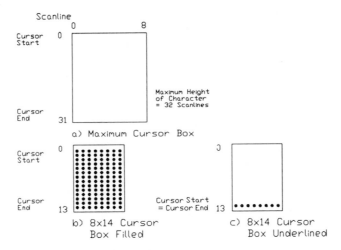

FIGURE 6.22 Cursor Shape

6.6.3 Enabling and Disabling the Cursor

In the VGA, the cursor may be turned off by setting the value in Cursor On/Off (COO) field of the Cursor Start Register. If the cursor start value is larger than the cursor end value, no cursor will be displayed. In the EGA, if the cursor start value is larger than the value in the cursor end value, two rectangles will be drawn within the character box. The first box will begin at the cursor start value and end at the bottom scan line of the cursor box. The second box will reside above the first box and will begin with the top scan line of the character box and end at the cursor end value.

It is possible to enable a cursor emulation mode in the VGA. This mode is enabled or disabled by a call to the Cursor Emulation BIOS call. If this mode is enabled, the type of cursor and the starting and ending values of the cursor may be adjusted depending on the values input to Set Cursor Type BIOS call, AH = 01. Various conditions are checked. If the conditions are met, specific cursor shapes will be drawn. This provides the programmer with a convenient way to draw underline cursors, full-block cursors, and half-block cursors.

An underline cursor is produced by setting the end value to be less than or equal to the start value plus 2. An overbar cursor is produced by setting the start value to be less than the end value, both of which are less than or equal to 3. A full-block cursor is produced by setting the start value to be less than or equal to 2 or the end value less than the start value. A half-block cursor is produced by setting the start value to be less than 2. Note that these cursor shapes were formed without the programmer's needing to be concerned with the current character box size.

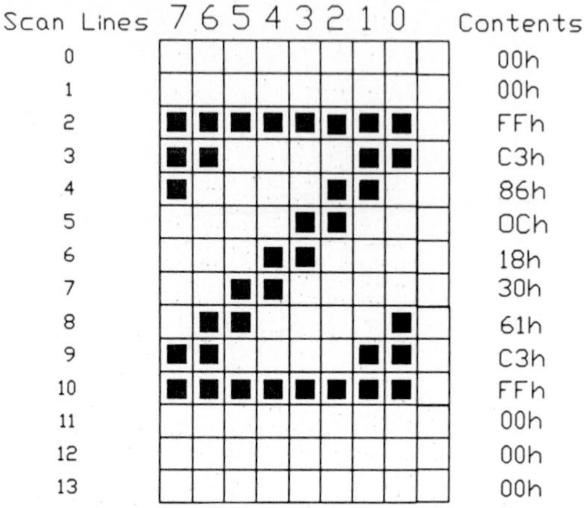

FIGURE 6.23   A Typical Character

6.7   DOWNLOADABLE CHARACTER SETS

The EGA/VGA is capable of utilizing downloadable character fonts. Two complete fonts and one supplemental font are supplied in the EGA BIOS ROM. Three complete fonts and one supplemental font are supplied in the VGA BIOS ROM. Additional fonts may be supplied by the user. Each character font consists of 256 characters. Each character is represented by a rectangular box filled with a grid of dots. Each dot in the box represents a pixel in the display memory and is represented by a bit in the character font.

The way that the character fonts are handled depends on whether the EGA/VGA is in an alphanumeric mode or a graphics mode.

6.7.1   Character Size

The character widths currently supported by the EGA/VGA are 8 pixels per character row in the color modes and 9 pixels per character row in the monochrome mode. Although the characters are nine pixels wide in the monochrome mode, the character sets store a horizontal line of a character as 8 pixels per character. A byte in the character set represents eight consecutive neighboring horizontal pixels. Consecutive bytes within a character represent vertical neighboring scan lines.

The character heights available in the character sets resident in BIOS range from 8 scan lines to 14 scan lines per character in the EGA and 8 to 16 scan lines per character in the VGA. The maximum height of a character to be accessed in the alphanumeric modes is 32 scan lines high. A typical character from character sets of each size is presented in Figure 6.23.

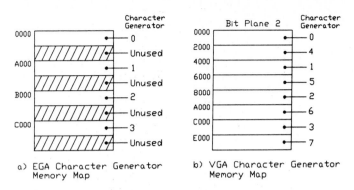

a) EGA Character Generator Memory Map

b) VGA Character Generator Memory Map

FIGURE 6.24   Resident Fonts in Bit Plane 2

6.7.2   Fonts Resident in Display Memory

When a character is referenced by an ASCII code, its bit pattern is found in the active resident display font. In the alphanumeric modes, four character sets may be resident in the EGA display memory and eight character sets may be resident in the VGA display memory. Each resident display font is 256 characters long. Two of these 256-long character sets may be active at a time, allowing any character to access any of 512 characters.

6.7.3   Fonts in the Alphanumeric Modes

In the alphanumeric modes, the EGA display memory planes store the character codes, character attributes, and character font bit patterns. The bit patterns corresponding to the character codes reside in bit plane 0; the character attributes reside in bit plane 1; and the character bit patterns reside in bit plane 2. Up to four character sets can be resident in the EGA bit plane 2. Up to eight character sets can be resident in the VGA bit plane 2. One or two of these character sets can be active, allowing a character set of either 256 or 512 characters.

In the EGA, bit plane 2 is subdivided into four blocks, each 16 Kbytes long. The 8 Kbytes of storage at the beginning of each of these blocks is reserved for the four resident fonts. In the VGA, bit plane 2 is subdivided into eight blocks, each 8 Kbytes long. Figure 6.24 illustrates the EGA/VGA resident fonts in bit plane 2.

In order to obtain higher-resolution character fonts, nonstandard EGA implementations have allocated bit plane 3 for the character font bit patterns. In these implementations, bit plane 3 is handled in a fashion similar to that used with bit plane 2. With these two planes chained together, a character width of 16 pixels can be achieved. With this increased character width, larger character fonts can be employed. Because each character has storage allocated for 32 scan lines, the largest a character can be is 16 by 32, four times the size of the 8-by-14 character set in the EGA/VGA.

6.7.4 The Location of a Character in Alphanumeric Modes

Regardless of the active font's character size, a single- sized block of memory is reserved for each character in the character set. Each character has 32 bytes reserved for it. Because each character set is 256 characters long, a total of 8,192 bytes of storage is required per font. This number—8,192 bytes—is referred to in computer terminology as *8 Kbytes*. Thus, 8 Kbytes literally means 8,192 bytes, not 8,000 bytes. These 32 bytes of storage refer to the maximum number of scan lines per character that can be displayed in an alphanumeric mode. It is computationally advantageous for this number to be a power of 2 because it facilitates rapid addressing. The character codes that are used to access these character bit patterns within the font follow the ANSII standard and vary from 00 hex to FF hex. In order to determine where the character shape exists in memory, it is necessary to multiply the character code number by the number of bytes per character and add in the base of the character font, as shown in Equation 6.3.

Equation 6.3 Determining the Address of a Character

$$\frac{\text{Character shape}}{\text{address}} = \frac{\text{Character base}}{\text{address}} + \left(\frac{\text{Font Character}}{\text{Code}} \times \frac{\text{\# of bytes}}{\text{per character}}\right)$$

It is possible to substitute a logical shift operation for the multiplication operation if the number of bytes per character is a power of 2. Because there are 32 bytes per character, the address of the character bit pattern can be determined by shifting the ASCII character code by 5 positions to the left. This left shift is equivalent to a multiplication by 32. Because the fonts do not overlap, it is possible to substitute a logical OR operation for the addition. Using these simplifications, the address of the character can be determined as shown in Equation 6.4.

Equation 6.4 Fast Determination of the Address of a Character

$$\frac{\text{Character shape}}{\text{address}} = \frac{\text{Font base}}{\text{address}} \mid [\,(\text{Character code} << 5\,)$$

The logical OR operation is denoted with the "|" symbol and the logical shift right operation is denoted with the "<<" symbol, which is consistent with the

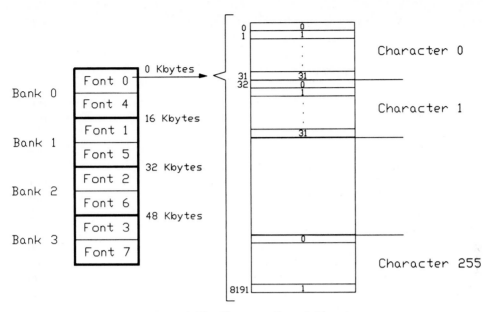

FIGURE 6.25 Character Font Addressing

notation used in the C language. The resulting 16-bit address points to the desired character bit pattern. It can be split up into three fields, as shown in Figure 6.25. This figure illustrates the logical operations from Equation 6.4.

6.7.5 Fonts in the Graphics Modes

In the graphics modes, pointers are provided to point to the active character set. This character set resides in host memory and can be one of either the ROM-based or the user-defined character sets. Only one 256-character-long character set may be active at a time.

6.7.6 The Location of a Character in the Graphics Modes

The location of a character in host memory is determined by locating the address of the starting location of the character set and adding the offset that points to the desired character, as shown in Equation 6.5.

Equation 6.5 Determining the Location of a Character

$$
\begin{array}{c}
\text{Address} \\
\text{of character}
\end{array}
=
\begin{array}{c}
\text{Pointer to} \\
\text{character set}
\end{array}
+
\begin{array}{c}
\text{Offset to} \\
\text{character}
\end{array}
$$

The pointer to the character set is located in the interrupt vector locations of interrupt INT 43 hex or interrupt INT 1F hex. These interrupts are located in host memory offset from address 0000:0000 hex by the interrupt number times 4. This occurs because each interrupt vector is four bytes long in order to store the long pointer. The long pointer must load both the segment and offset registers with 16-bit values. The vector at interrupt INT 1F hex contains the pointer to the upper 128 characters of the 256-character-long character set when the EGA/VGA is in display mode 4, 5, or 6.

The offset value that points to the desired character is determined by multiplying the number of bytes in each character by the ASCII character code, as shown in Equation 6.6.

Equation 6.6   Determining the Offset to a Character (Not Modes 4, 5, or 6)

$$\text{Offset} = \text{ASCII code} \times \text{Number of bytes per character}$$

If the display is in mode 4, 5, or 6, the bias is determined by multiplying the number of bytes in each character by the ASCII character code minus 128, as shown in Equation 6.7.

Equation 6.7   Determining the Offset to a Character (Modes 4, 5, and 6)

$$\text{Offset} = (\text{ ASCII code} - 128\text{ }) \times \text{Number of bytes per character}$$

6.7.7   Font-related BIOS Calls

Several BIOS calls are associated with the character fonts. These calls are listed in Table 6.14.

The programmer may load a user-defined or ROM-based character set in one of two ways. The first way, invoked by BIOS calls AL = 00 hex to AL = 04 hex, automatically issues a Set Mode without clearing the display memory. The second way, invoked by BIOS calls AL = 10 to AL = 14, requires the programmer to issue a Set Mode immediately before invoking one of these BIOS calls. In addition, display page 0 must be active. Once the BIOS call has been invoked, several of the character-related parameters and display registers will be modified to adjust to the new character set. The display registers affected in the EGA are listed in Figure 6.26.

The display parameters and display registers affected in the VGA are listed in Figure 6.27.

TABLE 6.14   BIOS-related Character Font Calls. AH = 11 Hex. Load Character Generator BIOS Routines

AL (Hex)	Title	Display Mode	Adapter
00	Load User Character Set	Alpha	EGA/VGA
01	Load ROM 9 by 14 Monochrome Set	Alpha	EGA/VGA
02	Load ROM 8 by 8 Color Set	Alpha	EGA/VGA
03	Set Block Specifier	Alpha	EGA/VGA
04	Load ROM 8 by 16 Character Set	Alpha	VGA
10	Load User Character Set	Alpha	EGA/VGA
11	Load ROM 9 by 14 Monochrome Set	Alpha	EGA/VGA
12	Load ROM 8 by 8 Color Set	Alpha	EGA/VGA
14	Load ROM 8 by 16 Character Set	Alpha	VGA
20	Load User 8 by 8 Color Set	Alpha	EGA/VGA
21	Load User Set	Graphics	EGA/VGA
22	Load ROM 8 by 14 Set	Graphics	EGA/VGA
23	Load Rom 8 by 8 Color Set	Graphics	EGA/VGA
24	Load Rom 8 by 16 Color Set	Graphics	VGA
30	Return Font Information	—	EGA/VGA

Maximum Scan Line = Bytes per character − 1

Cursor Start = Bytes per character − 2

Cursor End = 0

Vertical Display End = [(rows + 1) × bytes per character] − 1

Figure 6.26   EGA Register Modifications

Active Character Sets

The Set Block Specifier BIOS call, AH=11 hex AL=03 hex, allows the programmer to select two active character sets from the resident character sets. If two of the character sets are active, a character can select from 256 possible characters.

Resident Character Sets

The font-related BIOS calls provide a means of loading character sets into the resident slots available in bit plane 2 of display memory. In the EGA, up to four 256-long character sets may be resident at a time. In the VGA, up to eight 256-long character sets may be resident at a time.

Maximum Scan Line = Bytes per character − 1

Cursor Start = Bytes per character − 2

Cursor End = 0

For 400-scan-line modes:

Vertical Display End = [(rows + 1) × bytes/character] − 1

For 200-scan-line modes:

Vertical Display End = [(rows + 1) × bytes/character*2] − 1

ROWS = [(Number of Scan Lines) / bytes/character] − 1

CRT_LEN = (ROWS + 1) * CRT_COLS × 2

Figure 6.27 VGA Register Modifications

TABLE 6.15 Alphanumeric Default Character Sets at Mode Set

Mode (Hex)	Character Box Size	EGA Monitor	VGA # of Scan Lines
0 ,1	8 by 8	RGBI	200
0*,1*	8 by 14	RrGgBb	350
0+,1+	9 by 16	—	400
2 ,3	8 by 8	RGBI	200
2*,3*	8 by 14	RrGgBb	350
2+,3+	9 by 16	—	400
7	9 by 14	Mono/RrGgBb	350
7+	9 by 16	—	400

6.7.8 Character Sets in the Alphanumeric Modes

All of the alphanumeric modes load a default character set into display memory bit plane 2 at a Mode Set. The default character set chosen depends on the display mode selected and on the system configuration. Table 6.15 lists the default character sets selected during a Mode Set.

6.7.9 EGA Alphanumeric Default Character Sets

In the EGA, the configuration is determined by the type of monitor attached to the adapter. If an RGBI monitor is attached, the EGA is forced into a 200-scan-line mode and an 8-by-8 character set is employed. If an enhanced RrGgBb monitor is attached, the EGA goes into a 350-scan-line mode and an 8-by-14 character set is employed. In the monochrome mode, mode 7, either a monochrome monitor or the enhanced color monitor allows for 350 scan lines. The 9-by-14 character set is employed.

TABLE 6.16 Character Set Pointers for the BIOS Call Return Font Information

BH	Adapter	Pointer
0	EGA/VGA	User-defined graphics, 8-by-8 ASCII (128–255)
1	EGA/VGA	User-defined graphics
2	EGA/VGA	ROM 8 by 14
3	EGA/VGA	ROM 8-by-8 ASCII (0–127)
4	EGA/VGA	ROM 8-by-8 ASCII (128–255)
5	EGA/VGA	ROM alpha supplement 9 by 14
6	VGA	ROM 8 by 16
7	VGA	ROM alpha supplement 9 by 16

6.7.10 VGA Alphanumeric Default Character Sets

In the VGA, the configuration is determined by the number of scan lines selected. The number of scan lines is adjusted by the BIOS call Select Scan Line for Alphanumeric Modes, AH = 12 hex, BL = 30 hex. It can be set to 200, 350, or 400 scan lines. In the color alphanumeric modes, selecting 200 scan lines forces the VGA to use the 8-by-8 character set. Selecting 350 scan lines allows the VGA to use an 8-by-14 character set while selecting 400 scan lines allows use of the 8-by-16 character set. In these color modes, only the enhanced color monitor may be used. In the monochrome mode, mode 7, either the enhanced monochrome or the enhanced color monitor may be used. If 350 scan lines are selected, the 9-by-14 character set is used while if 400 scan lines are selected, the 9-by-16 character set is used. The 200-scan-line mode cannot be used while the VGA is in mode 7.

6.7.11 Loading Character Sets Into Display Memory

There are several character fonts resident in the BIOS ROM. These fonts may be accessed by the BIOS call Return Font Information. The pointer to the top of each of these character fonts is returned to the calling program by invoking this BIOS Call. Recall that the supplemental fonts are not complete fonts but rather a collection of character bit patterns. The various font pointers are presented in Table 6.16.

6.7.12 Character Sets in the Graphics Modes

The graphics modes do not load a character set into display memory—rather, these modes depend on a pointer that points to a character set bit pattern. The bit patterns reside in host memory address space, either in RAM or in BIOS ROM. In the graphics modes, the programmer provides the BIOS with a pointer to the desired character set bit patterns. Default pointers are used for the

TABLE 6.17 Alphanumeric Default Character Sets at Mode Set

Mode (Hex)	Character Box Size	Adapter Applicable	EGA Monitor	VGA Monitor
4,5	8 by 8	EGA, VGA	RGBI,RrGgBb	Color
6	8 by 8	EGA, VGA	RGBI,RrGgBb	Mono/color
D,E	8 by 8	EGA, VGA	RGBI,RrGgBb	Color
F	8 by 14	EGA, VGA	Mono,RrGgBb	Mono/color
10	8 by 14	EGA, VGA	RrGgBb	Color
11	8 by 16	VGA	—	Mono/color
12	8 by 16	VGA	—	Color
13	8 by 8	VGA	—	Color

different modes depending on the resolution of the selected mode. The default pointers select a specific-sized character set as indicated in Table 6.17.

A variety of character sets is available, including the 8-by-8 and 8-by-14 characters for the EGA/VGA and the 8-by-16 characters for the VGA. In addition, the user may provide pointers to user-defined character sets. A BIOS call, AL = 30 hex, is provided to return information to the calling program regarding the value of the pointers that reference the above-mentioned character sets. Table 6.16 lists the character set pointers.

The character set provided to the EGA/VGA when a graphics mode is active is pointed to by a pointer located in the Interrupt 43 hex vector. In all graphics modes, with the exception of modes 4, 5, and 6, this pointer points to the entire 256-character-long character set.

In the graphics modes 4, 5, and 6, the EGA/VGA is maintaining the CGA standard. In this standard, the pointer in the INT 43 hex vector points to the first 128 characters in the character set, ASCII 0 through 127. A second pointer is required to access the upper 128 characters of the character set. This pointer resides in the INT 1F hex vector. In these display modes, modes 4, 5, and 6, only the 8-by-8 character set is utilized.

6.7.13 Default Character Sets in the Graphics Modes

The pointer to the default character set is loaded into the proper interrupt vector location, as determined by the active display mode. In the EGA, a pointer to either the 8-by-8 character set or the 8-by-14 character set is selected depending on the display mode. In the VGA, a pointer to the 8-by-8, the 8-by-14, or the 8-by-16 character set is selected depending on the display mode. These character sets are presented in Table 6.18.

TABLE 6.18 Graphics Mode Default Character Sets at Mode Set

Mode (Hex)	Character Box Size	Adapter Applicable	EGA Monitor	VGA Monitor
0,1	8 by 8	EGA, VGA	RGBI,RrGgBb	Color
0,1	8 by 14	EGA, VGA	RrGgBb	Color
0,1	9 by 16	VGA	—	Color
2,3	8 by 8	EGA/VGA	RGBI,RrGgBb	Color
2,3	8 by 14	EGA/VGA	RrGgBb	Color
2,3	9 by 16	VGA	—	Color
7	9 by 14	EGA/VGA	Mono	Mono/Color
7	9 by 16	VGA	—	Mono/Color

Chapter 7
Graphics Processing

7.1 CHARACTERS

When the EGA/VGA is in a graphics mode, the display memory bit planes contain bit patterns that correspond directly to the dot patterns viewed on the screen. This is distinctly different from the configuration during an alphanumeric mode in which each bit plane has a specific function. The actual dot patterns displayed on the monitor are derived from the codes stored in the bit planes. In the graphics modes, these displayed dot patterns are output directly from the bit planes into the color lookup table and out to the monitor.

A character can be written to the display memory when the EGA/VGA is in a graphics mode by writing directly to the display or by going through the BIOS routines. Certainly, going to the display memory through the BIOS routines is the simpler, albeit slower, path. When writing single characters or character strings, the BIOS calls may be fast enough for many applications. However, applications that require rapid full-screen updates or scrolling windows of text may find the BIOS calls to be too slow.

7.1.1 Character Sets

The character-generation section of the EGA/VGA is based upon downloadable character fonts. To be called *downloadable*, the adapter must have the capability of accepting user-defined character fonts as well as its own. In the alphanumeric modes, bit plane 2, and in some cases bit plane 3, is reserved to hold the character font dot patterns. Thus, the fonts are downloaded to the display memory. Because the bit patterns reside within the display memory, special hardware within the EGA/VGA accesses the patterns in a rapid fashion.

Any font of the proper size may be loaded into the display memory and used as the active character set. These fonts may originate from an external source or may be one of the resident character fonts contained within the BIOS ROM. The display memory of the EGA is capable of storing four character sets simultaneously, and the VGA is capable of storing eight. Each character set is 256 characters long. The programmer may select either one or two of the 256 character fonts to be active at a time. The attribute byte associated with each character dictates which of the two fonts to use for that particular character.

228

7.1.2 Storing Characters in Display Memory

The display memory cannot be used to store the character fonts when the EGA is in a graphics mode because bit planes 2 and 3 are not available. All four bit planes are occupied in storing the bit-mapped graphics data. The programmer may write the characters directly into display memory or may use the character-related BIOS routines while the EGA/VGA is in one of the graphics modes.

The programmer has complete flexibility when writing characters directly to the display memory while the EGA/VGA is in a graphics mode. The characters may be any size, shape, color, or combination of colors. Suppose that the EGA/VGA is in display mode 10 hex and all four bit planes are active. A pixel is represented by one bit in each of the four bit planes. A character is constructed by loading the character's bit patterns into each bit plane. The Set/Reset Register may be used to write the character to the display memory. The Set/Reset Register writes one pixel to all bit planes simultaneously. Thus, an 8-by-14 character box can be written to the display memory in $14 \times 8 = 112$ byte move operations. If a full 80-×-25 screen is updated using this technique, nearly 224,000 bytes will be written to the display memory. Add in the necessary addressing operations associated with this data move operation and a full-screen write could take several seconds.

7.1.3 Writing Characters Quickly

If a few assumptions are made regarding the nature and orientation of the characters, the number of operations required to write characters to the display can be drastically reduced. The first assumption is that, in most cases, characters will be oriented horizontally, with each character displayed in one color. In addition, only the character foreground will be displayed, leaving the background transparent. A further assumption would be that the characters all fall on byte boundaries. Based on these assumptions, an 8-by-14 character can be written to the display memory in 14 byte operations. This reduces a full-screen write to 28,000 byte operations, providing an improvement of 8 to 1 over the previously described method.

The technique used to write characters takes advantage of these assumptions. It updates an entire character scan line in one byte move operation. All four bit planes are written to simultaneously. Because the character is 8 pixels wide, an entire character scan line can be contained in one byte. The byte that represents the bit pattern of one scan line is written into the Bit Mask Register. Each bit of the Bit Mask Register corresponds to one of the eight horizontal neighboring pixels of the display. Any bit set to a 1 in this register allows the corresponding pixel in the display memory to be modified. Likewise, any pixel reset to 0 protects the corresponding pixel in the display memory from being modified. The character foreground pixels are represented with a 1, and background pixels are represented with a 0. Thus, foreground pixels will overwrite the corresponding locations in the display memory, and background pixels will have no effect on the display memory.

The character color is loaded into the Set/Reset Register. All planes are configured to respond to this Register by loading an 0F hex into the Enable Set/Reset Register. Ultimately, only those planes selected in the Map Mask Register will actually be affected, regardless of the setting in the Enable Set/ Reset Register. The bit positions within each of the three Registers will correspond to a bit plane. All bit planes enabled by the Map Mask Register and set in the Enable Set/Reset Register will be updated by the subsequent write operation. A 0 in a bit position of the Set/Reset Register will cause the selected pixel in the corresponding bit plane to be overwritten with a 0. A 1 in a bit position will cause the pixel in the corresponding bit plane to be overwritten with a 1.

The Map Mask Register and the Enable Set/Reset Register are loaded to select the desired bit planes. The foreground color of the character is loaded into the Set/Reset Register. The first scan line from the character bit pattern is fetched and loaded into the Bit Mask Register. A byte, 00 hex, is written to the display memory using a MOV instruction to the desired position of the first scan line. All planes selected will be updated with the corresponding bit value in the Set/Reset Register. Because a Write Mode 0 is in effect, eight consecutive horizontal pixels will be written to the display. The Bit Mask Register assigns one bit per pixel. All pixels set to a 1 in the Bit Mask Register will cause the corresponding pixels to be loaded with the value from the Set/Reset Register. The single MOV instruction causes up to eight pixels in up to four bit planes to be updated with the value in the Set/Reset Register. The process is repeated for each character scan line by adjusting the address used in the MOV instruction so that it addresses the next scan line of the selected character. A new value that corresponds to the bit pattern of the second scan line of the character is written into the Bit Mask Register. Again, a 0 byte is written to display memory via a MOV instruction, updating the second scan line. This process repeats for all scan lines in the character.

If more sophisticated text output is desired, it is likely that the characters will not always fall on an even byte boundary. A single scan line in a character may take two byte write operations, requiring the Bit Mask Register and the address to be modified twice for each scan line output. A host buffer can be used to build up the character in a rectangular grid. Each bit can be written independently. Once constructed, the resultant two-dimensional matrix is output to the display one byte at a time. If a character string needs to be written to the display, a host buffer can be used to store an entire character line of data. Eight pixels at a time would still be written to the display. However, these eight pixels do not necessarily correspond to one character. The move string instructions MOVSB or MOVSW could be used to move the host buffer rapidly to the display.

Thus far, it has been assumed that the character strings are oriented horizontally. Writing characters that are not oriented in a horizontal direction is more difficult. Vertically oriented characters can be written by transposing the rows and columns of a character in a host buffer and then writing the host buffer to the display as if the characters were horizontal. A transposed 8-by-14 character box can be thought of as a 14-by-8 character box. Because 14 dots are written horizontally, two byte operations are necessary to output each character scan line for all eight scan lines. Other than this transposition, the character output process is identical to the horizontal character strings.

Angular orientations can be produced by first rotating the character bit patterns within a host memory array and then writing one horizontal line at a time. The maximum number of bytes for an 8-by-14 character would be two bytes per scan line for fourteen scan lines. By rotating the characters within a host buffer, strings can be output one byte at a time, and each byte may contain data from more than one character.

7.1.4   Graphics Text Processing through BIOS

The programmer may utilize the BIOS character routines to read and write characters to the display when the EGA/VGA is in a graphics mode. Because the downloadable character fonts are not located in display memory, the location of the desired font must be provided to the BIOS routine. This is done by one of the BIOS calls, as invoked by AH = 11, which is the Load Character Generator BIOS call. The parameter passed to the interrupt routine in the AL register determines the type of font loaded, as indicated in the Table 7.1.

The BIOS software must be told where the character set resides so that it can find the character bit patterns when drawing characters. These pointers may refer to user-defined downloadable character fonts located in host memory or to one of the character fonts located in the BIOS ROM. The character fonts are limited to 256 active characters at a time, because the attribute byte cannot contain the font selection bit as is done in the alphanumeric modes.

7.1.5   Finding a Character Set

When a character is accessed through a BIOS call, the character code and attribute byte are sent to the BIOS routine. The display memory address where the character will be placed is determined by the current cursor position of the selected page. Depending on the display mode, the pointer to the character font located at either the interrupt 43 hex or the 1F hex vector will be selected to point to the character bit pattern. If the current display mode is less than 7, a CGA emulation mode is in effect and the 8-by-8 character font is selected. If the character code is less than 80 hex, the vector at interrupt 43 hex is selected as the pointer to the base of the character bit patterns. Otherwise, the vector at interrupt 1F hex is selected.

TABLE 7.1 Load Character Generator BIOS Routines

AH=11 Hex

AL (Hex)	Title	Display Mode
21	Load User Set	Graphics
22	Load ROM 8-by-14 Set	Graphics
23	Load ROM 8-by-8 Color Set	Graphics

7.1.6 Locating a Bit Pattern within a Character Set

To determine the location of the selected character bit pattern, the character code is multiplied by 8 and added to the font base pointer found in the interrupt vector. If the current display mode is greater than 7, the vector at interrupt 43 hex is selected as the pointer to the base of the character bit patterns. To determine a character position, the number of bytes per character, as stored in host memory at 485 hex, is multiplied by the character code. This is necessary because a user-specified character size may be selected in these modes.

7.1.7 Writing the Bit Pattern to Display Memory

Once the bit pattern for the selected character is located within the character set, the pattern is written directly to the display memory at the current cursor position. The color of the character is determined by the attribute byte associated with the character. The foreground color ranges from 0 to 15 in bit positions 0 to 3 of the attribute byte. Bit 7 of the attribute byte is a flag that determines the type of write operation. If bit 7 is reset to 0, the write operation is straightforward. All pixels in the display memory corresponding to foreground pixels in the character are overwritten with the value indicated by the foreground color. If bit 7 of the attribute byte is set to a 1, the operation becomes an XOR logical operation. The new character data is XORed with the current data in the corresponding display memory location before the result is written to the display memory. The BIOS routine actually loads the Function Select (FS) field of the Data Rotate Register with a 3 to indicate that the XOR operation should take place.

With the XOR function enabled, the character will be written to the display memory without modifications if the area of the display memory selected contains all 0s. This occurs because any value XORed with a 0 remains unmodified. If the area of the display memory selected contains the same bit pattern as the new data being written, the character will be erased. This occurs because any value XORed with itself results in 0. The most common use of this XOR function is to draw and erase a character with minimal overhead. The programmer must simply output the character to the blank display, thereby writing the character to the display. Without modifying anything, the character can be rewritten to the display, causing the character to be erased.

If the area of the display memory to be modified contains all 1s, the resulting character color will be inverted. This occurs because any value XORed with 1 results in an inversion. This is a simple way to highlight a character on the screen. A character bit pattern of FF hex, all 1s, can be written to the display using the XOR feature. Any characters existing in the desired display memory locations will have their colors inverted. Color inversion means that all bits will be inverted. Thus, a character with color 5 (0101 binary) will be modified to color A hex (1010 binary). This process can be reversed by rewriting the same FF hex pattern to the character position with the XOR function enabled. The result in the above example is to redraw the character in its original color of 5.

If the data in the display memory is not all 0s, all 1s, or identical to the new data, the resultant character pattern written to the display will depend on the data present. If other data is present in the display area, the result will appear to be the original character overwritten with the new character. The result will be three colors, corresponding to the original character foreground color, the XOR of the original and the new character's foreground color, and the new character's foreground color.

7.2   GRAPHICS ATTRIBUTES

The character attributes are handled differently in graphics modes than in alphanumeric modes. In the graphics modes, the actual bit patterns for the character are stored in display memory. Each pixel is 1, 2, or 4 bits wide. The values loaded into the bits associated with each pixel are determined by the attribute byte. The attribute byte is interrogated as to the desired color or monochrome attribute for the character. The foreground portion of this attribute code is loaded into the pixels that correspond to the foreground of the character. Any background attribute value is ignored because the character is drawn in a transparent mode. All pixels associated with the background pixels of a character are ignored.

7.2.1   Two-color Mode

The two-color graphics mode in the EGA/VGA is invoked in mode 6. In addition, the VGA mode 11 uses the two-color mode. The foreground color of all characters is displayed in white. This white is obtained by setting all bits in each of the three colors to on. In the Palette Registers, this corresponds to a 17 hex. In the default Palette Register, all Palette Registers with the exception of Register 0 are loaded with a 17 hex. Any character attribute value other than 0 will result in the character being displayed in maximum intensity white. The 0 corresponds to the background color of the character.

TABLE 7.2 Monochrome Attributes

Character Attribute	Attribute
0,8	Black
1,9	Video
2,A	Black
3,B	Video
4,C	Blinking
5,D	Intensified Video
6,E	Blinking
7,F	Intensified Video

TABLE 7.3 Two-color Attributes

Attribute Value	Palette Number	Palette Value (Hex)	Resulting Color
0	0	00	Black
1	1	08	Video
4	4	18	Blinking
5	5	18	Intensified Video

7.2.2 Monochrome Mode

The monochrome mode emulates the EGA/VGA graphics on a monochrome display. This is associated with display mode F hex. Two bits are dedicated to each pixel in this mode. Thus, each character can be displayed with one of four attributes. The attributes associated with a character are derived from the two least significant bits of the foreground color in the attribute byte. The background color is ignored.

The two bits associated with each pixel are stored in bit planes 0 and 2. Bit planes 1 and 3 are disabled; thus, they do not contribute to the Palette Register address. This can be seen in the value of the Plane Select Register, index 12 hex, in the EGA or VGA Default Register Values Tables, found in Chapter 9, Tables 9.5 and 9.6, respectively. The value is 05, which corresponds to a 1 in bit positions 0 and 2 and a 0 in bit positions 1 and 3.

The standard monochrome attributes are listed in Table 7.2.

The possible attribute values, the associated Palette Register number, the default Palette Register value, and the resulting character attribute are listed in Table 7.3.

Note that the monochrome adapter uses bit 3 for the video and bit 4 for intensified. Thus, an 8 hex causes bit 3, the video bit, to be activated; a 10 hex causes bit 4, the intensified bit, to be activated. An 18 hex results in both being activated.

TABLE 7.4   Four-color Attributes

Attribute	Palette Value (Hex)	Color Select 1	Color Select 2
0	00	Black	Black
1	13	Light cyan	Green
2	15	Light magenta	Red
3	17	Intensified white	Brown

7.2.3   Four-color Mode

The four-color graphics modes in the EGA/VGA are invoked in modes 4 and 7. These modes emulate the CGA graphics standard. The color of each character is determined by the two least significant bits of the foreground portion of the attribute byte. Each pixel is represented by two bits. These two bits allow the pixel to access Palette Registers 0 through 3. These Palette Registers are loaded with values that allow the character to be displayed in one of the two standard CGA color selections. The attribute values, the associated default Palette Register values, and the associated colors are listed in Table 7.4.

7.2.4   Sixteen-color Mode

The sixteen-color graphics modes are modes D, E, and 10 hex for the EGA and VGA. In addition, mode 12 hex is available in the VGA. These modes assign four bits to each pixel. The four bits per pixel are loaded with the foreground attribute color of each character. Only the foreground pixel of each character is affected. The foreground attribute values, the associated Palette register value, and resultant colors are listed in Table 7.5.

7.2.5   256-color Mode

The 256-color mode is available through mode 13 hex of the VGA only. Eight pixels are reserved for each pixel. The attribute byte associated with each character contains four bits of foreground color. These four bits correspond to one of sixteen foreground colors. These sixteen values map to the sixteen palette registers. In the VGA, the outputs of the Palette Registers address the Color Registers. The actual color codes reside in the Color Registers.

This is the only mode in the VGA that requires that the Palette Registers not be changed. If a color needs to be changed, the associated Color Register, not the Palette Register, should be modified. According to the Default Palette Register Values, found in Chapter 9, in Table 9.6, the sixteen Palette Registers are loaded with incrementing values from 0 to 15.

The sixteen Color Registers selected by Palette Registers 0 through 15 are determined by the Color Select Register. The first sixteen Color Registers contain the EGA-compatible colors, as listed in Table 7.5. The second set of sixteen

TABLE 7.5 Sixteen-color Attributes

Attribute Value (Hex)	Palette Value (Hex)	Default Color
0	00	Black
1	01	Blue
2	02	Green
3	03	Cyan
4	04	Red
5	05	Magenta
6	06	Brown
7	07	White
8	38	Dark gray
9	39	Light blue
A	3A	Light green
B	3B	Light cyan
C	3C	Light red
D	3D	Light magenta
E	3E	Yellow
F	3F	Intensified white

registers contains gray scales. The remaining Color Registers contain combinations of colors based on the hue-saturation-intensity model.

7.3 DISPLAY MEMORY

The EGA/VGA display memory is constructed from dynamic read/write memory. It is segmented into four bit planes. These bit planes operate in a wide variety of ways depending on the display mode. In the literature, the four bit planes are also referred to as *bit maps*. Each bit plane may be from 16 Kbytes to 64 Kbytes long. Typical EGA/VGA implementations include four 64-Kbyte bit planes for a total of 256 Kbytes of memory. The organization of the display memory as four bit planes is shown in Figure 7.1.

7.3.1 Display Memory in Host Memory Address Space

The display memory is mapped into the host memory address space. It can occupy a maximum area of 128 Kbytes from A0000 hex to BFFFF hex in the host memory space per plane. The starting address is adjustable depending on the setting of the Memory Map (MM) field in the Miscellaneous Register. The possible values of this field, along with the corresponding starting addresses, are listed in Table 7.6.

Note that the fully-populated EGA/VGA cannot coexist with any other graphics board because a host memory and host port addressing conflict will occur. A half-populated EGA/VGA, which most such cards are, can coexist with an

TABLE 7.6 Memory Map Field

MM Field	Starting Address	Amount of Memory	Compatibility Emulation
0	A0000-BFFFF	128 Kbytes	Can't coexist
1	A0000-AFFFF	64 Kbytes	Can coexist
2	B0000-BFFFF	64 Kbytes	Hercules/MDA
3	B8000-BFFFF	16 Kbytes	CGA

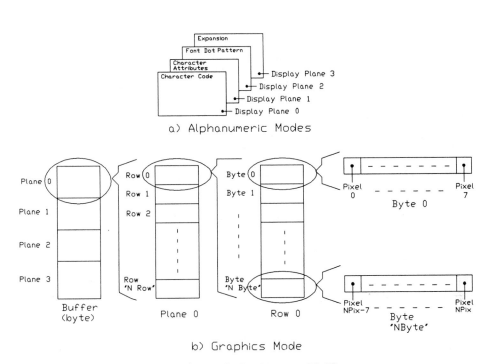

FIGURE 7.1 Display Memory Bit Planes

MDA, Hercules, or CGA board. If the EGA is configured in a color mode, however, only a monochrome or Hercules board may act as the other adapter. If the EGA/VGA is configured as a monochrome board, only a color adapter can coexist with it. The EGA/VGA memory can be mapped to look like a Hercules board when MM = 2; it can look like a CGA board when MM = 3.

A VGA adapter board can coexist with another VGA planar video. The planar video is contained on the host motherboard. Either can be selected as the active video device by invoking the Display Switch BIOS call, AH = 12 hex, BL = 35 hex.

TABLE 7.7 Display Pages: EGA/VGA Graphics Modes

Page	Mode 4,5 Hex	Mode D Hex	Mode E Hex	Mode 10 Hex
0	B8000	A0000	A0000	A0000
1	—	A2000	A4000	A8000
2	—	A4000	A8000	—
3	—	A6000	AC000	—
4	—	A8000	—	—
5	—	AA000	—	—
6	—	AC000	—	—
7	—	AE000	—	—

TABLE 7.8 Display Pages: VGA Graphics Modes

Page	Mode 11 Hex	Mode 12 Hex	Mode 13 Hex
0	A0000	A0000	A0000

TABLE 7.9 Display Pages: EGA/VGA Alphanumeric Modes

Page	Modes 0,1 Hex	Modes 2,3 Hex	Mode 7 Hex
0	B8000	B8000	B8000
1	B8400	B8800	B8800
2	B8800	B9000	B9000
3	B8C00	B9800	B9800
4	B9000	BA000	BA000
5	B9400	BA800	BA800
6	B9800	BB000	BB000
7	B9C00	BB800	BB800

7.3.2 Display Pages

The resolution of a single page and the total amount of display memory determine the number of display pages available in each display mode. Assuming 64 Kbytes per plane and a host starting address of A0000 hex, the starting addresses of the display pages are listed in Table 7.7. This table refers to the EGA/VGA graphics modes.

The VGA has three graphics modes that are not available on the EGA. Two of these modes, mode 11 hex and mode 12 hex, utilize a 640-by-480 resolution. One mode, mode 13 hex, uses a 320-by-200 resolution with eight bits dedicated to every pixel. These VGA-specific graphics modes are listed in Table 7.8.

Assuming 64 Kbytes per plane and a host starting address of B8000 hex, the starting addresses of the display pages when the EGA/VGA is in an alphanumeric mode are listed in Table 7.9.

7.3.3   Display Memory Organization

There are two basic types of display modes called the alphanumeric modes and the graphics modes. The functioning of the display memory is different depending on which of these modes is in effect. When in an alphanumeric mode, the display memory is used to hold character codes, attribute bytes, and character font bit patterns. Once decoded, the data in the display memory is converted to bit patterns that are sent to the monitor. When a graphics mode is in effect, the display memory is used to hold a bit-per-bit representation of the data being displayed on the monitor. The addressing is handled so that the bit stream coming from the display memory is output directly to be displayed on the monitor.

7.4   GRAPHICS DISPLAY MODES

The EGA/VGA graphics modes use each of the four bit planes to store the bit-mapped data to be displayed. The color of a pixel when viewed on the monitor is represented by one or more bits in one or more of the bit planes. The exact number of bits in different planes depends on the display modes. Table 7.10 lists the number of bits per plane and the number of planes that affect the color of a pixel.

7.4.1   Number of Colors versus Display Planes

The color determined from Table 7.10 above may be modified depending on whether a particular bit plane is enabled or disabled. This is controlled through the Color Plane Enable Register. Table 7.11 illustrates the increasing color resolution available by enabling bit planes.

7.4.2   CGA Emulation

The EGA/VGA can emulate the alphanumeric or graphics modes available in the CGA. This emulation includes the BIOS calls and the addressing of the display memory. Programs that command the CGA directly through the registers may not operate properly on the EGA/VGA. Some EGA/VGA implementations feature true CGA emulation. In the CGA modes, the EGA/VGA display memory is mapped into the host memory address space beginning at B8000 hex. The base address of the I/O ports is set at 3D4 hex.

7.4.3   CGA Graphics Modes

In the CGA emulation modes, the EGA display memory is organized in a packed display format. The 320-by-200 modes, 4 and 5, simulate the CGA low-resolution mode, and the 640-by-200 mode 6 simulates the CGA medium-resolution mode. In the low-resolution mode, each byte contains four neighboring horizontal pixels. In the medium-resolution mode, each byte contains eight neigh-

TABLE 7.10 Graphics Mode Pixels, Bits, and Bit Planes

Mode (Hex)	# of Colors	# Bits per Plane	Bit Planes Affected	Notes
4,5	4	2	0 or 1	1
6	2	1	0	2
D	16	1	0,1,2 and 3	3
E	16	1	0,1,2 and 3	3
F	4	1	0 and 2	4
10	16	1	0,1,2 and 3	3
11	2	1	0	2
12	16	1	0,1,2 and 3	3
13	256	8	0,1,2 or 3	5

Notes:
1. In modes 6 and 11 hex, each pixel consists of one bit in bit plane 0.
2. In modes 4 and 5, alternate bytes of data, each containing four pixels, are stored in bit plane 0 and bit plane 1. Bit plane 0 contributes the low-order bit, and bit plane 2 contributes the high-order bit of the two-bit pixel.
3. In modes D, E, 10, and 12 hex, each pixel corresponds to one bit in each of the four bit planes. Bit plane 0 contributes the low-order bit, followed by bit plane 1, and bit plane 2. Bit plane 3 contributes the high-order bit of the four bit pixel.
4. In mode F hex, bit plane 0 contributes the low-order bit and bit plane 2 contributes the high-order bit of the two bit pixel.
5. In mode 13 hex, all four bit planes are chained together and each pixel consists of eight bits. The plane in which a pixel resides depends on the position of the pixel on the display. Each plane holds one-quarter of the pixels.

TABLE 7.11 Number of Colors versus Planes Enabled

# of Display Planes Enabled	# of Colors
1	2
2	4
3	8
4	16

boring horizontal pixels. Notice that both display modes store an entire horizontal line in 80 bytes.

The CGA does not store display memory contiguously when operating in a graphics mode. Consecutive scan lines are separated by half of the display. Even-numbered scan lines are displayed at the scan line positions 0 to 99, and odd scan lines are displayed at the scan line positions 100 to 199.

Suppose that an image is stored in display memory in a contiguous byte array. The display format requires 80 bytes per horizontal line, with 200 horizontal lines per page. The array contains 80 × 200 = 1,600 bytes. The far left byte of

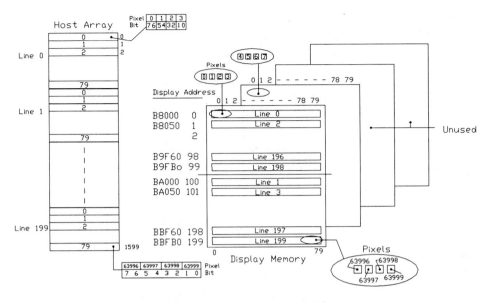

FIGURE 7.2   CGA Addressing Scheme

TABLE 7.12   CGA Graphics Emulation Modes

Display Mode (Hex)	Resolution Pixels	Number of Colors	Starting Address	Number of Pages
4,5	320 by 200	4	B8000	1
6	640 by 200	2	B8000	1
D	320 by 200	16	A0000	4/8
E	640 by 200	16	A0000	2/4

row *n+1* immediately follows the far right byte of row *n*. Each byte in the array is numbered continuously from 0 to 1,599. Figure 7.2 illustrates the way in which this contiguous display array is mapped onto the display. There are 80 characters per scan line and 200 scan lines per display. The Offset Register is set to 80, indicating that the virtual width of the image is 80 bytes.

The CGA graphics emulation modes are listed in Table 7.12. Modes 4, 5, and 6 actually emulate the memory configuration of the CGA, and modes D and E operate differently but also have 200 scan lines per screen.

7.4.4   Modes 4 and 5 (EGA/VGA)

Modes 4 and 5 are graphics modes that use display memory bit planes 0 and 1 to store the graphics information. As far as the EGA/VGA is concerned, there

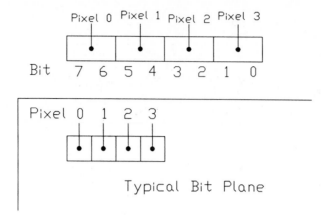

FIGURE 7.3 Modes 4,5: Pixel Packing

is no functional difference between modes 4 and 5. These modes use a display resolution of 320 horizontal pixels per scan line and 200 scan lines. The default character set invoked in these modes is the 8-by-8 character set.

Odd/even addressing techniques force even-numbered bytes to reside in bit plane 0 and odd-numbered bytes to reside in bit plane 1. There are four possible colors for each pixel, requiring two bits per pixel. The EGA/VGA display memory is organized in a packed display form as opposed to a bit-mapped format.

Each pixel is stored in two consecutive bits of a single byte in display memory. Each byte in display memory contains four neighboring horizontal pixels, as indicated in Figure 7.3. Pixel 0 is located to the immediate left of pixel 1, and so on. Only one page is available in either mode 4 or mode 5.

These modes allow a display resolution of 320 pixels per horizontal row by 200 rows per screen. This is equivalent to 64,000 pixels per page. There are four pixels per byte, totaling 16,000 bytes per page. Because two bit planes, bit planes 0 and 1, are used to store the data, only 8,000 bytes are required per page. Alternating bytes of data from the host memory are loaded into bit planes 0 and 1, as shown in Figure 7.4. Each byte of data contains four pixels; thus, one byte containing pixels 0 through 3 resides in bit plane 0; the following byte, containing pixels 4 through 7, resides in bit plane 1.

When display memory is read from or written to, the transfer of data to the two display bit planes occurs automatically because of special hardware in the EGA/VGA. This addressing mode is called *odd/even,* because data read from or written to even locations affects bit plane 0, and data read from or written to odd locations affects bit plane 1.

In Figure 7.5, a byte array in host memory called *data* is copied to display memory. The array consists of alternating character codes and attribute bytes. In the array, the "D" refers to the data byte and the "X" is the index number—

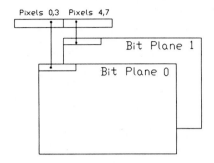

FIGURE 7.4 Modes 4,5: Mapping Data into Display Memory

Mapping Data to Display Memory

Host Array
"Data"

Data	Index
D0	0
D1	1
D2	2
D3	3
D158	158
D159	159
D160	160
D161	161
D162	162
D163	163
D15998	
D15999	

Column 4   7 12 15   316 319

| D1 | D3 | | D159 | Row 0 |
| D321 | D323 | | D479 | Row 2 |

Even Rows
Odd Addresses

| D161 | D163 | | D319 | Row 1 |

Odd Rows
Odd Addresses

Column 0   3 8   11   312   315

| D0 | D2 | | D158 | Row 0 |
| D320 | D322 | | D478 | Row 2 |

Even Rows
Even Addresses

| | | 15998 | Row 199 |

| D160 | D162 | | D318 | Row 1 |

Odd Rows
Even Addresses

| | | 15998 | Row 199 |

FIGURE 7.5 Modes 4,5: Moving Data from a Host Array to Display Memory

that is, 0, 1, 2, .. 79. The data in the data buffer is written to display memory bit planes 0 and 1, as indicated in Figure 7.5.

It should be noted that the memory in the bit plane is segmented into two halves. The upper half contains even scan rows, and the lower half contains odd scan rows. This is added to the fact that alternating bytes are contained in different bit planes. Figure 7.5 shows how four consecutive bytes of host memory, "D158", "D159", "D160", and "D161", are spread through display memory.

Although 16,000 bytes of memory are required per display page, only 8,000 bytes are required in each of the two bit planes because the alternating bytes

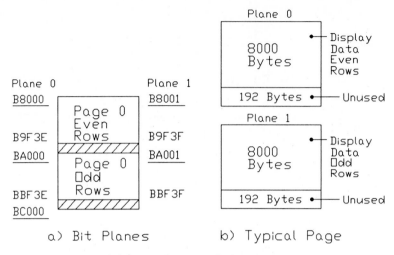

a) Bit Planes   b) Typical Page

FIGURE 7.6   Modes 4,5: Display Memory Map

are loaded into separate bit planes. Because odd/even memory mapping is in effect, only even addresses are accessible in bit plane 0, and only odd addresses are accessible in bit plane 1. A display page therefore requires 16,000 bytes and occupies 16,384 bytes of display memory address space. Up to two display pages can be resident in display memory simultaneously. The mapping of display pages into memory is illustrated in Figure 7.6.

7.4.5   Two-color Graphics Modes

Two display modes are available for performing two-color graphics. The first is mode 6 hex. It is available on both the EGA and the VGA. The second is mode 11 hex. It is available on only the VGA.

7.4.6   Mode 6

Mode 6 is a graphics display mode and uses display memory bit planes 0 and 1 to store the graphics information. It is compatible with the Monochrome Display Adapter (MDA). This mode uses a display resolution of 640 horizontal pixels per scan line and 200 scan lines. The default character set invoked in this mode is the 8-by-8 character set.

Odd/even addressing techniques force even-numbered bytes to reside in bit plane 0 and odd-numbered bytes to reside in bit plane 1. There are two possible colors for each pixel, so one bit is required per pixel.

Each pixel is stored in one bit position of a single byte in display memory. Each byte in display memory contains eight neighboring horizontal pixels, as

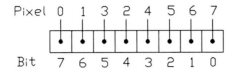

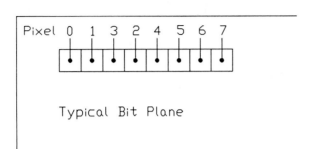

Typical Bit Plane

FIGURE 7.7 Mode 6: Pixel Packing

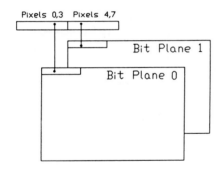

FIGURE 7.8 Mode 6: Mapping Data into Display Memory

indicated in Figure 7.7. Pixel 0 is located to the immediate left of pixel 1, and so on.

This mode allows a display resolution of 640 pixels per horizontal row by 200 rows per screen. This is equivalent to 128,000 pixels per page. Because there are eight pixels per byte, this totals 16,000 bytes per page. Because two bit planes, bit planes 0 and 1, are used to store the data, only 8,000 bytes are required per page. Alternating bytes of data from the host memory are loaded into bit planes 0 and 1, as shown in Figure 7.8. Each byte of data contains eight pixels; thus, one byte, containing pixels 0 through 7, resides in bit plane 0, and the following byte, containing pixels 8 through 15, resides in bit plane 1.

When display memory is read from or written to, the transfer of data to the two display bit planes occurs automatically because of special hardware in the EGA/VGA. This addressing mode is called *odd/even* because data read from or

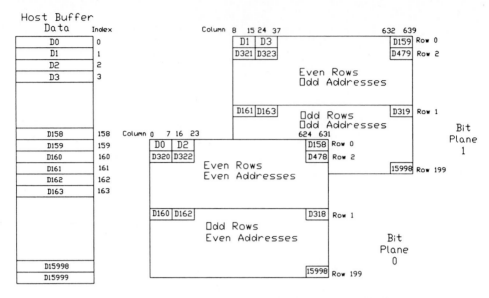

FIGURE 7.9 Mode 6: Moving Data from a Host Array to Display Memory

written to even locations affects bit plane 0, and data read from or written to odd locations affects bit plane 1.

In Figure 7.9, a byte array in host memory called *data* is copied to display memory. The array consists of alternating character codes and attribute bytes. In the array, the "D" refers to the data byte and the "X" is the index number—that is, 0, 1, 2, . . . 79. The data in the data buffer is written to display memory bit planes 0 and 1, as indicated in Figure 7.9.

It should be noted that the memory in the bit plane is segmented into two halves. The upper half contains even scan rows and the lower half contains odd scan rows. This is added to the fact that alternating bytes are contained in different bit planes. Figure 7.9 shows how four consecutive bytes of host memory, "D158", "D159", "D160", and "D161," are spread through display memory.

Although 16,000 bytes of memory are required per display page, only 8,000 bytes are required in each of the two bit planes because the alternating bytes are loaded into separate bit planes. Because odd/even memory mapping is in effect, only even addresses are accessible in bit plane 0, and only odd addresses are accessible in bit plane 1. A display page therefore requires 16,000 bytes and occupies 16,384 bytes of display memory address space. Up to two display pages can be resident in display memory simultaneously. The mapping of display pages into memory is illustrated in Figure 7.10.

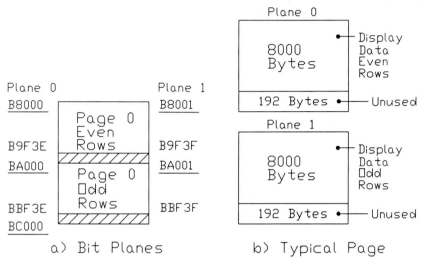

FIGURE 7.10 Mode 6: Display Memory Map

7.4.7 Mode 11 Hex (VGA)

Mode 11 hex is a graphics display mode that uses display memory bit plane 0 to store the graphics information. There are two possible colors for each pixel, so one bit per pixel is required. This mode uses a display resolution of 640 horizontal pixels per scan line and 480 scan lines. The default character set invoked in this mode is the 8-by-16 character set.

Each pixel is stored in one bit position of a single byte in display memory. Each byte in display memory contains eight neighboring horizontal pixels, as indicated in Figure 7.11. Pixel 0 is located to the immediate left of pixel 1, and so on.

This mode allows a display resolution of 640 pixels per horizontal row by 480 rows per screen. This is equivalent to 307,200 pixels per page. There are eight pixels per byte, totaling 38,400 bytes per page. Consecutive bytes in host memory map to consecutive bytes in display memory. The exception is when the offset value loaded into the Offset Register is different from the number of bytes per line. The memory mapping is illustrated in Figure 7.12.

In the following example, a data array in host memory called *data* is written to display memory. The host array is defined as a *char* array, so every element in the array is a byte wide. The elements in the data array each represent eight pixels. An element is named "D.X". The "D" refers to data and the "X" is the index number—that is, 0, 1, 2 . . . 159. If the data in the data buffer is written to display memory, it is loaded into bit plane 0, as indicated in Figure 7.13.

A single page requires 38,400 bytes of memory. Only one display page can

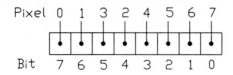

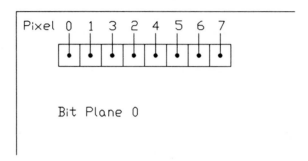

FIGURE 7.11   Mode 11 Hex: Pixel Packing

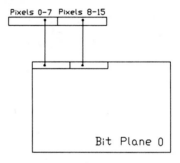

FIGURE 7.12   Mode 11 Hex: Mapping Data into Display Memory

be resident in display memory. However, display memory bit planes 1, 2, and 3 are unoccupied. The mapping of a display page into memory is illustrated in Figure 7.14.

7.4.8   Hercules/MDA Emulation

The EGA/VGA can emulate the Hercules or MDA standards to a certain degree, depending on the EGA implementation. The standard EGA can emulate the alphanumeric mode of the Hercules/MDA, and advanced boards can boast total compatibility. The monochrome graphics systems rely on a high-resolution display screen capable of displaying 720 by 350 pixels. The VGA allows a resolution of 720 by 400 pixels. A corresponding high-resolution character font size of 9 by 14 is used, producing the standard alphanumeric display format of 80 columns by 25 rows for the 350-scan-line mode. A 9-by-16 font is used to

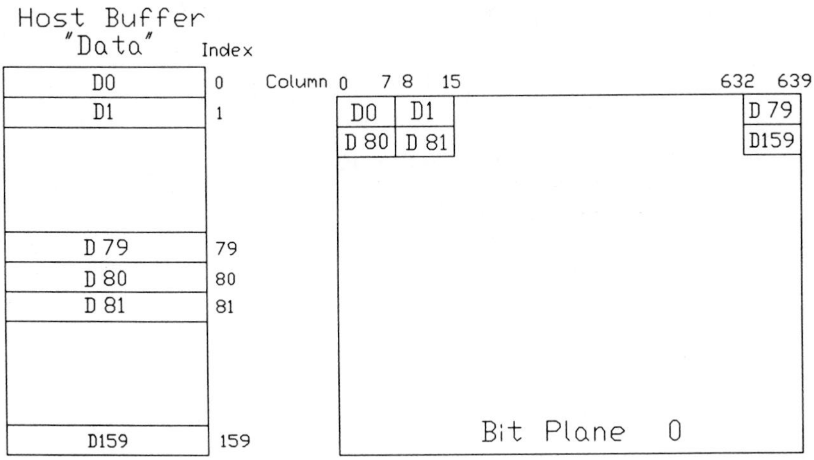

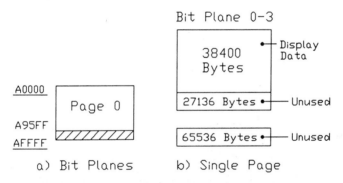

FIGURE 7.13   Mode 11 Hex: Moving Data from a Host Array to Display Memory

FIGURE 7.14   Mode 11 Hex: Display Memory Map

produce the same 80-by-25 character resolution when a 400-scan-line mode is active in the VGA.

The monochrome graphics half mode utilizes 32 Kbytes beginning at address B0000 hex; the full mode occupies 64 Kbytes, also beginning at B0000 hex. The Hercules operates with separate contiguous memory banks in a manner similar to that used by the CGA. However, the CGA splits the display into two banks, whereas the Hercules splits the display into four banks. Therefore, each scan line is separated from its nearest neighbors by one-quarter of the display.

When the EGA is emulating the Hercules, its memory is organized so that two of the four bit planes are used for display memory. Each byte in the display memory represents eight horizontal neighboring pixels. Each pixel is represented by one bit in bit plane 0 and one bit in bit plane 1. Each pixel may be displayed in one of two colors. Two display pages are available, called display

TABLE 7.13 Monochrome Graphics Emulation Modes

Display Mode (Hex)	Resolution	Number of Colors	Starting Address
F	640×350	3	A0000

TABLE 7.14 Monochrome Graphics Attributes

Plane 2	Plane 0	Pixel Color	Attribute Value
0	0	Black	0
0	1	Video	1
1	0	Blinking	4
1	1	Intensify	5

page 0 and display page 1. One of these is selected as the active display page in the Page Select field of the Hercules Mode Control Register.

There is only one monochrome graphics mode in the standard EGA/VGA implementation. It can be used as an enhanced Hercules/MDA graphics display mode. This mode can operate with either a monochrome monitor or an enhanced color monitor. The monochrome graphics display mode is listed in Table 7.13.

Note that the graphics mode F hex is not mapped at the same address as the Hercules graphics memory. In addition, this mode allows a 350-line resolution. Two bit planes, plane 0 and plane 2, are used to contain all of the display data. One bit from plane 0 and one from plane 2 are used together to represent the color. Table 7.14 illustrates the different monochrome attributes possible by representing a pixel in two planes.

If only 16 Kbytes are available per bit plane, two consecutive bit planes can be chained together to form a 32-Kbyte plane. Because four bit planes are available, plane 1 is chained to plane 0, and plane 3 is chained to plane 2. In this way, two 32-Kbyte bit planes are formed. This chaining is controlled in the Chain Odd/Even (COE) field of the Miscellaneous Register.

7.4.9 Mode F Hex (EGA/VGA)

Mode F hex is a four-color graphics display mode. On the EGA, it is designed to drive monochrome monitors that are capable of displaying black, video (white), blinking video, and intensified video. On the VGA, it is designed to drive the enhanced monochrome display monitor. This mode uses a display resolution of 640 horizontal pixels per scan line and 350 scan lines. The default character set invoked in this mode is the 8-by-14 character set.

Mode F hex assumes that a monochrome monitor is attached to the EGA.

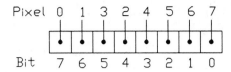

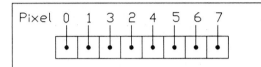

Typical Bit Plane

FIGURE 7.15 Mode F Hex: Pixel Packing

Any other monitor will not necessarily display the data correctly if mode F is active. The VGA can drive the enhanced color monitor or the enhanced mono-chrome monitor when mode F is active.

Mode F hex uses display memory bit plane 0 and bit plane 2 to store the graphics information. There are four possible colors for each pixel, so two bits per pixel are required.

Two bit planes are used to store the data. The attributes associated with this mode contain a video bit field and an intensity bit field. The video bit fields are stored in bit plane 0, and the intensity bit fields are stored in bit plane 2.

In EGA implementations of less than 64 Kbytes per plane, bit planes 0 and 1 are chained together, as are bit planes 2 and 3, in order to provide sufficient memory for an entire page.

Each pixel is stored in one bit position of a single byte in two bit planes of display memory. Each byte in display memory contains eight neighboring hor-izontal pixels, as indicated in Figure 7.15. Pixel 0 is located to the immediate left of pixel 1, and so on.

This mode allows a display resolution of 640 pixels per horizontal row by 350 rows per screen. This is equivalent to 224,000 pixels per page. There are eight pixels per byte, totaling 28,000 bytes per page. The two bit attributes associated with each pixel are mapped into separate bit planes. The video fields associated with each pixel are stored in bit plane 0, and the intensity fields associated with each pixel are stored in bit plane 2. The memory mapping is illustrated in Figure 7.16.

In the following example, a byte array in host memory called *data,* is written to display memory. The elements in the data array each represent four pixels.

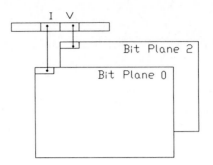

FIGURE 7.16 Mode F Hex: Mapping Data into Display Memory

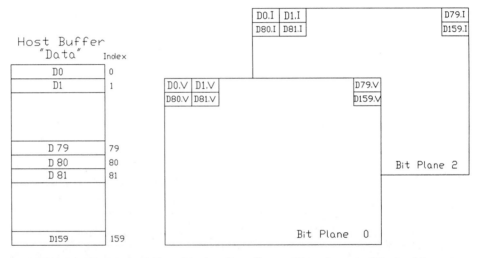

FIGURE 7.17 Mode F Hex: Moving Data from a Host Array to Display Memory

An element is named "D.X". The "D" refers to data and "X" is the index number—that is, 0, 1, 2 . . . 159. The video portion of the data in the data buffer is written to display memory bit plane 0, and the intensity portion of the data is written into bit plane 0. This is illustrated in Figure 7.17.

A single page requires 28,000 bytes of memory. Only one display page can be resident in display memory simultaneously. However, in EGA and VGA systems with 64 Kbytes per bit plane, display memory bit planes 1 and 3 are unoccupied. The mapping of the display page into memory is illustrated in Figure 7.18.

7.4.10 16-color Graphics Modes D, E, 10, and 12 Hex (D, E, 10 EGA/VGA; 12 VGA)

Modes D, E, 10 and 12 hex are graphics display modes that utilize all four display memory bit planes to store the graphics information. Each pixel is rep-

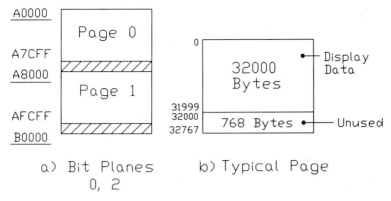

a) Bit Planes 0, 2   b) Typical Page

FIGURE 7.18   Mode F Hex: Display Memory Map

TABLE 7.15   Mapping Bit Position
to Bit Planes

Bit Position	Bit Plane
0	0
1	1
2	2
3	3

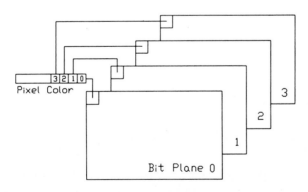

FIGURE 7.19   Modes D,E,10,12 Hex: Mapping Data into Display Memory

resented by four bits, one bit per bit plane. Each byte in display memory represents one bit of eight neighboring horizontal pixels. Because there are four bits per pixel, each pixel can be represented in one of 16 colors. The mapping of bit position to bit plane is shown in Table 7.15.

Each pixel is stored in one bit position of up to four bytes in display memory. This is illustrated in Figure 7.19.

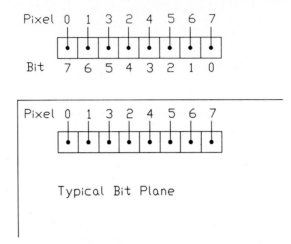

FIGURE 7.20   Modes D,E,10,12 Hex: Pixel Packing

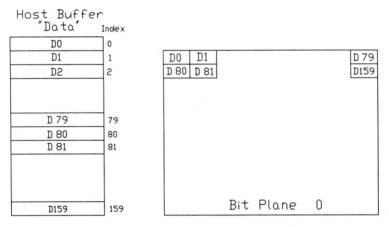

FIGURE 7.21   Modes D,E,10,12 Hex: Moving Data from a Host Array to Display Memory

Each byte in the four bit planes contains eight neighboring horizontal pixels, as indicated in Figure 7.20. Pixel 0 is located to the immediate left of pixel 1, and so on.

In the following example, a byte array in host memory called *data,* is written to display memory. The elements in the data array each represent four pixels. An element is named "D.X". The "D" refers to data and "X" is the index number—that is, 0, 1, 2 . . . 159. The video portion of the data in the data buffer corresponding to bit plane 0 is written to display memory bit plane 0. This is illustrated in Figure 7.21.

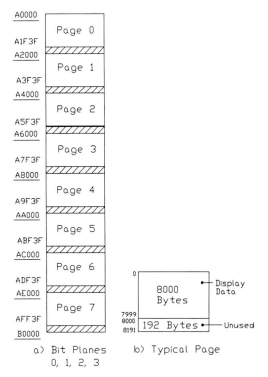

FIGURE 7.22   Mode D Hex: Display Memory Map

7.4.11   Mode D Hex (EGA/VGA)

This mode uses a display resolution of 320 horizontal pixels per scan line and 200 scan lines. This is equivalent to 64,000 pixels per page. There are eight pixels per byte, totaling 8,000 bytes per bit plane per page. Eight pages can reside in display memory simultaneously. The default character set invoked in this mode is the 8-by-8 character set. This allows 40 horizontal characters by 25 character rows. The mapping of display pages into memory is illustrated in Figure 7.22.

7.4.12   Mode E Hex (EGA/VGA)

Mode E hex uses a display resolution of 640 horizontal pixels per scan line and 200 scan lines. This is equivalent to 128,000 pixels per page. There are eight pixels per byte, totaling 16,000 bytes per bit plane per page. Four pages can reside in display memory simultaneously. The default character set invoked in this mode is the 8-by-8 character set. This allows 80 horizontal characters by 25

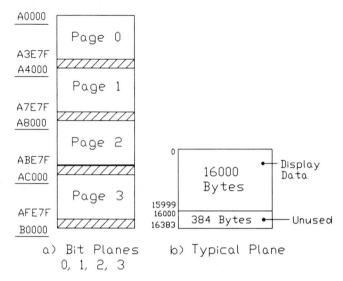

a) Bit Planes 0, 1, 2, 3 b) Typical Plane

FIGURE 7.23   Mode E Hex: Display Memory Map

character rows. The mapping of display pages into memory is illustrated in Figure 7.23.

7.4.13   Mode 10 Hex (EGA/VGA)

Mode 10 hex uses a display resolution of 640 horizontal pixels per scan line and 350 scan lines. This is equivalent to 224,000 pixels per page. There are eight pixels per byte, totaling 28,000 bytes per bit plane per page. Two pages can reside in display memory simultaneously. The default character set invoked in this mode is the 8-by-14 character set. This allows 80 horizontal characters by 25 character rows. The mapping of display pages into memory is illustrated in Figure 7.24.

7.4.14   Mode 12 Hex (VGA Only)

Mode 12 hex uses a display resolution of 640 horizontal pixels per scan line and 480 scan lines. This is equivalent to 307,200 pixels per page. There are eight pixels per byte, totaling 38,400 bytes per bit plane per page. Only one page can reside in display memory. The default character set invoked in this mode is the 8-by-16 character set. This allows 80 horizontal characters by 25 character rows. The mapping of display pages into memory is illustrated in Figure 7.25.

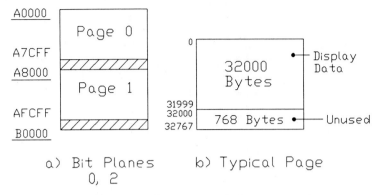

a) Bit Planes
0, 2

b) Typical Page

FIGURE 7.24 Mode 10 Hex: Display Memory Map

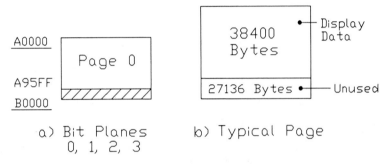

a) Bit Planes
0, 1, 2, 3

b) Typical Page

FIGURE 7.25 Mode 12 Hex: Display Memory Map

7.4.15 256-color Mode (VGA Only)

Only one mode is currently available that allows 256 simultaneous colors. This mode is available only on the VGA, and it is numbered mode 13 hex. The 256 Color Registers are accessed directly by the data in display memory. Each pixel is represented by eight bits, providing the 256 simultaneous colors.

7.4.16 Mode 13 Hex (VGA Only)

There are 256 possible colors for each pixel, so eight bits per pixel are required. Each pixel is stored in one byte of display memory. This byte can reside in any one of the four bit planes. The default character set invoked in this mode is the 8-by-8 character set. This allows 40 horizontal characters by 25 character rows.

This mode allows a display resolution of 320 pixels per horizontal row by 200 rows per screen. This is equivalent to 64,000 pixels per page. Because there is one pixel per byte, there are 64,000 bytes per page. Four bit planes are used

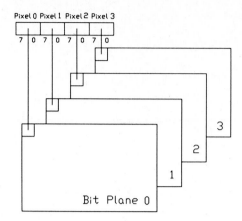

FIGURE 7.26 Mode 13 Hex: Mapping Data into Display Memory

to store the data, so only 16,000 bytes are required per page. Consecutive bytes of data from the host memory are loaded into bit planes 0, 1, 2, and 3 as shown in Figure 7.26. Each byte of data contains one pixel. The first byte, containing pixel 0, resides in bit plane 0, the second in bit plane 1, the third in bit plane 2, and the fourth in bit plane 3. A fifth byte would reside following pixel 0 in bit plane 0.

When display memory is read from or written to, the transfer of data from the host array to the four display bit planes in display memory occurs automatically because of special hardware in the VGA.

In the following example, a byte array in host memory called *data* is written to display memory. The elements in the data array each represent four pixels. An element is named "D.X". The "D" refers to data and "X" is the index number—that is, 0, 1, 2 . . . 159. The video portion of the data in the data buffer is written to display memory bit plane 0, 1, 2, and 3. This is illustrated in Figure 7.27.

A total of 16,000 bytes of memory is required per bit plane. Three out of four bytes in each bit plane are unused and cannot be accessed by the host in this display mode. Thus, the 16,000 bytes actually occupy 64,000 bytes of all four bit planes. At the end of each bit plane is an unused buffer of 1,535 bytes. Similarly, three out of four bytes are not available to the host. Only one display page can be resident in display memory. The mapping of this display page into memory is illustrated in Figure 7.28. Enhanced VGAs use this memory.

7.5 WRITING TO DISPLAY MEMORY

There are two general ways to write to display memory. The first, by far the simplest and slowest, is to use the BIOS call entitled Write Pixel. The second involves writing directly to the display memory.

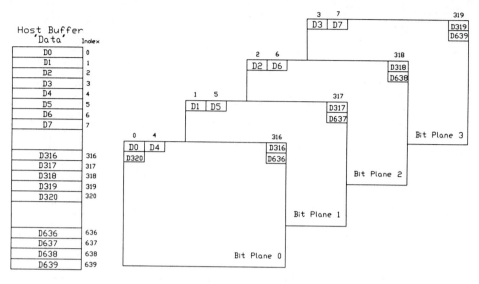

FIGURE 7.27 Mode 13 Hex: Moving Data from a Host Array to Display Memory

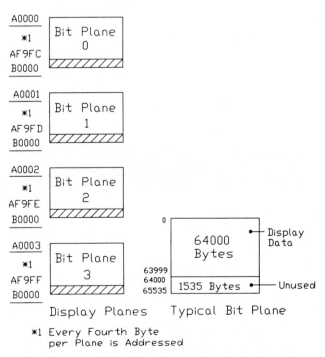

FIGURE 7.28 Mode 13 Hex: Display Memory Map

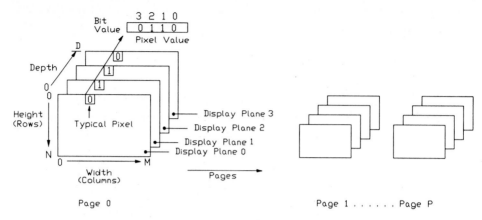

FIGURE 7.29   Four-dimensional Display Memory

The display memory can be thought of as a four-dimensional space. The two standard dimensions are height, or row, and width, or column. The third dimension is depth and relates to the intensity or color of the pixel. This depth value might be located in any or all of the four bit planes, depending on the display mode and the number of planes enabled. Figure 7.29 illustrates this generalized four-dimensional space.

In Figure 7.29, the height ranges from 0 to n rows; the width ranges from 0 to m columns; the depth ranges from 0 to 15; and the page number ranges from 0 to 7 pages.

7.5.1 Writing to Display Memory: BIOS

The Write Dot BIOS call, AH = 0C hex, modifies the value in one pixel location. Depending on the current display mode, this pixel may be represented by a one-bit, two-bit, or four-bit value. The programmer must provide the row number, column number, pixel value, and page number. These parameters correspond to the generalized four-dimensional graphic representation of display memory. A special feature is provided within the pixel value parameter. It causes the pixel value to be written directly into memory or to be logically XORed with the current value in that pixel location of display memory.

Although this BIOS call is simple to use and general enough to handle all display modes, it is extremely slow when a series of dots must be drawn.

7.5.2 Writing to Display Memory: Direct

The descriptions in the sections below involve writing directly to the display memory. To avoid repeating each description for each display format, the most commonly used display format was chosen. These descriptions are targeted for the display mode 10 hex, although they may be readily applied to the other graphics display modes.

7.5.3 Graphics Data Structures

Some general information about graphics data structures is appropriate before the details of writing to display memory are addressed. A pixel is the most primitive graphics element, and a bit is the most primitive computer element. A pixel may be represented by up to four bits in a 16-color system like the EGA.

When a computer has an 8-bit bus, the byte is the most primitive addressable element. A byte consists of eight bits. The smallest element that the computer can write to in a single instruction cycle is a byte.

The display memory is bit mapped and stores the image data in four separate bit planes. Each bit plane is organized into bytes, and each begins at the same host address. This provides an effective 32-bit display word, as illustrated in Figure 7.30.

This 32-bit bus is used in several display operations and may be accessed in a single instruction cycle. Note that at a single host address, one byte from each of the four bit planes contributes to form the 32-bit word. This 32-bit bus is the largest structure that the EGA can manipulate.

The EGA contains a byte-wide interface to the host. The VGA contains a 16-bit-wide bus interface to the host if the VGA is planar. In the Series/2 computers, the VGA is planar if it resides on the host backplane. The VGA contains an 8-bit-wide bus interface to the host if the VGA is an adapter plugged into a computer. This byte-wide bus is multiplexed by the dispatcher onto any or all of the four 8-bit bit plane buses. The Map Mask Register controls which of the planes the data will be written to. If all four planes are selected, the same eight bits will be written to each of the four bit planes. The byte-to-32-bit interface is illustrated in Figure 7.31.

7.5.4 Writing to a Pixel

Three write modes are available in the EGA/VGA. These are set in the Write Mode (WM) field of the Mode Register. The selected write mode dictates the nature of the write operation. Write modes 0, 2, and 3 are used when data is being transferred from the host to the EGA/VGA. Write mode 1 is used when data is being moved from one location in display memory to a second location. Write mode 2 is a convenient tool for writing to one or all bit planes of an individual pixel.

Two values must be determined in order to locate a pixel within the display memory. The first value corresponds to the byte address of display memory that contains the pixel. This value is determined by the row and column coordinates of the desired pixel.

The following example illustrates this process. Suppose that the display for-

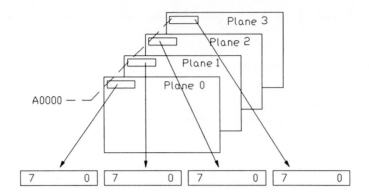

FIGURE 7.30 32-Bit Internal Display Bus

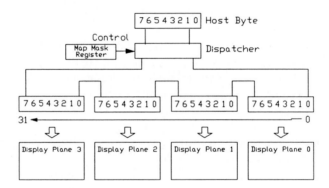

FIGURE 7.31 Host Byte to the 32-Bit Bus Display

mat is 640 horizontal dots by 350 vertical dots. Let the pixel location be at row number 85 and column number 243, resident on display page 0. The display memory address for display page 0 begins at A0000 hex. Each row of the display contains 80 bytes of information. Thus, row 85 corresponds to byte number 6,800 which is 1A90 hex. This is determined by multiplying 80 by 87. The address of the beginning of row 85 is A0000+1A90 hex, or A1A90 hex. Each byte in display memory corresponds to 8 pixels. Therefore, the byte that contains the pixel at column 243 is obtained by dividing the column number by 8. This gives the whole part of 30 with a remainder of 3. The whole part of 30, or 1E hex, is the offset from the start of the row to the byte that contains column 243. The address A1AAE is the address of the desired byte in display memory.

The second value that must be determined in order to find the desired pixel is the bit number within the byte A1AAE hex that corresponds to column 243. This is obtained from the remainder of 3. The byte at A1AAE corresponds to

TABLE 7.16 Pixels in Display Memory at Byte A000:1AAE

Bit	7	6	5	4	3	2	1	0
Column	240	241	242	243	244	245	246	247
Remainder	0	1	2	3	4	5	6	7
Mask (hex)	80	40	20	10	08	04	02	01

pixels 240 to 247. These pixels correspond to the remainders of 0 to 7 when using modulo 8 arithmetic. A remainder of 0 indicates that the far left pixel in the eight neighboring horizontal pixels is selected. This far left pixel is equivalent to the most significant bit of the byte. In this example, the remainder of 3 indicates the fourth pixel from the left in byte A1AAE. In order to enable only this pixel, the Bit Mask Register is used. It must be set to 10 hex to enable this pixel alone. The bit mask value of 10 hex is the second value required to access the pixel. Table 7.16 illustrates the values used to determine the bit mask value.

7.5.5 Write Mode 0 (EGA/VGA)

Write mode 0 is the most commonly used write mode when data is written from the host to the EGA. There are many options within write mode 0, depending on the setting of several of the EGA registers. The most general operation involves taking a byte from the host and writing it directly to one or more of the display memory planes. The data will pass through several hardware sections on its way from the host to the display memory. The path from the host to the display memory is illustrated in Figure 7.32.

7.5.6 Data Rotator

The first section through which the data passes is the barrel rotator. The barrel rotator is capable of shifting the input data from 0 to 7 bits to the right. Bits shifted out of the byte from the right are rotated back into the byte from the left. The number of bits that the input byte are rotated depends on the rotate count in the RC field of the Data Rotate Register. Figure 7.33 illustrates the operation of the barrel rotator, showing it shifting the input byte 3 bits.

7.5.7 Function Select

Once through the rotator, the data passes into the Arithmetic Logic Unit (ALU). Four 8-bit ALU sections are used to modify the data. Four logical operations may occur in the ALU as dictated by the Function Control (FC) field of the Data Rotate Register. These functions are listed in Table 7.17.

Functions 1, 2, and 3 logically combine the input byte with data stored in the

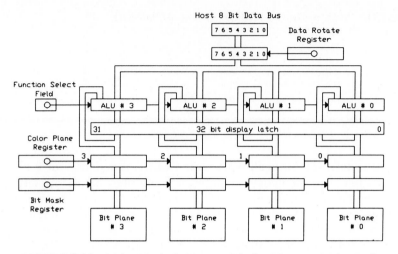

FIGURE 7.32 Write Mode 0: Host-to-Display-Memory Write Path

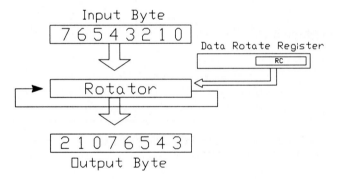

FIGURE 7.33 Barrel Rotator

32-bit processor latch. The 32-bit processor latch is loaded by performing a read operation from the display memory. Eight bits are loaded from each of the four bit planes. An assembly language MOV instruction can be used to read data from the display memory. The source field of this instruction should point to a byte location in display memory. Once this instruction has been executed, 32 bits of data from the four addressed bytes in the four bit planes will be accessed and loaded into the 32-bit processor latch. Each read operation updates this 32-bit register. The data in the latch remains unchanged until the next read operation.

A read-modify-write operation is normally used to logically modify data. For example, the equation $A = A \ \& \ B$ would be read "the value A is equal to the logical ANDing of A and B." To perform this operation, the value A would be

TABLE 7.17 Function Control Field

FC Field	Logical Function
0	Data unmodified
1	Data ANDed with latched data
2	Data ORed with latched data
3	Data XORed with latched data

read. This value is modified by logically ANDing it with *B*. The result is written in place of the original *A* value in display memory.

In assembly language, this operation could be accomplished without the display arithmetic logic unit by the following commands. Assume that the register pair DS:SI points to the selected byte in display memory and that the data to be used in the AND operation is in the AL register.

```
MOV   BL,DS:SI      ;move the display byte into the BL register
AND   AL,BL         ;AL = AL BL
MOV   DS:SI,AL      ;restore the display byte with the result
```

It should be noted that only one bit plane at a time can be accessed by a read operation. Thus, these instructions affect eight pixels in one and only one bit plane. If all four bit planes need to be modified, these instructions would be repeated four times, enabling a different bit plane before each iteration. The plane read is determined by the value in the Read Map Select Register.

This procedure can also be accomplished totally within the confines of the EGA/VGA as follows. A byte in display memory is read into the internal 32-bit EGA/VGA register. This value is ANDed with the data byte being transferred from the host. The result is written back to the display memory in place of the original data.

This technique is implemented in assembly language using the display ALU by first setting the Function Select (FS) field of the Data Rotate Register to the value 1. Again, assuming that the register pair DS:SI points to the desired location in display memory, the same operation can be performed as follows.

```
MOV   BL,DS:SI      ;move the data into the 32-bit register
MOV   DS:SI,AL      ;move the data back into the bit planes
```

The first instruction causes a read to occur. This loads the EGA/VGA 32-bit internal register with the four bytes from the addressed location in the display memory. The data is read into the BL register. However, the BL register in this example is actually a dummy register, since the value loaded into it will not be used. This is called a *dummy read* because it is unimportant whether the data gets to the host. The entire operation will occur within the EGA. The second instruction causes each of the four fields in the 32-bit register to be ANDed with the byte value in the AL register. The result is then written to all planes that are enabled in the Map Mask register. Remember that the AND operation occurs because of the FS field being previously set to 1.

It is important to realize that many instructions were saved using the second technique. The speed advantage was realized because of the internal EGA/VGA 32-bit register. This allows all four bit planes to be accessed in one instruction cycle.

In the previous example, both instructions accessed the same display data causing the $A = A \& B$ operation to be properly performed. If the address is changed between these instructions, the operation $C = A \& B$ will be performed. In this case, the result is not written over the original data because the data in the 32-bit latch remains there until another read operation from display memory occurs. At that time, it is overwritten with the new data. Thus, it is important not to change the address referencing the display memory in between the read and the write operations.

7.5.8 Plane Selection

The Map Mask Register was discussed above. It selects which bit planes will be affected in the write operation. Any plane selected will be modified according to the Function Select field. The logical operation selected by the Function Select field has two operands. The first operand is an 8-bit value provided to the ALU by the MOV instruction. This value will be replicated from one to four times, depending on the number of planes selected, in order to create the 32-bit word. The second operand is a 32-bit value having been loaded into the 32-bit display register.

Suppose that it is desired to XOR the value 55 hex with the byte values in each of the four bit planes at a desired address in the display memory. This byte is denoted in Equation 7.1 by "Byte(Bit Plane n)". All four display memory planes are enabled by loading a 0F hex into the Map Mask Register. An XOR operation is selected by loading a 03 into the Function Select field of the Data Rotate Register. Equation 7.1 illustrates this 32-bit XOR operation.

Equation 7.1 Using the XOR Function

Byte(bit plane 0) = 55 hex .XOR. byte(bit plane 0)

Byte(bit plane 1) = 55 hex .XOR. byte(bit plane 1)

Byte(bit plane 2) = 55 hex .XOR. byte(bit plane 2)

Byte(bit plane 3) = 55 hex .XOR. byte(bit plane 3)

TABLE 7.18 Color Plane Enable Field

CPE Field	Display Plane Enabled
Bit 0 = 1	Select display plane 0
Bit 1 = 1	Select display plane 1
Bit 2 = 1	Select display plane 2
Bit 3 = 1	Select display plane 3

Note that the second operand in each equation is unique, depending on the value in the display memory. Only one unique first operand, equal to 55 in this example, is possible for all four display planes.

The Color Plane Enable (CPE) field of the Color Plane Enable Register is a four-bit field. Each bit is associated with a bit plane, and any bit set to 1 causes the corresponding bit plane to be enabled. Table 7.18 lists the functions of the four bits within this register.

7.5.9 Bit Selection

Only selected bit positions within the four bit planes will be affected during a write operation. There are two levels of selection, the first being the bit plane selection and the second being the bit selection. The 32-bit data is organized as four parallel 8-bit buses, one bus to each of the bit planes. The Map Mask Register is used to determine which bit planes should be affected. The Bit Mask Register is used to determine which bits within all of the selected planes should be affected.

It is often desirable to enable only selected bits within the byte to be written to display memory. To accomplish this, it is necessary to mask certain bits from the write operation. A pixel is represented by a single bit in one or more of the bit planes. A byte is the smallest data structure that the host processor can update in a single instruction. Because a byte contains eight bits, masking is necessary if fewer than eight pixels are to be modified in a single instruction. The Set/Reset Register can also be used when writing to a single pixel. The Bit Mask Register is used to mask bits from the write operation.

Each bit in the Bit Mask Register corresponds to one of eight neighboring horizontal pixels. Any bit set to 1 enables that particular bit to be modified; likewise, any bit reset to 0 protects that bit. The most significant bit in the Bit Mask Register corresponds to the far left pixel on the display. All four bit planes are affected by the same bit plane mask, replicated from one to four times.

7.5.10 Set/Reset Function

The write mode 0 operation described above assumed that all four bits in the Enable Set/Reset Register were disabled. In effect, this disabled the Set/Reset function, and the selected bit planes were modified according to the data byte sent through the host MOV instruction. If one or more of the bits in the Enable Set/Reset Register were enabled, the write operation would take into account the value in the Set/Reset Register.

A single pixel often needs to be modified in all four bit planes. Using the direct approach, as illustrated above, four bytes would have to be sent to the display memory, one for each bit plane. Between each of these byte MOV operations, the Map Mask Register would be modified to select each of the four bit planes independently. The Bit Mask Register would mask out all bits other than the bit in the position associated with the desired pixel location. This requires a good many instructions and therefore a lot of processor time. A useful alternative is the Set/Reset function, which can modify a single pixel in all four bit planes with unique data. The direct approach could enable all four bit planes and thereby load all four bits of a pixel. However, each bit plane would be written with identical data—that is a 1 or a 0.

Suppose a pixel is to be loaded with the value A hex. The value A hex is equivalent to a 1010 binary. Table 7.19 illustrates which bits will be loaded into the four bit planes to achieve this color.

In order to load a pixel with the value A hex, using the Set/Reset approach, the value A hex would be written into the Set/Reset Register and the value F hex would be written into the Enable Set/Reset Register. The A hex corresponds to the desired color, and the value F hex causes all four bit planes to be selected for the Set/Reset function. Once these steps are taken, any write operation to display memory will invoke the Set/Reset function.

A pixel is loaded with the color A hex by writing a dummy value to the desired memory address. Both the address of the byte in display memory that contains the desired pixel and the pixel location within the byte must be determined. Using the same coordinates from the previous example, row 85 and column 243, the host address of A1AAE hex and the Bit Plane Mask value of 10 hex are used to access the desired pixel. Thus, a 10 hex is loaded into the Bit Mask Register. A MOV operation to address A1AAE hex causes the value A hex to be written to the desired pixel. A dummy write operation is used because all four planes will be updated from the Set/Reset Register rather than the host data path. The data coming from the host is ignored. The write instruction itself, regardless of the data, will cause the display update.

The operations that were described to occur on the host data will also modify the Set/Reset data. The Function Select field allows the Set/Reset data to be logically combined with the data resident in the display memory. The Map Mask Register controls which bit planes will be affected, and the Bit Mask Register determines which pixels within a given byte will be affected.

TABLE 7.19 Set/Reset Field

Bit Plane	Bit Value
0	0
1	1
2	0
3	1

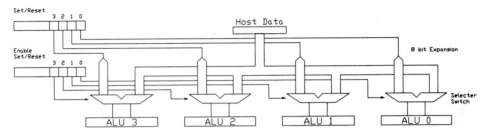

FIGURE 7.34 Set/Reset Example Data Flow

Figure 7.34 illustrates the Set/Reset data path. In this example the Enable Set/Reset Register is set to F hex, thereby selecting the data in the Set/Reset Register for all four data selectors. The value in each of the bit positions is replicated eight times before it is MASKed with the value in the Bit Mask Register. Note that each of the four bytes is MASKed with the identical byte loaded in the Bit Mask Register. Only the bit position enabled in the Bit Mask Register is modified in the bit planes. This bit position corresponds to the desired pixel. All four bit planes are enabled because the Map Mask Register is set to F hex. The write operation occurs directly because the Function Select Field of the Data Rotate Register is set to 0. As a result, no logical operations occur within the ALU.

It is possible to enable all planes in the Enable Set/Reset Register, yet not select desired planes in the Map Mask Register. The Map Mask Register takes precedence. No data will be modified in a bit plane that is not selected.

It is also possible to enable only selected planes in the Enable Set/Reset Register even though those bit planes are selected in the Map Mask Register. The effect is that all planes enabled in the Enable Set/Reset Register will be modified according to the corresponding value in the Set/Reset Register. The other planes will be modified depending on the data sent by the host. It therefore is possible to perform two independent operations in a single instruction cycle.

Suppose the Set/Reset Register contains an A hex and the Enable Set/Reset Register contains a 3 hex. The 3 in the Enable Set/Reset Register enables bit planes 0 and 1 for the Set/Reset Function. The corresponding bits in the Set/Reset register are 0 and 1 respectively. Further, suppose that the value of 40 hex is in the Bit Mask Register, thereby selecting one pixel. The Function Select field is assumed to be 0, thereby allowing a straight write operation. The following instruction would move the byte value BB hex to a byte in display memory addressed by DS:SI. Because the Bit Mask Register is a 40 hex, bit 6 of the host word will be copied to both display planes 2 and 3.

```
MOV   AL,OBBh        ;Load the AL register with BB hex
MOV   DS:SI,AL       ;Write BB hex to display memory
```

The effects on the pixel in display memory are shown in Table 7.20.

Programmers may find unique applications for this combined technique.

7.5.11   Write Mode 1 (EGA/VGA)

It is possible to move 32 bits of data from one display memory location to another in a single instruction cycle using write mode 1. This can greatly enhance the performance of the EGA by speeding up move operations. Combined with the MOV string instructions, large amounts of display memory can be moved rapidly. In the MOV string operation, both the source and destination fields must address display memory because this 32-bit move operation cannot be extended into the host memory, which is usually restricted to an 8-bit bus. The Data Rotator, the Set/Reset function, the ALU, and the bit mask are completely ignored in this write mode.

The internal bus of the EGA/VGA is 32 bits wide. This bus is written to during a processor read operation. The four bit planes contribute a byte of data each to the 32-bit latch when the processor reads a byte of information from display memory. The read operation occurs when a MOV instruction is executed with the source field addressing display memory. When write mode 1 is enabled, the data written to display memory in a MOV instruction comes from the display 32-bit latch; it is not presented by the host in the MOV instruction. All planes that are selected in the Map Mask Register will be updated with the data in the corresponding byte of the 32-bit display latch.

This powerful feature is a prime reason for having a display memory that is larger than the active display region. Images can be stored in nondisplayed regions of the display memory and then rapidly moved into the display region, 32 bits at a time. Using the MOV string operation, a contiguous block of data can be moved from one area of display memory to another. The host CX Register contains the number of bytes to move. The DS:SI Register pair points to the source data, and the ES:DI Register pair points to the destination data. Again, both must address display memory. This operation is illustrated in Figure 7.35.

The Move String Byte (MOVSB) instruction first reads a byte of data as

TABLE 7.20   Effects of the Set/Reset Function

Bit Plane	Pixel Value	Reason
0	0	Bit 0 of Set/Reset = 0
1	1	Bit 1 of Set/Reset = 1
2	0	Bit 6 of host byte = 1
3	0	Bit 6 of host byte = 1

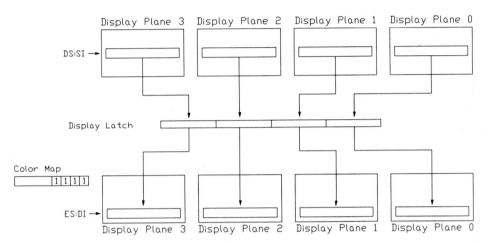

FIGURE 7.35   Write Mode 1

addressed by the source address field. The source address points to a byte in each of the display memory planes. These four bytes are written into the 32-bit display latch. The next function of the MOVSB instruction is to write the byte into memory as addressed by the destination address field. Again the data byte itself is ignored, and the 32-bit data in the display latch is loaded into the four bit planes. The CX count register is decremented and the process repeats until the count is zero, thereby moving a continuous block of data. The Move String Word (MOVSW) instruction could have been used. It operates identically to the Move String Byte (MOVSB) instruction except that a word is moved. Because the EGA has a byte interface to the host, this results in a slight speed improvement by reducing the instruction cycle time within the host. Because the internal display bus is 32 bits wide, it is not possible for the MOVSW instruction to result in 16 bits from each of the four bit planes being moved simultaneously.

A severe limitation of the write mode 1 feature is that each of the bytes in each bit plane represents eight pixels. Ideally, the 32-bit move instruction should shift the data before it is rewritten to the display memory. This would allow pixel alignment to occur. Without this ability, the source and destination blocks of data in the display memory are constrained to be byte-aligned data. This coarse movement results from the fact that each byte actually corresponds to eight pixels. It is only possible to move a group of pixels beginning at a pixel address that is a multiple of eight to a pixel address that is also a multiple of eight. The display can be considered as having a set of grid lines drawn every eighth pixel. The minimum block size that can be moved is 8 pixels, corresponding to the eight bits in a byte. The block size to be moved must be a multiple of eight, and the source and destination blocks must begin on the grid lines.

For example, suppose it is desirable to move a section of the image that begins at pixel 111 to a section that ends at pixel 317. The closest a programmer can come to pixel 111 is either 104 or 112. To include pixel 111 in the move operation, it is necessary to begin the move at pixel 104. The destination of the move must also be aligned to a multiple of eight. The nearest grid lines are 312 or 320. To include pixel 317, the best approximation to this move operation would be from pixel 104 to pixel 320.

7.5.12 Write Mode 2 (EGA/VGA)

The operation of write mode 2 is similar to the Set/Reset function in write mode 0. The purpose of this mode is to update a single pixel, represented in up to four bit planes. This mode, rather than the Set/Reset mode, would be selected when a group of pixels is to be updated. The group of bytes representing these pixels would be in a format where each byte would contain the four bits of the intensity to be loaded into each pixel. If 100 pixels are to be loaded, the host byte array would be 100 bytes long, and each byte would contain a four-bit value for each pixel. A MOVS string operation could copy this data quickly from the host array into the contiguous block of pixels. The data rotator and the Set/Reset function are ignored in this write mode.

The four-bit value to be loaded into the pixel is written to display memory via a MOV instruction in a similar fashion as the direct approach in write mode 0. For a single pixel to be modified, the Bit Mask Register must be loaded with the proper code byte to enable only that selected pixel. (Multiple pixels can be selected for the write operation by setting more than one bit in the Bit Mask Register.) Each bit in the four-bit value being moved to display memory is replicated eight times before it gets to the ALU. This is similar to the replication of the bits from the Set/Reset Register. This replication ensures that the data will be in the proper bit position for each of the four bit planes, regardless of which bit or bits are enabled in the Bit Mask Register. Figure 7.36 illustrates the functioning of write mode 2.

The destination field of the MOV instruction is contained in the DS:SI host register pair. The data to be moved in this example is B hex. The following instructions perform this operation, assuming that write mode 2 is in effect.

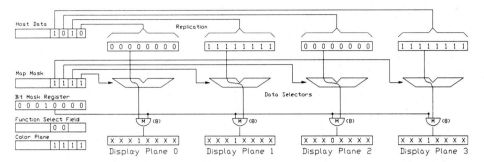

FIGURE 7.36   Write Mode 2

```
MOV   AL,0Bh         ;Move B hex into the AL register
MOV   DS:SI,AL       ;Move the B hex into all four bit planes
```

Note that up to eight pixels can be loaded with identical data if more than one bit in the Bit Mask Register is enabled.

7.5.13   Write Mode 3 (VGA Only)

Write mode 3 is relevant to the VGA only. Each plane is written to with eight identical bits. The bit value (1 or 0) selected for each of the four display planes (3–0) are derived from the corresponding bit positions in the SR field of the Set/Reset Register. Recall that the SR field has four bits, bits 3–0. The data written from the host is rotated according to the value in the Data Rotate Register. It is then ANDed with the Bit Mask Register to form an 8-bit value that acts as the Bit Mask for the write operation. The eight identical bits derived from the Set/Reset Register are masked with this resultant value before being written to the display memory. Figure 7.37 illustrates the operation of write mode 3.

7.6   READING FROM DISPLAY MEMORY

As is the case when writing to display memory, programmers may select to read from display memory using BIOS calls or by reading directly from the display memory.

7.6.1   Reading Display Memory: BIOS

The Read Dot BIOS call, AH=0D hex, reads the value in one pixel location. Depending on the current display mode, this pixel may be represented by a one-bit, two-bit, or four-bit value. The programmer must provide the desired page number and the row and column coordinates. These coordinates correspond to the generalized four-dimensional graphic representation. Although

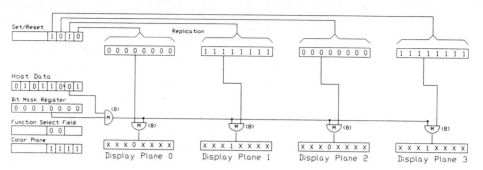

FIGURE 7.37 Write Mode 3

this BIOS call is simple to use and general enough to handle all display modes, it is extremely slow when a series of dots must be read.

7.6.2 Reading Display Memory: Direct

Two means can be used to read data from the display memory to the host. The first is a direct transfer from display memory to host, and the second reads the result of a comparison. These two read modes are selected through the Read Mode (RM) field of the Mode Register.

Only eight bits of information can be read back from the display memory at a time. The display memory is organized into four bit planes. A pixel may be represented by one or more bits in one or more of the bit planes. A read operation, invoked through a MOV instruction, reads from one of these four bit planes. The Read Map Select Register is used to select which of the bit planes will be selected. Only one bit plane may be read from the display memory to the host in a single instruction cycle. It is referred to as read mode 0.

A second type of read operation involves reading the result of a comparison. This is useful when color comparisons are being made. A great deal of time can be saved when it is necessary to determine if a pixel or group of pixels are a certain value. This comparison allows a maximum of eight pixels, each spanning up to four bit planes, to be compared to a selected color. The byte result of these comparisons is returned to the host as a byte value. Pixels that match the desired color cause a 1 to be returned in their corresponding bits of the returned byte. Pixels that do not match cause a 0 to be returned in their corresponding bit position.

7.6.3 Read Mode 0

Read mode 0 allows the programmer to read the contents of the display memory. Because each of the four bit planes is accessed at the same location in host address space, only one of the bit planes can be accessed in a read instruction.

TABLE 7.21 Read Map Register

Read Map Field	Display Plane Selected
0	0
1	1
2	2
3	3

A read operation can be initiated from the host via a MOV instruction with the source field addressing display memory. This instruction causes all four bit planes to be loaded simultaneously into the 32-bit EGA/VGA internal register. Although all four bit planes are read in the instruction, only one byte can be directed to the host via a MOV instruction. The Read Map Select Register is used to select which of the four bit planes will be read. The Read Map Select field contains a two-bit binary encoded value that determines which plane should be selected. Table 7.21 lists the possible options. Note that only one plane can be selected at a time. This contrasts with the Map Mask Register, in which any combination of planes can be enabled at one time during write operations.

A block diagram of read mode 0 is illustrated in the Figure 7.38.

In this example, the MOV instruction addresses the desired byte in all four planes through the DS:SI register pair. The Read Map Register is loaded with a 1, which selects bit plane 0. The byte value in bit plane 0 at DS:SI is transferred to the AL Register by the following instruction.

```
MOV  AL,DS:[SI]        ;read a byte from display memory to AL
```

Note that a block of display memory can be transferred readily to the host memory using the string instructions.

If the EGA/VGA has the odd/even addressing fields enabled, reading data from the bit planes may not produce the desired result. The odd/even addressing automatically directs bytes of data from the host that correspond to even addresses to even bit planes. Similarly, bytes of data that correspond to odd addresses are directed to odd bit planes. This is used in the alphanumeric modes so that the character codes are placed into bit plane 0 and the attribute bytes are placed in bit plane 1. Reading data in read mode 0 while the odd/even addressing mode is active will cause every other byte to be read from alternate planes, regardless of the setting of the Read Map Register. Thus, it is impossible to read 10 bytes of contiguous data from bit plane 0 with the odd/even mode in effect. Every other byte—that is, the odd addresses—of bit plane 0 will be ignored. These will be replaced with data corresponding to the even addresses from bit plane 1. To read these 10 contiguous bytes of memory, the display mode needs to be changed so that odd/even addressing is disabled.

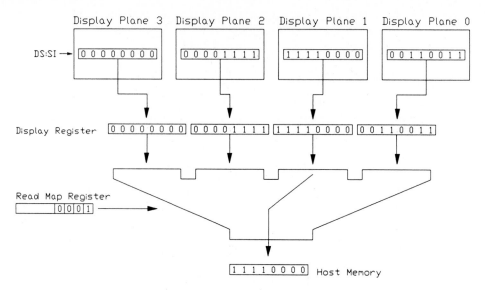

FIGURE 7.38 Read Mode 0

The odd/even addressing mode is complicated to control and it is perhaps best changed by getting out of the alphanumeric modes without a screen erase. The odd/even related fields are listed in Table 7.22.

Read mode 0 ignores the value in the Read Map Select Register when the VGA is in display mode 13 hex. In this mode, all four planes are chained together and a pixel is represented by one byte.

7.6.4   Read Mode 1

Read mode 1 returns the result of a comparison to the host via a MOV instruction. A block of comparisons can be invoked by using the move string instructions. The Color Compare Register holds a four-bit value corresponding to the four-bit value of a pixel. Each bit in the Color Compare Register represents the bit value in each of the four bit planes. The relationship between the bits in the Color Compare Register and the bit planes is illustrated in Figure 7.39.

In Figure 7.39, if the Color Compare Register is loaded with the value 6, and the pixel addressed in display memory also has a value of 6, the result of the comparison will be true.

A positive comparison will result in a 1 being loaded into the corresponding bit position of the byte returned to the host. Likewise, a negative comparison will result in a 0 being loaded into the corresponding bit position of the byte returned to the host. The results of eight comparisons, each up to four bits wide, can be returned to the host in a single instruction.

It is not necessary to use all of the four bits in the Color Compare Register

TABLE 7.22 Odd/Even Related Fields

Field	Register Name
O/E Odd/Even	Memory Mode
O/E Odd/Even Page	Misc. Output
O/E Odd/Even	Mode Register
COE Chain Odd to Even	Miscellaneous

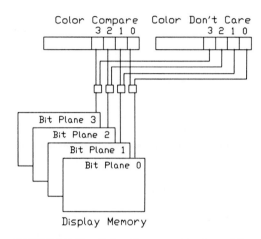

FIGURE 7.39 Color Compare Register Bits

when comparing the pixel values in display memory. Bit planes can be selected as being significant in the comparison or deselected as insignificant, depending on the corresponding values set in the Color Don't Care Register. Similar to the bit positions in the Color Compare Register, those in the Color Don't Care Register correspond to the bit planes. Thus, the value in bit position 0 dictates whether bit plane 0 should be considered in the comparison. Any bit set to a 1 in the Color Don't Care Register causes the corresponding bit in the Color Compare Register and the pixel value in the corresponding bit plane not to be used in the comparison. Likewise, any bit reset to a 0 in the Color Don't Care Register causes the corresponding bit plane to be used in the comparison. By selecting only desired planes, programmers can have comparisons performed on images that have pixels that are less than four bits deep. In addition, it is possible to compare classifications of pixels.

For example, a comparison can be made to determine all pixels whose most significant bit is a 1. To accomplish this, the Color Compare Register must be loaded with an 8, indicating that the comparison should look for a pixel whose value in bit plane 3 is a 1. In fact, this register could be loaded with any value whose most significant bit is a 1 because the other three bits will be ignored anyway. The Color Don't Care Register would be loaded with 7, indicating that only bit 3, the most significant bit, should be considered as being significant.

In the following example, a byte of display memory is accessed through a MOV instruction. The eight-bit result of the comparison will be loaded into the AL register. The DS:SI register pair points to the desired display memory address. Assuming that the Read Mode (RM) field of the Mode Register is set to 0, the following instruction would return the result of the comparison into the AL register.

```
MOV  AL,DS:[SI]       ;load the comparison result into AL
```

Each byte addressed in the four display memory planes contains eight pixels of information. All four planes are considered significant because a 0 is loaded into the Color Don't Care Register. The result of the comparison shows that there are three pixels in the group of eight pixels that compare true to the Color Compare value of A hex. This example is illustrated in Figure 7.40.

The Color Don't Care Register can be used to select which planes are significant. Table 7.23 illustrates some possible outcomes of the above example had the Color Don't Care Register contained different values.

7.7 DISPLAY MEMORY TIMING

The EGA/VGA controls the video bus sent to the monitor. This bus consists of the horizontal sync pulse, the vertical sync pulse, and the video signals. The video signals vary depending on the type of monitor being used. These signals are listed in Table 7.24 according to monitor type.

7.7.1 Sync Pulses

The horizontal and vertical sync pulses dictate the scan rate of the display. The horizontal sync pulse occurs once every horizontal line. The vertical sync pulse occurs once every screen refresh period. The monitor must be capable of operating at the frequencies being generated by the EGA or the VGA. In a low-resolution color mode with 320-by-200 or 640-by-200 resolution, most monitors expect the horizontal sync pulses to occur at a rate of 17.75 kHz with a vertical sync rate of 60 Hz. A high-resolution EGA monitor or a monochrome monitor expects the horizontal frequency to occur at a rate of 21.85 kHz with a vertical sync rate of 60 Hz. A VGA monitor must be capable of operating at a horizontal sync rate of 31.46 kHz with a vertical sync rate of 70.08 Hz.

It should be noted that at these rates a maximum of 262 horizontal lines is possible in the low-resolution case, with 364 lines possible in the EGA resolution. Because the monitor must allow time for the vertical refresh period, the maximum number of lines is limited to 200 and 350 for the EGA and 480 for the

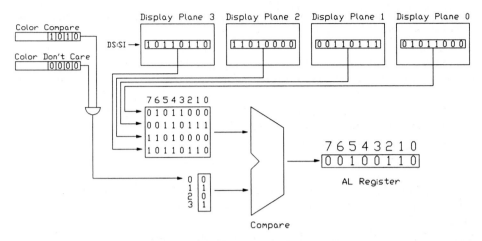

FIGURE 7.40 Read Mode 1 Example

TABLE 7.23 Color Don't Care Values

Color Don't Care Binary	Result of Comparison	Compare x = Either	Significant Planes
0111	10110110	1xxx	3
0011	10010000	10xx	3,2
1011	00101111	x0xx	2
1000	00100111	x010	2,1,0
0000	00100110	1010	3,2,1,0

TABLE 7.24 Monitor Types

Monitor Type	Video Signals	Type
Monochrome	Video, Intensity	Digital
RGBI Color	Red, Green, Blue, Intensity	Digital
RrGgBb Color	Red (2), Green (2), Blue (2)	Digital
RGB Color	Red, Green, Blue	Analog

VGA. The autosync monitors, called *multisync,* are capable of operating over a wide range of frequencies, allowing even higher resolutions than are currently output.

7.7.2 Horizontal Refresh Timing

The horizontal sync pulse synchronizes the monitor to the EGA/VGA. The EGA/VGA sends data on the video lines to the monitor. The serial data stream that feeds the monitor begins at the left of the screen and scans across to the right of the screen. At the end of a line, a horizontal sync pulse indicates the end of the line. Upon receiving this pulse, the monitor will send the electron beam back to the left border of the screen and begin scanning to the right again. The rate at which the monitor scans the electron beam across the phosphor is generated inside the monitor. This is one reason why the EGA/VGA and the monitor must be compatible. If the EGA/VGA is sending data too slowly, the monitor scanning will reach the right side of the screen and then wait for the next horizontal sync pulse. This results in the left portion of the data being displayed on the monitor. This section of data would appear to be stretched across the screen. Likewise, if the data is being output too quickly, the data will be squeezed on the right side of the screen. If the sync pulses are sent out too quickly, the monitor scanning will never refresh the right portion of the screen.

The horizontal timing pulses are illustrated in Figure 7.41.

The top part of Figure 7.41 represents the monitor screen. On the left of the screen is the border region, also called the *front porch*. It is followed by the displayed video data portion of the screen. The data representing one horizontal scan line is displayed in this portion of the display. This is followed by a right border, also called the *back porch*.

The EGA/VGA contains an internal character counter. It is reset to 0 when its value is equal to the value loaded into the Horizontal Total Register. The character counter increments by 1 for each character scan line output. In the EGA/VGA, the number of pixels per scan line in a character is typically eight or nine. Horizontal events are driven when the character counter equals one of the values set in the relevant horizontal registers. The basic horizontal events are horizontal sync, display enable, and horizontal blanking.

The horizontal sync pulse is the master timing pulse in the horizontal timing cycle. It is an active high pulse that begins when the character counter equals the value in the Start Horizontal Retrace Register. It ends when the low-order five bits of the character counter equal the value in the End Horizontal Retrace Register. The horizontal sync pulse signals the monitor to begin the retrace period.

The horizontal display enable signifies when the video data input from the display memory is being output to the display. The Horizontal Total Register dictates how many characters are present on a scan line. When the character counter reaches this value, the end of the scan line is issued and the character counter is reset. It is important to realize that the start of the horizontal timing period does not begin at the same time as when the display electron beam is at the left side of the screen. Intuitively, this would seem logical. However, displays are set up so that the start of the horizontal timing period coincides with the start of the display enable period. This positions the refresh period and left border after the right border.

Figure 7.42 illustrates the timing as it appears from the character counter.

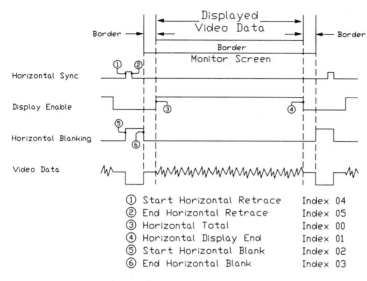

① Start Horizontal Retrace   Index 04
② End Horizontal Retrace   Index 05
③ Horizontal Total   Index 00
④ Horizontal Display End   Index 01
⑤ Start Horizontal Blank   Index 02
⑥ End Horizontal Blank   Index 03

FIGURE 7.41   Horizontal Timing

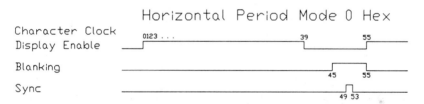

FIGURE 7.42   Horizontal Timing Mode 0

The numbers are the actual values used in the IBM EGA when the display is in a 40-character-per-line alphanumeric mode called display mode 0. Note that the active display region, which is indicated by the Display Enable signal being high, displays 40 characters numbered 0 to 39. The entire horizontal timing period consists of 55 characters, 40 displayed and 15 undisplayed.

Figure 7.43 shows the numbers used by the IBM during the 640-dots-per-line graphics mode called display mode 10 hex.

Note that the horizontal sync period takes up the entire horizontal blanking period. This is necessary when enhanced EGA multisync-type monitors are being driven.

7.7.3 Vertical Refresh Timing

The EGA/VGA controls the vertical refresh rate of the display system. The monitor must be properly synchronized with the EGA for the system to maintain proper vertical sync. The vertical timings are similar to the horizontal timings,

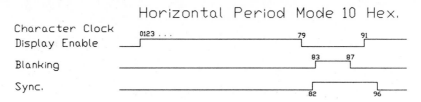

FIGURE 7.43 Horizontal Timing Mode 10 hex

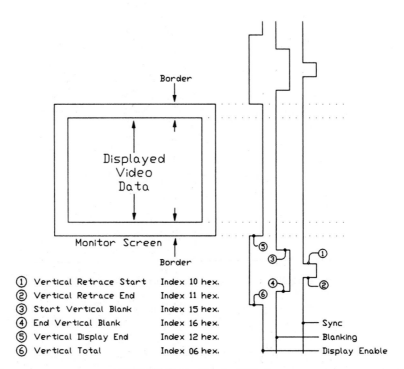

FIGURE 7.44 Vertical Timing

including a vertical sync pulse, vertical display enable, and vertical blanking. Figure 7.44 illustrates the vertical timing signals.

The left portion of this figure represents the monitor screen. On the top of the screen is the top border region, also called the *front porch*. It is followed by the displayed video data portion of the screen. The data representing each horizontal scan line is displayed in this portion of the display. This is followed by a bottom border, also called the *back porch*.

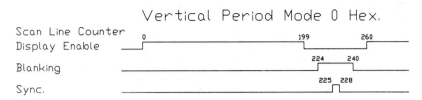

FIGURE 7.45   Vertical Timing Mode 0

Internal to the EGA/VGA is a horizontal scan line counter. When its value is equal to the value loaded into the Vertical Total Register it is reset to 0. The scan-line counter increments by one for each scan-line output. Vertical events are driven when the scan-line counter equals one of the values set in the relevant vertical registers. The basic vertical events are vertical sync, display enable, and vertical blanking. Each of these is represented in several of the EGA/VGA registers. It should be noted that the scan-line counter will get larger than 256, which is the largest value that can be stored in a byte register. An additional register called the Overflow Register is necessary to hold the ninth bit of the relevant vertical registers.

The vertical sync pulse is the master timing pulse in the vertical timing cycle. It is an active high pulse that begins when the scan-line counter equals the value in the Start Vertical Retrace Register. It ends when the low-order five bits of the scan-line counter equal the value in the End Vertical Retrace Register. The vertical sync pulse signals the monitor to begin a new screen, sending the electron beam back to the top left corner of the display.

The vertical display enable signifies when the horizontal lines of video data input from the display memory are being output to the display. The Vertical Total Register dictates how many scan lines are present on a display screen. When the scan-line counter reaches this value, the end of the scan line is issued and the scan-line counter is reset. It is important to realize that the start of the vertical timing period does not begin at the same time as when the display electron beam is at the top of the screen. Intuitively, it would seem logical. However, displays are set up so that the start of the vertical timing period coincides with the start of the display enable period. This positions the refresh period and top border after the bottom border. Figure 7.45 draws the timing as it appears from the character counter for display mode 0.

The numbers in this figure are the actual values used in the IBM EGA when the display is in a 200-scan-line alphanumeric mode called display mode 0. Note that the active display region, which is indicated by the Display Enable signal being high, displays 200 scan lines numbered 0 to 199. The entire vertical timing period consists of 260 scan lines, 200 displayed and 60 undisplayed.

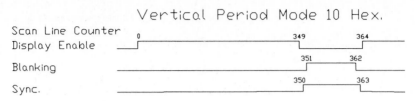

FIGURE 7.46 Vertical Timing Mode 10 hex

Figure 7.46 shows the numbers used by the IBM during the 350-scan-line graphics mode called display mode 10 hex.

Note that the vertical sync period takes up the entire vertical blanking period. This is necessary when enhanced EGA/VGA multisync-type monitors are being driven.

Chapter 8

Color Palette and Color Registers

8.1 COLOR PALETTE

A color palette is a lookup table that is used to convert the data associated with a pixel in the display memory into a color. A color palette provides a graphics adapter with a great deal of power and flexibility. In the VGA, the color palette is enhanced by the Color Registers.

A color palette allows the programmer to change the colors rapidly. For example, an image on the EGA/VGA can occupy 256 Kbytes of display memory. In a 16-color mode, only 16 colors can be displayed simultaneously. All 256 Kbytes of data in the display memory must be modified to change the colors on the display if a color palette is not present. With a color palette, only 16 bytes would have to be changed.

Another advantage of using a color palette is that the total number of possible colors can be greater than the number of colors that can be displayed simultaneously. In the 16-color modes, 16 colors can be displayed simultaneously. However, because of the Palette Registers in the EGA, these 16 colors can be selected from 64 possible colors. Each color in the Palette Registers is represented by six bits. In the VGA, this expansion is even more significant. In the 256-color mode, 256 simultaneous colors can be displayed. Each color is represented by 18 bits within the Color Registers, providing a selection from 256 Kcolors.

8.1.1 Palette Registers

The color palette consists of 16 Palette Registers. The data in the bit planes consists of from one to eight bits of information per pixel. The data corresponding to each pixel addresses one of the Palette Registers. In the EGA, the selected Palette Register produces a color that is output to the monitor. This path is illustrated in Figure 8.1.

In the VGA, the selected Palette Register produces another address, not a color code. This address is used to access one of the Color Registers which

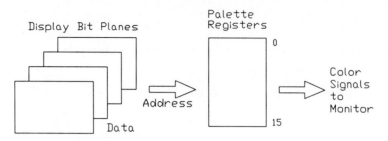

FIGURE 8.1 EGA Conversion of Data to Colors

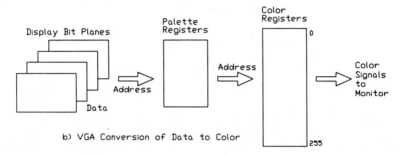

b) VGA Conversion of Data to Color

FIGURE 8.2 VGA Conversion of Data to Colors

contain the color codes. There are 256 Color Registers on the VGA. This process is illustrated in Figure 8.2.

In the alphanumeric modes, each character is represented by two values. One is for the foreground pixels of a character, and a second is for the background pixels. Each of these foreground and background values accesses a Palette Register. These values are stored in the character attribute.

In the graphics modes, each pixel is represented by one to eight bits in the display bit plane memory. The location of these bits, which represent a single pixel, depends on the active display mode. Figure 8.3 illustrates the palette addressing schemes used in the various display modes.

8.1.2   Codes Contained in the Palette Registers

Each of the Palette Registers contains six bits of information. In all of the display modes, with the exception of mode 13 hex in the VGA, these six bits define a color. In mode 13 hex, these six bits define a sequential address that accesses a Color Register. The color code contained in the Palette Register must conform to the monitor connected to the video system. For the EGA, a monochrome, RGBI color, or RrGgBb enhanced color monitor may be used. The color coding used in the EGA Palette Registers is illustrated in Figure 8.4.

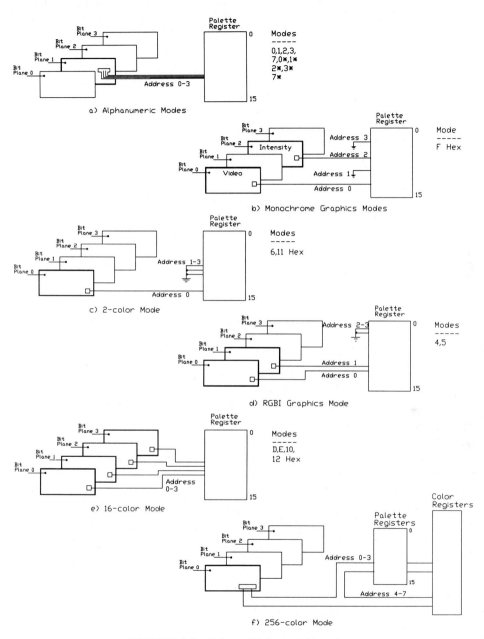

FIGURE 8.3   Palette Register Addressing

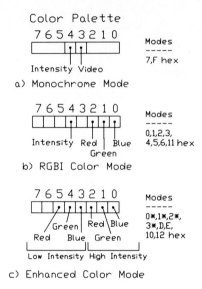

FIGURE 8.4 EGA Palette Register Color Codes

8.1.3 EGA Palette Register Outputs

In the EGA, the colors output to the monitor are contained in the Palette Registers according to the color codes in Figures 8.4A–C. Figure 8.5 illustrates the variety of output color codes presented to the monitors. The output format is determined by the configuration sense switch settings, which in turn depend on the monitor type.

8.1.4 VGA Palette Register Outputs

For the VGA, either an enhanced monochrome or enhanced color monitor may be used. The VGA automatically determines the monitor installed. The output format used in the VGA Palette Registers is illustrated in Figure 8.6.

In the VGA, the colors output to the monitor are contained in the Color Registers. These registers are accessed by the value in the Palette Registers, as illustrated in Figure 8.7.

8.1.5 Accessing the Palette Registers

The Palette Registers are contained in a dual-ported memory. The display memory requires access to the Palette Registers in order to refresh the display. The host requires access to the Palette Registers during read or write operations. The process of accessing the dual-ported Palette Registers is illustrated in Figure 8.8.

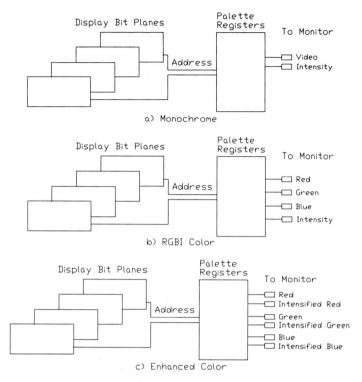

FIGURE 8.5 EGA Palette Outputs

This dual-ported memory is accessed through a host port register at host I/O address 3C0. This port has two different functions. One is to index the Palette Registers. In this mode, it is called the Attribute Address Register. A second is to act as a portal to the Palette Registers. In this mode, it may be thought of as a data register, similar to the data registers of the other EGA/VGA register groups.

An internal hardware flip-flop is used that multiplexes this port to load either this Attribute Address Register or one of the Attribute Registers. When the flip-flop is in the clear state, data output from the host to port 3C0 hex is directed to this Attribute Address Register. When the flip-flop is in the set state, data written to this port is directed to whichever Attribute Register index is loaded into the AA field of this register.

The flip-flop is controlled indirectly by the host. When a host assembly language input port instruction, IN, is issued to the Input Status #1 Register, the flip-flop is cleared. This register resides at port address 3BA hex for monochrome implementations or port addresses 3DA hex for color implementations. Once the flip-flop is cleared, the path is set so that outputs to this 3C0 hex port load an index that points to one of the Attribute Registers. This is equivalent

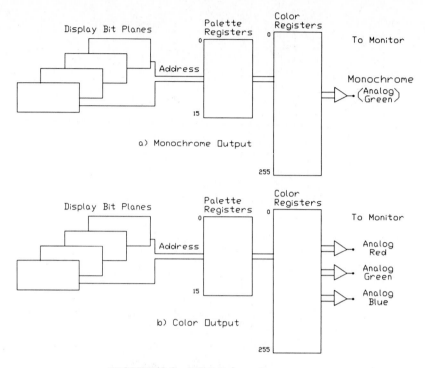

FIGURE 8.6 VGA Palette Outputs

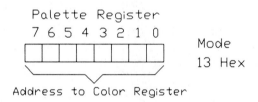

FIGURE 8.7 VGA Conversion of Data to Colors

to loading any of the other Address Registers. The next assembly language output port instruction written to this 3C0 hex port (OUT) will load the indexed Attribute Register. After the output occurs, the flip-flop automatically changes state. The following output will be directed once again to the Attribute Address Register.

In addition to the address field, the Attribute Address Register contains a Palette Address Source (PAS) field. This field is used to control the operation

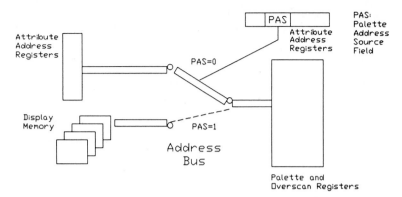

FIGURE 8.8 Accessing the Palette Registers

of the dual-ported palette RAM. If the host is to have control of the palette registers during a load operation, it must reset the PA field to 0. In order for the display memory to access this palette RAM, the PAS field must be set to a 1.

8.2 CONVERTING DATA TO COLORS

The variety of display modes available on the EGA/VGA provides a number of different possible color schemes. These include two-color modes, four-color modes, and 16-color modes. In addition, the VGA provides for a 256-color mode. The color modes and the bit planes affected are listed in Table 8.1.

8.2.1 Monochrome Modes

In the monochrome modes, the Palette Registers contain two fields, each one bit wide. These two bits are output to the monochrome monitor. The monochrome monitor requires two control signals that determine the intensity of the video signal. Together, these bits can produce four monochrome attributes. The possible monochrome intensities are shown in Table 8.2. The monochrome intensities are video (V) and intensify (I).

8.2.2 Monochrome Alphanumeric Mode

In the monochrome alphanumeric mode, mode 7, the code that determines the monochrome attribute for each character is contained in the attribute byte of the character. The attribute bytes are located in bit plane 2. The attribute byte may access any of the 16 Palette Registers. However, the values in the Palette Registers reflect the fact that only four codes are possible. The convention used is compatible with the monochrome adapter boards. The two-bit code resides in bits 3 and 4. Bits 7–5 and bits 2–0 are not relevant. Any attribute in display memory that has the video bit on—bit 3=1, for example—produces an output

TABLE 8.1 Palette Utilization

Display Mode (Hex)	Number of Colors	Palette Registers Affected
0,1	16	0–15
2,3	16	0–15
4,5	4	0,1,2,3
6	2	0,1
7	4	0,1,4,5
D	16	0–15
E	16	0–15
F	4	0,1,4,5
10	16	0–15
11	2	0,1
12	16	0–15
13	256	0–15

TABLE 8.2 Monochrome Intensity Values

Video	Intensify	Saturation
0	0	0% saturation = Black
0	1	50% saturation = Normal intensity
1	1	100% saturation = High intensity
1	0	Blinking normal intensity

that has the video bit on. Likewise, any attribute in display memory that has the intensity bit on—bit 4=1, for example—produces an output that has the intensity bit on. This occurs because the Palette Registers are loaded with the values indicated in Table 8.3.

8.2.3 Monochrome Graphics Mode

In the monochrome graphics mode, mode F hex, a two-bit-wide code is assigned to every pixel. This two-bit-wide field also represents the video and intensity bits of the monochrome attributes. Four of these two-bit-wide attributes are loaded into display memory, packed into a byte format. This is illustrated in Figure 8.9.

Each byte contains the attributes associated with four neighboring pixels. If all of the pixels are located on a line, attribute n is associated with the far left pixel. When display mode F hex is active, special hardware intercepts the data written to the display memory and loads all of the video attribute bits into bit plane 0 and all of the intensity attribute bits into bit plane 2. This is illustrated in Figure 8.3b above.

TABLE 8.3 Mode 7 Palette Default Values

Register	0	1	2	3	4	5	6	7	8	9	A	B	C	D	E	F
Value	0	8	8	8	8	8	8	8	10	18	18	18	18	18	18	18

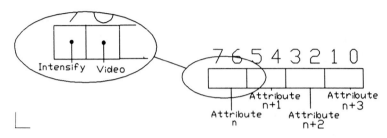

FIGURE 8.9 Monochrome Graphics Attribute Byte Packing

TABLE 8.4 Mode F Hex Palette Default Values

Register	0	1	2	3	4	5	6	7	8	9	A	B	C	D	E	F
Value	0	8	—	—	18	18	—	—	—	—	—	—	—	—	—	—

The 16 Palette Registers are addressed by two active bits, bit 0 and bit 2. Bits 1 and 3 are reset to 0, resulting in only four of the sixteen Palette Registers being relevant. The four Palette Registers accessed are registers 0, 1, 4, and 5, as shown in Table 8.4.

8.2.4 RGBI Color Mode

In the CGA-emulation modes, the Palette Registers contain the RGBI codes. This code is represented with four bits, which together can produce up to sixteen different colors. The three color bits—R=red, G=green, and B=blue—define eight colors, black included. The fourth bit, S=secondary dims the preceding eight possible colors.

The EGA is capable of driving an RGBI monitor directly in the 200-scan-line modes. Thus, the four-bit color code is output from the EGA adapter. The VGA cannot drive an RGBI monitor. However, the Palette Registers and the Color Registers are loaded with appropriate colors to provide compatibility. The bit positions in the palette registers contain the red, green, blue, and intensity fields, as listed in Figure 8.4b above.

8.2.5 RGBI Alphanumeric Modes

In the RGBI alphanumeric modes—modes 0, 1, 2, and 3—the code that determines the color attribute for each character is contained in the attribute byte of the character. The attribute bytes are located in bit plane 2. The attribute byte may access any of the sixteen Palette Registers. Each character can reference one Palette Register for the foreground color and one Palette Register for the background color.

In the EGA, either an RGBI monitor or an enhanced RrGgBb monitor is attached. If the RGBI monitor is attached, the lower four bits of the Palette output are output as the RGBI signals to the monitor. The Palette Registers represent a one-to-one mapping scheme, so that an attribute is output directly to the monitor. This is seen in the default values of the Palette Registers. All of the values in the Palette Registers are equal to the addresses of the Palette Register. The default values used for the RGBI modes are listed in Table 8.5.

If the RrGgBb monitor is attached, all six bits of the output of the Palette are output as the RrGgBb signals to the monitor. The Palette Registers simulate the color mapping used on the RGBI systems. The default values used for the RrGgBb modes are listed in Table 8.6. Because bit 4 is the intensity bit, all attributes that have the intensity bit set to 1 address Palette Registers number 8 through F hex. The values in these registers are all greater than or equal to 38 hex, which is 111xxx binary. Because bits 3, 4, and 5 are set to 1, the secondary R, G, and B bits are activated, producing less bright colors.

Palette Register 6 is loaded with a 14 hex instead of the expected 6 hex, and its intensified brother, Palette Register E hex, is loaded with a 3E hex as expected. Both of these values represent a brown or yellow, which is a combination of red and green. The 14 hex loaded into Palette Register 6 uses a secondary green with a primary red. A value of 6 in the Palette Register 6 would produce primary green and primary red.

8.2.6 RGBI Graphics Modes

In the RGBI graphics modes, modes 4 and 5, each pixel is represented by two color attribute bits. These four bits allow each pixel to be displayed in one of four colors. These graphics modes are compatible with the Color Graphics Adapter (CGA).

In the CGA adapter, these two attribute bits produce four colors, although the RGBI monitor is capable of displaying 16 colors. Two default palettes are present in the CGA. The programmer can select one of these two palettes to convert the two-bit attribute to an RGBI color. Table 8.7 lists the colors for each of the default palettes.

In the EGA/VGA, the two default colors can be loaded into the 16 Palette Registers through the Set Color Palette BIOS call, AH=0B hex. In the EGA/VGA, Palette Registers 0 through 3 are accessed by the two attribute bits. These four registers can be loaded with any colors desired.

TABLE 8.5   Modes 0, 1, 2, and 3 Palette Default Values

Register	0	1	2	3	4	5	6	7	8	9	A	B	C	D	E	F
Value	0	1	2	3	4	5	6	7	8	9	A	B	C	D	E	F

TABLE 8.6   Modes 0*, 1*, 2*, 3* Palette Default Values

Register	0	1	2	3	4	5	6	7	8	9	A	B	C	D	E	F
Value	0	1	2	3	4	5	14	7	38	39	3A	3B	3C	3D	3E	3F

* Enhanced graphics mode

TABLE 8.7   CGA-compatible Color Selection

ATR 1	ATR 0	Set 1	Set 0	EGA Palette Register
0	0	Background	Background	0
0	1	Cyan	Green	1
1	0	Magenta	Red	2
1	1	White	Brown	3

The two attribute bits associated with each pixel are named ATR1 and ATR0. The bit ATR1 is the most significant bit, and ATR0 is the least significant bit. The process used to convert a host address to a Palette Register address is not straightforward. The attribute bit ATR1 eventually becomes the color palette address bit 1. The attribute bit ATR0 becomes the color palette address bit 0.

In modes 4 and 5, the two attribute bits are located as neighbors in the same byte of data. This precludes simply loading one attribute bit in each of bit planes 0 and 1. Hardware controlled by the odd/even flags automatically directs even bytes of information to bit plane 0 and odd bytes of information to bit plane 1. Data input to the EGA/VGA when the EGA/VGA is in modes 4 or 5 is separated into bit planes 0 and 1, depending on the even or odd address of the data. The data present in these two planes is automatically unwrapped by more hardware, so that ATR1 and ATR0 address bits 1 and 0 of the color palette.

Four pixels are packed into each byte of the host byte buffer. Four consecutive bytes of display memory contain 16 pixels in host memory. When these four bytes are written to the display memory, the bytes located at the even host addresses are loaded into bit plane 0, and the odd host addresses are loaded into bit plane 1. The two attribute bits associated with each pixel are unwrapped and presented to the Palette Registers as address bits 0 and 1.

TABLE 8.8 Mode 6 Hex Palette Default Values

Register	0	1	2	3	4	5	6	7	8	9	A	B	C	D	E	F
Value	0	17	17	17	17	17	17	17	17	17	17	17	17	17	17	17

TABLE 8.9 Mode 11 Hex Palette Default Values

Register	0	1	2	3	4	5	6	7	8	9	A	B	C	D	E	F
Value	0	37	37	37	37	37	37	37	37	37	37	37	37	37	37	37

8.2.7 Two-color Modes

In the two-color graphics modes, modes 6 and 11 hex, each pixel is represented by one bit. Both of these modes are graphics modes, and there are no associated two-color alphanumeric modes. Mode 6 is meant to be compatible with the CGA graphics mode, and mode 11 hex is specially designed for the VGA to provide two-color graphics.

8.2.8 CGA Two-color Emulation

In mode 6 of the EGA/VGA, the one bit per pixel selects one of two palette locations. The default values loaded into the Palette Registers are listed in Table 8.8.

Eight consecutive pixels are packed into each byte of display memory. The processing is identical to the RGBI graphics modes 4 and 5 except that there are only two colors instead of four colors. As is true in the RGBI display modes, bit planes 0 and 1 in mode 6 are used to store even and odd bytes of the data. When the color palette is addressed, the single attribute bit for each pixel is presented to the Palette Registers as address bit 0.

8.2.9 VGA Two-color Emulation

In mode 11 of the VGA, the one bit per pixel selects one of two palette locations. The default values loaded into the Palette Registers are listed in Table 8.9.

Eight consecutive pixels are packed into each byte of display memory. The memory mapping is straightforward, using only bit plane 0 to store the data. When the color palette is addressed, the single attribute bit for each pixel is presented to the Palette Registers as address bit 0.

8.2.10 Enhanced Color Modes

In the enhanced color modes—modes D, E, 10, and 12 hex—a pixel is represented by four bits in display memory. These four bits reside in bit planes 0

TABLE 8.10 Color Intensities

Intensified Color Bit	Color Bit	Percentage of Saturation
0	0	0 % saturation
0	1	33 % saturation
1	0	66 % saturation
1	1	100 % saturation

TABLE 8.11 Modes D, E, 10, and 12 Hex Palette Default Values

Register	0	1	2	3	4	5	6	7	8	9	A	B	C	D	E	F
Value	0	1	2	3	4	5	14	7	38	39	3A	3B	3C	3D	3E	3F

through 3. One bit is assigned to each of the four bit planes. These four bits are combined to make the four-bit address to the Palette Registers. Any of these four bits can be disabled by using the Color Plane Enable Register. Any plane that is disabled causes the associated address bit to the Palette Registers to be reset to 0. Thus, if all four bit planes are disabled, all four address bits will be reset to 0, causing the color in Palette Register 0 to be displayed.

8.2.11 Enhanced Color: EGA

The EGA requires an enhanced color monitor that has six control lines to determine the color. Two lines are assigned for each of the red, green, and blue colors, which allows the monitor to display up to 64 different colors.

Each two-bit field in the Palette Registers corresponds to an intensity value of the three primary colors—red, green, and blue. The sum of these six bits determines the color displayed. Because each primary color is represented by two bits, each color can have four intensities. The possible values of a typical color are listed in Table 8.10.

The six bits are organized within the Palette Registers as shown in Figure 8.4c. The default values for the Palette Registers in these modes are identical to those for the RGBI color modes. The default values are repeated in Table 8.11.

8.2.12 Enhanced Color: VGA

The VGA requires an analog RGB monitor. There are three lines, one each of red, green, and blue, permitting the monitor to display an infinite number of colors. The VGA is restricted to six bits per color, which limits the possible number of colors to 256 Kcolors.

TABLE 8.12 Mode 13 Hex Palette Default Values

Register	0	1	2	3	4	5	6	7	8	9	A	B	C	D	E	F
Value	0	1	2	3	4	5	6	7	8	9	A	B	C	D	E	F

8.2.13 256-color Mode

The VGA provides mode 13 hex, which allows 256 colors. Every pixel is represented by eight bits of data. The eight bits when loaded into display memory are spread through the four bit planes. The eight bits are split into two four-bit fields. The first field, corresponding to the lower four bits (bits 0–3), addresses the Palette Registers. The four low-order outputs of the Palette Registers are used as the four low-order address bits, bits 0–3, for the Color Registers. The second field, corresponding to bits 4–7 from the display memory, are presented to the Color Registers as address bits 4–7.

The Palette Registers are restricted to provide a one-to-one transfer of address to data. The default values of the Palette Registers are listed in Table 8.12; they should not be modified by the programmer.

8.3 COLOR REGISTERS

The VGA is equipped with 256 Color Registers. A pixel or character in display memory consists of from one to eight bits of data. This data is used to address the 16 Palette Registers. The output of these Palette Registers is used in conjunction with the data in display memory to address the Color Registers. The Color Registers contain the color codes that are output to the digital-to-analog converters (DAC). The outputs of the DAC are sent to the monitor. Each of the Color Registers consists of a red, green, and blue component. Each of these color components is six bits wide.

8.3.1 Color Register Addressing

The Color Registers are addressed according to Figure 8.10.

Each of the sixteen Palette Registers contains six bits of data. In the EGA and in the VGA, with mode 13 hex excluded, these six bits are used as a color code. In mode 13 hex, these six bits are used as an address. They provide the low-order six bits of an eight-bit address that is presented to the Color Registers. Because there are 256 Color Registers, eight address bits are required.

The Palette Registers are present in the VGA to provide compatibility with the EGA. There is no need to have two layers of color conversion registers—

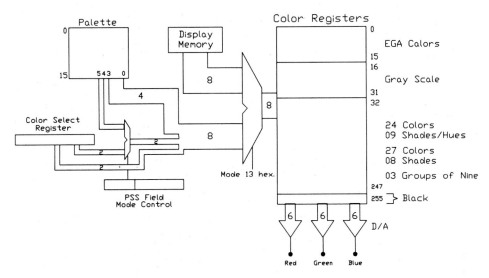

FIGURE 8.10 Color Register Addressing

that is, both the Palette Registers and the Color Registers. The Color Registers would be sufficient in themselves.

Suppose that Palette Register 5 contains a value of 3. The value 3 is a binary 000011, which translates to the color cyan, because both high-intensity blue and high-intensity green are active. Color Register 3 would be addressed if this value 3 is used as an address to present to the Color Registers. If Color Register 3 contains a value that activates a high-intensity green and a high-intensity blue, the resultant color will still be cyan. Thus, Palette Register 5 may be thought of either as containing a color 3 or as an address 3.

If the Palette Registers are thought of as an address for the Color Registers, a transparency should exist. An address presented to the Palette Registers should produce a value on the output of the Palette Registers that is identical to the address. The display bit planes provide the four low-order address bits to the Palette Registers. To provide transparency, the Palette Registers should provide four bits of output. These four bits access 16 of the Color Registers. Because there are 256 Color Registers, they may be segmented into 16 banks, each bank containing 16 registers. One bank is active at a time. The Palette Registers provide the address to an individual register in a bank.

If the Palette Registers are thought of as a color, six bits of output are provided. These six bits are used as the low-order six bits of the address provided to the Color Registers; they also access 64 of the Color Registers. Because there are 256 Color Registers, these may be segmented into 4 banks, each bank containing 64 registers. One bank is active at a time. The Palette Registers provide the address to an individual register in a bank.

8.3.2 Four Banks of 64 Color Registers

The Color Select Register provides two address bits, named bits C7 and C6. Combined with the six output bits from the Palette Registers, an eight-bit Color Register address is formed. In this configuration, the C7 and C6 fields of the Color Select Register act as a bank select. A bank, in this case, consists of 64 Color Registers. In the 16-color modes, 16 Color Registers must be reserved to hold the 16 colors. Each Palette Register contains a six-bit color code. Because the output of the Palette Registers address the Color Registers, these six bits can be used to select one of 64 Color Registers within a bank. The two high-order address bits, C7 and C6, are provided from the Color Select Register and act as a bank select. Rapid selections of other banks of Color Registers can be made by simply changing the value in the C7 and C6 fields.

This bank select mode is enabled by the Palette Size Select (PSS) field of the Mode Control Register. If this field is set to 1, the address bits C7 and C6 are used as the upper two bits of the address presented to the Color Registers. The six bits output from the Palette Registers are used as the six low-order address bits presented to the Color Registers. Thus, one of four banks can be selected. This color selection mode is illustrated in Figure 8.11.

8.3.3 Sixteen Banks of 16 Color Registers

In addition to fields C7 and C6, the Color Select Register provides two other address fields called C5 and C4. When these fields are combined with the four low-order output bits from the Palette Register, an eight-bit Color Register address is formed. In this configuration, the C7, C6, C5, and C4 fields of the Color Select Register act to select a bank. The four low-order output bits from the Palette Registers select a Color Register within a bank.

This bank-select mode is enabled by the Palette Size Select (PSS) field of the Mode Control Register. If this field is reset to 0, the address bits C5 and C4 are used in conjunction with C7 and C6 to form the four upper-order address bits presented to the Color Registers. Thus, one of sixteen banks can be selected. This color-selection mode is illustrated in Figure 8.12.

8.3.4 Color Register Organization

Each of 256 Color Registers is composed of three parts, corresponding to the red, green, and blue components. Each of these components is six bits wide, providing each of these three primary colors with 64 possible intensities or levels of saturation. When combined, the three primary colors provide the programmer with the opportunity to select any color from a possible selection of 256

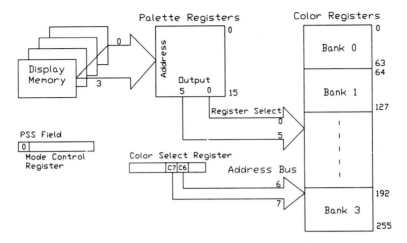

FIGURE 8.11   Four Banks of 64-color Registers

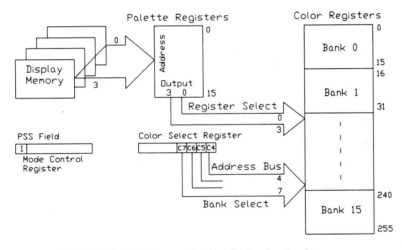

FIGURE 8.12   Sixteen Banks of 16-color Registers

Kcolors. The notation "256 Kcolors" actually translates into 262,144 possible colors.

The Color Registers may be set up to provide any combination of colors that appeals to the programmer. At initialization, the registers are set up as shown in Table 8.13.

8.3.5   Color Register Default Values

The Color Registers may be loaded with the initial values at a mode set by enabling the preload function. Likewise, the Color Registers may remain un-

TABLE 8.13 Initial State of the Color Registers

Registers	Color Scheme
0–15	Identical to the 16 EGA colors initially loaded into the EGA Palette Registers
16–31	16 evenly spaced shades of gray.
32–247	24 color groups, each consisting of nine shades of a color. Three intensity levels and three saturation levels are provided for each shade.
248–255	Preloaded with 0, for black

modified during a mode set if the preload function is disabled. The preload function is controlled by invoking the BIOS call named Default Palette Loading During Mode Set, AH = 12 hex, BL = 31 hex. A listing of the initial state of the Color Registers is given in Table 8.14. In this table, R = red, G = green, and B = blue.

8.3.6 Accessing the Color Registers

The Color Registers can be written to or read from by using the BIOS calls or by programming the Color Registers directly. The same arguments that apply to programming the control registers directly or through BIOS also apply to the programming of the Color Registers. Speed versus portability are the two key issues.

8.3.7 Modifying the Color Registers through BIOS

Several BIOS calls are available that relate to the Color Registers. All of these calls are found on the VGA only because there are no Color Registers on the EGA. Programmers may set or read a single Color Register or a group of Color Registers, or they may select or read the color page or bank. The Color Registers can be loaded during a mode set by enabling the Palette Loading function. Likewise, the Color Registers can remain unmodified during a mode set by disabling this function. These calls are invoked with interrupt INT 10 hex, with AH=10 hex or AH=12 hex. A listing of the Color Register BIOS-related calls is found in Table 8.15.

8.3.8 Modifying the Color Registers Directly

Four registers in the VGA are dedicated to the Video digital-to-analog converters. These registers are listed in Table 8.16.

Data is read from or written to the Color Registers through the PEL Address and PEL Data Registers. This register pair operates in a similar fashion to that used by the other EGA/VGA address and data register pairs. An index is set

TABLE 8.14 Initial Values in the Color Registers

Index	R	G	B	R	G	B	R	G	B	R	G	B
				Colors (R = Red, G = Green, B = Blue) (Values in Decimal)								
0	0	0	0	0	0	42	0	42	0	0	42	42
4	42	0	0	42	0	42	42	21	0	42	42	42
8	21	21	21	21	21	63	21	63	21	21	63	63
12	63	21	21	63	21	63	63	63	21	63	63	63
16	0	0	0	5	5	5	8	8	8	11	11	11
20	14	14	14	17	17	17	20	20	20	24	24	24
24	28	28	28	32	32	32	36	36	36	40	40	40
28	45	45	45	50	50	50	56	56	56	63	63	63
32	0	0	63	16	0	63	31	0	63	47	0	63
36	63	0	63	63	0	47	63	0	31	63	0	16
40	63	0	0	63	16	0	63	31	0	63	47	0
44	63	63	0	47	63	0	31	63	0	16	63	0
48	0	63	0	0	63	16	0	63	31	0	63	47
52	0	63	63	0	47	63	0	31	63	0	16	63
56	31	31	63	39	31	63	47	31	63	55	31	63
60	63	31	63	63	31	55	63	31	47	63	31	39
64	63	31	31	63	39	31	63	47	31	63	55	31
68	63	63	31	55	63	31	47	63	31	39	63	31
72	31	63	31	31	63	39	31	63	47	31	63	55
76	31	63	63	31	55	63	31	47	63	31	39	63
80	45	45	63	49	45	63	54	45	63	58	45	63
84	63	45	63	63	45	58	63	45	54	63	45	49
88	63	45	45	63	49	45	63	54	45	63	58	45
92	63	63	45	58	63	45	54	63	45	49	63	45
96	45	63	45	45	63	49	45	63	54	45	63	58
100	45	63	63	45	58	63	45	54	63	45	49	63
104	0	0	28	7	0	28	14	0	28	21	0	28
108	28	0	28	28	0	21	28	0	14	28	0	7
112	28	0	0	28	7	0	28	14	0	28	21	0
116	28	28	0	21	28	0	14	28	0	7	28	0
120	0	28	0	0	28	7	0	28	14	0	28	21
124	0	28	28	0	21	28	0	14	28	0	7	28
128	14	14	28	17	14	28	21	14	28	24	14	28
132	28	14	28	28	14	24	28	14	21	28	14	17
136	28	14	14	28	17	14	28	21	14	28	24	14
140	28	28	14	24	28	14	21	28	14	17	28	14
144	14	28	14	14	28	17	14	28	21	14	28	24
148	14	28	28	14	24	28	14	21	28	14	17	28
152	20	20	28	22	20	28	24	20	28	26	20	28
156	28	20	28	28	20	26	28	20	24	28	20	22
160	28	20	20	28	22	20	28	24	20	28	26	20
164	28	28	20	26	28	20	24	28	20	22	28	20

TABLE 8.14 *(cont.)*

Index	Colors (R = Red, G = Green, B = Blue) (Values in Decimal)											
	R	G	B	R	G	B	R	G	B	R	G	B
168	20	28	20	20	28	22	20	28	24	20	28	26
172	20	28	28	20	26	28	20	24	28	20	22	28
176	0	0	16	4	0	16	8	0	16	12	0	16
180	16	0	16	16	0	12	16	0	8	16	0	4
184	16	0	0	16	4	0	16	8	0	16	12	0
188	16	16	0	12	16	0	8	16	0	4	16	0
192	0	16	0	0	16	4	0	16	8	0	16	12
196	0	16	16	0	12	16	0	8	16	0	4	16
200	8	8	16	10	8	16	12	8	16	14	8	16
204	16	8	16	16	8	14	16	8	12	16	8	10
208	16	8	8	16	10	8	16	12	8	16	14	8
212	16	16	8	14	16	8	12	16	8	10	16	8
216	8	16	8	8	16	10	8	16	12	8	16	14
220	8	16	16	8	14	16	8	12	16	8	10	16
224	11	11	16	12	11	16	13	11	16	15	11	16
228	16	11	16	16	11	15	16	11	13	16	11	12
232	16	11	11	16	12	11	16	13	11	16	15	11
236	16	16	11	15	16	11	13	16	11	12	16	11
240	11	16	11	11	16	12	11	16	13	11	16	15
244	11	16	16	11	15	16	11	13	16	11	12	16
248	0	0	0	0	0	0	0	0	0	0	0	0
252	0	0	0	0	0	0	0	0	0	0	0	0

Note: All Color Register values are in decimal.

TABLE 8.15 Color Register BIOS-related Calls

AH (Hex)	AL (Hex)	Function of Call
10	10	Set individual Color Register
10	12	Set block of Color Registers
10	13	Select color page or paging mode
10	15	Read individual Color Register
10	17	Read block of Color Registers
10	1A	Read current color page number
12	BL = 31	Default palette loading during mode set

up in the address register that points to one of the internal Color Registers. This register is then accessed through the data register. Special hardware features included in the PEL Address and Data Registers can be used to speed up the read and write operations. This addressing is illustrated in Figure 8.13.

TABLE 8.16 Video Digital-to-Analog Converter Registers

Address	Read/Write	Function
3C8 hex	Read/write	PEL address during write
3C7 hex	Write only	PEL address during read
3C7 hex	Read only	DAC state
3C9 hex	Read/write	PEL Data Register
3C6 hex	Read/write	PEL mask

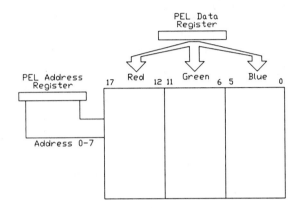

FIGURE 8.13 Direct Accessing of the Color Registers

PEL Address Register

The PEL Address Register is eight bits wide and addresses one of the 256 Color Registers. The PEL Address Register has two addresses in the host port I/O space. Writing to port address 3C8 hex provides an address to the Color Register and alerts the hardware that the host desires to write to the Color Registers. Similarly, writing to port address 3C7 hex provides an address to the Color Register and alerts the hardware that the host desires to read to the Color Registers.

The PEL Address Register autoincrements after three consecutive read or write operations to the PEL Data Register. This is provided so that consecutive Color Registers can be accessed without requiring the programmer to update the PEL Address Register.

PEL Data Register

The PEL Data Register contains a six-bit field that is used by the host to read data from or write it to the Color Registers. After the address to the Color Registers is set up in either of the ports associated with the PEL Address Register, the Color Register hardware is ready to accept three simultaneous read or write operations. The first read or write operation accesses the red field

TABLE 8.17   DAC State Register

Bits 0,1	Meaning
00 binary	DAC is currently in a read mode
11 binary	DAC is currently in a write mode

of the color register, the second accesses the green field, and the third accesses the blue field. It is important that a series of three read or write operations occurs before the index in the PEL Address Register is modified.

Due to hardware limitations, a slight delay is necessary between successive read or write operations performed to the PEL Data Register. The minimum period between successive accesses is 240 nanoseconds.

When the Color Registers are modified, "snow" may appear on the monitor. To eliminate this "snow," the programmer must insure that the display is not in an active refresh period. This can be accomplished in two ways. The programmer can modify the Color Registers only when the display is in a retrace period rather than an active display period, or the programmer can turn the refreshing off by using the Screen Off field in the Clocking Mode Register.

DAC State Register

The condition of the host interface section of the Color Registers can be monitored through the DAC State Register. This condition is important because the hardware expects three consecutive read or write operations after data is written to the PEL Address Register. Data corruption within the Color Registers can occur if a second write to the PEL Address Register occurs before the sequence of three read or write operations to the PEL Data Register has completed.

The status bits are located in bits 0 and 1 of the DAC State Register. The values returned during a read to this register reflect the state of the Color Register hardware. These states are listed in Table 8.17.

After the PEL Address Register is written to at one of its two addresses, the mode does not change until another write operation occurs to the alternate PEL Address Register port address. The mode stays in effect since sequential read or write operations are anticipated by the controller. The autoincrementing feature automatically updates index address.

PEL Mask Register

The PEL Mask Register is initialized to FF hex by the BIOS initialization procedure. This register should not be modified by the programmer.

8.3.9 Color Conversion

A variety of color-coding techniques is available with the EGA/VGA. These include using the two-bit color codes on the EGA and the six-bit color codes on the VGA. Color coding includes monochrome gray scales, RGBI color, RrGgBb color, and analog color. It is often necessary to convert from one color scheme to another.

Gray Scale

Gray shades are composed of equal amounts of red, green, and blue. White is the maximum gray scale value, and black is the minimum value. Thus, the number of gray scales is directly related to the number of bits reserved for each of the three primary colors.

The EGA allocates two bits per color. These two bits can produce four independent gray scales. The four levels of gray scale can be achieved using the color fields within the Palette Registers, as shown in Table 8.18.

The VGA allocates six bits per color which provides 64 possible gray scales. These 64 levels of gray scale are achieved using the six-bit color fields within the Color Registers, as shown in Table 8.19.

Converting RrGgBb, RGBI, and Monochrome

Thus far, three color schemes have been discussed. These include the monochrome intensities, the RGBI color outputs, and the enhanced color output, RrGbBb. It is sometimes necessary to convert the enhanced color outputs to the RGBI outputs or vice versa. Table 8.20 provides a conversion reference for the RrGbBb, RGBI, and monochrome formats.

Summing Colors to Gray Scale

In the VGA, the colors loaded into the Color Registers can be converted into gray scales. A formula is used to convert the intensity found in each of the three primary color components—red, green, and blue—into a gray scale value. The formula is listed in Equation 8.1.

Equation 8.1 Determining Gray Scale

$$\text{Gray Scale} = (.30 \times \text{red}) + (.59 \times \text{green}) + (.11 \times \text{blue})$$

Because the sum of the multipliers, .30 + .59 + .11, totals 1.00, gray scale values are preserved. In other words, a gray scale input to the equation produces a gray scale of the same intensity as an output.

The summing to gray scale function can be invoked automatically during a mode set if the summing feature is enabled. All 256 Color Registers will be summed to form the gray scales. If this summing feature is disabled, the Color

TABLE 8.18 EGA: Gray Scale Using the Color Registers

Intensified Color Bits			Color Bits			
SR	SG	SB	R	G	B	Gray Scale
0	0	0	0	0	0	0 % saturation
0	0	0	1	1	1	33 % saturation
1	1	1	0	0	0	66 % saturation
1	1	1	1	1	1	100 % saturation

TABLE 8.19 VGA: Gray Scale Using the Color Registers

Color Register Value			
Red	Green	Blue	Gray Scale
0	0	0	0 % saturation
1	1	1	1.6 % saturation
2	2	2	3.2 % saturation
.	.	.	.
.	.	.	.
.	.	.	.
63	63	63	100 % saturation

Registers will not be summed to a gray scale during a mode set. The programmer can cause a summing operation on any number of Color Registers to occur at command by using the BIOS routines. The BIOS calls that relate to the summing operation are listed in Table 8.21.

8.3.10 Selective Color Planes

The four bit planes address the color palette. However, not all of the planes will necessarily affect the address of a particular pixel. A logical AND operation occurs with the four-bit value in the Color Plane Enable Register and the four address bits coming from the four bit planes. This logical function is illustrated in Figure 8.14.

Any color palette address bit that equals 0 as a result of the AND operation (because a 0 existed in the corresponding bit field in the Color Plane Enable Register) is set to 0. For example, suppose the color palette address bits have a value of 7 (0111 binary) and the Color Plane Enable Register has a value of 3 (0011) binary. The AND operation would result in a 3 (0011 binary). Thus, Palette Register number 3 would be accessed.

TABLE 8.20 Converting RGBI and Monochrome

			RrGgBb						RGBI			Monochrome	
r	g	b	R	G	B	Code	I	R	G	B	I	V	
						Red							
0	0	0	1	0	0	4	0	1	0	0	0	1	
1	0	0	0	0	0	32	0	1	0	0	0	1	
1	0	0	1	0	0	36	1	1	0	0	0	1	
1	0	0	1	1	1	39	1	1	0	0	0	1	
1	1	1	1	0	0	60	1	1	0	0	0	1	
						Blue							
0	0	0	0	0	1	1	0	0	0	1	0	1	
0	0	1	0	0	0	8	0	0	0	1	0	1	
0	0	1	0	0	1	9	1	0	0	1	0	1	
0	0	1	1	1	1	15	1	0	0	1	0	1	
1	1	1	0	0	1	57	1	0	0	1	0	1	
						Green							
0	0	0	0	1	0	2	0	0	1	0	0	1	
0	1	0	0	0	0	16	0	0	1	0	0	1	
0	1	0	0	1	0	18	1	0	1	0	0	1	
0	1	0	1	1	1	23	1	0	1	0	0	1	
1	1	1	0	1	0	58	1	0	1	0	0	1	
						Violet							
0	0	0	1	0	1	5	0	1	0	1	0	1	
1	0	1	0	0	0	40	0	1	0	1	0	1	
0	0	1	1	0	0	12	0	1	0	1	0	1	
1	0	0	0	0	1	33	0	1	0	1	0	1	
0	0	1	1	0	1	13	1	1	0	1	0	1	
1	0	0	1	0	1	37	1	1	0	1	0	1	
1	0	1	0	0	1	41	1	1	0	1	0	1	
1	0	1	1	0	0	44	1	1	0	1	0	1	
1	0	1	1	1	1	47	1	1	0	1	0	1	
1	0	1	0	0	1	41	1	1	0	1	0	1	
1	1	1	1	0	1	61	1	1	0	1	0	1	
1	0	1	1	0	1	45	1	1	0	1	0	1	
						Cyan							
0	0	0	0	1	1	3	0	0	1	1	0	1	
0	1	1	0	0	0	24	0	0	1	1	0	1	
0	1	0	0	0	1	17	0	0	1	1	0	1	
0	0	1	0	1	0	10	0	0	1	1	0	1	
0	0	1	0	1	1	11	1	0	1	1	0	1	
0	1	0	1	1	1	19	1	0	1	1	0	1	

TABLE 8.20 *(cont.)*

		RrG	*gBb*					*RG*	*BI*		*Monochrome*	
r	*g*	*b*	*R*	*G*	*B*	*Code*	*I*	*R*	*G*	*B*	*I*	*V*
						Cyan						
0	1	1	0	0	1	25	1	0	1	1	0	1
0	1	1	0	1	0	26	1	0	1	1	0	1
0	1	1	1	1	1	31	1	0	1	1	0	1
1	1	1	0	1	1	59	1	0	1	1	0	1
0	1	1	0	1	1	27	1	0	1	1	0	1
						Yellow						
0	0	0	1	1	0	6	0	1	1	0	0	1
1	1	0	0	0	0	48	0	1	1	0	0	1
0	1	0	1	0	0	20	0	1	1	0	0	1
0	1	0	1	1	0	22	1	1	1	0	0	1
1	0	0	0	1	0	34	0	1	1	0	0	1
1	0	0	1	1	0	38	1	1	1	0	0	1
1	1	0	0	1	0	50	1	1	1	0	0	1
1	1	0	1	0	0	52	1	1	1	0	0	1
1	1	0	1	1	0	54	1	1	1	0	0	1
1	1	0	1	1	1	55	1	1	1	0	0	1
1	1	1	1	1	0	62	1	1	1	0	0	1
						Gray						
0	0	0	0	0	0	0	0	0	0	0	0	0
0	0	0	1	1	1	7	0	1	1	1	0	1
1	1	1	0	0	0	56	0	1	1	1	0	1
0	0	1	1	1	0	14	0	1	1	1	0	1
0	1	0	1	0	1	21	0	1	1	1	0	1
1	0	0	0	1	1	35	0	1	1	1	0	1
1	1	0	0	0	1	49	0	1	1	1	0	1
1	0	1	0	1	0	42	0	1	1	1	0	1
0	1	1	1	0	1	29	1	1	1	1	1	1
0	1	1	1	1	0	30	1	1	1	1	1	1
1	0	1	0	1	1	43	1	1	1	1	1	1
1	0	1	1	1	0	46	1	1	1	1	1	1
1	1	0	0	1	1	51	1	1	1	1	1	1
1	1	0	1	0	1	53	1	1	1	1	1	1
1	1	1	1	1	1	63	1	1	1	1	1	1
						Blinking						
—	—	—	—	—	—	—	1	0	0	0	1	0

TABLE 8.21 Summing to Gray Scale: Related BIOS Calls

AH (Hex)	Subcall (Hex)	Function of Call
10	AL = 1B	Sum color values immediately to gray scale
12	BL = 33	Enable/Disable summing to gray scale at mode set

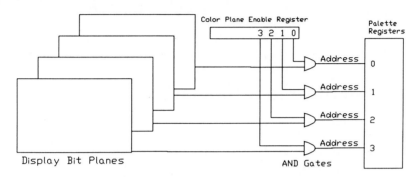

FIGURE 8.14 Selective Addressing of the Palette Registers

Chapter 9

Reading the State of the EGA and VGA

9.1 READING THE STATE OF THE ADAPTER

Programs must often read the state of the adapter to determine which graphics adapters are present in the computer system. Further, it is important to know which of these are active and what monitors are present. Once the adapter and monitor are known, it is frequently necessary to determine the mode and display parameters under which the adapter is currently operating.

The adapters present in the system can be ascertained by searching the host I/O ports for any active devices or by searching through BIOS ROM memory for adapter identifiers. Once the adapters are found, the attached monitor type can be determined from the state of the adapter. The display system configuration information can be obtained from tables that reside in the host memory. This information includes the starting address and the amount of display memory, the resolution of the display memory, the base port address of the control registers, the location of character fonts, and the state of the configuration switches. Information regarding the dynamic condition of the display can be determined by interrogating the display registers or from the BIOS tables stored in host memory. Typical parameters include the active display mode, the active display page, the cursor position, the number of rows and columns on the display, and the dimensions of the characters.

9.2 READING THE DISPLAY REGISTERS

The control registers resident on the EGA/VGA contain the most primitive information regarding the state of the graphics system. The EGA registers, for the most part, cannot be read. All of the VGA registers can be read. Both the EGA and the VGA maintain a table in BIOS that contains the default register values loaded into the registers during a Mode Set BIOS call.

9.2.1 Reading EGA Registers

The EGA adapter is limited in its ability to allow the programmer to read the state of its registers. The great majority of registers in the EGA are write-only.

TABLE 9.1   EGA Readable Registers

Register Name	Register Group	Index
Input Status # 0	Miscellaneous	—
Input Status # 1	Miscellaneous	—
Start Address High	CRTC	0C hex
Start Address Low	CRTC	0D hex
Cursor Location High	CRTC	0E hex
Cursor Location Low	CRTC	0F hex
Light pen High	CRTC	10 hex
Light pen Low	CRTC	11 hex

This is a severe limitation because memory resident programs have no way of determining the state of the EGA. This means that if a memory resident program desires to change the state of the EGA, it cannot restore the state back to the original condition. The readable EGA registers are listed in Table 9.1. Some EGA cards allow reading of the registers. The owner's manual should be consulted as to the readability of the EGA registers.

9.2.2   EGA Video Parameter Table

The default state of the EGA registers can be read from the Video Parameter Table in BIOS memory. The location of this table is pointed to by the Video Parameter Table Pointer, a double-word pointer that resides in the first location of the Table of Save Area Pointers. The Table of Save Area Pointers is pointed to by a second pointer. This pointer is called the Pointer to Table of Save Area Pointers. It resides in host memory at location 0000:04A8. Thus, it takes two pointers to arrive at the actual address of the Video Parameter Table.

The Video Parameter Table consists of a group of subtables, each 64 bytes long. Each subtable contains default values for the supported active modes. The number of modes present for the display adapter depends on the implementation. The standard EGA implementation contains 19 of these 64 subtables; one subtable for each of the display modes 0, 1, 2, 3, 4, 5, 6, 7, D, E, F, 10, F*, 10*, 0*, 1*, 2*, 3*. (The asterisk refers to the enhanced graphics modes.)

The form of these subtables is listed in Table 9.2.

The page length for each of these tables is listed in Table 9.3.

9.2.3   Initial Values of the EGA Registers

The values contained in this Video Parameter Table for the standard EGA implementation are listed in Table 9.4.

Also contained in the Video Parameter Table are the initial settings for all of the control registers. The initial settings are listed in Table 9.5.

TABLE 9.2 Form of the Video Parameter Table

Byte #	Description
0	Number of columns per page
1	Number of rows per page
2	Number of pixels per character
3,4	Page length
5–8	Sequencer Registers
9	Miscellaneous Register
10–34	CRTC Registers
35–54	Attribute Registers
55–63	Graphics Controller Registers

TABLE 9.3 Page Length According to Parameter Table

Mode (Hex)	Page Length (Decimal)
0	2,048
1	2,048
2	4,096
3	4,096
4	16,386
5	16,386
6	16,386
7	4,096
D	8,196
E	16,386
F	32,768
10	32,768
F*	32,768
10*	32,768
0*	2,048
1*	2,048
2*	4,096
3*	4,096

TABLE 9.4 Video Parameter Table

	Mode																	
	00	01	02	03	04	05	06	07	0D	0E	0F	10	0F*	10*	00*	01*	02*	03*
Col/Row	28	28	50	50	28	28	50	50	28	50	50	50	50	50	28	28	50	50
Row/Screen	18	18	18	18	18	18	18	18	18	18	18	18	18	18	18	18	18	18
Pel/Char	8	8	8	8	8	8	8	E	8	8	E	E	E	E	E	E	E	E
Col/Row	0	0	0	0	0	0	0	0	0	0	0	0	0	0	0	0	0	0

TABLE 9.5 Control Register Initial Values: EGA

Miscellaneous Register

								Mode									
0	1	2	3	4	5	6	7	D	E	F	10	0F*	10*	00*	01*	02*	03*
23	23	23	23	23	23	23	A6	23	23	A2	A7	A2	A7	A7	A7	A7	A7

Sequencer Registers

Index	0	1	2	3	4	5	6	7	D	E	F	10	0F*	10*	00*	01*	02*	03*
									Mode									
0	B	B	1	1	B	B	1	0	B	1	5	5	1	1	B	B	1	1
1	3	3	3	3	3	3	1	3	F	F	F	F	F	F	3	3	3	3
2	0	0	0	0	0	0	0	0	0	0	0	0	0	0	0	0	0	0
3	3	3	3	3	2	2	6	3	6	6	0	0	6	6	3	3	3	3
4	23	23	23	23	23	23	23	A6	23	23	A2	A7	A2	A7	A7	A7	A7	A7

CRTC Registers

Index	0	1	2	3	4	5	6	7	D	E	F	10	0F*	10*	00*	01*	02*	03*
									Mode									
0	37	37	70	70	37	37	70	60	37	70	60	5B	60	5B	2D	2D	5B	5B
1	27	27	4F	4F	27	27	4F	4F	27	4F	4F	4F	4F	4F	27	27	4F	4F
2	2D	2D	5C	5C	2D	2D	59	56	2D	59	56	53	56	53	2B	2B	53	53
3	37	37	2F	2F	37	37	2D	3A	37	2D	1A	17	3A	37	2D	2D	37	37
4	31	31	5F	5F	30	30	5E	51	30	5E	50	50	50	52	28	28	51	51
5	15	15	7	7	14	14	6	60	14	6	E0	BA	60	0	6D	6D	5B	5B
6	4	4	4	4	4	4	4	70	4	4	70	6C	70	6C	6C	6C	6C	6C
7	11	11	11	11	11	11	11	1F	11	11	1F	1F	1F	1F	1F	1F	1F	1F
8	0	0	0	0	0	0	0	0	0	0	0	0	0	0	0	0	0	0
9	7	7	7	7	1	1	1	D	0	0	0	0	0	0	D	D	D	D
A	6	6	6	6	0	0	0	B	0	0	0	0	0	0	6	6	6	6
B	7	7	7	7	0	0	0	C	0	0	0	0	0	0	7	7	7	7
C	0	0	0	0	0	0	0	0	0	0	0	0	0	0	0	0	0	0
D	0	0	0	0	0	0	0	0	0	0	0	0	0	0	0	0	0	0
E	0	0	0	0	0	0	0	0	0	0	0	0	0	0	0	0	0	0
F	0	0	0	0	0	0	0	0	0	0	0	0	0	0	0	0	0	0
10	E1	E1	E1	E1	E1	E1	E0	5E	E1	E0	5E	5E	5E	5E	5E	5E	5E	5E
11	24	24	24	24	24	24	23	2E	24	23	2E	2B	2E	2B	2B	2B	2B	2B
12	C7	C7	C7	C7	C7	C7	C7	5D	C7	C7	5D	5D	5D	5D	5D	5D	5D	5D
13	14	14	28	28	14	14	28	28	14	28	14	14	28	28	14	14	28	28
14	8	8	8	8	0	0	0	D	0	0	D	F	D	F	F	F	F	F
15	E0	E0	E0	E0	E0	E0	DF	5E	E0	DF	5E	5F	5E	5F	5E	5E	5E	5E
16	F0	F0	F0	F0	F0	F0	EF	6E	F0	EF	6E	A	6E	A	A	A	A	A
17	A3	A3	A3	A3	A2	A2	C2	A3	E3	E3	8B	8B	E3	E3	A3	A3	A3	A3
18	FF	FF	FF	FF	FF	FF	FF	FF	FF	FF	FF	FF	FF	FF	FF	FF	FF	FF
19	0	0	0	0	0	0	0	0	0	0	0	0	0	0	0	0	0	0

TABLE 9.5 *(cont.)*

Graphics Controller Registers

Index	0	1	2	3	4	5	6	7	D	E	F	10	0F*	10*	00*	01*	02*	03*
												Mode						
0	0	0	0	0	0	0	0	0	0	0	0	0	0	0	0	0	0	0
1	0	0	0	0	0	0	0	0	0	0	0	0	0	0	0	0	0	0
2	0	0	0	0	0	0	0	0	0	0	0	0	0	0	0	0	0	0
3	0	0	0	0	0	0	0	0	0	0	0	0	0	0	0	0	0	0
4	0	0	0	0	0	0	0	0	0	0	0	0	0	0	0	0	0	0
5	10	10	10	10	30	30	0	10	0	0	10	10	0	0	10	10	10	10
6	E	E	E	E	F	F	D	A	5	5	7	7	5	5	E	E	E	E
7	0	0	0	0	0	0	0	0	F	F	F	F	F	F	0	0	0	0
8	FF	FF	FF	FF	FF	FF	FF	FF	FF	FF	FF	FF	FF	FF	FF	FF	FF	FF

Attribute Controller Registers

Index	0	1	2	3	4	5	6	7	D	E	F	10	0F*	10*	00*	01*	02*	03*
												Mode						
0	0	0	0	0	0	0	0	0	0	0	0	0	0	0	0	0	0	0
1	1	1	1	1	13	13	17	8	1	1	8	1	8	1	1	1	1	1
2	2	2	2	2	15	14	17	8	2	2	0	0	0	2	2	2	2	2
3	3	3	3	3	17	17	17	8	3	3	0	0	0	3	3	3	3	3
4	4	4	4	4	2	2	17	8	4	4	18	4	18	4	4	4	4	4
5	5	5	5	5	4	4	17	8	5	5	18	7	18	5	5	5	5	5
6	6	6	6	6	6	6	17	8	6	6	0	0	0	14	14	14	14	14
7	7	7	7	7	7	7	17	8	7	7	0	0	0	7	7	7	7	7
8	10	10	10	10	10	10	17	10	10	10	0	0	0	38	38	38	38	38
9	11	11	11	11	11	11	17	18	11	11	8	1	8	39	39	39	39	39
A	12	12	12	12	12	12	17	18	12	12	0	0	0	3A	3A	3A	3A	3A
B	13	13	13	13	13	13	17	18	13	13	0	0	0	3B	3B	3B	3B	3B
C	14	14	14	14	14	14	17	18	14	14	0	4	0	3C	3C	3C	3C	3C
D	15	15	15	15	15	15	17	18	15	15	18	7	18	3D	3D	3D	3D	3D
E	16	16	16	16	16	16	17	18	16	16	0	0	0	3E	3E	3E	3E	3E
F	17	17	17	17	17	17	17	18	17	17	0	0	0	3F	3F	3F	3F	3F
10	8	8	8	8	1	1	1	E	1	1	B	1	B	1	8	8	8	8
11	0	0	0	0	0	0	0	0	0	0	0	0	0	0	0	0	0	0
12	F	F	F	F	3	3	1	F	F	F	5	5	5	F	F	F	F	F
13	0	0	0	0	0	0	0	8	0	0	0	0	0	0	0	0	0	0

9.2.4 Reading VGA Registers

The VGA, in contrast to the EGA, has given the programmer access to all of the registers. This important feature allows the programmer to read the status of any of the control registers. The Input Status #0 and Input Status #1 Registers are the only read-only registers on the VGA. All other registers are read/write. The typical default values of the VGA registers are listed in Table 9.6. All register values are listed in hex.

9.3 READING BIOS TABLES FROM MEMORY

The BIOS routines keep track of important video parameters in host RAM memory.

9.3.1 Reading Interrupt Vectors

The video-related interrupt parameters are stored in lower host memory, as indicated in Table 9.7.

In Table 9.7, note that the memory location is equivalent to four times the interrupt vector—that is, $4 \times 05 = 20 = 14$ hex. Multiplying by 4 is necessary because there are four bytes in each of the vector locations. There are four bytes because each location must contain a long pointer.

9.3.2 BIOS Storage in Host Memory

In addition to the vector locations, the BIOS routines store information in host memory. Memory locations range from 0000:0410 to 0000:04A8. Location 0000:0100 is reserved for print-screen status. Table 9.8 lists the relevant video memory storage locations.

These variables are critical to the programmer, especially in the EGA, because the majority of the EGA registers are write-only. Not being able to read the EGA registers forces the programmer to use these storage locations. Fortunately, all registers in the VGA are read/write, allowing the programmer to read the state of each register directly. Often, the variables stored in memory are the results of calculations based on the values in the EGA/VGA registers, and reading these locations is more convenient than calculating the value. The meaning of these memory variables is discussed in the following sections.

9.4 READING THE STATE OF THE EGA AND VGA ADAPTERS

Perhaps the greatest difference between the EGA and the VGA is the VGA's ability to provide information to the host program. This section describes how to access information to ascertain the state of the EGA and VGA.

TABLE 9.6 Control Register Initial Values: VGA

General Registers

							Mode								
Index	00	01	02	03	04	05	06	07	0D	0E	0F	10	11	12	13
0	63	63	63	63	63	63	63	A6	63	63	A2	A3	E3	E3	63
1	00	00	00	00	00	00	00	00	00	00	00	00	00	00	00
2	70	70	70	70	70	70	70	70	70	70	70	70	70	70	70
3	04	04	05	05	04	04	05	FF	04	04	FF	04	04	04	04

Sequence Registers

							Mode								
Index	00	01	02	03	04	05	06	07	0D	0E	0F	10	11	12	13
0	03	03	03	03	03	03	03	03	03	03	03	03	03	03	03
1	09	09	01	01	09	09	01	00	09	01	01	01	01	01	01
2	03	03	03	03	03	03	01	03	0F	0F	0F	0F	0F	0F	0F
3	00	00	00	00	00	00	00	00	00	00	00	00	00	00	00
4	02	02	02	02	02	02	06	02	06	06	06	06	06	06	0E

CRTC Registers

							Mode								
Index	00	01	02	03	04	05	06	07	0D	0E	0F	10	11	12	13
0	2D	2D	5F	5F	2D	2D	5F	FF	2D	5F	FF	5F	5F	5F	5F
1	27	27	4F	4F	27	27	4F	FF	27	4F	FF	4F	4F	4F	4F
2	28	28	50	50	28	28	50	FF	28	50	FF	50	50	50	50
3	90	90	82	82	90	90	82	FF	90	82	FF	82	82	82	82
4	2B	2B	55	55	2B	2B	54	FF	2B	54	FF	54	54	54	24
5	A0	A0	81	81	80	80	80	FF	80	80	FF	80	80	80	80
6	BF	BF	BF	BF	BF	BF	BF	FF	BF	BF	FF	BF	0B	0B	BF
7	1F	1F	1F	1F	1F	1F	1F	FF	1F	1F	FF	1F	3E	3E	1F
8	00	00	00	00	00	00	00	FF	00	00	FF	00	00	00	00
9	C7	C7	C7	C7	C1	C1	C1	FF	C0	C0	FF	40	40	40	41
A	06	06	06	06	00	00	00	FF	00	00	FF	00	00	00	00
B	07	07	07	07	00	00	00	FF	00	00	FF	00	00	00	00
C	00	00	00	00	00	00	00	FF	00	00	FF	00	00	00	00
D	00	00	00	00	00	00	00	FF	00	00	FF	00	00	00	00
E	00	00	00	00	00	00	00	FF	00	00	FF	00	00	00	00
F	31	31	59	59	31	31	59	FF	31	59	FF	59	59	59	31
10	9C	9C	9C	9C	9C	9C	9C	FF	9C	9C	FF	83	EA	EA	9C
11	8E	8E	8E	8E	8E	8E	8E	FF	8E	8E	FF	85	8C	8C	8E
12	8F	8F	8F	8F	8F	8F	8F	FF	8F	8F	FF	5D	DF	DF	8F
13	14	14	28	28	14	14	28	FF	14	28	FF	28	28	28	28
14	1F	1F	1F	1F	00	00	00	FF	00	00	FF	0F	00	00	40

TABLE 9.6   *(cont.)*

15	96	96	96	96	96	96	96	FF	96	96	FF	63	E7	E7	96
16	B9	B9	B9	B9	B9	B9	B9	FF	B9	B9	FF	BA	04	04	B9
17	A3	A3	A3	A3	A2	A2	C2	FF	E3	E3	FF	E3	C3	E3	A3
18	FF	FF	FF	FF	FF	FF	FF	FF	FF	FF	FF	FF	FF	FF	FF

Graphics Controller Registers

						Mode									
Index	*00*	*01*	*02*	*03*	*04*	*05*	*06*	*07*	*0D*	*0E*	*0F*	*10*	*11*	*12*	*13*
0	00	00	00	00	00	00	00	00	00	00	00	00	00	00	00
1	00	00	00	00	00	00	00	00	00	00	00	00	00	00	00
2	00	00	00	00	00	00	00	00	00	00	00	00	00	00	00
3	00	00	00	00	00	00	00	00	00	00	00	00	00	00	00
4	00	00	00	00	00	00	00	00	00	00	00	00	00	00	00
5	10	10	10	10	30	30	00	10	10	00	00	10	00	00	40
6	0E	0E	0E	0E	0F	0F	0D	0A	05	05	05	05	05	05	05
7	00	00	00	00	00	00	00	00	00	0F	05	00	05	0F	0F
8	FF	FF	FF	FF	FF	FF	FF	FF	FF	FF	FF	FF	FF	FF	FF

Attribute Controller Registers

						Mode									
Index	*00*	*01*	*02*	*03*	*04*	*05*	*06*	*07*	*0D*	*0E*	*0F*	*10*	*11*	*12*	*13*
0	00	00	00	00	00	00	00	00	00	00	00	00	00	00	00
1	01	01	01	01	13	13	17	08	01	01	08	01	3F	01	01
2	02	02	02	02	15	15	17	08	02	02	00	02	3F	02	02
3	03	03	03	03	17	17	17	08	03	03	00	03	3F	03	03
4	04	04	04	04	02	02	17	08	04	04	18	04	3F	04	04
5	05	05	05	05	04	04	17	08	05	05	18	05	3F	05	05
6	06	06	06	06	06	06	17	08	06	06	00	14	3F	14	06
7	07	07	07	07	07	07	17	08	07	07	00	07	3F	07	07
8	10	10	10	10	10	10	17	10	10	10	00	38	3F	38	08
9	11	11	11	11	11	11	17	18	11	11	08	39	3F	39	09
A	12	12	12	12	12	12	17	18	12	12	00	3A	3F	3A	0A
B	13	13	13	13	13	13	17	18	13	13	00	3B	3F	3B	0B
C	14	14	14	14	14	14	17	18	14	14	00	3C	3F	3C	0C
D	15	15	15	15	15	15	17	18	15	15	18	3D	3F	3D	0D
E	16	16	16	16	16	16	17	18	16	16	00	3E	3F	3E	0E
F	17	17	17	17	17	17	17	18	17	17	00	3F	3F	3F	0F
10	08	08	08	08	01	01	01	0E	01	01	0B	01	01	01	41
11	00	00	00	00	00	00	00	00	00	00	00	00	00	00	00
12	0F	0F	0F	0F	03	03	01	0F	0F	0F	05	0F	0F	0F	0F
13	00	00	00	00	00	00	00	00	00	00	00	00	00	00	00
14	00	00	00	00	00	00	00	00	00	00	00	00	00	00	00

TABLE 9.7 Interrupt Vectors

Memory Location (Hex)	Function
0000:0014	Interrupt INT 05 hex vector
0000:0028	Interrupt INT 0A hex vector
0000:0040	Interrupt INT 10 hex vector
0000:007C	Interrupt INT 1F hex vector
0000:0108	Interrupt INT 42 hex vector
0000:010C	Interrupt INT 43 hex vector

9.4.1 Reading the EGA State

Unlike the VGA, the EGA has no provision in the BIOS calls for returning the adapter state information. This information can be obtained from the memory locations reserved for the video system as listed in Table 9.8. The relevant values for each of the described display modes of the EGA are listed in Table 9.9. Note that this table does not contain elements that are relevant to the dynamic condition of these display modes. For example, the cursor position tables are not included in Table 9.9.

9.4.2 Reading the VGA State

The VGA BIOS provides a useful BIOS call that returns the current information regarding the state of the VGA. The BIOS call AH=1B hex invokes the Return Functionality/State Information. The programmer provides this BIOS call with a pointer to an array. The BIOS routine fills this array with the functionality and state information. The information returned to the calling program closely resembles the state table illustrated in Table 9.9. The values returned by this BIOS call and their associated offsets from the top of the array are listed in Table 9.10.

9.4.3 Functionality/State Information

Invoking the BIOS call to read the functionality/state information using a VGA planar system results in the information listed in Tables 9.11 through 9.15. Note that several parameters called out in the functionality/state specification from Table 9.15, are not included in this table. These parameters were eliminated from the Table 9.15 because they referred to non–mode-related functions. For example, cursor shape and cursor position are independent of the active display mode.

9.4.4 VGA Static Information Table

The static information table consists of a group of static parameters that describe the condition of the VGA. This table is called *static* because the values do not

TABLE 9.8 EGA: Host Memory Locations Reserved for Video

Memory Location (Hex)	Function
0000:0449	Active video mode
0000:044A	Number of character columns
0000:044C	Length of current display page
0000:044E	Start of current page in display memory
0000:0450	Cursor save area
0000:0450	Page 0: row / column
0000:0452	Page 1: row / column
0000:0454	Page 2: row / column
0000:0456	Page 3: row / column
0000:0458	Page 4: row / column
0000:045A	Page 5: row / column
0000:045C	Page 6: row / column
0000:045E	Page 7: row / column
0000:0460	Cursor mode: start / end
0000:0462	Current display page
0000:0463	Base host address of port I/O
0000:0465	Current mode
0000:0466	Current color
0000:0484	Number of characters rows on screen − 1
0000:0485	Bytes per character
0000:0487	Miscellaneous information
0000:0488	Configuration bits
0000:04A8	Pointer to Table of Save Area Pointers
0000:0100	Print-screen status

TABLE 9.9 EGA State Information

Active display mode = 0 hex

Number of character columns = 40
Length of display buffer = 800 hex
Start of active buffer = 0 hex
Cursor starting line = 7, ending line = 6

CRTC port address = 3D4 hex
Number of character rows per screen = 25
Character height = 14 rows

Active display mode = 1 hex

Number of character columns = 40
Length of display buffer = 800 hex
Start of active buffer = 0 hex
Cursor starting line = 7, ending line = 6

CRTC port address = 3D4 hex
Number of character rows per screen = 25
Character height = 14 rows

TABLE 9.9   *(cont.)*

Active display mode = 2 hex

Number of character columns = 80	CRTC port address = 3D4 hex
Length of display buffer = 1000 hex	Number of character rows per screen = 25
Start of active buffer = 0 hex	Character height = 14 rows
Cursor starting line = 7, ending line = 6	

Active display mode = 3 hex

Number of character columns = 80	CRTC port address = 3D4 hex
Length of display buffer = 1000 hex	Number of character rows per screen = 25
Start of active buffer = 0 hex	Character height = 14 rows
Cursor starting line = 7, ending line = 6	

Active display mode = 4 hex

Number of character columns = 40	CRTC port address = 3D4 hex
Length of display buffer = 4000 hex	Number of character rows per screen = 25
Start of active buffer = 0 hex	Character height = 8 rows
Cursor starting line = 0, ending line = 0	

Active display mode = 5 hex

Number of character columns = 40	CRTC port address = 3D4 hex
Length of display buffer = 4000 hex	Number of character rows per screen = 25
Start of active buffer = 0 hex	Character height = 8 rows
Cursor starting line = 0, ending line = 0	

Active display mode = 6 hex

Number of character columns = 80	CRTC port address = 3D4 hex
Length of display buffer = 4000 hex	Number of character rows per screen = 25
Start of active buffer = 0 hex	Character height = 8 rows
Cursor starting line = 0, ending line = 0	

Active display mode = 7 hex

Number of character columns = 80	CRTC port address = 3D4 hex
Length of display buffer = 1000 hex	Number of character rows per screen = 25
Start of active buffer = 0 hex	Character height = 14 rows
Cursor starting line = 12, ending line = 11	

Active display mode = D hex

Number of character columns = 40	CRTC port address = 3D4 hex
Length of display buffer = 2000 hex	Number of character rows per screen = 25
Start of active buffer = 0 hex	Character height = 8 rows
Cursor starting line = 0, ending line = 0	

TABLE 9.9   *(cont.)*

Active display mode = E hex

Number of character columns = 80

Length of display buffer = 4000 hex

Start of active buffer = 0 hex

Cursor starting line = 0, ending line = 0

CRTC port address = 3D4 hex

Number of character rows per screen = 25

Character height = 8 rows

Active display mode = F hex

Number of character columns = 80

Length of display buffer = 8000 hex

Start of active buffer = 0 hex

Cursor starting line = 0, ending line = 0

CRTC port address = 3D4 hex

Number of character rows per screen = 25

Character height = 14 rows

Active display mode = 10 hex

Number of character columns = 80

Length of display buffer = 8000 hex

Start of active buffer = 0 hex

Cursor starting line = 0, ending line = 0

CRTC port address = 3D4 hex

Number of character rows per screen = 25

Character height = 14 rows

TABLE 9.10   Functionality/State Information

Offset (Hex)	Notes	Length	Function
00	1	Word	Static Functionality Info. Table Offset
02	1	Word	Static Functionality Info. Table Segment
04		Byte	Active display mode
05		Word	Number of character columns per screen
07		Word	Length of current display page
09		Word	Start address of current display page
0B		Word	Cursor position table
0B		Word	Page 0: row / column
0D		Word	Page 1: row / column
0F		Word	Page 2: row / column
11		Word	Page 3: row / column
13		Word	Page 4: row / column
15		Word	Page 5: row / column
17		Word	Page 6: row / column
19		Word	Page 7: row / column
1B		Word	Cursor mode: start / end
1D		Byte	Current display page
1E		Word	Base host address of Port I/O
20		Byte	Current mode
21		Byte	Current color palette
22	2	Byte	Number of character rows on screen
23		Word	Bytes per character

TABLE 9.10 *(cont.)*

Offset (Hex)	Notes	Length	Function
25	3	Byte	Display combination code (DCC) (active)
26	3	Byte	Display combination code (DCC) (alternate)
27		Word	Number of colors supported in current mode
29		Byte	Number of pages supported in current mode
2A	4	Byte	Number of scan lines in current mode
2B	5	Byte	Primary active character block
2C	5	Byte	Secondary active character block
2D	6	Byte	Miscellaneous state information
2E–30			Reserved
31	7	Byte	Display memory installed
32	8	Byte	Save pointer state information
33–3F			Reserved

Notes:

1. The Static Information Table is pointed to by the Offset and Segment address located in offsets 00 and 02. (See the Static Information Table.)

2. The number of character rows on the screen is one greater than the similar value in the EGA. However, in the EGA, the value at host address 0000:0084 is one less than the number of columns.

3. The Display Combination Code signifies which type of monitor is installed in the active and alternate display adapter. (See the Display Combination Code.)

4. The number of scan lines in the current mode ranges from 200 to 480 scan lines depending on the active display mode. The code in this byte represents the number of scan lines, as indicated in Table 9.11.

5. The values in the primary and secondary active character block locations range from 0 to 259. These numbers represent block 0 to block 255, respectively.

6. The Miscellaneous state information is different from the Miscellaneous information byte of the EGA residing at host address 0000:0487. Each bit in the Miscellaneous state information byte has a special meaning. The function of each of these bits are listed in Table 9.12.

7. The amount of display memory installed can range from 64 Kbyte to 256 Kbytes. It is conceivable to load 512 Kbytes on the display adapter, because the PC memory map allows 512 Kbytes of storage between A000:0000 and BFFF:FFFF hex. Table 9.13 lists the possible display memory configurations.

8. Each bit in the save pointer state information byte contains a flag representing the active or inactive state of a variety of features in the VGA. Any bit set to 1 indicates that the respective state is active. Likewise, any bit reset to a 0 indicates an inactive state. The meaning of each bit is listed in Table 9.14.

TABLE 9.11 Number of Scan Lines in Alphanumeric Mode

Code	Number of Scan Lines
0	200
1	350
2	400
3	480

TABLE 9.12 Miscellaneous State Information Byte

Bit Number	Function
0	Monitor state =0 All modes on all monitors are inactive =1 All modes on all monitors are active
1	Color Register summing mode =0 Summing Mode inactive =1 Summing Mode active
2	Monochrome display =0 Monochrome display not attached =1 Monochrome display attached
3	Default palette loading during Mode Set =0 Palette, Color Registers not affected =1 Palette, Color Registers loaded
4	Cursor Emulation =0 Cursor emulation inactive =1 Cursor emulation active
5	Function of bit 3 of attribute byte =0 Use as part of background color =1 Use to signify blinking or non-blinking
6,7	Reserved

TABLE 9.13 Amount of Display Memory

Code	Amount of Display Memory
0	64 Kbytes
1	128 Kbytes
2	256 Kbytes
3	384 Kbytes
4-255	Reserved

TABLE 9.14 Save Pointer State Information Byte

Bit Number	Function (1 = Active)
0	512-character set
1	Dynamic save area
2	Alpha font override
3	Graphics font override
4	Palette override
5	Display combination code extension
6,7	Reserved

TABLE 9.15 Typical Functionality/State Information

Display mode = 0 hex

Number of character columns = 40
Length of display buffer = 800 hex
CRTC address = 3D4 hex
CRT_MODE_SET = 2C hex,
CRT_PALETTE = 30 hex
Number of character rows per screen = 25

Character height = 16
Number of colors = 16
Number of display pages supported = 8
Miscellaneous state information = 31 hex

Display mode = 1 hex

Number of character columns = 40
Length of display buffer = 800 hex
CRTC address = 3D4 hex
CRT_MODE_SET = 28 hex,
CRT_PALETTE = 30 hex
Number of character rows per screen = 25

Character height = 16
Number of colors = 16
Number of display pages supported = 8
Miscellaneous state information = 31 hex

Display mode = 2 hex

Number of character columns = 80
Length of display buffer = 1000 hex
CRTC address = 3D4 hex
CRTMODE_SET = 2D hex,
CRT_PALETTE = 30 hex
Number of character rows per screen = 25

Character height = 16
Number of colors = 16
Number of display pages supported = 8
Miscellaneous state information = 31 hex

Display mode = 3 hex

Number of character columns = 80
Length of display buffer = 1000 hex
CRTC address = 3D4 hex
CRTMODE_SET = 29 hex,
CRT_PALETTE = 30 hex
Number of character rows per screen = 25

Character height = 16
Number of colors = 16
Number of display pages supported = 8
Miscellaneous state information = 31 hex

Display mode = 4 hex

Number of character columns = 40
Length of display buffer = 4000 hex
CRTC address = 3D4 hex
CRT_MODE_SET = 2A hex,
CRT_PALETTE = 30 hex
Number of character rows per screen = 25

Character height = 8
Number of colors = 4
Number of display pages supported = 1
Miscellaneous state information = 11 hex

TABLE 9.15 *(cont.)*

Display mode = 5 hex

Number of character columns = 40 Character height = 8
Length of display buffer = 4000 hex Number of colors = 4
CRTC address = 3D4 hex Number of display pages supported = 1
CRT_MODE_SET = 2E hex, Miscellaneous state information = 11 hex
CRT_PALETTE = 30 hex
Number of character rows per screen = 25

Display mode = 6 hex

Number of character columns = 80 Character height = 8
Length of display buffer = 4000 hex Number of colors = 2
CRTC address = 3D4 hex Number of display pages supported = 1
CRT_MODE_SET = 1E hex, Miscellaneous state information = 11 hex
CRT_PALETTE = 3F hex
Number of character rows per screen = 25

Display mode = 7 hex

Number of character columns = 80 Character height = 16
Length of display buffer = 1000 hex Number of colors = 0
CRTC address = 3B4 hex Number of display pages supported = 8
CRT_MODE_SET = 29 hex, Miscellaneous state information = 31 hex
CRT_PALETTE = 30 hex
Number of character rows per screen = 25

Display mode = D hex

Number of character columns = 40 Character height = 8
Length of display buffer = 2000 hex Number of colors = 16
CRTC address = 3D4 hex Number of display pages supported = 8
CRT_MODE_SET = 29 hex, Miscellaneous state information = 11 hex
CRT_PALETTE = 30 hex
Number of character rows per screen = 25

Display mode = E hex

Number of character columns = 80 Character height = 8
Length of display buffer = 4000 hex Number of colors = 16
CRTC address = 3D4 hex Number of display pages supported = 4
CRT_MODE_SET = 29 hex, Miscellaneous state information = 11 hex
CRT_PALETTE = 30 hex
Number of character rows per screen = 25

TABLE 9.15 *(cont.)*

Display mode = F hex

Number of character columns = 80
Length of display buffer = 8000 hex
CRTC address = 3B4 hex
CRT_MODE_SET = 29 hex,
CRT_PALETTE = 30 hex
Number of character rows per screen = 25

Character height = 14
Number of colors = 0
Number of display pages supported = 2
Miscellaneous state information = 31 hex

Display mode = 10 hex

Number of character columns = 80
Length of display buffer = 8000 hex
CRTC address = 3D4 hex
CRT_MODE_SET = 29 hex,
CRT_PALETTE = 30 hex
Number of character rows per screen = 25

Character height = 14
Number of colors = 16
Number of display pages supported = 2
Miscellaneous state information = 11 hex

Display mode = 11 hex

Number of character columns = 80
Length of display buffer = A000 hex
CRTC address = 3D4 hex
CRT_MODE_SET = 29 hex,
CRT_PALETTE = 30 hex
Number of character rows per screen = 30

Character height = 16
Number of colors = 2
Number of display pages supported = 1
Miscellaneous state information = 11 hex

Display mode = 12 hex

Number of character columns = 80
Length of display buffer = A000 hex
CRTC address = 3D4 hex
CRT_MODE_SET = 29 hex,
CRT_PALETTE = 30 hex
Number of character rows per screen = 30

Character height = 16
Number of colors = 16
Number of display pages supported = 1
Miscellaneous state information = 11 hex

Display mode = 13 hex

Number of character columns = 40
Length of display buffer = 2000 hex
CRTC address = 3D4 hex
CRT_MODE_SET = 29 hex,
CRT_PALETTE = 30 hex
Number of character rows per screen = 25

Character height = 8
Number of colors = 0
Number of display pages supported = 1
Miscellaneous state information = 11 hex

TABLE 9.16   Static Information Table

Offset (Hex)	Notes	Length	Function
00	1	Byte	Video modes (BIOS call AH = 00)
01	1	Byte	Video modes (BIOS call AH = 00)
02	1	Byte	Video modes (BIOS call AH = 00)
03–06			Reserved
07	2	Byte	Scan lines of text available (BIOS call AH = 12 BL = 30 hex)
08		Byte	Character blocks available: alpha modes (BIOS call AH = 11)
09		Byte	Max. # of character blocks: alpha modes (BIOS call AH = 11)
0A	3	Byte	Miscellaneous functions (BIOS calls are bit dependent)
0B	3	Byte	Miscellaneous functions (BIOS calls are bit-dependent)
0C–0D			Reserved
0E	4	Byte	Save pointer functions

Notes:

1. The availability of the video modes is contained in three contiguous bytes of the static function table. The three bytes contain a total of 18 bits. Each bit is associated with a display mode. A bit position within one of these three bytes that is set to a 1 indicates that the respective mode is supported on this video system. The display modes and their associated bits are listed in Table 9.18.

2. In the VGA, it is possible to configure the alphanumeric display modes with 200, 350, or 400 lines as indicated in Table 9.19.

3. There are two bytes dedicated to miscellaneous functions of the VGA. In these two bytes, any bit set to a 1 indicates that the associated function is enabled. Likewise, any bit reset to a 0 indicates that the function is disabled. The meaning of each bit in the two bytes is listed in Table 9.20.

change during the operation of the VGA. Rather, this table lists the configuration of the VGA, which is similar to the information provided by sense switches. The values stored in the Static Information Table and their associated offsets from the start of the table are listed in Table 9.16.

9.4.5   Typical Static Function Block

A typical static function block is listed in Table 9.17. From the Functionality/State Information, it was determined that this block resides in BIOS ROM beginning at address E000:305F hex.

TABLE 9.17 Static Function Information Block

Video modes 0–7 = FF hex (1 = enabled)
Video modes 8–F = E0 hex (1 = enabled)
Video modes 10–13 = 0F hex (1 = enabled)
Scan lines available in text modes = 07 hex
Character blocks available in text modes = 2
Maximum # of active character blocks: alpha modes = 8
Miscellaneous functions = FF hex (1 = enabled)
Miscellaneous functions = 0E hex (1 = enabled)
Save Pointer functions = 0 hex (1 = enabled)

TABLE 9.18 Display Modes Available (BIOS Call AH = 00 Hex)

Byte	Bit	Display Mode (Hex) (1 = Supported 0 = Not supported)
00	0	Mode 0
00	1	Mode 1
00	2	Mode 2
00	3	Mode 3
00	4	Mode 4
00	5	Mode 5
00	6	Mode 6
00	7	Mode 7
01	0	Mode 8
01	1	Mode 9
01	2	Mode A
01	3	Mode B
01	4	Mode C
01	5	Mode D
01	6	Mode E
01	7	Mode F
02	0	Mode 10
02	1	Mode 11
02	2	Mode 12
02	3	Mode 13
02	4–7	Reserved

9.4.6 VGA Display Combination Code

The display combination code (DCC) contains information relevant to the type of display adapters installed in the computer and the monitors connected to the active and inactive display adapters. Because there can be two VGA systems installed in the same computer, one planar and one adapter, it is possible to

TABLE 9.19 Scan Lines Available in Alphanumeric Modes (BIOS Call AH = 12 Hex)

Bit	Number of Scan Lines
0	200
1	350
2	400
3–7	Reserved

TABLE 9.20 Miscellaneous Functions

Byte	Bit	Function (1 = Active)
00	0	All modes on all monitors
00	1	Color Registers summing (BIOS call AH = 10 AL = 1B hex) (BIOS call AH = 12 BL = 33 hex)
00	2	Character font loading (BIOS call AH = 11 hex)
00	3	Default palette loading on mode set (BIOS call AH = 12 BL = 31 hex)
00	4	Cursor emulation (BIOS call AH = 01, AH = 12 BL = 34 hex)
00	5	EGA palette (BIOS call AH = 10 hex)
	6	DAC color palette (BIOS call AH = 10 hex)
00	7	DAC color paging (BIOS call AH = 10 hex)
01	0	Light pen (BIOS call AH = 04 hex)
01	1	Save/restore (BIOS call AH = 1C hex)
01	2	Background intensity/blinking control (BIOS call AH = 11 hex)
01	3	Display combination code (DCC) (BIOS call AH = 1A hex)
01	4–7	Reserved

have any combination of monitors on either system. Both the active and the inactive display systems have their own DCC. The inactive display system is also called the *alternate display system*. The DCC codes and their meanings are listed in Table 9.21.

TABLE 9.21 Display Combination Code (BIOS Call AH = 1A Hex)

Code	Type of Adapter	Type of Monitor
0	None	None
1	Monochrome	Monochrome
2	Color Graphics Adapter	
7	PS/2 Display Adapter	Monochrome
8	PS/2 Display Adapter	Color

9.4.7 VGA: Saving and Restoring

A BIOS call is provided in the VGA which allows the video state to be saved or restored. This BIOS call, AH=1C hex, allows the programmer to load the video system with data provided in a buffer. The buffer can contain the video hardware state, the video data areas or the video palette state and color registers. This buffer can contain any combination of these groups of parameters. Upon invoking a save operation, a buffer provided by the programmer is loaded automatically by BIOS with the desired groups of parameters. Upon invoking a restore operation, the programmer provides the loaded buffer to BIOS and BIOS loads the groups of parameters into the VGA.

9.5 TESTING FOR HARDWARE

For software to operate in an environment that may contain different graphics adapters and monitors, it first must determine which hardware is present. Certain standardized techniques and some not-so-standard techniques are defined to assist the programmer in this task. The Micro Channel requires that the cards contain a registered ID number. In this case, it is necessary only to read the ID numbers on the bus to determine what hardware is present. This is not the case, however, for the EGA/VGA.

9.5.1 Testing for Adapters

Tests are often necessary to determine if an MDA, CGA, EGA, PGA, MEGA, or VGA is present. In addition, a system might have one adapter configured as a monochrome adapter and a second adapter configured as a color adapter. The System/2 computer family allows two VGA display systems to be resident in the same computer. In addition, both can be configured with color monitors. In the System/2, only one of these VGA systems, either the planar or the adapter, can be active at a time.

The EGA may be tested in a number of ways. One way to differentiate the MDA, CGA, and EGA is to read the system configuration word at host memory address 0040:0010. A primary display field is contained in bits 4 and 5 of the byte at this location. Table 9.22 lists the options for this field.

TABLE 9.22 Primary Display Field

Bit 5	Bit 4	Primary Display
0	0	EGA
0	1	CGA 40-column mode
1	0	CGA 80-column mode
1	1	MDA

TABLE 9.23 IBM Logo

Address	Character	Code (Hex)
C000:001E	I	49
C000:001F	B	42
C000:0020	M	4D

Another way to check for the EGA is to determine if the copyright information is present in the EGA BIOS ROM. The BIOS ROM starts at location A000:0000. The first two bytes contain the traditional BIOS identifiers 55 hex followed by AA. The copyright information begins at C000:0009. Although it is not a recommended method, an IBM identifier can be found at memory location C000:001E, as shown in Table 9.23.

Several software products use this flag to determine if an EGA is present. Compatible EGA adapters will usually contain these bytes in the proper memory locations.

If it is determined that an EGA monitor does not exist, it is possible to search for other adapters by writing to the appropriate Cursor Position Register for the other adapters. The monochrome and color adapters both rely on the 6845 graphics controller chip. A group of CRT Controller Registers are contained in this chip, one of which is the Cursor Location Register. This register is a read/write register because it is necessary to command the cursor to move to a desired location as well as reading the current location.

The monochrome adapter maps the CRTC Registers at host port address 3B4 hex, and the color adapter maps the register at 3D4 hex. This register must be loaded with a 0F hex in order to access the Cursor Location Register. The Cursor Position Register is then accessed, through host port 3B5 for monochrome adapters or host port 3D5 for color adapters. The programmer can read this register, saving the value for later, write a new value into this register, and then read it again. The register exists if the second read operation returns the same value as was written into the register. If the register exists, the adapter must be present. If the test is positive, the original data read from the cursor position can be returned to the Cursor Position Register.

9.5.2 Testing for Monitors

If the EGA is present, a test can be performed to determine whether a mono-chrome or monitor is attached to the adapter. A Miscellaneous Information Byte is located at memory address 0000:487. A monitor type field is kept in bit 1 of this byte. Table 9.24 lists the meaning of this field.

If an EGA is present with a monochrome monitor, it is possible that a second display adapter exists with a color monitor—for example, the CGA. Likewise, if the EGA is using a color monitor, a second display adapter may exist with a monochrome monitor—for example, the MDA or the Hercules.

9.5.3 Reading System Parameters

The EGA/VGA registers are accessed through the host input/output ports. If the system is configured as a monochrome system, certain ports will be config-ured at port addresses beginning with a 3Bx. Likewise, if the system is config-ured as a color system, certain ports will be configured at port addresses begin-ning with a 3Dx. The x refers to the least significant hexadecimal digit of the port address. Examples of these registers are the CRTC Address and Data Registers, the Feature Control Register, and the Input Status #1 Register. The other registers reside at host port addresses beginning with a 3Cx. It is possible to determine whether the ports can be accessed through ports 3Bx or 3Dx by the value in host memory address 0000:0463, called the Base Address of Active Video Interface Board. The value in this location will be loaded with a 3B4 or a 3D4, indicating the base port address.

It is possible to determine all relevant information regarding the EGA/VGA display memory. The base of the EGA display memory is at host address A000:0000. The amount of EGA display memory available can be obtained by a BIOS call. The Alternate Select BIOS call entitled Return Video Information can provide information regarding the amount of display memory installed on the board. Table 9.25 lists the possible memory configurations and the associated codes returned in the BL register. Most EGA implementations and all VGA implementations are configured with 256 Kbytes of display memory.

The EGA/VGA segments the display memory into display pages. The number of display pages available depends on the amount of display memory and the current display mode. The base address of the active display page relative to the host address of the EGA display memory can be determined from 0000:044E. This word contains the offset to the top of the current display page. The length of the display page is loaded into host address 0000:044C.

The horizontal and vertical resolution of a page can be measured in units of characters or pixels. The number of character rows minus 1 is loaded into host address 0000:0484, and the number of character columns is loaded into host address 0000:044A.

The number of vertical pixels can be determined by multiplying the number of rows per character by the number of character rows per screen. The number

TABLE 9.24 Monitor Field

Bit 1	Monitor Type
0	Color
1	Monochrome

TABLE 9.25 Amount of Display Memory

BL Register	Amount of Memory	Memory per Plane
0	64 Kbytes	16 Kbytes
1	128 Kbytes	32 Kbytes
2	192 Kbytes	48 Kbytes
3	256 Kbytes	64 Kbytes

of rows per character is loaded in host memory address 0000:0485, commonly called the number of bytes per character. This terminology is slightly confusing. The characters are stored in the character font bit patterns using a format that relies on one byte per character row. When displayed, however, a character does not necessarily represent eight horizontal pixels. Character sets whose characters are nine pixels wide are available.

The number of horizontal pixels can be determined by multiplying the number of character rows (as determined above) by 8. The nine-bit-wide characters do not have to be considered when a pixel coordinate system is used. The only time a pixel coordinate system would be used is when the EGA/VGA is in a graphics mode, and no graphics modes use nine-bit-wide character sets.

9.5.4 Reading the Cursor Status

Information regarding the cursor is kept in host memory and can be accessed through the Read Cursor Position BIOS call, AH = 03. The EGA display memory can be segmented into a maximum of eight display pages. The BIOS call returns the cursor position of any desired page.

A table of cursor row and column positions is kept in host memory beginning at host address 0000:0450. This table consists of eight row and column coordinate pairs, one for each possible display page. The row values are in the even byte addresses, and the column values are in the odd byte addresses. The values in each of the row and column positions refer to the character position instead of the pixel position. The shape of the cursor can be read from host memory address 0000:0460. The lower byte of this word contains the start scan line, and the upper byte contains the end scan line of the cursor block.

Table 9.26 Miscellaneous State Information

Bit Number	Information
0	Cursor emulation 0 = Direct cursor setting 1 = Emulate 8-by-8 cursor
1	Display monitor 0 = Color 1 = Monochrome
2	Display buffer access 0 = CPU can access memory at any time 1 = CPU must wait for display inactive
3	EGA status 0 = EGA active 1 = EGA inactive
4	(Reserved)
6,5	Amount of display memory 0 = 64 Kbytes 1 = 128 Kbytes 2 = 192 Kbytes 3 = 256 Kbytes
7	Status of display memory after mode set 0 = Display memory cleared 1 = Display memory preserved

9.5.5 Video Parameters

The current video mode number is contained in host memory address 0000:0449. The active video page number is contained in host memory address 0000:0462. Miscellaneous information is available in a byte at host address 0000:0487. Each bit in this byte refers to a specific function. These functions are listed in Table 9.26.

The video configuration can be determined by reading host memory address 0000:0488, called the configuration bits byte. The low-order four bits correspond to the sense switches on the EGA, and the high-order four bits correspond to the feature bits. The sense switches tell the EGA which monitor is attached and if the EGA is coexisting with any other display adapter. The meanings of these four bits of this memory byte are listed Table 9.27.

The EGA has a feature connector with two parallel inputs and two parallel outputs. The inputs to the feature connector are labeled FEAT 0 and FEAT 1. These inputs may be read in the Input Status #0 Register. The outputs are controlled through the Feature Control Register. The organization of these bits is listed in Table 9.28.

The EGA stores a list of double-word (long) pointers beginning at host

TABLE 9.27 Sense Switch Field of Video Configuration

Field (Hex)	Primary Display	Secondary Display
0	MDA Mono 80c	EGA RGBI 40c
1	MDA Mono 80c	EGA RGBI 80c
2	MDA Mono 80c	EGA RrGgBb 200p
3	MDA Mono 80c	EGA RrGgBb 350p
4	CGA RGBI 40c	EGA Mono 720p
5	CGA RGBI 80c	EGA Mono 720p
6	EGA RGBI 40c	MDA Mono 80c
7	EGA RGBI 80c	MDA Mono 80c
8	EGA RrGgBb 200p	MDA Mono 80c
9	EGA RrGgBb 350p	MDA Mono 80c
A	EGA Mono 720p	CGA RGBI 40c
B	EGA Mono 720p	CGA RGBI 80c

Legend:

MDA	= Monochrome Display Adapter
CGA	= Color Graphics Adapter
EGA	= Enhanced Graphics Adapter
Mono	= Monochrome monitor
RGBI	= 16-color monitor
RrGgBb	= Enhanced Color Monitor
#p	= Number of horizontal pixels per line
#c	= Number of horizontal characters per line

TABLE 9.28 Feature Control Field of Video Configuration

Bit Number	Information
4	Input value of FEAT 0 with FC1 ON
5	Input value of FEAT 1 with FC1 ON
6	Input value of FEAT 0 with FC1 OFF
7	Input value of FEAT 1 with FC1 OFF

memory address 0000:04A8. This table is called the Video Parameter Table Pointer. It consists of four pointers to other tables also resident in host memory. The four pointers address each of these other pointers. The Video Parameter Table Pointer is illustrated in Table 9.29.

The Video Parameter Table consists of 1,472 bytes of data organized as 23 blocks of information, each 64 bytes long. Each block is associated with a display mode and contains the values that are to be loaded into the EGA/VGA registers

TABLE 9.29 Video Table Pointer

Memory Address	Pointer
0000:04A8	Video Parameter Table
0000:04AC	Dynamic Save Area (optional)
0000:04B0	Alpha Aux Char Generator (optional)
0000:04B4	Text Aux Char Generator (optional)

TABLE 9.30 Video Parameter Table

Offset	Mode	Offset	Mode	Offset	Mode
000	0	040	1	080	2
0C0	3	100	4	140	5
180	6	1C0	7	200	8
240	9	280	A	2C0	B
300	C	340	D	380	E
3C0	F	400	10	440	F*
480	10*	4C0	0*	500	1*
540	2*	580	3*		

TABLE 9.31 Block Structure of Video Parameter Table

Offset	# Bytes	Contents
0	1	# columns
1	1	# rows
2	1	Pixels/character
3–4	2	Page length
5–8	4	Sequencer Registers
9	1	Miscellaneous Register
10–34	25	CRTC Registers
35–54	20	Attribute Registers
55–63	9	Graphics Controller Registers

during a Set Mode command. This table is typically located in the EGA BIOS ROM. Table 9.30 lists the modes and the offset from the long pointer in 0000:04A8 at which the register values can be found.

Each block of 64 bytes contains the values that will be loaded into the EGA registers. The meanings of the bytes within these blocks are listed in Table 9.31.

Chapter 10

The EGA/VGA Registers

10.1 THE EGA/VGA REGISTERS

All graphics functions of the EGA/VGA are controlled through a set of registers. The EGA/VGA standard dictates the placement and function of each of these registers. These registers are mapped into the host port address space and are accessed via assembly language IN and OUT instructions. Each of these registers is one byte wide and is segmented into one to eight independent fields. Graphics functions are controlled from these fields. A single function may require a field that spans more than one register. An example of this is seen in the Start Address Registers.

To specify the starting address of the display, it is necessary to load the Start Address Registers with a value that points to an individual byte within the display memory. Because there are 64 Kbytes possible, a 16-bit value is required to fully specify the start address. Thus, two registers, each a byte wide, are required. These are named the Start Address High and Start Address Low Registers.

In most cases, the EGA and VGA registers are identical. The VGA has added several features not available on the EGA, and many fields within the registers are specified for the VGA only. Some of the existing fields apply only to the EGA. Moreover, there are four fields that have one function for the EGA and a different function for the VGA.

10.1.1 Register Groups

The registers are grouped into five basic sets consisting of the General or External Registers, the Sequencer Registers, the CRTC Registers, the Graphics Registers, and the Attribute Registers. Note that certain registers exist at one of two host port addresses. These registers exist at host port address 3Bx hex if the VGA/EGA adapter is in a monochrome emulation mode and at host port address 3Dx hex if the adapter is in a color emulation mode. These registers are mapped in this manner to ensure downward compatibility. In addition, because the monochrome and color adapters are mapped into different I/O port addresses, a monochrome and color adapter can coexist in the same system. Table 10.1 illustrates the I/O port addresses used by these registers.

TABLE 10.1 Register Port Addresses

Register Groups	I/O Port Addresses (Hex)
General or External	3BA or 3DA, 3CA, 3C2, and 3CC
Sequencer	3C4, 3C5
CRTC	3B4, 3B5 or 3D4, 3D5
Graphics	3CE, 3CF
Attribute	3CO, 3C1

In many applications, it is advisable to use the BIOS routines to modify the registers in the EGA/VGA. All basic graphics functions can be programmed using the BIOS calls. However, several important features within the EGA/VGA can improve processing speed, and these are not implemented within the BIOS calls. In order to use these features, it is necessary for the programmer to access the registers directly. In addition, many of the graphics features that are programmed within the BIOS calls require a prohibitively long time to execute due to the BIOS overhead. In these cases, it is necessary to program the EGA/VGA by writing to the registers and display memory directly. It is possible to achieve a significant improvement in execution time by optimizing the data path to and from the host and the EGA/VGA.

Future graphics adapters may be compatible at the BIOS level, and direct programming of the registers may then cause erroneous results. However, the processing speed advantages of direct programming often outweigh the disadvantages of lost portability.

The EGA and VGA are compatible at the BIOS level. The VGA has additional features that can be accessed through the VGA BIOS calls but not through the EGA BIOS calls. All of the EGA BIOS calls are implemented in the VGA. The VGA is therefore downwardly compatible to the EGA. Code written for the EGA will run directly on the VGA if the code always uses the BIOS calls. Code that controls the EGA registers directly will not necessarily execute correctly on the VGA.

There are several cases in which the programmer should use the BIOS calls. Graphics functions that are performed once per session—for example, setting a mode or a color table—can be accomplished through the BIOS calls with little or no impact on processing time. Other functions may be called often throughout a program, yet the inherent BIOS delays may not be objectionable. Manipulating the cursor or writing a text string are two examples of situations in which BIOS calls can greatly simplify the programmer's task without causing significant delays. The programmer is well advised to use the BIOS calls for these operations.

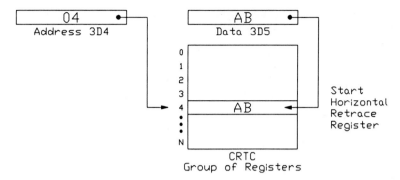

FIGURE 10.1 Accessing the EGA/VGA Registers

10.1.2 Accessing the Registers

The General Registers, also called the External Registers, and the Color Select Register in the Attribute Register group are accessed directly. Each of these registers has a unique host port I/O port address. Reading or writing data to these registers is accomplished by using the assembly language IN and OUT instructions. All of the other registers are accessed indirectly.

The indirect addressing technique uses two I/O host port locations to access a group of registers within the EGA/VGA. The two host port locations are called the index or address register and the data register. Each register within the group is assigned a unique index value. Registers within a group have index values that start at 0 and increment, ending with the last register in the group. The address register is used to point to one of the actual EGA/VGA registers within the group. If it is desired to write to a register, this register is loaded with the index value of the desired register. Once this is loaded, a byte is written from the host to the data register. The byte of data is automatically written to the selected register. This is illustrated in Figure 10.1.

In Figure 10.1, the index value, 03, is output to the address register. The data byte, AB hex, is then output to the data register. Because the address register contains an 03, register 03 is selected. The data byte, A5 hex, is automatically written to this register.

The registers are read in a similar manner. Again, the address register is loaded with the desired register index, and a data byte is read from the data register. The majority of registers within the standard EGA cannot be read. In contrast, all registers within the VGA can be read.

Reading and writing to the Attribute Registers is more complicated. Instead of the address and data register occupying two host port I/O addresses, they occupy the same port address. An internal flip-flop in the EGA/VGA is used to select either the Attribute Index Register or the Attribute Data Register. Both of these registers reside at I/O port address 3CO hex. The flip-flop is initialized to point to the index register by executing an I/O read instruction to either port 3BA or port 3DA hex. The actual address depends on whether the EGA is emulating a monochrome or a color adapter. After an output port instruction, OUT, is issued to the Attribute Index Register, the flip-flop toggles and points to the Attribute Data Register. Subsequent outputs to the Attribute Register at 3C0 hex cause the flip-flop to toggle repeatedly between the index and the data registers.

A problem exists because of this obscure addressing format. The state of the flip-flop cannot be interrogated or saved. Should a context switch occur, the state of this register is lost. If interrupts are a possible source of context changes, then interrupts should be disabled while the Attribute Registers are being accessed.

In the VGA, the lower seven registers in the CRTC Registers have a protect bit associated with them. It is located in the PR field of the Vertical Retrace End Register. If this field is set to a 1, CRTC registers 0 through 7 cannot be modified. The exception to this is the Line Compare (LC) field of the Overflow Register. This function protects the critical horizontal and vertical timing generator registers contained in these locations from modification. Programs that expect the EGA may attempt to load these registers with values that are appropriate for the EGA but not for the VGA. The Vertical Retrace Start Register, at index 10 hex, and the Vertical Retrace End Register, at index 11 hex, can be accessed only when the Compatible Read (CR) field of the End Horizontal Blanking Register is set to a 1.

10.1.3   The Register Diagrams

Each of the EGA/VGA register groups, registers, and fields is described in the following section. Each register is preceded by an illustration of the register. The fields within each register are indicated by an oval in the register. The placement of the oval dictates which bits within the register are dedicated to this field. Each oval contains a code of up to three letters that is used to identify the field. The functions of these fields are described in the text.

A field that applies only to the EGA is designated by a small square to the immediate left of the code. A field that applies only to the VGA is designated by a small square to the immediate right of the code. If a field has no squares, it applies to either the EGA or the VGA. A field with two codes separated by a square indicates that there are two separate meanings for the field, one for the EGA and one for the VGA.

10.2   THE GENERAL OR EXTERNAL REGISTERS

There are four General or External Registers in the EGA/VGA. These registers have their own port addresses. Because of these port assignments, the programmer accesses these registers directly, with no need of an index and data register pair. These registers are referred to as the External Registers in the EGA

TABLE 10.2 General or External Registers

Register Name	Write (Hex) (EGA/VGA)	Read (Hex) (EGA)	Read (Hex) (VGA)
Misc. Output	3C2		3CC
Feature Control	3DA/3BA		3CA
Input Status #0		3C2	3C2
Input Status #1		3DA/3BA	3DA/3BA

documentation and as the General Registers in the VGA documentation. Both implementations consist of the same four registers, although the fields within these registers vary. The General or External Registers are listed in Table 10.2.

Note that there are two addresses listed that allow writing to the Feature Control Register and the Input Status #1 Register. These two addresses are in the form 3Dx/3Bx. The first address, 3Bx, is applicable when the adapter is configured in a monochrome mode. The second address, 3Dx, is applicable when the adapter is configured in a color mode.

10.2.1 Miscellaneous Output Register

7	6	5	4	3	2	1	0
(VSP)	(HSP)	(PB)	(•DVD)	(CS)		(ER)	(IOA)

> EGA   Write Port 3C2 hex
> VGA   Write Port 3C2 hex
>   Read Port 3CC hex

VSP Vertical Sync Polarity   EGA, VGA **Bit 7**

Determines the polarity of the vertical sync pulse. Hardware manufacturers can use this field to control the pulse shape of the vertical sync pulse. On the VGA, this field is also used to control the vertical size of the monitor. The monitors that are supported by the VGA are autosynchronizing. These monitors must be capable of achieving vertical synchronization. To do so, they detect the polarity of the horizontal and vertical sync signals. The polarity of these sync pulses alerts the monitor as to how many vertical lines should be displayed. This is illustrated in Table 10.3.

=0 Select a positive vertical retrace sync pulse.

=1 Select a negative vertical retrace sync pulse.

TABLE 10.3 Vertical Size and Sync Polarity

Bit 7	Bit 6	Vertical Size	Active Lines
0(+)	0(+)	Reserved	Reserved
0(+)	1(−)	400 lines	414 lines
1(−)	0(+)	350 lines	362 lines
1(−)	1(−)	480 lines	496 lines

HSP Horizontal Sync Polarity   EGA, VGA **Bit 6**

Determines the polarity of the horizontal sync pulse. Hardware manufacturers can use this field to control the pulse shape of the horizontal sync pulse. On the VGA, this field is also used to control the vertical size of the monitor. The monitors that are supported by the VGA are autosynchronizing. They must be capable of achieving vertical synchronization. To do so, they detect the polarity of the horizontal and vertical sync signals. The polarity of these sync pulses alerts the monitor as to how many vertical lines should be displayed. This is illustrated in Table 10.3 above.

=0 Select a positive horizontal retrace sync pulse.

=1 Select a negative horizontal retrace sync pulse.

PB Page Bit for Odd/Even   EGA, VGA **Bit 5**

Selects the 64K page of memory when the system is in one of the odd or even modes. The display modes that utilize the odd/even modes are modes 0, 1, 2, 3 and 7.

=0 Select the low 64K page of memory.

=1 Select the high 64K page of memory.

DVD Disable the Video Drivers   EGA **Bit 4**

The video drivers on the EGA normally control the video direct drive video outputs. It is possible to utilize the direct drive video inputs from the feature connector. In order to use these feature connector inputs as the direct drive outputs, the internal video drivers must be taken off the bus. This field enables or disables the internal video drivers.

=0 Enable the internal video drivers.

=1 Disable the internal video drivers.

CS Clock Select   EGA, VGA **Bits 3,2**

The frequency of the clock used to drive the EGA hardware determines the overall speed of the graphics process. The horizontal frequency of the video

TABLE 10.4   Clock Source

Bit 3	Bit 2	EGA Clock Source	VGA Clock Source
0	0	14-mHz clock	25-mHz
0	1	16-mHz clock	28-mHz
1	0	external clock	Reserved

output controls the number of dots that may be displayed on a line and the number of lines that can be displayed on the screen. The mode of the display, color or monochrome, also determines the number of dots and lines possible.

The monitor type that is being utilized controls which clock frequencies may be used. For a standard color monitor, a 14-mHz clock signal is required to produce the desired horizontal frequency. For an EGA monitor, a 16-mHz clock signal may be utilized. If a multisync monitor is used, even higher clock frequencies may be implemented. Again, the higher the clock frequency, the greater the display resolution.

Anticipating the need for higher frequencies, the feature connector provides an input pin. A clock may be provided on this pin when higher horizontal resolutions are desired. For example, a 132-column display utilizing an 8-dot-wide character would require a higher frequency clock than 16mHz. This CS field determines the clock rate and, in the case of CS=2, the source of the clock. Table 10.4 illustrates the different clocks possible.

ER   Enable RAM   EGA, VGA   **Bit 1**

Enable Access of CPU to video memory. All display modes allow CPU access to the display memory.

=0   Disable access of the video memory from the CPU.

=1   Enable access of the video memory from the CPU.

IOA   Input/Output Address   EGA, VGA   **Bit 0**

The EGA may emulate either the monochrome or the color display adapters. This emulation exists only at the BIOS level on standard EGAs and may exist at the register level on specially equipped EGA boards. For monochrome emulation, the CRTC addresses are set to 3Bx. The Input Status #1 Register is set at 3B2, and the Feature Control Register is set at 3BA. For color adapters, the CRTC registers are set to 3Dx. The Input Status #1 Register is set to 3D2, and the Feature Control Register is set at 3DA.

=0   Monochrome emulation. Address based at 3Bx.

=1   Color emulation. Address based at 3Dx.

10.2.2 Feature Control Register

7	6	5	4	3	2	1	0
						•FC1	•FC0

> EGA Write Port 3BA hex Monochrome, 3DA hex Color
> VGA Write Port 3BA hex Monochrome, 3DA hex Color
> Read Port 3CA hex

The feature connector on the EGA provides two output pins called FC0 and FC1. The host processor can use these pins to convey information to the external devices in the same way that a parallel output port is programmed. Setting this bit to 1 causes the corresponding bit on the feature connector to go to a logical high state; setting it to a 0 causes the pin to go to a low state.

VSS Vertical sync select   VGA **Bit 3**

Controls the signal output to the vertical sync line that controls the monitor.

=0 Normal vertical sync output to the monitor.

=1 Vertical sync output to the monitor is the logical OR of the vertical sync and the vertical display enable.

FC1 Feature control bit 1   EGA **Bit 1**

Feature control bit 1 is on pin 20 of the feature connector.

=0 The logical state of FC1 is set to 0 (logical low).

=1 The logical state of FC1 is set to 1 (logical high).

FC0 Feature control bit 0   EGA **Bit 0**

Feature control bit 0 is on pin 21 of the feature connector.

=0 The logical state of FC0 is set to 0 (logical low).

=1 The logical state of FC0 is set to 1 (logical high).

10.2.3 Input Status #0 Register

7	6	5	4	3	2	1	0
•VRI	•FS1	•FS0	SS				

> EGA Read Port 3C2 hex
> VGA Read Port 3C2 hex

VRI Vertical Retrace Interrupt   EGA **Bit 7**

Reports the status of the Vertical Interrupt.

=0 Vertical retrace is occurring.

=1 Vertical retrace is not occurring. Video is being displayed.

FS1 Feature Status 1   EGA **Bit 6**

Reports the status of the feature 1 (FEAT1) on pin 17 of the feature connector.

=0 Feat1 = 0 (logical low level).

=1 Feat1 = 1 (logical high level).

FS0 Feature Status 0   EGA **Bit 5**

Reports the status of the feature 0 (FEAT0) on pin 19 of the feature connector.

=0 Feat0 = 0 (logical low level).

=1 Feat0 = 1 (logical high level).

SS Switch Sense   EGA, VGA **Bit 4**

Reports the status from one of the four sense switches as determined by the CS field of the Misc. Output Register.

=0 Selected sense switch = 0 (off).

=1 Selected sense switch = 1 (on).

10.2.4 Input Status #1 Register

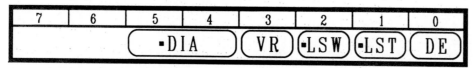

EGA Read Port 3BA hex monochrome, 3DA hex color.
VGA Read Port 3BA hex monochrome, 3DA hex color.

DIA Diagnostic   EGA **Bits 5,4**

Reports the status of two of the six color outputs. The values set into the VSM field of the Color Plane Enable Register determine which colors are input to these two diagnostic pins according to Table 10.5.

VR Vertical Retrace   EGA, VGA **Bit 3**

Reports the status of the display regarding whether the display is in a display mode or a vertical retrace mode. The occurrence of a 1 in this bit, indicating a

TABLE 10.5 DIA Field

DIA Field		Input Status #1 Register	
Bit 5	Bit 4	Bit 5	Bit 4
0	0	Red	Blue
0	1	I Blue	Green
1	0	I Red	I Green

vertical retrace, can generate a level-2 interrupt depending on the status of the Disable Vertical Interrupt (DVI) field of the Vertical Retrace End Register. This is used when software synchronization with the display is desired.

=0 Display is in the display mode.

=1 Display is in the vertical retrace mode.

LSW Light Pen Switch   EGA **Bit 2**

Monitors the status of the light pen switch. Light pens are all equipped with a switch that allows the operator another degree of control. The switch may be on the side of the light pen. More often, it is found on the tip of the pen. By pushing the pen against the screen, the user activates the pen switch.

=0 Light pen switch is pushed in (closed).

=1 Light pen switch is not pushed (open).

LST Light Pen Strobe   EGA **Bit 1**

Monitors the status of the light pen strobe. When the electron beam scans across the area of the screen where the light pen is pointing, the light pen's light sensitive device senses the light and produces a strobe pulse. The LST field monitors this pulse. By taking repeated rapid readings of this field, the software can determine the position of the pen with respect to the screen coordinates. When this field is active (LST = 1), the Light Pen Position Low and Light Pen Position High registers may be read to determine the position of the light pen.

=0 Light pen has not been triggered.

=1 Light pen is triggered (electron beam is at the light pen position).

DE Display Enable NOT   EGA, VGA **Bit 0**

Monitors the status of the display. Alerts the software that the display is in a horizontal or vertical retrace mode or in a display mode. Some older display adapters required that data in display memory be modified only during a retrace period. During a retrace period, no active display refreshing occurred. On these older displays, noise would occur on the screen if the display was modified

TABLE 10.6 Retrace Period

VR	DE	Display Status
0	0	Display mode
1	1	Vertical retrace time
0	1	Horizontal retrace time

during refreshing. This is not the case with the EGA/VGA. When DE is used in conjunction with the VR field of this register, it is possible to determine if the display is in a horizontal or vertical retrace period; see Table 10.6.

The horizontal retrace time can be used to synchronize the software with the horizontal scanning. This allows the programmer to update the color palette in a way that produces more than 16 simultaneous colors on the display.

=0 The display is in the display mode.

=1 The display is not in the display mode. Either the horizontal or vertical retrace period is active.

10.3 THE SEQUENCER REGISTERS

The Sequencer Registers consist of six registers. None of these registers has a unique host port address. Rather, the entire set of registers is accessed through an index and data register. These two registers exist in the host port address space. The ports are referred to as the Sequencer Address Register and the Sequencer Data Register.

The program accesses these registers by first loading the Sequencer Address Register with an index value ranging from 0 to 4. Next, it selects one of the five Sequencer Data Registers as the current active register. Reading or writing to this Sequencer Data Registers will repeatedly access the register selected by the index value until the Sequencer Address Register is modified. The Sequencer Address Register resides at port 3C4 hex, and the Sequencer Data Register resides at port 3C5 hex. All of the Sequencer Registers are write-only in the standard EGA and read/write in the VGA. The Sequencer Registers are listed in Table 10.7.

10.3.1 Reset Register

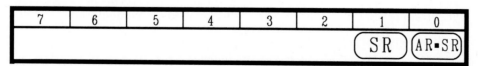

7	6	5	4	3	2	1	0
						SR	AR■SR

Index 00 hex

TABLE 10.7   Sequencer Registers

Register Name	Index	Write (Hex) (EGA/VGA)	Read Hex (VGA)
Address	—	3C4	3C4
Reset	0	3C5	3C5
Clocking Mode	1	3C5	3C5
Map Mask	2	3C5	3C5
Character Map Select	3	3C5	3C5
Memory Mode	4	3C5	3C5

The Reset register provides two ways to reset the processor. Either reset—SR or AR—will cause the sequencer to reset, thereby stopping the functioning of the EGA. Both resets must be off (logical 1) in order for the EGA to operate. Both cause a clear-and-halt condition to occur. All outputs are placed in a high-impedance state during a reset condition.

SR   Synchronous Reset   EGA, VGA   **Bit 1**

Control the state of the sequencer by producing a synchronous reset. A synchronous reset preserves memory contents. It must be used before changing the Clocking Mode Register in order to preserve memory contents.

   =0 Generate and hold the system in a reset condition.

   =1 Release the reset if bit 0 is in the inactive state.

SR   Synchronous Reset (No Asynchronous Reset on VGA)   VGA   **Bit 0**

Control the state of the sequencer by producing a synchronous reset. A synchronous reset preserves memory contents and must be used before changing the Clocking Mode Register to avoid loss of memory contents.

   =0 Generate and hold the system in a reset condition.

   =1 Release the reset if bit 1 is in the inactive state.

AR   Asynchronous Reset   EGA   **Bit 0**

Control the state of the sequencer by producing an asynchronous reset. An asynchronous reset may cause a loss of display memory contents.

   =0 Generate and hold the system in a reset condition.

   =1 Release the reset if bit 1 is in the inactive state.

10.3.2 Clocking Mode Register

7	6	5	4	3	2	1	0
		S0 ∙	S4 ∙	DC	SL	∙BW	8/9

Index 01 hex
Determine the clock timing.

SO Screen Off   VGA **Bit 5**

Turns the screen off along with the picture-generating logic. Because there is
no time spent refreshing the screen, the video processor has direct control of
the video memory, which facilitates rapid memory access.

=0 Screen is turned on.

=1 Screen is turned off.

S4 Shift Four   VGA **Bit 4**

Controls how often the video serializers should be loaded.

=0 Load the serializers every character clock cycle.

=1 Load the serializers every fourth character clock cycle.

DC Dot Clock   EGA, VGA **Bit 3**

The dot clock is the basic graphics clock of the system. It is generated from the
master clock input, the source of which is determined by the CS field of the
Misc. Output Register. If the Dot Clock is generated every input clock, high-
resolution outputs are possible. It also divides the master clock by 2 before
generating the Dot Clock. This has the effect of slowing down the system,
thereby stretching out the other timing signals. The divide-by-2 mode is used
when a horizontal resolution of 320 for the EGA or a horizontal resolution of
320 or 360 for the VGA is selected. Display modes 0, 1, 4, 5, and D utilize this
feature.

=0 Set the Dot Clock to the same frequency as the Master Clock.

=1 Divide the Master Clock by 2 to derive the Dot Clock.

SL Shift Load   EGA, VGA **Bit 2**

The EGA provides the two standard horizontal resolutions of 640 or 320 dots
per line. The display memory is organized in parallel words. The display output,
however, requires a serial output stream. Hardware associated with the EGA

converts this parallel data in a device called a video serializer. The high-resolution mode with 640 dots per line requires that the video serializers be loaded every character clock. The lower resolution mode of 320 dots per line allows the video serializers to be loaded every other character clock.

The VGA operates in a similar fashion to the EGA, except that this bit is significant only if the Shift Four (S4) field is set to a 0 to cause the serializers to be loaded every character clock. Combined, these two fields allow the serializers to be loaded every cycle, every other cycle, or every fourth cycle of the character clock.

=0 Load the video serializers every character clock. Use with 640 (EGA) or 720 (VGA) horizontal resolutions.

=1 Load the video serializers every other character clock. Use with 320 (EGA) or 360 (VGA) horizontal resolutions.

BW Bandwidth   EGA **Bit 1**

The video memory may be thought of as a triple-ported memory. This means that there are three devices attempting to access the memory. The CPU is one device. Its purpose is to load new data into the display memory or to read data out of the display memory. A second source desiring control of the display memory is the dynamic memory refresh timing. Because the EGA/VGA display memory is typically constructed from dynamic memory, the dynamic memory must be refreshed periodically or data will be lost. The addressing required to perform the dynamic memory refreshing must also share the memory bus. The third device is an output device. The video serializers must be loaded in order to refresh the display. The CRT display expects constant updating as the electron beam scans across its face. The serial data driving the electron beam must be read from the display memory.

The type of dynamic memory dictates how often the dynamic memory refreshing must take place on the memory bus. For every scan line, a certain amount of data must be read out into the video serializers. The amount of data is determined by the number of pixels being output per line. Therefore, the more data read out during this predetermined time, the more time the video serializers require the memory bus. This means that the CPU must wait for these two higher-priority devices before it can gain control of the memory bus.

The high-resolution modes require that the CRTC controller have four out of five memory cycles to fulfill the needs of the screen refresh. In lower-resolution modes, the CRTC can get by with two out of five memory cycles. Thus, in the high-resolution modes, the CPU must wait for one out of five memory cycles before it can read or write to memory. This slows down system throughput. However, it does allow for inexpensive dynamic memory to be used as display memory.

An equivalent field for the VGA is located in the BW field of the Horizontal Retrace End Register.

=0 The CRTC will control the memory bus on four out of five memory cycles. Used in all high-resolution modes.

=1 The CRTC will control the memory bus on two out of five memory cycles. Used in all lower resolution modes.

8/9 8/9 Dot Clocks   EGA, VGA **Bit 0**

The size of the character box determines the resolution of the resulting characters. The monochrome display mode 7 utilizes a 9-dot character. All other modes utilize an 8-dot character. Because 80 characters are desired, a total of 80×9, or 720, horizontal dots are necessary for mode 7. In all other modes with 80 dots per line, 80×8, or 640, dots per line are required. At times in the monochrome mode, the character font is 9 dots wide. Thus, two bytes are required to represent a single line of a character. It is also possible to represent the 9-dot character with an 8-dot matrix. Although this decreases the resolution of the character, it halves the amount of memory required to represent a single line, reducing it to 1 byte. In the case of graphics characters, character codes C0 hex to DF hex, it is desired that horizontal lines connect. Thus, it is necessary to extend the 8 dots to 9 dots. This is done by copying the dot representing the 8th dot, found in bit 7, into the position of the 9th dot. The effect is that horizontal lines are extended. A line in one character position will touch a character in the adjacent horizontal positions.

The EGA uses the 9-dots-per-character clock in mode 7, while the VGA uses the 9-dots-per-character clock in modes 0+, 1+, 2+, 3+, 7, and 7+.

=0 Character clocks 8 dots wide are generated. Used in all modes by mode 7, in which there are 320 or 640 horizontal dots.

=1 Character clocks 9 dots wide are generated. Used in the monochrome mode 7, in which there are 720 horizontal dots.

10.3.3 Map Mask Register

7	6	5	4	3	2	1	0
				EM3	EM2	EM1	EM0

Index 02 hex

The display memory is organized as nonstandard read/write memory with respect to the host processor. Each byte of memory represents from one to eight consecutive horizontal pixels. The display memory is viewed as being serial memory to the output drivers due to the video serializer. The CRTC controller views this memory through a 32-bit port. A 32-bit register sits between the CRTC graphics controller and the display memory.

The EGA/VGA consists of four display planes. Because each plane is organized as bytes, $4 \times 8 = 32$ bits. Each plane is mapped into the same host memory address space. When the host outputs a byte to display memory at a specific memory address, this byte may be written to any combination of the display memory planes. The Write Plane Mask Register determines which planes are written to. Any combination is allowed because the 32-bit-wide display memory path permits all four planes to be updated simultaneously. Because there are four display memory planes, one bit in this register is assigned to each plane; thus, four control bits are required. Each control bit corresponds to one memory plane. If the bit is disabled, the plane cannot be written to, and the plane is masked out of the system. Thus, this register is called the Plane Mask Register or the Map Mask Register.

On read operations, the 32-bit buffer register is also used. On a single read, all four memory planes can be read simultaneously. However, unlike the write operation, in which one byte is written to four bytes, the read operation can transfer only one byte to the host at a time The Read Map Select Register determines which plane is read back to the host.

There are write modes that allow the EGA to take advantage of this 32-bit memory path. For example, it is possible to copy EGA memory from one location to another 32 bits at a time. This is one reason for having display memory in excess of the display requirements. Patterns may be stored in the excess region and then copied at high speed to the portion of display memory being displayed. The write mode that selects this function is determined by the WM field of the Mode Register.

Another type of masking is possible. A byte references one to eight consecutive horizontal pixels, and it may be desired to modify only one pixel. This can be accomplished by masking out all pixels other than the desired pixel. This is done in the BM field of the Bit Mask Register.

The four memory planes are combined to produce a color for an individual pixel. The data bit from memory plane 0 is placed into the resulting four-bit word in bit position 0. It may be thought of as the least significant bit of the resulting color nibble. The data bit from memory plane 1 is placed into bit position 1, and so on, until memory plane 3 places a bit into bit position 3. Memory plane 3 may be thought of as the most significant memory plane.

EM3 Mask Memory Plane 3   EGA, VGA   **Bit 3**

=0 Disable memory plane 3 on CPU write operations.

=1 Enable memory plane 3 on CPU write operations.

EM2 Mask Memory Plane 2   EGA, VGA   **Bit 2**

=0 Disable memory plane 2 on CPU write operations.

=1 Enable memory plane 2 on CPU write operations.

EM1 Mask Memory Plane 1 EGA, VGA **Bit 1**

=0 Disable memory plane 1 on CPU write operations.

=1 Enable memory plane 1 on CPU write operations.

EM0 Mask Memory Plane 0 EGA, VGA **Bit 0**

=0 Disable memory plane 0 on CPU write operations.

=1 Enable memory plane 0 on CPU write operations.

10.3.4 Character Map Select Register

7	6	5	4	3	2	1	0
		SAH∙	SBH∙	SA		SB	

Index 03 hex

In the text modes, each character is represented by a character ASCII code and an attribute. The attribute determines the color of the character on a color system; on a monochrome system, the attribute sets any special features of the character—underline, blinking, or high intensity, for example. Bit 3 of the attribute is reserved for one of two purposes. In one configuration, it selects one of 16 colors as the foreground color of the character. In the second mode, it selects which of two character sets to use for the character. In this second mode, character sets of 512 characters may be used. This is possible because the ASCII character code is capable of selecting one of 256 characters. This additional attribute bit permits the character to be from one of two character sets.

In the EGA, the display planes are split into four banks, each being 16 Kbytes long. One font may be loaded into the first 8 Kbytes of each bank. In the VGA, the display planes are split into eight banks, each being 8 Kbytes long.

Suppose that a character is 8 bits per line wide and 32 lines long, each character requiring 32 bytes of memory. A 256-character set would then require 8 Kbytes of storage. If the character is wider than 8 dots per line, the upper byte of storage will be analogously stored into the first 8 Kbytes of each of the four banks of display plane 3. Restricting each character to 32 lines allows the characters to be aligned on 32-byte boundaries. Accessing a character is then a simple task of shifting the ASCII code 5 bits to the left.

Whether the system responds to bit 3 of the attribute byte as an intensity or as a character-set selector is determined by whether the two fields SB and SA are different. If these have the same value, the system assumes that bit 3 should be used to select the intensified colors. If they have different values, the system assumes that bit 3 should be used to select the character set. Although four fonts may be loaded simultaneously, only two can be active at a time.

TABLE 10.8 EGA Character Mapping

Bit 1	Bit 2	Map	Table Location
0	0	0	First 8K of bank 0 at 0–7 K
0	1	1	First 8K of bank 1 at 16–23 K
1	0	2	First 8K of bank 2 at 32–39 K
1	1	3	First 8K of bank 3 at 48–55 K

TABLE 10.9 VGA Character Mapping

Bits 5,4	Bits 3,1	Bits 2,0	Character Map	Address Offset to First Character
0	0	0	0	0 K
0	0	1	1	16 K
0	1	0	2	32 K
0	1	1	3	48 K
1	0	0	4	8 K
1	0	1	5	24 K
1	1	0	6	40 K
1	1	1	7	56 K

The character maps for the EGA are illustrated in Table 10.8.

The character maps for the VGA are illustrated in Table 10.9. It should be noted that bits 4 and 5 contain the third bit for each of the two character map fields.

SAH Select Character Generator A (High Order)   VGA **Bit 5**

Selects which of eight possible character sets to select when the attribute byte has bit 3 = 1. Combines with SA field.

SBH Select Character Generator B (High Order)   VGA **Bit 4**

Selects which of eight possible character sets to select when the attribute byte has bit 3 = 0. Combines with SB field.

SA Select Character Generator A   EGA, VGA **Bits 3,2**

Selects which of the eight possible character sets to select when the attribute byte has bit 3 = 1. Combines with SAH field for VGA.

SB Select Character Generator B   EGA, VGA **Bits 1,0**

Selects which of the eight possible character sets to select when the attribute byte has bit 3 = 0. Combines with SBH field for VGA.

10.3.5 Memory Mode Register

7	6	5	4	3	2	1	0
				C 4 •	O/E	E M	•A/G

Index 04 hex

This register contains several fields that control the way in which the display memory functions.

C4 Chain Four   VGA **Bit 3**

Controls the manner in which the display memory bit planes are accessed. In a write mode, the display bit plane is normally selected by the EM0–EM3 enable memory mask fields of the Map Mask Register. Any combination of the four display planes may be accessed simultaneously. In mode 13 hex, the four display memory bit planes are chained together, and only one can be selected at a time. In this mode, the two low-order address bits are used to select which of the four display bit planes are enabled. Thus, four sequential bytes written to the display memory are stored so that one byte occupies an identical addressed location in each of the four display planes.

In a read mode, only one display memory bit plane can be active at a time. The active bit plane is normally selected by the Read Map Select (RMS) field of the Read Map Select Register. In mode 13 hex, the operation is identical to the write operation above, with the Read Map Select Register being ignored and the display plane being selected by the low-order A1 and A0 address bits.

=0 The display planes are selected via the Map Mask and the Read Map Select Registers.

=1 The display planes are selected by the low-order A1 and A0 address bits; the four display planes are assumed to be chained.

O/E Odd/Even   EGA, VGA **Bit 2**

Determines whether the processor addresses a display memory plane sequentially, or whether odd addresses access display planes 1 and 3 and even addresses access display planes 0 and 2. The odd/even mode is enabled when memory addressing compatibility is desired between the EGA/VGA and the Color Graphics Adapter.

Note that the value of this bit should be the complement of the value in the OE field of the Mode Register.

=0 Enables the odd/even addressing mode.

=1 Directs the system to use a sequential addressing mode.

EM   Extended Memory   EGA,VGA   **Bit 1**

Alerts the graphics processors to the fact that extended memory is present. All EGA/VGA implementations with greater than 64 Kbytes should have this field enabled.

=0 No extended memory present. Display memory is less than 64 Kbytes.

=1 Extended memory is present. Display memory is greater than 64 Kbytes.

A/G   Alpha/Graphics Mode   EGA   **Bit 0**

Dictates whether the system is in an alphanumeric mode or a graphics mode. In an alphanumeric mode, characters are addressed by code and the memory planes are used to display the code, the attribute, and the character generators. In a graphics mode, the memory is used directly to display graphics data. A character would be represented by a two-dimensional series of dots.

In the EGA, three fields in the control registers redundantly control this function. The second and third fields are in the G/A field of the Mode Control Register and the G/A field of the Miscellaneous Register. Note that these values should be the complement of the A/G field in the appropriate register.

In the VGA, the alphanumeric and graphics modes are selected from the G/A fields in the Mode Control Register and the G/A field in the Miscellaneous Register.

=0 Select a graphics mode.

=1 Select an alphanumerics mode.

10.4   THE CRT CONTROLLER REGISTERS

The CRT Controller Registers, commonly called the CRTC Registers, consist of 26 registers in the EGA and 24 registers in the VGA. None of these registers has a unique host port address. Instead, an address and data register pair exists in the host port address space. The programmer accesses these registers by first loading the CRTC Address Register with an index value. This index value ranges from 0 to 24 decimal. However, the hexadecimal numbering convention of 0 to 18 hex is more commonly used.

In the EGA, the 26 registers map into 24 indexes because four registers share two identical indexes. Two of these are read-only registers dedicated to the light pen interface. Two other registers, at identical indexes (indexes 10 and 11 hex) are write-only registers. Thus, there is no addressing conflict.

In the VGA, there are no light pen registers, and all of the CRTC Registers are read/write. The CRTC Address Register selects one of the CRTC Data Registers as the current active register. Reading or writing to this CRTC Data

Register will repeatedly access the register selected by the index value, until the CRTC Address Register is modified.

The CRTC Address Register resides at port 3B4 hex for monochrome systems and port 3D4 hex for color systems. The CRTC Data Register resides at port 3B5 hex for the monochrome systems and port 3D5 hex for the color systems. The CRTC Registers are listed in Table 10.10.

10.4.1 Horizontal Total Register

7	6	5	4	3	2	1	0
				HT			

Index 00 hex

The Horizontal Total Register determines the horizontal scan time. It includes the borders, active display time, and horizontal retrace time. Internal to the CRT controller is a horizontal character counter. In the alphanumeric modes, this counter is initialized at the beginning of each scan line with a value of 0 and incremented after each character is output to the screen. In the graphics modes, the counter is incremented after either eight or nine pixels are output to the screen. These eight or nine pixels correspond to the width of the character in pixels as specified in the 8/9 field of the Clocking Mode Register.

The horizontal character counter counts from 0 to a maximum value indicated in the Horizontal Total Register. When the character counter reaches this value, it is reset to 0. This character counter overflow is the basis of all of the display timing. Because the horizontal counter increments on a character basis, a single byte is sufficient to store the number of characters per line. At the maximum value of 255 with eight pixels per character, the display can handle about 2,000 pixels per horizontal scan line.

In the EGA, the value loaded into this register is actually the total character count minus 2. Thus, if 90 characters are desired per line, the value 88 should be loaded into this register. In the VGA, the value loaded into this register is actually the total character count minus 5. If 90 characters are desired per line, a value of 85 should be loaded into this register.

HT Horizontal Total   EGA,VGA **Bits 7–0**

   EGA HT = The horizontal total − 2

   VGA HT = The horizontal total − 5

TABLE 10.10 CRT Controller Registers

Register Name	Index (Hex)	Write (Hex) (EGA/VGA)	Read (Hex) (EGA)	Read (Hex) (VGA)
Address	—	3D4/3B4	—	3D4/3B4
Horizontal Total	0	3D5/3B5	—	3D5/3B5
Horizontal Display End	1	3D5/3B5	—	3D5/3B5
Start Horizontal Blank	2	3D5/3B5	—	3D5/3B5
End Horizontal Blank	3	3D5/3B5	—	3D5/3B5
Start Horizontal Retrace	4	3D5/3B5	—	3D5/3B5
End Horizontal Retrace	5	3D5/3B5	—	3D5/3B5
Vertical Total	6	3D5/3B5	—	3D5/3B5
Overflow	7	—	—	3D5/3B5
Preset Row Scan	8	3D5/3B5	—	3D5/3B5
Max Scan Line	9	3D5/3B5	—	3D5/3B5
Cursor Start	A	3D5/3B5	—	3D5/3B5
Cursor End	B	—	—	3D5/3B5
Start Address High	C	3D5/3B5	3D5/3B5	3D5/3B5
Start Address Low	D	3D5/3B5	3D5/3B5	3D5/3B5
Cursor Location High	E	3D5/3B5	3D5/3B5	3D5/3B5
Cursor Location Low	F	3D5/3B5	3D5/3B5	3D5/3B5
Vertical Retrace Start	10	3D5/3B5	—	3D5/3B5
Light Pen High (EGA only)	10	—	3D5/3B5	—
Vertical Retrace Low	11	3D5/3B5	—	3D5/3B5
Light Pen Low (EGA only)	11	—	3D5/3B5	—
Vertical Display End	12	3D5/3B5	—	3D5/3B5
Offset	13	3D5/3B5	—	3D5/3B5
Underline Location	14	3D5/3B5	—	3D5/3B5
Start Vertical Blank	15	3D5/3B5	—	3D5/3B5
End Vertical Blank	16	3D5/3B5	—	3D5/3B5
Mode Control	17	3D5/3B5	—	3D5/3B5
Line Compare	18	3D5/3B5	—	3D5/3B5

10.4.2 Horizontal Display End Register

7	6	5	4	3	2	1	0
				HDE			

Index 01 hex

This register determines the number of displayed characters or character positions on a horizontal line. The internal horizontal character counter counts from 0 to the value indicated in the Horizontal Total register. However, not all of the characters on a horizontal line are to be displayed. The horizontal scan time consists of the border or porch, displayed data, and horizontal refresh times. Both the borders and the displayed data must fit into the horizontal display period.

At the end of each horizontal line, the CRT electron beam moves from the right extent of the current line to the left extent of the next lower line. The electron beam always scans from left to right on the screen in a top to bottom format. The time taken for the electron beam to get ready for the next line is called the horizontal retrace time. During this retrace time, no data should be written to the display. A display enable signal is generated to control when the display is enabled. Blanking occurs during the time that the display enable signal is inactive. The period of time surrounds the active display area on the screen and is called the border or porch. The overscan color is displayed during this border period and is controlled by the Overscan Register.

HDE Horizontal Display Enable   EGA,VGA **Bits 7–0**

The total number of displayed characters or character positions on a horizontal scan line.

EGA HDE = The number of displayed characters − 1.

VGA HDE = The number of displayed characters.

10.4.3   Start Horizontal Blanking Register

7	6	5	4	3	2	1	0
			S H B				

Index 02 hex

The horizontal blanking signal is generated when the horizontal character counter equals the value in the Start Horizontal Blanking Register. It ends when the value equals the value of the End Horizontal Blanking Register. The horizontal blanking signal is generated to stop the display of data during the CRT refresh time. Most blanking signals sent to the monitor are the composite of both the horizontal and vertical blanking times. The vertical blanking time is dictated by the Start Vertical Blanking and the End Vertical Blanking Registers. The blanking signal may be sent on its own line or combined into a composite signal that also includes either monochrome or color video data and sync information.

SHB Start Horizontal Blanking   EGA,VGA **Bits 7–0**

The value of the character counter at the time the horizontal blanking period should begin.

SHB = Start of Horizontal Blanking

10.4.4 End Horizontal Blanking Register

7	6	5	4	3	2	1	0
CR ▪	DES		EHB				

Index 03 hex

The end of the horizontal blanking period is determined by the value in this register. The character counter is an 8-bit counter. The start of the horizontal blanking period is determined by comparing the character counter and the value in the Start Horizontal Blanking Register. Both of these are 8-bit values. The width of the horizontal blanking period consists of the number of character positions that should be output during this period. The value in the End Horizontal Blanking (EHB) field of this register is used to determine the width of the blanking period.

In the EGA, the EHB field of this register is only 5 bits wide. These 5 bits represent the lower 5 bits of the character count that will cause the end of horizontal blanking. Thus, it represents a mod 32 counter. Because the three most significant bits of the character counter are not used, there will be eight times as many End Horizontal Blanking signals as there are Start Horizontal Blanking Signals. The only End Blanking pulse that is relevant is the pulse that occurs after the start of the blanking period. It is important to note that the value in this field does not represent the width of the blanking pulse. The width is determined by subtracting the beginning of the blanking signal from the end of the blanking signal, taking special care with the upper 3 bits. Note that the maximum length for the blanking signal is 31 character positions. The lower five bits of the value in the Start Horizontal Blanking Register should never equal the value in the End Horizontal Blanking field. The manner in which the width of the blanking period is determined is identical to the technique used to determine the width of the retrace period. The End Horizontal Retrace (EHR) field of the End Horizontal Retrace Register is also used for this purpose.

In the VGA, the functioning of this register is identical to its functioning in the EGA, with the exception that a sixth bit is added for the EHB field of the End Horizontal Retrace Register. Thus, a mod 64 counter is operating, allowing a blanking width of 63 character positions.

The Display Enable Skew Control field is used to compensate for hardware delays caused by accessing the attribute and character codes, accessing the character generator font, and reading the Pixel Panning Register. Certain modes require a one-character skew, and others use no character skew.

In the VGA, an additional field called the Compatible Read Field is used to enable access to the Vertical Retrace Start and the Vertical Retrace End Registers.

CR Compatible Read   VGA **Bit 7**

Enables or disables access to the Vertical Retrace Start and the Vertical Retrace End Registers.

=0 Disable access to these registers.

=1 Enable access to these registers.

DES Display Enable Skew   VGA, EGA **Bits 6,5**

The number of character clocks to skew the position of the horizontal timing to achieve proper synchronization. The two-bit binary value in this register represents the number of character clocks used to delay the timing.

EHB End Horizontal Blanking   VGA, EGA **Bits 4–0**

This field is used to determine the end of the horizontal blanking period as discussed above. In the VGA, a sixth bit is found in the EHB field of the End Horizontal Retrace Period.

10.4.5 Start Horizontal Retrace Register

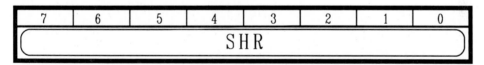

7	6	5	4	3	2	1	0
S H R

Index 04 hex

The horizontal sync pulse is the master horizontal synchronization reference used in the graphics system. The pulse begins when the character counter equals the value set in this register. Increasing this value causes the displayed area of the screen to be shifted horizontally to the right on the monitor.

The polarity of the horizontal sync pulse is set in the HSP field of the Miscellaneous Output Register.

SHR Start Horizontal Retrace.   EGA, VGA **Bits 7-0**

The value used to determine the start of the horizontal retrace period.

10.4.6 End Horizontal Retrace Register

7	6	5	4	3	2	1	0
SOM•EHB	— DES		EHR				

Index 05 hex

The value in this register determines where the end of the horizontal retrace period occurs. The width of the retrace period is determined in a manner similar to the technique used to determine the width of the blanking period. Unlike the EHB field, this field is a 5-bit value for both the EGA and the VGA. These 5 bits represents the lower 5 bits of the 8-bit character counter. When the lower 5 bits of the character counter equal the 5 bits in the End Horizontal Retrace field, the retrace time will end. See the End Horizontal Blanking Register for details.

SOM   Start Odd/Even Memory Address   EGA   **Bit 7**

Determines whether an odd or even memory address should be used as the first memory address after a horizontal refresh. This value is normally set to zero indicating that an even address should be used. This field is used during horizontal pixel panning operations.

=0 Start at an even memory address.

=1 Start at an odd memory address.

EHB   End Horizontal Blanking   VGA   **Bit 7**

The sixth bit of the EHB field found in the End Horizontal Blanking Register.

HRD   Horizontal Retrace Delay   EGA,VGA   **Bits 6–5**

The skew of the horizontal retrace signal used to synchronize the display adapter with the monitor. The high-resolution advanced EGA modes require retrace delays. The binary number in this 2-bit field determines the number of character clocks to skew the system.

EHR   End Horizontal Retrace   EGA,VGA   **Bits 4–0**

The 5-bit value used to determine the end of the horizontal retrace period as described above.

10.4.7 Vertical Total Register

7	6	5	4	3	2	1	0
VT							

Index 06 hex

This register determines the number of scan lines on the monitor, including both displayed and nondisplayed lines. It determines the frequency at which the vertical sync pulses will be generated. This is called the *vertical frequency*. Only the eight least significant bits of the vertical total are contained in this register. In the EGA, the ninth bit is found in the VT0 field of the Overflow Register. In the VGA, the ninth and tenth bits are found in the VT0 and VT1 fields of the Overflow Register respectively.

The vertical timing dictated by this register is similar to the horizontal timing dictated in the Horizontal Total Register. A line counter is used to count the horizontal scan lines. When the line counter equals the vertical total, a vertical retrace period begins.

VT Vertical Total   EGA,VGA **Bits 7–0**

The low-order eight bits of the value that determines the total number of vertical scan lines, including the vertical retrace period. The EGA has a ninth bit in the VT0 field of the Overflow Register. The VGA has a ninth and tenth bit in the VT1 field of the Overflow Register.

EGA VT = vertical retrace + # of horizontal scan lines.

VGA VT = vertical retrace + # of horizontal scan lines − 2.

10.4.8 Overflow Register

7	6	5	4	3	2	1	0
VRS∙	VDE∙	CL∙VT1	LC	VBS	VRS	VDE	VT

Index 07 hex

Certain registers associated with the vertical counter require field sizes larger than 8 bits. Several of the registers require 9 bits of accuracy because the vertical counter is greater than 256. In the VGA, the vertical total period requires a 10-bit value. The high-order bit fields of several of these registers are included in this register.

VRS Vertical Retrace Start Bit 9   VGA **Bit 7**

The ninth bit of the vertical retrace start value. The low-order 8 bits are found in the Vertical Retrace Start Register.

VDE Vertical Display Enable End Bit 9   VGA **Bit 6**

The ninth bit of the vertical display enable value. The low-order 8 bits are found in the Vertical Display Enable End Register.

CL Cursor Location Bit 8   EGA **Bit 5**

The ninth bit of the cursor location value. The low-order 8 bits are found in the Cursor Location Register.

VT1 Vertical Total Bit 9   VGA **Bit 5**

The tenth bit of the vertical total value. The low-order 8 bits are found in the Vertical Total Register. The ninth bit is found in the VT field of this register.

LC Line Compare Bit 8   EGA, VGA **Bit 4**

The ninth bit of the line compare value. The low-order 8 bits are found in the Line Compare Register.

VBS Start Vertical Blanking Bit 8   EGA, VGA **Bit 3**

The ninth bit of the start vertical blanking value. The low-order 8 bits are found in the Start Vertical Blanking Register.

VRS Vertical Retrace Start Bit 8   EGA, VGA **Bit 2**

The ninth bit of the start vertical retrace start value. The low-order 8 bits are found in the Vertical Retrace Start Register.

VDE Vertical Display Enable End Bit 8   EGA, VGA **Bit 1**

The ninth bit of the start vertical display end value. The low-order 8 bits are found in the Vertical Display End Register.

VT Vertical Total Bit 8   EGA, VGA **Bit 0**

The ninth bit of the start vertical total value. The low-order 8 bits are found in the Vertical Total Register. For the VGA, the tenth bit is found in the VT1 field of this register.

10.4.9 Preset Row Scan Register

7	6	5	4	3	2	1	0
		BP∎				PRS	

Index 08 hex

This register is used during scrolling operations in the EGA and the VGA. In the VGA, the BP field in this register is dedicated to panning operations. During scrolling, the first row of characters may not be full height. This occurs when the display is being panned and only a fraction of the top row of characters is visible. This register determines which scan line within the top row of characters should be displayed as the top scan line of that character row. This preset value is in effect only immediately after the vertical retrace period. The top row of data displayed on the monitor occurs immediately after the vertical retrace period.

The EGA/VGA is controlled as if the display consisted entirely of characters, even if the adapter is in a graphics mode. Each character is composed of a character box that consists of a matrix of dots equal to the number of rows in the character times the number of columns in the character. The rows in the character, also called scan lines, are numbered from the top down, beginning at zero and ending at the maximum row scan. The maximum row scan is equal to the number of scan lines in the character box and is contained in the Maximum Scan Line Register.

Scrolling is the effect achieved when the data on the screen appears to move up or down. The terminology in scrolling is reversed from the terminology used when viewing the screen as if through a window. When text is moved upward it is said that the text is "scrolled up." In a windows notation, one would view the window as moving downward through the text. This downward motion of the window would give the appearance of the displayed data moving upward.

There are two types of scrolling, a *character row scroll* (or *rough scroll*) and a *smooth scroll*. A character row scroll is used to scroll one complete row of characters at a time. For example, if the display were scrolling upward, the top row of characters on the display would disappear and the second row would become the top row. A new row of characters would appear at the bottom of the display. This would be a rough scroll because the entire group of scan lines representing a character was moved at one time.

A smooth scroll would scroll one scan line at a time. If a character consists of 14 scan lines, it would take 14 single-line scrolls before a new character row would appear. In this case, the characters in the first row would not be full height. The Preset Row Scan Register determines which scan line in the top

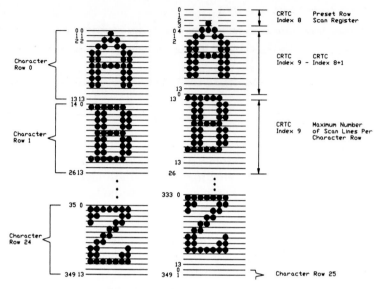

FIGURE 10.2 Smooth Scrolling

row of characters to output to the display as the top scan line of the top row of characters. Again, this is in effect only for the first row following a vertical retrace, which is the top row of the display. The maximum character matrix height is 32 rows. Therefore, this preset row scan can range from row 0 to row 31. Smooth scrolling is illustrated in Figure 10.2.

In the VGA, an additional field, BP, is present that enhances the control of the panning operation. It allows up to three characters to be panned, which corresponds to 24 pixels in an eight-pixel-per-character mode or 27 pixels in a nine-pixel-per-character mode.

BP Byte Panning   VGA **Bits 6–5**

This field controls the number of bytes to pan during a panning operation. The Horizontal Panning Register determines the number of pixels to pan, and this field determines the number of bytes to pan. Together, these fields allow up to three characters to be panned.

PRS Preset Row Scan   EGA,VGA **Bits 4–0**

The starting row of a character box displayed on the top row of characters on a screen. Normally, the value in this register is 0, which displays the entire vertical extent of the top row of characters.

10.4.10 Maximum Scan Line Register

7	6	5	4	3	2	1	0
2T4■	LC ■	VBS■	MSL				

Index 09 hex

The size of the rectangular character box is variable. The number of scan lines in a character ranges from 0 to 31 pixels. This register contains the maximum number of scan lines per character rows minus 1. This "minus 1" occurs because the topmost row of a character is row 0 rather than row 1.

The adapter can have only one maximum scan line count in effect at a time. If characters with different character heights are desired, the Maximum Scan Line Register should be set to the maximum character height. Because two character fonts may be active at a given time, it is possible to have one character set taller than the other. Each character in the shorter of the two character sets will be padded with zeros. When the smaller character set is selected, the character will be written to the screen with the additional rows of padded zeros as background. In the alphanumeric modes, the character background is displayed according to the background color. In the graphics modes, the background of the character is transparent and does not overwrite what is currently displayed. Therefore, the unused portion of the character, considered background, will not overwrite any data.

Regardless of the value selected for the maximum number of scan lines per character, the downloadable character fonts will be stored in display memory with each character consisting of 32 rows. If the character set contains 8 rows per character, the character would occupy the first 8 of the 32 available positions. The remaining 24 positions would be unused. These 32 rows are reserved for each character in order to achieve fast addressing of the character fonts. Because each character is 32 bytes apart in display memory, a shift operation is all that is required to determine the position of the character pattern. To determine the character position from the ASCII code, the code value is simply shifted five bits to the left. This is equivalent to a multiplication by 32.

In the VGA, the upper three bits of this register are used to allow 200 lines to be displayed as 400 lines and as additional overflow fields for the Line Compare and Start Vertical Blanking Registers.

2T4 200-to-400-line Conversion   VGA **Bit 7**

Allows a 200-line mode to be displayed on 400 display scan lines. This permits the 200-line display modes to fill the entire screen. Each line is duplicated twice by dividing the clock to the row scan counter by 2.

=0 Normal operation.

=1 Display 200 lines on the full display.

LC Line Compare Bit 9 VGA **Bit 6**

The tenth bit of the Line Compare value. The lower eight bits are in the Line Compare Register, and the ninth bit is in the LC field of the Overflow Register.

VBS Start Vertical Blanking Bit 9 VGA **Bit 5**

The tenth bit of the start vertical blanking value. The lower eight bits are in the Start Vertical Blanking Register, and the ninth bit is in the VBS field of the overflow register.

MSL Maximum Scan Line EGA, VGA **Bits 4–0**

The number of scan lines in a character row minus 1.

10.4.11 Cursor Start Register

7	6	5	4	3	2	1	0
		C O O▪			C S		

Index 0A hex

The hardware cursor is represented as a block of pixels occupying a character position. Like any character, the cursor is composed of a number of scan lines. In conjunction with the Cursor End Register, this register allows the height of the cursor to be variable. This register determines the first scan line within the character box that should be filled in. The scan lines within a character box are numbered from the top down. The count begins at 0, with the exception of the top scan line (see Preset Row Scan Register), and ends at the maximum character height defined in the Maximum Scan Line Register. A cursor that fills the entire character box should begin at scan line 0.

The cursor may be enabled or disabled by the COO field for the VGA.

COO Cursor On/OFF VGA **Bit 5**

Allows the cursor to be turned on or off.

=0 Turn the cursor off.

=1 Turn the cursor on.

CS Cursor Start EGA,VGA **Bits 4–0**

The number of the scan line within a character box that will be the first scan line displayed for the cursor. Because the maximum character size is 32 scan lines, this value may range from 0 to 31.

10.4.12 Cursor End Register

7	6	5	4	3	2	1	0
	C S K				C E		

Index 0B hex

The hardware cursor is represented as a block of pixels occupying a character position. Like any character, the cursor is composed of a number of scan lines. In conjunction with the Cursor Start Register, this register allows the height of the cursor to be variable. This register determines the last scan line within the character box that should be displayed as part of the cursor. The scan lines within a character box are numbered from the top down. The count begins at 0, with the exception of the top scan line (see Preset Row Scan Register), and ends at the maximum character height defined in the Maximum Scan Line Register. A cursor that fills the entire character box should end at the scan line equal to the maximum scan lines per character.

Because of the internal timing of the EGA, it is necessary in the high-resolution modes to skew the timing of the signals to achieve proper synchronization. The Cursor Skew field of this register is similar to the DES field in the End Horizontal Blanking Register and the HRD delay field in the End Horizontal Retrace Register.

CSK Cursor Skew   EGA, VGA **Bits 6–5**

The number of characters to delay the cursor data in order to achieve proper synchronization. The binary amount in this field is equal to the number of characters to skew.

CE Cursor End   EGA, VGA **Bits 4–0**

The bottom scan line to display per character row for the cursor.

10.4.13 Start Address High Register

7	6	5	4	3	2	1	0
			S A H				

Index 0C hex

The upper left corner of the display represents the origin of the display. The data to be displayed at this location is resident in the display buffer. The address of this data is determined by the 16-bit value found in the Start Address Registers. The maximum display buffer size is 64 Kbytes. Thus, a 16-bit address is required to address any given byte. Because the CRTC registers are 8 bits each, it takes two registers to fully specify the start address. The Start Address High Register represents the upper 8 bits of the 16-bit address, and the Start Address Low Register represents the lower 8 bits of the 16-bit address.

The screen may be considered to be a window through which data can be viewed. The size of the window is not necessarily the same as the size of the data. The maximum window size for a display would be the maximum resolution of the EGA/VGA. The display memory may be, and in fact often is, larger than this maximum resolution. If the starting address is modified, the window will move through the data, giving the effect of horizontal panning or vertical scrolling.

The display memory is 64 Kbytes per plane. Each plane begins with relative address 0. In the graphics modes, modifying the value in the starting address by 1 will change the position of the data to be displayed on the screen by one byte. In the EGA modes, this translates to 8 horizontal pixels because there are 8 pixels per byte, one pixel per bit. Thus, increasing the address by 1 will have the effect of shifting the display to the left by 8 pixels. Assuming that the dimensions of the display are not modified, the data corresponding to the left eight columns on the screen will no longer be displayed. New data will be displayed in the right 8 pixels of the screen.

Likewise, decreasing the starting address by 1 will cause the displayed data to shift 8 pixels to the right. If the starting address is increased by the number of horizontal pixels per row, the display will appear to scroll one row downward. The number of pixels in a horizontal row is determined by the number of character positions per row loaded in the Horizontal Display Enable End Register and the number of pixels per character loaded in the 8/9 field of the Clocking Mode Register. If there are 80 characters per row, corresponding to 640 pixels, increasing the starting address by 80 would cause the display to scroll one row upward. The previous top row of the display would no longer be displayed, and a new row would scroll into the bottom of the screen. Remember that this row represents one scan line, not a character row.

SAH Start Address High   EGA, VGA **Bits 7-0**

The high-order eight bits of the starting address that will determine the first data to be displayed after a vertical refresh. The low-order eight bits of the starting address are found in the Start Address Low Register.

10.4.14 Start Address Low Register

7	6	5	4	3	2	1	0
			SAL				

Index 0D hex

The upper left corner of the display represents the origin of the display. The data to be displayed at this location is resident in the display buffer. The address of this data is determined by the 16-bit value found in the Start Address Registers. The display buffer is 64 Kbytes long. Thus, a 16-bit address is required to address any given byte. Because the CRTC registers are 8 bits each, it takes two registers to fully specify the start address. The Start Address Low Register represents the lower 8 bits of the 16-bit address, and the Start Address High Register represents the higher 8 bits of the 16-bit address. See the Start Address High Register for details.

SAL Start Address Low   EGA, VGA **Bits 7–0**

The low-order 8 bits of the starting address that will determine the first data to be displayed after a vertical refresh. The high-order 8 bits of the starting address are found in the Start Address High Register.

10.4.15 Cursor Location High Register

7	6	5	4	3	2	1	0
			CLH				

Index 0E hex

The cursor position is determined by the 16-bit address that points to a byte in display memory. This register represents the upper 8 bits of the 16-bit address. The lower 8 bits of the 16-bit address are found in the Cursor Location Low Register. See the Start Address High Register for addressing details. It is necessary to specify the cursor address in this way because the cursor will nondestructively overwrite data on the screen. The EGA keeps track of which data is being overwritten by the cursor so that the original data occupying that location on the screen may be restored when the cursor moves. This allows the cursor to move about the screen without destroying data. The nondestructive activity of the cursor is transparent to the programmer. Note that the cursor location may point to a non-displayed location on the screen. In this case, the cursor would not be displayed.

CLH Cursor Location High   EGA, VGA   **Bits 7–0**

The 8 high-order bits of the 16-bit address that determines where the cursor will be located.

10.4.16 Cursor Location Low Register

7	6	5	4	3	2	1	0
			C L L				

Index 0F hex

The cursor position is determined by the 16-bit address that points to a byte in display memory. This register represents the lower 8 bits of the 16-bit address. The upper 8 bits of the 16-bit address are found in the Cursor Location High Register. See the Cursor Location High Register and the Start Address High Register for addressing details.

CLL Cursor Location Low   EGA, VGA   **Bits 7–0**

The 8 low-order bits of the 16-bit address which determines where the cursor will be located.

10.4.17 Vertical Retrace Start Register

7	6	5	4	3	2	1	0
			V R S				

Index 10 hex

In the VGA, this register may be accessed only if the Compatible Read (CR) field of the End Horizontal Blanking Register is set to a 1.

The vertical sync pulse is output when the scan line counter is equal to the value loaded into this register. The status of the display can be monitored through the VRI field of the Input Status #0 Register and through the DE or VR field of the Input Status #1 Register. These fields are used to indicate whether the system is in a vertical retrace, a horizontal retrace, or a display condition. As is true during the horizontal retrace, no information is drawn onto the screen during the vertical retrace.

The vertical retrace period is significantly longer than the horizontal retrace because of the longer distance that the electron beam needs to travel to get back to the top left corner of the monitor. Also, more time can be taken because the vertical retrace occurs only 50–60 times per second. This time can be utilized for internal display adapter housekeeping.

The sync pulse is a master timing pulse used internally for the display and externally to synchronize the monitor. Because the vertical counters are a minimum of nine bits, this register can hold only the low-order eight bits. The ninth bit is located in the VT field of the Overflow Register for the EGA. The ninth and tenth bits are located in the VT and VT1 fields of the Overflow Register for the VGA.

In the EGA, the occurrence of a vertical retrace period can generate an interrupt if the vertical retrace interrupt is enabled. It is enabled by resetting the DVI field of the Vertical Retrace End Register. The polarity of the vertical retrace period is set in the VSP field of the Miscellaneous Output Register.

VRS   Vertical Retrace Start   EGA, VGA   **Bits 7–0**

The low-order 8 bits of the value that determines when a vertical retrace pulse begins. The scan line counter is compared to this register at each horizontal retrace time. When the scan-line counter equals this value, the vertical retrace period begins.

10.4.18   Vertical Retrace End Register

7	6	5	4	3	2	1	0
PR▪	BW▪	▪DVI	▪CVI		EVR		

Index 11 hex

In the VGA, this register may be accessed only if the Compatible Read (CR) field of the End Horizontal Blanking Register is set to a 1.

The vertical sync pulse becomes inactive when the low-order five bits of the scan line counter, also called the horizontal scan count, is equal to this value. The vertical sync pulse begins when the scan count is equal to the value in the Vertical Retrace Start Register. The operation of this function is identical to the operation of the Horizontal Retrace End Register. Like that register, this register represents only the five low-order bits of the end value. After the vertical retrace begins, the five low-order bits of the scan line counter will be compared to this register. When they are equal, the retrace pulse will become inactive. See the Horizontal Retrace End Register for more details on this mod 32 counter.

In the EGA, the status of the display can be monitored through the VRI field of the Input Status #0 Register and through the DE or VR field of the

Input Status #1 Register. These fields are used to indicate whether the system is in a vertical retrace, a horizontal retrace, or a display condition. The occurrence of a vertical retrace signal can generate an interrupt if the interrupt is enabled. It is enabled by resetting the DVI field in this register. Note: The vertical interrupt is disabled if this field is equal to a 1. Thus, it is termed the Disable Vertical Interrupt field.

Further, in the EGA, when the vertical interrupt is enabled and a vertical retrace period occurs, an interrupt level 2 on a PC or level 9 on an AT is generated on the host processor. The CVI field of this register clears this vertical interrupt. Again, the notation is confusing because of the polarity of this field. A 0 in this field will cause the interrupt to be cleared. It is important for the interrupt service routine to reset the interrupt. The first thing that an interrupt service routine should do is to disable any further undesired interrupts from occurring. This insures that the interrupt service routine is not interrupted by undesired sources.

Disabling interrupts are particularly important in time-sensitive applications. Suppose that it is necessary to modify some parameter in the graphics system during the vertical retrace period, and the modification is to occur within the interrupt service routine. If non–time-sensitive interrupts such as keyboard or disk are serviced during this time, the vertical retrace period could well be over before control is returned to the vertical interrupt service routine. This could be avoided by disabling the disk and keyboard interrupts, along with any other undesirable interrupts.

At the end of the interrupt service routine, the interrupts are re-enabled. Because the EGA is generating the interrupt, as soon as the interrupts are re-enabled, the vertical interrupt will regenerate itself because the interrupt is still active. This occurs regardless of the fact that the interrupt was handled. The vertical interrupt signal does not go away when the vertical retrace period ends. It is necessary for the software to clear the interrupt. Thus, the second thing that the interrupt service routine should do is to clear the vertical interrupt by resetting a 0 into the CVI field of this register. This is done to ensure that a vertical interrupt is not missed.

If an event is to be synchronized with the vertical retrace period, it is not necessary to perform any function within the vertical retrace period itself, as long as the occurrence of the vertical retrace period is noted. Further, if a different time-sensitive interrupt occurs during the time that a vertical retrace period occurs, and if this time-sensitive interrupt service routine disables the level-2 interrupts and finishes after the vertical retrace period, the vertical retrace interrupt will still be pending. This would not be the case if the interrupt had been removed automatically at the end of the vertical retrace period.

In the VGA, bits 6 and 7 are used to protect the CRTC registers at indexes 0 through 7. The exception is the line compare field (LC) in the Overflow Register. The bandwidth of the system is also controlled for the VGA by allowing three or five dynamic RAM (DRAM) refresh cycles per horizontal line. A similar field is found in the BW field of the Clocking Mode Register for the EGA.

PR Protect Registers 0–7   VGA **Bit 7**

Protects CRTC registers at indexes 0 to 7 from being modified. The lower 8
registers in the CRTC contain sensitive horizontal and vertical timing settings.
Software expecting the EGA may program these registers unwittingly.

   =0 No protection is active.

   =1 Writing from the host to CRTC registers 0–7 is disabled.

BW Bandwidth   VGA **Bit 6**

Selects three or five DRAM refresh cycles per horizontal line.

   =0 Select three DRAM cycles.

   =1 Select five DRAM cycles.

DVI Disable Vertical Interrupts   EGA **Bits 5**

Controls the ability of the EGA to generate a level-2 interrupt on the occurrence
of a vertical interrupt.

   =0 Enable vertical interrupts.

   =1 Disable vertical interrupts.

CVI Clear Vertical Interrupts   EGA **Bit 4**

Removes a vertical interrupt when reset to 0. Note that setting this field to a 1
has no effect because it cannot generate an interrupt.

   =0 Clear the vertical interrupt.

   =1 No effect.

EVR Vertical Retrace End   EGA, VGA **Bits 3–0**

The low-order five bits of the value that will cause the vertical retrace period
to end. The horizontal scan line count is compared to the Vertical Retrace Start
Register. When the values are equal, a vertical retrace period is started. After
this time, the low-order five bits of the scan line count are compared to the five
bits in the **EVR** field. When they are equal, the vertical retrace period ends.

10.4.19 Light Pen High Register

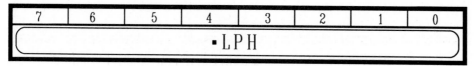

    Index 10 hex (EGA only)

The light pen interface generates a trigger pulse when the electron beam crosses
in front of the light pen. When this trigger occurs, the display memory address

of the current data being refreshed corresponds to the position of the light pen. This 16-bit value is automatically written into the two light pen registers. This register contains the high-order 8 bits of the 16-bit display memory address that corresponds to the current position of the light pen. The low-order 8 bits are automatically written into the Light Pen Low Register.

It is important to note that if the electron beam is not drawing any data onto the screen at the location of the light pen, no trigger will be generated. The electron beam must be exciting the screen phosphor before the light pen can detect the presence of light.

LPH Light Pen High   EGA **Bits 7–0**

The high-order 8 bits of the current position of the light pen as generated by the light pen trigger.

10.4.20 Light Pen Low Register

7	6	5	4	3	2	1	0
			•LPL				

Index 11 hex (EGA only)

This register contains the low-order 8 bits of the 16-bit display memory address that corresponds to the current position of the light pen. The high-order 8 bits are automatically written into the Light Pen High Register. See the Light Pen High Register for details.

LPL Light Pen Low   EGA **Bits 7–0**

The low-order 8 bits of the current position of the light pen as generated by the light pen trigger.

10.4.21 Vertical Display End Register

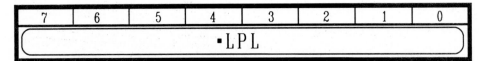

7	6	5	4	3	2	1	0
			VDE				

Index 12 hex

This register determines the number of the last horizontal scan line occurring on the bottom of the screen. The scan-line counter increments until the value in the Vertical Display Enable End Register is reached. Because this value is greater than 256, only the low-order eight bits of the enable end value can be stored in this register. The ninth bit is stored in the VDE field of the Overflow Register for the EGA. The ninth and tenth bits are stored in the VDE field of the Overflow Register for the VGA. The vertical blanking usually occurs before the value in the Vertical Display Enable End Register occurs. The horizontal lines that occur between these two values are considered to be the border area. The color of the border is determined by the value in the Overscan Register.

VDE Vertical Display End Enable   EGA, VGA **Bits 7–0**

The low-order 8 bits of the value in the Vertical Display Enable End Register. This determines the last horizontal line to be displayed on the bottom of the monitor, including the overscan region.

10.4.22 Offset Register

7	6	5	4	3	2	1	0
OFF							

Index 13 hex

This register specifies the width of the display. The EGA/VGA may be addressed in a byte mode or a word mode as specified in the CBT field of the Mode Control Register. This offset value corresponds to the difference between the addresses of two vertically neighboring pixels. This is often called *display pitch* in other graphic processors. The address of the next display row is computed by the current byte start address + (value in the Offset Register × K), where K = 2 for byte addressing and K = 4 for word addressing.

OFF Offset   EGA, VGA **Bits 7–0**

The difference in byte or words between vertically adjacent scan lines.

10.4.23 Underline Location Register

7	6	5	4	3	2	1	0
	DW•	CB4•	UL				

Index 14 hex

The EGA/VGA allows each character to be underlined as determined in each character's underline field. Each character is composed of up to 32 scan lines in the vertical dimension, as dictated in the Maximum Scan Line Register. The horizontal line used for the underlining will occur on one of these scan lines. The number of the scan line minus 1 is loaded into this register. The "minus 1" occurs because the scan lines are counted beginning with scan line number zero. Thus, the fourth scan line of the character is actually scan line number three.

The VGA uses bits 5 and 6 to enable double-word addressing and, when double-word addressing is enabled, to divide the character clock input to the memory address counter by 4. This is utilized when the four display modes are chained in mode 13 hex.

DW Double Word Mode   VGA   **Bit 6**

Allows normal addressing or double-word addressing.

=0 Normal word addressing.

=1 Double word addressing.

CB4 Count by Four   VGA   **Bit 5**

If the double-word addressing is enabled in the DW field of this register, this field controls the clock to the memory address counter. It is possible to divide this clock by 4, which would be done when the four display planes are chained in Mode 13 hex.

=0 Normal clocking.

=1 Divide the character clock to the memory address counter by 4.

UL Underline Location   EGA, VGA   **Bits 4–0**

The value in this field minus 1 determines the horizontal scan line within a character box on which the underline will occur.

10.4.24 Start Vertical Blank Register

7	6	5	4	3	2	1	0
			V B S				

Index 15 hex

The vertical blanking period begins when the horizontal scan line counter equals the start vertical blanking value. The vertical blanking period is used to turn off the data stream being output to the display during the vertical retrace period. The display enable period is normally concluded, as indicated by the value in the Vertical Display End Register, before the blanking begins. This allows a border region, the color of which is determined by the value in the Overscan Register. Because the horizontal scan line counter is greater than eight bits, only the low-order eight bits are contained in this register. The ninth bit is contained in the VBS field of the Overflow Register for the EGA. For the VGA, the ninth and tenth bits are contained in the VBS field of the Overflow Register and in the SVB field of the Maximum Scan Line Register.

VBS   Vertical Blank Start   EGA, VGA   **Bits 7–0**

The low-order 8 bits of the value that is compared to the horizontal scan line counter. When these two values are equal, the vertical blanking period begins.

10.4.25   End Vertical Blank Register

7	6	5	4	3	2	1	0
	VBE∎			VBE			

Index 16 hex

This register determines the end of the vertical blanking period. It is similar in operation to the End Horizontal Blanking, End Horizontal Retrace, and End Vertical Retrace Registers. In the EGA, the five-bit value in this register is compared to the low-order five bits of the horizontal scan line counter. The comparison causes the vertical blanking period to end after a vertical blanking period begins. It begins when the scan-line counter and the value in the Start Vertical Blanking Register are equal. Because only the low five bits are used, the comparison is based on mod 32 arithmetic. This limits the vertical blanking period to 32 character positions. In the VGA, this field is seven bits long, facilitating a mode 128 arithmetic.

VBE   End Vertical Blanking   EGA   **Bits 4–0**

The value that determines when the vertical blanking interval should end. This value is compared to the low-order five bits of the horizontal scan line counter.

VBE   End Vertical Blanking   VGA   **Bits 6–0**

The value that determines when the vertical blanking interval should end. This value is compared to the low-order seven bits of the horizontal scan line counter.

10.4.26 Mode Control Register

7	6	5	4	3	2	1	0
HR	W/B	AW	· OC	CBT	HRS	SRS	CMS

Index 17 hex

A multifunction register that assists in the control of the display. This register can generally be left alone by the programmer. When the mode of the display is changed, the BIOS commands will automatically adjust the value in this register to match the mode.

HR Hardware Reset   EGA, VGA **Bit 7**

Enables or disables the ability of the display to generate hardware horizontal and vertical retrace signals, display enable signals, and blanking signals.

=0 Places all horizontal and vertical control timings into a hold state, thereby forcing a reset condition.

=1 Enables the occurrence of the horizontal and vertical control signals.

W/B Word/Byte Mode   EGA, VGA **Bit 6**

Controls the way the internal addresses generated in the EGA are output to the display memory address bus. Word mode is used in CGA emulation.

=0 The word mode is selected, causing the addresses' bits to be shifted left one position before being output to the display memory. A more significant address bit is output on the least significant memory address line. This bit is either bit 13 or bit 15 depending on the value in the AW field in this register.

=1 The byte mode is selected, causing the addresses to be output to the display memory without being shifted.

AW Address Wrap   EGA, VGA **Bit 5**

Determines whether bit 13 or bit 15 should be output on the least significant address line to the display memory when the system is in a word mode, as indicated in the W/B field in this register. This field is used during CGA emulation. Shifting the address bits one position has the effect of halving memory. The CGA maps the even memory addresses in the first block of memory and the odd memory addresses in the second block of memory. This contrasts with using address bit 1 as a switch, as is done in the SRS field, which quarters the memory for Hercules emulation.

If bit 0 is substituted for memory address bit 13, consecutive scan lines are separated by 8 Kbytes. If bit 0 is substituted for memory address bit 15, successive scan lines are separated by 32 Kbytes.

=0   Select address bit 13 to be sent to the least significant address bit to the display memory. This should be used when 64K of memory is installed on the EGA/VGA board.

=1   Select address bit 15 to be sent to the least significant address bit to the display memory. This should be used when greater than 64K of memory is installed on the EGA board.

OC   Output Control   EGA   **Bit 4**

Enables or disables the output drivers. Note that this bit is used for alternative memory addressing by EGA/VGA chip manufacturers. Only the IBM EGA standard usage for this register is discussed here. Consult the manufacturers' specifications for the use of this bit on other EGA boards.

=0   Enable the EGA output drivers.

=1   Disable the EGA output drivers.

CBT   Count by Two   EGA, VGA   **Bit 3**

Determines whether the EGA/VGA memory address counter is clocked every character clock or every other character clock. This creates either a byte or a word refresh address for the display buffer. It determines the actual address difference in conjunction with the Offset Register.

=0   The memory address counter is clocked with the character clock input.

=1   The memory address counter is clocked with every other character clock input.

HRS   Horizontal Retrace Select   EGA, VGA   **Bit 2**

Controls the vertical resolution capability of the display. Normally, the vertical resolution of the display is limited to 512 horizontal lines because of the 9-bit scan-line counter in the EGA. In the VGA, it is limited to 1,024 horizontal lines because of the ten-bit scan-line counter in the VGA. If the scan-line counter is clocked with the horizontal retrace divided by 2, it will be clocked twice as often. This increases the possible vertical resolution to 1,024 horizontal scan lines in the EGA and 2,048 horizontal scan lines in the VGA.

=0   Clock the scan-line counter with every horizontal retrace.

=1   Clock the scan-line counter with every horizontal retrace divided by 2, allowing up to 1,024 addressable scan lines for the EGA and 2,048 horizontal scan lines for the VGA.

SRS   Select Row Scan Counter   EGA, VGA   **Bit 1**

This field allows the EGA/VGA to be compatible at the memory addressing level with a graphics system that uses a four-bank memory. The graphics system that most frequently uses such a four-bank memory is the Hercules mono-chrome adapter. The memory address bit 14 is multiplexed. The occurrence of the display enable period is indicated by the DE field of the Input Status #1 Register and is controlled by the Horizontal Display End Register and the Vertical Display End Register. During the display enable period, the memory address line corresponding to bit 14 is replaced with bit 1. This makes successive scan lines 16 Kbytes apart. This is similar to the multiplexing of bit 0 onto memory address bit 13 or bit 15 for CGA compatibility. In this mode, successive scan lines are 32 Kbytes apart. This function is controlled by the AW field of this register.

=0 Row scan counter bit 1 is placed on the memory address bus bit 14 during active display time. Bit 1, placed on memory address bit 14, has the effect of quartering the memory.

=1 Memory addresses are output sequentially.

CMS   Compatibility Mode Support   EGA, VGA   **Bit 0**

This field allows the EGA/VGA to address memory in a similar fashion to that used by the CGA. During the active display time, row scan address bit 0 is substituted for memory address bit 13. The CGA is controlled by the 6845 controller chip and uses the row scan address to increase the 6845 address potential. The 6845 normally can address only 128 lines. To achieve the desired 200-line resolution, the 6845 is programmed for a 100-scan-line resolution with two row scan addresses per character row. This chip places successive scan lines of the display memory in two separate odd and even memory banks. The CGA has 16 Kbytes of memory, and successive scan lines are placed 8 Kbytes apart. Row scan address bit 0 is used as the most significant address bit on the CGA to split up the memory into these two 8 Kbyte blocks. Bit 13 corresponds to the 8 Kbyte boundary, and row scan address bit 0 corresponds to odd and even scan lines. This causes the EGA/VGA to address memory in a similar fashion to that used by the CGA.

=0 Substitutes row scan address bit 0 for memory address bit 13, causing the memory of the EGA/VGA during the graphics modes to be compat-ible with the CGA's 6845 controller chip.

=1 Performs no substitution, causing the EGA to access memory sequen-tially.

10.4.27 Line Compare Register

7	6	5	4	3	2	1	0
			L C				

Index 18 hex

This register allows split-screen display. The low-order eight bits of a value are compared to the horizontal scan line counter. The ninth bit is located in the LC field of the Overflow Register for the EGA. In the VGA, the ninth bit is located in the LC field in the Overflow Register and the tenth bit is located in the LC field in the Overflow Register. When the scan line counter equals the value in this register, the line counter is cleared, causing the display to begin refreshing the top section of the display again. This causes the display to be split. The bottom portion of the display represents the difference between the value in the Line Compare Register and the value in the Vertical Display End Register. Split-screen operation is illustrated in Figure 10.3.

The starting address loaded into the Start Address High and Start Address Low Registers determines the location of the data that will be displayed in the upper right corner of the display. The length of each display is determined by the Horizontal Display End and Vertical Display End Registers. In normal operation, the Line Compare Register is loaded with a maximum value of 511 for the EGA and 1,023 for the VGA. This causes data to fill the entire screen. The line counter is not reset because it will never reach the maximum values in the Line Compare Register. The horizontal line counter, also called the vertical counter, will be reset only when the Vertical Display End value is reached at the bottom of the screen.

Now suppose that the Line Compare Register and its associated 9th bit are loaded with the value 175. In a 350-line display, this corresponds to a line halfway down the screen. When the vertical counter reaches 175, the memory address counter will be reset, causing the screen refreshing to begin at memory location 0. There will be no observable change to the top half of the screen if no other parameters have changed. The reason is that the starting address still dictates where the data begins for the top half of the display. The bottom half of the screen now reflects the data beginning at memory address 0, the beginning of the display planes. Thus, two screens are displayed on the monitor. The top half begins at the address in the Start Address High and Start Address Low Registers; the bottom half begins at memory location 0. If the Start Address registers are set to 0, a single screen will result.

This register is often used to provide split-screen operation that allows one portion of the screen to be scrolled independently of the other. If the Start Address registers are loaded with a new value, the top half of the screen will

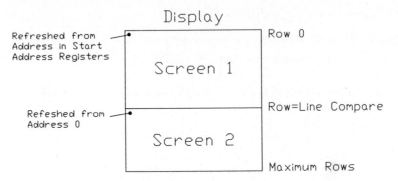

FIGURE 10.3 Split-screen Operation

reflect the change, and the bottom half will remain unchanged. See the Start Address High and Start Address Low Registers for addressing details.

LC Line Compare   EGA, VGA **Bits 7–0**

When the line counter is equal to the nine-bit line-compare value, the refresh address will be cleared, causing the horizontal display lines beneath the line compare value to be refreshed from display memory address 0. The effect is a dual-screen operation. This register contains the low-order eight bits of the line-compare value. This is illustrated in Figure 10.3.

10.5   THE GRAPHICS CONTROLLER REGISTERS

The Graphics Controller Registers consist of 9 registers. None of these registers has a unique host port address. Instead, an address and data register pair exists in the host port address space. The programmer accesses these registers by first loading the Graphics Address Register with an index value ranging from 0 to 8. The Graphics Address Register selects one of the Graphics Data Registers as the current active register. Reading or writing to this Graphics Data Register will repeatedly access the register selected by the index value, until the Graphics Address Register is modified. The Graphics Address Register resides at port 3CE hex, and the Graphics Data Register resides at port 3CF hex.

In addition to these indexed registers, the EGA contains two registers that have their own host port addresses. These registers are called the Graphics 1 Position and the Graphics 2 Position Registers. They reside at host port addresses 3CC and 3CA hex, respectively. The Graphics Controller Registers are listed in Table 10.11.

TABLE 10.11 Graphics Controller Registers

Register Name	Index (Hex)	Write (Hex) (EGA/VGA)	Read (Hex) (VGA)
Graphics 1 Position	—	3CC (EGA only)	—
Graphics 2 Position	—	3CA (EGA only)	—
Graphics Address	—	3CE	3CE
Set/Reset	0	3CF	3CF
Enable Set/Reset	1	3CF	3CF
Color Compare	2	3CF	3CF
Data Rotate	3	3CF	3CF
Read Map Select	4	3CF	3CF
Mode	5	3CF	3CF
Miscellaneous	6	3CF	3CF
Color Don't Care	7	3CF	3CF
Bit Mask	8	3CF	3CF

10.5.1 Graphics #1 Position Register (EGA only)

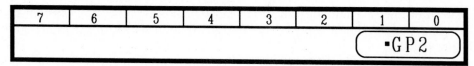

Write Port 3CC hex (EGA)

The EGA was originally implemented by IBM using two Graphics Controller Chips. It was necessary to program each to respond to a different set of two consecutive bits of the 8-bit host data bus. In the IBM EGA implementation, a 0 must be loaded into this register. In the VGA, there is no analogous register.

GP1 Graphics Position #1   **EGA Bits 2–1**

A zero should be loaded into this location to map host data bus bits 0 and 1 to display planes 0 and 1 respectively.

10.5.2 Graphics #2 Position Register (EGA only)

Write Port 3CA hex (EGA)

The EGA was originally implemented by IBM using two Graphics Controller Chips. This register is used to program the Graphics #2 chip. See the Graphics #1 Position Register for details.

GP2 Graphics Position #2.   EGA **Bits 1–0**

A 1 should be loaded into this location to map host data bus bits 2 and 3 to display planes 2 and 3, respectively.

10.5.3 Set/Reset Register

7	6	5	4	3	2	1	0
				S / R			

Index 00 hex

In normal display operation, the Set/Reset function is disabled through the Enable Set/Reset Register. Assuming a write mode of 0, as loaded in the MW field of the Write Mode Register, writing to display memory occurs in a horizontal block of up to eight consecutive pixels in one, two, three, or four planes. The data that is written into the display planes comes from the host processor data bus. The byte-wide data bus, bits 7–0, is sent to the EGA/VGA. It is interpreted as being eight neighboring horizontal pixels, where bit 7 corresponds to the far left pixel and bit 0 corresponds to the far right pixel. Depending on the value in the Bit Plane Mask Register, any or all of these bits might be written to the display memory. If more than one plane is enabled via the Map Mask Register, an identical pattern is written to each plane. This mode of writing to a display is termed *Bit Plane Mode* in the graphics world because unique data is written to consecutive locations in a single plane. Although multiple planes may be selected, these will be written with the same data as is written to a single plane.

It is sometimes desirable to write unique data to all display planes in a single operation. This mode of writing to a display is called *raster mode* because a multiplane pixel is written to in a single operation. The value in the Bit Plane Mask Register determines the number of horizontal neighboring pixels that will be affected in the byte addressed by the host processor. If more than one bit is enabled in the Bit Plane Mask Register, more than one pixel will be written to in a single operation. These multiple pixels will be loaded with the same data as presented in the Set/Reset Register.

In summary, the "Bit Plane Mode" writes unique information to horizontally neighboring pixels and copies this pattern to between 1 and 4 display planes. In the raster mode, unique information is written to between 1 and 4 display planes and copied to horizontally neighboring pixels.

The Set/Reset Register is loaded with the pattern that will be written to the display planes. There is a one-to-one correspondence between the bit positions in the Set/Reset register and the display plane numbers. Thus, bit 0 in the Set/Reset Register corresponds to memory plane 0, bit 1 corresponds to memory plane 1, and so on. Not all display planes need to be affected in a set/reset operation. The Enable Set/Reset Resister determines which planes should be affected in such an operation.

The bit locations in the Enable Set/Reset Register correspond to the bit locations in the Set/Reset register and the memory display plane numbers. Any bit that is set to 1 in the Enable Set/Reset Register causes the data in the corresponding display bit plane to be modified by the corresponding bit in the Set/Reset Register. If a bit is reset to 0 in the Enable Set/Reset Register, the corresponding display bit plane remains unmodified. Originally, all bits in the Enable Set/Reset Register were reset to 0, which had the effect of disabling the set/reset function. In this case, the data presented by the host processor was used to modify the data in the selected display planes as normal for write mode 0. The display planes that were modified in this case were those that were enabled in the Map Mask Register. Again, the bit positions (3–0) in the Set/Reset Register, Enable Set/Reset Register, and the Map Mask Register correspond to the display bit plane number (3–0).

It is also possible, and sometimes desirable, to combine the normal writing mode with the Set/Reset mode. In either mode, writing to the display memory requires data to be moved into the display memory address space. The specific address determines where the data will be written to with respect to the display. This data move is accomplished through an assembly language MOV instruction, either directly through assembly language or indirectly through a C command. This move command will move a byte of data to the desired location. A word move will simply write two consecutive bytes, similar to two consecutive byte move instructions.

Assume that all planes are enabled through the Map Mask Register. If the set/reset function is enabled in all four display planes, the data being referred to in the MOV instruction will be totally ignored. This occurs because all planes will be written to with the value in the Set/Reset Register. However, any planes that are not enabled in the Enable Set/Reset Register will ignore the data in the Set/Reset Register and will respond to the data in the MOV instruction in a normal manner. This is usually not desired unless the programmer is doing some very tricky programming. To get around the problem, the display planes that should not be modified must be disabled in the Map Mask Register before the set/reset function.

S/R Set/Reset   EGA, VGA **Bits 3–0**

The bit positions of this field correspond to the respective display planes and to the bit positions in the Enable Set/Reset Register. The display planes that correspond to the bits enabled in the Enable Set/Reset Register will be modified by the corresponding bits in this Set/Reset Register. This allows up to four display planes to be modified with unique data in a single operation. See the Enable Set/Reset Register.

10.5.4 Enable Set/Reset Register

7	6	5	4	3	2	1	0
					E S R		

Index 01 hex

Any bits set in this register will enable the set/reset write mode. This mode allows up to four display planes to be written with unique data in a single operation. See the Set/Reset Register for details.

ESR Enable Set Reset   EGA, VGA   **Bits 3–0**

The bit numbers in this field correspond to the respective display planes and to the bit positions in the Set/Reset Register. The display planes corresponding to the bits enabled in this field will be modified by the corresponding bits in this Set/Reset Register. This allows up to four display planes to be modified with unique data in a single operation.

10.5.5 Color Compare Register

7	6	5	4	3	2	1	0
					C C		

Index 02 hex

It is possible to read the result from a comparison of the data in the display planes with the value loaded into the Color Compare Register. The EGA has two read modes controlled by the RM field of the Mode Register. The more common read mode #0 causes data to be read from eight consecutive horizontal pixels from one of the four display memory planes. This data move is accomplished using an assembly language MOV instruction.

The memory plane selected is dictated by the binary value in the Read Map Select Register. The selected pixels are determined by the address referenced in the MOV instruction. In one byte move instruction, eight consecutive pixels will be read from one display plane. Word MOV instructions act similarly to two consecutive byte MOV instruction.

The second read mode (read mode #1), as loaded in the RM field of the Mode Register, is used when the result of a comparison is desired. A common computer graphics application is to fill a closed polygon or arbitrary shape. To fill the shape, it is necessary to know where the boundary of the shape is located. If the boundary is in a single color, it is necessary to determine which pixels correspond to that color. This can be done by reading the data using the read mode #0. Four consecutive reads are necessary, one from each display plane. Next, the data from the four reads must be reorganized into a word that represents the data from all four planes at one pixel's location. This must be compared to the boundary color. A positive comparison indicates that the specified pixel is the same color as the boundary color and is therefore part of the boundary. As is evident, a good deal of processing is necessary.

The internal hardware of the EGA/VGA uses a 32-bit data bus, and the host processor uses an 8-bit data bus. The 32-bit bus is composed of 8 bits from each display plane. A read operation actually loads all 32 bits simultaneously. A write also uses all 32 of these bits. All of the write modes utilize this 32-bit bus to speed writing operations. Read mode #1 also utilizes this 32-bit bus for compare operations. The EGA/VGA hardware also includes an internal 32-bit comparator. If read mode #1 is active, the 32-bit data read from the four display memory planes is compared on a pixel-by-pixel basis with the value in the Color Compare Register. Any or all planes may take part in the comparison, depending on the corresponding bits in the Color Don't Care Register. Each pixel is composed of up to four bits that correspond to the four display planes. The bit positions in the Color Compare Register and in the Color Don't Care Register correspond to the display bit plane numbers. Any bits in the Color Don't Care Register that are reset to 0 will cause the corresponding bit planes in the display memory to be compared to the data in the corresponding bit positions in the Color Compare Register. Any bits set to 1 in the Color Don't Care Register will not be considered in the comparison.

Suppose that the Color Don't Care Register contained a C hex, which is a 1100 binary. This value would indicate that display planes 0 and 1 should be compared to bit positions 0 and 1 in the Color Compare Register. Note that the 1 in bit positions 2 and 3 causes those corresponding bits in the Color Compare register not to be compared with the corresponding display planes. Also suppose that the Color Compare Register was loaded with the value A hex, which is 1010 binary. If the pixel addressed in the MOV instruction contained a color value of E hex, which is 1110 binary, a positive comparison would occur. This occurs because bits 0 and 1 are identical to bits 0 and 1 of the Color Compare Register, regardless of the values of bits 2 and 3.

Further, consider that the eight neighboring horizontal pixels as addressed by the MOV instruction have hex color values 0, 1, 2, 3, 4, 5, 6, and 7, from left to right. Using the same E hex in the Color Compare Register and C hex in the Color Don't Care Register would result in a comparison being read by the MOV instruction of 22 hex, which is 00100010. This occurs because only the pixel positions corresponding to colors 2 and 6 test positive. Both colors 2 and 6 have a 1 in bit position 1 and a 0 in bit position 0.

The read instruction, as commanded by the MOV byte instruction, reads 8 bits of information. The information read is the result of comparing the value in this Color Compare Register with the eight horizontal neighboring pixels addressed in the MOV instruction. All pixels that have the same color as the value in the Color Compare Register test positive and cause a 1 to be loaded into the corresponding bit position in the resultant byte of the MOV instruction. All pixels that are not the same color cause a 0 to be loaded into the corresponding bit position.

The speed benefit is obvious. A single MOV instruction utilizing read mode #1 performs the comparison of eight neighboring horizontal pixels.

CC Color Compare   EGA, VGA   **Bits 3–0**

The value in this register represents a four-bit color. This color value will be compared to eight neighboring horizontal pixels when read mode #1 is selected. The result of this comparison will be returned to the host processor through a MOV instruction. Not all four display planes need to take an active part in the comparison. The Color Don't Care Register determines which planes should be considered in the comparison. This read mode is contrasted to read mode #0, in which the MOV instruction would return the actual data located in the eight pixels of the selected display plane.

10.5.6 Data Rotate Register

7	6	5	4	3	2	1	0
		F S			R C		

        Index 03 hex

This register consists of two independent fields, both of which affect the data being written from the host processor to the display memory. The Rotate Count field consists of the binary value used as the number of bits to shift the data input from the host before writing the data to the display planes. This field is set to 0 by default, which causes the data not to be rotated. The binary number in the Rotate Count field determines the number of bits to rotate the byte to the right. The term *rotate* is used because the least significant bit in the byte, bit 0, will be shifted right out of the byte. It will then be rotated back into the byte from the most significant bit, bit 7. This rotate operation occurs before any other operations are performed on the data on its way from the host to the display memory.

Other functions that affect the data are the set/reset function controlled by the Set/Reset and Enable Set/Reset Registers, the write mode selected in the Mode Register, the logical read before write operations controlled by the Function Select field of this register, and the bit mask controlled in the Bit Mask Register. Again, the data rotate operation occurs before any of these other operations.

The rotate field is important because the display memory is organized into independent bit planes. Each byte of display memory consists of eight horizontal neighboring pixels. To write data to a desired bit, it is often necessary to shift the data to properly align the data with the bit position. For example, suppose a 1 needs to be written into horizontal pixel number 101 in the first row of the display. Pixel 101 will be found in the twelfth byte from the starting display address as loaded in the Start Address High and Start Address Low Registers. If the starting address is 0, pixel 101 will be located in byte number 11, which is the twelfth byte. The most significant bit of this byte, bit 7, corresponds to the far left pixel associated with that byte. This would be pixel number 96. Because pixel number 101 is five pixels to the left of pixel 96, the bit position that corresponds to pixel 101 would be five bits to the right of bit 7. This, of course, is bit 2.

The data byte to be written to pixel 101 is a 01 hex. Therefore, to write a 1 into this bit 2 location, it is necessary to shift into bit position 2 the 1 in bit 0 of the byte to be written. This can be done by rotating the data 7 positions to the right, creating 02 hex. This byte can then be written to the byte number 11, causing pixel 101 to be set to a 1. This operation also has the effect of writing a 0 to pixels 96 through 100 and a 0 in pixel 102 and 103. The Bit Plane Mask Register could be used to mask off all bit positions other than bit 2. This could be accomplished by loading the Bit Plane Mask Register with a 02 hex. This masking operation occurs after the rotation.

The EGA/VGA maintains a 32-bit internal data bus. Certain write modes, as loaded in the WM field of the Mode Register, take advantage of this wide bus to speed up operations. In write mode #2, a full 32 bits of data can be moved in a single instruction cycle from one location in display memory to another location in display memory. It would have been quite useful if the data rotater was placed in this path so that data could be shifted during the move operation. However, this is not the case, and the only place the rotater can be used is in the path from the host processor to the display memory.

The Function Select field modifies the data written by the host with data already in the display memory, before the data is written to the display memory. This operation occurs as the last step before the data is actually written to the display memory. The default setting for this field is 0, which causes the data to be unmodified by the data already present in the display memory. The logical functions possible all require read-before-write operations. The EGA/VGA uses the 32-bit internal latch to temporarily hold the data being read from all four display planes. This latch is then used to logically modify the new data before it is loaded into the display memory. The logical functions of AND, OR, or XOR can be performed on the new data with the data in the 32-bit internal latch. This latch must be preloaded with the correct display data if the logical operation is to perform correctly. This is usually accomplished by a read-before-write operation. Two consecutive move operations would be required, the first to read the data into some dummy register and the second to write the new data to the display.

The data that is read from the display memory can be loaded into a dummy register or memory location because it does not need to be used. The logical operation selected in this field occurs internal to the EGA/VGA. If data is read from the display memory at address A and is to be written into the display memory at address B, the logical operation will involve the data at address A being logically combined with the host data and then stored into the display at address B. This occurs because the read operation at address A loads the 32-bit internal latch with the data located at address A.

The AND operation may be used to reset individual pixels within a bit plane without modifying the neighboring pixels contained within the same byte. Any bits that correspond to a 0 in the host byte to be written will cause the associated bits in the display memory to be reset to 0 after the read-before-write operation. Any bits that are 1s in the host byte will cause the associated bits in the display memory to remain unchanged.

The OR operation may be used to set individual pixels within a bit plane without modifying the neighboring pixels contained within the same byte. Any bits that correspond to 1s in the host byte to be written will cause the associated bits in the display memory to be set to 1 after the read-before-write operation. Any bits that are 0 in the host byte will cause the associated bits in the display memory to remain unchanged.

The XOR operation may be used to invert individual pixels within a bit plane without modifying the neighboring pixels contained within the same byte. Any bits that correspond to 1s in the host byte to be written will cause the associated bits in the display memory to be inverted after the read-before-write operation. Any bits that are 0s in the host byte will cause the associated bits in the display memory to remain unchanged. Inversion means that bits in the display memory that are 1s will be changed to 0s; bits that are 0s in display memory will be changed to 1s.

FS Function Select   EGA, VGA   **Bits 5–4**

Data written from the host to the display memory may be logically modified with data already present in the display memory. The logical function selected is determined by the value in this field. The logical functions are listed in Table 10.12.

TABLE 10.12 Function Select Field

Bit 5	Bit 4	Logical Function
0	0	Data is written unmodified
0	1	Data is ANDed with the latched data
1	0	Data is ORed with the latched data
1	1	Data is XORed with the latched data

DR Data Rotate   EGA, VGA   **Bits 3–0**

Data written from the host to the display memory will be rotated to the right the number of bits indicated in this field. This rotation will occur before any other logical operations happen to this data on its way to the display memory.

10.5.7 Read Map Select Register

7	6	5	4	3	2	1	0
						R M S	

Index 04 hex

The value in this register determines which of the bit planes should be accessed during a read operation when the EGA/VGA is in read mode #0. The EGA/VGA has an internal bus that is 32 bits wide. A 32-bit register is used to latch eight bits of data from each of the four display planes during a read operation. This 32-bit bus must be narrowed to an 8-bit bus when transferring this data to the PC in a typical read operation.

When a bit plane is selected, eight bits from that plane are sent to the host through a multiplexor. When the EGA/VGA is in read mode #0, as set in the RM field of the Mode Register, the data located in the display memory will be sent to the host during a read operation. These eight bits correspond to the single bit values of eight horizontal neighboring pixels in that bit plane. Only one bit plane can be enabled at a time.

This register has no effect when the EGA/VGA is in the Read Mode #1 corresponding to the color compare mode.

RMS Read Map Select   EGA/VGA   **Bits 1-0**

Selects which plane to read in Read Mode 0.

10.5.8 Mode Register

7	6	5	4	3	2	1	0
	SR•		O/E	RM	•TC		WM

Index 05 hex

The Mode Register contains four fields used to control the EGA/VGA read and write modes. Differences exist in this register between the EGA and the VGA. The EGA has a Test Condition (TC) field in this register that is not present in the VGA. The VGA has a Shift Register Control Field (SR) and an additional bit reserved to allow special shift-register handling for mode 13 hex.

SR Shift Register   VGA   **Bit 6-5**

This field controls the output shift registers in order to format the data for straight EGA/VGA addressing, CGA compatibility, or VGA mode 13 hex addressing. The parallel data stored in the display memory must be serialized and placed onto the four bit planes. Data is accessed from display memory 32 bits at a time. The order in which the data is taken from the parallel display memory and placed onto the four serial bit plane outputs determines how the data is supplied.

In the EGA/VGA mode, the data is serialized so that the display memory in bit plane 0 is output on the serial output bit that corresponds to bit plane 0. Likewise, the display memory in bit plane 1 is output on the serial output bit that corresponds to bit plane 1. Bit planes 2 and 3 operate similarly. This is the normal direct addressing EGA/VGA mode of operation. The eight bits from display memory plane 0 are serialized and output so that the far right pixel in the horizontal group of pixels is shifted out first.

In the CGA emulation mode, the data is serialized so that the even bits in the four display bit planes are output on the even bit plane serial outputs, plane 0 and plane 2, and the odd bits are output on the odd bit plane serial outputs, plane 1 and plane 3. Bit plane 0 is output on both the plane 0 and plane 1 serial outputs. Bit plane 1 is also output on both the plane 0 and plane 1 serial outputs. Bit plane 2 is output on both the plane 2 and plane 3 serial outputs, and bit plane 3 is also output on bit plane 2 and bit plane 3. The resultant output to the monitor will be composed of a pixel from bit planes 0 and 1 followed by a pixel from bit planes 2 and 3. At any time, the four serial plane outputs represent two consecutive horizontally neighboring pixels. The two-bit binary code in these two bits determines the color to use. This emulates the CGA four-color mode.

In the VGA emulation mode for mode 13 hex, the shift registers are loaded with the four most significant bits of each plane, followed by the four least significant bits of the same plane. Display plane 0 is followed by display plane 1, plane 2, and plane 3. Each plane stores a byte that represents a single pixel. At an identical host address, the four display planes contain four neighboring pixels. All eight bits from each plane are shifted out in order.

=0 Output the data in a straightforward serial fashion with each display plane output on its associated serial output. This is the standard EGA/VGA format.

=1 Output the data in a CGA-compatible 320-by-200, four-color graphics mode. This is used in display modes 4 and 5.

=2 Output the data eight bits at a time from the four bit planes. This is the format for the VGA mode 13 hex.

SR Shift Register   EGA   **Bit 5**

This field controls the output shift registers to format the data for straight EGA addressing or for CGA compatibility. See the SR field above for details.

=0 Output the data in a straightforward serial fashion with each display plane output on its associated serial output. This is the standard EGA format.

=1 Output the data in a CGA compatible 320-by-200, four-color graphics mode. This is used in display modes 4 and 5.

O/E Odd/Even   EGA, VGA   **Bit 4**

Used to select between the EGA/VGA mode or the CGA-compatible mode of operation. This bit should always be the complement of the O/E field in the Memory Mode Register because that field requires the value to be 0 to select the CGA-compatible mode.

=0 Normal operating EGA/VGA mode.

=1 Controls the EGA/VGA so that even host addresses access even display planes, planes 0 and 2, and odd host address access odd display planes, planes 1 and 3.

RM Read Mode   EGA, VGA   **Bit 3**

This bit selects which read mode is active in the EGA/VGA. In the default read mode #0, the host processor reads data from the display memory through an assembly language MOV instruction. This instruction addresses eight consecutive horizontal neighboring pixels. The EGA/VGA has an internal 32-bit register that latches eight bits from each of the four display planes. These 32 bits are then multiplexed down to eight bits so that the data can be put onto the eight-bit host bus. Only one plane can be accessed at a time; the plane selected is determined by the Read Map Select Register. Consult this register for further details regarding reading data in the read mode #0.

In read mode #1, the host processor does not read the data from the display memory. Rather, it reads the result of a comparison. The comparison is made between the data in the display memory addressed by the assembly language MOV instruction and the value set in the Color Compare Register. Only those bits enabled in the Color Don't Care Register are used in the comparison. The Read Map Select Register has no effect when the EGA/VGA is in this mode. The resulting eight bits read by the MOV instruction represent eight comparisons. A 1 in a bit position indicates that the comparison is true; a 0 indicates that the comparison is false. See the Color Compare Register for details on read mode #1.

=0 Select read mode #0. Data read from the EGA/VGA represents eight neighboring horizontal pixels in one display plane, as specified in the Read Map Select Register.

=1 Select read mode #1. Data read from the EGA/VGA represents the result of a comparison made between the eight neighboring horizontal pixels from any or all display planes with the value in the Color Compare Register. The display planes selected for the comparison are determined in the Color Don't Care Register.

TC Test Condition   EGA **Bit 2**

This field was specified in the original IBM EGA to cause all EGA outputs to be placed in a high impedance state for testing purposes. Most implementations require that this bit always be set to a 0.

=0 Normal operation.

=1 Forces all EGA outputs to a high-impedance state for testing.

WM Write Mode   EGA, VGA **Bits 1–0**

The EGA/VGA features three write modes that control the manner in which data is written to the display memory.

=0 The default mode, write mode #0, provides several ways to get data from the host to the display memory. One technique allows eight consecutive neighboring horizontal pixels to be written to one or all selected display planes. The Bit Plane Mask Register determines which planes should be written to. The EGA maintains a 32-bit internal data bus. If all four planes are selected, the eight bits presented by the 8-bit host interface bus are copied into all four planes. This mode allows a unique pattern of eight bits to be written to one or all display planes. It does not allow eight pixels of unique data to be written simultaneously to more than one plane. Data written to more than one plane at a time must be identical.

On the way to the display, the data is passed through a pipeline of operations that occur transparently to the host. The first operation is a rotation of the data. The number of bits that the data is rotated to the right is dictated in the Rotate Register. The second operation either selects the data coming from the host and loads it onto the 32-bit bus or selects data from the Set/Reset Register.

The internal 32-bit bus will write to eight neighboring horizontal pixels in all four planes simultaneously. The Enable Set/Reset register determines which of the four planes are loaded with the eight bits from the host and which are written with the value in the Set/Reset register. Any plane not selected in the Enable Set/Reset Register will be loaded with the eight bits from the host. However, only those planes enabled in the Bit Plane Mask Register will actually be affected. Any plane that is selected by the Enable Set/Reset Register will be loaded with the corresponding bits in the Set/Reset Register. The Set/Reset function allows all four display planes to be written with unique data in a single operation. However, only one pixel may be written to with unique data. Eight neighboring pixels will be written to simultaneously with identical data in each pixel.

Once the 32-bit bus is primed, the pipeline passes through a 32-bit arithmetic unit. One input to the arithmetic logic unit is the 32-bit data just described. The second input is the 32-bit internal data latch that contains the last 32 bits of data that were loaded into it. Data is loaded into this read register when a read operation occurs from display memory.

When an assembly language MOV statement addresses display memory, eight consecutive horizontal pixels are read from all four planes into the 32-bit register. In normal operation, a read-before-write operation will occur through back-to-back MOV instructions. The first move instruction will refer to an address in the display memory address space as its source address. It can read this data into any dummy register because it will not be used. This operation is utilized only to load the 32-bit internal latch.

The second MOV instruction uses this same address as the destination field. The source for this instruction is the byte that is to be written to the display memory. If the Set/Reset mode is selected for all four bit planes, via the Enable Set/Reset Register, the source field of this MOV instruction may also be dummy data because it will not be used.

Once the 32-bit read register is primed, the arithmetic unit will perform an "AND," "OR," or "XOR" instruction depending on the Function Select field of the Data Rotate Register. The result of this arithmetic operation will be written to the display memory. However, only those bits selected in the Bit Mask Register will be affected by this arithmetic operation. All bits not selected in the Bit Mask Register will be unmodified.

Refer to the Data Rotate, Bit Plane Mask, Set/Reset, Enable Set/Reset, and Bit Mask Registers for more details on the writing operations related to write mode #0.

=1 Write mode #1. This mode allows eight unique neighboring horizontal pixels in all four bit planes to be moved from one display memory location to another display memory location. The EGA maintains a 32-bit data bus. When this bus is interfaced to the host 8-bit bus, it is restricted to eight unique bits. However, when the bus is used internally, 32 bits may be transferred at a time. This feature provides fast data-transfer operations when the data source and destination is display memory.

An assembly language move-string-of-bytes instruction, MOVSB, or move-string-of-words operation, MOVSW, is best suited for this write mode. The source address is set up in the host DS:SI registers to point to the address in display memory that corresponds to the source data. Likewise, the host ES:DI registers are set to point to the address in display memory that corresponds to the destination. The host CX register is set to the number of words or bytes to transfer, and the MOVSW or MOVSB instruction is executed. Data will be transferred 32 bits at a time.

=2 Write mode #2 writes to eight neighboring horizontal pixels in all four display planes simultaneously. The horizontal pixels are written to with eight identical values in a given plane. Bit plane 0 is written with eight bits of 0 or 1, as determined by the value in bit position 0 of the data byte sent to the EGA from the host. Likewise, planes 1, 2, and 3 are written with eight identical 0 or 1 values corresponding to the value in bit positions 1, 2, and 3 respectively in the data byte sent to the EGA from the host. The result is eight identical neighboring horizontal pixels. In this way, blocks of eight pixels can be written to quickly. However, this is not the purpose of this write mode.

This write mode is most effective when used in conjunction with the Bit Mask Register. If an individual pixel is to be written to, that pixel can be enabled in the Bit Mask Register. When write mode #2 is selected, the four bits of data can reside in the lower four bits of data being sent from the host to the display memory. A MOV instruction can be used for this purpose. Because this pixel's data will be replicated eight times because of the write mode, it is not necessary to shift the data. If more than one pixel is to be written to with the same value, a time savings can be achieved. The pixels do not need to be neighbors because any pattern of up to eight pixels can be enabled through the Bit Mask Register.

=3 Write mode #3 is relevant to the VGA only. Each plane is written to with eight identical bits. The bit value (1 or 0) selected for each of the four display planes (3-0) is derived from the corresponding bit positions in the SR field of the Set/Reset Register. Recall that the Set/Reset Field has four bits, bits 3–0. The data written from the host is rotated according to the value in the Data Rotate Register. It is then ANDed with the Bit Mask Register to form an eight-bit value that acts as the Bit Mask for the write operation. The eight identical bits derived from the Set/Reset Register are masked with this resultant value before being written to the display memory.

10.5.9 Miscellaneous Register

7	6	5	4	3	2	1	0
				M M		C O E	G / A

Index 06 hex

The Miscellaneous Register contains four fields used to control the EGA/VGA display mode, monochrome graphics emulation, and memory mapping.

MM Memory Map   EGA, VGA **Bit 3–2**

The display memory is mapped into the host processor's memory address space. The starting location and the length of the display memory are set in this field, as indicated in Table 10.13.

Memory mode 0 represents a full EGA/VGA. No other display adapter can be resident in the system. Memory mode 1 is also for the EGA/VGA, although other display adapters may reside in the system. Memory mode 2 is for Hercules emulation, and memory mode 3 is for CGA emulation. Some implementations of VGA cards allow up to 1 mbyte of memory.

COE Chain Odd-Even   EGA, VGA **Bit 1**

The host address bit 0 is replaced with a higher-order address bit, causing even host addresses to access planes 0 and 2 and odd CPU addresses to access planes 1 and 3. This mode is useful for Monochrome Graphics Adapter emulation. It allows a 128-Kbytes display buffer with two bits per pixel.

=0 Standard EGA/VGA addressing.

=1 Replace host address bit 0 with a higher-order address bit so that even host addresses access even planes and odd addresses access odd planes. Used for MDA emulation.

TABLE 10.13 Display Memory Starting Address

MM	Bit 3	Bit 2	Memory Location	Memory Length
0	0	0	A0000–BFFFF hex	128 K
1	0	1	A0000–AFFFF hex	64 K
2	1	0	B0000–B7FFF hex	32 K
3	1	1	B8000–BFFFF hex	32 K

G/A Graphics/Alphanumerics Mode   EGA, VGA **Bit 0**

Selects whether the system should be operating in a graphics or an alphanumeric mode. In the EGA, this field should be the complement of the A/G field in the Memory Mode Register.

=0 Select the alphanumeric mode of operation.

=1 Select the graphics mode of operation.

10.5.10 Color Don't Care Register

7	6	5	4	3	2	1	0
				C	D	C	

Index 07 hex

If the EGA/VGA is in read mode #1, as dictated by the RM field of the Mode Register, host reads from display memory will produce a bit pattern that represents the comparison of eight consecutive horizontal neighboring pixels with selected bits of a color loaded into the Color Compare Register. The bits included in the compare are determined by the bits that are reset in this register. Only bits that are reset to 0 in this register will be considered in the comparison between the display memory and the Color Compare Register. The read instruction is initiated via a MOV instruction.

The source field of this instruction is the desired starting address for the eight consecutive horizontal pixels in the display memory that are to be compared. The destination field is the place where the resultant bits from the eight comparisons should be loaded in the host. A 1 in a bit position corresponds to a positive comparison; a 0 corresponds to the associated bits not comparing. See the Read Mode (RM) field in the Mode Register and the Color Compare Register for more details.

Each of the four bits in this field operate independently, and each adheres to Table 10.14.

TABLE 10.14 Color Don't Care Fields

Bit #	Bit Plane Affected
0	0
1	1
2	2
3	3

=0 Do not consider the corresponding bit in the Color Compare register and the data from the corresponding bit plane in the comparison.

=1 Consider the corresponding bit in the Color Compare register and the data from the corresponding bit plane in the comparison.

10.5.11 Bit Mask Register

7	6	5	4	3	2	1	0
			B M				

Index 08 hex

The display memory is organized into bit four planes. Each pixel is represented by one bit in each bit plane. A byte of data in a bit plane in display memory corresponds to a single bit in eight horizontal neighboring pixels. The low-order bit of the byte represents the far right pixel in the group, and the high-order bit in the byte represents the far left pixel in the group. To write to a pixel or group of pixels within an eight-pixel group without disturbing the contents of the other pixels in the group, it is necessary to mask out the undesired pixels.

The undesired pixels can be masked from the write operation by setting the corresponding bits in this register to a 0. The low-order bit of this register corresponds to the far right pixel, and the high-order bit corresponds to the far left pixel. If all bits in this register are set to 0, writing data will have no effect in display memory because all bits will be masked out. Bit masking occurs as the last step before data is written to display memory.

In write mode 3, the value in the Bit Mask Register is ANDed with the host data byte before it is used as the bit mask. See the Memory Mode Register for details of Write Mode #3.

Each of the eight bits in this field operates independently, and each adheres to the following rule.

=0 All bits reset to 0 mask the corresponding bits in the display memory; thus, these pixels cannot be modified during a host write operation.

=1 All bits set to 1 allow the corresponding bits in the display memory to be modified by a write operation.

10.6 THE ATTRIBUTE CONTROLLER REGISTERS

The Attribute Controller Registers consist of 20 registers for the EGA and 21 registers for the VGA. None of these registers has a unique host port address. One register exists in the host port address space at 3C0 hex. This register represents both the Attribute Controller Address Register and the Attribute Controller Data Register. The programmer accesses the Attribute Controller Data Registers by alternately loading index values and data values into this 3C0 hex port address. The index values range from 0 to 13 hex for the EGA and 0 to 14 hex for the VGA. An additional register called the Color Enable Register is available on the VGA. The Attribute Address Register selects one of the Attribute Data Registers as the current active register. See the Attribute Address Register below for details. The Attribute Controller Registers are listed in Table 10.15.

10.6.1 Attribute Address Register

7	6	5	4	3	2	1	0
		PAS		ADR			

Write Port 3C0 hex (EGA)
Write Port 3C0 hex (VGA)
Read Port 3C1 hex (VGA)

This register selects the attribute controller registers that will be selected during a write operation for the EGA/VGA or a read operation for the VGA. This address register is different from the other EGA/VGA address registers. Unlike all other address/data port pairs, the attribute controller has only one port dedicated to it. This port resides at host location 3C0 hex. An internal hardware flip-flop is used to multiplex this port to load either this Address Attribute Register or one of the Attribute Registers. When the flip-flop is in the clear state, it causes data output from the host to port 3C0 hex to be directed to this Address Attribute Register. When the flip-flop is in the set state, data written to this port is directed to whichever Attribute Register index is loaded into the AA field of this register.

The Attribute Registers consist of the 16 Palette Registers, the Mode Control Register, the Overscan Color Register, the Color Plane Enable Register, and the

TABLE 10.15   Attribute Controller Registers

Register Name	Index (Hex)	Write (Hex) (EGA/VGA)	Read (Hex) (VGA)
Address	—	3C0	3C1
Palette	0–F	3C0	3C1
Mode Control	10	3C0	3C1
Overscan Color	11	3C0	3C1
Color Plane Enable	12	3C0	3C1
Horizontal Pixel Panning	13	3C0	3C1
Color Select (VGA only)	14	3C0	3C1

Horizontal Pixel Panning Register. The VGA also includes the Color Select Register.

The flip-flop is controlled indirectly by the host. When a host assembly language input port instruction, IN, is issued to the Input Status #1 Register, the flip-flop is cleared. This register resides at port address 3BA hex for monochrome implementations and 3DA hex for color implementations. Once cleared, the path is set so that outputs to this 3C0 hex port load an index that points to one of the Attribute Registers into the Address Register itself. This is equivalent to loading any of the other Address Registers. The next assembly language output port (OUT) instruction written to this 3C0 hex port will load the indexed Attribute Register. After the output occurs, the flip-flop automatically changes state. The following output will be directed once again to the Attribute Address Register.

In addition to the address field the Attribute Address Register contains a Palette Address Source (PAS) field. This field is used to control the operation of the dual-ported palette RAM. If the host is to have control of the palette registers during a load operation, it must reset the PA field to 0. In order for the display memory to access this palette RAM, the PAS field must be set to a 1.

PAS   Palette Address Source   EGA, VGA   **Bit 5**

Determines whether the palette dual-ported RAM should be accessed by the host or by the EGA display memory.

=0   Allows the host to access the palette RAM. Disables the display memory from gaining access to the palette.

=1   Allows the display memory to access the palette RAM. Disables the host from gaining access to the palette.

ADR   Attribute Address   EGA, VGA   **Bits 4–0**

Points to one of the Attribute Address Registers, as shown in Table 10.16.

TABLE 10.16 Attribute Address Registers

AA Field	Register
00–0F hex	Palette Registers 0–15
10 hex	Mode Control Register
11 hex	Overscan Color Register
12 hex	Color Plane Enable Register
13 hex	Horizontal Pixel Panning Register

10.6.2 Palette Registers

7	6	5	4	3	2	1	0
		SR	SG	SB	R	G	B

Index 00–0F hex

The color palette is a random access memory (RAM) that is used to indirectly map the data contained in the individual pixel locations of the display memory into colors. The palette consists of a RAM memory that is 16 locations long. It is addressed by the value in each pixel location of the display memory. From the host's perspective, the functioning of the palette in the EGA and VGA is identical. However, the manner in which a color is produced by the EGA or VGA is drastically different. The EGA Palette Registers contain the color codes. The output of the EGA palette drives the monitor directly. The VGA palette contains addresses. The output of the VGA palette addresses a second set of registers called the Color Registers. The actual color codes are stored in the Color Registers. This double level of registers serves no purpose other than providing compatibility between the VGA and EGA. One of the greatest advantages of the VGA is the extended set of Color Registers.

The concept of a palette greatly enhances a graphics system. A pixel in display memory is not associated with any color. Rather, the pixel simply contains a binary code. This binary value is used to address a particular location within the palette. Changing the value of the pixel merely changes the address presented to the color palette. The color codes reside inside the palette. The width of each location in the palette RAM determines the number of colors possible. The number of registers within the palette RAM determines the number of simultaneous colors that can be displayed.

A second advantage of the palette RAM is that colors may be modified without altering the actual data within the color table. For example, suppose several pixels have the value 1 and several others have the value 2. It might be desirable to map both the value 1 and value 2 pixels into the same color, say color 3. If no palette were available, a program would have to read all of the display memory, determine which pixels had values 1 or 2, and change them all to color 3. This process would be irreversible; there would be no way to get back to the original colors because it would not be possible to distinguish which of the color 3 values originally came from the value 1 colors and which came from the value 2 colors. By contrast, with the palette it is necessary only to change the values in palette locations 1 and 2 to the value 3. Reversing the process simply requires changing palette location 1 back to a 1 and changing location 2 back to a 2.

The number of bits per pixel determines the number of simultaneous colors that may be displayed. The four display planes of the EGA, or the EGA-compatible modes of the VGA, allow 16 simultaneous colors to be displayed. In the VGA advanced mode 13 hex, eight bits are assigned per pixel, allowing 256 simultaneous colors. The Color Registers are 18 bits wide with 6 bits assigned to each color. Thus, there are 32 possible levels of saturation for each color, or 256K possible colors. In this mode, the VGA palette acts as an index into the Color Registers and should not be modified.

In the EGA, an individual palette RAM location consists of a field dedicated to each of the three colors, red, green, and blue. Two bits are used for each color, totaling six bits per palette RAM location. As a result, the width of the palette is six bits. These red, green, and blue two-bit color codes produce the color code sent to the monitor. In the EGA, the two bits representing each color are sent to the monitor as six digital signals. This format is called *direct drive* or *digital RGB*. The term *RGB* stands for *red, green, and blue*.

In the VGA, each register in the palette consists of a six-bit field that addresses one of the first 64 Color Registers. The color codes are stored in these Color Registers. The output of the Color Registers drive three digital-to-analog (D/A) converters. These three analog signals are output to the monitor. This format is called *analog RGB*.

In the EGA and in the EGA-compatible modes of the VGA, the data in the Palette Registers determines the amount of red, green, and blue in the resultant color. Because there are two bits per color, there are four possible levels of saturation for each color. The coding is *R* for red and *SR* for secondary red. Likewise, *G* and *B* are for green and blue, and *SG* and *SB* are for secondary green and secondary blue. The two-bit code determines the intensity or saturation of the color, as listed in Table 10.17.

The colors may be combined to produce different hues or shades of colors. For example, if all six fields are set to 1, the resultant color would be highest-intensity white. If the secondary red (R) and the secondary green (G) are both set, the resultant color will be secondary yellow.

TABLE 10.17 16-color Intensity Saturation

(SR,SG,SB)	(R,G,B)	Color Saturation	
0	0	No intensity	0%
0	1	Lowest intensity	33%
1	0	Medium intensity	66%
1	1	Highest intensity	100%

SR Secondary Red   EGA, VGA **Bit 5**

0 = No secondary red present.
1 = Secondary red present.

SG Secondary Green   EGA, VGA **Bit 4**

0 = No secondary green present.
1 = Secondary green present.

SB Secondary Blue   EGA, VGA **Bit 3**

0 = No secondary blue present.
1 = Secondary blue present.

R Red   EGA, VGA **Bit 2**

0 = No red present.
1 = Red present.

G Green   EGA, VGA **Bit 1**

0 = No green present.
1 = Green present.

B Blue   EGA, VGA **Bit 0**

0 = No blue present.
1 = Blue present.

10.6.3 Mode Control Register

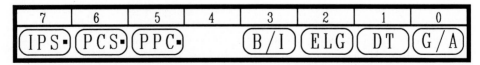

7	6	5	4	3	2	1	0
IPS▪	PCS▪	PPC▪		B/I	ELG	DT	G/A

Index 10 hex

This register contains four fields that control the EGA/VGA mode with respect to the attributes. It also contains three fields that control the VGA.

IPS   Internal Palette Size   VGA   **Bit 7**

The VGA Palette Registers each contain a field that is 6 bits wide. The output of the Palette Registers address the 256 Color Registers. The VGA contains four display planes that allow 16 simultaneous colors to be displayed.

It is possible to segment the Color Registers into 16 groups of registers, each group consisting of 16 registers. It is also possible to segment the Color Registers into 4 groups of registers, each group consisting of 64 registers. The first segmentation uses all 6 bits from the Palette Registers as the 6 low-order bits addressing the Color Registers. The upper-order two bits are provided through the C67 field of the Color Select Register. Thus, it is possible to select from four possible EGA-type palettes by simply changing the value in the C67 field. The second segmentation uses the 4 low-order bits in the Palette Registers as the 4 low-order address bits. It uses the C45 and C67 fields of the Color Select Register to obtain the four high-order address bits. In this way, the Color Registers can be used to rapidly select one of 16 possible color selections, each selection consisting of the 16 simultaneously displayed colors.

=0   The Palette Register's bits 4 and 5 provide the address bits 4 and 5 to the Color Registers.

=1   The C45 field of the Color Register provides the address bits 4 and 5 to the Color Registers.

PCS   Pixel Clock Select   VGA   **Bit 6**

Controls the clocking of the PELs to allow eight bits of data to select a color in mode 13 hex. This field is used in conjunction with the Shift Register (SR) field of the Mode Register. When the SR field is set to 2, data is loaded into the Shift Registers in two operations, providing eight bits of data from each display plane. This value of 2 is operative only during mode 13 hex. During this mode, the PCS field is set to 1.

=0   The pixel data is changed at each cycle of the dot clock.

=1   The pixel data is changed every second cycle of the dot clock.

PPC   Pixel Panning Compatibility   VGA   **Bit 5**

This field allows a section of the screen to be panned independently from the second section during a split-screen mode of operation.

=0   Prevents a line compare from affecting the output of the Pixel Panning Register.

=1   Allows a line compare to affect the output of the Horizontal Pixel Panning Register and the Byte Panning (BP) field of the Preset Row Scan Register.

B/I Enable Blink or Intensity   EGA, VGA **Bit 3**

This field controls whether the most significant bit of the character attribute byte, bit 7, is used to select background colors or to enable blinking. If it is used to enable blinking, whenever bit 7 of the character attribute byte is a 1, the character will blink. If bit 7 is a 0, the character will not blink. In this mode of operation, the background color is limited to one of eight possible colors. This occurs because the background color field of the character attribute byte is limited to three bits. These three bits address Color Palette Registers 0–7.

The blinking rate is determined from the vertical refresh period. In the standard implementations of the EGA, the vertical sync rate is divided by 32 to determine the blink rate. Because the vertical sync rate is normally on the order of 60 cycles per second, the resultant blink rate is about two blinks per second. Other implementations of the EGA may control the blinking in a different manner.

In monochrome modes, blinking causes the character to switch between on and off. In color modes, the most significant bit feeding the color palette is toggled. This causes the character color to switch between the lower and upper halves of the color palette. For example, a character with foreground color 3 and background color E hex would alternately change to foreground color D hex and background color 6 during the blinking cycle. In the graphics modes, the most significant bit addressing the color palette is switched, similarly altering the color codes.

The cursor blinks at its own rate. The standard implementations blink the cursor at twice the rate at which the character blinks. The vertical sync pulse is divided by 16 to derive this blink rate.

If this field is used to select a background intensity, bit 7 of the character attribute byte is used in conjunction with bits 4–6 to select a background color, and no blinking feature is available. The four most significant bits of the attribute byte are thus dedicated to the background color and are used to select one of 16 background colors in palette locations 0–15.

=0 Use bit 7 of the character attribute code to select a background color. Do not allow blinking.

=1 Use bit 7 of the character attribute code to enable or disable blinking. This is the default mode of operation.

ELG Enable Line Graphics Character Codes   EGA, VGA **Bit 2**

The line graphics character codes in the Monochrome Display Adapter are C0 hex to DF hex. These character codes represent graphics characters that include lines, corners, and some shapes. These were used to perform rudimentary graphics without relying on a graphics display adapter or forcing a display adapter to go into a graphics mode. When character fonts that are nine characters wide are used, as is common in the Monochrome Display Adapter, the ninth horizontal dot of the character in the graphics set should mimic the eighth dot of the same line. This extends the lines through the intercharacter spacing and connects horizontal lines from one character to the next.

When character sets are used that do not have special characters associated with line graphics in character codes C0 hex to DF hex, this field should be set to 0.

=0 Set the ninth dot of the character to the background color, regardless of the character code.

=1 Set the ninth dot of the character to the same value as the eighth dot of the character for all graphics line characters.

DT Display type   EGA, VGA **Bit 1**

Dictates whether the display attributes should be displayed as color display attributes or as IBM Monochrome Display Adapter attributes.

=0 Select color display attributes.

=1 Select IBM Monochrome Display Adapter attributes.

G/A Graphics/Alphanumeric   EGA, VGA **Bit 0**

Selects whether the display is in an alphanumeric or graphics mode. In the EGA, this field should be the inverse of the A/G field in the Memory Mode Register and the same value as the G/A field in the Miscellaneous Register. In the VGA, this field should be the same value as the G/A field in the Miscellaneous Register.

=0 Select alphanumeric mode.

=1 Select graphics mode.

10.6.4 Overscan Color Register

7	6	5	4	3	2	1	0
		SR	SG	SB	R	G	B

Index 11 hex

The border region or porch of the display surrounds the active display region. It exists on the top and bottom of the active display region. Its vertical size is determined by the distance between the vertical display enable period and the vertical blanking, as dictated by the Vertical Display End Register and the Start and End Vertical Blanking Registers. Its horizontal extent exists between the horizontal display enable period and the horizontal blanking, as dictated by the Horizontal Display End Register and the Start and End Horizontal Blanking Registers.

The border region occurs before the blanking begins in both the horizontal and vertical dimensions. Thus, a color needs to be selected for display during this period. Normally this color is 0, which is black. *Note:* Most EGA/VGA implementations do not operate satisfactorily when a color other than black is selected for the border region.

The color coding in this Overscan Register is identical to the color coding used in the Color Palette Registers. See the Color Palette Registers for details.

SR Secondary Red   EGA, VGA **Bit 5**

0 = No secondary red present.
1 = Secondary red present.

SG Secondary Green   EGA, VGA **Bit 4**

0 = No secondary green present.
1 = Secondary green present.

SB Secondary Blue   EGA, VGA **Bit 3**

0 = No secondary blue present.
1 = Secondary blue present.

R Red   EGA, VGA **Bit 2**

0 = No red present.
1 = Red present.

G Green   EGA, VGA **Bit 1**

0 = No green present.
1 = Green present.

B Blue   EGA, VGA **Bit 0**

0 = No blue present.
1 = Blue present.

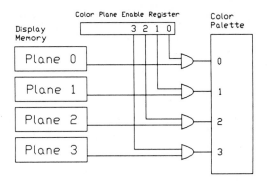

FIGURE 10.4 Selecting Colors

10.6.5 Color Plane Enable Register

7	6	5	4	3	2	1	0
		•VSM		CPE			

Index 12 hex

This register controls which plane will be enabled during the display process. Normally all planes are enabled, providing four address lines to the sixteen palette registers. If a plane is deselected, the corresponding data that addresses the palette registers is set to 0. Deselected planes can still be written to or read from in a normal fashion. This Color Plane Enable field affects only the output path between the display memory and the color palette. The effect of deselecting a plane is that the display will not contain any data located in that plane. Selecting color planes is illustrated in Figure 10.4.

If only plane 0 is selected, a 0 will address palette location 0 and a 1 will address palette location 1. If only plane 1 is selected, a 0 will address palette location 0 and a 1 will address palette location 2.

Table 10.18 illustrates this single-plane palette addressing. Note that a pixel in the selected plane that is a 0 always addresses palette location 0, regardless of the plane in which pixel is located. This occurs because all other planes are forced to 0.

The ability to select or deselect display planes is by no means limited to single planes. It is possible that at a given pixel location, neither plane will be on, either plane will be on, or both planes will be on. Table 10.19 illustrates the two plane possibilities using planes 1 and 2.

Table 10.20 illustrates the three plane possibilities using plane 1, 2, and 3.

This Color Plane Enable Register can also be used to display animation. One

TABLE 10.18 One-plane Palette Addressing

| | Palette Location | |
Single Plane Selected	Pixel=0	Pixel=1
0	0	1
1	0	2
2	0	4
3	0	8

TABLE 10.19 Two-plane Palette Addressing

Plane 2	Plane 1	Palette Location
0	0	0
0	1	2
1	0	4
1	1	6

TABLE 10.20 Three-plane Palette Addressing

Plane 3	Plane 2	Plane 1	Palette Location
0	0	0	0
0	0	1	2
0	1	0	4
0	1	1	6
1	0	0	8
1	0	1	10
1	1	0	12
1	1	1	14

plane can be selected while the other planes are being manipulated. If the selected display planes are changed periodically, motion effects can be achieved. Consider a case in which each display plane is enabled for a tenth of a second. The selecting sequence is planes 0, 1, 2, 3, 0, 1, 2, 3, ... enabled. In a motion picture, each frame on the film is shot in sequence. A figure moving across the screen moves a little bit in each successive frame. The frames on the film are numbered sequentially and never repeat. These frames could be mapped into a mod 4 picture plane counter to simulate the playback of this film.

Plane 0 would represent the image taken at t=0.0 second, plane 1 would represent the image taken at t=0.1 second, plane 2 at t = 0.2 second, plane 3 at t = 0.4 second, and plane 0 at t = 0.5 second. If the playback rate is slow enough to handle the time necessary to get the image being represented onto the next display plane, animation can be achieved. Again, this animation is not limited to one plane at a time.

In the EGA, this register also contains a Video Status MUX field. This selects two of the RGB direct-drive six-color outputs to be available on the DIA field of the Input Status #1 Register. This is used for diagnostic purposes.

VSM   Video Status MUX   EGA   **Bits 5–4**

Selects two of the six RGB outputs to be loaded into the DIA field of the Input Status #1 Register. See Input Status #1 Register for details on which colors get selected depending on this two-bit field.

CPE   Color Planes Enable   EGA, VGA   **Bits 3–0**

The display planes may be selected or deselected depending on the values in this field. Any combination of display planes can be selected simultaneously.

bit 0 = 0   Do not select display plane 0.
bit 0 = 1   Select display plane 0.
bit 1 = 0   Do not select display plane 1.
bit 1 = 1   Select display plane 1.
bit 2 = 0   Do not select display plane 2.
bit 2 = 1   Select display plane 2.
bit 3 = 0   Do not select display plane 3.
bit 3 = 1   Select display plane 3.

10.6.6   Horizontal Pixel Panning Register

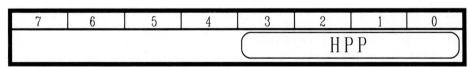

Index 13 hex

The display memory is organized into four bit planes. Each plane is organized as consecutive bytes with respect to the host processor and the graphics processor, and as individual pixels with respect to the output video refresh circuitry. Each byte of each of the four display planes has up to eight horizontally neighboring pixels. The first byte of information displayed on the screen in the upper left corner is determined by the value in the Start Address High and Start Address Low Registers. In an alphanumeric mode, the starting address

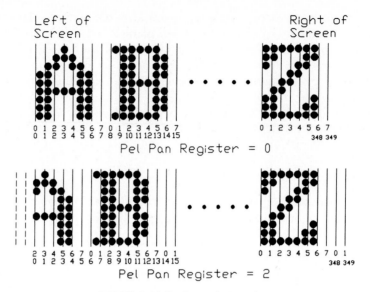

FIGURE 10.5 Smooth Panning

value corresponds to a character; in a graphics mode, this corresponds to eight neighboring horizontal pixels.

Panning is the term used when the display slides horizontally across the display. Using "windows" terminology, this would be stated as "moving the window horizontally across the data." It is possible to pan the display in an alphanumeric mode one character at a time by incrementing or decrementing the starting address.

If smooth panning is desired, this character-by-character panning will not suffice. It is therefore necessary to pan horizontally on a pixel-by-pixel basis. Smooth panning is illustrated in Figure 10.5.

In the standard font sizes, the character box is eight pixels wide. However, in larger character fonts or in the monochrome mode, the character box is greater than eight pixels wide. The standard EGA/VGA implementations allow a maximum character width of nine characters when in the monochrome alphanumeric mode. The standard selected for shifting the image is determined by the pixel size and is illustrated in Table 10.21.

This table is read as follows: If an eight-dot/character alphanumeric mode is selected and the HPP field is 0, the first dot shifted out will be the bit 0 in the word. This corresponds to the less significant bit and to the far right pixel displayed.

Likewise, if the nine-dot/character alphanumeric mode is selected and the HPP field is 4, the first dot to be shifted out will be the dot corresponding to the bit 3. Note that in the nine-dot/character mode, bit 8, which is the copy of

TABLE 10.21 Horizontal Pixel Panning

	Value in the HPP Field
Dots/Character	*0,1,2,3,4,5,6,7,8,9,A,B,C,D,E,F*
6	2,3,4,5,6,7
8	0,1,2,3,4,5,6,7
9	8,0,1,2,3,4,5,6,7
12	B,A,9,8,0,1,2,3,4,5,6,7
16	F,E,D,C,B,A,9,8,0,1,2,3,4,5,6,7

bit 7, is actually displayed on the right side of the character and bit 7 is displayed on the left side. This does not affect the display because neighboring character boxes touch anyway. The left side of one pixel touches the right side of the next pixel. In this table, the sequence from left to right of the bit positions corresponds to the shifting sequence. Because the CRT is refreshing from left to right, the first pixel out the shifter should be the far right pixel in the word. The far right pixel corresponds to the least significant bit.

In a graphics mode, incrementing or decrementing the starting address would shift the display eight pixels to the left or right. To achieve a smooth pan, the panning must also occur on a pixel-by-pixel basis. Graphics modes always assume an eight-dot/character size.

HPP Horizontal Pixel Pan   EGA, VGA **Bits 3–0**

The number of pixels to shift the video data horizontally to the left. This affects the starting far left pixel and the ending far right pixel on the screen. It is used in conjunction with the starting address for smooth panning applications.

10.6.7 Color Select Register

7	6	5	4	3	2	1	0
				C67 ▪		C45 ▪	

Index 14 hex

This register contains two fields which, combined with the output bits from the palette register, determine the eight-bit address used to select one of the 256 Color Registers. It is possible to segment the Color Registers into 16 groups with each group consisting of 16 registers. This is useful because in all but mode 13 hex, the maximum number of simultaneous colors that can be displayed is 16. Thus, it is possible to rapidly select from 16 different color palettes by simply modifying the C45 and C67 fields of this register.

A second technique segments the Color Registers into 4 groups with each group consisting of 64 registers. This is useful because the EGA palette is 64 colors long. Thus, it is possible to rapidly select from four different EGA palettes by modifying the C67 field of this register. See the Mode Control Register for details.

C67 Color Register Address Bits 6 and 7   VGA   **Bits 3–2**

Address bits 6 and 7 combine with the six output bits from the color palette to form the eight address bits to the Color Registers.

C45 Color Register Address Bits 4 and 5   VGA   **Bits 1–0**

Address bits 4 and 5 combine with the two address bits from the C67 field above and the four low-order output bits from the color palette to form the eight address bits to the Color Registers. This field is used only if the IPS field of the Mode Control Register is set to 1.

10.7   COLOR REGISTERS

10.7.1   PEL Address Write Mode Register

7	6	5	4	3	2	1	0
			A D R ▪				

VGA   Write Port 3C8 hex
Read Port 3C8 hex

ADR Address During Write Mode   VGA   **Bits 7–0**

This register contains the eight-bit address used to access one of the 256 Color Registers during a write operation. This register is similar to the address registers associated with the other register groups in that it occupies a location in the host I/O port address space and that it indexes one of the internal registers. It differs from the others in that it signifies that a write operation is to occur. A write operation consists of three byte outputs to the PEL Data Register. These three outputs load the red, green, and blue components of the indexed Color Register. The PEL Data Register can be thought of as an 18-bit-wide register that loads six bits during each output operation.

At the conclusion of the third output to the PEL Data Register, the address in this PEL Address Write Register automatically increments. This feature allows the programmer to output up to 768 consecutive bytes to the PEL Data Register without having to modify the PEL Address Write Register after its initial setting.

The PEL Address Write Register is a read/write register that allows the programmer to interrogate its current value. The operation of the PEL Address Register Write Register is identical to that of the PEL Address Read Register except that the latter is used for read operations and the former is a write-only register.

10.7.2 PEL Address Read Mode Register

7	6	5	4	3	2	1	0
			ADR ▪				

VGA   Write Port 3C7 hex

ADR Address During Read Mode   VGA   **Bits 7–0**

This register contains the eight-bit address used to access one of the 256 Color Registers during a read operation. This register is identical in function to the PEL Address Write Mode Register. It differs from this register in that it signifies that a read operation is to occur. A read operation consists of three byte inputs from the PEL Data Register. These three inputs read the red, green, and blue components of the indexed Color Register. The PEL Data Register can be thought of as an 18-bit-wide register. Six of these bits are loading into the PEL Data Register before each input operation. The first load occurs when the PEL Address Read Register is loaded.

At the conclusion of the third input from the PEL Data Register, the address in this PEL Address Read Register automatically increments. This feature allows the programmer to input up to 768 consecutive bytes from the PEL Data Register without having to modify the PEL Address Read Register after its initial setting.

10.7.3 PEL Data Register

7	6	5	4	3	2	1	0
			DATA ▪				

VGA   Write Port 3C9 hex
      Read Port 3C9 hex

DATA Data Value VGA **Bits 7–0**

This register is a 18-bit-wide register used to interface the host and the 256 Color Registers. This data register is similar to the other data registers except that it is 18 bits wide. Each Color Register contains three primary colors, each color represented by six bits. The host data bus is eight bits wide, and therefore only one of these components can be accessed at a time. The data written to and read from this register interacts with the Color Register that is indexed by the PEL Address Write or PEL Address Read Register. When the PEL Address Write Register is loaded with an index, internal hardware automatically selects the red component of the PEL Data Register. An output to this register loads this component with the six low-order bits. The hardware automatically changes to point to the green component of this register. Again an output loads this component with the six low-order bits. Similarly, the blue portion is loaded next. Once all three outputs have occurred, the PEL Address Write Register is autoincremented and the next output to the PEL Data Register will load the red portion once again. Because the address is incremented, the next higher Color Register will be affected. The function is identical in the read operations, with the PEL Address Read Register being affected.

10.7.4 DAC State Register

7	6	5	4	3	2	1	0
						S T A •	

VGA   Read Port 3C7 hex

STA DAC State Value VGA **Bits 1–0**

These two bits reflect whether a read or a write operation is in effect.

=0 A read operation is in effect. The PEL Address Read Register was accessed last.

=3 A write operation is in effect. The PEL Address Write Register was accessed last.

10.7.5   PEL Mask Register

7	6	5	4	3	2	1	0
			MASK •				

VGA   Write Port 3C6 hex
VGA   Read Port 3C6 hex

MASK Mask Value   VGA   **Bits 7–0**

This register is a read/write register; however, it is not to be modified by the programmer. It is initialized to FF hex by the BIOS Mode Set call.

Chapter 11

The EGA/VGA BIOS

11.1 EGA/VGA BIOS DESCRIPTIONS

The EGA/VGA Basic Input Output System (BIOS) resides in the host memory space beginning at address C0000 hex and extending to C4000 hex. This BIOS contains an initialization section invoked during bootstrap operations, code to control the EGA/VGA, and several character generators. The EGA BIOS source listings are provided in the IBM documentation. However, the BIOS source listings of the VGA are not provided. Because of the lack of source listings for the VGA, the EGA BIOS descriptions in this book are more comprehensive than are the VGA descriptions.

During the bootstrap operation, the host system BIOS scans the ROM space, looking for a ROM header that indicates that an EGA is present. If it finds this header, it performs a FAR CALL to address C0003 hex. This is the location of the start of the EGA BIOS initialization code. The first three bytes of ROM, beginning at address C0000 hex, contain a signature. At the starting address of C0003 hex resides a JMP SHORT instruction to the beginning of the EGA BIOS code. The jump is necessary because more signature information is present in the next several bytes, including the IBM copyright information and the BIOS creation date.

Once the short jump is taken, the code initializes the video vectors within the PC interrupt locations in the lower PC memory space. Next, it determines the configuration of the card and performs a hardware diagnostic. At the conclusion of the diagnostics, a tone will be issued indicating that the bootstrap operation was completed successfully. If this operation was not successful, a series of tones will signify the nature of the problem. At completion, a FAR RET instruction returns control to the host system's BIOS ROM.

The second section of the BIOS is dedicated to routines that provide all of the processing necessary to respond to the interrupt 10 hex calls. In this book, these interrupt calls are commonly referred to as the INT 10h calls. All INT 10h calls are directed to the BIOS through the interrupt vector located in the four bytes of memory beginning at 00040 hex in the interrupt vector table.

This interrupt was set up during initialization. Once the interrupt has been invoked, all registers are saved, and the AH register is interrogated to see which software handler to call. The AH register must contain a value from 0 to 13 hex for the EGA and from 0 to 1C hex for the VGA. This value determines which BIOS subroutine is invoked. If the value of the AH register is greater than 13 hex for the EGA or 1C hex for the VGA, another interrupt is invoked. This interrupt is number 42 hex. This gives the programmer the added facility of extending the EGA BIOS into a different BIOS or into host RAM memory.

If the value in the AH register is within the range of the EGA/VGA, it is used to determine which subroutine to invoke. In some cases, the AH register defines a group of similar functions, and the value in the AL register is used to determine which subroutine within the group should be invoked.

The host processor general-purpose registers—for example, BX, CX, and DX, are most often used to hold additional input parameters. At other times, these registers are used to hold output parameters passed back to the routine that invoked the BIOS. The SI or DI and DS or ES register pairs are sometimes used as input or output parameters. They traditionally hold pointers to some data buffer.

The third section of the BIOS is filled with the character tables. An 8-by-8 character table and an 8-by-14 dot table are available on the EGA. An 8-by-8 character table, an 8-by-14 character table, and an 8-by-16 character table are available on the VGA. The address within host memory at which these tables reside is made available to the programmer through a BIOS call.

11.2 DISPLAY MODES

11.2.1 AH = 00 Hex: Set Video Mode (EGA/VGA)

The EGA/VGA board has a standard set of display modes that control the resolution, type of display, and number of pages, along with several other features. These modes require a number of registers to be modified to achieve the desired result. It is advisable to use the interrupt 10 hex feature of the EGA/VGA BIOS when changing modes. This ensures that all of the features, some of which are redundant within several registers, are properly handled. However, it is possible to alter these registers individually to achieve similar modes or to create new modes. Caution is advised because modifying these registers incorrectly can, in some reported cases, damage the monitor and/or the EGA/VGA adapter board.

The current video mode is stored in host memory in the video buffer used by the BIOS interrupt routines. The mode is stored in location 449 hex. The selected display mode determines the number of characters in a scan row and is equivalent to the number of columns. The number of characters is loaded into memory location 44A hex. The mode also dictates the total length, in bytes, of the active display page. The total length is loaded into memory location 44C hex.

The key value sent to this interrupt routine in AL and the corresponding display mode that will become active are contained in Table 11.1 for the EGA and Table 11.2 for the VGA. Also included are the resolution of the screen in

TABLE 11.1 EGA Display Modes

AL (Hex)	Mode (Hex)	Resolution (# Cols. by # Rows)	Box Size	# Colors	# Pages	Display Format	Resolution in Pixels
00	0	40 by 25	8 by 8	16-color bw	8	Alpha	320 by 200
	0*	40 by 25	8 by 14	16-color bw	8	Alpha	320 by 350
01	1	40 by 25	8 by 8	16-color	8	Alpha	320 by 200
	1*	40 by 25	8 by 14	16-color	8	Alpha	320 by 350
02	2	80 by 25	8 by 8	16-color bw	8	Alpha	640 by 200
	2*	80 by 25	8 by 14	16-color bw	4,8	Alpha	640 by 350
03	3	80 by 25	8 by 8	16-color	8	Alpha	640 by 200
	3*	80 by 25	8 by 14	16-color	4,8	Alpha	640 by 350
04	4	40 by 25	8 by 8	4-color	1	Graph	320 by 200
05	5	40 by 25	8 by 8	4-color bw	1	Graph	320 by 200
06	6	80 by 25	8 by 8	2-color bw	1	Graph	640 by 200
07	7	80 by 25	9 by 14	bw	8	Alpha	720 by 350
0D	D	40 by 25	8 by 8	16-color	2,4,8	Graph	320 by 200
0E	E	80 by 25	8 by 8	16-color	1,2,4	Graph	640 by 200
0F	F	80 by 25	8 by 14	bw	1,2	Graph	640 by 350
10	10	80 by 25	8 by 14	16/64-color	1,2	Graph	640 by 350

columns and rows, the character box size, the total number of possible colors, the number of possible pages available in this mode, the display format, and the resolution of the display page.

The "Pages" column in Table 11.1 contains entries with more than one number—for example, "1,2,4". This indicates the number of pages available when the EGA is equipped with 64 Kbytes, 128 Kbytes, or 256 Kbytes of display memory, respectively.

The code "bw" stands for black and white or synonymously monochrome. The codes "16-color", "4-color", and "2-color" stand for the sixteen-, four-, and two-color modes normally associated with the Color Graphics Adapter (CGA). The code "16/64-colors" represents 16 simultaneously displayable colors out of the possible palette of 64 colors. This condition occurs when the monitor connected to the EGA is equipped with six color inputs—IR, IG, IB, R, G, and B.

The asterisk in the "Display Mode" column, indicates that an Enhanced Color Monitor is installed. The Enhanced Color Monitor must be capable of displaying 350 scan lines at a 21.85-kHz horizontal scan rate and a 60-Hz vertical scan rate. Modes 0, 1, 2, and 3 are automatically converted to modes 0*, 1*, 2*, or 3* when the EGA is configured for a high-resolution monitor. These advanced modes are invoked automatically through the settings of the sense switches on the EGA board.

The VGA has only one memory configuration. As a result, there is only one

TABLE 11.2 VGA Display Modes

AL (Hex)	Mode (Hex)	Resolution (# Cols by # Rows)	Box Size	Display Format	# Pages	Display Mode	Resolution in Pixels
00	0	40 by 25	8 by 8	16/256K bw	8	Alpha	320 by 200
	0*	40 by 25	8 by 14	16/256K bw	8	Alpha	320 by 350
	0+	40 by 25	9 by 16	16/256K bw	8	Alpha	360 by 400
01	1	40 by 25	8 by 8	16/256K	8	Alpha	320 by 200
	1*	40 by 25	8 by 14	16/256K	8	Alpha	320 by 350
	1+	40 by 25	9 by 16	16/256K	8	Alpha	360 by 400
02	2	80 by 25	8 by 8	16/256K bw	8	Alpha	640 by 200
	2*	80 by 25	8 by 14	16/256K bw	8	Alpha	640 by 350
	2+	80 by 25	9 by 16	16/256K bw	8	Alpha	720 by 400
03	3	80 by 25	8 by 8	16/256K	8	Alpha	720 by 200
	3*	80 by 25	8 by 14	16/256K	8	Alpha	640 by 350
	3+	80 by 25	9 by 16	16/256K	8	Alpha	720 by 400
04	4	40 by 25	8 by 8	4/256K	1	Graph	320 by 200
05	5	40 by 25	8 by 8	4/256K bw	1	Graph	320 by 200
06	6	80 by 25	8 by 8	2/256K bw	1	Graph	640 by 200
07	7	80 by 25	9 by 14	bw	8	Alpha	720 by 350
07	7+	80 by 25	9 by 16	bw	8	Alpha	720 by 400
0D	D	40 by 25	8 by 8	16/256K	8	Graph	320 by 200
0E	E	80 by 25	8 by 8	16/256K	4	Graph	640 by 200
0F	F	80 by 25	8 by 14	bw	2	Graph	640 by 350
10	10	80 by 25	8 by 14	16/256K	2	Graph	640 by 350
11	11	80 by 30	8 by 16	2/256K	1	Graph	640 by 480
12	12	80 by 30	8 by 16	16/256K	1	Graph	640 by 480
13	13	40 by 25	8 by 8	256/256K	1	Graph	320 by 200

entry per mode for the number of possible pages. The asterisk used in the "Display Mode" column indicates that the VGA is in a text mode with 350 vertical lines. The plus sign indicates that the VGA is in a text mode with 400 vertical lines. The number of vertical lines is controlled through the Vertical Size (VS) field of the Misc. Output Register.

Character Size

The alphanumeric modes, indicated by "Alpha" in Tables 11.1 and 11.2, use display memory plane 2 and, in some implementations, plane 3 for the character generator. Because these memory planes are random access memory (RAM), downloadable character fonts may be employed. The graphics modes, indicated by "Graph" in Tables 11.1 and 11.2, use the character generator programmed into the Read Only Memory (ROM). This generator typically shares the same

ROM as the EGA BIOS. Three character patterns are resident in most EGA implementations.

Erasure During Mode Change

It is possible to erase the display memory at the time of a mode change. The AL register is used to select the mode when the AH=0 (Set Mode) command is invoked. If the most significant bit of AL is set to 1, the display memory is not erased after a mode change. If the most significant bit of AL is reset to 0, the display memory is erased after a mode change. Thus, if mode 3 with a screen erasure is desired, the value in the AL register should be a 3 (Hex 3). If mode 3 with no screen erasure is desired, the value in the AL register should be set to a 131 (hex 83). When changing from an alphanumeric mode to a graphics mode, it is usually advisable to erase the display memory because the character ASCII codes, attributes, and the current character fonts are loaded into the four planes of display memory.

Display Mode Emulation

Display modes 0 through 6 emulate the Color Graphics Adapter (CGA). Mode 7 emulates the IBM Monochrome MDA or the Hercules Monochrome graphics standard. The modes with asterisks—0*, 1*, 2*, 3*, and 10*—are modes that are supported when a high-resolution monitor is being used. The only difference between modes 0 and 1 and modes 2 and 3 is the presence of a color burst signal, such as that used in a composite video.

The RCA video connectors on the back of most EGA boards were originally intended for composite video input and output. Most EGA implementations do not include any composite video output. As a result, these modes are identical. Mode 7, the monochrome alphanumeric mode, is the only mode that utilizes the 9-by-14-dot character cell.

Input Parameters
AL = The desired mode number. Note that setting bit 7 to one in the mode value contained in AL causes the screen not to be erased during a mode change. Resetting bit 7 to 0 causes the screen to be erased during a mode change.

Output Parameters
None.

EGA Registers Affected
Several of the fields in many of the EGA registers are affected.

Host Memory Affected
449 hex = Current video mode.
44A hex = Number of columns on screen.
44C hex = Length of active screen buffer.
44E hex = Start of current page.

450 = Cursor positions.
460 = Cursor mode.
462 = Current display page.
463 = Base host address of port.
465 = Current mode.
466 = Current color.
484 = Number of character rows.

11.3 CURSOR CONTROL

The shape of the cursor can be controlled by the programmer. A full character box or an underline is used as the common cursor shape. The row and column position of the cursor can be set or read by the programmer.

11.3.1 AH = 01 Hex: Set Cursor Type (EGA/VGA)

Set the shape of the cursor by setting the starting and ending scan lines of the cursor. The maximum character box height is 32 scan lines. The top of the character box is referred to as scan line 0. The bottom scan line is referred to as scan line 31. The cursor may be enabled or disabled in the alphanumeric modes through the Cursor On/Off (COO) field of the Cursor Start Register in the VGA. In the graphics modes the cursor is not displayed, although BIOS does keep track of its position.

It is possible to set the ending line of the cursor to be less than the starting scan line. In the EGA, this will cause the cursor box to start at the selected ending scan line, extend to the bottom of the character box, wrap around to the top of the character box, and end at the starting scan line. The effect is two disjoined boxes. In the VGA, setting the ending line of the cursor to be less than the beginning line causes no cursor to be displayed.

Certain memory locations within the host RAM are used to store graphics parameters. Location 460 hex in the host memory space contains the Cursor Mode Area. This area consists of two bytes of information corresponding to the current starting and ending scan lines of the cursor. This function loads these locations with the starting and ending cursor scan lines.

Input Parameters:
CH = The starting scan line for the cursor.
CL = The ending scan line for the cursor.

Output Parameters:
None.

EGA Registers Affected:
Cursor Start, Cursor End.

Host Memory Affected:
460 hex = Cursor ending scan line number.
461 hex = Cursor starting scan line number.

11.3.2   AH = 02 Hex: Set Cursor Position (EGA/VGA)

The cursor may be located at any character position in the display memory. Certain display modes have multiple display pages. The number of pages available for each mode depends on the amount of display memory installed. The number of pages per mode is listed in Tables 11.1 and 11.2 above.

The cursor position is a 16-bit word that corresponds to a character position. The display memory begins with character position 0 at the top left of the display and increments from left to right and then from the top down. The display mode determines the number of horizontal and vertical characters per page. Thus, an address in display memory can be translated to a page number, a horizontal row value, and a vertical column value. The cursor resides at one character position on one page only. If the cursor is on a display page other than the display page that is currently active, the cursor will not be visible.

This BIOS function uses the desired page, row, and column numbers rather than the character address. These input parameters, used in conjunction with the current display mode, determine the 16-bit cursor location. Remember that the cursor is not displayed in the graphics modes.

Certain memory locations within the host RAM are used to store graphics parameters. Location 450 hex contains the Cursor Save Area. This area consists of sixteen bytes of information segmented into eight sections, two bytes per section. Each section corresponds to one of the display pages. Eight sections are provided because the maximum number of display pages for any mode is eight. Each section consists of two bytes, one for the row position and one for the column position. This function loads the appropriate locations within the table.

Input Parameters:
BH = The page number where the cursor will reside.
DH = The row number to position the cursor.
DL = The column number to position the cursor.

Output Parameters:
None.

EGA Registers Affected:
Cursor Location High, Cursor Location Low.

Host Memory Affected:
450 hex + pagenumber × 2 = Cursor position column number.
451 hex + pagenumber × 2 = Cursor position row number.

11.3.3 AH = 03 Hex: Read Cursor Position (EGA/VGA)

This function provides information to the calling routine regarding the position and the cursor type. The functioning of the cursor position is described in the Set Cursor Position BIOS call (AH = 02). Reading the cursor position reverses the process used to write the cursor to a selected position. It converts the 16-bit cursor location into row and column numbers. It is necessary to provide the desired page number as an input parameter because each display page maintains its own cursor. The location of the cursor within each display page is stored in the Cursor Save Area of host RAM. The page number is necessary because the BIOS routine will check for the cursor position in the Cursor Save Area rather than deriving it from the Cursor Location Registers. The Cursor Location Registers store the location of the cursor associated with the current display page.

The Cursor Save Area resides in host RAM at location 450 hex. This area consists of sixteen bytes of information segmented into eight sections, two bytes per section. Each section corresponds to one of the display pages. Eight sections are provided because the maximum number of display pages for any mode is eight. Each section consists of two bytes, one for the row position and one for the column position. This function reads the appropriate locations within the table to determine the current cursor position.

Input Parameters:
   None.

Output Parameters:
   DH, HL = Row, column of cursor.
   CH, CL = Cursor type.

EGA Registers Affected:
   None.

Host Memory Affected:
   None.

11.4 LIGHT PEN POSITION

11.4.1 AH = 04 Hex: Read Light Pen Position (EGA)

The light pen is not the most popular of operator interactive devices for the PC, although as windows environments become more popular the light pen may see a resurgence in popularity. This function is available for the EGA only because the VGA has no light pen facilities. The function reports the status and position of the light pen to the calling program. The light pen position will be considered valid if the light pen has been triggered. The light pen triggers when the electron beam of the CRT excites the phosphor of the screen immediately in front of the light pen. When this occurs, the light pen trigger strobe (LST) field of the Input #1 Status Register is set.

It may be desirable to clear this field, indicating that the light pen strobe has not occurred. This BIOS routine clears this field upon completion. Clearing the light pen latch is accomplished in some implementations in the following manner. In an EGA mode, an I/O output instruction, OUT, must be executed to address 3DB hex to clear the light pen trigger field. In a CGA mode, this may be accomplished by reading or writing to this port through an IN or OUT instruction. In the Hercules modes, an I/O output to port 3BB hex is necessary.

The location of the light pen during the last trigger is returned as pixel locations.

Input Parameters:
   None.

Output Parameters:
   AH = 0   Light pen trigger has not occurred. No valid data.

   AH = 1   Light pen trigger has occurred. The data is valid.

   BX = Vertical pixel column in which light pen was located during the last trigger.

   CX = Horizontal pixel raster line in which light pen was located during the last trigger. This occurs in modes 4,5, and 6.

   DH = Horizontal character row in which light pen was located during the last trigger.

   DL = Vertical character column in which light pen was located during the last trigger.

EGA Registers Affected:
   The Light Pen Strobe (LST) field of the Input Status #1 Register is cleared, indicating that the data is no longer valid.

Host Memory Affected:
   None.

11.5   DISPLAY PAGE SELECTION

11.5.1   AH = 05 Hex: Select Active Display Page (EGA/VGA)

Depending on the current display mode and the amount of display memory, the EGA/VGA may be configured to have from 1 to 8 pages of full-screen graphics. Only one page may be selected at a time for display. This page is called the *active page*. A list of the number of display pages available for the display modes is found in Table 11.1 for the EGA and Table 11.2 for the VGA. The default active display page is page number 0.

The display memory contains more memory than is required for a single display page. In some cases, it is segmented into multiple display pages. The selected active display page dictates where the data to be displayed resides within the display memory. The EGA/VGA determines where to start refreshing the display by the values in the Start Address Registers. This BIOS routine will load the Start Address Registers with a value derived from the current video parameters and the new active display page requested.

The host memory video storage area contains a byte storage location for the active display page at 462 hex. The actual address of the starting location, as loaded in the EGA/VGA Start Address Register pair, is loaded into the two-byte location beginning at 44E hex.

In the alphanumeric modes, it is advantageous to store data on multiple pages. To view different pages, simply select a new active display page. A great deal of time can be saved this way because the BIOS call to change the active display page requires far less time than saving the current display page and rewriting another page in its place. This is especially useful for the diagnostic stages of programming. Variables, flags, and arrays can be easily stored on multiple pages, allowing a great deal of information to be readily available.

In the graphics modes, multiple graphs may be stored on separate pages to speed display operation or for pseudo-animation. It is possible to load one display page while another is being displayed. Alternate display and loading can achieve basic animation effects.

Input Parameters:
  AL = The page number for the new active display page.

Output Parameters:
  None.

EGA Registers Affected:
  Start Address High, Start Address Low.

Host Memory Affected:
  44E hex = Start of active display page.
  462 hex = Active display page number.

11.6 SCROLL SCREEN

A rectangular region of any size on the screen can be scrolled upward or downward any desired number of lines.

11.6.1 AH = 06 Hex: Scroll Active Page Up (EGA/VGA)

In a windows environment, it is often desirable to scroll selected areas of the screen without disturbing the rest of the screen. The BIOS interrupt allows a window to be defined on the screen by its upper left and lower right corners. Each of these corners is defined by its corresponding row and column value. These values represent the character positions at the corner locations.

Scrolling means the moving up or down of information on the screen. In addition to defining the position and size of the window, it is also necessary to define the number of scan lines that will be scrolled. If the number of scan lines requested is 0, the entire window will be blanked, providing a rapid means of clearing a portion of the display.

Character scrolling one line upward brings one new row of characters into the window at the bottom and scrolls one row of characters out of the window at the top. Similarly, scrolling two lines upward brings in two new lines at the bottom of the screen and scrolls the top two lines off the top of the window. This scroll routine does not bring in new text information at the bottom of the screen. Rather, it outputs blank lines with a new attribute for the new character lines being scrolled into the window. It is the programmer's responsibility to follow this scroll routine with a character string output to the selected line positions that have been scrolled onto the bottom of the screen.

It should be noted that this scrolling operation is totally unrelated to the hardware scrolling available through the Start Address Registers. For details see the scrolling section in Chapter 5.

Input Parameters:
AL = The number of scan lines to scroll. Note that if zero lines are requested, the entire window will be blanked.
BH = The attribute to be used on the new blank lines entering the window from the bottom.
CH = The upper left character row number of the window.
CL = The upper left character column number of the window.
DH = The lower right character row number of the window.
DL = The lower right character column number of the window.

Output Parameters:
None.

EGA Registers Affected:
None.

Host Memory Affected:
None.

Display Memory Affected:
The character codes of the display memory contained within the described window. The attribute codes of the display memory contained at the bottom of

the window. The number of lines to scroll, as input in AL, dictates how many lines will have their attribute bytes changed. The character codes reside in display memory plane 0, and the attributes reside in display memory plane 1.

11.6.2   AH = 07 Hex: Scroll Active Page Down (EGA/VGA)

This BIOS interrupt routine is similar in function to Scroll Active Page Up routine mentioned above. This routine scrolls the display window downward. New blank lines are input from the top of the window, and the data at the bottom of the window is lost. See the Scroll Active Page Up call above.

If the number of scan lines requested is 0, the entire window will be blanked. This provides a rapid means of clearing a portion of the display.

Input Parameters:
   AL = The number of scan lines to scroll. Note that if zero lines are requested, the entire window will be blanked.
   BH = The attribute to be used on the new blank lines entering the window from the top.
   CH = The upper left character row number of the window.
   CL = The upper left character column number of the window.
   DH = The lower right character row number of the window.
   DL = The lower right character column number of the window.

Output Parameters:
   None.

EGA Registers Affected:
   None.

Host Memory Affected:
   None.

Display Memory Affected:
   The character codes of the display memory contained within the described window. The attribute codes of the display memory contained at the top of the window. The number of lines to scroll, as input in AL, dictates how many lines will have their attribute bytes changed. The character codes reside in display memory plane 0, and the attributes reside in display memory plane 1.

11.7   READ/WRITE CHARACTERS

Three calls allow the programmer to read an attribute and character byte, write an attribute and character byte, or write a character only. These calls can be included into program loops that read or write strings of characters.

11.7.1   AH=08 Hex: Read Attribute/Character Pair (EGA/VGA)

This function returns the character code and attribute byte of the character located at the current cursor position. No attribute code is returned when the display is in one of the graphics modes. The page number input to this routine determines which display page will be used for the read operation. The cursor position is determined by the Cursor Save Area contained in the display information area buffer of host memory. See Set Cursor Position for a description of this area.

Character Storage

In the alphanumeric display modes, the character codes are stored in display page 0, and the character attributes are stored in display page 1. The current display mode, in conjunction with the desired page, determines the actual physical memory address corresponding to the cursor position. It is then a simple matter to read the character code from plane 0 and the attribute byte from plane 1.

In the graphics display modes, the problem is far more complicated. As in the alphanumeric modes, the current display mode and the desired page are used to determine the actual physical memory address corresponding to the cursor position. The next step involves determining which character is in the character box pointed to by the cursor position.

This BIOS function must determine which characters, if any, are written into a selected memory location corresponding to the cursor position. The cursor points to a rectangular area on the screen that contains a character box. The size of this area is dictated by the number of bytes per character. The character box contains a group of pixels. This routine must determine whether these pixels correspond exactly to one of the character pixel patterns in the active display font.

In the graphics mode, the characters are compared to a block of 128 characters in the character-generator section of the EGA BIOS ROM. It is often desirable to read a character code from the full 256 characters in the character generator. However, only the lower 128 characters of the character set can be accessed using this function. To access the upper 128 characters of the character set, the program must reset the interrupt 1F hex vector, located at 7C hex in host memory. This value must be set to point to the second set of character dot patterns associated with characters 128–256 of the selected character font.

The number of bytes per character is located in the display information area of host memory. This area, located in the host memory space, contains a byte at 485 hex that holds the current number of bytes per character.

To determine which character, if any, is present in this character box, it is necessary to compare the pixels in the character box with all of the possible character patterns in ROM. The Color Compare and Color No Care Registers and read mode #1 are used to speed up this function. If no character is found, a 0 code is returned in the character read position. Reading the character code at this position would return the "space" code of 20 hex, as expected.

Reading a Space

It is not possible to read a "space" in the graphics modes. Because a "space" character is all background, nothing will be present in that character position of the display memory. As a result, reading a character position corresponding to a "space" or a "tab" will return a 0 character code, indicating that no character was found.

Input Parameters:
BH = The page number.

Output Parameters:
AL = Character read. The character code of the character occupying the space in display memory corresponding to the current cursor position on the selected page.

AH = Character attribute. The attribute code of the character occupying the memory space at the current cursor position on the selected page.

EGA Registers Affected:
None.

Host Memory Affected:
None.

11.7.2   AH = 09 Hex: Write Attribute/Character Pair (EGA/VGA)

This function writes the character code and attribute byte to display memory at the current cursor position. The page number, an input parameter, determines which display page will be used for the write operation. The character count, also an input parameter, determines the number of times to replicate this character. In the alphanumeric modes, this number is limited to the number of characters left until the end of the current display page is reached. In the graphics modes, this number is limited to the number of remaining character positions to the right of the cursor position until the end of the line. The cursor position is determined by the Cursor Save Area contained in the display information area buffer of host memory. See Set Cursor Position for a description of this area.

Character Patterns

In the alphanumeric display modes, the character codes are written to display page 0, and the character attributes are written to display page 1. The current display mode, in conjunction with the desired page, determines the actual physical memory address corresponding to the cursor position.

In the graphics display modes, the character pattern is written to the display memory. As in the alphanumeric modes, the current display mode and the desired page are used to determine the actual physical memory address corresponding to the cursor position. In the graphics display modes, the characters are written into the display memory as a sequence of foreground dots. Writing a character to the display involves copying the character pattern that corresponds to the character code from the character generator into the display memory. This character generator is located in the EGA/VGA BIOS ROM. The size of the active font determines the size of the character box that contains the dot pattern of the selected character.

When a particular character is written onto the display, the character pattern corresponding to this character code is copied to the display memory at the selected position. The color of the character is determined by the attribute byte associated with the character to be written. The foreground color determines the color of the character, and thus, which display planes should be updated. If the foreground color is 0F hex, all planes will be requested for update. Likewise, if the foreground color is 1 hex, only plane 0 will be requested. It may not be possible to write into all planes requested. Only those planes enabled by the Map Mask Register may be modified.

In the graphics mode, the characters are formed from a block of 128 characters in the character-generator section of the BIOS ROM. It is often desirable to utilize the full 256 characters in the character generator. However, only the lower 128 characters of the character set can be accessed in this function. To access the upper 128 characters of the character set, the program must reset the interrupt 1F hex vector, located at 7C hex in host memory. This value must be set to point to the second set of character dot patterns associated with characters 128–256.

In the graphics modes, the most significant bit of the attribute byte, bit 7, determines the write mode. If this bit is 0, the dots in the foreground of the character overwrite the dots in the display memory. If this bit is a 1, the dots in the foreground of the character are logically XORed with the dots in the display memory. This XORing has the effect of erasing the character if it is already present in that location and writing the character if it is not present.

Writing a "Space" Character

Writing a "space" character to the display while the display is in an alphanumeric mode causes a 20 hex code to be written into display memory. The "space" character consists of a character box composed entirely of background dots. The attribute byte associated with this "space" character determines the color of the background dots. This background color fills the character box of the screen corresponding to the "space" position on the screen.

Writing a "space" character to the display while the display is in a graphics mode has no effect on the display. Nothing happens when a "space" is written because the graphics modes utilize a character transparency function. This function ignores all of the background pixels and writes only the foreground pixels associated with the selected character. The effect is that any data behind the background area of the character box will show through the character box.

Input Parameters:
BH = The page number.
AL = Character to write.   The character code of the character to be written to the display memory at the current cursor position on the selected page.
BL = Character attribute.   The attribute code of the character to be written to the display memory at the current cursor position on the selected page. Only the foreground pixels are written to the screen in the graphics modes. Note that bit 7 affects the way in which these foreground pixels modify the screen:

Bit 7=0   Overwrite whatever pixels are in the selected character box in display memory with the foreground pixels of the character.

Bit 7=1   Logically XOR the pixels in the selected character box in display memory with the foreground pixels of the character.

CX = Replication count.   The number of times to repeat this character/attribute pair.

Output Parameters:
None.

EGA Registers Affected:
None.

Display Memory Affected:
The display memory corresponding to the current cursor position. In the alphanumeric mode, planes 0 and 1 will be modified to contain the new character code and attribute byte, respectively. In the graphics modes, the display memory corresponding to the character box at the selected cursor position will be modified.

11.7.3   AH=0A Hex. Write Character Only (EGA/VGA)

This function writes a character to the display memory beginning at the current cursor position. The attribute byte of the character positions is not affected. The page number, an input parameter, determines which display page will be used for the write operation. The character count, also an input parameter, determines the number of times to replicate this character. In the alphanumeric modes, this number is limited to the number of characters left until the end of the current display page is reached. In the graphics modes, this number is limited to the number of remaining character positions to the right of the cursor position until the end of the line. The cursor position is determined by the Cursor Save Area contained in the display information area buffer of host memory.

See Set Cursor Position for a description of this area. See the Write Character/

Attribute call for details on writing characters in both the alphanumeric and graphics modes.

Input Parameters:

BH = The page number.

AL = Character to write. The character code of the character to be written to the display memory at the current cursor position on the selected page.

BL = Character attribute. In the alphanumeric modes, this field is ignored. In the graphics modes, bit 7 of this register affects the way in which the character foreground pixels modify the screen:

Bit 7=0 Overwrite whatever pixels are in the selected character box in display memory with the foreground pixels of the character.

Bit 7=1 Logically XOR the pixels in the selected character box in display memory with the foreground pixels of the character.

CX = Replication count. The number of times to repeat this character/attribute pair.

Output Parameters:

None.

EGA Registers Affected:

None.

Display Memory Affected:

The display memory corresponding to the current cursor position. In the alphanumeric mode, plane 0 will be modified to contain the new character code. In the graphics modes, the display memory corresponding to the character box at the selected cursor position will be modified.

11.8 COLOR PALETTE

11.8.1 AH = 0B Hex: Set Color Palette (EGA/VGA)

This function sets the color palette when the system is operating in modes 4 or 5, which are the 320-by-200 CGA display modes. This function is used to provide color compatibility with the CGA. In some nonstandard EGA implementations, mode 6, which corresponds to the 640-by-200 graphics mode, is also controlled by this function.

In the four-color mode, there are two bits that correspond to each pixel's color. These two bits are horizontal neighbors. Because these two bits can access only four locations in the palette, only four colors are possible. In the standard IBM implementation, one of two color schemes is loaded into the palette. Each of these palettes represents four colors. In some nonstandard implementations, the programmer may actually select which colors will be loaded into these palette registers.

In modes 4 or 5 (four-color modes), the palette color ID operates as follows: If the color ID = 0, the color value will select the background and intensity.

TABLE 11.3 Graphics Modes

Mode (Hex)	Adapter	Rows	Columns	Page	Color
4,5	EGA/VGA	0–199	0–319	0	0–3
6	EGA/VGA	0–199	0–639	0	0–1
D	EGA/VGA	0–199	0–319	0–7	0–15
E	EGA/VGA	0–199	0–639	0–3	0–15
F–10	EGA/VGA	0–349	0–639	0,1	0–15
11	VGA	0–479	0–639	1	0–1
12	VGA	0–479	0–639	1	0–15
13	VGA	0–199	0–319	1	0–255

The values from 0 to 15 select normal background colors, and the values 16–31 select the high-intensity background colors.

If the color ID = 1, the color value will select the four colors to be loaded into the first four positions of the color palette. The four colors that can be selected are as follows:

Color Value = 0
Select Palette #0

0 = black
1 = green
2 = red
3 = brown

Color Value = 1
Select Palette #1

0 = black
1 = cyan
2 = magenta
3 = white

Note that in certain implementations of this BIOS function, variations exist regarding how the color palette compatibility is set. Some implementations of this BIOS function allows the programmer to select the colors to be loaded into the palette. This function may also control the color selection of mode 6. In mode 6 (two-color mode), each pixel is represented by one pixel. In some cases a CGA Color Select Register at port address 3D9 hex is present. This register allows additional control to achieve CGA color compatibility.

Input Parameters:

BH = Color ID.   Selects the function of the Color Value.

BL = Color Value.   Controlled by the Color ID field above; provides the color for the background or the current palette number.

Output Parameters:

None.

EGA Registers Affected:

Color Palette Registers.

Host Memory Affected:
466 hex current color.

11.9   READ/WRITE PIXEL

Certainly the weakest aspect of the BIOS is the reading and writing of data while the display is in the graphics modes. There are only two routines, AH = 0C hex and AH = 0D hex. These read from or write to a pixel. These routines are notoriously slow when used in any graphics operations.

11.9.1   AH = 0C Hex: Write Pixel (EGA/VGA)

This function is a slow but sure way to write a pixel to the display memory when the EGA/VGA is in a graphics mode. The programmer provides the color, page number, row number, and column number. The possible values of these parameters are listed below.

Note that this function does not affect the cursor position. The position of the pixel to be modified is obtained by converting the mode and page number to a display memory address. The pixel written to is not necessarily on the current page, so it is possible that the write operation will have no effect on the displayed page. The active page does not change according to the page parameter sent to this function.

Input Parameters:
AL = Color value. Value to load into display memory at the desired position.

BH = Display page.   The display page that contains the pixel that should be written to by this function.

CX = Column number.   The horizontal pixel coordinate of the pixel. Note that this number represents a pixel number, not a character number. The columns count from 0, on the left of the screen, to a maximum value dictated by the display mode, on the right side of the screen.

DX = Row number.   The vertical pixel coordinate of the pixel. Note that this number represents a pixel number, not a character number. The rows count from 0, on the top of the screen, to a maximum row number dictated by the display mode, on the left side of the screen.

Output Parameters:
None.

EGA Registers Affected:
None.

Display Memory Affected.
The bit or bits corresponding to the display mode, the horizontal and vertical coordinate input parameters, the selected page, and the value of the Map Mask

Register. The Map Mask Register determines which planes are enabled for write operations.

11.9.2   AH = 0D Hex: Read Pixel (EGA/VGA)

This function is a slow but sure way to read the value in a pixel location in display memory when the EGA/VGA is in a graphics mode. The programmer provides the page number, row number, and column number as input parameters. The function returns the color of the pixel to the calling program as addressed by the input parameters. See the Write Pixel function above for more details.

The pixel read is not necessarily on the current page. The active page does not change according to the page number parameter sent to this function. Thus, if display page 0 is active, it is possible to read a pixel from display page 1.

Input Parameters:
BH = Display page.   The display page that contains the pixel that should be written to by this function.
CX = Column number.   The horizontal pixel coordinate of the pixel. Note that this number represents a pixel number, not a character number. The columns count from 0, on the left of the screen, to a maximum value dictated by the display mode, on the right side of the screen.
DX = Row number.   The vertical pixel coordinate of the pixel. Note that this number represents a pixel number, not a character number. The rows count from 0, on the top of the screen, to a maximum row number dictated by the display mode, on the left side of the screen.

Output Parameters:
AL = Color value.   Value to load into display memory at the desired position.

EGA Registers Affected:
None.

Display Memory Affected.
None.

11.9.3   AH = 0E Hex: Write TTY Character (EGA/VGA)

This function writes a character to the display memory. In addition to the regular characters that can be displayed, this function understands several carriage-control functions. It causes the display to operate in a similar manner to a TTY-type terminal. This write function operates on the carriage return, line feed, backspace, and bell key.

The TTY character is written to the display memory at the cursor position

TABLE 11.4 Cursor-control Keystrikes

Symbol	Name	Action
CR	Carriage Return	Moves the cursor to column 0 of the next character line.
LF	Line Feed	Moves the cursor down one character row. If the current character row is on the bottom of the screen, the entire screen is scrolled upward. The attribute of the new line is assigned to be the attribute of the previous last line's far left character. It is assumed that each line has only one attribute in these scrolling operations.
BS	Backspace	The cursor is moved to the left one character position. No action occurs if the cursor is at the far left column, column 0, of the line.
BELL	Bell	Causes the bell to ring.

on the active page. After the character is written, the cursor is advanced one position. When the end of the current horizontal line is reached, an effective carriage return and line feed are issued, thereby moving the cursor to column 0 of the next line. When a line feed is issued and the cursor is already on the bottom line, the entire screen is scrolled. The attribute of the new line being scrolled in from the bottom is the same as the attribute of the far left character in the bottom line of the display.

The attribute bytes associated with the characters when the display is in an alphanumeric mode remain unmodified, with the exception of a screen scroll previously discussed. In the graphics modes, it is necessary to specify the foreground color of the character.

Table 11.4 illustrates the operation of these cursor-control keystrikes.

The Write String BIOS call, AH = 13 hex, utilizes this Write TTY BIOS call when writing strings of characters to the display. Thus, character-control codes contained within the strings are treated as indicated in Table 11.4.

Input Parameters:

AL = Character code to write to the display at the current cursor position on the current page. The attribute byte of this character is not modified. This code may also be one of the four codes mentioned above.

BL = Foreground color for the graphics modes. If the display is in one of the graphics modes, this parameter contains the color that will be used to draw the character. Because there is no background color for characters in the graphics modes, this is the only color that needs to be specified.

Output Parameters:

None.

TABLE 11.5   Video State Memory Locations

Host Memory	Function
449 hex	Display mode
44A hex	Number of character columns
462 hex	Active display page

TABLE 11.6   Number of Character Columns

Mode (Hex)	# of Columns
0,1,4,5,D,13	40
2,3,5,6,7,E,F,10,11,12	80

Display Memory Affected:

If the character is a printable character, display memory is modified. The location of the modified display memory depends on the current cursor position, the active display page, and the display mode.

11.9.4   AH = 0F Hex: Read Current Video State (EGA/VGA)

This function reads the current state of the EGA/VGA, including the display mode, the number of character columns on the screen, and the current active display page. All of these values are located in the information buffer in host memory as shown in Table 11.5.

Input Parameters:

None.

Output Parameters:

AH = Number of character columns on the screen. Table 11.6 illustrates the number of character columns possible for the different display modes.

AL = Current display mode. The low-order seven-bit value in this register ranges from 0 to 10 hex in the standard EGA implementations. Bit 7 in the display mode corresponds to whether the display was cleared during the last mode change. If it was cleared, this bit will be a 0; if it was not cleared, this bit will be a 1. See the Set Mode Function for details on the display modes.

BH = Active display page. Table 11.7 illustrates the possible page values for the different display modes.

11.10   PALETTE REGISTERS

The 16 Palette Registers can be written to on the EGA. They can be written to and read from on the VGA. Individual registers or all 16 registers can be

TABLE 11.7 Possible Number
of Pages

Mode (Hex)	Page Numbers
4–6	0
D	0–7
E	0–3
F–10	0–7
11	1
12	1
13	1

accessed by the BIOS routines. Other functions within the Attribute Register Group, including the Intensity/Blinking Bit and the Overscan Register, are controlled in these BIOS calls.

11.10.1 AH = 10, AL = 0: Set Individual Palette Registers (EGA/VGA)

This function loads an individual Palette Register with a specified color. A better title for this BIOS function would be "Set Individual Attribute Registers," and the description would be "this function loads an individual Attribute Register with a specified value." The Palette Registers are only a subgroup of the Attribute Registers that can be programmed with this BIOS call. The Palette Registers are the first 16 of 20 Attribute Registers for the EGA and the first 16 out of 21 Attribute Registers for the VGA.

The colors loaded into the palette register determine the color output to the monitor. The EGA provides for 64 possible colors by allocating two bits per three primary colors—red, green, and blue. The coding of these six bits, according to the monitor type, is illustrated in Table 11.8.

The color palette consists of 16 registers that are used to map the values representing the intensity of each pixel into a color. The address of each palette register corresponds to the number of unique states available in the display memory. Table 11.9 illustrates the color palette addresses used according to the different display modes.

16-color Mode

In the 16-color mode, the color palette is accessed by one bit from each of the four memory planes. Bit plane 0 represents bit 0 of the four-bit address, bit plane 1 represents bit 1, bit plane 2 represents bit 2, and bit plane 3 represents bit 3. This four-bit address accesses a given location in the palette during the screen refreshing. Only those memory planes that are selected in the Enable Color Plane Register control the address feeding the palette. The bit planes that are deselected cause a 0 in that bit position of the four-bit address. Suppose

TABLE 11.8 Palette Color Codes

Bit #	Color EGA Monitor	Color RGBI Monitor	Monochrome Monitor
5	Secondary red	—	—
4	Secondary green	Intensity	Intensity
3	Secondary blue	—	Video
2	Red	Red	—
1	Green	Green	—
0	Blue	Blue	—

TABLE 11.9 Color Palette Utilization

Mode (Hex)	Color	Palette Addresses Used
0,1,2,3,D,E,10	16-color	0–15
4,5	4-color	0–3
6	2-color	0–1
7,F	Monochrome	0–1
11	2-color	0–1
12	16-color	0–15
13	256-color	0–15, VGA Color Registers

that bit plane 1 and 2 are disabled. This would mean that the only Palette Registers that could be accessed would be 0, 1, 8, and 9, as shown in Table 11.10.

256-color Mode

The 256-color mode is specific to the VGA and is associated with display mode 13 hex. The colors output to the monitor are derived from the 256 Color Registers on the VGA rather than the 16 Palette Registers used in all other display modes. In this mode, the 16 Color Palette Registers act as the low-order four bits of the address to the Color Registers. In this mode 13 hex, the 16 Palette Registers should not be modified. If it is desired to modify a color, the color code should be changed within the desired Color Register.

Nonpalette Attribute Registers

There are 20 registers in the EGA and 21 registers in the VGA that belong to the Attribute Registers. The first 16 are dedicated to the palette registers. The Attribute Registers are tricky to program because a single port address is used both to index the Attribute Registers and as the data port for them. It is sometimes more convenient to use this BIOS call rather than to program the registers directly.

TABLE 11.10 Examples of Palette Addressing

Bit Plane 3	Bit Plane 0	Palette Address
0	0	0
0	1	1
1	0	8
1	1	9

Register 10 hex is the Attributes Mode Control Register. This register controls several functions related to the output configuration of the EGA. See the Attributes Mode Control Register for further details.

Register 11 hex is called the Overscan Register. This register controls the color of the border region surrounding the graphics display area. The six-bit color coding of this register is identical to the color coding of the lower 16 palette registers that was described above. See the Overscan Register for further details.

Register 12 hex is the Color Plane Enable Register. This register controls the selecting and deselecting of display planes. Only selected display planes can be written to or can affect the output colors addressed by the lower 16 palette registers. See the Color Plane Enable Register for further details.

Register 13 hex is the Horizontal Pel Panning Register. This register is used when it is desired to smooth-pan the display area to the left or to the right. Rough panning moves the screen a character position at a time while smooth panning moves the screen one pixel location at a time. See the Horizontal Pel Panning Register for further details.

Register 14 hex is the Color Select Register. It is available only on the VGA. It selects either the upper two address bits or the upper four address bits, which select one of the 256 Color Registers.

Input Parameters:
  BH = Coded color value to be loaded into the palette.
  BL = Attribute Register address of the register to be loaded. The most commonly used registers in this group are the 16 Color Palette registers.

Output Parameters:
  None.

EGA Registers Affected:
  The selected Attribute Register.

11.10.2 AH = 10, AL = 1: Set Overscan Register (EGA/VGA)

This function loads the Overscan Registers with a color code. This color code will be displayed in the border region of the display. The border region is the region surrounding the graphics display area. It is bounded by the active display area and the horizontal and vertical blanking timing. The Overscan Register is actually Attribute Register 10 hex and can be also programmed by the Set Individual Palette Register above.

The EGA has great difficulty displaying colors other than black in the 350-line modes. This difficulty, related to timing, causes undesirable effects. The border region does operate properly in the 200-scan-line modes. To achieve a reasonable display, the Overscan Register should be set to 0 for the color black.

The VGA does not support overscan borders in the 40-column display modes. In other display modes, with the exception of mode 13 hex, all borders are restricted to one character wide.

The color codes in the Overscan Register use the same coding as that described in the Set Individual Palette Register BIOS call.

Input Parameters:
  BH = Color code for the border region.

Output Parameters:
  None.

EGA Registers Affected:
  Overscan Register.

11.10.3   AH = 10, AL = 2: Set All Palette Registers and Overscan Register (EGA/VGA)

This function loads all of the 16-color Palette Registers and the Overscan Register with the values in a 17-byte array. The values in the array are coded color values that are described in the Set Individual Palette Register BIOS call.

Input Parameters:
  ES:DX   Pointer to the 17-byte array containing the color codes for the 16 Palette Registers and for the Overscan Register. The ES Register is the segment register, and the DX register is the offset register. The actual 20-bit address is obtained by shifting the segment register by 4 bits to the left and ORing in the value in the offset register.

Output Parameters:
  None.

EGA Registers Affected:
  16 Palette Registers, Overscan Register.

11.10.4   AH = 10 Hex, AL = 3 Hex: Toggle Blink/Intensity Bit (EGA/VGA)

This function loads the Blink/Intensity field, B/I, of the Mode Control Register. This field defines whether bit 7 of the character attribute bytes controls blinking or background intensity.

It was desirable to maintain a one-byte character attribute. It was also desirable to allow the character to have one of sixteen foreground colors, to have one of sixteen background colors, and to be able to blink. This required nine bits of coded information, four for the foreground, four for the background and one for the blinking. A compromise was struck: the blinking field and the fourth bit of the background intensity bit share the same bit-7 position of the character attribute byte.

In order to select which function this bit 7 is controlling, a single bit in the Mode Control Register called the B/I field was created. This B/I field controls the blinking/intensity function for the entire display.

If the B/I field is set to 1, blinking is enabled, but only one of eight unique colors can be selected for the background intensity of the character. A character will blink if its associated attribute byte bit 7=1. The character will not blink if its associated attribute byte bit 7=0. Likewise, if the B/I field is reset to 0, blinking is disabled, but the background color can be represented by one of sixteen colors. Table 11.11 illustrates the possibilities.

Input Parameters:
BL = Value to load into the B/I field of the Mode Control Register, controlling the blinking/intensity function of bit 7 in the character attribute bit.
0 = Enable background intensities.
1 = Enable blinking.

Output Parameters:
None.

EGA Registers Affected:
B/I field of the Mode Control Register.

11.10.5 AH = 10 Hex, AL = 07 Hex: Read Individual Palette Register (VGA)

The Palette Registers may be read in the VGA. This very important feature allows programs to save the palette registers before modifying them. The original palette can then be restored after a program exits. This is useful when memory resident programs are competing for the display resource but have no way of communicating with one another regarding the state of the EGA.

The selected palette register color code is returned to the calling program.

Input Parameters:
BL = Palette Register to read.

Output Parameters:
BH = Color code read from the selected Palette Register.

EGA Registers Affected:
None.

TABLE 11.11 Blinking/Background Intensity

		Function	
B/I Field Mode Control	*Bit 7 Attribute*	*Blinking*	*Background Intensity*
0	0	No blink, 16 background colors	
0	1	No blink, 16 background colors	
1	0	No blink, 8 background colors	
1	1	Blink, 8 background colors	

11.10.6 AH = 10 Hex, AL = 08 Hex: Read Overscan Register (VGA)

The color code in the Overscan Register can be read with the value returned to the calling program.

Input Parameters:
None.

Output Parameters:
BH = Color code read from the Overscan Register

EGA Registers Affected:
None.

11.10.7 AH = 10 Hex, AL = 09 Hex: Read All Palette Registers and Overscan Register (VGA)

The color codes of the 16 Palette Registers and the Overscan Register can be read with the 17 byte values returned into a buffer pointed to by the output parameter register pair ES:DX.

Input Parameters:
ES = Segment Address pointing to the array that will contain the Palette and Overscan Register color codes.
DX = Offset Address pointing to the array that will contain the Palette and Overscan Register color codes.

Output Parameters:
None.

EGA Registers Affected:
None.

Host Memory Affected:
The 17-character array in host memory pointed to by the ES:DX register pair.

11.11 COLOR REGISTERS

The 256 Color Registers are available in the VGA but not the EGA. The BIOS routines can read from or write to individual registers or groups of them. The 256 Color Registers can be segmented into pages, and the active page can also be controlled. The colors present in these registers can be summed to produce gray scale values through one of these calls.

11.11.1 AH = 10 Hex, AL = 10 Hex: Set Individual Color Register (VGA)

This function allows the programmer to set one of the Color Registers. The VGA is equipped with 256 Color Registers that contain the actual color codes output to the monitor. Each contains three six-bit fields: one for the red intensity, one for the blue intensity and one for the green intensity. Because each field is six bits wide, it is possible to display 64 levels of intensity for each of the three primary colors. Because all three six-bit fields are combined to produce the resultant color code, an eighteen-bit field is used to create the color. These eighteen bits allow 256 K possible colors.

In the VGA display mode 13 hex, it is possible to exhibit all 256 of these Color Registers simultaneously. In all other modes, only a subset of 2,4, or 16 registers may be used simultaneously. By using the Color Select Register, it is feasible to rapidly select from groups of 16 or 64 Color Registers without having to modify the Color Registers.

Input Parameters:
    BX = Color Register number to set.
    CH = Intensity of the green color, ranging from 0–63.
    CL = Intensity of the blue color, ranging from 0–63.
    DH = Intensity of the red color, ranging from 0–63.

Output Parameters:
    None.

EGA Registers Affected:
    None.

11.11.2 AH = 10 Hex, AL = 12 Hex: Set Block of Color Registers (VGA)

This function permits the programmer to set a block of the Color Registers. The VGA is equipped with 256 Color Registers that contain the actual color codes output to the monitor. See the Set Individual Color Register for details.

The selected number of Color Registers are loaded from a buffer in host memory as addressed by the ES:DX register pair. Any number of registers, up to the maximum of 256, can be written, starting at an arbitrary register number. Thus, it is possible to write to two consecutive Color Registers beginning at Color Register number 100.

TABLE 11.12 Example of an Array of Colors

Byte Index	Color Value
0	Red intensity for Color Register 100
1	Green intensity for Color Register 100
2	Blue intensity for Color Register 100
3	Red intensity for Color Register 101
4	Green intensity for Color Register 101
5	Blue intensity for Color Register 101

The format of the data buffer consists of a sequence of three bytes per Color Register. The sequence is red, green, blue. This arrangement is followed by the next sequence, which corresponds to the next sequential Color Register. The buffer should be three times the number of Color Registers to be written. In the above example, the buffer would appear as indicated in Table 11.12.

Input Parameters:
    BX = Number of first Color Register to set.
    CX = Number of Color Registers to set.
    ES:DX = Segment/Offset Address of host array containing the color codes. The buffer should be three times the length of the number of Color Registers to set as indicated in the CX parameter.

Output Parameters:
    None.

EGA Registers Affected:
    Selected Color Registers.

11.11.3 AH = 10 Hex, AL = 13 Hex: Select Color Page (VGA)

There are 256 Color Registers, but only in mode 13 hex can all 256 be simultaneously displayed. There are two ways to segment the Color Registers. The first way segments the 256 registers into 16 blocks with 16 registers per block. This is useful when the VGA is in a 16-color mode. It allows the programmer to rapidly select from 16 possible palettes without having to reload any of the Color Registers. The second segmentation creates four blocks with 64 colors per block. This is useful when the programmer desires to modify the 64 possible colors accessed by the Palette Registers in the 16-color modes.

This BIOS call allows the programmer to select one of two functions. The first, selected with the input parameter BL = 0, allows the programmer to select the paging mode. The second, selected with BL=1, permits the programmer

TABLE 11.13 Selecting the Color Page

Input BL	Parameters (BH Function)	BH Possible Values
0	Select paging mode	0=4 pages of 64 Color Registers
		1=16 pages of 16 Color Registers
1	Select color page	0–3 if paging mode=0
		0–15 if paging mode=1

to change the active color page depending on the active color paging mode. The possible values for this call are illustrated in Table 11.13.

This BIOS call allows the programmer to select the page according to the current paging mode. The Internal Palette Size Select (IPS) field of the Mode Control Register is loaded depending on the input parameter to this BIOS call. This field is used in conjunction with the Color Select Register to determine the addressing technique used to select the Color Registers. See the IPS field of the Mode Control Register and the Color Select Register for details.

Input Parameters:
 BH = Paging mode or active color page.
   If BL = 0, Paging mode is selected.
     BH = 0   Select 4 pages of 64 Color Registers.
     BH = 1   Select 16 pages of 64 Color Registers.
   If BL = 1, Select page is selected.
     BH = 0–3 if in 4-page mode.
     BH = 0–15 if in 16-page mode.
 BL = Select function of this BIOS call
     BL = 0 Select Paging Mode
     BL = 1 Select Active Color Page Mode

Output Parameters:
 None.

EGA Registers Affected:
 Mode Control Register, Color Select Register

11.11.4   AH = 10 Hex, AL = 15 Hex: Read Individual Color Register (VGA)

This function allows the programmer to read one of the Color Registers. The VGA is equipped with 256 Color Registers that contain the actual color codes output to the monitor. See the Set Individual Palette Register for details.

Input Parameters:
 BX = Color Register number to read.

Output Parameters:
CH = Intensity of the green color, ranging from 0–63.
CL = Intensity of the blue color, ranging from 0–63.
DH = Intensity of the red color, ranging from 0–63.

EGA Registers Affected:
None.

11.11.5 AH = 10 Hex, AL = 17 Hex: Read Block of Color Register (VGA)

This function allows the programmer to read a block of the Color Registers. The VGA is equipped with 256 Color Registers that contain the actual color codes output to the monitor. See the Set Block of Color Register for details.

The selected number of Color Registers are loaded into a buffer in host memory that is addressed by the ES:DX register pair. Any number of registers, up to the maximum of 256, can be read, starting at an arbitrary register number.

The format of the data buffer consists of a sequence of three bytes per Color Register. The sequence is red, green, blue. This arrangement would be followed by the next sequence, which corresponds to the next sequential Color Register. The buffer should be three times the number of Color Registers to be written.

Input Parameters:
BX = Number of first Color Register to set.
CX = Number of Color Registers to set.

Output Parameters:
ES:DX = Segment/Offset Address of host array containing the color codes. The buffer should be three times the length of the number of Color Registers to set as indicated in the CX parameter.

Host Memory Affected:
The host memory that is addressed by the ES:DX register pair. Three times the number of bytes as input in the CX registers will be affected. The resultant array in no way reflects which registers are associated with the color sequences.

11.11.6 AH = 10 Hex, AL = 1A Hex: Read Current Color Page Number (VGA)

The 256 Color Registers may be configured either as 16 groups with 16 registers per group or as 4 groups with 64 registers per group. This is determined by the Internal Palette Size Select (IPS) field of the Mode Control Register and may be loaded through the Select Color Page BIOS CALL, AH=10 hex, AL=13 hex. Both the current paging mode and the active color page are returned to the calling routine. See the Select Color Page BIOS call for details.

Input Parameters:
None.

Output Parameters:
BH = Current active color page.
BL = Active paging mode.

EGA Registers Affected:
None.

11.11.7 AH = 10 Hex, AL = 1B Hex: Sum Color Values to Gray Scale (VGA)

This call converts the color values in the Color Registers into gray scale values. A weighted average is used to convert the intensity values of the three primary colors—red, green, and blue—into a gray scale according to the Equation 11.1. Any number of consecutive Color Registers can be converted using this call. The programmer provides the starting Color Register number and the number of Color Registers to convert.

Equation 11.1 Determining Gray Scale

$$\text{Gray Scale} = (.30 \times \text{Red}) + (.59 \times \text{Green}) + (.11 \times \text{Blue})$$

In creating the gray scale, 30 percent of the red intensity is added to 59 percent of the green intensity and added to 11 percent of the blue intensity. Because the resultant intensity is equal to 100 percent of the intensity of the three colors, the intensity of a gray scale will result in a gray scale of the same value. For example, assume that the three color values are 40, 40, and 40 for red, green, and blue respectively. This produces a gray scale of intensity 40. The resultant gray scale would be $(.30 \times 40) + (.59 \times 40) + (.11 \times 40) = 1.0 \times 40 = 40$.

This call is similar to the Summing to Gray Scales BIOS call, AH = 12 hex, BL = 33 hex. It differs in that the summing operation occurs automatically when this call is invoked. The Summing to Gray Scales call does not actually alter any Color Registers until subsequent mode sets occur and operations take place that access the Color Registers. If implemented in C, this operation would be similar to Listing 11.1. This example assumes that the three primary colors of each Color Register have been read from the Color Registers and loaded into the red, green, and blue arrays. The values start_reg and number_regs contain the starting Color Register number and the number of Color Registers to convert.

LISTING 11.1 Summing Selected Registers to Gray Scale

```
unsigned char Red[256], Blue[256], Green[256], Gray;
int i,start_reg,number_regs;
for (i=start_reg; i<=number_regs; i++)
 { Gray = (.30 * Red[i])+(.59 * Green[i])+(.11 * Blue[i]);
   Red[i] = Gray; Green[i] = Gray; Blue[i] = Gray;
 }
```

This BIOS call reads a set of the Color Registers, calculates the above equation, and rewrites the result into the red, green, and blue portions of the selected Color Registers. Any number of Color Registers, up to the maximum of 256, can be selected, beginning at any Color Register index.

Input Parameters:
 BX = First Color Register to be converted to gray scale.
 CX = Number of Color Registers to be converted.

Output Parameters:
 None.

EGA Registers Affected:
 The selected Color Registers.

11.12 CHARACTER GENERATION

Several BIOS routines allow the programmer to download ROM-based or user-based character sets into the display memory. Two sets of calls are provided for use during the alphanumeric modes. One set forces a mode set reset, and the second set automatically adjusts certain display parameters. In the graphics modes, the pointers to ROM-based or user-based character sets are loaded. Up to eight fonts can be resident in display memory. A BIOS call is provided that selects two of these fonts to be active. The active character font information can be returned to the programmer through one of these BIOS calls.

11.12.1 AH = 11, AL = 0: User ALPHA Load (with Reset) (EGA/VGA)

This function loads a character set into one of the font areas reserved in the display memory. The character set may consist of any number of bytes per character, up to the 32-byte limit. The programmer provides this routine with a long pointer that points to the character set that is to be loaded. All or any portion of a character set may be loaded into the display memory font area. This call can be used only when the EGA/VGA is in an alphanumeric mode.

Fonts in Display Memory

There are four areas reserved for the display fonts in the EGA and eight areas on the VGA. Before the character set is loaded, a Set Mode is automatically executed. See the Set Mode BIOS call for details. This Set Mode operation is executed without clearing the display. Thus, character codes and attributes located in display memory will not be erased. This feature of not erasing the display memory also allows the programmer to load partial fonts without erasing the original character fonts previously loaded in the display memory. The character fonts are located in bit plane 2 and, in some implementations, bit plane 3 of the display memory.

The memory plane, or planes, dedicated to holding the character sets, are each segmented into four blocks of 16 Kbytes each for the EGA and eight blocks of 8 Kbytes each for the VGA. In the EGA, the first 8 Kbytes of each of these four buffers is dedicated to a character font. Four fonts, each 256 characters long, may be loaded in memory simultaneously. In the VGA, all 8 Kbytes of each of the eight buffers are dedicated to the character fonts. In both the EGA and the VGA, only two of these four fonts may be active at a time, allowing a maximum of 512 different characters on the screen at one time.

In some implementations, character sets with character boxes wider than 8 bits are allowed. These characters may be up to 16 pixels wide. The left 8 bits of each scan line are stored in bit plane 2, and the right 8 bits of the scan lines are stored in bit plane 3.

Character Generator

The character generator consists of the dot patterns that represent each character in the character set. The character dot patterns are stored in character boxes, each of which is 32 bytes long. Bits set to 1 in the character font will be displayed in the foreground color, and bits reset to 0 will be displayed in the background color. The display memory consists of four display planes called bit planes, each being 32 Kbytes long. In the alphanumeric modes, bit plane 2 is used to hold the character generator. This limits the characters to an 8-bit-wide character box.

In the EGA, the single exception to this rule is the 9-by-14 monochrome character set. This 9-bit-wide character box is actually represented by 8 bits in the character generator. The ninth bit is derived from a copy of the eighth bit. For most characters, the 8-by-14 font is used to represent the 9-by-14 font. The difference, once displayed, is the additional column of background values in the 9-by-14 format.

Certain characters, however, require alternate font patterns to better utilize the 9-by-14 format. A supplemental character set is provided. The wider-bodied characters are represented in this new format and leave no blank column on the right side of the character. That is, the character foreground values extend to the far right limit of the character box. Once the character has been drawn, the ninth column of background colors will be drawn on the right of the character. Each character in this 9-by-14 supplement is represented in the BIOS character-generator bit patterns by 15 bytes of information. The first byte of each character is the ASCII code of the character that follows. These ASCII codes are necessary because all characters are not represented in the supplement. As a result, a simple indexed addressing scheme cannot be used. The characters included in the supplement include upper case *M, T, V, W, X, Y,* and *Z*. The lower case characters include *m, v,* and *w*. Symbolic characters including quotation marks, plus sign, and minus sign are included, along with six nonalphanumeric characters. The supplement is terminated with a 0 byte in the ASCII code location.

In the VGA, the characters sets are similar, with the exception of an additional 8-by-16 character set and a 9-by-16 alphanumeric supplement. These two fonts work in an identical fashion to that used by the 8-by-14 font and the 9-by-14 supplement in the EGA.

Input Parameters:

BH = The number of bytes per character. The maximum length of a character is 32 bytes. The character generator reserves 32 scan lines for each character, and each character will be stored in the 32 bytes regardless of the number of bytes per character. This facilitates rapid addressing. Because the number of bytes per character is specified, the BIOS routine knows how many bytes from the input user table to copy into each of the 32-byte character slots in the display memory.

BL = Block to Load. This dictates which of the four blocks of display memory dedicated to the character sets should be loaded.

CX = The number of characters to load. The number of characters is specified to let the BIOS routine know how many blocks of bytes associated with each character should be loaded into the display memory. The total number of bytes in the user array is equal to the number of bytes per character times the number of characters to load.

DX = The character offset into the selected block of memory. This value determines where in the display memory font area the incoming user character array should be loaded. The character patterns in the user character array are organized sequentially, with one character following the previous character. It is not necessary for the first character in the array to be the first character in the character set. This offset is specified to let the BIOS routine know where the user array should be loaded in the selected 8-Kbyte block in display memory.

ES:BP = The pointer to the user downloadable font contained in a sequential byte buffer. The ES register should contain the segment address of the array, and the BP register should contain the offset address of the array.

Output Parameters:

None.

Display Memory Affected:

Plane 2 of display memory beginning at the character offset times 32 and extending for the number of characters times 32. The "times 32" is needed because each character in the display buffer occupies 32 bytes, regardless of how many bytes it actually uses.

11.12.2   AH = 11, AL = 1: ROM Monochrome Set (with Reset) (EGA/VGA)

This subroutine loads the ROM-resident monochrome 9-by-14 character set into the selected 8-Kbyte block of memory in the display memory. It must be used only when the display is in an alphanumeric mode. Although the character width is 9 bits, the character box size is 8 bits wide. This function operates similarly to the Load User Character Set with Reset function above. Unlike that function, which loads a user-defined array into display memory, this function copies the 9-by-14 monochrome character set from ROM into the display memory. The entire character set is loaded into display memory.

The 9-by-14 monochrome character set consists of the 8-by-14 character set with supplemental 9-by-14 characters. Using this font size allows higher-resolution characters to be used when the display is operating in mode 7, which has a resolution of 720 dots per scan line. See the Load User Character Set with Reset BIOS call for details.

Input Parameters:

BL = The number of the block in display memory to load the 9-by-14 character font. This value may range from 0 to 3 in the EGA and from 0 to 7 in the VGA. It references the desired 8-Kbyte block of memory where this monochrome font should be loaded.

Output Parameters:

None.

Display Memory Affected:

The entire 8-Kbyte block of memory in display memory bit plane 2, and possibly bit plane 3, as specified in the Block Number parameter.

11.12.3   AH = 11, AL = 2: ROM 8x8 (with Reset) (EGA/VGA)

This function loads the ROM-resident 8-by-8 character set into the selected 8-Kbyte block of the display memory. This function operates similarly to the Load ROM Monochrome Character Set with Reset BIOS call. Unlike that function, which loads the 9-by-14 character set into display memory, this function copies the 8-by-8 character set into display memory. The entire character set is loaded.

This 8-by-8 font allows 43 lines of text to be displayed on a single screen when one of the 350-scan-line modes is active. It allows 60 lines of text to be displayed when the 480-line mode is active. All 8-bit-wide fonts allow 80 characters per line in the standard 640-pixel horizontal formats. See the Load ROM

Monochrome Character Set and the Load User Character Set with Reset BIOS calls for details.

Input Parameters:

BL = The number of the block in display memory to load the 8-by-8 character font. This value may range from 0 to 3 for the EGA and 0 to 7 for the VGA. It references the desired 8-Kbyte blocks of display memory where the 8-by-8 font should be loaded.

Output Parameters:

None.

Display Memory Affected:

The entire 8-Kbyte block in display memory bit plane 2, and possibly bit plane 3, as specified in the Block Number parameter.

11.12.4 AH = 11, AL = 3: Set Block Specifier (EGA/VGA)

This subroutine selects which of the character sets resident in the display memory should be used to determine the character dot pattern for a given character. In the EGA, four simultaneous character sets may be resident in display memory. In the VGA, eight simultaneous character sets may be resident in display memory. It is possible to have two of these resident character fonts loaded into display memory (active) at a time. Each character set is 256 characters long. When they are chained together, 512 unique characters can be displayed simultaneously.

Bit 3 of the character attribute byte is used either to select one of 16 foreground colors for the associated character or to choose from one of two resident character sets. Because each character set has 256 characters, an 8-bit-wide character code is required, thus utilizing the 8-bit character code. This leaves 8 bits in the character attribute byte to determine the character color, to determine the blinking status, and to select from one of the two character sets. All eight bits of the attribute byte can be dedicated to selecting the character color because it is possible to select one of 16 foreground colors and one of 16 background colors. In order to select blinking or not blinking and to select from one of the two character sets, it is necessary to double up on the function of two of the bits within the attribute byte. Bit 7 was selected to have the dual function of either being part of the background color code or being a switch for the blinking feature. Bit 3 was selected to have the dual function of either being part of the foreground color or being a switch for selecting one of the two character fonts.

When it is part of the foreground color, bit 3 is defined as the high-order bit of the four-bit foreground color field. If a 512-character set is desired, only eight unique foreground colors will be allowed, and the fourth bit, bit 3, will be dedicated to selecting one of the two active character sets. A switch in the attribute byte determines whether 16 foreground colors and one 256-character set or 8 foreground colors and two 256-character sets is used. Bit 3 of the attribute byte is used to select which of the two 256 character sets is selected if the values in the SA and SB fields are different.

The Character Map Select Register consists of two fields called the Character Generator Select A (SA) and the Character Generator Select B (SB) fields. Each of these fields may select one of the four or eight character fonts resident in display memory. If the values in both the SA and SB fields are identical, only one character set is active, and the system automatically considers bit 3 of the attribute byte to be part of the character foreground color code. Only one 256-character set is allowed. If the SA and SB fields are different, bit 3 is automatically assumed to be a switch that selects one of the two 256-character sets for its associated character code. Only one of eight foreground colors is possible per character.

In both the EGA and the VGA, it is recommended that the BIOS call at Int 10 hex, Set Palette Registers, be called before this Block Specifier call is invoked. The Set Individual Palette Register subfunction at AL = 00 hex should be used with the palette register number 12 hex selected by setting the BL Register to 12 hex. This register, number 12 hex, is not actually a palette register. It is the Color Plane Enable Register. If its value is set to 07 hex by setting the BH register to 07 hex, the value in the fourth bit, bit 3, of the character attribute byte is ignored when the color is generated. This is important because if bit 3 is being used to select one of the two character fonts, two character attribute bytes could have different values in bit 3, although both desire to be displayed in the same color.

Input Parameters:
BL = The value to load into the Character Map Select Register. This value contains the A and B fields. The format of this byte input parameter is identical to the bit fields of the Character Map Select Register. The map select fields in the Character Map Select Register on the EGA are shown in Figure 11.1.

In Figure 11.1, each of the fields SA and SB consists of two bits that allow the selection of one of four simultaneously loaded character sets.

The map select fields in the Character Map Select Register on the VGA are shown in Figure 11.2.

In Figure 11.2, each of the A and B select fields consists of three bits which allow the selection of one of eight simultaneously loaded character sets.

Output Parameters:
None.

EGA Registers Affected:
The Character Map Select Register.

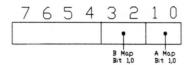

FIGURE 11.1 EGA Character Map Select Fields

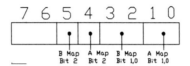

FIGURE 11.2 VGA Character Map Select Fields

11.12.5 AH = 11, AL = 04: ROM 8×16 Character Set (with Reset) (VGA)

This function loads the ROM-resident 8-by-16 character set into the selected 8-Kbyte block of the display memory. This function operates similarly to the Load ROM 8×8 Character Set with Reset BIOS call. Unlike that function, which loads the 8-by-8 character set into display memory, this function copies the 8-by-16 character set into display memory. The entire character set is loaded.

This 8-by-16 font allows 30 lines of text to be displayed on a single screen when one of the 480-scan-line modes is active. All 8-bit-wide fonts allow 80 characters per line in the standard 640-pixel horizontal formats. See the Load User Character Set with Reset BIOS calls for details.

Input Parameters:
BL = The number of the block in display memory to load the 8-by-8 character font. This value may range from 0 to 7 for the VGA. It references the desired 8-Kbyte blocks of display memory where the 8-by-16 font should be loaded.

Output Parameters:
None.

Display Memory Affected:
The entire 8-Kbyte block in display memory bit plane 2, and possibly bit plane 3, as specified in the Block Number parameter.

11.12.6 AH = 11, AL = 10: User Alpha Load (EGA/VGA)

This function loads a character set into one of the four or eight blocks of display memory reserved for the resident character sets. This function is nearly identical to the Load User Character Set AH = 11, AL = 0 function. The difference is that this function will recalculate several of the CRT Controller Registers (CRTC Registers) in the EGA/VGA. Recalculating these registers modifies the operational mode. It is modified according to the parameters input to this BIOS call. It should be noted that erratic results may occur if the recalculations are not close to the original values of the modified registers.

A second difference is that no Set Mode is automatically executed before the character set is downloaded. It is highly recommended to execute the Set Mode BIOS call immediately before invoking this function. In addition, the active display page must be 0 before this function is invoked. See the Load User Character Set with Reset function for details on downloading user character sets. Also see the Set Mode function for details on resetting the display mode.

Input Parameters:
BH = The number of bytes per character. The maximum length of a character is 32 bytes. Specifying the number of bytes per character lets the BIOS routine know how many bytes from the user table to copy into each of the 32-byte character slots in the display memory.

BL = Block to Load. This dictates which of the four or eight blocks of display memory dedicated to the character sets should be loaded.

CX = The number of characters to load. Specifying the number of characters lets the BIOS routine know how many blocks of bytes associated with each character to load into the display memory. The total number of bytes in the user array is equal to the number of bytes per character times the number of characters to load.

DX = The character offset into the selected block of memory. This value determines where to load the incoming user character array in the display memory font area. The character patterns in the user character array are organized sequentially, with one character following the previous character. It is not necessary for the first character in the array to be the first character in the character set. Specifying this offset lets the BIOS routine know where in the selected 8-Kbyte block in display memory the user array should be loaded.

ES:BP = The pointer to the user downloadable font contained in a sequential byte buffer. The ES register should contain the segment address of the array and the BP register should contain the offset address of the array.

Output Parameters:
None.

Display Memory Affected:
Plane 2 of display memory beginning at the character offset times 32 and extending for the number of characters times 32. The "times 32" is needed because each character in the display buffer occupies 32 bytes regardless of how many bytes per character are specified in the user array.

EGA Registers Affected:

Maximum Scan Line Register. The number of scan lines per character. Set equal to the bytes per character input parameter minus 1.

Cursor Start Register. Defines at which scan line in the character box to begin drawing the rectangular cursor block. In the EGA, this is set to the number of bytes per character parameter minus 1. This is the bottom line of the character box. In conjunction with the Cursor End Register (see below), this defines a cursor that fills the entire character box.

In the VGA, this is set to the number of bytes per character parameter minus 2. This is the next-to-the-bottom line of the character box. In conjunction with the Cursor End Register below, this defines a cursor that fills the bottom two lines of the character box.

Cursor End Register. Defines at which scan line in the character box to end drawing the rectangular cursor block. In the EGA, this is set to 0, which is the top line of the character box. In the VGA, it is set to the number of bytes per character parameter minus 1.

Vertical Display End Register. Determines the number of scan lines to include in the display portion of the screen. In the EGA/VGA, this is set according to the calculations in Equation 11.2 if the display is in a 350- or 480-scan-line display mode and according to the calculations in Equation 11.3 if the display is in a 200-scan-line display mode.

Equation 11.2 350 or 480-line Vertical Displacement

$$\text{Vertical Displacement} = (\text{the number of rows} + 1) \times (\text{the number of bytes per character}) - 1.$$

Equation 11.3 200-line Vertical Displacement

$$\text{Vertical Displacement} = (\text{the number of rows} + 1) \times (\text{the number of bytes per character} \times 2) - 1.$$

Overflow Register. The Vertical Display End (VDE) field of this register is adjusted. In the EGA, this field is bit 8 of the 9-bit Vertical Display End value. Bits 0–7 are contained in the Vertical Display End Register. In the VGA, this field is bits 8 and 9 of the 10-bit Vertical Display End value. Bits 0–7 are contained in the Vertical Display End Register.

In the VGA, two parameters are also affected by this BIOS call. The first is the number of character rows on the screen. It is modified according to Equation 11.4. In this equation, the number of scan lines is 200, 350, or 400. The 480-scan-line mode is applicable only in the graphics modes 11 hex and 12 hex. Thus, it is not relevant to this alphanumeric mode BIOS call.

Equation 11.4 Number of Rows on a Screen

Rows = (Number of Character rows / Character Height) − 1

The number of rows are calculated from Equation 11.4. The CRT length value, called CRT_LEN, is modified according to Equation 11.5.

Equation 11.5 CRT Length Parameter

CRT_LEN = (Rows+1) × (CRT_COLS × 2)

11.12.7   AH = 11 Hex, AL = 11 Hex: ROM Monochrome Set (EGA/VGA)

This function loads the ROM-resident monochrome 9-by-14 character set into the selected 8-KByte block of the display memory. It operates similarly to the Load ROM Monochrome Character Set with Reset BIOS call, number 01 hex, with the exception that the Set Mode function is not automatically invoked when this function is called. In addition, the active display page must be 0 before this function is invoked. Display parameters and registers will be modified according to the new font being loaded. See the Load ROM Monochrome Character Set with Reset BIOS call, number 01 hex, and the User Alpha Load BIOS call, number 10 hex, for details.

Input Parameters:
  BL = The number of the block in display memory to load the 9-by-14 character font. This value may range from 0 to 3 in the EGA and 0 to 7 in the VGA. It references one of 8-Kbyte blocks of memory reserved for the character fonts.

Output Parameters:
  None.

Display Memory Affected:
  The entire 8-Kbyte block of memory in display memory bit plane 2, and possibly bit plane 3, as specified in the Block Number parameter.

11.12.8   AH = 11 Hex, AL = 12 Hex: ROM 8×8 Set (EGA/VGA)

This call loads the ROM-resident 8-by-8 character set into the selected 8-Kbyte block of display memory. This call operates similarly to the Load ROM 8×8 Character Set with Reset BIOS call, 02 hex. Unlike that function, it does not automatically issue a Set Mode command. In addition, the active display page must be 0, and certain display parameters and registers will be modified. See the Load ROM Monochrome Character Set with Reset BIOS call, number 02 hex, and the User Alpha Load BIOS call, number 10 hex, for details.

Input Parameters:
  BL = The number of the block in display memory to load the 8-by-8 character font. This value may range from 0 to 3 for the EGA and 0 to 7 for the VGA. It references one of 8-Kbyte blocks of memory reserved for the character fonts.

Output Parameters:
  None.

Display Memory Affected:
  The entire 8-Kbyte block of memory in display memory bit plane 2, and possibly bit plane 3, as specified in the Block Number parameter.

11.12.9 AH = 11 Hex, AL = 14 Hex: ROM 8×16 Set (VGA Only)

This call loads the ROM-resident 8-by-16 character set into the selected 8-Kbyte block of display memory. This call operates similarly to the Load ROM 8×16 Character Set with Reset function, 04 hex. Unlike that function, it does not automatically issue a Set Mode command. In addition, the active display page must be 0, and certain display parameters and registers will be modified. See the Load ROM 8×16 Character Set with Reset BIOS call, number 04 hex, and the User Alpha Load BIOS call, number 10 hex, for details.

Input Parameters:
  BL = The number of the block in display memory to load the 8-by-16 character font. This value may range from 0 to 3 for the EGA and 0 to 7 for the VGA. It references one of the 8-Kbyte blocks of memory reserved for the character fonts.

Output Parameters:
  None.

Display Memory Affected:
  The entire 8-Kbyte block of memory in display memory bit plane 2, and possibly bit plane 3, as specified in the Block Number parameter.

11.12.10 AH = 11 Hex, AL = 20 Hex: User Graphics Characters INT 1FH 8×8 (EGA/VGA)

This call loads a pointer to an 8-by-8 user-defined character set. This pointer is loaded into the host memory as a vector to the second half of the 8-by-8 character font. This second half refers to characters with ASCII codes from 128 to 256. Only display modes 4, 5, and 6 utilize this pointer. The pointer can be read by invoking the Return Font BIOS call 30 hex with input parameter BH=01 hex. See the Return Font call for details.

In the graphics modes, it is necessary for the character set to reside in host memory because the display memory is dedicated to pixel graphics, and there is no room for character sets. Therefore, in order to allow downloadable character sets, the host memory must be used to store the character bit patterns. Either host RAM or BIOS memory space may be referenced by this pointer.

The character set pointer is a long pointer requiring a segment:offset register pair. In the special case of the 8 by 8 font, the character set pointer refers to the second 128 characters of the character set. The video interrupt 1F hex must be invoked to load the pointer to the second 128 characters, characters 128–255, of the character set. The Set Mode function should be invoked immediately preceding this function. See the Set Mode function for details.

In the EGA, a Parameter Table is maintained in host memory that provides a list of seven long pointers to other tables. Four of these tables are currently implemented, and three are reserved for future use. This Parameter Table is described in Table 11.14.

The Text Mode Auxiliary Character Generator Table and the Graphics Mode Auxiliary Character Generator Table apply to these character-set functions. The Text Mode Auxiliary Character Generator Table is described in Table 11.15.

This list is terminated when the mode value is equal to FF hex.

The Graphics Mode Auxiliary Character Generator Table is described in Table 11.16.

This list is terminated when the mode value is equal to FF hex.

Input Parameters:
ES:BP = The pointer to the user downloadable font contained in a sequential byte buffer. The ES register should contain the segment address of the array, and the BP register should contain the offset address of the array.

Output Parameters:
None.

Host Memory Affected:
The Graphics Mode Auxiliary Character Generator Table.

11.12.11   AH = 11 Hex, AL = 21 Hex: User Graphics Characters (EGA/VGA)

This call loads a pointer to a variable-sized user-defined character set. This pointer is loaded into the host memory through the Int 43 hex vector. This call is used in the graphics modes to point to the graphics characters. It is meant to be called immediately after a Set Mode command is issued. See the Load User Graphics Characters BIOS call 20 hex for details.

This pointer can be read by invoking the Return Font BIOS call 30 hex with input parameter BH=01 hex. See the Return Font call for details.

TABLE 11.14 Parameter Table

Offset (Hex)	Pointer Function (Long Pointer)
0	Video Parameter Table
4	Dynamic Save Area
8	Text Mode Auxiliary Character Generator Table
C	Graphics Mode Auxiliary Character Generator Table
10	Reserved
14	Reserved
18	Reserved

TABLE 11.15 Text Mode Auxiliary Character-Generator Table

Offset (hex)	Type	Function
0	Byte	Bytes per character
1	Byte	Block to load
2	Word	Count to store
4	Word	Character offset
6	Long	Font table pointer
A	Byte	Number of displayed rows. 0 = Maximum.
B	Byte	First mode value
C	Byte	Second mode value
.	.	.

TABLE 11.16 Graphics Mode Auxiliary Character-Generator Table

Offset (Hex)	Type	Function
0	Byte	Number of displayable rows. 0 = maximum.
1	Word	Bytes per character
3	Long	Font table pointer
7	Byte	First mode value
8	Byte	Second mode value
.	.	.

Input Parameters:

BL = Rows specifier. Defines how many character rows are to be on the screen. The standard number is 14, 25, or 43. In the EGA, the programmer may select any number by specifying a count of 0. The DL field then determines the number of rows. The possible row specifiers are listed in Table 11.17.

CX = The number of bytes per character. This dictates the height of the character box.

TABLE 11.17 User Row Specifier

Rows Specifier	Number of Rows
0 (EGA Only)	User-defined in the DL Register
1	14 rows
2	25 rows
3	43 rows

DL = In the EGA only, the number of character rows on the display if the rows specifier parameter is 0.

ES:BP = The pointer to the user downloadable font contained in a sequential byte buffer. The ES register should contain the segment address of the array, and the BP register should contain the offset address of the array.

Output Parameters:
None.

Host Memory Affected:
The Graphics Mode Auxiliary Character Generator Table.

11.12.12 AH = 11 Hex, AL = 22 Hex: Graphics Mode ROM 8×14 Character Set (EGA/VGA)

This call loads the long pointer to the 8-by-14 character set located in the EGA/VGA BIOS ROM. A description of the host memory parameter tables is discussed in Load User 8×8 Character Set Pointer BIOS call 20 hex. This pointer can be read back by invoking the Return Font BIOS call 30 hex with input parameter BH=02 hex. See the Return Font call for details.

Input Parameters:
BL = Rows specifier. Defines how many character rows are to be on the screen. The standard number is 14, 25, or 43. In the EGA, the programmer may select any number by specifying a count of 0. The DL field then determines the number of rows. The possible values for the row specifier are listed in Table 11.18.

In the VGA, the programmer is restricted to one of the three predetermined number of rows. Thus, the programmer must select 14, 25, or 43 rows on the screen.

DL = In the EGA, the number of character rows on the display if the rows specifier parameter is 0.

Output Parameters:
None.

Host Memory Affected:
The Graphics Mode Auxiliary Character Generator Table.

Table 11.18 8-by-14 Row Specifier

Rows Specifier	Number of Rows
0 (EGA Only)	User-defined in the DL register
1	14 rows
2	25 rows
3	43 rows

11.12.13   AH = 11 Hex, AL = 23 Hex: Graphics Mode ROM 8x8 Set (Double Dot) (EGA/VGA)

This call loads the long pointer to the lower half of the 8-by-8 character set located in the EGA/VGA BIOS ROM. A description of the host memory parameter tables is given in Load User 8x8 Character Set Pointer BIOS call number 12 hex. This pointer can be read by invoking the Return Font BIOS call 30 hex with input parameter BH = 03 hex. See the Return Font call for details.

Input Parameters:

BL = Rows specifier. Defines how many character rows are to be on the screen. The standard number is 14, 25, or 43. In the EGA, the programmer may select any number by specifying a count of 0. The DL field then determines the number of rows. The possible values for the row specifier are listed in Table 11.19.

In the VGA, the programmer is restricted to one of the three predetermined number of rows. Thus, the programmer must select 14, 25, or 43 rows on the screen.

DL = In the EGA, the number of character rows on the display if the rows specifier parameter is 0.

Output Parameters:

None.

Host Memory Affected:

The Graphics Mode Auxiliary Character Generator Table.

11.12.14   AH = 11 Hex, AL = 24 Hex: Graphics Mode ROM 8×16 Set (VGA)

This call loads the long pointer to the 8-by-16 character set located in the EGA BIOS ROM. A description of the host memory parameter tables is given in Load User 8x8 Character Set Pointer BIOS call number 12 hex. This pointer can be read by invoking the Return Font BIOS call 30 hex with input parameter BH = 08 hex. See the Return Font call for details.

TABLE 11.19 8-by-8 Row Specifier

Rows Specifier	Number of Rows
0 (EGA Only)	User-defined in the DL register
1	14 rows
2	25 rows
3	43 rows

TABLE 11.20 8-by-16 Row Specifier

Rows specifier	Number of rows
0	User-defined in the DL register
1	14 rows
2	25 rows
3	43 rows

Input Parameters:

BL = Rows specifier. Defines how many character rows are to be on the screen. The standard number is 14, 25, or 43. The possible values for the row specifier are listed in Table 11.20.

In the VGA, the programmer is restricted to one of the three predetermined number of rows. Thus, the programmer must select 14, 25, or 43 rows on the screen.

DL = In the EGA, the number of character rows on the display if the rows specifier parameter is 0.

Output Parameters:

None.

Host Memory Affected:

The Graphics Mode Auxiliary Character Generator Table.

11.12.15 AH = 11 Hex, AL = 30 Hex: Return Character Generator Information (EGA/VGA)

This call returns information related to the current character font to the calling program. The information returned includes the bytes per character, the number of character rows on the screen, and the pointer to one of the character sets. The programmer may select which of six pointers for the EGA or eight pointers for the VGA should be returned. These pointers indicate the starting location in host memory space of the respective character sets. The pointers returned to the calling program are listed in Table 11.21.

TABLE 11.21 Return Character Generator Information

Pointer Specifier	Adapter	Character Set Pointer Selected
0	EGA,VGA	Interrupt 1F hex (user 8-by-8 upper)
1	EGA,VGA	Interrupt 43 hex (user 8-by-8 lower, 8-by-14)
2	EGA,VGA	ROM 8-by-14
3	EGA,VGA	ROM 8-by-8 lower 128 characters
4	EGA,VGA	ROM 8-by-8 upper 128 characters
5	EGA,VGA	ROM 9-by-14 supplement
6	VGA	ROM 8-by-16
7	VGA	ROM 9-by-16 supplement

In addition to interrupt 10 hex, there are two video BIOS interrupts that affect the operation of the EGA/VGA font selection. These interrupts, 1F hex and 43 hex, specify the location of user-defined character sets resident in host memory. It is necessary to use host memory to store the downloadable character sets when in a graphics mode. This is necessary because all of the four display memory bit planes are reserved for graphics data. Unlike in the alphanumeric modes, in the graphics modes, bit planes 2 and 3 are not available to hold the character fonts.

The interrupt 1F hex pointer refers to the upper 128 characters of the 8-by-8 character set used in the graphics display modes 4, 5, or 6. The interrupt 43 hex pointer refers to the 8-by-14 character set or the lower 128 characters of the 8-by-8 character set.

There are three fonts loaded into the EGA ROM BIOS and five in the VGA ROM BIOS. The 8-by-8 font is special because it is split up into two character sets, one representing the lower 128 characters and the second representing the upper 128 characters. Initially, the 8-by-8 character font was split into two halves, each having 128 characters. It was believed that room could be saved by separating the graphics characters from the alphanumeric characters. In retrospect, this seems to have been a poor decision.

Input Parameters:
    BH = Pointer specifier. See Table 11.21.

Output Parameters:
    CX = The number of bytes per character in the selected character set.
    DL = In the EGA, the number of character rows on the screen; in the VGA, the number of character rows on the screen minus 1.
    ES = The segment pointer to the beginning of the selected character font. The entire address is specified in the ES:BP register pair.

BP = The offset pointer to the beginning of the selected character font. The entire address is specified in the ES:BP register pair.

11.13 ALTERNATE SELECT

The alternate select functions perform a variety of seemingly unrelated tasks. These tasks range from returning video information to selecting the number of scan lines in an alphanumeric mode.

11.13.1 AH = 12 Hex, AL = 0 Hex, BL = 10 Hex: Return Video Information (EGA/VGA)

This function returns information related to the current display mode and the configuration of the EGA/VGA. Information returned includes whether a color or monochrome mode is active, the amount of memory on the adapter, the status of the feature bits on the adapter feature connector, and the video configuration code. The video configuration code is determined from the four sense switches on the EGA and from the configuration set by the adapter POST on the VGA. There are no sense switches on the VGA.

Input Parameters:
  None.

Output Parameters:
  BH = Video Controller Mode.
  0 = Color. This indicates that several EGA/VGA registers are mapped into the host port space at 3Dx hex. The value of x depends on the selected register.
  1 = Monochrome. This indicates that several EGA/VGA registers are mapped into the host port space at 3Bx hex. The value of x depends on the selected register.
  BL = Memory Size. The two-bit code returned indicates the size of the display memory as follows:
  0 = 64 Kbytes
  1 = 128 Kbytes
  2 = 192 Kbytes
  3 = 256 Kbytes

  CH = Feature control bits. At power up, the feature bits FEAT0 and FEAT1, located on pin 19 and 17 respectively, are read and the values of these pins are recorded. This BIOS call returns the status of these bits as they appeared during power up. Subsequent changes made to these bits can be determined only by reading the DIA field of the Input Status #1 Register. See the Input Status #1 Register for details. This is valid on the EGA only.
  CL = Video configuration code. There are typically four sense switches located on the rear panel of EGA that dictate the desired configuration. Some EGA implementations utilize six sense switches, the additional two being used

for compatibility modes. The value returned as the configuration code indicates which display adapter is configured as the primary and secondary display adapter and which monitor is connected to it. Typical display adapters include the MDA, CGA, EGA, and VGA. Typical monitors include the monochrome, color RGBI, and enhanced color RrGgBb. Which adapters and monitors correspond to which configuration code varies with the particular manufacturer's version of the EGA/VGA adapter board.

11.13.2   AH = 12 Hex, AL = 0 Hex, BL = 20 Hex: Select Alternate Print Screen Routine (EGA/VGA)

This call allows a user-defined print-screen routine to be invoked instead of the print-screen handler normally invoked through the BIOS call. The normally used handler resides in host system BIOS and is called by the ROM interrupt 05 hex. This alternate print handler may be utilized to output the screen image to specific devices or to print all of the data on the screen if the EGA/VGA is in a nonstandard display mode that uses 43 rows per page or 132 columns per line.

When this Select Alternate Print Screen Routine function is invoked, the vector loaded into the EGA BIOS 05 hex interrupt is used to direct control to the proper print handler. It is the responsibility of the programmer to supply the print handler. In addition, the programmer must load the interrupt vector corresponding to interrupt 05 hex in location 14 hex of host memory.

The print-screen status is located in the EGA information buffer in host memory at address 500 hex. If the printer is offline or not ready, a timeout will occur and control will return to the calling program.

Input Parameters:
   None.

Output Parameters:
   None.

Host Memory Affected:
   500 hex = Print Screen Status. The codes in the status byte are described in the Table 11.22.

11.13.3   AH = 12 Hex, AL = 0 Hex, BL=30 Hex: Select Scan Lines for Alphanumeric Modes (VGA)

This call selects the number of scan lines and the default character set to use for an upcoming alphanumeric mode. The change takes effect at the next occurrence of a mode set. It is possible to configure the VGA to have either 200, 350, or 400 scan lines per screen in the alphanumeric modes. In addition, a 480-scan-line mode is possible in the graphics modes 11 hex and 12 hex. This feature provides some flexibility in the display modes.

TABLE 11.22 Print Screen Status Code

Value (Hex)	Meaning
0	Idle
1	Printing
FF	Error occurred during printing

Input Parameters:
　AL = The number of scan lines per page.
　=0　200 scan lines per page. (Can't be used in mode 7.)
　=1　350 scan lines per page.
　=2　400 scan lines per page.

Output Parameters:
　AL = Indicates that the call was valid or invalid.
　=12 hex　　　　Call was valid.
　=any other value.　Call was invalid.

Registers Affected:
　The Vertical Size (VS) field of the VGA Miscellaneous Output Register.

11.13.4　AH = 12 Hex, AL = 0 Hex, BL=31 Hex: Default Palette Loading During Mode Set (VGA)

This call selects whether the Palette Registers, Overscan Registers, and Color Registers will be loaded with default values during following mode sets. If this feature is disabled, these registers will remain untouched. Together with the clearing or not clearing of the display memory during a mode set, these calls provide the programmer with a certain amount of flexibility during mode sets.

Input Parameters:
　AL = Select or deselect the loading of the Palette Registers, Overscan Register, and Color Registers
　=0 Enable register loading during a mode set.
　=1 Do not load registers during a mode set.

Output Parameters:
　AL = Indicates that the call was valid or invalid.
　=12 hex　　　　Call was valid
　=any other value.　Call was invalid.

Registers Affected:
　Palette Registers, Overscan Registers, Color Registers, if enabled.

11.13.5 AH = 12 Hex, AL = 0 Hex, BL = 32 Hex: Video Enable/Disable (VGA)

This call selects whether the video should be enabled or disabled. The video input ports and the host address decoding are enabled or disabled as determined by this call. This is useful if more than one device is residing in the system with the same host port addresses or host memory addresses. It allows the VGA to be effectively pulled out of the system to avoid bus conflicts. This is especially important on systems where the VGA is part of the backplane.

Disabling the video can improve the data transfer speed when data is sent from the host to the VGA. The video refresh logic is not competing for the memory bus. When the video is enabled, both the host and the video refresh logic must compete for the display memory bus. Data transfer throughput increases of 3 to 1 were observed when loading the buffer with the video disabled as opposed to loading the buffer with the video screen enabled. A similar but less pronounced speed advantage is observed when the video screen is turned off. This can be accomplished by invoking the Video Screen On/Off BIOS call AH = 12 hex, BL = 36 hex.

Input Parameters:
   AL = Enable or disable the VGA video port and memory addressing.
   =0 Enable the video.
   =1 Disable the video.

Output Parameters:
   AL = Indicates that the call was valid or invalid.
   =12 hex   Call was valid
   =any other value.   Call was invalid.

Registers Affected

11.13.6 AH = 12 Hex, AL = 0 Hex, BL = 33 Hex: Summing to Gray Scales (VGA)

This call selects whether the colors in the Color Registers will be summed to convert the values in the Color Registers from colors to gray scales. The summing operation occurs during Mode Set and during calls that affect the Color Registers. All 256 Color Registers will be summed if this summing feature is enabled.

This call, like the Sum Color Values, performs a function similar to that performed by Gray Scale BIOS call AH=10 hex, AL = 1B hex. However, in this call no actual summing operation takes place. The composite color output from the Color Registers to the monitor is derived from the values of the three primary colors—red, green, and blue. These three primary color values are stored in each of the 256 Color Registers. Each primary color value ranges from

0 to 63. The higher the value is for each color, the brighter the color. The composite color observed on the monitor is derived by adding together the three values of red, green, and blue. When the values in each of the three primary colors are equal, the resultant color is a gray scale. The amount of intensity in each of the three colors determines the brightness value of the gray scale. This is similar to viewing a color video on a monochrome monitor.

A weighted sum is used to produce the gray scale value. The equation used is listed in Equation 11.6.

Equation 11.6 Summing to Gray Scale

$$Gray = (.30 \times Red) + (.59 \times Green) + (.11 \times Blue)$$

In this equation, the three primary colors refer to the values in the red, green, and blue components of each Color Register. The "gray scale" result of this equation is then loaded into the red, green, and blue components of the same Color Register. If the original color is a gray scale, the resultant color will also be a gray scale of the same intensity because the three multipliers sum to 1.0. When enabled, this operation modifies all 256 Color Registers.

The summing operation occurs during Mode Set and during operations that access the Color Registers. If implemented in C, this operation would be similar to Listing 11.2. The code in Listing 11.2 assumes that the three primary colors of each Color Register have been read from the Color Registers and loaded into the red, green and blue arrays.

LISTING 11.2 Summing to All Registers to Gray Scale

```
unsigned char Red[256], Blue[256], Green[256], Gray;
int i;
for (i=0; i<256; i++)
{ Gray = (.30 * Red[i])+(.59 * Green[i])+(.11 * Blue[i]);
  Red[i] = Gray;
  Green[i] = Gray;
  Blue[i] = Gray;
}
```

Input Parameters:
  AL = Enable or disable the Color Registers summing.
  =0 Enable the summing.
  =1 Disable the summing.

Output Parameters:
  AL = Indicates that the call was valid or invalid.

TABLE 11.23 Cursor Type During Cursor Emulation

Cursor Type	Parameters Set	Adjustable Cursor Type
Bit 5=1	None	No
Start End<=3	Overbar	No
Start+2>= End	Underline	Yes
Start <= 2 or End <		
Start	Full Block	Yes
Start > 2 Half	Half Block	Yes

=12 hex   Call was valid
=any other value.   Call was invalid.

Registers Affected:
If enabled, all 256 Color Registers.

11.13.7 AH = 12 Hex, AL = 0 Hex, BL = 34 Hex: Cursor Emulation (VGA)

This call selects whether the cursor will be drawn according to the current character definition. The cursor shape is initialized to be a horizontal line two scan lines wide at the bottom of the character box. If the emulation mode is active, the cursor will be drawn according to the current character height. Calls made to Set Cursor Type, the BIOS call at AH=01 hex, will cause software to be invoked automatically. This software will determine the type of cursor and whether any modifications are needed because of the new cursor height.

If there is no cursor or an overbar cursor, no modifications are made. If there is an underline cursor, a full-block cursor or a half-block cursor, adjustments are made. These states are determined by the Start and End parameters passed to the Set Cursor Type call. The values are listed in Table 11.23.

If the program detects that adjustments are active and the start or end of the cursor are out of bounds, adjustments are made until neither the Start Cursor nor End Cursor occur out of bounds. The adjustments made if the Start or End Cursor are out of bounds are listed in Table 11.24.

Input Parameters:
AL = Enable or disable the cursor emulation mode.
=0 Enable the cursor emulation.
=1 Disable the cursor emulation.

Output Parameters:
AL = Indicates that the call was valid or invalid.
=12 hex   Call was valid
=any other value. Call was invalid.

TABLE 11.24 Start and End Cursor Adjustments

Cursor Type	Start and End Cursor Adjustments.
Full Block	Modify End to the last line in the character box.
Half Block	Modify Start to be equal to the scan line half way in the character height. Modify End to the bottom scan line of the box.
Height > 16	An underline cursor is positioned on the last line in the character box.

11.13.8 AH = 12 Hex, AL = 0 Hex, BL = 35 Hex: Display Switch (VGA)

This call allows the programmer to select between the Personal System/2 Display Adapter and the video adapter that resides on the system motherboard. The system motherboard is also referred to as the *planar*. The addresses in the host I/O space of the input/output ports, the addresses in host memory address space of the display memory, and the BIOS routines may be configured to cause bus conflicts. If this is the case, it is necessary to disable one of the video systems before enabling the other.

At power-up, the power-on self-test (POST) determines if there are multiple display adapters resident. If there is an addressing conflict between the planar video and the adapter video, the POST initializes the adapter video and disables the planar video. If there is no addressing conflict, the POST initializes both video systems.

If the adapter video and the planar video are in conflict, only one can be active at a time. This BIOS call is used to select which video should be active and which should be inactive. In order for the BIOS routine to be able to make a system active or inactive, it must have access to a 128-byte buffer to save the current display state. It is necessary for the BIOS to store the current display state of each of the video systems in two such buffers. The programmer must call this BIOS routine twice to intitialize both buffers. This is accomplished by invoking this BIOS call with the AL input parameter set to a 0 for the adapter video and a 1 for the planar video. The programmer must provide the routine with a long pointer to a 128-byte buffer for both of these calls.

Subsequent switching of the active video can be accomplished by switching the active video off and switching the inactive video on. These functions are invoked by setting the AL input parameter to 2 and 3 respectively.

Input Parameters:

AL = Desired function of call.

=0 Switch off the adapter video. This also saves the system status in the buffer pointed to by the ES:DX register pair. The adapter video is enabled at the power-on self-test (POST). This call is useful when the display adapter is being changed for the first time after POST. It would be called first to disable the adapter video and to save the display state. It would then be followed by a call to this routine to switch on the planar video using the AL = 1 option.

=1 Switch on the planar video. This also saves the system status in the buffer pointed to by the ES:DX register pair. Because the planar video is disabled at POST, this call will be useful when changing the display adapter for the first time after POST.

=2 Switch off the active video. Assuming that either the planar video or the adapter video is active, a call to this routine switches whichever video is active to an inactive state. This would precede a call to this routine to switch on the inactive video using the AL=4 option.

=3 Switch on the inactive video. The inactive video will be made active. No buffers are initialized as they are in options AL = 0 and AL = 1.

Output Parameters:
AL = Indicates that the call was valid or invalid.
=12 hex   Call was valid
=any other value. Call was invalid.

11.13.9   AH = 12 Hex, AL = 0 Hex, BL = 36 Hex: Video Screen On/Off (VGA)

This call selects whether the video outputs to the display monitor should be enabled or disabled. This provides a convenient way for turning off the display which can improve the data-transfer speed from the host to the VGA by eliminating the video refresh logic's demand for the memory bus. When the video screen is turned on, both the host and the video refresh logic must compete for the display memory bus. Data transfer throughput increases of 2 to 1 are observed when the buffer is loaded with the video screen off as opposed to with the video screen on. A similar but even more pronounced speed advantage is observed when the entire video system is disabled. This can be accomplished by invoking the Video Enable/Disable BIOS call AH = 12 hex, BL = 32 hex.

Turning off the video screen is also beneficial to the monitor when the monitor is not in use. It protects the phosphor from being burned out at specific locations but does not require turning on and off the power to the monitor.

Several software products incorporate this video screen on/off feature into a memory resident program that senses when a specified amount of time has passed without a keyboard keystrike. The program concludes from the inactivity at the keyboard that the user is not at the monitor; it therefore turns off the screen. Any keystrike will turn it on again.

Input Parameters:
AL = Enable or disable the VGA video port and memory addressing.
=0 Turn on the video.
=1 Turn off the video.

Output Parameters:
    AL = Indicates that the call was valid or invalid.
    =12 hex   Call was valid
    =any other value. Call was invalid.

Registers Affected:
    The Screen Off (SO) field of the Clocking Mode Register.

11.14   WRITING A STRING OF CHARACTERS

11.14.1   AH = 13 Hex: Write String of Characters (EGA/VGA)

This call writes a string of one or more characters to the specified page of the display. This function uses the Write TTY function to write the data to the display. The Write TTY feature handles carriage returns (0D hex), line feeds (0A hex), backspace (08 hex) and bell (07 hex) characters as control characters rather than printable characters. The "line feed" control code causes the screen to be scrolled when it is encountered at the bottom of the active display page.

There are four variations of the Write TTY function; the appropriate variation is selected by the Format Code parameter in the AL register. Two of the four options consider the input character string to consist entirely of character codes. The string is written to the display with a common attribute byte. This value of this attribute byte is also input to the BIOS call. The other two options consider the input character string to consist of alternating character codes and attribute bytes. This allows each individual character to have its own unique attribute.

The Write TTY function normally moves the cursor one position to the right for every character that is output, somewhat as a typewriter does. Two of these options leave the cursor position unmodified. The other two options leave the cursor positioned at the end of the string just written to the display.

This function exhibits a few peculiarities. Although the function can write to pages other than the active page, the active page will scroll. When the host processor is an Intel 80286 microprocessor, as is the case in AT computers, the page parameter in BH is ignored, and the data is always written to the active page.

When the input character string consists of alternating character and attribute bytes, it is assumed that each character code is followed by an attribute byte. Together, each of these pairs determines the character dot pattern, colors, and blinking. The special carriage-movement characters are not printable on the screen and therefore require no attribute byte. These characters are loaded into the input character string with no attribute byte, causing strings of consecutive character codes to occur in the input parameter array with no separating attribute bytes.

TABLE 11.25 Write String Options

Format Code	Function	Cursor Motion
0	Character,character	None
1	Character,character	Moves to end of string
2	Character,attribute	None
3	Character,attribute	Moves to end of string

Input Parameters:

AL = Option code. The code selects which of the four types of write string operations is desired. The possible options and their associated functions are listed in Table 11.25.

BH = Page number. Directs the output to the selected page. The number of possible pages depends on the display mode and the amount of memory resident on the adapter.

BL = Attribute byte if the Format Code in AL is a 0 or 1. This attribute byte is associated with all of the printable characters in the string that are output to the display.

CX = Length of the string. In this function, as in the Write TTY function, the length is limited by the screen size in the alphanumeric modes and by the end of the current line if one of the display graphics modes is used.

DH = Cursor row position to begin writing the character string.

DL = Cursor column position to begin writing the character string.

ES = Pointer to the segment of the input string. The entire long pointer is input in the ES:BP register pair.

BP = Pointer to the offset of the input string. The entire long pointer is input in the ES:BP register pair.

Host Memory Affected:

450 Cursor position.

11.15 RETURN CONDITION OF THE VGA

Three BIOS calls are provided to return information regarding the state of the VGA. These include reading and writing the display combination code, returning the functionality/state information, and saving and restoring the video state.

11.15.1 AH = 1B Hex: Read/Write Display Combination Code (VGA)

This call reads or writes the Display Combination Code (DCC) into low memory. This call is meant to be used as a system function and typically is not invoked by the applications programmer. This call is invoked by the Power-on Self-test

TABLE 11.26 Display Combination Codes (DCC)

Code	Description	Monitor
0	Monochrome Display Adapter (MDA)	No monitor
1	Monochrome Display Adapter (MDA)	Monochrome
2	Color Graphics Adapter (CGA).	Color
7	Personal System/2 Display Adapter	Monochrome
8	Personal System/2 Display Adapter	Color

(POST) to initialize the BIOS. It reads or writes to the active video system and to the inactive video system.

The Display Combination Codes are listed in Table 11.26. The monitor information is not supported when the VGA is in a dual-screen configuration.

Input Parameters:
AL = Selects whether the call performs a read or write of the DCC.
=0 Read the Display Combination Code (DCC).
=1 Write the Display Combination Code (DCC).
BH = Inactive video system Display Combination Code (DCC).
BL = Active video system Display Combination Code (DCC).

Output Parameters:
AL = Indicates that the call was valid or invalid.
=1A hex   Call was valid
=any other value. Call was invalid.
BH = Inactive video system Display Combination Code (DCC).
BL = Active video system (DCC).

Registers Affected:
None.

Host Memory Affected:
Low memory storage location for the Display Combination Code (DCC).

11.15.2   AH = 1B Hex: Return Functionality/State Information (VGA)

This call reads the functionality/state table and returns the table to the calling routine. The table is loaded into a buffer that is pointed to by a long pointer passed to the call.

Input Parameters:
BX = Implementation type. Currently, this value must be 0.
ES = Pointer to the offset of the functionality/state table. The entire long pointer is input in the ES:DI register pair.

DI = Pointer to the segment of the functionality/state table. The entire long pointer is input in the ES:DI register pair.

Output Parameters:
AL = Indicates that the call was valid or invalid.
=1B hex   Call was valid
=any other value.   Call was invalid.

Host Memory Affected:
The array as pointed to by the ES:DI long pointer.

11.15.3   AH = 1C Hex: Save/Restore Video State (VGA)

This call either reads the active video state and returns the information from the video system to a host buffer or writes the active video state to the video system from the host buffer. The buffer is pointed to by the long pointer passed to this call in the ES:BX register pair. This call is not supported in dual-screen configurations when the active adapter is an alternate adapter—that is, the Monochrome Display Adapter or the Color Display Adapter.

This call has three options that allow the programmer to store any or all combinations of the video hardware state, the video data areas, and the video palette state and the Color Registers.

Input Parameters:
AL = Call option indicating desired function.

=0 Return the size of the save or restore buffer depending on the value passed in the selection field in the CX register.

=1 Save the video state by reading the desired values in the selection field in the CX registers and sending this data back to the host memory buffer. The host memory buffer is pointed to by the long pointer in the ES:BX register pair.

=2 Restore the video state by writing the desired values, as indicated in the selection field in the CX registers from the host buffer and loading this data into the video system. The host memory buffer is pointed to by the long pointer in the ES:BX register pair.

CX = Selection of areas of the video system to save or restore. Any or all of these areas can be saved by setting the associated bits 0 through 2 in CX register. Setting the bit to 1 causes the associated video area to be saved or restored. For example, if bits 0 and 1 are set, both the video hardware state and the video data areas will be saved or restored.

   bit 0 = Video hardware state.
   bit 1 = Video data areas.
   bit 2 = Video DAC state and Color Registers.

ES = Pointer to the offset of the save/restore buffer. The entire long pointer is input in the ES:BX register pair.

BX = Pointer to the segment of the save/restore buffer. The entire long pointer is input in the ES:BX register pair.

Output Parameters:

AL = Indicates that the call was valid or invalid.

=1C hex   Call was valid

=any other value. Call was invalid.

BX = The size block count of the save or restore buffer when the "return size" selection is invoked, which happens when the AL = 0 option is used.

Chapter 12

Programming Examples

12.1 LIST OF PROGRAM LISTINGS

EGA/VGA Control Routines

EGA/VGA Alphanumeric Routines

EGA/VGA Graphics Routines

EGA/VGA Window Routines

EGA/VGA Character Font Routines

EGA/VGA Character Font Routines

EGA/VGA Color-manipulation Routines

Special Effects Routines

Listing	Name	Applicable Adapter	Function	Page No.
12.78	LineComp	EGA/VGA	Load the Line Compare Register	593
12.78	StartAdr	EGA/VGA	Load the Starting Address Registers	593
12.78	PreRow	EGA/VGA	Load the Preset Row Scan Register	593
12.78	Offset	EGA/VGA	Load the Offset Register	593
12.79	PelPan	EGA/VGA	Load the Pel Panning Register	594

EGA/VGA General Register Routines

Listing	Name	Applicable Adapter	Function	Page No.
12.80	ModeReg	EGA/VGA	Set the Mode Register	595
12.80	MapMask	EGA/VGA	Set the Map Mask Register	595
12.80	SetRes	EGA/VGA	Set the Set/Reset Register	595
12.80	ESetRes	EGA/VGA	Set the Enable Set/Reset Register	595
12.80	ReadMap	EGA/VGA	Set the Read Map Register	595
12.80	BitMask	EGA/VGA	Set the Bit Mask Register	595

12.2 INTRODUCTION

The C and assembly language routines presented in this chapter illustrate the operation of the EGA/VGA and constitute the basis of a programmer's toolbox. The examples selected are in an understandable yet flexible format. More than 100 routines are included. These routines by no means form a complete toolbox; space would not allow one. Programmers can obtain a disk containing the source code to this toolbox for all of the routines presented in this chapter. Purchasing instructions are provided on the last page of this book.

The routines provide control of the EGA/VGA, read and write alphanumerics, points, lines, and images. Routines utilize the downloadable character fonts, the Palette and Color Registers, and the General Registers. The List of Program Listings at the beginning of this chapter enumerates the routines that are meant to be called by the programmer. Several other routines included in this chapter are invoked by these routines. These lower-order routines are also well documented and may be used by the programmer.

The assembly language routines rely on a macro file that contains a few useful macro expansions. This file is named macros.asm. The examples presented in this chapter should be preceded with the text shown in Listing 12.1. The "if1...endif" conditional assembly alerts the assembler to include the file in pass 1 of the assembly process.

LISTING 12.1 Including the Macro Expansions File

```
if1
include macros.asm
endif
```

Each assembly language file must also include a definition of the public variables and a definition of the code segment. A definition of the stack segment and data segment would also be necessary; however, none of the routines in this chapter require either a stack or data segment other than those defined by the C routines. The files must be closed with a declaration of the end of the code segment and the end of the program file. These definitions are shown in Listing 12.2.

LISTING 12.2 Defining Variables for Assembly Files

```
public _SetMode
codeseg segment byte public 'code'
assume cs:codeseg

        ... routine 1 ...
        ... routine 2 ...
        ... routine N ...

codeseg     ends
     end
```

The Microsoft C compiler Version 5 convention is assumed throughout this book. However, the C code is highly portable and should operate on any C compiler with little modification. The assembly language routines also assume the Microsoft C Version 5 interface conventions. Using other compilers may require the names of these routines and the code segment names to be modified.

The large model C compiler is assumed for all of the assembly language routines. Thus, the first parameter is found at [bp+6]. Byte and integer variables occupy two bytes on the stack, and array pointers require four bytes. These routines can be made to operate on medium model C compilers by modifying these references to the parameters on the stack.

12.3 NAMING CONVENTIONS

Trying to maintain order in naming routines is difficult if not impossible. Because of the file name limitations in DOS, the subroutine names in these examples are limited to eight characters. Most compilers can handle more than eight characters. However, files can become confused when DOS truncates the letters in the name to eight characters.

The display is considered as an external device on the system. Data is written from the host to the display. As a result, names of routines that involve transferring data from the host to the display usually begin with *Wr*. Similarly, names of routines that read data from the display to the host usually begin with *Rd*.

The names of routines that process along a horizontal direction contain an *H*; those that have a vertical orientation will contain a *V*. Rows are called *row*, and columns are called *col*. This can present a problem because colors can also be abbreviated as "col".

Routines that process alphanumerics contain an A; those that process graphics contain a *G* in a conspicuous location. An example of the former is *RdAWin*, which would stand for **Read** an **A**lphanumerics **Win**dow.

One source of common confusion is the mixing of rows and columns with *X* and *Y* addresses. Rows are measured along the vertical dimension, from top to bottom, and are thus associated with the *Y* dimension. Columns are measured along the horizontal dimension, from left to right, and are associated with the *X* dimension. Because the vertical dimension counts from top to bottom, the *Y* value increments as it goes down. This means that a 1 pixel beneath a second will have a greater *Y* value.

12.4 MACRO EXPANSIONS

The assembly language routines in this chapter rely on a set of macro expansions. These expansions help to simplify the code and do not require the processor overhead of a subroutine.

The two routines Prefix and Postfix in Listing 12.3 are used in nearly every assembly language routine in which parameters are accessed off of the stack or where the segment or index registers are modified.

LISTING 12.3 Setting Up and Closing Out Assembly Routines

```
; set up the assembly language program for "C" compatibility
; invoked by:
; Prefix

Prefix macro
     push bp            ;save the base pointer
     mov  bp,sp         ;copy the stack pointer
     push ds
     push es            ;save the registers
     push si
     push di
     endm

; close out the assembly language program consistent with "C"
```

```
;   conventions.
; invoked by:
;   Postfix

Postfix macro
    pop di
    pop si          ;restore the registers
    pop es
    pop ds
    mov sp,bp       ;restore the stack pointer
    pop bp          ;restore the base pointer
    ret             ;return from subroutine
    endm
```

When the size of the font is changed, it is necessary to set and reset the cursor-emulation bit of the miscellaneous byte in the BIOS storage area of host memory. The miscellaneous byte is located at 0000:0487 hex. The routines Set487 and Reset487 in Listing 12.4 perform these functions.

LISTING 12.4   Setting and Resetting the Cursor Emulation

```
; set the cursor emulation bit, bit 0 of the miscellaneous byte
; invoked by
;   Set487

Set487 macro
    sub ax,ax       ;set bit 0 of 0000:0487h
    mov ds,ax
    mov si,0487h
    or  byte    ptr ds:[si],01
    endm

;reset the cursor emulation bit, bit 0 of the miscellaneous byte
; invoked by
;   ReSet487

Reset487 macro
    sub ax,ax       ;reset bit 0 of 0000:0487h
    mov ds,ax
    mov si,0487h
    and byte ptr ds:[si],0FEh
    endm
```

12.5   CONTROLLING AND READING THE STATUS OF THE DISPLAY

The state of the EGA/VGA adapters is best controlled through the BIOS calls. The most fundamental element of control is to turn off and turn on the video drivers. This tends to save the screen during periods of non-use as well as speeding up data transfers. The routine OnVideo turns on the video, and OffVideo turns off the video. Both are listed in Listing 12.5.

LISTING 12.5   Turning the Video Screen On and Off

```
; Enable the video screen
; Calling protocol
; OnVideo();

_OnVideo proc far
    mov bl,36h      ;turn on the video
    mov ax,1200h
    int 10h
    ret
_OnVideo endp

; Disable the video screen
; Calling protocol
; OffVideo();

_OffVideo proc far
    mov bl,36h      ;turn off the video
    mov ax,1201h
    int 10h
    ret
_OffVideo           endp
```

The display mode and active display page can be set using the SetMode and SetPage routines in Listing 12.6. The BIOS calls are used in these routines because of the complexity involved in trying to perform the functions directly.

LISTING 12.6   Setting the Active Display Mode and Page

```
; Set the display mode
; Input parameters
;   mode            desired display mode

; Calling protocol
; SetMode(mode);

_SetMode proc far
    Prefix
    mov ah,00h      ;get current video state
    mov al,[bp+6]   ;get desired mode
    int 10h         ;interrupt 10
```

```
      Postfix
_SetMode endp

; Select a new active page
; Input parameters:
; page    desired page

; Calling protocol:
; SetPage(page);

_SetPage    proc    far
      Prefix
      mov al,[bp+6]    ;get active page
      mov ah,05        ;select page
      int 10h          ;call bios
      Postfix
_SetPage    endp
```

The EGA/VGA operational parameters can be determined by reading the control registers in the VGA, invoking the return parameter BIOS calls in the EGA/VGA, or reading the section of host RAM memory dedicated for the BIOS storage. The routines that follow utilize the BIOS calls.

It is far easier to determine the condition of the VGA than it is to determine the condition of the EGA. The VGA provides a much richer combination of routines for use in determining its state. All of the control registers on the VGA can be read; few of the EGA registers can be read.

Even though the registers can be read on the VGA, not all parameters are easily determined by the registers alone. The active display mode and active display page are two examples. These functions are not associated with a single register, but rather are determined by the combination of several of the registers.

Certain display parameters can be returned by calling the GetStat routine in Listing 12.7. It should be noted that this BIOS call requires the BP register. The assembly language routine must preserve the state of the BP register because it uses it to access parameters on the stack and to hold the value of the stack pointer. This is accomplished by PUSHing BP before the BIOS call and POPping BP after the BIOS call.

LISTING 12.7   Get the Display Status

```
; Determine the video state
; Output parameters:
;        buf[]      host "C" integer array containing the mode,
;                   number of columns and active page.
;        buf[0]     active display page
;        buf[1]     active display mode
```

```
;         buf[2]      number of character columns per row
;         buf[3]      number of rows per screen
; Calling parameters
;   GetStat(buf);
_GetStat proc far
    Prefix
    push bp          ;save the base pointer
    les  di,[bp+6]   ;point to the "C" buffer

; determine the mode, page, and number of columns
    mov ah,0fh       ;get current video state
    int 10h          ;interrupt 10
    mov dx,ax        ;save ah=number of chars al=mode
    xor ax,ax        ;clear AX

; send back page, mode and # columns
    mov  al,bh
    stosw            ;send back active page in buf[0]
    mov  al,dl
    stosw            ;send back mode in buf[1]
    mov  al,dh
    stosw            ;send back number of columns in buf[2]

; determine the rows per screen by calling the "Font Info" call
    push es
    mov  ax,1130h    ;font
    mov  bh,2        ;use any selection selection
    int  10h         ;NOTE this destroys ES:BP
    xor  dh,dh
    inc  dx          ;number of char rows = dl+1
    pop  es
    mov  es:[di],dx  ;send back the number or rows buf[3]

    pop  bp          ;restore the base pointer
    Postfix
_GetStat endp
```

The active display mode, the active display page, the number of character columns per row, and the number of rows on the screen can be read by calling this routine. Internally, the routine uses two BIOS calls to determine this information. The four parameters are provided in a four-integer-long C buffer, as shown in Table 12.1.

12.6 DETERMINING THE STATE OF THE VGA ADAPTER

The VGA adapter provides two BIOS calls that access control parameters. The first reads the functionality/state information, returning the values to a host buffer. This call is implemented in the routine RdInfo in Listing 12.8.

TABLE 12.1 Returned Parameters from the GetStat Routine

Buffer Index	Parameter
0	Active display page
1	Active display mode
2	Number of character columns per row
3	Number of rows per screen

LISTING 12.8 Read the Functionality/State Information

```
; Return the functionality/state information
; Output parameters:
; buf    "C" buffer to return state data
; Calling protocol:
; RdInfo(buf);

_RdInfo    proc far
    Prefix

    les di,[bp+6]    ;get buffer pointer
    mov bx,00        ;implementation type must be 0
    mov ah,1Bh       ;1B=return information
    int 10h          ;save data

    Postfix
_RdInfo endp
```

The second BIOS call, named Save/Restore Video State, allows the programmer to read the video state into a buffer, modify the state, and then return the state to normal by writing the state back to the adapter. Any combination of the video hardware, video data areas, or video Color Palette and Color Registers can be saved or restored, according to Table 12.2. Any combination of the bits in the CX register can be used in the same call to provide a concatenation of the different areas. When more than one area is selected, the order in which the data is read from or written to the table is determined by the precedence of Table 12.2. The first element in the table, the video hardware state, will always appear first if it is included. It will be followed by video data area, if it is present, followed by the Color Palette and Color Registers, if it is present.

The VState routine in Listing 12.9 can be used either to save or to restore these video areas.

TABLE 12.2 Areas of the Video Adapter to Save or Restore

Code (CX)	Area of Adapter
bit 0	Video hardware state
bit 1	Video data areas
bit 2	Video Color Palette and Color Registers

LISTING 12.9 Saving and Restoring the Video State

```
; Save or restore the video state
; Input parameters
; buf           "C" buffer which contains the video state data
;               during an AL=2, restore video state, request.
; state         desired data to save or restore
;                       01 = video hardware
;                       02 = video data areas
;                       03 = dac state and color registers
; operation     desired operation
;                       00 = return size of buffer
;                       01 = save video state
;                       02 = restore video state

; Output parameters
; buf        "C" buffer which will contain the video state data
;               during an AL=1, save video state, request.
; size          The size of the buffer, only returned during
;               a AL=0 selection requesting a return size

; Calling protocol
; size = Vidstate(buf,state,operation);

_VidState proc far
    Prefix

    les bx,[bp+6]    ;get buffer pointer
    mov cx,[bp+10]   ;get state to save
    mov ah,1Ch       ;1C=save/restore
    mov al,[bp+12]   ;desired operation
    int 10h          ;save data

    mov ax,bx        ;get return buffer size block count

    Postfix
_VidState        endp
```

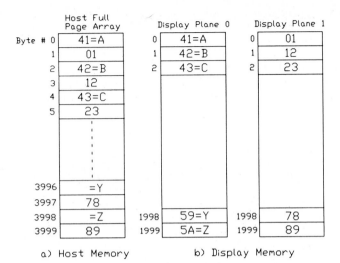

FIGURE 12.1 Alphanumeric Display Memory

12.7 ALPHANUMERICS

Alphanumeric processing involves reading and writing characters to the display. There are several ways in which the programmer can read or write single characters or character strings. The orientation of the character strings is typically horizontal; however, routines are presented that allow any orientation using variable intercharacter spacing.

Because the EGA/VGA allows color alphanumerics, each character is represented by a character code and attribute byte. The organization of the display memory is illustrated in Figure 12.1.

It is useful to write a string with one attribute for the entire string. At other times, it is useful to write a string with an attribute associated with each character. In addition, a string of characters can be written without modifying the attribute bytes.

12.7.1 Reading and Writing Characters

The most basic alphanumeric functions are reading and writing characters. The RdChar and WrChar routines in Listing 12.10 read and write a character to the display memory. The character is input or output through an integer whose lower byte contains the character code and whose upper byte contains the attribute byte.

LISTING 12.10 Reading and Writing a Character

```
; Read a character and its attribute.
; Input parameters
; page      desired display page
; row       desired row
; column    desired column

; Output parameters
; charatr   returned character and attribute.
;    The character code is returned in the lower byte.
;    The attribute byte is returned in the upper byte.

; Calling protocol:
; charatr = RdChar(page,row,column);

_RdChar proc far
    Prefix

    mov bh,[bp+6]    ;get active page
    mov dh,[bp+8]    ;get row
    mov dl,[bp+10]   ;get column
    mov ah,2         ;move Cursor to desired position
    int 10h

    mov ah,8    ;read character and attribute into ax
    int 10h     ;return with character/ attribute in ax

    Postfix
_RdChar endp

; Output a character and its attribute to the display
; Input parameters
; page      desired display page
; row       desired row
; column    desired column
; charatr   returned character and attribute.
;    The character code is in the lower byte.
;    The attribute byte is in the upper byte.

; Calling protocol:
; Wrchar(page,charatr,row,column);

_WrChar proc far
    Prefix

    mov bh,[bp+6]    ;get desired page
    mov dh,[bp+10]   ;get row to start string
    mov dl,[bp+12]   ;get column to start string
    mov ah,2         ;move Cursor to desired position
    int 10h
```

```
        mov ax,[bp+8]   ;get char in al, get attribute in ah
        mov bl,ah       ;attribute is in bl
        mov cx,01       ;one character
        mov ah,09       ;write character/attribute
        int 10h         ;display character/attribute

        Postfix
_WrChar endp
```

12.7.2 Character Strings

Writing a string of characters in any orientation is accomplished by the WrChars routine in Listing 12.11. The string of characters input to the routine is in a byte array containing only the character codes. Thus, the standard C string manipulation routines can be utilized. The string will be written in one color that is determined by the foreground and background colors also input to the routine. The first character is read at position row, column. The location of each subsequent character is determined by adding the row and column increment values.

LISTING 12.11   Writing a Character String in Any Orientation

```
; Write a string of characters in a given color on the display
; Input parameters:
; page      desired display page
; row       desired row
; column    desired column
; rowinc    # of vertical spaces to place between characters
; colinc    # of horizontal spaces to place between characters
; for       desired foreground color of the string
; back      desired background color of the string
; string    host "C" byte array of the character codes

; Calling protocol:
; WrChars(page,string,for,back,row,column,rowInc,colInc);

_WrChars proc     far
        Prefix

        mov dh,[bp+16]  ;get row
        mov dl,[bp+18]  ;get column
        mov ah,02       ;set cursor position
        mov bh,[bp+6]   ;desired page
        int 10h         ;set cursor row=dh

        lds si,[bp+8]   ;get address of string
        mov bl,[bp+12]  ;get foreground color
```

```
        and bl,0fh
        mov al,[bp+14]    ;get background color
        mov cx,04         ;put for and back into
        shl al,cl         ;attribute
        and al,0f0h
        or  bl,al         ;attribute is in bl
dloop:
        mov ah,09
        mov al,[si]       ;get character
        cmp al,00         ;last character in string ?
        jz  ddone         ;exit if done

        inc si            ;next char in string
        mov bh,[bp+6]     ;page #
        mov cx,01         ;one character
        int 10h           ;display
        add dh,[bp+20]    ;add row increment
        add dl,[bp+22]    ;add column increment
        mov ah,02         ;set cursor position
        mov bh,[bp+6]     ;get page
        int 10h           ;set cursor row=dh col=dl
        jmp dloop         ;display another if not

ddone:
    Postfix
_WrChars endp
```

Reading a string of characters in any orientation is accomplished by the RdChars routine in Listing 12.12. The string of characters output from this routine is sent to a C byte array. Because every character on the display is represented by a character and attribute byte, the array contains alternating character codes and attribute bytes. The first character is read at position row, column. The location of each subsequent character is determined by adding the row and column increment values.

LISTING 12.12   Reading a Character String in Any Orientation

```
; Read a string of characters and attributes from the display
; Input parameters:
; page      desired display page
; string    byte "C" array to place the characters and attribute
;           pairs. Even bytes as character and odd
;           bytes as attributes.
; numchar   number of characters to read from the display
; row       desired row
```

```
; column    desired column
; rowInc    # of vertical spaces to place between characters
; colInc    # of horizontal spaces to place between characters

; Calling protocol:
; RdChars(page,string,numchar,row,column,rowInc,colInc);

_RdChars           proc          far
      Prefix

      les di,[bp+8]    ;get pointer
      mov cx,[bp+12]   ;get number of characters
      mov bh,[bp+6]    ;get active page
      mov dh,[bp+14]   ;get row
      mov dl,[bp+16]   ;get column

re1:  mov ah,02        ;request set cursor
      int 10h          ;call bios

      mov ah,8         ;read character and attribute into ax
      int 10h

      stosw            ;return char and attribute
      add dh,[bp+18]   ;add row increment
      add dl,[bp+20]   ;add column increment
      loop re1         ;repeat til done

      Postfix
_RdChars    endp
```

Horizontal strings can be written to the character using either the WrStrCm routine in Listing 12.13 or the WrStrAm routine in Listing 12.14. The WrStrCm routine writes a character string in one color; the WrStrAm routine writes an attribute with each character.

A character string and an attribute byte are passed as parameters to the WrStrCm routine. The character string contains only the character codes, which makes it directly compatible with the C string-handling routines. The end of the character string is terminated by a *null* character, which is equivalent to a 0 and which may be invoked in C by using the "\0" notation within the string. The attribute byte is written into the display memory associated with each character. Note that the BP register must be saved because the BIOS call will modify it. The string is written beginning at the current cursor position.

The cursor position is moved at the end of the BIOS call to the position immediately following the last character output. If the last character represents the end of a line, the cursor is placed on the far left position of the following line. If the string fills the last line, the cursor is positioned down one line, forcing a scroll up one line. If this presents undesirable results, the BIOS call AH = 13 hex, AL = 01 hex can be changed to AH = 13 hex, AL = 00.

LISTING 12.13 Writing a String with a Single Attribute

```
; Write a string to the display at the current cursor position
;   and page. The cursor is moved to the end of the string at
;   completion.
; Input parameters:
; string Host "C" byte string of character codes terminated
;                 with a null=0 code.
; attr            Attribute for string of characters
; cursor          Determines whether the cursor will be moved
;                 or not
;                 at the end of the string output.
;                 0 = don't move cursor
;                 1 = move cursor
; calling protocol
; WrStrC(string,attr,cursor);

_WrStrC proc far
    Prefix
    push bp          ;save base point register
    mov di,bp        ;use di to access stack

;   determine # of characters in the string
    xor cx,cx        ;determine # of chars in string
    lds si,[di+6]    ;point to character array

a1: lodsb            ;get character and increment si
    cmp al,0         ;end of string
    jz  a2           ;exit if end
    inc cx
    cmp cx,500       ;character limit of 500
    jb  a1           ;exit if more than limit

a2: cmp cx,0
    jz  a3           ;exit if no characters
    push cx

    les bp,[di+6]    ;get pointer to string
    mov ah,0fh       ;get status
    int 10h          ;ah=# char, bh=page
    mov ah,03        ;get cursor position
    int 10h          ;dh,dl=position

    pop cx
    mov bl,[di+10]   ;get attribute
    mov al,[di+12]   ;get cursor control
    mov ah,13h       ;output string, move cursor
    int 10h

    pop bp           ;restore base point register
```

```
a3: Postfix
_WrStrC endp
```

A character string consisting of alternating character codes and attribute bytes is passed to the WrStrCA routine. The string is terminated by a *null* character in the character position at the end of the string. A null character is equivalent to a 0 and may be invoked in C by using the "\0" notation within the string.

LISTING 12.14 Writing a String of Character/Attribute Pairs

```
; Write a string to the display at the current cursor position
;    and page.
; Input parameters:
; charatr Host "C" array consisting of a string of character
;                  attribute pairs. The string is terminated by
;                  a null = 0 in the character position.
; cursor           Determines whether the cursor will be moved
;                  or not at the end of the string output.
;                  0 = don't move cursor
;                  1 = move cursor
; calling protocol
;    WrStrA(charatr,cursor);
_WrStrA proc far
        Prefix
        push bp          ;save base pointer

;    determine # of characters in the string
        xor cx,cx        ;determine # of chars in string
        lds si,[bp+6]    ;point to character array
        push ds
        push si

b1: lodsw                ;get character and increment si
    cmp al,0             ;end of string
    jz  b2               ;exit if end
    inc cx
    cmp cx,500           ;character limit of 500
    jb b1                ;exit if more than limit

b2: cmp cx,0
    jz  b3               ;exit if no characters
    push cx

    mov ah,0fh           ;get status
    int 10h              ;ah=# char, bh=page
```

```
        mov ah,03          ;get cursor position
        int 10h            ;dh,dl=position cx type

        pop cx
        pop bp
        pop es
        mov al,[bp+10]     ;get cursor control
        add al,2           ;make code be 2=no move or 3=move
        mov ah,13h         ;output string, move cursor
        int 10h

        pop bp             ;restore base pointer
b3: Postfix

_WrStrA endp
```

Two additional horizontal character string routines, WrString and RepChar, are provided in Listing 12.15. These routines write a character, repeated character, or string of characters but do not modify the character attribute bytes already in the display memory. For example, a character or string written at row 10 will be displayed in whatever attribute was previously assigned to the characters in row 10.

In the graphics mode, the attribute of a character must be supplied for each character drawn. An attribute is provided to these routines for the graphics modes. In the alphanumeric modes, the attribute is ignored.

In WrString, a character string is written to the display. The character string contains only the character codes, which makes it directly compatible with the C string-handling routines. The character string is terminated by a null character at the end of the character string. A null character is equivalent to a 0 and may be invoked in C by using the "\0" notation within the string. This routine utilizes the Write TTY BIOS call. Cursor-control characters present in the character string affect the positioning of the cursor, as shown in Table 12.3.

The RepChar routine writes a character a number of times into the display

TABLE 12.3 Cursor-control Characters

Character	*Action*
CR	Move the cursor to column 0 of the current row
LF	Move the cursor down one row. If the cursor is on the bottom row, scroll the screen up one row. The attribute of the new bottom row is the same as the attribute present in column 0 of the previous bottom row.
BS	Move the cursor one position to the left
BEL	Ring the bell

memory at the current cursor position. This routine is useful for initializing areas of the screen with a character pattern.

LISTING 12.15 Writing a String of Characters Only

```
; Output a character string. In the alphanumerics modes, no
;   attributes are modified. In the graphics modes, the
;   character string is written with the "grattr" attribute.
; Input parameters:
; page              desired display page
; string            character string containing character codes,
;                   terminated in a "null" character
; grattr            -graphics mode only- character attribute
; Calling protocol:
; WrString(page,string,grattr);

_WrString proc far
    Prefix

; select the active page
    mov al,[bp+6]   ;get desired page
    mov ah,05       ;select page
    int 10h

    lds si,[bp+8]   ;point to character array
    mov bl,[bp+12]  ;graphics mode attribute

runloop:
    lodsb           ;get the character into AL
    cmp al,0        ;end of string AL=null?
    jz  done        ;exit if end
    mov ah,0Eh      ;tty write character only
    int 10h
    jmp runloop     ;repeat til done
done:
    Postfix
_WrString endp

; Output a single character a multiple number of times.
;   In the alphanumerics modes, no attributes are modified.
;   In the graphics modes, the character string is written
;   with the "grattr" attribute.
; Input parameters:
; page              desired display page
; char              character to repeat
; numchar           number of times to write the character
; grattr            -graphics mode only- character attribute
```

```
; Calling protocol:
; RepChar(page,char,numchar,grattr);

_RepChar proc far
    Prefix
    mov cx,[bp+10]   ;get repeat count
    mov bh,[bp+6]    ;get desired page
    mov al,[bp+8]    ;get character
    mov bl,[bp+12]   ;graphics mode attribute
    mov ah,0Ah       ;write character only
    int 10h

    Postfix
_RepChar endp
```

12.8 CURSOR CONTROL

The programmer can do three basic things with the cursor: move it, read its position, and define its shape. The routines Cursor, RdCurs, and DefCurs in Listing 12.16 perform these functions. All three of these routines use the cursor-related BIOS calls.

LISTING 12.16 Cursor Control

```
; Set the position of the cursor
; Input parameters:
; row               = row number to position cursor
; column            = column number to position cursor
; page              = page number for cursor
; Calling protocol:
; Cursor(page,row,column);

_Cursor proc far
    Prefix

    mov ah,02        ;request set cursor
    mov bh,[bp+6]    ;page number
    mov dh,[bp+8]    ;row
    mov dl,[bp+10]   ;column
    int 10h          ;call BIOS to position cursor

    Postfix
_Cursor endp

; Read the cursor position
; Input parameters:
; page              current page to read cursor from
```

```
; Output parameters:
; RowCol              integer value containing the cursor position
;                     The row is returned in the low-order byte.
;                     The column is returned in the high-order byte


; Calling protocol:
; RowCol = RdCurs(page);

_RdCurs proc far
    Prefix
    mov ah,03         ;read cursor position
    mov bh,[bp+6]     ;page number
    int 10h           ;row in dh, col in dl

    mov al,dh         ;return row
    mov ah,dl         ;return column

    Postfix
_RdCurs endp

; Define the shape of the cursor.
; Input parameters:
; start               starting scan line for the cursor
; end                 ending scan line for the cursor

; Calling protocol:
; DefCurs(start,end);

_DefCurs proc far
    Prefix

    mov ch,[bp+6]     ;get Cursor start
    mov cl,[bp+8]     ;get Cursor end
    and cx,1fffh      ;assure bits (7-5) of high=0
    mov ah,01         ;read character and attribute into ax
    int 10h           ;define the cursor

    Postfix
_DefCurs endp
```

12.9 SCROLLING

Two scrolling routines are provided to scroll a window on the active display
page. The ScrollUp and ScrollDw routines in Listing 12.17 scroll a portion of
the display up or down. The upper left and lower right corner row and column
coordinates are passed to the routine, along with the number of lines to scroll.
For example, a window that consists of 20 character rows can be scrolled one
row up, causing all 20 rows to shift up one character row. In this example, the
top row would scroll out of the window, and the bottom row would be filled
with an attribute byte. The attribute byte consists of a foreground and background color that are also input as parameters.

LISTING 12.17 Scrolling Alphanumerics

```
; Scroll a window upward
; Input parameters:
; num                  number of lines to scroll the window upward
; ulRow,ulCol          upper left row, column coordinate of window
; brRow,brCol          bottom right row, column coordinate of window
; for                  foreground color to be scrolled in
; back                 background color to be scrolled in

; Calling protocol:
; ScrollUp(num,ulRow,ulCol,blRow,blCol,for,back);

_ScrollUp    proc     far
    Prefix
    mov bh,[bp+16]   ;get foreground color
    and bh,0fh
    mov al,[bp+18]   ;get background color
    mov cx,04        ;put for and back into
    shl al,cl        ;attribute
    and al,0f0h

    or  bh,al        ;attribute is in bh
    mov ah,06        ;request scroll screen up
    mov al,[bp+6]    ;get number of lines to scroll
    mov ch,[bp+8]    ;get upper left corner row
    mov cl,[bp+10]   ; get upper left corner column
    mov dh,[bp+12]   ; get lower right corner row
    mov dl,[bp+14]   ;get lower right corner column
    int 10h          ;call bios
    Postfix
_ScrollUp endp

; Scroll a window downward
; Input parameters:
; num                  number of lines to scroll the window
;                      downward
; ulRow,ulCol          upper left row, column coordinate of window
; brRow,brCol          bottom right row, column coordinate of window
; for                  foreground color to be scrolled in
; back                 background color to be scrolled in

; Calling protocol:
; ScrollDw(num,ulRow,ulCol,blRow,blCol,for,back);

_ScrollDw proc far
    Prefix
    mov bh,[bp+16]   ;get foreground color
    and bh,0fh
    mov al,[bp+18]   ;get background color
```

```
        mov cx,04          ;put for and back into
        shl al,cl          ;attribute
        and al,0f0h
        or  bh,al          ;attribute is in bh
        mov ah,07          ;request scroll screen down
        mov al,[bp+6]      ;get number of lines to scroll
        mov ch,[bp+8]      ;get upper left corner row
        mov cl,[bp+10]     ; get upper left corner column
        mov dh,[bp+12]     ; get lower right corner row
        mov dl,[bp+14]     ;get lower right corner column
        int 10h            ;call bios
        Postfix
_ScrollDw endp
```

12.10 DRAWING A POINT

A single point may occupy from one to four planes of memory. The BIOS call Draw Point utilizes the Set/Reset Register to access the point. Typically, points are drawn in combination with other points. In these cases, it may be appropriate to modify the point-drawing algorithm, bypassing the BIOS call to achieve faster throughputs.

This is the case in the line-drawing routine presented in section 12.11. Care must be taken to insure that the state of the display adapter is handled properly. For example, eliminating redundant loading or reloading of a register may achieve a time savings. However, doing so may leave the display adapter in an undesirable condition if these registers are not properly reset.

The point-drawing routine, named DrawPnt, uses the standard BIOS call. Similarly, the point-reading routine, named ReadPnt, also uses the standard BIOS call. Both are listed in Listing 12.18. Although straightforward, these are included here as examples of invoking a BIOS routine through an assembly language routine.

LISTING 12.18 Reading and Writing a Point

```
; Read a point from the display memory
; Input parameters:
; page display page to receive point
; x,y horizontal and vertical coordinates of point to read

; Output parameter:
; color color of point read

; Calling protocol
; color = ReadPnt(page,x,y);
```

```
_ReadPnt proc far
    Prefix              ;push appropriate registers

    mov bh,[bp+6]       ;get page number
    mov cx,[bp+8]       ;get x address column
    mov dx,[bp+10]      ;get y address row
    mov ah,0Dh          ;read dot
    int 10h             ;read the pixel
    xor ah,ah           ;return color in ax

    Postfix
_ReadPnt endp

; Draw a point into display memory
; Input parameters
; page                 display page to receive point
; x,y                  horizontal and vertical coordinates of point
; color                color to draw point

; Calling protocol
; DrawPnt(page,x,y,color);

_DrawPnt proc far
    Prefix              ;push appropriate registers

    mov bh,[bp+6]       ;get page number
    mov cx,[bp+8]       ;get x address column
    mov dx,[bp+10]      ;get y address row
    mov al,[bp+12]      ;get color
    mov ah,0Ch          ;write dot
    int 10h             ;draw the point

    Postfix
_DrawPnt endp
```

12.11 DRAWING A LINE

Probably the most important algorithm in computer graphics is the line-drawing algorithm. The algorithm included in this book is highly optimized for the EGA/VGA. This routine, called Line, is split up into three separate line-drawing algorithms. Two of these are special cases of line-drawing concerned with drawing horizontal and vertical lines. The third routine uses Bresenham's line algorithm and is used for all other lines. All three of these routines are specially written for optimal operation on the EGA/VGA.

The line algorithm is invoked by calling either the routine Line or the routine Line13. The Line routine operates in all display modes that use 16 colors. These modes utilize all four display modes to store a single pixel value. Eight pixels are represented in each byte of all four display planes. The Line13 routine is written specifically for the display mode 13 hex. This mode allows 256 simultaneous colors, with each byte containing the 8-bit color code for each pixel.

The Line and Line13 routine rely on special-purpose line-drawing routines to handle the horizontal and vertical lines. These horizontal and vertical line routines may be called directly if a horizontal or vertical line is required.

12.11.1 Horizontal Lines

The EGA/VGA configured in display modes D, E, F, or 10 hex, or the VGA configured in modes 11 or 12 hex, stores bits from eight neighboring horizontal pixels in a single byte of display memory. The smallest element that can be written to display memory is a single byte. Using a point-drawing routine to draw every point in the line would be wasteful because up to eight pixels can be handled in a single byte operation.

The algorithm used to draw horizontal lines calls upon one of three subroutines to actually draw the line. The routine DhLine in Listing 12.19 is called to draw horizontal lines.

LISTING 12.19 Drawing Horizontal Lines

```
/* Draw a horizontal line
Input parameters:
page                = desired page
x1                  = x-coordinate 1
x2                  = x-coordinate 2
y                   = y-coordinate
color               = desired color of line
Calling protocol: */
 HLine(page,x1,x2,y,color)

int x1,x2,y,color; char page;
{ int i,x,x1byte,x2byte,nbyte,address,dx,offset=80;
 char mask1,mask2;

ESetRes(15); SetRes(color);

if(x1>x2)
 {x=x1; x1=x2; x2=x;} /* reverse x-coordinates */

x1byte=x1>>3; x2byte=x2>>3;
dx=x2byte-x1byte; nbyte=(x2byte-x1byte)-1;
address = (y*offset) + x1byte;

switch (x1%8) {
case 0: mask1=0xff; break; case 1: mask1=0x7f; break;
case 2: mask1=0x3f; break; case 3: mask1=0x1f; break;
case 4: mask1=0x0f; break; case 5: mask1=0x07; break;
case 6: mask1=0x03; break; case 7: mask1=0x01; break; }
```

```
switch (x2%8) {
case 0: mask2=0x80; break; case 1: mask2=0xc0; break;
case 2: mask2=0xe0; break; case 3: mask2=0xf0; break;
case 4: mask2=0xf8; break; case 5: mask2=0xfc; break;
case 6: mask2=0xfe; break; case 7: mask2=0xff; break; }
  if(dx == 0)       Hsub1(address,mask1&mask2);
  if(dx == 1)       HSub2(address,mask1,mask2);
  if(dx>1)          HSub3(address,mask1,mask2,nbyte);
BitMask(255); ESetRes(0); MapMask(15); }
```

The first subroutine, named Hsub1, draws a horizontal line if the entire line is located in one byte. The second, named Hsub2, draws a horizontal line if the line fits in two bytes, and the third, Hsub3, draws a horizontal line when more than three bytes are contained. Dhline determines a bit mask for the single byte in Hsub1 and two masks, one for each end, for Hsub2 and Hsub3.

All of the bytes contained in the center of the line have a mask of FF hex because all bits represent pixels contained in the line. These mask values contain a 1 in the bit positions of pixels contained in the line and a 0 in the other bit positions. These masks are loaded into the Bit Mask Register. The Set/Reset Register and Enable Set/Reset Register are utilized in Write Mode 0 to actually draw the points. The Bit Mask Register and the Enable Set/Reset Register are reset by DhLine at completion of the line. Figure 12.2 illustrates these three cases.

The three assembly language routines used to draw a horizontal line are listed in Listing 12.20.

LISTING 12.20 Horizontal Line Subroutines

```
; Output a horizontal line containing one byte
; Input assumptions:
; Enable Set/Reset Register set to desired planes
; Set/Reset Register set to color

; Output assumptions:
; Enable Set/Reset Register reset to 0
; Bit Mask Register reset to 0xff

; Input parameters:
; address           = display memory offset address
; mask              = mask of single byte containing the line

; Calling protocol:
; Hsub1(addr,mask);
```

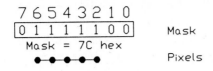

a) One Byte

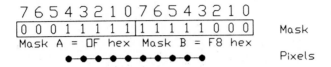

b) Two Bytes

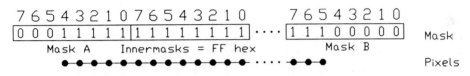

c) >Two Bytes

FIGURE 12.2 Drawing a Horizontal Line

```
_Hsub1 proc far
    Prefix

    mov ax,0A000h    ;point to display base
    mov ds,ax
    mov si,[bp+6]    ;get address

; load the Bit Mask Register
    mov ax,3ceh      ;point to mask address
    mov dx,ax
    mov al,8         ;8 for mask
    out dx,al
    inc dx           ;point to mask register
    mov al,[bp+8]    ;get mask
    out dx,al        ;load mask

    mov al,ds:[si]   ;dummy read before write
    mov ds:[si],al   ;output color

    Postfix
_Hsub1 endp

; Output a horizontal line contained within two bytes
; Input assumptions:
; Enable Set/Reset Register set to desired planes
```

```
; Set/Reset Register set to color

; Output assumptions:
; Enable Set/Reset Register reset to 0
; Bit Mask Register reset to 0xff

; Input parameters:
; address              = display memory offset address
; mask1                = first (left) mask for line
; mask2                = second (right) mask for line

; Calling protocol:
; HSub2(address,mask1,mask2);
_HSub2 proc far
    Prefix

    mov ax,0A000h    ;point to display base
    mov ds,ax
    mov si,[bp+6]    ;get address

; load the Bit Mask Register
    mov ax,3ceh      ;point to mask address
    mov dx,ax
    mov al,8         ;8 for mask
    out dx,al
    inc dx           ;point to mask register

; output first byte
    mov al,[bp+8]    ;get mask1
    out dx,al        ;load Bit Mask with mask1

    mov al,ds:[si]   ;dummy read
    mov ds:[si],al   ;output color

; output second byte
    mov al,[bp+10]   ;get mask2
    out dx,al        ;load Bit Mask with mask2

    inc si           ;increment address
    mov al,ds:[si]   ;dummy read
    mov ds:[si],al   ;output color

    Postfix
_HSub2 endp

; Output a horizontal line containing more than two bytes

; Input assumptions:
; Enable Set/Reset Register set to desired planes
; Set/Reset Register set to color

; Output assumptions:
; Enable Set/Reset Register reset to 0
; Bit Mask Register reset to 0xff
```

```
; Input parameters:
; address          = display memory offset address
; mask1            = first (left) mask for line
; mask2            = second (right) mask for line
; nbytes           = number of bytes in between end bytes
; Calling protocol:
; HSub3(address,color,mask1,mask2,nbyte);
_HSub3 proc far
    Prefix

    mov ax,0A000h   ;point to display base
    mov ds,ax
    mov si,[bp+6]   ;get address

; load the Bit Mask Register
    mov ax,3ceh     ;point to mask address
    mov dx,ax
    mov al,8        ;8 for mask
    out dx,al
    inc dx  .       ;point to mask register

; load the first byte
    mov al,[bp+8]   ;get mask1
    out dx,al       ;load Bit Mask with mask1

    mov al,ds:[si]  ;dummy read
    mov ds:[si],al  ;output color

; load the middle bytes
    mov al,0ffh
    out dx,al       ;load mask with FFh = all on

    mov cx,[bp+12]  ;get repeat count
o31: inc si         ;increment address
    mov al,ds:[si]  ;dummy read
    mov ds:[si],al  ;output color to a middle byte
    loop o31

; load the end byte
    mov al,[bp+10]  ;get mask2
    out dx,al       ;load Bit Mask with mask2

    inc si          ;increment address
    mov al,ds:[si]  ;dummy read
    mov ds:[si],al  ;output color

    Postfix
_HSub3 endp
```

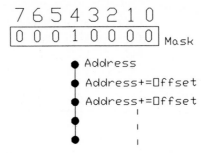

FIGURE 12.3 Drawing a Vertical Line

12.11.2 Vertical Lines

The address of a pixel in these specific display modes is determined by the byte address of display memory and the pixel location within this addressed byte. Drawing vertical lines involves setting up a mask that determines which pixel in the accessed bytes is affected. This mask does not have to change during the drawing of the line because the line is vertical. The address of each point in the line is determined by adding or subtracting, an offset value from the display address. This offset value represents the distance in bytes between two neighboring vertical pixels. Figure 12.3 illustrates the drawing of a vertical line.

Vertical lines are drawn by calling the routine VLine in Listing 12.21.

LISTING 12.21 Drawing a Vertical Line

```
/* Draw a vertical line.
Input Parameters:
 page                 = desired page
 x                    = x-coordinate
 y1                   = y-coordinate 1
 y2                   = y-coordinate 2
 color                = desired color

Calling Protocol:    */
 VLine(page,x,y1,y2,color)

int y1,y2,x,color,page;
{ int i,dy,address,offset=80,mask;

 mask = 0x80 >> (x&7); /* bit plane mask */

/* initialize the registers */
 ESetRes(0x0f); BitMask(mask); SetRes(color);
```

```
  if (y2>y1)
  { dy = 1+y2-y1; /* number of points to draw */
      address = (y1*offset)+(x>>3); /* starting address */
  }
  else
  { dy = 1+y1-y2; /* number of points to draw */
      address = (y2*offset)+(x>>3); /* starting address */
  }
  USub(address,dy,offset);
  BitMask(255); ESetRes(0);
}
```

The VLine routine determines the starting address of the line and calls the
assembly language routine VSub in Listing 12.22 to actually draw the line.

LISTING 12.22   Vertical Line Subroutine

```
; Draw a vertical line subroutine
; Input assumptions:
; Set/Reset Register is loaded with color.
; Enable Set/Reset Register has desired planes enabled.
; Bit Mask Register has correct bit enabled.

; Output assumptions:
; Enable Set/Reset Register reset to 0.
; Bit Mask Register reset to 0xFF.

; Calling protocol:
; VSub(address,dy,offset);

_VSub proc far
    Prefix

    mov ax,0A000h    ;set up the address
    mov ds,ax        ;get segment

;   load the working registers with the variables
    mov si,[bp+6]    ;load pointer to display memory
    mov cx,[bp+8]    ;load # of points into the CX
    mov bx,[bp+10]   ;get offset

; operational loop
runloop:
;   read before write
    mov ah,ds:[si]   ;dummy read
    mov ds:[si],ah   ;output color through set/reset

;   add the offset to the address pointer
    add si,bx        ;y (address) += offset
```

```
;   repeat til done
    loop runloop

    Postfix
_VSub endp
```

12.11.3 Bresenham's Algorithm

Bresenham's line algorithm is based on the fact that a line is composed of a series of connected pixels. An independent axis is selected, and a single pixel is drawn at each point on the independent axis between the two end points. Thus, the one coordinate of the point is determined by incrementing that variable. Because the points are connected, the dependent variable can either maintain the same value or change it by one. A decision variable is used to determine whether or not the dependent variable should change.

The independent variable is selected depending on the slope of the line. The line's slope is determined by dividing the number of pixels included in one direction by the number of pixels included in the other. The axis that has the greater number of pixels is elected as the independent axis. This process is illustrated in Figure 12.4.

In Figure 12.4, a line is drawn from coordinates $X = 20$, $Y = 10$ to the point $X = 32$, $Y = 18$. The difference is determined by Equation 12.1. Because the XDIF is larger, the X axis is selected as the independent variable.

Equation 12.1 Determining the Independent Axis

$$XDIF = ABS\ (X2 - X1) = ABS\ (32 - 20) = 12$$

$$YDIF = ABS\ (Y2 - Y1) = ABS\ (18 - 10) = 8$$

The line is drawn by incrementing the X variable from 20 to 32. At each point, a decision is made regarding the incrementing of the Y variable. The decision variable is modified at each point by one of two constants. The constants are determined by the slope of the line. These constants assume that the independent axis increments positively. This constrains the direction of the lines to positive motion along the independent variable. The dependent variable can move in a positive or negative direction. The difference of the independent variable, as calculated in Equation 12.1, must be positive. In other words, $X2$ or $Y2$ must be greater than $X1$ or $Y1$ respectively. It is a simple matter to reverse the coordinates, $X2 = X1$, $X1 = X2$, $Y1 = Y2$, and $Y2=Y1$, if the line moves in the wrong direction.

Implementing the algorithm for the EGA/VGA requires heuristic knowledge of the operation of the EGA/VGA. At each coordinate, along the independent axis, a point is drawn. The BIOS Draw Point call could be invoked to draw each point. This provides portability but imposes a heavy penalty because of

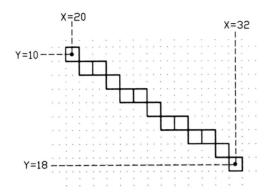

FIGURE 12.4   Drawing a Line

the unnecessary operations that occur. An optimum implementation is presented that minimizes the unnecessary operations.

Drawing a line on the EGA/VGA is accomplished using different techniques depending on which of the X or Y axes is the independent axis. The exception is display mode 13 hex on the VGA. This mode assigns one byte for every pixel, creating a symmetry between the horizontal and vertical axes. In all other modes, multiple pixels are represented in a single byte. A group of pixels—two, four, or eight—is accessed by a single address. An individual pixel within this byte is accessed by a bit position. When data is written to the display memory, a mask locates the pixel within the addressed byte. Moving to the left or right on the display involves shifting a pattern within the mask, and moving up or down involves adding an offset to the address. A single pixel can be accessed by representing the pixel with a 1 in one bit of the mask.

Moving one pixel to the left involves shifting this mask byte one bit to the left. Similarly, moving one pixel to the right involves shifting the mask one bit to the right. If an overflow occurs when shifting to the left, the address is decremented and the mask is reset to 01 hex. If an overflow occurs when shifting to the right, the address is incremented and the mask is reset to 80 hex. This is illustrated in Table 12.4 for the display modes D, E, F, 10, 11, and 12 hex. Shifting to the right is represented by reading from the top of the table downward, and shifting to the left is represented by reading from the bottom of the table upward.

In contrast, the Y axis is incremented by adding a constant value to the display address. The constant is equal to the number of bytes that separate two adjacent vertical bytes in the virtual image. This value is stored in the Offset Register, which cannot be read in the EGA. This value can be obtained by interrogating the system status through the BIOS call.

Because the mask value represents which pixel within the addressed byte is active, the mask value does not change when the Y axis is modified. In Table

TABLE 12.4 Changing the X Address

X *Coordinate*	X *Address*	Bit Mask (Hex)	Y Address × Offset
20	2	08	10
21	2	04	11
22	2	02	11
23	2	01	12
24	3	80	13
25	3	40	13
26	3	20	14
27	2	10	15
28	3	08	15
29	3	04	16
30	3	02	17
31	3	01	17
32	4	80	18

12.4, the *Y* byte address is observed to change from 10 to 18. If the offset is 80, this corresponds to addresses 800 to 1,440. The row number is multiplied by the offset to produce the *Y* address. The display memory address, which accesses a single byte in display memory, is obtained by adding the *X* address to the Y address. Moving in the positive *Y* direction is accomplished by adding to the display address a constant value that is equal to the display offset. Similarly, moving in the negative *Y* direction is accomplished by subtracting the offset from the display address.

The line-drawing routine, named Line in Listing 12.23, calls one of three assembly language subroutines. The Line routine sets up constants and determines which of these routines to call. The assembly language routines are called Xline, YpLine, and YnLine. One of these routines is selected according to the angle of the line. The selection process is illustrated in Figure 12.5.

LISTING 12.23 Drawing a Line

```
/* draw a line using Bresenham's algorithm
Input parameters:
 page            page
 ix1,iy1 first endpoint x,y coordinates of line
 ix2,iy2 second endpoint x,y coordinates of line
 color    color of the line

Calling protocol */
 Line(page,x1,y1,x2,y2,color)
```

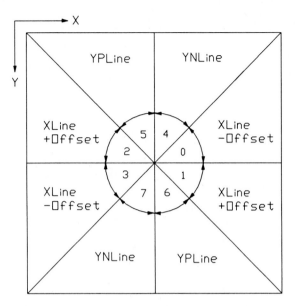

FIGURE 12.5   Selecting a Line-drawing Routine

```
int x1,y1,x2,y2; char color,page;
{ int dx,dy,d,d2,inc,incr1,incr2,xend,yend,
  x,y,offset=80,address,bmask,yinc,xinc;

dx = abs(x2-x1); /* length in the x direction */
if(dx == 0) /* is it a vertical line */
{ ESetRes(15); VLine(page,x1,y1,y2,color); }
else /* is it a horizontal line */
{ dy = abs(y2-y1); /* length in the y direction */
  if(dy == 0) HLine(page,x1,x2,y1,color);
else   /* neither vertical nor horizontal so do Bresenham's */
{
  ESetRes(15); SetRes(color); /* load registers */

/* determine if the slope is between 0 and 1 ie., dy>dx */
  if(dx>dy) /* slope<1 Quadrants 0, 1, 2, or 3 */
  {
    if(x1>x2)              /* Quadrant 0 or 1 */
      { x = x2; y = y2;
      if(y2>y1)  inc=-1; /* Quadrant 0 */
           else inc= 1; /* Quadrant 1 */
    }
    else                  /* Quadrant 2 or 3 */
      { x = x1; y = y1;
        if(y2>y1) inc=1;   /* Quadrant 2 */
```

```
                         else inc=-1;    /* Quadrant 3 */
                }
        d2 = dy<<1;              /* y distance times 2 */
         d = d2-dx;              /* init the decision variable to 2*dy-dx */
        incr1 = d2; /* increment for decision var, d' if d<0 */
        incr2 = (dy-dx)<<1; /* incr. for decision var if d>=0 */
        offset = 80; /* number of bytes per scan line */
        yinc = offset*inc; /* amount to change address */
        address = (y*offset)+(x>>3); /* starting address */
        bmask = 0x80 >> (x&7); /* bit plane mask */
        dx ++; /* number of points = 1+(x2-x1) */
        /* draw the line */
        XLine(d,dx,incr1,incr2,yinc,address,bmask);
        }
    else    /* slope >1 Quadrant 4, 5, 6 or 7 */
    {
    d2 = dx<<1;     /* x distance times 2 */
    d = d2-dy; /* init the decision variable to 2*dx-dy */
    incr1 = d2;     /* increment for decision var, d' if d<0 */
    incr2 = (dx-dy)<<1; /* incr. for decision var if d>=0 */
    offset = 80; /* number of bytes per scan line */
    dy ++;      /* number of points = 1+(y2-y1) */

    if(y1>y2) /* Quadrant 4 or 5 */
      {
        address = (y2*offset)+(x2>>3); /* starting address */
        bmask = 0x80 >> (x&7); /* bit plane mask */
        if(x2>x1) /* Quadrant 4 */
         YnLine(d,dy,incr1,incr2,offset,address,bmask);
        else /* Quadrant 5 */
          YpLine(d,dy,incr1,incr2,offset,address,bmask);
      }
     else /* Quadrant 6 or 7 */
      {
       address = (y1*offset)+(x1>>3); /* starting address */
       bmask = 0x80 >> (x&7);           /* bit plane mask */
       if(x2>x1) /* Quadrant 6 */
         YpLine(d,dy,incr1,incr2,offset,address,bmask);
       else /* Quadrant 7 */
         YnLine(d,dy,incr1,incr2,offset,address,bmask);
     }
    }
}BitMask(255); ESetRes(0); /* reset the EGA/VGA registers */
}
```

Figure 12.5 illustrates the eight quadrants that segment the 360 degrees surrounding a point. A line is drawn into one of these quadrants, depending on the slope of the line. If the line is drawn from the center point into quadrants 0, 1, 2, or 3, the Xline routine is called. If the line is drawn from the center point into quadrants 5 or 6, the YpLine routine is called. Consistently, if it is drawn into quadrants 4 or 7, the YnLine routine is called.

The XLine routine in Listing 12.24 is invoked when the X axis is determined to be the independent axis.

LISTING 12.24   Drawing a Line with *X* as the Independent Axis

```
; Draw a line with X as the independent axis.
; Assumptions on input:
; SetReset Register is pre-loaded with "color".
; Enable-SetReset Register is pre-loaded with the desired
; planes.

; Assumptions on output:
; Bit Mask Register and Enable-SetReset Register are reset.

; Input parameters:
; d                      decision variable
; dx                     number of pixels in x-dimension of line
; incr1                  increment #1 value for decision variable
; incr2                  increment #2 value for decision variable
; offset                 number of bytes per horizontal line
; address                starting offset address into display memory
; mask                   starting value of Bit Plane Mask Register

; Calling Protocol:
; XLine(d,dx,incr1,incr2,offset,address,mask)

_XLine proc far
 Prefix

 mov ax,0A000h      ;set up the address
 mov ds,ax          ;get segment

; set up the index to point to the Bit Mask Register
 mov ax,3ceh        ;point to address port
 mov dx,ax
 mov ax,8
 out dx,al          ;address bit plane mask
 inc dx             ;DX points to data port

; load the working registers with the variables
 mov si,[bp+16]     ;load pointer to display memory
 mov cx,[bp+8]      ;load # of points into the CX
 mov al,[bp+18]     ;get the bit mask in AL
 mov bx,[bp+6]      ;get the decision variable in BX
```

```
; operational loop
runloop:
  out dx,al           ;load the bit plane mask

; read before write
  mov ah,ds:[si]      ;dummy read
  mov ds:[si],ah      ;output color through set/reset

; adjust the bit mask for next right pixel
  shr al,1            ;bmask >> 1
  jnc same            ;jump if no overflow

; reset bit mask and increment address
  mov al,80h          ;bmask = 0x80
  inc si              ;address ++

same:
  cmp bx,0            ;d == 0 ?
  jl noinc            ;jump if d < 0

; adjust d += incr2 and increment y += inc
  add bx,[bp+12]      ;d += incr2
  add si,[bp+14]      ;y (address) += offset
  jmp check

; adjust d += incr1
noinc:
  add bx,[bp+10]      ;d += incr1

; repeat til done
check:
  loop runloop        ;repeat loop for each "x" until CX=0

  Postfix
_XLine endp
```

Each time the X variable is incremented, the mask value is shifted to the right. When the decision determines that the Y variable must be incremented, a positive offset is added to the Y address. When the Y variable is decremented, a negative offset is added to the Y address. Because the only difference in these two cases is the sign of the offset, it is possible to incorporate both positively and negatively incrementing Y values into the same routine. These two cases are illustrated in Figure 12.6.

This algorithm increments the X variable in each interaction by shifting the mask. It adds either a positive or a negative offset to the Y address depending on the condition of a decision variable. These two cases are illustrated in Figure 12.7.

The YpLine routine in Listing 12.25 is invoked when the Y variable is determined to be the independent axis and the X variable is increasing.

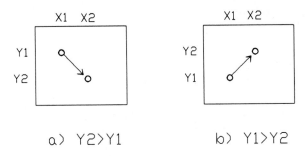

a) Y2>Y1 b) Y1>Y2

FIGURE 12.6 *X*-Axis Independent

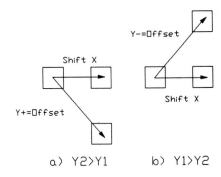

a) Y2>Y1 b) Y1>Y2

FIGURE 12.7 Incrementing along the *X*-Axis

LISTING 12.25 Drawing a Line with *Y* Independent and *X* Increasing

---

```
; Draw a line with X increasing and Y the independent variable
; Assumptions on input:
; SetReset Register is pre-loaded with "color".
; Enable-SetReset Register is pre-loaded with the desired
; planes.

; Assumptions on output:
; Bit Mask Register and Enable-SetReset Register are reset.

; Input parameters:
; d                     decision variable
; dy                    number of pixels in y-dimension of line
; incr1                 increment #1 value for decision variable
; incr2                 increment #2 value for decision variable
; offset                number of bytes in a horizontal line
; address               starting offset address into display memory
; mask                  starting value of Bit Plane Mask Register

; Calling Protocol:
; YpLine(d,dy,incr1,incr2,offset,address,mask)
```

```
        _YpLine proc far
            Prefix

    ; set up the address
        mov ax,0A000h
        mov ds,ax          ;load segment

    ; set up the index to point to the Bit Mask Register
        mov ax,3ceh        ;int to address port
        mov dx,ax
        mov ax,8
        out dx,al          ;address bit plane mask
        inc dx             ;DX points to data port

    ; load the working registers with the variables
        mov si,[bp+16]  ; load offset to display memory
        mov cx,[bp+8]   ; load # of points into the CX
        mov al,[bp+18]  ; get the bit mask in AL
        mov bx,[bp+6]   ; get the decision variable in BX

    ; operational loop
    runloop:
        out dx,al          ;load the bit plane mask
        mov ah,ds:[si]     ;dummy read before write
        mov ds:[si],ah     ;output color through set/reset

    ; always increment y (next row down) and test decision
        add si,[bp+14]  ;y (address) += offset
        cmp bx,0        ; d == 0 ?
        jl  noinc       ; jump if d < 0

    ; adjust d += incr2 and increment x
        add bx,[bp+12]  ; d += incr2

    ; increment x by adjusting the bit mask for next right pixel
        shr al,1        ; bmask >> 1
        jnc check       ; jump if no overflow

    ; reset bit mask since overflow and increment address
        mov al,080h     ; bmask = 0x80
        inc si          ; address ++
        jmp check

    ; adjust d += incr1
    noinc:
        add bx,[bp+10]  ; d += incr1

    ;    repeat til done
    check:
        loop runloop    ; repeat loop for each "x" until CX=0

        Postfix
    _YpLine endp
```

The YnLine routine in Listing 12.26 is invoked when the *Y* variable is determined to be the independent axis and the *X* variable is decreasing.

LISTING 12.26 Drawing a Line with *Y* Independent and *X* Decreasing

```
; Draw a line with X decreasing and Y the independent variable
; Assumptions on input:
; SetReset Register is pre-loaded with "color".
; Enable-Set Reset Register is pre-loaded with the desired
;    planes.

; Assumptions on output:
; Bit Mask Register and Enable-SetReset Register are reset.

; Input parameters:
; d                    decision variable
; dy                   number of pixels in y-dimension of line
; incr1                increment #1 value for decision variable
; incr2                increment #2 value for decision variable
; offset               number of bytes per horizontal line
; address              starting offset address into display memory
;  mask                starting value of Bit Plane Mask Register

; Calling Protocol:
; Ynline(d,dy,incr1,incr2,offset,address,mask)

_Ynline proc far
    Prefix

; set up the address
    mov ax,0A000h
    mov ds,ax        ;load segment

; set up the index to point to the Bit Mask Register
    mov ax,3ceh      ;point to address port
    mov dx,ax
    mov ax,8
    out dx,al        ;address bit plane mask
    inc dx           ;DX points to data port

; load the working registers with the variables
    mov si,[bp+16]   ; load offset to display memory
    mov cx,[bp+8]    ; load # of points into the CX
    mov al,[bp+18]   ; get the bit mask in AL
    mov bx,[bp+6]    ; get the decision variable in BX

; operational loop
runloop: out dx,al   ;load the bit plane mask
    mov ah,ds:[si]   ;dummy read before write
    mov ds:[si],ah   ;output color through set/reset
```

```
; always increment y (next row down) and test decision
    add  si,[bp+14]  ;y (address) += offset
    cmp  bx,0        ; d == 0 ?
    jl   noinc       ; jump if d < 0
; adjust d += incr2 and decrement x
    add  bx,[bp+12]  ; d += incr2
; decrement x by adjusting the bit mask for next left pixel
    shl  al,1        ; bmask << 1
    jnc  check       ; jump if no overflow
; reset bit mask since overflow and decrement address
    mov  al,01h      ; bmask = 0x01
    dec  si          ; address --
    jmp  check
; adjust d += incr1
noinc:
    add  bx,[bp+10]  ; d += incr1
; repeat til done
check:
    loop runloop     ;jump if y <= yend

    Postfix
_Ynline endp
```

Two routines are necessary because in one case the mask is shifted to the left, and in the other case the mask is shifted to the right. In addition, overflows are handled differently. Both of these cases are illustrated in Figure 12.8.

This algorithm increments the *Y* variable in each interaction by adding a positive offset to the display address. It moves one pixel to the right or to the left, depending on the subroutine selected. These two cases are illustrated in Figure 12.9.

12.11.4 Drawing a Line in Mode 13 Hex

Mode 13 hex is a 256-color mode associated with the VGA. The line-drawing routines for this mode are presented in Listing 12.27. The main routine, Line13, is used to draw the line. All routines parallel the line drawing routines used in the 16-color modes. Notice how much simpler the process of line drawing is when a pixel is represented by a single byte.

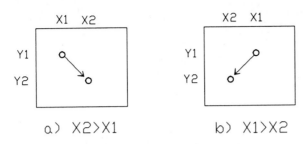

FIGURE 12.8 *Y-Axis Independent*

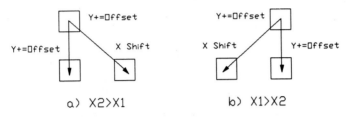

FIGURE 12.9 Incrementing along the *Y*-Axis

LISTING 12.27 Drawing a Line in Mode 13 Hex

```
/* Draw a line in Mode 13 hex
   Input parameters:
   page                   page
   ix1,iy1                first endpoint x,y coordinates of line
   ix2,iy2                second endpoint x,y coordinates of line
   color                  color of the line
Calling protocol */
Line13(x1,y1,x2,y2,color)

int x1,y1,x2,y2,color;
{ int dx,dy,d,d2,xinc,yinc,incr1,incr2,x,y,address, offset=320;

dx = abs(x2-x1); /* length in the x direction */
if(dx == 0) /* is it a vertical line */
  VLine13(x1,y1,y2,color);
else /* is it a horizontal line */
  { dy = abs(y2-y1); /* length in the y direction */
    if(dy == 0) HLine13(x1,x2,y1,color, offset);
  else /* neither vertical or horizontal so do Bresenham's */
  {/* determine if the slope is between 0 and 1 i.e., dy>dx */
    if(dx>=dy)     /* slope<1 Quadrants 0, 1, 2, or 3 */
```

```
    { if(x1>x2)                              /* Quadrant 0 or 1 */
       { x = x2; y = y2;
           if(y2>y1) yinc=-offset;      /* Quadrant 0 */
               else yinc= offset; } /* Quadrant 1 */
        else                        /* Quadrant 2 or 3 */
          { x = x1; y = y1;
             if(y2>y1) yinc= offset;        /* Quadrant 2 */
                 else yinc=-offset; } /* Quadrant 3 */
   address = (y*offset)+x;          /* starting address */
   d2 = dy<<1;                      /* y distance times 2 */
   d = d2-dx; /* init the decision variable to 2*dy-dx */
   incr1 = d2;         /* increment for decision var, d' if d<0 */
   incr2 = (dy-dx)<<1; /* incr. for decision var if d>=0 */
   XLine13(d,dx+1,incr1,incr2,yinc,address,color);
    }
   else           /* slope >1 Quadrant 4, 5, 6 or 7 */
     { if(y1>y2)                    /* Quadrant 4 or 5 */
        { x = x2; y = y2;
           if(x2>x1) xinc=-1;       /* Quadrant 4 */
               else  xinc= 1; }     /* Quadrant 5 */
       else
         { x = x1; y = y1;          /* Quadrant 6 or 7 */
            if(x2>x1) xinc= 1;      /* Quadrant 6 */
                else  xinc=-1; }    /* Quadrant 7 */
   address = (y*offset)+x;     /* starting address */
   d2 = dx<<1;           /* x distance times 2 */
   d = d2-dy;     /* init the decision variable to 2*dx-dy */
   incr1 = d2;     /* increment for decision var, d' if d<0 */
   incr2 = (dx-dy)<<1; /* incr. for decision var if d>=0 */
   YLine13(d,dy+1,incr1,incr2,xinc,address,color,offset);
   }   /* end of quadrants 0,1,2,3 or 4,5,6,7 */
  }}  /* end of not horizontal or vertical */
}
```

The line-drawing routine calls the XLine13 routine in Listing 12.28 to draw the line if the *X* axis is independent.

LISTING 12.28 Drawing a Line: *X* Is the Independent Variable

---

```
; Draw a line in Mode 13 hex with X the independent variable.
; Input parameters:
; d                      decision variable
; dx                     number of pixels in x-dimension of line
```

```
; incr1              increment #1 value for decision variable
; incr2              increment #2 value for decision variable
; yinc               amount to add to y variable per point
; address            starting offset address into display memory
; color              desired color

; Calling Protocol:
; XLine13(d,dx,incr1,incr2,yinc,address,color)

_XLine13 proc far
    Prefix

    mov ax,0A000h    ; set up the address
    mov es,ax        ;get segment

;   load the working registers with the variables
    mov di,[bp+16]   ; load display offset address
    mov cx,[bp+8]    ; load # of points into the CX
    mov bx,[bp+6]    ; get the decision variable in BX
    mov ah,[bp+18]   ; get color

; operational loop
runloop:
;   send the first point
    mov es:[di],ah   ; write to display memory

; increment the x variable
    inc di

    cmp bx,0         ; d == 0 ?
    jl  noinc        ; jump if d < 0

; adjust d += incr2 and increment y += inc
    add bx,[bp+12]   ; d += incr2

    add di,[bp+14]   ;y (address) += offset
    jmp check

; adjust d += incr1
noinc:
    add bx,[bp+10]   ; d += incr1

;   repeat til done
check:
    loop runloop     ; repeat loop for each "x" until CX=0

    Postfix
_XLine13 endp
```

The line-drawing routine calls the YLine13 routine in Listing 12.29 to draw the line if the *Y* axis is independent.

LISTING 12.29   Drawing a Line: *Y* Is the Independent Variable

```
; Draw a line in Mode 13 hex with Y the independent variable.
; Input parameters:
; d                      decision variable
; dy                     number of pixels in y-dimension of line
; incr1                  increment #1 value for decision variable
; incr2                  increment #2 value for decision variable
; xinc                   amount to add to x variable per point
; address                starting offset address into display memory
; color                  desired color
; offset                 display offset
; Calling Protocol:
; YLine13(d,dy,incr1,incr2,xinc,address,color,offset)

 _YLine13 proc far
    Prefix

    mov ax,0A000h   ; set up the address
    mov es,ax       ;get segment

;   load the working registers with the variables
    mov di,[bp+16]  ; load display offset address
    mov cx,[bp+8]   ; load # of points into the CX
    mov bx,[bp+6]   ; get the decision variable in BX
    mov ah,[bp+18]  ; get color

; operational loop
runloop:
;   send the first point
    mov es:[di],ah  ; write to display memory

; increment the y variable
    add di,[bp+20]  ;y (address) += offset (always positive)

    cmp bx,0        ; d == 0 ?
    jl  noinc       ; jump if d < 0

; adjust d += incr2 and increment y += inc
    add bx,[bp+12]  ; d += incr2

    add di,[bp+14]  ;increment the x variable
    jmp check

; adjust d += incr1
noinc:
    add bx,[bp+10]  ; d += incr1

;   repeat til done
check:
    loop runloop    ; repeat loop for each "x" until CX=0

    Postfix
_YLine13 endp
```

If the line routine determines that the line is horizontal, it calls the HLine13 routine in Listing 12.30. This routine relies on an assembly language routine called VSub13, presented in Listing 12.31, to actually interact with the display memory.

LISTING 12.30 Drawing a Horizontal Line in Mode 13 Hex

```
/* Draw a horizontal line in VGA Mode 13 hex.
Input Parameters:
 x           = x-coordinate
 y1          = y-coordinate 1
 y2          = y-coordinate 2
 color       = desired color
 offset      = display offset

Calling Protocol: */
HLine13(x1,x2,y,color,offset)

int x1,x2,y,color;
{ int x,dx,address;

if(x1>x2)
 {x=x1; x1=x2; x2=x;} /* reverse x-coordinates */

dx = (x2-x1) +1; /* number of x pixels */
address = (y*offset) + x1;
HSub13(address,dx,color); /* draw the horizontal line */
}
```

LISTING 12.31 Horizontal Line Subroutine

```
; Horizontal line subroutine for Mode 13 hex
; input parameters
; address          starting display offset address
;                  segment=A000hex
; dx               number of pixels to write
; color            color of pixels

; Calling protocol:
; HSub13(address,dx,color);

_HSub13 proc far
    Prefix

    mov ax,0A000h    ;segment address
    mov es,ax
```

```
        mov di,[bp+6]    ;segment address
        mov cx,[bp+8]    ;get number of pixels
        mov al,[bp+10]   ;get color

  rep stosb              ;draw the line

        Postfix
  _HSub13 endp
```

If the line routine determines that the line is vertical, it calls the VLine13 routine in Listing 12.32. This routine relies on an assembly language routine called VSub13, presented in Listing 12.33, to actually interact with the display memory.

LISTING 12.32   Drawing a Vertical Line in Mode 13 Hex

```
/* Draw a vertical line in VGA Mode 13 hex.
Input Parameters:
  x          = x-coordinate
  y1         = y-coordinate 1
  y2         = y-coordinate 2
  color      = desired color
  offset     = display offset

Calling Protocol: */
  VLine13(x,y1,y2,color,offset)

int y1,y2,x,color,offset;
{ int t,dy,address;

  if (y1>y2)
   {t=y2; y2=y1; y1=t;}
   dy = y2-y1+1; /* number of points to draw */
   address = (y1*offset)+x; /* starting address */

  VSub13(address,dy,color);
}
```

LISTING 12.33   Vertical Line Subroutine

```
; write a vertical line in Mode 13 hex
; Input parameters:
; address          starting display offset address
                   segment=A000hex
; dy               number of pixels to write
; color            color of pixels
; offset           display offset
```

```
; Calling protocol:
;   VSub13(address,dy,color,offset);

_VSub13 proc far
    Prefix

    mov ax,0A000h    ;segment address
    mov es,ax

    mov di,[bp+6]    ;segment address
    mov cx,[bp+8]    ;get number of pixels
    mov al,[bp+10]   ;get color

runloop:
    mov es:[di],al   ;draw the line
    add di,[bp+12]   ;add offset for mode 13 hex
    loop runloop

    Postfix
_VSub13 endp
```

12.12   DRAWING A CIRCLE

A circle exhibits an eight-quadrant symmetry, as shown in Figure 12.10. Thus, the points on the circumference of a circle need only be calculated from 0 to 45 degrees.

Bresenham's circle algorithm is implemented in the routine called Circle, presented in Listing 12.34. This routine operates in a similar fashion to that used by the line-drawing routine. Because the circle is symmetric about the X and Y axis, either the X or Y axis may be chosen as the independent variable. The initial condition sets the first point according to Equation 12.2.

Equation 12.2   Initial Conditions for the Circle

$X = X$ center
$Y = Y$ center + radius

This positions the point at the 270-degree point. The 45-degree span that will be calculated travels from this 270-degree point to the 315 degree point. In this routine, the X axis is selected as the independent variable, and it increments for each point. A decision variable is used to determine whether the Y axis should be decremented for every point. Remember that decrementing the address corresponds to an upward motion along the Y axis on the EGA/VGA. The process of drawing a circle is illustrated in Figure 12.11.

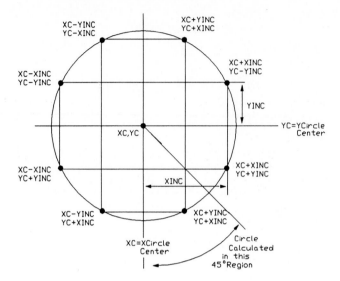

FIGURE 12.10 Eight-point Symmetry

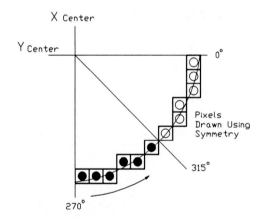

FIGURE 12.11 Drawing a Circle

LISTING 12.34 Drawing a Circle

```
/* draw the outline of a circle.
Input parameters:
 xc horizontal center coordinate
 yc vertical center coordinate
 radius radius of circle
 color color of circle
```

```
Calling protocol: */
 Circle(page,xc,yc,radius,color)

int radius,xc,yc,page,color;
{ int x=0,y,d;

 y = radius; /* initialize y to radius */
 /* with x=0 and y=radius, first point is at 270 degrees */
 d = 3 - (2*radius); /* initialize the decision variable */

while (x<y)
 { CircPnt(page,x,y,xc,yc,color); /* draw in 4 quadrants */
    if(d<0) /* don't decrement y */
      d += (4 * x) + 6; /* update the decision variable */
      else
      { d += 4*(x-y) + 10; /* update the decision variable */
       y --; } /* decrement y */
    x++; /* increment the x variable */
 } /* end of while (x<y) */
 if(x==y) CircPnt(page,x,y,xc,yc,color); /* draw a point in
four quadrants */

 }
```

Each *X* and *Y* coordinate pair is drawn in eight places on the display by calling the routine CircPnt shown in Listing 12.35. This routine calculates the eight symmetric points that are shown in Figure 12.10 and writes the eight points to the screen using the DrawPnt routine.

LISTING 12.35   Determining the Eight-point Symmetry

```
/* draw eight points symmetrically around a circle
Input parameters:
 page                   = desired page
 x,y                    = coordinate of point to replicate eight
                          times
 xc,yc                  = center of circle
Calling protocol: */
 CircPnt(page,x,y,xc,yc,color)

int page,x,y,xc,yc,color;
{ int xxcp,xxcm,xycp,xycm,yxcp,yxcm,yycp,yycm;

 /* draw points using eight point symmetry */
xxcp = xc+x; xxcm = xc-x; xycp = xc+y; xycm = xc-y;
yxcp = yc+x; yxcm = yc-x; yycp = yc+y; yycm = yc-y;
DrawPnt(page,xxcp,yycp,color);
DrawPnt(page,xxcp,yycm,color);
```

```
DrawPnt(page,xxcm,yycp,color);
DrawPnt(page,xxcm,yycm,color);
DrawPnt(page,xycp,yxcp,color);
DrawPnt(page,xycp,yxcm,color);
DrawPnt(page,xycm,yxcp,color);
DrawPnt(page,xycm,yxcm,color);
}
```

12.13   DRAWING AN IMAGE

An image, also called a *window*, consists of a rectangular area filled with pixels of any value. The windows are written to the screen in horizontal lines. Each pixel may have its own color. This is different from the line-drawing routine, in which the entire horizontal line was drawn in a single color.

The window may be associated with an alphanumeric or graphics display mode. In the alphanumeric display modes, its dimensions are measured in character positions along both the horizontal and vertical axes. In the graphics display modes, its dimensions are measured in pixels along the horizontal axis and in scan lines along the vertical axis.

The data that resides inside the window fills a two-dimensional space in the display memory. Lines are not necessarily contiguous because the width of the window does not necessarily correspond to the width of the virtual display. The width of the virtual display is stored in the Offset Register, as illustrated in Figure 12.12.

The buffer may be declared as a one-dimensional or a two-dimensional C array. The format used for the data in the window routines is identical to the C data convention. The elements of each row are stored sequentially, each row loaded contiguously in the C array.

12.13.1   Writing to a Window

The routine WrWin in Listing 12.36 writes a data buffer to the display memory at a specified location. The calculations that determine the position of the window in the display memory vary depending on the active display mode. The position and size of the window are determined by the horizontal and vertical dimensions passed to the routine. The parameters passed to this routine represent the horizontal and vertical coordinates of the upper left and lower right corners of the window.

LISTING 12.36   Writing a Window to Display Memory

```
/* write a rectangular window to the display memory.
Input parameters:
 page           desired display page
```

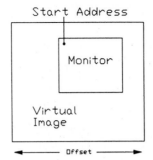

FIGURE 12.12   The Monitor Window within a Virtual Image

```
x1,y1          upper-left coordinates of the window
x2,y2          lower-right coordinates of the window
buf     host "C" byte buffer which will be loaded with the data
Calling protocol: */
WrWin(page,x1,y1,x2,y2,buf)

int page,x1,y1,x2,y2; unsigned char buf[];
{ char *pntbuf;
 int segment,address,ncol,nrow,numbyte,offset,gstat[4],t;

 ncol = (x2-x1)+1; nrow = (y2-y1)+1;
 /* protect for reversed windows */
 if(ncol<0)
 { ncol = -ncol; t=x2; x2=x1; x1=t; }
 if(nrow<0)
 { nrow = -nrow; t=y2; y2=y1; y1=t; }

 GetStat(gstat);   /* determine the current display mode */
 switch(gstat[1])  /* operate depending on mode */
 {
 case 0: case 1: case 2: case 3: case 7:
    WrAWin(page,buf,y1,x1,y2,x2);
    break;

 case 4: case 5:
    numbyte = ncol >> 2; /* four pixels per byte */
    /*    do even rows (y/2) * 40 * 2 = y*40 */
    address = (y1*40) + (x1>>2);
    WrGWin(0xB800,address,buf,numbyte,nrow/2,80);
    /* do odd rows */
    WrGWin(0xBA00,address,buf,numbyte,nrow/2,80);
    break;

 case 6:
    numbyte = ncol >> 3; /* eight pixels per byte */
```

```
      /*   do even rows (y/2) * 80 = y*40 */
      address = (y1*40) + (x1>>3);
      WrGWin(0xB800,address,buf,numbyte,nrow/2,80);
      /* do odd rows */
      WrGWin(0xBA00,address,buf,numbyte,nrow/2,80);
      break;

  case 0x0D:
      numbyte = ncol >> 3; /* eight pixels per byte */
      address = (page&7) * 0x2000 + (y1*40) + (x1>>3);
      PlaneWr(0xA000,address,buf,numbyte,nrow,40);
      break;

  case 0x0E:
      numbyte = ncol >> 3; /* eight pixels per byte */
      address = (page&3) * 0x4000 + (y1*80) + (x1>>3);
      PlaneWr(0xA000,address,buf,numbyte,nrow,80);
      break;

  case 0x0F:
      numbyte = ncol >> 3; /* eight pixels per byte */
      address = (page&1) * 0x8000 + (y1*80) + (x1>>3);
      WrGWin(0xA000,address,buf,numbyte,nrow,80);
      break;

  case 0x10:
      numbyte = ncol >> 3; /* eight pixels per byte */
      address = ((page&1)*0x8000) + (y1*80) + (x1>>3);
      PlaneWr(0xA000,address,buf,numbyte,nrow,80);
      break;

  case 0x11:
      numbyte = ncol >> 3; /* eight pixels per byte */
      address = (y1*80) + (x1>>3);
      WrGWin(0xA000,address,buf,numbyte,nrow,80);
      break;

  case 0x12:
      numbyte = ncol >> 3; /* eight pixels per byte */
      address =(y1*80) + (x1>>3);
      PlaneWr(0xA000,address,buf,numbyte,nrow,80);
      break;

  case 0x13:
      numbyte = ncol; /* one pixel per byte */
      address =(y1*320) + x1;
      WrGwin(0xA000,address,buf,numbyte,nrow,320);
      break;
  }
}
```

In the alphanumeric modes, the routine WrAWin in Listing 12.37 is called to output the data to the screen. In this case, the buffer is assumed to be composed of character and attribute pairs for each character. This routine relies on the WrChars routine in Listing 12.11 above to perform the character output a horizontal line at a time.

LISTING 12.37 Writing an Alphanumeric Window

```
/* write a rectangular window of character attribute pairs
Input parameters:
  page          desired display page
  buf           buffer which contains char/attribute pairs
  row1,col1     character coordinates of upper-left corner
  row2,col2     character coordinates of lower-right corner

Calling protocol: */
WrAWin(page,buf,row1,col1,row2,col2)

int page,row1,col1,row2,col2; unsigned char buf[];
{unsigned int charatr,row,column,i=0;

  for (row=row1; row<=row2; row++)
    for (column=col1; column<=col2; column++)
      { charatr = buf[i] + (buf[i+1]<<8);
        WrChar(page,charatr,row,column); i+=2;
      }
}
```

In the graphics modes, the WrWin routine writes to a single display plane by calling the WrGWin routine. It calls the routine PlaneWr to write to all four display planes. This routine also calls the WrGWin routine to write to each display plane.

The routine PlaneWr, shown in Listing 12.38, writes the data to all four display planes. The data may be considered as a three-dimensional data set, the first dimension being the pixels per row, the second being the rows, and the third being the display bit planes. Because the data is stored in a contiguous buffer, one plane after another, a pointer, rather than an array, is passed to the WrGWin routine. This pointer is incremented by the number of bytes per plane each time the WrGWin routine is called.

LISTING 12.38   Writing a Window to Four Display Planes

```
/* write the data to all four bit planes
Input Parameters:
  segment        segment portion of the display memory address
  address        offset portion of the display memory address
  buf            buffer containing the data
  numbyte        number of bytes per row
  nrow           number of rows in the window
  offset         number of bytes per horizontal display line
Calling protocol: */
PlaneWr(segment,address,buf,numbyte,nrow,offset)

int segment,address,numbyte,nrow,offset;
unsigned char buf[];
{ char *pntbuf; int byteperwin;

pntbuf = &buf[0]; /* pointer pntbuf points to buf */
byteperwin = numbyte * nrow;
MapMask(1);
WrGWin(segment,address,pntbuf,numbyte,nrow,offset);

pntbuf += byteperwin; /* plane 1 after plane 0 in buf */
MapMask(2);
WrGWin(segment,address,pntbuf,numbyte,nrow,offset);

pntbuf += byteperwin; /* plane 2 after plane 1 in buf */
MapMask(4);
WrGWin(segment,address,pntbuf,numbyte,nrow,offset);

pntbuf += byteperwin; /* plane 3 after plane 2 in buf */
MapMask(8);
WrGWin(segment,address,pntbuf,numbyte,nrow,offset);
MapMask(0x0f);          /* enable all planes */
}
```

In the graphics modes in which multiple pixels are stored per byte, a simplification is used in these routines. This simplification speeds up the data transfer. The window is always assumed to reside on even byte boundaries. In the graphics modes that store eight pixels per byte, this means that the window corners will be drawn beginning in the far left pixel of a byte and ending in the far right pixel of a byte. The horizontal line-drawing routines can be modified and used to produce routines that can process windows at any pixel location.

The routine WrGWin, shown in Listing 12.39, writes a window to any selected planes in display memory. The display memory segment and offset addresses passed to this routine represent the upper left corner of the window. The number of bytes per row and the number of rows per window are passed as parameters. In addition, because the window does not necessarily correspond to the width of the virtual display, the number of bytes in a horizontal scan line of the virtual display is also passed as a parameter. This virtual width does not necessarily correspond to the number of bytes displayed on a horizontal line.

LISTING 12.39 Writing an Image to Display Memory

```
; Write a plane of data to the display memory
; Input Parameters
; segment          segment address of starting coordinates
; offset           offset address of starting coordinates
; buffer           host "C" buffer containing the data
; nbyte            number of bytes per row
; nrow             number of rows
; bpvrow           bytes per virtual row

; Calling protocol
; WrGWin(segment,offset,buffer,nbyte,nrow,bpvrow);

_WrGWin proc far
 Prefix

; load the segment:offset address to display memory in ES:DI
 mov ax,[bp+6]      ;get segment to display memory
 mov es,ax          ;load into ES
 mov di,[bp+8]      ;get offset to display memory

; load the segment:offset address of the "C" buffer in DS:SI
 lds si,[bp+10]     ;get segment and offset of buffer

; set up constants for the data moving
 mov dx,[bp+16]     ;get the number of rows per window
 mov bx,[bp+18]     ;get window bytes per row
 sub bx,[bp+14]     ;(virtual - window )bytes per row
 mov ah,[bp+14]     ;get bytes per window
 xor ch,ch          ;clear the CH

; move one row per loop
runloop:
 mov cl,ah          ;number of bytes per row
rep movsb           ;move the data
 add di,bx          ;add offset for display address
 dec dx             ;decrement the row counter
 jg runloop         ;repeat for all rows

 Postfix
_WrGWin endp
```

12.13.2 Reading from a Window

Reading a window from display memory is accomplished in a similar fashion as writing the window to display memory. The descriptions associated with the write routines apply to the read routines. The parameters are identical, with the exception of the plane parameter. Unlike the write operation, the read operation can read only one bit plane at a time. The desired bit plane is selected in the plane parameter as a binary number. Thus, if the parameter 1 is sent to the MapMask routine, bit plane 0 will be selected. However, if the parameter 1 is sent to the ReadMap routine, bit plane 1 is selected. Because this routine is also meant to be used with the larger-resolution display modes, it is limited to reading from either page 0 or page 1.

The routine RdWin in Listing 12.40 reads a window from the display memory and returns the data to a C buffer. The format of this buffer is identical to the format of the buffer passed to the WrPlane routine.

LISTING 12.40 Reading an Image from Display Memory

```
/* Read a rectangular window to the display memory.
Input parameters:
  page                   desired display page
  x1,y1                  upper-left coordinates of the window
  x2,y2                  lower-right coordinates of the window

Output parameter:
  buf                    host "C" byte buffer which will be loaded
                         with the data

Calling protocol:    */
RdWin(page,x1,y1,x2,y2,buf)

int page,x1,y1,x2,y2; unsigned char buf[];
{ char *pntbuf;
  int segment,address,ncol,nrow,numbyte,offset,t,gstat[4];

ncol = (x2-x1)+1; nrow = (y2-y1)+1;
  /* protect for reversed windows */
  if(ncol<0)
  { ncol = -ncol; t=x2; x2=x1; x1=t; }
  if(nrow<0)
  { nrow = -nrow; t=y2; y2=y1; y1=t; }

GetStat(gstat);
  switch(gstat[1]) /* operate depending on mode */
  {
  case 0: case 1: case 2: case 3: case 7:
  RdAWin(page,buf,y1,x1,y2,x2);
  break;
```

```
case 4: case 5:
 numbyte = ncol >> 2; /* four pixels per byte */
 /*    do even rows (y/2) * 40 * 2 = y*40    */
     address = (y1*40) + (x1>>2);
 RdGwin(0xB800,address,buf,numbyte,nrow/2,80);
 /* do odd rows */
 RdGwin(0xBA00,address,buf,numbyte,nrow/2,80);
 break;

case 6:
 numbyte = ncol >> 3; /* eight pixels per byte */
 /*    do even rows (y/2) * 80 = y*40    */
     address = (y1*40) + (x1>>3);
 RdGwin(0xB800,address,buf,numbyte,nrow/2,80);
 /* do odd rows */
 RdGwin(0xBA00,address,buf,numbyte,nrow/2,80);
 break;

case 0x0D:
 numbyte = ncol >> 3; /* eight pixels per byte */
 address = (page&7) * 0x2000 + (y1*40) + (x1>>3);
 PlaneRd(0xA000,address,buf,numbyte,nrow,40);
 break;

case 0x0E:
 numbyte = ncol >> 3; /* eight pixels per byte */
     address = (page&3) * 0x4000 + (y1*80) + (x1>>3);
 PlaneRd(0xA000,address,buf,numbyte,nrow,80);
 break;

case 0x0F:
 numbyte = ncol >> 3; /* eight pixels per byte */
 address = (page&1) * 0x8000 + (y1*80) + (x1>>3);
 RdGwin(0xA000,address,buf,numbyte,nrow,80);
 break;

case 0x10:
 numbyte = ncol >> 3; /* eight pixels per byte */
 address = (page&1)*0x8000 + (y1*80) + (x1>>3);
 PlaneRd(0xA000,address,buf,numbyte,nrow,80);
 break;

case 0x11:
 numbyte = ncol >> 3; /* eight pixels per byte */
 address = (y1*80) + (x1>>3);
 RdGwin(0xA000,address,buf,numbyte,nrow,80);
 break;

case 0x12:
 numbyte = ncol >> 3; /* eight pixels per byte */
 address =(y1*80) + (x1>>3);
```

```
  PlaneRd(0xA000,address,buf,numbyte,nrow,80);
  break;

case 0x13:
  numbyte = ncol; /* one pixel per byte */
  address =(y1*320) + x1;
  RdGwin(0xA000,address,buf,numbyte,nrow,320);
  break;
  }
}
```

In the alphanumeric modes, the window is read by calling the RdAWin routine in Listing 12.41.

LISTING 12.41   Reading a Window in the Alphanumeric Modes

```
/* read a rectangular window of character attribute pairs.
Input parameters:
  page               desired display page
  buf                buffer to contain char/attribute pairs
  row1,col1          character coordinates of upper-left corner
  row2,col2          character coordinates of lower-right corner
Calling protocol: */
RdAwin(page,buf,row1,col1,row2,col2)

int page,row1,col1,row2,col2; unsigned char buf[];
{unsigned int charatr,row,column,i=0;

for (row=row1; row<=row2; row++)
   for (column=col1; column<=col2; column++)
 { charatr = RdChar(page,row,column);
   buf[i] = charatr & 0xff; i++;
   buf[i] = (charatr>>8) & 0xff; i++;
 }
}
```

In the graphics modes, the RdWin routine either calls the subroutine RdGWin in Listing 12.42 directly in order to read a plane, or it calls the routine PlaneRd in Listing 12.43, which reads all four display bit planes.

LISTING 12.42   Read a Window in the Graphics Modes

```
; Read a plane of data from the display memory
; Input Parameters
```

```
; segment              segment address of starting coordinates
; offset               offset address of starting coordinates
; buffer               host "C" buffer containing the data
; nbyte                number of bytes per row
; nrow                 number of rows
; bpvrow               bytes per virtual row

; Calling protocol
; RdGWin(segment,offset,buffer,nbyte,nrow,bpvrow);

_RdGWin proc far
 Prefix

; load the segment:offset address to display memory in DS:SI
 mov ax,[bp+6]        ;get segment to display memory
 mov ds,ax            ;load into DS
 mov si,[bp+8]        ;get offset to display memory

; load the segment:offset address of the "C" buffer in ES:DI
 les di,[bp+10]       ;get segment and offset of buffer

; set up constants for the data moving
 mov dx,[bp+16]       ;get the number of rows per window
 mov bx,[bp+18]       ;get window bytes per row
 sub bx,[bp+14]       ;(virtual - window )bytes per row
 mov ah,[bp+14]       ;get bytes per window
 xor ch,ch            ;clear the CH

; move one row per loop
runloop:
 mov cl,ah            ;number of bytes per row
 rep movsb            ;move the data
 add si,bx            ;add byte increment
 dec dx               ;decrement the row counter
 jg  runloop          ;repeat for all rows

 Postfix
_RdGWin endp
```

LISTING 12.43 Read a Window from Display Memory

```
/* read the data to all four bit planes
Input Parameters:
  segment              segment portion of the display memory
                       address
  address              offset portion of the display memory address
  buf                  buffer which will contain the data
  numbyte              number of bytes per row
  nrow                 number of rows in the window
  offset               number of bytes per horizontal display line
```

```
Calling protocol: */
 PlaneRd(segment,address,buf,numbyte,nrow,offset)

int segment,address,numbyte,nrow,offset;
 unsigned char buf[];
{ char *pntbuf; int byteperwin;

pntbuf = &buf[0]; /* pointer pntbuf points to buf */
 byteperwin = numbyte * nrow;
 ReadMap(0);
 RdGwin(segment,address,pntbuf,numbyte,nrow,offset);

pntbuf += byteperwin; /* plane 1 after plane 0 in buf */
 ReadMap(1);
 RdGwin(segment,address,pntbuf,numbyte,nrow,offset);

pntbuf += byteperwin; /* plane 2 after plane 1 in buf */
 ReadMap(2);
 RdGwin(segment,address,pntbuf,numbyte,nrow,offset);

pntbuf += byteperwin; /* plane 3 after plane 2 in buf */
 ReadMap(3);
 RdGwin(segment,address,pntbuf,numbyte,nrow,offset);
}
```

12.14 DATA DECODING

In the sixteen-color modes, each pixel is represented by a four-bit value. Multiple pixels can be stored in a byte array, with each byte containing a four-bit intensity. This data format is called pixel-packed because each pixel is represented within a single byte. Eight bytes of data, each byte consisting of four relevant bits, total 32 bits of data to represent eight pixels. The data resident in the display bit planes is stored in a bit-mapped format because a single pixel can be located in up to four display planes. Reading four bytes, one from each of the display bit planes, produces 32 bits that represent eight pixels. Two routines are presented to convert data from the bit-mapped into the pixel-packed format and vice-versa.

The routine Demux in Listing 12.44 converts four bytes in bit-mapped format into an array of eight bytes in which each byte contains a single pixel intensity. The most significant bit in each of the four bytes, bit 7, represents a bit from the far left pixel in the eight neighboring horizontal pixels. The value determined from the four bit 7s is returned in the output buffer element 0. The value determined from the four bit 6s is returned in the output buffer element 1. Similarly, the value from the four bit 0s is returned in the output buffer element 7. Upon completion, the eight-byte array contains eight pixel elements reading from left to right across the screen.

LISTING 12.44 Demultiplexing Four Bytes into Eight Pixels

```
; Demultiplex four bytes which contain eight pixels in a bit
;   mapped format, into eight color values.
; Input parameters:
; inbuf[]        input buffer containing four bytes

; Output parameters:
; outbuf[]     output buffer containing eight bytes

; Calling protocol
; DeMux(inbuf,outbuf);

_DeMux proc far
    Prefix

    les di,[bp+10]  ;point to the output buffer
    mov cx,8        ;zero that buffer
    xor al,al       ;zero al
rep stosb           ;zero all eight values

    lds si,[bp+6]   ;point to the input buffer DS:SI
    mov dx,04
    mov bl,01       ;set up mask

runloop:
    Call Fill8      ; process Bit Plane 0,1,2,3
    shl bl,1        ; shift the mask
    dec dx
    jne runloop     ; repeat til done with four bytes

    Postfix
_DeMux endp
```

The routine Mux in Listing 12.45 converts an eight-byte array, each element of which contains a pixel value, into four bytes, each byte containing a bit-mapped format. The first byte in the output array, element 0, represents bit plane 0, element 1 represents bit plane 1, etc. The most significant bit in the output bytes, bit 7, represents a bit in the far left pixel in the eight neighboring horizontal pixels. The value loaded into the four bit 7s is determined from the input buffer element 0. The value loaded into the four bit 6s is determined from the input buffer element 1. Similarly, the value loaded into the four bit 0s is determined from the output buffer element 7. Upon completion, the four-byte array contains the data representing each of the four bit planes.

LISTING 12.45 Multiplexing Eight Pixels into Four Bytes

```
; Multiplex four bytes in a Bit Mapped format, into eight color
;   values.
```

```
; Input parameters:
; inbuf[]    buffer containing eight pixel values

; Output parameters:
; outbuf[]    output buffer containing four bytes

; Calling protocol
; Mux(inbuf,outbuf)

_Mux proc far
    Prefix

; zero the four output bytes
    les di,[bp+10]  ;point to output
    xor al,al       ;zero al
    mov cx,04       ;do for all four output bytes
rep stosb

    lds si,[bp+6]   ;point to the input buffer
    mov dx,08       ;do for all eight bytes
    mov bl,80h      ;process bit 0

runloop:
    les di,[bp+10]  ;point to the output buffer
    Call Fill4      ;multiplex one byte into four bytes
    shr bl,1        ;shift left mask
    dec dx
    jne runloop     ;repeat til done

    Postfix
_Mux endp
```

The DeMux and Mux routines each call a subroutine to perform the shifting operation; these subroutines are called Fill8 and Fill4, respectively. They are listed in Listing 12.46.

LISTING 12.46 Multiplexing and Demultiplexing Subroutines

```
; Subroutine called by "DeMux" to fill the eight output bytes.
; Input parameters:
; DS:SI        points to word in buffer to multiplex
; bl register  contains the bit mask

; Output parameters:
; ES:DI        points to output word

; Assembly Language Calling protocol:
;    Call Fill8

Fill8 proc near
    les di,[bp+10]  ;point to the output buffer ES:DI
```

```
    lodsb              ;get the input, inc DS:SI
    mov cx,8           ;eight pixels in a byte
loop8:
    rcl al,1           ;get bit into carry
    jnc zero8      ;jump if bit is 0
; set the bit in the output buffer
    or   es:[di],bl ;or in a 1 into the output buffer

zero8:    inc di     ;increment the output array ES:DI
    loop loop8         ;finish plane 0

    ret
Fill8    endp
```

```
; Subroutine called by "Mux" to fill the four output bytes.
; Input parameters:
; DS:SI          points to word in buffer to multiplex
; bl register   contains the bit mask

; Output parameters:
; ES:DI          points to output word

; Assembly Language Calling protocol:
;     Call Fill4

Fill4    proc near
    lodsb              ;get the byte into AL, inc DS:SI
    mov cx,04          ;four bits in a word

loop4:
    rcr al,1           ;get bit into carry
    jnc zero4          ;jump if bit is 0
    or es:[di],bl      ;or in a 1 into the output

zero4:    inc  di      ;point to next byte in output
    loop loop4

    ret
Fill4    endp
```

12.15   CLIPPING

The Cohen-Sutherland algorithm is implemented for clipping a line. It is based upon the divide-and-conquer technique of continually segmenting a line until the entire line can be either accepted or rejected. A set of endpoints is provided to the routine, and a reject flag or a new set of endpoints is returned from this routine. The reject flag indicates that none of the line is contained within the specified window. The new set of endpoints indicate the portion of the line that does fit into the window. These endpoints may then be used to draw the line, improving performance because only the points actually contained in the window are calculated.

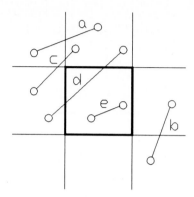

FIGURE 12.13   Clipping a Line

The Clipper routine in Listing 12.47 performs this clipping operation. The coordinates of the endpoints of the line are passed to the routine in an *X* and *Y* array. The upper-left and lower-right coordinates of the window are also passed to the routine. If the line is rejected, the return variable is set to 1. If it is accepted, the return variable is reset to 0, and the new coordinates are returned in the *X* and *Y* arrays.

The clipping operation is illustrated in Figure 12.13. Lines *a* and *b* are rejected by the reject routine without segmentation because both set of endpoints violate a single border line. Line *c* is rejected after calculation because both endpoints violate two border lines. Line *d* is accepted after calculation because a portion of the line resides in the window. The original endpoints of both lines *c* and *d* are in the same quadrants; thus, segmentation is required before a decision can be made. Line *e* is accepted without calculation because both endpoints reside in the window.

LISTING 12.47   Clipping a Line

```
/* clip a line so that it fits into a rectangular window
input parameters:
x[]           = x-coordinates of endpoints of line x[0],x[1]
y[]           = y-coordinates of endpoints of line y[0],y[1]
xmin,ymin  = coordinates of lower left corner of rectangular
xmax,ymax  = coordinates of upper right corner of rectangular

output parameters:
x[]           = clipped x-coordinates x[0],x[1] of line
y[]           = clipped y-coordinates y[0],y[1] of line
function returns a 1 if line is trivially rejected
```

```
   calling protocol:
reject = CLIPPER(x,y,xmin,xmax,ymin,ymax) */

CLIPPER(x,y,xmin,xmax,ymin,ymax)
int x[],y[],xmin,xmax,ymin,ymax;

{ int code1,code2,rejected,accepted,done=0,t1,t2,t3;

do
{
 /* determine the OutCode of point 1 */
code1=OutCode(x[0],y[0],xmin,xmax,ymin,ymax);
 /* determine the OutCode of point 2 */
code2=OutCode(x[1],y[1],xmin,xmax,ymin,ymax);

if((rejected=Reject(code1,code2))!=0) return(1);
 else {
  if((accepted=Accept(code1,code2))!=0) return(0);
   else {
     if(code1==0)
       { t1=x[0]; t2=y[0]; t3=code1;
          x[0]=x[1]; y[0]=y[1]; code1=code2;
          x[1]=t1; y[1]=t2; code2=t3; }

     if((code1 & 0x01)!=0) {
x[0]+=(x[1]-x[0])*(float)(ymax-y[0])/(y[1]-y[0]);
y[0]=ymax; }

     else if((code1 & 0x02)!=0) {
x[0]+=(x[1]-x[0])*(float)(ymin-y[0])/(y[1]-y[0]);
y[0]=ymin; }

     else if((code1 & 0x04)!=0) {
y[0]+=(y[1]-y[0])*(float)(xmax-x[0])/(x[1]-x[0]);
x[0]=xmax; }

     else if((code1 & 0x08)!=0) {
y[0]+=(y[1]-y[0])*(float)(xmin-x[0])/(x[1]-x[0]);
x[0]=xmin; }

}} /* end of elses */
 } while (1==1);
}
```

The Clipper routine calls upon three subroutines. The first, named OutCode, is used to determine the quadrant where a point exists with respect to the window. The OutCode values depend on the quadrant and are shown in Figure 12.14.

The other routines, Accept and Reject, are used to determine if a point can be trivially accepted or rejected. These routines are listed in Listing 12.48.

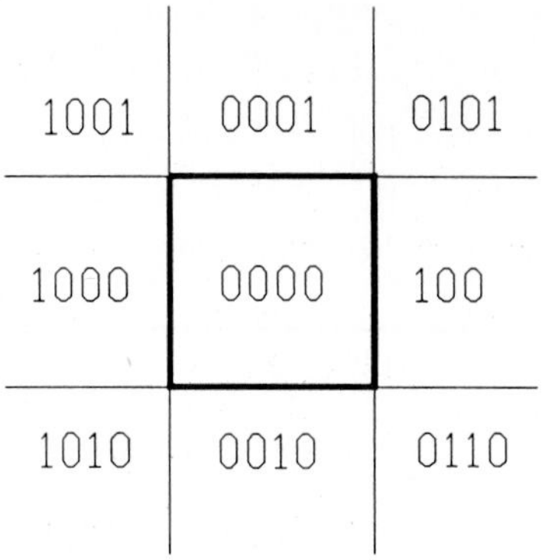

1001	0001	0101
1000	0000	100
1010	0010	0110

FIGURE 12.14 Definition of the OutCodes

LISTING 12.48 Clipping Subroutines

```
/* determine the outcode of a point at x,y with respect to a
      window which is limited by xmin,ymin and xmax,ymax
Input parameters:
 x,y           = point to determine outcode
xmin,ymin      = coordinates of lower left corner of rectangle
 xmax,ymax     = coordinates of upper right corner of rectangle
Output parameter:
 Function Returns a binary four bit code as follows:
  bit 0 = point is to top of window
  bit 1 = point is to bottom of window
  bit 2 = point is to right of window
  bit 3 = point is to left of window
Calling protocol */
code = OutCode(x,y,xmin,xmax,ymin,ymax)

OutCode(x,y,xmin,xmax,ymin,ymax)
int x,y,xmin,xmax,ymin,ymax;
{ int code; code=0;
if(y>ymax) code |= 0x01;        /* beneath window */
 else if(y<ymin) code |= 0x02; /* above window */
if(x>xmax) code |= 0x04;        /* to right of window */
 else if(x<xmin) code |= 0x08; /* to left of window */
return(code);
}

/* determine if a code can be rejected trivially
Input parameters:
 code1     = out code of point 1
 code2     = out code of point 2
```

```
Output parameter:
 Function Returns a 0 if cannot reject and a 1 if reject

Calling protocol:
 rejected = Reject(code1,code2) */

Reject(code1,code2)
int code1,code2;
{ if ((code1 & code2)==0) return(0); /* cannot reject */
                  else return(1); /* reject the line */
}

 /* determine if a code can be accepted trivially
Input parameters:
 code1       = out code of point 1
 code2       = out code of point 2

Calling protocol:
 accepted = Accept(code1,code2) */

Accept(code1,code2)
int code1,code2;
{ if ((code1 | code2)==0) return(1); /* accept the line */
                  else return(0); /* cannot accept */
}
```

12.16 CLEARING DISPLAY MEMORY

Clearing the display memory is actually a special case of setting the display memory to a constant value. Routines are provided to clear a character line, a group of character lines, a rectangular window, or an entire page. The techniques employed to clear alphanumerics are different from those employed to clear graphics. Clearing alphanumerics is accomplished by setting character codes to a "space" and by setting the attributes to a desired value. Clearing graphics is accomplished by setting all pixels to a desired value.

12.16.1 Clearing a Character Row

A character row consists of a set of characters in a horizontal line. The length of a character row is determined by the virtual window defined in the Offset Register. The height of a character row is determined by the number of scan lines in the active character font, as set in the Maximum Scan Line Register.

A character row or multiple character rows can be cleared by using the ClrLine routine in Listing 12.49. This routine is useful when displaying text on the screen. The selected lines are cleared, and the cursor is positioned to the far left character position of the top line cleared. The lines can be cleared on any display page, not necessarily the active display page. The desired page number is passed to the routine; however, this page does not become the active display page. The line number and the number of lines to clear are also passed to the routine as parameters.

LISTING 12.49   Clearing a Line or Multiple Lines

```
/* Clear a line of text in any mode. Positions the cursor at the
      first position of the first line cleared.
Input parameters:
 line     desired character line
 numline  number of lines to clear
 page     desired page
Calling protocol: */
 ClrLine(page,line,numline)

int page,line,numline;
{ int i,buf[4];

 GetStat(buf); /* determine the current display mode*/
 switch(buf[1])
 {
 case 0: case 1: case 2: case 3: case 7:
    AClear(page,line,numline,7); break;
 case 4: case 5: case 6:
 case 0x0D: case 0x0E: case 0x0F: case 0x10:
 case 0x11: case 0x12: case 0x13:
    AClear(page,line,numline,0); break;
 }
Cursor(page,line,0);
}
```

The ClrLine routine operates in any of the alphanumeric or graphics modes. In the alphanumeric modes, an attribute of 07 hex is written to the cleared region of the display. This translates into a 0 background color, typically black, and a 7 foreground color, typically white. In the graphics modes, an attribute of 00 hex is written to the cleared region. The foreground color is 0, typically black, and there is no background color written to the display in the alphanumeric modes. Not writing a background color produces a transparent effect.

The ClrLine routine calls an assembly language routine AClear, shown in Listing 12.50, which actually clears the lines. This routine utilizes the scroll-up command. The starting row and column coordinates and the number of rows are passed to the routine as parameters. The number of characters per line is automatically determined and is used as the number of columns to scroll. Because the scroll operation operates only on the active display page, it is necessary to change the active display page before executing the scroll operation. The original active display page is reactivated at the conclusion of this routine.

LISTING 12.50 Clearing Alphanumeric Lines

```
; Clear the display by scrolling in blanks
; Input parameters:
; page           = desired display page
; row            = starting row to clear
; numrow         = number of rows to clear
; attribute      = attribute to scroll into window
;                  =7 for alpha modes
;                  =0 for graphics modes

; Calling protocol:
; AClear(page,row,numrow,attribute);

_AClear    proc far
    Prefix

;   determine state, page=bh ah=number of columns
    mov  ah,0fh
    int 10h
    push bx          ;save page in bh
    dec  ah          ;number of columns -1
    push ax          ;save number of columns in ah

;   select new page
    mov al,[bp+6]    ;get page into al
    mov ah,05        ;select active display page
    int 10h          ;select active page

    mov ah,07        ;request scroll screen down
    mov bh,[bp+12]   ;attribute
    mov al,[bp+10]   ;get number of rows to clear
    xor cl,cl        ;starting column number = 0
    mov ch,[bp+8]    ;get starting row number
    pop dx           ;get number of columns in dh
    mov dl,dh        ;ending column in dl
    mov dh,al        ;get number of rows
    add dh,ch        ;end row = start row + # of rows
    dec dh           ;minus 1
    int 10h          ;call bios for scroll

;   reset to original page
    pop ax
    mov al,ah        ;get page number in al
    mov ah,05        ;select active display page
    int 10h          ;select active page

    Postfix
_AClear  endp
```

12.16.2 Clearing a Window

A window consists of a rectangular region on the display. It is defined by the upper-left coordinate and the lower-right coordinate. If the window is an alphanumeric window, the coordinates are character positions. This occurs in the alphanumeric display modes 0, 1, 2, 3, and 7. If the window is a graphics window, the coordinates are pixels. This occurs in the graphics display modes 4, 5, 6, D, E, 10, 11, 12, 13 hex.

The techniques used to perform the clearing operation are determined by the active display mode. The routine ClrWin in Listing 12.51 clears a window by determining the active display mode and taking the appropriate action. The page number is passed to this routine. Like the ClrLine routine, ClrWin can clear a page that is not the active page. The corner coordinates are passed to the routine along with the desired color that will be loaded into the cleared window. If an alphanumeric mode is active, the coordinates are measured in character positions and the color represents the character attribute. If a graphics mode is active, the coordinates are measured in pixels and the color represents the data to be loaded into each pixel within the window. Typically, the coordinates of the first corner—the upper right—are lower than the coordinates of the second corner—the lower left. If this is not the case, the routine switches the coordinates to compensate.

LISTING 12.51 Clearing a Window

```
/* preset a window in display memory to a specific color.
Input parameters:
   page        desired page
   x1,y1       top left corner of window
   x2,y2       bottom right corner of window
   color       desired color
Calling protocol: */
ClrWin(page,x1,y1,x2,y2,color)

int page,color,x1,y1,x2,y2;
{ char bmask; int buf[4],address,numbyte,nrow,ncol,t;

ncol = (x2-x1)+1; nrow = (y2-y1)+1;

/* protect for reversed windows */
if(ncol<0)
  { ncol = -ncol; t=x2; x2=x1; x1=t; }
if(nrow<0)
  { nrow = -nrow; t=y2; y2=y1; y1=t; }
```

```
GetStat(buf);
switch(buf[1]) /* operate depending on mode */
{
 case 0: case 1: case 2: case 3: case 7:
    if(page != buf[0]) /* change only if new page */
     { SetPage(page); /* select the new page */
       ClrAWin(color,y1,x1,y2,x2);
       SetPage(buf[0]); /* reselect the old page */
     }
    else
        ClrAWin(color,y1,x1,y2,x2);
    break;

 case 4: case 5:
   numbyte = ncol >> 2; /* four pixels per byte */
   switch(color & 0x03) /* only use foreground color 0-2 */
   {case 0: bmask = 0x00; break;
   case 1: bmask = 0x55; break;
   case 2: bmask = 0xAA; break;
   case 3: bmask = 0xFF; break; }
/*     do even rows (y/2) * 40 * 2 = y*40 */
address = (y1*40) + (x1>>2);
ClrGWin(0xB800,address,bmask,numbyte,nrow/2,80);
/* do odd rows */
ClrGWin(0xBA00,address,bmask,numbyte,nrow/2,80);
break;

 case 6:
    numbyte = ncol >> 3; /* eight pixels per byte */
    if (color==0) bmask = 0; else bmask = 0xff;
    /* do even rows (y/2) * 80 = y*40 */
    address = (y1*40) + (x1>>3);
    ClrGWin(0xB800,address,bmask,numbyte,nrow/2,80);
    /* do odd rows */
    ClrGWin(0xBA00,address,bmask,numbyte,nrow/2,80);
    break;

 case 0x0D:
    mbyte = ncol >> 3; /* eight pixels per byte */
    address = (page&7) * 0x2000 + (y1*40) + (x1>>3);
    Clear4(0xA000,address,color,numbyte,nrow,40);
    break;

 case 0x0E:
    numbyte = ncol >> 3; /* eight pixels per byte */
    address = (page&3) * 0x4000 + (y1*80) + (x1>>3);
    Clear4(0xA000,address,color,numbyte,nrow,80);
    break;
```

```
    case 0x0F:
        numbyte = ncol >> 3; /* eight pixels per byte */
        address = (page&1) * 0x8000 + (y1*80) + (x1>>3);
        if (color!=0) bmask = 0xff; else bmask = 0;
        ClrGWin(0xA000,address,bmask,numbyte,nrow,80);
        break;
    case 0x10:
        numbyte = ncol >> 3; /* eight pixels per byte */
        address = ((page&1)*0x8000) + (y1*80) + (x1>>3);
        Clear4(0xA000,address,color,numbyte,nrow,80);
        break;
    case 0x11:
        numbyte = ncol >> 3; /* eight pixels per byte */
        address = (y1*80) + (x1>>3);
        if (color!=0) bmask = 0xff; else bmask = 0;
        ClrGWin(0xA000,address,bmask,numbyte,nrow,80);
        break;
    case 0x12:
        numbyte = ncol >> 3; /* eight pixels per byte */
        address =(y1*80) + (x1>>3);
        Clear4(0xA000,address,color,numbyte,nrow,80);
        break;
    case 0x13:
        numbyte = ncol; /* one pixel per byte */
        address =(y1*320) + x1;
        ClrGWin(0xA000,address,color,numbyte,nrow,320);
        break;
    }
}
```

The ClrWin routine calls a subroutine that clears the four display planes; this subroutine, named Clear4, is presented in Listing 12.52. This is called in display modes D, E, 10, and 12 hex. It is assumed that all four display planes are used to store the pixel color, producing a 16-color display. If this is not the case, the subroutine Clear4 has to be modified.

LISTING 12.52 Clearing Multiple Planes

```
/* clear all four display planes

Input parameters:
    segment      segment address of display memory
    address      offset address of display memory
```

```
color          desired color to load into cleared area
numbyte        number of bytes per row in the window
nrow           number of rows in the window
offset         number of bytes in a row of the virtual display
```

Calling protocol: */
Clear4(segment,address,color,numbyte,nrow,offset)

```
 int color,segment,address,numbyte,nrow,offset;
{ char bmask;

 if ((color&1)!=0) bmask = 0xff; else bmask = 0;
MapMask(0x01);
ClrGWin(segment,address,bmask,numbyte,nrow,offset);
 if ((color&2)!=0) bmask = 0xff; else bmask = 0;
MapMask(0x02);
ClrGWin(segment,address,bmask,numbyte,nrow,offset);
 if ((color&4)!=0) bmask = 0xff; else bmask = 0;
MapMask(0x04);
ClrGWin(segment,address,bmask,numbyte,nrow,offset);
 if ((color&8)!=0) bmask = 0xff; else bmask = 0;
MapMask(0x08);
ClrGWin(segment,address,bmask,numbyte,nrow,offset);
MapMask(0x0f);
}
```

The ClrWin routine calls an assembly language routine called ClrAWin, shown in Listing 12.53, to clear a window in the alphanumeric modes. This routine performs the scrolling operation on the desired window.

LISTING 12.53 Clearing an Alphanumeric Window

```
; Clear the display at the current page by scrolling in blanks
; Input parameters:
; attribute      attribute to scroll into window
; row1,col1      top-left corner of window
; row2,col2      bottom-right corner of window

; Calling protocol
; ClrAWin(attribute,row1,col1,row2,col2);

_ClrAWin        proc        far
    Prefix

    mov bh,[bp+6]   ;attribute to scroll in
    mov ch,[bp+8]   ;get top-left row
    mov cl,[bp+10]  ;get top-left column
    mov ax,[bp+12]  ;get bottom-right row
```

```
        mov dl,[bp+14]   ;get bottom-right column
        mov dh,al        ;get bottom-right row
        sub al,ch        ;bottom row - top row in AL
        inc al           ;number of rows +1
        mov ah,06h       ;request scroll screen
        int 10h          ;call bios

        Postfix
_ClrAWin endp
```

The ClrWin routine calls an assembly language routine called ClrGWin, shown in Listing 12.54, to clear a window in the graphics modes. This routine moves the desired color into the pixels contained within the desired window.

LISTING 12.54   Clearing a Graphics Window

```
; Write a plane of data to the display memory.
; Input Parameters
; segment        segment address of starting coordinates
; offset         offset address of starting coordinates
; color          bit to fill into window
; nbyte          number of bytes per row
; nrow           number of rows
; bpvrow         bytes per virtual row

; Calling protocol
; ClrGWin(segment,offset,color,nbyte,nrow,bpvrow);

_ClrGWin proc far
    Prefix

; load the segment:offset address to display memory in ES:DI
    mov ax,[bp+6]    ;get segment to display memory
    mov es,ax        ;load into ES
    mov di,[bp+8]    ;get offset to display memory

; set up constants for the data moving
    mov dx,[bp+14]   ;get the number of rows per window
    mov bx,[bp+16]   ;get window bytes per row
    sub bx,[bp+12]   ;(virtual - window )bytes per row
    mov cx,[bp+12]   ;get bytes per window
    mov al,[bp+10]   ;get color

; move one row per loop
runloop:
    push cx          ;save number of bytes per line
rep stosb            ;load with constant
    pop cx           ;restore number of bytes per line
    add di,bx        ;add byte increment
```

```
    dec dx          ;decrement the row counter
    jg  runloop     ;repeat for all rows

    Postfix
_ClrGWin endp
```

This routine utilizes the store byte instruction (STOSB) with a repeat field to
clear a line. The display memory address is incremented automatically because
of the instruction. At the end of each row, a constant is added to the address
so that the next row will be accessed. This constant is equal to the width of the
virtual image minus the width of the desired window. The constant is stored in
the BX register.

12.16.3 Clearing a Page

The entire page can be cleared using the ClrPage routine in Listing 12.55. This
routine simply sets up the end coordinates for the ClrWin routine.

LISTING 12.55 Clearing a Page

```
/* Clear a page of text in any mode.
Input parameters:
 page    desired page to clear
 attr    attribute

Calling protocol: */
ClrPage(page,attr)

int page; char attr;
{ int buf[4];

 /* determine the current display mode*/
 GetStat(buf); /* mode is in buf[1] */

switch(buf[1])
 {
  case 0: case 1: case 2: case 3: case 7:
   ClrWin(page,0,0,buf[2],buf[3],attr); break;
  case 4: case 5: case 0x0D: case 0x13:
   ClrWin(page,0,0,319,199,attr); break;
  case 6: case 0x0E:
   ClrWin(page,0,0,639,199,attr); break;
  case 0x0F: case 0x10:
   ClrWin(page,0,0,639,349,attr); break;
  case 0x11: case 0x12:
   ClrWin(page,0,0,639,479,attr); break;
 }
}
```

12.17 DOWNLOADING CHARACTER FONTS

In the alphanumeric modes, four character fonts can reside in the EGA simultaneously, and eight can reside in the VGA. These fonts reside in bit plane 2, which is segmented into four or eight blocks. Fonts, either user-defined or ROM-resident, are loaded into these blocks.

12.17.1 Writing a Font in the Alphanumeric Modes

User-defined character sets are loaded into display memory by using the routine WrFont in Listing 12.56. The font bit patterns are passed to this routine in a byte array along with the number of scan lines per character. Each block in display memory can contain 256 characters, each character occupying up to 32 bytes. This routine can download any number of characters, beginning at any character position within the block. For example, three characters can be loaded into ASCII positions 65 through 67, thus overwriting A, B, and C. The BIOS call Load User Text Set at AH = 11 and AL = 10 is used. This does not force a mode set.

LISTING 12.56 Writing a Character Set to Display Memory

```
; Write a font into one of the font blocks in display memory
; Input parameters:
; input       array containing character bit patterns
; blknum      block number
;         (0-3) for EGA
;         (0-7) for VGA
; numline     number of scan lines per character

; Calling protocol:
; WrFont(input,blknum,numline);
_WrFont proc far
    Prefix
    push bp          ;save the base point register

    mov bl,[bp+10]   ;get block number
    and bl,07        ;limit to 0-7 block number

    les ax,[bp+6]    ;point to "C" buffer es:ax
    mov bh,[bp+12]   ;# bytes per character
    mov bp,ax        ;load offset to "C" buffer es:bp
    mov cx,100h      ;do for 256 characters
    xor dx,dx        ;begin at 0
    mov ax,1110h     ;load font
    int 10h
```

```
    pop bp              ;restore the base point register
    Postfix
_WrFont endp
```

The programmer may select to download a character set into the display memory by using one of the BIOS calls. The selected font is loaded into one of the blocks of bit plane 2 reserved for the character sets. The programmer may download a user-defined character set or a ROM-resident character set. The routines UserSet, Rom8×8, Rom8×14, and Rom8×16 in Listing 12.57 perform this function. A parameter passed to these routines dictates whether a mode set will occur during the loading process.

LISTING 12.57 Loading ROM-Resident Character Sets

```
; Load a pointer to a user defined alphanumerics character set
; Input parameters:
; segment          segment address of font
; offset           offset address of font
; numchar          number of characters to load
; bpc              bytes per character
; block            desired block
;                      0-3 EGA
;                      0-7 VGA
; modeset          Mode set flag 0=No Mode Set 1=Mode Set
; Calling protocol:
; UserSet(segment,offset,numchar,bpc,block,modeset);
_UserSet proc far
    Prefix
    push    bp         ;save the base point register
    mov es,[bp+6]      ;get segment address
    mov bp,[bp+8]      ;get offset address
    mov cx,[bp+10]     ;get number of characters
    mov bh,[bp+12]     ;get bytes per character
    mov bl,[bp+14]     ;get block number
    mov dl,[bp+16]     ;get mode flag
    mov al,00h         ;assume no mode set
    cmp dl,1           ;test for mode       set
    je   u0
    mov al,10h         ;no mode set
u0: mov ah,11h         ;load font pointer
    int 10h
    pop bp             ;restore the base point register
```

```
        Postfix
_UserSet endp


; Load a pointer to an 8×8 (lower 128) graphics character set
; Input parameters:
; block       block number to load font into.
;                   0-3 EGA
;                   0-7 VGA
; modeset     Mode set flag 0=No Mode Set 1=Mode Set

; Calling protocol:
; Rom8×8(segment,modeset);

_Rom8×8 proc far
        Prefix

        mov bl,[bp+6]     ;get block number
        mov dl,[bp+8]
        mov al,02h        ;assume no mode set
        cmp dl,1          ;test for mode set
        je  u2
        mov al,12h        ;no mode set
u2: mov ah,11h            ;load font pointer 8×8
        int 10h

        Postfix
_Rom8×8 endp

; Load a pointer to an 8x14 alphanumerics character set
; Input parameters:
; block       block number to load font into.
;                   0-3 EGA
;                   0-7 VGA
; modeset     Mode set flag 0=No Mode Set 1=Mode Set

; Calling protocol:
; Rom8×14(block,modeset);

_Rom8×14 proc far
        Prefix

        mov bl,[bp+6]     ;get block number
        mov dl,[bp+8]
        mov al,01h        ;assume no mode set
        cmp dl,1          ;test for mode      set
        je  u1
        mov al,11h        ;no mode set

u1: mov ah,11h            ;load font pointer 8×8
        int 10h

        Postfix
_Rom8×14 endp
```

```
; -VGA ONLY- load a pointer to an 8x16 graphics character set
; Input parameters:
; block        block number to load font into.
;              0-3 EGA
;              0-7 VGA
; modeset      Mode set flag 0=No Mode Set 1=Mode Set

; Calling protocol:
; Rom8×16(block,modeset);

_Rom8×16 proc far
     Prefix

     mov bl,[bp+6]    ;get block number
     mov dl,[bp+8]
     mov al,04h       ;assume no mode set
     cmp dl,1         ;test for mode       set
     je  u4
     mov al,14h       ;no mode set

u4:  mov ah,11h       ;load font pointer 8×8
     int 10h

     Postfix
_Rom8×16 endp
```

12.17.2 Writing a Font in the Graphics Modes

In the graphics modes, it is not necessary—or possible—to load the character sets into bit plane 2 because bit plane 2 is used for graphics information. Two pointers are provided through interrupt vector 1F hex and interrupt vector 43 hex. Only one character set can be active at a time. The 8-by-8 character set is actually split into two character sets, each 128 characters long. This is done to provide downward compatibility to the 7-bit ASCII code; it has no other real purpose. This pointer references either a user-defined font in RAM memory or a preprogrammed ROM-resident font. BIOS must be told the number of character rows that are present on a single image. This value is necessary so that BIOS can determine the location of a character row in display memory.

The BIOS character string routines operate in the graphics modes as well as the alphanumeric modes. In the graphics modes, the BIOS string-related routines are asked to write characters on the display at specified row and column positions. The BIOS routines are passed the ASCII character code, the row and column, and the foreground color of the character. In order to draw the character, the BIOS routine must know where to begin drawing the character and how many characters to draw. In the graphics modes all characters are eight bits wide.

In the graphics modes, pointers to either user-defined character sets or ROM-based character sets can be passed to BIOS by using the GUser8×8, GUserSet, GRom8×8, GRom8×14, and GROM8×16 routines in Listing 12.58.

LISTING 12.58 Loading Graphics Modes Character Sets

```
; Load a pointer to a user defined 8x8 (upper 128) graphics
;   character set for interrupt INT 1F hex.
; Input parameters:
; segment           segment address of font
; offset            offset address of font

; Calling protocol:
; GUser8×8(segment,offset);

_GUser8x8 proc far
    Prefix
    push bp          ;save the base point register

    mov es,[bp+6]    ;get segment address
    mov bp,[bp+8]    ;get offset address
    mov ax,1120h     ;load font pointer 8x8
    int 10h

    pop bp           ;restore the base point register
    Postfix
_GUser8x8 endp

; Load a pointer to a user defined graphics character set
; Input parameters:
; segment           segment address of font
; offset            offset address of font
; numrow            number of scan lines on the display
;             1=14 scan lines
;             2=25 scan lines
;             3=43 scan lines
; bpc               bytes per character

; Calling protocol:
; GUserSet(segment,offset,numrow,bpc);

_GUserSet proc far
    Prefix
    push bp          ;save the base point register

    mov es,[bp+6]    ;get segment address
    mov bp,[bp+8]    ;get offset address
    mov bl,[bp+10]   ;get number of scan lines per display
    mov cx,[bp+12]   ;get bytes per character
    mov ax,1121h     ;load font pointer
    int 10h

    pop bp           ;restore the base point register
    Postfix
_GUserSet endp
```

```
; Load a pointer to an 8x8 (lower 128) graphics character set
; Input parameters:
; segment          segment address of font
; offset           offset address of font
; numrow           number of scan lines on the display
;                1=14 scan lines
;                2=25 scan lines
;                3=43 scan lines
; Calling protocol:
; GRom8×8(segment,offset,numrow);

_GRom8×8 proc far
    Prefix
    push bp          ;save the base point register

    mov es,[bp+6]    ;get segment address
    mov bp,[bp+8]    ;get offset address
    mov cx,[bp+10]   ;get bytes per character
    mov ax,1123h     ;load font pointer 8×8
    int 10h

    pop bp           ;restore the base point register
    Postfix
_GRom8×8 endp

; Load a pointer to an 8x14 graphics character set
; Input parameters:
; segment          segment address of font
; offset           offset address of font
; numrow           number of scan lines on the display
;                1=14 scan lines
;                2=25 scan lines
;                3=43 scan lines
; Calling protocol:
; GRom8×14(segment,offset,numrow);

_GRom8x14 proc far
    Prefix
    push bp          ;save the base point register

    mov es,[bp+6]    ;get segment address
    mov bp,[bp+8]    ;get offset address
    mov cx,[bp+10]   ;get bytes per character
    mov ax,1123h     ;load font pointer 8x14
    int 10h

    pop bp           ;restore the base point register
    Postfix
_GRom8×14 endp
```

```
; -VGA ONLY- load a pointer to an 8x16 graphics character set
; Input parameters
; segment              segment address of font
; offset               offset address of font
; numrow               number of scan lines on the display
;                1=14 scan lines
;                2=25 scan lines
;                3=43 scan lines

; Calling protocol:
; GRom8×16(segment,offset,numrow);

_GRom8×16 proc far
    Prefix
    push bp          ;save the base point register

    mov es,[bp+6]    ;get segment address
    mov bp,[bp+8]    ;get offset address
    mov cx,[bp+10]   ;get bytes per character
    mov ax,1124h     ;load font pointer 8x16
    int 10h

    pop bp           ;restore the base point register
    Postfix
_GRom8×16 endp
```

12.17.3 Reading the Font Information

The location of the characters sets can be determined by calling the routine FontInfo in Listing 12.59.

LISTING 12.59 Return Font Information

```
; Return the font related information.
; Input parameters:
;   choice           particular information desired (0-9)

; Output parameters:
; buf    integer return information buffer
;           [0]      pointer segment
;           [1]      pointer offset
;           [2]      bytes per character regardless of choice
;           [3]      number of rows regardless of choice

; Calling protocol:
; FontInfo(buf,choice);

_FontInfo proc far
    Prefix
```

```
        push bp             ;save the base pointer
        lds si,[bp+6]       ;point to buffer
        mov ah,11h          ;font
        mov al,30h          ;return character generator info
        mov bh,[bp+10]      ;get selection
        int 10h

        mov ax,es
        mov ds:[si],ax      ;return segment
        inc si
        inc si
        mov ax,bp
        mov ds:[si],ax      ;return offset
        inc si
        inc si
        mov ds:[si],cx      ;return bytes per character
        inc si
        inc si
        xor dh,dh
        inc dx              ;number of char rows = dl+1
        mov ds:[si],dx      ;return rows per screen

        pop bp              ;restore the base pointer
        Postfix
_FontInfo endp
```

The FontInfo routine is passed a font number, 0–7, that specifies which of the pointers should be returned. Table 12.5 lists the possibilities for this routine.

A long pointer is returned to the calling program to point to the top of the current font buffer. The ROM-resident fonts are usually located in the EGA/ VGA BIOS ROM, which is located in host memory space C000:xxxx. In addition to the font pointer, information regarding the current number of character rows on the screen and the number of scan lines per character is also returned to the calling routine.

It should be noted that these parameters refer to the active character set, not the character set referenced in this subroutine call. For example, if an 8-by-14 character set is active, and information is requested regarding an 8-by-8 character set, the number of bytes per character returned from this subroutine will be 12, reflecting the active mode.

12.17.4 Selecting a Character Set

Once the fonts are downloaded in the alphanumeric modes, the programmer can select which font or fonts are active. Up to two fonts, each 256 characters long, can be active at a time, providing a 512-character resident set. The ASCII code for each character is 8 bits wide, which allows a single character to be selected from the 256 characters in one set. An additional bit, bit 3, is provided

TABLE 12.5 Return Font Information

Font #	Font Size	Adapter	Mode
0	Int 1F hex	EGA/VGA	Graphics
1	Int 43 hex	EGA/VGA	Graphics
2	8-by-14	EGA/VGA	Alphanumeric
3	8-by-8 (Lower)	EGA/VGA	Alphanumeric
4	8-by-8 (Upper)	EGA/VGA	Alphanumeric
5	9-by-14	EGA/VGA	Alphanumeric
6	8-by-16	VGA	Alphanumeric
7	9-by-16	VGA	Alphanumeric

in the character attribute byte that can select from among eight of these sets of characters.

These two resident sets are called *A* and *B*. The Character Map Select Register, is provided to associate each of the *A* and *B* active fonts with one of the four or eight resident fonts. The default condition is *A* = 0 and *B* = 0 which results in all characters referencing the 256 characters in block 0. Block 0 is the only resident block of memory loaded with a character set at a mode set initialization command.

The active character sets, *A* and *B*, are modified by calling the WrBlock routine. The VGA can interrogate this register by using the RdBlock routine. Both are listed in Listing 12.60.

LISTING 12.60 Read and Write the Character Set Block

```
/* -VGA Only- Returns A font # in buf[0] and B font # in buf[1]
Input parameters:
  buf[]  buffer which contains the A font and B font block
numbers
          buf[0] = A font number
          buf[1] = B font number
Calling protocol: */
 RdBlock(buf)

int buf[];
{ int block,a,b;
outp(0x3c4,3); block = inp(0x3c5);
b = (block >>2) & 0x03;
a = block & 0x03;
```

```
if((block & 0x20)!=0) b += 4;
if((block & 0x10)!=0) a += 4;
buf[0] = a; buf[1] = b;
}
/* set the block specifier from "a" and "b" block #'s
Input parameters:
 ablock        block number for font a
 bblock        block number for font b

Calling Protocol */
 WrBlock(a,b)

int a,b;
{ int block;

block = (a&3)|((b&3)<<2);
if((a & 0x4)!=0) block += 0x10;
if((b & 0x4)!=0) block += 0x20;
BlockVal(block);
}
```

The WrBlock routine calls an assembly language routine named BlockVal, presented in Listing 12.61, to actually invoke the BIOS call.

LISTING 12.61 Invoking the Set Block BIOS Call

```
; Set the value for the A and B active blocks
; input parameters
; block  desired block code containing A and B block numbers

; calling parameters
; BlockVal(block);

_BlockVal proc far
    Prefix

    mov bl,[bp+6]    ;get desired mode
    mov ax,1103h     ;set blocks
    int 10h          ;interrupt 10

    Postfix
_BlockVal endp
```

If both the *A* and *B* block pointers are loaded with the value 1, both active sets refer to the character set resident in block 1. Loading an 8-by-8 character set into block 1 while an 8-by-14 character set is in block 0 will result in an 8-by-8 character being displayed when block 1 is active and an 8-by-14 character set being displayed when block 0 is active. However, the Max Scan Line Register must be set each time the block is changed; otherwise, the wrong number of scan lines per character will be displayed. Because there is only one Max Scan Line Register, two character sets that have a different number of scan lines per character cannot be used simultaneously. The Max Screen Line Register can be loaded through the MaxLine routine in Listing 12.62.

LISTING 12.62 Loading the Max Scan Line Register

```
/* Load the Max Scan Line Register with the number of scan lines
        per character.
Input parameters:
 numline                the number of scan lines per character

Calling protocol: */
MaxLine(numline)
int numline;
{
numline --; /* the register stores the number of lines -1 */
outp(0x3d4,9); outp(0x3d5,numline);
}
```

Three routines are provided to handle all of the necessary parameters to set the screen to a format that has 25, 43, or 50 lines per screen. The cursor shape and the underline locations are related to the number of scan lines per character. The routine F25row in Listing 12.63 sets up an 8-by-14 character set, and the routines F43row (Listing 12.64) and F50row (Listing 12.65) set up an 8-by-8 character set in display formats that have 43 and 50 character rows. The cursor shape and the underline location must be modified to be compatible with these display formats. Note that this routine sets and resets the Cursor Emulation bit of the Miscellaneous byte stored in the BIOS storage area of host memory at location 0040:0087.

LISTING 12.63 Setting Up a 25-row Display

```
; Set up the display for a 25 row format.
; Input parameters:
;   block       block number to load font
;                   0-3 for EGA
;                   0-7 for VGA

; Calling protocol:
;   F25row(block);
```

```
_F25row proc far
    Prefix

; determine the active page
    mov ah,0fh
    int 10h          ;bh=page
    mov bl,bh        ;get page in lower
    push bx          ;save the current page in upper

; make page 0 active
    mov ax,0500h     ;set active page to 0
    int 10h

; load the 8×14 character set
    mov ax,1111h     ;set to 8x14 character set
    mov bl,[bp+6]    ;into desired block
    int 10h

; set to 1 bit 0 of the Miscellaneous Information byte in
; host memory to enable the cursor emulation.
    Set487           ;set bit 0 of 0000:0487h

; set the cursor position to a three line underline
    mov cx,0B0Dh     ;set cursor to begin at 11
    mov ah,01        ;and end at 13
    int 10h

; reset to 0 bit 0 of the Miscellaneous Information byte in
; host memory to disable the cursor emulation.
    Reset487         ;Reset bit 0 of 0000:0487h

; adjust the underline location
    mov dx,03d4h
    mov al,14h
    out dx,al
    inc dx
    mov al,0Dh
    out dx,al

; reset the active page to its previous value
    pop ax           ;get original page
    mov ah,05h       ;set original active page
    int 10h

    Postfix
_F25row endp
```

A similar routine called F43row, presented in Listing 12.64, resets the display to a 43-row format.

LISTING 12.64 Setting Up a 43-row Display

```
; Set up the display for a 43 row format.
; Input parameters
;   block       block number to load font
;                   0-3 for EGA
;                   0-7 for VGA

; Calling protocol:
; F43row(block);

_F43row proc far
    Prefix

; determine the active page
    mov ah,0fh
    int 10h             ;bh=page
    mov bl,bh           ;get page in lower
    push bx             ;save the current page in upper

; make page 0 active
    mov ax,0500h        ;set active page to 0
    int 10h

; load the 8x8 character set
    mov ax,1112h        ;set to 8x8 character set
    mov bl,[bp+6]
    int 10h

; set to 1 bit 0 of the Miscellaneous Information byte in
; host memory to enable the cursor emulation.
    Set487              ;set bit 0 of 0000:0487h

; set the cursor position to a block
    mov cx,0600h        ;begin at 6 end at 0
    mov ah,01
    int 10h             ;set the cursor

; reset to 0 bit 0 of the Miscellaneous Information byte in
; host memory to disable the cursor emulation.
    Reset487            ;Reset bit 0 of 0000:0487h

; adjust the underline location
    mov dx,03d4h        ;adjust underline location
    mov al,14h
    out dx,al
    inc dx
    mov al,07h          ;set underline to line 7
    out dx,al

; reset the active page to its previous value
    pop ax              ;get original page
```

```
    mov ah,05h      ;get old active page
    int 10h

    Postfix
_F43row endp
```

A similar routine called F50row, presented in Listing 12.65, resets the display to a 50-row format.

LISTING 12.65   Setting Up a 50-row Display

```
; Set up the display for a 50 row format.
; Input parameters:
;    block       block number to load font
;                    0-3 for EGA
;                    0-7 for VGA
; Calling protocol:
; F50row(block);

_F50row proc far
    Prefix

; determine the active page
    mov ah,0fh
    int 10h         ;bh=page
    mov bl,bh       ;get page in lower
    push bx         ;save the current page in upper

; make page 0 active
    mov ax,0500h    ;set active page to 0
    int 10h

; select 50 lines
    mov ax,1202h    ;select 400 scan lines
    mov bl,30h
    int 10h

; perform a mode set without changing display mode
    mov ah,0fh      ;determine the current mode
    int 10h         ;mode returned in al
    mov ah,00h      ;set mode
    int 10h

; load the 8×8 character set
    mov ax,1112h    ;set to 8×8 character set
    mov bl,[bp+6]   ;get block number
    int 10h
```

```
        ; set to 1 bit 0 of the Miscellaneous Information byte in
        ; host memory to enable the cursor emulation.
            Set487            ;set bit 0 of 0000:0487h

        ; set the cursor position to a block
            mov cx,0600h      ;begin at 6 end at 0
            mov ah,01
            int dh            ;set the cursor

        ; reset to 0 bit 0 of the Miscellaneous Information byte in
        ; host memory to disable the cursor emulation.
            Reset487          ;Reset bit 0 of 0000:0487h

        ; adjust the underline location
            mov dx,03d4h      ;adjust underline location
            mov al,14h
            out dx,al
            inc dx
            mov al,07h        ;set underline to line 7
            out dx,al

        ; reset the active page to its previous value
            pop ax            ;get original page
            mov ah,05h        ;get old active page
            int 10h

            Postfix
    _F50row endp
```

In the VGA, it is possible to set the number of scan lines per display to 200, 350, or 400. The number of scan lines per page divided by the number of scan lines per character yields the number of character rows per screen. The routine called SetLines, presented in Listing 12.66, performs this function.

LISTING 12.66   Setting the Number of Scan Lines per Page

```
        ; - VGA Only -Set the number of scan lines for the alphanumerics
        ;    modes
        ; Input parameters:
        ; numlines    number of lines per screen
        ;               0 = 200 scan lines (not available in mode 7)
        ;               1 = 350 scan lines
        ;               2 = 400 scan lines

        ; Calling protocol:
        ; SetLines(numlines);

    _SetLines proc far
            Prefix
```

```
        mov al,[bp+6]    ;get number of scan lines
        mov ah,12h       ;set number of scan lines
        mov bl,30h       ;part of definition
        int 10h

        Postfix
_SetLines        endp
```

12.17.5   Reading a Character Font

It is possible to read a font bit pattern into a C buffer by calling the RdFont routine in Listing 12.67. This routine performs a move string operation that transfers a specified number of characters from one memory location to another. In this case, the source of the move is the character font and the destination is the C buffer. The pointer to the character font bit patterns to read, the number of characters, and the number of bytes per character are also provided to this routine. The character set bit patterns are returned to the C buffer. The pointer to desired bit patterns can be provided by the FontInfo routine.

LISTING 12.67   Reading a Font

```
; Read a font from one memory location to another
; Input parameters:
;  input_segment    array segment address to read from
;  input_offset     array offset address to read from
;  output           output array to write to
;  nchar            number of characters to read
;  bpc              bytes per character

; Calling protocol:
; RdFont(input_segment,input_offset,output,nchar,bpc);

_RdFont proc far
        Prefix

        mov ax,[bp+14]  ;do for "nchar" characters
        mul word ptr [bp+16] ;# character * bytes/character
        mov cx,ax       ;into counter for number of bytes
        mov ds,[bp+6]   ;point to source segment
        mov si,[bp+8]   ;point to source offset
        les di,[bp+10]  ;point to destination
        rep movsb

        Postfix
_RdFont endp
```

12.17.6 Modifying a Character Set

The character set bit patterns, once entered into the C buffer, can be modified and written back to the display. One popular technique involves shifting the bit patterns in a character set so that an italic effect is achieved. The Ital14 routine in Listing 12.68 illustrates a typical shift operation for a 14-byte-long character set. The modified bit patterns can be written back to the display memory by using the "WrFont" routine.

LISTING 12.68 Creating an Italic Character Set

```
/* shift the bit patterns to create an italics effect
Input parameters:
 buf[]          buffer containing the bit patterns
 nchar          number of characters in the buffer

Calling Protocol: */
Ital14(buf,nchar)

unsigned char buf[]; int nchar;
{ int i,j;

for (i=0; i<nchar; i++)
{ j = i*14;
buf[j]=buf[j]>>3;         buf[j+1]=buf[j+1]>>3;
buf[j+2]=buf[j+2]>>2;     buf[j+3]=buf[j+3]>>2;
buf[j+4]=buf[j+4]>>1;     buf[j+5]=buf[j+5]>>1;
buf[j+6]=buf[j+6];        buf[j+7]=buf[j+7];
buf[j+8]=buf[j+8]<<1;     buf[j+9]=buf[j+9]<<1;
buf[j+10]=buf[j+10]<<2;   buf[j+11]=buf[j+11]<<2;
buf[j+12]=buf[j+12]<<3;   buf[j+13]=buf[j+13]<<3;
 }
}
```

12.17.7 Writing Characters without BIOS

In the graphics modes, it is possible to write a bit pattern directly to memory without going through BIOS. This provides the programmer with additional flexibility. The routine called GraphChr, presented in Listing 12.69, provides a means of writing a character to a specified address in display memory. It utilizes write mode 2 to achieve a high data-transfer rate. A character bit pattern of a specified number of scan lines is written to a specified address in display memory. The character color is also passed to this routine. The offset parameter refers to the number of bytes per scan line in the virtual display.

LISTING 12.69   Writing a Character Directly to the Display

```
; Load a graphics character into display memory directly
; Input assumptions:
;    The display is in a graphics mode
;    Write mode 2 is in effect

; Output assumptions:
;    Write Mode reset to 0

; input parameters
; charbuf[]  array containing bit pattern
; address    display address to load character
; offset     display offset
; bpc        bytes per character
; color      foreground color of character

; calling protocol
; GraphChr(charbuf,address,offset,bpc,color);

_GraphChr proc far
    Prefix

; point to the Bit Plane Mask
    mov ax,3ceh      ;point to address port
    mov dx,ax
    mov al,8
    out dx,al        ;load bit plane mask index
    inc dx           ;DX points to data port

    lds si,[bp+6]    ;character bit pattern in DS:SI
    mov ax,0A000h    ;segment to display memory
    mov es,ax        ;display memory offset in ES
    mov di,[bp+10]   ;display memory segment in DI
    mov bx,[bp+12]   ;offset in BX
    mov cx,[bp+14]   ;bytes per character in CX
    mov ah,[bp+16]   ;get color

runloop:
    mov al,ds:[si]   ;get bit pattern byte
    inc si           ;increment source SI
    out dx,al        ;load Bit Plane Mask Register
    mov es:[di],ah   ;write color
    add di,bx        ;add offset to DI destination

    loop runloop     ;repeat for bpc characters

    Postfix
_GraphChr endp
```

12.18 COLOR PALETTE

A color, when displayed on the video monitor, is composed of red, green, and blue components. In the Palette Registers, two bits are assigned to each of these three primary colors. Each primary color ranges in intensity from 0 to 3. Because the final color value is composed from a 6-bit word, there can be 64 possible colors. The 6 bits are located in the lower 6 bits in each of the 16 Palette Registers. Each Palette Register is 1 byte wide.

12.18.1 Encoding and Decoding Colors

It is common for the programmer to consider each of these primary color intensities as independent values. The EnCol routine encodes a color from the three intensities of red, green, and blue to a single coded value. The coding of this value is compatible with the Palette Registers. The DeCol routine decodes a single color byte, coded in the Palette Register format, into the three primary intensities. Because there are 16 Palette Registers, two additional routines—EnCols and DeCols—are provided to encode or decode a buffer of 16 colors. These four routines are listed in Listing 12.70.

LISTING 12.70 Encoding and Decoding Colors

```
/* encode a color (using the palette encoding scheme) from the
   RGB inputs.
Input parameters:
 red       red (0-3)
 green     green (0-3)
 blue      blue (0-3)

Output parameters:
 code      The encoded color is returned as the character
           function return parameter.

Calling protocol:
 code = EnCol(red,green,blue); */

char EnCol(red,green,blue)
 char red,green,blue;

{ char g0,b0,r0,g1,b1,r1,color;
  green&=3; blue&=3; red&=3;          /* limit inputs to 0-3 */
  g0=(green&2); g1=(green&1)<<4;      /* position green */
  r0=(red&2)<<1;    r1=(red&1)<<5;    /* position red */
  b0=(blue&2>>1;    b1=(blue&1)<<3;   /* position blue */
  color=g0+g1+r0+r1+b0+b1;            /* resultant coded color */
```

```
    return(color);
}
```

```
/* decode a color, coded in the palette encoding scheme, into
   the three primary colors "red", "green" and "blue".
Input parameters:
 color     coded color containing red, green, and blue
```

```
Output parameters:
 buf       output buffer where buf[0]=red, buf[1]=green,
           buf[2]=blue
```

```
Calling protocol:    */
 DecCol(color,buf)
```

```
char color,buf[];
```

```
{ buf[0] = ((color & 0x20)>>5)+((color&4)>>1); /* red */
 buf[1] = ((color & 0x10)>>4)+(color&2); /* green */
 buf[2] = ((color & 0x08)>>3)+((color&1)<<1)    /* blue */
}
```

```
/* Encode an array of colors, using the palette encoding scheme,
   from the RGB inputs.
Input parameters:
 red       buffer of 16 red (0-3) values
 green     buffer of 16 green (0-3) values
 blue      buffer of 16 blue (0-3) values
```

```
Output parameters:
 buf    Encoded color buffer containing 16 coded colors.
```

```
Calling protocol: */
EnCols(buf,r,g,b)
```

```
 char r[],g[],b[],buf[];
```

```
{ int i;
 for (i=0; i<16; i++) buf[i] = Encol(r[i],g[i],b[i]);
}
```

```
/* Decode an array of 16 colors from "inbuf", using the palette
   encoding scheme, into three primary color byte arrays "red",
   "green" and "blue".
Input parameters:
 inbuf[]     buffer containing 16 encoded color values
```

```
Output parameters:
 red[]       buffer containing 16 red intensities
 green[]     buffer containing 16 green intensities
 blue[]      buffer containing 16 blue intensities
```

```
Calling protocol: */
 DecCols(inbuf,red,green,blue)
```

```
char inbuf[],green[],blue[],red[];
{ int i; char colbuf[3];

 for (i=0; i<16; i++)
 { DecCol(inbuf[i],colbuf);
    red[i] = colbuf[0];
    green[i] = colbuf[1];
    blue[i] = colbuf[2]; }
}
```

12.18.2 Writing to the Palette Registers

An individual Palette Register can be loaded with the routine WrPal; the entire group of 16-color registers can be loaded with the routine WrPals. Both of these routines are listed in Listing 12.71.

LISTING 12.71   Loading the Palette Registers

```
; Set an individual palette register
; Input parameters
; regnum      desired palette register
; color       color to load into the palette register

; Calling protocol
;   WrPal(regnum,value);
_WrPal    proc far
    Prefix
    mov bl,[bp+6]    ;load palette register
    mov bh,[bp+8]    ;load palette value
    mov ax,1000h     ;load palette register
    int 10h
    Postfix
_WrPal    endp

; Load all color palette registers
; Input parameters
; colorbuf    host "C" byte array containing the 16 color
;             registers

; Calling protocol
; WrPals(colorbuf);

_WrPals    proc far
    Prefix

    lds si,[bp+6]    ;load address of byte buffer
    mov cx,16        ;do for 16 registers
    xor bl,bl        ;start at 0 register
```

```
wr1: mov bh,[si]      ;get color byte
     mov ax,1000h     ;load palette register
     int 10h          ;load a value
     inc si           ;point to next value
     inc bl           ;point to next register
     loop wr1

     Postfix
_WrPals  endp
```

12.18.3   Reading from the Palette Registers

It is not possible to read the Palette Registers in the EGA, but it is possible to read them in the VGA. The RdPal and RdPals routines in Listing 12.71 read one or all of the Palette Registers. It should be noted that the RdPals routine actually returns 17 bytes, the last byte being the overscan color code. This can be a source of errors if the C array is only 16 bytes long.

LISTING 12.72   Read the Palette Registers

```
; Read a Palette Register
; Input parameters
; palnum       number of the desired palette register

; Return parameters
; color       color value read from the selected Palette Register

; Calling protocol
; color = RdPal(palnum);

_RdPal    proc far
     Prefix

     mov bl,[bp+6]    ;get palette number
     mov ax,1007h     ;read a Palette Register
     int 10h          ;save data

     xor ah,ah
     mov al,bh        ;return palette value

     Postfix
_RdPal    endp

; Read all Palette Registers and Overscan
; Input parameters
; palnum number of desired palette register

; Return parameters
; palbuf      A 17 byte "C" buffer which will contain the values
; in the 16 Palette Registers and the Overscan Register.
```

```
; Calling protocol
; RdPals(palbuf);

_RdPals     proc far
    Prefix

    les dx,[bp+6]    ;point to "C" buffer
    mov ax,1009h     ;read Palette Registers
    int 10h          ;save data

    Postfix
_RdPals     endp
```

12.18.4 Displaying the Palette and Color Registers

The user may desire to view the palette colors on the monitor similar to a "pull-down" menu. Two useful routines are provided to write 16 boxes along the right side of the screen. Each of these boxes contains a single color; each color represents one of the Palette Registers. The boxes represent Palette Register 0 on the top to Palette Register 15 on the bottom. The data residing behind the color boxes is read into a buffer before the boxes are drawn. This original data can be redrawn into the original positions when the viewing is finished. These routines make use of the window routines WrWin, RdWin, and ClrWin.

These routines operate in any of the EGA/VGA graphics display modes except modes 4 and 5. The VGA mode 13 hex displays 256 colors using the Color Registers. In this mode, these Color Registers are displayed in place of the palette registers, using 8 columns of 32 boxes. Each box represents one Color Register, counting from the top left box downward from 0 to 31. The next box, number 32, is the top box on the next column to the right. The counting continues downward and to the right until the last box, number 255, is displayed in the bottom right box.

The ShowPal routine draws the boxes onto the right portion of the screen. The data currently resident in that portion of display memory is written to a buffer and passed back to the calling routine. The RemovPal routine is used to write this data back into its original location. In this way, the view boxes can be enabled or disabled without disturbing the original data. The ShowPal and RemovPal routines are listed in Listing 12.73.

LISTING 12.73 Viewing the Color Palette

```
/* display 16 color boxes showing the Palette Register values on
   the right side of the screen.
Input parameters:
page     desired display page
buf      "C" buffer which will contain the data which is
```

currently occupying the space where the color boxes will be drawn.

```
Calling protocol: */
 ShowPal(page,buf)
int page; unsigned char buf[];
{ int i,j,x1,y1,x2,y2,y3,yy1,yy3,yinc,ybox,mode[4],dum;

 GetStat(mode);
 switch(mode[1]) /* operate depending on mode */
  {
case 0x0D:
 x1=290; x2=x1+23; y1=10; y2=y1+180;
 y3=y1+6; yinc=11; ybox=16; break;

case 0x0E:
 x1=600; x2=x1+31; y1=10; y2=y1+180;
 y3=y1+6; yinc=11; ybox=16; break;

case 0x10:
 x1=600; x2=x1+31; y1=20; y2=y1+309;
 y3=y1+9; yinc=20; ybox=16; break;

case 0x12:
 x1=600; x2=x1+31; y1=20; y2=y1+437;
 y3=y1+17; yinc=28; ybox=16; break;

case 0x13:
 x1=264; x2=x1+55; y1=4; y2=y1+191;
 y3=y1+4; yinc=6; ybox=32; break;

 }
RdWin(page,x1,y1,x2,y2,buf); /* save what's there */
ClrWin(page,x1,y1,x2,y2,0); /* clear a background */

if(mode[1]!=0x13)
 for (i=0; i<ybox; i++)
  { ClrWin(page,x1,y1,x2,y3,i);
    y1 += yinc; y3 += yinc; }
 else
 for (j=0; j<8; j++)
  { yy1 = y1; yy3 = y3;
    for (i=0; i<ybox; i++)
     { ClrWin(page,x1,yy1,x1+5,yy3,i+(j*32));
       yy1 += yinc; yy3 += yinc; }
    x1 += 7; x2 +=7;
  }
}
```

/* remove 16 color boxes showing the current palette register values on the right side of the screen. Replace it with the original data.

```
    Input parameters:
    page      desired display page
    buf       "C" buffer which will contain the data which is
              currently occupying the space where the color boxes
              will be drawn.

    Calling protocol: */
    ErasePal(page,buf)

    int page; unsigned char buf[];
    { int x1,y1,x2,y2,mode[4];

     GetStat(mode);
     switch(mode[1]) /* operate depending on mode */
     {
    case 0x0D:
     x1=290; x2=x1+23; y1=10; y2=y1+180; break;

    case 0x0E:
     x1=600; x2=x1+31; y1=10; y2=y1+180; break;

    case 0x10:
     x1=600; x2=x1+31; y1=20; y2=y1+309; break;

    case 0x12:
     x1=600; x2=x1+31; y1=20; y2=y1+437; break;

    case 0x13:
     x1=264; x2=x1+55; y1=4; y2=y1+191; break;

     }
    WrWin(page,x1,y1,x2,y2,buf);
    }
```

12.19 COLOR REGISTERS

The VGA is equipped with 256 Color Registers. These Color Registers are similar in function to the Palette Registers. Each contains a red, green, and blue component. Each is 18 bits long, requiring three host read or write cycles.

12.19.1 Reading from the Color Registers

The operator can read from or write to one or more of these Color Registers. The routines RdColor and RdColors in Listing 12.74 read the red, green, and blue components from one or more of the Color Registers.

LISTING 12.74 Reading or Writing to the Color Registers

```
; Read a Color Register
; Input parameters:
```

```
; numreg      number of registers to read.

; Output parameters:
;   buf    "C" byte buffer which will contain the selected Color
; Register. The Color Register is represented by three bytes.
; The order is red, followed by green, followed by blue.

; calling protocol
; RdColor(buf,regnum);

_RdColor  proc far
    Prefix

    les di,[bp+6]    ;get buffer pointer
    mov bx,[bp+10]   ;register number
    mov ax,1015h     ;read a color registers
    int 10h
    mov al,dh        ;return red
    stosb
    mov al,ch        ;return green
    stosb
    mov al,cl        ;return blue
    stosb

    Postfix
_RdColor  endp

; Read any number of Color Registers
; Input parameters:
; first      number of the first Color Register to read.
; numreg     number of registers to read.

; Output parameters:
; buf[]       "C" byte buffer which will contain the selected
;             Color Registers. Each value representing a Color
;             Register occupies three bytes in this array. The
;             order is red, followed by green, followed by blue.
;             The first byte in the array is the red component
;             of the first element selected. The length of the
;             buffer is three times the number of registers.

; calling protocol
;  RdColors(buf,first,numreg);

_RdColors          proc far
    Prefix

    les dx,[bp+6]    ;get buffer pointer
    mov bx,[bp+10]   ;starting register
    mov cx,[bp+12]   ;number of registers to read
    mov ax,1017h     ;read block of color registers
    int 10h
```

```
        Postfix
    _RdColors endp
```

12.19.2 Writing to the Color Registers

Writing to the Color Registers is similar to reading from the Color Registers.
The routines WrColor and WrColors in Listing 12.75 write the red, green, and
blue components to one or more of the Color Registers.

LISTING 12.75 Writing to the Color Registers

```
; Write to a single Color Register
; Input parameters:
; regnum     number of the Color Register to load.

;   buf[]     "C" byte buffer which contains the selected Color
;             Register. The Color Register is represented by
;             three bytes. The first is red, followed by green,
;             followed by blue.
; calling protocol
; WrColor(buf,regnum);

_WrColor  proc far
    Prefix

        lds si,[bp+6]     ;get buffer pointer
        lodsb
        mov dh,al         ;load red
        lodsb
        mov ch,al         ;load green
        lodsb
        mov cl,al         ;load blue

        mov bx,[bp+10]    ;register number
        mov ax,1010h      ;write a color register
        int 10h
        Postfix

_WrColor  endp

; Write any number of Color Registers
; Input parameters:
; first      number of the first Color Register to write.
; numreg     number of registers to write.

; Output parameters:
;   buf    "C" byte buffer which contains the selected Color
```

```
; Registers. Each value representing a Color Register occupies
; three bytes in this array. The order is red, followed by
; green, followed by blue. The first byte in the array is the
; red component of the first element selected. The length of the
; buffer is three times the number of registers selected.

; Calling protocol:
;  WrColors(buf,first,numreg);

_WrColors  proc far
    Prefix

    les dx,[bp+6]    ;get buffer pointer
    mov bx,[bp+10]   ;starting register
    mov cx,[bp+12]   ;number of registers to read
    mov ax,1012h     ;read block of color registers
    int 10h

    Postfix
_WrColors endp
```

12.19.3 Summing to Gray Scale

The values in the Color Registers can be summed to produce a gray scale. The routine SumGray in Listing 12.76 sums the values in any number of the Color Registers.

LISTING 12.76 Summing Colors to Gray Scale

```
; Sum a block of color registers to gray scale
; Input parameters:
; first      number of the first Color Register to sum.
; numreg     number of registers to sum.

; calling protocol
; SumGray(first,numreg);

_SumGray  proc far
    Prefix

    mov bx,[bp+6]    ;starting register
    mov cx,[bp+8]    ;number of registers to write
    mov ax,101Bh     ;set block of color registers
    int 10h

    Postfix
_SumGray         endp
```

12.19.4 Default Loading of the Palette and Color Registers

The Palette Registers and the Color Registers can be loaded with default values at a mode set. The DefaultP routine in Listing 12.77 enables or disables this function.

LISTING 12.77 Default Palette and Color Register Loading

```
; Enables or disables the loading of the Palette and Color
; Registers during a Mode Set.
; Input parameters:
; choice      Enable or disable default color loading
;          0 = Enable default color loading
;          1 = Disable default color loading
; Calling protocol
; DefaultP(choice);

_DefaultP proc far
    Prefix

    mov al,[bp+6]    ;get choice
    mov bl,31h       ;select default palette load
    mov ah,12h
    int 10h

    Postfix
_DefaultP endp
```

12.20 SPECIAL EFFECTS

Programming special effects on the EGA/VGA usually involves complex utilization of simple routines. Instead of long program examples that smooth pan a screen of data, only the basic routines are presented in this book. As long as the principles are understood, these modules can be connected together to form special effects.

The special effects presented in this section include smooth panning, smooth scrolling, and split-screen operation. Smooth panning is accomplished by manipulating the Pixel Panning, Offset Register, and Starting Address Registers. The Pixel Panning Register handles the panning at the pixel level, the Starting Address Registers control the panning at the character size level, and the Offset Register determines the overall dimension of the virtual image.

Smooth scrolling is accomplished similarly, except that the Preset Row Register is used to handle the scrolling at the pixel level. Split-screen operation is accomplished by loading the Line Compare Register with the row number at which the screen should be split. Smooth-scrolling and split-screen manipulation are accomplished by using the routines in Listing 12.78. Smooth panning is accomplished by using the routine in Listing 12.79.

LISTING 12.78 Special Effects C Routines

```
/* load the Line Compare Register
Input parameters:
 splitrow      row at which the screen should be split

Calling protocol: */
 LineComp(splitrow)

int splitrow;
{ char mode,ovflow; int buf[4];
/* determine the mode to determine the correct value to load
into the Overflow Register. This register can be read in the
VGA. */
GetStat(buf); mode = buf[1];

 switch(mode)
   {
 case 0: case 1: case 2: case 3: case 7: case 15: case 16:
    ovflow = 0x1F; break;
 case 4: case 5: case 6: case 13: case 14:
    ovflow = 0x11; break;
 }
if(splitrow < 256) ovflow &= 0x2f; else ovflow |= 0x10;

 outp(0x3d4,0x18); outp(0x3d5,splitrow); /* load Line Compare */
 outp(0x3d4,0x07); outp(0x3d5,ovflow); /* load Overflow */
 }

/* load the start address high and low with a 16 bit value
Input parameters:
 start        Address to load into the Start Address Register

Calling protocol: */
 StartAdr(start)

int start;
{char slow,shigh;
 slow = start & 0xff;
 shigh = (start >> 8) & 0xff;
 outp(0x3d4,0x0C); outp(0x3d5,shigh);
 outp(0x3d4,0x0D); outp(0x3d5,slow);
}

/* load the Preset Row Scan Register
Input parameters:
 firstrow      first row of the top character row to display
```

```
Calling protocol: */
 PreRow(firstrow)

char firstrow;
{ outp(0x3d4,0x08);
 outp(0x3d5,firstrow);
}

/* load the Offset Register
Input parameters:
 bperline       number of bytes per virtual display row
Calling protocol: */
 Offset(bperline)

char firstrow;
{ outp(0x3d4,0x13);
 outp(0x3d5,bperline);
}
```

LISTING 12.79 Special Effects Assembly Language Routines

```
; Load the Pixel Panning Register
; Input parameters:
;   firstpel        The far left pixel of the far left
;                   character to display

; Calling protocol:
; PelPan(firstpel);
_PelPan  proc far
    Prefix
    mov dx,3dah       ;status register 1 bit 3=retrace

bo1: in  al,dx
    test al,08h       ;test for vertical retrace
    jz   bo1          ;wait for retrace

    in   al,dx        ;reset ATC addressing (dummy input)
    mov dx,3c0h       ;ATC index register
    mov ah,[bp+6]     ;get pel pan value
    mov al,33h        ;palette address source=1 reg address=13
    out dx,ax         ;output the pel pan value

    Postfix
_PelPan  endp
```

12.21 WRITING TO THE EGA/VGA REGISTERS

Several of the routines in this chapter write directly to the EGA/VGA registers.
The techniques employed to write to these EGA/VGA registers are nearly

identical from register to register. The routines output an index to the selected address register and output the data to the selected data register. The exceptions to this are the Attribute Registers. All of the Attribute Registers are handled through BIOS calls.

Because the routines are so similar, only the routines required by the programs provided in this chapter are included in Listing 12.80.

LISTING 12.80 Writing to Several EGA/VGA Registers

```
/* load the "mode" register with the byte "mode" */
ModeReg(mode)
 char mode;
{ outp(0x3ce,5); outp(0x3cf,mode); }

/* load the map mask register with the byte "plane" */
MapMask(plane)
 char plane;
{ outp(0x3c4,2); outp(0x3c5,plane); }

/* load the "set reset" register with byte "value" */
SetRes(value)
char value;
{ outp(0x3ce,0); outp(0x3cf,value); }

/* load the enable set reset register with "mask" */
ESetRes(mask)
char mask;
{ outp(0x3ce,1); outp(0x3cf,mask); }

/* load the "read map select" register */
ReadMap(mapcode)
 char mapcode;
{ outp(0x3ce,4); outp(0x3cf,mapcode); }

/* this sets the "bit mask" register to the byte "val" */
BitMask(val)
char val;
{ outp(0x3ce,8); outp(0x3cf,val); }
```

Chapter 13

The Super VGA

13.1 THE SUPER VGA CARD

The VGA graphics controller reigns as the most popular color graphics system for the IBM PC family of computers. A staggering number of VGAs and related software are in use. Although new graphics controllers are knocking at the door, the momentum gained by the VGA has kept it firmly in place as the graphics adapter of choice.

Nearly all VGA cards manufactured today exceed the VGA standard (as described in Chapters 1-12) in some significant way. These new and improved VGAs have been labeled *Super VGAs, Extended VGAs* or *Advanced VGAs.* For the remainder of this book I will refer to these cards as *Super VGAs.*

With no *super* standards to go by, VGA chip designers have developed their own specific implementations. As a result, each super card implementation is different. Whatever the superlative title, a programmer must have an understanding of the techniques used to program these cards.

13.1.1 Super VGA Terminology

Several different manufacturers produce VGA cards. Each of these VGA cards are based upon a VGA controller chip. The performance of the card depends on the particular VGA controller chip and the supporting implementation. While each chip set is different, most of these cards are based upon one of several VGA chips sets from seven major manufacturers. This solves some problems for the programmer. Cards using the same chip can be programmed identically.

To help the programmer even further, the performance features of each of these cards are very similar. Display resolutions, for the most part, are the same for each card (that is, 640 by 480, 800 by 600, 1024 by 768). Other features are also similar. For example, memory is mapped (memory squeezing) into the PC address space through paging registers for each implementation.

The Video Electronics Standards Association (VESA) has made an after-the-fact attempt to create a set of standards for the Super VGAs. These standards are beginning to trickle down.

In summary, the Super VGA cards surpass the VGA standard by doing more, doing it faster, in less space and for less money. A summary of the improvements is found in Table 13.1.

13.1.2 Super VGA Feature Enhancements

The Super VGA now boasts resolutions and processing speeds which can adequately perform many graphics tasks. The most important advance is unquestionably the higher spatial resolutions. To support these display resolutions, VGA controllers can now directly access 1 and 2 megabyte of display memory. The higher resolutions in the 16-color modes have made CAD and desktop publishing much more effective. The higher resolutions in the 256-color modes have brought a whole new collection of imaging applications to the VGA arena.

The penalty for increased resolution is additional memory. For example, a 1024 by 768 256-color graphics image requires 786,432 bytes. Two problems occur when using this much memory. The first problem arises because the size

TABLE 13.1   Super VGA Features

Description	Super VGA	Standard VGA
More functionality	1024 by 768 16-color 1024 by 768 256-color 8-bit per color DACs 1 Megabyte memory Hardware cursor Larger and smaller fonts Interrupt capability Downward compatibility	640x480 16-color 320x200 256-color 6-bit per color DACs 256 Kbytes memory Software cursor
Faster	16-bit bus Interface queue Dual paging Video RAM Shadow RAM BIOS Linear address space	8-bit bus

Smaller	Single VLSI ASIC chip
	Higher level of integration
	1 megabit memory chips
	
	Programmable clock chip
	
	Surface mount technology
		Chip sets
		Lots of support chips
		64K or 256K memory
		    chips
		Multiple crystal
		    oscillators

Cheaper	Large production runs Shorter design cycles Cheaper memory Fewer parts	

of the image—in fact the size of most sub-windows—is larger than 64 Kbytes. Sixteen-bit addressing no longer suffices, and 32-bit addressing arithmetic must be employed. The second problem is that there is only one 64 Kbyte chunk of memory available at A0000 hex for the VGA display memory in the PC/DOS environment. Thus, display memory has to be overlayed.

Additional color acuity is available through new color DACs featuring 8-bits per color, as opposed to the 6-bit per color DACs, on the standard VGAs. With more computer programmers desiring to do imaging applications on the VGA, it is likely that systems utilizing 16-bit color per pixel will become available for the VGA.

Programmers will appreciate several other features. Hardware cursors are ideal for mouse interaction due to their high speed responsiveness. These cursors also allow for a variety of effects due to their programmability. The ability to generate and handle vertical retrace interrupts has also been included. Improved character handling permits larger character fonts (up to 32 by 32) to be used in the alphanumeric modes and smaller character fonts to be used in 143-character/line applications. Anti-aliasing techniques are used to improve the readibility of the smaller fonts.

13.1.3 Super VGA Speed Enhancements

The Super VGAs can move pixels and text around on the screen considerably faster than the first generation VGAs. A much larger memory makes this possible. To achieve the same effective processing rate on a 1024 by 768 image as opposed to a 320 by 200 image, the electronics system must be over 12 times faster. Speed enhancements are present in the host to VGA interface, the display memory to VGA controller interface, and the graphics operations themselves. The 16-bit bus interface greatly reduces the wait-states imposed with 8-bit systems. It allows twice the data to be transferred per operation. Caches are present in several of the Super VGAs to speed data transfers.

The real bottleneck in graphics operations is the multi-ported display memory. The host, the VGA controller, the video refresh circuitry and the dynamic memory refresh cycles, all vie for time on the precious display memory bus. Faster display memory and video RAM memory help reduce the delays.

Graphics operations are also enhanced when the VGA BIOS is executed from RAM memory (shadow RAM)—as opposed to the EPROMs—because the RAM has inherently faster access times. Graphics operations can also be accelerated by implementing the features in hardware. Several new features, including hardware bit masking and rotate registers, allow data to be transferred to selected bit positions, bit-planes or non-byte aligned memory locations without the need for CPU data manipulations.

With the 286, 386, and operating systems such as OS/2, Windows, and DOS extensions, the potential exists to improve the speed performance of the VGA by getting the VGA out of the A0000 segment and into upper memory. The additional space eliminates the cumbersome overlapped memory schemes and the display memory can be accessed using a linear address scheme. In addition, the 32-bit addressing instructions in the 80386 can be utilized in conjunction with this linear addressing. No VGA currently supports this feature.

13.1.4   Super VGA Cost Reductions

Without a doubt, a major factor contributing to the VGA's success is cost. Not only have the Super VGAs improved performance, but they have done so without an increase in cost. The costs associated with a graphics system include the graphics adapter card, the display memory, the monitor, and the software which runs on it. With increased production runs, the production cost per card decreases as do the amortized design and non-recurring engineering costs. Programmers can rely on the VGA for high-performance, low-cost graphics.

The same principle applies to the display monitors. The display memory cost is dictated by density, size, speed and the principle of supply and demand. Because VGAs utilize the same memory chips already used in computer memory, graphics users can ride the coat-tails of the computer industry and benefit from the low costs and competitive environment for this memory. The VGA was based upon this principle. Last, but by no means least, is the reduced cost of software.

13.1.5   Super VGA Popularity

The Super VGAs are popular, first and foremost, because they are VGAs and build upon the VGA standard. By definition, they are downwardly compatible to the standard VGA. Thus, software applications can use the VGA even if they do not utilize the super features. The improvements present in contemporary VGAs are incremental. Hardware and software designers, already familiar with the inner workings of the VGA, do not have to jump off into the unknown to modify their designs and utilize the new chips. The super features are easily integrated into the VGA standard software. Even though there is a lack of standards, code is easily converted from one VGA implementation to another.

The VGA is a dumb frame buffer and has a limited number of graphics-processing capabilities built onto the graphics card. Unlike its competition, which uses graphics coprocessors, the VGA relies on the host processor. This has actually worked out quite well for those who favor the VGA. The majority of VGA users utilize the DOS operating system. The DOS operating system is a single-user system, and it is unclear what the host processor would be doing during the time that the coprocessor is performing the graphics operations.

The end-user is eventually motivated by economy and has likely already paid for a 10, 12 or 16 MHz 80286 or a 16, 20, 25 or 33 MHz 80386 not to mention the 80287 or 80387 coprocessors. And sure enough, here comes the 80486. Fortunately, the price of these general-purpose processors has fallen at the same time that their speed has increased. The dumb frame buffer VGA is still outperforming the competition for the majority of graphics operations. This will change as more graphics-oriented or multi-tasking operating systems (Windows, OS/2 Presentation Manager, X-Windows) become popular.

Competing standards must provide downward compatibility. Most Super VGAs sport downward compatibility to MDA, CGA, Hercules and EGA software. This is no small feat as it entails a considerable amount of hardware, software and elbow grease. A question arises for new graphics cards: Should they maintain downward compatibility? If they do, they necessarily increase their costs and complexities. The new graphics card can employ downward compatibility directly, can have a standard display daughterboard or can have a feedthrough. Either of these choices allows the user to utilize a single monitor. Although this can reduce costs, it can place unrealistic demands upon the monitor. This can eventually force compromises in graphics performance. If the new graphics card implementation does not conform to the older standards, the user is forced to have a second display adapter resident which means a second monitor.

The VGA maintains a position because the consumer will not purchase hardware which does not have an installed base of software. The software industry itself does not really favor rapid change. For all practical purposes, every software application that uses demanding graphics has a VGA interface or driver. In fact, due to the non-standardized Super VGAs, most have several VGA drivers for each application.

Imagine that a graphics software package must run in DOS, OS/2, Windows, and Gem and that it must operate in four display modes for each. Further, imagine that it uses the super features of the VGA on five, distinct chips sets. A company that has created or purchased 80 drivers is not going to be thrilled about the costs of developing more for a new graphics system. This is especially true if the perceived marketplace for the new product is not overwhelming. Concurrently, a user who has spent $500 for a VGA card and $700 for monitor is not inclined to run to the computer store to purchase a costly new graphics system. The reticence of both seller and buyer to spend more money results in marketplace inertia. Few applications developers are this ambitious.

13.1.6   Competing Graphics Standards

The principle difference between the Super VGAs and the competition (beyond the fact that the Super VGA benefits from the VGA standard) is the VGA has no coprocessor on board. The coprocessor reduces the workload of the CPU by speeding up graphics performance. Three competitors are the 8514/A standard by IBM, the Texas Instruments Graphics Architecure (TIGA) by Texas Instruments, and cards built upon the HD63484 Advanced CRT Controller (ACRTC) by Hitachi. All three are based upon coprocessors.

The 8514/A standard from IBM is a dedicated processor. It is not programmable, but it handles certain operations, like drawing lines and moving image data, very well. The goal of IBM was to force software developers to utilize the Applications Interface (AI) software interface by not publishing the register definitions. Unfortunately, graphics applications typically demand high speed, and most software developers go directly to the hardware, therefore bypassing software interfaces like the BI0S or 8514 AI. In an attempt to keep down the cost of the 8514/A, IBM designed the video interface to operate at a resolution of 1024 by 768 interlaced. This interlaced feature is very troublesome, causing highly perceptible flicker.

Some hardware manufacturers have built 8514/A software emulators for their graphics systems. The 8514/A software interface is well documented. Other hardware manufacturers have reverse engineered the 8514/A down to the register level for hardware compatibility. These have re-engineered the video interface to utilize non-interlaced 1024 by 768 resolutions. This reversal can cause confusion when a user attempts to purchase a monitor which is 8514/A compatible. The VESA group is establishing a standard for the 8514/A in an attempt to standardize this hardware interface.

The Texas Instrument (TIGA) standard is based upon the TI-34010 and the 34020 graphics processor. These processors are specialized graphics processors and have rather extensive instruction sets. This means that a software interface that operates on today's 34010 will be compatible with tomorrow's 34030 processor. Some argue that this compatibility is undesirable since the old software will not take advantage of the new generation 34010 or 34020 features. Texas Instruments has also released graphics support chips and floating-point coprocessors which enhance the 34010 or 34020 performance. The progammability of these processors make them seductive. However, it is expensive for software developers to use the power of these complex graphics processors.

13.2   COMPONENTS OF THE SUPER VGA

The VGA card is really a graphics system unto itself. The components of a standard VGA and Super VGA are shown in Figure 13.1. Both systems rely on a clock oscillator, a VGA chip, display memory, video output, and a host interface. Each component in the Super VGA, Figure 13.1b, contains improvements and refinements over the same component in the standard VGA, Figure 13.1a. Some implementations place the VGA chip on the host computer mother board, as shown in Figure 13.1c.

13.2.1   Clock Oscillators

The *clock oscillator* is the heart of the VGA, generating the principle clock. The speed of the clock generated dictates the performance of the graphics card. In synchronous VGA implementations, the higher the speed of the clock, the more operations the system can perform in a unit of time. This translates directly into the amount of data per unit time that can be moved around the system. As the clock ticks faster, the resolutions can get larger. The resolution includes both spatial and color resolution. The eventual data rate is based upon the number of bits per second that can be thrown at the monitor. In asynchronous VGA implementations, separate clock oscillators are used, one for the CPU interface and one for the CRTC.

Suppose that a spatial resolution of 1024 by 768 pixels with 8 bits per pixel is desired. This translates to 786,432 bytes per screen. Further, suppose that the system is to be non-interlaced with refreshes 60 times a second. The data rate has to be 47,185,920 bytes per second.

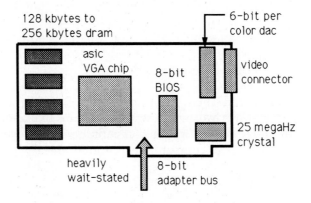

a) Standard VGA Adapter

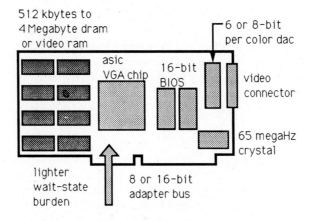

b) Super VGA Adapter

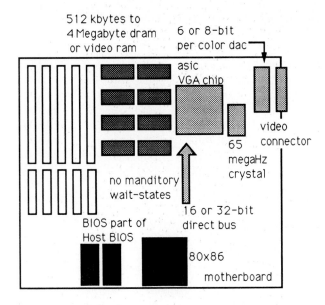

c) Motherboard Implementation
of Super VGA

FIGURE 13.1   Three VGA Implementations

Typical oscillator frequencies are shown in Table 13.2. In order to achieve each designated frequency, a unique oscillator set to each frequency must be present on the card. A highly compacted surface mount card with four crystal oscillators is a rare sight. Since the oscillator's activities interfere with radio transmissions, it is doubtful if designers, aware of the stringent rules for Federal Communications Commission (FCC) approval regarding radio transmission, readily comply to construct such a product. New advances in electronic circuitry incorporate these multiple frequencies into a single device.

13.2.2   VGA ASIC Chip

The VGA controller is a dedicated *graphics controller chip*, and it is programmable to a certain degree. However complicated, it is not classified as a graphics coprocessor because it lacks the general progammable capabilities of a coprocessor. The programmer can select specific graphics operations (that is, write mode, read mode, bit mask), but cannot combine these into a *program* through which the VGA controller can sequence.

TABLE 13.2 Clock Frequencies for Display Modes

# colors	character resolution	pixel resolution	mode	VGA clock	EGA clock
16	40x25	360x400	0,1	28 MHz	14 MHz
16	80x25	640x200	0*1*	25 MHz	16 MHz
16	80x25	640x350	0+,1+	25 MHz	14 MHz
16	80x25	720x400	2,3	28 MHz	16 MHz
16	40x25	320x200	2*,3*	25 MHz	14 MHz
16	80x25	720x400	2+,3+	28 MHz	14 MHz
4	40x25	320x200	4,5	25 MHz	14 MHz
2	80x25	640x200	6	25 MHz	14 MHz
2	80x25	720x350	7	28 MHz	16 MHz
2	80x25	720x400	7+	28 MHz	–
16	40x25	320x200	D	25 MHz	14 MHz
16	80x25	640x200	E	25 MHz	14 MHz
2	80x25	640x350	F	25 MHz	14 MHz
16	80x25	640x350	10	25 MHz	16 MHz
2	80x25	640x480	11	25 MHz	–
16	80x25	640x480	12	25 MHz	–
256	40x25	320x200	13	25 MHz	–
16	132x25	1056x400	*	40 MHz	–
16	100x37	800x600	6A (VESA)	50 MHz	–
16	120x45	960x720	*	50 MHz	–
16	128x48	1024x768	*	65 MHz	–
256	80x25	640x400	*	50 MHz	–

* non-standard mode
– not an EGA mode

Application Specific Integrated Circuits

The VGA controllers are implemented in *Application Specific Integrated Circuits* (ASICs). An EPROM is probably the most simple of the ASICs. An EPROM is application specific, and it is certainly an integrated circuit. A Programmable Array Logic (PALs) is another example of a simple application-specific, integrated ciruit. EPROMs and PALs are not typically called ASICs. Instead, they are usually referred to as programmable logic. Confusing? Perhaps, but let it suffice that EPROMs and PALs are not complicated enough to be called ASICs. Both rely on a program, or some sort of fuse, to mold the design of a circuit.

Next in the chain of complexity is the programmable gate array. Gate arrays can be thought of as generalized PALS, or circuit boards on a chip. The non-reprogammable gate arrays use fuses to form links among the logic elements while the reprogrammable gate arrays use RAM elements. Certainly there are advantages to both, but the non-reprogrammable gate arrays are typically faster and yield higher densities. Programmable gate arrays are getting complex enough to be classified as ASICs. Although the densities and performance of the programmables are increasing, they still lag far behind the features of the non-programmable gate arrays.

Integrated circuit designers have a broad range of platforms to work from when actually designing silicon. Designers use three technologies when producing VGA chips. The lowest level of silicon design uses a full custom method. The second level uses standard cells. The designer can design the chip from the base up, using predefined elements, called standard cells. These elements include memory, gates, counters, FIFOs, shift registers, and adders. Standard cell designs yield all sorts of circuits, including the powerful microprocessors. Standard cell design is expensive and entails large non-recurring engineering fees, ranging from $100,000 to several million dollars.

The next level down is the gate array. The gate array already has the lowest levels of silicon laid down on the chip, and the designer is constrained to work with this configuration. Different gate arrays have different basic architectures. Again, the designer has a selection of gates to design with including most of the standard cell elements, with the exception of random access memory elements. Gate arrays can be typically designed with non-recuring engineering costs of between $30,000 and $100,000, depending on their complexity.

Designing memory elements into a gate array is costly in terms of space and used gates. Typically a designer selects either standard-cell or gate-array technology, based upon whether the application requires memory. If an application requires memory, the designer can use a gate array and interface it to a standard SRAM. Now, however, pin-out becomes a problem, because the ASICs have limitations on the number of pins a package can support. The VGA chips typically come in 144 and 160 pin packages.

The VGA ASIC

The VGA, standard or super, has a set of functions that it must perform. These include memory management, pixel processing, host interface and CRT control, and sequence and attribute control. The *VGA ASIC* determines the performance features and details of each VGA implementation. In most cases, compatibility with the IBM VGA has been strictly observed.

The Super VGA ASICs, shown in Figure 13.2 have gone far beyond this standard and are really considered in a class by themselves. Six manufacturers of Super VGAs are presented in this book, and most have more than one Super VGA chip. Each chip is different and must be dealt with separately.

Memory Management

The *memory management* portion of the VGA is a complex mechanism. It must provide memory control timing and sequence control, including dynamic memory refresh control, memory address control, and memory data. The

VGA ASIC Chip

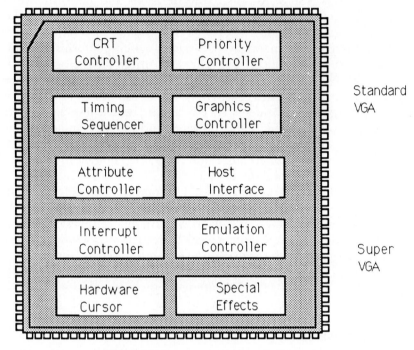

FIGURE 13.2   The VGA ASIC Chips

memory address bus is formed by two 8-bit buses which interface to memory while the data bus is 32 bits wide, accommodating the four 8-bit planes. The memory and data bus architecture was designed to fit well into the standard memory sizes. Suppose memory chips are configured with 1 megabyte locations by 1 bit per location, as shown in Figure 13.3a. In this case, the chip would require 20 bits of address and 1 bit of data.

Another configuration would be 256 Kbytes locations by 4 bits per location as shown in Figure 13.3b. This configuration would require 18 bits of address and 4 bits of data.

If the VGA is configured in a 16-color mode, each pixel is represented by four bits, and these bits could be located in each of the four RAM chips. Thus, it would be simple to gate in data into one bit-plane (one RAM) while leaving the other bits (other 3 RAMs) untouched. This would take four chips. There would be enough memory with these four chips to store a 1024 by 1024 pixel image (1 megabyte of 4 bit words). With the second configuration, the four-bit planes could reside in one chip. This would mean that a single chip could be used to

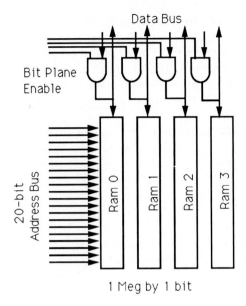

a) Using four 1 Meg x 1bit RAM
for a 1024x1024 16-color display buffer

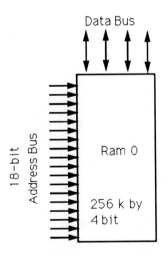

b) Using a single 256k x 4bit
RAM for a 640x400 16-color display buffer

FIGURE 13.3 Small System Implementation of VGA Display Mode

store an image that is 640 by 400 pixels. Of course, it would take four chips to store the 1024 by 1024 image. However, it is no longer an easy task to store data in one bit without disrupting the other three bits since the memory chip accesses all four bits at a time. Thus, a read-modify-write operation would be required, using two memory accesses per operation. If a 256-color mode is in effect, each pixel is 8 bits. There is little need to write into a single-bit position within the byte.

If a 16 bit wide display memory data bus is desired, sixteen 1-bit memory chips would be required, as shown in Figure 13.4a. Better suited to this 16-bit memory, only four 4-bit per memory chips would be required, as shown in Figure 13.4b.

Host Interface

As listed in Chapter 10, all of the standard registers are implemented within the VGA gate array. In addition, the Super VGA registers are also implemented in the gate arrays. These registers form the *host interface* between the host and the VGA. All host-modified functions which the VGA performs are controlled through these registers. The VGA must decode the addresses from the host address bus and the I/O bus to determine whether the VGA is being accessed. The range of memory and port addresses are fixed, based upon the VGA standard.

The Super VGAs extend the port addresses to accomodate the new registers. An especially interesting feature of some of the Super VGAs is their ability to remap the memory and I/O addresses to other places. Remapping the memory allows the VGA to reside in upper memory, out of the A0000 hex segment. This feature will be used by non-DOS operating systems which can access this upper memory.

Some VGA host interfaces have cache memory between the host and VGA. This allows data or control instructions to be queued up and can reduce the wait-states interjected into the host's system timing.

Super VGAs can typically interface with the host through the16-bit, AT bus or through the standard 8-bit bus. Some are programmable, regardless of whether they have 8- or 16-bit bus interfaces. Others automatically sense whether the VGA card is plugged into an 8-bit or 16-bit slot.

Timing Sequencer

The *Timing Sequencer* provides basic timing control for both the CRT Controller and the Attribute Controller. The timing control includes the following: horizontal count resolution (8 or 9 dots/character), the various dot clocks and their divide down cousins, and the video loading circuitry which determines whether data should be loaded at every 8, 16, or 32 dot clock. The Timing Sequencer is controlled through the Timing Sequencer registers discussed in Chapter 10.4.

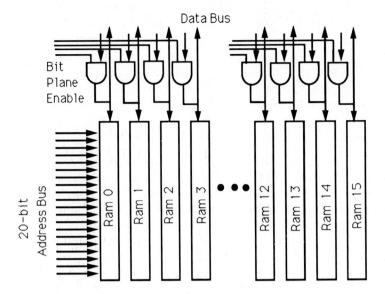

a)   Implementing a 16-bit data bus using 1-bit
1Meg memory chips

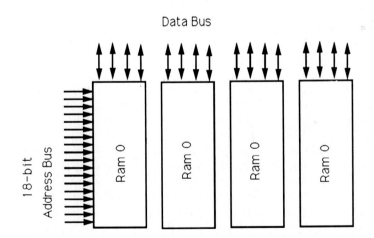

b)   Implementing a 16-bit data bus using 4-bit
1Meg memory chips

FIGURE 13.4   Large System Implementation of VGA Display Memory

CRT Controller

The *CRT controller* (CRTC) provides an 18-bit linear address, vertical and horizontal sync signals and cursor addresses to control the raster-scan CRT displays. Internal to the VGA, the addresses and timing are stored in two-dimensions, horizontal and vertical, while externally the memory is sequential. This control is derived from the CRTC registers in Chapter 10.4.

Attribute Controller

The internal *Attribute Controller* provides high-speed video shifting and processing for the alphanumeric and graphics modes. The attribute controller handles 8 or 9 bit font data widths in the alphanumeric modes and must reformat pixel data into 1, 2, or 8 bits of adjacent data for the graphics modes. Some Super VGAs can reformat the pixel data into 16 bits of adjacent data per pixel. In either mode, this data is translated through an internal lookup table called the palette and sent out to the color lookup table. The Attribute Registers are described in Chapter 10.6; the Color Registers are described in Chapter 10.7. The standard VGA Attribute Registers support *Plane* (16-color) or *Byte* (256 color modes). Some VGAs support *Word* (65,536 color) pixel structures.

Graphics Display Controller

The *graphics controller,* described in Chapter 10.5, helps the host CPU in graphics-related operations. These include rotate, bit masking, and z-plane operations with four boolean operations in response to a single CPU write. In a sense, this controller may be thought of as a primitive graphics coprocessor. Placing bitmap operations in the gate array high-speed hardware improves the graphics performance of the VGA significantly over a dumb frame buffer. This processing is restricted to Plane operations and cannot be used in byte or word operations. This limits the effectiveness of using the 16-bit host interface.

13.2.3   Display Memory

Display memory causes bottle neck in the system because there is competition for this memory. To a large extent, the speed of the display memory dictates the performance of the system. When the EGA was first introduced, systems utilized 256K bit DRAM chips. The highest EGA mode was 640 by 350 with 16-color using a total of 128 Kbytes, thereby requiring 4 memory chips. The 1024 by 768 256-color resolution of the Super VGA requires 786,432 bytes as well as eight 1-megabit chips or two 4-megabit chips.

There are three types of memory chips which would fit the bill for video memory. These are dynamic RAM (DRAM), video-RAM (VRAM) and Static Ram (SRAM). Both the DRAM and the VRAM require memory refresh while the SRAM does not. Typically, SRAM is not used due to the lower density and higher cost penalties paid for this memory.

In the standard VGA, 256K bytes of memory is needed in the display buffer to support both 4-bit per pixel and 8-bit per pixel. In some of the Super VGAs, a 16- bit per pixel configuration is also possible.

Dynamic Memory

Dynamic memory is by far the most popular memory used in VGA systems. Dynamic memory requirements are outlined in Table 13.3. There are three tyrants competing for this memory resource. The first is the VGA chip itself. It must read the memory, write the memory and perform the ever-present memory refresh necessary for dynamic memory. The second is the host computer. It must read and write into the memory. The third, and most persistent, is the video circuitry which must read the memory and use the contents to refresh the CRT tube. The host computer can turn off the port to the video circuitry, thereby cutting it off from the display memory. Consequently, the video screen goes blank.

Video Memory

Some VGAs have gone the extra half-mile to support *video memory*, VRAM. In and of itself, VRAM is dual-ported. It anticipates the requirements of the video circuitry and provides a special serial port just for that purpose. It knows that the video circuitry never wants to write to this memory. The video frame grabber is an exception. VRAM also knows that the video circuitry desires a sequential output from this memory.

The density of VRAMs track the density of DRAMs closely, since the memory elements are the same in each case. The problem centers on cost and availability. Typically, the cost of the VRAM is twice that of the DRAM.

TABLE 13.3 Dynamic Memory Requirements

# Colors	Pixel Resolution	# 256K x 4 Dram memory chips	# 1Meg x 4 Dram memory chips	Memory speed
16	640x480	2	1	100 nsec
256	640x480	4	1	100 nsec
16	800x600	2	1	80 nsec
256	800x600	8	2	100 nsec
16	1024x768 *1	4	2	100 nsec
256	1024x768 *1	8	2	100 nsec
16	1024x768	4	2	80 nsec
256	1024x768	8	2	80 nsec

*1 interlaced

Static RAM

SRAMs are beautiful. As long as power is present, they remember what they are doing, and no refreshing is necessary. They are also exceedingly fast. The only problem is that their densities are lower, their power requirements greater, and their cost even higher. Typically, the cost of the SRAM is five times that of the DRAM, and advances usually lag behind DRAM by one generation.

13.2.4   Video Output Circuitry

The *Video Output Refresh Circuitry* must feed a near-constant stream of data to the CRT. Typically 80 percent of the memory accesses must be dedicated to the Video Refresh Circuitry. The host is prevented from accessing memory during memory refreshing. If, in the worst case, 80 percent of the memory accesses are for video refresh, only one out of five host memory accesses will get through. The host is told that the VGA is not ready if it attempts to read too quickly. This "not ready" signal comes to the host in the form of wait-states. Be aware that the speed of the graphics system is principally dependent on the wait-states generated by the host interface and the inability of the host to access display memory.

The interface to the CRT monitor is through the video output circuitry. The immediate buffer between the video memory and the CRT is the color palette chip. The width of the palette dictates the number of colors per pixel while the length of the palette dictates the number of simultaneous colors that can be displayed. Super VGAs can easily interface to palettes that can display eight bits per color totalling 24 bits per pixel. This is compared to six bits per color for the standard VGA. Note this is not what is termed 24 bit color, since the length of the palette is still restricted to 256 registers, that is, 256 simultaneous colors. True color, 24-bit color, means 24 bits per color with 16 million simultaneous colors.

The new generation of color palette chips allow more colors and feed through modes which provide access to 16-bit and 24-bit true color images. These chips are significantly better for imaging applications. A 16-bit color per pixel allows 64 Kbytes color possibilities per pixel. Typically, this is split between 32 shades of red and blue and 64 shades of green. Others split these 16 bits into 64 shades of red and green and 16 shades of blue. Blue is always given the least resolution because human vision is less sensitive to the blue spectrum of color but highly sensitive to green and red spectrums.

True color has 24 bits per pixel images. It allows 16.8 million colors to be displayed. The resultant colors really are staggering. The difference between the green of a dollar bill and the green of grass are subtle, yet significant.

13.2.5   Host Interface

The *host interface* affects the performance of any graphics system. It has a profound affect on graphics systems that have no coprocessor. The host interface also has an impact on the VGA. Every command, every byte, every pixel must pass through the hands of the host interface. Like any middle-man, the interface keeps a little for itself.

Graphics systems with coprocessors can get by with sending a single command through the interface. This sets in motion thousands of operations within the graphics system. A little tax paid here and there may appear to be scant. The VGA, however, must send everything through the interface, and the penalties are striking. The design generalities and idiosyncrasies of the IBM PC environment compound the problem.

The IBM "true blue" VGA was first introduced on the system board of the PS/2 family of computers. The interface relied on the MCA, the microchannel bus. The non-IBM, but standard VGAs, were designed to interface to the host processor through the PC/AT bus. Severe penalties are paid when one ventures through the PC/AT bus in the form of wait-states. Wait-states occur when some external device wants the host to slow down. The device might have slow memory or be a slow I/O device unable to keep up with the host. The inserted and sometimes unnecessary wait-states can bring the graphics system to its knees. One would expect the IBM VGA to have an advantage and to operate faster than the adapter card VGA versions. In a sense it does because bus wait-states are not interjected. However, unfortunately, the IBM VGA is so slow that the increased performance due to fewer wait-states has been eaten by the graphics processor and memory.

The Super VGAs rely on the 16-bit AT bus, as opposed to the 8-bit PC bus of the original VGA adapters. (Most of the first VGAs relied on the 8-bit PC bus to interface to the host processor.) The latter creates an unnecessary slowdown since the AT automatically inserts six additional cycles of wait-states when accessing an 8-bit device. The PC was designed as a 4.77 MHz bus. The AT assumes that it has to slow down to this bus rate for an 8-bit card. The AT inserts only two additional cycles of wait-states when accessing a 16-bit device. In addition, a 16-bit transfer also transfers twice as much data as an 8-bit transfer. Thus, theoretically, the 16-bit VGAs should outperform the 8-bit VGAs by 2–6 : 1. Unfortunately, this is not the case, since the VGA is inherently an 8-bit device. A bottleneck occurs further down the line, which forces the interjection of additional wait-states.

The VGA is based on an 8-bit architecture. Designers have done a great deal of creative "souping up" to help the chips take advantage of the 16-bit transfers. Especially suited to the 16-bit transfers are the alphanumeric mode, where a character is represented by an 8-bit ASCII code and an 8-bit attribute totaling 16 bits. Other operations vary, depending upon speed advantages when using the 16-bit interface, and are highly chip-implementation specific.

The BIOS routines associated with interrupt 10 hex are usually located in EPROMs on the VGA adapter card. Utilizing 16-bit word wide, EPROMs can help speed things up since, once again, 16-bit transfers are occurring out of the inherently slow EPROMs. Most Super VGAs include two EPROMs to ensure 16-bit transfers.

Another popular technique employs shadow RAM. Shadow RAM is popular in the 80386 systems where the data resident in the VGA EPROMs is copied to RAM, and the BIOS operates from this location. Yet another technique uses RAM-resident BIOS device drivers which reside in host memory. The device drivers get loaded as terminate and stay resident programs. They redirect the video interrupt 10 hex from the VGA EPROM to the RAM location to which they are loaded.

13.2.6   16-bit Memory Transfers

Designing a 16-bit interface for memory transfers is not trivial on the AT bus. The PC bus was designed by IBM. Once it was carved in stone there was no turning back. There is a problem with the latched and unlatched address bus on the AT. These two address buses are passed to the adapters through the AT connectors. When 16-bit memory accesses are desired, a tri-stated line called MEM16 must be pulled low by the adapter, indicating to the host processor that a 16-bit transfer is desired. The host has to do some fancy footwork to determine whether it should output two 8-bit bytes on data lines 0–7 or one 16-bit word on data lines 0–15. In order to have enough time, the AT bus requires that the MEM16 line be asserted shortly after the address lines settle. The address lines are used by the adapter to determine whether it should respond at all to the bus address. Thus, it has to be decoded by the adapter.

Consider the following example. The VGA display memory resides at address A0000–B0000 hex in the PC memory address space. The host wants to read a word from the VGA at address A1000. It exerts the address A1000 on the bus and waits for a bit. During this time, all devices on the memory bus have to look at the address, A1000, to determine if they should respond. In this case, the VGA address decoder would detect that A1000 resides between A0000 and Affff and so gears itself up. It still does not know if the host wants to read or write. Since this VGA is a 16-bit device, it wants to exert MEM16 to alert the host to this fact. As soon as it decodes the A0000 hex, it sends out the low signal on the MEM16 line. The host in turn identifies the MEM16 line and sends its memory read pulse. Then it waits for a bit before it reads the 16-bit data on the data bus bits 0–15. During this second wait, this VGA has to use the read pulse to enable the output of its memory (previously addressed at a1000) and send the 16-bit signal onto the data bus bits 0–15.

The problem is that decoding the address takes time for the VGA, and it has to send out the MEM16 line quickly. The address cannot be decoded until the address lines settle. On the PC, there are two sets of address lines on the PC being latched and unlatched. The unlatched lines settle before MEM16 has to be asserted, while the latched lines settle after MEM16 has to be asserted. We can rule out using the latched address lines. The problem is that no complete set of unlatched address lines are available, the lowest being address bit 17. As a result, the address decoding circuitry cannot detect memory locations that are smaller than 128 Kbytes. Therefore, the VGA can only detect that a memory access is required somewhere between A0000 and Bffff before it can decide whether to respond with a MEM16 signal. Unfortunately, in dual monitor systems, a Hercules card may well be residing at B0000 with unpredictable results. I have yet to see a 16-bit Hercules implementation.

The MEM16 line is another reason why 16-bit VGAs will operate in an 8-bit mode, while in AT systems with bus speeds greater than 8 MHz, they will not operate in a 16-bit mode. The increased speed of the bus and the subsequent decreased time for the MEM16 line to be asserted exceeds the decoding rate of the VGA.

13.2.7 System Throughput

The pipeline existing between the host and the VGA is primarily limited by the serial connection of the host interface and the display memory bottlenecks. In such instances, the system performance is dictated by the worse of the two. For example, if the host can only pass data across the bus at 1.5 megabyte/second rate and the display memory can only allow data into display memory at a 1.5 megabyte/second rate, the system throughput will be around 1.5 megabytes/second. If the host bus passes 10 megabytes/second while the display memory still operates at 1.5 megabytes per second, then the throughput rate will still be approximately 1.5 megabytes/second.

13.2.8 Graphics Displays

The output of the video circuitry must drive some type of display. These include monochrome, color, digital, analog, fixed frequency, multi-syncing, and monochrome or color flat panel displays. Table 13.4 lists some common monitor types.

TABLE 13.4 Common Display Types

Display	*Characteristics*	*Graphics Card Compatibility*
Monochrome	Black and White	Hercules/MDA
Color <= 200 lines	Digital 16-color	CGA
Fixed Freq. <= 350 lines	Digital 64-color	EGA
Fixed Freq. <= 480 lines	Analog color	VGA
Enhanced Monochrome	Analog monochrome	VGA
Multi-syncing interlaced	Analog color	8514/A, Super VGA
Multi-syncing	Analog color	Super VGA
Mono flat panel	4 shades of gray	Laptops CGA, EGA, VGA
Color flat panel	64 colors	Laptops EGA, VGA

Monitors and Emulation

The Super VGAs share the ability to perform some type of downward compatibility. It is necessary to ensure that the proper monitor is installed. Otherwise damage can occur to the monitor. Some Super VGAs check to see the monitor type and report the findings. Others leave it to the user to ensure that the proper monitor is in place.

Fixed Frequency Monitors

The MDA, Hercules, CGA, EGA, VGA and 8514/A are *fixed frequency monitors*. They provide a standardized set of display resolutions. The simpler cards provide fewer resolutions from which to choose. For example, the CGA or Hercules has only one resolution and, consequently, only requires the monitor to synchronize at one known set of horizontal and vertical frequencies. As the number of required frequencies has increased and the industry has lost its apparent fear of non-standard frequencies, the fixed frequency monitors have given way to multi-syncing monitors.

Multi-syncing Monitors

With the EGA, the number of possibilities increased and the concept of multi-syncing monitors became popular. The *multi-syncing monitors* have lower and upper bounds on the synchronization frequencies. This has raised some problems regarding downward compatibility. It is not cost effective to design a monitor to sync to both high and low frequencies. Consequently, high performance monitors cannot necessarily display low resolution images which conform to the timing specifications of the low performance monitors.

Interlaced and Non-interlaced Monitors

Interlaced monitors are cheaper to build than non-interlaced monitors in the same range of performance. The issue came up when IBM decided to formalize the interlaced 1024 by 768 graphics mode of the 8514/A. It is virtually agreed by all that the interlacing has an annoying flicker. The 8514/A clones do not follow suit. These have predominantly incorporated non-interlaced 1024 by 768 modes. Unfortunately, for these clones to be *compatible* they should also be capable of supporting an interlaced 1024 by 768 mode. Most of the later generation Super VGA chips do support the interlaced display modes in addition to the non-interlaced display modes.

NTSC compatibility

Interlacing also plays a part in the display of images on televisions and VCRs which adhere to the NTSC standard. Several new cards are now available which convert the VGA modes to the NTSC standard and allow the output of the VGA to be displayed on a television or recorded on a VCR. However, the designers work under great restrictions in order to reduce the costs of production. I have yet to see a system to recommend. More expensive graphics systems, designed specifically for broadcast-quality video, do a great job. For instance, the TARGA or VISTA cards produce beautiful video. On the other hand, these same cards cannot come close to competing with the VGA as far as high-resolution display modes are concerned.

Flat Panels

Flat-panel displays can be either monochrome or color. The monochrome systems are based upon liquid LCD or gas discharge technologies. These can be made to display gray scale by time-modulating the signal. For example, suppose the frame rate is divided into four cycles. A pixel can be set to *on* in none, one, two, three or four of these time cycles producing five possible shades of gray. Dithering is another technique used. However, using it means decreased resolution.

Color displays are based on the active matrix Thin Film Transistor (TFT) or the Super Twist (STN) Technologies. Currently, 64 colors can be produced on these color flat panels.

A typical panel consists of 640 by 240 pixels. Mounting one panel on top of the other provides a 640 by 480 display resolution. The number of horizontal and vertical pixels filling a screen is fixed. Thus, there can be no compensation in timing to affect screen size or position. For example, a 640 by 350 display cannot be continuously stretched to fill a 640 by 480 pixel flat panel. Special techniques called *vertical compensation* must be used to fill the screen.

One vertical-compensation technique involves offsetting the display so that the 350 lines are at least centered. Another repeats lines or inserts blank lines evenly spaced through the display. It is be possible to stretch the display through interpolation. However, the calculation requirements on the processor to perform interpolation rule out this technique.

Clever color compression techniques must be employed to reduce the amount of colors inherent in the VGA to a number which can be displayed on the flat panel. In addition, contrast enhancement techniques must be used when mapping color to gray scale. Colors can have the same monochromic value, meaning they would look very different on a color monitor but identical on the monochrome flat panel. Some VGAs have algorithms implemented in hardware to perform the color compression and contrast enhancement.

13.3 SUPER VGA BIOS

The standard VGA BIOS is described in Chapter 11. Some of the Super VGAs have added additional calls to the video BIOS. These additional calls allow the user to set up extended graphics modes, access extended registers, save and restore the state of the VGA extended registers, set up emulation modes, return VGA information, and set power on video conditions. The VESA standards

TABLE 13.5   VESA BIOS Recommendations

Function	Function number	Section
Return Super VGA Information	0	13.5.3
Return Super VGA Mode Information	1	13.5.4
Set Super VGA Video Mode	2	13.5.5
Return Current Video Mode	3	13.5.6
Save/Restore Super VGA State	4	13.5.7
CPU Video Memory Window Control	5	13.5.8

group has recommended that a new set of BIOS calls be mandatory as listed in Table 13.5. More discussion of the VESA BIOS recommendations will follow in the next section.

The VGA BIOS is resident in one or two EPROMs located on the VGA adapter card. If only one EPROM is present, an 8-bit BIOS interface is used. If two are present, a 1-bit BIOS interface is present. The BIOS memory is mapped into PC memory space at c0000 to c5fff and at c6800–c7fff hex. providing 30 Kbytes of code space for the BIOS memory. When this occurs, the video BIOS is located on the motherboard. In this case, the VGA controller typically has to be alerted so that it can map out the aforementioned address space. In addition, many computers have the facility to copy the video BIOS into shadow RAM. When this function is enabled, execution of BIOS calls occurs from RAM memory as opposed to the slower ROM memory. This shadow RAM is non-DOS memory specifically dedicated for this purpose.

A potential problem involving a clash between the VGA BIOS and the 8514/A BIOS was headed off at the pass by the VESA committee. The base address of the ROM for the 8514/A depends on the ROM size, the type of host interface, and the base address field of the 8514/A Extension Register 2. The ROM size might be 8K or 32K. The Host interface might be a PC/AT or a microchannel. If the 8514/A is in a microchannel, its ROM exists at C6800 to C7FFF. The VESA committee recommends that this base address be used when the 8514/A is installed in a microchannel system while the default address of C8000 to C9FFF be used in the PC/AT systems.

13.4   THE SUPER VGA STANDARDS

The Super VGA cards have improved upon the VGA standard, but unfortunately, they have done so in a non-standard way. Each implementation is similar to the others; all try and accomplish basically the same things. Yet each is slightly different from the others and none stand out as the clear champion with the slickest solution.

All of the Super VGAs take advantage of the VGA standard and remain downwardly compatible. However, they all suffer from this compatibility since many of the additions must be patched in. This process is often awkward and slow.

Some Super VGAs actually have two modes. The first conforms to the VGA standard. The second does not conform, but it is better suited to fast programming. Luckily, the paths taken by the VGA manufacturers have not diverged very much. It is not that difficult to modify the code that drives one Super VGA while allowing it to operate on any other. Chapter 14 and 15 contain details on just how to do this.

VESA is a consortium of electronic manufacturers spearheaded by NEC. They have attempted to standardize some display modes and BIOS calls for the Super VGAs. The VESA standards will be discussed in detail in Section 13.5 of this chapter.

13.4.1 Standardizing the Super VGA

Every programmer should be familiar with the five major areas in the Super VGAs. These five are terminology, identifying the VGA card and its capabilities, accessing the extended registers, accessing the display modes, and accessing the display memory.

13.4.2 Standardizing Terminology

The Super VGA terminology is shrouded in problems. The first problem relates to labelling a VGA which functions beyond the standard VGA. Some call them *extended*, others *advanced* and others *super*. I have selected the terminology *super*.

The second problem has to do with defining the terms *page, plane, bank* and *window*. There is general agreement regarding the use of plane. Display memory is overlayed into four display planes, each 8 bits wide. This creates an effective data bus which is 32 bits wide. This *planar* memory configuration was ideal for the 16-color modes.

In the standard VGA, the terminology page is used to indicate when more than one display screen fits into display memory. For example, in the alphanumeric display mode 3, the resolution is 80 by 25 characters and totals 2,000 characters. Each character occupies one byte in each of the four display planes. Since each plane is 64 Kbytes long, it is possible to fit 32 display pages in the 256 Kbyte VGA display memory. Thus, like a book, the VGA has multiple pages. Within each page it has multiple planes. This is illustrated in Figure 13.5.

From here the terminology goes out to pasture. As more memory was added to the VGA, it had to be further overlayed to fit into the 64 Kbyte segment. Terms for the resultant sub-page, sub-plane units elluded the terminology departments at the VGA manufacturers. Some called them pages while others called them banks. As described in Section 13.5, VESA has named these windows. VESA may have selected a neutral term to avoid siding with any one of the manufacturers. I prefer and use banks throughout this book since pages was

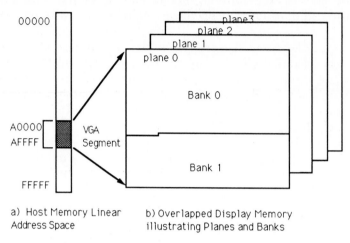

00000

A0000
AFFFF

FFFFF

VGA
Segment

plane 3
plane 2
plane 1
plane 0

Bank 0

Bank 1

a) Host Memory Linear
Address Space

b) Overlapped Display Memory
illustrating Planes and Banks

FIGURE 13.5   VGA Memory Technology

already taken and *windows* means too many things. Besides, Apple, Microsoft or Xerox do not take kindly to the use of the word *windows* without a trademark.

13.4.3   Identifying the VGA and Card Capabilities

Some Super VGA cards have well-defined functions for determining the chip type and capabilities of the card. Others do not. In some cases, it is necessary to poke around with registers and memory locations. Writing patterns and reading them back can help determine what is and is not present. Techniques for identifying the VGA and its capabilities are presented in Chapters 14 and 15.

13.4.4   Accessing the Super VGA Extended Registers

All Super VGAs have Extended registers in addition to the standard VGA registers. Where these registers reside and how the programmer accesses them varies from one implementation to another. Some are grouped within the standard VGA register groups. Others are in an address space by themselves. The Extended registers are often locked and access to them can require special programming. Complete listings of several manufacturers' Extended registers are presented in Chapters 14, 15 and in Appendix A.

13.4.5   Using the Super VGA Display Modes

The implementations of the Super VGAs support several Extended display modes, each with their own spatial and color resolutions. Not every card supports every display mode. Most support the high resolution 16-color modes.

Several cards do not extend beyond 640 by 480 for the 256-color modes. Common display modes, and some not so common ones, are listed in Table 13.6 and Table 13.7. In certain implementations, the display modes are accessed through the standard AH=0 Set Mode BIOS call described in Section 11.2.1. Some of the display modes are accessed through a separate BIOS call. The actual mode numbers for each of these resolutions vary according to the particular implementation. The more common screen resolutions are displayed in Figure 13.6.

13.4.6 Accessing the Super VGA Display Memory

All Super VGAs support at least 512 Kbytes of memory. This means that the 512 Kbytes must be overlayed in some fashion, or in several ways, to fit within the 64

TABLE 13.6 Commonly Used Super VGA Graphics Display Modes

Resolution	# of Colors	Display Memory	# of Banks
640 by 400	256	256 Kbytes	4
640 by 480	256	512 Kbytes	5
800 by 600	16	256 Kbytes	1
800 by 600	256	512 Kbytes	8
1024 by 768	16	512 Kbytes	2
1024 by 768	256	1 Megabyte	12
640 by 350	256	256 Kbytes	4
752 by 410	16	256 Kbytes	1
720 by 540	16	256 Kbytes	1
720 by 540	256	512 Kbytes	6
960 by 720	16	256 Kbytes	1
800 by 600	2	256 Kbytes	1

TABLE 13.7 Commonly Used Super VGA Alphanumerics Display Modes

Resolution	# of Colors	Display Memory	# of Banks
132 by 25	2,4 or 16	256 Kbytes	1
132 by 28	2,4 or 16	256 Kbytes	1
132 by 44	2,4 or 16	256 Kbytes	1
132 by 50	2,4 or 16	256 Kbytes	1
80 by 60	16	256 Kbytes	1
100 by 40	16	256 Kbytes	1
100 by 60	16	256 Kbytes	1

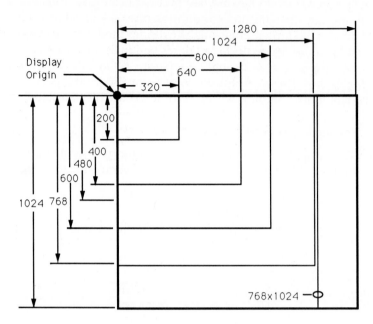

FIGURE 13.6 Super VGA Spatial Resolutions

Kbyte segment in host memory address space at A0000 hex. To access this memory, paging or bankswitching techniques are employed.

Each implementation has defined its own locations for these Bank Switching registers. Some have placed them in more than one location. Some have one Bank Switch Register, while others have separate registers for read and write. Some have two general registers, and unfortunately, others have split up the single feature into several locations.

In the 16-color modes, these 512 Kbytes are overlayed into four display planes, each being 128 Kbytes. The 128 Kbytes is further overlayed into the 64-Kbyte segment A0000 hex in the PC memory address space. The 1024 by 768 pixel resolution in the16-color display mode is the only currently implemented 16-color mode which requires more than 256 Kbytes of total display memory. This translates into a single 64-Kbyte segment per display plane.

In the 256-color modes, the overlaying is more severe. The four display planes are chained together, called *chain 4,* and extend in a linear address space within a 64-Kbyte segment. In a 640 by 400 display mode, 256,000 bytes are required. This fits within 256 Kbytes of total display memory. However, it must be overlayed into four banks to fit within the 64-Kbyte host address space at A0000 hex.

13.4.7 Other Super VGA Features

Not all features are shared by the Super VGA cards. The exclusive features are downward compatibility, hardware cursors, large character fonts in alphanumeric modes, anti-aliased character sets also for the alphanumeric modes, interrupt counters, sliding registers, and bit masking.

Downward compatibility means that the VGA can emulate either the MDA, Hercules, CGA or EGA. One Super VGA even emulates the 8514/A standard. The techniques and levels of emulation vary according to each implementation. Typically, a set of registers is specifically present for emulation use. In some cases, BIOS calls are present to set up the emulation. Sophisticated duplication of CRT Controller timing registers is provided so that emulation modes do not have to overwrite the normal values for these registers when in a VGA mode.

Hardware cursors are very important in graphical interface environments and are included in two of the Super VGA implementations discussed in this book. A cursor pattern is software generated and is stored in high display memory. This pattern will be displayed at a specified position. A mouse or another pointing device typically dictates the position to load the cursor. The position of the cursor can also be interrogated.

The cursor can be thought of as containing a foreground and a background. For example, the cursor is surrounded by a rectangular region. If the cursor shape is an arrow, then the arrow could be considered foreground while the space in the rectangular box, not covered by the arrow itself, could be considered the background. The application can specify a color for the foreground and background of the cursor.

It is also possible to program how the cursor affects the pixels that it overlays. For example, the cursor can overwrite or be drawn in an opaque or transparent color. It can also be quickly enabled or disabled, caused to blink at varying rates, or zoom in dimension.

The "hot-spot" of the cursor is also programmable. This allows any point within the cursor pattern to be programmed as the coordinates to return when the cursor position is queried. A hardware cursor and its relevant terminology are illustrated in Figure 13.7.

Large character fonts are also available on several of the Super VGAs. Character sizes up to 32 pixels by 32 scan lines can be programmed to operate in the alphanumeric modes. Of course, any character size can be programmed in the graphics modes, but the alphanumeric modes will operate much quicker when text is the only output desired. It is certainly possible, to load non-character symbols within these large character boxes. This permits the eloquent use of icons within the alphanumeric modes.

Small character sets are also advantageous, especially when high resolution screens are desired. The problem is readability. One solution is called *anti-aliased* character fonts, available on at least one Super VGA. Aliasing is a term borrowed

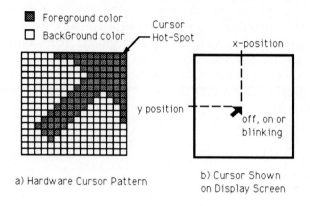

a) Hardware Cursor Pattern

b) Cursor Shown
on Display Screen

c) Location of Cursor Pattern
in Display Memory

FIGURE 13.7 Hardware Cursor

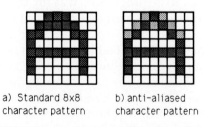

a) Standard 8x8
character pattern

b) anti-aliased
character pattern

FIGURE 13.8 Anti-aliased Character Pattern

from signal processing. It has to do with violating the constraints set up when sampling continuous signals into a digital format. In imaging, it may be thought of as an undesirable effect associated with *pixelation*. A character which suffers from not having enough pixels can be enhanced by adding gray scale to the character. This is illustrated in Figure 13.8.

13.5 VIDEO ELECTRONICS STANDARDS ASSOCIATION (VESA)

The corsortium of graphics card and video monitor manufacturers (VESA) has made an attempt to standardize the Super VGAs. Unfortunately, this attempt comes after most of the damage has already been done. VESA has recommended that an 800 by 600 16-color graphics mode be standardized. Hopefully, 1024 by 768 16-color and 640 by 480, 800 by 600 and 1024 by 768 256-color mode standards will follow. In addition, VESA has recommended several new video BIOS calls.

13.5.1 VESA Display Mode 6a hex

The standard defines a common BIOS interface to the VGA 800 by 600 16-color mode. This interface is an extension to the standard VGA interface.

The mode is invoked by the Set Mode video BIOS function as normal, using the mode number 6a hex to indicate the 800 by 600 16-color mode. The BIOS data area changes are listed in Table 13.8.

13.5.2 VESA Video BIOS Extensions

The two goals of the VESA BIOS Extension are to return information about the video environment to the application and to assist the application in initializing and programming the hardware. A software application has no standardized mechanism for determining the presence of a particular video card. To make this determination, the application must read specific I/O registers within the

TABLE 13.8   Video BIOS Data Area Changes with Mode 6a hex

Name	Address	Size	Description	New Value
CRT Mode	40:0049	Byte	Current BIOS video mode	Not Specified
CRT Cols	40:004a	Word	Number of video columns	64hex = 100
CRT Len	40:004c	Word	Size of video buffer	F000h = 61,440
Rows	40:0084	Byte	# of character rows-1	Not Specified
Points	40:0085	Word	# of bytes per character	Not Specified

VGA and the extended VGA register space. A set of routines for determining the video card is provided in Chapters 14 and 15. Without a close-up knowledge of the particular VGA chip used on the interrogated card and the surrounding features of the card, the application cannot take advantage of the card's special features.

The VESA BIOS Extension provides functions to return information about the video environment. These functions return system level information and video mode specific details. These functions are listed in Table 13.9 and are further described in Table 13.10.

TABLE 13.9   VESA BIOS Extensions

Function	Name	Description
00	Return Super VGA Information	Return general system information about the general capabilities of the Super VGA environment. A 256-byte buffer is return to the caller.
01	Return Super VGA Mode Information	Return information about a specific Super VGA video mode. A 256-byte buffer is return to the caller.
02	Set Super VGA Video Mode	Initialize a Super VGA video mode in a similar way that the standard Set Mode BIOS call operates.
03	Return Current Video Mode	Return the current video mode number in a similar way that the standard Read Current Video State BIOS call operates.
04	Save/Restore Video State	Save or restore the Super VGA video state, including all registers, DAC registers, and BIOS Data Area.
05	CPU Video Memory Control	Provide access to the video memory through bank switching.

TABLE 13.10   Return Status Information

Register	Value	Description
AL	== 4F hex	Function is supported
AL	!= 4F hex	Function is NOT supported
AH	== 00 hex	Function call was executed successfully
AH	!= 00 hex	Function call was NOT executed successfully

Details of each of these functions follow in the following four sections. The status word returned by the following BIOS calls is described in Table 13.10. This code applies to all of the VESA Extended BIOS function calls.

13.5.3   BIOS Return Super VGA Information

The AH = 4f hex, Al=00h function 00h provide information regarding the general capabilites of the Super VGA environment. The function fills an information block structure at the address specified by the caller. The information block size is 256 bytes.

Output Parameters:
  ES:DI = segment:offset far pointer to calling routine buffer where the
          information block should be loaded.
  AX = Status as indicated in Table 13.10

  The VGA block information is described in Table 13.11.

TABLE 13.11   The VGA Information Block Structure

Name	Size	Value	Description
VESASignature	4 bytes	'VESA'	4 byte signature indicating this is a valid VESA structure.
VESAVersion	word	?	Current VESA BIOS version number
OEMStringPtr	long	?	Far pointer to OEM string identifying the VGAimplementation
Capabilities	4 bytes	?	Capability of the video environment indicating the supported features.
VideoModePtr	long	?	Far pointer to supported VGA mode list.

The *VESASignature* field contains the character string *VESA* if this is a valid VESA structure. (Note: The string is not terminated with a NULL character to indicate the end of a string.)

The *VESAVersion* field is the VESA standard to which the Super VGA BIOS conforms. The higher byte specifies the major version number while the lower byte specifies the minor version number. The intial VESA version number is 1.0. VESA versions are upwardly compatible.

The *OEMStringPtr* field is a far pointer to a NULL terminated OEM-defined string. The string may be used to identify the video chip, video board, memory configuration and others. The only restriction for the format of the string is the NULL termination.

The *Capabilities* field describes the general features supported in the video environment. The long integer contains 32 bits, and none have been defined.

The *VideoModePtr* field is a far pointer to a list of supported Super VGA mode numbers. These mode numbers may be VESA standard modes or manufacture specific mode numbers. Each mode number is one 16-bit word long. (Note: The list is terminated with a–1 value FFFF hex. This list might be a static list located in ROM or a dynamic list loaded in RAM. The mode numbers as defined by VESA are described in Table 13.11.)

The standard mode numbers are 7 bits wide and the standard VGA modes range from 0 to 13 hex. The extended modes, as defined by the manufacturers, range from 14 hex to 7f hex. Values greater than 7f hex = 127 cannot be used since bit 7 indicates to the BIOS mode Set command, whether the display memory to be used in the desired mode will be cleared or not.

The VESA mode numbers are 15 bits wide, as shown in Table 13.12. Note that the VESA mode numbers range from 100 hex to 1FF hex. There can only be 256 possible VESA modes since bit 8 is a flag which indicates whether the mode is a VESA-defined mode.

The one mode which VESA has defined, mode 6A hex, is an 800 by 600 16-color mode. The official VESA mode number for this mode is 102 hex. Additional modes defined by VESA are listed in Table 13.13.

TABLE 13.12 VESA Mode Number Format

Bit Position	Description	Value
Bit 15	Reserved	set to 0
Bit 14–9	Reserved by VESA for future expansion	set to 0
Bit 8	VESA mode	0 = Not a VESA mode 1 = VESA mode
Bit 7–0	Mode number	0–ff hex

TABLE 13.13   VESA Defined Modes

VESA Mode Number	7 bit Mode Number	Pixel Resolution	Number of Colors
100 hex	—	640x400	256
101 hex	—	640x480	256
102 hex	6A hex	800x600	16
103 hex	—	800x600	256
104 hex	—	1024x768	16
105 hex	—	1024x768	256
106 hex	—	1280x1024	16
107 hex	—	1280x1024	256

13.5.4   BIOS Return Super VGA Mode Information

The AH = 4f hex, Al=01h function 00h provides information to the calling program about a specific Super VGA video mode. The function fills an information block structure at the address specified by the caller. The information block size is a maximum of 256 bytes. Both a VESA-defined mode and a non-VESA-defined mode can be queried for using this BIOS mode. Note that some implementations may not support the non-VESA defined modes.

Input Parameters:

CX = super VESA or non-VESA VGA video mode of which information is desired

Output Parameters:

ES:DI = segment:offset far pointer to calling routine buffer where the information block should be loaded.

AX = Status as indicated in Table 13.10

The mandatory mode information block is described in Table 13.14. The optional Mode Information Block is described in Table 13.15. The optional mode information block will be present if bit 1 of the ModeAttributes bit is set to 1.

The mode attribute field, *ModeAttributes*, describes certain important characteristics of the video memory, as indicated in Table 13.15. The window attributes fields, *WinAAttributes* and *WinBAttributes* describe characteristics of the windowing scheme, as described in Table 13.16.

Examples of optional information which can be found in the mode information block are included in Table 13.17.

TABLE 13.14   Mandatory Information Structure Describing a Video Mode

Name	Size	Description
ModeAttributes	word	Mode attributes describing important characteristics of the video mode
WinAAttributes	byte	Describe characteristics of the CPU windowing scheme for window A
WinBAttributes	byte	Describe characteristics of the CPU windowing scheme for window B
WinGranularity	word	Defines the smallest boundary, in Kbytes, on which the window can be placed in video memory.
WinSize	word	Specifies the size of the window in Kbytes
WinASegment	word	Segment address of where the window A is located in host address space
WinBSegment	word	Segment address of where the window B is located in host address space
WinFuncPtr	long	Far Pointer to the function which actually performs the windowing.
BytesPerScanLine	word	Number of bytes that each logical scanline consists of. A logical scan line can be equal or greater than the displayed scanline.

TABLE 13.15   Mode Attribute Bit Fields

Bit	Function
0	Specifies whether this mode can be initialled in the present video configuration. This bit can block access to a video mode if there is some environmental condition precluding its usage, that is, the monitor attached to the VGA is not sufficient to handle the blocked mode's resolution.
1	Specifies whether the extended mode information is available. Video modes defined by VESA will have certain known characteristics. This extended information is an optional provision in the information block as described in Table 13.14. It is optional due to the space constraints for ROM based implementations of the VESA BIOS Extensions. Since the VESA-defined modes are standardized, this optional information is already known and need not be included.
2	Indicates whether the BIOS has support for output functions. Some typical output functions include TTY output, scrolling, and pixel. VESA recommends that the BIOS support all output functions.
3	Indicates whether the mode is a monochrome or color mode. Monochrome modes, as indicated by a 0 in bit 3 of Table 13.12, maps the CRTC register pairs to addresses 3B4/3B5 hex. Color modes, as indicated by a 1 in bit 3 of Table 13.12, maps the CRTC register pairs to addresses 3D4/3D5.

TABLE 13.15 (*continued*)

Bit	Function
	0 = monochrome mode
	1 = color mode
4	Indicates whether the mode is a text mode or a graphics mode. Text modes utilize bit planes 0 and 1 for character and attribute codes respectively. They utilize bit planes 2 and 3 for the character font bit patterns.
	0 = text mode
	1 = graphics mode

TABLE 13.16 Window Attribute Bit Fields

Bit	Function
0	Whether the window A or B is supported.
	0 = Window A or B is not supported
	1 = Window A or B is supported
1	Whether the window A or B is readable
	0 = Window A or B is not readable
	1 = Window A or B is readable
2	Whether the window A or B is writeable
	0 = Window A or B is not writeable
	1 = Window A or B is writeable
3–15	Reserved for future expansion.

TABLE 13.17 Optonal Information in the Mode Information Block

Name	Size	Description
XResolution	word	Horizontal resolution in pixels
YResolution	word	Vertical resolution in pixels
XCharSize	byte	Character cell width
YCharSize	byte	Character cell height
NumbeofPlanes	byte	Number of memory planes
BitsPerPixel	byte	Number of bits per pixel
NumberofBanks	byte	Number of banks. The bank size is indicated in the BankSize field.
MemoryModel	byte	Memory model type. See Table 13.17.
BankSize	byte	Size of each memory bank in Kbytes. Modes that do not use scan line banks would set this field to 0.

The memory model field, MemoryModel describes the memory organization, as indicated in Table 13.18.

The number of banks field, *NumberOfBanks*, contains the number of banks in which the scan lines are grouped. For example, the CGA and Hercules have distinct banks of memory which are not sequentially mapped to the screen. CGA graphics modes have two banks while the Hercules graphics modes have four banks. If the scan line number is divided by the number of banks, the remainder is the bank that contains the scan line. The resultant quotient is the scan line number within the bank.

Consider the following example. Suppose a CGA mode with two banks is in effect. To locate scan line 131, divide 131 by two. This yields a quotient of 65 and a remainder of 1. Thus, the scan line is in bank 1 and is located in scan line 65 within that bank.

The bank size field, *BankSize*, specifies the size of each bank as previously described in units of Kbytes. The CGA-compatible modes and the Hercules compatible modes each have 8192 bytes per bank. Thus, the value of this field would be set to 8. Modes which do not have scanline banks would set this field to 0.

13.5.5   BIOS Set Super VGA Video Mode

The AH = 4f hex, Al=02h function 02 initializes a super video mode. The BX register contains the Super VGA mode to set. The format of the VESA mode numbers is described in Table 13.11. If the mode cannot be set, the BIOS should leave the video environment unchanged. An error code is returned as described in Table 13.10.

Input Parameters:
BX   Video Mode
            Bit 0–14 = video mode as per Table 13.10
            Bit 15 is a flag indicating whether the display memory which
            will be affected by this mode should be cleared.
                        Bit 15=1   Clear video memory
                        Bit 15=0   Do not clear video memory

Output Parameters:
AX   Status as described in Table 13.10

13.5.6   AH = 4f Hex, Al=03h: Return Current VGA Video Mode

Function 03 returns the current video mode. The BX Register contains the desired VGA mode to return. The format of the VESA mode numbers is described in Table 13.10. This function is similar to the Read Current Video State BIOS call, AH=0F hex, described in Chapter 11.9.4. The main difference is that

TABLE 13.18   Memory Model Types

Code	Memory Type
00 hex	Text mode
01 hex	CGA mode
02 hex	Hercules graphics mode
03 hex	4 plane planar mode
04 hex	Packed pixel mode
05 hex	Non-chain 4, 256-color mode
06-0F hex	Reserved for future use by VESA
10-FF hex	To be defined by the card or chip manufacturer

the video mode is returned in the AL Register as a byte, while this function returns the mode as a word in the BX Register. A second difference is that the clear option is not indicated in the mode number. The BIOS Set Mode, Function 00 hex described in Chapter 11.2.1, and the VESA Set Super VGA Video Mode, Function 02 hex just described in Section 13.5.5, allow the user to optionally clear the memory. In the AH=0F BIOS call, the state of the display memory clearing is returned in bit 7. This is not the case in this VESA Function 03 hex call. The Memory-Clear bit will not be returned in the BX Register since the purpose of this call is to return the mode number. If the clear state is desired, the application should inquire through bit 7 of the mode value in the BIOS state area of host memory at byte location 40:0087. It can also be determined by calling the BIOS Read Current Video Mode function 0F.

Output Parameters:
BX	Video Mode
	Bit 0–14 = video mode as per Table 13.10
AX	Status as described in Table 13.10

13.5.7   BIOS Save/Restore Super VGA Video State

The AH = 4f hex, Al=04h function 04 hex provides a means to save and restore the Super VGA video state. The functions are a superset of the three subfunctions of the standard VGA BIOS call Function 1C hex described in Section 11.15.3. There are three subfunctions within this BIOS call. These determine the actual operation of this call and are selected through the DL Register. The three subfunctions allow the return of the size of the save/restore state buffer. This saves the Super VGA video state and restores the Super VGA video State described in Table 13.19.

TABLE 13.19   Save/Restore Super VGA Video States Subfunctions

Subfunction	Description
00 hex	Return the size of the buffer to be loaded with data if a save state is called or read from if a restore state is called. The size indicates the number of 64-byte blocks needed to hold the data. For example, if the size, as returned in the BX register, is 15, the buffer should be 15*64=960 bytes long.
01 hex	Save the Super VGA video state. The state of the VGA will be read as indicated in the requested states field described in Table 13.17. When the states are combined, the data relevant to these states will be loaded into the buffer in a specific order. This same order will be used for the analogous Restore State Function.
02 hex	Restore the Super VGA video state. The state of the VGA will be written as indicated in the requested states field described in Table 13.17. When the states are combined, the data relevant to these states will be read from the buffer in a specific order. This same order would have been used by the analogous Save State function.

TABLE 13.20   Save/Restore Function Requested States

Blt	Requested State
0	Save/restore the video hardware state
1	Save/restore the video BIOS data state
2	Save/restore the video DAC state
3	Save/restore the Super VGA state

There are four possible states that can be saved. These include the video hardware state, the video BIOS data state, the video DAC state and the Super VGA state. The first three are identical to the three states stored in the standard BIOS Save/Restore Video State function AH=1C hex call described in Section 11.15.3. The fourth handles the Super VGA states. These are described in Table 13.20. The first three states should be the same from one VGA adapter to another while the fourth state should not be assumed to be compatible across different VGA adapters.

The four possible requested states can be combined to form sixteen possible combinations. For example, a request state code of A hex = 1010 binary would indicate that the data in the save/restore buffer would contain the Super VGA state and the video hardware state.

Subfunction DL=00

Subfunction DL=00 returns the size of the buffer in 64-byte blocks necessary for a save state or expected for a restore state BIOS call. The size is determined by the requested states.

Input Parameters:

DL=0	Return the buffer size of the save/restore buffer
CX	Requested states as indicated in Table 13.19

Output Parameters:

AX	Status as indicated in Table 13.10
BX	Number of 64-byte blocks which are required for the size of the buffer as in order to store/restore the requested states.

Subfunction DL=01

Subfunction DL=01 saves the Super VGA state. The requested states, as indicated in the CX Register, will determine the areas of the VGA to be saved and the order in which they will be loaded into the buffer. It is possible to determine the size of each area and the order in which each is saved in the buffer by experimentation. The size, in 64-byte blocks, of each state can be determined by calling subfunction 1 four times with one state requested for each call. The order within the buffer can be determined by searching through the data for matching patterns. This really should not be necessary as long as the same states are requested for complimentary save and restore calls.

Input Parameters:

DL=1	Save the Super VGA state
CX	Requested states as indicated in Table 13.17
ES:BX	Segment:Offset address of buffer which will contain the data as saved from the Super VGA. The size and ordering of this buffer conforms to the requested states.

Output Parameters:

AX	Status as indicated in Table 13.10

Subfunction DL=02

Subfunction DL=2 restores the Super VGA state. The requested states, as indicated in the CX Register, will determine the areas of the VGA to be restored and the order in which they will be loaded into the buffer. It is possible to determine the size of each area and the order in which each is saved in the buffer by experimentation. The size, in 64-byte blocks of each state, can be determined by calling subfunction 1 four times with one state requested for each call. The order within the buffer can be determined by searching through the data for matching patterns. This should not be necessary as long as the same states are requested for complimentary Save and Restore calls.

Input Parameters:

DL=2	Restore the Super VGA state
CX	Requested states as indicated in Table 13.17
ES:BX	Segment:Offset address of buffer which is expected to contain the data which will be restored into the Super VGA. The size and ordering of this buffer conforms to the requested states.

Output Parameters:

AX	Status as indicated in Table 13.10

13.5.8   BIOS CPU Video Memory Window Control

The AH = 4f hex, Al=05h function 04 hex provides a means to set or get the position of a specified window in the video memory. This function allows direct access to the hardware paging registers. To use this function, the application can obtain the size, location and granularity of the desired window through the Return Super VGA mode information, VESA BIOS function 01 hex described in Section 13.5.4. This function has two sub-functions for selecting the video memory window or the returning of the window position.

Two windows are possible — windows A and B. These are described and defined in Table 13.11. The two windows exist because several of the Super VGAs use two-paging schemes. The ability to use two pages is important because speed is usually an issue.

When moving memory from one location to another it is necessary to maintain two sets of pointers, one for the source data and another for the destination data. In the host, this is accomplished by the DS:SI source address register pair and ES:DI for the destination address register pair. These segment:offset registers describe the 18-bit address necessary to completely describe the address. In the VGA, when mapped into the PC address space A0000–AFFFF space, this is a bit more complex. Paging or Bank registers are necessary to hold the upper address because the display memory is no longer contiguous. Maintaining two Page registers allows data to be transferred without constantly fiddling with the page (bank) registers.

An example is when the MOVSx instruction is used. If dual paging is engaged, the DS and ES registers are set to the display memory segment address A000. The DI and SI offset registers point to the offset of the data within each segment. The Page (bank) registers are set to their respective banks. At this point all necessary pointers are initialized, and a REP MOVSx instruction can be executed. Up to 64 Kbytes can be transferred without ever touching a Page (bank) Register.

The two Page (bank) registers correspond to the windows A and B pointers described below. If only one Page Register is used, only one window should be utilized. Otherwise, both windows A and B should point to identical locations.

Both windows A & B functions can be directly accessed through a far call from the application. The address of the BIOS function may be obtained from the VESA BIOS function 01 as described in Section 13.5.4. A field in the ModeInfoBlock, described in Table 13.11, contains the far pointer address to this function. The location of this function may change when the VGA is in different video modes. Therefore, the location of this function should be interrogated after each mode set. Note that even this direct function call might be too time consuming. It may be desirable to directly access the Super VGA registers responsible for the bank setting. Techniques vary for each VGA implementation. Several techniques are described in Chapter 15.

In the far call version, the AX and DX registers are not preserved. The application must load the input parameters in the BX and DX registers for the set window command. However, it is not necessary to load the AX Register when using the far call version of this function. When using the direct, register-setting techniques described in Chapter 15, each function must be scrutinized to determine the specific registers involved.

Subfunction BH=00

Subfunction BH=00 selects a Super VGA window memory window. There are two possible windows, either A or B. The window number, window A or B, is input to this subfunction. The window position in video memory, according to the window granularity units, is returned.

In the following example, the window granularity is 4 Kbytes and 64 windows would describe the full 1 megabyte space. This is the case when a 256-color mode is engaged, and the 4 Kbyte segment corresponds to 4 Kbytes in each of the four planes totalling 16 Kbytes. Thus, 16 Kbytes * 64 = 1 megabyte. When the window points to 512 K, it is equivalent to half way into memory which corresponds to a window location of 32.

Input Parameters:

BH=00	Select Super VGA video memory window
BL	Window number
	0 = Window A
	1 = WindowB
DX	Window position in video memory. This value is according to window granularity.

Output Parameters:

AX	Status as indicated in Table 13.10

Subfunction BH=01

Subfunction BH=01 return the Super VGA window memory window number. Windows A and B are the only two possible windows. The window number for one of these two is input to this subfunction, and the window position in video memory, according to the window granularity units, is returned. This function returns the current window number of the selected window.

Input Parameters:
BH=00	Return Super VGA video memory window
BL	Window number
	0 = Window A
	1 = Window B

Output Parameters:
AX	Status as indicated in Table 13.10
DX	Window position in video memory. This value is according to window granularity.

13.6   IDENTIFYING THE GRAPHICS ENVIRONMENT

Each implementation of the VGA has its own specific potential and programming specifics. However, there are many similarities. Section 13.6 presents the theory and background of some of the similarities. Chapter 14 provides application specific details. Chapter 15 contains program examples that implement these basic features.

The discussions in this section provide details about the following: definitions, techniques and problems associated with identifying the VGA, controlling the VGA, saving and restoring the state of the VGA, memory addressing techniques, writing to display memory and selecting a start address.

The first three items, identifying the VGA, controlling the VGA and saving and restoring the state of the VGA, will become much simpler when the VGA adapter manufacturers and the BIOS programmers implement the VESA standards associated with identifying which VGA chip is present, the capabilities of the adapter surrounding the chip, and a BIOS call to save and restore the Extended registers. Section 13.6.1, 13.6.2 and 13.6.3 help describe these functions. The corresponding VESA definitions are found in Sections 13.5.

The last three items, memory addressing techniques, writing to display memory, and selecting a starting address, will describe in detail how memory is actually organized. The reader may select to use these techniques and the program examples provided in Chapter 15 instead of the VESA standard BIOS call which handles changing banks (pages, windows). The principle reason for this choice is speed. Although the Al=05h BIOS call named *CPU Video Memory Window Control* described in Section13.5.8 has an associated direct function call, this may still be too slow for several applications.

Any program which intends to use the advanced features of the Super VGAs will have to determine the graphics environment installed on the host computer. This can be a simple or a complex task. In general, the pertinent questions that must be answered about the graphics environment are which other cards beside the VGA are present, which VGA chip is present, and the potentials of the VGA card itself. Several of these important issues are listed in Table 13.21.

13.6.1   The Graphics Environment

Most computer systems contain one graphics card, although some contain none or multiple cards. It is assumed that at least one VGA is present. Other graphics cards can coexist with the VGA card. There are monochrome graphics cards, MDA and Hercules, less powerful color graphics cards, CGA, EGA, other VGA graphics cards, and cards including 8514/A, TIGA or special purpose cards.

If a monochrome card coexists with the VGA, the VGA must be configured in a color mode. By configuring the VGA into a color mode, the CRTC registers will be located at 3D4/3D5. Other registers in the Super VGA register sets may be affected by this setting. The monochrome memory will reside at B0000–B7FFF hex while the VGA memory will reside between A0000–AFFFF hex. There are exceptions to this location, as certain VGA cards will allow their memory, when configured in a color mode, to be mapped into A0000–BFFFF hex. Details are discussed in Chapter 14.

TABLE 13.21   Assessing the Graphics Environment

Question	Possibilities
Other graphics cards	Yes, No
Which graphics cards	CGA, MDA, VGA, multiple VGAs, 8514/A, TIGA, other
VESA Supported ?	No, Yes
VESA Version Implemented	Integer
Manufacturer of VGA Chip	ATI, Chips and Tech, Genoa, Paradise, Trident, Tseng, Video7
Chip Identification Number	Integer
Chip Version	Integer
Location	Motherboard or Adapter Card
Host Interface	8 bit, 16 bit or 32 bit
Amount of Display Memory	256 Kbytes, 512 Kbytes, 1 megabyte, 2 megabyte, 4 megabyte
16-Color Display Modes Accommodated ?	800x600, 1024x768, 1280x1024, etc. interlaced or non-interlaced?
256-Color Display Modes Accommodated ?	640x400, 640x480, 800x600, 1024x768 etc.
Emulation Modes Available ?	No, CGA, MDA, Hercules, EGA, 8514/A
Color DAC ?	6-bit, 8-bit, 16-bit, 24-bit per color
Type of Monitor ?	Monochrome, Standard Frequency, Multi-syncing

There seem to be no 16-bit monochrome cards. This can cause a problem if 16-bit memory accesses are desired to and from the VGA. Since the VGA has no way of enabling 16-bit address to addresses A0000–AFFFF without including B0000–BFFFF, 16-bit accesses will be forced upon the poor and unexpecting monochrome card. This can cause bus conflicts and/or unpredictable results.

The author finds that using a monochrome monitor in conjunction with a VGA card is essential when debugging graphics applications. This is especially true when using a debugger, like Microsoft's *CodeView*, which has the facility to handle two simultaneous graphics systems.

Some VGA manufacturers claim that no other graphics card can coexist with their VGA. In these cases, I recommend using the monochrome card with their VGA anyway. This restriction was created by IBM designers who designed the AT bus with such a major limitation as 128 Kbyte accesses limited to 16-bit transfers.

If a color graphics card, CGA, coexists with the VGA in question, that VGA must be set up in a monochrome mode. The CRTC registers will be mapped to 3B4/3B5, and the memory will reside at B0000–B7FFF hex. Once again, unpredictable results will occur if the VGA is configured in a 16-bit memory access mode.

The EGA, being so similar to the VGA, cannot coexist with the VGA unless the VGA card can be disabled. This situation is similar to having multiple VGAs in the same system. The IBM PS/2 VGA was designed on the motherboard and had the capability of being disabled. Several of the Super VGAs share this capability, allowing multiple VGA systems to operate in parallel. One can immediately see the importance of this feature once multi-user operating systems, such as UNIX, hit the PC platforms with graphical interfaces such as X-Windows.

There are three ways of approaching multiple monitors. The first is to utilize a high-speed data link such as ethernet going to an ethernet-compatible user station. This link is standard in the workstation environment. Currently, monitors supporting X-Windows are available. They eliminate the need for multiple processors on the network. It would be possible to interface a microprocessor, ethernet adapter, some memory and a VGA chip to a monitor and keyboard and have a remote VGA workstation. This would be especially well suited to applications requiring remote stations.

A second possibility is to have multiple VGAs with only one active at a time on the host bus. In this case, all but one VGA would be "asleep" with respect to the host. Each could have the same port and memory addresses and a single control register with a ID code. Most VGAs have the ability to be asleep. Of course, all monitors would have to be within video monitor cable distance from the VGA cards. Some cards are equipped with multiple VGAs on a single card.

A third and preferable condition is for the VGAs to map into different memory and I/O space when distances are not an issue . With the 80386 address space, there is enough elbow room for about a thousand or so VGAs. In some cases, the Super VGAs can remap memory and I/O address space to accommodate multiple VGA implementations. Typically, this re-mapping would be used in conjunction with a restructuring of the VGA address space to remove overlapping memory. The advantages of the linear address space with the 80386's 32 bit instructions are significant.

The 8514/A adapter is compatible with the VGA and requires a VGA to operate. In 1987, IBM introduced the VGA and the 8514/A at the same time. The hooks for the 8514/A are designed into the IBM standard video BIOS on the VGA. Similar to the TIGA graphics adapters described in the following paragraph, the 8514/A requires a standard DOS adapter. This is certainly a drawback. 8514/A cards have either a feedthrough capability for a VGA or an on-board VGA. Transfer of control from one display mode which runs of the VGA to one which runs on the 8514/A is easily and eloquently accomplished through the BIOS on the VGA. This is one advantage that the 8514/A has over the TIGA based cards.

The TIGA graphics adapters, based on the Texas Instruments TI34010 and TI34020 coprocessors, coexist with the VGA. Currently, the PC has to have a standard adapter in order to boot up. This might be an MDA, Hercules, CGA, EGA, VGA or 8514/A. Several of the TIGA cards have an onboard VGA, or a feedthrough path for the VGA. Having a separate VGA card means a separate monitor. Having a feedthrough path allows the user to utilize the same monitor. Of course, the monitor has to have syncing capabilities to handle both the VGA and the TIGA adapter.

There is no simple technique to inquire as to which cards are available on the system. In the case of an MDA or Hercules card, the VGA is set up in a color mode, and its display memory is typically mapped at A0000–AFFFF or from B8000–BFFFF. The CRTC registers is mapped at 3D4/3D5. The Hercules or MDA display memory is located at B0000–B0FFF, and its control registers are located between 3B0–3BF. It is possible to read a value in this memory space, replace it with another value, read it again and see if the value changed. If this can be performed, a Hercules or MDA is present. The original value should then be replaced. Another technique is to read/modify/re-write one of the control registers in a similar fashion as was done to the memory.

If a CGA is present, the VGA will be set up as a monochrome system with its display memory at B0000–B7FFF and the CRTC registers located at 3B4/3B5. The CGA display memory resides at B8000–B8FFF, and its Control registers reside at 3D4/3D5. Similar techniques to those used in the preceding paragraph could be used to determine whether a CGA card is present.

If multiple VGAs are present, the specific VGA card documentation must be consulted to determine how the VGA discriminates between the multiple VGAs.

13.6.2   Is VESA Supported?

Luckily, VESA has a well-defined BIOS call which identifies whether VESA is present and if so, which version. This is outlined in Table 13.10.

13.6.3 Determining Which VGA Is Present

Each Super VGA has a fingerprint which can be traced by looking for certain clues. A message may be hiding in BIOS; a particular register may be present which is not present in the other Super VGA implementations.

Chapters 14 through 19 provide detailed descriptions for identifying six of the popular VGA chips. The chips selected include ATI, Chips and Technologies, Paradise, Trident, Tseng Labs, and the Video7 VGA Chips. In certain cases, these manufacturers have more than one VGA chip and it is necessary to distinguish which particular chip is present. The chips described in this book are listed in Table 13.22.

13.6.4 Determining the VGA Host Interface

It is necessary to identify the type of host interface in order to interface to these chips. In some cases, registers will be located in different locations depending on whether the VGA is on the motherboard or on an adapter. The speed advantages inherent with the motherboard-located VGAs is significant, and the future will certainly see a growing popularity of VGA implementations on the motherboard.

A second reason to determine the type of host interface deals with the 8 and 16-bit interfaces. All Super VGA chips can handle the 16-bit host interface. The three aspects of this interface include the BIOS, the I/O ports and the display memory. All 16-bit cards can be configured to operate in either the 8-bit or 16-bit mode. Some have auto sensing; others have switch settings or jumpers. Still others have programmable registers which control the interface; a few more have a combination of the above.

It is not always true that "more is better." Quite often more means more trouble. In cases when the width of the interface uses automatic sensing through switch settings or through jumpers, the programmer is relinquished of responsibility. However, a programmable interface is another story and defies solution.

Here is the problem. The PC bus interface can either transfer memory or

---

TABLE 13.22 Super VGA Chips Detailed in this Book

Manufacturer	Chip Number
ATI	18800
Chips and Technologies	451, 452, 453, 455
Paradise/Western Digital	PVGA1a, PVGA1b
Trident	8800, 8900
Tseng Labs	ET3000, ET4000
Video7/Headland Tech	V7VGA

I/O. Both are presented with a 16-bit enable control line called "MEM16" and "IO16" respectively. The I/O ports are the easiest to interface. Typically they interface to hardware registers which are fast and simple. The host has considerable time to set up a 16-bit I/O transfer, and the adapter can decode all of the slow address lines. Thus, every port address can be decoded individually to determine if that particular port address is an 8- or 16-bit port. Usually the speed of the host bus will not affect the operation of the 16-bit ports.

The memory transfers are more complicated. These encompass both the BIOS instruction execution transfers and the display memory data transfers. The host does not have much time to set up the 8- or 16-bit transfer, and consequently, the adapter can not decode all of the address lines. Chunks of address space in 128 Kbyte increments have to be decoded as one entity. The problem is that there are no 128 Kbyte segments dedicated just to the VGA. The host memory address space utilization is generally mapped in Table 13.23.

As for BIOS transfers, Table 13.22 shows that the Video BIOS area shares the 128 Kbyte space with the Hard Disk BIOS and host BIOS. Typically, the host BIOS and the disk BIOS are not a source of problems. The Host BIOS is not a problem since it is typically 16 bits wide and does not depend on the MEM16 line since it is not on an adapter card. The disk BIOS is typically not a problem because most disk controllers used in 16-bit bus systems utilize the 16-bit interface.

The MEM16 and IO16 line are open-collector lines. This means that more than one source can pull the line down at a time without any hardware conflicts. Thus, it is likely that both the Super VGA and the hard disk controller are always both pulling down MEM16.

A problem does exist in the non-defined memory area between the Video BIOS, which starts at C000 hex, and the Hard Disk BIOS, which starts at C8000. Industrious third-party manufacturers have squeezed their BIOS codes into this area. If their 8-bit or 16-bit card cannot support an 8-bit BIOS, their card will not function properly.

TABLE 13.23 16-bit Memory Address Decoding Map

Host Address Range	Typical Usage
00000 – 1FFFF	Interrupt Vectors, ROM BIOS Communications Area, DOS Communications Area
20000 – 3FFFF	DOS
40000 – 5FFFF	Device Drivers, Resident command.com
60000 – 7FFFF	RAM, random buffers, control blocks
80000 – 9FFFF	RAM
A0000 – BFFFF	Video Display Memory for Monochrome and Color
C0000 – DFFFF	Video BIOS, Hard Disk BIOS and host BIOS
E0000 – FFFFF	Host BIOS

Consider the following example. Suppose the VGA in question is just sitting idle while a third- party scanner card is being accessed. Further suppose the scanner sends an interrupt, and the host interrupt vector sends the program counter to location C6000, location of the scanner BIOS. The scanner BIOS is only 8 bits wide and does not even interface to the connector which contains the MEM16 signal. It is innocent. It is just in the wrong place at the wrong time. The address C6000 gets exerted onto the bus and before the scanner can respond, the superfast decoding logic on the Super VGA determines that the address did reside within C0000 and DFFFF. It exerts MEM16 and then remains off the bus since it has no business with C6000. Unfortunately, the damage is already done! The host has sensed the MEM16 line and reads in an instruction from the scanner which it is expecting to be 16 bits wide. Nobody is responding to C6000 and so the upper eight bits of the bus are in a tri-stated condition. The instruction makes no sense to the host and trouble results.

So, what is a programmer to do? Perhaps an interactive operator setup procedure is necessary before engaging the 16-bit interface. More typically, an application will simply kick-in the 16-bit interface and let the buyer sort it out.

13.6.5   Determining Which Modes are Supported

A Super VGA BIOS can have defined several high resolution modes and will respond to commands to install these modes. However, the VGA card may not be equipped with enough memory or the monitor attached to the VGA may not be sufficient to handle all of the display modes.

Let us consider the issue of having enough memory. The Super VGAs are equipped with either 256 Kbytes, 512 Kbytes or one megabyte. Soon versions will appear with four megabytes. Each Super VGA has its own display modes, but not all defined modes will run on a given implementation. This is due to variations in the amount of display memory present, as well as the type of adapter and monitor. It is a simple issue to perform a start-up test to determine the amount of memory residing on the card. One performs read/modify writes through the various banks until the memory runs out.

The monitor is more difficult to detect. The VESA standard includes a table indicating valid display modes. This table can be interrogated to determine whether a mode can be used. In some Super VGAs, a register contains information regarding the monitor type. These cards perform automatic monitor sensing and set up themselves at power on. Warnings are provided to ensure that a different monitor is not attached while power is on. These user-friendly cards do not allow display modes inappropriate for the monitor type. The programmer can attempt to set a mode and look for an error in the return parameter.

13.6.6   Determining the Emulation Modes

The techniques used for setting up downward compatibility vary from one Super VGA card to another. It is necessary to consult the documentation of individual cards to set up their emulation modes. Some cards provide BIOS calls; others provide set-up programs. Still others provide registers which can be programmed for proper emulation. In any case, the appropriate monitor has to be installed for these emulation modes to function well.

13.6.7   Determining the Resolution of the Color DAC

VGAs operate in either a 2-, 4-, 16- or 256-color mode. In any of these modes, the 2, 4, 16 or 256 colors can be either 18-bit or 24-bit color. Unfortunately, there is no standard way to set up the final color resolution. The DAC chips are compatible pin for pin. For a few extra dollars, one can have 24-bit color. Note that this is not "true color" which is also called 24-bit color. There can only be 256 different colors.

It is not the responsibility of the VGA chip to keep track of the type of DAC chip present. The cards which do support the 8-bit-per-color DACS have external decoding, and their documentation should be consulted for details on selecting or determining the DAC color resolution.

13.7   CONTROLLING THE SUPER VGA

Techniques used to control the Super VGAs range in complexity from turning the VGA *on* to setting up complex emulation states. Fortunately, the manufacturers have helped programmers by coding many control features in the BIOS. Hardware engineers have implemented the features in hardware.

Some of the control aspects are performed immediately at power up while others occur inside a tight and frequently-used loop. Thus, the speed at which these control functions must be executed varies. The word control is, of course, very broad. Almost anything can be lumped into the category of control. Table 13.24 includes those features of the Super VGAs categorized as control features.

TABLE 13.24   Controlling The Super VGA

Feature	Technique
Enabling and disabling the VGA	Register, Switch, Autosense
Configuring up the host interface	Register
Accessing the VGA registers	Register, BIOS
Setting display modes	BIOS
Controlling Emulation	BIOS, Register
Locking out or protecting registers	Register
Controlling vertical interrupts	Register
Saving and restoring the VGA state	BIOS, Register

13.7.1 Enabling and Disabling the VGA

There are several on/off switches for the VGA. The many techniques for taking firm control of the standard VGA are listed in Table 13.25. Each item is discussed in the following paragraphs. References are made to the appropriate sections in Chapters 1–12 when features are part of the VGA standard.

As discussed in Section 10.3.2, the standard VGA allows the screen to be turned off by setting bit 5 of the Clocking Mode Register. When turned off, the programmer can achieve maximum bandwidth transfers to the display memory since the host will not be wait-stated due to display refresh cycles. The display monitor is still provided with horizontal and vertical sync pulses and a blanking color. In most implementations, this blanking color is black, while in some this color can be programmed.

To adjust the Clocking Mode Register without destroying memory contents, the sequencer must first be reset through a synchronous reset, using the Reset Register. As discussed in Section 10.3.1, this is accomplished by writing a 0 to bit 1 followed by writing a 1 to bit 1. This causes a synchronous reset pulse to be issued. A similar pulse written to Bit 0 causes an asynchronous reset. This, in turn, causes data loss in the display memory. Recall that the display memory is constructed of dynamic RAM memory.

The display memory can be cut off from the host through the Miscellaneous Output Register. As presented in Section 10.2.1, this is one way in which to

TABLE 13.25 Resetting and Enabling The Standard VGAs

Function	Purpose	Technique
Asynchronous Reset	Reset sequencer	Reset Register Bit 0=0
Synchronous Reset	Reset sequencer	Reset Register Bit 1=0
Turn off the screen	Fast memory access	Clocking Mode Register Bit 5=1
Turn on the screen	Display Image	Clocking Mode Register Bit 5=0
Enable RAM	Enable host access to RAM	Miscellaneous Output Register Bit 1=1
Disable RAM	Disable host access to RAM	Miscellaneous Output Register Bit 1=0
Disable Display	Blank the screen	Attribute Address Register Bit 5=0
Enable Display	Normal operation	Attribute Address Register Bit 5=1

TABLE 13.26 Controlling the Super VGAs

Feature	Typical Implementation Technique
Enable or Disable VGA	Register
Put VGA Asleep or Awake	Register
Enter/Exit Setup Mode	Register

allow multiple VGAs to reside in the same host system with their respective memories mapped to the same host memory addresses. Only one VGA would have its memory enabled at a time. The rest would be put "to sleep."

The display can be enabled or disabled through the Attribute Address Register. As indicated in Section 10.6.1, the palette and other attribute registers are dual-ported. Either the host or the display video circuitry has access to them. One can inadvertently cut the video drivers off, thereby blanking the screen, by keeping Bit 5 of this reset after indexing the attribute registers.

Mismanaging the registers in any number of ways can cause the display to go blank. In addition, all of display memory could be loaded with black color, or all of the color registers could be set to black. If the programmer desires to blank the screen, one of these techniques can be used.

Some of the Super VGAs have additional facilities to enable and disable the card. In addition, the card can be awoken or put to sleep. These cases are shown in Table 13.26. Detailed descriptions can be found in Chapters 15–21.

13.7.2 Configuring the Host Interface

The Super VGAs have the ability to handle 16-bit transfers. The three types of controlled transfer include the display memory accesses, the ROM accesses, and the I/O port accesses. The Super VGAs cards can be inserted into 8- or 16-bit card slots. The user can often select 8- or 16-bit I/O accesses, 8- or 16-bit display memory addresses, or 8- or 16-bit BIOS accesses by setting switches or by placing or removing jumpers. Some cards are auto-configurable. These automatically adapt to an 8- or 16-bit card. In addition, the user can select to enable or disable on-card BIOS. Typical cases are listed in Table 13.27. Detailed descriptions for each Super VGA manufacturer are found in Chapters 15–21.

Most of the Super VGAs have a facility for fine-tuning the speed of the host to VGA interface. Typical features are fast decoding, fast writing and fast scrolling. Some host systems do not allow fast decoding. The features of fast writing and scrolling release the host as soon as the instruction is completed; they do not generate host wait-states.

TABLE 13.27 Configuring the Host Interface

Feature	Typical Implementation Technique
Select 8- or16-bit I/O	Register, switch, autosense
Select 8- or 16-bit memory	Register, switch, autosense
Select 8- or 16-bit BIOS	Register, switch, autosense
Enable on-card BIOS	Register, switch
Select Slow/Fast Address Decode	Register, switch
Fast Write	Register
Fast Scroll	Register

TABLE 13.28 Accessing the Super VGA Registers

Feature	Typical Implementation Technique
Enter Set Up Mode	Register at 46E8 for PC/AT or 3C3 for Microchannel
Enable Extended Registers	Register
Lock Registers	Register
Accessing Extended Registers	Register, BIOS

13.7.3 Accessing the VGA Registers

As we know by now, the VGA is composed of the standard VGA registers, emulation registers and extended or super registers. A programmer must know how to access these registers while preventing other applications from accessing them. Table 13.28 lists some issues related to accessing registers.

The VGA is assumed to be awake. Otherwise, no registers will be accessible as discussed in the preceding paragraphs. The BIOS Mode Set command accesses nearly all of the registers as does the Save/Restore State BIOS call. Both of these are described in the remaining sections of this chapter.

In certain implementations, an extended BIOS call is provided to access the extended registers. One chip manufacturer provides a disclaimer as to where the enable key is for the extended registers. The manufacturer may want to move it around in the future; an indirect memory location in BIOS for this address has been provided.

Chapter 10 described how to access the standard VGA registers. Accessing the extended or Super VGA registers is typically accomplished through additional port addresses in the same range of port addresses as the standard VGA registers. Usually there is a technique for enabling and disabling access to these registers.

In addition, several of the Super VGAs have a setup mode that acts as a key to the Extended registers. This setup facility was designed and specified by IBM because its VGA is designed onto the motherboard and the use of multiple VGAs in a single system was anticipated. The setup concept is well-suited to putting VGAs to sleep. Some manufacturers have followed suit and implemented a 46E8 register.

The Extended register addresses vary according to whether the implementation is on a microchannel or an AT bus. The Setup Control Register was placed at 4CE8 hex in the I/O space for the PC/AT and at 3C3 hex for the microchannel. The value 4CE8 was selected based on the result of an extensive search through computer history that concluded that no one has ever used the port address 4CE8 willingly.

There are several cases where it is desirable to lock out applications from getting to registers. Of course, this lock-out facility is not meant to keep out the user. Just the applications which were designed before all of this sophistication. Consider this example. Due to downward compatibility, an old game program might be running on a Super VGA which is operating in a CGA emulation mode. The application will probably want to write to the CGA registers. However, the emulation is not exact. It is therefore advisable to keep the old application out of certain registers. Locking the registers creates the illusion in old applications that they are in control, despite reality.

The first example of a lock-out is in the standard VGA mode set. I stumbled around trying to restore registers after a mode set. The display was not correct unless the mode remained unchanged. After considerable effort combined with some guidance, I found that the CRTC registers 0-7 are locked automatically after a mode set. These registers must be unlocked through the Vertical Sync End Register bit 7 as discussed in Section 10.4.18 of this book!

The reason for this write protection is to enable EGA applications to function on a VGA. Some EGA applications write directly to the EGA CRT controller. Such applications will fail on a VGA since the EGA and VGA monitors require different timing signals.

A second reason to lock registers is to protect the hardware and software from inadvertently messing them up. By locking the registers, it is less likely that a program will mistakenly unlock the registers. There are several levels of locking, and several groups of registers can be locked or unlocked. This provides a great deal of flexibility for the programmer who is dealing with emulation or older applications.

13.7.4   Setting the Display Mode

Typically, the display modes are set through a BIOS call. There are over fifty registers which must be set up to perform a correct mode set. In addition, a BIOS data area in host memory must be considered. The values loaded into the VGA registers, both standard and extended for a mode set depend on the particular implementation and are not standard across different VGA cards. This is true, even if the same VGA chip is used. It is best to leave mode sets up to the BIOS. There is nothing mystical about a mode set. An effective mode set can be achieved by copying and restoring the proper registers and BIOS data area. However, many have tried and failed.

Most of the Super VGAs utilize the Mode Set BIOS call AH=0, as described in Section 11.2.1. In certain instances, a special BIOS call is necessary to activate the non-standard VGA display modes. Some routines return a parameter which indicates if the mode set was successful. Others simply ignore the command if the mode number is invalid. A parametric mode set BIOS call is also available, which allows the programmer to enter the desired horizontal and vertical resolutions and the number of colors. If a predefined mode equivalent to these parameters is available, the corresponding mode will be set. This would be a useful way to initialize a particular mode when the VGA chip manufacturer is unknown. Unfortunately, not all video chips support this function, and it needs to be universally accepted to be useful. The VESA standard does take care of this problem for you through a BIOS call.

The majority of modes are standard. Sixteen color modes are stored in a planar fashion, while 256-color modes are stored in a packed fashion. The four-color modes of the CGA have been left behind. In some cases, two-color modes have made it to the big time of higher resolutions. There are exceptions to these rules.

In one case, a four-color 1024 by 768 mode is provided, and the same manufacturer provides a 1024 by 768 16-color mode, where the pixels are stored in a packed fashion. The packed technique is advantageous when a natural separation into display planes is not evident. For example, suppose the source of image data is a photograph, and the image is represented in sixteen colors. The smallest logical element into which the pixel can be decomposed is the four bit element representing each of the sixteen colors. In contrast, suppose the source of the image was a CAD package, and the image represents four overlayed line drawings. Each of these line drawings is represented in one plane and is therefore bimodal (0 or 1). The smallest logical element in this instance is a single bit, where a pixel would be represented as a combination of four such bits. In a packed mode, it would be possible to draw one plane at a time (one bit per pixel), without spending time transferring data relevant to the other planes. In a packed mode, it would be necessary to transfer all information relevant to the pixel (four bits per pixel), even if just one plane needed to be drawn.

In this sixteen-color display mode, two consecutive pixels are stored in a single byte. This creates problems when the transfer is not byte-aligned. For example, suppose there was a horizontal row of 100 pixels stored in a 50-byte array with bytes 0 and 1 stored together, 2 and 3 stored together, and so on. In this case, pixel 0 would be in the upper four bits and pixel 1 would be in the lower four bits of the byte. Further, suppose it was desired to move the data to the display beginning at pixel 201. Now pixel 201 is in the lower four bits of byte

100 relevant to that display row. Thus, there is a shifting of four bits required to align the input data to the destination. This is very time consuming. Those familiar with the planar modes are familiar with this problem. A solution is presented in Chapter 16 on Chips and Technologies.

13.7.5 Controlling Emulation

A common feature amongst the Super VGAs is the ability to emulate the MDA, Hercules, CGA and EGA. Some treat the EGA as a special case of the VGA. As is shown in Chapter 10, nearly all fields of the EGA are contained in the VGA. However, there are a few minor exceptions. A new ability is to emulate the 8514/A. I am not convinced that this will prove to be important because any application having an 8514/A driver also has a VGA driver. The VGA driver will be faster than the 8514/A emulation.

The emulation modes are controlled by directly accessing the registers. In some cases, it is wise to also lock register groups after the emulation is set up. BIOS calls to set up emulation are also provided for some of the Super VGAs.

13.7.6 Controlling Vertical Interrupts

Certain VGAs have the facility for generating interrupts when a vertical retrace period is encountered. Typically, the application interrupt service routine will count down from this 30 frame per second (approximately) rate, and perform some function. Animation would be one example. One Super VGA has the facility to generate vertical interrupts after a prescribed number of vertical retrace periods. This is very useful since it limits unnecessary processing time for countdown to occur from the 30-frame-per-second rate. Vertical interrupts are handled through the standard VGA registers. These include the Input Status Register, described in Section 10.2.3, and the Vertical Retrace End Register, described in Section 10.4.18.

If no interrupt-generation facility is provided, the vertical retrace period can be determined by reading bit 3 of the Input Status One Register, described in Section 10.2.4.

13.7.7 Saving and Restoring the VGA State

Last but not least in the control category is the tricky issue of saving and restoring the VGA state. The standard VGA has three areas considered unique by the BIOS Save and Restore State function described in Section 11.15.3. These are the video hardware registers, the video data areas, and the video DAC state and color registers. The Super VGAs do not have any standardized areas reserved in the BIOS data area of host RAM to store information, nor do they have any additional DAC registers. All that is necessary to save or restore the super state is to save or restore the super registers.

The Save and Restore Video State BIOS call has a peculiar characteristic. The

Save function actually alters the original contents of the registers or data areas involved. To maintain the original state after a Save BIOS call, the programmer should immediately perform a Restore BIOS call using this same function.

The information in the hardware-state area is described in Table 13.29 and totals 70 bytes.

The video data definition area resides in the host memory address space 400 hex–500 hex. This is typically referred to as *locations in segment 40 hex*. The Save state command reads the consecutive memory locations beginning at segment 40 hex : offset 49 hex and ending with segment 40 hex : offset A9 hex. This totals 96 bytes. This information is described in Table 9.8.

The DAC storage area contains the values of the DAC registers and the DAC color registers themselves. This is described in Table 13.30. The DAC storage area requires 772 bytes.

The possible combinations of storage and the number of types required for each are listed in Table 13.31. Also presented in this table is the number of bytes requested by the BIOS call. Remember that the BIOS call returns the number of 64-byte data chunks. Thus, the BIOS total is equal to the closest multiple of 64 greater or equal to the actual number of bytes.

TABLE 13.29   Hardware State Save Area

Offset into Save Buffer (hex)	Registers
0	Sequencer Index
1	CRT Controller Index
2	Graphics Controller Index
3	Attribute Controller Index
4	Feature Control Register
5–8	Sequencer Registers Index 1–5
9	Sequencer Register Index 0
A–22	CRT Controller Registers 0–8 hex
23–32	Palette Registers 0–F hex
33–36	Attribute Registers 10–3hex
37–3F	Graphics Controller Registers 0–8
40	CRTC Base Address low
41	CRTC Base Address high
42	Plane 0 Latch
43	Plane 1 Latch
44	Plane 2 Latch
45	Plane 3 Latch

TABLE 13.30 DAC Storage Area

Offset	Value
0	Read/Write mode Dac
1	Pixel Address
2	Pixel Mask
3–302 hex	256 pairs of 3-color registers totalling 768 bytes
303 hex	Color Select Register

TABLE 13.31 Bytes Required to Save the Standard State

DAC Area Requested	BIOS Data Requested	Hardware Requested	# of Bytes Required	# Returned From BIOS Call
No	No	Yes	70	128
No	Yes	No	96	128
No	Yes	Yes	166	192
Yes	No	No	772	832
Yes	No	Yes	842	896
Yes	Yes	No	868	896
Yes	Yes	Yes	938	960

13.8 MEMORY ADDRESSING TECHNIQUES

The most important and frequently used feature of the Super VGAs is the display memory. In the DOS environment there are128 Kbytes of memory space at A0000-BFFFF, reserved for display memory. The VGA has to share this area with the MDA, Hercules or CGA. It is left with the single 64-Kbyte segment from A0000 to AFFFF. This is not a big sacrifice since the 8086 or 80286 registers are 16 bits wide; 64 Kbytes is a natural size for a chunk of memory anyway.

This is not the case with the 80386 running in its native mode. (This point will be discussed later in this book.) The VGA memory address controller has to fit one megabyte or more of memory into a single 64-Kbyte segment. It does this by overlaying the memory into multiple banks, none greater than 64 Kbytes.

13.8.1 Single Paging Systems

Figure 13.9 illustrates a paging technique. In this figure, and in subsequent figures, the amount of VGA memory can vary from 1 to 4 megabytes. The principles remain the same. It just takes more banks for more memory.

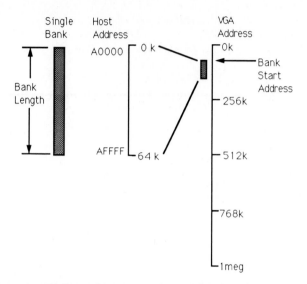

FIGURE 13.9 Single-Bank (Paging) System

A bank start address determines where the bank resides within the VGA one megabyte address space. The length of the bank and the bank start address completely describe the bank as far as the host address generation is concerned. In this figure, a bank is 64 Kbytes long and maps directly into the host address space between A0000 and AFFFF hex. To read or write into this bank from the host, one simply sets the ES Segment Register to A0000 and the DI offset register to the desired location within the bank. To access memory outside of the current bank, the programmer changes the Bank Start Address so that the desired memory locations fall within the newly located bank.

This technique is a bit cumbersome copying memory from one location to another. Suppose the source of the data resided between 768 Kbytes and 832 Kbytes and the destination of the data resided between 0 Kbytes and 64 Kbytes. The program would have to set the Bank Start Address to the source area, read a value, change the Bank Start Address to the destination area, and write the value. This cycle would repeat for every value copied. The value might be a byte, a 16-bit word, or a 32 bit word depending on the write mode.

In the preceding example, we are accessing one megabyte of memory requiring 20 address bits. Assuming that the bank length is 64 Kbytes, sixteen of these address bits are used to span a segment, called intra-segment. This leaves the high four address bits to describe the bank number.

There are several techniques that one can employ to read/write to this memory. One technique would be to restrict each data transfer to 64 Kbytes. Thus, the total transfer would be accomplished by segmenting it into several chunks of transfers, one leaving off where the previous one ended and none crossing a bank boundary. The Bank Start Address would be loaded before each transfer. This technique is especially well-suited for BITBLT's since it allows the use of the move string DMA instructions.

A second technique uses 32-bit arithmetic for the address generation and checks for overflows. When an overflow occurs, the Bank Start Address is incremented. This technique is well-suited for writing lines which are not horizontal. This type of structure can not take advantage of the DMA string instructions anyway as there is no pre-calculation.

Constrained to one Bank Start Address Register, a programmer would design this register so that it resides in a place which is both fast and easy to access. Unfortunately, this is not always the case. In one early implementation, the four bits were split up into four different registers so that the number of instructions per pixel became quite ridiculous.

13.8.2 Dual Paging Systems

Dual-paging systems alleviate the problem of moving data from one display location to another by keeping two Bank Start Addresses as shown in Figure 13.10. The process would be to set up the one Bank Start Address to the start of the source segment and the second to the start of the destination segment. With both the ES and DS registers set to A0000, the SI and DI registers pointing to their respective source and destination offsets and the CX Register containing the number of words to transfer, it is then possible to transfer data through the repeat move string DMA instruction.

Like the single paging system, the value moved during each cycle of the DMA instruction could be a byte, 16-bit word or 32-bit word. The only limiting element here would be the wait-states issued by the display memory. If the display can withstand being disabled (see Section 13.7.1), wait-states can be minimized. If the VGA is mounted on the motherboard and the display memory is fast enough, zero-wait-state data transfers can be accomplished. Since 32 bits can be moved at a time, this translates into respectable data transfers. Unfortunately, there are a lot of "ifs" between zero-wait-states and the reality of today's implementations.

13.8.3 Banks, Planes and Pages

There are several ways to organize memory within the VGA, depending on the display mode. Some common techniques used in the Super VGAs' advanced modes are given in Table 13.32. The first mode has four colors per pixel and is unique. Its organization is reminiscent of the CGA modes using odd and even banks. It is included here for completeness. Note, however, that it will not be discussed further. All remaining modes implemented in the Super VGAs fit into

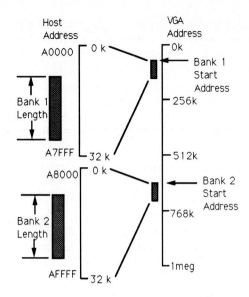

FIGURE 13.10 Dual-Bank (Paging System)

the planar or packed format. The second mode, which uses 16 colors in a packed mode, is also unique with the 16 colors represented in a packed format. Thus, two pixels adjoin in a single byte instead of the one pixel per byte in the 256-color modes. Other than this, it fits into the packed memory organization category.

The Macintosh uses a similar organization for its 16-color mode. The rest of this section will discuss only the third and fourth modes. These assume that a 16-color mode is planar and a 256-color mode is packed.

13.8.4 16-color Mode Planar Memory Organization

As a review, planar memory means that a pixel is represented by bits of information spread out across a set of planes. When this occurs, 16 colors are possible, requiring four bits. The four display planes, have the pixel represented by one bit per plane. Display memory is organized as bytes. There are eight pixels per byte. The memory planes are overlayed in the host memory address space so that each plane occupies exactly the same host addresses. These can be accessed independently by virtue of the read and write plane select registers.

The Map Mask Register, described in Section 10.3.3, controls the plane selection during write operations. The four bit field allows any combination of the four planes to be written to at the same time. The Read Map Select Register, described in Section 10.5.7, on the other hand allows the selection of one of the

TABLE 13.32 Super VGA Advanced Display Modes

# of Colors	Bits per plane	Planes per pixel	Bytes per bank	Plane Organization	Terminology
4	2	1	256 Kbytes	Sequential	Unique
16	4	1	64 Kbytes	Sequential	Packed
16	1	4	256 Kbytes	Overlapped	Planar
256	8	1	64 Kbytes	Sequential	Packed

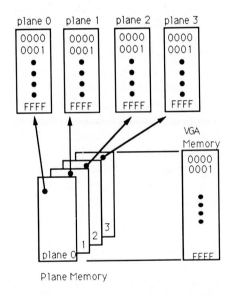

FIGURE 13.11 Planar Memory Organization in 16-color Mode

four planes with a two bit-field. This prevents bus conflicts on read operations, no conflict occurs on write operations. The planar organization is illustrated in Figure 13.11.

There can be greater than 64 Kbytes of memory on the Super VGAs. As a result, additional memory segmentation is necessary. This is where the banks come in. In Figure 13.12, a one-Megabyte system is shown. Note that each plane, 0–3, is drawn so that it is overlayed to span the address range from A0000 to AFFFF hex. The four memory banks, 0–3, are shown across the figure. Each consists of a set of four planes. Important to note from this figure is that each bank actually consists of 256 Kbytes of memory. This is an important fact and distinguishes the planar from the packed memory organizations.

Suppose a programmer wants to write to a byte at the location 400 hex, in plane 0 of bank 3. In host memory space this is accomplished by enabling plane 0, accessing bank 3, setting the ES segment register to A0000 hex, setting the DI register to 400 hex, and writing the byte through the ES:[DI] registers. The question is how does one access bank 3?

Each Super VGA is different but similar. As was mentioned in the previous section, each bank has a Bank Length and a Bank Start Address. Suppose the bank is 64 Kbytes long and the Start Address can increment in chunks of 64 Kbytes. This incremental value is referred to as the *granularity*. Although each bank is 256 Kbytes long with respect to the VGA memory, these banks are only 64 Kbytes long with respect to the host. Thus, this location would be located in the fourth bank, bank 3. The Bank Start Address would be loaded with a three. Programmers should again note that this is a very important point and feature-specific to the planar VGA display modes.

The granularity mentioned above is "pretty granular" at 64 Kbytes. Most VGA implementations set the granularity to 4 Kbytes while keeping the Bank Length at 64 Kbytes. This causes the banks to overlap by 60 Kbytes. Figure 13.13 illustrates this case. The right-most column is the one megabyte address space with respect to the VGA. The second column from the right is the 256-Kbyte memory space with respect to a single plane. The third column from the right shows that there are four display planes which accounts for the scale factor of four. Each

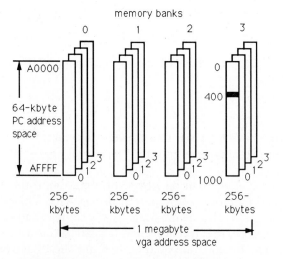

FIGURE 13.12 Planar Memory Banks

bank is 64 Kbytes long; each overlaps its neighbor by 60 Kbytes, stepping 4 Kbytes at a time. It takes 16 overlapped banks to span one 64 Kbyte plane segment, which translates into one 256 VGA Kbyte segment. Sixty-four banks are required to span the entire 256-Kbyte plane memory space. This translates into the entire one megabyte VGA memory space.

13.8.5   Common 16-Color Planar Display Modes

This section contains maps of the display memory for all common Super VGA modes. The basic organization of the 16-color planar modes are shown in Figure 13.14. This figure illustrates a display mode utilizing two banks of memory across the four display planes as shown in Figure 13.14a. Note that the boundary between bank 0 and bank 1 does not occur at the start of a scan line but rather somewhere in the middle. This is the case when the number of bytes per scan line is not an integer divisor of 64 Kbytes, which is 65536 bytes in actuality. Later in this section, a technique is described which ensures that all 16-color planar modes which can be displayed in two banks can be made to have bank transitions at the beginning of a scan row. This can simplify code considerably.

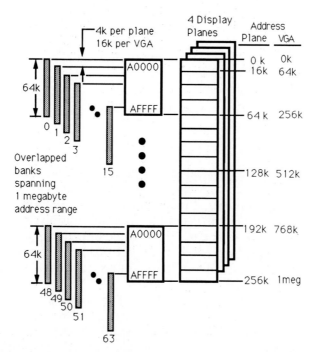

FIGURE 13.13   Overlapped Banks in a Planar Display Mode

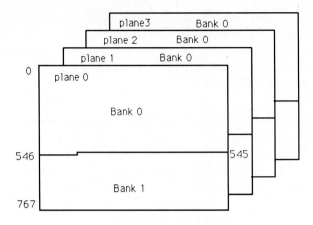

a) Two Banks and Four Display Planes

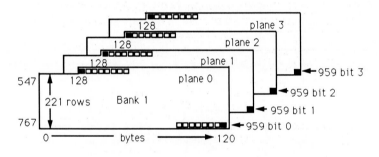

b) Bank 1 Exploded View

FIGURE 13.14   Typical 16-color Planar Memory Map

Figure 13.14b shows an exploded view of Bank 1. Note that bank boundary occurs at pixel 128, which translates to byte 16, of scan line 546. Pixel 128 is actually located in bit position 7 in all four planes of the byte at this location. When writing to this pixel, the byte which contains this pixel would be written to the first byte in bank 1. The last pixel in the displayed portion of bank 1 is labeled pixel 959, indicating that there are 960 pixels per scan line. This pixel is actually in bit position 0 of all four planes of the 120th byte in the 767th scan line. This would be byte 26,623 in bank 1.

The number 26,623 is derived as follows: The image has a resolution of 960 pixels (120 bytes) by 768 scan lines. It requires two banks of memory, the first occupying 545+ scan lines. If 65536 is divided by 120, the result is 546, with a remainder of 16. Thus, there are 546 complete scan lines (0-545) plus one scan line which contains 16 bytes (128 pixels). The second bank must contain the remaining 104 bytes of scan line 546 and 221 full scan lines to reach the scan line total of 768. The 120th byte of scan line 767 would be

(221*120) + 104 = 26,624 bytes

which is byte number 26,623 in bank 1.

There is a set of common VGA 16-color resolutions ranging from 320 by 200 to 1024 by 768 and proposed 1280 by 1024. A pictoral map of each of these display modes follow. These maps are useful when writing code or trying to understand the code presented in Chapter 15. These maps are presented in Figures 13.15–13.20 as itemized in Table 13.33.

In Figure 13.15, a 320 by 200 pixel display mode is presented. This mode requires 320/8 = 40 bytes per scan line per plane. A single bank can contain

TABLE 13.33   16-color Planar Display Memory Maps

Figure Number	Resolution pixels	Memory Required	# of Pages with 1 meg	# of Banks
13.15	320 by 200	32,000	2	1
13.16	640 by 480	153,600	6	1
13.17	800 by 600	240,000	4	1
13.18	960 by 720	345,600	3	2
13.19	1024 by 768	393,216	2	2
13.20	1280 by 1024	655,360	1	3

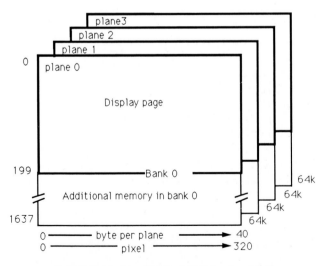

FIGURE 13.15   320 by 200 16-color Mode

65536/40 =1,638 scan lines. There are four display planes. Thus, 40*4=160 bytes per scan line is the total for all display planes. A single image would occupy 32,000 bytes of display memory, 8000 bytes per plane. This image is considered a page. Of course, the effective or virtual resolution of the image could be much larger than 320 by 200, and the user could pan or scroll to see other 320x200 windows.

Figures 13.16 and 13.17 are similar, in that an image fits in a single bank. No

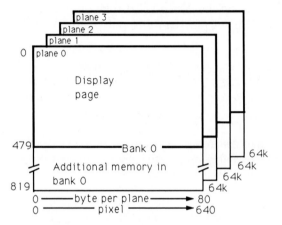

FIGURE 13.16   640 by 480 16-color Mode

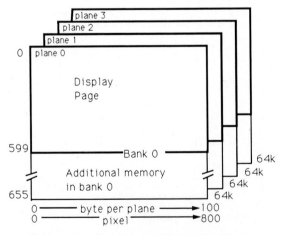

FIGURE 13.17   800 by 600 16-color Mode

bank switching is necessary if the virtual image size fits within this single bank as well. Image manipulation is much quicker if the arithmetic and graphics instructions do not have to worry about bank switching.

Figure 13.18 is a 960 by 720 display mode. This display mode is possible because monitors which can not keep up with a full 1024 by 768 non-interlaced can sometimes keep up with a 960 by 720 mode. Note that the image in this mode does span two banks and that the bank transition does not occur at the start of a scan line.

Figure 13.19 and FIgure 13.20 illustrate the high-resolution 16-color modes. The 1280 by 1024 mode requires three banks of memory.

Aligning Banks to the Start of Scan Lines

If the display mode, be it 16-color planar or 256-color packed, can fit in two banks, the boundary of the two banks can be forced to align to the start of a scan line by adjusting the start address. The start address is a 16-bit address. This address dictates which byte contains the first pixel which will be displayed. The Start Address Low and High registers are described in Section 10.4.13 and 10.4.14 respectively. The start address is typically set to 0, but can be modified to create a panning or scrolling effect. In this case, it is desirable to align the bank boundary.

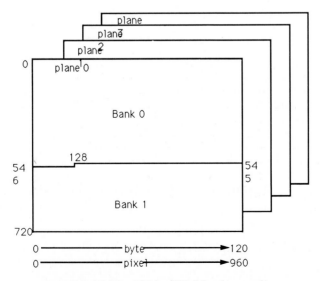

FIGURE 13.18 960 by 720 16-color mode

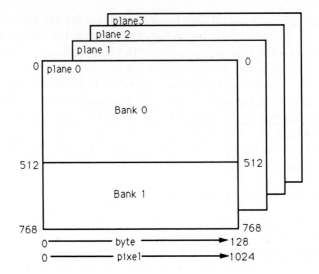

FIGURE 13.19   1024 by 768 16-color Mode

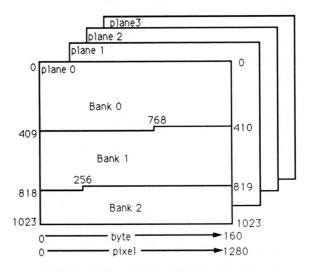

FIGURE 13.20   1280 by 1024 16-color Mode

If there are only two banks, there are two boundaries. One is at the start of the first bank; the second is at the transition between the first and second bank. It is always assumed that the start of the first bank is aligned to the beginning of a scan line since it starts at the start of scan line 0. If the number of bytes per scan line does not divide evenly into 65,536, the transition boundary will not align to the start of a scan line. If the start address is set equal to the number of bytes which occur as the remainder in the divide of 65,536 / (# of bytes per scan line), the fractional part is accounted for and the number of bytes per scan line will divide equally into (65,566 - remainder). First encountered through ATI, I have found no penalty in doing this neat little trick.

13.8.6 Common 256-Color Packed Display Modes

The 256-Color modes are stored in memory as one byte per pixel, contained in a single plane. This is called *packed* since a pixel is packed into a single byte. In the 16-color packed mode, two pixels are packed into a byte, as opposed to being spread across the various planes. The memory is still organized as planes. However, the addressing is completely different from the 16-color planar modes described in Section 13.8.5. Figure 13.21 illustrates the packed memory organization in a packed display mode. Note that the four display planes are organized so that sequential addressing jumps from plane 0, to 1, to 2, to 3 and back to plane 0 again. As a result, 8 consecutive pixels are actually loaded so that

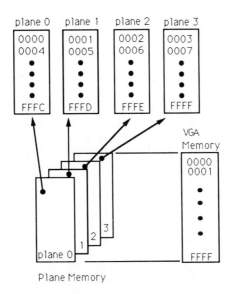

FIGURE 13.21 Packed Memory Organization in 256-color Modes

pixels 0 and 4 are in plane 0, pixels 1 and 5 are in plane 1, pixels 2 and 6 are in plane 2, and pixels 3 and 7 are in plane 3.

Fortunately, the memory address controller takes care of all this. The programmer does not even need to consider which plane memory would be going into. In the above example, it would only be necessary to write out 8 bytes to consecutive display memory locations. The only time that a programmer must consider the display planes is when data is read or written in a packed mode and written or read in a planar mode.

It is interesting and important to note that a 64-Kbyte segment in host memory address space actually encompasses 16 Kbytes in each display plane. The Super VGAs support resolutions which extend beyond a single 64-Kbyte segment. Thus, as with the 16-bit planar examples, paging is necessary. The requirement for paging is far more stringent with respect to the packed display modes for two reasons. First, the packed mode considered uses 8 bits per pixel in the 256-color modes as opposed to 4 bits per pixel in the 16-color modes. Thus, twice the memory must be stored for the same spatial resolution image. Secondly, the display planes are not overlapped with respect to the host memory address space. This causes a 64-Kbyte segment in host memory address space to access 64 Kbytes of memory in the VGA memory address space. This is four times less than the planar alternative where 256 Kbytes of VGA memory address space is spanned by the single 64-Kbyte segment in host memory address space. Consequently, there are a lot more banks required in the 256-color modes.

The packed memory banks organization is illustrated in Figure 13.22. This figure is similar to and should be compared to Figure 13.12. In Figure 13.22, the planes are numbered 0 to 3 and are shown as being overlapped. The single 64-

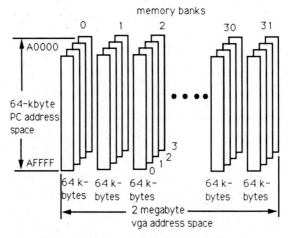

FIGURE 13.22   256-color Overlapped Memory

Kbyte segment A0000–AFFFF hex is shown to span all four display planes as opposed to the single display plane in Figure 13.12. A bank of four display planes is shown to contain 64 Kbytes as opposed to the 256 Kbytes in the planar example of Figure 13.12. One last difference is that there are 32 memory banks in the packed mode as opposed to the 4 memory banks in the planar example. This factor of 8 is derived from the 2 times as much data factor in the 8 versus 4 bits per pixel ratio multiplied by the 4 display planes.

Once again, similar to the 16-color planar mode, there is a need to reduce the granularity of a bank. The question is how much. If a 4-Kbyte granularity is selected, it would require 256 banks to span the one megabyte host address space. Due to the planar organization of memory (even in the packed modes) of the Super VGAs, the decision was made to have a packed granularity of 16-Kbytes. Thus, the total number of banks is 64, analogous to the planar case. The catch is that the terminology is such that the granularity can still be considered to be 4 Kbytes, if one is operating in the plane address space. Programmers should be careful with the terminology and the corresponding VGA implementation. It is important to understand both the difference and the sameness of the 4-Kbyte planar granularity and the 16-Kbyte VGA granularity. This is illustrated in Figure 13.23. This figure should be compared to Figure 13.13 which portrays the analogous, 16-color planar situation.

A typical 256-color packed memory map is pictorially represented in Figure 13.22. The relationship of the four display planes and the five banks necessary to represent a single image are shown in this figure. Note that the bank boundaries do not align to the start of scan lines. This figure should be compared to Figure 13.14 which portrays the analogous planar representation. The text associated with Figure 13.14 also applies to the location of a pixel within a bank.

In this packed case, the right-most four pixels in the last scan line of an image are labeled byte *n* through *n+3*. A scan line containing 640 pixels translates into 640 bytes per scan line. Since 640 does not divide evenly into 65,536, the bank boundaries will not be aligned to the start of a scan line. Since there are more than two planes in this relatively low-resolution image, there is no chance of forcing the alignment by using the start address technique discussed in Section 13.8.5. A typical 256-color memory map is shown in Figure 13.24.

There are a set of common VGA 16-color resolutions ranging from 320 by 200 to 1024 by 768 and proposed 1280 by 1024. A pictoral map of each of these display modes follow. These maps are useful when writing code or trying to understand the code presented in Chapters 15–21. The maps are presented in Figures 13.15–13.20 as itemized in Table 13.34.

In Figure 13.25, a 320 by 200 pixel display mode is presented. This mode requires 320 bytes per scan line per plane. A single bank can contain 65536/320 = 204 scan lines. This image is considered a page. Of course, the effective or virtual resolution of the image could be much larger than 320 by 200, and the user could pan or scroll to see other 320 by 200 windows.

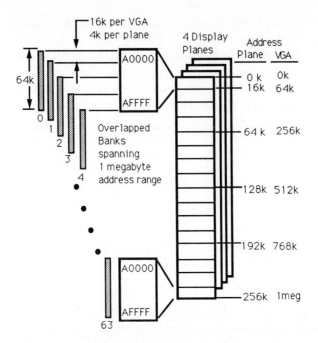

Note: Address increments by one in VGA address space and it increments by four in the plane address space

FIGURE 13.23 Overlapped Banks in a Packed Mode

TABLE 13.34 256-color Packed Display Memory Maps

Figure Number	Resolution pixels	Bytes Required	# of Pages with 1 Meg	# of Banks
13.24	320 by 200	64,000	16	1
13.25	640 by 400	256,000	4	4
13.26	640 by 480	307,200	3	5
13.27	800 by 600	80,000	2	7
13.28	1024 by 768	86,432	1	12
13.29	1280 by 1024	1,310,720	0 (*1)	20

Note: *1 1280 by 1024 mode requires 2 Meg implementation

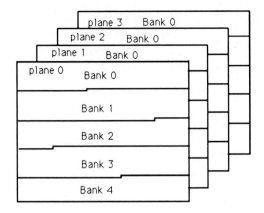

a) Five Banks and Four Display Planes

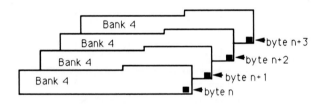

b) Bank 4 Exploded View

FIGURE 13.24 Typical 256-color Packed Memory Map

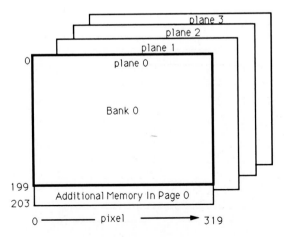

FIGURE 13.25 320 by 200 256-color Mode

In Figures 13.26–13.29, typically 256-color display modes are displayed. Note that the only display mode used, an even divisor into 65,536, is the 1024 pitch of Figure 13.28. The 1280 by 1024 mode displayed in Figure 13.29 would require a VGA with more than one megabyte as shown in Table 13.34.

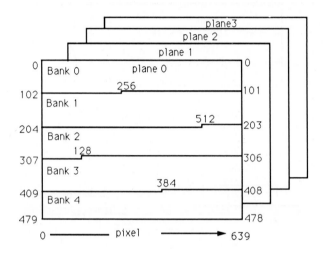

FIGURE 13.26 640 by 400 or 640 by 480 256-color Mode

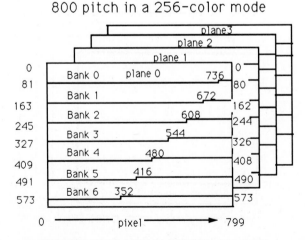

FIGURE 13.27 800 by 600 256-color Mode

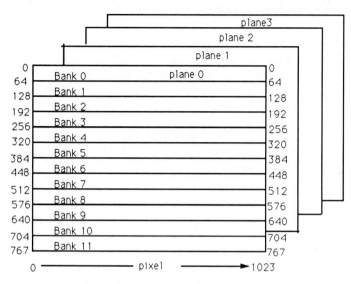

FIGURE 13.28 1024 by 768 256-color Mode

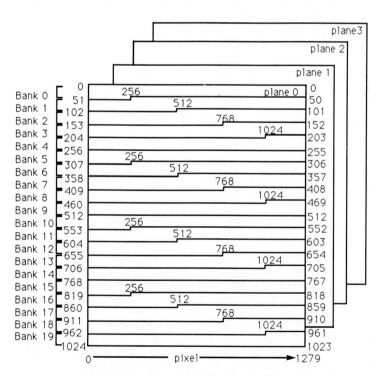

FIGURE 13.29 1280 by 1024 256-color Mode

13.8.7   16-bit Color Display Modes

An exciting advancement in several of the Super VGA chips is the ability to control memory so that a pixel can be displayed in either a 16-bit per color or 24-bit per color display mode. These display modes are very important. They have several user applications. The Macintosh II family of computers has the most popular array, which include color desk top publishing, color layout, color separations, color slide and page scanning, imaging, broadcast quality video, high-quality presentation graphics, solid CAD modeling and many more. With inexpensive 16-bit per color and 24-bit per color display systems, the software applications which currently run on the Macintosh will be rapidly ported over to the PC.

The 16-bit per color mode can produce 65,536 different colors. To achieve these 65,536 colors, each pixel is represented by 16 bits. This provides a quantum leap from the maximum of 256 different colors available on the 8-bit per pixel mode. Even more colors are achieved by the 24-bit per color mode. These modes allow 16,777,216 different colors to be displayed at a time.

It should be noted that though the 16-bit/color display modes allow more colors to be displayed at a time, they do not allow a finer color granularity. In the 16-color and 256-color modes, the 4-bit or 8-bit value representing the color is mapped through a color lookup table, commonly referred to as the *Color registers*. The Color registers map each of these 16 or 256 values into a color. This color is formed by a combination of a red value, a blue value, and a green value. The Color registers are commonly called Digital to Analog converters (DACs). These DACs typically create a color based on 6 bits per color component (red, green or blue) or 8-bits per color component. In the 6-bit case, a single color is represented by 18-bits which can produce one of 262,144 colors. Even more pronounced is the 8-bit per color component which produces a 24-bit color value which can produce one of 16,777,216 colors. Therefore, the new 16-bit per color display mode is less than either of the color granularities of the 6-bit or 8-bit color DACs. The 24-bit per color mode equals the current color granularity of the 8-bit color DACs.

Another commonly used display mode is the 32-bit per color mode. In this mode, the three color components are each represented by 8 bits. The remaining four bits can be used to represent something else. Its typical usage is an alpha-numeric overlay channel. At other times, it is used to represent a monochrome 8-bit per color version of the image. Another option is for representing the image in 8-bit color. This parallel representation of the same image could be very useful for rapid display of the compressed image while maintaining the high-color-resolution image in memory.

The organization of these 16-bit, 24-bit and 32-bit per color memory modes are displayed in Figure 13.30–13.32 respectively. These display modes are very similar to the 256-color memory configurations with an exception occurring when a single pixel is represented by more than one byte.

In Figure 13.30, a single pixel is represented by two consecutive bytes of memory. However, these two bytes reside in separate display planes. Table 13.35 describes the location of four pixels referred to in Figure 13.30.

In Figure 13.31, a single pixel is represented by three bytes. The location of the four pixels referred to in Figure 13.31 are described in Table 13.36.

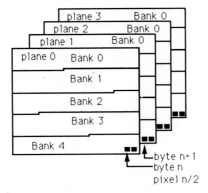

FIGURE 13.30   16-bit per Pixel Memory Map

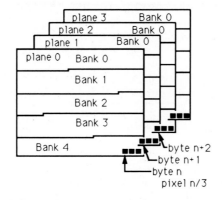

FIGURE 13.31   24-bit per Pixel Memory Map

TABLE 13.35   Memory Locations of Four Pixels in Figure 13.30

Pixel	Bytes	
n/2	n	n+4
n/2 + 1	n+1	n+5
n/2 + 2	n+2	n+6
n/2 + 3	n+3	n+7

In Figure 13.32, a single pixel is represented by four bytes producing a 32-bit per pixel mode. The location of the four pixels referred to in Figure 13.32 are described in Table 13.37.

13.8.8 16-bit Color Palette DAC

Several manufacturers have palette DAC chips which can interface to 16-bit and 24-bit true-color inputs. Sierra Semiconductor has released a high color palette DAC chip which can perform 16-bit color. What makes this chip especially relevant to the VGA is that it is pin-for-pin compatible to the palette DAC chips currently used on VGA cards. This means that as long as the Super VGA manufacturers can conform to its timing requirements, 16-bit color can be a reality without printed circuit board modifications. The chip can support 6-bit per color or 8-bit per color outputs in the 16- or 256-color modes. In addition, the chip can provide 5-bits per color in a 16-bit per pixel mode.

Control of the 16-bit per pixel mode occurs through a new register in the Color Register Set. This register can be accessed through an external pin on the DAC chip or through an internal technique. The internal technique allows the chip to be pin-per-pin compatible with existing DAC chips.

The Control Register is shown in Figure 13.33. The HCE field enables or disables the 16-bit color mode. If the HCE field is set to 1, the 16-bit per pixel color mode is enabled. If it is set to 0, the normal pseudo-color modes are

TABLE 13.36 Memory Locations of Four Pixels in a 24-bit per Pixel Mode

Pixel	Bytes		
$n/2$	n	n+4	n+8
$n/2 + 1$	n+1	n+5	n+9
$n/2 + 2$	n+2	n+6	n+10
$n/2 + 3$	n+3	n+7	n+11

TABLE 13.37 Memory Locations of Four Pixels in a 32-bit per Pixel Mode

Pixel	Bytes			
$n/2$	n	n+4	n+8	n+12
$n/2 + 1$	n+1	n+5	n+9	n+13
$n/2 + 2$	n+2	n+6	n+10	n+14
$n/2 + 3$	n+3	n+7	n+11	n+15

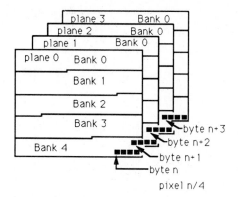

FIGURE 13.32   32 bit per Pixel Memory Map

High-Color DAC Control Register

7	6	5	4	3	2	1	0
(HCE)							

Indexed by 4 consecutive reads   Written to by the fifth
from the Pixel Address Read   write to the Pixel Address
Mode Register   Read Mode Register

FIGURE 13.33   High-color DAC Control Register. The HCE field enables the high-color 16-bit per pixel mode.

active. In order to maintain compatibility with existing hardware, the DAC Control Register does not have its own port address. It is accessed indirectly through the PEL Mask Register discussed in Section 10.7.5.

An internal switch can point to the DAC Control Register or to the PEL Mask Register. The switch normally points to the PEL Mask Register. If four consecutive reads occur to the PEL Mask Register, the switch changes position and the next write to the PEL Mask Register will actually be directed to the DAC Control Register. The four reads must be sequential with no intervening instructions.

Once enabled, the color sent to the monitor is derived from the 16-bit word. Currently, only five bits of color from each of the three red, green and blue components are used. The color is derived as shown in Table 13.38 and is shown in Figure 13.34a. Also included in Figure 13.34b is an example of a 32 bit per pixel implementation. The eight bits, 24–31 do not directly drive a color gun.

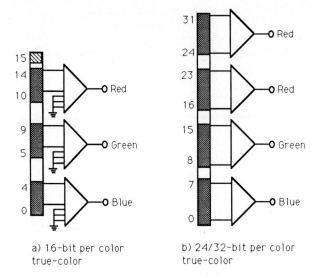

a) 16-bit per color true-color

b) 24/32-bit per color true-color

FIGURE 13.34 True Color DAC Outputs

TABLE 13.38 16-bit per Pixel Color

Bits	Color
0–4	Blue 0–4
5–9	Green 0–4
10–15	Red 0–4

It should be noted that there are three distinct signals feeding the DAC convertors. These are the 6-bit code in the normal VGA applications, the 8-bit code for the extended DACs and the 5-bit code from the 16-bit true color. Each of these signals is fed into the most significant bits of the 8-bit DAC. The least significant bits not covered by the 5- or 6-bit signals are set to 0. This means that in the case of the 6-bit DAC, the maximum brightness is approximately 2.8 percent less than the fully saturated 8-bit input. This is due to the two least-significant bits being set to 0. A maximum code is therefore 255-7=248. In the case of the 5-bit color code from the 16-bit per pixel mode, the problem is worse. Since the lowest three bits are forced to zero, the maximum code is 255-15=240, representing a 5.9 percent less than a fully saturated signal. A 6-bit RAM output feeding an eight bit DAC is shown in Figure 13.35a. An 8-bit RAM output is shown in Figure 13.35b.

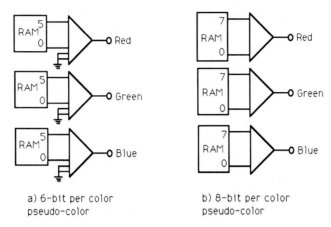

a) 6-bit per color
pseudo-color

b) 8-bit per color
pseudo-color

FIGURE 13.35 Pseudo-color DAC Outputs

13.9 FEATURES OF THE SUPER VGA CHIPS

The majority of Super VGA cards are based upon integrated circuits produced by one of six manufacturers. In addition, each of these manufacturers have several chips within its Super VGA product line. Each of these VGA chips are different yet each performs similar functions. As would be expected, the chips from different manufacturers contrast more with each other than the different chips from the same manufacturer. Highly similar chips from the same manufacturer are referred to as having come from the same product line.

There are several basic features which the programmer must understand in order to program these Super VGA chips. These basic features include controlling the VGA, polling the VGA for status information, utilizing the super display modes, reading and writing to the extended display memory, and controlling the display start address. Chapters 14–20 provide a discussion of these features and details for respective manufacturers' implementation techniques. It is assumed that the reader is familiar with the relevant descriptions presented in this chapter before the details of each implementation are tackled.

13.9.1 VGA Chip Manufacturers Detailed in this Book

This book includes chapters, provided in alphabetical order, for the following manufacturers: ATI Technologies, Chips and Technologies, Genoa, Paradise/Western Digital, Trident, Tseng Labs and Video7/Headland Technologies. The Super VGA chip numbers for each of these manufacturers is included in Table 13.39.

TABLE 13.39   VGA Chip Manufacturers and Chip Numbers

Chip Manufacturer	Chip Numbers
ATI Technologies	18800,28800
Chips and Technologies	82C451, 82C452, 82C453, 82C455, 82C456
Genoa	5000 seies, GVGA
Paradise/Western Digital	PVGA1a, WD90C00, WD90C10, WD90C11
Trident	8800, 8900
Tseng Labs	ET3000, ET4000
Video7/Headland Technologies.	V7VGA

13.10   STANDARD VGA REGISTERS REVISITED

There are several registers in the standard VGA register set which affect memory accessing. These are described in detail in Chapter 10 and are listed in Table 13.40. Many of these registers are referred to in Chapters 14–19. Comments are provided for the reader's convenience. The Offset Register, described in Section 10.4.22, controls the virtual width of the screen. For example, the display mode might be 640 by 480, while the actual image might be 1024 by 768. The offset register dictates the number of bytes or words between vertically adjacent scan lines can be controlled by setting the offset field to the ac of the image. This offset is derived by the equation:

$$\text{OFF field} = \text{Desired Offset} / K$$

In this equation, K is 2 for byte addressing and 4 for word addressing. The VGA system is typically in a word addressing mode as controlled by the W/B field of the Mode Control Register. Thus, in word mode, an offset of 800 would translate to an OFF value of 200. It can readily be seen from the above equation that virtual offsets greater or equal to 1024 will require additional bits for the offset field. These additional bits are provided in the Extended registers for each implementation.

The Mode Control Register, described in Section 10.4.26, contains a bit, field W/B, which controls word or byte accesses. If the W/B field is 0, word accessing occurs. If it is1, byte addressing occurs.

The Miscellaneous Register described in Section 10.5.9 is also relevant. The Memory Map field, *MM*, controls where the memory resides within the host memory address space. The Memory Map Field is described again in Table 13.41.

TABLE 13.40   Standard VGA Control Registers Used During Memory Accesses

Function	Register Name	Port	Index	Bits	Value
Virtual Width of Display	Offset	3D4	13	7–0	0–255
Memory Map Mode	Miscellaneous	3CE	6	3–2	0–3
Word or Byte Addressing	Mode Control	3CE	17	6	0–1
Display Start Address Low	Start Address Low	3D4	C	7–0	0–255
Display Start Address High	Start Address High	3D4	D	7–0	0–255
Cursor Address Low	Cursor Location Low	3D4	E	7–0	0–255
Cursor Address High	Cursor Location High	3D4	F	7–0	0–255

TABLE 13.41   Memory Map Field, MM, in the Miscellaneous Register

Memory Map	Address Range	Usage
0	A0000–BFFFF	128 Kbyte segments
1	A0000–AFFFF	64 Kbyte segments
2	B0000–B7FFF	Monochrome emulation
3	B8000–BFFFF	Alphanumeric modes

The display start address as well as the cursor start address is a 16-bit value which determines the location within a 64-Kbyte segment. The display start address points dictates the display memory location which will be displayed as the first pixel in the upper-left corner of the display. Similarly, the cursor start address determines the location of the cursor.

Chapter 14

Super VGA
Code Basics

14.1   INTRODUCTION

The programmer faces a true challenge when trying to create a fast and eloquent program that accommodates multiple display modes, pages, planes, and banks. In addition, the programmer must make this program operate under a variety of VGA chips, each with its own operational specifics.

Two basic functions encountered repeatedly are the bitblt and the single-pixel operations. The bitblts are common in imaging applications when manipulating a rectangular region. The single-pixel operations are most commonly encountered when objects are based on non-horizontal or vertical lines. Several techniques are available for each of these two cases. Some some of them are presented in this section. Details and program examples for particular implementations on different Super VGAs can be found in Chapters 16–21.

It is the philosophy of this book that similar functions must be written in order to optimize performance. These similar routines need to handle planar or packed display modes. They must be further segmented into two cases according to whether or not bank boundaries are involved. These cases are then repeated for each Super VGA implementation. This encompasses a number of functions. However, it eliminates the need for decisions at the time-critical, low-level functions.

14.1.1   Determining Where the Super VGA Ports are Mapped

In most cases, the Super VGA cards have their standard VGA ports mapped into the same locations. Their extended ports are spread through the immediate vicinity of the standard VGA port addresses. The ports at 3B4/3D4 hex and 3B5/3D5 hex are the exceptions. In monochrome configurations, the 3Bx hex mapping is used. In color configurations, the 3Dx configuration is used. The macro provided in Listing 14.1 determines whether these ports are located at 3Bx or 3Dx hex.

LISTING 14.1   Determining if the VGA is in a Monochrome or Color Mode

```
Function: Determine if the VGA is in a monochrome or color mode
;       Is VGA in a monochrome or color mode
;               bit 0=0 monochrome 3Bx
;               bit 0=1 color 3Dx
; Output Parameters:
;       dx              either 3D0 or 3B0
; Calling Protocol:
;       mono_or_color
mono_or_color  macro

        push    ax
        mov     dx,3cch         ;point to miscellaneous register
        in      al,dx           ;get byte
        test    al,1            ;test bit 0
        jz      mono            ;is zero so monochrome

;       is color
        mov     dx,3d0h         ;color port at 3dx
        jmp     go_on

;       is monochrome
mono:
        mov     dx,3b0h         ;color port at 3dx
go_on:
        pop     ax
endm
```

In some Super VGA configurations, the Attribute registers can be mapped differently from the VGA standard. The 3C0/3C1 hex register pair can be configured to act as an index/data pair as opposed to the standard VGA configuration. The state of the Attribute Index or internal attribute flip-flop can be read in certain Super VGAs.

Due to port mapping conflicts, it is also possible to map the VGAs into the 2xx hex address space instead of the 3xx hex port address space.

14.2   TRANSFERRING DATA WITHIN A SINGLE BANK

A block transfer typically involves a rectangular region consisting of a number of rows and columns. The most simple special case of this block transfer occurs when the number of rows is equal to one. In this case, the transfer involves all or part of a single row. Since the row is organized contiguously in display memory, a DMA Repeat Move String instruction can be used.

14.2.1   Determining the Starting Address

The starting address can be thought of as either a linear address or an x, y coordinate pair. The linear address, assumed to be a long integer (32 bits), is determined from the x, y coordinate pair by the Equation 14.1.

Equation 14.1   Determining Linear Address

```
Linear_Address = x + (Y * bytes_per_row)
```

The bank number, assuming the bank granularity is 64 kbytes, can be determined by the Equation 14.2.

Equation 14.2   Determining a Bank Address

```
Bank Number = (Linear_Address & 0x00FF ) >> 16;
```

Thus, the whole part of a mod 65536 operation produces the bank address. The bank address is equivalent to the high-order 16 bits of the long integer. Typically, a maximum of one megabyte of display memory is provided on the Super VGAs. This translates into a four-bit bank number (bits 20–17).

The fractional part of this arithmetic produces the intra-segment offset address of the pixel. The fractional part is equivalent to the low-order 16 bits of the long integer. This is termed the pixel offset and can be calculated from Equation 14.3.

Equation 14.3   Determining a Pixel Offset Address

```
Pixel Offset = Linear_Address & 0x0000FFFFF;
```

This equation can be coded concisely in assembly language by the code examples in Listings 14.2 and 14.3. The starting, left-most, x-coordinate is used in Listing 14.2 while the ending, right-most, x-coordinate is used in Listing 14.3. This assembly language code determines the (long) linear address from the equation (y * bytes_per_row) + x. This can be used to determine the bank and offset values of the start and end of the single scanline block to be transferred. The long arithmetic places the 64-Kbyte bank number in DX Register and the lower 16-bit intra-bank offset in the AX Register.

LISTING 14.2   Calculating an Offset and a Bank Address of the Starting Point

```
;Function:
; Calculate the bank number and offset address

;Input Parameters:
;       bytes_per_row           = bytes per row
;       x_start_coordinate      = starting x coordinate (left-most)
;       y_coordinate            = y coordinate

;Output Parameters:
;       dx                      = Start_Bank_Number (64-Kbyte granularity)
;       ax                      = Start_Offset address

Start_Address           macro   bytes_per_row, x_start_coordinate,
                                y_coordinate

; determine the starting location
        mov     ax,bytes_per_row        ; get bytes_per_line in ax
        mov     bx,y_coordinate         ; get y in bx
        mul     bx                      ; y*bytes_per_line in dx:ax
        add     ax,x_start_coordinate   ; add x_coordinate
endm
```

LISTING 14.3   Calculating an Offset and a Bank Address of the Ending Point

```
; Function
; Enter with:
;       bytes_per_row           = bytes per row
;       x_end_coordinate        = ending x coordinate (right-most)
;       y_coordinate    = y coordinate

; Exit with:
;       dx                      = Start_Bank_Number (64-kbyte granularity)
;       ax                      = Start_Offset address

End_Address     macro   bytes_per_row, x_end_coordinate, y_coordinate

; determine the starting location
        mov     ax,bytes_per_row        ; get bytes_per_line in ax
        mov     bx,y_coordinate         ; get y in bx
        mul     bx                      ; y*bytes_per_line in dx:ax
        add     ax,x_end_coordinate     ; add x_coordinate
endm
```

The *Bank_Off* function determines the starting bank number and offset address within the bank that corresponds to a given x, y and the number of bytes per row. This function can be called from a C program and is provided in Listing 14.4.

LISTING 14.4 Determining the Bank Number and Offset of a Point in Memory

```
; Function:
;   Determining the bank number and offset of a point in an x,y
;   space with a given number of bytes per row

; Input Parameters:
; x,y                       horizontal and vertical coordinates of point
; bytes_per_row             display bytes_per_line = # of bytes in a row

; Output Parameters:
;   offset      Offset of point within bank
;   segment     Bank value that contains point

; Calling protocol
; Bank_Off(x,y,bytes_per_line,&offset,&bank);

 Bank_Off proc far USES ES DI, arg1,arg2,arg3,arg4:FAR PTR,arg5:FAR PTR

; determine the (long) address =( y * offset )+ x where the segment
; is in dx and the offset is in ax
        mov     ax,arg3         ; get offset
        mov     bx,arg2         ; get y
        mul     bx              ; y * offset
        add     ax,arg1         ; (y * offset) + x (lower 16 bits)
        adc     dx,0            ; (y * offset) + x (upper n bits)

        les     di,arg4         ;get point to return offset
        mov     es:[di],ax      ;send back ax=offset
        les     di,arg5         ;get pointer to return bank
        mov     es:[di],dx      ;send back ax=bank
        ret
Bank_Off endp
```

14.2.2 Writing to a Single Bank

In the simplest case of transfers contained within a single bank, data can be written to display memory without concern for long arithmetic or bank crossing. The *Wr_Part* function loads a block of data into display memory and is provided in Listing 14.5.

In some cases, the Super VGAs will be configured as 128-Kbyte segments ranging from A0000–BFFFF hex in host address space. It is necessary to pass the display segment address, A0000h or B0000h, to the write function in these cases. In the majority of cases, the display memory is configured as 64 Kbytes between A0000–AFFFF. In these cases it is not necessary to pass the segment address since A0000 will always suffice. A second function, *Wr_Part_128* is provided in Listing 14.6 to handle the 128-Kbyte segmentation.

LISTING 14.5 Writing to a Portion of Display Memory Assuming a 64-Kbyte Memory Map

```
; Function:
;  Writing to a portion of a display segment beginning at a start ;
;  address from a "C" array assuming a 64-Kbyte memory map.

; Input Parameters:
; buf_ptr       pointer to host "C" buffer containing data
; npix          number of pixels
; start         offset of window into display memory

; Calling protocol
; Wr_Part(buf_ptr,npix,start);

 Wr_Part proc far USES DS ES DI, arg1:FAR PTR,arg2,arg3

;        source of data is from a C buffer
         lds    si,arg1         ;get pointer to top of array

;        destination of data is into the A0000 display segment offset
;        by the start address
         mov    ax,0a000h
         mov    es,ax           ;point to base of display
         mov    di,arg3         ;starting address of display

;        move desired number of words
         mov    cx,arg2         ;desired number of bytes
         rep    movsb           ;write to memory
         ret

 Wr_Part endp
```

LISTING 14.6   Writing to a Portion of Display Memory Assuming a 128-Kbyte Memory Map.

```
; Function:
;  Writing to a portion of a display segment from a "C" array
;  assuming a 128-Kbyte memory map

; Input Parameters:
; buf_ptr              pointer to host "C" buffer containing data
; npix                 number of pixels
; start                offset of window into display memory
; segment              display memory offset, either A000 or B000

; Calling Protocol:
;  Wr_Part_128(buf_ptr,npix,start,segment);

 Wr_Part_128 proc far USES DS ES DI, arg1:FAR PTR,arg2,arg3,arg4

;       source of data is from a C buffer
        lds     si,arg1          ;get pointer to top of array

;       destination of data is into the display segment offset by
;       the start address
        mov     ax,arg4          ;get segment address
        mov     es,ax            ;point to base of display
        mov     di,arg3          ;starting address of display

;       move desired number of words
        mov     cx,arg2          ;desired number of bytes
        rep     movsb            ;write to memory
        ret

Wr_Part_128 endp
```

14.2.3   Reading from a Single Bank

Nearly identical to the write function, data can be read from a single plane using the *Rd_Part* function. The *Rd_Part* function reads a block of data from display memory, assuming a 64-Kbyte memory map, and is provided in Listing 14.7. A 128-Kbyte memory map is provided in Listing 14.8.

LISTING 14.7   Read From a Portion of Display Memory Assuming a 64-Kbyte Memory Map

```
;  Function:
;   Read from a portion of a display segment from a "C" array
;   assuming a 64-Kbyte memory map.

;  Input Parameters:
;  buf_ptr              pointer to host "C" buffer that will contain
                        data
;  npix                 number of pixels
;  start                offset of window to start at

;  Calling Protocol:
;  Rd_Part(buf_ptr,npix,start);

  Rd_Part proc far USES DS ES DI, arg1:FAR PTR,arg2,arg3

;        source of data is from a C buffer
         les    di,arg1          ;get pointer to top of array

;        destination of data is into the A0000 display segment offset
         by the start address
         mov    ax,0a000h
         mov    ds,ax            ;point to base of display
         mov    si,arg3          ;starting address of display

;        move desired number of words
         mov    cx,arg2          ;desired number of bytes
         rep    movsb            ;write to memory
         ret

  Rd_Part endp
```

LISTING 14.8   Read From a Portion of Display Memory Assuming a 128-Kbyte Memory Map

```
;  Function:
;   Read from a portion of a display segment from a "C" array,
;   assuming a 128-Kbyte memory map.

;  Input Parameters:
;  buf_ptr              pointer to host "C" buffer that will contain data
;  npix                 number of pixels
```

```
; start                  offset of window to start at
; segment                segment address A000 or B000 hex

; Calling Protocol:
; Rd_Part_128(buf_ptr,npix,start,segment);

    Rd_Part_128 proc far USES DS ES DI, arg1:FAR PTR,arg2,arg3,arg4

;       source of data is from a C buffer
        les    di,arg1            ;get pointer to top of array

;       destination of data is into the A0000 display segment offset
;       by the start address
        mov    ax,arg4            ;get segment address
        mov    ds,ax              ;point to base of display
        mov    si,arg3            ;starting address of display

;       move desired number of words
        mov    cx,arg2            ;desired number of bytes
        rep    movsb              ;write to memory
        ret
Rd_Part_128 endp
```

14.2.4   Clearing a Single Bank

The Read and Write functions require a buffer since every pixel can be different. When clearing a window, only one color is necessary. The *Clr_Part* function loads a single color into a display memory window, assuming a 64-Kbyte memory map, and is provided in Listing 14.9. A 128-kbyte memory map is provided in Listing 14.10.

LISTING 14.9   Clearing a Portion of Display Memory Assuming a 64-Kbyte Memory Map

```
; Function:
;   Clearing a portion of a display bank beginning at a start
;   address to a specific color assuming a 64-Kbyte memory map

; Input Parameters:
; color           color to preset window
; npix            number of pixels
; start           offset of window to start at

; Calling Protocol:
; Clr_Part(color,npix,start);
```

```
Clr_Part proc far USES ES DI, arg1:byte,arg2,arg3

;           destination of data is into the A0000 display segment offset
;           by the start address
            mov     ax,0a000h
            mov     es,ax           ;point to base of display
            mov     di,arg3         ;starting address of display
            mov     al,arg1         ;get color

;           move desired number of bytes
            mov     cx,arg2         ;desired number of bytes
            rep     stosb           ;write to memory
            ret

Clr_Part  endp
```

LISTING 14.10   Clearing a Portion of Display Memory Assuming a 128-Kbyte Memory
Map

```
; Function:
;   Clearing a portion of a display bank beginning at a start
;   address to a specific color assuming a 128-Kbyte memory map

; Input Parameters:
; color         color to preset window
; npix          number of pixels
; start         offset of window to start at

; Calling Protocol:
; Clr_Part_128(color,npix,start);

Clr_Part_128 proc far USES ES DI, arg1:byte,arg2,arg3

;           destination of data is into the A0000 display segment offset
;           by the start address
            mov     ax,0a000h
            mov     es,ax           ;point to base of display
            mov     di,arg3         ;starting address of display
            mov     al,arg1         ;get color

;           move desired number of bytes
            mov     cx,arg2         ;desired number of bytes
            rep     stosb           ;write to memory
            ret

Clr_Part_128 endp
```

A special case of the Clear function is useful when the entire bank is to be cleared. This function, *Clr_Bank*, clears an entire bank, assuming a 64-Kbyte memory map, and is provided in Listing 14.11. A 128-Kbyte memory map is provided in Listing 14.12.

LISTING 14.11   Clearing an Entire Bank assuming a 64-byte memory map

```
; Function:
; Clear an entire bank assuming a 64-byte memory map

; Input Parameters:
;  color              color to set segment

; Calling Protocol:
; Clr_Bank(color);

Clr_Bank proc far USES ES DI, arg1:byte
        mov     ax,0a000h
        mov     es,ax           ;point to base of display
        xor     di,di           ;start at base of segment
        mov     cx,0ffffh       ;65536 bytes in a bank
        mov     al,arg1         ;get color
        rep     stosb           ;fill memory
        stosb                   ;one more time for 65536
        ret

Clr_Bank endp
```

LISTING 14.12   Clearing an Entire Bank Assuming a 128-byte Memory Map

```
; Function:
; Clearing an entire bank assuming a 128-byte memory map

; Input Parameters:
;  color              color to set segment

; Calling Protocol:
; Clr_Bank_128(color);

Clr_Bank_128 proc far USES ES DI, arg1:byte
        mov     ax,0a000h
        mov     es,ax           ;point to base of display
        xor     di,di           ;start at base of segment
```

```
        mov     cx,0ffffh       ;65536 bytes in a bank
        mov     al,arg1         ;get color
        rep     stosb           ;fill memory
        stosb                   ;one more time for 65536

        mov     ax,0b000h
        mov     es,ax           ;point to base of display
        xor     di,di           ;start at base of segment
        mov     cx,0ffffh       ;65536 bytes in a bank
        mov     al,arg1         ;get color
        rep     stosb           ;fill memory
        stosb                   ;one more time for 65536
        ret

Clr_Bank_128 endp
```

14.2.5 Writing to Four Display Planes

The function provided in Listing 14.13 writes data from an array into all four planes of display memory. The number of bytes involved in the transfer to each display plane is input to the function in the *num_bytes* variable. The data resides in a character buffer pointed to by *buf_ptr*. The data in the buffer is 4 * *num_bytes* bytes long since the buffer contains distinct data for all four display planes. The data is organized so that the num_bytes relevant to plane 0 are first, followed by *num_bytes* of data for plane 1, plane 2 and plane 3.

Four calls to the W*r_Part* function follow the enabling of the appropriate write plane. Since all four display planes can be enabled at once, only one plane is enabled at a time through the codes, 01, 02, 04 and 08. The *MapMask* function is provided in Listing 12.80. After each output, the buffer pointer, *buf_ptr* is incremented by the number of bytes output *num_bytes*.

LISTING 14.13   Writing to Four Display Planes

```
/*
Function:
Writing a horizontal line in a 16-bit mode. The lines worth of data
consists of 4 * dx bytes. The line is embedded within a buffer
pointed to by the buf_ptr.

Input Parameters:
num_bytes       number of bytes in the transfer to each plane
off_addr        offset address into current bank of display memory
buf_ptr         pointer to character buffer containing a line at a time in
```

a single plane. Thus, each byte contains one bit of eight pixels. It consists of num_bytes bytes of plane 0 followed by num_bytes bytes of plane 1,2, and 3.

```
Calling Protocol: */
Wr_Part_16(buf_ptr,num_bytes,off_addr)
char *buf_ptr; unsigned int off_addr; int num_bytes;

{
MapMask(1);    /* write to bit plane 0 */
Wr_Part(buf_ptr,num_bytes,off_addr); buf_ptr += num_bytes;

MapMask(2);    /* write to bit plane 1 */
Wr_Part(buf_ptr,num_bytes,off_addr); buf_ptr += num_bytes;

MapMask(4);    /* write to bit plane 2 */
Wr_Part(buf_ptr,num_bytes,off_addr); buf_ptr += num_bytes;

MapMask(8);    /* write to bit plane 3 */

Wr_Part(buf_ptr,num_bytes,off_addr);
}
```

14.2.6 Reading from Four Display Planes

Reading from all four display planes is accomplished through the code in Listing 14.14. This code is very similar to the write function in Section 14.2.4. The main difference is the coding to the Read Map Register. Only one display plane can be read from at a time, and consequently, the codes are *01, 02, 03,* and *04.* The ReadMap function is provided in Listing 12.80.

14.2.7 Clearing Four Display Planes

Clearing all four display planes is similar to writing to the display planes except that a single color is used for the transfer. As a result, there is no input buffer or buffer pointer. Code that clears all four display planes is presented in Listing 14.15. Since all four display planes can be written to simultaneously, only one call to Wr_Part is necessary. All four display planes are enabled by the code *0x0F.* The MapMask function is provided in Listing 12.80.

LISTING 14.14 Reading from Four Display Planes

```
/*
Function:
Reading a horizontal line in a 16-bit mode. The lines worth of data
consists of 4 * num_bytes bytes. The line is embedded within a
buffer pointed to by the buf_ptr.

Input Parameters:
        num_bytes       number of bytes in the transfer to each plane
        off_addr        offset address into current bank of display
                        memory
        buf_ptr         pointer to character buffer containing a line
                        at a time in a single plane. Thus, each byte
                        contains one bit of eight pixels. It consists
                        of num_bytes bytes of plane 0 followed by
                        num_bytes bytes of plane 1,2, and 3.

Calling Protocol: */
 Rd_Part_16(buf_ptr,num_bytes,off_addr)
 char *buf_ptr; unsigned int off_addr; int num_bytes;

{
 ReadMap(0);    /* Read from plane 0 */
 Rd_Part(buf_ptr,num_bytes,off_addr);   buf_ptr += num_bytes;

 ReadMap(1);    /* Read from plane 1 */
 Rd_Part(buf_ptr,num_bytes,off_addr);   buf_ptr += num_bytes;

 ReadMap(2);    /* Read from plane 2 */
 Rd_Part(buf_ptr,num_bytes,off_addr);   buf_ptr += num_bytes;

 ReadMap(3);    /* Read from plane 3 */
 Rd_Part(buf_ptr,num_bytes,off_addr);
 }
```

LISTING 14.15 Clearing Four Display Planes

```
/*
Function:
        Clearing a horizontal line in a 16-bit mode to all four
        display planes.
```

```
        Input Parameters:
              num_bytes              number of bytes in the transfer to
                                     each plane
              off_addr               offset address into current bank of
                                     display memory
              color                  color to set display window

Calling Protocol: */
Clr_Part_16(color,num_bytes,off_addr)
unsigned char color; unsigned int num_bytes,off_addr;


{
MapMask(0x0f);          /* write to bit planes 0, 1, 2 and 3 */
Clr_Part(color,num_bytes,off_addr);

}
```

14.3 TRANSFERRING DATA TO TWO BANKS

If the banks associated with the first and last points in a window are not equal, special care must be taken to ensure that the upper-order bank addresses and lower-order bank offset addresses are handled properly. The special case when only two banks are crossed is considered in this section.

In the case of a rectangular window, the transfer of data that crosses a single bank boundary can be split into two transfers. The first transfer starts at the beginning of the window and ends with the last pixel contained in the window that falls in the first bank. The second transfer starts with the first pixel in the window that falls into the second bank and ends with the last pixel contained in the window.

The most simple example occurs when the width of the window is equal to the virtual width of the display. The number of pixels in the first bank can be derived by determining the distance from the starting pixel to the last pixel in the bank. The number of pixels in the second bank is equal to the offset of the last pixel in the window. Two DMA transfers can be initiated to accomplish the entire transfer. Note that the start offset of the first DMA transfer will be the offset address of the first pixel. The offset of the second bank is 0 (It begins at the bank boundary by default). The number of pixels in the first bank and the starting offset address of the first bank can be calculated by the Equations 14.4 and 14.5, respectively.

Equation 14.4   Calculating the Number of Pixels in the First Bank

```
    Pixels_in_First_Bank = 65536 - Start_Offset
```

Equation 14.5   Calculating the Starting Offset Address in the First Bank

$$Start\_Offset\_First\_Bank = Start\_Offset$$

The number of pixels in the second bank and the starting offset address of the second bank can be calculated by the Equations 14.6 and 14.7, respectively.

Equation 14.6   Calculating the Number of Pixels in the Second Bank

$$Pixels\_in\_Second\_Bank = Enbytes\_per\_rowset$$

Equation 14.7   Calculating the Starting Offset Address in the Second Bank

$$Start\_Offset\_Second\_Bank = 0$$

14.4   TRANSFERRING DATA TO MULTIPLE BANKS

Transferring data to multiple banks using the simplification where the width of the rectangular window to be transferred is equal to the virtual width of the display, is handled in a similar fashion. Additional DMA instructions are issued, one for each intermediate bank. The start address of all intermediate banks is 0, and the number of bytes to transfer is 65536.

When the width of the window is less than the virtual width of the display, separate DMA instructions are issued, one for each horizontal line in the window.

14.4.1   Techniques

There is a technique for moving blocks of data across bank boundaries. It involves pretesting where the bank transitions will occur before any data is moved. This can be accomplished by comparing the start and end points of the window against the bank transition points.

14.4.2   Single-Row Transfers

The simplest case occurs when the rectangular window is only one scan-line high. There are four special circumstances considered in this section, as illustrated in Figure 14.1.

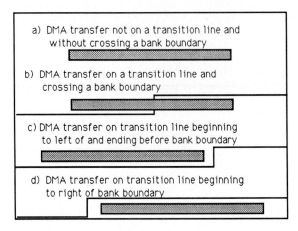

FIGURE 14.1 Single Row DMA Transfers

The first, shown in Figure 14.1a, occurs when the transfer does not happen at a bank transition row. This is the most elementary of the four cases. The bank start address and the intra-bank offset address are determined, and the number of pixels in the single line are transferred to the display memory. Since the line is not on a bank transition row, no bank crossing is possible.

The remaining three circumstances, shown in Figure 14.1b–d, occur when the block transfer is on a bank transition line. Figure 14.1b illustrates what happens when the actual transfer crosses the boundary. Figure 14.1c–d show the cases when the actual transition is not crossed. In this case, the entire transfer occurs to the left or right of the point of transition and is functionally equivalent to the case where the line does not occur on a bank transition line. Determining whether the scan row is on a bank transition line may seem cumbersome for a single-line transfer. However, this technique is very useful when generalizing to non-single, scan-line transfers.

14.4.3 Multiple-Row Transfers

Next, we consider the case when the window is more than one line high. Like the single-row case, the first example of this occurs when the width of the scan line is the same as the virtual width of the display. This is the simplest case since the first (left-most) pixel of scan line $n+1$ immediately follows the last (right-most) pixel of scan line n. This case is illustrated in Figure 14.2. Note that the virtual image size, as loaded into the Offset Register, is not necessarily the number of bytes per displayed scan line. The virtual width of the display is based

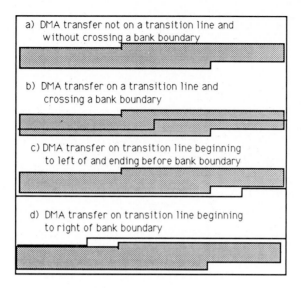

FIGURE 14.2   Multiple Full-Row DMA Transfers

on the number of pixels per byte and whether the addressing mode is byte, word or double word. The Offset Register is described in Section 10.4.22.

The starting and ending bank numbers involved in the transfer are determined by left-top and bottom-right coordinates of the window. The bank starting address and the number of pixels to transfer are determined as shown in Equations 14.8 and 14.9, respectively.

Equation 14.8   Calculating of the Number of Pixels in the First Bank

```
Pixels_in_First_Bank = 65536 - Start_Offset
```

Equation 14.9   Calculating of the Starting Offset Address in the First Bank

```
Start_Offset_First_Bank = Start_Offset
```

If the transfer spans more than two banks, all intermediate banks are full, 64-Kbyte transfers. These fill the entire bank as shown in Equations 14.10 and 14.11, respectively.

Equation 14.10   Calculating the Number of Pixels in the Middle Banks

```
Pixels_in_Middle_Banks = 65536
```

Equation 14.11   Calculating the Starting Offset Address in the Middle Banks

```
Start_Offset_Middle_Bank = 0
```

The number of pixels and the starting offset address for the last bank can be determined by Equations 14.12 and 14.13, respectively.

Equation 14.12   Calculating the Number of Pixels in the Last Bank

```
Pixels_in_Last_Bank = Enbytes_per_rowset
```

Equation 14.3   Calculating the Starting Offset Address in the Last Bank

```
Start_Offset_Second_Bank = 0
```

14.5   TRANSFERRING WINDOWS

The last case considered here occurs when the transfer height is not limited to a single row and the width is not equal to the virtual display width. There are, once again, three cases to be considered as shown in Figure 14.3.

14.5.1   Transfers Within a Single Bank

The first case, illustrated in Figure 14.3a, transfers data to one block. The start and ending bank numbers are the same. The length of a DMA transfer is limited to the width of the window since the right-most pixel of one scan line is NOT contiguous to the left-most pixel of the following scan line. These transfers can be accomplished through the code in Listing 14.16.

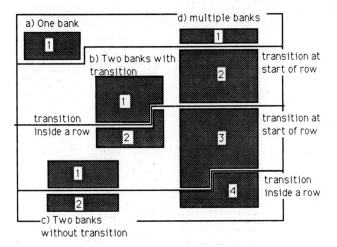

FIGURE 14.3 Transfering Rectangular Blocks

LISTING 14.16 Writing a Window to the Display Within a Single Bank

```
/*
Function:
        Writing a window to the display within a single bank

Input Parameters:
        x_start,x_end           starting and ending horizontal
                                coordinates
        y_start,y_end           starting and ending vertical
                                coordinates
            buffer      data buffer containing image data

Calling Protocol: */
 Write_Interbank_Window(x_start,y_start,x_end,y_end,buffer,bytes_per_row)
int x_start,y_start,x_end,y_end,bytes_per_row; char buffer[];

{ char *buf_pointer;
  unsigned int length; int scan_line;

        buf_pointer = &buffer[0];          /* point to the start
                                           of the data buffer */
        length = 1 + (x_end - x_start);    /* determine the
                                           length of a single
                                           scan-line */
```

```
                                                    single plane. Thus, each by
/* loop through the entire block with one dma transfer per scan-
   line */
for (scan_line=y_start; scan_line<=y_end; scan_line++)
 {
   /* transfer "length" bytes to the selected bank in display memory */
   DMA_Transfer(x_start,scan_line,length,buf_pointer,bytes_per_row);
   buf_pointer += length;       /* point to the next lines data */
 }
}
```

The routine *DMA_Transfer* moves *length* bytes of image data into the selected
bank beginning at a *start_offset* as determined by the Equation 14.14. The
start_offset variable can be an unsigned single precision integer since overflow
is guaranteed not to occur within a single bank.

Equation 14.14   Calculating a Starting Offset Address

```
start_offset = (y * bytes_per_row) + x;
```

14.5.2   Transfers Crossing Multiple Banks

The second and third cases, shown in Figure 14.3b–c, are special cases of the
fourth case shown in Figure 14.3c. The transfer either crosses two bank boundaries or more than two bank boundaries respectively. If it crosses two bank
boundaries, the transfer operation could be accomplished through two DMA
loops, one for each bank. If it crosses more than two boundaries, the first and
last transfer are identical to the first and second transfer in the two bank cases of
Figure 14.3b–c. Each has to account for the possibility of encountering a bank
transition at either the bottom line (for the top window) or the top line (of the
bottom window). The intermediate transfers have to account for the possibility
of encountering a bank transition at both the top and bottom lines. Section
14.6 provides a discussion of the more general cases.

14.6   CROSSING BANK BOUNDARIES AT THE END OF A LINE

 In Figure 14.3b, the bank boundary does not occur between x_start and x_end.
The code in Listing 14.17 will transfer image data into one or more banks
under this constraint. This could happen if the bank boundaries occurred in
between scan lines or if these occurred within a scan line but not within x_start
and x_end. The example in Listings14.17 through 14.19 assume that the bank

transitions occur at the start of scan lines. This is always the case when the display virtual offset is 1024 bytes. This forces each bank boundary to be aligned to the start of a scan lines since 1024 divides into 65,536 evenly.

In these examples, the buffer must be large enough to hold the data. In cases where the buffer is larger than 64 Kbytes, a "huge" buffer must be employed. A different technique could have been used that requires multiple 64-Kbyte buffers. The image data would be split into 64-Kbyte chunks, each residing in its own buffer. These buffers could then map directly into their respective 64-Kbyte banks of display memory. This is very useful when LIM memory is used since it maps into 64-Kbyte chunks anyway.

The Write–, Read–, and Clear–Window functions call upon a few other functions. These determine the banks and offset addresses of the starting and ending points in the window, set the appropriate bank register, and Write–, Read– or Clear–data within a bank. These are entitled *Bank_Off, Set_Write_Bank* or *Set_Read_Bank* and *Wr_Part, Rd_Part* or *Clr_Part*.

The Bank_Off function returns the bank number and offset that corresponds to a given x,y coordinate and the number of bytes per row. This function is based upon banks that are 64 Kbytes long. Since the addressing is the same across the different Super VGAs, this function is not Super VGA implementation specific.

The Set_Write_Bank or Set_Read_Bank function loads the write or read bank switching register assuming a bank granularity of 64 Kbytes. There are three basic types of bank switching modes. The first is a single bank mode where all accesses to display memory utilize the bank register as the upper order address bits into display memory. The second and third type utilize dual bank switching. Using dual banks can speed up display memory transfers requiring fewer bank switches. A direct analogy can be found in the ES and DS segment registers.

The second bank switching mode segments the 64-Kbyte window into two banks. Typically the lower bank ranges from A0000–A7FFF, and the upper bank ranges from A8000–AFFFF hex. All read-and-write operations that fall into one of these two 32-Kbyte regions are directed into display memory by the appropriate lower or upper bank.

The third bank switching mode utilizes one bank for read operations and the other for write operations. These functions are specific to Super VGA and they are provided in Chapters 15–21 for each Super VGA implementation.

The Wr_Part, Rd_Part, and Clr_Part functions are based on a single segment and are not dependent on the particular Super VGA implementation.

14.6.1 Writing a Window in 256-color Mode Aligned Bank Transitions

The function in Listing 14.17 writes to a window, assuming a 256-color graphics mode is in effect. In addition, the bank transitions must occur in between rows, termed aligned. Each row could be 512 or 1024 bytes wide.

The offset address, *b_offset* and bank number, *b_bank* of the left-top corner window coordinate, is used to initialize the pointers. The width of the window, *dx*, is calculated from the x2 and x1 coordinates.

The data transfer has a source and destination. The source buffer is the b*uf* array that is pointed to by *buf_ptr*. The destination pointer is the display memory, and an offset index into this memory is kept in display_ptr. Every row transferred requires that the source pointer, *buf_ptr* be incremented by dx. The destination pointer, *display_ptr*, is incremented by the number of bytes per virtual display of the display, *bytes_per_row*.

A long integer, d*isplay_offset* is maintained to track bank crossings. Bank crossings occur when display_offset exceeds the bank limit of 65,536. The lower 16 bits of this long integer are used as the offset into the current bank of display memory.

A do...while loop is executed which outputs one row of window data to the display. After each output, the source pointer, buf_ptr, and destination pointer, display_offset, are incremented by dx and bytes_per_row respectively. If the long integer display_offset exceeds 65,536, a bank crossing occurs between the line just output and the next line. Therefore, a bank switch is necessary. The current bank number, *bank_num*, is incremented and output to the bank register. In addition, the source pointer, display_offset, must be initialized. Since the first row of the bank is being accessed, the offset value is equal to x1.

The row counter, *row*, is incremented and the do...while loop is executed until the last row is output.

LISTING 14.17   Writing to a Window Assuming Aligned Bank Transitions

```
/*
Function:
 Writing data to a window in display memory.

Input Parameters:
 x1,y1                   top-left corner coordinates
 x2,y2                   bottom-right corner coordinates
 buf                     "C" byte buffer containing colors
 bytes_per_row           number of bytes per row

Calling Protocol: */
 Wr_Win_Aligned(x1,y1,x2,y2,buf,bytes_per_row)

int x1,y1,x2,y2; char buf[];
{ unsigned int b_offset,display_ptr;
  int b_bank,dx,bank_num,row;
  char *buf_ptr;
  long display_offset;
```

```
/* determine the starting bank and offset */
 Bank_Off(x1,y1,bytes_per_row,&b_offset,&b_bank);

 dx = (x2-x1)+1; /* determine the width of the window */
 display_offset = b_offset;
 buf_ptr = &buf[0]; /* point to top of buffer */
 bank_num=b_bank;
 Set_Write_Bank(bank_num); /* increment bank */
 row = y1;                          /* start with starting row
                                       number */


do
{

 display_ptr = display_offset;
 Wr_Part(buf_ptr,dx,display_ptr);
 buf_ptr += dx;            /* increment source buffer pointer */
 display_offset += bytes_per_row;     /* inc display offset */

/* check to see if a bank transition occurred */
 if(display_offset>=65536L)
  { bank_num++;                       /* it occurred so increment
                                         bank */

   Set_Write_Bank(bank_num);          /* load bank */
   display_offset = x1;               /* set up next banks display
                                         offset address */

  }
  row ++;                             /* increment row counter */
} while (row<=y2);      /* repeat til last row */

}
```

14.6.2   Reading a Window in 256-color Mode Aligned Bank Transitions

Reading a window assuming the banks are aligned, is nearly identical to writing a window. The major difference is in the function call that accesses the Read Bank Register instead of the Write Bank Register. In actuality, these might be the same.

A second difference is the source of data now refers to the display memory and is accessed by display_offset and display_ptr while the destination is the C buffer, *buf*, pointed to by "buf_ptr". Listing 14.18 presents code that reads a window under this constraint.

LISTING 14.18   Reading from a Window Assuming Aligned Bank Transitions

```
/*
Function:
Reading data to a window in display memory.

Input Parameters:
x1,y1                   top-left corner coordinates
x2,y2                   bottom-right corner coordinates
buf                     "C" byte buffer containing colors
bytes_per_row           number of bytes per row

Calling Protocol: */
 Rd_Win_Aligned(x1,y1,x2,y2,buf,bytes_per_row)

int x1,y1,x2,y2,bytes_per_row; char buf[];
{ unsigned int b_offset,display_ptr;
 int b_bank,dx,bank_num,row;
 char *buf_ptr;
 long display_offset;

/* determine the starting bank and offset */
 Bank_Off(x1,y1,bytes_per_row,&b_offset,&b_bank);

 dx = (x2-x1)+1; /* determine the width of the window */
 display_offset = b_offset;   /* setup display offset address */
 buf_ptr = &buf[0];           /* point to top of buffer */
 bank_num=b_bank;
 Set_Read_Bank(bank_num);     /* set up bank */
 row = y1;                     /* start with starting row number */

do
{
   display_ptr = display_offset;
   Rd_Part(buf_ptr,dx,display_ptr);
   buf_ptr += dx;               /* increment source buffer pointer */
   display_offset += bytes_per_row;   /* inc display offset */

/* check to see if a bank transition occurred */
 if(display_offset>=65536L)
 { bank_num++;                          /* it occurred so increment
                                        bank */

   Set_Read_Bank(bank_num);           /* load bank */
   display_offset = x1;               /* set up next banks display
```

```
                                          offset address */
     }
     row ++;                              /* increment row counter */
     } while (row<=y2);    /* repeat til last row */

     Set_Read_Bank(0); /* restore the bank to bank 0 */
     }
```

14.6.3   Clearing a Window in 256-color Mode Aligned Bank Transitions

Clearing a window is nearly identical to writing a window. The difference is that only one color is written to all pixels within the window. Therefore, there is no *buf* or buf_ptr. This allows windows of any size to be cleared since there are no C buffer restrictions. Since data is being written to display memory, the write bank register is used. Code that clears a window under this constraint is presented in Listing 14.19.

LISTING 14.19   Clearing a Window Assuming Aligned Bank Transitions

```
/*
Function:
Clearing data to a window in display memory.

Input Parameters:
x1,y1           top-left corner coordinates
x2,y2           bottom-right corner coordinates
color   byte value containing color
bytes_per_row   number of bytes per row

Calling Protocol: */
 Clr_Win_Aligned(x1,y1,x2,y2,color,bytes_per_row)

int x1,y1,x2,y2; char color;
{ unsigned int b_offset,display_ptr;
 int b_bank,dx,bank_num,row;
 long display_offset;

/* determine the starting bank and offset */
 Bank_Off(x1,y1,bytes_per_row,&b_offset,&b_bank);

 dx = (x2-x1)+1; /* determine the width of the window */
 display_offset = b_offset;            /* setup display offset
                                          address */
 bank_num=b_bank;
```

```
      Set_Write_Bank(bank_num);              /* Setup bank */
      row = y1;                              /* start with starting row
                                                number */


    do
    {
    display_ptr = display_offset;            /* load the display offset */
    Clr_Part(color,dx,display_ptr);          /* clear a line */
    display_offset += bytes_per_row;         /* increment display offset*/

    /* check to see if a bank transition occurred */
     if(display_offset>=65536L)
      { bank_num++;                          /* it occurred so increment bank */
        Set_Write_Bank(bank_num);  /* load bank */
        display_offset = x1;       /* set up next banks display offset
                                      address */
      }
    row ++;                                  /* increment row counter */
    } while (row<=y2);    /* repeat til last row */
    }
```

14.7 TRANSFERRING DATA ACROSS GENERALIZED BANK TRANSITIONS

The following code which writes, reads or clears a window makes no assumptions regarding where bank transitions occur. The bank transitions can occur in between rows, to the left of the window, to the right of the window or somewhere within the window. In Figure 14.3c, the transfer crosses a bank boundary that is within the block, that is, x_start <= x_bank_transfer <= x_end.

There are four types of bank transitions as shown in Figure 14.4. The first type of transition, illustrated in Figure 14.4a, occurs in between rows, termed row-aligned. The second, illustrated in Figure 14.4b, occurs to the left of the window. The third, shown in Figure 14.4c, occurs within the window. The fourth, shown in Figure 14.4d, occurs to the right of the window. These have to be differentiated in order to correctly determine the offset address within a given bank. In this figure, there are four bank crossings each with a left-most pixel marked *X1*. The bank transition occurs at the x-coordinate *xt* in each case. Each case represents two vertically neighboring lines, labeled *1* and *2*.

In the first case, the offset address of the line 2 begins at X1. In the second case, the beginning of offset address of line 2 is determined by Equation 14.15.

Equation 14.15 Offset Address When Transition is to Left of Window

```
offset_address = X1 - xt
```

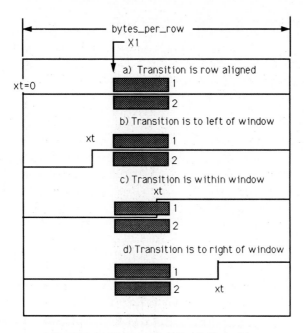

FIGURE 14.4   Crossing Bank Transitions

In the third case, there would be two offset addresses associated with line 2. The first represents the portion of the line still in the top-most bank. The second represents the portion of the line in the bottom-most bank. The first portion's offset would be bytes_per_row bytes beyond line 1; the second portion's offset would be zero. In the fourth case, the offset of line 2 would be determined by the Equation 14.16.

Equation 14.16   Offset Address When Transition is to Right of Window

```
offset_address = x1 + (bytes_per_row- xt)
```

14.8   HANDLING A WINDOW IN 256-COLOR MODES

In the 256-color modes, a single pixel consists of one byte. Three functions follow that write to, read from or clear a window. No assumptions are made as to where the bank transition occurs.

14.8.1 Writing a Window in 256-color Modes

Writing a window with generalized bank transitions is very similar to the aligned bank transition case described in Section 14.6.1. An additional step is required since a bank transition can occur in the middle of a line. The implementation presented in Listing 14.20 bases its operation on a line-by-line basis within a do...while loop, similar to the aligned case. Within the loop a test is made before each line is output. This test determines if the line to be output will cross a bank boundary. Separate code is executed according to whether it will or will not.

If the line to be drawn will cross the bank boundary, two lines must be drawn. The first line extends to the end of the bank from the current offset. The second line extends to the end of the line from the start of the next bank. The display and buffer pointers, display_ptr and buf_ptr accurately reflect the buffer locations. The length of the two line segments, length_1 and length_2 are calculated based on the example in Figure 14.4 and Equations 14.15 and 14.16. The first line segment is drawn, and the source buffer pointer, buf_ptr, incremented.

At this point it is necessary to change banks. The bank number, bank_num, is incremented and output to the Write Bank Register. Since the transition occurred within a bank, the first pixel drawn in the second line segment corresponds to the first pixel in the next bank. The display buffer offset pointer, display_ptr, is thus set to 0. The second line segment is drawn and the display buffer pointer, display_ptr, adjusted.

The second case occurs when a transition will not happen during the drawing of the next line. The line is drawn and the buffer pointer, buf_ptr is incremented. The number of bytes per row, bytes_per_row, is added to the long integer display offset variable, display_offset. If the resultant number exceeds 65,536, a transition occurs before the next line is drawn. If this is the case, the bank must be switched, and the offset of the first pixel of the next line must be determined. The bank counter is incremented and output to the Write Bank Register.

Calculation of the offset to the first pixel in the next line is dependent on where the bank transition occurs. This is described in Figure 14.4 and Equations 14.15 through 14.16. To reduce calculation, a table is constructed that contains the x-axis bank transition points. These points vary depending on the number of bytes per row of the display. Three examples are given for 640, 800 and 1024 bytes per row. Note that the bank transitions in the 1024-byte case always occur at x=0. This is due to the fact that the banks are aligned. The code presented in Section 14.6 is better suited to the task.

The x-axis transition of the new bank, found in *sx[bank_num]*, is compared to the left-most pixel of the window, x1. The appropriate display pointer offset is determined according to whether the bank transition occurs to the left or to the right of the window. It is already known that the bank transition will occur outside of the last drawn line. This insures that if the bank transition occurs to the right of x1, that it will actually occur to the right of x2.

The display pointer is adjusted, the row counter is incremented, and the do...while loop continues until the last row is drawn.

LISTING 14.20   Writing a Window in a 256-color Mode

```
/*
Function:
 Writing data to a window in display memory.

Input Parameters:
 x1,y1          top-left corner coordinates
 x2,y2          bottom-right corner coordinates
 buf            byte containing color

Calling Protocol: */
 Wr_Win_256(x1,y1,x2,y2,buf,bytes_per_row)

int x1,y1,x2,y2,bytes_per_row; char buf[];
{ unsigned int b_offset,display_ptr;
 int b_bank,dx,length_1,length_2,bank_num,row,sx[12],i;
 long end_of_line,display_offset;
 char *buf_ptr;

/* determine the offsets and banks of the starting and ending
points */
 Bank_Off(x1,y1,bytes_per_row,&b_offset,&b_bank);
 dx = (x2-x1)+1; /* determine the width of the window */

switch(bytes_per_row)
  {
   case 640:
        sx[0]=0;   sx[1]=256; sx[2]=512; sx[3]=128; sx[4]=384;
        sx[5]=0;break;
   case 800:
        sx[0]=0;   sx[1]=736; sx[2]=672; sx[3]=608; sx[4]=544;
        sx[5]=480; sx[6]=416; sx[7]=352; break;
   case 1024:
        for (i=0; i<12; i++) sx[i]=0;
  }

/* initialize the bank and pointers */
 row = y1;                              /* start with starting row
                                          number */
```

```
display_offset = b_offset;     /* load the intra-window offset
                                  address */
display_ptr = display_offset;
buf_ptr = &buf[0]; /* point to top of buffer */
bank_num=b_bank;
Set_Write_Bank(bank_num); /* setup first bank */

do
{

/* does this line cross a bank */
 end_of_line = (long)display_ptr + dx;
 if(end_of_line>=65536L)
 {
 /* must draw line as two line segments. Draw first segment */
 length_2 = end_of_line - 65536L; /* length of second line segment */
 length_1 = dx - length_2; /* length of first line segment */
 Wr_Part(buf_ptr,length_1,display_ptr);  /* write the line */
 buf_ptr += length_1;  /* increment buffer pointer */

/* change banks */
 bank_num ++;   /* increment to next bank */
 Set_Write_Bank(bank_num); /* setup first bank */
 display_ptr = 0;       /* setup display offset */
/* draw second line segment */
 Wr_Part(buf_ptr,length_2,display_ptr); /* write the line */
 buf_ptr += length_2;  /* increment buffer pointer */
 display_ptr = bytes_per_row - length_1;   /* inc display offset */
 }
else
 { /* draw a single line */
 Wr_Part(buf_ptr,dx,display_ptr);
 buf_ptr += dx;/* increment buffer pointer */

/* check to see if this was the last line in the bank */
 display_offset = (long)display_ptr + bytes_per_row;
 if(display_offset>=65536L)
 {
/* change banks */
 bank_num ++;   /* increment to next bank */
 Set_Write_Bank(bank_num); /* setup first bank */

        if(sx[bank_num]<=x1)
         display_ptr = x1-sx[bank_num];       /* display offset */
       else
```

```
            display_ptr = x1+(bytes_per_row-sx[bank_num]); /* display
            offset */
    }
    else
      display_ptr += bytes_per_row;
  }
 row ++;                                    /* increment row counter */
 } while (row<=y2);
}
```

14.8.2 Reading a Window in 256-color Modes

A similar routine, presented in Listing 14.21, reads the data from the display
and places it into the *buf* buffer. There is only difference between the read
routine and the write function. This is the call to Rd_Part as opposed to Wr_Part
and the setting of the read bank as opposed to the write bank.

LISTING 14.21 Reading a Window in a 256-color Mode

```
/*
Function:
 Reading data to a window in display memory.

Input Parameters:
 x1,y1                 top-left corner coordinates
 x2,y2                 bottom-right corner coordinates
 buf                   byte containing color

Calling Protocol: */
 Rd_Win_256(x1,y1,x2,y2,buf,bytes_per_row)

int x1,y1,x2,y2,bytes_per_row; char buf[];
{ unsigned int b_offset,display_ptr;
 int b_bank,dx,length_1,length_2,bank_num,row,sx[12],i;
 long end_of_line,display_offset;
 char *buf_ptr;

switch(bytes_per_row)
  {
    case 640:
```

```
            sx[0]=0;   sx[1]=256; sx[2]=512; sx[3]=128; sx[4]=384;
            sx[5]=0;  break;
      case 800:
            sx[0]=0;   sx[1]=736; sx[2]=672; sx[3]=608; sx[4]=544;
            sx[5]=480; sx[6]=416; sx[7]=352; break;
      case 1024:
            for (i=0; i<12; i++) sx[i]=0;
}


/* determine the offsets and banks of the starting and ending
points */
 Bank_Off(x1,y1,bytes_per_row,&b_offset,&b_bank);
 dx = (x2-x1)+1; /* determine the width of the window */


/* initialize the bank and pointers */
 row = y1;                                 /* start with starting row
                                               number */
 display_offset = b_offset;    /* load the intra-window offset
                                         address */
 display_ptr = display_offset;
 buf_ptr = &buf[0]; /* point to top of buffer */
 bank_num=b_bank;
 Set_Read_Bank(bank_num); /* setup first bank */


 do
 {

 /* does this line cross a bank */
  end_of_line = (long)display_ptr + dx;
  if(end_of_line>=65536L)
  {
    /* must draw line as two line segments. Draw first segment */
   length_2 = end_of_line - 65536L; /* length of second line segment */
   length_1 = dx - length_2; /* length of first line segment */
   Rd_Part(buf_ptr,length_1,display_ptr); /* Read the line */
   buf_ptr += length_1;            /* increment buffer pointer */

   /* change banks */
   bank_num ++;   /* increment to next bank */
   Set_Read_Bank(bank_num); /* setup first bank */
   display_ptr = 0;     /* setup display offset */

 /* draw second line segment */
 Rd_Part(buf_ptr,length_2,display_ptr); /* Read the line */
 buf_ptr += length_2; /* increment buffer pointer */
```

```
      display_ptr = bytes_per_row - length_1;      /* inc display offset */
     }
  else
   {
     /* draw a single line */
     Rd_Part(buf_ptr,dx,display_ptr);
     buf_ptr += dx;      /* increment buffer pointer */

  /* check to see if this was the last line in the bank */
   display_offset = (long)display_ptr + bytes_per_row;
   if(display_offset>=65536L)
  {
     /* change banks */
     bank_num ++;   /* increment to next bank */
     Set_Read_Bank(bank_num); /* setup first bank */

           if(sx[bank_num]<=x1)
           display_ptr = x1-sx[bank_num];      /* display offset */
          else
           display_ptr = x1+(bytes_per_row-sx[bank_num]); /* display
           offset */
    }
  else
       display_ptr += bytes_per_row;
  }
   row ++;                                       /* increment row counter */
  }   while (row<=y2);

  }
```

14.8.3   Clearing a Window in 256-color Modes

The Clear function, presented in Listing 14.22, is nearly identical to the Write Window function. Since the Clear function sends a single color to every pixel within the window, no buffer or buffer pointer are required. Consequently, there is no addressing problem, and the window can be any size.

LISTING 14.22   Clearing a Window in a 256-color Mode

```
/*
Function:
Clear a window in display memory.

Input Parameters:
 x1,y1        top-left corner coordinates
 x2,y2        bottom-right corner coordinates
 color     byte containing color

Calling Protocol: */
 Clr_Win_256(x1,y1,x2,y2,color,bytes_per_row)

int x1,y1,x2,y2,bytes_per_row; char color;
{ unsigned int b_offset,display_ptr;
 int b_bank,dx,length_1,length_2,bank_num,row,sx[12],i;
 long end_of_line,display_offset;

switch(bytes_per_row)
  {
    case 640:
        sx[0]=0;   sx[1]=256; sx[2]=512; sx[3]=128; sx[4]=384;
        sx[5]=0; break;
    case 800:
        sx[0]=0;   sx[1]=736; sx[2]=672; sx[3]=608; sx[4]=544;
        sx[5]=480; sx[6]=416; sx[7]=352; break;
    case 1024:
      for (i=0; i<12; i++) sx[i]=0;
  }

/* determine the offsets and banks of the starting and ending
points */
 Bank_Off(x1,y1,bytes_per_row,&b_offset,&b_bank);
 dx = (x2-x1)+1; /* determine the width of the window */


/* initialize the bank and pointers */
row = y1;                                /* start with starting row
                                            number */
display_offset = b_offset;     /* load the intra-window offset
                                    address */
display_ptr = display_offset;
bank_num=b_bank;
Set_Write_Bank(bank_num); /* setup first bank */
```

```
  do
  {

   /* does this line cross a bank */
   end_of_line = (long)display_ptr + dx;
   if(end_of_line>=65536L)
   {
     /* must draw line as two line segments. Draw first segment */
     length_2 = end_of_line - 65536L; /* length of second line segment */
     length_1 = dx - length_2; /* length of first line segment */
     Clr_Part(color+1,length_1,display_ptr); /* write the line */

     /* change banks */
     bank_num ++;   /* increment to next bank */
      Set_Write_Bank(bank_num); /* setup first bank */
     display_ptr = 0;      /* setup display offset */

     /* draw second line segment */
      Clr_Part(color+3,length_2,display_ptr); /* write the line */
      display_ptr = bytes_per_row - length_1;      /* inc display offset */
   }
  else
   {
     /* draw a single line */
      Clr_Part(color,dx,display_ptr);

     /* check to see if this was the last line in the bank */
      display_offset = (long)display_ptr + bytes_per_row;
      if(display_offset>=65536L)
   {
     /* change banks */
     bank_num ++;   /* increment to next bank */
     Set_Write_Bank(bank_num); /* setup first bank */

         if(sx[bank_num]<=x1)
           display_ptr = x1-sx[bank_num];      /* display offset */
         else
           display_ptr = x1+(bytes_per_row-sx[bank_num]); /* display offset */
         }
         else
          display_ptr += bytes_per_row;
         }
         row ++;                            /* increment row counter */
         } while (row<=y2);
         }
```

14.9 HANDLING A WINDOW IN 16-COLOR MODES

These same Write, Read and Clear functions could be used in the 16-color modes by dividing the x-coordinates by 8 and using 16-bit versions of the Wr_Part function. However, this is not necessary since the only popular 16-color display mode that crosses a bank boundary is the 1024 by 768 mode. This mode has only one bank crossing, between lines 511 and 512, so the write, read and clear functions are much simpler. These are provided in Listings 14.23 through 14.25 respectively.

The buffer used in the Write and Read functions consists of data from all four display planes. It is organized so that the first (top-most) line of the window is at the start of the buffer. The length of each line is a given number of bytes. The data from the first line of all four display planes is loaded contiguously, followed by the data from the next scan line's four display planes.

Imagine that there are N bytes per line. The data that resides in the buffer is described in Table 14.1. It assumes that the first scan line is at row 0. Thus, the length of the buffer is equal to four times the number of pixels in the window.

14.9.1 Writing a Window in 16-color Modes

In the code of Listing 14.23, data is written to display memory in a 16-color mode. It is assumed that a 1024 x 768 display mode is active. The code in Listing 14.23 also assumes that the left-most and right-most edges of the window, x1 and x2, are byte-aligned. Code presented in Chapter 12 can be incorporated to handle non-byte-aligned cases.

The byte addresses of the left and right-most edges of the window are determined by dividing the x1 and x2 coordinates by 8. This accounts for the eight pixels per byte (in one plane). The function has two cases. In the first, the

TABLE 14.1   Data Format in the 16–color Window Buffer

Byte	Row	Plane
0 to (N–1)	0	0
N to (2N–1)	0	1
2N to (3N–1)	0	2
3N to (4N–1)	0	3
4N to (5N–1)	1	0
5N to (6N–1)	1	1
6N to (7N–1)	1	2
7N to (8N–1)	1	3

window extends across the bank boundary. In the second, the window is completely contained in one bank.

In the first case, the first write bank, bank 0, is selected. The destination display pointer, display_ptr, is set to the starting location and the buffer pointer, buf_ptr, is initialized to the top of the buffer. The transfer of data is accomplished through two do...while loops. The first outputs data to the first bank, bank 0, and the second outputs data to bank 1. One line is output at a time. The Wr_Part_16 function outputs 4 * dx bytes, dx bytes to each of the four display memory planes. Thus, the display offset pointer is incremented by 4 * dx. The first loop outputs data until line 512 is reached.

At line 512, the bank is switched to bank 1, and a similar do..while loop is executed. The display pointer, display_ptr is initialized to the left-most byte of the window since it will be starting at the first row in the bank.

The single-bank case is identical to the dual bank case with the exception that only one do...while loop is executed, either to bank 0 or bank 1.

LISTING 14.23   Writing to a Window to a 1024 by 768 16-color Mode

```
/*
Function
Writing a window to display memory from a "C" buffer.

Input parameters:
 x1,y1         top-left corner coordinates
 x2,y2         bottom-right corner coordinates
 buf           host buffer containing data

Calling protocol: */
 Wr_Win_1024_16(x1,y1,x2,y2,buf)

int x1,y1,x2,y2; char buf[];
{ int row,dx,bytes_per_row=128; unsigned int display_ptr;
 char *buf_ptr;

/* there are 8 bits per pixel in the 16-color mode */
 x1 = x1>>3;   x2 = x2>>3;
 dx = (x2-x1)+1; row = y1;

if((y1<512)&(y2>=512))  /* does it span both banks */
  {
    /* write to the first bank */
    Set_Write_Bank_16(0);
    display_ptr = y1*bytes_per_row + x1;           /* starting offset */
```

```
    buf_ptr = &buf[0];                          /* point to start of
                                                buffer */

    do
    {
       Wr_Part_16(buf_ptr,dx,display_ptr);      /* write a line */
      buf_ptr += 4*dx;                          /* increment buffer
                                                pointer */
         display_ptr+=bytes_per_row;            /* increment display
                                                pointer */
      row++;                                     /* increment row
                                                counter */
    } while (row<512);                           /* repeat til end of
                                                bank */


/* write to the second bank */
 Set_Write_Bank_16(1);
 display_ptr = x1;                              /* starting offset */
 do
 {
    Wr_Part_16(buf_ptr,dx,display_ptr);         /* write a line */
   buf_ptr += 4*dx;                             /* increment buffer
                                                pointer */
      display_ptr+=bytes_per_row;               /* increment display
                                                pointer */
   row++;                                        /* increment row
                                                counter
 } while (row<=y2);                              /* repeat til end of
                                                window */
}

else /* contained in one segment */
{ if(y1<512) /* contained in bank 1 */
      {
        Set_Write_Bank_16(0);
          display_ptr = y1*bytes_per_row + x1;  /* starting
                                                offset */
      buf_ptr = &buf[0];                        /* point to
                                                top of buffer */
      do
      {
        Wr_Part_16(buf_ptr,dx,display_ptr);     /* write a line */
        buf_ptr += 4*dx;                        /* increment
                                                buffer pointer */
          display_ptr+=bytes_per_row;           /* increment
                                                display pointer */
        row++;                                  /* increment row
                                                counter */
```

```
        } while (row<=y2);              /* repeat til end of window */
    }

else   /* contained in bank 2 */
        {
          Set_Write_Bank_16(1);
          display_ptr = (y1-512)*bytes_per_row + x1; /* starting offset */
          buf_ptr = &buf[0];                  /* point to top of
                                                 buffer */

        do
        {
            Wr_Part_16(buf_ptr,dx,display_ptr); /* write a line */
          buf_ptr += 4*dx;                    /* increment
                                                buffer pointer */

            display_ptr+=bytes_per_row;        /* increment display
                                                pointer */

        row++;                                 /* increment row
                                                counter */
        } while (row<=y2);                     /* repeat til end of
                                                window */

        }
    }
}
```

14.9.2   Reading a Window in 16-color Modes

The Read function is presented in Listing 14.24. It is similar to the Write function, with the source and destination pointers reversed. In addition, the Read bank is used instead of the Write bank.

LISTING 14.24   Reading a Window to a 1024 by 768 16-color Mode

```
/*
Function:
 Reading a window to display memory from a "C" buffer.

Input Parameters:
 x1,y1          top-left corner coordinates
 x2,y2          bottom-right corner coordinates

Output Parameters:
 buf            host buffer that will contain data
```

```
Calling protocol: */
 Rd_Win_1024_16(x1,y1,x2,y2,buf)

int x1,y1,x2,y2; char buf[];
{ int row,dx,bytes_per_row=128; unsigned int display_ptr;
 char *buf_ptr;

/* there are 8 bits per pixel in the 16-color mode */
x1 = x1>>3;   x2 = x2>>3;
dx = (x2-x1)+1; row = y1;

if((y1<512)&(y2>=512))  /* does it span both banks */
{
   /* write to the first bank */
   Set_Read_Bank_16(0);
   display_ptr = y1*bytes_per_row + x1;           /* starting offset */
   buf_ptr = &buf[0];                             /* point to start of
                                                  buffer */
 do
 {
     Rd_Part_16(buf_ptr,dx,display_ptr);          /* read a line */
    buf_ptr += 4*dx;                              /* increment buffer
                                                  pointer */

     display_ptr+=bytes_per_row;                  /* increment display
                                                  pointer */

  row++;                                          /* increment row
                                                  counter */

 } while (row<512);                               /* repeat til end of
                                                  window */

/* write to the second bank */
 Set_Read_Bank_16(1);
 display_ptr = x1;                                /* starting offset */
 do
 {
   Rd_Part_16(buf_ptr,dx,display_ptr);            /* read a line */
   buf_ptr += 4*dx;                               /* increment buffer
                                                  pointer */

   display_ptr+=bytes_per_row;                    /* increment display
                                                  pointer */

  row++;                                          /* increment row
                                                  counter */

 } while (row<=y2);                               /* repeat til end of
                                                  window */

}
```

```
else /* contained in one segment */
 { if(y1<512) /* contained in bank 1 */
      {
        Set_Read_Bank_16(0);
         display_ptr = y1*bytes_per_row + x1; /* starting offset */
       buf_ptr = &buf[0];                     /* point to top of
                                                 buffer */

      do
      {
         Rd_Part_16(buf_ptr,dx,display_ptr);/* read a line */
          buf_ptr += 4*dx;                   /* increment buffer
                                                pointer */

           display_ptr+=bytes_per_row;       /* increment display
                                                pointer */

         row++;                              /* increment row
                                                counter */

        } while (row<=y2);                   /* repeat til end of
                                                window */

      }
   else /* contained in bank 2 */
        {
            Set_Read_Bank_16(1);
            display_ptr = (y1-512)
          *bytes_per_row + x1;             /* starting offset */
            buf_ptr = &buf[0];             /* point to
                                             top of buffer */

        do
        {
          Rd_Part_16(buf_ptr,dx,display_ptr);/* read a line */
          buf_ptr += 4*dx;                   /* increment buffer
                                                pointer */

          display_ptr+=bytes_per_row;        /* increment display
                                                pointer */

         row++;                             /* increment row
                                                counter */

        } while (row<=y2);                  /* repeat til end of
                                                window */

        }
 }
 }
```

14.9.3 Clearing a Window in 16-color Modes

The Clear function, presented in Listing 14.25 is nearly identical to the Write function. The difference is that there is no buffer or buffer pointer. Consequently, no restriction regarding window size is imposed on this function.

LISTING 14.25 Clearing a Window in a 1024 by 768 16-color Display Mode

```
/*
Function:
 Clearing a window in display memory to a color.

Input parameters:
 x1,y1          top-left corner coordinates
 x2,y2          bottom-right corner coordinates
 color          byte containing color

Calling protocol: */
 Clr_Win_1024_16(x1,y1,x2,y2,color)

int x1,y1,x2,y2; char color;
{ int row,dx,bytes_per_row=128; unsigned int display_ptr;

/* there are 8 bits per pixel in the 16-color mode */
 x1 = x1>>3;   x2 = x2>>3;
 dx = (x2-x1)+1; row = y1;

 if((y1<512)&(y2>=512))  /* does it span both banks */
 {
 /* write to the first bank */
 Set_Write_Bank_16(0);
 display_ptr = y1*bytes_per_row + x1;          /* starting offset */
 do
 {
     Clr_Part_16(color,dx,display_ptr);        /* clear a line */
     display_ptr+=bytes_per_row;               /* increment display
                                               pointer */
  row++;                                       /* increment row
                                               counter */
 } while (row<512);                            /* repeat til end of
                                               window */

/* write to the second bank */
   Set_Write_Bank_16(1);
   display_ptr = x1;                           /* starting offset */
  do
```

```
    {
        Clr_Part_16(color,dx,display_ptr);         /* clear a line */
        display_ptr+=bytes_per_row;                /* increment display
                                                      pointer */

      row++;                                       /* increment row
                                                      counter */

    } while (row<=y2);                             /* repeat til end of
                                                      window */

}
else /* contained in one segment */
{ if(y1<512) /* contained in bank 1 */
        {
            Set_Write_Bank_16(0);
            display_ptr = y1*bytes_per_row + x1;   /* starting offset */
          do
              { Clr_Part_16(color,dx,display_ptr); /* clear a line */
               display_ptr+=bytes_per_row;         /* increment display
                                                      pointer */

          row++;                                   /* increment row
                                                      counter */

          } while (row<=y2);                       /* repeat til end of
                                                      window */

        }

else   /* contained in bank 2 */
        {
            Set_Write_Bank_16(1);
            display_ptr = (y1-512)*bytes_per_row + x1;   /* starting
                                                            offset */
          do
              { Clr_Part_16(color,dx,display_ptr); /* clear a line */
           display_ptr+=bytes_per_row;             /* increment display
                                                      pointer */

          row++;                                   /* increment row
                                                      counter */

          } while (row<=y2);                       /* repeat til end of
                                                      window */

        }

    }

}
```

14.10 DRAWING SINGLE PIXELS

Transferring single pixels is easier than transferring blocks. There are several techniques. One technique determines the bank number and offset of the pixel in question by referencing the x,y coordinate-pair inputs and the offset of the display. It then loads the bank and transfers the pixel. Code that draws a pixel in a planar mode is more complicated than code that draws a pixel in a packed mode. Examples of each follow.

A packed display mode is organized so that each pixel occupies one byte. Typical code for drawing a pixel in such a mode is provided in Listing 14.26. The Chips and Technologies 452 Super VGA chip is used as an example.

Note that the granularity of the page register is actually 16 Kbytes long. The overflow condition that signals a bank transition occurs on a 64-Kbyte boundary. This accounts for the shift left by two operations. The loading of the bank register is the only Super VGA specific code in this function. It is simple to have this code to operate on other Super VGAs. The only necessary modification is to replace this bank register selection code with the other specific bank register code for other Super VGAs.

14.10.1 Drawing a Pixel in 256-color Modes

LISTING 14.26 Example of drawing a point in a 256-Color Mode

```
; Function:
;   Draw a point into display memory in extended resolution 256   ;
;   color modes for the Chips.

; Input parameters
; arg1: x                         horizontal coordinate of point
; arg2: y                         vertical coordinate of point
; arg3: color                     color to draw point
; arg4: bytes_per_line            number of bytes per line

; Calling protocol
; DrawPix_256(x,y,color,bytes_per_line);

  DrawPix_256 proc far USES ES SI ,arg1,arg2,arg3:byte,arg4

; determine the (long) address = ( y * bytes_per_line ) + x
; where the segment is in dx and the bytes_per_line is in ax
        mov     ax,arg4           ; get bytes_per_line in ax
        mov     bx,arg2           ; get y in bx
        mul     bx                ; y*bytes_per_line in dx:ax
        add     ax,arg1           ; (y*bytes_per_line)+x lower 16 bits
                                  in ax
```

```
        mov     di,ax               ; load as display offset for es:di

;       determine page register
        adc     dx,0                ; (y*bytes_per_line)+x upper n bits in dx
        mov     ah,dl               ;put page value into cl for port output

;       set up the bank register
        Load_Single_Bank_256    ;load the write bank

; send the data to the display memory
        mov     ax,0a000h           ; point to display memory base
        mov     es,ax
        mov al,arg3                 ; get color
        mov     es:[di],al          ; store color in display memory

        ret
DrawPix_256 endp
```

This routine could be simplified if it is known that the bank will not need to change, and the linear address determination cannot overflow a 64-Kbyte boundary, as provided in Listing 14.27.

LISTING 14.27   Example of Drawing a Pixel Within a Single Bank in a 256-color Mode

```
; Function:
;   Drawing a point into display memory in extended resolution 256
color modes for the Chips.

; Input parameters
; arg1: x                       horizontal coordinate of point
; arg2: y                       vertical coordinate of point
; arg3: color                   color to draw point
; arg4: bytes_per_line          number of bytes per line

; Calling protocol
; DrawPic_256(x,y,color,bytes_per_line);

DrawPic_256 proc far USES ES SI ,arg1,arg2,arg3:byte,arg4

; determine the address = ( y * bytes_per_line ) + x
        mov     ax,arg4             ; get bytes_per_line in ax
        mov     bx,arg2             ; get y in bx
        mul     bx                  ; y*bytes_per_line in dx:ax
        add     ax,arg1             ; (y*bytes_per_line)+x lower 16 bits in ax
        mov     di,ax               ; load as display offset for es:di
```

```
; send the data to the display memory
        mov     ax,0a000h       ; point to display memory base
        mov     es,ax
        mov     al,arg3         ; get color
        mov     es:[di],al      ; store color in display memory


        ret
DrawPic_256 endp
```

14.10.2 Drawing a Pixel in 16-color Modes

A planar display mode is organized for each byte to contain multiple pixels and
be distributed across all four display planes. The Set/Reset register and Enable
Set/Reset Register can be used to write to all display planes simultaneously. The
Bit Mask register can be used to mask off the bits corresponding to other pixels
in the byte.

Two functions are provided that write a pixel in the planar display modes.
The first handles the Set/Reset and Enable Set/Reset registers while the second
does not. In the case of a single-color line drawing routine, the Set/Reset and
Enable Set/Reset registers can be set once before the line is drawn.

Listing 14.28 provides typical code to draw a pixel in handling the Set/Reset
and Enable Set/Reset Registers. Code that does not handle these registers is
provided in Listing 14.29. Again, the 452 Super VGA chip from Chips and
Technologies is used as an example. Note that the granularity of the Page
Register is actually 8 Kbytes long. The overflow condition that signals a bank
transition occurs on a 64-Kbyte boundary. This accounts for the shift left by
three operation. The loading of the Bank Register is the only code specific to
Super VGA in this function. For this code to operate on other Super VGAs,
replace this bank register selection code with the other specific bank register
code for other Super VGAs.

LISTING 14.28   Drawing a Pixel Using the Set/Reset Function

```
; Function:
; Drawing a point into display memory in extended resolution 16
color modes for the Chips.

; Input parameters
; arg1: x                     horizontal coordinate of point
; arg2: y                     vertical coordinate of point
; arg3: color                 color
; arg4: bytes_per_line        number of bytes per line
```

```
; Calling protocol
; DrawPic_16(x,y,color,bytes_per_line);

DrawPic_16 proc far USES ES DI,arg1,arg2,arg3:byte,arg4

; Enable all planes in the Enable Set/Reset Register
        mov     dx,3ceh
        mov     ah,0fh          ;set all planes to 1
        mov     al,1            ;index Enable Set/Reset Register
        out     dx,ax

; Load the Set/Reset Register with the color
        mov     ah,arg3         ;get color
        mov     al,0            ;index Set/Reset Register
        out     dx,ax

; get the x index and divide by 8 for 16-color
        mov     ax,arg1         ; get the x address
        shr     ax,1            ; divide by 8
        shr     ax,
        shr     ax,1
        push    ax              ;save byte address for later

; set up the Bit Mask Register
        mov     ax,3ceh         ;point to address port
        mov     dx,ax
        mov     ax,8
        out     dx,al           ;address bit plane mask
        inc     dx              ;DX poits to data port

;       load the Bit Mask Register
        mov     cx,arg1         ;get x address
        and     cx,0007h        ;only want bit position
        mov     al,80h          ;bit mask
        shr     al,cl           ;put bit mask into proper position
        out     dx,al           ;output bit plane mask

; determine the (long) address = ( y * bytes_per_line ) + x
; where the segment is in dx and the bytes_per_line is in ax
        mov     ax,arg4         ; get bytes_per_line in ax
        mov     bx,arg2         ; get y in bx
        mul     bx              ; y*bytes_per_line in dx:ax
        pop     cx              ; get the x byte address
        add     ax,cx           ;(y*bytes_per_line)+x lower 16 bits in ax
        mov     di,ax           ;load as display offset for es:di
```

```
;           determine bank register
            adc     dx,0                ;(y*bytes_per_line)+x upper n bits in dx
            mov     ah,dl               ;put page value into cl for port output

;           set up the bank register
            Load_Single_Bank_16    ;load the write bank

; send the data to the display memory through set reset
            mov     ax,0a000h           ; point to display memory base
            mov     es,ax
            mov     al,es:[di]          ; dummy read from display memory
            mov     es:[di],al          ; store color in display memory

            ret
DrawPic_16 endp
```

LISTING 14.29   Draw a Pixel Assuming the Set/Reset function is already Loaded

```
; Function:
; Draw a point into display memory in extended resolution 16-color
modes for the Chips.

; NOTE: Assumes that Set/Reset and EnableSet/Reset Register are
;                  preset with color.

; Input parameters
; arg1: x                     horizontal coordinate of point
; arg2: y                     vertical coordinate of point
; arg3: bytes_per_line        number of bytes per line

; Calling protocol
; DrawPix_16(x,y,color,bytes_per_line);

DrawPix_16 proc far USES ES DI,arg1,arg2,arg3

; get the x index and divide by 8 for 16-color
            mov     ax,arg1             ; get the x address
            shr     ax,1                ;divide by 8
            shr     ax,1
            push    ax                  ;save byte address for later

; set up the Bit Mask Register
            mov     ax,3ceh             ;point to address port
            mov     dx,ax
            mov     ax,8
```

```
        out     dx,al           ;address bit plane mask
        inc     dx              ;DX points to data port

;       load the Bit Mask Register
        mov     cx,arg1         ;get x address
        and     cx,0007h        ;only want bit position
        mov     al,80h          ;bit mask
        shr     al,cl           ;put bit mask into proper position
        out     dx,al           ;output bit plane mask

; determine the (long) address = ( y * bytes_per_line ) + x
; where the segment is in dx and the bytes_per_line is in ax
        mov     ax,arg3         ; get bytes_per_line in ax
        mov     bx,arg2         ; get y in bx
        mul     bx              ; y*bytes_per_line in dx:ax
        pop     cx              ; get the x byte address
        add     ax,cx           ; (y*bytes_per_line)+x lower 16 bits in ax
        mov     di,ax           ; load as display offset for es:di

;       determine bank register
        adc     dx,0            ; (y*bytes_per_line)+x upper n bits in dx
        mov     ah,dl           ;put page value into cl for port output

;       set up the bank register
        Load_Single_Bank_16     ;load the write bank

; send the data to the display memory through set reset
        mov     ax,0a000h       ; point to display memory base
        mov     es,ax
        mov     al,es:[di]      ; dummy read from display memory
        mov     es:[di],al      ; store color in display memory
        ret

DrawPix_16 endp
```

14.11 DRAWING A LINE

Drawing a generalized line is accomplished by calling upon the draw pixel functions described in Section 14.5. Two functions are provided. One that draws a line in a 256-color mode. Another draws a line in a 16-color mode.

14.11.1 Drawing a Line in 256-color Modes

Drawing a line in a 256-color mode is accomplished by the code in Listing 14.30. Since one pixel occupies one byte, there is no need for bit masking.

LISTING 14.30 Drawing a Line in One of the 256-color Modes

```
/*
Input parameters:
 page       page
 x1,y1          first endpoint x,y coordinates of line
 x2,y2          second endpoint x,y coordinates of line
 color     color of the line
 bytes_per_row          offset of display
 extended       extended register port address

Calling protocol */
 Line_256(x1,y1,x2,y2,color,bytes_per_row,extended)

int x1,y1,x2,y2,bytes_per_row,extended; char color;
{ int dx,dy,incr1,incr2,d,x,y,xend,yend,yinc,xinc;

/* determine slope of line */
dx = abs(x2-x1);
dy = abs(y2-y1);

if(dx>=dy) /* slope < 1 */
 {if(x1>x2)
   { x = x2; y = y2; xend = x1;
      if(dy==0) yinc=0;
      else { if(y2>y1) yinc = -1; else yinc = 1; }}
  else
   { x = x1; y = y1; xend = x2;
      if(dy==0) yinc=0;
      else { if(y2>y1) yinc = 1; else yinc = -1; }}

incr1 = 2*dy; d = incr1-dx; incr2 = 2*(dy-dx);
DrawPix_256(x,y,color,bytes_per_row,extended);

while (x<xend)
   { x ++;
      if (d<0) d += incr1;
      else { y +=yinc; d = d + incr2; }
      DrawPix_256(x,y,color,bytes_per_row,extended);
 }
}
else
{
 if(y1>y2)
```

```
    { x = x2; y = y2; yend = y1;
        if(dx==0) xinc=0;
        else { if(x2>x1) xinc = -1; else xinc = 1; }}
    else
    { x = x1; y = y1; yend = y2;
        if(dx==0) xinc=0;
        else {if(x2>x1) xinc = 1; else xinc = -1; }}

incr1 = 2*dx; d = incr1-dy; incr2 = 2*(dx-dy);
DrawPix_256(x,y,color,bytes_per_row,extended);

while (y<yend)
  { y ++;
      if (d<0) d += incr1;
      else { x +=xinc; d = d + incr2; }
      DrawPix_256(x,y,color,bytes_per_row,extended);
  }
 }
}
```

14.11.12 Drawing a Line in 16-color Modes

Code that draws a line in a 16-color mode is provided in Listing 14.31. Since a single pixel is spread across four display planes and a single byte contains data for eight pixels, the mapping from pixels to bytes is not as straightforward as the example in Listing 14.30. The function Draw_Pix_16 is used to draw in the single pixel, across all four display banks, without disturbing neighboring pixels. The four display planes are handled by utilization of the Set/Reset and Enable Set/Reset registers. The Draw_Pix_16 function assumes that the Set/Reset and Enable Set/Reset registers are preset. This can be accommodated since the line is drawn in only one color. At the end of this function the Bit Mask, Set/Reset and Enable Set/Reset registers are reset to their normal operating condition.

LISTING 14.31   Drawing a Line in One of the 16-color Modes

```
/*
Input parameters:
 page       page
 x1,y1          first endpoint x,y coordinates of line
 x2,y2          second endpoint x,y coordinates of line
 color      color of the line
bytes_per_row          offset of display
```

```
Calling Protocol */
 Line_16(x1,y1,x2,y2,color,bytes_per_row)

int x1,y1,x2,y2,bytes_per_row; char color;
{ int dx,dy,incr1,incr2,d,x,y,xend,yend,yinc,xinc;

/* enable the set reset function and load the color */
ESetRes(15); SetRes(color); /* load registers */
dx = abs(x2-x1);
dy = abs(y2-y1);

if(dx>=dy) /* slope < 1 */
 {if(x1>x2)
   { x = x2; y = y2; xend = x1;
       if(dy==0) yinc=0;
       else { if(y2>y1) yinc = -1; else yinc = 1; }}
  else
   { x = x1; y = y1; xend = x2;
       if(dy==0) yinc=0;
       else { if(y2>y1) yinc = 1; else yinc = -1; }}

incr1 = 2*dy; d = incr1-dx; incr2 = 2*(dy-dx);
DrawPix_16(x,y,color,bytes_per_row);

while (x<xend)
 { x ++;
   if (d<0) d += incr1;
     else { y +=yinc; d = d + incr2; }
       DrawPix_16(x,y,color,bytes_per_row);
 }
}
else
{
 if(y1>y2)
 { x = x2; y = y2; yend = y1;
     if(dx==0) xinc=0;
     else { if(x2>x1) xinc = -1; else xinc = 1; }}
  else
   { x = x1; y = y1; yend = y2;
       if(dx==0) xinc=0;
       else { if(x2>x1) xinc = 1; else xinc = -1; }}

incr1 = 2*dx; d = incr1-dy; incr2 = 2*(dx-dy);
DrawPix_16(x,y,color,bytes_per_row);
 while (y<yend)
  { y ++;
```

```
    if  (d<0)  d  +=  incr1;
     else  {  x  +=xinc;  d  =  d  +  incr2;  }
      DrawPix_16(x,y,color,bytes_per_row);
  }
 }
 BitMask(255);  ESetRes(0);  /*  reset  the  EGA/VGA  registers  */
 }
```

Care must be taken to set the banks correctly. If an address overflow is not detected and the bank is not adjusted properly, incorrect results will occur. Figure 14.5a shows a correctly drawn line that crosses a bank boundary. The data will be *aliased* back into the same bank instead of being mapped into the new bank. In the case of a line, this appears similar to the line in Figure 14.5b.

This figure demonstrates that the aliasing is deterministic. Suppose the line in Figure 14.5a crosses the scan line containing the bank transition at pixel 364. This x and y location translates into a linear host address of 65,100 in that bank. This is 436 pixels from the end of the bank and assumes that the width of the display is 800 pixels. The next point drawn on the line would be at 65,100 + 800 + 1. This summation occurs since the last pixel was at 65,100. The next pixel occurs on the next scan line that is 800 pixels away. Assuming that the line is drawn at a 45 degree angle, the x coordinate will be incremented, yielding an address of 65901 that is 365 pixels into the next bank, bank 1. If the bank is not switched to bank 1, the next point will be drawn 365 pixels into bank 0 resulting in the alias as shown in Figure 14.5b.

14.12   SELECTING A START ADDRESS

The display memory is typically larger than the image being displayed on the monitor. This additional memory may be unused, contain other images, or contain unseen areas of the displayed image, when the displayed image virtual size is larger than the display image size. A pointer is provided to allow the programmer to move the viewable window port around within the larger display memory.

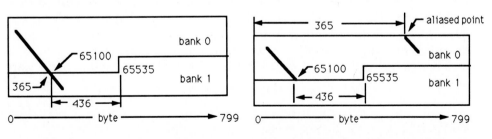

a) Line with Proper Bank Transition   b) Line with Improper Bank Transition

FIGURE 14.5   Lines Crossing Bank Transistions

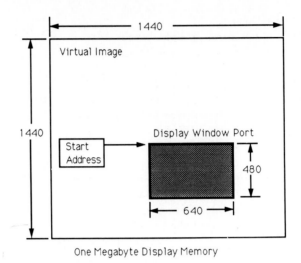

FIGURE 14.6 Virtual 16-color Image in One Megabyte of Display Memory

Figure 14.6 illustrates a 640 by 480 16-color image residing in a Super VGA equipped with one megabyte of display memory. The one megabyte is actually 1,048,756 bytes of memory. It can hold 2,097,152 16-color pixels. The virtual image could be 1440 by 1440 pixels.

The standard VGA starting address is a 16-bit register described in Sections 10.4.13 and 10.4.14. These 16-bits can access any point within a single 64 Kbytes of memory. Additional address bits are required to address any point within the one megabyte of memory space. In the 16-color mode, this requires an additional 2 bits of upper start address. These two bits select between one of the four banks of memory. In the 256-color mode, four additional start address bits are required to create the 20-bit address necessary for the one megabyte of memory. A virtual image is shown mapped into a one-megabyte display address space in Figure 14.6.

As you may now suspect, each of the Super VGAs has its own unique way to control the start address of the display. Some allow only 18-bits of start address and force the 256-color modes to begin on a plane 0 pixel, that is, mod 4 pixel. This is a logical simplification and is probably due to the address generation circuitry not being able to start on any plane other than plane 0.

A macro is provided in Listing 14.32 which loads the lower 16-bits of the start address.

LISTING 14.32 Load the lower 16-bits of the Start Address

```
;  Input parameters:
;       bx              16-bit start address
```

```
;   Output  Parameters:
;        dx                       pointing  to  CRTC  data  register


;   Calling  Protocol:
;        set_start_address
         (space  line)
         set-start  address   macro
         mono_or_color   ;determine  if  at  3Bx  or  3Dx
         add      dx,04               ;access  3x4/3x5
;        send  out  low  byte
         mov      al,0dh              ;start  address  low
         out      dx,al               ;index  start  address  low
         inc      dx                  ;point  to  data
         mov      al,bl               ;get  integer
         out      dx,al               ;send  out  low


;        send  out  high  byte
         dec      dx
         mov      al,0ch              ;start  address  high
         out      dx,al               ;index  start  address  high
         inc      dx                  ;point  to  data
         mov      al,bh               ;get  high  order  byte
         out      dx,al               ;send  out  high
endm
```

14.13   POSITIONING THE CURSOR

The cursor is positioned with a start address similar to the display start address described in Section 14.11. The lower 16 bits of the start address are in the standard VGA Cursor Position High and Low Register described in Sections 10.4.11 and 10.4.12.

Certain VGAs have one or two extended bits to position the cursor into upper memory. This is very useful in certain applications. Typically, the alphanumeric modes rely on the cursor position and no alphanumeric modes extend above the first 64 Kbytes of memory.

The VGAs that do provide extended cursor addressing allow alphanumeric pages to extend beyond the lower 64 Kbytes.

A macro is provided in Listing 14.33 which loads the lower 16-bits of the cursor position.

LISTING 14.33   Load the lower 16-bits of the Cursor Position
_____

```
;   Input  parameters:
;        bx                   16-bit  cursor  position

;   Output  Parameters:
```

```
;       dx                pointing to CRTC data register

; Calling Protocol:
;       position_cursor

        mono_or_color  ;determine if at 3Bx or 3Dx
        add    dx,04             ;access 3x4/3x5

;       send out low byte
        mov    al,0fh            ;start address low
        out    dx,al             ;index cursor position low
        inc    dx                ;point to data
        mov    al,bl             ;get integer
        out    dx,al             ;send out low

;       send out high byte
        dec    dx
        mov    al,0eh            ;start address high
        out    dx,al             ;index cursor position high

        inc    dx                ;point to data
        mov    al,bh             ;get high order byte
        out    dx,al             ;send out high
endm
```

14.14 DISPATCHING TO THE SPECIFIC SUPER VGAS

Chapters 15–21 provide details for the different manufacturers of the Super VGA chips. In addition, several manufacturers produce multiple VGA chips that must be handled separately. As seen in these chapters, identifying the VGA chip in question is not trivial. It can be time consuming if the identification is done in a low-level function.

Four techniques are presented in this section. The first identifies the VGA environment during a setup mode. At that point, only code relevant to the VGA installed in the system is used. A second technique involves identifying the VGA at the low-level functions. A third technique selects the appropriate code for the specific VGA at a high-level function. This decision is based upon a table of VGA chips. Each high-level function would be passed the appropriate VGA code. The fourth technique selects the appropriate code based on the active display mode.

14.14.1 Identifying the VGA During Setup

The VGA chip can be determined at setup, either automatically or through operator interaction. The functions necessary for automatic detection are provided in Chapters 15–21. At setup, either linkable or run-time libraries may be created that would include only the appropriate routines. No further decisions must be made as long as the VGA chip does not change.

14.14.2   Identifying the VGA at Low-level Functions

It is most logical to design a graphics system as a top-down tree. The top portion of the tree should contain the code that was not VGA manufacturer or chip specific. The bottom portion of the tree should contain the implementation specific code.

The advantages to this design process are obvious. One line drawing routine, window write or read routine could handle all of the Super VGAs. Only the lowest function, for example, the bank switching function, would need to deal with the VGA specifics.

This is the tack the VESA committee is taking with their Super VGA standards. Unfortunately, the proposal requires decision making at a very low level and could result in undesirable performance.

14.14.3   Sending Identification to Each Function

The active VGA could be identified as a part of the program's start-up initialization. All possible VGAs could be coded with a number. Each high-level function would select the appropriate lower-level functions based on this code. A typical list of VGA codes is provided in Table 14.2.

TABLE 14.2   Coded List of Super VGAs

Code	Chip Manufacturer	Chip Numbers
10	ATI	18800
11	ATI	28800
20	Chips and Technologies	82c451
21	Chips and Technologies	82c452
22	Chips and Technologies	82c453
23	Chips and Technologies	82c455
24	Chips and Technologies	82c456
30	Genoa	5000 series
31	Genoa	GVGA
40	Paradise	PVGA1a
41	Paradise	WD90C00
42	Paradise	WD90C10
43	Paradise	WD90C11
50	Trident	8800
51	Trident	8900
60	Tseng Labs	ET3000
61	Tseng Labs	ET4000
70	Video7	VEGA VGA
71	Video7	V7VGA

Chapter 15

ATI Technologies

15.1 INTRODUCTION TO THE ATI TECHNOLOGIES SUPER VGA CHIPS

ATI Technologies has two Super VGA chips. The first version of the first-generation 18800 chip version provided 1024 by 768 sixteen-color and four-color modes and up to 800 by 600 256-color modes. The sixteen-color, high-resolution mode utilized a packed format with two pixels per byte. This provided programmers with a challenge since it was not planar and consequently did not port easily to other 1024 by 768 sixteen-color Super VGA cards. A later version added an additional display mode which did provide the planar 1024 by 768 sixteen-color mode.

The VGA Wonder card is based on the 18800 chip. Version 3 of this chip contained no clock chip. Version 4 was titled the 18800-1. It did not include a clock chip. Version 5 was titled the 18800-1 and it did contain a clock chip.

The VGA Wonder+ card is based on thie 28800 chip with a clock chip. The VGA Edge is based on the 18800-1 without a clock chip while the VGA Edge-16 has a clock chip. The EGA Wonder+ is based on the 18800-1 without a clock chip.

The second generation ATI Super VGA chip, the 28800, provides a fine-tuned VGA environment for high performance. Utilizing high-speed DRAMs and FIFO buffers, the 18800 provides nearly a two-to-one speed advantage over the 28800. From a programmer's perspective the 28800 is nearly identical to the 18800.

The ATI cards also include non-volatile RAM and when used in conjunction with the VSetup program, the cards can be optimized for the desired system performance.

15.1.1 Non-Standard Display Modes

Using clever implementations, the version 1 18800 chip from ATI utilized uncommon high-resolution display modes. These modes incorporated a hybrid combination of planar and packed modes. A four-color 1024 by 768 mode was introduced and was essentially the only four-color non-CGA type mode available in the VGA. There are some clear advantages to four-color modes, and it would be useful for the industry to standardize such a mode.

Many programmers favor the sixteen-color mode implemented in a packed format. Unfortunately, it is unique to ATI Technologies. Instead of a pixel spreading its bits across the four display planes, the four bits are packed into half of a byte. This packed sixteen-color technique is the standard sixteen-color technique on the Macintosh. Fortunately, the 18800 and the 28800 Super VGA chips also includes a planar (standard) sixteen-color high-resolution mode. This is described in Section 15.7.4.

15.1.2   Locating the Extended Register Set

It is important to note where ATI Technologies locates the Extended Register Set registers. The Extended Register Set is based on indexed register pairs common to many VGA register sets. ATI has provided an indirect pointer to the location of the Index Register of this register pair (one less than the data register) in BIOS ROM at location C000:0010. To determine the address, a programmer must retrieve this address from BIOS memory. ATI warns against hard-coding the address of the Extended Register based on the company's stated prerogative to "change the location in future BIOS releases." It seems if there is a need to alter it, the change would be in future VGA chip versions and not BIOS releases.

Typically, this index address is loaded into the DX register for an output port instruction. To fetch this location without disrupting other registers, the following macro code is necessary. In the code examples which follow, it is assumed that this value is stored in a variable called *EXT* as shown in Listing 15.1.

LISTING 15.1   Get Extended Register Set Index Register Port Address Macro

```
;  Function:
;  Returns  the  value  of  the  extended  register  in  the  DX  register

;  Output  Parameters:
;      dx       Extended  Register  Set  Index  Register  Port  Address

;  Calling  Protocol:
;  get_ATI_extended

get_ATI_extended        macro
        push    es
        push    bx                      ;  save  the  two  registers  used
                                        in  this  code
        mov     ax,0c000h
        mov     es,ax           ;  load  the  BIOS  ROM  segment
```

```
        mov     bx,10h          ; load the offset to the indirect
                                  pointer
        mov     dx,es:[bx]      ; get the location of the extended
                                  registers
        pop     bx              ; restore the two registers used in
                                  this code
        pop     es
endm
```

The extended registers are at the core of every Super VGA function and the above code can take a considerable amount of time. As a result, hard coding seems inevitable.

15.1.3 Describing the ATI Extended Registers

ATI Technologies views the extended register locations and functions as proprietary information. Details regarding these registers are not readily released. It is common knowledge that each of the Super VGA manufacturers reverse-engineered the IBM VGA. ATI has done some innovative things with its implementation. However, protecting the register locations seems counter-productive. This book offers the best explanation of these extended registers given the manufacturer's constraints.

15.2 CONFIGURING THE ATI SUPER VGA

15.2.1 Configuration Fields and Setup Program

The ATI Super VGA can be configured to operate in the PC/AT bus or in the Microchannel bus. In the PC bus, a setup program is used to determine whether 8- or 16-bit ROM accesses. Auto detection hardware and software is provided to determine whether an 8- or 16-bit data path should be used. The chip is put into an interlaced mode if an interlaced monitor is sensed by the auto selection test at power-up. These features are listed in Table 15.1.

TABLE 15.1   Configuring the ATI Technologies Super VGAs

Function	Technique
Select 8-bit ROM	VSETUP program option [G]
Select 16-bit ROM	VSETUP program option [G]
Select 8-bit data path	Auto Detect 8-bit slot
Select 16-bit data path	Auto Detect 16-bit slot
Vertical NON-Interlace	Auto Monitor Select at Power-up
Vertical Interlace	Auto Monitor Select at Power-up

15.3 CONTROLLING THE ATI SUPER VGA

There are no Extended registers dedicated to enabling or disabling the VGA. The Extended registers are always enabled. Having these always enabled means that there is no "pure" VGA mode. Of special concern with the ATI VGA is the location of the extended registers. The extended register location can be determined by reading the value at C000:0010 hex. An assembly macro call is provided in Listing 15.1 to return the Extended Register in the DX Register. It returns it in the DX Register because in most cases the location is needed for port access and the DX Register contains the port address during port accesses.

15.4 INQUIRING FOR THE ATI SUPER VGA CONFIGURATION

ATI provides information in BIOS memory regarding the VGA card ID, card definition, chip revision number, monitor type, and memory size as indicated in Table 15.2.

15.4.1 Identifying the ATI VGA Card

The ATI card is identified by checking a string starting at C000:0031-003A for the following characters: 761295520. This can be accomplished through the Listings 15.2 and 15.3.

TABLE 15.2 Determining ATI Technologies Display Status

Function	Register Name	Port	Index	Bits	Value
Identify Card	9 Characters at C000:003—003A				
Card Definition	1 byte at C000:0042				
VGA Chip Revision Number	1 byte at C000:0043				
Monitor Type	Statu	Ext	BB	0–3	0–15
Memory Size	Status	Ext	BB	5	0–1

LISTING 15.2 Determining if the Card is an ATI

```
/*
Function:
 determining if the card is an ATI card

Output Parameters:
 1 card is an ATI
 0 card is NOT an ATI
```

```
Calling Protocol:
 ATI= Is_It_ATI() */

#include <string.h>
int Is_It_ATI()
{ char key[9],signature[9]; int result;

  strncpy(key,"761295520",9); /* put ATI key into string */
  Get_ATI_Key(signature); /* get ATI key */

/* compare the two strings and return the result */
 result = strncmp(key,signature,9);
 if(result=0) return(1);
    else return(0);
}
```

LISTING 15.3   Returning the ATI Signature string

```
; Function:
;       Returning the 9 bytes at C000:0031 The ATI card is
;       identified by checking a string starting at
;       C000:0031-003A for the following characters: 761295520.

; Output Parameters
;       signature       output string to load 9 characters into

; Calling Protocol:
; Get_ATI_Key(signature)

Get_ATI_Key proc far USES ES DI DS SI, arg1:FAR PTR, arg2

;       set up source pointer
        mov     ax,0c000h       ;point to VGA BIOS segment
        mov     ds,ax
        mov     si,0031h        ;location of signature

;       set up destination pointer
        les     di,arg1

;       set up for number of bytes to transfer and transfer
        mov     cx,9
        rep     movsb
        ret
Get_ATI_Key     endp
```

15.4.2 Identifying Which ATI Chip

The first and second version of the ATI 18800 chip and the 28800 chips are discussed in this book. Consequently, it is necessary to determine which version of the 18800 is present or whether the 28800 is present. The 28800 and the 18800–2 appear identical to the programmer and consequently do not need to be differentiated. The 18800–1 can be identified by its lack of a display mode 55 hex as shown in Listing 15.4. In addition, the difference can be determined by identifying the version number as discussed in the following section.

LISTING 15.4   Determine if an ATI Mode is Available

```
; Function:
; Determine if an ATI mode is available

; Input Parameters:
;       AH=12 hex                 Extended VGA Control
;       BX=5506 hex               Get Mode information
;       BP=FFFF hex               Setup for return argument
;       AL= Mode                  Desired mode number of which status
;                                 is desired


; Output Parameters:
;       BP=return                 Return argument
;                                 FFFF hex        Mode not supported
;                                 ! FFFF hex Mode supported. Value
;                                 returned is the offset into the CRTC
;                                 table for that mode. The
;                                 segment to this table is C000 hex.


; Calling Protocol:
;       response=Is_ATI_Mode_Available();

Is_ATI_Mode_Available proc far USES BP ES, arg1:byte

mov    al,arg1        ;get desired mode value
       mov    ah,12h
       mov    bx,5506h
       mov    bp,0ffffh
       int    10h            ;is mode available?
       mov    ax,bp
       ret
Is_ATI_Mode_Available endp
```

15.4.3 Identifying the ATI Chip Revision

The chip-revision number is determined by checking the byte located at C000:0043. This number increments with each revision. At this point in time, revisions 1, 2 and 3 exist. The chip version, and identification byte are determined in Listings 15.5 and 15.6. The identification byte is described in Section 15.4.4.

LISTING 15.5   Returning the ATI Information and Chip Revision

```
/*
Function:
 Determining the ATI card version number and identification

Output Parameters:
 identity pointer to ATI identity
 chip_version pointer to ATI chip version

Calling Protocol:
 Which_ATI(identity) */

 Which_ATI(identity)

char identity[2];
{ unsigned int environment;

 environment = Get_ATI_Version_ID();
 identity[0] = environment & 0xff; /* identity in lower byte */
 identity[1] = (environment>>8) & 0xff; /* chip version in upper
                                           byte*/
}
```

LISTING 15.6   Returning the ATI Version and ID Information

```
; Function:
;        Returning the identification and chip version bytes.

; Output Parameters
;        environment      integer containing Chip revision number in
;                         upper byte and identification code in lower
;                         byte
```

```
; Calling Protocol:
; environment = Get_ATI_Version_ID()

Get_ATI_Version_ID proc far USES DS SI, arg1:FAR PTR, arg2
;       set up source pointer
        mov     ax,0c000h       ;point to VGA BIOS segment
        mov     ds,ax
        mov     si,0042h        ;location of identification

;       set up for number of bytes to transfer and transfer
        mov     ax,ds:[si]      ;get 42 and 43 and return to caller
        ret
Get_ATI_Version_ID      endp
```

15.4.4 Identifying the VGA Environment

The card identity byte, located at C000:0042, provides further information about the VGA enviroment and is described in Table 15.3. This identification byte can be determined though the Listing 15.7.

Additional configuration information can be determined through Listing 15.7. This function returns the amount of memory and the current active monitor.

TABLE 15.3 ATI Identification Byte

Bit	Value	Meaning
0	0	16-bit VGA
0	1	8-bit VGA
1	1	mouse port present on display adapter
2	1	supports non-interlaced 1024x768
3	0	AT/PC
3	1	microchannel
4	1	contains programmable video clock chip
5–7		undefined

LISTING 15.7 Determining the Monitor and Memory Size

```
; Function:
;       Determining the memory size and monitor type
; Output Parameters:
;       configuration           configuration word
```

```
;                               memory definition      lower byte
;                                    0=256 Kbytes
;                                    1=512 Kbytes
;                               monitor definition     upper byte
;                                         See Table 15.4

; Calling Protocol:
;       configuration = Get_ATI_Information();

Get_ATI_Information proc far
        get_ATI_Extended                        ;load the extended
                                                 port address in dx
        mov     al,0bbh                 ;index of monitor/memory
        out     dx,al                   ;index monitor/memory port
        inc     dx
        in      al,dx                   ;get monitor and memory
                                         configuration
        mov     ah,al                   ;copy monitor into upper
        and     ah,0fh                      ;isolate monitor
        and     al,20h                      ;memory is in bit 5
        mov     cx,5
        shr     al,cl                   ;put memory bit into bit 0
        ret
Get_ATI_Information endp
```

The monitor is automatically sensed at power-up, and the card is configured accordingly. To determine the current monitor configuration, the Status register can be read and the monitor values are contained in bits 0–3, denoted by the *MON* field in Figure 15.1. The memory size, denoted by *DEF* field, returns either a 0 in bit 5 indicating 256 Kbytes of memory or a 1 in bit 5 indicating 512 Kbytes of memory. This is loaded into the upper byte of the return variable from Listing 15.7.

Status Register

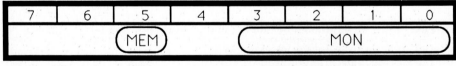

Index BB at Port EXT   Port EXT+1 Read/Write

FIGURE 15.1 ATI Status Register. The Monitor type resides in the MON field. The amount of memory is indicated in the MEM field.

The monitor configurations are listed in Table 15.4. These codes are returned in the lower byte of the return parameter from Listing 15.4.

It is possible to set the monitor to a specific code through software as shown in Listing 15.8. This function will work when switching between analog monitor types or digital monitor types. It cannot be used to switch between analog and digital monitor type.

TABLE 15.4 Monitor Configuration Codes

Status Register Bits 0–3	Monitor Type
0	EGA
1	PS/2 monochrome
2	TTL monochrome
3	PS/2 color
4	RGB color
5	Multisync
7	PS/2 8514
8	Seiko 1430
9	NEC Multisync 2A
A	Crystalscan 860/Tatung 1439
B	NEC Multisync 3D
C	TVM 3M
D	NEC MultiSync XL
E	TVM 2A
F	TVM 3A

LISTING 15.8 Load the Monitor Status Field to a Specified Monitor Type

```
; Function:
;       Load the monitor

; Input Parameters:
;       code            monitor code

; Calling Protocol:
;       Load_Monitor(code);
Load_Monitor proc far arg1:byte
```

```
              get_ATI_Extended        ;load the extended port address in dx
              mov    al,0bbh                  ;index of monitor/memory
              out    dx,al             ;index monitor/memory port
              inc    dx
              in     al,dx             ;get monitor and memory
                                       configuration

;             now load up the monitor
              mov    ah,al             ;copy monitor into upper
              and    ah,0f0h           ;isolate monitor
              or     ah,arg1           ;monitor code
              mov    al,0bbh           ;index of monitor/memory

              dec    dx                ;point back to index
              out    dx,ax             ;output new monitor/memory

              ret
Load_Monitor endp
```

15.5   ATI TECHNOLOGY DISPLAY MODES

The Super VGA alphanumeric modes are 132 columns wide, from 25 to 44 lines. All operate in the standard sixteen-color mode. Four different display fonts are utilized. These are listed in Table 15.5.

The Super VGA graphics modes span the common 16- and 256-color display modes. Two unique modes are provided, as mentioned in Section 15.2.1. These are modes 55 hex and 65 hex. The display modes 53 and 54 appear identical. Mode 53 is downwardly compatible to the ATI EGA Wonder Card which supported an 800 by 600 EGA display mode. These modes are listed in Table 15.6.

15.5.1   Display Mode 65 hex

Mode 65 hex is the 1024 by 768 sixteen-color mode which utilizes packed memory organization. This was the first technique employed by ATI Technologies to implement a 1024 by 768 mode. Another 1024x768 sixteen-color mode is mode 55h. This mode uses a planner memory organization common to all the other Super VGA chips. Older cards may not support the newer mode 55 hex.

The display memory is organized in a packed fashion, with a pair of pixels represented in each byte of display memory. A typical byte is displayed in Figure 15.2. Outside of the fact that there are two pixels per byte, the memory organization is identical to the packed display modes described in Section 15.8.6.

A major difference occurs between this mode and either the 256-color packed modes or the sixteen-color planar modes with respect to accessing the color palette. The sixteen-color planar modes utilize the 16 palette registers located

TABLE 15.5 ATI   Technologies Alphanumerics Modes

Mode	Rows	Columns	Font	Resolution	Colors	Chip
23	25	132	8x14*	1056x350	16	18800
27	25	132	8x14*	1056x350	2	18800
33	44	132	8x8	1056x352	16	18800
27	44	132	8x18	1056x352	2	18800

* 8x16 on 1056by 400 modes with analog monitor on a V5 VGA Wonder+

TABLE 15.6   ATI Technologies Graphics Modes

Mode	Resolution	Colors	Chip	Memory
53	800x600	16	18800	256 Kbytes
54	800x600	16	18800	256 Kbytes
55	1024x768	16 (planar)	18800-1	512 Kbytes
61	640x400	256	18800	256 Kbytes*
62	640x480	256	18800	512 Kbytes
63	800x600	256	18800	512 Kbytes
65	1024x768	16 (packed)	18800	512 Kbytes

* 512 Kbytes required for VGA Wonder+

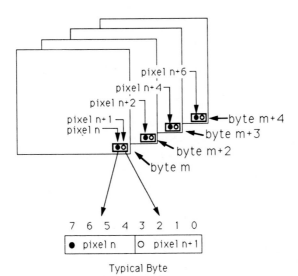

Typical Byte

FIGURE 15.2   Memory Organization for ATI MOde 65 hex. Illustrates 16-color packed organization.

in the Attribute Registers at 3C0 as described in Section 10.6. The packed mode utilizes fifteen of the locations in the color registers. Thus, this mode could be considered a pseudo 31-color mode.

Two groups of registers within the 256 color registers are used in this display mode. The first set of color registers are indexed from 0–0F, incrementing by 1. These correspond to the pixel located in the lower nibble of the byte. This pixel is labeled *pixel n+1* in Figure 15.1. This is the standard way in which a sixteen-color mode accesses the color registers.

The second group of color registers are indexed from 0–F0 incrementing by 10 hex. These correspond to the pixel located in the upper nibble of the byte. This pixel is labeled *pixel n* in Figure 15.1. This is described in Table 15.7.

It should be noted that there is no way to distinguish between the 00 of the low order pixel and the 00 of the high order pixel. ATI recommends that this pixel be left at black because the 00 palette register controls the color of the border region. I agree, since the border regions are typically problematic, and it is a good idea to keep this color black. Many VGAs allow the border region to be assigned a specific color other that one in the color palette. This is the best approach since there are times one does not want to dedicate palette register 0 to black (or any fixed color for that matter).

The external color registers can be programmed directly or through the Set Color Register BIOS calls described in Section 11.11. One simply uses the indexes 00–0F or the indexes 00–F0.

TABLE 15.7   Color Registers Used in Mode 65 hex

Low Order Pixel Index	High Order Pixel Index	Default Color Value *1
00	00	black
01	10	blue
02	20	green
03	30	cyan
04	40	red
05	50	magenta
06	60	brown
07	70	white
08	80	dark gray
09	90	light blue
0A	A0	light green
0B	B0	light cyan
0C	C0	light red
0D	D0	light magenta
0E	E0	yellow
0F	F0	bright white

15.5.2   Display Mode 67 hex

Display mode 67 hex is a 1024 by 768 four-color mode. These four colors are reminiscent of the CGA modes. This mode can best be described as a planar mode utilizing odd-even bank switching. Each pixel is represented by two bits spread across two display planes. Even pixels are represented in planes 0 and 1 while odd pixels are stored in planes 2 and 3. This is illustrated in Figure 15.3.

Locating a pixel is accomplished by first multiplying the vertical, y, coordinate by the number of bytes per display line. In this case there are 1024 pixels per scan line and eight pixels per byte. Therefore, there are 128 bytes per scan line. Each plane is 64 Kbytes long—thus single precision unsigned arithmetic

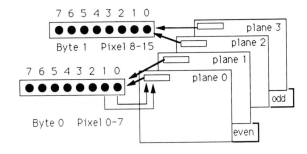

a) Planar Organization Showing 8 Pixels per Byte Resident in 2 Planes Organized in an Odd/Even Fashion. Note: Reverse pixel to display ordering. Pixel in bit 0 is left-most pixel on display.

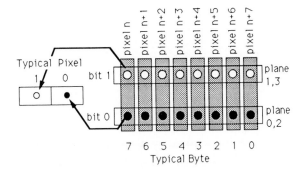

b) Memory Organization Showing a Pixel Resident in Two Display Planes

FIGURE 15.3   Memory Organization for ATI Mode 67 hex. Illustrates 4-color planar odd-even addressing.

will suffice. This number , *base_address*, forms the base address of the byte containing the eight left-most pixels in the proper scan line. Next, the horizontal pixel number, x, is divided by eight. Both the whole and the fractional parts should be calculated. The whole part of the division provides the byte number *byte_number*, which contains the pixel in question. The fractional part, *pixel_place* is saved for later. If this byte number, byte_number, is even, the pixel resides in a byte which is located in display planes 0 and 1. If the byte number is odd, the pixel resides in a byte which is located in display planes 2 and 3. Next, dividing the byte number, byte_number, by two provides the byte offset, *byte_offset*, within the selected pair of planes. Finally, the fractional part, pixel_place is used to find the bit position within the selected byte. The pixel_place resulting from the division of x/8 is used to find the actual bit position of the pixel in question. This division is also a mod 8 operation. A mask can be formed by shifting the constant 01 hex left by the number pixel_place. This occurs because the most significant bit in each byte represents the right-most pixel when mapped to the display.

The two bits refer to one of four predefined colors in one of four-color sets. The color sets are selected by setting bits 0 and 1 in the Color Select register described in Section 10.6.7. The color selections possible are shown in Table 15.8.

The palette registers are loaded with the standard index values allowing them to point to their respective color registers. The SET field, an additional field, is present in these sixteen palette registers as shown in Figure 15.4.

TABLE 15.8 Four-Color Mode Color Values

Color Set	C0=0,C1=0	C0=1,C1=0	C0=0,C1=1	C0=1,C1=1
0	black	white	gray	bright white
1	black	cyan	red	white
2	black	green	yellow	red
3	black	cyan	magenta	white

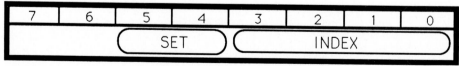

Typical Palette Register

Index 0-15 at Port 3C0   Port 3C0 Read/Write

FIGURE 15.4 ATI Palette Registers in Mode 67 hex. The palette index is stored in the INDEX field. The color set is stored in the SET field.

This SET field must contain the color set for each of the sixteen registers. Code which performs this function is provided in Listing 15.9.

LISTING 15.9   Setting up the Palette for a Four-color Color Set

```
; Function:
;       Setting up the Palette Registers for a new color set

; Inputs:
;       color_set              color set number from 0-3

; Outputs:
;       Loads the palette Registers with the color set

; Calling Protocol:
;       Set_Palette_Mode_67(color_set)

Set_Palette_Mode_67    proc far arg1:byte

;       wait for start vertical retrace period
        mov     dx,3dah                    ; load input status register
                                                 one

;       first wait for active period
wait_active:
        in      al,dx
        test    al,8                       ; look for bit = 0
        jz      wait_active     ;wait for start of vertical retrace
                                period

;       now wait for retrace period
wait_retrace:
        in      al,dx
        test    al,8                       ;look for bit 3=1
        jnz     wait_retrace    ;wait for start of vertical retrace
                                period

;       set up for transfer to palette registers
        mov     ah,arg1                    ;get color set
        mov     cl,4
        shl     ah,cl                      ;shift into the SET
                                           field bits 6-5
        mov     dx,3c0h                    ;palette register address
        xor     bl,bl                      ;start at zero
        mov     cx,16                      ;load all 16 palette registers
```

```
; load the color index value in bits 6-5 of each index register
load_all:
        mov     al,bl              ;get the palette index
        out     dx,al              ;output index
        or      al,ah              ;put in the color set bits in ah

        out     dx,al              ;output to the palette register
        inc     bl                          ;increment the
                                            index

        loop    load_all

        ret
Set_Palette_Mode_67     endp
```

15.6   ACCESSING THE ATI DISPLAY MEMORY

The ATI Technologies VGA chip maps display memory into host memory address space by using one or two bank registers. These are listed in Table 15.9. Each page maps a 64-Kbyte segment of display memory into the host address space. The values range from 0 to 15. Currently, only eight display pages are supported with the 512K maximum memory configuration.

The one-megabyte of address space, currently limited to 512K, can be mapped into the host address space through a single or dual bank mode. This feature is controlled by the E2B field in the ATI Technologies # Register. If this bit is zero, the single bank mode is selected. If one, the dual bank mode is selected. This register is shown in Figure 15.5.

In both cases, the registers are aligned to 4 Kbyte segments, providing a granularity of 4 Kbytes. The 20-bit memory address is formed by the sixteen bit address generated by the CRT addressing (low order 16-bits) added to the four bits in the Bank Select Register (high order 4 bits) shown in Figure 15.6.

15.6.1   Single Bank Mode

In the single-bank mode, one bank field, Bank in the Bank Register is used to access the bank memory in 64-Kbyte banks. This register is shown in Figure 15.7.

TABLE 15.9   Reading and Writing to ATI Technologies Display Memory

Function	Register Name	Port	Index	Bits	Value
Select Write Bank	Bank Select	Ext	B2	4–1	0–7
Select Read Bank	Bank Select	Ext	B2	7–5	0–7
Single/Dual Bank Mode	ATI Technologies				
	Register E	Ext	BE	3	0,1

ATI Register E

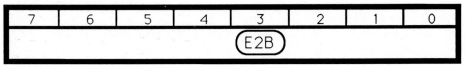

Index BE at Port EXT   Port EXT+1 Read/Write

FIGURE 15.5 ATI Register E. The E2B field enables the single or dual bank memory accessing modes.

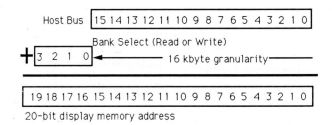

FIGURE 15.6 Creation of a 20-bit Address Using Bank Selection

Bank Register Single Bank Mode

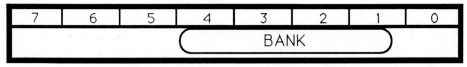

Index B2 at Port EXT   Port EXT+1 Read/Write

FIGURE 15.7 Bank Select Register in Single Bank Mode

The single-bank field, Bank, of the Bank Select Register can be loaded through the macro code in Listing 15.10. The C-callable function is provided in Listing 15.11.

LISTING 15.10   Loading the Single-bank Register Macro

```
;  Function:
;        Loading the single-bank register with a bank value of 0-15
;          representing a 64 Kbyte bank.

;  Input Parameters:
;        bl                                        bank number (0-15)

Load_Single_Bank_ATI    macro
               get_ATI_extended         ;point to extended registers in dx
               mov      al,0b2h          ;al=b2h for index to bank select
               out      dx,al            ;output to extended register index b2

;              input the current value in the bank register
               inc      dl               ;point to data of index/data pair
               in       al,dx            ;read bank select register
               mov      ah,al            ;save for later

;              put the new bank value into bits 4-1
               and      ah,0e1h          ;zero out bank bits 4-1
               shl      bl,1             ;shift left 1 bit for bits 4-1
               or       ah,bl            ;OR in bank value

mov       al,0b2h                        ;index bank register again
          dec      dl                    ;point back to index/data pair
          out      dx,ax                 ;output new value back to register
endm
```

LISTING 15.11   Loading the Single-bank Field

```
;  Function:
;  Loading the Single Bank Register

;  Input parameters
;  arg1: bank              0-7 bank value

;  Calling protocol
;  Set_Write_Bank_ATI(bank);

Set_Write_Bank_ATI proc far, arg1:byte

mov       bl,arg1         ;get bank number
          Load_Single_Bank_ATI                    ;load bank
          ret
Set_Write_Bank_ATI        endp
```

15.6.2 Dual-Bank Mode

The dual-bank mode is only supported on the 18800–1 and 28800 chip sets. In the dual-bank mode, the Bank Select Register maps 64-Kbyte segments into the host memory address space. One field is dedicated to read operations and the second is dedicated to write operations. The write bank starting address field, WB, is located in bits 3–0 while the read bank starting address field, RB, is located in bits 7–5 of the Select Bank Register as shown in Figure 15.8 and listed in Table 15.9. This register is located at Port Ext and index B2. Since each register is dedicated to a read or write operation, both can be mapped into the same host address space. An operation which writes anywhere between A0000-AFFFF will automatically use the WB field. Similarly, an operation which reads anywhere between A0000–AFFFF will automatically use the RB field.

The Dual-bank registers provide a mechanism for transferring data from one display memory location to another. The read and write fields of the Bank Select Register need to be written to only once for every time a 64-Kbyte bank is crossed.

Suppose a programmer wants to move a bank from one location to another in the display memory. It is desirable to use the REP MOVSW instruction. It is only necessary to load the Bank Select Register, set up the segment registers to both point to A000, set up the offset registers to point to the source and destination offset, and the CX Register with the number of words to move. This setup is followed by the REP MOVSW instruction. The maximum number of pixels that can be moved in one REP MOVSW sequence would be determined by the distance to the next 64-Kbyte boundary. It is necessary to set up the Bank Select Register before crossing these boundaries. This is illustrated in Figure 15.9.

Code to load the write bank address would perform a read, modify, and write operation putting the new write bank number into the Bank Select Register as shown in Listing 15.12.

Bank Register Dual Bank Mode

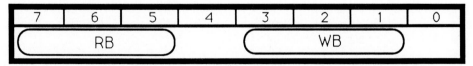

Index B2 at Port EXT   Port EXT+1 Read/Write

FIGURE 15.8 ATI Bank Register in a Dual Bank Mode. The write bank pointer is in the WB field and the read bank pointer is in the RB field.

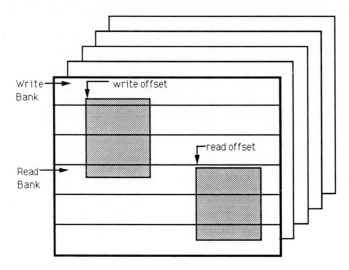

FIGURE 15.9   Display Memory Address Generation. Read/Write operations utilizing the read and write bank registers. A 20-bit address is formed by the four-bit bank value and the 16-bit offset value.

LISTING 15.12   Loading Write Bank Number In Dual Bank Mode

```
;  Function:
;        Loading the Write Bank with a new start address in dual bank
mode

;  Input with:
;        bl               Bank_Number
;                              0-7 bank number indicating desired
;                              64-Kbyte bank

;  Calling Protocol:
;  Load_Write_Bank_ATI

Load_Write_Bank_ATI      macro

;        save the registers that are used in this macro
         push    ax
         push    dx

;        set up index to Bank Select Register
         get_ATI_extended
```

```
        mov     al,0b2h
        out     dx,al               ;output index

;       Read... read Bank Select Register
        inc     dl                  ;point to data
        in      al,dx               ;read Bank Select Register
        mov     ah,al               ;put Bank Select Register
        and     ah,0f0h             ; zero out bits 3-0

;       Modify... put bank value and index into ax.
        shl     bl, 1               ;put into bit 1
        or      ah,bl               ;put Bank Value into high order byte
        mov     al,0b2h             ;put index into low order byte

;       Write.... output New Bank Register
        dec     dl                  ;point to extended index
        out     dx,ax               ;output new Bank Value Register

;       Return registers to original state
        pop     dx
        pop     ax
endm
```

Code to load the read bank address would perform a read, modify, and write operation. It puts the new read bank number into the Bank Select Register as shown in Listing 15.13.

LISTING 15.13   Loading Read Bank Number in Dual Bank Mode

```
; Function:
;       Load the Read Bank with a new start address in Dual Bank
Mode

; Input with:
;       bl              Bank_Number             0-7 bank number
                                                indicating desired
;                                               64-Kbyte bank

; Calling Protocol:
; Load_Read_Bank_ATI

Load_Read_Bank_ATI      macro

;       save the registers that are used in this macro
        push    ax
```

```
            push    dx
;           set up index to Bank Select Register
            get_ATI_extended
            mov     al,0b2h
            out     dx,al           ;output index

;           Read... read Bank Select Register
            inc     dl              ;point to data
            in      al,dx           ;read Bank Select Register
            mov     ah,al           ;put Bank Select Register
            and     ah,0f0h         ; zero out bits 7-4

;           Modify... put bank value and index into ax
            ror     bl,1
            ror     bl,1
            ror     bl,1            ;shift into bit positions 7-5
            or      ah,bl           ;put Bank Value into high order byte
            mov     al,0b2h         ;put index into low order byte

;           Write.... output New Bank Register
            dec     dl              ;point to extended index
            out     dx,ax           ;output new Bank Value Register

;           Return registers to original state
            pop     dx
            pop     ax
endm
```

The C-callable functions, which load the write and read banks in the dual paging mode, are provided in Listings 15.14 and 15.15 respectively.

LISTING 15.14   Loading the Write Bank Register in a Dual-bank Mode

```
; Function
; Load the Write Bank Register in a Dual Bank Mode

; Input parameters
; arg1: bank           0-7 bank value

; Calling protocol
; Set_Write_Bank_Dual_ATI(write_bank);

Set_Write_Bank_Dual_ATI proc far, arg1:byte
```

```
        mov     bl,arg1         ;get bank number
        Load_Write_Bank_ATI                     ;load bank
        ret
Set_Write_Bank_Dual_ATI         endp
```

LISTING 15.15 Loading the Read Bank Register in a Dual-bank Mode

```
; Function:
; Loading the Read Bank Register in a Dual Bank Mode

; Input parameters
; arg1: bank          0-7 bank value

; Calling protocol
; Set_Read_Bank_Dual_ATI(write_bank);

Set_Read_Bank_Dual_ATI proc far, arg1:byte

        mov     bl,arg1         ;get bank number
        Load_Read_Bank_ATI      ;load bank
        ret
Set_Read_Bank_Dual_ATI endp
```

The ATI dual bank mode can be enabled through the function provided in Listing 15.16. The ATI single bank mode can be enabled through the function in Listing 15.17.

LISTING 15.16 Set Up for Dual-bank mode Macro

```
;Function:
:       Enable dual bank switching
;       bank mode is single or dual based on bit 3 of ATI Extended E
;             bit 3=0 single bank
;             bit 3=1 dual bank
; Calling Protocol:
;       Enable_Dual_Bank_ATI();

Enable_Dual_Bank_ATI proc FAR
        get_extended_ATI                ;load the extended port
                                         address in dx
        mov al, 0beh                    ;index of dual paging enable
        out dx,al
```

```
            inc dl
            in al, dx                ;input value from ATI Extended E
            mov ah,al
            or ah, 08h               ;set bit 3 to 1
    ;       rewrite the new port
            dec dl
            mov al, Obeh             ;index of dual paging enable
            out dx,ax                ;output new value to ATI register E
            ret
Enable_Dual_Bank_ATI endp
```

LISTING 15.17   Set Up for Dual-bank Mode Macro

```
;Function:
;       Enable dual bank switching
;       bank mode is single or dual based on bit 3 of ATI Extended E
;               bit 3=0 single bank
;               bit 3=1 dual bank

; Calling Protocol:
;       Enable_Single_Bank_ATI();

Enable_Single_Bank_ATI proc FAR
        get_extended_ATI         ;load the extended port address in dx
        mov al, obeh             ;index of dual paging enable
        out dx, al
        inc dl
        in al, dx                ;input value from ATI Extended E
        mov ah, al
        and ah, 0f7h             ;set bit 3 to 0
;       rewrite the new port
        dec dl
        mov al, Obeh             ;index of dual paging enable
        out dx, ax               ;output new value to ATI register E
        ret
Enable_Single_Bank_ATI endp
```

15.7   CONTROLLING THE CRT ADDRESS GENERATION

15.7.1   Controlling the Start Address

The host cannot extend control of the start address of the display or of the cursor past the 64-byte segment controlled through the Start Address Low and

Start Address High registers. The ATI start address can be loaded through the function in Listing 15.18. This function utilizes the "set_start_address" macro in Listing 14.32.

Sixteen-color Modes Start Address

The memory is configured as four overlapped planes in the sixteen-color modes. Each plane is 64 Kbytes long. There is one such set of planes in the 256-Kbyte implementations and there are two groups of these planes in the 512 Kbyte configurations. These groups are called *pages*. The sixteen bits of the Start Address Low and High registers, therefore, actually point to a pixel within the 256 Kbyte page of memory. The granularity of the start address is four bytes.

Two sixteen-color display mode extend into the second bank of memory. This are the 1024 by 768 sixteen-color modes. Both of these modes, 55 hex and 65 hex, will automatically cross the page boundary during display cycles. It is not possible to set the start address beyond a location if the first page. Since the first page consists of 64 Kbytes and a single line requires 1024/8 = 128 bytes, a total of 512 scan lines can fit in the first page. Thus, the start address can not extend beyond scan line 511.

256-Color Mode Start Address

The memory is physically divided among four display planes in the 256-color modes. However, unlike the sixteen-color modes, the memory is not logically split between these four display planes in the 256-color modes. Due to the

LISTING 15.18   Loading the ATI Start Address

```
;  Function:
;       Loading the ATI Start Address

;  Input Parameters
;       address           unsigned integer starting address

;  Calling Protocol:
;       Load_Start_ATI(address)

Load_Start_ATI proc far        arg1
        mov     bx,arg1
        set_start_address          ;load the lower 16-bits of the address
        ret
Load_Start_ATI endp
```

memory organization (sequential locations being loaded across the four display pages), the 64-Kbyte span of the start addresses only covers 64 Kbytes. The 256-color modes include the 640 by 400, the 640 by 480 and the 800 by 600 resolutions. These require 256,000 bytes, 307,200 bytes and 480,000 bytes respectively. This means that the starting address can not exceed scanlines 102 for the 640-pixel-wide-display-modes and scanline 81 for the 800-pixel-wide-display-mode.

15.7.2 Cursor Control

The alphanumeric modes do not have a problem with page crossing since none extend beyond the first 256-Kbyte page. The cursor can be controlled in the alphanumeric modes by using the 16-bit cursor start address contained in the Cursor Start Address High and Cursor Start Address Low registers. These registers are discussed in Sections 10.4.15 and 10.4.16, respectively.

There is no hardware cursor capability in the ATI chip. Therefore, the hardware cursor has to be positioned through read/modify/write operations. Controlling the cursor can be done through the BIOS cursor control functions in Section 11.3.2 and 11.3.3. In addition, the programmer can use the same techniques used in accessing the memory to draw the cursor anywhere on the screen. The cursor can be positioned through the function in Listing 15.19 using the "set_cursor_position" macro found in Listing 14.33.

15.7.3 Controlling the Display Offset

The display offset determines the size of the virtual image. The 8-bit value stored in the Offset Register in the CRTC Register Group, is described in

LISTING 15.19 Positioning the ATI Cursor

```
; Function:
;      Positioning the ATI Cursor

; Input Parameters
;      address          unsigned integer starting address

; Calling Protocol:
;      Position_Cursor_ATI(address)

Position_Cursor_ATI    proc far        arg1
        mov    bx,arg1
        Set_cursor_position
        ret
Position_Cursor_ATI endp
```

Section 10.4.22. In the word mode, which is typically the case, display offsets up to 1024 bytes can be defined.

15.8   ATI TECHNOLOGY BIOS EXTENSIONS

One new BIOS call is provided called Is Mode Available?. Several modes do not support certain alphanumeric functions. Most notably, there are no graphics BIOS calls for the extended and non-standard 1024 by 768 modes. These BIOS differences are listed in Table 15.10.

The new BIOS call is accessed through AH=12 hex. This mode returns a coded value indicating whether the desired mode is available.

15.8.1   Is Mode Available?

```
Inputs:
        AH=12 hex              Extended VGA Control
        BX=5506 hex           Get Mode information
        BP=FFFF hex           Setup for return argument
        AL= Mode              Desired mode number of which status
                              is desired


Output Parameters

        BP=return             Return argument
                              FFFF hex      Mode not supported
                              Not FFFF hex  Mode is supported and
                                            value returned is the
                                            offset into the CRTC
                                            table for that mode.
                                            The segment to this
                                            table is C000 hex.
```

TABLE 15.10   ATI Technologies Super BIOS

Function	AH	Feature
Is Mode Available	12	Returns whether mode is supported
Scroll Active Page Up	06	Not Supported in Modes 61, 62, 63, 65, 67
Scroll Active Page Down	07	Not Supported in Modes 61, 62, 63, 65, 67
Read Character at Cursor	0C	Not Supported in Modes 65, 67
Write Dot	0D	Not Supported in Modes 65, 67
Read Dot	0D	Not Supported in Modes 65, 67
Write TTX	0E	Not Supported in Modes 65, 67

Chapter 16

Chips and Technologies

16.1 INTRODUCTION TO THE CHIPS AND TECHNOLOGIES CHIP SET

Chips and Technologies manufactures five Super VGA chips as listed in Table 16.1. The low-end 82c451 is intended for minimum Super VGA configurations. The 82c452 is designed for demanding graphics applications. The high-resolution 82c453 is capable of driving VRAM. Finally, the 82c455 and 82c456 are meant for the flat-panel displays.

For the most part, the chips are compatible at the register level. Unless otherwise noted, the reader may assume that documentation in this section refers to all chips in Table 16.16. Chip-specific features are indicated and multiple definitions are provided when differences occur. The 82c451 provides the core for these registers.

Chips and Technologies offers a generous set of extension registers. These allow functions to remain isolated in specific registers. Thus, the programmer is not faced with the constant problem of having to read/modify/write everything, constantly having to shift around bit fields.

The Chips and Technologies chips provide the greatest number of functions and special features of any of the Super VGAs. The 82c451 provides the basic Super VGA format. It forms the foundation for the later generation of chips. The 82c455 and 82c456 are based upon the 82c451. These are specially designed to interface to flat-panel displays.

The 82c452 is the second-generation Super VGA with an impressive array of feature. It contains just about everything that one could hope for in a Super VGA. The only major drawback is that it cannot support VRAM, nor display resolutions much greater than 640 by 480 in the 256-color modes.

The 82c453 was designed to be very fast. It is meant specifically for VRAM. It supports the high-resolution, 256-color modes.

These processors provide a high level of integration when interfaced to the PC/AT or to the microchannel bus. All processors are configured with the ability to eloquently coexist in a system with multiple Super VGAs of the same product line. Each can operate in a variety of 8- or 16-bit bus width modes.

TABLE 16.1 Chips and Technologies Super VGA Product Line

Chip	Memory	Features
82c451	256 Kbytes DRAM	Low Cost
82c452	1 Meg DRAM	Lots of features 640x480 maximum 256-color modes
82c453	1 Meg VRAM	Fast VRAM, high resolution 256-color modes
82c455	256 KDRAM	Flat Panel Display Compatible
82c456	256 KDRAM	Enhanced Flat Panel Display Compatible

16.1.1 Emulation

Downward compatibility is provided to the MDA, Hercules, CGA, and EGA through BIOS calls or direct access to the emulation registers. The programmer can choose to protect a wide variety of registers through a sophisticated selection of Write Protect fields within several Write Protect registers. Trap registers are also provided for generating traps or access to specific registers. Compatibility is also enhanced by the provision of an alternate set of CRTC registers, providing display timing control. When an emulation mode is engaged, these registers can contain the relevant timing for the specified emulation mode without disrupting the VGA timing registers.

The general trend in Super VGAs is to move away from the non-maskable interrupts and their associated traps. One problem which plagues these implementations occurs in a program like Microsoft Word. This application queries to see what adapter is present. The only way to find out if an adapter is present is to try and access a register in the questioned adapter. As soon as this query occurs, the auto-sensing VGA detects the access to the register and flags it in an attempt to access a non-VGA card. The VGA then traps and sets itself up to emulate that adapter.

The newer generation Super VGAs have implemented downward compatibility through the use of registers and special software. By using a second set of timing registers and exhaustive write protection, it is possible to emulate the other adapters without generating traps. However, this precludes auto-emulation.

16.1.2 Processing Speed

Each new chip has increased display memory. Consequently, there is need for speed in graphics processing. Hardware assist on frequently-used graphics functions, VRAM support, and fast host interfaces have dramatically improved the performance of the Super VGAs.

These chips sport several levels of pipelining and cache memories. They provide a fast interface to the host interface and to the graphics memory. The 82c453 claims to operate at the AT 8 MgHz bus rates.

16.1.3 82c451 Chip

The 82c451 is the first generation Super VGA. It provides the basic platform for the chips of a later generation. The 82c451 can support downward emulation, bank switching 132-column text modes, and up to 800 by 600 16-color modes. The VGA-standard bus interface is provided for either 8- or 16-bit transfers to the PC/AT bus and 16-bit transfers to the PS/2 via the motherboard or microchannel. The 82c451 includes a single bank register for bank switching (paging). The flat-panel controllers, the 82c455 and 82c456, are based upon this 82c451 engine.

16.1.4 82c452 Chip

The 82c452 is the second generation Super VGA chip designed to access up to one Megabyte of DRAM and to display 1024 by 768 16-color non-interlaced graphics modes. The 82c452 chip has many features not present in any of the other VGA chips. However, the 82c452 cannot support interlaced display modes.

One of the most important new features of this chip set is the ability to do non-byte aligned data transfers. This only applies to the planar modes where multiple pixels reside in each byte. The traditional technique shifts data to get it to byte align, read the data from display memory, mask off the appropriate bits, and write the data byte aligned. If eight pixels were to be written, beginning at pixel four of one byte and ending in pixel 3 of the next byte, these operations would have to be performed twice.

Chips and Technologies allows the programmer to do non-byte aligned transfers transparently. The programmer merely loads a direction and shift count before the transfer. From then on, subsequent read and write operations act as if there were no byte boundaries. Using the same example as above, a single write would suffice to send four bits to the first byte and four bits to the second byte, without disrupting the undesired bits.

Another feature is the ability to generate interrupts during vertical refresh cycles with frame interrupt counting. By using this feature, the VGA can interrupt the host processor only after a preset number of vertical refresh cycles have occurred. Other processors which allow the generation of vertical interrupts require that one interrupt be generated at each vertical refresh cycle.

16.1.5 82c453 Chip

The 82c453 is the "hot rod" of the Chips and Technologies family of Super VGA chips. It is designed specifically for VRAM memory and utilizes the VRAM capabilities better than any other implementation. Several features were sacrificed in order to fit this into silicon, that is, the hardware cursor present in the 82c452. Chips and Technologies claims that the speed of the 82c453 allows adequate control of a programmable cursor through standard read/write operations. The 82c453 has extended its banking to provide a quadruple improvement in granularity. The granularity of the bank addressing is now 4 Kbytes as opposed to the 16 Kbytes in the 82c451 and 82c452.

Certain other features were not carried over from the 82c452. These include interrupt skipping, sliding data transfers, and the hardware cursor. In many instances, the speed advantages of the 82c453 accomplish the same tasks in comparable amounts of time. For example, standard memory accessing techniques can be used to implement the non-byte aligned transfers or the hardware cursor.

Features in the 82c453 which provide the speed enhancements include uncompromised VRAM control, hardware bit masking to the display memory, and enhanced character manipulations in the 256-color graphics modes. In addition, internal data paths are filled with caches and FIFOS. The host interface has also been improved. Together, these enhancements provide a remarkably fast graphics processor.

16.1.6 82c455 Chip

Displaying VGA to a flat panel requires special implementation due to the feature differences and hardware variations between the CRT monitor and the flat panels. Supported flat panels include LCD, plasma and electroluminescent panels of varying resolutions. In addition, the 82c455 can control analog or digital CRT monitors. The 82c455 is the first generation flat-panel controller, and it is based on the 82c451 register set. Several additional registers are incorporated to assist in the control of the flat-panels. Other registers and features are included to handle the mapping of colors from the VGA color modes to the flat-panel displays. The flat-panel displays are either black and white or have limited color capabilities. The 82c455 cannot drive either.

Features in the 82c455 include 16 gray scales, text enhancements and vertical compensation for EGA modes. The 256-color Mode 13 display mode is not directly supported. Instead, it requires a special software driver.

The 82c455 can produce gray scales on panels which do not support gray levels directly, for example, LCD panels. This is accomplished through the use of linear Frame Rate Control (FRC). The 82c455 can produce gray scales on panels which do support gray levels directly, for example, on most plasma panels. This is accomplished through the use of Pulse Width Modulation (PWM).

16.1.7 82c456 Chip

The 82c456 is the second-generation flat-panel Controller and is based on the 82c455. It differs from the 82c455 in several ways. It produces a true 64 gray-scale representation of color, has hardware support for the 256-color mode, Mode 13, and produces 64 colors for the Super Twist (STN) color flat panels.

The 82c456 can support resolutions up to 800 by 600 in the 16-color modes. Extended BIOS tables are provided which allow special control parameters to accommodate the wide variety of flat-panel displays.

The 82c456 is equipped with two additional registers to handle the color mapping on panels which do not directly support gray scale, for example, LCDs. The 82c456 enhances this by the use of polynomial-based FRC counters, in addition to the linear-based FRC counters in the 82c455.

16.2 CONFIGURING THE CHIPS AND TECHNOLOGIES SUPER VGA

The Chips and Technologies Super VGA chips can be configured in a variety of ways, depending on the particular chip. Most of the configuration features either speed up the graphics operation, or provide additional flexibility.

Speed enhancements include 16-bit data and program transfers and fast address decoding. Additional flexibility allows the system to be used in a PC/AT or PS/2 , on a motherboard or adapter card, with other VGAs and in lower one Megabyte memory or upper memory.

16.2.1 Configuring the Chips and Technologies VGAs

Two registers contain the bit fields necessary to configure the VGA with respect to 8- or 16-bit transfers. These include 8/16-bit I/O or memory transfers, and the ability to enable or disable the on-card BIOS ROM as shown in Table 16.2.

The CPU Interface Register for the 82c451, 2, 4 and 5 controls the data bus width as shown in Figure 16.1. If the I16 field is set to 1, 16-bit I/O transfers are enabled. If 0, 8-bit I/O transfers are enabled. If the M16 field is set to 1, 16-bit memory transfers are enabled; if 0, 8-bit memory transfers are enabled. The ATR field provides readback information on the status of the Attribute Register flip-flop and is discussed in Section 16.4.3.

The I/O Addressing can include all 16 address bits or it can include only 10 address bits. The EGA/VGA can be accessed by 10 bits for addresses under 3FF hex. If the I/O field is set to 1, only 10 bits are used. If the I/O field is set to 0, all 16 bits are used.

16.2.2 Configuring the Flat Panel VGAs

There are several configuration fields necessary to control the flat panels. The Display Type Register shown in Figure 16.2 contains five such fields as indicated in Table 16.3.

The PD field configures the VGA to interface to a single- or double-drive flat panel. If the PD field is set to 1, the VGA is configured for a double drive. If it is 0, a single drive is expected. A double-drive system requires two distinct data ports while a single-drive system requires one port to access both panels. There is no such thing as a single panel, dual-drive system. The PO field configures the VGA to control a single- or dual-panel display. The PO field is set to 0 for a

CPU Interface

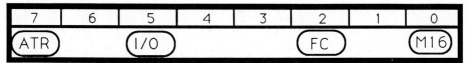

Index 02 at Port 3D6   Port 3D7 Read/Write

FIGURE 16.1 CPU Interface Register. The M16 and I16 fields select 8- or 16-bit memory cycles respectively. The FC field enables proprietary fast cycles for MCA interface only. The ATR field is a read-only field containing the attribute flip-flop status.

Panel Type 82c455/6

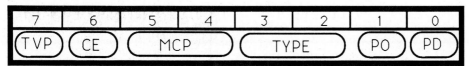

Index 51 at Port 3D6   Port 3D7 Read/Write

FIGURE 16.2 Panel Type Register for 82c455/456. The PD field configures the single/ dual drive. The PO field configures for single/dual panels. The TYPE field configures for the type of display. The MCP configures for the mono/color panels. The CE controls the compatibility Mode Enable. The TVP controls the text video output polarity.

TABLE 16.2 Configuring the Chips and Technologies Super VGAs

Function	Register Name	Port	Index	Bits	Value
Slow Decoding	CPU Interface	3D6	2	2	0
Fast Decoding	CPU Interface	3D6	2	2	1
Select 8-bit I/O	CPU Interface	3D6	2	1	0
Select 16-bit I/O	CPU Interface	3D6	2	1	1
Select 8-bit data path	CPU Interface	3D6	2	0	0
Select 16-bit data path	CPU Interface	3D6	2	0	1
Enable on-card ROM	ROM Interface	3D6	3	0	0
Disable on-card ROM	ROM Interface	3D6	3	0	1
Attribute port pairing	CPU Interface 82c453	3D6	2	4–3	0–3
16-bit I/O decoding	CPU Interface 82c453	3D6	2	5	0
10-bit I/O decoding	CPU Interface 82c453	3D6	2	5	1
Pel Panning Control	CPU Interface 82c453	3D6	2	6	0,1

TABLE 16.3   Configuring the Chips and Technologies Flat-panel Super VGAs

Function	Register Name	Port	Index	Bits	Value
Single/Dual Drive	Display Type	3D6	51	0	0–1
Single/Dual Panel	Display Type	3D6	51	1	0–1
Panel Type	Display Type	3D6	51	3–2	0–3
Mono/Color Type	Display Type	3D6	51	5–4	0–3
Horizontal Panel Size	Panel Size	3D6	52	2–0	0–7
Vertical Panel Size	Panel Size	3D6	52	4–3	0–7

TABLE 16.4   Display Types

TYPE	Display Type
0	LCD
1	CRT (default)
2	Plasma, Electroluminescent

TABLE 16.5   Monochrome or Color Panel Select

TYPE	Display Type
0	Color Panel 3 bit data pack
1	Color Panel 1 bit data pack
2	Monochrome panel

single panel and 1 for a double panel. The Type field configures the VGA for the type of display. A TTL or analog display is the reset default. Table 16.4 lists the display types.

The MCP field configures the VGA for a monochrome or color panel. Table 16.5 lists the possible Monochrome or color selections for the MCP field. The TVP field configures the system for the proper polarity of video data in the text mode. This field is only relevant to flat panels and determines whether normal or inversed video is displayed (that is, white on black or black on white).

The VGA is alerted to the size of the flat panel through the Panel Size Register shown in Figure 16.3. The horizontal size is reported in the HSIZE field, and the vertical size field is reported in the VSIZE field. The supported horizontal and vertical sizes are listed in Tables 16.6 and 16.7 respectively.

TABLE 16.6 Flat Panel Horizontal Size

HSIZE	Horizontal Size
1	640 pixels
2	720 pixels

TABLE 16.7 Flat Panel Vertical Size

VSIZE	Vertical Size
1	200 lines
2	350 lines
4	400 lines
8	480 lines

Panel Size 82c455/6

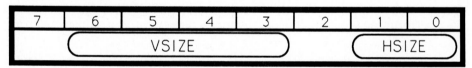

Index 51 at Port 3D6   Port 3D7 Read/Write

FIGURE 16.3 Panel Size Register for 82c455/456. The HSIZE field controls the panel horizontal resolution. The VSIZE field controls the vertical resolution.

16.2.3 On-Card ROM

The on-card can be enabled or disabled through the ROM field of the ROM Interface Register as displayed in Figure 16.4. If the ROM field is 1, the on-card ROM is enabled. If 0, the on-card ROM is disabled. In the PC/AT the default condition enables the on-card ROM. In the PS/2 microchannel interface the default condition disables the on-card ROM.

ROM Interface

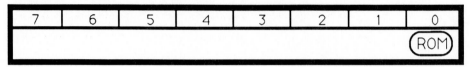

7	6	5	4	3	2	1	0
							(ROM)

Index 03 at Port 3D6   Port 3D7 Read/Write

FIGURE 16.4   ROM Interface Register. The ROM field enables the on-card ROM.

16.3   CONTROLLING THE CHIPS AND TECHNOLOGIES SUPER VGAS

16.3.1   Setup Mode

The Chips and Technologies VGA can be controlled by several registers as listed in Table 16.8. These chips are equipped with the industry-standard 46E8 and 3C3 hex registers which enable or disable the VGA and allow it to be put into a setup mode. If the VGA resides on a PC/AT adapter card, the port address for the Setup Control Register is at 46E8 hex. If the VGA resides on the motherboard, presumably in a microchannel system, it resides at port address 3C3 hex. The Setup Control Register is shown in Figures 16.5 and 16.6 for the PC/AT and motherboard respectively.

The Setup Mode can be entered and exited through Listings 16.3 and 16.4 respectively. It should be noted that no other registers in the Chips VGA register set can be accessed when the VGA is in the Setup Mode. Listings 16.1 and 16.2 perform the same functions implemented as assembly language macros.

TABLE 16.8   Resetting and Enabling the Chips and Technologies Super VGAs

Function	Register Name	Port	Index	Bits	Value
Index Extended Registers	Extended Index	3D6			0–FF
Enable VGA PC/AT	Setup Control	46E8		3	1
Disable VGA PC/AT	Setup Control	46E8		3	0
Enable VGA Microchannel	Setup Control	3C3		0	1
Disable VGA Microchannel	Setup Control	3C3		0	0
VGA Awake	Global Enable	102		0	1
VGA Asleep	Global Enable	102		0	1
Enter Setup PC/AT	Setup Control	46E8		4	1
Exit Setup PC/AT	Setup Control	46E8		4	1
Enter Setup Microchannel	Setup Control	3C3		4	1
Exit Setup Microchannel	Setup Control	3C3		4	1
Multiple VGA Enable	Extended Enable	103		4–0	0–31

Setup Control PC/AT Register

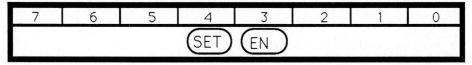

Port 46E8 Read Only

FIGURE 16.5 Setup Control PC/AT Register. Adapter Card Implementation at Port 46E8 hex. The EN field enables or disables the VGA. The SET field enters or exits the Setup mode.

Setup Control PS/2 Register

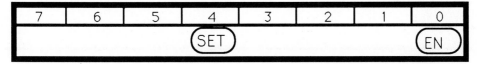

Port 3C3 Read/Write

FIGURE 16.6 Setup Control PS/2 Register. Motherboard Implementation at Port 3C3 hex. The EN field enables or disables the VGA. The SET field enters or exits the Setup mode.

LISTING 16.1 Entering into the Setup Mode

```
;  Function:
;  Entering into the setup mode

;  Calling Protocol:
;  Into_Setup_Chips()

Into_Setup_Chips proc far
        into_setup
        ret
Into_Setup_Chips endp
```

LISTING 16.2 Exit from Setup Mode

```
;  Function:
;  Exit into the setup mode
;  Calling Protocol:
;  Exit_Setup_Chips()
```

```
Exit_Setup_Chips proc far

        out_of_setup
        ret
Exit_Setup_Chips endp
```

LISTING 16.3   Going into Setup Mode Macro

```
; Function:
;       Going into of setup mode
; Calling Protocol:
;       into_setup

into_setup macro
        mov     dx, 46e8h
        mov     al, 1eh
        out     dx, al
endm
```

LISTING 16.4   Going Out of Setup Mode Macro

```
; Function:
;       Going out of setup mode
; Calling Protocol:
;       out_of_setup

out_of_setup macro
        mov     dx, 46e8h
        mov     al, 0eh
        out     dx, al
endm
```

16.3.2   Enabling and Resetting the Super VGAs

The VGA can be enabled through the EN field, bit 3, of the Setup Control Register at 46E8 or through the EN field, bit 0, at 3C3. The VGA can also be put into the setup mode through the SET field of either the 46E8 or 3C3 implementation. In the either implementation, the setup registers, xx2, 103 and 104 hex can only be accessed when the setup mode is active. Once in the setup mode, only the setup registers can be accessed.

The Extended registers are normally locked and must be turned on if access is desired. The extended registers all reside at the 3C6/3C7 indexed address pair. These can be enabled or disabled through the macros in Listings 16.5 and 16.6 respectively.

LISTING 16.5 Enabling Extensions Macro

```
; Function:
;       Enabling Extensions

; Calling Protocol:
;       enable_extensions

enable_extensions macro
        into_setup
        mov     dx,103h
        mov     al,80h
        out     dx,al
        out_of_setup
endm
```

LISTING 16.6 Disable Extensions Macro

```
; Function:
;        Disable Extensions

; Calling Protocol:
;        disable_extensions

disable_extensions macro
        into_setup
        mov     dx,103h
        mov     al,00h
        out     dx,al
        out_of_setup

endm
```

The extended registers can be turned on or off through a C function provided in Listings 16.7 and 16.8 respectively.

LISTING 16.7 Enabling the Extended Registers

```
; Function:
; Enabling the extended registers

; Calling Protocol:
;       Extended_On_Chips();
```

```
Extended_On_Chips proc far arg1:byte

        into_setup
        enable_extensions
        out_of_setup

        ret
Extended_On_Chips endp
```

LISTING 16.8   Disable the Extended Registers

```
; Function:
 ; Disable the extended registers

; Calling Protocol: */
; Extended_Off_Chips()

Extended_Off_Chips proc far arg1:byte

        into_setup
        disable_extensions
        out_of_setup

        ret
Extended_Off_Chips endp
```

16.3.3   Setup Registers

The Setup registers include the Global Enable Register, the Extended Enable Register and the Global ID Register, as shown in Figures 16.7 through 16.9, respectively.

The two principle functions of these Setup registers are to enable the extended registers and to determine the ID of the VGA. The Extended registers are an extensive set of registers which surpass the standard VGA register set as discussed in Chapter 10. These Extended registers may be enabled through the EXT field of the Extended Enable Register.

16.3.4   Controlling the Flat Panel VGAs

There are several control functions specific to the flat-panel controllers. These are listed in Table 16.9. A compatibility mode can be enabled through the CE field of the Panel Type Register shown in Figure 16.2 above. When compatibility is enabled, the display is adjusted according to three factors. These are the

Global Enable (Setup)

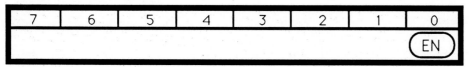

Port xx2 and Setup Mode Read/Write

FIGURE 16.7   Global Enable Register, accessed only in Setup Mode at port address xx2 indicates that any address ending in 2, within the setup registers, will access this register. Allows enabling and disabling the VGA through EN.

Extended Enable (Setup)

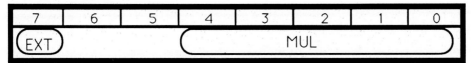

Port 103 and Setup Mode Read/Write

FIGURE 16.8   Extended Enable Register, accessed only in Setup Mode at port address 103. Allows use of multiple VGAs through MUL, and access to Extended Registers through EXT.

Global ID (Setup)

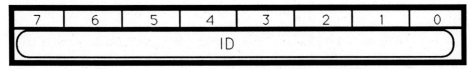

Port 104 and Setup Mode Read Only

FIGURE 16.9   Global ID Register, accessed only in Setup Mode at port address 104. The Chips I/D number resides in the ID field.

TABLE 16.9 Controlling the Chips and Technologies Flat-panel Super VGAs

Function	Register Name	Port	Index	Bits	Value
Compatibility	Display Type	3D6	51	6	0–1
Frame Rate Control	Panel Format	3D6	50	1–0	0–1
Pulse Width Mod. Control	Panel Format	3D6	50	3–2	0–1
Color Threshold	Color Mapping	3D6	63	3–0	0–1
256 Color mapping	Color Mapping	3D6	63	4	0,1
Color Lookup Enable	Color Mapping	3D6	63	5	0,1
Color Lookup Protect	Color Mapping	3D6	63	6	0,1
Graphics Output Polarity	Color Mapping	3D6	63	7	0,1
Text Video Polarity	Display Type	3D6	51	7	0–1
Blink Rate	Blink Rate Control	3D6	60	5–0	0–63
Blink Cycle	Blink Rate Control	3D6	60	7–6	0–3

Panel Format 82c455/6

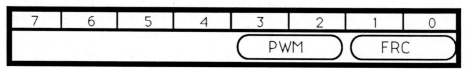

Index 50 at Port 3D6   Port 3D7 Read/Write

FIGURE 16.10 Panel Format Register for 82c456. The FRC field controls the frame rate control. The PWM controls the pulse width modulation.

panel size, current display mode and the contents of the compensation registers. The compensation registers are discussed in Section 16.3.4. If the CE field is set to 1, the compatibility mode is enabled. If 0, the compatibility mode is disabled.

It is possible to produce gray scales using flat panels. Some panels have inherent gray scale or color capabilities while others do not. The Panel Format Register, shown in Figure 16.10, controls the type of gray scale. If the panel does not support gray levels, internally gray scale is achieved through FRC. In the 82c455, linear FRC is available. In the 82c456, both linear and polynomial FRCs are possible. If the flat panel does internally support gray levels, Pulse Width modulation (PWM) is used to produce the gray scale.

The Frame Rate Control (FRC) is controlled through the FRC field of the Panel Format Register. Table 16.10 lists the possible frame rate control options.

TABLE 16.10 Frame Rate Control

FRC	Meaning
0	No gray scale simulated for monochrome systems. Eight colors for color displays.
1	Four simulated colors for color panels only. (64 colors are displayed).
2	64 gray levels simulated on monochrome panels only.

TABLE 16.11 Pulse Width Modulation

PWM	Meaning
0	No gray scales for monochrome or color systems.
1	Four colors supported by the color panels only. (64 colors are displayed).
2	Sixteen gray levels supported by the monochrome panels only.
3	256 gray levels supported by the color single panels only.

FRC performs the same function as Pulse Width Modulation. A pixel is allowed to be on or off during five cycles. For example, a pixel can be on 0, 20, 40, 60, 80 or 100 percent of the time.

The Pulse Width Modulation (PWM) is controlled through the PWM field of the Panel Format Register. Table 16.11 lists the possible pulse width modulation options.

16.3.5 Gray Levels and Color Attributes for Flat Panel VGAs

The Graphics Color Mapping Control Register shown in Figure 16.11 and the Panel Type Register shown in Figure 16.2 control the color and gray scale mapping for the flat panels.

The Text Mode Video Polarity is controlled in the TVP field of the Display Type Register. The analogous polarity for the graphics modes is controlled by the GVP field of the Graphics Color Mapping Control Register.

When no gray levels are supported, the display is bistable. This is the case when the FRC and PWM fields in the Panel Format Register are set to 0. In a bistable display, it is necessary to threshold a color so all values less than that threshold are mapped to a 0, and all values equal or above the threshold are mapped to a 1. The Color Threshold Value is controlled through the THRESH field of the Graphics Color Mapping Control Register.

Graphics Color Mapping Control 82c455/6

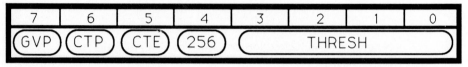

Index 63 at Port 3D6   Port 3D7 Read/Write

FIGURE 16.11   Graphics Color Mapping Control Register for 82C455/6. The THRESH field contains the grapics threshold value. The 256 field controls which nibble to use for the 8-bit color. The CTE field enables the color table lookup. The CTP field write protects the color lookup table. The GVP field controls the graphics video polarity.

When the VGA is in a 256-color mode, either the low four bits or the upper four bits of the 8-bits-per-pixel value can be used to generate a four-bit value. If the 256 field of the Graphics Color Mapping Control Register is set to 1, the upper four bits are used to generate a 16-level color. If the 256 field is set to 0, the lower four bits are used.

The internal color lookup table can be enabled or disabled through the CTE field. If the CTE field is set to 1, the internal color table is enabled. If 0, the internal color table is disabled. The internal color table can be write protected through the CTP field. If the CTP field is set to 1, the internal color table is enabled. If 0, the color table is disabled. Write protecting the internal color lookup table is contingent on the attribute registers being write-protected.

The blink rate of the the cursor, characters and pixels can be controlled though the Blink Rate Control Register shown in Figure 16.12.

The cursor blink rate determines the frequency of the character and dot blink rates. The blink rate is determined by the number of vertical sync periods during which the cursor will be on and off. The cursor blink duty cycle is fixed at a 50 percent duty cycle. The character and blink period will be twice that of the cursor blink period. This means it will blink twice as slow. The equation used to determine the blink rate uses the value in the RATE field as follows:

```
Cursor Blink Frequency = Vertical Sync Frequency * 2 * (RATE+1)
```

The blink duty cycle determines the brightness of the character or pixel that is blinking. The duty cycle is controlled through the CYCLE field as shown in Table 16.12. Note that the cursor is restricted to a 50 percent duty cycle.

16.3.6   Frame Rate Control in the 82c456

The 82c456 can use either linear or polynomial-based FRC to generate gray scales on flat panel displays which do not have internal gray levels. FRC is based on time sharing the pixel. This is identical to the PWM features of the internal gray scale panels. Time sharing is sufficient for the 16-color modes.

Blink Rate Control 82c455/6

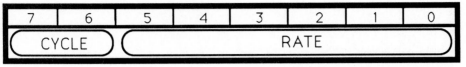

Index 60 at Port 3D6   Port 3D7 Read/Write

FIGURE 16.12 Blink Rate Control Register for 82c455/6. The RATE field controls the blink rate. The CYCLE field controls the blink duty cycle.

TABLE 16.12 Attribute Blink Duty Cycle

CYCLE	Duty Cycle
1	25 percent
2	50 percent
3	75 percent

In addition to time sharing, it is possible to dither the image to produce subjective gray scale. Since mode 13 hex is 320 by 200 pixels, dithering can be used to zoom this resolution to 640 by 400. Each pixel in the Mode 13 space can be represented by four pixels in the 640 by 400 space. The pattern generator which produces the dither is controlled through the polynomial generator.

The FRC and Palette Control Register, shown in Figure 16.13, controls the type of frame rate control and selects the palette. If the EN field of the FRC and Palette Control Register is set to 1, the polynomial FRC counters are used. If the EN field is set to 0, the linear FRCs are used.

If the polynomial-based FRC option is engaged, the polynomial N and M values determine the offset in row and columns of the FRC count. The N and M values are controlled through the PN and PM fields respectively of the Polynomial FRC Control Register shown in Figure 16.14. Trial and error can produce a variety of effects. Programmers are encouraged to experiment with different values of N and M.

16.3.7 Flat Panel Palette

To produce the color or gray level, the 82c456 can bypass the external palette, always use the external palette, utilize the external palette only during 256-color modes, or always employ 64 gray levels for the 256-color modes and 16 gray levels for all other modes. This ability is controlled through the PS field. The PS field is described in Table 16.13. The 82c455 always bypasses the external flat-panel palette.

FRC and Palette Control 82c456

Index 6D at Port 3D6   Port 3D7 Read/Write

FIGURE 16.13   FRC and Palette Control Register for 82c456. The EN field enables the FRC mode. The LC field controls the maximum number of gray levels. The PS field selects the Palette.

Polynomial FRC Control 82c456

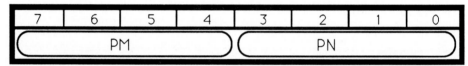

Index 6E at Port 3D6   Port 3D7 Read/Write

FIGURE 16.14   Polynomial FRC Control Register for 82c456. The PN and PM fields control the values in the polynomial counters.

TABLE 16.13   Flat Panels Palette

PS	External Palette	16-color modes	256-color modes
0	Bypass	bypass	bypass
1	Conditional	bypass	use
2	Use	use	use
3	Use	16 gray levels	64 gray levels

16.3.8   Flat Panel SmartMap

The compression from the 16-color modes to gray scale requires an intelligent algorithm. The algorithm used by the 82c455 and 82c456 is called *Smartmap*. The Smartmap feature is used when 16 gray levels are supported. This is indicated by the FRC=2 and PWM=2 values in the Panel Format Register. It is controlled through the Smartmap Control Register shown in Figure 16.15. The Smartmap feature is enabled by setting the EN field of this register to 1. If 0, the Smartmap feature is disabled. If the Smartmap feature is disabled, the color-lookup table is used. If the Smartmap feature is enabled, the color-lookup table is bypassed.

Smartmap Control 82c455/6

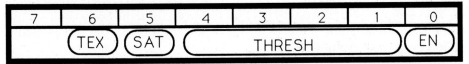

7	6	5	4	3	2	1	0
	TEX	SAT		THRESH			EN

Index 61 at Port 3D6   Port 3D7 Read/Write

FIGURE 16.15 Smart Map Control Register for 82c455/6. The EN field enables or disables the Smartmap function. The THRESH field contains the background and foreground color difference threshold. The SAT field contains the Smartmap saturation value. The TEX field enhances the text by reversing the 7 and F text attributes on the 82c456.

Smartmap Shift Parameter 82c455/6

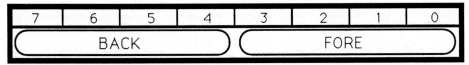

7	6	5	4	3	2	1	0
		BACK				FORE	

Index 62 at Port 3D6   Port 3D7 Read/Write

FIGURE 16.16 Smartmap Shift Parameter Register for 82c455/6. The FORE field contains the number of levels to shift the foregound color. The BACK field contains the number of levels to shift the background color.

The Smartmap threshold defines the minimum difference between the foreground and background colors. If the difference is zero, it may not be possible to differentiate the colors. It is desirable to spread apart the foreground and background colors to achieve a sufficient contrast. The amount of desirable contrast depends on the application.

The THRESH field of the Smartmap Control Register defines the minimum difference between the foreground and background colors before they are spread apart. If the threshold is not crossed, the foreground and background colors are spread apart. These are spread by an amount indicated in the FORE and BACK fields of the Smartmap Shift Parameter Register shown in Figure 16.16.

The FORE field controls the number of levels to shift the foreground color when the THRESH value is not crossed. If the foreground color is greater than the background color, the FORE field is added to the foreground color. If the foreground color is less than the background color, the FORE field is subtracted from the foreground color.

The BACK field controls the number of levels to shift the background color when the THRESH value is not crossed. If the foreground color is greater than the background color, the BACK field is subtracted from the background color. If the foreground color is less than the background color, the BACK field is added to the background color.

The text attributes can be enhanced by the TEX field of the Smartmap Control Register. If the TEX field is set to 1, the text attributes 07 and 0F hex are reversed. The text attribute 07 hex is normally bright gray while the attribute 0F hex is darker gray. If the TEX field is 0, the text attributes are not altered.

16.3.9 Flat Panel Compensation

When controlling a CRT, the VGA provides the master timing. If the CRT can accommodate the scan rates and bandwidth, the VGA can produce a wide variety of pixel resolutions on the screen. The VGA also controls the timing of the display data which allows the image to be moved on the screen. Positioning, centering and filling the screen with the image are relatively straightforward tasks.

Unlike the continually variable CRTs, the flat-panel displays have a fixed number of horizontal and vertical pixels. The VGA has few options regarding positioning the image on the display. A pixel can be written to or skipped. Similarly, a scan line can be written to or skipped.

This presents difficulties when a VGA controller has to provide multiple resolutions. The flat panels are typically 640 pixels wide. This works out very well since the common widths are 320 and 640. Obviously, one would not want to use an 800 or 1024 wide scan line. The 320-pixel width is accommodated by simply writing each pixel twice to fill the 640 flat-panel width. The MDA modes use 720 pixels wide with 9-pixel-wide characters. This can be rectified by dropping the resolution to 640 pixels and utilizing 8-pixel wide characters. If all display accesses go through the BIOS, this works out well. However, graphics modes which utilize the Hercules standard will have problems fitting the 720 pixels into the 640 flat-panel width.

A common height for flat panels is 240 scan lines. Placing two flat panels together provides 480 scan lines. This is a good match for the 480 scan line modes. However, the VGA commonly uses the 350 and 400 scan line modes. To fit the 350 or 400 lines into the 480 scan-line display, the 82c455 and 82c456 use compensation.

There are two types of compensation—text-mode and graphics-mode compensation. It is possible to disable text and use graphics-mode compensation even if the VGA is in a text mode.

Compensation either compresses or stretches the image to fit the image into the flat-panel display space. In a text mode, only compression is allowed. An example of text-mode compensation is shown in Figure 16.17.

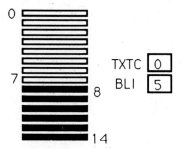

FIGURE 16.17 Text-mode Compressing Compensation. For example, a 200-line mode on a 350-line panel.

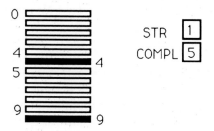

FIGURE 16.18 Graphics -mode Vertical Compensation. For example, 350 lines on a 380-line pane

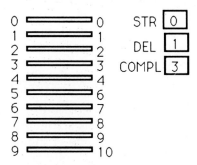

FIGURE 16.19 Graphics-mode Stretching Compensation. For example, program every line except fourth to repeat. 200 lines on a 350-line panel.

In a graphics mode, either compression or stretching is allowed. Compression is illustrated in Figure 16.18, and stretching is illustrated in Figure 16.19. Programmers should recall that graphics-mode compensation can be used in a text mode.

Text-mode compensation is controlled by three registers. One register corresponds to 350 line modes when the number of scan lines per character row is greater than 8. A second corresponds to 350 line modes when the number of scan lines per character row is less than or equal to 8. The third corresponds to 400 line modes. Text-mode compensation can insert a programmable amount of blank lines in between each displayed row of data.

The three registers which which control text-mode compensation are identical in operation. When there are 350 scan lines and a character is represented by greater than 8 lines, text mode compensation is controlled through the Text Mode 350_A Compensation Register shown in Figure 16.20. When there are 350 scan lines and a character is represented by 8 or less scan lines, text-mode compensation is controlled through the Text Mode 350_B Compensation Register shown in Figure 16.21. When there are 400 scan lines, text-mode compensation is controlled through the Text Mode 400 Compensation Register shown in Figure 16.22.

In each of these three registers, the type of compensation is controlled through the TXTC field. If the TXTC field is set to 0, text-mode compensation is enabled and blank lines are inserted after each row. The inserted blank lines are the color of the border color. If the TXTC field is set to 1, the text-mode compensation is disabled and graphics compensation will be used if it is enabled.

The number of blank lines inserted is controlled through the BLI field. The BLI field contains the number of blank scan lines + 1 to insert after each row. This field is effective only when the text-mode compensation is enabled, TXTC=0.

Graphics mode compensation is controlled through two registers, one corresponds to 350 line graphics modes while the second register corresponds to 400 scan line modes. Three techniques may be used. One technique allows a blank scan line to be interjected after a programmable number of displayed scan lines. A second technique allows a scan line to be periodically replicated after a programmable number of scan lines. A third allows a scan line to be periodically deleted after a programmable number of scan lines. A qualifier to all these modes allows the programmable number, used in the three described techniques, to be incremented every other period.

The two graphics compensation registers are identical in their functioning. The Graphics Mode 350 Compensation Register shown in Figure 16.23 is used when a 350-line graphics mode is active. The Graphics Mode 400 Compensation Register shown in Figure 16.24 is used when a 400-line graphics mode is active.

The two types of compensation allow stretching or compressing the vertical display. The stretch feature is controlled through the STR field. If the STR field is set to 1, vertical stretching is enabled and a scan line is replicated periodically every N lines. The compress feature is enabled through the DEL field. If the DEL field is set to 1, vertical deletion is enabled and a scan line is deleted periodically every N lines.

The number of lines, N between a stretch or compress is controlled through

Text Mode 350_A 82c455/6

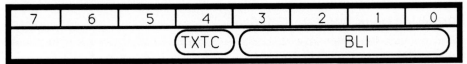

Index 55 at Port 3D6   Port 3D7 Read/Write

FIGURE 16.20 Text Mode 35O_A Register for 82c455/6. The BLI field controls the number of blank lines+ 1 inserted after each row. The TXTC field is the compensation type for fonts larger than eight lines.

Text Mode 350_B 82c455/6

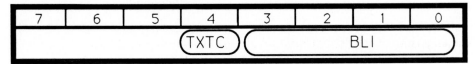

Index 56 at Port 3D6   Port 3D7 Read/Write

FIGURE 16.21 Text Mode 350_B Register for 82c455/6. The BLI field controls the number of blank lines+ 1 inserted after each row. The TXTC field is the compensation type for fonts eight lines or smaller.

Text Mode 400 82c455/6

Index 57 at Port 3D6   Port 3D7 Read/Write

FIGURE 16.22 Text Mode 4000_B Register for 82c455/6. The BLI field controls the number of blank lines+ 1 inserted after each row. The TXTC field is the compensation type.

Graphics Mode 350 82c455/6

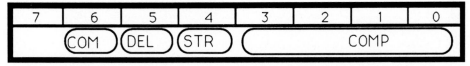

Index 58 at Port 3D6   Port 3D7 Read/Write

FIGURE 16.23 Graphics Mode 350 Register for 82c455/6. The COMP field controls the number of displayed scan lines between replication or skip. The STR field enables the vertical stretch function. The DEL field enables the vertical delete function. The COM field controls an increment of the COMP field every other period.

Graphics Mode 400 82c455/6

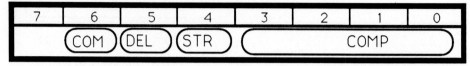

Index 59 at Port 3D6   Port 3D7 Read/Write

FIGURE 16.24 Graphics Mode 400 Register for 82c455/6. The COMP field controls the number of displayed scan lines between replication or skip. The STR field enables the vertical stretch function. The DEL field enables the vertical delete function. The COM field controls an increment of the COMP field every other period.

the COMP field. The COMP field contains the number of displayed scan lines between a stretch or compress. In addition, double scanning can represent a single line by two displayed scan lines.

16.4 INQUIRING ABOUT THE CHIPS AND TECHNOLOGIES CONFIGURATION

The programmer can acquire information about the Super VGA chips. The chip identification, amount of memory, and card ID can be identified as indicated in Table 16.14.

16.4.1 Identifying the Chips and Technologies VGA

The VGA ID can be found through the ID field of the Global ID register. This field can be used to identify the chip as indicated in Table 16.15.

A Chips and Technologies Super VGA can be identified through the code in Listing 16.9.

TABLE 16.14 Determining Chips and Technologies Display Status

Function	Register Name	Port	Index	Bits	Value
Chip Version	Chip Version	3D6	0	7–0	0–255
Memory Map	Memory Mapping	3D6	4	1–0	0–3
Card ID Microchannel	Microchannel ID high	101		7–0	0–255
Card ID Microchannel	Microchannel ID low	100		7–0	0–255
PC/AT Bus	Configuration	3D6	26	0	1
PS/2 Bus	Configuration 82c453	3D6	26	0	0
VRAM Memory	Configuration 82c453	3D6	26	2–1	0–3

TABLE 16.15   Chips and Technologies Identification Numbers

ID Field	Meaning
A5 hex	Chips and Technologies Chip

LISTING 16.9   Determining if the Chip is a Chips and Technologies Super VGA

```
/*
Function:
 Determining if the chip is a Chips and Technologies Super VGA

Output Parameters:
 1 card is an Chips
 0 card is NOT an Chips

Calling Protocol:
 Chips= Is_It_Chips()  */

int Is_It_Chips()
{ unsigned char value; int flag;
into_setup();

value = inp(0x104); /* input Global ID register */
if(value==0xa5) flag=1;
        else flag=0;

exit_setup();
return(flag);
}
```

16.4.2   Identifying Which Chips and Technologies VGA

The chip version can be found in the Chip field of the Chip Version Register shown in Figure 16.25. The first version is Number 11 hex. This number increments for every revision. The chip number may be a 82c451, 452, 453, 455 or 456. Which Chips and Technologies Super VGA is in place can be identified through Listing 16.10. The chip number can be identified by the returned identity through the codes in Table 16.16.

Chip Version

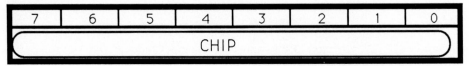

Index 00 at Port 3D6   Port 3D7 Read/Write

FIGURE 16.25   Chip Version Register. The chip version number is located in the CHIP field.

LISTING 16.10   Determining Which Chips and Technologies Super VGA Chip

```
/*
Function:
 Determining the Chips and Techologies chip Number

Output Parameters:
  identity      integer containing chip code. The version register
                contains two hex character. The hex character in
                the upper nibble is a chip code.
                        1 = 82c451
                        2 = 82c452
                        3 = 82c453
                        5 = 82c455
                        6 = 82c456
                The hex character in the lower byte is the version
                number.

Calling Protocol:
  identity = Which_Chips() */

int Which_Chips()

{ int answer; unsigned char old_value,value,version;

Extended_On_Chips(); /* turn on extensions */

outp(0x3d6,00); /* Chip Version Register */
version = inp(0x3d7)&0xf0;    /* get chip id but remove version */

switch(version)
{
  case 0x10: /* must differentiate between 451 and 452 */
```

```
outp(0x3D6,0x3a); /* see if Graphics Cursor Color 1 is there */
old_value = inp(0x3D7);
outp(0x3d7,0xaa);       /* modify register */
value = inp(0x3D7);     /* read back register */
outp(0x3d7,old_value); /* restore register */
if(value==0xaa) answer=2;
          else answer=1;

break;
  case 0x20: answer=5; break;
  case 0x30: answer=3; break;
  case 0x50: answer=6; break;
}

Extended_Off_Chips();
return(answer);
}
```

TABLE 16.16   Identifying the Chips
and Technologies Chip Number

Code	Chip Number
1	82c451
2	82c452
3	82c453
5	82c455
6	82c456

16.4.3   Determining the Attribute Flip-Flop Status

Accessing the Attribute Index Register, as described in Section 10.6, controls a flip-flop which determines whether the port address 3C0 is an Index or Data register. The status of this flip-flop can be read in the ATR field of the CPU Interface Register shown in Figure 16.1. This field is the same for the 82c451,2,3,5 and 6.

16.4.4   Addressing the Attribute Registers

The I/O addressing of the Attribute Registers is strange due to the internal flip-flop. This can be rectified through the ACM field of the CPU Interface Register shown in Figure 16.1. If the ACM field is set to 1, the Attribute register index/

Configuration 82c453

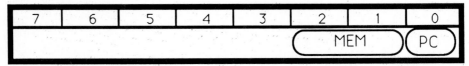

Index 26 at Port 3D6   Port 3D7 Read/Write

FIGURE 16.26 Configuration Register for 82c453. The PC field describes whether the 453 is in a PC/AT or Microchannel. The MEM field describes teh VRAM memory configuration.

TABLE 16.17 VRAM Memory

MEM field	Amount of memory	# Chips	Chip Configuration
0	512 Kbytes	16	64 Kbyte x 4
1	512 Kbytes	4	256 Kbyte x 4
2	1 Megabyte	8	256 Kbyte x 4
3	512 Kbytes	8	64 Kbyte x 4

data pair is accessed through 3C0 and 3C1 respectively. This works for either 8-bit or 16-bit port accesses. If the ACM field is set to 2, the Attribute register index/data pair is also accessed through 3C0 and 3C1 respectively. However, this only works for 8-bit port accesses. This is non-standard and will not work for all of the other Super VGAs. On the other hand, it is simpler and faster to use. Several Super VGAs have such a feature. If the ACM field is set to 0, normal addressing at 3C0 for both the index and data occurs.

16.4.5 VRAM Memory 82c453

The 82c453 supports VRAM memory. The amount and configuration of this memory can be determined through the MEM field of the Configuration Register for the 82c453 shown in FIgure 16.26. The MEM field is described in Table 16.17.

16.4.6 82c453 on a PC or AT

The host computer can be determined through the PC field of the Configuration Register for the 82c453 shown in Figure 16.26. If the host computer is a PC/AT the PC field will return a 1. If the host computer is a PS/2, the PC field will return a 0.

TABLE 16.18   Chips and Technologies Alphanumerics Modes

Mode	Rows	Columns	Font	Resolution	Colors	Chip
60	25	132	8x8	1056x400	16	451/452/453
61	50	132	8x8	1056x400	16	451/452/453

TABLE 16.19   Chips and Technologies Graphics Modes

Mode	Resolution	Colors	Chip	Memory Organization
25	640x480	16	451/452/453	planar
6A	800x600	16	451/452/453	planar
70	800x600	16	451/452/453	planar
71	960x720	16	452	planar
72	1024x768	16	452/453	planar
78	640x400	256	451/452/453	packed
79	640x480	256	452/453	packed
7A	768x576	256	452	packed
7C	800x600	256	453	paked
7E	1024x768	256	453	packed

16.5   CHIPS AND TECHNOLOGIES DISPLAY MODES

Chips and Technologies supports all of the standard super display modes as shown in Tables 16.18 and 16.19. The alphanumeric modes support 132 column displays; the graphics modes go up to 1024x768 256-color. All 16-color display modes operate in the Planar Display Mode. All 256-color modes operate in the Packed Display Mode.

16.6   ACCESSING CHIPS AND TECHNOLOGIES DISPLAY MEMORY

The Chips and Technologies solution to accessing the extended memory is simple and effective. It should be clear by now that the objective is to map the display memory into a 64-Kbyte host memory address segment. Control of the memory access is accomplished through manipulation of the extended registers.

TABLE 16.20 Bank Granularity

Chip	Memory	Mode	Granularity
82c451,5,6	256 Kbytes	packed	64 Kbytes
82c451,5,6	256 Kbytes	planar	not applicable
82c452	1 Megabyte	packed	16 Kbytes
82c452	1 Megabyte	planar	4 Kbytes
82c453	1 Megabyte	packed	4 Kbytes
82c453	1 Megabyte	planar	1 Kbytes

The bank registers described in the following sections provide three distinct granularities as shown in Table 16.20.

The bank granularity for the 451, 455 and 456 only relates to the Packed Display Mode due to the 256 Kbyte memory limit. The planar modes are orgainized as four planes, each 64 Kbytes long. The only packed mode which fits into the 256 Kbytes is Mode 13 hex. Mode 13 hex is a 320 by 200 display mode requiring 64 Kbytes. The bank selection therefore allows Mode 13 hex to access all 256 Kbytes of memory.

The bank granularity for the 452 is 16 Kbytes for the Packed Display Modes and 4 Kbytes for the Planar Display Modes. The factor of four difference is again based on the four overlapped display planes.

The bank granularity for the 453 is 4 Kbytes for the Packed Display Modes and 1 Kbyte for the Planar Display Modes. The factor of four difference is again based on the four overlapped display planes. The factor of four improvement over the 452 is due to the two additional bits in the bank registers.

16.6.1 Accessing 82c451 Display Memory

The 82c451 is configured with 256 Kbytes of display memory. The registers relevant to memory accessing are listed in Table 16.21. The memory mapping register has one field in the 82c451, shown in Figure 16.27 The MEM field of Figure 16.11 controls the memory addressing. If 0, the memory is VGA compatible. If 1, the extended memory is mapped as four pages of 64 Kbytes each or two pages of 128 Kbytes each.

Either the 64-Kbyte or 128-Kbyte addressing is in effect, based on the page number field (PN field) 82c451 CPU Paging Register as show in Figure 16.28. This two-bit page number defines which of the 64-Kbyte banks of display memory is to be mapped into CPU address space. Thus, all 256 Kbytes of memory on the 82c451 can be accessed.

TABLE 16.21   Accessing Chips and Technologies Display Memory in the 82c451

Function	Register Name	Port	Index	Bits	Value
Select VGA Compatibility	Memory Mapping	3D6	4	2	0
Memory Quad Mode	Memory Mapping	3D6	4	2	0
Memory Map Mode	Miscellaneous	3CE	6	3–2	0–3
Bank Switching	CPU Paging	3D6	B	1–0	0–3

Memory Mapping 82c451, 455, 456

Index 04 at Port 3D6   Port 3D7 Read/Write

FIGURE 16.27   Memory Mapping Register for the 82c451 allows access to extended memory through the MEM field.

CPU Paging 82c451, 455, 456

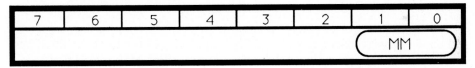

Index 0B at Port 3D6   Port 3D7 Read/Write

FIGURE 16.28   CPU PagingRegister for the 82c451selects one of four 64 kbyte segments to be mapped into CPU address space through the MEM field.

16.6.2   Accessing 82c452/453 Display Memory

The 82c452 and 82c453 provide the programmer with a great deal of flexibility and control over the display memory. The relevant registers used to map the display memory into the host memory space are listed in Table 16.22.

In the 82c452/453 implementations, the host CPU can access the display memory through bank switching. The programmer can select to utilize one or

TABLE 16.22   Reading and Writing to Chips and Technologies Display Memory

Function	Register Name	Port	Index	Bits	Value
Single Bank	CPU Paging	3D6	B	1	0
Dual Banks	CPU Paging	3D6	B	1	1
VGA Standard Memory	CPU Paging	3D6	B	0	0
512k or 1 Meg Memory	CPU Paging	3D6	B	0	1
Display Address Don't Divide	CPU Paging	3D6	B	2	0
Display Address Divide by 4	CPU Paging	3D6	B	2	1
Single/Low Bank Start Adr.	Single/Low Map	3D6	10	5–0	0–63
High Bank Start Address	High Map	3D6	11	5–0	0–63

CPU Paging 82c452,453

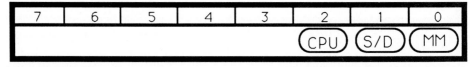

Index 0B at Port 3D6   Port 3D7 Read/Write

FIGURE 16.29   CPU Register for the 82c453. The divide by 4 mode is enabld by CPU. The Single/Dual mode is controlled by S/D and the Extended Memory is controlled by MM.

two bank registers. Three registers permit utilization of the bank facility. These are the CPU Paging, the Single/Low Map and the High Map registers as shown in Figures 16.29 to 16.31.

The CPU Paging Register controls memory compatibility mapping through the MM field, whether the system is in a single- or dual-bank (paging) mode through the "S/D" field. It also controls how the CPU should access memory in display mode 13 hex.

If the MM field is a 0, the memory is configured as 256 Kbytes of VGA-compatible memory. If 1, the memory is configured for the extended modes and enables access to the 512K or one-megabyte memory configurations. If the S/D field is 0, only the Single/Low Map Register is used to page through the memory. If 1, two bank registers can be used in parallel. These are both the Single/Low Map and the High Map registers. If the CPU field is 0, no divide by four occurs, and the display memory in Mode 13 hex is accessed as normal. If 1, the CPU addresses are divided by four. This allows access to all of the display memory in Mode 13 hex and permits display memory to be accessed sequentially.

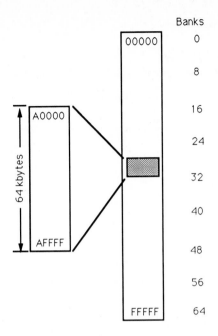

FIGURE 16.30 Single Map Single/Low Map = 100 addressing a 64-byte segment from 64000 to 73FFF.

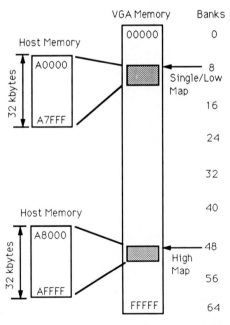

FIGURE 16.31 Dual Map Single/Low = 32 to address a 32-Kbyte segment from 20000-27FFF and High Map=192 to address 32-Kbyte segment from C0000 to C7FFF.

Single/Low Map 82c452

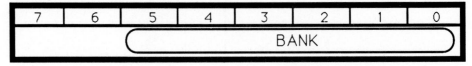

Index 10 at Port 3D6   Port 3D7 Read/Write

FIGURE 16.32 Single/Low Map Register for the 82c452. Contains bank starting address for full single or dual mapping modes in the BANK field.

High Map 82c452

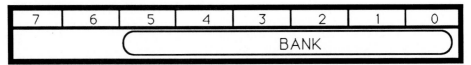

Index 11 at Port 3D6   Port 3D7 Read/Write

FIGURE 16.33 High Map Register for the 82c452. Contains bank starting address for full single or dual mapping modes in the BANK field.

The bank (page) registers of Figures 16.32 and 16.33 control the bank selection of the display memory. The Single/Low Register contains the bank starting address when the system is configured for one bank register when the S/D field is set to 0. It also controls the bank starting address of the lower 32 Kbytes of display memory when the S/D field is set to 1. If the S/D field is set to 1, the upper 32 Kbytes of display memory is accessed through the bank start address in the High Map Register.

16.6.3 Accessing 82c453 Display Memory

The 82c453 handles bank switching in a fashion similar as the 82c452. The major difference is that the 453 provides finer granularity. As can be seen in Figures 16.34 and 16.35, the BANK fields are each 8-bits wide. This provides a 1-Kbyte granularity in the planar display modes and a 4-Kbyte granularity in the packed modes.

16.6.4 Single Paging

The 82c451, 455 and 456 are always in a single-paging mode. The 82c452 and 82c453 can be put into a dual-paging mode. If the system is configured in a single map mode, the Single/Low Map Register contains the bank start address.

Single/Low Map 82c453

Index 10 at Port 3D6   Port 3D7 Read/Write

FIGURE 16.34 Single/Low Map Register for the 82c452. Contains bank starting address for full single or dual mapping modes in the BANK field.

High Map 82c453

Index 11 at Port 3D6   Port 3D7 Read/Write

FIGURE 16.35 High Map Register for the 82c452. Contains bank starting address for full single or dual mapping modes in the BANK field.

The value in the MAP field ranges from 0 to 63. It indicates the 4-Kbyte starting boundary. For example, a 1 in the MAP field causes the host 64-Kbyte memory beginning at A0000 to be mapped into display memory, beginning at memory address 4096. This is illustrated in Figure 16.30. The granularity of the bank mapping is 4 Kbytes.

Single-mode paging is enabled through the code in Listing 16.11.

LISTING 16.11   Setting up for single-mode paging

```
; Function:
;       Setting up for single-mode paging

; Calling Protocol:
;       Set_Single_Paging_Chips();

Set_Single_Paging_Chips proc far
```

```
;        set up index to CPU Paging Register
         mov    dx,3d6h        ;point to CPU Paging Register
         mov    al,0bh
         out    dx,al

;        input the current value for non-destructive output
         in     al,dx          ;input CPU Paging Register
         and    al,0fdh        ;zero bit 1 for single page
         out    dx,al          ;output control
         ret
Set_Single_Paging_Chips  endp
```

16.6.5 Bank Switching for the 82c451,455,456

A macro is provided in Listing 16.12 that loads the Single Bank Register for the 82c451,455 or 456. These chips can only access 256 Kbytes of memory. The bank field can be 0–3, providing a 64-Kbyte granularity. It allows access to the entire 256 Kbytes of memory during Mode 13 hex.

Listings 16.13 and 16.14 load the Single Bank Register with a bank value which assumes a granularity of 64 Kbytes. These functions are called when a 16-bit planar mode is active. Since the Single Bank Register does not differentiate between reading and writing, the two listings are identical. They are both provided to facilitate code calling protocol compatibility with the listings in the other Super VGA chapters.

LISTING 16.12 Loading the Bank Register for the 82c451,455 and 456

```
; Function:
;       Loading the Single Bank with a new start address for 256-
;       color modes

; Input with:
;       bl      Single Bank_Number
;               0-3 bank number indicating desired 64-kbyte bank

; Calling Protocol:
;       Load_Bank_Chips

Load_Bank_Chips macro

;        set up index to Bank Select Register
```

```
mov     dx,3d6h        ;point to CPU Paging Register
mov     al,0bh
mov     ah,bl
out     dx,ax    ;output bank
```

```
endm
```

LISTING 16.13 Loading Write Bank Number for the 82c451,455 and 456

```
; Function:
;       Loading the Write Bank with a new start address for the
;       82c451,455 and 456

; Input with:
;       write_bank      Write Bank_Number
;                  0-3 bank number indicating desired 64-kbyte bank

; Calling Protocol:
;       Set_Write_Bank_Chips(write_bank);

Set_Write_Bank_Chips proc far arg1:byte

        mov     bl,arg1        ;get argument
        Load_Bank_Chips

        ret
Set_Write_Bank_Chips endp
```

LISTING 16.14 Loading Read Bank Number for the 82c451,455 and 456

```
; Function:
;       Loading the Read Bank with a new start address for the
;       82c451,455 and 456

; Input with:
;       read_bank      Read Bank_Number
;                      0-3 bank number indicating desired 64 Kbyte
;                      bank

; Calling Protocol:
;       Set_Read_Bank_Chips(read_bank);
```

```
Set_Read_Bank_Chips     proc  far        arg1:byte

        mov     bl,arg1 ;get  argument
        Load_Bank_Chips
        ret
Set_Read_Bank_Chips endp
```

16.6.6   Bank Switching for the 82c452 and 82c453

Two macros are provided for the 82c452 that load the single bank register depending on whether a Planar or Packed Display Mode is active. The Bank Register has a different granularity, depending on whether the display mode is a 16-bit planar or a 256-color packed mode.

Listing 16.15 contains a macro to load the Single Bank Register with a value in a 16-bit planar mode. Listing 16.16 contains a macro to load the Single Bank Register with a value in a 16-bit packed mode.

LISTING 16.15   Loading the Single Bank Register Bank Number 16-color modes 82c452/3 Macro

```
; Function:
;       Loading the Single Bank with a new start address for 16-
;               color modes for the 82c452/3

; Input with:
;       bl      Single Bank_Number
;               0-63 bank number indicating desired 16-kbyte bank

; Calling Protocol:
;       Load_Single_Bank_16_Chips

Load_Single_Bank_16_Chips macro
;       set up index to Bank Select Register
        mov     dx,3d6h ;point to Single/Low Map Register
        mov     al,10h
        mov     ah,bl
        shl     ah,1
        shl     ah,1
        shl     ah,1
        shl     ah,1    ;shift left 4 for 64 kbyte banks
        out     dx,ax   ;output bank

endm
```

LISTING 16.16   Loading the Single Bank Register Bank Number 256-color Modes 82c452/3 Macro

```
;  Function:
;        Loading the Single Bank with a new start address for 256-;
;        color modes 82c452/3

;  Input with:
;        bl        Single Bank_Number
;                    0-63 bank number indicating desired 16-kbyte bank

;  Calling Protocol:
;        Load_Single_Bank_256_Chips

Load_Single_Bank_256_Chips macro

;        set up index to Bank Select Register
         mov     dx,3d6h          ;point to Single/Low Map Register
         mov     al,10h
         mov     ah,bl
         shl     ah,1
         shl     ah,1     ;shift left 2 for 64 kbyte banks
         out     dx,ax    ;output bank

endm
```

Listings 16.17 and 16.18 load the Single Bank Register with a bank value which assumes a granularity of 64 Kbytes. These functions are called when a 16-bit Planar Mode is active. Since the Single Bank Register does not differentiate between reading and writing, the two listings are identical. They are both provided to facilitate code-calling protocol compatibility with the listings in the other Super VGA chapters.

LISTING 16.17   Loading the Write Bank Number 256-color Modes for the 82c452/3

```
;  Function:
;        Loading the Write Bank with a new start address 256-color
;        modes for the 82c452/3

;  Input with:
;        write_bank     Write Bank_Number
;                    0-63 bank number indicating desired 64-kbyte bank
```

```
; Calling Protocol:
;       Set_Write_Bank_256_Chips(write_bank);

Set_Write_Bank_256_Chips proc far arg1:byte
mov     bl,arg1         ;get argument
        Load_Single_Bank_256_Chips

        ret
Set_Write_Bank_256_Chips endp
```

LISTING 16.18   Load Read Bank Number 256-color Modes for the 82c452/3

```
; Function:
;       Load the Read Bank with a new start address 256-color modes
;       for the 82c452/3

; Input with:
;       read_bank       Read Bank_Number
;                       0-63 bank number indicating desired 64-kbyte
;                       bank

; Calling Protocol:
;       Set_Read_Bank_256_Chips(read_bank);

Set_Read_Bank_256_Chips proc far arg1:byte

        mov     bl,arg1         ;get argument
        Load_Single_Bank_256_Chips

        ret
Set_Read_Bank_256_Chips endp
```

Listings 16.19 and 16.20 load the Single Bank Register with a bank value which assumes a granularity of 64 Kbytes. These functions are called when a 16-bit planar mode is active. Since the Single Bank Register does not differentiate between reading and writing, the two listings are identical. They are both provided to facilitate code calling protocol compatibility with the listings in the other Super VGA chapters.

LISTING 16.19 Loading Write Bank Number 16-color mModes for the 82c452/3

```
; Function:
;       Loading the Write Bank with a new start address 16-color
;       modes for the 82c452/3

; Input with:
;       write_bank      Write Bank_Number
;                               0-63 bank number indicating desired
;                               64-kbyte bank

; Calling Protocol:
;       Set_Write_Bank_16_Chips(write_bank);

Set_Write_Bank_16_Chips proc far arg1:byte

        mov     bl,arg1         ;get argument
        Load_Single_Bank_16_Chips

        ret
Set_Write_Bank_16_Chips endp
```

LISTING 16.20 Loading Read Bank Number 16-color Modes for the 82c452/3

```
; Function:
;       Loading the Read Bank with a new start address 16-color ;
;       modes for the 82c452/3

; Input with:
;       read_bank       Read Bank_Number
;                               0-63 bank number indicating desired
;                               64-kbyte bank

; Calling Protocol:
;       Set_Read_Bank_16_Chips(read_bank);

Set_Read_Bank_16_Chips proc far arg1:byte

        mov     bl,arg1         ;get argument
        Load_Single_Bank_16_Chips

        ret
Set_Read_Bank_16_Chips endp
```

16.6.7 Dual Paging

The 82c452 and 82c453 can be placed into a dual-paging mode. In the Dual-paging Mode, the bank-switching operation is a bit more complex. Two bank start address registers are provided. The VGA hardware knows which one to use based on the memory addressing. In a typical scenario, the display memory is mapped into the host through a 64-Kbyte segment at A0000. This 64-Kbyte segment is split into a lower portion (A0000–A7FFF) and an upper portion (A8000–AFFFF), each 32 Kbytes long. If a memory transfer is addressed within the A0000–A7FFF range, the Single/Low Map Register is engaged. Similarly, if the A8000–AFFFF range is addressed, the High Map Register is engaged.

Dual-mode paging is enabled through the code in Listing 16.21.

LISTING 16.21 Setting up for Dual-mode Paging for the 82c452/3

```
;  Function:
;        Set up for dual-mode paging for the 82c452/3

;  Calling Protocol:
;        Set_Dual_Paging_Chips();

Set_Dual_Paging_Chips proc far

;        set up index to CPU Paging Register
         mov     dx,3d6h          ;point to CPU Paging Register
         mov     al,0bh
         out     dx,al

;        input the current value for non-destructive output
         in      al,dx   ;input CPU Paging Register
         or      al,02h  ;set bit 1 for dual page
         out     dx,al   ;output control
         ret
Set_Dual_Paging_Chips endp
```

The values in the BANK fields of these registers range from 0–63. These indicate a 4-Kbyte increment within one display plane, of which there are four.

In the planar display modes, the display memory address of a pixel, within a plane, is pointed to by this register. The address is determined by multiplying the bank number by 4 Kbytes. This accounts for the 4-Kbyte granularity.

In the packed display modes, the display memory address of a pixel in plane 0 is pointed to by this register. The memory in display planes 1–3 follows sequentially and cannot be accessed by the bank register. The address is determined by multiplying the bank number by 16 Kbytes. This accounts for the 4-Kbyte granularity and 4 display planes. Note that although the bank is 64 Kbytes long, only 32-Kbyte transfers can occur in one transfer. This limitation occurs because the boundary at A8000 must be crossed. Otherwise, a wrap-around would occur.

Dual-paging is accomplished using the same functions as were used in Section 16.6.6. The Single Bank Register is used for the low address map which is 32 Kbytes long, ranging from A0000–A7FFF hex. The High Bank Register is used for the high address map which is 32 Kbytes long ranging from A8000–AFFFF hex. Accessing these registers is accomplished through Listings 16.22 and 16.23. These are identical to the listings in Section 16.6.6 with the exception that the Single/Low Map Bank Select Register is located at index 10 hex while the High Map Bank Select Register is located at 11 hex.

LISTING 16.22 Loading the High Map Bank Register in 16-color Modes for the 82c452/3 Macro

```
;  Function:
;       Loading the High Map Bank with a new start address for 16-;
;       color  modes  for  the    82c452/3

;  Input  with:
;       bl      Single Bank_Number
;               0-63 bank  number  indicating  desired  16-kbyte  bank

;  Calling  Protocol:
;       Load_High_Bank_16_Chips

Load_High_Bank_16_Chips macro

;       set  up  index  to  Bank  Select  Register
        mov     dx,3d6h         ;point  to  Single/Low  Map  Register
        mov     al,11h
        mov     ah,bl
        shl     ah,1
        shl     ah,1
        shl     ah,1
        shl     ah,1    ;shift  left  4  for  64  kbyte  banks
        out     dx,ax   ;output  bank

        endm
```

LISTING 16.23   Loading High Map Bank Register in 256-color for the 82c452/3

```
; Function:
;       Loading the High Bank with a new start address for 256-color
;       modes for the 82c452/3

; Input with:
;       bl                      Single Bank_Number
;                               0-63 bank number indicating desired
;                               16-kbyte bank

; Calling Protocol:
;       Load_High_Bank_256_Chips

Load_High_Bank_256_Chips macro

;       set up index to Bank Select Register
        mov     dx,3d6h         ;point to Single/Low Map Register
        mov     al,11h
        mov     ah,bl
        shl     ah,1
        shl     ah,1    ;shift left 2 for 64 kbyte banks
        out     dx,ax   ;output bank

endm
```

Listings 16.24 and 16.25 load the Single Bank Register with a bank value which assumes a granularity of 64 Kbytes. These functions are called when a 16-bit planar mode is active. Since the Single Bank Register does not differentiate between reading and writing, the two listings are identical. They are both provided to facilitate code calling protocol compatibility with the listings in the other Super VGA chapters.

LISTING 16.24   Loading Write Bank Number 256-color Dual-paging Modes for the 82c452/3

```
; Function:
;       Load the Write High Bank with a new start address 256-color
;       dual-paging modes for the 82c452/3

; Input with:
;       write_bank      Write Bank_Number
;                               0-63 bank number indicating desired
;                               64-kbyte bank
```

```
; Calling Protocol:
;       Set_Write_High_Bank_256_Chips(write_bank);

Set_Write_High_Bank_256_Chips proc far arg1:byte

        mov     bl,arg1         ;get argument
        Load_High_Bank_256_Chips

        ret
Set_Write_High_Bank_256_Chips endp
```

LISTING 16.25   Loading Read High Bank Number 256-color Dual-paging Modes for the 82c452/3

```
; Function:
; Load the Read High Bank with a new start address 256-color dual-
; paging modes for the 82¢452/3

; Input with:
;       read_bank       Read Bank_Number
;                               0-63 bank number indicating desired
;                               64-kbyte bank

; Calling Protocol:
;       Set_Read_High_Bank_256_Chips(read_bank);

Set_Read_High_Bank_256_Chips proc far arg1:byte
        mov     bl,arg1         ;get argument
        Load_High_Bank_256_Chips

        ret
Set_Read_High_Bank_256_Chips endp
```

Listings 16.26 and 16.27 load the Single Bank Register with a bank value which assumes a granularity of 64 kbytes. These functions are called when a 16-bit planar mode is active. Since the Single Bank Register does not differentiate between reading and writing, the two listings are identical. They are both provided to facilitate code calling protocol compatibility with the listings in the other Super VGA chapters.

LISTING 16.26 Loading Write High Bank Number 16-color Dual-paging Modes for the 82c452/3

```
; Function:
; Load the Write High Bank with a new start address 16-color dual-
; paging modes for the 82c452/3

; Input with:
;       write_bank      Write Bank_Number
;        0-63 bank number indicating desired 64-kbyte bank

; Calling Protocol:
;       Set_Write_High_Bank_16_Chips(write_bank);

Set_Write_High_Bank_16_Chips proc far arg1:byte

        mov     bl,arg1         ;get argument
        Load_High_Bank_16_Chips

        ret
Set_Write_High_Bank_16_Chips endp
```

LISTING 16.27 Load Read Bank Number 16-color dual-paging modes for the 82c452/3

```
; Function:
; Load the Read Bank with a new start address 16-color modes in
; dual-paging modes for the 82c452/3

; Input with:
;       read_bank       Read Bank_Number
;                           0-63 bank number indicating desired
;                           64-kbyte bank

; Calling Protocol:
;       Set_Read_High_Bank_16_Chips(read_bank);

Set_Read_High_Bank_16_Chips proc far arg1:byte

        mov     bl,arg1         ;get argument
        Load_High_Bank_16_Chips

        ret
Set_Read_High_Bank_16_Chips endp
```

16.6.8 Hardware Bit Masking 82c453

In the planar configurations, a pixel is represented by data which resides in more than one display plane. In addition, the data associated with more than one pixel is stored in a single byte of display memory within a plane. Bit masking is required when writing to one or more pixel without affecting the other pixels in a given byte. A hardware bit-mask feature is provided in the 82c453. It provides a very fast technique for bit masking.

In the standard VGA, a Bit Mask Register is provided to facilitate this bit masking operation. However, this requires a read/modify/write to display memory, and the read operations are typically very slow. The Bit Mask Register is described in Section 10.5.11.

In the 82c453, two registers are provided to facilitate fast bit masking. These utilize the organization of the video RAM memory to provide bit masking without requiring read/modify/writes. The Write Bit Mask Control Register, shown in Figure 16.36, controls the bit masking operation.

The EM field of this register enables the Bit Mask Function. If the EM field is set to a 1, the hardware bit masking is enabled. If 0, this feature is disabled. If the feature is enabled, the SRC field controls the source of the bit-mask pattern. The SRC field is described in Table 16.23.

Write Bit Mask Control 82c453

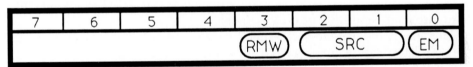

Index 23 at Port 3D6   Port 3D7 Read/Write

FIGURE 16.36 Write Bit Mask Control Register for 82c453. The EM field enables or disables the VRAM write mask function. The SRC field controls the source of the pattern for the write mask function. The RMW field enables the fast read/modify/write function.

TABLE 16.23 The Source of Bit Mask Patterns

SRC	Source
0	Write Bit Mask Pattern Register
1	Graphics Controller Bit Mask Register
2	Rotated CPU byte

Write Bit Mask Pattern 82c453

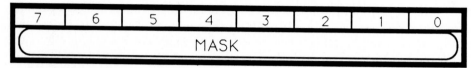

Index 24 at Port 3D6   Port 3D7 Read/Write

FIGURE 16.37   Write Bit Mask Pattern Register for 82c453. The MASK field contains the mask pattern for the write bit mask function when enabled by the SRC field of the Write Bit Mask Pattern Register.

As shown in Figure 16.37, the Bit Mask Pattern Register is used to provide the mask if the SRC field is 0. If the SRC field is 1, the Bit Mask Register described in Section 10.5.11 provides the mask pattern. This is very useful when older code is converted since it provides a simple porting task. If the SRC field is a 2, the rotated CPU byte is used as the mask. This is useful for character generation.

16.6.9   Hardware Read/Modify/Write Cycles 82c453

The 82c453 also provides a hardware assist for read/modify/write cycles. This is enabled through the EM field in the Write Bit Mask Control Register. If the EM field is set to 1, the hardware read/modify/write cycle feature is enabled. It must be pointed out that a CPU read operation cannot be performed when this hardware read/modify/write cycle is enabled.

This feature reduces the time to perform the read/modify/write cycles by 50 percent. This feature is very effective for logical operations. It is possible to perform a read/modify/write using this hardware assist at the same time that the hardware Bit Mask function is enabled.

16.6.10   Hardware Fast Font Paint 82c453

The 82c453 supports the high resolution 1024 by 768 256-color mode. This powerful mode contains 3/4 of a megabyte of memory. If this mode is displaying alphanumerics, a simple screen scroll involves moving 3/4 megabyte of memory! This, of course, is due to the fact that in a graphics mode each character is stored as a bit pattern. Fortunately, the 82c453 has provided an eloquent path for speeding up alphanumerics processing in the high resolution graphics modes.

The actual bit pattern for the character font is not stored in display memory. The bit patterns are interjected into the video data path further down stream. A typical character is 8 bits wide by 16 scan lines high. This requires 16 bytes of data for a single character.

In the packed pixel graphics modes, the 82c453 makes it possible to display alphanumerics characters as character codes. In the Packed Pixel Mode, four bytes are consecutively loaded into the four display planes. These four bytes produce a 32-bit display memory word which resides in the display latches. In a 256-color mode, an 8x16 pixel character is represented by 128 bytes of information corresponding to the 128 pixels covered by the character.

The technique implemented in the Fast Font Paint Mode can increase the graphics character map painting by a factor of four or eight. The 82c453 require two write operations per byte of character font. Since a byte of character font contains eight pixels, a 4:1 enhancement is achieved.

The Fast Font Paint Mode is enabled through the FFP field of the CPU Interface Register for the 82c453 shown in Figure 16.38. If the FFP field is set to 1, the Fast Font Paint Mode is enabled. If it is set to zero, the mode is disabled.

In the early 82c453 versions, if the Fast Font Paint Mode is enabled, the byte written to display memory consists of a nibble of information. This nibble corresponds to the left-most or right-most four pixels in the particular character scan line. Four memory-write operations to display memory are accomplished by this one host write operation. Instead of the four bits being written into display memory, the foreground color is written to all pixels which correspond to a 1 in the nibble. Similarly, the background color is written to all pixels which correspond to a 0 in the nibble.

Figure 16.39a illustrates the mapping of a single scan line of a character into the four display memory planes. Since a horizontal scan line contains eight pixels, two pixels are shown in each plane. In Figure 16.39b a typical character

CPU Interface 82c453

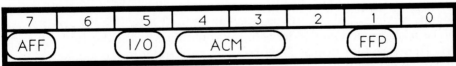

Index 02 at Port 3D6   Port 3D7 Read/Write

FIGURE 16.38 CPU Interface Register for 82c453. The FFP field enables the Fast Font Paint function. The ACM field controls the Attribute Controller Mapping. The I/0 field selects either 1O-bit or 16-bit I/0 address decoding. The AFF field contains the Attribute Flip-Flop Status.

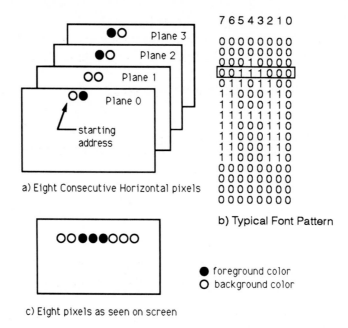

a) Eight Consecutive Horizontal pixels

b) Typical Font Pattern

c) Eight pixels as seen on screen

● foreground color
○ background color

FIGURE 16.39   Fast Font Paint

font pattern is shown. In Figure 16.39c the corresponding display shows the foreground and background colors for each pixel.

The attribute of the pixel consists of a foreground color and a background color. Since a 256-color Packed Display Mode is active, both the foreground and background color are eight bits. The foreground color is stored in the Scratch #1/Foreground Color Register shown in Figure 16.40. If the fast font painting mode is disabled, this register can be used as scratch storage.

The background color is derived from the values in the display latch registers. There are four display latch registers corresponding to the four display planes. In the 256-color modes, these four display planes translate into four horizontal consecutive pixels. If all four display latch registers are loaded with the same value, all four consecutive pixels will have the same background color. This would be used in an opaque character paint operation. If the four display latches are loaded with the current colors of the four consecutive pixels, a transparent character map will result since only the pixels corresponding to the foreground of the character will be changed.

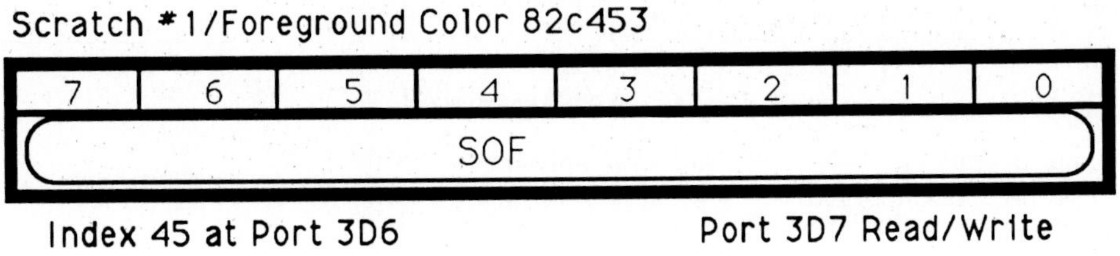

Scratch #1/Foreground Color 82c453

7	6	5	4	3	2	1	0
			SOF				

Index 45 at Port 3D6   Port 3D7 Read/Write

FIGURE 16.40   Scratch #1/Foreground Color Register for 82c453. The SOF field contains either the scratch value that can be used as a scratchpad or the foreground color when in the Fast Font Paint Mode.

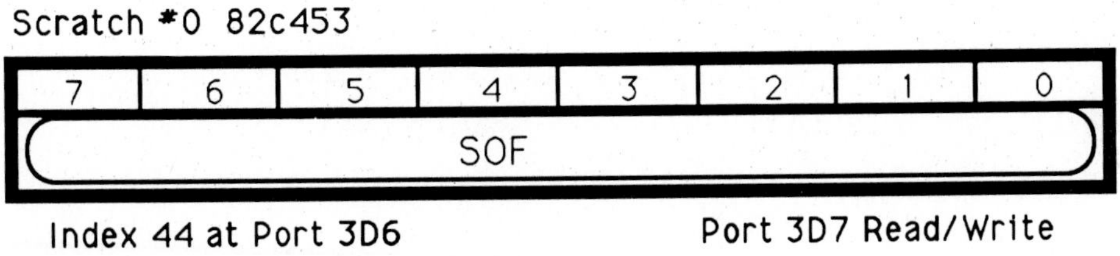

Scratch #0 82c453

7	6	5	4	3	2	1	0
			SOF				

Index 44 at Port 3D6   Port 3D7 Read/Write

FIGURE 16.41   Scratch #0 Register for 82c453. The SCRATCH field contains the scratch value that can be used by application software.

16.6.11   Scratch Registers on 82c453

There are two scratch registers available on the 82c453. The first is discussed in conjunction with the Fast Font Paint function described in Section 16.6.8. This scratch register is called the Scratch #1/Foreground Color Register shown in Figure 16.41. The second register is totally undedicated and may be used by application software. This register is shown in Figure 16.40.

16.7   CONTROLLING THE CRT ADDRESS GENERATION

16.7.1   Controlling the Display Start Address

The manner in which the display memory is mapped to the screen is controlled through the CRT address generation circuitry. The operating characteristics of this memory is controlled through the Memory Mapping Register while added addressing bits are provided for the start address, cursor and offset as listed in Table 16.24.

TABLE 16.24   Chips and Technologies Display Address Control

Function	Register Name	Port	Index	Bits	Value
Wrap Around	Memory Mapping	3D6	4	2	0
Cross Bank Boundaries	Memory Mapping	3D6	4	2	1
Start Address Bits 17–16	Start Address Top	3D6	C	1–0	0–3
Cursor Address Bits 17–16	Cursor Address Top	3D6	A	1–0	0–3
Fine Granularity for Offset	Auxiliary Offset Register	3D6	D	0	0–1

TABLE 16.25   Memory Size as Found in the Memory Mapping Register

MEM field	Display Memory Size
00	256 Kbytes
01	512 Kbytes
10	1 Megabyte
11	Not Used

The Memory Mapping Register is shown in Figures 16.42. The MEM field in the Memory Mapping Register indicates the amount of memory present as listed in Table 16.25. The three popular configurations are provided with one field available for future expansion (more memory hopefully). If 256 Kbytes are present, the memory is organized into four planes of 64 Kbytes each. If 512 Kbytes is present, the memory is organized into 2 banks and 4 planes of 64 Kbytes each. If one Megabyte is present, the memory is organized into four planes, 256 Kbytes each. Each plane can either be divided into 64-Kbyte banks in planar modes, or the entire one Megabyte can be divided into 64-Kbyte banks in packed modes.

The WRP field controls wrap around. If this bit is set to 0, the CRT address generation will wrap around at the 64-Kbyte boundary. The CRT address generation controls what is seen on the display. If the WRP bit is 0, the CRT address will wrap around since the display memory address bits 17 and 16 will be generated by the CRT address counter. If the WRP field is 1, the CRT address will cross banks since the address bits 17 and 16 will be generated by the TOP field of the Top Address Register.

Memory Mapping 82c452

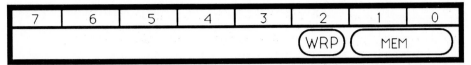

Index 04 at Port 3D6   Port 3D7 Read/Write

FIGURE 16.42   Memory Mapping Register for the 82c452 provides access to the amount of display memory through the "MEM" field and controls CRT wrap around through the "WRP" field.

Start Address Top 82c452, 82c453

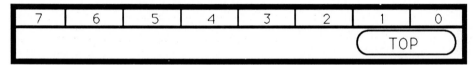

Index 0C at Port 3D6   Port 3D7 Read/Write

FIGURE 16.43   Start Address Top. The display start address bits 17–16 are located in the TOP field.

Due to one Megabyte of display memory space, additional address bits are required for the display start address, cursor start address, and display offset. The Start Top Address Register provides the additional address bits 16 and 17 as shown in Figure 16.43.

The extended memory beyond 256 Kbytes must be enabled if it is to be accessed by the CRT controller. If it is disabled, wrap around on the display will occur at the 256 Kbyte boundary. It can be enabled or disabled through Listings 16.28 and 16.29 respectively.

LISTING 16.28   Enabling Extended Memory Addressing

```
/*
Function:
  Enabling extended memory CRT addressing. Memory above 256 kbytes
  can be displayed.

Calling Protocol: */
Enable_Ext_Memory_Access()
```

```
{ unsigned char value;
  Extended_On_Chips();

outp(0x3d6,0x04);         /* memory map register */
value = inp(0x3d7);        /* read register */
value |= 0x04;            /* set bit 2=1 for extended memory
                             addressing */
outp(0x3d7,value);

Extended_Off_Chips();
}
```

LISTING 16.29   Disable Extended Memory Addressing Causing Wrap Around.

```
/*
Function:
 Disable extended memory CRT addressing. Memory above 256 kbytes
cannot be displayed. Wrap around will occur.

Calling Protocol: */
 Disable_Ext_Memory_Access()

{ unsigned char value;
  Extended_On_Chips();

outp(0x3d6,0x04);         /* memory map register */
value = inp(0x3d7);        /* read register */
value &= 0xfb;            /* reset bit 2=0 for extended memory
                             addressing */
outp(0x3d7,value);

  Extended_Off_Chips();
}
```

The 20-bit start address is loaded by sending the lower 16-bits to the Start Address High and Low Registers and the upper two bits to the Start Address Top Register as shown in Listing 16.30. This function utilizes the set_start_address macro in Listing 14.31.

LISTING 16.30 Loading the Display Start Address

```
;  Function:
;       Loading the 20-bit Display Start Address

;  Input Parameters
;       address          unsigned integer starting address
;       top                        top two bits of address

;  Calling Protocol:
;       Load_Start_Chips(address,top)

Load_Start_Chips        proc far       arg1,arg2:byte

        mov     bx,arg1
        set_start_address         ;load the lower 16-bits of the start
                                  address

;       send out top address
        enable_extensions         ; enable extensions
        mov     dx,3d6h
        mov     al,0ch            ;index Extended Start Address
        mov     ah,arg2
        out     dx,ax
        disable_extensions        ; disable extensions

        ret
Load_Start_Chips        endp
```

16.7.2 Controlling the Cursor Start Address

Due to the one Megabyte of display memory space, additional address bits are required for the display start address, cursor start address, and display offset. The Cursor Address Top Register provides the additional address bits 16 and 17 as shown in Figure 16.44.

The term *offset* determines the virtual width of the display. The standard VGA Offset Register is eight bits and can handle virtual, display widths of up to 1024. To provide for wider virtual images up to 2048 pixels, an additional bit is provided as shown in Figure 16.45. This bit, field O8, acts as the ninth offset address bit. Also included in this register is an analogous bit for the alternate offset register used during emulation.The 20-bit cursor address is loaded by sending the lower 16-bits to the Cursor Address High and Low Registers and the upper two bits to the Cursor Address Top Register as shown in Listing 16.31. This function utilizes the position_cursor macro in Listing 16.32.

Cursor Address Top

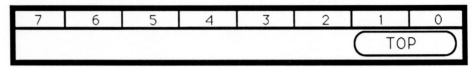

Index OA at Port 3D6   Port 3D7 Read/Write

FIGURE 16.44 Cursor Address Top. The cursor display start address bits 17–16 are located in the TOP field.

Auxiliary Offset Register

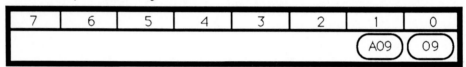

Index OD at Port 3D6   Port 3D7 Read/Write

FIGURE 16.45 Auxiliary Offset Register. Offset address bit located in 09 and alterate emulation offset bit in A09.

LISTING 16.32 Position the Cursor

```
; Function:
;       Load the 20-bit Cursor Position

; Input Parameters
;       position        unsigned integer position
;       top             top two bits of address

; Calling Protocol:
;       Position_Cursor_Chips(position,top)

Position_Cursor_Chips  proc far        arg1,arg2:byte

        mov    bx,arg1
        position_cursor          ;position cursor

;       send out top cursor address
        enable_extensions        ; enable extensions
        mov    dx,3d6h
        mov    al,0ah            ; index Cursor Address Top
        mov    ah,arg2
```

```
       out     dx,ax
       disable_extensions      ; disable extensions

       ret
Position_Cursor_Chips endp
```

16.7.3   Controlling the Display Offset

The display offset determines the size of the virtual image. The eight-bit value stored in the Offset Register of the CRTC Register Group is the only control for the display offset. This register is described in Section 10.4.22.

16.8   CHIPS AND TECHNOLOGIES BIOS EXTENSIONS

Extended BIOS calls are accessed through the AH=5F code as listed in Table 16.26.

16.8.1   Get Controller Information

This provides the programmer with information about the graphics chip and memory configuration.

Inputs:
AH=5F	Extended VGA Control
AL=00	Get Controller Information

Outputs:
AL=5F	Extended VGA control function supported
BL= Chip Type	bits 7–4 Chip Type
	0 = 82c451
	1 = 82c452
	2 = 82c455
	? = 82c453
	bits 3-0 Revision Number
BH= Memory Size	video memory size

TABLE 16.26   Chips and Technologies Extended BIOS Calls

Function	AH	AL	Feature
Get Controller Information	5F	00	Returns Chip Information
Set Emulation Mode	5F	01	Set Emulation Mode
Auto Emulation Control	5F	02	Enable/Disable auto emulation
Power-On Video Conditions	5F	03	Sets Power-on conditions
Enhanced Save/Restore State	5F	90–92	Handles standard and Super states

> 0 = 256 kbytes
> 1 = 512 kbytes
> 2 = 1 megabyte

CX=Miscellaneous   Miscellaneous Information
>15–2 = reserved
>1 = System Environment
>>0=PC/AT
>>1=PS/2
>2 = Dac Size
>>0=6-bit
>>1=8-bit

16.8.2   Set Emulation Mode

This allows the programmer to set up emulation modes.

Input:
AH=5F	Extended VGA Control
AL=00	Get Controller Information
BL=Operation Mode	Operation Mode

> 0-1=reserved
> 2 =Enable CGA Emulation
> 3 =Enable MDA Emulation
> 4 =Enable Hercules Emulation
> 5 =Enable EGA Emulation
> 6 =Enable VGA Emulation

Outputs:
AL=5F	Extended VGA control function supported
AH=Return Status	Return Status

> 0=Function Unsuccessful
> 1=Function Successful

16.8.3   Auto Emulation Control

Auto Emulation Control makes it possible to enter into an emulation mode automatically. Thus, any application which attempts to access non-VGA registers will cause the VGA chips to generate non-maskable interrupts causing the system to jump into an emulation mode.

Inputs:
AH=5F	Extended VGA control
AL=2	Auto emulation control
BL=selection	Enable or disable auto emulation

> 0=enable auto emulation
> 1=disable auto emulation

Outputs:

AL=5F	Extended VGA control function supported
AH=Return Status	Return Status
	0=Function Unsuccessful
	1=Function Successful

16.8.4   Set Power-on Video Conditions

Set Power-on Video Conditions permits the saving of start-up parameters for automatic installation during power up. The VGA implementation requires non-volatile storage for the memory associated with these selections. If this feature is available, the bits 13–10 of the Miscellaneous Information 0 data would should be set.

Inputs:

AH=5F	Extended VGA control
AL=3	Set Power-on video conditions
BL=Configuration	Configuration selection
	0=Set display mode as specified in the cx register to boot up at power-up.
	1=Set emulation mode as specified in the cx register to boot up at power-up.
if(BL==0)	
CL=mode	Display Mode
CH=mode	Options
	Bits 1-0 = Scanlines
	0=200
	1=350
	2=400
	Bit 7 = Performance
	0=Reset after next boot
	1=Set until changed
if(BL==1)	
CL=mode	Emulation Mode (See extended BIOS emulation call above)
CH=mode	Options
	Bit 7 = Performance
	0=Reset after next boot
	1=Set until changed

Outputs:

AL=5F	Extended VGA control function supported
AH=Return Status	Return Status
	0=Function Unsuccessful
	1=Function Successful

16.8.5   Enhanced Save/Restore Video State Function

This function is similar to the Save/Restore BIOS function 1C described in Sections 11.16.3 and 13.7.7. The capacity to store the Super VGA state has been added to this function through bit 15 of the CX input parameter. This BIOS function is split into three sub-functions. One returns the amount of storage necessary or expected for the save/restore functions respectively. The other two sub-functions actually perform the Save or Restore functions.

Subfunction 90   Determine size of buffer

Inputs:

AL=5F hex	Extended VGA control function
AL=90 hex	Return Save/Restore buffer size
CX=Mask State	States of Save/Restore
	bit 0 = save/restore video hardware
	bit 1 = save/restore BIOS data state
	bit 2 = save/restore DAC state
	bit 15 = save/restore type
	0 = save/restore all state information
	1 = save/restore super state only

Outputs:

AL=5F	Extended VGA control function supported
bx = blocks required	Number of 64-byte blocks required for the save or expectedfor the restore.

Subfunction 91   Save the State

Inputs:

AL=5F hex	Extended VGA control function
AL=91 hex	Save state
CX=Mask State	States to Save
	bit 0 = save video hardware
	bit 1 = save BIOS data state
	bit 2 = save DAC state
	bit 15 = save type

                                        0 = save all state information
                                        1 = save super state only
ES:BX   Segment:Offset pointer to buffer which
                               will contain the stateinformation at the
                               successful conclusion of this call.

Outputs:
  AL=5F   Extended VGA control function supported

Subfunction 90   Determine size of buffer

Inputs:
  AL=5F hex   Extended VGA control function
  AL=92 hex   Restore state
  CX=Mask State   States to Restore
                                        bit 0 = restore video hardware
                                        bit 1 = restore BIOS data state
                                        bit 2 = restore DAC state
                                        bit 15 = restore type
                                                0 = restore all state information
                                                1 = restore super state only
  ES:BX   Segment:Offset pointer to buffer which should
                               contain the state information for the restore
                               function.

Outputs:
  AL=5F   Extended VGA control function supported

16.9   CHIPS AND TECHNOLOGIES SPECIAL FEATURES

Several special features available on the Chips and Technologies chip are listed
in Table 16.27.

16.9.1   Anti-Aliased Display Fonts

The 82c452 and 82c453 support a font mode which utilizes 2 bits/pixel. The
fonts are stored in corresponding addresses in display planes 2 and 3. The most
significant bit is stored in display plane 2 and the least in display plane 3 as
shown in Figure 16.46.

The anti-aliased fonts are controlled by the Text Mode Register shown in
Figure 16.47. The 2BP field of this register enables (2BP=1) or disables (2BP=0)
the anti-aliased font feature. If 2BP is set to 0, the feature is disabled and normal
font patterns are utilized. The font bit patterns are stored in bit plane 2 under

TABLE 16.27   Chips and Technologies Special Features

Feature	Supporting Chips	Description
Anti-Aliased Fonts	452	Allows gray scale alphanumeric fonts
Downward Emulation	451,452,453,455,456	Emulates MDA, Hercules, CGA,EGA
Interrupt skipping	452	Interrupts after n vertical cycles
Hardware Cursor	452	Hardware cursor
Hardware Write Mask	453	Hardware write mask
Hardware Fast Font	453	Hardware fast font drawing

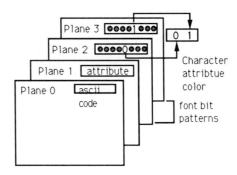

FIGURE 16.46   Anti-aliased Font Storage

Text Mode

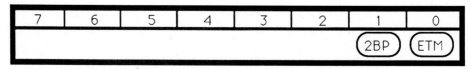

Index 0E at Port 3D6   Port 3D7 Read/Write

FIGURE 16.47   Text Mode Register. Extended Text Mode Controlled by ETM and 2 bits/pixel enable by 2BP.

TABLE 16.28 Anti-Aliased Bit Colors

Bit Plane 2	Bit Plane 3	Color	Percent Foreground
0	0	0 Background	$0 <= x < .25$
0	1	1 Foreground 1	$.25 <= x < .50$
1	0	2 Foreground 2	$.50 <= x < .75$
1	1	3 Foreground 3	$.75 <= x < 1.0$

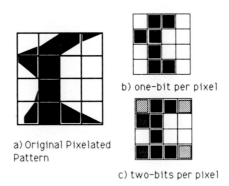

a) Original Pixelated Pattern

b) one-bit per pixel

c) two-bits per pixel

FIGURE 16.48 Anti-aliased Four-color Font

normal VGA conditions. Each pixel in the foreground of a character is represented by a 1, while the background pixels in the rectangular pixel pattern box are 0.

If the anti-aliased fonts are enabled, each pixel in the rectangular character box is represented by two bits instead of the standard one bit per pixel. The font bit pattern for each character is stored with one bit of each pixel in bit plane 2 and one bit in bit plane 3. The lower order bit is stored in bit plane 3 while the higher order bit is stored in bit plane 2. The meaning of the four possible colors are described in Table 16.28. A typical character pattern is shown in Figure 16.48.

16.9.2 Downward Emulation

The 82c450 family can emulate the MDA, Hercules, CGA and EGA cards through BIOS calls or through several extended registers. It is beyond the scope of this

Frame Interrupt Count

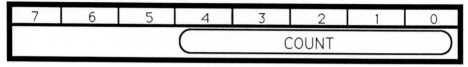

Index 2A at Port 3D6   Port 3D7 Read/Write

FIGURE 16.49   Frame Interrupt Count. COUNT vertical refresh cycles occur before vertical interrupt is generated.

TABLE 16.29   Interrupt Count Timing

Count field	Interrupt Timing
0	Interrupt every vertical refresh cycle
1	Interrupt every other vertical refresh cycle
31	Interrupt every 32nd vertical refresh cycle

book to detail the many registers involved in this complex project. The registers include the emulation control, alternate timing, and trap status registers. It is useful to reference the Set Emulation BIOS call detailed in Section 16.3.6.

16.9.3   Interrupt Skipping

Interrupt skipping is a useful feature for those who utilize the vertical interrupts. The Frame Interrupt Count Register is shown in Figure 16.49.
The COUNT field determines the time period between vertical interrupts. A hardware counter counts down from the COUNT value to zero, at zero generates an interrupt, and resets the COUNT field once again. The possible time periods are listed in Table 16.29. If the vertical refresh period occurs at 30 frames a second, the maximum value of 31 in the COUNT field will cause an interrupt approximately every second.

16.9.4   Hardware Cursor

The Hardware Cursor is available on the 82c452. It provides an excellent cursor compatible to the Windows Presentation Manager standards. Its features are outlined in Table 16.30. Details of the eleven registers and memory location of this cursor are beyond the scope of this book.

TABLE 16.30   Hardware Cursor Features

Feature	Description
Size	32 pixels wide and 512 pixels high
Positioning	Pixel resolution anywhere on the screen
Zoom	Horizontally zoomed by factor of 2
Colors	Foreground color, background color, transparencies
Color Resolution	2 bits/pixel
Attributes	Blink at 8 or 16 blink frames per on and off period

Chapter 17

Genoa Systems

17.1 INTRODUCTION TO THE GENOA SUPER VGA CHIPS

Genoa has manufactured two Super VGAs. The first was based on a Tseng
ET3000 chip while the second is based on a Genoa chip. The first series of VGAs
based on the ET3000 are found on cards in the 5000 series. All other cards are
based on the Genoa chip.

The Genoa VGA chip, called the GVGA, provides a wide variety of Super
VGA display modes. The GVGA supports up to 512 Kbytes of memory. Both
interlaced and non-interlaced monitors are supported. Some 30 enhanced display modes are provided. Resolutions extend to 1024 by 768 16-color modes
and 800 by 600 256-color modes. Alphanumerics modes include 132 columns in
both the color and monochrome modes. Non-standard graphics resolutions
abound, including 512 by 512 and 720 by 512 16-color and 256-color modes.
Also included is a 1024 by 768 4-color display mode.

Emulation is provided by loading appropriate timing values into the VGA
registers. This allows the GVGA to function as a MDA, Hercules, CGA or EGA.
The Extended registers can not be locked. Non-maskable interrupts can be
automatically generated through access to 3D8 for color systems, or through
3B8 for monochrome systems.

Extended memory-accessing is provided through dual-bank registers. One
register is dedicated to read operations while the second is dedicated to write
operations. The display memory can be configured into 64-Kbyte or 128-Kbyte
banks.

A special vertical refresh rate of 70 MHz is provided for those who have
monitors which will support this scan rate. This 70 MHz operation provides less
perceivable flicker due to its higher scan rate.

17.1.1 Non-Standard Display Modes

Genoa provides a 4-color mode at the 1024 by 768 resolution. This graphics
display mode, Mode 7F hex, is organized in a Link 4 Mode, which organizes
memory as eight banks of 32 Kbytes each.

17.2 CONFIGURING THE GENOA SUPER VGA

17.2.1 Bus Data Widths and Switch Configurations

The Genoa Super VGA can be configured to operate in the PC/AT bus or in the microchannel bus. A set of DIP switches are provided on the cards which enable 8- or 16-bit transfers, type of monitor or CGA emulation. These are listed in Table 17.1. If a CGA game is played off of a floppy disk, the switch position 6 should be placed in the down position.

The ROM bus width and memory data bus width can be configured through sense switches on the VGA card as indicated in Table 17.1. The status of these switches can be determined through the Configuration Register discussed in Section 17.4.4.

In addition to the bus width, the monitor type is also programmed through the sense switches. The monitor types are provided in the *User's manual*. Some software, namely CGA game software, requires the card to be configured in a CGA compatible mode at power up. A switch is dedicated to this purpose.

If the monitor will handle a 70 MHz vertical scan rate, the GVGA can be placed into a flicker-free state. A 70 MHz vertical scan rate will be output to the monitor during specific display modes. This feature is enabled through the FF field of the Enhanced Control #3 Register shown in Figure 17.3. If the FF field is set to 1, the flicker-free state is enabled. If it is set to 0, the flicker-free state is disabled and normal vertical scan rates are output to the monitor.

The M16 field of the Enhanced Control #2 Register sets the bus width to either 8-bit or 16-bit operation. This bit affects both the BIOS I/O and the memory data bus. If the EN field is set to 1, a 16-bit host interface bus is used. If it is set to 0, an 8-bit bus is used.

TABLE 17.1 Configuring the Genoa Super VGAs

Function	Technique/Register	Port	Index	Bit	Value
Select 8-bit ROM	Switch Position 8 = Up				
Select 16-bit ROM	Switch Position 8 = Down				
Select 8-bit data path	Switch Position 7 = Up				
Select 16-bit data path	Switch Position 7 = Down				
Monitor Type	Switch Positions 4-1				
CGA Game Emulation	Switch Position 6 Down				
Normal VGA	Switch Position 6 Up				
Vertical Interlace	Enhanced Control #1	3x5	2F	3,0	0–3
8-bit data path	Enhanced Control #2	3C5	07	2	0
16-bit data path	Enhanced Control #2	3C5	07	2	1
Flicker free	Enhanced Control #2	3C5	07	2	0
Normal vertical scan rate	Enhanced Control #3	3C5	08	2	1

17.2.2 Speed Enhancements

The VGA can be fine tuned through an application software package. The tuning functions are listed in Table 17.2. Not all systems can handle the increased bandwidth generated by the fine tuning. It is necessary to experiment to achieve optimum system performance.

The speed enhancement features are controlled through the Enhanced Control Register #4 as shown in Figure 17.1. The FS field enables fast no-wait-state-access to display memory during scrolling operations. When the host issues a BIOS call to initiate a scroll operation, the GVGA returns control to the host as soon as the BIOS call is initiated. Thus, the host does not have to wait for the scroll operation to be complete. If the FS field is set to 1, fast scrolling is enabled. If 0, normal bandwidth scrolling occurs. The FA field allows fast address decoding on host read and write operations. If the FA field is set to 1, fast accesses are enabled. If 0, normal bandwidth memory accesses occur.

Not all motherboards can handle the fast address decoding. The TBE field enables two banks memory access. Two-bank memory access is specific to one card manufacturer and should not be modified by the programmer. If the TBE field is set to 1, the two-bank memory access mode is enabled. If 0, a normal single-bank access occurs.

The PW field enables the Pre-Wait function. There are times when the dynamic RAM resident on the VGA can be pushed to run a bit faster. By enabling Pre-Wait, sometimes the memory will run a little faster. If the PW field is set to 1, the Pre-Wait function is enabled. If 0, the Pre-Wait function is disabled. The FW field enables the Fast Write function. Fast writing releases the host bus as soon as the memory write operation is issued. The data from the host is latched, and the bus is released. If the FW field is set to 1, fast write operations are enabled. If 0, wait-states are issued to the host processor.

TABLE 17.2   Fine Tuning Performance

Function	Technique/Register	Port	Index	Bit	Value
Fast Write	Enhanced Control #4	3C5	10	6	1
Normal Write	Enhanced Control #4	3C5	10	6	0
Pre_Wait	Enhanced Control #4	3C5	10	3	1
No Pre_Wait	Enhanced Control #4	3C5	10	3	0
Fast Decode	Enhanced Control #4	3C5	10	1	1
Normal Decode	Enhanced Control #4	3C5	10	1	0
Fast Scroll	Enhanced Control #4	3C5	10	0	1
Normal Scroll	Enhanced Control #	3C5	10	0	0

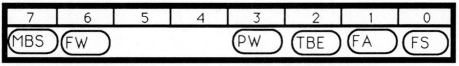

Enhanced Control #4 Register

7	6	5	4	3	2	1	0
MBS	FW			PW	TBE	FA	FS

Index 10 at Port 3C4   Port 3C5 Read/Write

FIGURE 17.1 Enhanced Control #4 Register. The FS field controls fast scrolling. The FA field controls fast accesses. The TBE fleld enables twobank memory access. The PW fleld controls the prewait function. The FW field controls fast writing. The MBS field selects memory bank 0 or 1.

TABLE 17.3 Monitor Selection (D=down U=Up)

Switches

1	2	3	4	Monitor Type	Typical Monitor
D	D	D	U	800 by 600	Sony 1302
U	D	D	U	1024 by 768 Non-interlaced	Sony 1304
U	U	D	U	1024 by 768 Non-interlaced	Nanao 9070
U	D	U	U	1024 by 768 Non-interlaced	NEC XL
D	U	U	U	1024 by 768 Interlaced	NEC 3D
D	D	U	U	800 by 600	NEC 2A
U	U	U	U	1024 by 768 Interlaced	8514/A
U	D	D	D	70 Hz vertical Sync Rate	——

17.2.3 Monitor Type

The monitor type is selected via four sense switches as shown in Table 17.3. Care must be taken to ensure that the proper setting is provided. As noted in the last switch setting of this table, a 70 Hz vertical frequency is provided. This is effective in reducing perceived flicker. However, care must be taken to insure that the monitor interfaced to the GVGA-based VGA card is adequate to handle this higher vertical frequency. Extensive lists of monitors are provided in the *User's Manual*. The monitor type can also be determined by reading bits 6–4 of the data byte in the BIOS storage area at 0040:0488 hex.

Enhanced Control #1 Register

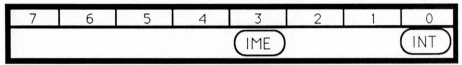

Index 2F at Port 3B4/3D4   Port 3B5/3D5 Read/Write

FIGURE 17.2 Enhanced Control #1 Register. The IME field selects between the interlaced alphanumerics and graphics modes. The INT field enables interlaced operation.

TABLE 17.4 Emulation

Function	Register Name	Port	Index	Bits	Value
NMI Enable	Enhanced Control #2	3C5	7	6	1
NMI Disable	Enhanced Control #2	3C5	7	6	0
Color Autoswitch	Enhanced Control #3	3C5	8	2	1
No Color Autoswitch	Enhanced Control #3	3C5	8	2	0
Mono Autoswitch	Enhanced Control #3	3C5	8	1	1
No Mono Autoswitch	Enhanced Control #3	3C5	8	1	0
VGA and EGA modes	Enhanced Control #3	3C5	8	0	0
MDA Hercules or CGA	Enhanced Control #3	3C5	8	0	1
VGA operation	Enhanced Control #3	3C5	8	3	0
EGA operation	Enhanced Control #3	3C5	8	3	1

The Interlaced mode is enabled through the INT field of Enhanced Control #1 Register shown in Figure 17.2. If the INT field is set to 1, the interlaced mode is active. If it is set to 0, the interlaced mode is not active.

17.2.4 Emulation

The GVGA provides emulation of the Hercules or CGA through register settings or auto detection and non-maskable interrupts. Emulation features are listed in Table 17.4. Non-maskable interrupts can be enabled through the NMI field of the Enhanced Control #2 Register shown in Figure 17.3. If the NMI field is set to 1, non-maskable interrupts are generated when writing occurs to the ports at 3x8 hex. If the NMI field is 0, no non-maskable interrupts are generated.

The VGA is differentiated from the EGA through the EOV field of the Enhanced Control #3 Register shown in Figure 17.4. If the EOV field is set to 0, the VGA is active. If it is set to 1, the EGA emulation is active.

Enhanced Control #2 Register

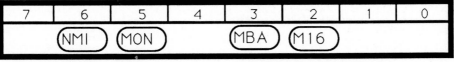

Index 7 at Port 3C4   Port 3C5 Read/Write

FIGURE 17.3 Enhanced Control #2 Register. The M16 field controls 8- or 16-bit memory accesses. The MBA field reports whether the VGA is on a mother board or on an adapter card. The NMl field enables non-maskable interrupts when accessing 3x8.

Enhanced Control #3 Register

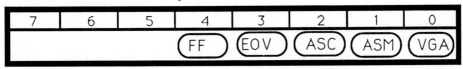

Index 8 at Port 3C4   Port 3C5 Read/Write

FIGURE 17.4 Enhanced Control #3 Register. The VGA field selects either an EGA/VGA mode or an MDA, CGA or Hercules Mode. The ASM and ASC fields control the monochrome and color autoswitching emulation. The EOV field selects either an EGA or VGA. The FF field controls 70 Hz refresh.

17.2.5 VGA/EGA/MDA/Hercules Emulation

The VGA/EGA modes are differentiated from the MDA/Hercules and CGA modes through the VGA field. If the VGA field is set to 1, the MDA/Hercules and CGA mode is enabled. If the VGA field is set to 0, the EGA/VGA field is enabled. This field is used when configuring the Memory Segment Register discussed in Section 17.6.2.

The EGA and VGA can be differentiated through the EOV field of the Enhanced Control #3 Register. If the EOV field is set to 0, the VGA mode of operation is enabled. If it is set to 1, the EGA mode of operation is enabled.

Autoswitching is enabled through the ASC field when a color mode is used. Any attempt to write to 3D8 will cause a non-maskable interrupt to be generated. Setting the ASC field to 1 enables this function. If the ASC field is set to 0, no autoswitching on 3D8 hex will occur.

Autoswitching is enabled through the ASC field when a monochrome mode is used. Any attempt to write to 3B8 will cause a non-maskable interrupt to be generated. Setting the ASC field to 1 enables this function. If the ASC field is set to 0, no autoswitching on 3B8 hex will occur.

Herchi Register

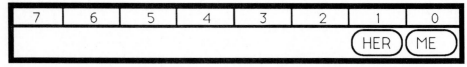

Index 2E at Port 3B43D4   Port 3B5/3D5 Read/Write

FIGURE 17.5 Herchi Register. The ME field enables the CGA access to the Maximum Scan Line Register 1. The HER field enables Chinese applications under Hercules mode.

17.2.6 CGA Emulation

The CGA can be emulated for games through a sense switch shown in Table 17.4 and through a ME field of the Herchi Register. The Herchi Register is shown in Figure 17.5.

If the ME field is set to 1, the Maximum Scan Line Register, discussed in Section 10.4.10, is programmable under CGA modes. This is mostly used for several CGA games which require access to this register. This bit has no effect when a VGA mode is active.

If the ME field is set to 0, normal VGA operation occurs. Another aspect of the Herchi Register is the HER field. It is a specific field relevant only to a Chinese card manufacturer. If the HER field is set to 1, the Chinese application can run under the Hercules mode. This bit has no effect when a normal VGA mode is active. When the HER field is set to 0, the Chinese application can not run.

17.3 CONTROLLING THE GENOA SUPER VGA

The VGA cannot be globally enabled or disabled. The GVGA extended registers are always enabled. Having these continually enabled means that there is no "pure" VGA mode. The registers are distributed through the normal VGA register port space utilizing non-standard VGA indexes.

The standard Global Enable registers are located at 3C3 hex for PS/2 systems and at 46E8 hex for PC/AT systems. These registers are shown in Figures 17.6 and 17.7 respectively. If the EN field is set to a 1, the VGA is enabled. If the EN field is set to a 0, the VGA is disabled.

17.4 INQUIRING FOR THE GENOA SUPER VGA CONFIGURATION

Genoa provides information in BIOS memory regarding the VGA card ID, card definition, chip revision number, monitor type, and memory size as indicated in Table 17.5.

Global Enable PC/AT Register

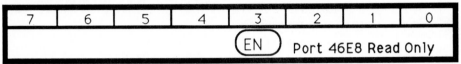

FIGURE 17.6   Global Enable Register. Adapter Card Implementation at Port 46E8. The EN field enables or disables the VGA.

Global Enable PS/2 Register

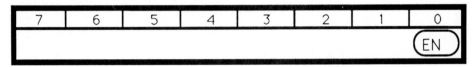

FIGURE 17.7   Setup Control Register. Motherboard Implementation at Port 3C3. The EN field enables or disables the VGA.

TABLE 17.5   Determining Genoa Display Status

Function	Register Name	Port	Index	Bits	Value
Identify Card	Indirect through C000:0037				77 hex
ROM BIOS Size	Configuration Register	3C5	05	6–5	0–3
I/O Address	Configuration Register	3C5	05	4	0–1
8-bit ROM	Configuration Register	3C5	05	2	1
16-bit ROM	Configuration Register	3C5	05	2	0
8-bit Bus	Configuration Register	3C5	05	6-5	1
16-bit Bus	Configuration Register	3C5	05	6-5	0
PC/AT System	Configuration Register	3C5	05	0	1
PS/2 System	Configuration Register	3C5	05	0	0
Motherboard	Enhanced Control #2	3C5	07	3	1
Adapter Card	Enhanced Control #2	3C5	07	3	0
Analog Monitor	Enhanced Control #2	3C5	07	5	0
TTL Monitor	Enhanced Control #2	3C5	07	5	1

17.4.1   Identifying the Genoa VGA Card

The Genoa family of VGA cards can be identified through the four data bytes in BIOS memory space. The start address offset byte of these four bytes is at C000:0037. This offset byte is added to the base address C000:0000 to deter-

TABLE 17.6   Genoa Signature

Byte Location Segment	Byte Location Offset	Value
C000:	0000 + (C000:0037)	77
C000:	0001 + (C000:0037)	xx (See Table 17.7)
C000:	0002 + (C000:0037)	66
C000:	0003 + (C000:0037)	99

mine the long pointer to the identification bytes. The four-byte identification is as follows (in hex): 77 xx 66 99. The xx field identifies which card and chip are present while the 77, 66 and 99 fields identify the Genoa VGA. The byte ordering is described in Table 17.6.

A Genoa chip or card can be identified by using the code provided in Listing 17.1. This C function calls upon the assembly language function in Listing 17.2.

LISTING 17.1   Determining if the chip is a Genoa Super VGA

```
/*
Function:
   Determining if the chip is a Genoa Super VGA

Output Parameters:
   1 card is an Genoa
   0 card is NOT an Genoa

Calling Protocol:
   Genoa= Is_It_Genoa() */

int Is_It_Genoa()
{ char signature[4];

Get_Genoa_Key(signature); /* get Genoa key */

if(( signature[0] == 0x77) & ( signature[2] == 0x99) &
   ( signature[3] == 0x66) ) return(1);
        else return(0);

}
```

LISTING 17.2 Returning the Genoa Signature String

```
; Function:
;    Returning the Genoa ID.
;    The Genoa card is identified by checking a byte which is
;    pointed to by the byte at C000:0037. The byte is added to
;    C000:0000 to find the Genoa ID which should be 77 hex.

; Output Parameters
;       signature                        in AX

; Calling Protocol:
;    Get_Genoa_Key(signature)

Get_Genoa_Key proc far USES DS SI ES DI, arg1:FAR PTR

;       set up source pointer
        mov     ax,0c000h         ;point to VGA BIOS segment
        mov     ds,ax
        mov     si,0037h          ;location of signature

;       get pointer offset
        xor     ax,ax             ;zero upper byte
        mov     al,ds:[si]        ;get pointer to id
        mov     si,ax             ;put into offset register

;       get pointer to destination
        les     di,arg1

;       get id
        mov     cx,4                         ;move four bytes

        rep     movsb
        ret

Get_Genoa_Key  endp
```

17.4.2 Identifying Which Genoa Chip

Only the Genoa GVGA chip is discussed in this book. Earlier Genoa cards were based on the Tseng Labs' ET3000 chip. The chip and card number are determined by referencing the third byte in the four-byte string described in Section 17.4.1. The Genoa cards and their associated codes are listed in Table 17.7. The four bytes are (in hex) as follows: 77 xx 99 66.

If an older Genoa card — 5100, 5200, 5300 or 5400 — is detected, code should conform to the code provided in Chapter 19 for the ET3000. The ET3000 is produced by Tseng Labs. Code to identify the resident Genoa card, and consequently VGA chip, is provide in Listing 17.3.

TABLE 17.7 Genoa Card and Chip Identification

Card	Chip	xx Field
5100	Tseng ET3000	33
5200	Tseng ET3000	33
5300	Tseng ET3000	55
5400	Tseng ET3000	55
6100	Genoa GVGA	22
6200	Genoa GVGA	00
6300	Genoa GVGA	00
6400	Genoa GVGA	11
6600	Genoa GVGA	11

LISTING 17.3 Determining Which Genoa Super VGA Chip

```
/*
Function:
    Determining Which Genoa Super VGA chip

Output  Parameters:
            33 hex      Card is 5100 or 5200
            55 hex      Card is 5300 or 5400
            22 hex      Card is 6100
            00 hex      Card is 6200 or 6300
            11 hex      Card is 6400 or 6600

Calling  Protocol:
  Card = Which_Genoa()  */

int  Which_Genoa()
{ char  signature[4];  int  card;

  Get_Genoa_Key(signature);  /* get Genoa key */

card=signature[1];
return(card);
}
```

Configuration Register

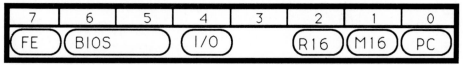

Index 5 at Port 3C4   Port 3C5 Read/Write

FIGURE 17.8 Configuration Register. The PC field reports whether the host is a PC/ AT or PS/2. The M16 and R16 fields report whether the memory and ROM bus are 8- or 16-bits. The 1/0 field reports whether the I/0 is at 2xx or 3xx. The BIOS field defines the BIOS size.

17.4.3   Identifying the Genoa chip Revision

Genoa Systems does not provide any methodology for returning the GVGA chip version number.

17.4.4   Identifying the VGA Environment

Status can be returned to the programmer via the Configuration Register shown in Figure 17.8.

The PC field indicates when the VGA is in a PC/AT or PS/2 host system. The PC field is read only. If the PC field returns a 0, the VGA is in a PS/2 system. If it returns a 1, the VGA is in a PC/AT system.

The M16 field indicates when the VGA is interfaced to the host through an 8- or 16-bit bus. The M16 field is read only. If the M16 field returns a 0, a 16-bit external bus is active. If it returns a 1, an 8-bit bus is active.

The R16 field indicates the width of the BIOS ROM bus. The BIOS field is read only. If the BIOS field returns a 0, a 16-bit external bus is active. If it returns a 1, an 8-bit bus is active. The I/O field reports whether the VGA I/O port address space resides in the 2xx or 3xx hex address space. If the I/O field returns a 0, then the I/O mapping is at 2xx. If the I/O field returns a 1, then the I/O mapping is at 3xx hex. This 3xx mapping is the VGA standard. The BIOS size field returns information about the size of the BIOS ROM. The default BIOS size is 24 Kbytes, beginning at C000:0000 in host memory address space. The BIOS size field should also be considered a read-only field. The meaning of this field is indicated in Table 17.8.

Additional status can be returned in the Enhanced Control #2 Register shown in Figure 17.3. The MON field reports the type of monitor as set by the sense switches. If the MON field contains a 1, a TTL monitor is installed. If 0, an analog monitor is installed.

The MBA field reports when the GVGA is installed on a motherboard or on an adapter card. If the MBA field is set to 1, the GVGA is on a motherboard. If 0, the GVGA is on an adapter card.

TABLE 17.8 BIOS ROM Size

BIOS field	ROM BIOS Size
0	24 Kbytes (default)
1	30 Kbytes
2	32 Kbytes
3	24 Kbytes

The FE field enables either two or eight simultaneously displayable fonts. If the FE field is set to 1, eight simultaneously displayable fonts are enabled. These maps are controlled by the Character Map Select Register described in Section 10.3.4 with the mapping described in Table 10.10.

17.5 GENOA TECHNOLOGY DISPLAY MODES

The Super VGA alphanumeric modes are 132-column width, from 25 to 44 lines. All operate in the standard 16-color mode. Four different display fonts are utilized. These are listed in Table 17.9.

The Super VGA graphics modes span the common 16 and 256-color display modes. Two unique modes are provided, as mentioned in Section 17.2.1. These are modes 55 hex and 65 hex. Missing is a 1024 by 768 256-color mode. These modes are listed in Table 17.10.

17.5.1 Display Mode 7F hex

Display mode 7F hex is a 1024 by 768 4-color mode. These four colors are reminiscent of the CGA modes. This mode can best be described as a planar mode utilizing odd-even bank switching. Each pixel is represented by two bits spread across two display planes. Even pixels are represented in planes 0 and 1 while odd pixels are stored in planes 2 and 3. This is illustrated in Figure 17.9. It can be seen that a contiguous set of data values would be written to planes 0,1,2,3,0,1,...and so on.

To locate a pixel, first multiply the vertical, y, coordinate by the number of bytes per display line. In this case, there are 1024 pixels per scan line and eight pixels per byte. Therefore, there are 128 bytes per scan line. Each plane is 64-Kbytes long. Thus, single precision unsigned arithmetic will suffice. This number , base_address, forms the base address of the byte containing the eight left-most pixels in the proper scan line.

The second step is to divide the horizontal pixel number, x, by eight. Both the whole and fractional parts should be calculated. The whole part of the

TABLE 17.9 Genoa Super VGA Alphanumeric Display Modes

Resolution	# of colors	Manufacturer	Chip	Mode
80 by 29	2	Genoa	all	43
80 by 32	2	Genoa	all	44
80 by 44	2	Genoa	all	45
132 by 25	2	Genoa	all	46
132 by 29	2	Genoa	all	47
132 by 32	2	Genoa	all	48
132 by 44	2	Genoa	all	49
80 by 32	16	Genoa	all	58
100 by 42	16	Genoa	all	5A
132 by 25	16	Genoa	all	60
132 by 29	16	Genoa	all	61
132 by 32	16	Genoa	all	62
132 by 44	16	Genoa	all	63
132 by 60	16	Genoa	all	64
80 by 60	16	Genoa	all	72
80 by 66	16	Genoa	all	74
100 by 75	16	Genoa	all	78/6B

TABLE 17.10 Genoa Super VGA Graphics Display Modes

Resolution	# of colors	Manufacturer	Chip	Mode
720 by 512	16	Genoa	all	59
640 by 350	256	Genoa	all	5B
640 by 480	256	Genoa	all	5C
720 by 512	256	Genoa	all	5D
800 by 600	256	Genoa	all	5E
1024 by 768	16	Genoa	all	5F
800 by 600	16	Genoa	all	6A
800 by 600	256	Genoa	all	6C
640 by 480	16	Genoa	all	73
800 by 600	16	Genoa	all	79
512 by 512	16	Genoa	all	7C
512 by 512	256	Genoa	all	7D
640 by 400	256	Genoa	all	7E
1024 by 768	4	Genoa	all	7F

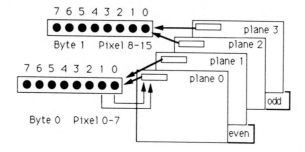

a) Planar Organization Showing 8 Pixels per Byte Resident
in 2 Planes Organized in an Odd/Even Fashion. Pixel in bit 7 is
left-most pixel on display.

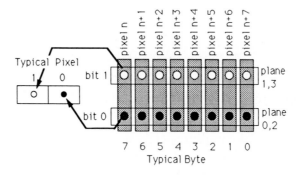

b) Memory Organization Showing a Pixel
Resident in Two Display Planes

FIGURE 17.9 Memory Organization for Genoa Mode 7F hex. Illustrates 4-color planar odd-even addressing.

division provides the byte number, byte_number, which contains the pixel in question. The fractional part, pixel_place is saved for later. If this byte number, byte_number, is even, the pixel resides in a byte which is located in display planes 0 and 1. If the byte number is odd, the pixel resides in a byte which is located in display planes 2 and 3.

The third step is to divide the byte number, byte_number, by two. This provides the byte offset, byte_offset, within the selected pair of planes.

Finally, the fractional part, pixel_place is used to find the bit position within the selected byte. The pixel_place resulting from the division of x/8 is used to find the actual bit position of the pixel in question. This division is also a mod 8 operation. A mask can be formed by shifting the constant 80 hex right by the number pixel_place. This occurs because the most significant bit in each byte represents the left-most pixel when mapped to the display.

The two bits encoded into each pixel select one of four colors. There are eight color combinations in one of eight color sets. The color sets are selected by setting bits 0 and 1 in the Color Select register described in Section 10.6.7.

There are two additional fields of interest to mode 7F hex. These are both contained in the Enhanced Control #5 Register shown in Figure 17.10. These fields are extremely useful when the Mode 7F is used. The display mapping is peculiar and the programmer might desire to read or write to display memory in a format other than the Mode 7F format. Similarly, the programmer might desire to display the data in a format other than the Mode 7F format.

The RWM field enables the memory read/write mapping to be compatible with the 1024 by 768 Mode 7F hex display mode. If the RWM field is set to 1, this mapping is engaged. If the RWM field is set to 0, it is disabled and normal memory accessing occurs.

The data, which will eventually be displayed in Mode 7F, can be more conveniently read or written in a different way. Thus, if the system is in a Mode 7F configuration, data can be read or written to memory in a different format. Conversely, while the display is in a display mode other than Mode 7F, the memory can be read or written to in the Mode 7F format.

The GOM field enables the CRT graphics output to be compatible with the 1024 by 768 Mode 7F hex display mode. If the GOM field is set to 1, this display format is used. If the GOM field is set to 0, this display format is not used and the normal display output occurs.

The programmer might not want information to be displayed in the Mode 7F format while the system is in a Mode 7F configuration. For example, a portion of the display memory might be written in a Mode 7F format while another portion is written in a planar 16-color format. The display output format can be rapidly switched back and forth between the Mode 7F format and the planar 16-color format.

The display palette is organized so that all 16 locations of the color palette must be loaded to produce the four possible colors. The palette is organized as four groups of four colors each. The four colors reside in palette locations 0, 1, 2 and 3. These are repeated in palette locations 4,5,6 and 7, again in 8, 9, 10 and 11 and finally in 12, 13, 14 and 15. Thus, color 0 resides in palette locations 0, 4, 8 and 12. Color 1 resides in 1, 5, 9 and 13, and so on.

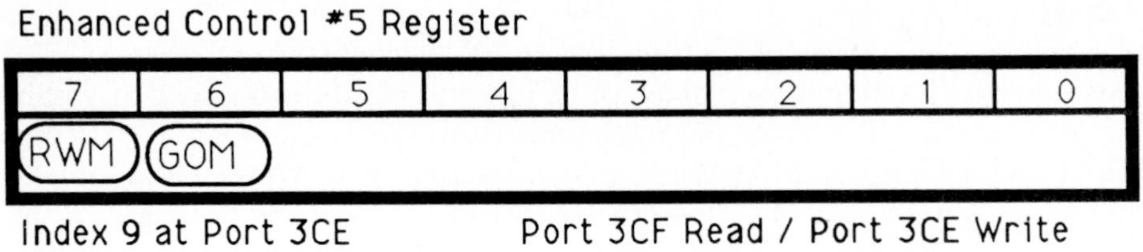

Enhanced Control #5 Register

7	6	5	4	3	2	1	0
(RWM)	(GOM)						

Index 9 at Port 3CE   Port 3CF Read / Port 3CE Write

FIGURE 17.10   Enhanced Control #5 Register. The GOM field and the RWM field control the graphics output mapping and the memory read/write mapping for the mode 7F hex.

17.6   ACCESSING THE GENOA DISPLAY MEMORY

The Genoa VGA chip maps display memory into host memory address space by using a single-bank register which contains a read and write bank (segment). These are listed in Table 17.11. Both the read and write banks map a 64-Kbyte segment of display memory into the host address space. The values range from 0 to 7, allowing 512 Kbytes of memory to be accessed.

17.6.1   Bank Select

The bank select feature is specific to a particular card manufacturer and the MBS field should not be modified by the programmer. The memory bank selection is controlled through the MBS field of the Enhanced Control Register #4. If the MBS field is set to 0, memory bank 0 is selected. If the MBS field is set to 1, memory bank 1 is selected.

The bank registers are aligned to 64-Kbyte segments, providing a granularity of 64 Kbytes. The 19-bit memory address is formed by the sixteen-bit address generated by the CRT addressing (low order 16-bits) added to the three bits in the Bank Select Register (high order 3 bits) shown in Figure 17.11.

Two macros are provided to load the write and read banks in Listings 17.4 and 17.5 respectively.

17.6.2 Memory Configuration

The memory configuration is controlled by three distinct fields listed in Table 17.13. The EGA/VGA mapping is controlled through the VGA field of the Enhanced Control #3 Register shown in Figure 17.4. If the VGA field is set to 1, MDA/Hercules or CGA emulation is in effect. If this is the case, memory is accessed regardless of bank (segment) switching. If the VGA field is 0, EGA or VGA operation is in effect.

The Miscellaneous Register, discussed in Section 10.5.9, contains a two-bit field which controls the memory mapping. This field is set to 0 or 1 for the graphics modes which affect bank switching. If this field is set to 0, the memory

TABLE 17.11   Reading and Writing to Genoa Display Memory

Function	Register Name	Port	Index	Bits	Value
Write Bank	Memory Segment	3C4	6	5–3	0–7
Read Bank	Memory Segment	3C4	6	2–0	0–7
Memory Configuration	Memory Segment	3C4	6	6	0,1
Select EGA/VGA mode	Enhanced Control #3	3C4	8	0	0
Select /Herc/CGA mode	Enhanced Control #3	3C4	8	0	1
128 Kbytes at A000	Miscellaneous	3CE	6	3–2	0
64 Kbytes at A000	Miscellaneous	3CE	6	3–2	1
Page Select	Miscellaneous Output	3C2	–	5	0,1
Bank Select	Enhanced Control #4	3C4	10	7	0,1

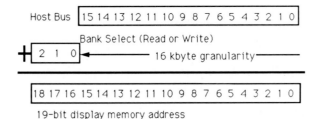

FIGURE 17.11   Creation of a 19-bit Address Using Bank Selection

is organized as 128 Kbytes at A0000 hex. If the memory mapping field is set to 1, the memory is organized as 64 Kbytes at A0000 hex.

In the 64-Kbyte instance, address bit 16 is used to generate the 17th address bit for display memory. The bank-select bits 2–1 are used to generate the address bits 18 and 17 respectively.

In the 128-Kbyte instance, either page select bit, PB, of the Miscellaneous Register is used as address bit 16 or the read or write bank bit-0 is used to generate the address bit 16 for display memory. The Miscellaneous Output Register, discussed in Section 10.2.1. The bank select bits 2–1 are used to generate the address bits 18 and 17 respectively.

These memory mapping options are listed in Table 17.12.

TABLE 17.12 Memory Mapping in the GVGA

Address 19	Address 18	Address 17	Enhanced Control#3	Miscellaneous MM field	En. Control 3 MEM field
A2	A1	Hercules	1 (Hercules)	don't care	don't care
Bank2	Bank1	A16	0 (VGA)	1 (64-Kbyte)	don't care
Bank2	Bank1	PB	0 (VGA)	0 (128-Kbyte)	0
Bank2	Bank1	Bank0	0 (VGA)	0 (128-Kbyte)	1

Memory Segment Register

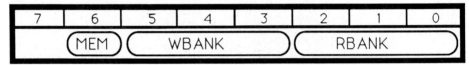

Index 6 at Port 3C4   Port 3C5 Read/Write

FIGURE 17.12 Memory Segment Register. The WBANK field selects the 64 or 128-Kbyte segment during write operation. The RBANK field selects the 64- or 128-Kbyte segment during read operations. The MEM field provides configuratlon information for memory mapping.

The MEM field of the Memory Segment Register, shown in Figure 17.12, controls the source of address bit 17. If the MEM field is set to 0, the page bit, PB, of the Miscellaneous Output register acts as address bit 17. If the MEM field is set to 1, the least significant bit of the bank fields, Bank0, acts as address bit 17.

17.6.3 Read/Write Bank Switching

The Dual bank registers provide a mechanism for rapidly transferring data from one display memory location to another. The read and write fields of the Memory Segment Register needs to be written to only once every time a 64-Kbyte bank is crossed.

Suppose a programmer wants to move a bank from one location to another in the display memory. It is desirable to use the REP MOVSW instruction. It is necessary only to load the Bank Select Register. Then it is necessary to set up both the segment registers to point to A000, the offset registers to point to the source and destination offset, and the cx register with the number of words to move. This setup is followed by the REP MOVSW instruction. The maximum

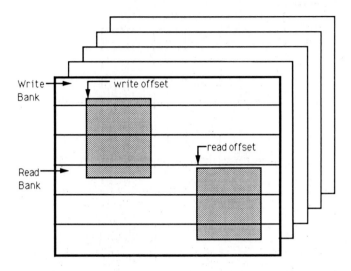

FIGURE 17.13   Disply Memory Addressing. Read/Write operations utilizing the read and write bank registers. A 19-bit address is formed by the three-bit bank value and the 16-bit offset value.

number of pixels that can be moved in one REP MOVSW sequence is determined by the distance to the next 64-Kbyte boundary. It is necessary to set up the Memory Segment Register before crossing these boundaries. This is illustrated in Figure 17.13.

Macro code to load the write and read bank address performs a read, modify, and write operation, putting the new write bank number into the Bank Select Register as shown in Listings 17.4 and 17.5 respectively.

LISTING 17.4   Loading the Write Bank Numbe Macro

```
; Function:
;       Loading the Write Bank with a new start address

; Input with:
;       bl                      Write Bank_Number
;                                  0-7 bank number indicating desired
;                               64-Kbyte bank
```

```
; Calling Protocol:
;       Load_Write_Bank_Genoa

Load_Write_Bank_Genoa macro
;       set up index to Bank Select Register
        mov     dx,3c4h          ;point to memory Segment Register
        mov     al,06h
        out     dx,al            ;output index

;       input value so Configuration bit is preserved
        inc     dx
        in      al,dx            ;input value
        and     al,0c7h                  ;zero write bank bits 5-3

;       load in the new bank value
        and     bl,07h                   ;only want 3 bits
        shl     bl,1             ;put desired write bank into bits 5-3
        shl     bl,1             ;put desired write bank into bits 5-3
        shl     bl,1             ;put desired write bank into bits 5-3

        or      al,bl            ;or in write bank
        out     dx,al            ;output bank

endm
```

LISTING 17.5   Loading the Read Bank Number Macro

```
; Function:
;       Loading the Read Bank with a new start address

; Input with:
;       bl      Read Bank_Number
;                  0-7 bank number indicating desired 64-Kbyte bank

; Calling Protocol:
;       Load_Read_Bank_Genoa

Load_Read_Bank_Genoa macro

;       set up index to Bank Select Register
        mov     dx,3c4h                  ;point to memory Segment
                                          Register
```

```
        mov     al,06h
        out     dx,al           ;output index

;       input value so Configuration bit is preserved
        inc     dx
        in      al,dx           ;input value
        and     al,0f8h             ;zero write bank bits 2-0

;       load in the new bank value
        and     bl,07h              ;only want 3 bits

        or      al,bl       ;or in write bank
        out     dx,al       ;output bank


    endm
```

The C-callable functions to load the write and read banks are provided in Listings 17.6 and 17.7 respectively.

LISTING 17.6   Loading the Write Bank Number

```
;  Function:
;       Loading the Write Bank with a new start address

;  Input with:
;       write_bank      Write Bank_Number
;                               0-7 bank number indicating desired
;                               64-Kbyte bank

;  Calling Protocol:
;       Set_Write_Bank_Genoa(write_bank);

Set_Write_Bank_Genoa proc far arg1:byte

;       load in the new bank value
        mov     bl,arg1         ;get argument
        Load_Write_Bank_Genoa

        ret
Set_Write_Bank_Genoa endp
```

LISTING 17.7   Loading the Read Bank Number

```
; Function:
;       Loading the Read Bank with a new start address

; Input with:
;       read_bank       Read Bank_Number
;                               0-7 bank number indicating desired
                                64-Kbyte bank

; Calling Protocol:
;       Set_Read_Bank_Genoa(read_bank);

Set_Read_Bank_Genoa proc far arg1:byte

;       load in the new bank value
        mov     bl,arg1         ;get argument
        Load_Read_Bank_Genoa

        ret
Set_Read_Bank_Genoa endp
```

17.7   CONTROLLING THE CRT ADDRESS GENERATION

17.7.1   Controlling the Start Address

The host cannot extend control of the start address of the display or of the cursor past the 64-byte segment controlled through the Start Address Low and Start Address High registers. The Genoa start address can be loaded through the function in Listing 17.8. This function utilizes the set_start_address macro in Listing 14.32.

LISTING 17.8   Loading the Genoa Start Address

```
; Function:
;       Loading the Display Start Address

;InputParameters
;       address         unsigned integer starting address

; Calling Protocol:
;       Load_Start_Genoa(address)

Load_Start_Genoa        proc far        arg1,arg2:byte
```

```
        mov     bx,arg1
        set_start_address       ;load the 16-bit start address
        ret
Load_Start_Genoa        endp
```

16-Color Modes Start Address

The memory is configured as four overlapped planes in the 16-color modes. Each plane is 64 Kbytes long. There is one such set of planes in the 256-Kbyte implementations. There are two groups of these planes in the 512-Kbyte configurations. These groups are called pages. The sixteen bits of the Start Address Low and High registers, therefore, actually point to a pixel within the 256-Kbyte page of memory. The granularity of the start address is four bytes.

Two sixteen-color display mode extend into the second bank of memory. This are the 1024 by 768 16-color modes. Both of these modes, 55 hex and 65 hex, will automatically cross the page boundary during display cycles. It is not possible to set the start address beyond a location if the first page. Since the first page consists of 64 Kbytes and a single line requires 1024/8 = 128 bytes, a total of 512 scan lines can fit in the first page. Thus, the start address cannot extend beyond scan line 511.

256-Color Mode Start Address

The memory is physically divided among four display planes in the 256-color modes. However, unlike the 16-color modes, the memory is not logically split between these four display planes in the 256-color modes. Due to the memory organization (sequential locations being loaded across the four display pages), the 64-Kbyte span of the start addresses only covers 64 Kbytes. The 256-color modes include the 640 by 400, the 640 by 480 and the 800 by 600 resolutions. These require 256,000bytes, 307,200 bytes and 480,000 bytes respectively. This means that the starting address can not exceed scanlines 102 for the 640 pixel wide display modes and scanline 81 for the 800 pixel wide display mode.

17.7.2 Cursor Control

The alphanumeric modes do not have a problem with page crossing since none extend beyond the first 256-Kbyte page. The cursor can be controlled in the alphanumeric modes by using the 16-bit cursor start address contained in the Cursor Start Address High and Cursor Start Address Low registers. These registers are discussed in Sections 10.4.15 and 10.4.16 respectively.

Code to position the cursor is provided in Listing 17.9. This function utilizes the position_cursor macro in Listing 14.33.

LISTING 17.9   Position the Cursor

```
; Function:
;       Load the Cursor Position

; Input Parameters
;       position                unsigned integer position

; Calling Protocol:
;       Position_Cursor_Genoa(position)

Position_Cursor_Genoa           proc far        arg1,arg2:byte

        mov     bx,arg1
        position_cursor                 ;load the 16-bit cursor position

        ret
Position_Cursor_Genoa endp
```

17.7.3   Controlling the Display Offset

The display offset determines the virtual image size. The eight-bit value stored in the Offset Register in the CRTC Register Group, is described in Section 10.4.22. In the word mode, which is typically the case, display offsets up to 1024 bytes can be defined.

Chapter 18

The Paradise Super VGA Chips

18.1 INTRODUCTION TO THE PARADISE/WESTERN DIGITAL VGA

The Paradise, trademark of Western Digital, Super VGA family of chips includes the PVGA1A, the WD90C00, the WD90C10 and the WD90C11. The features of each are described in Table 18.1. Each chip is downwardly compatible to the newer generations. The first generation PVGA1A chip provides the framework for the second-generation WD90C00 chip. The WD90C00 builds upon the basic framework of the PVGA1A by adding additional Extended registers and providing higher display resolutions. Similarly, the WD90C10 and WD90C11 are later versions of the WD90C00.

The WD90C10 is a stripped-down version of the WD90C00, not an enhancement. The WD90C10 will exist mainly on motherboard implementations of the VGA. This chip only supports the basic VGA modes, no 256-color modes other than Mode 13 hex. It will have a total of 256 Kbytes DRAM, providing the capability of 800 by 600 16-color, 1024 by 768 2- and 4-color graphics and 132 column text modes. It will not do 640 by 400 or 640 by 480 in the 256-color modes as did the PVGA1A and WD90C00.

The WD90C11 is the enhanced version of the WD90C00. It provides improved data paths and memory addressing. Both of these provide improved performance. The WD90C11 will support 512Kbytes of memory allowing it to support the 640 by 400, 640 by 480, 800 by 600 in the 256-color mode, and 1024 by 768 in the 16-color mode. It will have twice the speed performance of the WD90C00.

18.1.1 The PVGA1A Super VGA Chip

The first-generation Super VGA chip, the PVGA1A, is straightforward and easy to program. This VGA implementation supports the high-resolution 800 by 600 16-color display modes but is limited to 640 by 480 in the 256-color mode. The VGA card is equipped with a maximum of 512 Kbytes of memory. Some vendors have implemented the PVGA1A with one megabyte.

The PVGA1A has seven Extended registers as indicated in Table 18.2. Access to these registers is typically locked, with the exception of the PR5 register. This

TABLE 18.1   Paradise/Western Digital Chips

Chip Name	16-color Max Resolution	256-color Max Resolution	Memory Capability
PVGA1A	800 by 600	640 by 480	512 Kbytes or 1 Megabyte
WD90C00	1024 by 768	800 by 600	512 Kbytes or 1 Megabyte
WD90C10	640 by 480	320 by 200	256 Kbytes
WD90C11	1024 by 768	800 by 600	512 Kbytes

TABLE 18.2   Paradise Extended Registers

Name	Usage	Designation	Port	Index	
Address Offset A	Bank Switch A	PR0A		3CE	9
Address Offset B	Bank Switch B	PR0B		3CE	A
Memory Size	Memory Configuration	PR1		3CE	B
Video Select	Video Configuration	PR2		3CE	C
CRT Control	CRT Address Control	PR3		3CE	D
Video Control	Video Control	PR4		3CE	E
General Purpose	Enable Extended Registers	PR5		3CE	F

register contains the enable key to the other Extended registers. It is always unlocked.

MDA and CGA emulation is available. EGA emulation is not handled separately from the VGA operation. Utilities are provided that change the display controller to emulate the 6845 CRT controller. This path was chosen over implemention of non-maskable interrupts (NMI) and autoswitching. This path was chosen to eliminate the problem which occured when "smart" software would check to see what graphics cards were present. For example, the software would issue a CGA command which would cause the hardware to switch state in an attempt to emulate the CGA card.

Both single and dual-paging schemes are available to the programmer. The paging scheme is unique in that the banks are not fixed to 64-Kbyte intervals. Instead, they are controlled by the addition of the host address and the bank registers. This is very useful if a data transfer is known to be under 64 Kbytes. The bank register can be set up to point to the closest 4-Kbyte boundary and the 64-Kbyte transfer can proceed.

The 512 Kbytes of memory can be accessed through bank switching. A standard bank switching technique is available which utilizes either one- or two-bank registers. The memory can be configured into 64-Kbyte or 128-Kbyte segments.

The VGA BIOS contains extended function calls that allow extended mode setting, emulation and access to the Extended registers.

18.1.2   The WD90C00 Super VGA Chip

The second-generation Super VGA chip, the WD90C00, improves upon the performance of the PVGA1A chip by increasing display resolutions and providing support for interlaced and non-interlaced monitors. Like the PVGA1A, the chip can support up to one megabyte of DRAM memory. Although a 16-bit host data path is provided, it only operates in the packed display modes. The planar display modes rely on the 8-bit data path.

In addition to the seven Extended registers available in the PVGA1A, eight additional Extended registers are provided in the WD90C00. These registers control interlaced timing and EGA hardware emulation. They also provide additional register locking, a software scratchpad, and additional addressing capabilities. These registers are located in the CRTC register group instead of residing within the same register group as the earlier Extended registers.

Three new sixteen-color modes were added at the 1024 by 768 resolution. These provide a four-color and two-color graphics mode. Output timing can be constrained to be completely compatible with the 8514/A interlaced monitors.

18.1.3   The WD90C10 Super VGA Chip

The WD90C10 is a stripped-down version of the WD90C00. Functionally, these two chips are very similar. The WD90C10 has four additional extended registers which provide additional control and status information. The WD90C00 provides enhanced system configuration ability to the hardware designer for inexpensive motherboard implementations. All features of the WD90C00 are directly applicable to the WD90C10 except some of the higher display modes.

18.1.4   The WD90C11 Super VGA Chip

The WD90C11 is the enhanced version of the WD90C00 and WD90C10. Due to improved memory accessing, the WD90C11 provides an 800 by 600 256-color display mode. One major WD90C11 enhancement is the ability to configure the PR0A and PR0B extended bank select registers. In the PVGA1A and WD90C00, these registers perform identically. Bank switching can be accomplished using the single PR0A Register or the dual PR0A/PR0B registers. In the 64-Kbyte memory dual mapping case, the PR0B Register is used when memory accesses occur to the 32-Kbyte host memory address space A0000–A7FFF. The PR0A Register is used when memory accesses occur to the 32-Kbyte host memory address space A8000–AFFFF. In the 128-Kbyte memory dual map case, the PR0B register is used when memory accesses occur to the 64-Kbyte host memory address space A0000 to A7FFF. The PR0A register spans the 64-Kbyte space between A8000 to AFFFF. Read or write operations can occur through either Bank Selection Register.

In the WD90C11, the PR0A and PR0B registers can be configured so both are used when memory accesses occur to the 64-Kbyte host memory address space A0000-AFFFF. All read operations utilize the PR0A Register while all write operations utilize the PR0B Register.

18.2   CONFIGURING THE PARADISE SUPER VGA

The memory, I/O, and ROM can be configured for 8- or 16-bit transfers. In addition, on-card ROM can be enabled or disabled and 30- or 32-Kbyte mapping of the ROM is configurable. These features are shown in Table 18.3.

18.2.1   8- or 16-bit Bus Interface

The Paradise card can be configured for 8- or 16-bit transfers as indicated in Table 18.3. Transfers occur between the host to display memory and between the host and the ROM through the M16 and R16 fields of the PR1 register. In addition, the on-card ROM can be enabled or disabled through the ENR field of the PR1 register. The PR1 register is shown in Figure 18.1. Additional fields include MEM, MAP and ENB. These are discussed in Section 18.6.2.

18.2.2   BIOS ROM Bus Width

The Paradise card also has jumpers and switches for configuring the card's data width. An autosense feature through Switch 5 will automatically determine whether 8- or 16-bit ROM access should be allowed. This is determined at power up. The decision is based on detection of the 16-bit extension connector and testing the bus speed. The WI jumper deinstalled will force the autosense feature to be 16-bit ROM. This may cause conflicts between C0000 and DFFFF. Other 8-bit cards can cause conflicts, and the autosense feature might not work.

18.2.3   BIOS ROM Mapping

The WD90C00,10 and 11 can be configured to allow the BIOS ROM to span the entire 32-Kbyte ROM address space from C0000 to C7FFF through the Miscellaneous Control #3 Register. It is also possible to disable access to the 2 Kbytes of BIOS ROM between C6000-C67FF. If the MOR field is set to 1, the 2 Kbytes between C6000 and C67FF are not decoded. If the MOR field is 0, all 32 Kbytes are decoded. The PR17 register is shown in Figure 18.2. If a Western Digital BIOS is used, always set this to 32-Kbyte ROM address.

The EBR and M04 fields are available only on the WD90C10 and WD90C11. The EBR field enables EBROMN to decode 64-Kbyte BIOS from C0000 to CFFFF hex. If the EBR field is set to 1, the 64-Kbyte BIOS is enabled. The M04

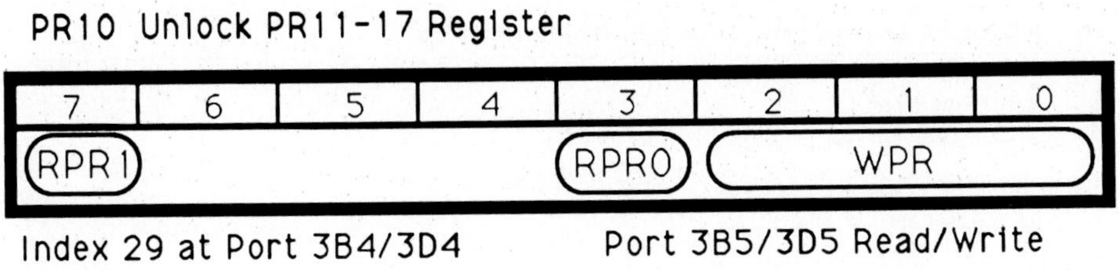

PR10 Unlock PR11-17 Register

7	6	5	4	3	2	1	0
(RPR1)				(RPR0)		WPR	

Index 29 at Port 3B4/3D4   Port 3B5/3D5 Read/Write

FIGURE 18.6 PR10 Unlock PR 11–17 Register. The RPR0 and RPR1 fields protect the PR10–PR17 registers from being read. The WPR field protect sthe PR11–PR17 registers from being written to.

TABLE 18.5 Write Protection of PR10-18

W 2	P 1	R 0	PR10–PR17
0	X	X	Write protected
X	1	X	Write protected
X	X	0	Write protected
1	0	1	Write protected

TABLE 18.6 Write Protection of PR10–18

RPR1	RPR0	PR10–PR17
0	X	Read protected
X	1	Read protected
1	0	Read enabled

The WPR field controls the write protection as listed in Table 18.5. This field allows the protection of registers PR11–PR18. The WPR field write protects the registers PR11–PR17 as shown in Table 18.5. PR10 cannot be write-protected. If it were, there would be no way to unlock it for use.

The RPR0 and RPR1 fields form together to create the read protection code as listed in Table 18.6. These registers protect registers PR10–PR18. It is recommended to write 85 hex into PR10 to enable read and write access.

The Paradise VGA extensions can be enabled or disabled through the macro code provided in Listings 18.1 and 18.2 respectively.

LISTING 18.1 Enabling Paradise Control Extensions

```
; Function:
;     Enabling Paradise extensions

; Calling Protocol:
;     Extensions_On_Paradise();

Extensions_On_Paradise macro

;   extensions on
    mov dx,3ceh          ;address PR5
    mov al,0fh           ;index F = PR5
    mov ah,05h           ;turn on extensions
    out dx,ax

;   unlock PR10-PR17
    mono_or_color
    add dx,4
    mov al,29h           ;address PR10
    mov ah,85h           ;unlock read and write
    out dx,ax

;   unlock extended sequencer
    mov dx,3c4h
    mov al,06h           ;index Unlock Sequencer Register
    mov ah,48h           ;unlock extended sequencer
    out dx,ax

endm
```

LISTING 18.2 Disabling Paradise Extensions

```
; Function:
;     Disabling Paradise extensions

; Calling Protocol:
;     Extensions_Off_Paradise();

Extensions_Off_Paradise macro
    mov dx,3ceh          ;address PR5
    mov al,0fh           ;index F = PR5
    mov ah,00h           ; turn on extensions
    out dx,ax
```

```
;   lock PR10-PR17
    mono_or_color
      add dx,4
      mov al,29h              ;address PR10
      mov ah,00h               ;lock read and write
      out dx,ax

;   unlock extended sequencer
    mov dx,3c4h
      mov al,06h             ;index Unlock Sequencer Register
      mov ah,00h             ;unlock extended sequencer
      out dx,ax
endm
```

The C-callable functions to enable or disable the extensions are provided in Listings 18.3 and 18.4 respectively.

LISTING 18.3   Enabling Paradise Extensions

```
;  Function:
;     Enabling Paradise extensions

;  Calling Protocol:
;  Extended_On_Paradise();

Extended_On_Paradise proc far
    Extensions_On_Paradise
  ret
Extended_On_Paradise endp
```

LISTING 18.4   Disabling Paradise Extensions

```
;  Function:
;     Disabling Paradise extensions;

Calling Protocol:
;     Extended_Off_Paradise();

Extended_Off_Paradise proc far
     Extensions_Off_Paradise
  ret
Extended_Off_Paradise endp
```

PR12 Scratch Pad Register

Index 2B at Port 3B4/3D4   Port 3B5/3D5 Read/Write

FIGURE 18.7 PR12 Scratch Pad Register. The SCRATCH field can be used for any purpose.

PR14 Interlace H/2 End Register

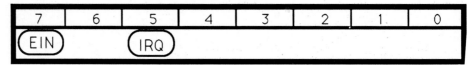

Index 2D at Port 3B4/3D4   Port 3B5/3D5 Read/Write

FIGURE 18.8 PR14 Interlace H/2 End Register. The EIN field enables interrupts.The INT field enables interlaced mode.

18.3.2   WD90C00,10 and 11 Scratch Pad

PR12 is the Scratch Pad Register. This register is reserved for BIOS and is shown in Figure 18.7.

18.3.3   WD90C11 Scratch Pad

Additional scratch space is provided in the Display Configuration Status Register shown in Figure 18.8. The Scratch field in this register is four bits wide and can be used by the programmer. This field is also reserved for BIOS.

18.3.4   WD90C00,10 and 11 Vertical Interrupts

Vertical interrupts can be enabled through the Interlace H/2 End Register. Strictly speaking, the VGA standard does not require vertical interrupts, and they should not be used in microchannel applications. The EGA did include vertical interrupts as part of the standard. If the EIN field is set to 1, vertical interrupts are enabled. If 0, vertical interrupts are disabled. This register is shown in Figure 18.8.

Global Enable Register

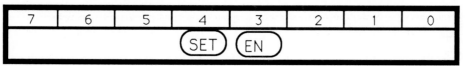

Port 46E8 Read/Write

FIGURE 18.9 Global Enable Register. Adapter Card Implementation at Port 46E8. Controls enabling and disabling of the VGA through the EN field. The SET field allows access to the 102 hex Wake Up Port.

Global Enable Register

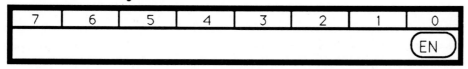

Port 3C3 Read/Write

FIGURE 18.10 Global Enable Register. Motherboard Implementation at Port 3C3. Controls enabling and disabling of VGA through the EN field.

18.3.5 Control of 46E8 Global Enable

The Global Enable registers control the enabling and disabling of the VGA chip. If the chip is on an adapter card, the location of this register is at 46E8. If it is on a microchannel card or on the motherboard, the location is at 3C3. Both of these registers are shown in Figures 18.9 and 18.10, respectively.

The 46E8 register can be enabled to be read at the E46 field of PR15. Typically, the 46E8 Register is a Write-only Register. The PR15 and PR16 registers are shown in Figures 18.11 and 18.12 respectively. The PM field of the Miscellaneous #1 Register is discussed in Section 18.6.6. The DB field is discussed in Section 18.7.6.

18.3.6 WD90C10/11 Cursor Control

The WD90C10 and WD90C11 can enable or disable cursor blinking through the BLN field of the Miscellaneous Controls Register shown in Figure 18.13. If the BLN field is 1, cursor blinking is disabled in the text modes. If 0, cursor blinking is enabled.

PR15 Miscellaneous Control *1 Register
7
6
5
4
3
2
1
0
E46
INC
PM
DB
Index 2E at Port 3B4/3D4
Port 3B5/3D5 Read/Write

FIGURE 18.11 PR15 Miscellaneous Control #1 Register.The E46 field enables port 46E8 to be read.The INC field provides interlaced compatibility to 8514/A timing. The PM field enables page mode addressing in alphanumeric modes. The DB field disables borders.

PR16 Miscellaneous Control *2 Register
7
6
5
4
3
2
1
0
MOD
TOP
MEM
Index 2F at Port 3B4/3D4
Port 3B5/3D5 Read/Write

FIGURE 18.12 PR16 Miscellaneous Control #2 Register. The MEM field selects standard VGA memory. The TOP field provides the top bits 16 and 17 for the display start address. The MOD field provides the limits to how high the CRTC address counter will count.

Miscellaneous Controls WD91C10,11
7
6
5
4
3
2
1
0
BLN
Index 12 at Port 3C4
Port 3C5 Read/Write

FIGURE 18.13 Miscellaneous Controls Register WD91C10 ,11. The BLN field controls cursor blinking.

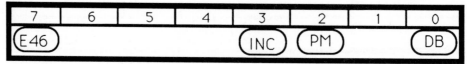

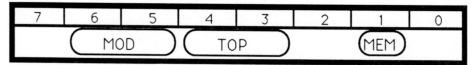

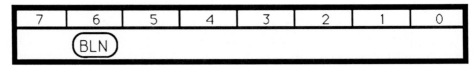

TABLE 18.7   Speed Enhancements in the WD90C11

Field	Bit	Value	Function
TBL	6	1	Enhance speed for blank lines
TMT	5	1	Enhance text operations
RDY	4–3	0	Enhance speed for 12 MHz host
RDY	4–3	1	Enhance speed for 10 MHz host
RDY	4–3	2,3	Enhance speed for 8 MHz host
EWB	2	1	Enhance write operations

18.3.7   Enhanced WD90C10/11 Speed Control

The WD90C11 can provide additional speed enhancements in either text or alphanumerics modes. The System Interface Control Register, shown in Figure 18.3, provides four fields which can enhance speed performance. These are listed in Table 18.7

The TBL field can enhance performance 10 percent by removing extra memory cycles during blank lines. Setting the TBL field to 1 enables blank line removal. Setting it to 0 disables this feature. Setting the TMT field to 1 enhances text operations.

The RDY fields take control when the ready line is released. The ready line is used to signal to the host processor that wait-states are desired. The sooner this ready line is released, the fewer wait-states will be requested. The EWB field enables a 16-bit write buffer. This nearly eliminates wait-states for CPU writes to display memory. If the EWB field is set to 1, the write buffer is enabled. If only 256 Kbytes of DRAM exist in either the WD90C10 or WD90C11, the 800 by 600 mode should set this bit to 0.

18.4   INQUIRING ABOUT THE PARADISE SUPER VGA CONFIGURATION

The programmer can determine the memory size and memory map through the PR1 Extended register. It can identify the VGA through data written into the ROM memory. Details for selecting the VGA status are presented in Table 18.8.

18.4.1   Identifying the Paradise Card

The programmer can sense the Paradise card by looking at the VGA identification string at host memory address C000:007D. This string should be four

TABLE 18.8   Determining Paradise Display Status

Function	Register Name	Port	Index	Bits	Value
Memory Size	PR1	3CF	0B	7–6	0–3
Memory Map	PR1	3CF	0B	5–4	0–3
VGA Identification	Byte at C000:007D				"VGA="
BIOS Date	String at C000:0009				
BIOS Version	Byte at C000:0035				
Compatibility	Display Configuration	3C5	7	2–1	0,1
Mono/Color Mode	Display Configuration	3C5	7	3	0,1

characters long from 7D–80 and should contain VGA=. Code to identify the Paradise VGA is provided in Listing 18.5. This function calls upon the assembly language function in Listing 18.6. This code utilizes the assembly language function which actually acquires the string from memory.

LISTING 18.5   Determining If the Card is a Paradise

```
/*
Function:
 Determining if the card is a Paradise card

Output Parameters:
 1 card is a Paradise
 0 card is NOT a Paradise

Calling Protocol:
 Paradise= Is_It_Paradise() */

#include <string.h>

int Is_It_Paradise()
{ char key[9],signature[9]; int result;

    strncpy(key,"VGA=",4); /* put Paradise key into string */
    Get_Paradise_Key(signature); /* get signature */

    /* compare the two strings and return the result */
    result = strncmp(key,signature,4);
    if(result==0) return(1);
    else return(0);
}
```

LISTING 18.6 Returning the Paradise Signature String

```
;     Function:
;     Returning the Paradise ID.
;     The Paradise chips are identified by checking a string which is
;     located at C000:007D.

; Output Parameters
;     signature   character string

; Calling Protocol:
;     Get_Paradise_Key(signature)

Get_Paradise_Key proc far USES DS SI ES DI, arg1:FAR PTR

;     set up source pointer
      mov ax,0c000h ;point to VGA BIOS segment
      mov ds,ax
      mov si,007Dh ;location of signature

       les di,arg1     ;set up destination "c" buffer signature

;   get id
      mov cx,4      ;move 4 bytes
      rep movsb
      ret
Get_Paradise_Key     endp
```

18.4.2   Identifying the Paradise Chip

The Paradise Chip can be a PVGA1A, a WD90C00, WD90C10 or WD90C11.
These are differentiated by the presence of specific registers. Each chip builds
upon the register set of its predecessor. Each chip adds new registers. The
presence of these registers determines which VGA chip is installed. Code to
perform this function is provided in Listing 18.7.

  Differentiating the WD90C00, WD90C10 and the WD90C11 is a bit problematic. The WD90C00 is differentiated from the WD90C10 and WD90C11 through
the Miscellaneous Control Register at index 12 hex of the register pair 3C4/
3C5 hex. It is necessary to load bit 6 with a 1 and then a 0, and check to see
whether the port responds with a 1 and 0. If it does not, the chip is a WD90C00.
Similarly, the WD90C10 is differentiated from the WD90C11 by the WD90C11
Register at index 10 hex of the register pair 3C4/3C5 hex. The WD90C10 only

responds to bits 1–0 of this register. It is necessary to load bit 3 with a 1 and then
a 0, and check to see whether the port responds with a 1 and 0 in return. If it
does not, the chip is a WD90C10.

LISTING 18.7 Determining the Paradise Chip

```
/*
Function:
     Determining the Paradise chip

Output Parameters:
     identity               integer containing chip code
                                  1 = PVGA1A
                                  2 = WD90C00
                                  3 = WD90C10
                                  4 = WD90C11

NOTE:   A subsequent consequence of this call is that the mode
        control registers are put into their new state.

Calling Protocol:
     identity = Which_Paradise() */

   Which_Paradise()

{    int base;
     unsigned char old_value,new_value,wd90c10;

 Extended_On_Paradise();
if( (inp(0x3CC) & 0x01)==1) base = 0x3D0; else base = 0x3B0;

/* first find out if it is a PVGA1A */
outp(base+4,0x2B); old_value = inp(base+5); /* get old value */
outp(base+5,0xAA); new_value = inp(base+5); /* try new value */

outp(base+5,old_value);        /* restore old value */
if(new_value!=0xAA) return(1); /* it is a PVGA1A */

/* now distinguish between WD90C00 and WD90C10 by loading bit 6 of
the Miscellaneous Control to a 0 */
outp(0x3C4,0x12); old_value = inp(0x3C5);

/* set bit 6 to a 0 */
```

```
outp(0x3C5,old_value&0xbf); new_value=inp(0x3C5)&0x40;
if(new_value!=0); return(2); /* its a wd90c00 */

outp(0x3C5,old_value|0x40); new_value=inp(0x3C5)&0x40;
if(new_value==0); return(2); /* its a wd90c00 */

outp(0x3c5,old_value);
if(new_value==0) return(2); /* if it is a 0 then WD90C00 */

/* now distinguish between a WD90C10 and a WD90C11 by loading the
extended register at 3C4/3C5 index 10 hex bit 3 with a 0 and then a
1 */

wd90c10=0; /* assume its a wd90c11 */
outp(0x3C4,0x10); old_value = inp(0x3c5);
outp(0x3C5,old_value&0xfb); new_value=inp(0x3C5)&0x04;
if(new_value!=0); wd90c10=1;

outp(0x3C5,old_value|0x04); new_value=inp(0x3C5)&0x04;
if(new_value==0); wd90c10=1;

outp(0x3C5,old_value);
if(wd90c10==1) return(3); /* if it is a 0 then WD90C10 */
              else return(4); /* if not then WD90C11 */
}
```

18.43   Identifying the WD90C11 Configuration

Additional status information can be determined in the WD90C11 though the Display Configuration Status Register shown in Figure 18.14.

Emulation status can be determined through the 6845 and EGA fields. The 6845 field is used to indicate whether the WD90C11 is in a 6845 emulation mode. A 1 returned in the 6845 field indicates that the 6845 compatibility is in effect. A 0 is returned if an EGA or VGA mode is in effect. The 6845 emulation can indicated MDA, Hercules, or CGA emulation. The EGA field indicates the status of the EGA emulation. A 1 returned in the EGA field indicates EGA emulation.

The VGA can be configured in a monochrome or color mode. This determines where certain registers are mapped. In addition, it can be used with the 6845 field to determine whether CGA or MDA/Hercules modes are in effect. A 1 returned in the MOC field indicates that the system is in a color mode. Consequently, the CRTC addresses are at 3Dx. If the 6845 emulation is in effect, a CGA is being emulated. A 0 in the MOC field indicates that a monochrome

Display Configuration Status

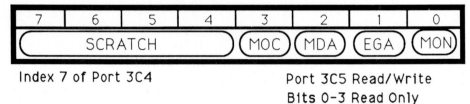

Index 7 of Port 3C4

Port 3C5 Read/Write
Bits 0-3 Read Only

FIGURE 18.14 Display Configuration Status Register. The SCRATCH field provides four bits of scratch space. The MOC field reflects whether the system is in a monochrome or color mode. The MDA field reflects 6845 compatibility. The EGA field reflects EGA compatibility. The MON field reflects the type of monitor.

mode is in effect. The CRTC addresses are at 3Bx, and if the 6845 emulation is in effect, an MDA/Hercules is being emulated.

18.5 PARADISE DISPLAY MODES

18.5.1 Alphanumeric Modes

The Paradise adapter has four alphanumeric modes available to allow 25 and 43 lines of 132-column text in either the 4- or 16-color configuration. These modes are listed in Table 18.9. The PVGA1A-based character font bit patterns will be 7 pixels wide when a fixed frequency monitor is present. These will be 8 pixels wide when a multi-frequency monitor is detected. The monitor type is based upon the setting of a DIP switch. With the WD90C00, C10, and C11, the character font patterns will be 9 dots wide. The resolution changes accordingly in both multi-frequency and fixed frequency monitors.

18.5.2 132-Column Alphanumerics Modes

In PVGA1A-based VGAs, because the 132-column modes utilize different fonts, the mode set command does not perform the font loading automatically when a 7-bit font is needed. The 8-bit font resides in the ROM, and the mode set can load this font with no problem. The 7-bit font resides on disk. A special driver is necessary to load this font as shown in Listing 18.8. The application needs to read the state of Dip Switch #1 status after a mode set to determine whether a fixed frequency monitor is resident. If it is, the application will have to load the 7-bit font. The dip switch number 1 status is located in the PR5 register in the

TABLE 18.9 Paradise Alphanumerics Modes

Mode	Rows	Columns	Font	Resolution	Colors	Monitor
54	43	132	8x9	924x387	16	fixed
54	43	132	8x9	1056x387	16	multi-sync
55	25	132	7x16	924x400	16	fixed
55	25	132	8x16	1056x400	16	multi-sync
56	43	132	7x9	924x387	4	fixed
56	43	132	8x9	1056x387	4	multi-sync
57	25	132	7x16	924x400	4	fixed
57	25	132	8x16	1056x400	4	multi-sync

SWITCH field shown in Figure 18.5. Switch number 1 is found in bit position 7. The following code will load the appropriate font according to the monitor present and mode set. A utility program provided with the Western Digital Card, when used to set 132 columns, will load the 7-dot wide font. One can access this font in bit plane 2 after loading 132 columns. Later versions of the card did not include this 7 dot wide font code.

LISTING 18.8 Loading a 7-bit Wide Character Font

```
; Function:
;       Loading the 7-bit font if necessary

; Inputs:
;       size = 5 for 5x7 font size
;       size = 7 for 7x16 font size
;       Must have defined the memory locations for the 5x7 or 7x16
;       fonts in the code segment
;               f5x7            ; location of 5x7 font
;               f7x16   ; location of 7x16 font

; Outputs:
;       If a multi-sync monitor, don't do anything
;       If a fixed frequency monitor, load either a 5x7 or 7x16 font

; Calling Protocol:
;       Handle_7_bit_font       size
```

```
    Handle_7_bit_font       macro   size

        mov     ax,007fh                ;Use extended SetMode
        mov     bh,1Fh                  ;to look at PR5
        int     10h

        test    bl,80h                  ;check bit 7
        jne     quit                    ;a multi-syncing monitor is
                                        ;present

;       a fixed frequency monitor is present. Load the 7-bit font

;       determine whether a 5x7 or 7x16 font is necessary
        mov     ax,size
        test    ax,5                    ;see if it is a 5x7 font
        jne     load_7x16               ;if is a 7x16 font
;       a 5x7 font is required (Mode 54 or 56)
        mov     ax,offset f5x7          ; load address of font for
                                        ; modes 54 and 56
        mov     bh,9h                   ; load 9 bytes per character
        jmp     load_it

;       a 7x16 font is required (Mode 55 or 57)
load_7x16:
        mov     ax,offset f7x16;        load address of fonts for
                                        modes 55h and 57 hex
        mov     bh,10h                  ; load 16 bytes per character

;       load the font via BIOS Call User Alpha Load 11h (See Section
;       11.12.6) The BIOS call wants ES:BP to point to the font
load_it:
        push    cs
        pop     es                      ; point es segment to code
                                        ; segment

        push    ax
        pop     bp                      ; put offset into BP register


        mov     ax,1100h                ; BIOS call AH=11 AL=10
        mov     bl,00h                  ; load into block 0
        mov     cx,256                  ; load all 256 characters in
                                        ; set
        xor     dx,dx                   ; start with character 0
        int     10h
    endm
```

TABLE 18.10   Paradise Graphics Modes

Mode	Resolution	Colors	Chip	Char Size	Characters
58	800x600	16	pVGA1,WDC90Cxx	8x8	100x75
59	800x600	2	pVGA1,WDC90Cxx	8x8	100x75
5E	640x400	256	pVGA1,WDC90Cxx	8x16	80x25
5F	640x480	256	pVGA1,WD90Cxx	8x16	80x25
5A	1024x768	2	WD90Cxx	8x16	128x48
5B	1024x768	4	WD90Cxx	8x16	128x48
5D	1024x768	16	WD90Cxx, C11 (512K)	8x16	128x48
5C	800x600	256	WD90C11 (512K)	8x8	100x75

18.5.3   Paradise Graphics Modes

The paradise family of Super VGA chips provide a wide variety of graphics display modes as indicated in Table 18.10. Included are two, four, sixteen and 256-color display modes ranging in resolutions up to 1024 by 768.

18.5.4   PVGA1A Graphics Modes

The PVGA1A supports a limited number of graphics modes with a maximum resolution of 800x600 in the 16-color modes and 640 by 400 in the 256-color modes. A 640 by 480 256-color mode is available with 512 Kbyte DRAM. An 800 by 600 2-color mode is also provided.

18.5.5   WD90Cxx Graphics Modes

The WD90C00, WD90C10, and WD90C11 provide three high-resolution 1024 by 768 graphics modes. The 16-color mode 5D uses the VGA standard 16-color planar memory organization. The 2-color and 4-color modes 5A and 5B use a unique scheme of memory mapping.

18.5.6   Mode 5B 1024 by 768 Four-Color Display Mode

Mode 5B is a 1024 by 768 four-color graphics mode. It uses two bits per pixel. Thus, four pixels reside in the same display byte. This qualifies as a packed display mode. The display planes are chained together in a fashion similar to the 256-color modes. The basic difference is that there are four pixels per byte instead of one pixel per byte. This is illustrated in Figure 18.15.

The four colors reference palette registers 0–3. If the default palette registers for this mode are in place, these will reference color registers 0–3.

This chained mode has a 16-bit data path. Consequently, speed improvements can be realized if the 16-bit host data path is engaged.

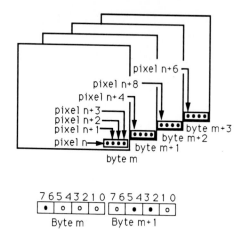

FIGURE 18.15 Memory Organization for Mode 5B hex. Illustrates four-color packed organization.

18.5.7 Mode 5A 1024 by 768 Two-Color Display Mode

The display mode 5A is a two-color packed mode which has eight pixels per byte. It utilizes an odd-even plane addressing scheme utilizing two display planes. Suppose that byte address m contains eight pixels, n,n+1,...,n+7, and this byte resides in plane 0. The neighboring (to the right) eight pixels would reside at byte address m+1, in plane 1.

A similar odd-even technique can be used in planes 2 and 3 to allow a second page to reside in display memory. This odd-even scheme is illustrated in Figure 18.16.

Accessing the display memory is accomplished by selecting the desired pair of display planes. If the image data resides in display plane 0 and 1, the Map Mask Register, discussed in Section 10.3.3, enables both planes 0 and 1. Similarly, the Read Map Register, discussed in Section 10.5.7, accesses either plane 0 or 1. If the image data resides in display plane 2 and 3, the Write Map Register enables both planes 2 and 3. Similarly, the Read Map Register accesses either plane 2 or 3. Enabling all planes 0,1,2 and 3 causes identical data to be written into both images simultaneously.

Displaying an image which resides in plane 0 is accomplished by enabling planes 0 and 1 through the Color Plane Enable Register. This register was discussed in Section10.6.5. An image which resides in planes 2 and 3 is displayed by enabling plane 2 through the Color Plane Enable Register. Enabling both planes 0 and 2 causes both images to be simultaneously displayed.

If planes 0 and 1 are used, the two colors reference palette registers 0 and 1. If planes 2 and 3 are used, the two colors reference palette registers 0 and 4. If the default palette registers for this mode are in place, these will reference color

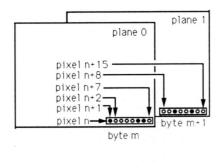

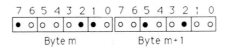

FIGURE 18.16 Memory Organization for Mode 5A hex. Illustrates two-color-packed organization.

registers 0, 1 and 4. Note that color register 1 and 4 are selected since only plane 0 or 2 is selected to produce a color. By selecting both planes 0 and 2 through the Color Plane Enable Register, the images can both be overlayed producing a three-color mode. Only three colors can be achieved since only color registers 0, 1 and 4 can be accessed.

This chained mode has a 16-bit data path. Consequently, speed improvements can be realized if the 16-bit host data path is engaged.

18.6 ACCESSING THE PARADISE DISPLAY MEMORY

The display memory can be accessed through single- or dual-bank registers. The memory size and mapping fields are configurable. In the WD90C00, the memory can be organized as the standard 256 Kbytes of VGA memory and a special feature allows paged alphanumerics modes. The register fields relevant to memory accessing are listed in Table 18.11.

In addition, the WD90C11 can configure the PR0A and PR0B registers to a dual-bank selection state where the PR0B Register is used exclusively for write operations and the PR0A Register is used exclusively for read operations by using 3C5 index 11 bit 7.

18.6.1 Bank Addressing

The 512 Kbytes of display memory can be mapped into a 64-Kbyte or a 128-Kbyte host address space at A0000–AFFFF or A0000–BFFFF, respectively. The 512 Kbytes of memory are overlayed into this address space through the bank

TABLE 18.11   Reading and Writing to Paradise Display Memory

Function	Register Name	Port	Index	Bits	Value
Bank Register A	PR0A	3cF	09	6–0	0–127
Bank Register B	PR0B	3cF	0A	6–0	0–127
Enable Dual Banks	PR1	3cF	0B	3	1
Enable PR0A Bank	PR1	3cF	0B	3	0
Memory Size	PR1	3cF	0B	7–6	0–3
Memory Map	PR1	3cF	0B	5–4	0–3
Enable Paged					
Alphanumerics	PR15	3x5	2E	2	1
Standard Alphanumerics	PR15	3x5	2E	2	0
Standard VGA Memory	PR16	3x5	2F	1	1
Extended Memory	PR16	3x5	2F	1	0
Read/Write Bank Select	System Interface				
	Control	3c5	11	7	1
32k Bank Select	System Interface				
	Control	3c5	11	7	0

registers. There are three Extended registers, PR0A, PR0B, PR1, and 3C5 index 11 bit 7, which control the bank switching. These registers are described in Table 18.12. The PR1 register, as shown in the previous Figure 18.16 , contains three fields relevant to accessing display memory.

The programmer can select to utilize either one or two bank registers based on the EN field of PR1. If the ENB field is set to 1, both the PR0A and PR0B registers are engaged. If 0, only the PR0A Register is engaged. Both the PR0A and PR0B registers contain a BANK field as shown in Figures 18.17 and 18.18.

The BANK field contains a bank value from 0–127 which is added to the system bus address bits 18–12. This provides a 4-Kbyte granularity, and the 128 * 4 Kbytes spans the entire 512-Kbyte display memory address range. The value in the BANK field is added to the host bus address as shown in Figure 18.19.

There are three distinct bank selection modes in the WD90C10 and WD90C11. The first uses just PR0A for the bank select. This applies to read or write operations. The second uses PR0A for the lower 32 Kbytes from host memory address space A0000–A7FFF and uses PR0B for the upper 32 Kbytes from A8000–AFFFF hex. The third mode is a read/write mode where PR0A is used for all read operations which occur within the 64 Kbytes from A0000–AFFFF hex. In addition, PR0B is used for the write operations in the 64 Kbytes from A0000–AFFFF hex. Three macros are provided in Listings 18.9–18.11 which set up the VGA for the Single, Dual and Read/Write modes respectively.

PROA Address Offset A

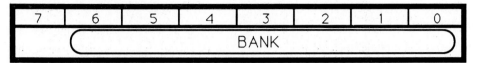

Index 09 at Port 3CE   Port 3CF Read/Write

FIGURE 18.17   PROA Address Offset A Register. The BANK field controls the address bits 18–12 of the display memory providing a 4K granularity.

PROB Address Offset B

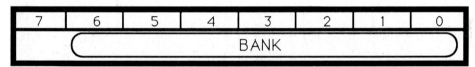

Index 0A at Port 3CE   Port 3CF Read/Write

FIGURE 18.18   PROB Address Offset B Register. The BANK field controls the address bits 18–12 of the display memory address providing a 4K granularity.

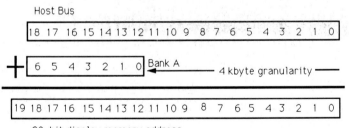

FIGURE 18.19   Creation of a display address using PROA. A 20-bit address accesses 512 Kbytes of display memory.

LISTING 18.9 Setup for Single Bank Mode

```
; Function:
;   Setup for Single Bank Mode

; Calling Protocol:
;   Single_Bank_Paradise();

Single_Bank_Paradise proc far arg1:byte

    Extensions_On_Paradise      ; turn on extensions
;        disable read/write mode
 mov dx,3c4h   ; fix System Interface Register just in case a WD
                    chip is present
 mov al,11h
 out    dx,al

;   non-destructive reset of bit 7
 inc    dx
 in     al,dx
 and al,7fh             ;zero bit 7
 out    dx,al           ;restore

;        disable PROB
 mov dx,3ceh            ;fix Memory Size Register
 mov al,0bh
 out dx,al

;        non-destructive reset of bit 3
 inc    dx
 in     al,dx
 and al,0f7h                    ;zero bit 3
 out    dx,al           ;restore

 ret
Single_Bank_Paradise endp
```

LISTING 18.10 Setup for Dual Bank Mode

```
; Function:
;   Setup for Dual Bank Mode

; Calling Protocol:
;   Dual_Bank_Paradise();
```

```
Dual_Bank_Paradise proc far arg1:byte

    Extensions_On_Paradise              ; turn on extensions
;       disable read/write mode
    mov dx,3c4h ;       fix System Interface Register just in case a
                        WD chip is present
    mov al,11h
    out dx,al

;   non-destructive reset of bit 7
    inc dx
    in  al,dx
    and al,7fh          ;zero bit 7
    out dx,al           ;restore

;       enable PR0B
    mov dx,3ceh         ;fix Memory Size Register
    mov al,0bh
    out dx,al

;       non-destructive set of bit 3
    inc dx
    in al,dx
    or al,08h           ; set bit 3
    out dx,al           ; restore

    ret
Dual_Bank_Paradise endp
```

LISTING 18.11   Setup for Read/Write Bank Mode

```
; Function:
;   Setup for Read/Write Bank Mode

; Calling Protocol:
;   Read/Write_Bank_Paradise();

ReadWrite_Bank_Paradise proc far arg1:byte

    Extensions_On_Paradise              ; turn on extensions

;       enable read/write mode
```

```
        mov dx,3c4h          ;fix System Interface Register just in case a
                             WD chip is present
     mov al,11h
     out dx,al

;    non-destructive set of bit 7
     inc dx
     in  al,dx
     or  al,80h              ;set bit 7
     out dx,al               ;restore

;        enable PR0B
     mov dx,3ceh             ;fix Memory Size Register
     mov al,0bh
     out dx,al

;        non-destructive set of bit 3
     inc dx
     in  al,dx
     or  al,08h              ; set bit 3
     out dx,al               ; restore

     ret
ReadWrite_Bank_Paradise endp
```

In the single or dual bank mode, the write and read banks can be loaded through the macros provided in Listings 18.12 and 18.13 respectively. These functions are identical and are both provided for functional compatibility with other VGA software provided in this book.

The C callable functions to control the write bank and read bank fields are provided in Listing 18.14 and 18.15.

LISTING 18.12   Macro to Load Write Bank Number

```
; Function:
;     Load the Write Bank with a new start address

; Input with:
; bl    Write Bank_Number
;         0-7 bank number indicating desired 64-Kbyte bank
```

```
; Calling Protocol:
;       Load_Write_Bank_Paradise

Load_Write_Bank_Paradise macro

;   set up PR0A Register
      mov dx,3ceh          ;point to PR0A Register
      mov al,09h
      mov ah,bl
      shl ah,1             ;adjust to 64 Kbyte bank size
      shl ah,1
      shl ah,1
      shl ah,1
      out dx,ax ;output bank

endm
```

LISTING 18.13   Macro to Load Read Bank Number

```
;
 Function:
;      Load the Read Bank with a new start address

; Input with:
; bl            Read Bank_Number
;                   0-7 bank number indicating desired 64-Kbyte bank

; Calling Protocol:
;      Load_Read_Bank_Paradise

Load_Read_Bank_Paradise macro

;      set up PR0A Register
      mov dx,3ceh          ;point to PR0A Register
      mov al,09h
      mov ah,bl
      shl ah,1             ;adjust to 64 Kbyte bank size
      shl ah,1
      shl ah,1
      shl ah,1
      out dx,ax            ;output bank

endm
```

LISTING 18.14   Load Write Bank Number

```
; Function:
;     Load the Write Bank with a new start address

; Input with:
;     write_bank        Write Bank_Number
;                   0-7 bank number indicating desired 64-Kbyte bank

; Calling Protocol:
;     Set_Write_Bank_Paradise(write_bank);

Set_Write_Bank_Paradise proc far arg1:byte

;     set up index to Bank Select Register
      mov bl,arg1 ;get page
      Load_Write_Bank_Paradise


      ret
Set_Write_Bank_Paradise endp
```

LISTING 18.15   Load Read Bank Number

```
; Function:
;     Load the Read Bank with a new start address

; Input with:
;     read_bank Read Bank_Number
;                   0-7 bank number indicating desired 64-Kbyte bank

; Calling Protocol:
;     Set_Read_Bank_Paradise(read_bank);

Set_Read_Bank_Paradise proc far arg1:byte

;     set up index to Bank Select Register
      mov bl,arg1 ;get page
      Load_Read_Bank_Paradise

      ret
Set_Read_Bank_Paradise endp
```

In the read/write mode, the write and read banks can be loaded through the macros provided in Listings 18.16 and 18.17 respectively. These functions are identical and are both provided for functional compatibility with other VGA software provided in this book.

The C callable functions to load the write and read banks in the read/write mode are provided in Listings 18.18 and 18.19 respectively.

LISTING 18.16 Macro to Load Write Bank Number in Read/Write Bank Mode

```
; Function:
; Load the Write Bank with a new start address in Read/Write Bank
; Mode

; Input with:
; bl   Write Bank_Number
;        0-7 bank number indicating desired 64-Kbyte bank

; Calling Protocol:
;  Load_Write_Bank_RW_Paradise

Load_Write_Bank_RW_Paradise macro

;    set up PR0A Register
    mov dx,3ceh  ;point to PR0B Register
    mov al,0Ah
    mov ah,bl
    shl ah,1     ;adjust to 64 Kbyte bank size
    shl ah,1
    shl ah,1
    shl ah,1
    out dx,ax    ;output bank
endm
```

LISTING 18.17 Macro to Load Read Bank Number in Read/Write Bank Mode

```
; Function:
;    Load the Read Bank with a new start address in Read/Write Bank
;    Mode

; Input with:
; bl          Read Bank_Number
;               0-7 bank number indicating desired 64-Kbyte bank

; Calling Protocol:
;    Load_Read_Bank_RW_Paradise
```

```
Load_Read_Bank_RW_Paradise macro

;       set up PR0A Register
        mov dx,3ceh                 ;point to PR0A Register
        mov al,09h
        mov ah,bl
        shl ah,1                    ;adjust to 64 Kbyte bank size
        shl ah,1
        shl ah,1
        shl ah,1
        out dx,ax                   ;output bank

endm
```

LISTING 18.18   Load Write Bank Number in read/write bank mode

```
; Function:
;   Load the Write Bank with a new start address read/write bank ;
;   mode

; Input with:
;       write_bank          Write nank number
;                           0-7 bank number indicating desired 64-Kbyte
                            bank

; Calling Protocol:
;       Set_Write_Bank_RW_Paradise(write_bank);

Set_Write_Bank_RW_Paradise proc far arg1:byte

;       set up index to Bank Select Register
        mov bl,arg1 ;get page
      Load_Write_Bank_RW_Paradise

 ret
Set_Write_Bank_RW_Paradise endp
```

LISTING 18.19   Load Read Bank Number read/write bank mode

```
; Function:
;   Load the Read Bank with a new start address read/write bank mode

; Input with:
; read_bank     Read bank number
;               0-7 bank number indicating desired 64-Kbyte bank
```

```
;  Calling Protocol:
;       Set_Read_Bank_RW_Paradise(read_bank);

Set_Read_Bank_RW_Paradise proc far arg1:byte
;       set up index to Bank Select Register
      mov bl,arg1 ;get page
        Load_Read_Bank_RW_Paradise

   ret
Set_Read_Bank_RW_Paradise endp
```

TABLE 18.12   Memory Size Field MEM

MEM	Memory Size	Configuration
0	256 Kbytes	VGA standard
1	256 Kbytes	PVGA bank switching
2	512 Kbytes	PVGA bank switching
3	1 megabyte	PVGA bank switching

TABLE 18.13   Memory Configuration Field MAP

MEM	Memory Map	Configuration
0	A0000–BFFFF	VGA standard
1	0–3FFFF	1st 256 out of 1 megabyte Kbytes address space
2	0–7FFFF	1st 512 out of 1 megabyte Kbytes address space
3	0–FFFFF	1st 1 Megabyte address space

18.6.2 Memory Size and Mapping

The memory size is controlled through the MEM field of the PR1 register. Table 18.12 describes this field. It contains the amount of memory present and the configuration. Only the 256 Kbytes of memory can be configured as the VGA standard.

The memory map field of the PR1 Register is described in Table 18.13. The 20-bit address associated with the one Megabyte of display memory address space ranges from 0 to FFFFF hex. If 256 Kbytes are present, the memory will be resident between 0 and 3FFFF hex. Similarly, 512 Kbytes will be resident between 0 and 7FFFF hex.

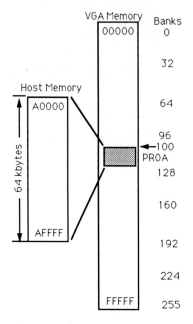

FIGURE 18.20   Using a Single Bank Register PR0A= 100 decimal to address 64 Kbyte segment from 64000 to 73FFF.

In addition, the WD90C00 allows the memory to be configured as the standard 256 Kbytes IBM VGA mapping through the MEM field of the Miscellaneous Control #2 Register displayed in Figure 18.12. If the MEM field is set to 1, the IBM standard memory configuration is selected regardless of the memory size bits described in the MEM field in Table 18.14. Typically, these bits will be set to 0 for VGA applications. Other values will cause memory conflicts in the PC environment.

18.6.3   Single Page Register Mode

If the PR0A Register is selected in a single page mode, the 19-bit address necessary to access the 512 Kbytes of display memory or the 20-bit address necessary for the one Megabyte of display memory is obtained by using the PR0A Register as a bank address in conjunction with the host address. The host address is a 20-bit address in the form A0000–AFFFF for a 64-Kbyte segment and A0000–BFFFF for a 128-Kbyte segment. The 64–Kbyte segment pointed to by PR0A is mapped into the host memory space at A0000. This is illustrated in Figure 18.20.

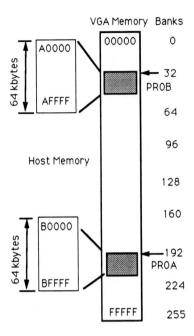

FIGURE 18.21   Using Dual Banks in a 128 -Kbyte Configuration. PROB=32 to address a 64 Kbyte segment from 20000–2FFFF and PROA= 192 to address 64 Kbyte segment from COOOO to CFFFF.

18.6.4   32-Kbyte Dual Page Registers Mode

When the dual bank registers are engaged, the programmer can perform efficient memory transfers. The display memory space is configured into either 128 or 64-Kbyte segments. Figure 18.21 illustrates the 128-Kbyte configuration. Note that data transfers to A0000-AFFFF utilize the bank register PR0B while transfers to B0000-BFFFF utilize the PR0A bank register.

Figure 18.22 illustrates the 64-Kbyte configuration. Note that data transfers to A0000–A7FFF utilize the bank register PR0B while transfers to A8000–AFFFF utilize the PR0A bank register.

18.6.5   Read/Write Dual Page Registers Mode

The WD90C10 and WD90C11 allow an additional bank selection mode. This mode utilizes dual bank registers, PR0A and PR0B. The memory can be configured so all write operations are directed through the PR0B register and all read operations are directed through the PR0A register. The memory is mapped into the host address space through a 64-Kbyte segment at A0000–AFFFF. The display memory is segmented into 64-Kbyte banks. The PR0A and PR0B regis-

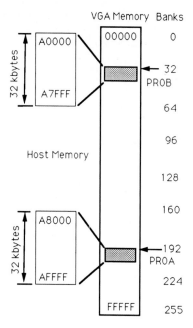

FIGURE 18.22 Using Dual Bank Registers in a 64-KbyteConfiguration. PROB=32 to address a 32-Kbyte segment from20000–27FFF and PROA=192 to address 32-Kbyte segment from COOOO to C7FFF.

ters can be used to access memory in any of these banks through the 64-Kbyte segment. When a read operation occurs to the host memory space between A0000 and AFFFF, the PR0A register is automatically invoked. Similarly, a write operation to the host memory space between A0000 and AFFFF, invokes the PR0B register. This mapping is illustrated in Figure 18.23.

This bank selection technique is controlled through the R/W field of the System Interface Control Register shown in Figure 18.3. The PR0B register must be enabled through the ENB field of the PR1 Memory Size Register shown in Figure 18.1. If the R/W field is set to 1, the PR0A register is used for reads and the PR0B register is used for writes. If the R/W field is set to 0, either 64-Kbyte or 32-Kbyte dual bank or single bank selection is in effect.

18.6.6 Page Mode Alphanumerics

It is possible in the WD90C00, WD90C10 and WD90C11 to speed up alphanumeric transfers by forcing screen refresh memory read cycles to use the page mode addressing techniques. This page mode addressing is identical to the page mode addressing automatically used in graphics mode. Speed improvements of 30 to 40 percent can be achieved using this mode.

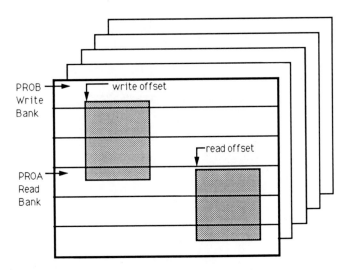

FIGURE 18.23 Read/Write Dual Bank Mapping. Display Memory Addressing in the WD91COO. Read/write operations utilizing the PROA and PROB Bank registers. The R/W field of the System Interface Control Register must be set to 1 for this bank addressing mode.

The PM field of the Miscellaneous Control #1 Register controls this function. If the PM field is set to 1, the page mode addressing scheme is enabled. If the PM field is 0, the page mode is disabled. Make sure that after setting this bit, the font is reloaded into planes 2 and 3. That is, this bit should be set before the font is loaded.

The 132-column character mode requires that the page mode addressing be enabled. When enabled, the configuration and functioning of the Character Map Select Register is modified. The normal configuration for this register is described in Section 10.3.4. The new configuration is shown in Figure 18.24.

In this new configuration, the MEMSEG field selects one of eight memory segments within planes 2 and 3. The host addresses for both planes are identical due to the plane overlapping. Each of these segments is 8 Kbytes long, filling the entire 64-kbyte segment.

A pair of character maps exist for each segment. One resides in plane 2 and the second in plane 3. This is illustrated in Figure 18.25.

There are a total of 16 character maps. The character maps are labeled [0–7].[2-3]. Thus, the character map in segment 0 and in plane 2 has the name 0.2. The selection of the map from either plane 2 or plane 3 is accomplished redundantly through the SEL field and the bit 3 of the character attribute bit. The selection is detailed in Table 18.14.

Reconfigured Character Map Select Register

7	6	5	4	3	2	1	0
			SEL		MEMSEG		

Index 3 of Port 3C4   Port 3C5 Read/Write

FIGURE 18.24   Reconfigured Character Map Select Register. When the page mode alphanumeric addressing is engaged, the Character Map Select Register is reconfigured. Refer to Section 10.3.4 for original mapping. The MEMSEG field selects one of eight 8-Kbyte memory segments. The SEL field selects a character map.

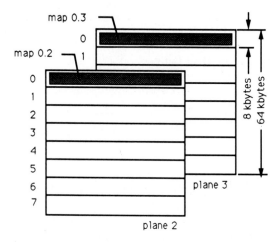

FIGURE 18.25   Page Mode Character Map. A pair of character maps exist in each of the eight segments in planes 2 and 3. In Segment O, the banks are labeled bank 0.2 and 0.3.

TABLE 18.14   Character Map Selection

SEL Field	Attribute Bit 3	Plane Selected
0	X	2
1	0	3
1	1	2
2	0	2
2	1	3
3	X	3

18.7 CONTROLLING THE CRT ADDRESS GENERATION

The PRVGA1a and the WD90C00, WD90C10 and WD90C11 permit positioning the starting address and cursor address in any location in the extended display memory space. The relevant fields are listed in Table 18.15.

18.7.1 Display and Cursor Start Address Generation

To position any portion of the image memory onto the display, it is necessary to provide an extended start address. Bits 16 and 17 are programmed through the STRT field in the PR3 CRT Control Register described in Figure 18.26 .

The display starting address can be loaded through the code provided in Listing 18.20. This function utilizes the "set_start_address" macro in Listing 14.32. It is often advisable to wait for vertical refresh before loading the start address.

18.7.2 Controlling the Display Offset

The cursor position can be loaded through the code provided in Listing 18.21. This function utilizes the "position_cursor" macro in Listing 14.33.

TABLE 18.15 Paradise Display Address Control

Function	Register Name	Port	Index	Bits	Value
Start Address Bit 17–16	PR3	3CF	0D	4–3	0–3
Disable Border	PR15	3x5	2E	0	1
Enable Border	PR15	3x5	2E	0	0
Modulus of Address Counter	PR16	3x5	2F	6–5	0–3
Address Counter Offset	PR16	3x5	2F	4–3	0–3

PR3 CRT Control

| 7 | 6 | 5 | 4 | 3 | 2 | 1 | 0 |

STRT   MB2

Index 0D at Port 3CE   Port 3CF Read/Write

FIGURE 18.26 PR3 CRT Control Register. The STRT field contains bits 17–16 for the CRT address generation. CRT address can be multiplied by 2 through the MB2 field. The remaining fields are used to lock/unlock access to various registers.

LISTING 18.20   Load the Display Start Address

```
;       Function:
; Load the Display Start Address

; Input Parameters
;     address    unsigned integer starting address
;     top        top two bits of address

; Calling Protocol:
;       Load_Start_Paradise(address,top)

Load_Start_Paradise proc far arg1,arg2:byte

        mov bx,arg1
           set_start_address        ;load the 16-bit start address

;      send out top address
        mov dx,3c4h
        mov al,0dh ;index PR3 CRT Control
        out dx,al

;      read current value
        inc dx
        in al,dx          ;get value
        and al,0e7h       ;zero out start address 17-16 bits 4-3

;      or in new start address
        mov bl,arg2       ;get top address
        and bl,03h        ;only want 2 bits
        mov cx,3
        shl bl,cl         ;shift left 3 to get bit in proper position
        or al,bl
        out dx,al         ;output top address
   ret
Load_Start_Paradise endp
```

LISTING 18.21   Load the Cursor Position

```
; Function:
;     Load the Cursor Position

; Input Parameters
;     address    unsigned integer starting address
;     top        top two bits of address
```

```
; Calling Protocol:
;        Position_Cursor_Paradise(address,top)

Position_Cursor_Paradise proc far arg1,arg2:byte

        mov bx,arg1
          position_cursor    ;load the 16-bit cursor position

;      send out top address
        mov dx,3c4h
        mov al,0dh              ;index PR3 CRT Control
        out dx,al

;      read current value
        inc dx
        in al,dx    ;get value
        and al,0e7h          ;zero out start address 17-16 bits 4-3

;        or in new cursor position (CRTC Top Address)
        mov bl,arg2          ;get top address
          and bl,03h         ;only want 2 bits
          mov cx,3
        shl bl,cl            ;shift left 3 to get bit in proper position
        or al,bl
        out dx,al              ;output top address
  ret
Position_Cursor_Paradise endp
```

18.7.3   Controlling the Display Offset

The display offset determines the virtual image size. The eight-bit value stored in the Offset Register in the CRTC Register Group, described in Section 10.4.22. In the word mode, which is typically the case, display offsets up to 1024 bytes can be defined.

18.7.4   Address Counter Modulus

The WD90C00, WD90C10 and WD90C11 allow the CRT address counter width to be controlled. The address counter can count to 64 K or 128 K of bytes words or double-words. It may be desirable to utilize this modulus counter when virtual images exceed the resolution of the display mode. The MOD field of the Miscellaneous Control #2 Register in the WD90Cxx determines the modulus as indicated in Table 18.16.

TABLE 18.16 CRTC Address Counter Width

MOD field	Counter Width
0	256 K
1	128 K
2	64 K

TABLE 18.17 CRTC Address Counter Offset

TOP field	Counter Width
0	0 K
1	64 K
2	128 K
3	192 k

18.7.5 The Display Offset

The upper address bits, bits 17 and 16, of the CRTC address counter can be offset to one of four 64-Kbyte boundaries spanning 256 Kbytes of display memory. The TOP field of the Miscellaneous Control #2 Register in the WD90Cxx controls this offset as indicated in Table 18.17. These bits are summed with bits 4 and 3 of PR16.

18.7.6 Border Display

The border region of the screen is often problematic. The WD90C00, WD90C10 and WD90C11 have the ability to force the video outputs to 0 during the time that the border region is being displayed. The border, also called overscan region, can be forced to 0 by setting the DB field of the Miscellaneous Control #1 Register in the WD90Cxx to 1. If the DB field is 0, the border region is displayed as normal with the overscan color. The overscan color is located in the Overscan Color Register described in Section 10.6.4.

18.8 BIOS Extensions

Paradise provides a set of 10 BIOS Calls as shown in Table 18.18. These have to do with setting the display modes, emulation modes, reading the status of a mode set and reading the extended PR registers.

TABLE 18.18   Paradise Super BIOS

Function	AH	AL	BH	Feature
Parametric Mode Set	0	7E	0	Set a mode based on parameters
Set VGA Mode	0	7F	0	Old Set a VGA mode
Set Non-VGA Mode	0	7F	1	Old Set a non-VGA mode
Extended Mode Status	0	7F	2	Return status of last mode call
Lock VGA or Non-VGA mode	0	7F	3	Lock VGA into current mode
Set MDA Mode	0	7F	4	Set MDA emulation
Set CGA Mode	0	7F	5	Set CGA emulation
Set VGA Mono	0	7F	6	Set VGA into a mono mode
Set VGA Color	0	7F	7	Set VGA into a color mode
Write PR Register (1)	0	7F	09-0F	Write a PR Register
Read PR Register	0	7F	19-1F	Read a PR Register
Set Analog EGA Emulation (1)	0	7F	20	Sets analog EGA emulation

Notes: (1) WD90C00 or WD90C11

18.8.1   Parametric Mode Set

The alphanumeric and graphic display modes, listed in Tables 18.10 and 18.11, can be invoked by using the Parametric Mode Set BIOS Call. The programmer provides the horizontal, vertical and color resolution to the BIOS call. If a mode is supported which matches these resolutions, a mode set will be issued. It is not recommended to use this mode. The AH=00 Set Mode command described in Section 11.2 should be used to set the standard or extended display modes.

Inputs:

AH=00h	Mode Set BIOS Call
AL=7E hex	Parametric Mode Set Subfunction
BX=Horizontal Resolution	Horizontal Resolution
	pixels if a graphics mode
	columns if an alphanumeric mode
CX=Vertical Resolution	Vertical Resolution
	pixels if a graphics mode
	rows if an alphanumeric mode

DX=Color Resolution   Number of colors

0=monochrome

2,4,16,256 = number of colors

Outputs:

Selected matching mode is set

18.8.2   Set VGA Mode

This function is an old BIOS function designed to bring the VGA controller into a VGA emulation state after a soft boot operation. The technique involves setting up the desired mode using the standard Mode Set BIOS call. Next, this Set VGA Mode BIOS call is issued. This sets up the VGA so a soft boot will cause the chip to initialize in a VGA state.

Inputs:

AH=00 hex	Mode Set BIOS Call
AL=7F hex	Extended Mode Set Subfunction
BH=00 hex	Set Non-Extended VGA Mode

Outputs:

BH=return	Return parameter
	7F = valid call
	Not 7F = invalid call

18.8.3   Set Non-VGA Mode

This function is an old BIOS function designed to bring the VGA controller into a non-VGA emulation state after a soft boot operation. The technique involves setting up the desired mode using the standard Mode Set BIOS call. Next, this Set Non-VGA Mode BIOS call is issued. This sets up the VGA so a soft boot will cause the chip to initialize in a non-VGA state. If a monochrome mode is desired, set to MDA/Hercules emulation. If a color mode is desired, set to CGA emulation.

Inputs:

AH=00 hex	Mode Set BIOS Call
AL=7F hex	Extended Mode Set Subfunction
BH=01 hex	Set VGA Mode

Outputs:

BH=return	Return parameter
	7F = valid call
	Not 7F = invalid call

18.8.4 Extended Mode Status

The Extended Mode Status returns the status of the last mode call.

Inputs:

AH=00 hex	Mode Set BIOS Call
AL=7F hex	Extended Mode Set Subfunction
BH=02 hex	Query Mode Status

Outputs:

BH=return	Return parameter
	7F = valid call
	Not 7F = invalid call
BL=status	Status parameter
	0 if a VGA mode
	1 if a non-VGA mode
CH=memory present	Amount of memory present in 64-Kbyte chunks
CL=memory required	Amount of memory used for current mode

18.8.5 Lock VGA or Non-VGA Mode

The current mode can be locked so the VGA system will default to the locked mode after a soft reset. Some applications require the soft reset initialization to work properly.

Inputs:

AH=00 hex	Mode Set BIOS Call
AL=7F hex	Extended Mode Set Subfunction
BH=03 hex	Lock Current Mode

Outputs:

BH=return	Return parameter
	7F = valid call
	Not 7F = invalid call

18.8.6 Set Non-VGA MDA/Hercules Mode

This function brings the VGA system into a MDA/Hercules emulation mode. It emulates the 6845 graphics controller. It does not require soft booting and can be invoked at any time.

Inputs:

AH=00 hex	Mode Set BIOS Call
AL=7F hex	Extended Mode Set Subfunction
BH=04 hex	Set Non-VGA MDA/Hercules Mode

Outputs:

BH=return	Return parameter
	7F = valid call
	Not 7F = invalid call

18.8.7 Set Non-VGA CGA Mode

This function brings the VGA system into a CGA emulation mode. It emulates the 6845 graphics controller. It does not require soft booting and can be invoked at any time.

Inputs:

AH=00 hex	Mode Set BIOS Call
AL=7F hex	Extended Mode Set Subfunction
BH=05 hex	Set Non-VGA CGA Mode

Outputs:

BH=return	Return parameter
	7F = valid call
	Not 7F = invalid call

18.8.8 Set VGA Mono Mode

This function brings the VGA system into a VGA monochrome mode. It does not require soft booting and can be invoked at any time.

Inputs:

AH=00 hex	Mode Set BIOS Call
AL=7F hex	Extended Mode Set Subfunction
BH=06 hex	Set Non-Extended VGA Mode

Outputs:

BH=return	Return parameter
	7F = valid call
	Not 7F = invalid call

18.8.9 Set VGA Color Mode

This function brings the VGA system into a VGA color mode. It does not require soft booting and can be invoked at any time.

Inputs:

AH=00 hex	Mode Set BIOS Call
AL=7F hex	Extended Mode Set Subfunction
BH=07 hex	Set Non-Extended VGA Mode

Outputs:

BH=return	Return parameter
	7F = valid call
	Not 7F = invalid call

18.8.10 Write a PR Register

This function allows the programmer to write to one of the PR registers as shown in Table 18.19. This is available on the WD9xCxx generation of Paradise Super VGAs.

Inputs:

AH=00 hex	Mode Set BIOS Call
AL=7F hex	Extended Mode Set Subfunction
BH=desired register	Number of PR register to read. Refer to Table 18.20.
BL=register value	Value of PR register

Outputs:

BH=return	Return parameter
	7F = valid call
	Not 7F = invalid call

18.8.11 Read a PR Register

This function returns the contents of one of the PR registers as shown in Table 18.20.

Inputs:

AH=00 hex	Mode Set BIOS Call
AL=7F hex	Extended Mode Set Subfunction
BH=desired register	Number of PR register to read. Refer to Table 18.21.

Outputs:

BH=return	Return parameter
	7F = valid call
	Not 7F = invalid call
BL=register value	Value of PR register

18.8.12 Set Analog EGA Emulation

The EGA can be emulated when the VGA card is attached to an analog monitor. This is available on the WD9xC00 generation of Paradise Super VGAs.

Inputs:

AH=00 hex	Mode Set BIOS Call
AL=7F hex	Extended Mode Set Subfunction
BH=20 hex	Emulate EGA with Analog Monitor
BL=EGA switches	low nibble is EGA switches.

Outputs:

BH=return	Return parameter
	7F = valid call
	Not 7F = invalid call

TABLE 18.19   PR Register Codes for Write Operations

Code	Register	Chip
9	PROA	PVGA1A or WD90Cxx
A	PROB	PVGA1A or WD90Cxx
B	PR1	PVGA1A or WD90Cxx
C	PR2	PVGA1A or WD90Cxx
D	PR3	PVGA1A or WD90Cxx
E	PR4	PVGA1A or WD90Cxx
F	PR5	PVGA1A or WD90Cxx

TABLE 18.20   Read PR Register Codes

Code	Register	Chip
19	PROA	PVGA1A or WD90Cxx
1A	PROB	PVGA1A or WD90Cxx
1B	PR1	PVGA1A or WD90Cxx
1C	PR2	PVGA1A or WD90Cxx
1D	PR3	PVGA1A or WD90Cxx
1E	PR4	PVGA1A or WD90Cxx
1F	PR5	PVGA1A or WD90Cxx
29	PR10	WD90C00, WD90C10, WD90C11
2A	PR11	WD90C00, WD90C10, WD90C11
2B	PR12	WD90C00, WD90C10, WD90C11
2C	PR13	WD90C00, WD90C10, WD90C11
2D	PR14	WD90C00, WD90C10, WD90C11
2E	PR15	WD90C00, WD90C10, WD90C11
2F	PR16	WD90C00, WD90C10, WD90C11
30	PR17	WD90C00, WD90C10, WD90C11

Chapter 19

The Trident Super VGA Chip Sets

19.1 INTRODUCTION TO THE TRIDENT VGA

The two Trident Super VGA chips are the TVGA 8800 and 8900. As one would suspect, the 8800 is a second-generation 8900. The 8800 is very similar to the 8900 with a few minor differences. Most notably is the different default condition used for accessing the display memory. The 8800 default maps the display memory into host address space A0000–BFFFF hex through a 128-Kbyte bank-selection technique. The 8900 default maps the display memory into host address space A0000–AFFFF hex through a 64-Kbyte bank selection technique. In either case, the chip can be controlled such that either a 64-Kbyte or 128-Kbyte mapping is used. In addition, the 8800 can only access 512 Kbytes of memory while the 8900 can access one Megabyte of display memory.

The 8800 can accommodate 1024 by 768 16-color display resolutions and 640 by 480 256-color display modes. The 8900 can accomodate 1024 by 768 in both the 16-color and 256-color modes. Neither chip can support VRAM implementations.

The 8900 supports emulation of the MDA, CGA and Hercules standards. The 8800 supports a unique feature called super fonts. These super fonts allow up to 16 Kbytes of character codes to be stored in display memory. Each character can be up to 32 bytes, supporting 16 x 16 character sets.

One further note. Older versions of the Trident 8800 chip, called the BR version, do not support 64 Kbyte segments. These chips are very rare and they can, for all intents and purposes, be ignored.

19.2 CONFIGURING AND CONTROLLING THE TRIDENT VGA

19.2.1 Configuring the Trident Super VGAs

Both the Trident 8800 and the 8900 are designed to use either the 8- or 16-bit PC/AT interface and the PS/2 microchannel conventions. As of this writing, no MCA cards exist which use either the 8800 or 8900 VGA chip.

The Trident 8800 and 8900 provide a variety of programmable controls

TABLE 19.1 Configuring the Trident Super VGAs

Function	Register Name	Port	Index	Bits	Value
Disable on-card ROM	Power-up Mode 2	3C4	F	6	0
Enable on-card ROM	Power-up Mode 2	3C4	F	6	1
Select 8-bit ROM	Power-up Mode 2	3C4	F	7	0
Select 16-bit ROM	Power-up Mode 2	3C4	F	7	1
Select 8-bit video memory	Switch position 6				on
Select 16-bit video memory	Switch position 6				off
Select 8-bit bus interface	Mode Control 1	3C4	E	3	0
Select 16-bit bus interface	Mode Control 1	3C4	E	3	1
Auto Bus Size detection	Jumper J2 pins 2-3				connected
Manual Bus Size detection	Jumper J2 pins 1-2				connected
Fast Address Decode	Switch position 5				off
Slow Address Decode	Switch position 5				on
Vertical NON-Interlace	CRTC Module Testing	3D4	1E	2	0
Vertical Interlace	CRTC Module Testing	3D4	1E	2	1

through the Power-Up Mode 2 Register. The card is configured through a combination of jumpers, switch position and programmable registers as shown in Table 19.1.

For 1024 by 768 modes, the interlaced versus non-interlaced control is selected by DIP switch SW3. Jumper J2 enables or disables the card's ability to detect auto bus size. This feature is put onto a jumper because it can be problematic. The auto selection has no way of knowing what other cards lurk in the shadows of the same address space on the PC/AT bus. If the auto selection is unsuccessful, it can be disabled. This allows individual control of memory bus width and ROM bus width. A switch (SW5) allows the card to be configured for slow or fast memory address decoding. A second switch (SW6) can configure the card for 8- or 16-bit video memory path. The autodetection feature detects 8- or 16-bit bus as reflected in the BUS field of Mode Control 1 Register as shown in Figure 19.1.

The ROM configuration features are present in the Power-up Mode 2 Register shown in Figure 19.2. The on-card ROM can be enabled or disabled through the ER field of this register. The 8- or 16-bit ROM interface can be selected through the ROM field of this register.

Power-up Mode Register 2

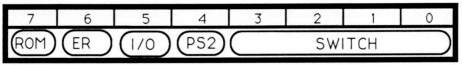

Index OF at Port 3C4   Port 3C5 Read/Write

FIGURE 19.1   Power-up Mode Register 2. The on-card switch values reside in the SWITCH field, the bus definition is in the PS2 field, the ROM enable is in the ET field and the ROM data width is in the ROM field. The I/O field selects port addressing at 3xx or 2xx hex.

Module Testing Register

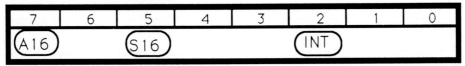

Index 1E at Port 3C4   Port 3C5 Read/Write

FIGURE 19.2   Module Testing Register. The interlaced mode is controlled through the INT field. The CRT starting address bit-16 is controlled through the S16 field. The host address bit-16 is controlled through the A16 field (8900only).

The system can be configured to operate in an interlaced or non-interlaced mode through the INT field of the CRTC Module Testing Register.

19.3   CONTROLLING THE TRIDENT 8800 AND 8900

The Trident 8800 and 8900 can be enabled and disabled in either the PC/AT or the PS/2 microchannel implementations. The techniques are compatible with the IBM standard and are listed in Table 19.2.

TABLE 19.2   Resetting and Enabling the Trident 8900

Function	Register Name	Port	Index	Bits	Value
Enable VGA adapter	Display Adapter Enable	46E8		3	0
Disable VGA adapter	Display Adapter Enable	46E8		3	1
Enable VGA motherboard	Video Subsystem Enable	3C3		0	0
Disable VGA motherboard	Video Subsystem Enable	3C3		0	1

Display Adapter Enable Register

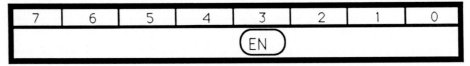

Port 46E8 Read Only

FIGURE 19.3 Display Adapter Enable Register. Adapter Card implementation at Port 46E8. Allows enabling and disabling of VGA through the EN field.

Video Subsystem Enable Register

Port 3C3 Read/Write

FIGURE 19.4 Video Subsytem Enable Register. Motherboard implementation at Port 3C3. Allows enabling and disabling of VGA through the EN field.

The PC/AT implementation utilizes the EN field of the Display Adapter Enable shown in Figure 19.3. The PS/2 microchannel implementation utilizes the EN field of the Video Subsystem Enable Register, shown in Figure 19.4.

19.4 DETERMINING THE STATUS OF THE TRIDENT SUPER VGAS

The status of the Trident Super VGAs can be determined by reading the BIOS identification or writing and reading from the extended registers. In the case of the 8900, a Chip Version register is provided. The 8800 can be identified through the Trident trademark in the BIOS area or through the Hardware Version Register value. The 8900 provides the chip identification in a CHIP field of the Chip Version Register or through the microchannel ID registers as shown in Table 19.3.

19.4.1 Identifying the Trident VGA

The Trident 8800 or 8900 can be identified by the presence of an inverting bit field in the Mode Control #1 register. The PAGE field at bit position 1 in this register is unique in that it inverts the data written into it, when the data is read out. In other words, writing a 1 into the PAGE field will result in a 0 being read.

TABLE 19.3 Determining Trident Display Status

Function	Register Name	Port	Index	Bits	Value
Chip Version	Hardware Version	3C4	B	3–0	0–15
Card ID Microchannel	Microchannel ID high	101		7–0	0–255
Card ID Microchannel	Microchannel ID low	100		7–0	0–255
Memory Size	Software Programming	3C4	1F	1–0	0–1
Bus Type	Power–Up Mode #2	3C4	F	4	0–1
Switch Settings	Power–Up Mode #2	3C4	F	3–0	0–15

All of the VGA manufacturers are rapidly filling the space in the 3B0–3DF port range and it is typically not safe to rely on a register as the sole source of evidence to indicate the presence of the VGA card. In this case, however, the probability that another manufactuer will have an inverting bit in this location is very small.

The Trident 8800 or 8900 can be identified through the code in Listing 19.1. The Hardware Version Register can also be used to identify the chips. The register should be read twice to avoid changing the *old* and *new* definitions of other registers.

LISTING 19.1 Determining if the VGA chip is a Trident

```
/*
Function:
        Determining if the VGA card is a Trident card

Output Parameters:
        1 card is a Trident
        0 card is NOT a Trident

Calling Protocol:
        Trident= Is_It_Trident() */

int Is_It_Trident()
{ unsigned char new_value,old_value,value;

    outp(0x3C4,0x0E);           /* read the Mode Control #1 Register */
    old_value = inp(0x3C5);

    outp(0x3C5,0x00);           /* write a new value bit 1=0 all other
                                   bits 0 */

    value = inp(0x3C5)&0x0F;    /* read the new value */
```

```
outp(0x3C5,old_value);              /* write the old value */

if(value==0x02) return(1);          /* check for bit 1=1 and all other bits
                                       0 */

            else return(0);
}
```

19.4.2   Identifying Which Trident VGA

The chip identification is located in the CHIP field of the Hardware Version Register as illustrated in Figure 19.5. The chip number can be determined through the code in Listing 19.2.

LISTING 19.2   Determining the Trident Chip
_____

```
/*
Function:
        Determining the Trident chip number

Output Parameters:
        identity            integer containing chip code
                                     8800 = Trident 8800 chip
                                     8900 = Trident 8900 chip

NOTE:    A subsequent consequence of this call is that the mode
                control registers are put into their new state.

Calling Protocol:
   identity = Which_Trident() */

Which_Trident()

{
  unsigned char value;

outp(0x3C4,0x0B); /* Version Register */
  outp(0x3c5,0); /* dummy write to put system into old definitions */

value > = inp(0x3C5); /* read causes new definitions */

if(value>=0x03) return(8900);
        else return(8800);

}
```

Hardware Version Register

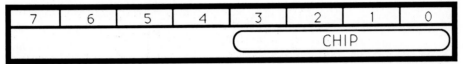

Index 0B at Port 3C4   Port 3C5 Read/Write

FIGURE 19.5   Hardware Version Register. The chip version resides in the CHIP field. The mode Control registers assume their "old" definitions when a write occurs to this register. The Mode Control Registers toggle definitions when a read occurs.

Software Programming Register 8900 Only

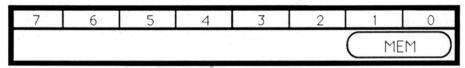

Index 1F at Port 3C4   Port 3C5 Read/Write

FIGURE 19.6   Software Programming Register 8900 Only. The memory size is controlled through the MEM field.

19.4.3   Determining the Trident VGA Environment

The memory size can be read in the MEM field of the Software Programming Register shown in Figure 19.6. The bus type can be read in the PS/2 field of the Power-Up Mode #2 Register. The switch settings also reside in this register in the SWITCH field.

19.5   TRIDENT DISPLAY MODES

The Trident Super VGAs support a wide variety of high-resolution display modes. The 8800 can display up to 1024 by 768 in the 16-color modes and 640 by 480 in the 256-color modes. The 8900 can display up to 1024 by 768 in both the 16- and 256-color modes interlaced or non-interlaced. In addition, the 8800 and 8900 have a unique mode which displays 768 by 1024 in the 16-color mode. The 1024 raster lines require a special monitor capable of keeping up with the high bandwidth. The alphanumeric display modes are listed in Table 19.4 while the graphics display modes are listed in Table 19.5.

TABLE 19.4   Trident Alphanumerics modes

Mode	Rows	Columns	Font	Resolution	Colors	Chip
50	30	80	8x16	640 by 480	16	8800,8900
51	43	80	8x11	640 by 480	16	8800,8900
52	60	80	8x8	640 by 480	16	8800,8900
53	25	132	8x14	1056 by 350	16	8800,8900
54	30	132	8x16	1056 by 480	16	8800,8900
55	43	132	8x11	1056 by 473	16	8800,8900
56	60	132	8x8	1056 by 480	16	8800,8900
57	25	132	9x14	1188 by 350	16	8800,8900
58	30	132	9x16	1188 by 480	16	8800,8900
59	43	132	9x11	1188 by 473	16	8800,8900
5A	60	132	9x8	1188 by 480	16	8800,8900

TABLE 19.5   Trident Graphics Modes

Mode	Resolution	Colors	Chip	Alpha	Character
5B	800x600	16	8800,8900	100x75	8x8
5C	640x400	256	8800,8900	80x25	8x16
5D	640x480	256	8800,8900	80x30	8x16
5E	800x600	256	8900	100x75	8x8
5F	1024x768	16	8800,8900	128x43	8x16
61	768x1024	16	8800, 8900	96x64	8x16
62	1024x768	256	8900	128x48	8x16

19.6   ACCESSING THE TRIDENT DISPLAY MEMORY

The 8800 and 8900 are both mapped into the host address space through a bank overlapped system. Either chip can be configured to operate in a 128-Kbyte bank mode or a 64-Kbyte bank mode. The 8800 defaults to a 128-Kbyte bank map at power up. The 8900 defaults to a 64-Kbyte bank map at power up. A 128-Kbyte bank memory map is shown in Figure 19.7.

Most likely, the chips the programmer will choose to configure the memory into 64-Kbyte segments in the host address space from A0000–AFFFF. This is a much simpler technique than was involved in the 128-Kbyte memory map. The 8800 can only access 512 Kbytes of memory while the 8900 can access one Megabyte of display memory. The 512 Kbytes of display address space are mapped into 8 of these 64-Kbyte banks (segments). The one Megabyte of display address space is mapped into 16 of these 64-Kbyte banks (segments). The registers

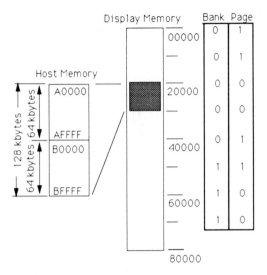

FIGURE 19.7 128-Kbyte Bank Memory Map. Segment ranges from A0000–BFFFF. Page = 0, Bank = 0.

TABLE 19.6 Reading and Writing to Trident Display Memory in a 64-Kbyte Memory Map

Function	Register Name	Port	Index	Bits	Value
Enable Extended Memory	Mode Control 2	3C4	D	4	1
Disable Extended Memory	Mode Control 2	3C4	D	4	0
Select 256K Bank, 128K page	Mode Control 1	3C4	E	2–1	0–3
Select 256K Bank, 64K page	New Mode Control 1	3C4	E	3–2	0–3
Select 128K Page	New Mode Control 1	3C4	E	1	0–1
Select 64K Segment, 64K page	New Mode Control 1	3C4	E	0	0–1

involved in accessing display memory are listed in Table 19.6. The register terminology, as defined by Trident, are called Old Mode Control #1 and Old Mode Control #2 or New Mode Control #1 and New Mode Control #2. A 64-Kbyte memory map is illustrated in Figure 19.8

The technique for accessing these registers creates additional problems. The old and new versions of each of these Mode Control registers reside at the same port addresses. They are differentiated by an internal switch. The switch is

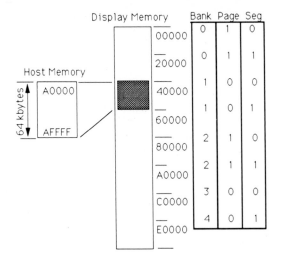

FIGURE 19.8   64Kbyte Bank Memory Map. Segment = 0, Page = 0, Bank = 1

initialized and activated by reading and writing to a completely separate register. This could lead to problems if the exact state needs to be saved and restored. Figure 19.9 illustrates this internal switching.

Trident provides additional registers which provide the value of the attribute index and attribute state. Recall that the Attribute registers are controlled in a similar fashion. The Attribute registers are described in Section 10.6.

The technique used to access the *old* or *new* registers involves writing to and reading the Hardware Version Register. The Hardware Version Register is shown in Figure 19.5. The CHIP field of this register provides information as to the chip version number. This would normally be considered a read-only field, and indeed it is. Writing to this register does not effect the bits in any way.

The switch can be toggled between the old and new states through the code in Listings 19.3 and 19.4 respectively.

LISTING 19.3   Enabling the Old Definition of Mode Registers

```
; Function:
;       Enabling Old Definition of Mode Registers

; Calling Protocol:
;       Old_Mode_Trident();

Old_Mode_Trident proc far
        mov     dx,3c4h
```

```
mov     ax,000bh              ;index the Version Register
        out     dx,ax         ;perform write to cause old
                              definition


ret
Old_Mode_Trident  endp
```

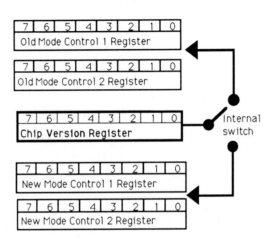

FIGURE 19.9 Old/New Internal Switch. Reading and writing to the Chip Version Registers controls access to the Old or New Mode Control Registers.

LISTING 19.4   Enabling New Definition of Mode Registers

```
;  Function:
;       Enabling New Definition of Mode Registers

;  Calling Protocol:
;       New_Mode_Trident();

New_Mode_Trident  proc far
        mov     dx,3c4h
```

```
        mov     ax,000bh                ;index the Version Register
        out     dx,ax           ;perform write to cause old
                                definition
        in      ax,dx           ;read to cause new definitions
        ret
New_Mode_Trident endp
```

Old Mode Control Register #1

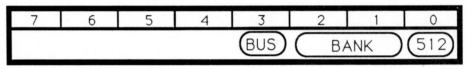

Index OE at Port 3C4   Port 3C5 Read/Write

FIGURE 19.10 Old Mode Control Register #1. The *old* definition of the Mode Control Register #1. Extended CRT Display Addressing in the 512 field. The Memory bank addressing is controlled through the BANK field. The 8- or 16-bit host bus is selected through the BUS field.

When a read instruction accesses the Version Register the internal switch which accesses either the *old* or *new* Mode Control 1 and 2 Registers will toggle. When a write occurs to this register, the switch will be positioned so the *old* Mode Control 1 and 2 registers will be accessed.

The Old Mode Control 1 Register is shown in Figure 19.10. It contains fields which control the VGA and provides access to display memory. The 512 field is used as address bit 17 of the CRTC controller. If the 512 field is 0, the lower 512 Kbytes of display memory are enabled. If 1, the upper 512 Kbytes of display memory are enabled. This implies that there can be no automatic crossing of this 512-Kbyte boundary. Thus, it is not possible to display part of the lower 512 Kbytes of display memory at the same time as part of the upper 512 Kbytes of memory are being displayed. The exception to this rule is the 1024 by 768 256-color display mode. Both banks of memory are required to display a single image in this display mode.

The BANK field of the Old Mode Control 1 Register selects one of four banks of 256 Kbytes of display memory for CPU operations. This page switching mechanism is relevant to the 128-Kbyte paging scheme which is activated when the internal switch is in the *old* position.

The Old Mode Control 2 Register is shown in Figure 19.11. It contains fields which control the VGA. The emulation modes are selected through the EMU

Old Mode Control Register #2

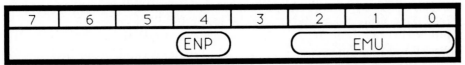

Index 0D at Port 3C4   Port 3C5 Read/Write

FIGURE 19.11 Old Mode Control Register #2. The *old* definition of the Mode Control Register #2 enables emulation through the EMU field. It also enables or disables the page switching mode through the ENP field.

New Mode Control Register #1

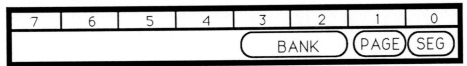

Index 0E at Port 3C4   Port 3C5 Read/Write

FIGURE 19.12 New Mode Control Register #1. The *new* definition of the Mode Control Register #1 provides a three-bit bank start address through the SEG, PAGE, and BANK fields. Note that the PAGE field is inverted.

TABLE 19.7 Emulation Mode Control

EMU field	Emulation
0	VGA
3	EGA
5	CGA, MDA, Hercules

field of Old Mode Control 1 Register as listed in Table 19.7. The Bank Selection (paging) Mode can be enabled or disabled through the ENP field. If the ENP field is 0, the paging is disabled, and the memory is compatible with the standard VGA. If the ENP field is 1, the paging mode is enabled and access to the display memory above 256 Kbytes is enabled.

The New Mode Control 1 Register is shown in Figure 19.12. It is active when the system is in a 64-Kbyte paging scheme. The four bits necessary to access the sixteen 64-Kbyte pages are resident in this register. The segment selection accesses 64-Kbyte segments and is found in the SEG field. The page selection accesses 128-Kbyte segments and is found in the PAGE field. (NOTE: Like the 8800, the page field is inverted. A 0 in the PAGE field would access the upper 128-Kbyte page while a 1 would access the lower 128-Kbyte page for write operations. Read operations are not inverted.) The 256-Kbyte banks (0-3) are located in the BANK field of this register. These three fields can be considered as one bank address field. This register can be programmed in a fashion compatible to other VGA systems which use 64-Kbyte segments. However, before the 64-Kbyte bank number can be loaded into this register, the bit value in the bit 1 position must be inverted.

The New Mode Control 2 Register contains clock control information which is not relevant for this book.

Bank selection typically occurs through the New Mode Control #1 Register. The bank value is different depending on whether the host operation reads or writes to display memory. If the operation is a write, the PAGE field of this register should be inverted. This can be seen in Listing 19.5 in the XOR BL,2 instruction. If the operation is a read, the PAGE field should not be inverted. Two macros are provided in Listings 19.5 and 19.6 to perform the loading of the bank value.

LISTING 19.5 Loading the Write Bank Number for the 64 Kbyte

```
; Function:
;       Loading the Write Bank with a new start address for the 64
;       Kbyte

; Input with:
;       bl                        Write Bank_Number
;                                  0-15 bank number indicating desired
;                         64-Kbyte bank

; Calling Protocol:
;       Load_Write_Bank_Trident

Load_Write_Bank_Trident macro

;       set up index to Bank Select Register
        mov     dx,3c4h          ;point to Mode Control #1 Register
        mov     al,0eh
        xor     bl,02            ;adjust page bit
        mov     ah,bl
        out     dx,ax            ;output bank

endm
```

LISTING 19.6 Loading the Read Bank Number for the 64-Kbyte Memory Map

```
; Function:
;       Loading the Read Bank with a new start address for the 64-
;       Kbyte memory map

; Input with:
;       bl                          Read Bank_Number
;                                   0-15 bank number indicating desired
;                                   64-Kbyte bank


; Calling Protocol:
;       Load_Read_Bank_Trident

Load_Read_Bank_Trident macro

;       set up index to Bank Select Register
        mov     dx,3c4h          ;point to Mode Control #1 Register
        mov     al,0eh
        mov     ah,bl
        out     dx,ax            ;output bank

endm
```

Loading the Bank registers from a C routine is accomplished through the code in Listings 19.7 and 19.8 for write and read operations respectively.

LISTING 19.7 Loading the Write Bank Number for the 64-Kbyte memory map

```
; Function:
;       Loading the Write Bank with a new start address for the 64-
;       Kbyte memory map

; Input with:
;       write_bank      Write Bank_Number
;                               0-7 bank number indicating desired
;                               64-Kbyte bank

; Calling Protocol:
;       Set_Write_Bank_Trident(write_bank);
```

```
Set_Write_Bank_Trident proc far arg1:byte

;         set up index to Bank Select Register
          mov    bl,arg1          ;get page
          Load_Write_Bank_Trident
          ret
Set_Write_Bank_Trident endp
```

LISTING 19.8   Loading the Read Bank Number for the 64-Kbyte Memory Map

```
;  Function:
;       Loading the Read Bank with a new start address for the 64-
;       Kbyte memory map
;  Input with:
;       read_bank       Read Bank_Number
;                                 0-7 bank number indicating desired
;                                 64-Kbyte bank

;  Calling Protocol:
;       Set_Read_Bank_Trident(read_bank);

Set_Read_Bank_Trident proc far arg1:byte

;         set up index to Bank Select Register
          mov    bl,arg1          ;get page
          Load_Read_Bank_Trident

          ret
Set_Read_Bank_Trident endp
```

19.7   CONTROLLING THE CRT ADDRESS GENERATION

19.7.1   Controlling the Display Start Address

To display the one Megabyte onto the screen, it is necessary to utilize the Old Mode Control 1 Register and the CRTC Module Testing Register. These registers are described in Table 19.8.

The CRTC Module Testing Register, shown in Figure 19.2, contains two fields which augment the 16-bit start addresses provided in the CRTC registers. The 16-bit addressing can be enabled through the A16 field of this register. If the A16 field is a 0, the address bit 16 function is disabled. This is the standard VGA implementation and will cause wrap around at the 64-Kbyte segment. If

TABLE 19.8 8900 Trident Display Address Control

Function	Register Name	Port	Index	Bits	Value
Select lower 512K Bank	Old Mode Control 1	3C4	E	0	0
Select higher 512K Bank	Old Mode Control 1	3C4	E	0	1
Start Address Bit 16	CRTC Module Testing	3D4	1E	5	0–1
Address Bit 16 Enable	CRTC Module Testing	3D4	1E	7	0–1

the A16 field is a 1, the address bit 16 function is enabled.

The address bit 16 is provided to the CRT addressing through the S16 field of this register. This allows access to 128 Kbytes of display memory. The display start address can be loaded through the code in Listing 19.9. This function utilizes the set_start_address macro in Listing 14.32.

LISTING 19.9 Loading the Display Start Address

```
; Function:
;       Loading the Display Start Address

;InputParameters
;       address         unsigned integer starting address
;       top             top two bits of address

; Calling Protocol:
;       Load_Start_Trident(address,top)

Load_Start_Trident      proc far        arg1,arg2:byte

        mov     bx,arg1
        set_start_address       ;load the 16-bit start address

;       send out top address
        dec     dx
        mov     al,1eh          ;index Module Testing Register
        out     dx,al
```

```
;       read current value
        inc     dx
        in      al,dx           ;get value
        and     al,0dfh         ;zero out start address-16 bit 5
;       or in new start address
        mov     bl,arg2         ;get top address
        and     bl,01h          ;only want 1 bit
        mov     cx,5
        shl     bl,cl           ;shift left 5 to get bit in proper position
        or      al,bl
        or      al,80h          ;set bit 1 for enable bit 16
        out     dx,al           ;output top address
        ret
Load_Start_Trident      endp
```

19.7.2 Controlling the Cursor Start Address

The cursor start address can not be extended beyond the 16-bit cursor address contained in the Cursor Start Address High and Low Registers. This does not create a problem since the alphanumerics modes do not extend beyond the first 64-Kbyte segment. The graphics modes require read/modify/write memory accesses as described in Section 19.4.

Listing 19.10 provides the code to position the cursor. This function utilizes the position_cursor macro in Listing 14.33.

LISTING 19.10   Positioning the Cursor

```
;  Function:
;       Loading the Cursor Position

;  Input Parameters
;       position                unsigned integer position

;  Calling Protocol:
;       Position_Cursor_Trident(position)

Position_Cursor_Trident         proc far        arg1,arg2:byte

        mov     bx,arg1
        position_cursor         ;load the 16-bit cursor position
        ret
Position_Cursor_Trident endp
```

19.7.3 Controlling the Display Offset

The display offset determines the virtual image size. The eight-bit value stored in the Offset Register in the CRTC register group, described in Section 10.4.22. In the word mode, which is typically the case, display offsets up to 1024 bytes can be defined.

19.8 TRIDENT BIOS EXTENSIONS

The only addition to the standard VGA BIOS functions is the enhanced Mode Set command. This extension of the AH=0 BIOS function returns an argument in the AH register, if a Super VGA mode is invoked. The Set Mode BIOS function is described in Section 11.2.1. The returned value passed back in the AH register is described in Table 19.9.

TABLE 19.9 Trident Enhanced Mode Set BIOS Function

Returned Value in AH	Description
0	Set mode was successful
80	Fail. Wrong switch setting
81	Insufficient video memory
82	The 36 MHz crystal cannot support the mode 8800
82	Mode not supported 8900
83	The 40 MHz crystal cannot support the mode 8800
83	Mode not supported 8900
84	The 44.9 MHz crystal cannot support the mode 8800
84	Mode not supported 8900
85	Dead crystal or no crystal 8800
86	Wrong CRTC base for dual screen 8900
87	Text mode not supported 8900

Chapter 20

The Tseng Labs
Super VGA Chip

20.1 INTRODUCTION TO THE TSENG LABS VGA

Tseng Labs has manufactured two Super VGA Chips named the ET3000 and ET4000. As one would expect, the ET4000 is an advanced version of the ET3000. Its features include faster processing, the ability to handle VRAM memory, a generous helping of caches and FIFOS to speed up graphics operations, and the capacity to access more display memory. Both the ET3000 and ET4000 are simple processors to program.

Along with the capacity to access more display memory comes the higher resolution display modes. The ET3000 is capable of 1024 by 768 16-color and 800 by 600 256-color while the ET4000 is capable of 1024 by 768 16-color and 1024 by 768 256-color modes. The ET4000 can emulate the MDA, Hercules, CGA, and EGA graphics cards. Either can reside in the PC/AT bus or on a microchannel bus and both can generate interrupts to the host.

One major difference between the ET3000 and ET4000 is the field locations for the Read and Write Bank Selection registers. The need to provide additional banks for the higher resolution display modes in the ET4000 forced the redefinition of the read and write bank. Thus, software which utilizes the dual-bank configuration must determine whether a ET3000 or ET4000 is present before setting the Read Bank Register. The hardware zoom window available on the ET3000 is not available on the ET4000.

20.1.1 ET3000 Chip

The ET3000 is the first-generation Super VGA from Tseng Labs. Table 20.1 describes the different versions of the ET3000. The ET3000-AX and ET3000-BX versions are discussed in this chapter. Both are register-level compatible to the standard VGA and are downwardly compatible to the MDA/ Hercules and CGA. Each supports 132-column alphanumerics display modes, multiple windows and multiple simultaneous soft fonts. In addition, both support hardware pan and zoom in graphics and text modes.

The hardware, zoom feature is an interesting special effect which allows the

926

TABLE 20.1 ET3000 Versions

Chip Name	Capabilities	Host Bus	16-bit Resolution	256-bit Resolution
ET3000-AX	Most Powerful	8/16	1024x768	800x600
ET3000-BX	Less Powerful	8	800x600	640x480
ET3000-Bp	Basic VGA chip	8	800x600	320x200

creation of an independent window on the screen. This window contains a zoomed representation of a portion of display memory. The starting x and y location of the zoomed window is programmable. Its size is determined by the data which is to be zoomed. A rectangular region within the display memory is targeted as the window to zoom. Finally, a horizontal and vertical zoom factor, one to eight, is specified. At this point, the system is primed, and all that remains is to enable the zoom function. The zoom window overlays the normal display window.

20.1.2 ET4000 Chip

The ET4000 is the second-generation Super VGA chip from Tseng Labs. The major improvement of the ET4000 over the ET3000 is speed and resolution. The improved data paths, fast cache and FIFO memories, and VRAM control all lead to faster graphics processing. The hardware, zoom feature of the ET3000 was not included in the ET4000. Additional registers are provided in the ET4000 for enhanced control.

The ET4000 is extremely fast. It supports VRAM memory and has highly-optimized memory control for the DRAM memory. Speed tests have shown that the DRAM memory configuration can run nearly the speed of the 8 MHz PC/AT bus. This, of course, is based on the wait-states imposed on the PC/AT bus. Tseng recommends the DRAM configuration on cards that plug into this bus. When the ET4000 is mounted on a motherboard, it does not have the forced wait-states imposed upon it from the host. The VRAM memory configuration is recommended in this application.

The ET4000 takes full advantage of the VRAM dual-ported memory. One port is used for data input while the second port is used for data output. The memory is configured with a 16-bit wide data bus from the ET4000 to the display memory. The display memory can consist of two chips totalling 256 Kbytes, four chips totalling 512 Kbytes, or eight chips totaling one Megabyte of memory. The VRAM chips are 256K x 4 bits each. Four chips comprise a bank. Each bank utilizes a 16-bit data bus in and out to the host and a 16-bit data bus out to the video refresh circuitry. The 16-bit bus is not extended to 32-bits when eight chips are used. Rather, a second bank is placed in parallel to the first bank. This limits the bandwidth to the 16-bit bus rate instead of increasing the bandwidth to a 32-bit bus rate.

The ET4000 dedicates 25 percent of its silicon to FIFO memory, cache memory and memory management. This silicon is well used and translates into very fast graphics.

20.2   CONFIGURING THE TSENG LABS VGA

The ET4000 provides the standard capabilities for configuring the card as shown in Table 20.2.

20.2.1   8- or 16-bit Bus Interface

Both the memory and I/O data paths are designed to be either 8 or 16 bits wide through the Video System Configuration #1 Register. The I/O bus width is controlled through the I16 field. The display memory bus width is controlled through the D16 field. This register is shown in Figure 20.1.

The on-card ROM can be configured for 8- or 16-bit operation through the R16 field of the Video System Configuration #2 Register shown in Figure 20.2. If the R16 field is set to 1, 16-bit ROM accesses will be enabled. If the R16 field is

TABLE 20.2   Configuring the Tseng Labs Super VGAs

Function	Register Name	Port	Index	Bits	Value
Enable segment addressing	Video System Config. 1	3D4	36	4	0
Enable linear addressing	Video System Config. 1	3D4	36	4	1
Select 8-bit I/O	Video System Config. 1	3D4	36	7	0
Select 16-bit I/O	Video System Config. 1	3D4	36	7	1
Select 8-bit data path	Video System Config. 1	3D4	36	6	0
Select 16-bit data path	Video System Config. 1	3D4	36	6	1
Enable 8-bit ROM	Video System Config. 2	3D4	37	4	0
Enable 16-bit ROM	Video System Config. 2	3D4	37	4	1
Read Speed Performance	RAS/CASVideo Config.	3D4	32	7–0	0–255
Vertical NON-Interlace	Overflow High	3D4	35	7	0
Vertical Interlace	Overflow High	3D4	35	7	1
Disable On-Card ROM	TS Auxiliary Mode	3C4	7	3	0
Disable On-Card ROM	TS Auxiliary Mode	3C4	7	5	1
Enable VGA compatibility	TS Auxiliary Mode	3C4	7	7	1
Enable EGA compatibility	TS Auxiliary Mode	3C4	7	7	0

Video System Configuration 1

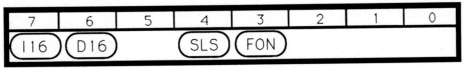

Index 36 at Port 3B4/3D4   Port 3B5/3D5 Read/Write

FIGURE 20.1   Video System Configuration Register 1. The 8- or 16-bit bus selection for display memory resides in the D16 field and for I/O memory in the I16 field. The addressing scheme can be linear or segmented controlled by the SLS field. The font width is controlled through the FON field.

Video System Configuration 2

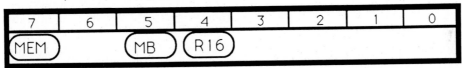

Index 37 at Port 3B4/3D4   Port 3B5/3D5 Read/Write

FIGURE 20.2   Video System Configuration Register 2. The R16 field controls whether a 16-bit BIOS is installed. The MB field optimizes memory bandwidth and the MEM field selects either VRAM or DRAM.

0, 8-bit ROM accesses will be enabled. Typically, this field would not be modified by the programmer. Other hardware on the VGA card would have to be configured for the 8- or 16-bit ROM accesses. This might be in the form of jumpers or switches. The programmer may find it useful to determine whether 8- or 16-bit accesses are currently being used.

All other fields within the Video System Configuration #2 Register are related to hardware configuration. As with the R16 field, these should not be modified. The MEM field controls whether DRAM or VRAM is installed. If the MEM field is 1, VRAM is installed. If MEM is set to 0, DRAM is installed. The MB field controls memory bandwidth. A 0 value in the MB field indicates better performance than if the MB field is set to 1. The BRA field enables block read-ahead. A 0 value in the BRA field enables block read-ahead and indicates better performance than if the BRA field is set to 1.

The RAS/CAS Configuration Register can provide information regarding the bandwidth of the system. This field should not be altered by the programmer. It is likely that it is already optimized for the specific card. The TIME field is really a combination of six fields which reside in this register. It is beyond the scope of

RAS/CAS Configuration

Index 32 at Port 3B4/3D4   Port 3B5/3D5 Read/Write

FIGURE 20.3   RAS/Configuraton Register. The TIME field is a composite field that configures memory speed performance.

this book to describe each field but suffice it to say that a 1 in any bit position in the TIME field will degrade performance. The RAS/CAS Configuration Register is displayed in Figure 20.3. Table 20.2 lists some common configurations and their respective TIME fields. Each bit in the TIME field effects memory in a unique way. Calculating memory performance is complex. The fewer 1s in this TIME field the better.

One caveat regarding Table 20.2 concerns the relationship between the TIME field and the video boards system clock. If the system clock is slow, this value will be smaller than if the system clock is fast. Table 20.2 lists two entries, one for 28 MHz system clock and a second for a 36 MHz system clock. The 28 MHz system clock has a smaller value in the TIME field. However, the 36 MHz version is likely to run faster.

The memory speed certainly affects processing speed and the value in the TIME field. Typically, memory comes in either 80 or 100 nanosecond access-time versions. If the DRAM of VRAM memory is 80 nanosecond memory, the value in the TIME field is likely to be smaller than if the memory is 100 nanosec-ond memory. This occurs because the memory has added headroom. If the values in the TIME field are the same, it is likely that the faster 80 nanosecond memory is not being utilized. In Table 20.3, a VRAM entry with 80 nanosecond memory has a TIME value of 0 (ideal), while the 100 nanosecond memory has a value of 09.

20.2.2   On-Card ROM

The on-card BIOS ROM can be enabled or disabled through the R0 and R1 fields of the TS Auxiliary Mode ET3000 Register and TS Auxiliary Mode ET4000 Register shown in Figure 20.4 and Figure 20.5 respectively. These two fields combine to form a two-bit control code which configures the ROM, as shown in Table 20.4. The combination R1=0 and R0=1 disables the ROM. The power-on default is R1=1, R0=1. The ET3000 or ET4000 can also be placed into a VGA emulation or into an EGA emulation mode through the VGA field. If the VGA field is 1, the VGA compatibility is enabled; if 0, the EGA compatibility is en-abled. The power-on default condition is VGA emulation.

TS Auxiliary Mode ET3000

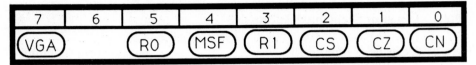

Index 7 at Port 3C4   **Port 3C5 Read/Write**

FIGURE 20.4 TS Auxiliary Mode Register. The VGA field enables VGA or EGA compatibility. The R1,R0 fields select the ROM BIOS address space. The CN, CZ, and CX fields complement the function of the three possible windows. These are the normal, zoom, and split screen windows respectively. The MSF field enables multiple soft fonts.

TS Auxiliary Mode ET4000

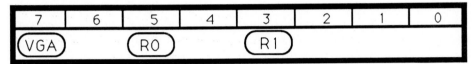

Index 7 at Port 3C4   **Port 3C5 Read/Write**

FIGURE 20.5 TS Auxiliary Mode ET4000 Register. The VGA field enables VGA or EGA compatibility. The R1,R0 fields select the ROM BIOS address space.

TABLE 20.3 RAS/CAS Configuration Register Typical Values

Memory Type	Memory Speed	System Clock	TIME Field
Ideal			00
VRAM memory	80 nsec		00
VRAM memory	100 nsec		09
VRAM memory		28 MHz	00
VRAM memory		36 MHz	08
DRAM memory		40 MHz	70

TABLE 20.4 Configuring the BIOS ROM

R1	R0	ROM BIOS Addresses	Total Memory
0	0	C0000–C3FFF	16 Kbytes
0	1	ROM disabled	0 Kbytes
1	0	C0000–C5FFF; C6800–C7FFF	30 Kbytes
1	1	C0000–C7FFF	32 Kbytes

20.2.3 Linear or Segmented Addressing

The VGA can be configured to access memory in a linear or in a segmented fashion through the SLS field. The linear addressing mode forces all display memory to be continuous. This is a much more efficient way to utilize the ET4000. If the SLS Field is 1, this linear mapping scheme is enabled. If 0, the standard VGA segmented memory mapping scheme is enabled.

In extended DOS or OS/2 applications, it is possible to place the VGA into high memory where there is room to place one Megabyte of display memory into a contiguous address space. This allows the ET4000 to ignore the bank selection registers. There are two advantages to this approach. The first ensures faster programs; the second ensures continuous high-speed operation from a hardware perspective.

The software advantage requires an extended operating system and access to the memory through the 80286, 80386 or 80486 processors. The software advantage becomes pronounced when 32-bit instructions can handle the one megabyte without segment registers.

The hardware advantage is primarily aimed at video frame-grabbers where the hardware has a continuous stream of data coming at the ET4000 display memory, and the ET4000 cannot afford to perform bank switching.

20.2.4 Interlaced or Non-interlaced Control

The ET3000 and ET4000 can interface to either interlaced or non-interlaced monitors. This is accomplished through the Overflow High Register for the ET3000 and ET4000 This register contains several extended address and control fields as shown in Figures 20.16 and 20.17. (See page 951.) The ET3000 and ET4000 can control either an interlaced or a non-interlaced monitor through the INT field of the Overflow High Register. If the INT field is 1, the interlaced mode is engaged. If 0, the non-interlaced mode is engaged.

20.2.5 Extended Vertical Timing

The extended address bits extend the address range of the Vertical Blank, Vertical Total, Vertical Display End, Vertical Sync Start and the Line Compare register. These five fields, located in the Overflow High Register, are described in Table 20.5. The Overflow High Register for the ET3000 and ET4000 are shown in Figures 20.16 and 20.17, respectively. Each acts as bit 10 of the respective fields. Note that bit 8 of these registers reside in the same bit positions of the Overflow Low Register. The Overflow Low Register is described in Section 10.4.8. Also in the Overflow Low Register is bit 9 of the Vertical Total, Vertical Display End and Vertical Sync Start . Bit 9 of the Vertical Blank Start and Line

TABLE 20.5   Overflow High Register Fields

Bit	Field	Feature	Usage
7	INT	Vertical Interlace	1=vertical interlace
6	RMW	Read/Modify/Write	1=enable Read/Modify/Write
5	GL	Gen-lock	1=enable gen-lock
4	LC10	Line Compare Bit 10	
3	VS10	Vertical Sync Start Bit 10	
2	VD10	Vertical Display End Bit 10	
1	VT10	Vertical Total Bit 10	
0	VB10	Vertical Blank Start Bit 10	

Compare Register are found in the Maximum Row Address Register described in Section 10.4.10.

These extended address bits in bit positions 0–4 extend the address range for the vertical timing to 11 bits. The standard VGA representations of these vertical timing functions are 10 bits thereby allowing access of up to 1024 scan lines. Extending this to 11 bits allows accessing of up to 2048 scan lines.

20.3   CONTROLLING THE TSENG LABS VGA

The ET4000 uses the VGA-compatible control registers located at port address 46E8 for the PC/AT systems and 3C3 for the PS/2 motherboard microchannel systems. The EN field enables the VGA if set to 1 and disables the VGA if set to 0 as illustrated in Table 20.6 and in Figures 20.6 and 20.7.

20.3.1   Enabling the VGA

Only one of these two Video Subsystem Enable registers are enabled at a time. This is controlled through the ENVS field of the Compatibility Control Register

Video Subsytem Register for PC/AT

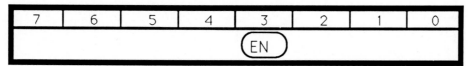

Port 46E8   Read Only

FIGURE 20.6   Display Adapter Enable Register. Adapter card implementation at Port 46E8. Allows enabling and disabling of VGA through the EN field.

Video Subsystem Register for PS/2 Microchannel

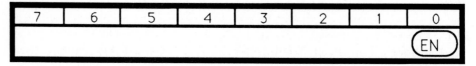

Port 3C3 Read/Write

FIGURE 20.7 Video Subsystem Enable Register. Motherboard implementation at Port 3C3. Allows enabling and disabling of VGA through the EN field.

TABLE 20.6 Resetting and Enabling the Tseng Super VGAs

Function	Register Name	Port	Index	Bits	Value
Enable VGA PC/AT	Video Subsystem Enable	46E8		3	1
Disable VGA PC/AT	Video Subsystem Enable	46E8		3	0
Enable VGA Microchannel	Video Subsystem Enable	3C3		0	1
Disable VGA Microchannel	Video Subsystem Enable	3C3		0	0
Enable Card Microchannel	Setup Control	102		0	0
Disable Card Microchannel	Setup Control	102		0	1
Switch Normal Window	TS Auxiliary Mode ET3000	3C5	7	0	1
Same Normal Window	TS Auxiliary Mode ET3000	3C5	7	0	1
Switch Zoom Window	TS Auxiliary Mode ET3000	3C5	7	1	1
Same Zoom Window	TS Auxiliary Mode ET3000	3C5	7	1	1
Switch Split Window	TS Auxiliary Mode ET3000	3C5	7	2	1
Same Split Window	TS Auxiliary Mode ET3000	3C5	7	2	1

shown in Figure 20.8. If the ENVS field is 1, the system is configured so that this register will reside at the 46E8 port address. If 0, the system is configured for the 3C3 port address. This is the power-up default position so that the Video Subsystem Enable Register is located at port address 3C3.

Compatibility Control Register

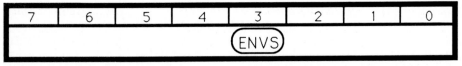

Index 34 at Port 3B4/3D4   Port 3B5/3D5 Read/Write

FIGURE 20.8 Compatibility Register. The ENVS field controls whether the Video Subsystem Enable Register is mapped to 3C3 or 46E8.

20.3.2 Switching Alphanumeric/Graphic Modes

The ET3000 provides a technique for switching the mode of each of three independent windows. The ET3000 can have a normal display window, split screen display window, and zoom window. These windows do not have to be displayed in the same fashion as the current display mode. Since each window is independent, it can be programmed to be in either a graphics or a text mode. This is accomplished through the CN, CZ and CS fields in the TS Auxiliary Mode ET3000 Register as shown in Figure 20.4. It should be noted that these fields have different functions in the corresponding TS Auxiliary Mode ET4000 Register as shown in Figure 20.5. If the CN field is 1, the mode in the normal display window is changed from text to graphic or vice versa. If the CN field is 0, no change occurs. The CZ and CS fields operate similarly for the zoom and split screen windows respectively.

20.4 INQUIRING ABOUT THE TSENG CONFIGURATION

Other than the standard VGA registers and the Extended registers described in this chapter, there are no additional register fields dedicated to Tseng configuration. The microchannel Card ID registers can only be accessed when the system is in a setup mode. Table 20.7 lists some registers used to acquire information.

20.4.1 Identifying the Tseng Chips

The Tseng chip family can be identified by accessing the Miscellaneous Register shown in Figure 20.9. This register is located in the Attribute Register group at index 16 hex. Bits 4 and 5, the HIGH field of this register are used to select the high-resolution timings. The programmer can read this HIGH field, re-write it with a different value, read it and verify that the re-write operation was successful. If it was successful, the card is based on a Tseng Labs chip. At this point, the original value in the HIGH field should be restored.

The Tseng Chip family can be identified through the code in Listing 20.1.

TABLE 20.7 Inquiring about the Tseng Configuration

Function	Register Name	Port	Index	Bits	Value
Identify Card	Microchannel Id. Low	POS 100		7–0	0–255
Identify Card	Microchannel Id. High	POS 101		7–0	0–255
Identify Tseng	Miscellaneous	3C0	16	4	0,1
Identify Chip	Extended Start	3x4	33	0–3	0–15

ATC Miscellaneous

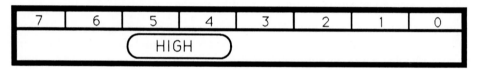

7	6	5	4	3	2	1	0

HIGH

Index 16 at Port 3C0   Port : Write 3C0 Read 3C1

FIGURE 20.9 ATC Miscellaneous Register. The high resolution and high-color mode resides in the HIGH field.

LISTING 20.1 Determining if the VGA is a Tseng Labs Super VGA

```
/*
Function:
    Determining if the card is a Tseng card

Output Parameters:
    1 card is a Tseng
    0 card is NOT a Tseng

Calling Protocol:
  Tseng= Is_It_Tseng() */

int Is_It_Tseng()
{ unsigned char new_value,old_value,value;

At enable "key" if ET4000 */
        outp(0x3bf, 3);
        if ((inp(0x3cc)d1)outp(0x3d8, 0xa0);
            else outp(0x3B8, 0xA0);
```

```
/* read the old value */
inp(0x3DA); /* dummy read to set up attribute index */
outp(0x3C0,)x16); /* index ATC Miscellaneous Register */
old_value = inp(0x3C1);

/* write a new value */
inp(0x3DA); /* dummy read to set up attribute index */
outp(0x3C0,0x16); new_value = old_value ^0x10;
outp(0x3C0,new_value);

/* read the new value */
inp(0x3DA); outp(0x3C0,0x16); /* index ATC Miscellaneous Register */
value = inp(0x3C1);

/* write the old value */
inp(0x3DA); outp(0x3C0,0x16); /* index ATC Miscellaneous Register */
outp(0x3C0,old_value);

if(value==new_value) return(1);
     else return(0);

}
```

20.4.2   Identifying which Tseng Chips

The ET4000 can be distinguished from the ET3000 by the availability of the
Extended Start Address Register shown in Figure 20.15. This register is located
in the CRTC register group at port address 3x4/3x5 index 33 hex. The x refers
to D if a color mode is active and B if a monochrome mode is active. The
programmer can read this register, re-write it with a different value, read it and
verify that the re-write operation was successful. If it was successful, the card is
based on an ET4000 chip. If it was unsuccessful, the card is based on an ET3000
chip. At this point, the original value in the register should be restored.

The ET3000 can be differentiated from the ET4000 by the code in Listing
20.2.

LISTING 20.2   Determining which Tseng Labs Super VGA Chip

```
/*
Function:
         Determining the Tseng chip

Output Parameters:
         identity        integer containing chip code
```

```
                                        3000 = ET3000
                                        4000 = ET4000
Calling Protocol:
   identity = Which_Tseng()  */


Which_Tseng()


{
 int base; unsigned char new_value,old_value;
if( (inp(0x3CC) & 0x01)==1) base = 0x3D0; else base = 0x3B0;

/* get old value */
outp(base+4,0x33); old_value = inp(base+5);

/* change value */
outp(base+5,old_value ^0x0f); new_value = inp(base+5);

/* restore old value */
outp(base+5,old_value);

if(new_value==old_value 10x0f) return(4000);
                else return(3000);


}
```

20.5   TSENG LABS DISPLAY MODES

The ET4000 supports the standard alphanumerics modes which incorporate a variety of 132-column display modes. In addition, two alphanumeric modes allow 60 by 80 and 40 by 100 character resolutions. These modes are described in Table 20.8.

TABLE 20.8   Tseng Labs Alphanumerics modes

Mode	Rows	Columns	Font	Resolution	Colors	Chip
18	44	132	8x8	1056x352	2	4000
19	25	132	9x14	1188x350	2	4000
1A	28	132	9x13	1188x364	2	4000
22	44	132	8x8	1056x352	16	4000
23	25	132	8x14	1056x350	16	4000
24	28	132	8x13	1056x364	16	4000
26	60	80	8x8	640x480	16	4000
2A	40	100	8x15	800x600	16	4000

TABLE 20.9   Tseng Graphics Modes

Mode	Resolution	Colors	Chip
25	640x480	16	4000
29	800x600	16	4000
2D	640x350	256	4000
2E	640x480	256	4000
2F	640x400	256	4000
30	800x600	256	4000
37	1024x768	16	4000
38	1024x768	256	4000

The ET4000 supports the standard graphics modes which extend to 1024 by 768 in both the 16-color and 256-color modes. These modes are described in Table 20.9.

20.6   ACCESSING THE TSENG LABS DISPLAY MEMORY

The ET3000 can access up to 512 Kbytes of display memory while the ET4000 can access up to one Megabyte of display memory. Tseng Labs implemented the traditional technique of overlaying the display memory into 64-Kbyte banks. To provide rapid transfers of data from display memory to display memory, dual-bank registers are implemented. One bank register is dedicated to write operations, and the other is dedicated to read operations. This allows both to be mapped into the same memory space. The optimum size with respect to the host is 64 Kbytes. The PC standard dictates that this should reside between A0000 and AFFFF hex.

Tseng wanted to provide a granularity of 16 Kbytes. This requires a three-bit bank field for the fully populated ET3000 and a four-bit bank field for the fully populated ET4000. Unfortunately, when the field was defined for the ET3000, only three bits were allocated for the Write Bank Select, immediately adjoined by the three bits of the Read Bank Select. When it was time to extend the memory for the ET4000, there was no adjacent bit in the register for the fourth bit required for the field. The two extra bits in the register were located in bit positions 6 and 7.

Fortunately, Tseng Labs reacted with the correct decision. They chose to move the read field over one bit to the left, thereby providing the additional bit position. While this causes compatibility problems, it means that programs which access the heavily-utilized Write Bank Select Register are not split up by the Write Bank value. One can simply load the 64-Kbyte bank value into the register as opposed to shifting the lone bank bit to the proper position.

TABLE 20.10 Reading and Writing to Tseng Labs Display Memory

Function	Register Name	Port	Index	Bits	Value
Enable Segment Addressing	Video System Config. 1	3D5	36	4	0
Enable Linear Addressing	Video System Config. 1	3D5	36	4	1
Write Bank ET3000	GDC Segment Select	3CD		2–0	0–7
Read Bank ET3000	GDC Segment Select	3CD		5–3	0–7
Write Bank ET4000	GDC Segment Select	3CD		3–0	0–15
Read Bank ET4000	GDC Segment Select	3CD		7–4	0–15

An important feature of the ET4000 is its ability to map its display memory into a linear address space instead of a segmented address space. The one megabyte of display memory is mapped into a linear one Megabyte address space in the host. Obviously, this would be placed above the lower one Megabyte memory space currently used by DOS. A protected mode-operating system must be used to utilize this mode. The performance of the graphics system based on the linear addressing mode, a 32-bit addressing processor (80386, 80486), zero wait-state video RAM, and a motherboard implementation of the chip would be outstanding. In addition, software would be easy to write and highly compatible across different display adapters, given that the one Megabyte of host address space was standardized.

20.6.1 Reading and Writing to the Display Memory

There are two Extended VGA registers relevant to reading and writing to the display memory as shown in Table 20.10.

The Video System Configuration #1 register is illustrated in Figure 20.1. The bank-selection techniques are described in the following section.

20.6.2 ET3000 Bank Addressing

A Bank (segment) Selection Register, called the GDC Segment Select Register, contains two bank-selection fields. One field, WSP, is the Write Bank field while the other, RSP, is the Read Bank field. The WSP field controls the upper three bits of address which are provided to the display memory by the host during write operations. The RSP field controls the upper three bits of address which are provided to the display memory by the host during read operations. This register is shown for the ET3000 in Figure 20.10.

A destructive but fast way to load the Write Bank Select field is through the

Segment Select ET3000

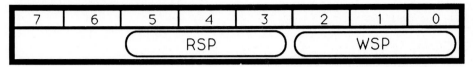

Port 3CD Read/Write

FIGURE 20.10   Segment Select Register ET4000. The Write Bank (segment) pointer resides in the WSP field. The Read Bank (segment) pointer resides in the RSP field.

macro in Listing 20.3. This macro can be used as a fast way to load the Write Bank while destroying the current Read Bank. It can also be used to load both the Write and Read banks simultaneously.

The Write and Read banks can be loaded non-destructively through the macro code in Listings 20.4 and 20.5 respectively.

LISTING 20.3   Loading the Write Bank Field for the ET3000

```
;  Function:
;      Loading the Read and Write banks with a new start address for
;          the ET3000.

;  Input with:
;      bl                              Write Bank_Number
;                                      0-7 bank number indicating desired
;                                      64-Kbyte bank

;  Calling Protocol:
;      Load_Banks_Tseng_3000

Load_Banks_Tseng_3000 macro

;      set up index to Bank Select Register
       mov     dx,3cdh         ;point to memory Segment Register
       mov     al,bl
       or  al, 40h             ;normal value for bit 6 with 64-Kbyte
                               segment
       out     dx,al           ;output bank

endm
```

LISTING 20.4 Loading the Write Bank for the ET3000 Macro

```
; Function:
; Loading the Write Bank with a new start address for the ET3000

; Input with:
;      bl                       Write Bank_Number
;                               0-7 bank number indicating desired
;                               64-Kbyte bank


; Calling Protocol:
;       Load_Write_Bank_Tseng_3000

Load_Write_Bank_Tseng_3000 macro

;       set up index to Bank Select Register
        mov     dx,3cdh        ;point to memory Segment Register

;       input value so Read Bank is preserved
        in      al,dx          ;input value
        and     al,0f8h        ;zero write bank bits 2-0

;       load in the new bank value
        and     bl,07h         ;only want 3 bits of bank

        or      al,bl          ;or in write bank
        out     dx,al          ;output bank

endm
```

LISTING 20.5 Loading the Write Bank for the ET4000 Macro

```
; Function:
; Loading the Read Bank with a new start address for the ET3000

; Input with:
;      bl                       Read Bank_Number
;                               0-7 bank number indicating desired
;                               64-Kbyte bank

; Calling Protocol:
;       Load_Read_Bank_Tseng_3000

Load_Read_Bank_Tseng_3000 macro
```

```
;       set up index to Bank Select Register
        mov     dx,3cdh         ;point to memory Segment Register

;       input value so Write Bank preserved
        in      al,dx           ;input value
        and     al,0c7h         ;zero read bank bits 5-3

;       load in the new bank value
        and     bl,07h          ;only want 3 bits
        shl     bl,1            ;put desired write bank into bits 5-3
        shl     bl,1
        shl     bl,1
        or      al,bl           ;or in read bank
        out     dx,al           ;output bank
endm
```

The Bank Select Register can be accessed by C programs using the functions in Listings 20.6 and 20.7. These two functions change the write or read bank without disturbing the other bits in the register.

LISTING 20.6   Loading Write Bank Number for the ET3000

```
; Function:
;       Loading the Write Bank for the ET3000 with a new start
;       address

; Input with:
;       write_bank      Write Bank_Number
;                               0-7 bank number indicating desired
;                               64-Kbyte bank

; Calling Protocol:
;       Set_Write_Bank_Tseng_3000(write_bank);

Set_Write_Bank_Tseng_3000 proc far arg1:byte

;       load in the new bank value
        mov     bl,arg1         ;get argument
        Load_Write_Bank_Tseng_3000

ret
Set_Write_Bank_Tseng_3000 endp
```

LISTING 20.7 Loading Read Bank Number for the ET3000

```
;  Function:
;       Loading the Read Bank for the ET3000 with a new start
;       address
;  Input with:
;       read_bank       Read Bank_Number
;                               0-7 bank number indicating desired
;                               64-Kbyte bank
;  Calling Protocol:
;       Set_Read_Bank_Tseng_3000(read_bank);

Set_Read_Bank_Tseng_3000 proc far arg1:byte

;       load in the new bank value
        mov     bl,arg1         ;get argument
        Load_Read_Bank_Tseng_3000

        ret
Set_Read_Bank_Tseng_3000 endp
```

20.6.3 ET4000 Bank Addressing

A Bank (segment) Selection Register, called the GDC Segment Select Register, contains two bank selection fields. One field, WSP, is the write bank field while the other, RSP, is the Read Bank field. The WSP field controls the upper four bits of address which are provided to the display memory by the host during write operations. The RSP field controls the upper four bits of address which are provided to the display memory by the host during read operations. This register is shown for the ET4000 in Figure 20.11.

A destructive but fast way to load the Write Bank Select field is through the macro in Listing 20.8. This macro can be used as a fast way to load the Write Bank while destroying the current Read Bank. It can also be used to load both the Write and Read banks simultaneously.

LISTING 20.8 Loading the Banks Number for the ET4000

```
;  Function:
;       Loading the read and write banks with a new start address
;       for the ET4000.

;  Input with:
;       bl                      Write Bank_Number
;                               0-15 bank number indicating desired
;                               64-Kbyte bank
```

```
; Calling Protocol:
;       Load_Write_Bank_Tseng_4000


Load_Write_Bank_Tseng_4000 macro


;       set up index to Bank Select Register
        mov     dx,3cdh         ;point to memory Segment Register
        mov     al,bl
        out     dx,al       ;output bank


endm
```

Segment Select ET4000

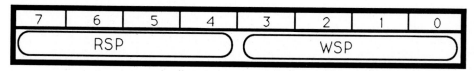

Port 3CD Read/Write

FIGURE 20.11 Segment Select Register ET4000. The Write Bank (segment) pointer resides in the WSP field. The Read Bank (segment) pointer resides in the RSP field.

The Write and Read banks can be loaded non-destructively through the macro code in Listings 20.9 and 20.10, respectively.

LISTING 20.9 Loading the Write Bank with a New Start Address for the ET4000 Macro

```
; Function:
;     Loading the Write Bank with a new start address for the ET4000


; Input with:
;       bl                      Write Bank_Number
;                                   0-7 bank number indicating desired
                                    64-Kbyte bank


; Calling Protocol:
;       Load_Write_Bank_Tseng_4000


Load_Write_Bank_Tseng_4000 macro
```

```
;       set up index to Bank Select Register
        mov     dx,3cdh         ;point to memory Segment Register

;       input value so Read Bank is preserved
        in      al,dx           ;input value
        and     al,0f0h             ;zero write bank bits 3-0

;       load in the new bank value
        and     bl,0fh          ;only want 4 bits
        or      al,bl           ;or in write bank
        out     dx,al           ;output bank

endm
```

LISTING 20.10 Loading the Write Bank with a New Start Address for the ET4000
Macro

```
; Function:
;       Loading the Read Bank with a new start address for the ET4000

; Input with:
;       bl                              Read Bank_Number
;                                       0-7 bank number indicating desired
;                           64-Kbyte bank

; Calling Protocol:
;       Load_Read_Bank_Tseng_4000

Load_Read_Bank_Tseng_4000 macro

;       set up index to Bank Select Register
        mov     dx,3cdh         ;point to memory Segment Register

;       input value so Write Bank preserved
        in      al,dx           ;input value
        and     al,0fh          ;zero read bank bits 7-4

;       load in the new bank value
        and     bl,0fh          ;only want 4 bits
        shl     bl,1            ;put desired write bank into bits 7-4
        shl     bl,1
        shl     bl,1
        shl     bl,1
        or      al,bl           ;or in read bank
        out     dx,al           ;output bank
endm
```

946

The Bank Select Register can be accessed by C programs, using functions in Listings 20.11 and 20.12. These two functions change the write or read bank without disturbing the other bits in the register.

LISTING 20.11   Loading Write Bank Number for the ET4000

```
; Function:
;       Loading the Write Bank for the ET4000 with a new start
;       address

; Input with:
;       write_bank      Write Bank_Number
;                               0-7 bank number indicating desired
;                               64-Kbyte bank

; Calling Protocol:
;       Set_Write_Bank_Tseng_4000(write_bank);

Set_Write_Bank_Tseng_4000 proc far arg1:byte

;       load in the new bank value
        mov     bl,arg1         ;get argument
        Load_Write_Bank_Tseng_4000

        ret
Set_Write_Bank_Tseng_4000 endp
```

LISTING 20.12   Loading Read Bank Number for the ET4000

```
; Function:
;       Loading the Read Bank for the ET4000 with a new start
;       address

; Input with:
;       read_bank       Read Bank_Number
;                               0-7 bank number indicating desired
;                               64-Kbyte bank

; Calling Protocol:
;       Set_Read_Bank_Tseng_4000(read_bank);

Set_Read_Bank_Tseng_4000 proc far arg1:byte
```

```
;       load in the new bank value
        mov     bl,arg1         ;get argument
        Load_Read_Bank_Tseng_4000
        ret
Set_Read_Bank_Tseng_4000 endp
```

20.6.4   Granularity

The granularity of these Read and Write Bank fields in the GDC Segment Select Register is 64 Kbytes. In both the ET3000 and ET4000 implementations, the display memory is split into four display planes. A granularity of 64 Kbytes was selected to map this 512 Kbytes of memory into the 64-Kbyte host segment. Eight banks are required for this granularity. In the 1 Megabyte configuration, each plane is 256 Kbytes long. A granularity of 64 Kbytes was selected to map this one megabyte of memory into the 64-Kbyte host segment. Sixteen banks are required for this granularity. Consequently, a three-bit bank field was required for the fully populated ET3000 and a four-bit bank field is required for the fully populated ET4000. The 20-bit address presented to the display memory is illustrated in Figure 20.12.

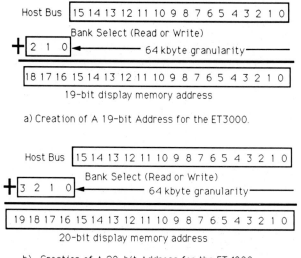

FIGURE 20.12   Creation of an Address Using Bank Selection for the ET3000 and ET4000.

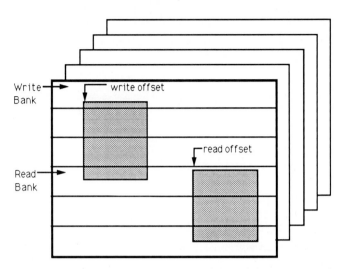

FIGURE 20.13 Display Memory Addressing. Read/write operations utilizing the Read and Write Bank registers. A 20-bit address is formed by the four-bit bank value and the 16-bit offset value.

20.6.5 Dual Bank Selection

The dual-bank registers provide a mechanism for transferring data from one display memory location to another. The Read and Write fields of the GDC Segment Select Register need to be written to only once for every time a 64-Kbyte bank is crossed.

Suppose it is desired to move a bank from one location to another in the display memory. It is desired to use the REP MOVSW instruction. It is only necessary to load the GDC Segment Select Register, set up the segment registers to both point to A000, set up the offset registers to point to the source and destination offset, and the cx register with the number of words to move. This setup would be followed by the REP MOVSW instruction. The maximum number of pixels that can be moved in one REP MOVSW sequence would be determined by the distance to the next 64-Kbyte boundary. It is necessary to set up the GDC Segment Select Register before crossing these boundaries. This is illustrated in Figure 20.13.

20.7 CONTROLLING THE CRT ADDRESS GENERATION

Both the ET3000 and the ET4000 allow for extended CRT address control through an Extended Start Address registers shown in Figures 20.14 and 20.15 respectively. Note that both are contained in the CRTC register group. However, each has a different CRTC index value. Since the ET3000 can access only

Extended Start Address for the ET4000

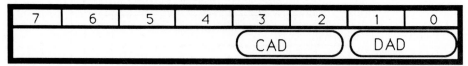

Index 33 at Port 3B4/3D4   Port 3B5/3D5 Read/Write

FIGURE 20.14   Extended Start Address Register for the ET4000. Contains bits 17–16 for the CRT addressing. These display start address bits reside in the DAD field and the cursor start address bits reside in the CAD field.

Extended Start Address for the ET3000

Index 23 at Port 3B4/3D4   Port 3B5/3D5 Read/Write

FIGURE 20.15   Extended Start Address Register for the ET3000. Contains bits 16 for the CRT addressing. The display start address bits resides in the DA field. The cursor start address bit resides in the CA field. The zoom start address bit resides in the ZA field.

half of the memory that the ET4000 can access, only one bit is required for the ET3000 while two are required for the ET4000. Also, there is no hardware zoom in the ET4000. Thus, there are no zoom extended bits. Registers used for address control are listed in Table 20.11.

It should be noted that the Overflow High registers for the ET3000 and ET4000, shown in Figures 20.16 and 20.17 respectively, are accessed through different indexes. It is indexed in the ET3000 at 25 hex while it is indexed at 35 hex in the ET4000. The Vertical Blank Start Bit 10 is contained in the VS10 field. The Vertical Total Bit 10 is contained in the VT10 field. The Vertical Display End Bit 10 is contained in the VD10 field. The Vertical Sync Start Bit 10 is contained in the VS10 field. The Line Compare Bit 10 is contained in the LC10 bit. The ET4000 has an additional high speed read/modify write bit in the RMW field. This feature is currently not supported.

20.7.1   ET3000 Display Start Address

The Tseng Labs ET3000 provides one additional bit of addressing to set up the CRT Addressing. The lower 16 bits of the display start address are controlled

TABLE 20.11 Tseng Labs' Display Address Control

Function	Register Name	Port	Index	Bits	Value
Start Address Bit 16	Extended Start ET3000	3x4	23	0	0,1
Cursor Address Bit 16	Extended Start ET3000	3x4	23	1	0,1
Zoom Address Bit 16	Extended Start ET3000	3x4	23	2	0,1
Start Address Bits 17–16	Extended Start ET4000	3x4	33	1–0	0–3
Cursor Address Bits 17–16	Extended Start ET4000	3x4	33	3–2	0–3
Bit 10 of CRT Address High	Overflow High ET3000	3x4	25	4–0	0–31
Bit 10 of CRT Address High	Overflow High ET4000	3x4	35	4–0	0–31

Overflow High Register ET3000

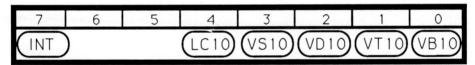

Index 25 at Port 3B4/3D4   Port 3B5/3D5 Read/Write

FIGURE 20.16 Overflow High Register. Bits 10 of the Vertical Blank Start, Vertical Total, Vertical Display End, Vertical Sync Start and Line Compare fields are contained in the VB10, VT10, VD10, VS10, and LC10 fields respectively. Vertical interlace is enabled through the INT field.

Overflow High Register ET4000

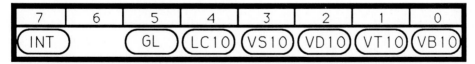

Index 35 at Port 3B4/3D4   Port 3B5/3D5 Read/Write

FIGURE 20.17 Overflow High Register. Bits 10 of the Vertical Blank Start, Vertical Total, Vertical Display End, Vertical Sync Start, and Line Compare fields are contained in the VB10, VT10, VD10, VS10, and LC10 fields respectively. Vertical interlace is enabled through the INT field. External syncing for gen-lock is enable through the GL field.

through the Display Start Address registers in the standard VGA register set. These are described in Sections 10.4.13 and 10.4.14. Code which loads the display start address for the ET3000 is provided in Listing 20.13. This function utilizes the set_start_address macro in Listing 14.32.

LISTING 20.13 Loading the Display Start Address for the ET3000

```
; Function:
;       Loading the Display Start Address for the ET3000

; Input Parameters
;       address     unsigned integer starting address
;       top             top two bits of address

; Calling Protocol:
;       Load_Start_Tseng_3000(address,top)

Load_Start_Tseng_3000  proc far        arg1,arg2:byte

        mov     bx,arg1
        set_start_address       ;load the 16-bit start address

;       send out top address
        dec     dx
        mov     ah,33h          ;index Extended Start Address
        out     dx,al

;       read current value
        inc     dx
        in      al,dx     ;get value
        and     al,0fch         ;zero out start address

;       or in new start address
        mov     cl,arg2         ;get top address
        and     cl,03h          ;only want two bits
        or      al,cl
        out     dx,al       ;output top address
        ret
;       send out top cursor address
        dec     dx
        mov     al,23h          ;index Extended Start Address
        out     dx,al

;       read current value
```

```
        inc    dx
        in     al,dx          ;get value
        and    al,0fdh        ;zero out start address bit 1

;       or in new start address
        mov    cl,arg2         ;get top address
        and    cl,01h          ;only want one bit
        shl    cl,1            ;put into bit position 1
        or     al,cl
        out    dx,al           ;output top address
Load_Start_Tseng_3000  endp
```

20.7.2 ET4000 Display Start Address

The Tseng Labs ET4000 provides two additional bits of addressing, similarly provided to set up the Display Start Address. The lower 16 bits of the display start address are controlled through the Display Start Address registers in the standard VGA register set. These are described in Sections 10.4.13 and 10.4.14. Two additional bits, bits 16 and 17, are provided in the CAD field of the Extended Start Address Register. This register is displayed in Figure 20.16. Code to load the start address for the ET4000 is provided in Listing 20.14. This function utilizes the set_start_address macro in Listing 14.32.

LISTING 20.14 Loading the Display Start Address for the ET4000

```
; Function:
;       Loading the Display Start Address for the ET4000

; Input Parameters
;       address         unsigned integer starting address
;       top                     top two bits of address

; Calling Protocol:
;       Load_Start_Tseng_4000(address,top)

Load_Start_Tseng_4000  proc far        arg1,arg2:byte

        mov    bx,arg1
        set_start_address       ;load the 16-bit start address

;       send out top address
        dec    dx
        mov    al,33h                   ;index Extended Start Address
        out    dx,al
```

```
;       read current value
        inc     dx
        in      al,dx           ;get value
        and     al,0fch          ;zero out start address

;       or in new start address
        mov     cl,arg2          ;get top address
        and     cl,03h           ;only want two bits
        or      al,cl
        out     dx,al            ;output top address
        ret
Load_Start_Tseng_4000   endp
```

20.7.3   ET3000 Cursor Start Address

The Tseng Labs ET3000 provides one additional bit of addressing to set up the CRT Addressing. The lower 16 bits of the cursor start address are controlled through the Cursor Address registers in the standard VGA register set. These are described in Sections 10.4.15 and 10.4.16.

Since the display memory is split into four display planes, only 17 address bits are required for the CRT addresses as shown in Listing 20.15. This function utilizes the position_cursor macro in Listing 14.33.

LISTING 20.15   Positioning the Cursor for the ET3000

```
; Function:
;       Loading the Cursor Position for the ET3000

Input Parameters
;       position                unsigned integer position
;       top                     top one bit of address

; Calling Protocol:
;       Position_Cursor_Tseng_3000(position,top)

Position_Cursor_Tseng_3000      proc far        arg1,arg2:byte

        mov     bx,arg1
        position_cursor          ;load the 16-bit cursor position

;       send out top cursor address
        dec     dx
        mov     al,23h           ;index Extended Start Address
        out     dx,al
```

```
;       read current value
        inc     dx
        in      al,dx       ;get value
        and     al,0feh         ;zero out cursor address bit 0

;       or in new start address
        mov     cl,arg2         ;get top address
        and     cl,01h          ;only want one bit
        or      al,cl
        out     dx,al       ;output top address

        ret
Position_Cursor_Tseng_3000 endp
```

20.7.4 ET4000 Cursor Start Address

The Tseng Labs ET4000 provides two additional bits of addressing, similarly provided to set up the Cursor Start Address. The lower 16 bits of the cursor start address are controlled through the Cursor Start Address registers in the standard VGA register set. These are described in Sections 10.4.15 and 10.4.16. Two additional bits, bits 16 and 17, are provided in the CAD field of the Extended Start Address Register. This register is displayed in Figure 20.16. Code to position the cursor for the ET4000 is provided in Listing 20.16. This function utilizes the position_cursor macro in Listing 14.33.

LISTING 20.16   Positioning the Cursor for the ET4000

```
;  Function:
;       Loading the Cursor Position for the ET4000

;  Input Parameters
;       position                unsigned integer position
;       top                     top two bits of address

;  Calling Protocol:
;       Position_Cursor_Tseng_4000(position,top)

Position_Cursor_Tseng_4000      proc far        arg1,arg2:byte

        mov     bx,arg1
        position_cursor;  load the 16-bit cursor position
```

```
;        send out top cursor address
         dec     dx
         mov     al,33h           ;index Extended Start Address
         out     dx,al

;        read current value
         inc     dx
         in      al,dx           ;get value
         and     al,0fch         ;zero out cursor address

;        or in new start address
         mov     cl,arg2         ;get top address
         and     cl,03h          ;only want two bits
         shl     cl,1            ;put into bit positions 3-2
         shl     cl,1
         or      al,cl
         out     dx,al           ;output top address

         ret
Position_Cursor_Tseng_4000 endp
```

20.7.5   Controlling the Display Offset

As described in Section 10.4.22, no additional bits are provided for the offset address beyond the eight bits provided in the Offset Register. With word addressing, these bits can cover 2040 pixels in the 256-color mode and 4080 pixels in the 16-color mode on the ET4000.

20.8   TSENG LABS BIOS EXTENSIONS

There are no extended BIOS calls specified or recommended by Tseng Labs regarding the Super VGA functions of either the ET3000 or ET4000.

20.9   TSENG LABS EXTRA FEATURES

20.9.1   Character Font Width

The ET4000 can be configured to operate with 8, 9, 10, 11, 12, and 16-bit wide character fonts. These are selected through the FON field of the Video System Configuration #1 Register and additional registers in the Timer Sequencer. This is discussed in detail in the Tseng Labs Data Book. If the FON field is set to 1, the 16-bit wide fonts are enabled. It set to 0, the 8-bit wide fonts are selected. In a 1024 wide display mode, one could display 64 characters, each 16-bits wide.

20.9.2   Gen-lock

Actual gen-lock is complicated and requires additional external hardware. The term *gen-lock* is used in reference to the ET4000 to merely indicate that it can be externally synchronized. External synchronization is used primarily for frame-grabbing, where the need to provide external synchronization is important.

The ET4000 can be configured to operate with an external sync. This external sync, provided on a special input line to the ET4000, resets the internal line and character counter asynchronously. This feature allows an external device to control the vertical sync timing of the ET4000. It allows an external device to be the master of the video timing. This is called gen-lock. The gen-lock capability is controlled through the GL field of the Overflow High Register described in Figure 20.17.

20.9.3   Read/Modify/Write

The ET4000 has a special mode which allows Read/Modify/Write operations to occur after a read operation. This feature is currently not supported.

20.9.4   Hardware Zoom and Pan

The ET3000 is equipped with hardware zoom capability. An independent destination window, or *zoom window* can be defined. This window is overlayed onto the screen as an independent window. The zoom window can be in a text or graphics mode, independent of the normal display window. The image data which is displayed in this zoom window is derived from data in a portion of display memory. Thus, a source window contains data to be zoomed, and a destination window contains the zoomed data. The destination window is referred to as the zoom window. This is illustrated in Figure 20.18.

The hardware zoom feature is enabled through the ZEN field of the Zoom Control Register. If the ZEN field is set to 1, the hardware zoom feature is enabled. The Zoom Control Register is shown in Figure 20.19.

The amount of zoom is programmable in both the horizontal and vertical dimension, as controlled by the XZOOM and YZOOM fields in the Zoom Control Register. In the horizontal dimension, the XZOOM field defines an X zoom factor of 0 to 7. This defines the number of times each pixel is to be repeated horizontally within the active zoom window. A 0 in the XZOOM field causes a 1:1 zoom. In the vertical dimension, the YZOOM field defines a Y zoom factor of 0 to 7. This defines the number of times each scan line is to be repeated horizontally within the active zoom window. A 0 in the YZOOM field causes a 1:1 zoom. It should be noted that vertical zooming is only allowed in the graphics modes.

The source window is specified by a zoom start address. This zoom start address is identical to the display start address and the cursor start address. It points to a starting location in display memory. Like the display and cursor start

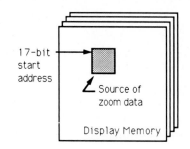

17-bit
start
address

Source of
zoom data

Display Memory

a) Source of Zoom Data. Size of source zoom
window is determined by the x and y zoom factors

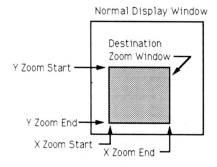

Normal Display Window

Destination
Zoom Window

Y Zoom Start →

Y Zoom End →

X Zoom Start

X Zoom End

b) Destination of zoom window specified by
corners of rectangular box.

FIGURE 20.18 Hardware Zoom. Source and destination zoom definitions

address, the zoom start address must be 17 bits to access the 512 Kbytes of memory. Actually, 17 bits accesses the 128 Kbytes in each of the four display plane. The zoom start address register resides in the Zoom Start Address Low and Zoom Start Address High registers shown in Figures 20.20 and 20.21, respectively. Bit 16 is found in the Z16 field of the Extended Start Address Register shown in Figure 20.10.

The zoom window is completely defined by the four corners of a rectangular window. These four corners are defined by the X Zoom Start and X Zoom End registers in the horizontal dimension shown in Figures 20.22 and 20.23 respectively. The XSTRT and XEND fields in these registers refer to the character counter. Thus, in a graphics mode, this field represents 8 pixels in the 16-color modes.

The vertical corners are defined by the YSTRT and YEND fields in the Y Zoom Start and Y Zoom End registers in the vertical dimension shown in Figures

Zoom Control ET3000

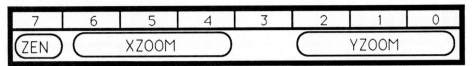

Index 6 at Port 3C4   Port 3C5 Read/Write

FIGURE 20.19   Zoom Control Register. The ZEN field enables the zoom function. The XZOOM and YZOOM control the horizontal and vertical zoom factors respectively.

Zoom Start Address Low ET3000

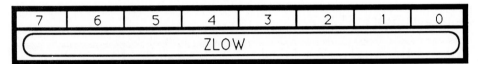

Index 20 at Port 3B4/3D4   Port 3B5/3D5 Read/Write

FIGURE 20.20   Zoom Start Address Low Register. The ZLOW field contains the eight low-order address bits that determine where the zoom data should come from in display memory.

Zoom Start Address Middle ET3000

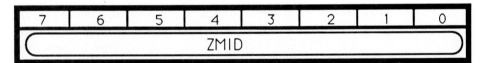

Index 21 at Port 3B4/3D4   Port 3B5/3D5 Read/Write

FIGURE 20.21   Zoom Start Address Middle Register. The ZMID field contains the eight mid-order address bits that determine where the zoom data should come from in display memory.

X Zoom Start ET3000

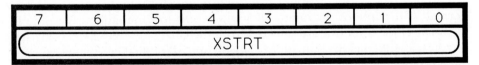

Index 1B at Port 3B4/3D4   Port 3B5/3D5 Read/Write

FIGURE 20.22   X Zoom Start. The XSTART field contains the horizontal start address of the zoom window.

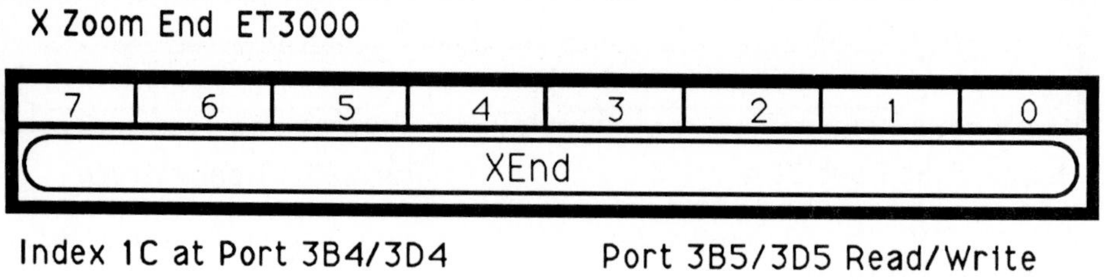

X Zoom End ET3000

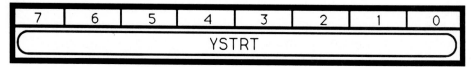

7	6	5	4	3	2	1	0
			XEnd				

Index 1C at Port 3B4/3D4   Port 3B5/3D5 Read/Write

FIGURE 20.23   X Zoom End. The XEND field contains the horizontal end address of the zoom window.

Y Zoom Start ET3000

7	6	5	4	3	2	1	0
			YSTRT				

Index 1D at Port 3B4/3D4   Port 3B5/3D5 Read/Write

FIGURE 20.24   Y Zoom Start. The YSTART field contains the vertical start address of the zoom window.

20.24 and 20.25. These values refer to scan lines. Two additional bits are required to address a maximum of 1024 scan lines. These two high order bits, bits 8 and 9, are found in the YSTRTH and YENDH fields of the Y Zoom Start and End High Register shown in Figure 20.26.

20.9.5   Multiple Soft Fonts

The ET3000 allows up to eight soft fonts to simultaneously reside in display memory. This function is enabled through the MSF field of the TS Auxiliary Mode ET3000 Register shown in Figure 20.4. If the MSF field is set to 1, multiple simultaneous fonts are enabled. If the MSF field is 0, normal font selection occurs.

The bits 6–3 of the attribute byte determine which font is selected. The normal VGA mode of operation allows two fonts to simultaneously reside in memory. These two fonts are selected from the Character Map Select Register which is described in Section 10.3.4. The SA and SB of this register are ignored if the simultaneous font mode is in effect. In this case, the font is selected by the attribute bits 6, 4, and 3 as shown in Table 20.12. Note that bit 5 is actually the inverse of bit 6 and only provides redundant information. If bit 6 is the same as bit 5, two simultaneous fonts can be selected, using bit 3 as shown in Table 20.13.

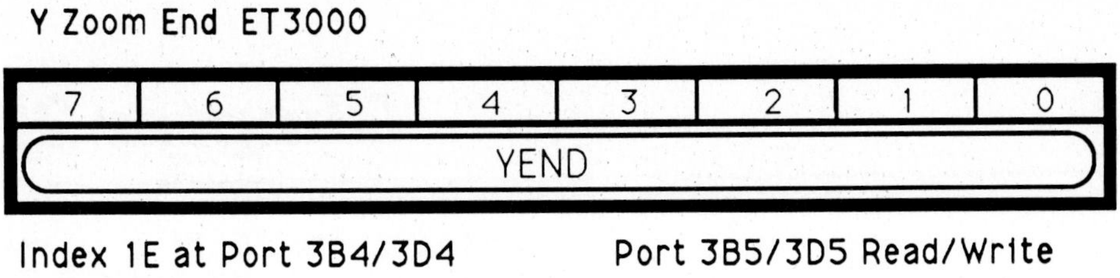

Y Zoom End ET3000

7	6	5	4	3	2	1	0
YEND							

Index 1E at Port 3B4/3D4   Port 3B5/3D5 Read/Write

FIGURE 20.25 Y Zoom End. The YEND field contains the vertical end address of the zoom window.

Y Zoom Start and End High ET3000

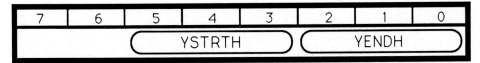

7	6	5	4	3	2	1	0
		YSTRTH			YENDH		

Index 1F at Port 3B4/3D4   Port 3B5/3D5 Read/Write

FIGURE 20.26 Y Zoom Start and End High Register. The YSTRTH and YENDH fields contain the top three bits of address, bits 10–8, for the vertical start and end address of the zoom window.

TABLE 20.12   Selecting One Of Eight Simultaneous Fonts

Attribute Bits 6 5 4 3	Selected Font	Resides at
0 1 0 0	0	0 Kbytes
0 1 0 1	1	16 Kbytes
0 1 1 0	2	32 Kbytes
0 1 1 1	3	48 Kbytes
1 0 0 0	4	8 Kbytes
1 0 0 1	5	24 Kbytes
1 0 1 0	6	40 Kbytes
1 0 1 1	7	56 Kbytes

TABLE 20.13   Selecting One Of Two Simultaneous Fonts

Attribute Bits 6 5 4 3	Selected Font	Resides at
0 0 0 0	0	0 Kbytes
0 0 0 1	1	16 Kbytes
1 1 0 0	0	0 Kbytes
1 1 0 1	1	16 Kbytes

Chapter 21

The Video7 Super VGA Chip Sets

21.1 INTRODUCTION TO THE VIDEO7/HEADLAND TECHNOLOGIES VGA

Video7/Headlands Technologies manufacturers the V7VGA Super VGA chip and uses it in several of its Super VGA cards. The V7VGA chip is very powerful and supports several special effects. Depending on the implementation, the chip can support resolutions up to 1024 by 768 in the 16-color mode and 800 by 600 in the 256-color modes. The chip can access up to one Megabyte of display memory. A wide variety of display modes are available. The chip can support DRAM or VRAM implementations

The standard MDA, Hercules and CGA emulations are available through an emulation register and an extended BIOS function. This emulation includes write protection of three register groups and non-maskable interrupt enables.

Both the PC/AT or the PS/2 standards are adhered to by the V7VGA. It includes the standard Display Enable registers with a setup mode. The Extended registers are grouped together and can be enabled or disabled. Extended address bits are provided for the CRT address generation and the split-screen function.

Dual-bank selection is provided with separate Read and Write Bank Select registers. In the Version 3 of the V7VGA chip, the implementation was very poor. The bits of these Read and Write banks were spread across three registers. In addition, the Read and Write Bank registers share the same two low order bits, so read and write windows must be separated by 16 Kbytes. In Version 4 of the V7VGA chip, this was rectified by putting the Read and Write banks into separate registers with no bits in common. In addition, all four bits of each bank are contiguous.

Several extended BIOS functions are provided which give information about the system, set up the extended display modes, and handle emulation modes.

The V7VGA is known for its special features which include masked bit-plane writing, hardware cursor, foreground and background color control for drawing characters, and dithering.

TABLE 21.1 Configuring the Video7 Super VGAs

Function	Register Name	Port	Index	Bits	Value
Select 8-bit memory	16-bit Interface	3C5	FF	0	0
Select 16-bit memory	16-bit Interface	3C5	FF	0	1
Select 8-bit I/O	16-bit Interface	3C5	FF	1	0
Select 16-bit I/O	16-bit Interface	3C5	FF	1	1
Enable Fast-Write	16-bit Interface	3C5	FF	2	1
Disable Fast-Write	16-bit Interface	3C5	FF	2	0
Select 8-bit ROM	16-bit Interface	3C5	FF	3	0
Select 16-bit ROM	16-bit Interface	3C5	FF	3	1
Enable VGA PC/AT	Rom Map & Video Subsytem	46E8		2–0	0–7

16-Bit Interface Control

Index FF at Port 3C4   Port 3C5 Read/Write
                              BS field is Read Only

FIGURE 21.1   16-bit Interface Control Register. The M16, R16, and I16 control the 8- or 16-bit interface to memory, ROM, and I/O respectively. The FWE field enables fast write cycles. The BS field is read only and returns whether the card is plugged into an 8- or 16-bit slot. The BE field enables or disables the bank selection.

21.2   CONFIGURING THE VIDEO7 VGA

The V7VGA is configured through the 16-bit Interface Register and a field in the ROM Mapping and Video Subsystem Control Register. This register is described in Table 21.1 and shown in Figure 21.1.

21.2.1   8- or 16-bit Bus Interface

This register allows the selection of 8- or 16-bit memory, ROM or I/O data paths through the M16, R16 and I16 fields respectively. The on-card BIOS ROM can be enabled or disabled through the ROM field. Fast write cycles can be enabled through the FWE field. If the fast write mode is enabled, the address and data are latched internally in the V7VGA from the host address and data bus. This releases the host and the CPU can execute additional instructions.

Suppose a host instruction attempts to write to display memory. Memory delays are likely and releasing the host through this fast write mode eliminates the need to impose a wait-state. If the host attempts to access the display memory before the subsequent write operation is completed, wait-states are imposed. In the case of an instruction sequence such as REP MOVSX, where data is being moved to display memory, the fast write mode will have little effect. However, write to display memory instructions, interspersed with other instructions, result in speed advantages.

The BS field provides bus-status information on whether the card is plugged into an 8- or 16-bit bus. This field is described in Section 21.2.3 below.

21.2.2   On-Card ROM

The V7VGA allows the on-card ROM to be mapped into the host address space. The host reserves the memory space between C0000 and C7FFF for video BIOS. The 4-Kbyte range from C7000 to C7FFF maps to one of the 4-Kbyte banks of the 32-Kbyte BIOS ROM based on the value in the RBC field of the ROM Mapping and Video Subsystem Control Register. This mapping is linear from C0000 to C7FFF.

21.3   CONTROLLING THE VIDEO7 VGA

The Video7 VGA can be controlled by several registers, as listed in Table 21.2. Note that the port address 3x5 refers to either 3D5 or 3B5, depending on whether the system is configured in a color or monochrome mode. These chips are equipped with the industry standard 46E8 and 3C3 registers which enable or disable the VGA and which allow the VGA to be put into a setup mode. The 46E8 register is non-standard, in the sense that it also contains a ROM Bank Control field, RBC. This field is described in Section 21.2.1.

21.3.1   Enabling the VGA

If the VGA resides on a PC/AT adapter card, the register used to enable and disable the video adapter is the ROM Map and Video Subsystem Register, located at port address 46E8 hex. This register is illustrated in Figure 21.2.

If the VGA resides on the motherboard, presumably in a microchannel system, the register used to enable and disable the video adapter is the Video Subsystem Enable Register, located at port address 3C3 hex. This register is illustrated in Figure 21.3.

A third register for enabling and disabling the card is the Alternate Video Subsystem Enable Register, shown in Figure 21.4. This register is located at port address 102 hex.

The VGA can be enabled through the EN field of the Video Subsystem Enable Register, the Alternate Video Subsystem Enable Register, or the ROM Mapping and Video Subsystem Register. The differences between these three fields are listed in Table 21.3.

TABLE 21.2 Resetting and Enabling the Video7 Super VGAs

Function	Register Name	Port	Index	Bits	Value
Enable Video Microchannel	Video Subsystems Enable	3c3		0	1
Disable Video Microchannel	Video Subsystems Enable	3c3		0	0
Enable VGA PC/AT	ROM Map & Video Subsystem	46E8		3	1
Disable VGA PC/AT	ROM Map & Video Subsystem	46E8		3	0
Enable Video	Alt Video Subsystems Enable	102		0	1
Disable Video	Alt Video Subsystems Enable	102		0	0
Enter Setup Mode PC	ROM Map & Video Subsystem	46E8		4	1
Exit Setup Mode PC	ROM Map & Video Subsystem	46E8		4	0
Disable Video	Clear Vertical Display	3x5	30-3F	0	0,1
Enable Extensions	Extensions Control	3C5	6	—	EA
Disable Extensions	Extensions Control	3C5	6	—	AE

ROM Mapping and Video Subsystem Control

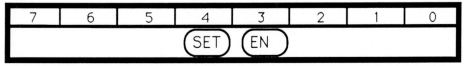

Port 46E8   Port 46E8 Write Only
                             Typically PC/AT

FIGURE 21.2 ROM Mapping and Video Subsystem Control Register. The video system can be enabled through the EN field. The Setup Mode can be entered through the SET field.

Video Subsystem Enable

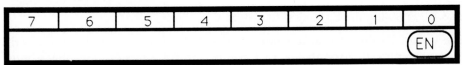

Port 3C3   Port 3C3 Read/Write
                             Typically PS/2

FIGURE 21.3 Video Subsystem Enable Register. The EN field enables the VGA card when the ARM field of the Compatibility Control Register is armed.

Alternate Video Subsystem Enable

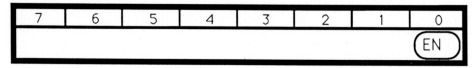

Port 102 and Setup

Port 102 Read/Write
Typically PC/AT

FIGURE 21.4 Alternate Video Subsystem Enable Register. The EN field enables the VGA card. The system must be in the Setup mode fo the host to access this register.

TABLE 21.3 Enabling the VGA

Register	Platform	Constraints
ROM Mapping and Video Subsystem	PC/AT	none
Video Subsystem Enable	PS/2	must be armed
Alternate Video Subsystem Enable	PC/AT PS/2	must be in setup mode or armed

The setup mode is enabled in the PC/AT systems by setting the SET field of the ROM Mapping and Video Subsystem Register to 1. Once in the setup mode, only ports 102 hex, 3C3 hex and 46E8 hex will be active.

Arming of the enable function occurs in the ARM field of the Compatibility Control Register. This register is illustrated in Figure 21.5. If the ARM field is set to 1, the enable field in either the Video Subsystem Enable Register or the Alternate Video Subsystem Enable Register are active. If the ARM field is set to 0, these EN fields are inactive.

21.3.2 Enabling the Extended Registers

The Video7 Extended registers must be enabled before access will be granted. They are enabled through the Extensions Control Register. The Extensions Control Register does not reflect the data written to it. It is a read only register. It has one field which returns the status of whether the extensions are enabled or not. The ENE field returns a 0 if the extensions are disabled. A 1 is returned if the extensions are enabled.

Writing a code of EA hex to this register enables extensions. Writing a code of AE hex disables extensions. All other writes to this register are ignored. The

Compatibility Control

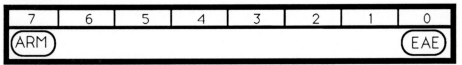

Index FC at Port 3C4   Port 3C5 Read/Write

FIGURE 21.5 Compatibility Control Register. The ARM field controls whether the VSE field of the Video Subsystem Enable register is armed. The EAE field controls the extended attribute function.

Extensions Control

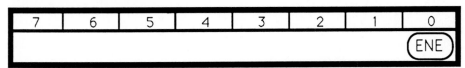

Index 06 of Port 3C4   Port 3C5 Read/Write

FIGURE 21.6 Extensions Control Register. The ENE field enables access to the extension registers. The extension registers are located at indexes 80–FF of the indexed register pair 3C4/3C5.

Extensions Control Register, displayed in Figure 21.6, is in fact a read only register; however, writing to this register does cause extensions to be enabled or disabled.

The extensions can be enabled or disabled through the macros provided in Listings 21.1 and 21.2 and from the C-callable functions in Listings 21.3 and 21.4.

LISTING 21.1 Enabling Video 7 Extensions Macro

```
; Function:
;       Enabling Video 7 Extensions

; Calling Protocol:
;       Extensions_On_V7

Extensions_On_V7 macro
        mov     dx,3c4h         ;address Extensions Control Register
        mov     al,6
        mov     ah,0eah         ; turn on extensions
        out     dx,ax
endm
```

LISTING 21.2   Disabling Video 7 Extensions Macro

```
; Function:
;       Disabling Video 7 extensions

; Calling Protocol:
;       Extensions_Off_V7

Extensions_Off_V7 macro
        mov     dx,3c4h         ;address Extensions Control Register
        mov     al,6
        inc     dx
        mov     ah, 0aeh        ; turn off extensions
        out     dx,ax
endm
```

LISTING 21.3   Enabling Video 7 extensions

```
; Function:
;       Enabling Video 7 extensions

; Calling Protocol:
;       Extended_On_V7();

Extended_On_V7 proc far
        Extensions_On_V7
        ret
Extended_On_V7 endp
```

LISTING 21.4   Disabling Video 7 extensions

```
; Function:
;       Disable Video 7 extensions

; Calling Protocol:
;       Extended_Off_V7();

Extended_Off_V7 proc far
        Extensions_Off_V7
        ret
Extended_Off_V7 endp
```

Clear Vertical Display

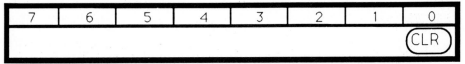

Index 30-3F at Port 3B4/3D4   Port 3B5/3D5 Write Only

FIGURE 21.7 Clear Vertical Display Register. The CLR field controls the screen blanking, allowing more display memory cycles to be dedicated to the CPU.

21.3.3 Speeding up Transfers

A special feature enhancing the operation of the V7VGA is the ability to prematurely clear the vertical display. This can be accomplished by writing a 1 to the CLR field of the Clear Vertical Display Register shown in Figure 21.7.

This causes a longer vertical retrace period. The reason for doing this is to give the host processor more access to the display memory. It gains this access since the display memory is fighting to refresh the display. The effect is that a minor visual disturbance occurs.

21.4 INQUIRING FOR THE VIDEO7 SUPER VGA CONFIGURATION

The V7VGA has made identification very easy and thorough as listed in Table 21.4. Note that the port address 3x5 refers to either 3D5 or 3B5, depending on whether the system is configured in a color or monochrome mode. The microchannel ID value is available at the Card ID Microchannel High and Low registers as per the PS/2 microchannel standard.

21.4.1 Chip Identification

The chip identification code is available in the Identification Register, as illustrated in Figure 21.8. A unique and clever technique was designed by Video7 to allow the programmer to identify the chip, regardless of the chip's mode.

The Start Address High Register, described in Section 10.4.13, and its associated CRTC Index Register are available in any configuration, that is, EGA, VGA, CGA, and MDA. This register can be read in any situation without causing damage to the current mode. The technique used to identify the V7VGA is to read the value of the Start Address High Register and to read in the Identification Register. The Identification register contains an ID field, the result of the logical XOR function taking on the value in the Start Address High Register and the constant value EA. The XOR function is an exclusive-OR operation, as described in Table 21.5. If the inputs are different, the output is a 1. Similarly, if the inputs are the same, the output is a 0.

TABLE 21.4 Determining Video 7 Display Status

Function	Register Name	Port	Index	Bits	Value
Card ID Microchannel	Microchannel ID high	101		7-0	0-255
Card ID Microchannel	Microchannel ID low	100		7-0	0-255
Identification	Identification	3x5	1F	7-0	0-255
Chip Revision	Chip Revision	3C5	8E	7-0	0-255
Bus Status	16-bit Interface	3C5	FF	3	0,1
Copy the switches	Switch Strobe	3C5	EA	—	—
Location of switches	Switch Readback	3C5	F7	7-0	0-255
Attribute Index	Graphics Controller Data	3x5	24	4-0	0-31
Palette Source	Graphics Controller Data	3x5	24	5	0,1
Index or Display	Graphics Controller Data	3x5	24	7	0,1
Extensions Enabled	Extensions Control	3C5	6	0	1
Extensions Disabled	Extensions Control	3C5	6	0	0

TABLE 21.5 Exclusive OR operation

Input	Input	Output
0	0	0
0	1	1
1	0	1
1	1	0

Identification

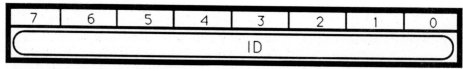

Index 1F at Port 3B4/3D4   Port 3B5/3D5 Read Only

FIGURE 21.8 Identification Register. The V7VGA is identified through the ID field. The ID field is EA hex XORed with the SAH field of the Start Address High Register.

Suppose that the value in the Start Address High Register is a 8F hex. If the 8F hex value is exclusive ORed with the constant EA hex from above, the result is 65 hex. This value, 65 hex should show up in the Identification register.

The Video7 VGA can be identified through the code in Listing 21.5.

LISTING 21.5   Determining the Video 7 Card

```
/*
Function:
 Determining the Video 7 Card

Output Parameters:
 1 card is a Video7
 0 card is NOT a Video7

Calling Protocol:
 value = Is_It_V7() */

int Is_It_V7()
{ unsigned char new_value,old_value,value,id;
  int base;

Extended_On_V7();

/* determine if monochrome or color */
if( (inp(0x3CC) & 0x01)==1) base = 0x3D0; else base = 0x3B0;

/* get old value of start high register */
outp(base+4,0x0C); old_value = inp(base+5);

/* change value */
outp(base+5,0x55); new_value = inp(base+5);

/* read the ID register */
outp(base+4,0x1f); id = inp(base+5);  /* read the ID Register */

/* restore old value */
outp(base+4,0x0C); outp(base+5,old_value);

Extended_Off_V7();
/* ID = (Start_High XOR EA hex) */
  if(id==(0x55^0xEA)) return(1);
  else return(0);
}
```

21.4.2   Which Video7 VGA

The specific VGA chip can be determined through the chip-revision number in the CHIP field of the Chip Revision Register, as illustrated in Figure 21.9. The chip name can be accessed through the code in Listing 21.6 .

Chip Revision

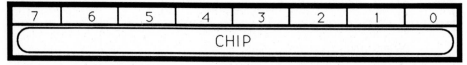

Index 8E-8F at Port 3C4   Port 3C5   Read Only

FIGURE 21.9 Chip Revision Register. The chip revision level is returned in the CHIP field.

LISTING 21.6 Determining the Video7 Chip

```
/*
Function:
 Determining the Video7 chip

Output Parameters:
 identity        integer containing chip code
                            1 = VEGA VGA
                            2 = V7VGA FASTWRITE/VRAM
                            3 = V7VGA Version 5
                            4 = 1024i

Calling Protocol:
 identity = Which_V7() */

int Which_V7()

{ int result;
 unsigned char value;

Extended_On_V7();

  outp(0x3C4,0x8E); /* Version Register */
  value = inp(0x3C5); /* read version */

Extended_Off_V7();

if( (value<0xFF) & (value>=0x80)) result=1;
if( (value<0x7F) & (value>=0x70)) result=2;
if( (value<0x5A) & (value >=0x50)) result=3;
If ((value <0x4A) & (value > 0x40)) result=4
return(result);
}
```

Switch Strobe

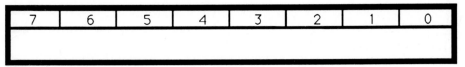

Index EA at Port 3C4   Port 3C5   Write Strobe Only

FIGURE 21.10 Switch Strobe Register. Providing a write to this port produces a strobe that copies the on-card switches into the SWITCH field of the Switch Readback Register.

Switch Readback

Index F7 at Port 3C4   Port 3C5 Read/Write

FIGURE 21.11 Switch Strobe Register. The positions of the on-card switches can be read from the SWITCH field in conjunction with an output to the Switch Strobe Register.

TABLE 21.6 Acquiring Information through Extended BIOS Functions

BIOS Function Name	Section
Inquire into Super Condition	10.7.1
Get Information	10.7.2
Get Mode/Screen Resolution	10.7.3
Get Video Memory Configuration	10.7.6

21.4.3 Sense Switches

The sense switches can be interrogated by writing to the Switch Strobe Register. Any value can be used in the write operation since only the write strobe to this port is used. At this time, the sense switches are written into the SWITCH Switch Readback Register. These two registers are illustrated in Figures 21.10 and 21.11 respectively.

21.4.4 Inquiring through BIOS

Four extended BIOS functions are provided for assisting the programmer in acquiring information from the VGA. These are listed in Table 21.6 and are described in Section 21.7.

Information relevant to the active display mode can be acquired through the Get Information BIOS call as provided in Listing 21.7.

LISTING 21.7 Getting Information About the Current Active Display Mode

```
; Function:
;   Getting Video7 extensions mode (Video-7 Only)

; Output Parameters:
;       buf[]             "C" integer array containing the mode
;                              number of rows, columns and active page.
;              buf[0]          active display page
;              buf[1]          active display mode
;              buf[2]          number of character columns per row
;              buf[3]          number of rows per screen

; Calling Protocol:
;   Get_Status_V7(buf);

Get_Status_V7 proc far USES ES DI, arg1:FAR PTR
         les    di,arg1     ;point to output array

    mov    ah,0fh                      ;get current video state for page
         int    10h                    ;interrupt 10
         xor    bl,bl
         mov    ax,bx
         stosw                   ;store active page in BUF[0]

    mov    ax,6f04h                ;extended V7 function
         int    10h                    ;to get status
         xor    ah,ah
         stosw               ; store mode in BUF[1]
         mov    ax,bx              ;store horizontal columns in BUF[2]
         stosw
         mov    ax,cx              ; store vertical rows in BUF[3]
         stosw

         ret
Get_Status_V7 endp
```

21.4.5 Inquiring About Attribute Status

One of the problematic areas when trying to acquire the state of the VGA has been the attribute controller. The Attribute Controller Index Register, described in Section 10.6.1 has several functions, one of which is that it acts as

Graphics Controller Data Latch

Index 22 at Port 3B4/3D4   Port 3B5/3D5 Read Only

FIGURE 21.12 Graphics Controller Data Latch Register. The DATA field contains one of the four bit-plane data latches. The latch is selected through the RMS field of the Read Map Select Register.

both the Index Register and the Data Register. An internal switch is toggled each time the register is written to, switching it from the Index Register to the Data Register. Reading the complete state of the VGA would require reading the state of this internal switch.

Video7 provides the ability to read this switch through the I/D field of the Graphics Controller Data Latch illustrated in Figure 21.12.

The INDEX field represents the index value, which points to one of the Palette or Attribute registers. The PAS field indicates whether the palette registers are pointing to the index or to the display memory. Both the INDEX and PAS fields mimick the same fields in the actual Attribute Controller Index Register, which can be read at Port 3C0 hex.

21.5 VIDEO7 DISPLAY MODES

The V7VGA is equipped with the Super VGA standard, 132-column alphanumeric modes, along with several 80- and a 100-column modes. The Super VGA graphics modes include 2-, 4-, 16- and 256-color modes, spanning to 1024 by 768 in the 16-color mode, and 800 by 600 in the 256-color mode. Only the VRAM supports the 800 by 600 256-color mode. The VRAM is non-interlaced at the 1024 by 768 resolution. The 1024 is interlaced at the 1024 by 768 resolution. The alphanumerics and graphics modes are listed in Tables 21.7 and 21.8, respectively. It should be noted that these extended display modes cannot be entered through the standard AH=00 Set Mode BIOS call. Rather, a special function is provided to set the extended modes. The calling protocol of this BIOS call is presented in Section 21.7.4. An example of its useage is provided in Listing 21.8.

LISTING 21.8 Setting a Video7 Extended Display Mode

```
;   Function:
;   Setting Video7 extended display mode

;   Input Parameters:
;       mode            desired extended display mode
;
```

```
; Calling Protocol:
;    Set_Mode_V7(mode);

Set_Mode_V7 proc far arg1
        mov     bx,arg1
        mov     ax,6f05h
        int     10h
        ret
Set_Mode_V7 endp
```

TABLE 21.7 Video7 Alphanumerics Modes

Mode	Rows	Columns	Font	Resolution	Colors	Chip
40	43	80	8x8	640x344	2	V7VGA
41	25	132	8x14	1056x350	2	V7VGA
42	43	132	8x8	1056x344	2	V7VGA
43	60	80	8x8	640x480	16	V7VGA
44	60	100	8x8	800x480	16	V7VG
45	28	132	8x14	1056x392	16	V7VGA

TABLE 21.8 Video7 Graphics Modes

Mode	Resolution	Colors	Chip
60	752x410	16	V7VGA
61	720x540	16	V7VGA
62	800x600	16	V7VGA
63	1024x768	2	V7VGA
64	1024x768	4	V7VGA
65	1024x768	16	V7VGA
66	640x400	256	V7VGA
67	640x480	256	V7VGA
68	720x540	256	V7VGA
69	800x600	256	V7VGA

21.6 ACCESSING THE VIDEO7 DISPLAY MEMORY

Unfortunately, accessing the Video7 display memory in Version 3 is complex and time-consuming. The functions which control the process are based on several fields dispersed between several registers. In addition, certain differences exist, depending on whether DRAM or VRAM memory is installed. En-

TABLE 21.9 Reading and Writing to Video 7 Display Memory

Function	Register Name	Port	Index	Bits	Value
Write Bank Start Address	1 Mbyte RAM Bank Select	3C5	F6	1–0	0–3
Read Bank Start Address	1 Mbyte RAM Bank Select	3C5	F6	3–2	0–3
Select Page	Page Select	3C5	F9	0	0,1
Enable Bank Selection	16-bit Interface Control	3C5	FF	4	0,1
Dual Bank Selection	Dual Bank Select (Ver 4)	3C5	E0	7	0,1
Single/Write Bank	Write Bank (Ver 4)	3C5	E8	7–4	0–15
Read Bank	Read Bank (Ver 4)	3C5	E9	7–4	0–15

TABLE 21.10 Bank Selection

Bank Bit	Register	Field	
0	Page Select Register	PS	Figure 21.15
1	Miscellaneous Output	PB	Section 10.2.1
2–3 (Write)	Bank Select	WB	Figure 21.16
2–3 (Read)	Bank Select	RB	Figure 21.16

abling the high-resolution modes can be accomplished through mode sets, so the control functions do not really need to be considered. The registers involved in accessing the display memory are listed in Table 21.9.

Fortunately, Version 5 of the V7VGA chip rectifies this problem. A single field exists for the bank address. In addition, a dual-bank mode can be engaged, providing separate bank selection for read and write operations.

21.6.1 Reading and Writing to the Display Memory

The Video7 display memory is accessed through the standard bank selection techniques. Up to one megabyte of display memory can be acesed through a 64-Kbyte segment mapped into the host address space at A0000–AFFFF hex. In 512-Kbyte configurations, there are eight 64-Kbyte banks, while in the one Megabyte configuration there are sixteen such banks.

In either the 512-Kbyte or one Megabyte configurations, the field is split between three separate registers. This provides for slow bank switching. The three fields involved in this bank switching are listed in Table 21.10 and displayed in Figure 21.13.

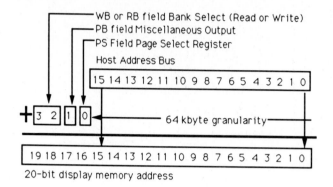

FIGURE 21.13 Creation of a 20-bit Address using Bank Selection.

Page Select

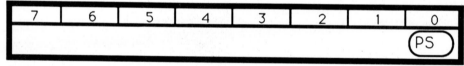

Index F9 at Port 3C4   **Port 3C5 Read/Write**

FIGURE 21.14 Page Select Register. The PS field controls the linear address mapping of the 256-color high-resolution modes into a single 64-Kbyte address space.

21.6.2 V7VGA Versions 1–3

The least significant bit in the bank pointer, bit 0, is the PS field of the Page Select Register, shown in Figure 21.14. This field determines the 4-Kbyte granularity. Currently, no other fields share this register; consequently, no read/modify/write operation is required.

The second, least significant bit in the bank pointer, bit 1, is in the PB field of the Miscellaneous Output Register. This register is described in Section 10.2.1 and the PB field resides in bit position 5. A read/modify/write operation will be required to preserve the other bit fields in this register.

Bits 0 and 1 are the same, whether a read or write operation is in effect. Thus, the display memory location must be separated by a minimum of 16 Kbytes.

The two most significant bits of the bank pointer, bits 3–2, reside in the Bank Select Register, illustrated in Figure 21.15. Two bank selection fields are pro-

Bank Select

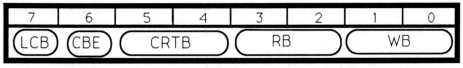

Index F6 at Port 3C4   Port 3C5 Read/Write

FIGURE 21.15 Bank Select Register. The WB field controls the Write Bank. The RB field controls the Read Bank and the CRTB controls the CRT bank. The WRP field controls bank wrap-around. The LCB field contains the enable bit allowing bank control of the line compare function.

vided in this register . The WB field of this register contains the two-bit for write operations, while the RB field contains the two-bit fields for the read operations. Writing to either of these fields requires read/modify/write operations, to preserve the other fields.

The values loaded into the respective fields in the Bank Select Register are always used to access the display memory when 1 megabit, DRAM memory chips are used. The host read, host write and CRTC addresses use these fields. The BE field of the 16-bit Interface Register typically enables bank selection; however, it has no effect when DRAM memory is used. The 16-bit Interface Register is illustrated in Figure 21.15.

When the VGA is equipped with VRAM, the bank selection process is activated when the BE field of the 16-bit Interface Register is set to 1. If the BE field is set to 0, the fields in the Bank Register have no effect. If the BE field is 0, up to four virtual VGA screens can be loaded in the one megabyte of address space.

Loading the Read and Write banks is accomplished differently for the 16-color and 256-color modes. The Read Bank and Write Bank fields for the 16-color modes are loaded through the code in Listings 21.9 and 21.10, respectively.

LISTING 21.9 Loading Write Bank Number 16-color

```
;  Function:
;        Loading the Write Bank with a new start address. Assumes
;           that the extensions are enabled. The bank bits are split
;           into three fields in three separate registers as follows:
;
;        Bank Bit   Register          Address          Index     Write
;        3-2        Bank Select          3C4          F6           1-0
;        1          Miscellaneous Out    3CC          -            5
;        0          Ext. Page Select     3C4          F9           0
```

```
;  Input  Parameters:
;      bl                              Write Bank_Number
;                                      0-15  bank  number  indicating  desired
;                                      64-Kbyte  bank


;  Calling  Protocol:
;      Load_Write_Bank_16_V7


Load_Write_Bank_16_V7 macro

;      set  up  the  Bank  Select  Regsiter  bits  0  with  address  bits  17
;      non-destructively
       mov     dx,3c4h        ;access  Bank  Select  Register
       mov     al,0f6h
       out     dx,al          ;index  Bank  Select  Register
       inc     dx
       in      al,dx          ;get  its  current  value

;      put  bits  17  into  bit  0  of  Bank  Select  Register
       mov     ah,al
       and     ah,0fch        ;zero  bit  0-1
       and     bl,1           ;only  want  bit  0  of  bank
       or      ah,bl
       mov     al,ah
       out     dx,al          ;load  Bank  Select  Register
endm
```

LISTING 21.10   Loading Read Bank Number 16-color

```
;  Function:
;      Loading  the  Read  Bank  with  a  new  start  address.  Assumes  that
;      the  extensions  are  enabled.  The  bank  bits  are  split  into
;      three  fields  in  three  separate  registers  as  follows:

;      Bank  Bit   Register            Address         Index  Read
;      3-2         Bank  Select        3C4      F6      3-2
;      1           Miscellaneous  Out  3CC      -       5
;      0           Ext.  Page  Select  3C4      F9      0

;  Input  Parameters:
;      bl                              Read Bank_Number
;                                      0-15  bank  number  indicating  desired
;                                      64-Kbyte  bank
;  Calling  Protocol:
;      Load_Read_Bank_16_V7
```

```
Load_Read_Bank_16_V7 macro

;        set up the Bank Select Regsiter bits 0 with address bits 17
;        non-destructively
        mov     dx,3c4h         ;access Bank Select Register
        mov     al,0f6h
        out     dx,al           ;index Bank Select Register
        inc     dx
        in      al,dx           ;get its current value

;        put bits 17 into bit 2 of Bank Select Register
        mov     ah,al
        and     ah,0fch         ;zero bit 3-2
        and     bl,01h                  ;only want bits 1
        shl     bl,1
        shl     bl,1            ;put into bit position 2
        or      ah,bl
        mov     al,ah
        out     dx,al           ;load Bank Select Register
endm
```

The Read Bank and Write Bank fields for the 256-color modes are loaded through the code in Listings 21.11 and 21.12 respectively.

LISTING 21.11   Loading the Write Bank Number 256-color

```
; Function:
;       Loading the Write Bank with a new start address. Assumes
;       that the extensions are enabled. The bank bits are split
;       into three fields in three separate registers as follows:

;       Bank Bit   Register          Address        Index Write

;       3-2        Bank Select       3C4      F6     1-0
;       1          Miscellaneous Out 3CC      -      5
;       0          Ext. Page Select  3C4      F9     0

; Input Parameters:
;       bl                          Write Bank_Number
;                                   0-15 bank number indicating desired
;                                   64-Kbyte bank

; Calling Protocol:
;       Load_Write_Bank_256_V7
```

```
Load_Write_Bank_256_V7 macro

;       set up the Extended Page Select Register for bit 16
        mov     dx,3c4h         ;bank bit 0
        mov     ah,bl
        and     ah,1            ;only concerned with bit 16 (bank bit 0)
        mov     al,0f9h         ;index Extended Page Select
        out     dx,ax           ;load bit 0

;       set up the Miscellaneous Output Register with bit 21.
;       Load it into bit 5 without disrupting other values
        mov     ah,bl                   ;bank bit 1
        and     ah,2                    ;bit 1 contains bit 17
        shl     ah,1                    ;bit 2 "         " "
        shl     ah,1                    ;bit 3 "         " "
        shl     ah,1                    ;bit 4 "         " "
        shl     ah,1                    ;bit 5 "         " "
        mov     dx,3cch                 ;address Miscellaneous
                                        ;Register
        in      al,dx           ;read value
        and     al,0dfh                 ;zero bit 5
        mov     dx,3c2h                 ;address Miscellaneous
                                        ;Register
        or      al,ah           ;load the page bit (bit 5)
        out     dx,al           ;output page bit 17

;       set up the Bank Select Regsiter bits 0 and 1 with address
;       bits 18 and 19 non-destructively
        mov     dx,3c4h         ;       access Bank Select Register
        mov     al,0f6h
        out     dx,al           ;index Bank Select Register
        inc     dx
        in      al,dx           ;get its current value

;       put bits 19-18 into bits 1-0 of Bank Select Register
        mov     ah,al
        and     ah,0fch                 ;zero bits 1-0
        shr     bl,1                    ;put address bits 19-18 into
                                        ;bits 1-0
        shr     bl,1
        and     bl,3                    ;only want bits 1-0
        or      ah,bl
        mov     al,ah
        out     dx,al           ;load Bank Select Register
endm
```

LISTING 21.12   Loading the Read Bank Number 256-color

```
; Function:
;       Loading the Read Bank with a new start address. Assumes that
;       the extensions are enabled. The bank bits are split into
;       three fields in three separate registers as follows:
;       Bank Bit    Register            Address  Index   Read
;       3-2         Bank Select         3C4      F6      3-2
;       1           Miscellaneous Out   3CC      -       5
;       0           Ext. Page Select    3C4      F9      0


; Input Parameters:
;       bl                              Read Bank_Number
;                                       0-15 bank number indicating desired
;                                       64-kbyte bank


; Calling Protocol:
;       Load_Read_Bank_256_V7

Load_Read_Bank_256_V7 macro

;       set up the Extended Page Select Register for bit 16
        mov     dx,3c4h         ;bank bit 0
        mov     ah,bl
        and     ah,1            ;only concerned with bit 16 (bank bit 0)
        mov     al,0f9h         ;index Extended Page Select
        out     dx,ax           ;load bit 0


;       set up the Miscellaneous Output Register with bit 21.
;       Load it into bit 5 without disrupting other values
        mov     ah,bl           ;bank bit 1
        and     ah,2            ;bit 1 contains bit 17
        shl     ah,1            ;bit 2 "          " "
        shl     ah,1            ;bit 3 "          " "
        shl     ah,1            ;bit 4 "          " "
        shl     ah,1            ;bit 5 "          " "
        mov     dx,3cch         ;address Miscellaneous Register
        in      al,dx           ;read value
        and     al,0dfh         ;zero bit 5
        mov     dx,3c2h         ;address Miscellaneous Register
        or      al,ah           ;load the page bit (bit 5)
        out     dx,al           ;output page bit 17


;       set up the Bank Select Regsiter bits 0 and 1 with address
;       bits 18 and 19 non-destructively
```

```
        mov     dx,3c4h         ;access Bank Select Register
        mov     al,0f6h
        out     dx,al           ;index Bank Select Register
        inc     dx
        in      al,dx           ;get its current value

;       put bits 19-18 into bits 3-2 of Bank Select Register
        and     al,0f3h         ;zero bits 3-2
        and     bl,0ch                  ;only want bits 3-2
        or      al,bl
        out     dx,al           ;load Bank Select Register
endm
```

Functions which control the Read and Write Banks for the 16-bit color modes are provided in Listings 21.13 and 21.14, respectively.

LISTING 21.13 Loading Write Bank Number 16-color

```
; Function:
;       Loading the Write Bank with a new start address

; Input with:
;       write_bank      Write Bank_Number
;                               0-7 bank number indicating desired
;                       64-Kbyte bank

; Calling Protocol:
;       Set_Write_Bank_16_V7(write_bank);

Set_Write_Bank_16_V7 proc far arg1:byte

;       set up index to Bank Select Register
        mov     bl,arg1         ;get page
        Load_Write_Bank_16_V7

        ret
Set_Write_Bank_16_V7 endp
```

LISTING 21.14 Loading Read Bank Number 16-color

```
; Function:
;       Loading the Read Bank with a new start address
```

```
; Input with:
;       read_bank        Read Bank_Number
;                                 0-7 bank number indicating desired
;                                 64-Kbyte bank


; Calling Protocol:
;       Set_Read_Bank_16_V7(read_bank);

Set_Read_Bank_16_V7 proc far arg1:byte

;       set up index to Bank Select Register
        mov     bl,arg1          ;get page
        Load_Read_Bank_16_V7


        ret
Set_Read_Bank_16_V7 endp
```

Functions which control the Read and Write banks for the 256-bit color modes are provided in Listings 21.15 and 21.16, respectively.

LISTING 21.15   Loading the Write Bank Number 256-color

```
; Function:
;       Loading the Write Bank with a new start address

; Input with:
;       write_bank       Write Bank_Number
;                                 0-7 bank number indicating desired
;                                 64-Kbyte bank

; Calling Protocol:
;       Set_Write_Bank_256_V7(write_bank);

Set_Write_Bank_256_V7 proc far arg1:byte

;       set up index to Bank Select Register
        mov     bl,arg1          ;get page
        Load_Write_Bank_256_V7


        ret
Set_Write_Bank_256_V7 endp
```

LISTING 21.16 Loading the Read Bank Number 256-color

```
;  Function:
;       Loading the Read Bank with a new start address

;  Input with:
;       read_bank       Read Bank_Number
;                               0-7 bank number indicating desired
;                       64-Kbyte bank

;  Calling Protocol:
;       Set_Read_Bank_256_V7(read_bank);

Set_Read_Bank_256_V7 proc far arg1:byte

;       set up index to Bank Select Register
        mov     bl,arg1         ;get page
        Load_Read_Bank_256_V7

        ret
Set_Read_Bank_256_V7 endp
```

21.6.3 V7VGA Version 4

The default condition for the Version 4 V7VGA chip is the single-bank mode. In the single-bank mode the Single/Write Bank Register, shown in Figure 21.16, provides the bank address. In the dual-bank mode, the Read Bank Register, shown in Figure 21.17, provides the bank address. The BANK field in each register is four bits wide, providing a 16-Kbyte granularity.

Single/Write Bank Register (Version 5+)

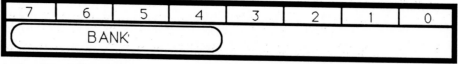

Index E8 at Port 3C4   Port 3C5 Read/Write

FIGURE 21.16 Single/Write Bank Register. The BANK field contains the four-bit bank value providing 16-Kbyte granularity.

Read Bank Register (Version 4+)

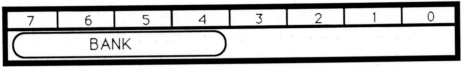

Index E8 at Port 3C4   Port 3C5   Read/Write

FIGURE 21.17 Read Bank Register. The BANK field contains the four-bit bank value providing 16-Kbyte granularity for read operations when in split-bank mode.

Miscellaneous Control Register (Version 4+)

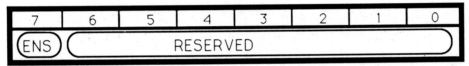

Index E8 at Port 3C4   Port 3C5   Read/Write

FIGURE 21.18 Miscellaneous Control Register. The ENS field enables split-bank mode.

The single- or dual-bank mode, is selected by the ENS field of the Miscellaneous Control Register shown in Figure 21.18. If the ENS field is set to 1, the split-bank mode is enabled. If it is set to 0, the single-bank mode is selected.

The Read Bank and Write Bank fields for the Version 4 V7VGA chip are loaded through the code in Listings 21.17 and 21.18, respectively.

LISTING 21.17 Loading the Single/Write Bank Number (Version 4)

```
; Function:
;       Loading the Single/Write Bank with a new start address.
;       Assumes that the extensions are enabled.

; Input Parameters:
;       bl                      Write Bank Number
;                               0-15 bank number indicating desired
;                               64-Kbyte bank

; Calling Protocol:
;       Load_Write_Bank_V74
```

```
Load_Write_Bank_V74 macro
        mov     ah,bl
        shl     ah,1            ;put bank into bits 7-4
        shl     ah,1
        shl     ah,1
        shl     ah,1
        mov     al,0e8h         ;point to write bank register
        mov     dx,3c4h         ;in extended registers
        out     dx,ax
endm
```

LISTING 21.18   Loading the Read Bank Number (Version 4)

```
; Function:
;       Load the Read Bank with a new start address. Assumes
;       that the extensions are enabled.

; Input Parameters:
;       bl                              Read Bank Number
;                                       0-15 bank number indicating desired
;                                       64-Kbyte bank

; Calling Protocol:
;       Load_Read_Bank_V74

Load_Read_Bank_V74 macro

        mov     ah,bl
        shl     ah,1            ;put bank into bits 7-4
        shl     ah,1
        shl     ah,1
        shl     ah,1
        mov     al,0e9h         ;point to read bank register
        mov     dx,3c4h         ;in extended registers
        out     dx,ax
endm
```

The single- or dual-bank modes for the Version 4 V7VGA chip are enabled through the code in Listings 21.19 and 21.20, respectively.

LISTING 21.19   Enabling Dual-Bank Mode (Version 4)

```
; Function:
;       Enabling Dual-Bank Mode in Version 4 silicon.
```

```
; Calling Protocol:
;       Enable_Dual_Bank_V74();

Enable_Dual_Bank_V74 proc far
        Extensions_On_V7
        mov     dx,3c4h         ;point to extension registers
        mov     al,0e0h         ;point to Miscellaneous Control
        out     dx,al
        inc     dx
        in      al,dx           ;don't disturb other bits

        or      al,80h          ;set bit 7=1
        out     dx,al
        Extensions_Off_V7
        ret
Enable_Dual_Bank_V74 endp
```

LISTING 21.20   Enabling Single- Bank Mode (Version 4)

```
; Function:
;       Enabling Single-Bank Mode in Version 4 silicon.

; Calling Protocol:
;       Enable_Single_Bank_V74();

Enable_Single_Bank_V74 proc far
        Extensions_On_V7
        mov     dx,3c4h         ;point to extension registers
        mov     al,0e0h         ;point to Miscellaneous Control
        out     dx,al
        inc     dx
        in      al,dx           don't disturb other bits

        and     al,7fh          ;set bit 7=0
        out     dx,al
        Extensions_Off_V7
        ret
Enable_Single_Bank_V74 endp
```

Functions which control the Read and Write banks for the Version 4 V7VGA in a 16-bit color mode are provided in Listings 21.21 and 21.22, respectively.

LISTING 21.21   Loading the Write Bank Number 16-color

```
; Function:
;       Loading the Write Bank with a new start address

; Input with:
;       write_bank      Write Bank_Number
;                               0-7 bank number indicating desired
;                               64-Kbyte bank

; Calling Protocol:
;       Set_Write_Bank_16_V74(write_bank);

Set_Write_Bank_16_V74 proc far arg1:byte

;       set up index to Bank Select Register
        mov     bl,arg1         ;get page
        Load_Write_Bank_V74

        ret
Set_Write_Bank_16_V74 endp
```

LISTING 21.22   Loading the Read Bank Number 16-color

```
; Function:
;       Loading the Read Bank with a new start address

; Input with:
;       read_bank       Read Bank_Number
;                               0-15 bank number indicating desired
;                               64-Kbyte bank

; Calling Protocol:
;       Set_Read_Bank_16_V74(read_bank);

Set_Read_Bank_16_V74 proc far arg1:byte

;       set up index to Bank Select Register
        mov     bl,arg1         ;get page
        Load_Read_Bank_V74

ret
Set_Read_Bank_16_V74 endp
```

Functions which control the Read and Write banks for the Version 4 V7VGA in a 256-bit color mode are provided in Listings 21.23 and 21.24, respectively.

LISTING 21.23   Loading the Write Bank Number 256-color

```
; Function:
;        Loading the Write Bank with a new start address

; Input with:
;        write_bank       Write Bank_Number
;                                0-15 bank number indicating desired
;                                64-Kbyte bank

; Calling Protocol:
;        Set_Write_Bank_256_V74(write_bank);

Set_Write_Bank_256_V74 proc far arg1:byte

;        set up index to Bank Select Register
         mov     bl,arg1        ;get page
         Load_Write_Bank_Video74

         ret
Set_Write_Bank_256_V74 endp
```

LISTING 21.24   Loading the Read Bank Number 256-color

```
; Function:
;        Loading the Read Bank with a new start address

; Input with:
;        read_bank        Read Bank_Number
;                                0-15 bank number indicating desired
;                                64-Kbyte bank

; Calling Protocol:
;        Set_Read_Bank_256_V74(read_bank);

Set_Read_Bank_256_V74 proc far arg1:byte

;        set up index to Bank Select Register
         mov     bl,arg1        ;get page
         Load_Read_Bank_V74
         ret
Set_Read_Bank_256_V74 endp
```

21.7 CONTROLLING THE CRT ADDRESS GENERATION

The CRT address generation handles the transfering of display memory to the monitor. This register fields associated with the CRT address generation are listed in Table 21.11.

21.7.1 CRT Display and Cursor Address Generation

When enabled, the CRTB field of the Bank Select Register contains the upper order address bits, bits 17 and 16, for the CRT address generation. While reading and writing to single megabytes of display memory requires 20 bits, only 18 bits are required for displaying the data on the screen. The lower-order 16 bits are found in the Start Address High and Low registers and in the Cursor Location High and Low registers. These registers are described in Sections 10.4.13 through 10.4.21. The upper-order two bits, bits 17 and 16, are contained in the CRTB field of the Bank Select Register. The selection of bits 17 and 16 is illustrated in Figure 21.19.

Enabling the CRTB field and bank selection is accomplished through the CBE and LCB fields which enable the bank selection process. Wraparound occurs when these fields are disabled and a maximum of 256 Kbytes of display memory is displayed.

The Counter Bank Enable field, CBE, determines where bits 16 and 17 of the generated display address, used during CRT operations, comes from. It can either come from the memory address counter or from the bank select field, CRTB in this register

If the CBE field is set to 1, the bank memory addressing mode is disabled and the address bits 17 and 16 are generated by the memory address counter. In this case wraparound occurs and the bank pointer has no effect. If the CBE field is set to 0, the bank address bits 17 and 16 are generated by the CRTB field of this register. In this case bank selection is engaged.

Fonts cannot cross bank boundaries and thus the bank select field, CRTB, associated with CRT operations should always be engaged. The address counter will simply wraparound at 64 Kbytes. The CBE field should be set to 0 in text modes so the font and character/attribute pairs are guaranteed to come from the same bank.

The LCB field similary enables the bank registers for the line compare function. If the LCB field is set to 0, the bank memory addressing mode is enabled. Thus, address bits 16 and 17 will be generated by the CRTB field. When the scan line number is reached and the split screen needs to be refreshed, the top line displayed will come from the top of the current bank, as indicated in the CRTB field.

If the LCB field is set to 1, the bank pointers have no effect and the split screen function displays data from the top of display memory. In this case, the address bits 16 and 17 are reset to 0.

TABLE 21.11   Video 7 Display Address Control

Function	Register Name	Field	Port	Index	Bits	Value
Enable Bank Selection	16-bit Interface	BE	3C5	FF	4	1
Disable Bank Selection	16-bit Interface	BE	3C5	FF	4	0
Write Bank Start Address	Bank Select	CRTB	3c5	F6	5–4	0–3
Bank Wrap Around	Bank Select	CBE	3c5	F6	6	1
Cross Bank Boundariess	Bank Select	CBE	3c5	F6	6	0
Line Compare Wrap	Bank Select	LCB	3c5	F6	7	1
Line Compare Cross Banks	Bank Select	LCB	3c5	F6	7	0

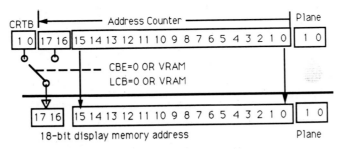

FIGURE 21.19   Creation of an 18-bit CRT address. If VRAM is present, CRTB is always selected. If DRAM is present, the CBE and LCB fields control whether CRTB or the Address Counter is selected for bits 17–16. The Address Counter always is selected for bits 15–0.

21.7.2   Display Starting Address

The display starting address can be controlled through the code in Listing 21.25. This function utilizes the set_start_address macro in Listing 14.32.

LISTING 21.25   Loading the Display Start Address

```
;  Function:
;        Loading the Display Start Address

;  Input Parameters
;        address            unsigned integer starting address
;        top                top two bits of address
```

```
;  Calling  Protocol:
;        Load_Start_V7(address,top)

Load_Start_V7   proc  far       arg1,arg2:byte

        mov     bx,arg1
        set_start_address     ;load  the  16-bit  start  address

;       send  out  top  address
        Extensions_On_V7      ;turn  on  extensions
        mov     dx,3c4h
        mov     al,0f6h        ;Bank  Select  Register
        out     dx,al

;       read  current  value
        inc     dx
        in      al,dx     ;get  value
        and     al,0cfh        ;zero  out  start  address  17-16  bit  5-4

;       or  in  new  start  address
        mov     bl,arg2        ;get  top  address
        and     bl,03h         ;only  want  2  bits
        mov     cx,4
        shl     bl,cl     ;shift  left  4  to  get  bit  5-4
        or      al,bl
        out     dx,al     ;output  top  address
        Extensions_Off_V7      ;turn  on  extensions
        ret
Load_Start_V7   endp
```

21.7.3 Positioning the Cursor

The cursor position can be controlled through the code in Listing 21.26. This function utilizes the position_cursor macro in Listing 14.33.

LISTING 21.26 Position the Cursor

```
;  Function:
;        Position  the  Cursor

;  Input  Parameters
;       address          unsigned  integer  starting  address
;       top              top  two  bits  of  address

;  Calling  Protocol:
;        Position_Cursor_V7(address,top)
```

```
Position_Cursor_V7      proc  far        arg1,arg2:byte

        mov    bx,arg1
        position_cursor    ;load the 16-bit cursor position

;       send out top address
        Extensions_On_V7       ;turn on extensions
        mov    dx,3c4h
        mov    al,0f6h         ;Bank Select Register
        out    dx,al

;       read current value
        inc    dx
        in     al,dx           ;get value
        and    al,0cfh         ;zero out start address 17-16 bit 5-4

;       or in new start address
        mov    bl,arg2         ;get top address
        and    bl,03h          ;only want 2 bits
        mov    cx,4
        shl    bl,cl           ;shift left 4 to get bit 5-4
        or     al,bl
        out    dx,al           ;output top address
        Extensions_Off_V7      ;turn on extensions
        ret
Position_Cursor_V7     endp
```

21.7.4 Controlling the Display Offset

No additional bits are provided for the offset address, beyond the eight bits provided in the Offset Register as described in Section 10.4.22. With word addressing, these eight bits can cover 1024 pixels. Having no additional offset bits limits the virtual display width to 1024 pixels.

21.8 VIDEO7 BIOS EXTENSIONS

The Video7 cards are equipped with six extended BIOS functions listed in Table 21.12. These assist the programmer in setting the extended display modes, setting up emulation and returning display status.

21.8.1 Inquire into Super Condition

Returns whether the Video7 extensions are enabled.

TABLE 21.12 Video7 Super BIOS

Function	AH	AL	Feature
Inquire into Super Condition	6F	00	Returns whether extensions are enabled
Get Information	6F	01	Returns video information
Get Mode/Screen Resolution	6F	04	Returns mode and screen size
Set Super Mode State	6F	05	Allows setting of super modes
Select Autoswitch Mode	6F	06	Automatically enters emulation mode
Get Video Memory Configuration	6F	07	Returns memory configuration

Inputs:

AH=6F hex	Extended BIOS Functions
AL=00 hex	Inquire into super condition

Outputs:

BX=return parameter	Return parameter
	'V7' = indicates Video7 extensions are available
	Not 'V7' = No Video7 extended functions

21.8.2 Get Information

Returns video information regarding the diagnostic bits, display type, monitor resolution, vertical sync, light pen, and display enabled. It should be noted that the last four values in postions 0–3 can be read directly from the Input Status #1 Register, as discussed in Section 10.2.4. These fields tend to be temporal and would likely change state before the BIOS could return. The programmer should not use this BIOS call for determining the status of these fields but rather should interrogate Input Status #1 directly.

Inputs:

AH=6F hex	Extended BIOS Functions
AL=01 hex	Get Information

Outputs:

AH=return parameter	Return parameter. See Table 21.13
	Valid Byte returned.
	2 = Invalid BIOS call

21.8.3 Get Mode/Screen Resolution

Returns current video mode and screen size in either columns versus rows or pixels versus pixels depending on whether the current mode is a text or graphics mode respectively.

TABLE 21.13   Get Information Return Status

Bit	Meaning	0	1
7–6	Diagnostic Bits		
5	Display type	Color	Monochrome
4	Monitor Resolution	>200 lines	<=200 lines
3	Vertical Sync	Display	Retrace
2	Light Pen Switch	Active	Not Active
1	Light Pen Flip Flop	Not Set	Set
0	Display Enabled	Enabled	Retrace

Inputs:

AH=6F hex	Extended BIOS functions
AL=04 hex	Get current mode and screen resolution

Outputs:

AL=current video mode	Mode number
BX=horizontal resolution	Columns if alphanumeric mode, Pixels if graphic mode
CX=vertical resolution	Rows if alphanumeric mode, Pixels if graphic mode
AH=return parameter	Return parameter. !2 = Valid BIOS call 2 = Invalid BIOS call

21.8.4   Set Super Mode State

Allows the setting of one of the Super VGA modes. The standard AH=0 Set Mode BIOS function will not handle these extended modes. This function however will handle the standard VGA calls.

Inputs:

AH=6F hex	Extended BIOS functions
AL=05hex	Set Mode
BL=mode value	

Outputs:

AH=return parameter	Return parameter. !2 = Valid BIOS call 2 = Invalid BIOS call

21.8.5   Select Autoswitch Mode

Selects the type of emulation autoswitched and bootup modes. This function can be invoked repeatidly to enable and disable different functions. More than one selection can be enabled at a time.

Inputs:

AH=6F hex	Extended BIOS functions
AL=06hex	Enter emulation mode
BL=autoswitch mode	Selection
	00 = Select EGA/VGA only modes
	01 = Select Autoswitched VGA/EGA/ CGA/MDA
	02 = Select 'Bootup' CGA/MDA
BH=function	Function to perform on selection
	0 = enable selection
	1 = disable selection

Outputs:

AH=return parameter	Return parameter.
	!2 = Valid BIOS call
	2 = Invalid BIOS call

21.8.6   Get Revision Code/Video Memory Configuration

Returns memory configuration as DRAM or VRAM, amount of memory present, and chip revision. The chip revision code can also be determined directly through the chip revision registers at Index 8E and 8F hex of the extended register 3C4/3C5 port. The chips are described in Table 21.14. The VEGA VGA is the older Video7 card and can be identified by a revision code between 80–8F hex. The Fast Write and VRAM card can be identified by revision codes between 70–79 hex. They can be differentiated by the memory code. If bit 7 of the memory configuration is 1, the memory is VRAM and the card must be a VRAM card. If bit 7 is a 0, the card must be a Fast Write card. The 1024i card can be identified by a revision code of 42 hex. In addition, the V7VGA version 5 chips will be identified by a code of 50 to 5F hex.

Inputs:

AH=6F hex	Extended BIOS functions
AL=07hex	Return Memory Configuration

Outputs:

AH=Memory configuration	Memory configuration
	Bit 7=0 DRAM
	Bit 7=1 VRAM
	Bit 6–0 # of 256 Kbyte blocks of memory

TABLE 21.14 Chip Revisions

Code	Chip
00–41	Reserved for future chips
40–49	1024i card
50–59	V7VGA Version 5.0
70–7F	V7VGA Chip revision 3
80–FF	VEGA VGA chip

BH=Chip Revision	Revision code for S/C chip
BL=Chip Revision	Revision code for G/A chip

21.9 VIDEO7 SPECIAL FEATURES

The Video7 processor is rich in extended features. These features include extended alphanumeric underlining, enhanced graphics operations, hardware cursor and fast character drawing.

21.9.1 Alphanumerics Extended Attributes

Extended attributes allows for underlining to occur regardless of the attribute byte of a character. This is accomplished by providing for a character attribute code to be represented by a 16-bit value. Any texture of underlining is possible since any bit in the 8-bit extended attribute byte can be set or reset.

Typically, the attribute code is eight bits and is stored in display memory plane 1. Its analogous ASCII code is stored in display memory plane 0. Extended attribute codes are stored at the same address in display memory plane 3. This extended attribute feature allows any attribute to be underlined. Any bit which is set to 1 in the extended attribute byte will result in the corresponding character. Any bit which is 0 will not cause an underline. If the byte is set to FF hex, the entire eight bits of the character pattern will be underlined.

The extended attributes function is enabled through the EAE field of the Compatibility Control Register illustrated in Figure 21.5. If the EAE field is set to 1, the extended text attributes are enabled. If it is set to 0, the extended attributes are disabled. Each character can have its own extended attribute byte. This is accomplished by writing the extended attribute code to display plane 3. The Map Mask Register, described in Section 10.3.3 can be used to enable only plane 3. The address of the attribute byte would correspond to the attribute of the character code.

Masked Write Control VRAM Only

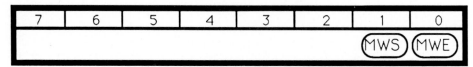

Index F3 at Port 3C4   Port 3C5 Read/Write

FIGURE 21.20 Masked Write Control Register. The write masking function is enabled through the MWE field. When enabled, the MWS field selects whether the rotated CPU bit is selected or the MASK field of the Masked Write Mask Register is used for the mask.

Masked Write Mask VRAM Only

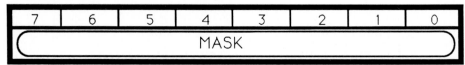

Index F4 at Port 3C4   Port 3C5 Read/Write

FIGURE 21.21 Masked Write Mask Register. The write mask is controlled through the MASK field.

21.9.2 Masked Writes

It is often desirable to write to selected bit positions within a selected byte without disturbing other bit positions within the same byte. This is possible in a standard VGA by using Bit Mask Register as described in Section 10.5.11. However, this requries a read cycle followed by a write cycle. This is very time-consuming due to the burden of wait-states placed on write operations which immediately follow read operations. If the VGA configuration includes VRAM memory, it is possible to perform masked write operations without using read instructions. Masked write operations are accomplished by using the Masked Write Control Register and the Masked Write Mask Register illustrated in Figures 21.20 and 21.21, respectively.

The MWE field of the Masked Write Control Register enables or disables the masked write function. If the MWE field is set to 1, the masked writes are enabled. If it is set to 0, the masked writes are disabled and all bit positions will be affected. The MWS field selects the source for the masked write mask. The mask is 8 bits wide. If a bit in the mask is set to 1, the corresponding bit in display memory will be affected by the write operation. If a bit in the mask is a 0, the corresponding bit in display memory will not be affected. If the MWS field is set to 1, the rotated CPU byte is selected as the source for the masked write mask. If the MWS field is set to 0, the mask value present in the Masked Write

Mask Register is selected as the source for the mask. Both of these can be very useful depending on the application.

21.9.3   Fast Character Drawing

It is often desirable to draw characters onto a colored background. This can be accomplished by specifying a foreground color and a background color. Any bit in the character pattern which is set to a 1 (foreground) will be written into display memory with the foreground color. Similarly, any character pattern set to a 0 (background) will be written into display memory with the background color.

Video7 provides several alternate techniques to perform this task through a set of several foreground/background registers. It is beyond the scope of this book to describe this process. The V7VGA technical reference manual can be consulted for more details.

21.9.4   Hardware Cursor

The hardware cursor provides a fast technique for non-destructive cursor placement. The cursor can be any pattern or color and can be positioned anywhere on the screen. It is beyond the scope of this book to describe this hardware cursor. The V7VGA technical reference manual can be consulted for more details.

Super VGA
Display Modes

The Super VGAs are equipped with the standard VGA display modes from 0 to A. Each has text and graphics display modes beyond these standard modes. The first set of tables provide the alphanumeric modes for each manufacturer detailed in this book. The second set lists the graphics modes for each manufacturer. The third set lists display modes organized by number of colors.

A.1   ALPHANUMERIC MODES ACCORDING TO MODE NUMBER

Alphanumeric modes use the dislay memory to contain the alphanumeric codes, attributes, and character fonts. The IBM standard and Super VGA alphanumeric modes are listed in Table A.1. These modes are ordered according to mode number. As can be seen, several manufacturers have used the same mode numbers for different display modes.

TABLE A.1   VGA Alphanumeric Display Modes Ordered by Mode Number

Resolution	# of colors	Manufacturer	Chip	Mode	Common
40 x 25	16	IBM	standard	0,1	
80 x 25	16	IBM	standard	2,3	
80 x 25	2	IBM	standard	7	
132 x 44	4	Tseng	all	18	
132 x 25	4	Tseng	all	19	
132 x 28	4	Tseng	all	1A	
132 x 44	16	Tseng	all	22	
132 x 25	16	Tseng	all	23	*2
132 x 25	16	ATI	all	23	*2
132 x 28	16	Tseng	all	24	
80 x 60	16	Tseng	all	26	
132 x 25	2	ATI	all	27	
100 x 40	16	Tseng	all	2A	

Resolution	# of colors	Manufacturer	Chip	Mode	Common
132 x 44	16	ATI	all	33	
132 x 44	2	ATI	all	37	
80 x 43	16	Video7	all	40	
132 x 25	16	Video7	all	41	
132 x 43	16	Video7	all	42	
80 x 60	16	Video7	all	43	*2
80 x 29	2	Genoa	all	43	*2
80 x 32	2	Genoa	all	44	*2
100 x 60	16	Video7	all	44	*2
80 x 44	2	Genoa	all	45	*2
132 x 28	16	Video7	all	45	*2
132 x 25	2	Genoa	all	46	
132 x 29	2	Genoa	all	47	
132 x 32	2	Genoa	all	48	
132 x 44	2	Genoa	all	49	
80 x 30	16	Trident	all	50	
80 x 43	16	Trident	all	51	
80 x 60	16	Trident	all	52	
132 x 25	16	Trident	all	53	
132 x 43	16	Paradise	all	54	*2
132 x 30	16	Trident	all	54	*2
132 x 43	16	Trident	all	55	*2
132 x 25	16	Paradise	all	55	*2
132 x 43	4	Paradise	all	56	*2
132 x 60	16	Trident	all	56	*2
132 x 25	16	Trident	all	57	*2
132 x 25	4	Paradise	all	57	*2
132 x 30	16	Trident	all	58	*2
80 x 32	16	Genoa	all	58	*2
132 x 43	16	Trident	all	59	
100 x 42	16	Genoa	all	5A	*2
132 x 60	16	Trident	all	5A	*2
132 x 25	16	Chips	all	60	*2
132 x 25	16	Genoa	all	60	*2
132 x 50	16	Chips	all	61	*2
132 x 29	16	Genoa	all	61	*2
132 x 32	16	Genoa	all	62	
132 x 44	16	Genoa	all	63	
132 x 60	16	Genoa	all	64	
80 x 60	16	Genoa	all	72	
80 x 66	16	Genoa	all	74	
100 x 75	16	Genoa	all	78/6B	

Note:

*2 indicates two chips share the same mode number

A.2 ALPHANUMERIC MODES ACCORDING TO MANUFACTURER

The display modes listed in Table A.1 are repeated again in Tables A.2–A.9 below. The IBM standard includes 3 alphanumeric display modes as shown in Table A.2. Each Super VGA manufacturer has added their own set of extended alphanumerics display modes as shown in Tables A.2–A.9.

TABLE A.2 IBM Standard VGA Alphanumeric Display Modes

Resolution	# of colors	Manufacturer	Chip	Mode
40 x 25	16	IBM	standard	0,1
80 x 25	16	IBM	standard	2,3
80 x 25	2	IBM	standard	7

TABLE A.3 ATI Super VGA Alphanumeric Display Modes

Resolution	# of colors	Manufacturer	Chip	Mode
132 x 25	16	ATI	all	23
132 x 25	2	ATI	all	27
132 x 44	16	ATI	all	33
132 x 44	2	ATI	all	37

TABLE A.4 Chips and Technologies Super VGA Alphanumeric Display Modes

Resolution	# of colors	Manufacturer	Chip	Mode
132 x 25	16	Chips	all	60
132 x 50	16	Chips	all	61

TABLE A.5 Genoa Super VGA Alphanumeric Display Modes

Resolution	# of colors	Manufacturer	Chip	Mode
80 x 29	2	Genoa	all	43
80 x 32	2	Genoa	all	44
80 x 44	2	Genoa	all	45
132 x 25	2	Genoa	all	46
132 x 29	2	Genoa	all	47
132 x 32	2	Genoa	all	48

Resolution	# of colors	Manufacturer	Chip	Mode
132 x 44	2	Genoa	all	49
80 x 32	16	Genoa	all	58
100 x 42	16	Genoa	all	5A
132 x 25	16	Genoa	all	60
132 x 29	16	Genoa	all	61
132 x 32	16	Genoa	all	62
132 x 44	16	Genoa	all	63
132 x 60	16	Genoa	all	64
80 x 60	16	Genoa	all	72
80 x 66	16	Genoa	all	74
100 x 75	16	Genoa	all	78/6B

TABLE A.6   Paradise Super VGA Alphanumeric Display Modes

Resolution	# of colors	Manufacturer	Chip	Mode
132 x 25	4	Paradise	all	57
132 x 25	16	Paradise	all	55
132 x 43	4	Paradise	all	56
132 x 43	16	Paradise	all	54

TABLE A.7   Trident Super VGA Alphanumeric Display Modes

Resolution	# of colors	Manufacturer	Chip	Mode
80 x 30	16	Trident	all	50
80 x 43	16	Trident	all	51
80 x 60	16	Trident	all	52
132 x 25	16	Trident	all	53
132 x 25	16	Trident	all	57
132 x 30	16	Trident	all	54
132 x 30	16	Trident	all	58
132 x 43	16	Trident	all	55
132 x 43	16	Trident	all	59
132 x 60	16	Trident	all	56
132 x 60	16	Trident	all	5A

TABLE A.8   Tseng Labs Super VGA Alphanumeric Display Modes

Resolution	# of colors	Manufacturer	Chip	Mode
80 x 60	16	Tseng	all	26
100 x 40	16	Tseng	all	2A
132 x 25	4	Tseng	all	19

TABLE A.8   *(continued)*

Resolution	# of colors	Manufacturer	Chip	Mode
132 x 28	4	Tseng	all	1A
132 x 44	4	Tseng	all	18
132 x 25	16	Tseng	all	23
132 x 28	16	Tseng	all	24
132 x 44	16	Tseng	all	22

TABLE A.9   Video7 Super VGA Alphanumeric Display Modes

Resolution	# of colors	Manufacturer	Chip	Mode
80 x 43	16	Video7	all	40
80 x 60	16	Video7	all	43
100 x 60	16	Video7	all	44
132 x 25	16	Video7	all	41
132 x 43	16	Video7	all	42
132 x 28	16	Video7	all	45

A.3   GRAPHICS MODES ACCORDING TO MODE NUMBER

Graphics modes use memory to display information on a pixel-by-pixel basis. The IBM standard and Super VGA graphics modes are listed in Table A.10. These modes are ordered according to mode number. As can be seen, several manufacturers have used the same mode numbers for different display modes.

TABLE A.10   VGA Graphics Display Modes According to Mode Number

Resolution	# of colors	Manufacturer	Chip	Mode	Common
640 x 200	2	IBM	standard	06	
320 x 200	16	IBM	standard	0D	
640 x 200	16	IBM	standard	0E	
640 x 350	4	IBM	standard	0F	
640 x 350	16	IBM	standard	10	
640 x 480	2	IBM	standard	11	
640 x 480	16	IBM	standard	12	
320 x 200	256	IBM	standard	13	
640 x 480	16	Tseng	all	25	
800 x 600	16	Tseng	all	29	
640 x 350	256	Tseng	all	2D	
640 x 480	256	Tseng	all	2E	

Resolution	# of colors	Manufacturer	Chip	Mode	Common
800 x 600	256	Tseng	all	30	
1024 x 768	16	Tseng	all	37	
1024 x 768	256	Tseng	ET4000	38	
800 x 600	16	ATI	all	53	
800 x 600	16	ATI	all	54	
800 x 600	2	Paradise	all	59	
800 x 600	16	Paradise	all	58	
1024 x 768	2	Paradise	00,10,11	5A	
1024 x 768	4	Paradise	00,10,11	5B	*2
800 x 600	16	Trident	all	5B	*2
800 x 600	256	Paradise	11	5C	*2
640 x 400	256	Trident	all	5C	*2
1024 x 768	16	Paradise	00,10,11	5D	*2
640 x 480	256	Trident	all	5D	*2
640 x 400	256	Paradise	all	5E	
640 x 480	256	Paradise	all	5F	*2
1024 x 768	16	Trident	all	5F	*2
1024 x 768	4	Trident	8900	60	*2
752 x 410	16	Video7	all	60	*2
720 x 540	16	Video7	all	61	*3
768 x 1024	16	Trident	8900	61	*3
640 x 400	256	ATI	all	61	*3
640 x 480	256	ATI	all	62	*3
1024 x 768	256	Trident	8900	62	*3
800 x 600	16	Video7	all	62	*3
800 x 600	256	ATI	all	63	*2
1024 x 768	2	Video7	all	63	*2
1024 x 768	4	Video7	all	64	
1024 x 768	16	Video7	all	65	*2
1024 x 768	4	ATI	all	65	*2
640 x 400	256	Video7	all	66	
640 x 480	256	Video7	all	67	*2
1024 x 768	16	ATI	all	67	*2
720 x 540	256	Video7	all	68	
800 x 600	256	Video7	all	69	
800 x 600	16	Chips	all	6A	
800 x 600	16	Chips	all	70	
1024 x 768	16	Chips	452,453	72	
640 x 400	256	Chips	all	78	
640 x 480	256	Chips	452,453	79	
768 x 576	256	Chips	452,453	7A	
800 x 600	256	Chips	453	7B	

Notes:
*2 indicates two chips share the same mode number
*3 indicates three chips share the same mode number

A.4 GRAPHICS MODES ACCORDING TO MANUFACTURER

The IBM standard includes eight graphics modes as shown in Table A.10. Each Super VGA manufacturer has added their own graphics modes as shown in Tables A.11–A.18.

TABLE A.11 IBM Standard VGA Graphics Display Modes

Resolution	# of colors	Manufacturer	Chip	Mode
640 x 200	2	IBM	standard	06
640 x 350	4	IBM	standard	0F
640 x 480	2	IBM	standard	11
320 x 200	16	IBM	standard	0D
640 x 200	16	IBM	standard	0E
640 x 350	16	IBM	standard	10
640 x 480	16	IBM	standard	12
320 x 200	256	IBM	standard	13

TABLE A.12 ATI Super VGA Graphics Display Modes

Resolution	# of colors	Manufacturer	Chip	Mode
800 x 600	16	ATI	all	53
800 x 600	16	ATI	all	54
800 x 600	256	ATI	all	63
1024 x 768	4	ATI	all	65
1024 x 768	16	ATI	all	67
640 x 400	256	ATI	all	61
640 x 480	256	ATI	all	62

TABLE A.13 Chips and Technologies Super VGA Graphics Display Modes

Resolution	# of colors	Manufacturer	Chip	Mode
800 x 600	16	Chips	all	6A
800 x 600	16	Chips	all	70
800 x 600	256	Chips	453	7B
1024 x 768	16	Chips	452,453	72
640 x 400	256	Chips	all	78
640 x 480	256	Chips	452,453	79
768 x 576	256	Chips	452,453	7A

TABLE A.14   Genoa Super VGA Graphics Display Modes

Resolution	# of colors	Manufacturer	Chip	Mode
720 x 512	16	Genoa	all	59
640 x 350	256	Genoa	all	5B
640 x 480	256	Genoa	all	5C
720 x 512	256	Genoa	all	5D
800 x 600	256	Genoa	all	5E
1024 x 768	16	Genoa	all	5F
800 x 600	16	Genoa	all	6A
800 x 600	256	Genoa	all	6C
640 x 480	16	Genoa	all	73
800 x 600	16	Genoa	all	79
512 x 512	16	Genoa	all	7C
512 x 512	256	Genoa	all	7D
640 x 400	256	Genoa	all	7E
1024 x 768	4	Genoa	all	7F

TABLE A.15   Paradise Super VGA Graphics Display Modes

Resolution	# of colors	Manufacturer	Chip	Mode
800 x 600	2	Paradise	all	59
800 x 600	16	Paradise	all	58
640 x 400	256	Paradise	all	5E
640 x 480	256	Paradise	all	5F
1024 x 768	2	Paradise	WD90C00	5A
1024 x 768	4	Paradise	WD90C00	5B
1024 x 768	16	Paradise	WD90C00	5D

TABLE A.16   Trident Super VGA Graphics Display Modes

Resolution	# of colors	Manufacturer	Chip	Mode
800 x 600	16	Trident	all	5B
640 x 400	256	Trident	all	5C
640 x 480	256	Trident	all	5D
1024 x 768	16	Trident	all	5F
1024 x 768	4	Trident	8900	60
768 x 1024	16	Trident	8900	61
1024 x 768	256	Trident	8900	62

TABLE A.17   Tseng Labs Super VGA Graphics Display Modes

Resolution	# of colors	Manufacturer	Chip	Mode
640 x 480	16	Tseng	all	25
800 x 600	16	Tseng	all	29
640 x 350	256	Tseng	all	2D
640 x 480	256	Tseng	all	2E
800 x 600	256	Tseng	all	30
1024 x 768	16	Tseng	all	37
1024 x 768	256	Tseng	ET4000	38

TABLE A.18   Video7 Super VGA Graphics Display Modes

Resolution	# of colors	Manufacturer	Chip	Mode
640 x 400	256	Video7	all	66
640 x 480	256	Video7	all	67
752 x 410	16	Video7	all	60
720 x 540	16	Video7	all	61
720 x 540	256	Video7	all	68
800 x 600	16	Video7	all	62
800 x 600	256	Video7	all	69
1024 x 768	2	Video7	all	63
1024 x 768	4	Video7	all	64
1024 x 768	16	Video7	all	65

A.5   VGA GRAPHICS MODES ACCORDING TO NUMBER OF COLORS

A.5.1   Two-Color Modes

The two-color modes are designed for black and white emulation of the MDA/ Hercules cards or for high resolution black and white system. The IBM standard includes two of these two-color modes as shown in Table A.19. Super VGA two-color modes include 800 by 600 and 1024 by 768 modes as shown in Table A.20.

TABLE A.19   2-color IBM Standard VGA Graphics Display Modes

Resolution	# of colors	Manufacturer	Chip	Mode
640 x 200	2	IBM	standard	06
640 x 480	2	IBM	standard	11

TABLE A.20 2-color Super VGA Graphics Display Modes

Resolution	# of colors	Manufacturer	Chip	Mode
800 x 600	2	Paradise	all	59
1024 x 768	2	Paradise	WD90C00	5A
1024 x 768	2	Video7	all	63

A.5.2 4-Color Modes

The four-color modes were originally designed for CGA emulation. IBM has provided one four-color mode in the VGA standard, as shown in Table A.21. Super VGA manufacturers have utilized the four-color mode to provide high resolution graphics while minimizing display memory, as shown in Table A.22.

TABLE A.21 4-color IBM Standard VGA Graphics Display Modes

Resolution	# of colors	Manufacturer	Chip	Mode
640 x 350	4	IBM	standard	0F

TABLE A.22 4-color Super VGA Graphics Display Modes

Resolution	# of colors	Manufacturer	Chip	Mode
1024 x 768	4	ATI	all	67
1024 x 768	4	Paradise	WD90C00	5B
1024 x 768	4	Trident	8900	60
1024 x 768	4	Video7	all	64
1024 x 768	4	Genoa	all	7F

A.5.3 16-Color Modes

Probably the most common VGA graphics modes are the 16-color modes. The IBM standard has provided four such modes, as shown in Table A.23. The VESA committee has standardized an 800x600 16-color mode. Nearly every Super VGA manufacturer has included a 1024 by 768 16-color mode. The most common 16-color modes include the 800 by 600 modes shown in Table A.24 and the 1024 by 768 modes shown in A.25. Some non-standard Super VGA modes utilizing the 16-color are shown in Table A.26.

TABLE A.23 16-color IBM Standard VGA Graphics Display Modes

Resolution	# of colors	Manufacturer	Chip	Mode
320 x 200	16	IBM	standard	0D
640 x 200	16	IBM	standard	0E
640 x 350	16	IBM	standard	10
640 x 480	16	IBM	standard	12

TABLE A.24 800 x 600 16-color Super VGA Graphics Display Modes

Resolution	# of colors	Manufacturer	Chip	Mode
800 x 600	16	ATI	all	53
800 x 600	16	ATI	all	54
800 x 600	16	Chips	all	6A
800 x 600	16	Chips	all	70
800 x 600	16	Paradise	all	58
800 x 600	16	Trident	all	5B
800 x 600	16	Tseng	all	29
800 x 600	16	Genoa	all	6A
800 x 600	16	Genoa	all	79

TABLE A.25 1024 x 768 16-color Super VGA Graphics Display Modes

Resolution	# of colors	Manufacturer	Chip	Mode
1024 x 768	16	ATI	all	65
1024 x 768	16	Chips	452,453	72
1024 x 768	16	Paradise	WD90C00	5D
1024 x 768	16	Trident	all	5F
1024 x 768	16	Tseng	all	37
1024 x 768	16	Video7	all	65
1024 x 768	16	Genoa	all	5F

TABLE A.26   Non-standard 16-color Super VGA Graphics Display Modes

Resolution	# of colors	Manufacturer	Chip	Mode
640 x 480	16	Tseng	all	25
768 x 1024	16	Trident	8900	61
752 x 410	16	Video7	all	60
720 x 540	16	Video7	all	61
720 x 512	16	Genoa	all	59
640 x 480	16	Genoa	all	73
512 x 512	16	Genoa	all	7C

A.5.4   256-Color Modes

The IBM standard 256-color mode was only 320 by 200 pixels as shown in Table A.27. Since then Super VGA manufacturers have brought the resolutions all the way up to 1024 by 768. The common modes are 640 by 400 as shown in Table A.28, 640 by 480 as shown in Table A.29, 800 by 600 as shown in Table A.30 and 1024 by 768 as shown in Table A.31. Some non-common 256-color modes are shown in Table A.32.

TABLE A.27   256-color IBM standard VGA Graphics Display Modes

Resolution	# of colors	Manufacturer	Chip	Mode
320 x 200	256	IBM	standard	13

TABLE A.28   640 x 400 256-color Super VGA Graphics Display Modes

Resolution	# of colors	Manufacturer	Chip	Mode
640 x 400	256	ATI	all	61
640 x 400	256	Chips	all	78
640 x 400	256	Paradise	all	5E
640 x 400	256	Trident	all	5C
640 x 400	256	Video7	all	66
640 x 400	256	Genoa	all	7E

TABLE A.29   640 x 480 256-color Super VGA Graphics Display Modes

Resolution	# of colors	Manufacturer	Chip	Mode
640 x 480	256	ATI	all	62
640 x 480	256	Chips	452,453	79
640 x 480	256	Paradise	all	5F
640 x 480	256	Trident	all	5D
640 x 480	256	Tseng	all	2E
640 x 480	256	Video7	all	67
640 x 480	16	Genoa	all	73

TABLE A.30   800 x 600 256-color Super VGA Graphics Display Modes

Resolution	# of colors	Manufacturer	Chip	Mode
800 x 600	256	ATI	all	63
800 x 600	256	Chips	453	7B
800 x 600	256	Tseng	all	30
800 x 600	256	Video7	all	69

TABLE A.31   1024 x 768 256-color Super VGA Graphics Display Modes

Resolution	# of colors	Manufacturer	Chip	Mode
1024 x 768	256	Trident	8900	62
1024 x 768	256	Tseng	ET4000	38

TABLE A.32   Non-standard 256-color Super VGA Graphics Display Modes

Resolution	# of colors	Manufacturer	Chip	Mode
640 x 350	256	Tseng	all	2D
768 x 576	256	Chips	452,453	7A
512 x 512	256	Genoa	all	7D
640 x 350	256	Genoa	all	5B
720 x 512	256	Genoa	all	5D

VGA and Super VGA Registers

From the host's perpective, the VGA consists of a set of ports and display memory. The port address space used by the VGA resides in the 3Bx, 3Cx, and 3Dx port space. The Super VGA manufacturers have spread out in the same basic address space to find room for their Extended registers. In some cases, they have found unique addresses while in other cases, manufacturers use the same port address and index for different purposes.

B.1 PC/AT VGA INTERFACE REGISTERS

The PC/AT interface utilizes the register at 46E8 as shown in Table B.1. Different manufacturers refer to this register with different names. In Table B.1, it is referred to as ...*Global Enable*. If the VGA is mounted on an adapter card this register typically resides at port address 3C3 hex. If it resides on the motherboard the address is typically at 3C3 hex. The port register 102 hex is typically resident in PS/2 systems; however, in certain circumstances, the 102 port is mapped into the PC/AT systems.

TABLE B.1   PC/AT VGA Interface Registers

Chip	Register Name	Write	Read	Index
PC/AT card	...Global Enable	46E8		
PC/AT motherboard	...Global Enable	3C3		
all	Card Enable	102	102	

B.2 PS/2 VGA INTERFACE REGISTERS

The PS/2 interface uses the POS 93, 100, 101 and 102 registers, as indicated in Table B.2.

TABLE B.2 PS/2 VGA Interface Registers

Chip	Register Name	Write	Read	Index
all	Card ID low		POS 100	
all	Card ID high		POS 101	
all	Card Enable	POS 102	POS 102	

B.3 IBM STANDARD VGA

The IBM Standard VGA register locations are listed in Table B.3.

TABLE B.3 Standard VGA Registers

Chip	Register Name	Write	Read	Index
Standard VGA	Misc. Output	3C2	3CC	
Standard VGA	Feature Control	3xA	3CA	
Standard VGA	Input Status #1		3C2	
Standard VGA	Input Status #2		3xA	
Standard VGA	EGA Position #1	3CC		
Standard VGA	EGA Position #2	3CA		
Standard VGA	Sequencer	3C4/3C5	3C4/3C5	00–04
Standard VGA	CRT Controller	3x4/3x5	3x4/3x5	00–18
Standard VGA	Graphics Controller	3CE/3CF	3CE/3CF	00–08
Standard VGA	Attribute	3C0	3C1	00–14
Standard VGA	PEL Address Read	3C7		
Standard VGA	DAC State		3C7	
Standard VGA	PEL Address Write	3C8	3C8	
Standard VGA	PEL Data	3C9	3C9	0–FF
Standard VGA	PEL Mask	3C6	3C6	

B.4 ATI TECHNOLOGIES

The ATI Technologies VGA register locations are listed in Table B.4. Due to ATI's proprietary view of their registers, the registers listed in Table B.4 are not meant to be complete. The register location of the Extended registers is termed *Ext.* This is due to the ATI philosophy that the register may change location in future ATI releases.

TABLE B.4 Standard VGA Registers

Chip	Register Name	Write	Read	Index
18800,28800	Extended	Ext/Ext+1	Ext/Ext+1	B0–BE
18800,28800	Monitor Type	Ext/Ext+1	Ext/Ext+1	BB
18800,28800	Bank Select	Ext/Ext+1	Ext/Ext+1	B2
18800,28800	ATI Register #E	Ext/Ext+1	Ext/Ext+1	BE
18800,28800	Extended	Ext/Ext+1	Ext/Ext+1	B0–BE

B.5 CHIPS AND TECHNOLOGIES

Chips and Technologies has staked out a register space at 3D6/3D7 for all of their Extended registers. All Extended registers reside in this indexed port address pair, as shown in Table B.5.

TABLE B.5 Standard VGA Registers

Chip	Register Name	Write	Read	Index
451,2	Extended	3D6/3D7	3D6/3D7	00–06
451,2	Extended	3D6/3D7	3D6/3D7	08–0E
451,2	Extended	3D6/3D7	3D6/3D7	28–2F
451,2,3,5,6	Extended	3D6/3D7	3D6/3D7	7F
451,2,3,5,6	Extended	3D6/3D7	3D6/3D7	14–1E
451,2	CGA/Hercules	3x8	3x8	
451,2	CGA	3D9	3D9	
451,2	Hercules	3BF	3BF	
452	Extended	3D6/3D7	3D6/3D7	30–3A
453	Extended	3D6/3D7	3D6/3D7	00–03
453	Extended	3D6/3D7	3D6/3D7	05
453	Extended	3D6/3D7	3D6/3D7	0B–0D
453	Extended	3D6/3D7	3D6/3D7	10–11
453	Extended	3D6/3D7	3D6/3D7	20
453	Extended	3D6/3D7	3D6/3D7	23–29
455,6	Extended	3D6/3D7	3D6/3D7	41–45
455,6	Extended	3D6/3D7	3D6/3D7	08–09
455,6	Extended	3D6/3D7	3D6/3D7	0B
455,6	Extended	3D6/3D7	3D6/3D7	0D
455,6	Extended	3D6/3D7	3D6/3D7	28
455,6	Extended	3D6/3D7	3D6/3D7	2B
455,6	Extended	3D6/3D7	3D6/3D7	50–6C
455,6	Extended	3D6/3D7	3D6/3D7	7E
456	Extended	3D6/3D7	3D6/3D7	6D–6E

B.6 PARADISE/WESTERN DIGITAL

Paradise/Western Digitial has placed their Extended registers in the 3CE/3CF, 3x4/3x5 and 3C4/3C5 address space, as shown in Table B.6.

TABLE B.6 Paradise/Western Digital VGA Registers

Chip	Register Name	Write	Read	Index
all	Extended	3CE/3CF	3CE/3CF	09–0F
C00,C10,C11	Extended	3x4/3x5	3x4/3x5	29–30
C10,C11	Extended	3x4/3x5	3x4/3x5	31–3F
C10,C11	Extended	3C4/3C5	3C4/3C5	06–07
C10,C11	Extended	3C4/3C5	3C4/3C5	11–12
C11	Extended	3C4/3C5	3C4/3C5	10

B.7 GENOA

Genoa has placed their Extended registers in the 3CE/3CF, 3x4/3x5 and 3C4/3C5 address space as shown in Table B.7.

TABLE B.7 Genoa VGA Registers

Chip	Register Name	Write	Read	Index
GVGA	Extended	3CE/3CF	3CE/3CF	09–0B
GVGA	Extended	3x4/3x5	3x4/3x5	2E–2F
GVGA	Extended	3C4/3C5	3C4/3C5	05–08
GVGA	Extended	3C4/3C5	3C4/3C5	10

B.8 TRIDENT

Trident has placed their Extended registers in the 3x4/3x5 and 3C4/3C5 address space as shown in Table B.8.

TABLE B.8   Trident VGA Registers

Chip	Register Name	Write	Read	Index
8800	Extended	3C4/3C5	3C4/3C5	1E
8800	Extended	3C4/3C5	3C4/3C5	0D–0E
8800, 8900	Extended	3C4/3C5	3C4/3C5	0B
8900	Extended	3C4/3C5	3C4/3C5	0D–0F
8900	Extended	3x4/3x5	3x4/3x5	1E–1F
8800, 8900	Extended	3x4/3x5	3x4/3x5	22
8800, 8900	Extended	3x4/3x5	3x4/3x5	24
8800, 8900	Extended	3x4/3x5	3x4/3x5	26

B.9   TSENG LABS

Tseng has placed their Extended registers in the 3x4/3x5, 3C4/3C5, 3CE/3CF and 3C0/3C1 indexed address space. In addition, three port registers at 3CB, 3CD are also used as shown in Table B.9.

TABLE B.9   Standard VGA Registers

Chip	Register Name	Write	Read	Index
3000,4000	Extended	3C4/3C5	3C4/3C5	05–07
3000	Extended	3x4/3x5	3x4/3x5	1B–21
3000	Extended	3x4/3x5	3x4/3x5	23
3000	Extended	3x4/3x5	3x4/3x5	25
3000,4000	PEL Add/Dat	3CB	3CB	
3000,4000	Segment Select	3CD	3CD	
3000,4000	Miscellaneous	3C0	3C1	16
3000,4000	Extended	3CE/3CF	3CE/3CF	0D–0E
4000	Extended	3x4/3x5	3x4/3x5	32–37

B.10   VIDEO7/HEADLAND TECHNOLOGY

Video7/Headland has placed their Extended registers in the 3C4/3C5 indexed address space, as shown in Table B.10. This table shonws that Video7 has requested all registers between 80–FF hex in the 3C4/3C5 register set. The registers currently used by Video7 are shown beneath this first entry.

TABLE B.10   Standard VGA Registers

Chip	Register Name	Write	Read	Index
Requested	Extended	3C4/3C5	3C4/3C5	80–FF
V7VGA	Extended	3C4/3C5	3C4/3C5	83
V7VGA	Extended	3C4/3C5	3C4/3C5	8E–8F
V7VGA	Extended	3C4/3C5	3C4/3C5	94
V7VGA	Extended	3C4/3C5	3C4/3C5	9C–A5
V7VGA	Extended	3C4/3C5	3C4/3C5	EA–FF
V7VGA	Extended	3x4/3x5	3C4/3C5	1F,22,24
V7VGA	Cache Control	4BC4	4CB4	
V7VGA	Cache Control	4BC5	4CB5	

B.11   TABLES OF VGA AND SUPER VGA REGISTERS

Maps are provided in Figures B.1 through B.8 which show the positioning of the VGA and Super VGA Registers within the host I/O port address space. The legend of Figures B.2–B.8 is provided in Figure B.1.

The Figures B.2 through B.9 are described in Table B.11.

TABLE B.11   Description of Figures

Figure #	I/O Index Space
B.2	00–1F hex
B.3	20–3F hex
B.4	40–5F hex
B.5	60–7F hex
B.6	80–9F hex
B.7	A0–BF hex
B.8	C0–DF hex
B.9	E0–FF hex

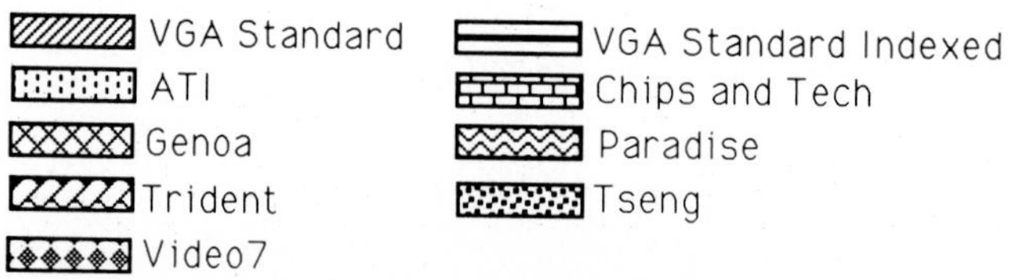

VGA Standard   VGA Standard Indexed

ATI   Chips and Tech

Genoa   Paradise

Trident   Tseng

Video7

FIGURE B.1   I/O Map Legend

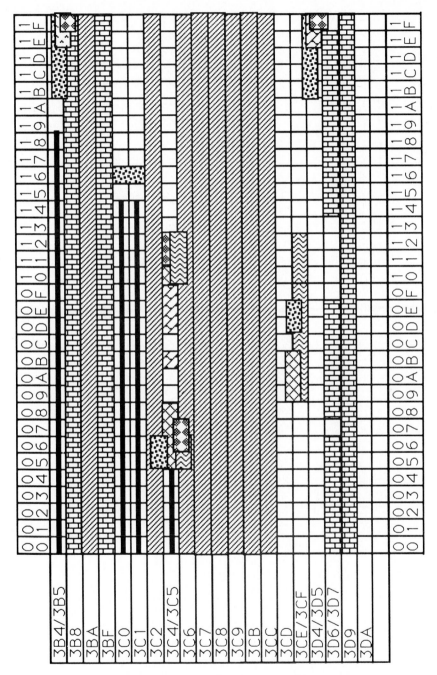

FIGURE B.2   I/O Registers 00–1F hex.

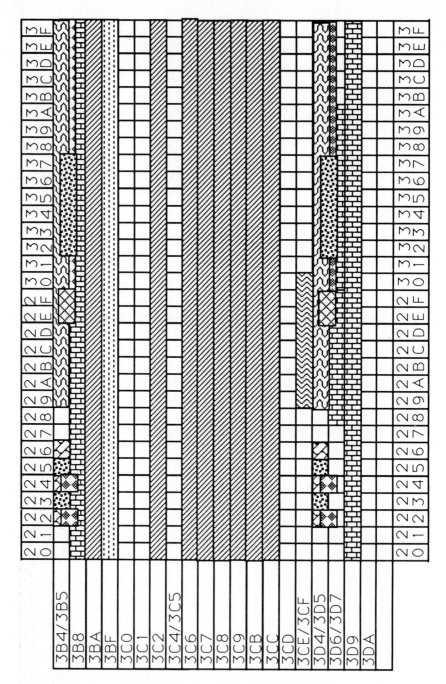

FIGURE B.3 I/O Registers 20–3F hex.

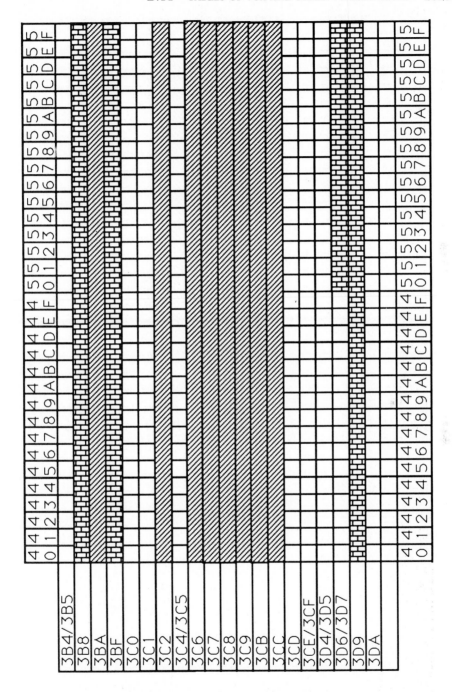

FIGURE B.4 I/O Registers 40–5F hex.

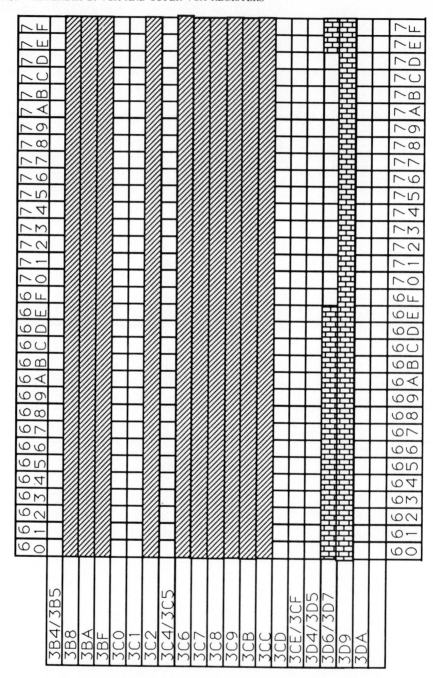

FIGURE B.5   I/O Registers 60–7F hex.

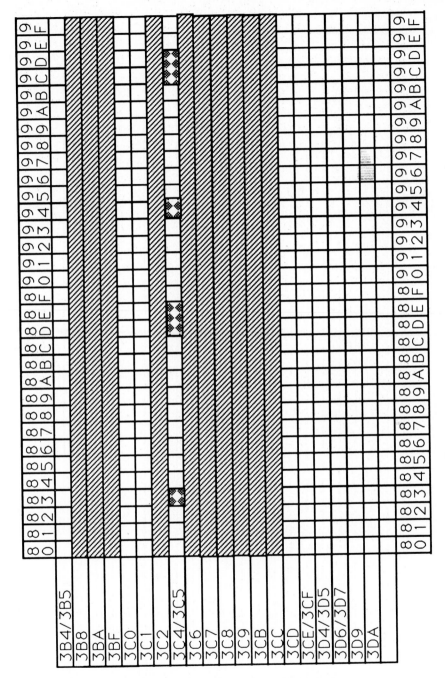

FIGURE B.6   I/O Registers 80–9F hex.

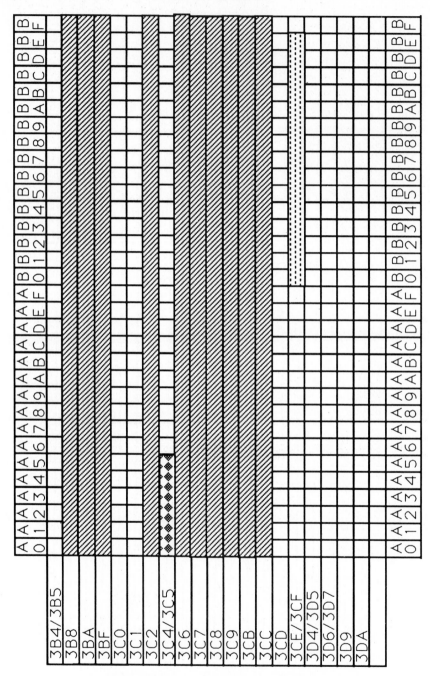

FIGURE B.7   I/O Registers A0–BF hex.

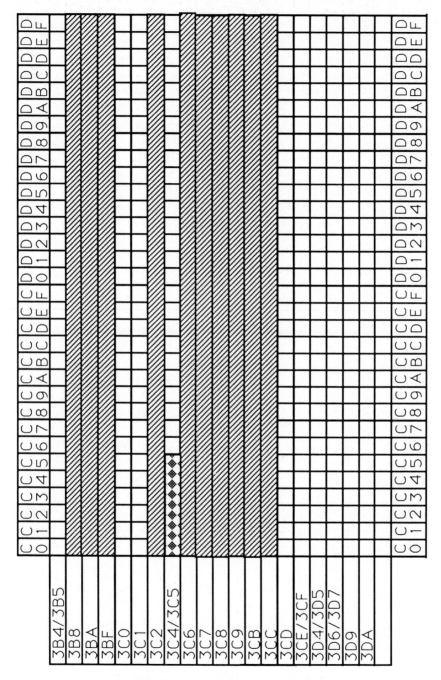

FIGURE B.8   I/O Registers C0–DF hex.

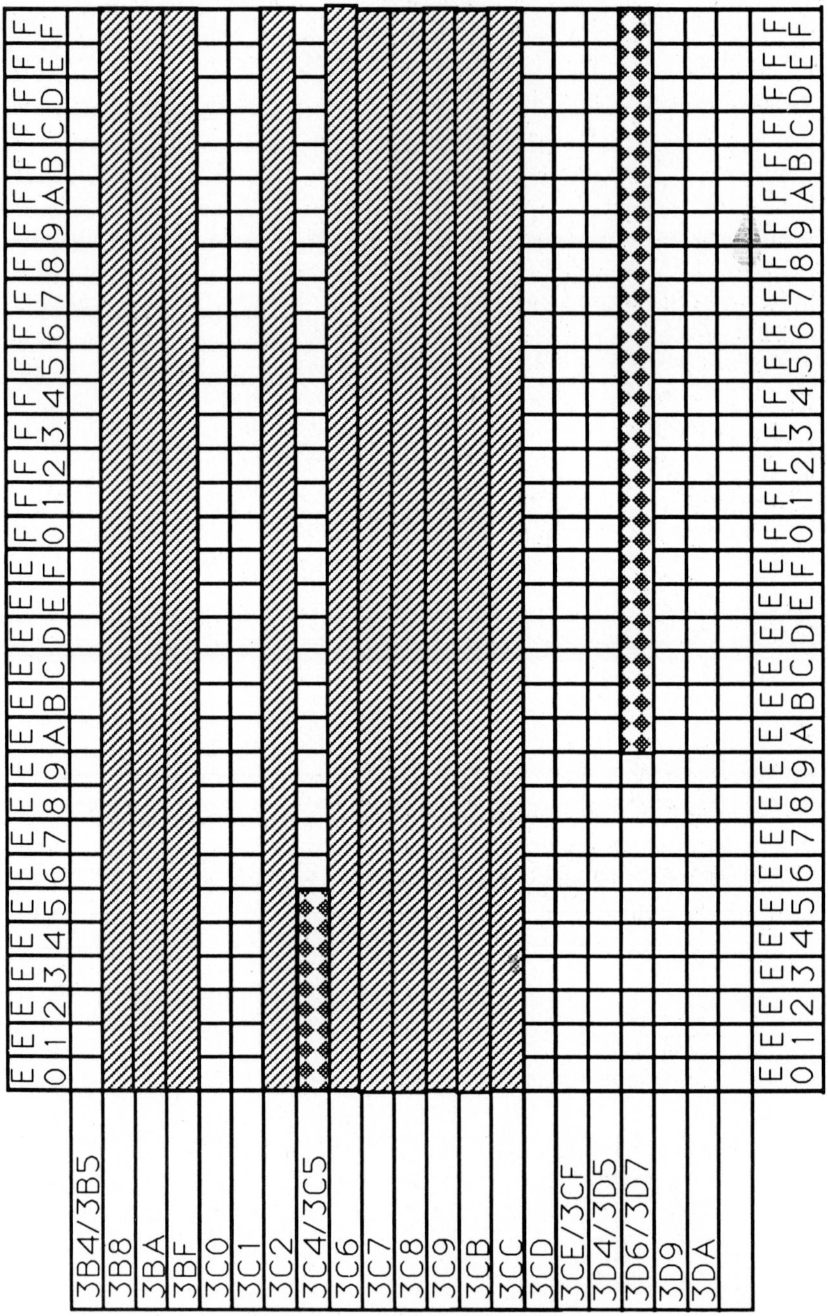

FIGURE B.9 I/O Registers E0–FF hex.

Index

Special Offer for Software

Programmer's Guide Companion Disk and the Super VGA Toolbox

Software companion disks are available to help programmers save time and ensure accuracy. Written by Richard Ferraro, all code is written in C and Assembly Language. All software is well-documented and royalty free.

Programmer's Guide Companion Disk includes all of the 150 source code listings contained in this book.

Super VGA Toolbox contains an additional 300 source code functions. Included in the *Super VGA Toolbox* are a **Standard VGA Library** and a **Global VGA Library**. The **Standard VGA Library** provides over 150 source code functions which control the EGA/VGA cards. The **Global VGA Library** provides over 150 source code functions capable of controlling all of the most popular Super VGA cards. A 100-page manual is included with the *Super VGA Toolbox*.

Programmers may also wish to purchase one or more **Specific Libraries. These are specially optimized for each of the Super VGA chips for programmers desiring optimally coded functions and special effects specific to each chip.**

For additional information call (206) 362-2520. Orders may be placed by mailing the completed order form below. Full payment must be received prior to shipping. No warranty for this product is implied or expressed.

- -

Mail orders (Check / Money Order)
Payment should be made to:
Richard Ferraro
2568 NE 188th, Seattle, WA 98155

Name_____ Company_____

Address_____

City_____ State _____ Zip _____

Country_____

Daytime phone_____ Desired Disk Format: _____ 5 1/4 _____ 3 1/2

_____ copies of *Programmer's Guide Companion Disk* @ $29.99 = $_____

_____ copies of *Super VGA Toolbox* @ $199.99 = $_____

_____ copies of a *Specific VGA Toolbox* @ $29.99 = $_____

_____copies of *Programmer's Guide to the EGA/VGA Cards* (Second Edition, 1990) @ 29.99 = $_____

Specific VGA Libraries (check each desired)

☐ ATI 18800 Version 1	☐ Paradise PVGA1a	☐ Video7 V7VGA Version 1-3
☐ ATI 18800 Version 1, 28800	☐ Paradise WD90C11	☐ Video7 V7VGA Version 4
☐ Chips&Tech 82c452	☐ Trident 8800	☐ ZYMOS ZYVGA
☐ Chips&Tech 82c453	☐ Trident 8900	☐ Cirrus 510/520/5320
☐ Genoa 5000 series	☐ Tseng ET3000	☐ _____
☐ Genoa GVGA	☐ Tseng ET4000	☐ _____

Shipping/Handling: *Please Note: Shipping rates are subject to change.*

Subtotal from above_____

UPS Domestic Ground @ $3.90_____

UPS Domestic 2nd Day Air (Except AK & HI) @ 4.90_____

UPS Domestic 2nd Day Air AK & HI @ $8.50_____

Federal Express Next Afternoon Delivery @ 16.75_____

U.S. Express Mail Domestic $14.25_____

U.S Express Mail Foreign (except Philippines, Eastern Europe and Iran) @19.75_____

Call or write if your country is not included above._____

Washington State residents add 8.1% sales tax_____

Total_____